Lecture Notes in Computer Science　900

Edited by G. Goos, J. Hartmanis and J. van Leeuwen

Advisory Board: W. Brauer　D. Gries　J. Stoer

Ernst W. Mayr   Claude Puech (Eds.)

STACS 95

12th Annual Symposium
on Theoretical Aspects of Computer Science
Munich, Germany, March 2-4, 1995
Proceedings

 Springer

Series Editors

Gerhard Goos
Universität Karlsruhe
Vincenz-Priessnitz-Straße 3, D-76128 Karlsruhe, Germany

Juris Hartmanis
Department of Computer Science, Cornell University
4130 Upson Hall, Ithaca, NY 14853, USA

Jan van Leeuwen
Department of Computer Science, Utrecht University
Padualaan 14, 3584 CH Utrecht, The Netherlands

Volume Editors

Ernst W. Mayr
Institut für Informatik, Technische Universität München
Arcisstraße 21, D-80290 München, Germany

Claude Puech
iMAGIS-IMAG
BP 53, F-38041 Grenoble Cedex 09, France

CR Subject Classification (1991):F, D.1, D.4, G.1-2, I.3.5, E.3

ISBN 3-540-59042-0 Springer-Verlag Berlin Heidelberg New York

CIP data applied for

© Springer-Verlag Berlin Heidelberg 1995
Printed in Germany

Typesetting: Camera-ready by author
SPIN: 10485406   45/3140-543210 - Printed on acid-free paper

Preface

The Symposium on Theoretical Aspects of Computer Science (STACS) is held annually, alternating between France and Germany. The STACS meeting is organized jointly by the Special Interest Group for Theoretical Computer Science of the Gesellschaft für Informatik (GI) in Germany and the Special Interest Group for Applied Mathematics of Association Française des Sciences et Technologies de l'Information et des Systèmes (afcet) in France.

STACS'95 is the twelfth in this series, held in München March 2–4, 1995. The locations of the preceding symposia were:

1984 Paris	1985 Saarbrücken
1986 Orsay	1987 Passau
1988 Bordeaux	1989 Paderborn
1990 Rouen	1991 Hamburg
1992 Cachan	1993 Würzburg
1994 Caen	

For all of these symposia, the proceedings have been published in the Lecture Notes for Computer Science series of Springer Verlag, as are the proceedings for this 12th STACS.

STACS has become one of the most important annual meetings in Europe for the Theoretical Computer Science community. This time, 180 submissions with authors from (at least) 36 countries made the deadline of August 15, 1994. Each submission was sent to at least four members of the program committee. In addition, each member of the program committee received the abstracts of all of the submitted papers. The program committee then met for two days (October 21/22) in München and selected 53 out of the 180 submissions (29%) to be presented at the conference. Because of the constraints imposed by the format of the conference ($2\frac{1}{2}$ days), a number of good papers did not make it. As a whole, the program committee was impressed by the high scientific quality of the submissions as well as the broad spectrum of topics they covered within the area of Theoretical Computer Science. As in the previous years, there was no way to organize the talks other than to have parallel sessions and allot a mere 25 minutes for each regular talk!

We would like to express our immense gratitude to all the members of the Program Committee, which consisted of

M. Ben-Or (Jerusalem)	P. Pudlák (Praha)
I. Castellani (Valbonne)	C. Puech (Grenoble, co-chair)
J.-P. Delahaye (Lille)	A. Restivo (Palermo)
M. Dietzfelbinger (Dortmund)	P. Schmitt (Karlsruhe)
Z. Ésik (Szeged)	U. Schöning (Ulm)
H. Ganzinger (Saarbrücken)	J. Stern (Paris)
D. Krob (Paris)	M. Yung (Yorktown Heights)
E.W. Mayr (München, chair)	

They and the many subreferees they enlisted put a lot of work into reviewing the submissions, judging their significance and scientific merits.

We also thank the three invited speakers of this meeting for accepting our invitation and sharing with us their insights on some interesting developments in our area.

We acknowledge the support of the following institutions and corporations for this conference: Bayerische Motorenwerke AG, Cray-Research Deutschland GmbH, Deutsche Forschungsgemeinschaft, Europäische Union, IBM Deutschland, Sun Microsystems, and Technische Universität München.

Finally, we would like to thank particularly the members of the Organizing Committee consisting of E. Bayer, V. Heun, R. Holzner, U. Koppenhagen, K. Kühnle, E.W. Mayr, A. Schmidt, H. Stadtherr, and I. Wohlrab.

München, January 1995   Ernst W. Mayr
                                                               Claude Puech

List of Reviewers

J.-P. Allouche
K. Ambos-Spies
A. Arnold
L. Babai
E. Badouel
J.P. Bahsoun
P. Balbiani
A. Bar-Noy
D. Basin
D. Bauer
H. Baumeister
D. Beauquier
J. Bečvář
C. Beeri
G. Berry
J. Berstel
P. Berthomé
M. Bertol
C. Bertram-Kretzberg
E. Best
N. Blum
A. Bockmayr
P. Boldi
B. Bollig
A. Bouali
S. Boucheron
G. Boudol
G. Brassard
H. Braun
D. Breslauer
V. Bruyère
J. Burghardt
H.-J. Burtschick
A. Carpi
B. Carre
O. Carton
B. Chlebus
P. Chrétienne
M. Clerbout
H. Comon
A. Cornuejols
M. Cosnard
B. Courcelle

N. Creignou
S. Crespi-Reghizzi
L. Csirmaz
E. Csuhaj-Varjú
L. Czaja
M. Dam
C. Damm
F. d'Amore
P. Darondeau
J. Dassow
C. De Felice
F. Del Cerro
M. Delest
C. Delorme
J. Demetrovics
R. De Nicola
F. Denis
M. de Rougemont
J. Despeyroux
P. Devienne
M. Dezani
V. Di Gesù
W. Dittrich
J. Dix
O. Dubois
A. Durand
B. Durand
D. Fehrer
P. Fischer
P. Flajolet
P. Fraigniaud
P. Franciosa
M. Franklin
R. Freund
K. Friedl
Z. Fülöp
T. Gaizer
D. Gardy
M. Garzon
P. Gastin
S. Gaubert
B. Gaujal
J. Gergo

A. Giambruno
D. Giammarresi
R. Giancarlo
J. Giesl
M. Goessel
P. Goralcik
E. Goubault
D. Gouyou-Beauchamps
S. Graf
E. Grandjean
D. Grőger
R. Grosu
I. Guesarian
Y. Gündel
T. Hagerup
R. Hähnle
P. Hajnal
G. Hansel
M. Hanus
R. Heckmann
M. Hennessy
V. Heun
Th. Hofmeister
R. Holzner
G. Horváth
G. Hotz
M. Huber
M. Hühne
G. Italiano
M. Ito
L. Iturrioz
G. Ivanyos
M. Jantzen
J. Karhumäki
C. Kenyon
J. Kincses
R. Klasing
J. Köbler
U. Koppenhagen
J. Krajíček
I. Kramosil
M. Krause
H.-J. Kreowski

Th. Kropf
L. Kučera
M. Kudlek
U.-M. Kuenzi
K. Kühnle
M. Kummer
A. Labella
T. Lacoste
C. Laneve
S. Lange
M. Latteux
C. Lecoutre
T. Lecroq
H. Lefmann
A. Leitsch
B. Le Saëc
Th. Lettmann
N. Levy
M. Löbbing
G. Longo
G. Lüttgen
E. Madelaine
B. Mahr
J. Makowsky
M. Marrensakis
J. Matoušek
G. Mauri
A. Mayer
J. Mazoyer
C. Meinel
F. Meyer auf der Heide
P. Michel
F. Mignosi
M. Moinard
M. Morvan
M. Mukund
H. Müller
A. Muscholl
N. Nisan
A. Nonnengart
H.J. Ohlbach
E.-R. Olderog
P. Orponen
Th. Ottmann

O. Paterson
E. Pelz
A. Petit
A. Pietracaprina
G. Pighizzini
J.E. Pin
M. Piotrow
A. Pluhár
G. Pucci
K. Reinhardt
R. Reischuk
W. Reissenberger
A. Rensink
G. Richomme
Y. Roos
D. Rooß
P. Rossmanith
J.-C. Routier
B. Rozoy
Y. Sagiv
K. Salomaa
M. Santha
M. Sauerhoff
P. Savický
C. Scheideler
S. Schirra
G. Schnitger
R. Schuler
P. Schupp
A. Schuster
O. Schwarzkopf
D. Seese
H. Seidl
G. Sénizergues
P. Sewell
J. Sgall
D. Sieling
J. Šíma
H. Simon
J. Simon
R. Sloan
M. Soria
D. Sotteau
E. Speckenmeyer

H. Stadtherr
B. Steffen
M. Steinby
V. Stemann
G. Struth
R. Studer
K. Sutner
V. Švejdar
A. Szalas
P.S. Thiagarajan
C. Thiel
Th. Thierauf
W. Thomas
E. Timmerman
S. Tison
A. Tönne
D. Troeger
A. Tsantilas
T. Tsantilas
G. Turán
C. Uhrig
S. Varricchio
Z. Vavřín
R. Venkatesan
C. Verhoef
V. Vialard
W. Vogler
F. Voisin
H. Vollmer
H. Wagener
F. Wagner
A. Weber
G. Weikum
P. Weil
C. Weise
E. Weydert
R. Wiehagen
Th. Wilke
J. Wuertz
S. Žák
A. Zundel
J. Zwiers

Contents

Graph Theory, Data Bases

Automata Theory IV

Theory of Parallel Computing II

Complexity Theory III

XIII

Computational Geometry

Complexity Theory IV

Invited Talk

On the synthesis of strategies in infinite games *

Wolfgang Thomas

Institut für Informatik und Praktische Mathematik
Christian-Albrechts-Universität Kiel, D-24098 Kiel
wt@informatik.uni-kiel.d400.de

Abstract. Infinite two-person games are a natural framework for the study of reactive nonterminating programs. The effective construction of winning strategies in such games is an approach to the synthesis of reactive programs. We describe the automata theoretic setting of infinite games (given by "game graphs"), outline a new construction of winning strategies in finite-state games, and formulate some questions which arise for games over effectively presented infinite graphs.

1 Introduction

One of the origins of automata theory over infinite strings was the interest in verifying and synthesizing switching circuits. These circuits were considered as transforming infinite input sequences into output sequences, and systems of restricted arithmetic served as specification formalisms ([Ch63]). With Büchi's decision procedure for the monadic second-order theory S1S of one successor ([Bü62]), it turned out that the "solution problem" (in more recent terminology: the verification problem or model checking problem) for circuits with respect to specifications in S1S was settled. Büchi's proof showed that S1S specifications can be turned into ω-automata, whence the verification problem amounts to an inclusion test for ω-languages defined by automata. In the context of nonterminating reactive (finite-state) programs, this result was refined and extended in many ways during the past decade, especially for several systems of temporal logic (in place of S1S), and with the aim of obtaining more efficient decision procedures for program verification. See [CGL94] for a survey of the state-of-the-art.

However, this approach does not fully exploit the available automata theoretic results: Büchi and Landweber presented in their fundamental work [BL69] an algorithm which decides the realizability of a given specification and in this case synthesizes a circuit (or finite-state reactive program) from the specification. This result is "better" than the decidability of S1S in the sense that it is better to automatically construct a correct reactive program than to verify an existing one.

---

* This work was supported by the ESPRIT Basic Research Action 6317 ASMICS ("Algebraic and Syntactic Methods in Computer Science")

One may consider a nonterminating reactive program as a player in a two-person game against the "environment" (the second player). A play of the game is an infinite sequence of actions performed in alternation by the two players. The decision who wins is provided by a set S of plays (given by the specification, and containing plays with certain desirable properties). If for any choice of actions by the environment the program builds up a play in S, it is "correct" with respect to S. This approach was pursued in [ALW89], [PR89], among others (for more background and references we recommend [NYY92a]). However, the theory of infinite games still lacks a development regarding applications as this has been achieved for finite-state program verification. Especially more efficient algorithms for the construction of winning strategies would be useful, e.g. in control theory and "discrete event systems" ([RW89]).

We shall start with an introduction to the automata theoretic framework for studying infinite games. Here a game is specified by a "game graph" (a transition system in which the two players perform their transition steps) together with a "winning condition". We present a new proof of the Büchi-Landweber Theorem (as a construction of finite-state strategies in games over finite graphs with a winning condition of Muller type) and discuss some problems which arise for games over effectively presented infinite graphs.

I thank H. Lescow, S. Seibert and Th. Wilke, as well as the participants of the ASMICS Workshop "Transition systems with infinite behavior" (Bordeaux, November 1994), for many helpful discussions.

2 Definitions

2.1 State-based games

An abstract *infinite game* is given by an ω-language $\Gamma \subseteq A^\omega$ over an alphabet A (which is assumed to be finite in this paper). A *play* of the game is an ω-word $\alpha = a_0 a_1 a_2 \ldots$ over A, built up by two players 0 and 1 as follows: Player 0 picks a_0, player 1 picks a_1, player 0 picks a_2, and so on in alternation. The play α is won by 0 if $\alpha \in \Gamma$, otherwise the play is won by 1.

Often infinite games arise in a more concrete form than just by a set Γ of infinite words. A standard situation in computer science is the consideration of a transition system over a set of states, where actions induce steps from states to states, and plays are describable as state sequences. When ω-languages are specified by automata, this view is natural. It allows to model phenomena which are hidden in the abstract setting (assumed usually in descriptive set theory). For example, by means of states, periodicities in plays may be immediately captured by state repetitions, and also different potentials of performing actions (depending on the momentary state) are simply describable. In the following we introduce state-based games, using terminology from [Bü77], [Bü83], [GH82], [McN93], and [Ze94].

A *game graph* is of the form $G = (Q, Q_0, Q_1, A, \delta, \Omega)$ where Q is a finite or countable set of "states", Q_0, Q_1 define a partition of Q (Q_i containing the states where it is the turn of player i to perform an action), A is a finite set (of "actions"), and $\delta : Q \times A \to Q$ is a partial transition function. We require that the underlying graph is bipartite with respect to these transitions; formally, we have $\delta(Q_i \times A) \subseteq Q_{1-i}$ for $i = 0, 1$. Also for any $q \in Q$ some $a \in A$ is required where $\delta(q, a)$ is defined. Sometimes we designate a state q as "start state" and indicate the game graph by G_q.

The item Ω is an "acceptance component". In the sequel, we shall consider the cases where Ω is a state-set $F \subseteq Q$, a finite collection $\mathcal{F} = \{F_1, \ldots, F_m\}$ of state-sets, or a sequence $(E_1, F_1, \ldots, E_m, F_m)$ of sets of states from Q. We may view the states of the game graph "colored" correspondingly: a state q is colored by the 0-1-vector $c(q)$ of length 1, resp. m, resp. $2m$, where a 1 in the i-th component indicates that q belongs to the i-th set given in Ω. For a sequence $\gamma \in Q^\omega$ let $c(\gamma)$ be the sequence $c(\gamma(0))c(\gamma(1)) \ldots$ of associated colors.

For a game graph G over Q, the decision who wins a play is fixed by a subset $\mathcal{C}$ of Q^ω, which we call *winning predicate*. We write "$\mathcal{C}(\gamma)$" if γ belongs to $\mathcal{C}$. If the acceptance component of G determines a coloring in $\{0, 1\}^m$, we require that membership of γ in $\mathcal{C}$ is already fixed by the color sequence $c(\gamma) \in (\{0, 1\}^m)^\omega$. The pair $(G, \mathcal{C})$ (or $(G_q, \mathcal{C})$) is a *state-based game*. A *play* in this game is a sequence $\gamma \in Q^\omega$ such that for any two succeeding states $\gamma(i), \gamma(i+1)$ there is an action a with $\delta(\gamma(i), a) = \gamma(i+1)$ (and such that $\gamma(0) = q$ if we deal with G_q). Player 0 *wins* the play γ if $\gamma \in \mathcal{C}$, otherwise player 1 wins.

A game $(G_q, \mathcal{C})$ may be considered as a (possibly infinite) ω-automaton, defining the ω-language which consists of all sequences $\alpha \in A^\omega$ which induce a play won by player 0.

A useful representation of a game $(G_q, \mathcal{C})$ is the unravelling of G_q in tree form, as *game tree* $t(G_q)$, which is again a game graph: Its states are the sequences $q_0 \ldots q_r$ which are possible initial segments of plays in G_q, and its transition function δ' is defined by $\delta'(q_0 \ldots q_r, a) = q_0 \ldots q_r \delta(q_r, a)$. The winning set $\mathcal{C}$ is adapted accordingly (referencing only q_r from a state $q_0 \ldots q_r$, but indicated again by $\mathcal{C}$). We call the game $(t(G_q), \mathcal{C})$ the *tree representation* of $(G_q, \mathcal{C})$.

2.2 Winning conditions

A *winning condition* is a formula (involving atomic formulas $c(\gamma(i)) = c_l$ for colors c_l) which defines a winning predicate $\mathcal{C}$. The most basic conditions refer to acceptance components of the form $\Omega = F$ (inducing a coloring in $\{0, 1\}$):

- $\mathcal{C}(\gamma) :\equiv \exists i \; \gamma(i) \in F$ (formally: $\exists i \; c(\gamma(i)) = 1$)   ($\Sigma_1^0$-*condition*),
- $\mathcal{C}(\gamma) :\equiv \forall i \; \gamma(i) \in F$ (Π_1^0-*condition*),
- $\mathcal{C}(\gamma) :\equiv \exists j \forall i \geq j \; \gamma(i) \in F$ (short: $\forall^\omega i \; \gamma(i) \in F$)   ($\Sigma_2^0$-*condition*),
- $\mathcal{C}(\gamma) :\equiv \forall j \exists i > j \; \gamma(i) \in F$ (short: $\exists^\omega i \; \gamma(i) \in F$)   ($\Pi_2^0$-*condition*).

For $k = 1, 2$, a game specified with a Σ_k^0-condition (Π_k^0-condition) is called a Σ_k^0-game (Π_k^0-game). More general winning conditions are first-order formulas with atomic formulas $R(i_1, \ldots, i_n)$ for any numerical relations R besides the atomic formulas $c(\gamma(i)) = c_l$; they define the finite-Borel games (where the winning predicate occurs on a finite level of the Borel hierarchy). The prefix of unbounded quantifiers in the prenex normal form of such a formula gives a bound for the level of the defined winning predicate in the Borel hierarchy.

An important class of games consists of the $\mathcal{B}(\Sigma_2^0)$-games, where the winning sets are defined by Boolean combinations of Σ_2^0-conditions. We use here two forms, namely, for acceptance components $\mathcal{F} = \{F_1, \ldots, F_m\}$

$$\mathcal{C}(\gamma) :\equiv \{f \mid \exists^\omega i \; \gamma(i) = f\} \in \mathcal{F} \quad (\textit{Muller condition}),$$

and for acceptance components $(E_1, F_1, \ldots, E_m, F_m)$

$$\mathcal{C}(\gamma) :\equiv \bigvee_{k=1}^m (\exists^{<\omega} \gamma(i) \in E_k \wedge \exists^\omega i \; \gamma(i) \in F_k) \quad (\textit{Rabin condition}).$$

These $\mathcal{B}(\Sigma_2^0)$-conditions are of special interest because they allow the specification of many properties which are relevant in concurrent systems (e.g. fairness properties, cf. [MP92]). Moreover, if games are considered as ω-automata, and games defining the same ω-language are regarded as equivalent, it is possible for finite-state games to reduce arbitrary S1S definable winning conditions to the Rabin condition and to the Muller condition (see, for example, [Th90]).

2.3 Strategies and Determinacy

A *strategy* for player 0, resp. 1, in the game $(G_q, \mathcal{C})$ as given above is a function σ which associates with any node $q_0 \ldots q_r$ of the game tree $t(G_q)$ (where $q_r \in Q_0$, resp. $q_r \in Q_1$) one of its successors in the game tree. A strategy σ thus determines a *fragment* of the game tree, obtained from the game tree by deleting all nodes ending in Q_1, resp. Q_0, which are not values of σ, together with their descendants. Let us denote this *strategy tree* by $t_\sigma(G_q)$. The function σ is called *winning strategy* for 0, resp. 1 in $(G_q, \mathcal{C})$ if for all paths γ through $t_\sigma(G_q)$ we have $\gamma \in \mathcal{C}$. (In this paper we do not consider *nondeterministic strategies*, as done in [GH82], [YY90], [Ze94].)

The existence of winning strategies is a central subject in descriptive set theory (see e.g. [Mos80]). The predominant question there is that of *determinacy*: For which games is it possible to guarantee that one of the two players has a winning strategy? If this holds the game is called *determined*. Determinacy is a powerful principle of complementation and hence important in mathematical logic: Nonexistence of a winning strategy for one player implies existence of a winning strategy for the other player. By a deep result of Martin [Ma75], a game is determined if its winning predicate is Borel. The games considered in this paper are all given with Borel winning predicates and hence determined.

In the questions of determinacy and complementation, the two players are handled symmetrically. For most applications in distributed systems, however, one identifies the players with two parties which are handled asymmetrically: one of them represents the program (or "control", here identified with player 0), the other represents the environment (or "disturbance", here identified with player 1). Then it is more interesting that player 0 has a winning strategy than just one of the two players. For example, an operating system (player 0) should function in an arbitrary or even hostile environment (player 1). Determinacy is helpful or necessary, however, in proofs that a strategy construction is complete, or when an induction refers to "smaller" games where a strategy can be guaranteed just for one of the players (and not for a fixed one).

We are mainly interested in the effective presentation and the easy execution of strategies for a given player, assuming that the games are presented as finite objects. For instance, we consider recursive games. (Such a game would be specified by an algorithm which allows to compute predecessors and successors of the nodes in the game tree, their colors, and their association with players 0 and 1.) For effectively presented games (of a given type), the following questions arise:

1. Does player 0 have a winning strategy?
2. Is there an effective (or efficient) construction of winning strategies for player 0 from game presentations?
3. How to construct winning strategies of low computational complexity?

The second question is concerned with the *construction* of winning strategies, the third one with the *execution* of strategies. In the former case an effective or efficient transformation from representations of games to representations of strategies is required, while in the latter case efficient algorithms to compute values of strategies (i.e., values of word functions σ over the state space) are asked for.

In the simplest case, where a value $\sigma(q_0 \ldots q_r)$ of a strategy only depends on the last state q_r, we speak of a *no-memory strategy*. Such strategies are representable as fragments of the game graphs: For example, a no-memory strategy for player 0 is specified by keeping only a single edge from any state of Q_0 in a game graph over Q. If a strategy σ is computable by a finite automaton (say by a Moore automaton), it is called a finite-memory strategy or *finite-state strategy*. Another important type of strategy is that of *recursive* (effectively executable) strategies.

3　Finite-state games

In this section we outline an "incremental" proof of the Büchi-Landweber Theorem of [BL69]: Given a finite-state game with Muller winning condition, the partition of the state space into the sets of states from which player 0, resp. player 1, wins is computable, and corresponding winning strategies are effectively constructible as finite-state strategies. We proceed in four steps, covering winning conditions of inceasing difficulty (Σ_1^0- and Π_2^0-condition, a special type of Rabin condition, and the Muller condition).

3.1　Σ_1^0- and Π_2^0-games

The first step deals with Σ_1^0-games. For a game graph $G = (Q, Q_0, Q_1, A, \delta, F)$, we have to determine the set of those states from which player 0 can force a visit of some state in F. This is done by computing, for $i \geq 0$, the sets W_i of states from which a visit in F can be forced in at most i steps. Clearly we have $W_0 = F$ and

$$W_{i+1} = W_i \cup \{p \in Q_0 \mid \exists a \in A\; \delta(p, a) \in W_i\}$$
$$\cup \{p \in Q_1 \mid \forall a \in A\; \delta(p, a) \in W_i \text{ if defined}\}.$$

Since the sequence (W_i) is increasing and Q is finite, there is some k where this sequence becomes constant and is the union of the W_i. Let Reach(F) be W_k for the first such k. It is easy to see this set contains the states from which 0 wins the game. The winning strategy is best described by the ranking of states as determined by the sets W_i (the rank of $p \in$ Reach(F) being the smallest i such that $p \in W_i$). Now the strategy just has to ensure that the rank decreases with each step, which can be done by deleting all edges violating this condition. We obtain a no-memory strategy. A no-memory strategy for the opposite player 1 applies to any state in $Q_1 \setminus$ Reach(F), specifying a transition to a target state again outside Reach(F) (which exists by definition of Reach(F)).

In the second step we treat Π_2^0-games, again given by game graphs of the form $G = (Q, Q_0, Q_1, A, \delta, F)$. We determine the states from which infinitely many visits of F can be forced by player 0 (and skip here the proof that player 1 wins from the remaining states). For this, we first compute the states from F (forming a set Recur(F)) which allow player 0 to force infinitely many revisits of F. In an auxiliary step we define, for any given state set V, the set of states from which a single revisit in V can be forced in ≥ 1 steps. For this purpose, one modifies the definition of the sets W_i above. Let

$$W_1' = \{p \in Q_0 \mid \exists a \in A\; \delta(p, a) \in V\}$$
$$\cup \{p \in Q_1 \mid \forall a \in A\; \delta(p, a) \in V \text{ if defined}\}$$

and obtain W_{i+1}' from W_i' as W_{i+1} from W_i above. Let us denote by Reach$^+(V)$ the first set W_k' such that $W_k = W_{k+1}'$; precisely from its states a visit of V can be forced by player 0 in ≥ 1 steps. Now let V_i be the set of states from which player 0 can force at least i visits to F. We have

$$V_1 = F, \quad V_{i+1} = V_i \cap \text{Reach}^+(V_i)$$

The sequence (V_i) is decreasing. Let Recur(F) be their intersection, i.e., V_l for the smallest l with $V_l = V_{l+1}$. In the considered Π_2^0-game, player 0 has now a winning strategy from those states which are in Reach(Recur(F)). Again it is a no-memory strategy by the inductive definition of the sets W_i' (where one imposes to stay within V_l when it is entered).

3.2 $\mathcal{B}(\Sigma_2^0)$-games

We discuss $\mathcal{B}(\Sigma_2^0)$-games in two stages. The first refers to the so-called *Rabin chain condition* ([Mst84]), the second to the Muller condition. A Rabin chain condition over a state set Q is given by a sequence $(E_1, F_1, \ldots, E_m, F_m)$ with the extra property that $E_1 \subset F_1 \subset \ldots \subset E_m \subset F_m\ (\subseteq Q)$. As in Section 2.2, the winning condition requires for a play $\gamma \in Q^\omega$ that for some k, infinitely visits in F_k occur but only finitely many visits in E_k (finally excluding E_k).

The construction of no-memory strategies for games with such winning conditions works by induction on the size of the state space. We follow a construction of McNaughton ([McN93, Thm. 6.2]), given there for winning conditions of a related form (Muller conditions "without splits"). The claim is that any game graph with Rabin chain winning condition allows a partition into two sets W_0, W_1 such that player i has a no-memory winning strategy from the states in W_i.

Consider the game graph $G = (Q, Q_0, Q_1, A, \delta, \Omega)$ with acceptance component $\Omega = (E_1, F_1, \ldots, E_m, F_m)$. If $|Q| \le 2$ the claim is trivial. In the induction step, assume that $E_1 = \emptyset$, i.e., F_1 is the first nonempty entry in Ω (otherwise switch players 0 and 1). Pick $q \in F_1$. Then infinitely many visits of q suffice to ensure a win of player 0. (Note that, by the chain condition and minimality of F_1, there is no way to extend $\{q\}$ to a set of infinitely often visited states that causes a win of player 1.) One verifies that $Q \setminus \text{Reach}(\{q\})$ is again a game graph G_0; thus the induction hypothesis yields a partition of this game graph into sets V_0, V_1 such that player i has a no-memory winning strategy in G_0 playing from states in V_i.

We now distinguish the following two (complementary!) cases: Either player 0 can force a direct transition from q to $Q \setminus V_1$, or player 1 can force a direct transition to V_1. We claim that in the first case, the states from which 0 wins are those in $Q \setminus V_1$ (which is the set $\text{Reach}(\{q\}) \cup V_0$): Player 0 works from any state in $\text{Reach}(\{q\})$ towards q and (by case 1) proceeds to V_0 where the existing winning strategy is applied as long as player 1 allows to stay in V_0. If 1 chooses to leave V_0, then necessarily by a transition into $\text{Reach}(\{q\})$ which means 0 can force a visit to q again. (Transitions from V_0 to V_1 by player 1 are impossible by the induction hypothesis on the game graph G_0.) Thus, player 1 only has the options to remain in V_0 from some moment onwards or to pass through q again and again. In either option, player 0 wins (using an extension of the given no-memory strategy on V_0 to a no-memory strategy also on $\text{Reach}(\{q\})$). The required winning strategy for 1 is the one given by the induction hypothesis.

It remains to treat the case that player 1 can force a direct transition from q into V_1. Consider all states (including q, of course) from which player 1 can force a visit in V_1 over the game graph G. Call this set V; on V there is a no-memory winning strategy for 1. The complement of V in G turns out to be a game graph to which (by absence of q) again the induction hypothesis can be applied. Its decomposition into two sets U_0, U_1 yields the desired partition of G, namely U_0 as the set of states from which 0 wins, and $V \cup U_1$ as the set of states from which 1 wins, both by a no-memory strategy.

Finally, we consider $\mathcal{B}(\Sigma_2^0)$-games presented with the Muller winning condition. Here a collection $\mathcal{F} = \{F_1, \ldots, F_m\}$ of state sets is given, and the winning condition for player 0 requires that the states visited infinitely often in a play form one of the sets F_k. (Thus, only loops, i.e. strongly connected state sets, are reasonable candidates of such sets F_k.) Let us verify that winning strategies without memory do not suffice, by considering the example game graph displayed in the figure. The even-numbered circles represent the states in Q_0, the odd-numbered boxes those of Q_1. We suppress the labels on edges (actions).

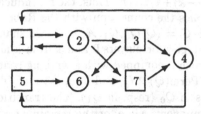

Since all possible loops are uniquely determined by their odd-numbered states, we name the final state sets just by their odd-numbered elements. Suppose the loops $\{1,3\}$ and $\{1,3,5,7\}$ are those in which player 0 wins (defining the set $\mathcal{F}$). Then a no-memory strategy would have to select one edge at state 4, but any of the two possible choices would enable player 1 to win (obviously for the choice of 5, and for the choice of state 1 by passing from 3 to 6 when state 3 is reached).

A little contemplation will show that at state 4 it should be known how it was reached: If 4 was reached directly from 3, then a good choice is to go to state 1 and from 2 always to 3, which means that upon repetition of this process the loop $\{1,3\}$ is assumed forever and player 0 wins. If, however, state 4 is reached from 3 via 6 and 7, then it is advisable to force a visit of all odd-numbered states: first 5 and again 7, then 1 and 3. This can be executed, for example, by a memory which always records the last two visits to odd-numbered states. (Assuming that player 0 moves from 2 always to 3, there are three possibilities of last visits at state 4: $(1,3)$, $(5,7)$, and $(3,7)$. The first two cases require a transition to state 1, the last case a transition to 5.) Altogether the strategy is implementable by a Moore automaton and hence finite-state.

The record on last visits of states is a basic tool for building strategies: it is found under the name *later appearance record* LAR in [GH82], *order-vector* in [Bü83], and *latest visitation record* in [McN93]. For a general construction, we shall use the LAR here in an extended form following [Bü83]: Over the state-set $Q = \{1,\ldots,n\}$, an LAR with *hit position* is a permutation $(i_1,\ldots,i_n)$ of $(1,\ldots,n)$ together with a number h from $\{1,\ldots,n\}$ (the "hit"). We write this as an n-tuple where position h is underlined and identify the set of all these extended vectors with $\mathrm{Perm}(Q) \times Q$. Formally, we introduce the extended LAR of a finite state-sequence inductively: For the empty sequence ε over $Q = \{1,\ldots,n\}$, $\mathrm{LAR}(\varepsilon)$ is $(1,\ldots,\underline{n})$. For a state sequence $s.q$, $\mathrm{LAR}(s.q)$ is obtained by taking q from its position j in $\mathrm{LAR}(s)$ towards the end, and setting the hit to be j. So the hit records from which place onwards in an LAR a change has just occurred. In our example above (disregarding again all even-numbered states), a repeated tour through the loop $\{1,3\}$ will lead to LAR-values $(5,7,\underline{1},3)$ and $(5,7,\underline{3},1)$, whereas the repeated tour through all states will set the hit to the first position again and again. Using the hit position, a set F can be fixed as containing precisely the states visited infinitely often, in the following way (assuming $|F| = k$): From some moment onwards, the hit stays $\geq (n - k) + 1$, and infinitely often the hit is $(n - k) + 1$ with the elements of F (in some order) on the LAR positions $(n-k)+1, \ldots, n$. Thus, the hit induces a scale for the final sets by size (which supplies the connection with the Rabin chain condition).

Given a game graph $G = (Q, Q_0, Q_1, A, \delta, \mathcal{F})$, we shall extract the desired finite-state winning strategies for players 0 and 1 from a new game graph $G' = (Q', Q'_0, Q'_1, A, \delta', \Omega)$, which is equipped with a winning condition in Rabin chain form. We set $Q' = Q \times \mathrm{Perm}(Q) \times Q$, and let a state of Q' be in Q'_0 (resp. Q'_1) iff its first component is in Q_0 (resp. in Q_1). The transition function δ' copies δ regarding the first component, while for the remaining components δ' realizes the update of the LAR as explained above. A play γ over G thus corresponds to a play γ' over G', using the initial LAR for the first state $\gamma'(0)$. We shall define the acceptance component Ω in Rabin chain form such that the following equivalence holds:

A play γ over G is won by player 0 (resp. player 1) iff the corresponding play γ' over G' is won by player 0 (resp. player 1).

Using this, we can apply the previous strategy construction to G' (since over G' the winning condition is in Rabin chain form) and obtain a no-memory strategy for any $q' \in Q'$ where there is a winning strategy for player 0 (resp. player 1) in $G'_{q'}$ at all. The strategy is obtained by deleting certain transitions in G', which in turn defines the desired finite-state strategy over G (since the storage and updates of the extended LAR can be realized by a finite automaton).

It remains to establish the above equivalence. For this, we assume $|Q| = n$ and define a chain $\Omega = (E_1, F_1, \ldots, E_n, F_n)$ of subsets of Q. Let E_j contain all states from Q' where the LAR part has a hit value smaller than j, and let F_j be the union of E_j with the set of states from Q' where this hit value is precisely j and the LAR-entries from the hit position onwards form a set in $\mathcal{F}$. (We obtain a proper inclusion chain by merging E_j and E_{j+1} if $F_j \setminus E_j = \emptyset$, resp. F_j and F_{j+1} if $E_{j+1} \setminus F_j = \emptyset$.) It is now easy to verify the claimed equivalence, which completes the strategy construction for finite-state $\mathcal{B}(\Sigma_2^0)$-games.

In our example above, we could work just with the set of odd-numbered states in place of Q. In [McN93], such a set W of "relevant states" is introduced in general: It contains just enough states for the distinction between final and non-final loops. We see from the proof above that in a game over Q with a Muller condition over a set W of relevant states, the winner has a winning strategy requiring a memory of size $|W|! \cdot |W|$. A recent (and quite different) proof of S. Seibert ([Se94]) gives a proper exponential upper bound of $4^{|W|}$ for the memory. Examples of H. Lescow and S. Seibert show that for some constant c, $c^{|W|}$ is a lower bound for the memory size of the winner. It would be interesting to know classes of games (or winning conditions) where the winner has a polynomial size (however non-zero memory) winning strategy.

The proof above shows that the Rabin chain condition is a useful intermediate step in handling games (or automata) with the Muller condition. We see how the game presentations are related to the memory-size in winning strategies: When game graphs are considered as ω-automata, the transformation of automata with Muller acceptance to those with Rabin chain acceptance involves a blow-up in the state space which supplies exactly the memory suitable to win games with Muller winning condition as compared to the (zero) memory for games with Rabin chain condition.

The Rabin chain condition was introduced by Mostowski in [Mst84] but remained rather unnoticed. It was applied independently for obtaining no-memory strategies in [Mst91a] and [EJ91] (where it is called "parity condition"). The simulation of Muller acceptance using Büchi's version of the LAR, as presented here, yields smaller transition graphs with Rabin chain condition than previous constructions in [Mst91b] and [Ca94].

Gurevich and Harrington showed the much more general result that strategies with an LAR memory suffice for $\mathcal{B}(\Sigma_2^0)$-games even over infinite graphs ("Forgetful Determinacy Theorem" [GH82], [YY90], [Ze94]). By lack of space we cannot enter this interesting subject here. For example, fixed point constructions (as above in Section 3.1 for the finite-state case) require now ordinal-indexed sets. Games of this form can be applied to obtain the complementation of Rabin tree automata (as proposed by Büchi [Bü77], [Bü83]). Several approaches have been developed to obtain transparent proofs; as recent references, besides the papers listed above, we mention [EJ91], [Mu92], [Kl94], [MS94].

4   Games over pushdown transition graphs and recursive graphs

The subject of this section is still in its beginnings: effective winning strategies (and their construction) for games on effectively presented infinite graphs.

A natural first step after finite-state games is to consider games over transition graphs of deterministic pushdown automata. Here each node corresponds to a global state of a pushdown automaton, given by the content of the pushdown store and the state of the finite control. These are *context-free graphs* in the sense of Muller and Schupp ([MS85]), also called "context-free processes" in semantics of concurrency, and their unravellings in tree form are the *algebraic trees* in the sense of [Co83]. As Courcelle has shown in [Co94], the monadic second-order theory of an algebraic tree is decidable. This result can be applied to games over algebraic trees where the winning conditions are expressible in monadic second-order logic. In this case, the existence of a winning strategy is expressed by a monadic second-order sentence about the game tree, saying "there is a fragment of the game tree defining a strategy, such that for each path through the fragment, the winning condition is satisfied". (Analogously, the Büchi-Landweber-Theorem can be shown using finite tree automata over infinite trees and the effective solution of their emptiness problem, cf. [Ra72].) One should expect that from the decidability proof of [Co94] also an effective construction of a winning strategy can be extracted (if such a strategy exists); however, this sharpened claim and a complexity analysis are presently open.

In contrast to the finite-state case, there are now natural winning conditions which are no more monadic second-order definable and occur at higher Borel levels than $\mathcal{B}(\Sigma_2^0)$. An example is the winning condition on paths through a pushdown transition graph which requires that some pushdown content (possibly with an extra property) occurs infinitely often. The condition is in Σ_3^0-form, and it seems interesting to decide the existence of winning strategies for a given player, to analyze if and when these strategies are recursive, and to construct the strategies effectively. So far, only Büchi's work [Bü83] on $(\Sigma_3^0 \cap \Pi_3^0)$-games seems to be available on this subject. (In such games, it can also be appropriate to admit infinitely many colors, e.g. representing the infinitely many pushdown contents, in order to reformulate the winning condition.)

In *recursive games*, the construction of effective strategies may fail even for Π_2^0-winning conditions. To verify this, consider the following game tree t:

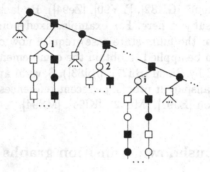

The tree is defined using the halting problem for Turing machines in the following way: Below the node named i in the figure, we have a switch of colors (as indicated) on the k-th level of the two branches iff the i-th Turing machine M_i halts on the empty tape after k steps. Clearly the tree t is recursive. Consider the game $(t, \mathcal{C})$ with winning condition "$\mathcal{C}(\gamma) :\equiv \exists^\omega n \ \gamma(n)$ is colored black". It is obvious that a winning strategy for 0 in this game is recursive iff the halting problem for Turing machines is recursive (because at node i a strategy has to fix a decision which is equivalent to the decision whether M_i eventually halts).

A more drastic statement can be obtained from the following recursion theoretic result: There is a nonempty Π_2^0-ω-language $L \subseteq \{0,1\}^\omega$ such that no ω-word $\gamma \in L$ is hyperarithmetical, i.e., for any $\gamma \in L$ the numbers i with $\gamma(i) = 1$ form a set of natural numbers outside Δ_1^1. (See e.g. [Mos80, 4.D.10], using that in the Cantor space $\{0,1\}^\omega$, Σ_1^1-sets are projections of Π_2^0-sets.) Such an ω-language L contains the ω-words $\alpha \in \{0,1\}^\omega$ such that $\exists^\omega i \ \alpha(0) \ldots \alpha(i) \in R$ for a certain recursive set R; L induces a full binary recursive game tree t_L where the root is associated with player 0 and a node $a_1 a_2 \ldots a_{2i} a_{2i+1} \in \{0,1\}^+$ is colored "black" iff $a_1 a_3 \ldots a_{2i+1} \in R$. A strategy for 0 defines a path γ through t_L and is of the same recursion theoretic degree as γ. Using again the winning condition "$\mathcal{C}(\gamma) :\equiv \exists^\omega n \ \gamma(n)$ is black", there is a winning strategy for 0 (because $L \neq \emptyset$), but none which is hyperarithmetical.

As above for context-free games, special but natural classes of recursive games should be found such that there are recursive winning strategies, which moreover should be obtained effectively from the game presentations.

5 Conclusion

We conclude with a remark on two general research directions which were not touched in this paper.

For applications in control systems, it is important to connect the discrete model considered above with the possibility of continuous changes of parameters in time. References on games over such "hybrid systems" are [NYY92b] and [MPS94].

Finally, we mention a somewhat vague problem: Is there a logical framework for the specification of games such that winning strategies can be built up in a "compositional" manner? The present automata theoretic methodology uses two nontrivial and often impractical transformations when starting from logical specifications: First the conversion of logical formulas to automata (and game graphs), which is costly when the specifications involve many quantifier alternations, secondly the conversion of game graphs to strategies, which can be costly for games with $B(\Sigma_2^0)$-winning conditions. A logic of system specification which would allow to construct strategies more directly (at least in some interesting cases) would be both of theoretical and practical value.

References

[ALW89] M. Abadi, L. Lamport, P. Wolper, Realizable and unrealizable specifications of reactive systems, in: *Proc. 17th ICALP* (G. Ausiello et al., eds.), Lecture Notes in Computer Science **372** (1989), Springer-Verlag, Berlin 1989, pp. 1-17.

[Bü62] J.R. Büchi, On a decision method in restricted second order arithmetic, in: *Proc. Int. Congr. Logic, Method. and Philos. of Science* (E. Nagel et al., eds.), Stanford Univ. Press, Stanford 1962, pp. 1-11.

[Bü77] J.R. Büchi, Using determinacy to eliminate quantifiers, in: *Fundamentals of Computation Theory* (M. Karpinski, ed.), Lecture Notes in Computer Science 56, Springer-Verlag, Berlin 1977, pp. 367-378.

[Bü83] J.R. Büchi, State-strategies for games in $F_{\sigma\delta} \cap G_{\delta\sigma}$, *J. Symb. Logic* **48** (1983), 1171-1198.

[BL69] J.R. Büchi, L.H. Landweber, Solving sequential conditions by finite-state strategies, *Trans. Amer. Math. Soc.* **138** (1969), 295-311.

[Ca94] O. Carton, Chain automata, in: *Technology and Applications*, Information Processing '94, Vol. I (B. Pherson, I. Simon, eds.), IFIP, North-Holland, Amsterdam 1994, pp. 451-458.

[Ch63] A. Church, Logic, arithmetic and automata, *Proc. Intern. Congr. Math. 1962*, Almqvist and Wiksells, Uppsala 1963, pp. 21-35.

[CGL94] E. Clarke, O. Grumberg, D. Long, Verification tools for finite-state concurrent systems, in: *A Decade of Concurrency* (J.W. de Bakker et al., eds.), Lecture Notes in Computer Science **803**, Springer-Verlag, Berlin 1994, pp. 124-175.

[Co83] B. Courcelle, Fundamental properties of infinite trees, *Theor. Comput. Sci.* **25** (1983), 95-169.

[Co94]   B. Courcelle, The monadic second-order theory of graphs IX: Machines and their behaviours, Techn. Report, LaBRI; Université Bordeaux I, 1994.

[EJ91]   E.A. Emerson, C.S. Jutla, Tree automata, Mu-calculus and determinacy, in: *Proc. 32th Symp. on Foundations of Computer Science* (1991), 368-377.

[GH82]   Y. Gurevich, L. Harrington, Trees, automata, and games, in: *Proc. 14th ACM Symp. on the Theory of Computing*, San Francisco, 1982, pp. 60-65.

[Kl94]   N. Klarlund, Progress measures, immediate determinacy, and a subset construction for tree automata, *Ann. Pure Appl. Logic* **69** (1994), 243-168.

[Ma75]   D. Martin, Borel determinacy, *Ann. Math.* **102** (1975), 363-371.

[McN93] R. McNaughton, Infinite games played on finite graphs, *Ann. Pure Appl. Logic* **65** (1993), 149-184.

[MP92]   Z. Manna, A. Pnueli, *The Temporal Logic of Reactive and Concurrent Programs*, Springer-Verlag, Berin, Heidelberg, New York 1992.

[Mos80] Y. N. Moschovakis, *Descriptive Set Theory*, North-Holland, Amsterdam 1980.

[MPS94] O. Maler, A. Pnueli, J. Sifakis, On the synthesis of discrete controllers for timed systems, these Proceedings.

[Mst84] A.W. Mostowski, Regular expressions for infinite trees and a standard form of automata, in: A. Skowron (ed.), *Computation Theory*, Lecture Notes in Computer Science **208**, Springer-Verlag, Berlin 1984, pp. 157-168.

[Mst91a] A.W. Mostowski, Games with forbidden positions, Preprint No. 78, Uniwersytet Gdański, Instytyt Matematyki, 1991.

[Mst91b] A.W. Mostowski, Hierarchies of weak automata and weak monadic formulas, *Theor. Comput. Sci.* **83** (1991), 323-335.

[Mu92]   A. Muchnik, Games on infinite trees and automata with dead-ends. A new proof for the decidability of the monadic second-order theory of two successors, *Bull. of the EATCS* **48** (1992), 220-267.

[MS85]   D.E. Muller, P.E. Schupp, The theory of ends, pushdown automata, and second-order logic, *Theor. Comput. Sci.* **37** (1985), 51-75.

[MS94]   D.E. Muller, P.E. Schupp, Simulating alternating tree automata by nondeterministic automata: new results and new proofs of the theorems of Rabin, McNaughton and Safra, *Theor. Comput. Sci.* (to appear).

[NYY92a] A. Nerode, A. Yakhnis, V. Yakhnis, Concurrent programs as strategies in games, in: *Logic from Computer Science* (Y. Moschovakis, ed.), Springer, 1992.

[NYY92b] A. Nerode, A. Yakhnis, V. Yakhnis, Modelling hybrid systems as games, in: *Proc. 31st IEEE Conf. on Decision and Control*, Tucson, pp. 2947-2952.

[PR89]   A. Pnueli, R. Rosner, On the synthesis of a reactive module, in: *Proc. 16th ACM Symp. on Principles of Progr. Lang.*, Austin, pp. 179-190.

[Ra72]   M.O. Rabin, Automata on infinite objects and Church's Problem, Amer. Math. Soc., Providence, RI, 1972.

[RW89]   P.J.G. Ramadge, W.M. Wonham, The control of discrete event systems, *Proc. of the IEEE* **77** (1989), 81-98.

[Se94]   S. Seibert, Doctoral Thesis, in preparation.

[Th90]   W. Thomas, Automata on infinite objects, in: J. v. Leeuwen (ed.), *Handbook of Theoretical Computer Science*, Vol. B., Elsevier Science Publ., Amsterdam 1990, pp. 133-191.

[YY90]   A. Yakhnis, V. Yakhnis, Extension of Gurevich-Harrington's restricted memory determinacy theorem: A criterion for the winning player and an explicit class of winning strategies, *Ann. Pure Appl. Logic* **48** (1990), 277-297.

[Ze94]   S. Zeitman, Unforgettable forgetful determinacy, *J. Logic Computation* **4** (1994), 273-283.

Finding the Maximum with Linear Error Probabilities: a sequential analysis approach

Guy Louchard

Université Libre de Bruxelles - Département d'Informatique, Boulevard du Triomphe CP 212, B-1050 Bruxelles (Belgique), louchard@ulb.ac.be

Abstract. Assume that n players are represented by n reals, uniformly distributed over the unit interval.

We assume that the error probability of a comparison game between two players depends linearly on the distance between the players. Using sequential analysis approach, we present an algorithm to estimate the maximum ξ of the players with an error less than ε.

Mean cost, variance and centered moments generating function are analyzed.

1 Introduction

The usual tournament used for finding ξ, the best of n players assumes that each game played is won by the better of the two players involved. Our concern here is to deal with occasional errors. One question is how to define a model for the errors. Several people have done work on the topic. In particular, Feige et al. [3] have studied a probabilistic model, where the outcome of games are independent, random and correct with fixed probability $1 - p$. However, this is somewhat unrealistic: the outcome of a game between the best and second best players should clearly be much more random than between the best and the worst players.

Other authors (see for instance Adler et al. [1], where a rather complete bibliography can be found that we don't reproduce here) use preference scheme based on a winning matrix $p_{i,j}$. They usually assume: $p_{best,j} > \frac{1}{2}$ (no draws). But the best two players can be very close together.

In this paper, we study a model in which the error of a game depends on the values of the players involved.

More precisely, the players are n reals between 0 and 1; all the games are independant; a game between x and z gives x as the winner with probability $(1 + (x - z))/2$. Thus if x is better than z, then x will win with probability barely more than $1/2$ if z is very close to x, and with probability almost 1 if z is the worst player and x the best player.

For the purpose of our analysis, we will in addition assume that the players are uniformly distributed over the unit interval. The operations are (possibly erroneous) comparisons between players.

Of course, one cannot compute the maximum ξ with certainty, since there is always a slight probability that most of the comparisons will be erroneous. Thus our goal is to compute an element which is the maximum with probability at least $1 - \varepsilon$, where ε is a parameter.

Another important difference with other results in the literature is that we want to obtain a detailed asymptotic analysis for the cost $\mathcal{T}$: not only the mean but, when possible, the variance (when $\mathcal{T}$ is a random variable) and even the complete distribution. Usually, only $O(\varphi(n, \varepsilon))$ are derived for $E[\mathcal{T}]$ in classical results (and sometimes, only worst case is considered).

We shall use here a sequential analysis approach (see Sec.4 for a short description).

In the second Section, we study how classical tournament algorithms perform in this model of errors. We show that they behave really poorly in term of the cost $\mathcal{T}$.

In Sections 3, 4 and 5 we present an algorithm for finding the maximum with confidence $1 - \varepsilon$, based on sequential analysis, which, after several refinements leads to a mean cost $E[\mathcal{T}] = C[\frac{n \log_2^2 n}{\varepsilon}(ln^{(2)}(n) + ln(1/\varepsilon))]$.

In Section 6 we analyze the variance and in Section 7 the centered moments generating functions. Section 8 concludes the paper.

MAPLE was in great help in computing several complicated expansions.

2 Poor performance of classical tournaments

In this section, we analyze classical tournaments, mainly in order to set up the probabilistic tools and to pave the way to further sequential analysis techniques.

2.1 Algorithm I

All n values (or keys) are assumed to be uniform $[0, 1]$ i. i. d. random variables (R.V), $\xi :=$ maximum value of the n keys. At each comparison, we assume that the probability p of correct answer is given by $p = (y + 1)/2$, where y is the difference of the values of the players being compared. Let us analyze the following algorithm, which is a variation on the classical tournament: the n keys (we assume $n = 2^H$) are divided into pairs. Each pair plays a number of games, and the player who loses the most games is eliminated. The winners are again divided into pairs, and so on. We can picture the tree as shown in Figure 1. We note that $j = n/2^i :=$ number of leafs descending from each node.

We will use indifferently i or j, following ease of formulation. At each level i, the max ξ (if it has won all previous competitions) is compared to the winner of $j = n/2^i$ keys (independent of ξ). If we make a large number $N(j)$ of comparisons, then we obtain an error probability $\varepsilon(j)$ by choosing $N(j)$ in the following way. Let $K_1 > K_2$. We make N comparisons and decide that $K_1 > K_2$ if the total number Y of Yes-answers is $> N/2$. Let $y = K_1 - K_2$.

(In the sequel the distance between two compared keys will always be denoted by y). Then the number Y of correct answers is a Bernoulli variable, which

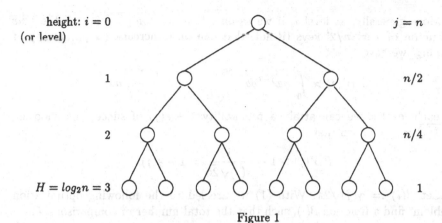

Figure 1

approaches a normal distribution, with mean value $N(j)(1+y)/2$ and variance $N(j)(1-y^2)/4$.

$$\tilde{Y} := \frac{Y - N(j)(1+y)/2}{\sqrt{N(j)}\sqrt{(1-y^2)/4}} \overset{\mathcal{D}}{\sim} \mathcal{N}(0,1)$$

where $\mathcal{N}(m,\sigma^2)$ is the standard Gaussian R.V. with mean m and variance σ^2 and $\overset{\mathcal{D}}{\sim}$ means convergence in distribution. So we must choose $N(j)$ so that

$$Pr\{Y > N(j)/2\} = Pr\{\tilde{Y} > -y\sqrt{N(j)}/\sqrt{1-y^2}\} = 1 - \varepsilon$$

Let $PW(j)$ be the probability that ξ wins at level i, conditioned on the value of ξ. At level H, we compare ξ with a key with uniform distribution in $[0,\xi]$. But $\xi \sim 1 - O(\frac{1}{n})$. Unless other mention, $\sim$ means: asymptotic to, $n \to \infty$. So $PW(1)$ is given by

$$PW(1) \sim \int_0^1 dx \int_{-y\sqrt{N(1)}/\sqrt{1-y^2}}^{\alpha} \frac{e^{-z^2/2}}{\sqrt{2\pi}} dz,$$

with $y = (1-x)\xi$. For ease of notation, we define

$$M(j) := N(j)\xi^2. \tag{1}$$

Since $\sqrt{1-y^2} < 1$, we have:

$$PW(1) > \int_0^1 dx \int_{-\sqrt{M(1)}(1-x)}^{\alpha} \frac{e^{-z^2/2}}{\sqrt{2\pi}} dz$$

The contribution of $\sqrt{1-y^2}$ is analyzed in [6].

More generally, at level i, if we assume that we compare ξ with the *true* maximum of $j := n/2^i$ keys (if not, that can only increase ξ's probability of winning, we have

$$PW(j) > \int_0^1 jx^{j-1}dx \int_{-\sqrt{M(j)}(1-x)}^{\propto} \frac{e^{-z^2/2}}{\sqrt{2\pi}}dz.$$

At each level i, we can attain a probability $1 - \varepsilon(j)$ of success by choosing $\sqrt{M(j)} = \gamma(j)j$ such that

$$PW(j) > 1 - \frac{1}{\gamma(j)\sqrt{2\pi}} = 1 - \varepsilon(j).$$

Let $\beta(i) := \gamma(j)\sqrt{2\pi}$. With (1) we are led to the following optimization problem: find a function $\beta(\cdot)$, such that the total number of comparisons T:

$$T = \sum_{i=1}^H \frac{M(j)}{\xi^2}\frac{2^i}{2} = \sum_1^H \frac{n^2}{2^i}\beta^2(i)/(4\pi\xi^2) \text{ is minimum,} \tag{2}$$

under the constraint

$$\prod_1^H \left(1 - \frac{1}{\beta(i)}\right) = 1 - \varepsilon \quad \text{or} \quad \sum_1^H \left(-\frac{1}{\beta(i)}\right) \sim -\varepsilon.$$

By Euler summation formula, and Euler-Lagrange (E.L.), the number of comparisons is given by

$$N(j) \sim 9n^2 / \left[2\pi 2^{2/3}\xi^2\varepsilon^2 ln^2 2 \ 2^{4i/3}\right]$$

and the total cost, by (2), is given by

$$T \sim \frac{n^2 27}{8\pi ln^3 2 \ \varepsilon^2\xi^2}. \tag{3}$$

2.2 Algorithm II

Instead of letting two nearly equal players play together, it has been noticed by several authors (see for instance Adler et al. [1] Sec.1) that it can be more discriminating to let them play against a weak third player.

Assume that we compare two keys, $u \le v, (v - u = y \ge 0)$ with a third key $z < u$. We make each comparison $\frac{N}{2}$ times, with Y_2 Yes-answers for $v(Y_1$ for $u)$. We derive

$$\frac{2(Y_2 - Y_1) - \frac{N}{2}y}{\sqrt{N/2}\sqrt{\varphi(u,v,z)}} \overset{\mathcal{D}}{\sim} \mathcal{N}(0,1) \tag{4}$$

$\varphi(u,v,z) := 1 - (v - z)^2 + 1 - (u - z)^2$.

Obviously, to compare v and u with the best efficiency, we must use, when possible, $z = 0$. Assume that we possess this null key. We obtain

$$N(j) \sim \frac{2}{\pi\xi^2}\left(\frac{log_2 n}{\varepsilon}\right)^2 \left(\frac{1}{n} + \frac{1}{j}\right)j^2 = \frac{2}{\pi\xi^2}\left(\frac{log_2 n}{\varepsilon}\right)^2 \frac{n(2^i + 1)}{2^{2i}}$$

and $T \sim nlog_2^3 n/(\xi^2\pi\varepsilon^2)$.

2.3   Algorithm III

Of course, we usually don't possess key $z = 0$. Let us, in a first stage, estimate z, the min of n^α keys, $(\alpha < 1)$ with Algorithm I. From (3) this costs $O\left(\frac{n^{2\alpha}}{\varepsilon^2}\right)$.

After that, in a second stage, we use Algorithm II. $\varphi(u, v, z)$ in (4) becomes

$$\sim 1 - \left(1 - \frac{1}{n} - \frac{1}{n^\alpha}\right)^2 + 1 - \left(1 - \frac{1}{j} - \frac{1}{n^\alpha}\right)^2 \sim 2\left(\frac{1}{j} + \frac{2}{n^\alpha}\right).$$

The cost leads to

$$\mathcal{T} \sim \frac{n^2}{\xi^2 \pi} \sum_1^H \frac{\beta^2(i)}{2^i}\left[\frac{2}{n^\alpha} + \frac{2^i}{n}\right]$$

and we finally derive $\mathcal{T} = O(\frac{n^{4/3}}{\varepsilon^2})$ which is only a small improvment on Algorithm I.

2.4   Algorithm IV

Let us try to improve Algorithm III in the following way. We start as Algorithm I on the bottom of the tree, estimating together the max and the min, until we reach some level I. After that, we use Algorithm II, at each level i, with $z :=$ any value among the estimated min at level i (we keep computing the min at each level with Algorithm II). At level i we do not yet know the min at this level (for that, we need the max ξ at level i) but min at level $i + 1$ is asymptotically equivalent for using Algorithm II.

Theorem 2.1 *To compute the maximum ξ of n keys with an error less than ε, the total cost $\mathcal{T}$ is given by the table:*

Algorithm	I	II	III	IV
Cost	$\frac{27n^2}{8\pi ln^3 2\varepsilon^2 \xi^2}$	$\frac{n log_2^3 n}{\xi^2 \pi \varepsilon^2}$	$\frac{27n^{4/3}}{8\pi ln^3 2\varepsilon^2 \xi^2} + \frac{C_4^3 n^{4/3}}{\pi \varepsilon^2 \xi^2}$	$\frac{2C_7^3 n log_2^3 n}{\pi \xi^2 \varepsilon^2}$

□

Obviously Algorithm IV is the best but still not very efficient: ε^2 induces an unbearable cost.

3   Sequential approach-Algorithm SI

Let us first describe a classical sequential approach to discriminate between to possible values p and $1 - p$ of a Binomial R.V. parameter (See for instance Gosh and Sen [4] for a general description of sequential analysis).

If we fix p and we if compute $D_k := \#(\text{Yes}) - \#(\text{No})$ after k tests, the sequential approach chooses two barriers a and $-a$ and stop when D_k reaches a or $-a$. From results on Brownian motions (see for instance Darling and Siegert [2]), we know that $(p > q, q := 1 - p)$

$$a = \frac{2pq}{p - q} ln\left(\frac{1 - \varepsilon}{\varepsilon}\right)$$

if we want a level of confidence $1 - \varepsilon$.

The presence of a $ln(\frac{1}{\varepsilon})$ factor is classical in standard tournaments. However, here, we have a density which does not exclude two equal players. We will see that this induces a $1/\varepsilon$ factor in our final best algorithm.

Let us return to our sequential analysis approach. More generally, for a random walk with mean μ and variance σ^2 for each step, the asymptotic probability of reaching the barrier a before $-a$ is given, for $a \gg 1$, by $1 - \frac{1}{\alpha+1}$. With $\alpha := e^{2a\mu/\sigma^2}$, the mean hitting time (i.e. the cost) is given by

$$E(T_{a,a}) = \frac{a}{\mu}\left[\frac{\alpha-1}{\alpha+1}\right] \qquad (5)$$

Darling and Siegert have computed the Laplace Transform of the Brownian Motion hitting time $T_{a,b}$ for two barriers $a > 0, b < 0$. With

$$\xi_1, \xi_2 := \frac{\mu \pm \sqrt{\mu^2 + 2\sigma^2\lambda}}{\sigma^2}$$

they obtain

$$E[e^{-\lambda T_{ab}}] = (e^{\xi_1 b} - e^{\xi_2 b} - e^{\xi_1 a} + e^{\xi_2 a})/(e^{\xi_2 a + \xi_1 b} - e^{\xi_1 a + \xi_2 b}). \qquad (6)$$

From (6), setting $b = -a$, we derive

$$S_2 := E[T_{a,a}^2] = a[-6a\mu\alpha + \alpha^2(a\mu + \sigma^2) - \sigma^2 + a\mu]/[(1+\alpha)^2\mu^3] \qquad (7)$$

3.1 Comparing ξ with the maximum of j keys

a) Let us first consider the case $j \gg 1$ and choose for D_k the barriers $a(j)$ and $-a(j)$. It is well known that the density jx^{j-1} can be approximated by e^{-u}, with $1 - x = u/j$. (As in Sec.2, $y = (1-x)\xi$). This gives

$$p = \frac{1}{2}\left[\frac{u}{j}\xi + 1\right], \qquad \mu = p - q = y = \frac{u}{j}\xi, \qquad \sigma^2 = 4pq \sim 1$$

So we obtain

$$1 - \varepsilon(j) \sim \int_0^\infty du\, e^{-u}[1 - e^{-2a(j)u\xi/j}] = 1 - \frac{1}{1 + 2a(j)\xi/j}$$

$$\sim 1 - \frac{j}{2a(j)\xi} \qquad (8)$$

and we immediately see that we must have $j = o(a(j))$. This can be checked with Section 3.3 results.

About the mean hitting time, we derive, by setting $u = \frac{jz}{a(j)}$,

$$E[T(j)] \sim \frac{a(j)j}{\xi}\int_0^\infty e^{-zj/a(j)}\left(1 - e^{-2\xi z}\right)\left/\left(1 + e^{-2\xi z}\right)\frac{dz}{z}\right.$$

After detailed analysis (given in [6]), this leads to

$$E(T(j)) \sim \frac{a(j)j}{\xi}ln(a(j)/j) = \frac{a(j)n}{2^i\xi}ln(a(j)2^i/n) \qquad (9)$$

b) Let us now turn to the case $j = O(1)$. We obtain, with the same notations as in a)

$$\varepsilon(j) \sim \int_o^j du \left(1 - \frac{u}{j}\right)^{j-1} e^{-2a(j)u\xi/(j4pq)}$$

Again, a detailed analysis leads to the same asymptotic expression as (9). A similar computation can be done for $\mathcal{T}$.

3.2 Comparing two (independent) maxima of j keys: x_1 and x_2

Remark that, now, costs are R.V. So we must analyze these R.V. at each node, and not only on the node involving ξ. We consider both cases $j \gg 1$ and $j = O(1)$. It is shown in [6] that we get the same asymptotic expressions as in Section 3.1.

3.3 Optimization

We must choose $a(j)$ in order to minimize $E(\mathcal{T})$. By E.L. this gives

$$E(\mathcal{T}) \sim -\frac{n^2}{\varepsilon\xi^2} C_{11} ln(\varepsilon)$$

with $C_{11} := \frac{C_{10}}{2} \int_1^\infty \frac{2^{-t/2}}{\sqrt{t}} dt$.

4 Sequential approach - Algorithm SII

We will only need to consider the case $j \gg 1$. (Algorithm SII will only be used under this condition).

4.1 Comparing ξ will be the maximum of j keys

Each step involves two comparisons: we compare ξ with the min $\zeta(j)$ of j keys ($Y_2 = 1$ if we obtain a Yes-answer) and we compare the maximum of j keys with $\zeta(j)$ ($Y_1 = 1$ if we obtain a Yes-answer).

Then, it is easily checked that $E(Y_2 - Y_1) = y/2$, $\text{VAR}(Y_2 - Y_1) \sim \frac{1}{2}(\frac{1}{n} + \frac{3}{j})$. It is shown in [6] that this leads to

$$1 - \varepsilon(j) \geq 1 - \frac{2}{\xi a(j)} \tag{10}$$

and

$$E[\mathcal{T}(j)] \sim \frac{4a(j)j}{\xi} ln[a(j)]. \tag{11}$$

4.2 Comparing two (independent) maxima of j keys

This leads again to (11). Note that, by (5), we obtain

$$E[\mathcal{T}_{a,a}] \sim \frac{ja^2(j)}{2}, z \to 0, \qquad E[\mathcal{T}_{a,a}] \sim \frac{2ja^2(j)}{\xi z}, z \to \infty \tag{12}$$

5 Sequential approach - Algorithm SIV

Now we combine both algorithms: on the bottom of the tree ($i := H..I$), we use Algorithm SI, estimating together the max and the min. After that ($i := I..1$) we use Algorithm SII at each level i, with $\zeta(j) =$ any value among the estimated min at level i. Then the expected cost becomes, by (11)

$$E[T] \sim 2 \left[\sum_1^I \frac{4n^2}{2\xi} b(i) ln[nb(i)] + \frac{n^2}{2\xi} \sum_I^H b(i) ln[b(2^i) 2^i] \right]$$

with the constraint (see (8) and (10)

$$\varepsilon = \sum_1^I \frac{2}{\xi n b(i)} + \sum_I^H \frac{1}{2\xi b(i) 2^i}$$

A rather long analysis (see [6]) leads to the following theorem (C_{12} and C_{13} are constants which are detailed in [6]).

Theorem 5.1 *The expected cost of Algorithm SIV is given by*
$n \geq 1/\varepsilon$:

$$E[T] \sim \frac{2n log_2^2 n ln 2 \sqrt{2C_{12}}}{\varepsilon \xi} (ln^{(2)}(n) + ln(1/\varepsilon))$$

$n = (1/\varepsilon)^\kappa, \kappa < 1$:

$$E[T] \sim \frac{2n log_2^2 n ln 2 \sqrt{C_{13}}}{\varepsilon \xi} \left(\sqrt{2} + \frac{1}{(ln2)^{3/2}} \right) (ln^{(2)}(n) + ln(1/\varepsilon))$$

6 Variance of the cost T

Let us first analyze the variance for a fixed drift μ. (5) and (7) lead to

$$\mathrm{VAR}[T_{a,a}] = \frac{a(\sigma^2 \alpha^2 - 4a\mu\alpha - \sigma^2)}{(1+\alpha)^2 \mu^3}$$

and asymptotically, $\mathrm{VAR}[T_{a,a}] \sim \frac{a\sigma^2}{\mu^3}$, $a \to \infty$, $\mu > 0$. But this is obvious: this is exactly the asymptotic variance for the hitting time T_a of a classical B.M., with drift μ, to a *single* barrier a (see Louchard et al. [5]). It is also proved, in the same paper that, the distribution of T_a is asymptotically Gaussian and the distribution remains asymptotically Gaussian even in the presence of another barrier. But here, the drift $\downarrow 0$ as we approach the root and the analysis is more delicate. We will only treat the subcase $n \geq \frac{1}{\varepsilon}$ (see Sec.6.1), the other subcase is similarly analyzed and leads to the same asymptotic results.

6.1 Using Algorithm SI

If $j \gg 1$, we proceed as in Sec.4.1 a) and 4.2 a): we set $\mu = \xi z/a, \sigma^2 = 1$, and $\alpha = e^{2\xi z}$. It is easily checked that (7) leads to

$$S_2 \sim \frac{5}{3}a^4 - \frac{6}{5}a^4\xi^2 z^2 + .., z \to 0 \quad \text{and} \quad S_2 \sim \frac{a^4(1+\xi z)}{\xi^3 z^3}, z \to \infty.$$

So

$$E[S_2(j)] \sim \frac{j}{a(j)} \int_0^\infty e^{-zj/a(j)} S_2 dz \sim ja^3(j)f_1(\xi)\left[1 + O(\frac{1}{a^2(j)})\right]$$

with

$$f_1(\xi) := \int_0^\infty \frac{-6\alpha\xi z + \xi z\alpha^2 + \alpha^2 - 1 + \xi z}{(1+\alpha)^2(\xi z)^3}dz.$$

A similar analysis can be done if $j = O(1)$.

6.2 Using Algorithm SII

a is constant in this case. We consider only the subcase $j \gg 1$. We set here $\mu = \frac{\xi z}{2ja}, \sigma^2 = \frac{2}{j}, \alpha = e^{\xi z/2}$. This leads to

$$E[S_2(j)] \sim \frac{1}{a}\int_0^\infty e^{-z/a} S_2 dz \sim a^3 j^2 f_2(\xi)$$

with

$$f_2(\xi) := \int_0^\infty \frac{-6\alpha\xi z/2 + \xi z\alpha^2/2 + 2\alpha^2 - 2 + \xi z/2}{(1+\alpha)^2(\xi z/2)^3}dz.$$

6.3 Algorithm SIV

It is immediately checked, with (9) for Algorithm I and (11) for Algorithm II that, in both cases,

$$\text{VAR}[T(j)] \sim E[T^2(j)] = E[S_2(j)]$$

Remember also that we make two comparisons per step and that we estimate the maximum and the minimum.

To simplify the analysis, we assume that R.V. are independent from one level to the next, this is not quite correct: if we compare a very large key with a smaller one, it will win with a high probability and will win the game on the next level also with high probability. The effect of the correlation will be considered in a further work. After all computations, we obtain

$$\text{VAR}[T] \sim \frac{4C_{12}^{3/2}}{\varepsilon^3}ln^3(n)f_2(\xi)n^2 \cdot \frac{1}{2^{3/2}2ln2} \tag{13}$$

An important conclusion can be drawn from our analysis: clearly, for $i = 1..I$, the first R.V. dominate: we don't have the condition of infinite smallness (see Petrov [7] Chap. IV) which would lead to an infinitely divisible distribution (for instance a Gaussian R.V.).

So we must consider all moments of T.

7 Distribution of the cost $\mathcal{T}$

Let us return to (6) and analyze Algorithm II, $j \gg 1$.
So $\mu = \frac{\xi z}{2ja}$, $\sigma^2 = \frac{2}{j}$, $\alpha = e^{\xi z/2}$.

To obtain the distribution of $\tilde{T}(j,z) := T_{a,a}(j,z)/a^2 j$, we set $\lambda = \theta/a^2 j$. This
gives, with $R := \xi z \sqrt{1 + 16\theta/(\xi z)^2}$

$$E[e^{-\theta \tilde{T}(j,z)}] = \varphi_1(\theta, z),$$

with

$$\varphi_1(\theta, z) := \frac{(e^{-\xi z/4 - R/4} - e^{-\xi z/4 + R/4} - e^{\xi z/4 + R/4} + e^{\xi z/4 - R/4})}{e^{-R/2} - e^{R/2}}$$

For $z \to 0$, we obtain

$$\varphi_1(\theta, 0) = 2 \frac{e^{-\sqrt{\theta}} - e^{\sqrt{\theta}}}{e^{-2\sqrt{\theta}} - e^{2\sqrt{\theta}}} \sim 1 - \frac{\theta}{2} + \frac{1}{2}\frac{5}{12}\theta^2 + \cdots$$

This of course confirms (12).
For $z \to \infty$, we obtain

$$\varphi_1(\theta, z) \sim -\frac{2\theta}{\xi z} + \frac{\theta^2}{2}\left[\frac{4}{(\xi z)^2} + \frac{16}{(\xi z)^3}\right] - \frac{4}{3}\frac{48/z^2 + 12\xi/z + \xi^2}{z^3 \xi^5}\theta^3 + \cdots \quad (14)$$

which confirms (12).

Again, with (9) and (11), we immediately check that all moments are actually
asymptotically centered moments and even cumulants. So we set ($\alpha = e^{\xi z/2}$):

$$\varphi_2(\theta, z) := \varphi_1(\theta, z) - \frac{2\theta}{\xi z}\frac{\alpha - 1}{\alpha + 1} - 1$$

and $\varphi_3(\theta) = \int_0^\infty \varphi_2(\theta, z)dz$ which converges by (14), $\varphi_3(\theta) \sim \frac{\theta^2}{2}f_2(\xi) - \frac{\theta^3}{6}f_3(\xi) + \cdots$.

So the centered transform

$$E[e^{-\theta[\tilde{T}_j - E[\tilde{T}_j]]}] \sim 1 + \frac{1}{a}\int_0^a e^{-z/a}\varphi_2(\theta, z)dz \sim 1 + \frac{\varphi_3(\theta)}{a}.$$

We have seen that, for $\mathcal{T}$, the dominant contribution is due to $i = 1..I$. So
we obtain (again we assume that maximum and minimum lead to independent
R.V.).

$$E[e^{-\lambda[\mathcal{T} - E[\mathcal{T}]/2]}] \sim \prod_{i=1}^\infty [1 + \frac{1}{a}\varphi_3(\lambda a^2 \frac{n}{2^i})]^{2^i} \sim \exp[\int_1^\infty \frac{1}{a}\varphi_3(\lambda a^2 n/2^t)2^t dt]$$

or

$$E[\exp\{-\lambda[\mathcal{T} - E[\mathcal{T}]]/(2a^2 n)\}] \sim \exp[2\int_1^\infty \frac{1}{a}\varphi_3(\lambda/2^t)2^t dt] \quad (15)$$

Set $\frac{\lambda}{2^t} = w$. (15) becomes

$$\exp\left[\frac{\lambda}{aln2}\int_0^{\lambda/2}\frac{\varphi_3(w)}{w^2}dw\right] \sim 1 + \frac{\lambda}{aln2}\int_0^{\lambda/2}\frac{\varphi_3(w)}{w^2}dw \qquad (16)$$

(Remember that, asymptotically, cumulants and centered moments are equivalent). First term of (16) gives $f_2(\xi)\lambda^2/(4aln2)$ which of course confirms (13). All other moments can be immediately computed from (16). We can summarize our results in the following theorem.

Theorem 7.1 *Variance and centered moments generating function of T, for Algorithm SIV, are given by*

$$VAR(T) \sim \frac{C_1^{3/2}}{\sqrt{2}\varepsilon^3 ln2}ln^3(n)f_2(\xi)n^2$$

$$E[\exp\{-\lambda[T - E[T]]/(2a^2n)\}] \sim 1 + \frac{\lambda}{aln2}\int_0^{\lambda/2}\frac{\varphi_3(w)dw}{w^2}.$$

8 Conclusion

Using a sequential analysis approach, we have devised an algorithm for estimating the maximum among n players, represented by uniform $[0,1]$ R.V.

Many problems remain to be solved: analysing the effect of comparing ξ with the winner among j keys (instead of the true maximum of j keys), considering non-linear correct answer probability in the general algorithm, studying the correlation between levels etc. This will be the object of future work. Parallelism of some parts of the algorithm should also be considered.

Acknowledgment The author wishes to thank C. Kenyon for early comments on a preliminary version of this paper and T. Bruss for discussion on sequential analysis.

References

1. M. ADLER, P. GEMMELL, M. HARCHOL, R.M.KARP and Cl.KENYON
   Selection in the Presence of Noise: The Design of Playoff Systems
   Proc. SODA 1994, San Francisco.
2. D.A. DARLING and J.F. SIEGERT
   The First Passage Problem for a Continuous Markov Process
   An. Math. Stat. 1953, 624-639.
3. U. FEIGE, D. PELEG, P. RAGHAVAN and E. UPFAL
   Computing with Unreliable Information. In *Symposium on Theory of Computing*, 1990, 128-137.
4. B.K. GOSH and P.K. SEN
   Handbook of Sequential Analysis. Marcel Dekker, 1991.

5. G. LOUCHARD, R. SCHOTT
   Probabilistic Analysis of Some Distributed Algorithms. Wiley, Random Structures
   and Algorithms **2**, 2, 1991, 151-186.
6. G. LOUCHARD
   Finding the maximum with linear error probabilities: a sequential analysis approach, Département d'Informatique, TR-297, 1994.
7. V.V. PETROV
   Sums of Independent Random Variables
   Ergebnisse der Mathematik und ihrer Grenzgebiete. Band 82, Springer-Verlag,
   1975.

Completeness and Weak Completeness Under Polynomial-Size Circuits*

David W. Juedes[1] and Jack H. Lutz[2]

[1] Department of Computer Science, Ohio University, Athens, Ohio 45701, U.S.A.,
juedes@ohiou.edu
[2] Department of Computer Science, Iowa State University, Ames, Iowa 50011,
U.S.A., lutz@cs.iastate.edu

Abstract. This paper investigates the distribution and nonuniform complexity of problems that are complete or weakly complete for ES-PACE under nonuniform many-one reductions that are computed by polynomial-size circuits (P/Poly-many-one reductions). Every weakly P/Poly-many-one-complete problem is shown to have a dense, exponential, nonuniform complexity core. An exponential lower bound on the space-bounded Kolmogorov complexities of weakly P/Poly-Turing-complete problems is established. More importantly, the P/Poly-many-one-complete problems are shown to be *unusually simple* elements of ESPACE, in the sense that they obey nontrivial *upper* bounds on nonuniform complexity (size of nonuniform complexity cores and space-bounded Kolmogorov complexity) that are violated by almost every element of ESPACE. More generally, a Small Span Theorem for P/Poly-many-one reducibility in ESPACE is proven and used to show that every P/Poly-many-one degree —including the complete degree — has measure 0 in ESPACE. (In contrast, almost every element of ESPACE is weakly P-many-one complete.) All upper and lower bounds are shown to be tight.

1 Introduction

The most prominent structural aspect of a complexity class is the presence or absence of complete problems under efficient reducibilities. A complete problem, when it is present, contains complete information about all problems in the class, and this information is organized in such a way as to be accessible by efficient reductions.

A measure-theoretic generalization of completeness, called *weak completeness*, was proposed by Lutz [31] and has recently been a subject of several investigations [20, 34, 33, 30, 19, 4, 21, 18, 37]. Briefly, if $\leq_{\mathcal{R}}$ is an efficient reducibility and $\mathcal{C}$ is a complexity class, then a *weakly $\leq_{\mathcal{R}}$-complete* problem for $\mathcal{C}$ is a decision problem (i.e., language) $C \subseteq \{0,1\}^*$ such that $C \in \mathcal{C}$ and all the problems in a non-measure 0 subset of $\mathcal{C}$ (in the sense of resource-bounded

---

* This work was supported in part by National Science Foundation Grant CCR-9157382, with matching funds from Rockwell International, Microware Systems Corporation, and Amoco Foundation.

measure [32, 29]) are $\leq_{\mathcal{R}}$-reducible to $\mathcal{C}$. That is, a problem $C \in \mathcal{C}$ is weakly $\leq_{\mathcal{R}}$-complete for $\mathcal{C}$ if C contains complete information about all the problems in a non-negligible subset of $\mathcal{C}$, and this information is organized in such a way as to be accessible by $\leq_{\mathcal{R}}$-reductions. For classes such as $E = \mathrm{DTIME}(2^{\mathrm{linear}})$, $E_2 = \mathrm{DTIME}(2^{\mathrm{polynomial}})$, and $\mathrm{ESPACE} = \mathrm{DSPACE}(2^{\mathrm{linear}})$, that have well-understood measure structure, Lutz [30] has shown that weak $\leq_m^P$-completeness is a proper generalization of $\leq_m^P$-completeness. (See sections 2 and 3 for precise definitions of notation and terminology used in this introduction.)

Juedes and Lutz [20] began the systematic investigation of the complexity and distribution of problems that are $\leq_m^P$-complete or weakly $\leq_m^P$-complete for the exponential time complexity classes E and E_2. Main results of [20] (in the case of E) include

(i) a proof that every weakly $\leq_m^P$-complete problem for E has a dense exponential complexity core;

(ii) a proof that almost every problem in E has $\{0,1\}^*$ as an exponential complexity core;

(iii) a proof that (essentially) every exponential complexity core of every $\leq_m^P$-complete problem for E has a dense complement, whence by (ii) the set $\mathcal{C}_m^P(E)$, consisting of all problems that are $\leq_m^P$-complete for E, has measure 0 in E; and

(iv) a Small Span Theorem, which implies (among other things) that *every* $\leq_m^P$-degree has measure 0 in E.

In the present paper, we conduct a similar investigation, but we now focus on nonuniform reductions that are computed by polynomial-size circuits. Such reductions are "combinatorially efficient," even though they need not be algorithmically computable. As noted by Skyum and Valiant [42], the investigation of such reductions sheds light on the "purely combinatorial" aspects of the completeness phenomenon.

We work in the complexity class ESPACE. There are two related reasons for this choice. First, ESPACE has a rich structure that is well enough understood that we can prove absolute results, unblemished by oracles or unproven hypotheses. In particular, much is known about the Kolmogorov complexity and circuit-size complexity of languages in ESPACE[22, 32], while little is known at lower complexity levels. Our second reason for this choice is that the structure of ESPACE is closely related to the structure of polynomial complexity classes. For example, Hartmanis and Yesha [15] have shown that

$$E \subsetneq \mathrm{ESPACE} \Longleftrightarrow P \subsetneq P/\mathrm{Poly} \cap \mathrm{PSPACE}. \qquad (1.1)$$

This, together with the first reason, suggests that the separation of P from PSPACE might best be achieved by separating E from ESPACE. We thus seek a detailed, quantitative account of the nonuniform structure of ESPACE.

We work with the P/Poly-many-one reducibility ("$\leq_m^{P/\mathrm{Poly}}$-reducibility"), a nonuniform extension of the P-many-one reducibility ("$\leq_m^P$-reducibility") that was first defined by Karp [23]. The $\leq_m^{P/Poly}$-reductions are precisely those many-one reductions that can be computed by polynomial-size circuits.

Returning to the question at hand, let C be the set of all languages that are $\leq_{\mathcal{R}}$-complete for ESPACE, where $\leq_{\mathcal{R}} \in \{\leq_m^P, \leq_m^{P/Poly}\}$. Similarly, let $\mathcal{H}$ be the set of all languages that are $\leq_{\mathcal{R}}$-hard for ESPACE, so that $C = \mathcal{H} \cap$ ESPACE. We show that *every* element of $\mathcal{H}$ must obey strict upper and lower bounds on its nonuniform complexity. Moreover, (i) the upper bounds are violated by almost every language in ESPACE (in the sense of resource-bounded measure), and (ii) the bounds are tight, even when attention is restricted to C. These results imply that the $\leq_{\mathcal{R}}$-complete languages for ESPACE are *unusually simple* languages in ESPACE.

We use two measures of nonuniform complexity. These two measures are stated in terms of the density of nonuniform complexity cores and space-bounded Kolmogorov complexity. For the first measure, we use the density of a language's "largest" nonuniform complexity core. Intuitively, a *complexity core* is a set of *uniformly hard instances*. This concept was introduced by Lynch[35] and has been investigated by many others [11, 13, 38, 39, 8, 17, 40, 9, 12, etc.]. Roughly speaking, a complexity core for a language A is a fixed set K of inputs such that *every* machine whose decisions are consistent with A fails to decide efficiently on almost all elements of K.

Space-bounded Kolmogorov complexity is our second measure of nonuniform complexity. Kolmogorov complexity was introduced by Solomonoff[43], Kolmogorov[26], and Chaitin[10]. Resource-bounded Kolmogorov complexity has been investigated extensively [26, 14, 41, 27, 28, 5, 16, 25, 1, 2, 3, 31, 32, etc.]. We work with the *space-bounded Kolmogorov complexity* of languages. Roughly speaking, for $A \subseteq \{0,1\}^*$, $n \in \mathbf{N}$, and a space bound t, the space-bounded Kolmogorov complexity $KS^t(A_{=n})$ is the length of the shortest program that prints the 2^n-bit characteristic string of $A_{=n} = A \cap \{0,1\}^n$, using at most t units of workspace. Similarly, $KS^t(A_{\leq n})$ is the length of the shortest program that prints the $(2^{n+1} - 1)$-bit characteristic string of $A_{\leq n} = A \cap \{0,1\}^{\leq n}$, using at most t units of workspace.

Let us now be more precise about our main results. In section 3 we prove two new almost everywhere lower bounds on the nonuniform complexity of languages in ESPACE. First, we show that, for all $c \in \mathbf{N}$ and $\epsilon > 0$, almost every language A in ESPACE has

$$KS^{2^{cn}}(A_{=n}) > 2^n - n^\epsilon \text{ a.e.} \tag{1.2}$$

This improves the $2^n - 2^{\epsilon n}$ lower bound of [32]. Second, we show that, for all $c \in \mathbf{N}$, almost every language in ESPACE has $\{0,1\}^*$ as a DSPACE(2^{cn})/Poly-complexity core. (A language is P-bi-immune if and only if it has $\{0,1\}^*$ as a P-complexity core [7], so this can be regarded as a very strong bi-immunity property.)

In section 4 we exhibit tight lower bounds on the space-bounded Kolmogorov complexity and density of complexity cores of hard languages for ESPACE. Huynh [16] has already proven a lower bound on the Kolmogorov complexity of $\leq_T^P$-hard languages for ESPACE, namely that, for any such hard language H, there exists $\epsilon > 0$ such that

$$KS^{2^{n^{\epsilon}}}(H_{\leq n}) > 2^{n^{\epsilon}} \text{ a.e.} \tag{1.3}$$

Here we strengthen Huynh's result by proving that (1.3) holds for every *weakly* $\leq_T^{P/Poly}$-*hard* language H for ESPACE, i.e., for every H to which more than a measure 0 set of the languages in ESPACE are $\leq_T^{P/Poly}$-reducible.

Lower bounds on the densities of complexity cores for hard languages have already been proven by Orponen and Schöning [39] and Huynh [17]. In particular, Huynh [17] proved that every language that is $\leq_m^P$-hard for ESPACE has a dense P/Poly-complexity core. In section 4, we strengthen Huynh's result by proving that, for every weakly $\leq_m^{P/Poly}$-hard language H for ESPACE, there exists $\epsilon > 0$ such that H has a dense DSPACE($2^{n^{\epsilon}}$)/Poly-complexity core.

In section 5 we exhibit tight upper bounds on the nonuniform complexity of hard languages for ESPACE. We prove that for every $\leq_m^{P/Poly}$-hard language H for ESPACE, there exists $\epsilon > 0$ such that $KS^{2^{2n}}(H_{=n}) < 2^n - 2^{n^{\epsilon}}$ i.o. We also prove that every DSPACE(2^{2n})/Poly-complexity core of every $\leq_m^{P/Poly}$-hard language for ESPACE has a dense complement.

By combining our upper bound results from section 5 with the almost everywhere lower bound results of section 3, we conclude that the $\leq_m^{P/Poly}$-complete languages are *unusually simple* languages in ESPACE. Hence the $\leq_m^{P/Poly}$-complete languages form a measure 0 subset of ESPACE. More generally, in section 5, we prove a Small Span Theorem for $\leq_m^{P/Poly}$-reducibility in ESPACE. Given a language A, the *lower* $\leq_m^{P/Poly}$-*span* of A is the set of all languages that are $\leq_m^{P/Poly}$-reducible to A, and the *upper* $\leq_m^{P/Poly}$-*span* of A is the set of all languages to which A is $\leq_m^{P/Poly}$-reducible. Our Small Span Theorem says that, for every $A \in$ ESPACE, at least one of these spans has measure 0 in ESPACE. This result implies that *every* $\leq_m^{P/Poly}$-degree — including the complete $\leq_m^{P/Poly}$-degree — has measure 0 in ESPACE.

Although our results are similar *in form* to those of [20], the nonuniform nature of the reductions and complexity measures force us to use quite different methods in the present paper.

2 Preliminaries

When a property $\phi(n)$ of the natural numbers is true for all but finitely many $n \in \mathbf{N}$, we say that $\phi(n)$ holds *almost everywhere (a.e.)*. Similarly, $\phi(n)$ holds *infinitely often (i.o.)*, if $\phi(n)$ is true for infinitely many $n \in \mathbf{N}$. We write $[\![\phi]\!]$ for the Boolean value of a condition ϕ. That is, $[\![\phi]\!] = 1$ if ϕ is true, 0 if ϕ is false.

If $x \in \{0,1\}^*$ is a string, we write $|x|$ for the *length* of x. If $A \subseteq \{0,1\}^*$ is a language, then we write A^c, $A_{\leq n}$, and $A_{=n}$ for $\{0,1\}^* - A$, $A \cap \{0,1\}^{\leq n}$, and $A \cap \{0,1\}^n$ respectively. The sequence of strings over $\{0,1\}$, $s_0 = \lambda, s_1 = 0, s_2 = 1, s_3 = 00, ...$, is referred to as the standard enumeration of $\{0,1\}^*$.

The *characteristic sequence* of a language $A \subseteq \{0,1\}^*$ is the infinite binary sequence $\chi_A \in \{0,1\}^\infty$ defined by $\chi_A[i] = [\![s_i \in A]\!]$ for all $i \in \mathbf{N}$. The *characteristic string* of $A_{\leq n}$ is the N-bit string $\chi_{A_{\leq n}} = \chi_A[0..N-1]$, where $N = |\{0,1\}^{\leq n}| = 2^{n+1} - 1$. Similarly, the characteristic string of $A_{=n}$ is the 2^n-bit string $\chi_{A_{=n}} = \chi_A[2^n - 1..2^{n+1} - 2]$.

If A is a finite set, we denote its cardinality by $|A|$. A language D is *dense* if there exists some constant $\epsilon > 0$ such that $|D_{\leq n}| > 2^{n^\epsilon}$ a.e. A language S is *sparse* if there exists a polynomial p such that $|S_{\leq n}| \leq p(n)$ a.e..

We work primarily with the class $\text{ESPACE} = \bigcup\limits_{c=0}^{\infty} \text{DSPACE}(2^{cn})$. The exponential time class is $\text{E} = \bigcup\limits_{c=0}^{\infty} \text{DTIME}(2^{cn})$. The complexity classes P, NP, and PSPACE that were mentioned in section 1 have standard definitions. (See [6], for example.)

We model nonuniform computation in terms of machines that take advice. An *advice function* is a function $h : \mathbf{N} \to \{0,1\}^*$. If M is a machine and h is an advice function, then language accepted by the *machine/advice pair* M/h is the set $L(M/h) = \{x \in \{0,1\}^* \mid \langle x, h(|x|) \rangle \in L(M)\}$. We use the functions $time_{M/h}(x)$ and $space_{M/h}(x)$ to denote the number of steps and tape cells, respectively that the machine M takes on input $\langle x, h(|x|) \rangle$.

We are especially interested in machines that take polynomially bounded advice. If $t : \mathbf{N} \to \mathbf{N}$ is a time-bound, then $\text{DTIME}(t(n))/\text{Poly}$ is the set of languages A for which there exists a machine M, constant c, and polynomially bounded advice function h such that $L(M/h) = A$ and $time_{M/h}(x) \leq c \cdot t(|x|) + c$ for every $x \in \{0,1\}^*$. The classes $\text{DSPACE}(s(n))/\text{Poly}$, $\text{DTIME}^A(t(n))/\text{Poly}$, and $\text{DSPACE}^A(t(n))/\text{Poly}$ are defined similarly. The class P/Poly is defined as the union over all polynomials p of the $\text{DTIME}(p(n))/\text{Poly}$ classes. It is well-known [24] that P/Poly consists exactly of those languages that are computed by polynomial-size Boolean circuits.

3 The Distribution of Nonuniform Complexity

In this section we investigate the distribution of languages that have *high nonuniform complexity*. We use space-bounded Kolmogorov complexity and nonuniform complexity cores as measures of nonuniform complexity. The main results of this section show that almost every language in ESPACE is very complex with respect to each of these measures. Specifically, we prove that almost every language A in ESPACE has space-bounded Kolmogorov complexity $KS^{2^{cn}}(A_{=n}) > 2^n - \sqrt{n}$ for almost every n and that almost every language in ESPACE has $\{0,1\}^*$ as a $\text{DSPACE}(2^{cn})/\text{Poly}$-complexity core.

The distribution of languages in ESPACE with high Kolmogorov complexity was first investigated in [32]. Here we strengthen the results of [32] in two directions. First, we show that the almost everywhere lower bound of $2^{n+1} - 2^{\epsilon n}$ on $KS^{2^{cn}}(A_{\leq n})$ is tight and cannot be improved (see Theorem 3.3). Next, we improve the almost everywhere lower bound on $KS^{2^{cn}}(A_{=n})$ from $2^n - 2^{\epsilon n}$ to

$2^n - n^\epsilon$ (Corollary 3.5). (Recall from the introduction that $KS^{2^{cn}}(A_{=n})$ and $KS^{2^{cn}}(A_{\leq n})$ are the 2^{cn}-space bounded Kolmogorov complexities of $\chi_{A_{=n}}$ and $\chi_{A_{\leq n}}$, respectively.)

Theorem 3.1 (Lutz [32]). Let $c \in \mathbf{N}$ and $\epsilon > 0$.

(a) If $X = \{A \subseteq \{0,1\}^* \mid KS^{2^{cn}}(A_{=n}) > 2^n - 2^{\epsilon n} \text{ a.e.}\}$, then $\mu_{\text{pspace}}(X) = \mu(X \mid \text{ESPACE}) = 1$.

(b) If $Y = \{A \subseteq \{0,1\}^* \mid KS^{2^{cn}}(A_{\leq n}) > 2^{n+1} - 2^{\epsilon n} \text{ a.e.}\}$, then $\mu_{\text{pspace}}(Y) = \mu(Y \mid \text{ESPACE}) = 1$.

Here we ask the natural question: Can the almost everywhere lower bounds of Theorem 3.1 be improved? Consider Theorem 3.1(b). Martin-Löf [36] has shown that, for every real $a > 1$, almost every language $A \subseteq \{0,1\}^*$ has space-bounded Kolmogorov complexity

$$KS^{2^{cn}}(A_{\leq n}) > 2^{n+1} - an \text{ a.e.} \tag{3.1}$$

(In fact, Martin-Löf showed that this holds even in the absence of a space bound.) The following known bounds show that the lower bound (3.1) is relatively tight.

Theorem 3.2. There exist constants $c_1, c_2 \in \mathbf{N}$ such that every language A satisfies the following two conditions.

(i) $KS^{2^n}(A_{\leq n}) < 2^{n+1} + c_1$ for all n.
(ii) $KS^{2^{c_2 n}}(A_{\leq n}) < 2^{n+1} - \log n + c_1$ i.o.

(Part (i) of Theorem 3.2 is well known and obvious. Part (ii) extends a result of Martin-Löf [36].)

Since the bound of Theorem 3.1(b) is considerably lower than that of (3.1), one might expect to improve Theorem 3.1(b). However, the following upper bound shows that Theorem 3.1(b) is also tight. (In comparing Theorems 3.1(b) and 3.3 it is critical to note the order in which A and ϵ are quantified.)

Theorem 3.3. For every language $A \in \text{ESPACE}$, there exists a real $\epsilon > 0$ such that $KS^{2^{2n}}(A_{\leq n}) < 2^{n+1} - 2^{\epsilon n}$ a.e.

Thus we cannot hope to improve Theorem 3.1(b).

An elementary counting argument shows that, for every $c \in \mathbf{N}$, there *exists* a language $A \in \text{ESPACE}$ with $KS^{2^{cn}}(A_{=n}) \geq 2^n$ for all $n \in \mathbf{N}$. This suggests that the prospect for improving Theorem 3.1(a) may be more hopeful. In fact, we have the following almost everywhere lower bound result. (The notion of p-convergence of a series is defined in [32].)

Theorem 3.4. Let $c \in \mathbf{N}$ and let $f : \mathbf{N} \to \mathbf{N}$ be such that $f \in \text{pspace}$ and $\sum_{n=0}^{\infty} 2^{-f(n)}$ is p-convergent. If $X = \{A \subseteq \{0,1\}^* \mid KS^{2^{cn}}(A_{=n}) > 2^n - f(n) \text{ a.e.}\}$, then $\mu_{\text{pspace}}(X) = \mu(X \mid \text{ESPACE}) = 1$.

Corollary 3.5. Let $c \in \mathbf{N}$ and $\epsilon > 0$. If $X = \{A \subseteq \{0,1\}^* \mid KS^{2^{cn}}(A_{=n}) > 2^n - n^\epsilon \text{ a.e.}\}$, then $\mu_{\text{pspace}}(X) = \mu(X \mid \text{ESPACE}) = 1$.

Corollary 3.5 is a substantial improvement of Theorem 3.1(a).

We now turn our attention to complexity cores. The notion of nonuniform complexity cores was first defined and investigated by Huynh [17]. Here we use a modified version of the original definition.

Given a machine M, an advice function h, and an input $x \in \{0,1\}^*$, we write $M/h(x) = 1$ if M accepts $\langle x, h(|x|) \rangle$, $M/h(x) = 0$ if M rejects $\langle x, h(|x|) \rangle$, and $M(x) = \perp$ in any other case (i.e., if M fails to halt or M halts without deciding $\langle x, h(|x|) \rangle$). If $M(x) \in \{0,1\}$, we write $space_{M/h}(x)$ for the number of steps used in the computation of $M(\langle x, h(|x|) \rangle)$. If $M(x) = \perp$, we define $space_{M/h}(x) = \infty$. We partially order the set $\{0,1,\perp\}$ by $\perp < 0$ and $\perp < 1$, with 0 and 1 incomparable. A machine/advice pair M/h is *consistent* with a language $A \subseteq \{0,1\}^*$ if $M/h(x) \leq [x \in A]$ for all $x \in \{0,1\}^*$.

Definition (Huynh [17]). Let $s : \mathbf{N} \to \mathbf{N}$ be a space bound and let $A, K \subseteq \{0,1\}^*$. Then K is a DSPACE($s(n)$)/Poly-*complexity core* of A if, for every $c \in \mathbf{N}$ the following holds. For every machine M and polynomially bounded advice function h, if M/h is consistent with A, then the fast set

$$F = \{x \mid space_{M/h}(x) \leq c \cdot s(|x|) + c\}$$

has the property that $|F \cap K|$ is sparse.

Intuitively, very complex languages must have large nonuniform complexity cores. This intuition is supported by the following technical lemma.

Lemma 3.6. If $s : \mathbf{N} \to \mathbf{N}$ is space constructible and p is a polynomial, then every language A with $KS^{n \cdot s(n)}(A_{=n}) > 2^n - p(n)$ a.e. has $\{0,1\}^*$ as a DSPACE($s(n)$)/Poly-complexity core.

Since almost every language in ESPACE has high space-bounded Kolmogorov complexity almost everywhere, Lemma 3.6 allows us to conclude that almost every language in ESPACE has maximal nonuniform complexity cores.

Corollary 3.7. Fix $c \in \mathbf{N}$. Then, almost every language in ESPACE has $\{0,1\}^*$ as a DSPACE(2^{cn})/Poly-complexity core.

4 Nonuniform Complexity of Weakly Hard Problems: Lower Bounds

In the previous section we saw that almost every language in ESPACE is maximally complex with respect to two measures of nonuniform complexity. In this section we show that every weakly $\leq_m^{P/Poly}$-hard language for ESPACE obeys tight lower bounds on its complexity in terms of these complexity measures. (Recall that a language H is weakly $\leq_m^{P/Poly}$-hard for ESPACE if the set

$$P/Poly_m(H) = \{A \subseteq \{0,1\}^* \mid A \leq_m^{P/Poly} H\}$$

does not have measure 0 in ESPACE.) Our first result shows that every weakly $\leq_m^{P/Poly}$-hard language for ESPACE has a dense DSPACE(2^{n^ϵ})-complexity core. This result extends work of Huynh [17].

Theorem 4.1. For every weakly $\leq_m^{P/Poly}$-hard language H for ESPACE, there is a real $\epsilon > 0$ such that H has a dense DSPACE(2^{n^ϵ})/Poly complexity core.

Corollary 4.2 (Huynh [17]). Every $\leq_m^P$-hard language for ESPACE has a dense P/Poly-complexity core.

Our next theorem provides a lower bound on the Kolmogorov complexity of weakly $\leq_T^{P/Poly}$-hard languages for ESPACE. This result extends another result of Huynh [16].

Theorem 4.3. For every weakly $\leq_T^{P/Poly}$-hard language H for ESPACE, there exists an $\epsilon > 0$ such that $KS^{2^{n^\epsilon}}(H_{\leq n}) > 2^{n^\epsilon}$ a.e.

Corollary 4.4 (Huynh[16]). For every $\leq_T^P$-hard language H for ESPACE, there exists an $\epsilon > 0$ such that $KS^{2^{n^\epsilon}}(H_{\leq n}) > 2^{n^\epsilon}$ a.e.

Note that Theorems 4.1 and 4.3 cannot be significantly improved.

5 Nonuniform Complexity of Hard Problems: Upper Bounds

In the previous section, we saw that each weakly $\leq_m^{P/Poly}$-hard language for ESPACE obeys an exponential lower bound on its nonuniform complexity. This fact is not too surprising, since each weakly hard language contains complete information about a nonnegligible subset of ESPACE. Here we show a more surprising fact, namely, that each $\leq_m^{P/Poly}$-hard language obeys a nontrivial *upper* bound on its nonuniform complexity. This upper bound, in combination with the almost-everywhere lower bound from section 3, allows us to conclude that the $\leq_m^{P/Poly}$-hard languages for ESPACE are *unusually simple*.

In Theorem 5.1, we show that every $\leq_m^{P/Poly}$-hard language for ESPACE is DSPACE(2^{2n})/Poly-decidable on a dense, DSPACE(2^{2n})/Poly-decidable set of inputs. This implies that that every DSPACE(2^{2n})/Poly-complexity core of every $\leq_m^{P/Poly}$-hard language for ESPACE has a dense complement. In Theorem

5.3, we show that every $\leq_m^{P/Poly}$-hard language has space-bounded Kolmogorov complexity

$$KS^{2^{3n}}(H_{=n}) < 2^n - 2^{n^\epsilon} \text{ i.o.}$$

for some $\epsilon > 0$. Our results allow us to conclude in Theorem 5.5 that the $\leq_m^{P/Poly}$-complete languages for ESPACE form a measure 0 subset of ESPACE.

In the latter part of this section we show that Theorem 5.5 is a special case of a more general phenomenon. Specifically, we prove a Small Span Theorem (Theorem 5.6), which states that every language $A \in$ ESPACE has a least one of following two properties:

(i) The lower $\leq_m^{P/Poly}$-span of A, consisting of all languages that are $\leq_m^{P/Poly}$-reducible to A, has measure 0 in ESPACE.

(ii) The upper $\leq_m^{P/Poly}$-span of A, consisting of all languages to which A is $\leq_m^{P/Poly}$-reducible, has pspace-measure 0, hence measure 0 in ESPACE.

The Small Span Theorem has several immediate consequences. First, it implies that *every* P/Poly-many-one degree has measure 0 in ESPACE (Theorem 5.7). Second, it implies that P/Poly has measure 0 in ESPACE, a fact that was originally proven by Lutz [32]. Finally, it implies that the set of $\leq_m^{P/Poly}$-complete languages for ESPACE has measure 0 in ESPACE.

We begin this section by establishing a nontrivial upper bound on the size of nonuniform complexity cores for the $\leq_m^{P/Poly}$-hard languages for ESPACE. We start by presenting the following useful theorem, which says that every $\leq_m^{P/Poly}$-hard language for ESPACE is DSPACE(2^{2n})/Poly-decidable on a dense, DSPACE(2^{2n})/Poly-decidable set of inputs.

Theorem 5.1. For every $\leq_m^{P/Poly}$-hard language H for ESPACE, there exist $B, D \in$ DSPACE(2^{2n})/Poly such that D is dense and $B = H \cap D$. □

We now have our upper bound on the sizes of complexity cores of $\leq_m^{P/Poly}$-hard languages for ESPACE.

Theorem 5.2. Every DSPACE(2^{2n})/Poly-complexity core K of every $\leq_m^{P/Poly}$-hard language for ESPACE has a dense complement. □

We also use Theorem 5.1 to show that every $\leq_m^{P/Poly}$-hard language for ESPACE has unusually low space-bounded Kolmogorov complexity infinitely often.

Theorem 5.3. For every $\leq_m^{P/Poly}$-hard language H for ESPACE, there exists an $\epsilon > 0$ such that

$$KS^{2^{3n}}(H_{=n}) < 2^n - 2^{n^\epsilon} \text{ i.o.}$$

Theorems 5.2 and 5.3 cannot be significantly improved.

By Corollaries 3.5 and 3.7, almost every element of ESPACE fails to obey the upper bounds given by Theorems 5.2 and 5.3. Thus, with respect to the size of nonuniform complexity cores and space-bounded Kolmogorov complexity, the $\leq_{\mathrm{m}}^{\mathrm{P/Poly}}$-complete languages are *unusually simple* elements of ESPACE.

Ambos-Spies, Terwijn, and Zheng [4] showed that almost every language in E is weakly $\leq_{\mathrm{m}}^{\mathrm{P}}$-complete for E. Their method can be routinely adapted to show that almost every language in ESPACE is weakly $\leq_{\mathrm{m}}^{\mathrm{P}}$-complete for ESPACE. It follows that upper bounds on nonuniform complexity given by Theorems 5.1 and 5.2 do *not* hold for all weakly $\leq_{\mathrm{m}}^{\mathrm{P}}$-complete languages for ESPACE. This also yields the following.

Corollary 5.4. There is a language that is weakly $\leq_{\mathrm{m}}^{\mathrm{P}}$-complete, but not $\leq_{\mathrm{m}}^{\mathrm{P/Poly}}$-complete, for ESPACE.

As we have seen in Corollaries 3.5 and 3.7, almost every language in ESPACE has very high space-bounded Kolmogorov complexity almost everywhere and the set $\{0,1\}^*$ as a DSPACE(2^{cn})/Poly-complexity core. In this section we have shown that the $\leq_{\mathrm{m}}^{\mathrm{P/Poly}}$-hard languages do not satisfy these conditions. We conclude that the $\leq_{\mathrm{m}}^{\mathrm{P/Poly}}$-hard languages are unusually simple.

Theorem 5.5. Let $\mathcal{H}_{\mathrm{ESPACE}}$, $\mathcal{C}_{\mathrm{ESPACE}}$ be the sets of languages that are $\leq_{\mathrm{m}}^{\mathrm{P/Poly}}$-hard, $\leq_{\mathrm{m}}^{\mathrm{P/Poly}}$-complete, respectively, for ESPACE. Then $\mathcal{H}_{\mathrm{ESPACE}}$ has pspace-measure 0, and hence $\mathcal{C}_{\mathrm{ESPACE}}$ is a measure 0 subset of ESPACE.

An examination of the proofs leading up to Theorem 5.5 reveals that there is a fixed language A with the property that the set of languages that A is $\leq_{\mathrm{m}}^{\mathrm{P/Poly}}$-reducible to has measure 0 in ESPACE. This fact is a special case of a more general phenomenon. For any fixed language $A \in$ ESPACE, either the set of languages that A is $\leq_{\mathrm{m}}^{\mathrm{P/Poly}}$-reducible to or the set of languages that are $\leq_{\mathrm{m}}^{\mathrm{P/Poly}}$-reducible to A has measure 0 in ESPACE. We refer to this phenomenon as the "small span phenomenon." Before we present our "small span" result we require some notation. Recall from section 5 that we defined the *lower span* of a language $B \subseteq \{0,1\}^*$ under an arbitrary reducibility $\leq_{\mathcal{R}}$ to be $\mathcal{R}(B) = \{A \subseteq \{0,1\}^* \mid A \leq_{\mathcal{R}} B\}$. Here we define the *upper span* of a language $B \subseteq \{0,1\}^*$ under an arbitrary reducibility $\leq_{\mathcal{R}}$ to be $\mathcal{R}^{-1}(B) = \{A \subseteq \{0,1\}^* \mid B \leq_{\mathcal{R}} A\}$. Furthermore, we define the $\mathcal{R}$-*degree* of a language $B \subseteq \{0,1\}^*$ to be $\deg_{\mathcal{R}}(B) = \mathcal{R}(B) \cap \mathcal{R}^{-1}(B)$.

Theorem 5.6 (Small Span Theorem). For every $A \in$ ESPACE, either
(a) $\mu_{\mathrm{pspace}}((\mathrm{P/Poly})_{\mathrm{m}}^{-1}(A)) = \mu((\mathrm{P/Poly})_{\mathrm{m}}^{-1}(A) \mid \mathrm{ESPACE}) = 0$ or
(b) $\mu((\mathrm{P/Poly})_{\mathrm{m}}(A) \mid \mathrm{ESPACE}) = 0$.

The Small Span Theorem has several consequences. Most notably, Theorem 5.6 implies that *every* P/Poly-many-one degree has measure 0 in ESPACE.

Theorem 5.7. For all $A \subseteq \{0,1\}^*$, $\mu(\deg_{\mathrm{m}}^{\mathrm{p/poly}}(A) \mid \mathrm{ESPACE}) = 0$.

Note that $\deg_{\mathrm{m}}^{\mathrm{p/poly}}(\{0\}) = \mathrm{P/Poly}$, so Theorem 5.7 generalizes the known fact [32] that P/Poly has measure 0 in ESPACE.

References

1. E. Allender and R. Rubinstein. P-printable sets. *SIAM Journal on Computing*, 17:1193–1202, 1988.
2. E. W. Allender. Some consequences of the existence of pseudorandom generators. *Journal of Computer and System Sciences*, 39:101–124, 1989.
3. E. W. Allender and O. Watanabe. Kolmogorov complexity and degrees of tally sets. *Information and Computation*, 86:160–178, 1990.
4. K. Ambos-Spies, S. A. Terwijn, and Zheng Xizhong. Resource bounded randomness and weakly complete problems. In *Proceedings of the Fifth Annual International Symposium on Algorithms and Computation*, pages 369–377. Springer-Verlag, 1994.
5. J. L. Balcázar and R. V. Book. Sets with small generalized Kolmogorov complexity. *Acta Informatica*, 23:679–688, 1986.
6. J. L. Balcázar, J. Díaz, and J. Gabarró. *Structural Complexity I*. Springer-Verlag, Berlin, 1988.
7. J. L. Balcázar and U. Schöning. Bi-immune sets for complexity classes. *Mathematical Systems Theory*, 18:1–10, 1985.
8. R. Book and D.-Z. Du. The existence and density of generalized complexity cores. *Journal of the ACM*, 34:718–730, 1987.
9. R. Book, D.-Z Du, and D. Russo. On polynomial and generalized complexity cores. In *Proceedings of the Third Structure in Complexity Theory Conference*, pages 236–250, 1988.
10. G. J. Chaitin. On the length of programs for computing finite binary sequences. *Journal of the Association for Computing Machinery*, 13:547–569, 1966.
11. D.-Z. Du. *Generalized complexity cores and levelability of intractable sets*. Ph.D. thesis, University of California, Santa Barbara, 1985.
12. D.-Z. Du and R. Book. On inefficient special cases of NP-complete problems. *Theoretical Computer Science*, 63:239–252, 1989.
13. S. Even, A. Selman, and Y. Yacobi. Hard core theorems for complexity classes. *Journal of the ACM*, 35:205–217, 1985.
14. J. Hartmanis. Generalized Kolmogorov complexity and the structure of feasible computations. In *Proceedings of the 24th IEEE Symposium on the Foundations of Computer Science*, pages 439–445, 1983.
15. J. Hartmanis and Y. Yesha. Computation times of NP sets of different densities. *Theoretical Computer Science*, 34:17–32, 1984.
16. D. T. Huynh. Resource-bounded Kolmogorov complexity of hard languages, *Structure in Complexity Theory*, pages 184–195. Springer-Verlag, Berlin, 1986.
17. D. T. Huynh. On solving hard problems by polynomial-size circuits. *Information Processing Letters*, 24:171–176, 1987.
18. D. W. Juedes. *The Complexity and Distribution of Computationally Useful Problems*. Ph.D. thesis, Iowa State University, 1994.
19. D. W. Juedes. Weakly complete problems are not rare. submitted, 1994.
20. D. W. Juedes and J. H. Lutz. The complexity and distribution of hard problems. *SIAM Journal on Computing*, 24, 1995. to appear.
21. D. W. Juedes and J. H. Lutz. Weak completeness in E and E_2. *Theoretical Computer Science*, 1995. to appear.
22. R. Kannan. Circuit-size lower bounds and non-reducibility to sparse sets. *Information and Control*, 55:40–56, 1982.

37

23. R. M. Karp. Reducibility among combinatorial problems. In R. E. Miller and J. W. Thatcher, editors, *Complexity of Computer Computations*, pages 85–104. Plenum Press, New York, 1972.
24. R. M. Karp and R. J. Lipton. Some connections between nonuniform and uniform complexity classes. In *Proceedings of the 12th ACM Symposium on Theory of Computing*, pages 302–309, 1980.
25. K. Ko. On the notion of infinite pseudorandom sequences. *Theoretical Computer Science*, 48:9–33, 1986.
26. A. N. Kolmogorov. Three approaches to the quantitative definition of 'information'. *Problems of Information Transmission*, 1:1–7, 1965.
27. L. A. Levin. Randomness conservation inequalities; information and independence in mathematical theories. *Information and Control*, 61:15–37, 1984.
28. L. Longpré. *Resource Bounded Kolmogorov Complexity, a Link Between Computational Complexity and Information Theory*. Ph.D. thesis, Cornell University, 1986. Technical Report TR-86-776.
29. J. H. Lutz. Resource-bounded measure. in preparation.
30. J. H. Lutz. Weakly hard problems. *SIAM Journal on Computing*. to appear. See also *Proceedings of the Ninth Structure in Complexity Theory Conference*, 1994, pp. 146–161. IEEE Computer Society Press.
31. J. H. Lutz. Category and measure in complexity classes. *SIAM Journal on Computing*, 19:1100–1131, 1990.
32. J. H. Lutz. Almost everywhere high nonuniform complexity. *Journal of Computer and System Sciences*, 44:220–258, 1992.
33. J. H. Lutz and E. Mayordomo. Cook versus Karp-Levin: Separating completeness notions if NP is not small. *Theoretical Computer Science*. to appear. See also *Proceedings of the Eleventh Symposium on Theoretical Aspects of Computer Science*, Springer–Verlag, 1994, pp. 415–426.
34. J. H. Lutz and E. Mayordomo. Measure, stochasticity, and the density of hard languages. *SIAM Journal on Computing*, 23:762–779, 1994.
35. N. Lynch. On reducibility to complex or sparse sets. *Journal of the ACM*, 22:341–345, 1975.
36. P. Martin-Löf. Complexity oscillations in infinite binary sequences. *Zeitschrift für Wahrscheinlichkeitstheory und Verwandte Gebiete*, 19:225–230, 1971.
37. E. Mayordomo. *Contributions to the study of resource-bounded measure*. Ph.D. thesis, Universitat Politècnica de Catalunya, 1994.
38. P. Orponen. A classification of complexity core lattices. *Theoretical Computer Science*, 70:121–130, 1986.
39. P. Orponen and U. Schöning. The density and complexity of polynomial cores for intractable sets. *Information and Control*, 70:54–68, 1986.
40. D. A. Russo and P. Orponen. On P-subset structures. *Mathematical Systems Theory*, 20:129–136, 1987.
41. M. Sipser. A complexity-theoretic approach to randomness. In *Proceedings of the 15th ACM Symposium on Theory of Computing*, pages 330–335, 1983.
42. S. Skyum and L. G. Valiant. A complexity theory based on boolean algebra. *Journal of the ACM*, 32:484–502, 1985.
43. R. J. Solomonoff. A formal theory of inductive inference. *Information and Control*, 7:1–22, 224–254, 1964.

Communication Complexity of Key Agreement on Small Ranges
(Preliminary Version)

Jin-Yi Cai[1] and Richard J. Lipton[2] and Luc Longpré[3] and Mitsunori Ogihara[4] and Kenneth W. Regan[1] and D. Sivakumar[1]

[1] Department of Computer Science, State Univ. of NY at Buffalo, Buffalo NY 14260-2000. E-mail: cai|regan|sivak-d@cs.buffalo.edu Cai was supported in part by NSF Grants CCR-9057486 and CCR-9319093, and by an Alfred P. Sloan Fellowship.
[2] Department of Computer Science, Princeton University, Princeton, NJ 08544. E-mail: rjl@cs.princeton.edu. Supported in part by NSF Grant CCR-9304718.
[3] Computer Science Department, University of Texas at El Paso, El Paso, TX 79968. Email: luc@cs.utep.edu. Supported in part by NSF Grant CCR-9211174.
[4] Department of Computer Science, University of Rochester, Rochester, NY 14627. E-mail: ogihara@cs.rochester.edu. Supported in part by the NSF under grant CCR-9002292 and the JSPS under grant NSF-INT-9116781/JSPS-ENG-207.

Abstract. We study a variation on classical key-agreement and consensus problems in which the key space S is the range of a random variable that can be sampled. We give tight upper and lower bounds of $\lceil \log_2 k \rceil$ bits on the communication complexity of agreement on some key in S, using a form of Sperner's Lemma, and give bounds on other problems. In the case where keys are generated by a probabilistic polynomial-time Turing machine, we show agreement possible with zero communication if every fully polynomial-time approximation scheme (fpras) has a certain symmetry-breaking property.

1 Introduction

A fundamental problem in key agreement between two parties, commonly called "Alice" and "Bob," is for Alice to communicate some string w to Bob over an expensive, noisy, and/or insecure channel. Most previous work places no restriction on w, or considers w to be drawn uniformly at random from strings of some length n. We study cases in which w comes from a relatively small set $S \subseteq \{0,1\}^n$, namely the set of possible outputs of a random variable G. Alice and Bob have identical copies of G, which is regarded as a randomized *key generator*. Each can *sample* the private copy of G, can use a private coin for other purposes, and can send messages to the other. They wish to *agree* on some key $w \in S$, while exchanging much fewer than n bits. Several kinds of problems we consider are:

1. *Any-key agreement.* Upon the end of their conversation, Alice commits to a string $s_A \in S$, Bob commits to $s_B \in S$, and they succeed if $s_A = s_B$.
2. *Selected-key agreement.* Alice commits to a designated key $w \in S$ before the conversation, and they succeed if after the conversation, Bob also commits to w.
3. *Subset agreement.* At end of conversation, Alice commits to a subset S_A of S of some pre-determined size m, Bob commits to S_B, and they succeed if $S_A = S_B$.
4. *Weak subset agreement.* Same as last item, but with success if $S_A \cap S_B \neq \emptyset$.

These problems have a practical motivation that is speculative but suggestive: Consider Alice and Bob to be users at remote sites. There are many applications that call for generating, say, one or a few primes of large length n having special properties, and they want to make sure that with high probability they generate the same primes. The simple method where Alice generates a prime p and sends it to Bob costs n bits. Somewhat more economical is for Alice to send the *rank* of p in the set S of admissible primes, costing $\log_2 \|S\| < n$ bits. However, this requires both computing and inverting the *ranking function* of S as defined on all of $\{0, 1\}^n$, which can be (NP-) hard even in cases where S has cardinality two (see [6]).

Suppose, however, that the range S of G is fairly small. This is not unreasonable: consider either the way that a good pseudorandom generator used as input to other processes restricts the range of observed outputs by virtue of its small seed space, or the possibility of restricting the size of S by setting switches inside G (done blindly by the party supplying G and known to no one). Our point in this paper is that Alice and Bob can gain enough information about S by privately sampling G that they can reach agreement on the basis of ranking information. So long as the same copy of G does not fall into enemy hands, the transmitted information on ranks within S itself should give away little information about the actual values in S.

The first problem is relevant when it is sufficient for Alice and Bob to agree on *some* key in S. The latter three arise when it is important that one or m keys be selected from S "at random"; our intent is that Alice would build the designated key or keys, and then assist Bob in building the same one(s). The statistical idea used to solve the problems resembles, albeit on a smaller scale, the methods for *learning discrete distributions* in [15, 16].

A second point of interest in our work is that it gives a new twist on much-studied distributed-consensus problems. In a typical consensus problem involving k processors, each processor is given some value, and the goal is for the processors to agree on one of the values that were initially input. We can extend our setting from Alice and Bob to k parties, and the difference is that now the keys are given as outcomes of a random variable, rather than being pre-set. In this abstract we concentrate on the two-party case, without faulty parties. Like the methods for distributed-consensus lower bounds in [5, 3, 25, 10, 11], our lower bounds use a form of *Sperner's Lemma*, but with the difference that the nodes in the simplicial complex used are labeled by random variables, rather than by processor IDs and features of local communication graphs (see [5] or "views" in [3]).

Our work also differs from that of Maurer [17, 18] and Ahlswede and Csiszàr [1] in its emphasis on the *communication complexity* of the problems: Do restrictions on the size or structure of the key space help Alice and Bob to agree while exchanging substantially fewer than n bits? We treat questions of secrecy and channel noise as secondary, regarding them as factors that can make communication expensive. Orlitsky and others [24, 21, 22, 23, 20] have studied communication complexity in settings where Alice observes a random variable X, Bob observes a random variable Y (often dependent on X), and the object is for them to exchange single outcomes each has seen. For example, Y may select two "teams" i and j from a "league" $S = \{1, \ldots, k\}$, while X reveals the winner to Alice. In [21] it is shown that $\lceil \log_2 k \rceil$ bits are necessary and sufficient for a one-message protocol in which Alice tells Bob the winner. If two messages beginning with Bob are allowed, however, Bob can tell

Alice the index l of the first bit where the binary representations of i and j differ, and Alice sends the lth bit of her number, making at most $\lceil \log\log k \rceil + 1$ bits; both of these protocols are error-free. Our setting has several differences: (i) the ability for Alice and Bob to take repeated samples of the random variable G, (ii) the lack of advance knowledge by Alice and Bob of the universe $S \subseteq \{0,1\}^n$, and (iii) the inherent role of randomness and error. The selected-key problem can be represented in their framework, with Y null, but there are still differences in the representation and non-rankability of S.

Section 2 proves our main theorems, which combine to give an absolutely tight figure of $\lceil \log_2 k \rceil$ bits for the any-key agreement problem, where $k = \|S\|$. The upper bound is obtained by a one-message protocol with runtime polynomial in n and k, while the identical lower bound holds for arbitrary protocols, even when Alice is computationally omnipotent and knows the distribution of G. Upper and lower bounds are given for the other three problems, and tightening these is open.

This lower bound holds under the assumption that the source G is a "black box" random variable, one that Alice and Bob can interact with only by sampling. When G is a *feasible generator*, namely one computed by a probabilistic polynomial time Turing machine (PPTM), we are led to the problem of whether every feasible G has a "monic refinement," as defined in Section 3. There we prove that breaking the symmetry between two adjacent round-off values of a *fully-polynomial time randomized approximation scheme* suffices to compute a monic refinement of a feasible generator G, and hence to solve any-key agreement for G in expected polynomial time with *zero* communication, regardless of the size of S. This presents an interesting contrast between the sharp lower bound in the case of arbitrary G versus the difficulty that proving even non-zero lower bound against a feasible G entails proving $P \neq \#P$.

2 Main Results

In this version we assume familiarity with interactive protocols, the formalization of an r-round *conversation* $(\alpha_1, \beta_1, \ldots, \alpha_r, \beta_r)$ between Alice and Bob (beginning with Alice, and with β_r possibly null), and unambiguous encodings of conversations by binary strings α. (Details may be found in [8].) The case $r = 1$, β_r null is a *one-message protocol*. Each of Alice and Bob is allowed to interact privately with the random variable G by making "sample requests." Each sample request returns some string in $\{0,1\}^n$ according to the distribution of G, and costs n time units. Alice and Bob may also use their private coin in computations. Neither is allowed to see the other's coinflips or sample strings; i.e., there is no "common randomness." When G is fixed we write p_y as short for $\text{Prob}[G = y]$. The set $S = \{y : p_y > 0\}$ is called the *support set* of G, and the number k stands for an upper bound on its cardinality. We express time bounds in terms of n, k, and the *error tolerance* ϵ of the protocol on the problem at hand. The numbers n, k, and ϵ are known by both Alice and Bob. A function $\epsilon(n)$ that is $o(n^{-c})$ for every fixed $c > 0$ is said to be *negligible*, and if it is $o(2^{-cn})$ for some $c > 0$, then it is *exponentially vanishing*.

The idea for the upper bounds is to form a "histogram" of the strings received in sample requests, and look for reproducible "gaps" in the observed frequencies.

Theorem 1. *Any-key agreement, for any G with range $S \subseteq \{0,1\}^n$ of size k, can be achieved with exponentially-vanishing error by a protocol in which Alice sends one message of at most $\lceil \log_2 k \rceil$ bits, and in which Alice and Bob run in time polynomial in n, k, and $\log(1/\epsilon)$.*

Proof Sketch. Let N be large enough so that for each element $y \in S$, the probability that the observed frequency of y in N independent trials belongs to the interval $[p_y - 1/k^2 \ldots p_y + 1/k^2]$ is greater than $1 - \epsilon/2$. N is bounded by a polynomial in k and $\log(1/\epsilon)$ independent of p_y. Alice makes N sample requests and observes some number $k' \leq k$ of distinct strings returned by G. Let $f_1, \ldots, f_{k'}$, in nonincreasing order, stand for the observed frequencies of the strings in her histogram, and for convenience put $f_{k'+1} = 0$. Then there exists some i, $1 \leq i \leq k'$, such that $f_i - f_{i+1} > 2/k^2$. This represents a "non-negligible gap" in her histogram. Alice chooses any such i (e.g., the least one) and sends i to Bob.

Then Bob makes N sample requests, and forms his own histogram with frequencies $f_1', \ldots, f_l'$; here l may differ from k'. Then with error at most ϵ, the set S_A of the i most-frequent strings observed by Alice is the same as the set S_B observed by Bob. Thus if Alice commits to the *lexicographically* greatest member of S_A, and Bob likewise with S_B, they succeed with probability at least $1 - \epsilon$. $\qquad\square$

The case where all elements of S are equally likely makes $i = k$ and meets the stated upper bound $\lceil \log_2 k \rceil$ in the protocol. Note that on the promise that this is the case, or even that all elements of S occur with probability that is non-negligible in k, Alice and Bob can agree with *zero* communication by doing polynomially-many samples until, with high probability, each sees all k distinct elements. In general, Alice and Bob can try the strategy of doing some pre-determined (or communicated) numbers of trials and committing to the lex greatest string each sees. This may fail when S has elements of probability $1/k^c$ for many different values of c. A different strategy is for Alice and Bob to choose their most-frequent elements, and this can be augmented with communication about lex high or low or otherwise "distinctive" elements among the frequent ones. With all of this latitude even for 0-bit and 1-bit protocols, it seems surprising that the upper bound in Theorem 1 cannot be lowered even by 1 bit. This is so even when Alice knows the *true* distribution of G and is computationally omnipotent! We first prove this in the case of a 1-message protocol.

Theorem 2. *The best success probability in a one-message protocol, where Alice has u distinct available messages and Bob is polynomial-time, is bounded above by u/k.*

Proof. Let a PPTM B representing "Bob" be fixed. It is enough to consider random variables G whose range S is a subset of k elements $e_1, \ldots, e_k$ whose identities are known to both Alice and Bob in advance. The one important point is that if $e_i \notin S$, i.e. if $\text{Prob}[G = e_i] = 0$, and Alice and Bob commit to e_i, they are considered *not* to succeed, in accordance with the stipulation that they agree on a member of S.

We furthermore consider random variables G with the property that for some $m > 0$, and all i, $\text{Prob}[G = e_i]$ is a multiple of $1/2^m$. (We use m and 2^m this way for notational uniformity with the next section, and to relate Bob's time bound to m.) The space of all such random variables forms a *simplicial complex* S_k embedded in the nonnegative orthant of the $(k-1)$-dimensional hyperplane of points in $\mathbf{R}^k$ whose coordinates sum to 1. Two nodes in S_k are adjacent iff they differ by $1/2^m$ in two coordinates, and agree in all the others. The maximum clique size in this graph is k, and a k-clique is called a *simplex* in S_k. S_k has k-many extreme nodes G_i defined by $\text{Prob}[G_i = e_i] = 1$, and the nodes G where $\text{Prob}[G = e_i] = 0$ are said to form the *opposite facet* of G_i. Every interior node, i.e. where all elements have nonzero probability, has $k^2 - k$ neighbors, and belongs to $2k$-many simplexes.

Now we define a "coloring function" $C : S_k \to \{1,\dots,k\}$ for all nodes G by: Take some $i \in S$ and message x_t $(1 \le t \le u)$ that maximizes the probability that Bob, given message x_t and sampling G, commits to i. (If i is not unique, any such i will do.) This probability is well-defined since there is no further interaction after x_t is transmitted, and a computationally omnipotent Alice can do no better than committing to i. Then define $C(G) = i$. This coloring satisfies the hypotheses of *Sperner's Lemma*, using the statement in [5], namely:

Suppose for each i, $C(G_i) = i$, and for every node G in the opposite facet to i, $C(G) \ne i$. Then there exists at least one simplex whose k mutually-adjacent nodes are given k distinct colors by C.

Since there are only u different messages Alice can send, at least k/u of these nodes are optimized by sending the same message x_t. Since these nodes represent random variables whose component probabilities differ by $1/2^m$ at most, Bob cannot statistically distinguish them in the polynomially-many trials he is allowed. Hence for any element e_j, the differences among these nodes G in the probability that Bob receiving x_t commits to e_j are at most $\delta(m)$, where $\delta(m)$ is exponentially vanishing in m. Since an optimal Alice commits to a different element at each node, there is one at which Bob is correct with probability at most $u/k + \delta(m)$. Letting $m \to \infty$ and exploiting metric completeness and closure yields the conclusion. $\square$

If we restricted attention to r.v.'s G with range S of cardinality exactly k, then the argument trivially fails if Alice and Bob know S in advance, but it goes through for the case of arbitrary $S \subseteq \{0,1\}^n$ if $k \ll 2^n$. The proof works even if Bob runs in sub-exponential time, so long as m can be chosen large enough (e.g. $m = \Theta(n)$) that Bob cannot distinguish the adjacent nodes in his time bound.

The reduction from multi-round protocols to one-message protocols can lower the success probability and blow up the running time by moderate amounts.

Theorem 3. *For every b-bit protocol (A,B) for any-key agreement that runs in time t and succeeds with probability p, and $\delta > 0$, there is a one-message protocol (A',B') that succeeds with probability $p - \delta$, and that runs in time linear in t, nearly-linear in 2^b, and polynomial in $1/\delta$.*

Proof Sketch. There are at most $N = 2^b$ possible conversations under the unambiguous encoding. For each i, $1 \le i \le N$, let q_i denote the probability that Alice and Bob have conversation α_i, and let p_i be the success probability conditioned on α_i occurring. Then $p = \sum_i p_i q_i$. Elementary calculation shows that there exists some i such that $p_i \ge p - \delta$ and $q_i \ge Q = \delta/N(1 - p + \delta)$.

Both A' and B' are given copies of the old Alice A and the old Bob B to simulate. A computationally-omnipotent A' who knows the distribution of G could calculate i herself and send α_i to B'. We observe that a polynomial-time A' can do almost as well: she can simulate enough runs of the (A, B) protocol so that with confidence at least $1 - \delta/2$, she finds a conversation α_i that gives $q_i > Q/2$ and $p_i > p - 2\delta$. The number of runs needed is on the order of:

$$N \log N (1 - p + \delta)(p - \delta)(1 - p + \delta) \log^3(1/\delta)/\delta^3. \tag{1}$$

When B' receives α_i from A', he does multiple runs of the old (A, B) protocol until conversation α_i occurs, and chooses the same value B did in the first such run. With probability at least $1 - \delta/2$, this happens in the first $(1/q_i) \log_e(2/\delta)$ runs, so the time taken by the new Bob upon receiving a message from Alice can be bounded by a constant times $tN \log_2(1/\delta) \cdot (1 - p)/\delta$, which is less than the time for A'. □

Note that if p is close to 1, and δ is about $(1 - p)/2$ in Equation 1, then then the number of trials needed works out roughly to $N \cdot (1/\delta)$. In any event, if we tolerate a falloff in the success probability of the form 1/polynomial, then A' and B' still run in polynomial time. When the new Alice is computationally omnipotent and knows the distribution, however, the hit on the running time is only a factor of $\log(1/\delta)$, which is polynomial even when $1 - p$ is exponentially vanishing. This suffices to prove our lower bound, while the upper bound is deferred to the next subsection.

Theorem 4. *To attain success probability $1/2^a - 1/2^n$ for any-key agreement with a polynomial-time Bob, where $a > 0$, $\lceil log_2 k \rceil - a$ bits are necessary and sufficient.* □

2.1 Other Agreement Problems

Now we study the communication complexity of the other three problems in the Introduction, namely selected-key agreement, subset agreement, and weak subset agreement. Where the allowed error probability ϵ on the protocol is unstated, it is assumed to be exponentially vanishing.

Theorem 5. *Agreement on a selected key w can be achieved in expected polynomial time (in n, k, and $1/p_w$) by a one-message protocol that communicates at most $2 \lceil \log_2 k \rceil$ bits.*

Proof Sketch. Let w denote the element that Alice wishes to communicate. Let c be such that $p_w > 1/k^c$. Assume further that Alice knows the value of c (if not, she can sample in increasing powers of k until she obtains a good estimate of p_w). Let N be large enough so that the probability that the observed frequency of w in N independent trials is in the interval $[p_w - 1/4k^2 \ldots p_w + 1/4k^2]$ is greater than $\epsilon/2$. Alice makes N sample requests and chooses a "gap" of at least $1/k^d$ in her histogram, for some $d > c$. Note that such a gap must exist since $p_w > 1/k^d$. Let f_i and f_{i+1} denote the observed frequencies on either side of the gap, so that $f_i - f_{i+1} > 1/k^d$. Let S_A denote the elements whose observed frequencies are at least f_i. As before, Alice sends to Bob the index i of the gap. In addition, Alice sends the lexicographic rank of w in the set S_A.

Bob samples until he sees all i elements promised by Alice and knows their frequencies with enough confidence to perceive the gap, and then deduces w from the rank information in Alice's message. □

(*Remarks:* If we want Bob to shut himself off in polynomial time in all possible computations, it seems we need Alice also to communicate c to Bob, taking an extra $\log c = \log\log(1/p_w)$ bits. When c is fixed; i.e., when the probability of the selected key is non-negligible, the time bounds are polynomial in k.)

This leaves an interesting question about the gulf between $2\lceil \log_2 k \rceil$ bits in the upper bound and the lower bound of $\lceil \log_2 k \rceil$ bits that carries over from Theorem 2. If Bob were able to compute the ranking function of S, as obtains in other cases of key-transfer we know in the literature, then clearly $\lceil \log_2 k \rceil$ bits would suffice. Our *point* is that when S is an arbitrary subset of $\{0,1\}^n$ of moderate size ($\log_2 k < n/2$), we see no way for Alice to tell Bob what to look for without taking samples and communicating some robust feature of the results, in addition to the ranking information. We suspect our upper bound is tight, but have been unable to prove it.

For the problem of subset agreement, let m denote the sizes of sets S_A and S_B that Alice and Bob must commit to. We first observe that m can be at most k', where $k' \leq k$ denotes the number of elements that occur with non-negligible probability.

Corollary 6. *For subset agreement in expected polynomial time, $\lceil \log_2 k \rceil$ bits are necessary and sufficient.*

Proof Sketch. The lower bound follows immediately from Theorem 2. The protocol used in the proof of Theorem 1 can be modified to work for the subset agreement case. Alice samples sufficiently many times, and chooses a gap i such that there are at least m elements with observed frequencies at least f_i. Such a gap must exist, since there are at least m elements with non-negligible probability. Alice then sends the number of elements above the "chosen gap." Finally Alice and Bob commit to the lexicographically largest m strings from this set. $\square$

(*Remarks:* Again, if Bob is required always to shut himself off in a given time bound, we have Alice send an additional $\log\log(1/p_m)$ bits, where p_m is the frequency of the mth most likely element.)

Before proceeding to the problem of weak subset agreement, we prove the upper bound in Theorem 4, re-stated in the following way. Let $\ell = \lceil \log_2 k \rceil$.

Proposition 7. *With b bits of communication, Alice and Bob can achieve any-key agreement with success probability at least $1/2^{\ell - b} - 1/2^n$, in polynomial time.*

As in the proof of Theorem 1, Alice finds an index i, $1 \leq i \leq k'$, such that the observed frequencies f_i and f_{i+1} satisfy the "gap" requirement $f_i - f_{i+1} > 1/k^2$. Instead of sending i to Bob, Alice sends the *most significant* b bits of the binary representation of i. Bob "fills in" the least significant $\ell - b$ bits of the index i randomly. Clearly, the probability that Bob hits Alice's intended index is at least $1/2^{\ell - b}$. $\square$

Using similar ideas, we provide an upper bound for weak subset agreement.

Corollary 8. *Weak subset agreement can be achieved with $\lceil \log_2 k - \log_2 m \rceil$ bits.*

Proof. Alice chooses a "gap index" i and sends the binary string x that represents the most significant $\lceil \log_2 k - \log_2 m \rceil$ bits of i. Alice and Bob, respectively, initialize S_A and S_B to $\emptyset$. For each possible binary string y of $\lceil \log_2 m \rceil$ bits, Alice and Bob consider the index $j = xy$ obtained by concatenation. Let e_A^j and e_B^j, respectively, denote the lexicographically largest members of the set of elements that Alice and Bob observe to have frequencies at least f_j. Alice and Bob add e_A^j and e_B^j, respectively, to S_A and S_B. Clearly, S_A and S_B have m elements each. Moreover, both Alice and Bob must consider the index i that Alice picked initially; by the proof of Theorem 1, $e_A^i = e_B^i$ with very high probability, so $S_A \cap S_B \neq \emptyset$ with high probability. The running times are similar to those in Theorem 1. □

Next we prove that $\lceil \log_2 k - 2 \log_2 m \rceil$ bits are necessary for weak-subset agreement. Whether either of these bounds can be improved to meet the other is open.

Corollary 9. *Weak subset agreement requires at least* $\lceil \log_2 k - 2 \log_2 m \rceil$ *bits.*

Proof. Let ϵ be an exponentially vanishing quantity. Suppose to the contrary that there is a protocol P that uses $\log_2 k - 2 \log_2 m - 1$ bits of communication to succeed with probability $1 - \epsilon$ on any random variable G. Then Alice and Bob can use P to beat the lower bound of Theorem 2: Run P to commit to sets S_A and S_B of size m, and then pick elements $s_A \in S_A$ and $s_B \in S_B$ uniformly at random. The probability that $s_A = s_B$ equals $1/m^2$, which is greater than the upper bound of $1/2m^2$ promised in Theorem 2 by a non-negligible quantity. □

3 Feasible Generators

In this section we remove the assumption that the generator G is a "black box," and instead suppose that it is modeled by a probabilistic polynomial-time Turing machine (PPTM) M_G. Without much loss of generality we may suppose that M_G has a binary fair coin, and makes m coinflips in any computation. Then M_G can be regarded as an ordinary deterministic Turing machine computing a function from $\{0,1\}^m$ to $\{0,1\}^n$, with uniform distribution over strings $u \in \{0,1\}^m$.

In order to talk about asymptotic complexity in a uniform manner, we give n to M_G on its input tape, and we also suppose that $m(n) = n^{O(1)}$. For a useful extension of generality, we allow the input tape of M_G to hold an *argument string* $x \in \{0,1\}^n$. Then M_G represents an *ensemble* of random variables G_x, with valid key-sets S_x. Formally, for any language S, let $S_x := \{y : \langle x, y \rangle \in S\}$, where $\langle \cdot, \cdot \rangle$ is a fixed polynomial-time pairing function.

Definition 10. A *feasible generator* consists of a set S and a PPTM M, such that for all arguments x, M makes $m(|x|)$ coinflips and $\mathrm{Prob}_u[M(x, u) \in S_x] > 3/4$.

Note that it is not the case that every random seed u leads to a valid key, but the probability of failure is not too large. If S is polynomial-time decidable, we can equivalently suppose $M(x, u) = \perp$ if $M(x, u) \notin S_x$. Sanchis and Fulk [26] give evidence that there are languages S in P such that no deterministic polynomial time algorithm on inputs 0^n can *generate* a member of S of length n. It is still unknown whether *certified primes* of the form $\langle p, c \rangle$, where c is a short proof that p is prime, can be generated in deterministic polynomial time, although several feasible generators for them are known.

Jerrum, Valiant, and Vazirani [13] considered generators in which x stands for a graph, and S_x is e.g. the set of perfect matchings in x. They were interested in generating elements with uniform or nearly-uniform distribution on S_x. We pose intuitively the opposite question: can the distribution on S_x be heavily biased in favor of one element, or a small number of elements?

Definition 11. A feasible generator (M, S) has a *monic refinement* M' if for all arguments x, there exists a single $y \in S_x$ such that $\text{Prob}_u[M'(x, u) = y] > 3/4$.

Here the "3/4" is amplifiable by majority vote to give exponentially-vanishing error in polynomially-many trials. The function mapping x to y then belongs to the class BPPSV defined by Grollmann and Selman [9]. Having a monic refinement is different from the notion of probabilistically "isolating a unique element" in Chari, Rohatgi, and Srinivasan [4]. They use the method from [19] of assigning random weights to edges so that with high probability, there is a unique minimum-weight perfect matching. However, different random weightings can yield different matchings.

Now we reconsider the problems of Section 1 when the generator is feasible, and when Alice and Bob *share* the argument string x. This models the situation of two remote users working on the same problem who want to generate the same primes without common randomness or heavy communication. In these examples the size k of the key sets S is exponential in n, and so the sampling methods for the upper bounds in the last section take too long. Instead:

Proposition 12. *Any-key agreement with a feasible G is solvable with no communication (and success probability $3/4$) iff G has a monic refinement.* □

We show, however, that the question of monic refinements is hard even when $k = 2$, using a natural class of PPTMs. A function $f : \Sigma^* \to \mathbf{N}$ is said to have a *fully polynomial time randomized approximation scheme* (fpras) [14, 13] if there is a PPTM M such that for all $x \in \Sigma^*$ and $c > 0$, taking $\epsilon := 1/c$:

$$\text{Pr}_u\left[\frac{f(x)}{(1+\epsilon)} \leq M(\langle x, 0^c \rangle, u) \leq f(x)(1+\epsilon)\right] > 3/4. \tag{2}$$

Jerrum and Sinclair [12] showed that the permanent function for "dense" 0-1 matrices, which is still #P-complete, has an fpras.

Note that M is multi-valued. We observe that the approximation can be done by a total function which is at most 2-valued. The "3/4" here and in (2) can be amplified to give exponentially vanishing error.

Proposition 13. *Let f have an fpras. Then there is a p-machine M' such that for all $x \in \Sigma^*$ and $c > 0$, there are two values y_1, y_2 such that $f(x)/(1+\epsilon) \leq y_1 \leq y_2 \leq f(x)(1+\epsilon)$ and $\text{Pr}_r[M'(x, 0^c) \in \{y_1, y_2\}] > 3/4$.*

The proof idea is to let $a = M(x, u)$ and round a off to the nearest of appropriately-chosen gridpoints. However, if the true value of $f(x)$ is midway between gridpoints, then we may expect "equal scatter" between the two values, with no non-negligible advantage for either. If instead we always "round down," then we have a similar situation when $f(x)$ is close to a gridpoint. We call the problem of whether M' can be made single-valued the "symmetry-breaking problem for fpras." We first show:

Theorem 14. *If every 2-valued feasible generator has a monic refinement, then all feasible generators with $S \in P$ have monic refinements.*

The proof is not so simple as for analogous results about NP-machines in [27]. One attempt is to let M be given, and by analogy with the next-ID function of an NP-machine, define $g(x,v) \mapsto b$ if $(\exists u \sqsupseteq vb) M(x,u) \in S$. (Here $b \in \{0,1\}$.) However, v might be a node in the tree of M with very few valid outputs below it, and hence the valid outputs of g may not have high enough probability. A second attempt is to define $g(x,v) \mapsto 1$ if $\mathrm{Pr}_{u \sqsupseteq v}[M(x,u) \in S_x] \geq 1/4$, and $g(x,v) \mapsto 0$ if $\mathrm{Pr}_{u \sqsupseteq v}[M(x,u) \in S_x] \leq 3/4$. Then g does meet the requirements of two-valuedness and high probability, so by hypothesis there is a total single-valued restriction g' and an M' which computes it with high probability. However, depth-first backtrack search on '1' values of g' might take exponential time. Our proof modifies the second attempt to make the search halt in expected polynomial time, using a trick analogous to the "method of conditional probabilities" in [2].

Proof Sketch. Given f and the PPTM M, let $q(n) = 2p(n) + 5$. For all a, $0 \leq a \leq p(n) + 1$, and all $v \in \{0,1\}^{<p(n)}$, define

$$g(x,v) \mapsto a \quad \text{if} \quad \mathrm{Pr}_{u \sqsupseteq v}[M(x,u) \in S_x] \in [\frac{2a}{q(n)} \cdots \frac{2a+3}{q(n)}].$$

This covers $[0 \ldots 1]$ with $p(n)+1$ intervals so that adjacent intervals overlap, but no point is in more than two intervals and there is a large gap between every second interval. Then g is total. Since $graph(f) \in P$, one can estimate $\mathrm{Pr}_{u \sqsupseteq v}[M(x,u) \in S_x]$ to within an additive term of $1/p(n)^2$ with high probability by taking polynomially many trials. Hence g meets the requirements of two-valuedness and high probability. By hypothesis, g has a monic refinement g'. The probability of error in g' can be made exponentially vanishing in polynomial time, so that with high probability, a search which requests polynomially many values of g' never obtains an erroneous one. The conclusion follows from the observation that if $g'(x,v) = a$, then at least one child w of v has $g'(x,w) \geq a - 1$. The root has value $g'(x,\lambda) = p(n) + 1$. Hence the path which takes the left child iff its value is at most one less than the current node hits the bottom before the probability reaches zero. □

The attempt to do the left-leaning path directly with g again runs into symmetry-breaking problems if the value $g(x,w)$ of the left child of v is in the overlap between "one less" and 'two less." Now we observe:

Theorem 15. *If the symmetry-breaking problem can be solved for fpras, then every feasible generator M with $S \in P$ has a monic refinement.*

Proof Sketch. Let M be given, and with reference to the last proof, define

$$h(x,v) = 2^{p(n)} + 2^{|v|} \cdot \|\{ u \in \{0,1\}^{p(n)} : u \sqsupseteq v \wedge M(x,u) \in S_x \}\|.$$

Then $h \in \#P$. We claim that thanks to the padding term $2^{p(n)}$, h has an fpras computable by sampling polynomially many values as in the previous proof. (Before, g only estimated the number of witnesses below node u additively, not up to a multiplicative factor of $(1 + \epsilon)$, and might give zero if the number were small, but now that the numbers are between $2^{p(n)}$ and $2^{p(n)+1}$, the factor pulls off a large interval.) Taking $\epsilon \approx 1/p(n)$ makes it possible to cover $[2^{p(n)} \ldots 2^{p(n)+1}]$ by $p(n) + 1$ overlapping intervals of roughly equal size whose endpoints are powers of $(1 + \epsilon)$. Symmetry breaking for the fpras allows monic selection of these endpoints, which then plays the role of g' in the previous proof. $\qquad\qquad\qquad\qquad\qquad\qquad$ □

The question of whether the lower bounds on any-key agreement in Section 2 carry over to the case of feasible generators motivates the following two hypotheses:

(1) There exist feasible generators (M, S) that have no monic refinement.
(2) (stronger) There exist feasible generators (M, S) such that for every PPTM M', if M satisfies $(\forall^{\infty} x)(\exists y \in S_x)\, \mathrm{Prob}_u[M'(x,u) = y] \geq 1/k + \epsilon(n)$, where $k = \|S_x\|$, then $\epsilon(n)$ is exponentially vanishing.

Here $S \in P$. We have been unable to show that the failure of the weaker hypothesis (1) causes any "drastic" collapse of complexity classes, even of BPP into RP or ZPP, or relating to knowledge complexity (e.g. in [7]). Moreover, there seems to be no straightforward connection between hypothesis (2) and the hypothesis that good pseudorandom number generators exist. This raises interesting new problems.

4 Conclusion

Besides the open problems given in Section 2 and above, there appear to be several avenues for significant further work. One concerns the difference between "arbitrary" distributions and computable distributions. It is interesting that while the lower bound in Theorem 2 holds for arbitrarily-powerful Alice, the upper bound is achieved by polynomial-time computation, and applies in the worst case over all possible distributions of G. This leaves open the possibility that when G has the structure of a feasible generator, or when the distribution of keys has some smoothness properties, better upper bounds on both time and communication can be obtained.

We observe that the upper bounds also carry over to k-party environments, with fault-free processors, by having one designated party play the role of "Alice" while each of the other $k - 1$ plays the role of "Bob." In the fault-free case, it remains to ask whether the same lower bounds still apply. The introduction of either "noise" or systematic faults in the communicated sampling data leads to a completely new problem. The combination of ideas in our work, the noise-tolerant learning model developed by Kearns [15], and the work on distributed protocols described in the Introduction may have important consequences.

References

1. R. Ahlswede and I. Csiszàr. Common randomness in information theory and cryptography—part I: Secret sharing. *IEEE Trans. Info. Thy.*, 39:1121–1132, 1993.
2. N. Alon and J. Spencer. *The Probabilistic Method*. Wiley, 1992. With an appendix by P. Erdős.
3. E. Borowsky and E. Gafni. Generalized FLP impossibility result for t-resilient asynchronous computations. In *Proc. 25th STOC*, pages 91–100, 1993.

4. S. Chari, P. Rohatgi, and A. Srinivasan. Randomness-optimal unique element isolation, with applications to perfect matching and related problems. In *Proc. 25th STOC*, pages 458–467, 1993.

5. S. Chaudhuri, M. Herlihy, N. Lynch, and M. Tuttle. A tight lower bound for k-set agreement. In *Proc. 34th FOCS*, pages 206–215, 1993.

6. A. Goldberg and M. Sipser. Compression and ranking. *SIAM J. Comput.*, 20, 1991.

7. O. Goldreich, R. Ostrovsky, and E. Petrank. Computational complexity and knowledge complexity. In *Proc. 26th STOC*, pages 534–543, 1994.

8. S. Goldwasser, S. Micali, and C. Rackoff. The knowledge complexity of interactive proof systems. *SIAM J. Comput.*, 18:186–208, 1989.

9. J. Grollmann and A. Selman. Complexity measures for public-key cryptosystems. *SIAM J. Comput.*, 17:309–335, 1988.

10. M. Herlihy and N. Shavit. The asynchronous computability theorem for t-resilient tasks. In *Proc. 25th STOC*, pages 111–120, 1993.

11. M. Herlihy and N. Shavit. A simple constructive computability theorem for wait-free computation. In *Proc. 26th STOC*, pages 243–252, 1994.

12. M. Jerrum and A. Sinclair. Approximating the permanent. *SIAM J. Comput.*, 18:1149–1178, 1989.

13. M. Jerrum, L. Valiant, and V. Vazirani. Random generation of combinatorial structures from a uniform distribution. *Theor. Comp. Sci.*, 43:169–188, 1986.

14. R. Karp and M. Luby. Monte-Carlo algorithms for enumeration and reliability problems. In *Proc. 24th FOCS*, pages 56–64, 1983.

15. M. Kearns. Efficient noise-tolerant learning from statistical queries. In *Proc. 25th STOC*, pages 392–401, 1993.

16. M. Kearns, Y. Mansour, D. Ron, R. Rubinfeld, R. Schapire, and L. Sellie. On the learnability of discrete distributions. In *Proc. 26th STOC*, pages 273–282, 1994.

17. U. Maurer. Perfect cryptographic security from partially independent channels. In *Proc. 23rd STOC*, pages 561–572, 1991.

18. U. Maurer. Secret key agreement by public discussion from common information. *IEEE Trans. Info. Thy.*, 39:733–742, 1993.

19. K. Mulmuley, U. Vazirani, and V. Vazirani. Matching is as easy as matrix inversion. *Combinatorica*, 7:105–113, 1987.

20. M. Naor, A. Orlitsky, and P. Shor. Three results on interactive communication. *IEEE Trans. Info. Thy.*, 39:1608–1615, 1993.

21. A. Orlitsky. Worst-case interactive communication I: Two messages are almost optimal. *IEEE Trans. Info. Thy.*, 36:1111–1126, 1990.

22. A. Orlitsky. Worst-case interactive communication II: Two messages are not optimal. *IEEE Trans. Info. Thy.*, 37:995–1005, 1991.

23. A. Orlitsky. Average-case interactive communication. *IEEE Trans. Info. Thy.*, 38:1534–1547, 1992.

24. A. Orlitsky and A. El Gamal. Average and randomized communication complexity. *IEEE Trans. Info. Thy.*, 36:3–16, 1990.

25. M. Saks and F. Zaharoglou. Wait-free k-set agreement is impossible: The topology of public knowledge. In *Proc. 25th STOC*, pages 101–110, 1993.

26. L. Sanchis and M. Fulk. On the efficient generation of language instances. *SIAM J. Comput.*, 19:281–296, 1990.

27. A. Selman. A taxonomy of complexity classes of functions. *J. Comp. Sys. Sci.*, 48:357–381, 1994.

Pseudorandom Generators and the Frequency of Simplicity*

Yenjo Han** and Lane A. Hemaspaandra***

Department of Computer Science, University of Rochester,
Rochester, NY 14627 USA.

Abstract

Allender [All89] showed that if there are dense P languages containing only a *finite* set of Kolmogorov-simple strings, then all pseudorandom generators are insecure. We extend this by proving that if there are dense P (or even BPP) languages containing only a *sparse* set of Kolmogorov-simple strings, then all pseudorandom generators are insecure.

1 Introduction

A pseudorandom generator is a deterministic polynomial-time algorithm that takes a short random seed and produces a long output. A pseudorandom generator is *secure* if the ensemble of its outputs is indistinguishable from a truly random distribution of strings. The existence of secure pseudorandom generators has been a subject of keen interest to many researchers ever since Yao [Yao82] formally defined secure pseudorandom generators. Blum and Micali [BM82] showed that secure pseudorandom generators can be constructed under the assumption that the discrete logarithm problem is hard. Yao [Yao82] showed how to construct a secure pseudorandom generator from any one-way permutation. Thereafter, many results on the relationship between pseudorandom generators and one-way functions showed that pseudorandom generators can be constructed from less restrictive one-way functions [Lev87,GKL93,ILL89,Hås90]. This line of research culminated with results proving, in both the nonuniform model (Impagliazzo, Levin, and Luby (1989)) and the uniform model (Håstad (1990)), that the existence of secure pseudorandom generators is equivalent to the existence of one-way functions.

In contrast, the study of the relationship between the existence of secure pseudorandom generators and the frequency of Kolmogorov-simple strings in dense languages was undertaken much later. Allender [All89] showed that if there are dense P languages containing only a *finite* set of Kolmogorov-simple strings, then all pseudorandom generators are insecure. In this paper, we continue this line of research by showing that if there are dense P (or even BPP) languages

---

* Supported in part by grants NSF-CCR-8957604, NSF-INT-9116781/JSPS-ENG-207, and NSF-CCR-9322513.
** Email: han@cs.rochester.edu.
*** Work done in part while visiting the University of Electro-Communications–Tokyo. Email: lane@cs.rochester.edu.

containing only a *sparse* set of Kolmogorov-simple strings, then all pseudorandom generators are insecure. We do this by first establishing that the injectivity (degree of "many-to-one"-ness) of secure pseudorandom generators is bounded by an arbitrary polynomial fraction. We also establish similar bounds on the injectivity of secure pseudorandom extenders and the injectivity of pseudorandom string generators derived from any secure pseudorandom extender.

The rest of the paper consists of three sections. In Section 2, we introduce definitions and state some useful lemmas. In Section 3, we establish results on the injectivity of secure pseudorandom generators and extenders. In Section 4, we study the relationship between the existence of secure pseudorandom generators and the frequency of simplicity in dense P (and BPP) languages.

2 Preliminaries

Throughout this paper, we use the alphabet $\Sigma = \{0, 1\}$. For any set L and any integer n, $L^{=n}$ denotes the set of all length n strings in L. P denotes the class of languages that can be recognized by deterministic polynomial-time Turing machines (see, e.g., [HU79] for the definitions of Turing machines and other standard notions used in this paper). For any finite set A, we use $\|A\|$ to denote the cardinality of A. A set L is *dense* if there is a constant d such that, for infinitely many values of n, $\|L^{=n}\| \geq n^{-d}2^n$. A set L is *sparse* if there is a constant s such that, for all $n \geq 2$, $\|L^{=n}\| \leq n^s$.

A pseudorandom generator is a deterministic polynomial-time function that, for some constant $k > 1$ and for each n, has the property that, when given an input of length n, the function outputs a string of length n^k. A pseudorandom extender is a deterministic polynomial-time function that, when given an input of length n, outputs a string of length $n + 1$. A pseudorandom generator or extender is considered secure if the distribution of its outputs is indistinguishable from a truly random distribution. The formalization of security is done in terms of statistical tests [Yao82]. A statistical test is a probabilistic polynomial-time decision algorithm. Let Π be a statistical test. $\mathrm{P}_\Pi(\Sigma^n)$ is the probability with which Π accepts an input string that is drawn uniformly from Σ^n. Let g be a pseudorandom generator or extender. $\mathrm{PS}_\Pi(g, \Sigma^n)$ is the probability with which Π accepts $g(x)$, when $g(x)$ is formed by drawing x uniformly from Σ^n.

Definition 1. (Secure Pseudorandom Generator) [Yao82] Let g be a pseudorandom generator that, for some constant $k > 1$ and every n, maps each input of length n to an output string of length n^k. Given a statistical test Π and a positive constant p, g *passes the statistical test Π with precision n^{-p}* if there exists an integer n_0 such that for all $n \geq n_0$, it holds that

$$|\mathrm{P}_\Pi(\Sigma^{n^k}) - \mathrm{PS}_\Pi(g, \Sigma^n)| < n^{-p}.$$

g is *secure* if for all statistical tests Π and for all constants p, it passes the statistical test Π with precision n^{-p}.

The security of a pseudorandom extender is defined similarly [BH89]. It is known that there exist secure pseudorandom generators if and only if there exist secure pseudorandom extenders [BH89]. Since pseudorandom extenders are more convenient in proving our results, we, following the approach of Allender [All89], consider only pseudorandom extenders in Section 4 of this paper. Nevertheless, the resulting theorems are valid even when stated in terms of pseudorandom generators.

Given a pseudorandom extender g, the following definition of g_b provides a method for generating pseudorandom strings of arbitrary length. Note that since g_b outputs only strings of one length, g_b does not qualify as a pseudorandom generator. Nonetheless, g_b generates perfectly good pseudorandom strings if g is secure and the length of the input is smaller than b. Henceforward, we will refer to g_b as a "pseudorandom string generator" derived from the pseudorandom extender g.

Definition 2. [BH89]   Let g be a pseudorandom extender. For any string x and any $b \in \{0, 1, 2, \ldots\}$, $g_b(x)$ is defined as

$$g_b(x) = c_1(x)c_2(x) \cdots c_b(x),$$

where

$$c_i(x) = \text{head} \circ g(t_i(x))$$

and

$$t_i(x) = (\text{tail} \circ g)^{i-1}(x)$$

and head(x) is the first character of the string x and tail(x) is the remainder of x after the first character is taken off of it.

Note that the time complexity of g_b is $\mathcal{O}(bt_g(n))$ where $t_g(n)$ is the time complexity of g.

Obviously, a polynomial-time algorithm M_L that recognizes a language L can be considered a statistical test. Allender [All89], via a generalization of a technique used in the earlier literature [BH89,Yao82,BM84], showed that given a language L, there is a statistical test $T(L, g, b)$ that effectively "boosts" a test of a pseudorandom extender g to a test of the "generator" g_b. (See Lemma 4 below.) If b is sufficiently greater than the length of the input string, then, since g_b maps a short string to a much longer string, the output string has low Kolmogorov complexity, and thus, it is easy to apply Kolmogorov complexity argumentation to the test of g_b. It turns out that the boosting effect remains unchanged even if we replace M_L with an arbitrary probabilistic polynomial-time decision algorithm A. Below, we introduce the statistical test $T(A, g, b)$ and the "boosting lemma" in a slightly generalized form that we will need later.

Definition 3. [All89]   Let A, g, and b be a statistical test, a pseudorandom extender, and a positive integer, respectively. Given an input x of length $n + 1$, the statistical test $T(A, g, b)$ performs the following algorithm:

Probabilistically choose $i \in \{0, \ldots, b-1\}$.
Probabilistically choose $z \in \Sigma^{b-i-1}$.
Let $y = g_i(\mathrm{tail}(x))$, and let $c = \mathrm{head}(x)$.
Accept iff A accepts zcy.

Note that it is not necessarily true that i can be chosen from $\{0, \ldots, b-1\}$ with equal probability regardless of the value of b. Nonetheless, it is easy to design a polynomial-time approximation algorithm that chooses i with very small error that is negligible for our purposes. Since the error does not affect the validity of our results in this paper, we will ignore it and assume that i can be chosen from $\{0, \ldots, b-1\}$ with equal probability.

Lemma 4. (Boosting Lemma) *Let A and g be a statistical test and a pseudorandom extender, respectively. For all n and b, it holds that*

$$\mathrm{P}_{T(A,g,b)}(\Sigma^{n+1}) - \mathrm{PS}_{T(A,g,b)}(g, \Sigma^n) = \frac{1}{b}(\mathrm{P}_A(\Sigma^b) - \mathrm{PS}_A(g_b, \Sigma^n)).$$

The proof of Lemma 4 is a straightforward generalization of the proof of the corresponding result of Allender [All89].

The following lemma shows that when a polynomial number of pinpoints are randomly dropped on the unit interval, any interval collection of "meaningful" size is hit by at least one of the pinpoints with very high probability. This lemma plays an important role in establishing the injectivity results in Section 3.

Definition 5. Let n be a positive integer. Consider a collection of mutually disjoint intervals in $[0, 1]$ the total length of which is n^{-l}. Let $\gamma_l(n)$ denote the probability with which no interval in the collection is hit by any of n^{2l} pinpoints that are randomly dropped on $[0, 1]$.

Lemma 6. (Pin Dropping Lemma) *For all $l \in Z^+$, $\gamma_l(n) = \mathcal{O}(2^{-n^l})$.*

Proof: Clearly, $\gamma_l(n) = \left(1 - n^{-l}\right)^{n^{2l}}$. Since $\lim_{n \to \infty} (\gamma_l(n))^{n^{-l}} = e^{-1} < \frac{1}{2}$, it follows that $\gamma_l(n) = \mathcal{O}(2^{-n^l})$. ∎

Kolmogorov complexity (see [LV93]) provides an important tool to describe the complexity of each individual string. The Kolmogorov complexity of a given string x is the length of the shortest code that as input to a (certain) universal Turing machine, yields output x. The short code, in a sense, plays the role of a *description* of the longer string x. In order to describe sets of strings with low Kolmogorov complexity, we adopt the time-bounded Kolmogorov complexity set notation of Hartmanis ([Har83], see also [Sip83], and, generally, [LV93] for a discussion of the history). Let M_v be a Turing machine. $K_v[s(n), t(n)]$ is the set

$$\{\, x \in \Sigma^* \mid (\exists y \in \Sigma^*)[|y| \leq s(|x|) \wedge M_v(y) \text{ prints } x \text{ in time } t(|x|)] \,\}.$$

Hartmanis [Har83] showed that there is a *universal* Turing machine u such that for all v there is a constant c such that for all s and t,

$$K_v[s(n), t(n)] \subseteq K_u[s(n) + c, ct(n) \log t(n) + c].$$

In the rest of the paper, we use $K[s(n), t(n)]$ to mean $K_u[s(n), t(n)]$.

54

3 Injectivity of Pseudorandom Generators

We establish an upper bound on the injectivity of secure pseudorandom generators and pseudorandom extenders. We also establish that the same bound applies to the pseudorandom string generators that are derived from a pseudorandom extender using the method of Definition 2.

Theorem 7. *Let g be a secure pseudorandom generator. Then, for any integer l, there exists an integer n_0 such that it holds that for any integer $n \geq n_0$,*

$$\max_{x \in \Sigma^n} \|g^{-1}(g(x))\| \leq n^{-l} 2^n.$$

Theorem 8. *Let g be a secure pseudorandom extender. Then, for any integer l, there exists an integer n_0 such that it holds that for any integer $n \geq n_0$,*

$$\max_{x \in \Sigma^n} \|g^{-1}(g(x))\| \leq n^{-l} 2^n.$$

The following theorem on the injectivity of pseudorandom string generators derived from a pseudorandom extender will be useful in proving the results of Section 4.

Definition 9. Let g be a secure pseudorandom extender and let k be a positive integer. Let $\rho_{g,k}(n)$ denote the maximum injectivity of g_b in the range $n^k \leq b < n^{k+1}$ for inputs of length n; that is,

$$\rho_{g,k}(n) = \max_{\substack{x \in \Sigma^n \\ n^k \leq b < n^{k+1}}} \|(g_b^{-1}(g_b(x)))^{=n}\|.$$

Theorem 10. *Let g be a secure pseudorandom extender. Then, for any positive integers $k \geq 2$ and l, there exists an integer n_0 such that it holds that for any integer $n \geq n_0$,*

$$\rho_{g,k}(n) \leq n^{-l} 2^n.$$

4 The Frequency of Simplicity

Allender [All89] showed that if a secure pseudorandom extender exists, every dense language L in P has infinitely many easy strings. Allender stated this result using a Kolmogorov complexity notation of Levin ([Lev84], see also [All92]) that blurs together description length and time complexity. The following theorem restates his result using the now standard time-bounded Kolmogorov complexity notation [Har83].

Theorem 11. *[All89] If there are a dense set $L \in$ P and $\epsilon > 0$ such that $L \cap K[n^\epsilon, 2^{n^\epsilon}]$ is finite, no pseudorandom extender is secure.*[4]

---

[4] In an earlier conference paper [All87], Allender originally made the following claim that is stronger than Theorem 11: if there are a dense set $L \in$ P, $\epsilon > 0$, and $t > 1$ such that $L \cap K[n^\epsilon, n^t]$ is finite, no pseudorandom extender is secure. However, the lemma

With the help of Lemma 4, one can easily sketch the proof idea as follows. Let g be a pseudorandom extender. Let M be a P machine that accepts L. We show that g is insecure by applying the statistical test M to g_b. Since L is dense, there is a number $d > 0$ such that $P_M(\Sigma^b)$ (i.e., $\|L^{=b}\|/2^b$) is greater than b^{-d} for infinitely many b. Thus, in order to pass the statistical test M with precision n^{-p} for an arbitrary p, $PS_M(g_b, \Sigma^n)$ must be close to $P_M(\Sigma^b)$ and certainly greater than zero for infinitely many values of b that are within reach of an arbitrary polynomial in n. However, since $L \cap K[n^\epsilon, 2^{n^\epsilon}]$ is finite, for all but finitely many n and for $b \geq n^{1/\epsilon}$, $L \cap g_b(\Sigma^n)$ is empty and, consequently, $PS_M(g_b, \Sigma^n)$ is zero. Thus, g fails the statistical test M with precision n^{-p} for sufficiently large values of p. Therefore, g is not secure.

Starting from the same assumption as Allender's, we now draw a stronger conclusion: if a secure pseudorandom extender exists, every dense language in P has a non-sparse subset of easy strings. The proof below synthesizes the above proof idea and the injectivity result of Theorem 10.

Theorem 12. *If there are a dense set $L \in$ P, $\epsilon > 0$, and $t > 1$ such that $L \cap K[n^\epsilon, n^t]$ is sparse, then no pseudorandom extender is secure.*

Proof: Let g be a pseudorandom extender. We will show that g is not secure by using the test Π defined below. Let j be a constant such that the running time of g is in $\mathcal{O}(n^j)$. Let h be an integer that satisfies $h > 1/\epsilon$ and $1 + j/h < t$. Let $f(n) = n^h$. Since L is dense, there exists a positive integer d such that $\|L^{=n}\| \geq n^{-d} 2^n$ infinitely often. Let M be a polynomial-time decision algorithm that recognizes L. Given an input x of length $n + 1$, Π executes the following algorithm:

> Probabilistically chooses $b \in \{ f(n), \ldots, f(n+1) - 1 \}$.
> Run $T(M, g, b)$ on x.

Note that as n spans all lengths, b covers all lengths, too. It is not hard to see that Π is a polynomial-time algorithm. Let

$$\Delta(n) = P_\Pi(\Sigma^{n+1}) - PS_\Pi(g, \Sigma^n).$$

To prove that g is not secure, it suffices to show that there is an integer p such that $|\Delta(n)|$ is greater than n^{-p} for infinitely many values of n. From the definition of Π, it is easy to see that

$$\Delta(n) = \frac{1}{f(n+1) - f(n)} \sum_{b=f(n)}^{f(n+1)-1} (P_{T(M,g,b)}(\Sigma^{n+1}) - PS_{T(M,g,b)}(g, \Sigma^n)).$$

---

that was used to establish this claim had an invalid proof. The proof overlooked the fact that the range of a function $r(n)$ with the integral domain may miss infinitely many integers in case $r(n) = \Omega(n)$. Nonetheless, Allender's original claim holds as it is a restricted version of Theorem 12.

Applying the Boosting Lemma (Lemma 4), we get

$$\Delta(n) = \frac{1}{f(n+1) - f(n)} \sum_{b=f(n)}^{f(n+1)-1} \frac{1}{b} (\mathrm{P}_M(\Sigma^b) - \mathrm{PS}_M(g_b, \Sigma^n)).$$

Since $\mathrm{P}_M(\Sigma^b)$ and $\mathrm{PS}_M(g_b, \Sigma^n)$ in the sum satisfy

$$\mathrm{P}_M(\Sigma^b) = \frac{\|L^{=b}\|}{2^b}$$

and

$$\mathrm{PS}_M(g_b, \Sigma^n) = \sum_{x \in \Sigma^n} \frac{\mathrm{Prob}(M(g_b(x)) \text{ accepts})}{2^n}$$

$$\leq \sum_{y \in g_b(\Sigma^n)} \frac{\rho_{g,h}(n) \, \mathrm{Prob}(M(y) \text{ accepts})}{2^n},$$

we get the following after simple rewriting.

$$\Delta(n) \geq \frac{1}{(f(n+1))^2} \left[\max_{f(n) \leq b < f(n+1)} \frac{\|L^{=b}\|}{2^b} - \sum_{b=f(n)}^{f(n+1)-1} \frac{\rho_{g,h}(n)}{2^n} \|L \cap g_b(\Sigma^n)\| \right].$$

It is not hard to see that for almost all n, if $b \geq n^h$, then $g_b(\Sigma^n) \subseteq K[n^\epsilon, n^t]$. Since $L^{=n} \cap K[n^\epsilon, n^t]$ is sparse, it follows that there exists an s that satisfies $\|L \cap g_b(\Sigma^n)\| \leq b^s$ for all sufficiently large b. Recall that $\|L^{=b}\| \geq b^{-d} 2^b$ for infinitely many values of b. Thus, choosing $l = (s + d + 1)h + 1$ in Theorem 10, it follows that for infinitely many values of n,

$$\Delta(n) \geq \frac{1}{(n+1)^{2h}} \left[\frac{1}{n^{dh}} - \frac{(n+1)^{sh+1}}{n^l} \right] \geq n^{-(d+2)h-1}.$$

Hence, g is not secure. ∎

BPP [Gil77] is the class of languages that can be recognized by probabilistic polynomial-time Turing machines whose accuracy is at least $\frac{1}{2} + \lambda$ for all inputs, where λ is any constant in the range $0 < \lambda < \frac{1}{2}$. That is, if L is a set in BPP, then there is a probabilistic polynomial-time Turing machine M such that, for each x,

$$x \in L \text{ iff } \mathrm{Prob}(M \text{ accepts } x) \geq 0.5 + \lambda, \text{ and}$$
$$x \notin L \text{ iff } \mathrm{Prob}(M \text{ rejects } x) \geq 0.5 + \lambda.$$

It is well-known that the accuracy of a BPP set can be greatly amplified. Given a polynomial q, the accuracy of a BPP-machine can be made to exceed $1 - 2^{-q(|x|)}$ for all inputs x (see, e.g., [ZH86]). With such a small error bound possible for BPP, it is not hard to see that a slight modification of the above proof leads to the following result.

Theorem 13. *If there are a dense set $L \in$ BPP, $\epsilon > 0$, and $t > 1$ such that $L \cap K[n^\epsilon, n^t]$ is sparse, then no pseudorandom extender is secure.*

It would be interesting if we could show the existence of easy strings at each length where the density of strings is high. Though such existence remains an open question, Allender showed a related positive result by employing (a somewhat idiosyncratic definition of) *a.e. dense* sets, instead of *dense* sets.

Definition 14. [All89]   A set L is *a.e. dense* if L is infinite and for some d and for all large n, $L^{=n} \neq \emptyset \Rightarrow \|L^{=n}\| \geq n^{-d}2^n$.

Theorem 15. *[All89]   If secure pseudorandom extenders exist, then for each a.e. dense* P *set* L *and for all* k, *there exists* c *such that for almost all* n, *it holds that*

$$L^{=n^k} \neq \emptyset \Rightarrow \|L^{=n^k} \cap K[cn^{1/k}, 2^{cn^{1/k}}]\| > 0.$$

Using the proof technique developed in this paper, Theorem 15 can be strengthened as follows.

Theorem 16. *If secure pseudorandom extenders exist, then for each a.e. dense* BPP *set* L *and for all* k, *there exists* t *such that for all* s *and for almost all* n, *it holds that*

$$L^{=n^k} \neq \emptyset \Rightarrow \|L^{=n^k} \cap K[n^{1/k}, n^t]\| > n^{sk}.$$

All the results of this paper so far are with respect to security against probabilistic polynomial-time statistical tests. One might ask whether this paper's generalizations also hold with respect to security against circuit-based nonuniform statistical tests in P/poly. It turns out that such a generalization is trivial. Consider the following theorem.

Theorem 17. *[All89]   If there exist pseudorandom extenders that are secure against statistical tests in* P/poly, *then for each a.e. dense* P/poly *set* L *and for all* $\epsilon > 0$, *there exists* c *such that for almost all* n, *it holds that*

$$L^{=n} \neq \emptyset \Rightarrow \|L^{=n} \cap K[cn^{\epsilon}, 2^{cn^{\epsilon}}]\| > 0.$$

This theorem can be generalized as Theorem 18. The generalization is indeed trivial because the "generalization" from 0 to n^s can be handled by coding polynomially many strings into a circuit, and the generalization from P/poly to BPP/poly is trivialized by the fact[5] that

$$\mathrm{P/poly} = \mathrm{BPP/poly} = \bigcup_{S \in \mathrm{SPARSE}} \mathrm{BPP}^S,$$

where SPARSE denotes the class of sparse sets.

---

[5] The fact is clear as all these are in (P/poly)/poly = P/poly. Note that it is not in general the case that C/poly = $\bigcup_{S \in \mathrm{SPARSE}} C^S$, and, in fact, some "promise classes" may not meet this equality [GB91], though as we have just shown, the promise class BPP does satisfy the equality, and so, similarly, do the promise classes R, coR, and ZPP.

Theorem 18. *If there exist pseudorandom extenders that are secure against statistical tests in* P/poly, *then for each a.e. dense* BPP/poly *set L and for all* $\epsilon > 0$, *there exists t such that for all s and for almost all n, it holds that*

$$L^{=n} \neq \emptyset \;\Rightarrow\; \|L^{=n} \cap K[n^\epsilon, n^t]\| > n^s.$$

Note that Theorem 18 subsumes the nonuniform versions of Theorems 12 and 16. It is an open question whether the uniform equivalent of Theorem 18 holds.

Acknowledgments

We are very grateful to Osamu Watanabe, Mitsunori Ogihara, and Seinosuke Toda for hosting a visit to Tokyo during which this work was done in part, and to Eric Allender for literature pointers, helpful comments and suggestions, and for a discussion that helped to strengthen Theorem 12 to its current form. We are also grateful to Marius Zimand for proofreading the paper.

References

[All87] E. Allender. Some consequences of the existence of pseudorandom generators, preliminary version. In *Proceedings of the 19th ACM Symposium on Theory of Computing*, pages 151–159, 1987.

[All89] E. Allender. Some consequences of the existence of pseudorandom generators. *Journal of Computer and System Sciences*, 39:101–124, 1989.

[All92] E. Allender. Applications of time-bounded kolmogorov complexity in complexity theory. In O. Watanabe, editor, *Kolmogorov Complexity and Computational Complexity*, EATCS Monographs on Theoretical Computer Science, pages 4–22. Springer-Verlag, 1992.

[BH89] R. Boppana and R. Hirschfeld. Pseudorandom generators and complexity classes. In *Advances in Computing Research*, volume 5, pages 1–26. JAI Press Inc., 1989.

[BM82] M. Blum and S. Micali. How to generate cryptographically strong sequences of pseudo-random bits. In *Proceedings of the 23rd IEEE Symposium on Foundations of Computer Science*, pages 112–117, 1982. Final version appears as [BM84].

[BM84] M. Blum and S. Micali. How to generate cryptographically strong sequences of pseudo-random bits. *SIAM Journal on Computing*, 13(4):850–864, 1984.

[GB91] R. Gavaldà and J. Balcázar. Strong and robustly strong polynomial-time reducibilities to sparse sets. *Theoretical Computer Science*, 88:1–14, 1991.

[Gil77] J. Gill. Computational complexity of probabilistic Turing machines. *SIAM Journal on Computing*, 6(4):675–695, 1977.

[GKL93] O. Goldreich, H. Krawczyk, and M. Luby. On the existence of pseudorandom generators. *SIAM Journal on Computing*, 22(6):1163–1175, 1993.

[Har83]   J. Hartmanis. Generalized Kolmogorov complexity and the structure of feasible computations. In *Proceedings of the 24th IEEE Symposium on Foundations of Computer Science*, pages 439–445. IEEE Computer Society Press, 1983.

[Hås90]   J. Håstad. Pseudo-random generators under uniform assumptions. In *Proceedings of the 22nd ACM Symposium on Theory of Computing*, pages 395–404, 1990.

[HU79]   J. Hopcroft and J. Ullman. *Introduction to Automata Theory, Languages, and Computation.* Addison-Wesley, 1979.

[ILL89]   R. Impagliazzo, L. Levin, and M. Luby. Pseudo-random generation from one-way functions. In *Proceedings of the 21st ACM Symposium on Theory of Computing*, pages 12–24, 1989.

[Lev84]   L. Levin. Randomness conservation inequalities; information and independence in mathematical theories. *Information and Control*, 61:15–37, 1984.

[Lev87]   L. Levin. One way functions and pseudorandom generators. *Combinatorica*, 7(4):357–363, 1987.

[LV93]   M. Li and P. Vitanyi. *An Introduction to Kolmogorov Complexity and Its Applications.* Springer-Verlag, 1993.

[Sip83]   M. Sipser. A complexity theoretic approach to randomness. In *Proceedings of the 15th ACM Symposium on Theory of Computing*, pages 330–335, 1983.

[Yao82]   A. Yao. Theory and applications of trapdoor functions. In *Proceedings of the 23rd IEEE Symposium on Foundations of Computer Science*, pages 80–91, 1982.

[ZH86]   S. Zachos and H. Heller. A decisive characterization of BPP. *Information and Control*, 69:125–135, 1986.

Classes of Bounded Counting Type and their Inclusion Relations*

Ulrich Hertrampf

Theoretische Informatik, Universität Würzburg,
Am Exerzierplatz 3, D-97072 Würzburg, Germany

Abstract. Classes of bounded counting type are a generalization of complexity classes with finite acceptance types. The latter ones are defined via nondeterministic machines whose number of accepting paths up to a certain maximum is responsible for the question of acceptance of the input. For the classes of bounded counting type each computation path may have one of k possible results from the set $\{0, \ldots, k-1\}$ ($k \geq 2$), and we count the number of paths having result 1, as well as the number of paths having result 2, etc. Each result (except 0) is counted up to a certain maximum, and the vector formed by these numbers is responsible for the acceptance question.

In this paper we design and prove correctness of an algorithm deciding the question "Is there an oracle separating C_1 from C_2?" for arbitrary classes C_1 and C_2 of bounded counting type. For the special case of classes of finite acceptance types we can give a direct solution to the separability question, thus solving an open problem from [H94a].

Moreover, we note that a surprising consequence on relativizable closure properties of #P can be obtained from these investigations [H94c].

1 Introduction

During the past four or five years several techniques have been developed to uniformly describe many complexity classes by appropriate models. One such technique is the model of locally definable acceptance types (LDA types), which motivated by a suggestion of Wagner [W90] was developed in [H92a, H92b, NR93]. This model, using a finite set of k-valued functions to evaluate the computation tree generated by nondeterministic machines, was able to characterize nearly all well known classes between P and PSPACE, except for those involving probabilistic elements.

A different model, which is even more general, was developed by Bovet, Crescenzi, and Silvestri [BCS91, BCS92]. This model is nowadays called the leaf language model (cf. [HLSVW93, JMT94, H94b, HVW94]).

Both of these techniques are able to describe a certain special set of complexity classes in a very general way: if we consider LDA types consisting of one

---

* This research was supported by Deutsche Forschungsgemeinschaft, Grant number Wa 847/1-1, "k-wertige Schaltkreise".

binary associative function, where the underlying structure is a finite commutative aperiodic monoid, then we obtain the same variety of complexity classes as if we consider leaf languages over an alphabet $\{0, \ldots, k-1\}$, where the membership of a string x in the leaf language only depends on the values $\max(|x|_i, m)$ for $i = 1, \ldots, k - 1$ and a fixed threshold m. These complexity classes are called classes of bounded counting type, since it suffices to perform some kind of bounded counting on the results of a nondeterministic machine's computation paths.

One special case of such classes is given by the finite acceptance type classes, considered in [GW87, GNW90, H94a]. These classes appear, if the finite commutative aperiodic monoid defining an associative LDA type is generated by one element, or equivalently, if the above described leaf language is defined over the alphabet $\{0, 1\}$. In this paper we push forward the work begun in [H94a] considerably: we not only solve the problem left open there about classes of the type $\{a, b\}P$; instead we give a very general result, characterizing all classes with finite acceptance types and completely solving the problem whether one such class is (relativizably) contained in another one. This is done in Section 7. All these results are special cases of an even more general solution to the case of classes of bounded counting type, which will be solved in Section 6. Before that we will formally define the classes we deal with (Section 2) and provide the ingredients needed to prove our main result, namely the theorem of Bovet, Crescenzi, and Silvestri (Section 3), the hypergraph method (Section 4), and the theorem of Ramsey (Section 5). Finally, we mention an important and surprising result on the class #P that can be obtained from our main result (Section 8), and we close with some concluding remarks (Section 9).

2 Classes of Bounded Counting Type

In this section we will formally define the classes of bounded counting type. We will deal with nondeterministic machines, whose computation paths may have one of a set of k possible "results". Thus we generalize the usual definition of the functions $\mathrm{acc}_M(x)$ and $\mathrm{rej}_M(x)$, being the number of accepting (rejecting, resp.) paths of machine M on input x, as follows:

Definition 1. Let M be a nondeterministic machine, where paths produce results from the set $\{0, \ldots, k-1\}$. Then for $i \in \{0, \ldots, k-1\}$ we define $\#_M(x, i)$ as the number of paths produced by machine M on input x having result i.

Definition 2. A class of bounded counting type is a class $\mathcal{C}$, such that there are numbers $k, m \in \mathbb{N}$, $k \geq 2$, $m > 0$, and a set $\alpha \subseteq \{0, \ldots, m\}^{k-1}$ with the property that a language L is in $\mathcal{C}$ if and only if there exists a polynomial time machine M with

$$x \in L \Leftrightarrow (\max(\#_M(x, 1), m), \ldots, \max(\#_M(x, k - 1), m)) \in \alpha.$$

We will denote the so defined class $\mathcal{C}$ by $\mathcal{C}_{(k,m,\alpha)}$.

Note that, according to this definition, membership of x in L does not depend on the number of paths with result 0.

Like the classes with finite acceptance types, also the classes of bounded counting type are all subclasses of BH, the boolean hierarchy over NP:

Proposition 3. *Let C be a class of bounded counting type, $C = C_{(k,m,\alpha)}$. Let $|\alpha| = r$. Then $C \subseteq NP(2r)$.*

Proof. Similar to Proposition 2 in [H94a].

To every class $C_{(k,m,\alpha)}$ we can define a leaf language $A_{(k,m,\alpha)}$ (cf. [HLSVW93, JMT94, H94b] for the definition of a leaf language):

Definition 4. Let $k, m \in \mathbb{N}$, $k \geq 2$, $m > 0$, $\alpha \subseteq \{0, \dots, m\}^{k-1}$. Then the set $A_{(k,m,\alpha)}$ is defined as the set

$$\{x \in \{0, \dots, k-1\}^* \mid (\max(|x|_1, m), \dots, \max(|x|_{k-1}, m)) \in \alpha\}.$$

That is, a string is in $A_{(k,m,\alpha)}$ if and only if the vector formed by the numbers of occurrences of symbols $1, \dots, k-1$, each counted up to m, belongs to α.

The following lemma follows immediately from the definitions (see [JMT94] for a definition of $\text{Leaf}^P(.)$ and $\text{BalancedLeaf}^P(.)$):

Lemma 5. $\text{Leaf}^P(A_{(k,m,\alpha)}) = \text{BalancedLeaf}^P(A_{(k,m,\alpha)}) = C_{(k,m,\alpha)}$

Our main result will be obtained from three important ingredients, the theorem of Bovet, Crescenzi, and Silvestri [BCS91, BCS92], the hypergraph method [H94a], and the theorem of Ramsey [R30], which are stated in the following sections.

3 The BCS Theorem

We will in the subsequent sections mainly use the leaf languages model, because it provides a very useful connection between the existence of an oracle separating two classes and the non-existence of a special kind of reduction between the corresponding leaf languages.

Definition 6. A language $A \subseteq \Sigma_1^*$ is plt-reducible to $B \subseteq \Sigma_2^*$, $A \leq_m^{\text{plt}} B$, if there exist two functions f and g, each computable in polylogarithmic time on a deterministic machine with random access to the input, $f: \Sigma_1^* \times \mathbb{N} \to \Sigma_2$, $g: \Sigma_1^* \to \mathbb{N}$, such that

$$x \in A \Leftrightarrow f(x,1)f(x,2)\dots f(x,g(x)) \in B.$$

Using this definition the main result from [BCS91] can be stated as follows. (It should be noted here that a similar result has been obtained independently by Vereshchagin [V93].)

Theorem 7 (Bovet et al.). *Let C_1 and C_2 be two complexity classes with leaf languages A_1 and A_2, respectively. Then A_1 is plt-reducible to A_2 if and only if C_1 is contained in C_2 in all relativizations.*

The functions f and g used in the definition of plt-reductions induce a function h that maps every word x to the string $h(x)$ defined by

$$h(x) = f(x,1)f(x,2)\ldots f(x,g(x)).$$

Thus we can also talk about a plt-reduction h, such that $x \in A \Leftrightarrow h(x) \in B$, keeping in mind that the polylogarithmic time constraint applies to the computation of the length $|h(x)|$ from x, and of each single bit $h(x)_i$, not to the computation of the whole string $h(x)$.

4   The Hypergraph Method

The preceding section recalled a very useful criterion for the separability question of leaf language defined complexity classes. Unfortunately, applying this criterion is still very hard in very many cases. In order to make the application easier, a general method was developed in [H94a] to more or less visualize the essential parts of plt-reductions in question. We repeat the main definitions and generalize the result from [H94a], which for many cases connects plt-reductions to hypergraphs.

Definition 8. A hypergraph H on n vertices is a mapping $H \colon 2^{[n]} \to \mathbb{N}$. Here, $[n]$ denotes the set $\{1,\ldots,n\}$. We call the elements of $[n]$ vertices of the hypergraph H, and the subsets $I \subseteq [n]$ satisfying $H(I) = k > 0$ are called hyperedges of multiplicity k.

To each hypergraph H on n vertices, we define another mapping $\overline{H} \colon 2^{[n]} \to \mathbb{N}$ by $\overline{H}(I) = \sum_{J \subseteq I} H(J)$.

Definition 9. A hypergraph sequence (also called an H-sequence) is an infinite sequence $H_1, H_2, \ldots$ where H_n is a hypergraph on n elements.

Definition 10. An (r,s)-hypergraph H on $n \cdot r$ vertices and an (r,s)-H-sequence $H_1, H_2, \ldots$ are defined analogously to the above definitions, but using r different sorts of vertices and s different sorts of edges (thus, $H \colon 2^{[n] \times [r]} \to \mathbb{N}^s$ is an (r,s)-hypergraph on $n \cdot r$ vertices).

The main result on hypergraphs in connection with plt-reductions is the following:

Theorem 11. *Let $A_1 = A_{(k,m,\alpha)}$ and $A_2 = A_{(k',m',\alpha')}$ be two leaf languages defining the classes C_1 and C_2 of bounded counting type, and let $A_1 \leq_m^{\mathrm{plt}} A_2$. Then there is a $(k-1, k'-1)$-H-sequence $H_1, H_2, \ldots$ such that for large enough n, and for all $J \subseteq [n] \times [k-1]$ we have*

$$\max((|J_1|,\ldots,|J_{k-1}|),m) \in \alpha \Leftrightarrow \max(\overline{H}(J),m') \in \alpha'.$$

Here, $J_i = J \cap ([n] \times \{i\})$ $(i = 1, \ldots, k - 1)$, and the maxima of vectors with numbers are taken componentwise.

Proof. An extension of the proof of Lemma 17 in [H94a]; refer to the full paper for a complete proof.

So we can obtain the impossibility of a plt-reduction (and thus the existence of an oracle separation) by showing that a certain kind of hypergraphs cannot exist. We want to illustrate this by the following example:

Let $A_1 = A_{(2,3,\{1,2\})}$ and $A_2 = A_{(2,3,\{2\})}$. Assume that $A_1 \leq_m^{\text{plt}} A_2$ (and thus $\{1,2\}\text{P} \subseteq 1\text{-NP}$ under all relativizations). Thus for all large n there has to exist a hypergraph H, such that for all $J \subseteq [n]$ we have

$$|J| \in \{1,2\} \Leftrightarrow \overline{H}(J) = 2.$$

But then, since $\overline{H}(\{a,b\}) = H(\{a,b\}) + H(\{a\}) + H(\{b\}) + H(\emptyset) = 2$ and $\overline{H}(\{a\}) = H(\{a\}) + H(\emptyset) = 2$, we have $H(\{a,b\}) = H(\{b\}) = 0$ for all $a, b \in [n]$. Thus, $\overline{H}(\{a,b\}) = H(\emptyset) = 2$. But then, also $\overline{H}(\emptyset) = 2$, which would imply $|\emptyset| \in \{1,2\}$, certainly a contradiction. Consequently, there is an oracle X, such that $\{1,2\}\text{P}^X \nsubseteq \{2\}\text{P}^X = 1\text{-NP}^X$.

5 The Theorem of Ramsey

We state the Ramsey theorem in terms of hypergraphs, because this is the way we will use it.

Theorem 12 (Ramsey, 1930). *Let (H_n) be an H-sequence. For a fixed number k let the value $H_n(I)$ for all n and all I with $|I| = k$ be bounded by the constant m. Further let a number n_0 be given. Then there is a number N, such that for all $n > N$, in $[n]$ there is a subset J such that $|J| = n_0$ and for all I, I' with $I, I' \subseteq J$ and $|I| = |I'| = k$ we have: $H_n(I) = H_n(I')$.*
We write $R(k, m, n_0)$ for the smallest such number N.

The proof is given in the original work of Ramsey, but one can find a nice presentation of the proof in the book of Graham, Rothschild and Spencer [GRS80] too. Let us remark that applying a Ramsey argument in complexity theory is certainly not a new idea. As only one of many examples let us mention here the recent paper by Verbitsky [V94].

We need the following (r, s)-version of the Ramsey theorem.

Theorem 13. *Let (H_n) be an (r, s)-H-sequence. For a fixed r-tuple $(k_1, \ldots, k_r)$ let all components of $H_n(I)$ for all I with $|I \cap ([n] \times \{i\})| = k_i$ $(1 \leq i \leq r)$ be bounded by the constant m (for all n). Further let a number n_0 be given. Then there is a number N, such that for all $n > N$, in $[n] \times [r]$ there is a subset J with $|J \cap ([n] \times \{i\})| = n_0$ such that for all I, I' with $I, I' \subseteq J$ and $|I \cap ([n] \times \{i\})| = |I' \cap ([n] \times \{i\})| = k_i$ $(1 \leq i \leq r)$ we have: $H_n(I) = H_n(I')$.*

Proof. The proof can be given using two inductions, refer to the full paper for details.

We will use this theorem in the following form, which can be obtained by iterated application:

Corollary 14. *Let (H_n) be an (r,s)-H-sequence with the property that for sets I with $|I| \leq k$ the value of $H_n(I)$ in all components is bounded by m. Then for any given value of n_0 one can find for large n a subgraph of H_n of size n_0 such that inside the subgraph for all I with $|I| \leq k$ the value of $H_n(I)$ is determined by the values $|I \cap ([n] \times \{i\})|$ $(1 \leq i \leq r)$.*

6 Main Result on Separability of Bounded Counting Type Classes

In this section we will prove our main result in the most general form. We need two definitions:

Definition 15. A function $f\colon \{0,\ldots,m\}^{k-1} \to \mathbb{N}^{k'-1}$ is called a (k,m,k',m')-function, if for all $z \in \{0,\ldots,m\}^{k-1}$ all components of $f(z)$ are bounded by m'.

Note that for given values k, m, k', m' there are at most

$$(m'+1)^{(k'-1)(m+1)^{k-1}}$$

different (k,m,k',m')-functions, and these can be easily enumerated.

Definition 16. Let $\alpha \subseteq \{0,\ldots,m\}^{k-1}$ and $\alpha' \subseteq \{0,\ldots,m'\}^{k'-1}$, and let f be a (k,m,k',m')-function. We say that f respects the pair (α,α'), if for all $z \in \{0,\ldots,m\}^{k-1}$ we have

$$z \in \alpha \Leftrightarrow \max\left(\sum_{z' \leq z} \binom{z}{z'} \cdot f(z'), m'\right) \in \alpha'.$$

Here, the z' are taken from $\{0,\ldots,m\}^{k-1}$ (the $\leq$ relation is taken componentwise), $\binom{z}{z'}$ is a multinomial coefficient, and the maximum of the vector sum with m' is taken componentwise too.

Theorem 17. *Let $C_1 = C_{(k,m,\alpha)}$, and $C_2 = C_{(k',m',\alpha')}$ be two classes of bounded counting type. Then there is an oracle X such that $C_1{}^X \not\subseteq C_2{}^X$ if and only if all (k,m,k',m')-functions f do not respect the pair (α,α').*

Proof. Assume that for all X, $C_1{}^X \subseteq C_2{}^X$. Then by Theorem 7 we know that $A_{(k,m,\alpha)} \leq^{\text{plt}}_m A_{(k',m',\alpha')}$. Consequently, by Theorem 11 we have arbitrarily large $(k-1, k'-1)$-hypergraphs corresponding to that plt-reduction. Then by Corollary 14 we can find arbitrarily large uniform subgraphs. View such a subgraph of size $m \cdot (k-1)$ as a $(k-1, k'-1)$-hypergraph H. Then H has the property

$$\forall J \subseteq [m] \times [k-1]: |J| \in \alpha \Leftrightarrow \max(\overline{H}(J), m') \in \alpha'. \qquad (*)$$

But since H is uniform, we have a function $g \colon \mathbb{N}^{k-1} \to \mathbb{N}^{k'-1}$, such that $H(J) = g(|J|)$ for all $J \subseteq [m] \times [k-1]$, and thus

$$\overline{H}(J) = \sum_{J' \subseteq J} g(|J'|) = \sum_{z \leq |J|} \binom{|J|}{z} \cdot g(z),$$

where z is taken from $\{0, \ldots, m\}^{k-1}$ and $\binom{|J|}{z}$ is a multinomial coefficient. Now take $f(z) = \max(g(z), m')$, the maximum taken componentwise. Then f is a (k, m, k', m')-function, which by equivalence $(*)$ respects the pair (α, α').

Conversely, if there is a (k, m, k', m')-function f that respects the pair (α, α'), then we can easily construct a simulation of a machine for a C_1-language by a C_2-machine: For every vector $(r_1, \ldots, r_{k-1}) \in \{0, \ldots, m\}^{k-1}$ guess $k-1$ groups of computation paths of the simulated machine, the i-th group consisting of r_i different paths. If for all $i \in \{1, \ldots, k-1\}$ all paths guessed in group i have result i, then produce $f_j(r_1, \ldots, r_{k-1})$ paths of result j $(j \in \{1, \ldots, k'-1\})$, otherwise produce one output of value 0. (Here, the f_j are the component functions of f, i.e. $f(.) = (f_1(.), \ldots, f_{k'-1}(.))$.) Obviously, this yields the desired relativizable simulation.

Corollary 18. *The following algorithm on input $(k, m, \alpha, k', m', \alpha')$ correctly decides, whether there is an oracle X such that $C^X_{(k,m,\alpha)} \not\subseteq C^X_{(k',m',\alpha')}$:*

```
algorithm oracle separation:
    result := yes;
    for all (k,m,k',m')-functions f do
        if f respects (α,α') then
            result := no;
    if result=yes then output YES
    else output NO
```

7 The Special Case of Classes with Finite Acceptance Types

Now we want to look at the special case of $k = k' = 2$, $\max(\alpha) < m$, $\max(\alpha') < m'$. Then α and α' are finite sets of nonnegative integers, $C_{(k,m,\alpha)}$ and $C_{(k',m',\alpha')}$ are the finite acceptance type classes $(\alpha)\text{P}$ and $(\alpha')\text{P}$, and the theorem of the preceding section becomes:

Corollary 19. *Let $\alpha, \alpha' \subseteq \mathbb{N}$, $|\alpha| < \infty$, $|\alpha'| < \infty$. Then there is an oracle X such that $(\alpha)\mathrm{P}^X \not\subseteq (\alpha')\mathrm{P}^X$ if and only if all $(2, m, 2, m')$-functions f do not respect the pair (α, α').*

Further restricting ourselves to the case $|\alpha| = |\alpha'| = 2$ we can by an easy case inspection prove the following solution to the open problem from [H94a]:

Theorem 20. *Let $a < b$ and $c < d$. Then $\{a, b\}\mathrm{P} \subseteq \{c, d\}\mathrm{P}$ in all relativizations, if and only if*

$$[(a \leq c) \wedge (b - a \leq d - c)] \ \vee \ \left[(1 \leq c) \wedge \left(\binom{b}{a} - 1 \leq d - c\right)\right].$$

The completed graph from [H94a], indicating all inclusionship relations between classes of this kind, is reproduced in Figure 1.

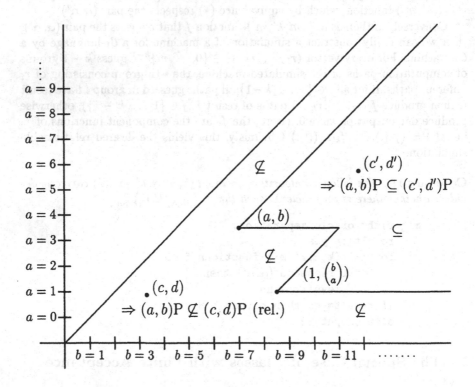

Figure 1: The classes of type $\{a, b\}\mathrm{P}$.

For the more general case of arbitrary finite acceptance type classes we observe the following consequence of Corollary 19:

Corollary 21. *Let* $\alpha, \alpha' \subseteq \mathbb{N}$, $|\alpha| < \infty$, $|\alpha'| < \infty$. *Then we have for all oracles* X, $(\alpha)\mathrm{P}^X = (\alpha')\mathrm{P}^X$ *if and only if one of the following conditions is satisfied:*

1) $\alpha = \alpha'$.

2) $\exists r_1, r_2 \geq 0 : \alpha = \{0, \ldots, r_1\} \wedge \alpha' = \{0, \ldots, r_2\}$.

3) $\exists r_1, r_2 > 0 : \alpha = \{r_1\} \wedge \alpha' = \{r_2\}$.

In the first case, obviously both classes are identical. In the second case, one can show that both classes equal coNP, *and in the third case both classes equal* 1-NP.

8 Closure Properties of #P

We learn from the technique developed in this paper that relativizable simulations, which are useful to prove inclusions of bounded counting type classes, can only be of the form: Guess a certain number of computation paths, check whether some predicted results appear there in fact, and if so, then output a certain given result, otherwise reject (i.e. output 0).

Extending this technique a little more, an interesting fact on closure properties of #P was proven in [H94c]. Theorem 23, given below, is taken from there.[1]

Definition 22. A function $f \colon \mathbb{N}^r \to \mathbb{N}$ is called a closure property of #P, if for all functions $g_1, \ldots, g_r \in$ #P, the function h, which is defined by $h(x) = f(g_1(x), \ldots, g_r(x))$ is again in #P. We call f a strong closure property, if it is a closure property of #P in all relativizations.

Theorem 23. *Let* $f \colon \mathbb{N}^r \to \mathbb{N}$, *then* f *is a strong closure property of* #P, *if and only if* f *can be represented as*

$$f(z) = \sum_{z' \leq z_0} \alpha_{z'} \binom{z}{z'}$$

for some $z_0 \in \mathbb{N}^r$ *and fixed values* $\alpha_{z'}$ *for all* $z' \leq z_0$. *Here,* z, z_0, *and* z' *are elements of* $\mathbb{N}^r$, *and* $\binom{z}{z'}$ *is a multinomial coefficient.*

9 Conclusion

We used Ramsey's theorem in connection with the theorem of Bovet et al. and the hypergraph method to obtain an easy algorithm that decides whether two given classes of a certain type can be separated by an oracle. This is interesting, because the type of classes (namely those of bounded counting type) includes a nontrivial variety of complexity classes, among others all levels of the boolean hierarchy over NP, as well as all levels of boolean hierarchies over arbitrary finite or co-finite acceptance type classes.

---

[1] Note that the formula cited in the survey article [H94b] from an earlier version of [H94c] was wrong.

Moreover, we could completely solve the relationships among classes of type $\{a, b\}$P and more general among all classes with finite acceptance types explicitly.

Finally, a surprising characterization of all reasonable (i.e. relativizable) closure properties of #P, which are of the form $f \colon \mathbb{N}^r \to \mathbb{N}$, can be obtained from our result.

Acknowledgement.

Thanks are due to the participants of the 1994 Burg Rothenfels week, Klaus Wagner, Heribert Vollmer, Gerhard Buntrock, Diana Rooß, and Herbert Baier for stimulating discussions on the topics of this paper.

References

[BCS91]   D. P. Bovet, P. Crescenzi, R. Silvestri, Complexity Classes and Sparse Oracles; 6th *Structure in Complexity Theory Conference* (1991), pp. 102–108.

[BCS92]   D. P. Bovet, P. Crescenzi, R. Silvestri, A Uniform Approach to Define Complexity Classes; *Theoretical Computer Science* **104** (1992), pp. 263–283.

[GRS80]   R. Graham, B. Rothschild, J. Spencer, *Ramsey Theory;* John Wiley & Sons (New York, 1980).

[GNW90]   T. Gundermann, N.A. Nasser, G. Wechsung, A Survey on Counting Classes; 5th *Structure in Complexity Theory Conference* (1990), pp. 140–153.

[GW87]   T. Gundermann, G. Wechsung, Counting Classes of Finite Acceptance Types; *Computers and Artificial Intelligence* **6** (1987), pp. 395–409.

[H92a]   U. Hertrampf, Locally Definable Acceptance Types for Polynomial Time Machines; 9th *Symposium on Theoretical Aspects of Computer Science* (1992), LNCS 577, pp. 199–207.

[H92b]   U. Hertrampf, Locally Definable Acceptance Types - The Three-Valued Case; 1st *Latin American Symposium on Theoretical Informatics* (1992), LNCS 583, pp. 262–271.

[H94a]   U. Hertrampf, Complexity Classes with Finite Acceptance Types; 11th *Symposium on Theoretical Aspects of Computer Science* (1994), LNCS 775, pp. 543–553.

[H94b]   U. Hertrampf, Complexity Classes Defined via k-valued Functions; 9th *Structure in Complexity Theory Conference* (1994), pp. 224–234.

[H94c]   U. Hertrampf, On Simple Closure Properties of #P; *Technical Report No. 90, Universität Würzburg* (1994).

[HLSVW93]   U. Hertrampf, C. Lautemann, T. Schwentick, H. Vollmer, K. W. Wagner, On the Power of Polynomial Time Bit-Reductions; 8th *Structure in Complexity Theory Conference* (1993), pp. 200–207.

[HVW94]   U. Hertrampf, H. Vollmer, K. W. Wagner, On Balanced vs. Unbalanced Computation Trees; *Mathematical Systems Theory,* to appear.

[JMT94]   B. Jenner, P. McKenzie, D. Thérien, Logspace and Logtime Leaf Languages; 9th *Structure in Complexity Theory Conference* (1994), pp. 242–254.

[NR93]   R. NIEDERMEYER, P. ROSSMANITH, Extended Locally Definable Acceptance Types; 10th *Symposium on Theoretical Aspects of Computer Science* (1993), LNCS 665, pp. 473–483.

[R30]   F. P. RAMSEY, On a Problem of Formal Logic; *Proceedings London Math. Society* **30** (1930), pp. 264–286.

[V94]   O. VERBITSKY, Towards the Parallel Repitition Conjecture; 9th *Structure in Complexity Theory Conference* (1994), pp. 304–307.

[V93]   N. K. VERESHCHAGIN, Relativizable and Nonrelativizable Theorems in the Polynomial Theory of Algorithms; *Izvestija Rossijskoj Akademii Nauk* **57(2)** (1993), pp. 51-90.

[W90]   K. W. WAGNER, personal communication, 1990.

Lower Bounds for Depth-Three Circuits With Equals and Mod-Gates

Frederic Green

Department of Mathematics and Computer Science, Clark University
Worcester, Massachusetts 01610, fgreen@black.clarku.edu

Abstract. We say an integer polynomial p, on Boolean inputs, weakly m-represents a Boolean function f if p is non-constant and is zero (mod m) whenever f is zero. In this paper we prove that if a polynomial weakly m-represents the Mod_q function on n inputs, where q and m are relatively prime and m is otherwise arbitrary, then the degree of the polynomial is $\Omega(n)$. This generalizes previous results of Barrington, Beigel and Rudich [BBR] and Tsai [Tsai], which held only for constant (or slowly growing) m. The proof technique given here is quite different and somewhat simpler. We use a method in which the inputs are represented as complex q^{th} roots of unity (following Barrington and Straubing [BS]). The representation is used to take advantage of a variant of the inverse Fourier transform and elementary properties of the algebraic integers. As a corollary of the main theorem and the proof of Toda's theorem, if q, p are distinct primes, any depth-three circuit which computes the Mod_q function, and consists of an equals gate at the output, Mod_p-gates at the next level, and AND-gates of small fan-in at the inputs, must be of exponential size. In terms of Turing machine complexity classes, there is an oracle A such that $\text{Mod}_q\text{P}^A \not\subseteq \text{C}_=\text{P}^{\text{Mod}_p\text{P}^A}$.

1 Introduction

One of the challenges facing circuit complexity is to prove lower bounds on bounded-depth circuits with Mod_m gates (that determine if the number of inputs is not divisible by the number m). If m is prime, exponential lower bounds are known for general bounded-depth circuits including AND's and OR's in addition to the MOD's [Sm]. Unfortunately the proof techniques for these results make essential use of the fact that $\mathbf{Z}/m\mathbf{Z}$ is a field if m is prime, and the situation for composite m (in which case $\mathbf{Z}/m\mathbf{Z}$ is a ring which is not even an integral domain) has proved to be more difficult. Algebraic or combinatorial techniques other than those used in [Sm] or [Raz] appear to be necessary.

Recently, progress has been made in the simple but important case of a single Mod_m-gate over small AND's [BBR], [Tsai]. This paper, for the most part, continues this line of investigation. Since this computational model is really based on polynomials, we formulate the problem accordingly. Let $p : \{0,1\}^n \to \mathbf{Z}$ be an integer polynomial, and $q, m \geq 2$ be relatively prime natural numbers. What is the minimum degree of p such that for all $(x_1, ..., x_n) \in \{0,1\}^n$, $p(x_1, ..., x_n) \equiv 0 \ (m)$ iff $\sum_{i=1}^{n} x_i$ is divisible by q? This question was studied by Barrington,

Beigel and Rudich [BBR], and, in subsequent work, by [Tsai]. The strongest lower bound, obtained by Tsai, states that the polynomial must have degree linear in n, if m is a constant or a slowly growing function of n. But what if m is some arbitrary function of n, where the only constraint on m is that it is prime to q? This question has a number of motivations; below we will see that it is related to lower bounds for depth-3 circuits as mentioned in the title. It is also of some intrinsic interest, since allowing m to vary in this way gives a considerably stronger computational model. Intuitively it would make sense that the degree lower bound has nothing to do with m's dependence on n, and is only due to the relative primality of q and m. However, it is not clear how the techniques of [BBR] and [Tsai] can be adapted to handle this more general case. In this paper we introduce techniques that do.

Here we therefore consider a generalization of the problems studied in [BBR], [Tsai]. The most significant lower bounds will be for the *modulo* functions,

$$\mathrm{Mod}_{m,r}(x_1, ..., x_n) = \begin{cases} 0 \text{ if } \sum_{i=1}^{n} x_i \equiv r \ (m) \\ 1 \text{ otherwise,} \end{cases}$$

or their negations (for example, a Mod_m gate computes the function $\neg \mathrm{Mod}_{q,0}$). Let f be any Boolean function on n inputs. We say an integer polynomial p on n Boolean inputs m-*represents* f if for all input settings of $x_1, ..., x_n$, $f(x_1, ..., x_n) = 0$ iff $p(x_1, ..., x_n) \equiv 0 \ (m)$. The *MOD-degree* of f is the smallest degree of a polynomial which m-represents f for some m. Let f_q be any one of the functions $\mathrm{Mod}_{q,r}$ or $\neg \mathrm{Mod}_{q,r}$. Define the *relatively prime MOD-degree* (or *rp-MOD-degree*, for short) of f_q as the smallest degree of a polynomial which m-represents f_q for some m which is relatively prime to q. Some functions have large MOD-degrees (for example, the AND function; see Proposition 9 below). Trivially, the MOD-degree of any f_q is 1. Our main theorem is,

Theorem 1. *For any* $n \in \mathbf{N}$, *the rp-MOD-degree of any of the functions* $\mathrm{Mod}_{q,r}(x_1, ... , x_n)$ *or* $\neg \mathrm{Mod}_{q,r}(x_1, ... , x_n)$ *is at least* $\lfloor \frac{n}{2(q-1)} \rfloor$.

Actually a stronger result is proved. Introducing terminology analogous to that of [ABFR], say a polynomial *weakly* m-represents a Boolean function f if p is not a constant function and $f(x_1, ..., x_n) = 0 \implies p(x_1, ..., x_n) \equiv 0 \ (m)$. Define the *weak rp-MOD-degree* in the obvious way. Theorem 5 says that the weak rp-MOD-degree of the modulo functions is $\Omega(n)$. As a by-product (see Corollary 6), we present a new proof that, if m is independent of n and is not a prime power, the minimal degree of a polynomial which m-represents the $\neg \mathrm{Mod}_m$ function is $\Omega(n)$, a result originally obtained in [Tsai].

The proof strategy is substantially different than those used in [BBR] and [Tsai]. We make use of the representation of Boolean inputs by complex roots of unity, introduced by Barrington and Straubing [BS]. There the goal was to show that the *sign* of p could not agree with $\mathrm{Mod}_{q,r}$. Related results, via similar techniques, for lower bounds on circuits consisting of one threshold over Mod_q gates, have been obtained recently by Krause and Pudlák [KP]. The main difference between the setting here and that of [BS] is that here we work in a finite ring (i.e., $\mathbf{Z}/m\mathbf{Z}$) rather than an infinite field (i.e., the complex numbers). This introduces some interesting technical twists to the argument of [BS]. It also, unfortunately, introduces some difficulties which we have not been able to overcome. Barrington and Straubing show that the sign of p can't agree with $\mathrm{Mod}_{q,r}$ even for a constant fraction of the input settings. We have not been able to show this type of non-approximability result in the present context, mainly because, working in a ring which is not a field, it is not always possible to find non-trivial solutions to a system of linear equations.

The topic of this paper was originally motivated by some questions about depth-3 circuits involving both threshold and mod gates. As is well known, threshold and parity gates are a potent combination. Inspired by Toda's theorem [Tod] that $\mathrm{PP}^{\mathrm{PH}} \subseteq \mathrm{PP}^{\oplus \mathrm{P}}$, Allender [Al] showed that any quasi-polynomial size "generalized preceptron," consisting of a threshold gate over $\mathrm{AC}^{(0)}$-type circuits, can be simulated by a quasi-polynomial-size depth-three circuit consisting of a threshold gate at the root, parity gates at the next level and AND gates of polylog size connected to the inputs (which we refer to here as "threshold-of-$\oplus^+$" circuits). On the negative side, drawing on work of Hajnal et al. [HMPST] and Boppana and Håstad [Has], it was shown in [Gre 91] that generalized perceptrons cannot compute the parity function (in terms of complexity classes, that there is an oracle A such that $\oplus \mathrm{P}^A \not\subseteq \mathrm{PP}^{\mathrm{PH}^A}$). Improvements and generalizations have appeared in [Bei], [BRS], [BS]. However, as of this writing, no non-polynomial lower bounds are known for the more powerful threshold-of-$\oplus^+$ circuits (and hence no oracle is known separating $\mathrm{PP}^{\oplus \mathrm{P}}$ from PSPACE). In fact the best one can do, by Smolensky's theorem [Sm], is $\Omega(n^{1/2-o(1)})$ for threshold-of-Mod_q^+ circuits computing parity (q an odd prime). Although this problem has not received as much press as the ACC problem [Bar], it shares at least some of its difficulty.

Some progress has been made in a restricted version of the problem in [CGT], in which the functions computed by the parity sub-circuits are symmetric. Here we consider a different kind of restriction: the parity sub-circuits are general, but the top gate is an "exact threshold" or "equals" gate (the resulting circuit may be referred to as an "equals-of-$\oplus^+$" circuit). In terms of Turing machine complexity classes, we thus consider the relativized power of classes such as $\mathrm{C}_=\mathrm{P}^{\oplus \mathrm{P}}$. While the resulting problems appear to be considerably simpler than those associated with $\mathrm{PP}^{\oplus \mathrm{P}}$, it is hoped that some insight will be gained towards attacking the more general problem.

It is natural to conjecture that if q and p are distinct primes, that an equals-of-Mod_p^+ circuit which computes the Mod_q function would have to be of exponential size. We prove this in the current paper. By the proof of the second part of Toda's theorem (see Theorem 7), this problem reduces to Theorem 1.

We conclude the introduction with some remarks on notation. Following the convention of [GKRST], if G is a Boolean gate, G^+ denotes a family of circuits with G at the root and AND gates of polylog fan-in at the input level. An *equals* gate over n Boolean inputs $x_1, ..., x_n$ with weights $w_i \in \mathbf{N}$ ($1 \le i \le n$) and threshold $t \in \mathbf{N}$, with $0 \le t \le n$, returns 1 iff $\sum_{i=1}^n w_i x_i = t$. All our results apply to equals gates with arbitrary integer weights. Finally, if R is a ring and $m \in \mathbf{N}$, $a \equiv b\ (mR)$ means that for some $x \in R$, $a = b + mx$. When it is clear which R is being used (usually $R = \mathbf{Z}$), we use the notation $a \equiv b\ (m)$.

2 Lower Bounds for the rp-MOD-degree of Modulo Functions

We start by reviewing the formulation of [BS] to express circuit inputs as complex roots of unity. Let q be a natural number ≥ 2 and ζ denote the primitive complex root of unity $e^{\frac{2\pi i}{q}}$ (q will be fixed in this section). Let $D = \{1, \zeta, \zeta^2, ..., \zeta^{q-1}\}$. Note that

$$\sum_{y \in D} y^k = \begin{cases} q \text{ if } k \equiv 0\ (q) \\ 0 \text{ otherwise.} \end{cases}$$

We will consider polynomials over n variables $y_1, ..., y_n \in D$. Let V denote $\{0, ..., q-1\}$. Since $y^q = 1$ for any $y \in D$, a monomial will have the general form $\prod_{i \in S_e} y_i^{e_i}$, where $e \in V^n$, and by definition S_e denotes the set $\{i | e_i \neq 0\}$. Define $\prod_{i \in \emptyset} y_i^{e_i} = 1$. The integer $|S_e|$ is called the *weight* of the monomial.

The first crucial observation to make here is that the sum of a monomial of non-zero weight less than n over all values of the y_i's subject to the constraint $\prod_{i=1}^n y_i = \zeta^r$ (for any integer r) is zero. Let "$y : \prod y = \zeta^r$" denote that $y \in D^n$ varies subject to the constraint $\prod_{i=1}^n y_i = \zeta^r$.

Lemma 2. *Let r, n be integers. Let e_i ($i \in \{1, ..., n\}$) be integers such that for each i, $0 \leq e_i \leq q - 1$. Define S_e as above and suppose $|S_e| < n$. Then*

$$\sum_{y: \prod y = \zeta^r} \prod_{i \in S_e} y_i^{e_i} = \begin{cases} q^{n-1} \text{ if } S_e = \emptyset \\ 0 \quad\ otherwise. \end{cases}$$

Proof. If $S_e = \emptyset$, the result is obvious. Suppose $S_e \neq \emptyset$. Let $y_i = \zeta^{k_i}$ for each i. Since $|S_e| < n$, there is an $i' \in \{1, ..., n\} - S_e$. The constraint $\prod_{i=1}^n y_i = \zeta^r$ is equivalent to,

$$\sum_{i=1}^n k_i \equiv r\ (q).$$

This determines $k_{i'}$ uniquely in terms of the other k_i's. We can then perform the sum over the k_i's ($i \neq i'$) independently. Hence for any $i \in S_e$, the sum has a factor,

$$\sum_{k_i=0}^{q-1} \zeta^{k_i e_i},$$

which is zero, since $e_i \not\equiv 0\ (q)$. ∎

For any integer r, it will be convenient to define the r-*inner product* $\langle f, g \rangle_r$ for functions f, g over D^n as,

$$\langle f, g \rangle_r = \frac{1}{q^{n-1}} \sum_{y: \prod y = \zeta^r} \overline{f}(y_1, ..., y_n) g(y_1, ..., y_n).$$

Lemma 2 says that $\langle 1, \prod_{i \in S_e} y_i^{e_i} \rangle_r$ is zero unless $S_e = \emptyset$, in which case it is 1. More generally, the set of monomials of weight $< n/2$, under the r-inner product, form an orthonormal basis for polynomials of weight $< n/2$ over D^n.

Lemma 3. *Let* $e', e \in V^n$ *and* $|S_e \cup S_{e'}| < n$. *Then,*

$$\left\langle \prod_{i \in S_{e'}} y_i^{e'_i}, \prod_{i \in S_e} y_i^{e_i} \right\rangle_r = \begin{cases} 1 \text{ if } e = e' \\ 0 \text{ otherwise.} \end{cases}$$

Proof. Define,

$$S(e, e') = \left\langle \prod_{i \in S_{e'}} y_i^{e'_i}, \prod_{i \in S_e} y_i^{e_i} \right\rangle_r.$$

The inner product can be written as,

$$S(e, e') = \frac{1}{q^{n-1}} \sum_{y: \prod y = \zeta^r} \prod_{i \in S_{e'} - S_e} y_i^{q - e'_i} \prod_{i \in S_e - S_{e'}} y_i^{e_i} \prod_{i \in S_{e'} \cap S_e} y_i^{e_i - e'_i}.$$

Because $|S_e \cup S_{e'}| < n$, we can apply Lemma 2. By that lemma, if $S_e \Delta S_{e'} \neq \emptyset$, $S(e, e') = 0$. If $S_e \Delta S_{e'} = \emptyset$, $S(e, e') = 0$ unless $e = e'$. If $e = e'$ then the sum is q^{n-1}, so $S(e, e') = 1$. ∎

The main result concerns integer polynomials which take on values in the ring $\mathbf{Z}/m\mathbf{Z}$ for some m. Since we work with roots of unity, it is convenient to extend this to $\Omega/m\Omega$, where Ω is the ring of algebraic integers. We then use the elementary property that an algebraic integer is a rational number if and only if it is a rational integer. Because of this fact, the notation $a \equiv b \ (m)$ means $a \equiv b \ (m\Omega)$ as well as $a \equiv b \ (m\mathbf{Z})$ if a and b are integers. Nevertheless, we usually resort to the more precise notations $a \equiv b \ (m\Omega)$ or $a \equiv b \ (m\mathbf{Z})$. (See [IR] (chapter 6) for a compact treatment of all the relevant notions.)

In the following lemma, we show, for a polynomial with algebraic integer coefficients $t : D^n \to \Omega$ of weight $< n/2$, that we can solve for the coefficients in terms of special values of t, namely, exactly those values of $t(y_1, ..., y_n)$ such that $\prod_{i=1}^n y_i = \zeta^r$, for any r. The idea of the proof of the main theorem is to use this lemma to show that the coefficients are zero when $t(y_1, ..., y_n) \equiv 0 \ (m)$ for the indicated values of $\mathbf{y}$.

Lemma 4. *Let m be a natural number relatively prime to q. Suppose $t : D^n \to \Omega/m\Omega$ is a polynomial with algebraic integer coefficients and weight $< n/2$, i.e., of the form,*

$$t(y_1, ..., y_n) \equiv \sum_{e \in V^n : |S_e| < n/2} c_e \prod_{i \in S_e} y_i^{e_i} \quad (m\Omega) \tag{1}$$

where $c_e \in \Omega$. Then for any natural number r and $e \in V^n$ with $|S_e| < n/2$,

$$c_e \equiv \langle \prod_{i \in S_e} y_i^{e_i}, t(y_1, ..., y_n) \rangle_r \quad (m\Omega). \tag{2}$$

Proof. Note that since q and m are relatively prime, q has an inverse in $\mathbf{Z}/m\mathbf{Z}$, and hence also in $\Omega/m\Omega$. Hence the r-inner product is well-defined in $\Omega/m\Omega$. Let $e' \in V^n$ be such that $|S_{e'}| < n/2$. Take the r-inner product of both sides of equation 1 with $\prod_{i \in S_{e'}} y_i^{e'_i}$. We obtain,

$$\langle \prod_{i \in S_{e'}} y_i^{e'_i}, t(y_1, ..., y_n) \rangle_r \equiv \sum_{e \in V^n : |S_e| < n/2} c_e \langle \prod_{i \in S_{e'}} y_i^{e'_i}, \prod_{i \in S_e} y_i^{e_i} \rangle_r \quad (m\Omega).$$

Note $|S_{e'} \cup S_e| < n$. Apply Lemma 3 to the above equation to obtain equation 2.
∎

We now state and prove the main theorem. Theorem 1 is then immediate.

Theorem 5. *Fix any natural number q and let N be any positive natural number. Let $p : \{0, 1\}^N \to \mathbf{Z}$ be a polynomial over the Boolean variables $x_1, ..., x_N$ with integer coefficients, and let $m \in \mathbf{N}$ be such that q and m are relatively prime. Suppose that for some integer $0 \le r \le q - 1$, for any $x_1, ..., x_N$ it holds that,*

$$\sum_{i=1}^N x_i \equiv r \ (q) \implies p(x_1, ..., x_N) \equiv 0 \ (m),$$

and that p is not a constant function mod m. Then the degree of p is at least $\lfloor \frac{N}{2(q-1)} \rfloor$.

Proof. The result is trivial if $N < 2(q - 1)$, so suppose wlog that $N \ge 2(q - 1)$. Let d be the degree of the polynomial p. Suppose $d < \lfloor \frac{N}{2(q-1)} \rfloor$. Then we will show that, under the given hypotheses, p is always zero mod m.

Define ζ, D, V as in the discussion above. Exactly as in [BS], we restrict the input settings so that p can be regarded as a polynomial over inputs in D. For this purpose, assume wlog that $(q-1)|N$; other values of N can be reduced to this by restricting $< q - 1$ of the inputs to 1 (this is the origin of the floor in the degree lower bound). Let $n = \frac{N}{q-1}$. Group the N inputs into n sets of size $q - 1$, each of the form $\{x_{(q-1)i+1}, ..., x_{(q-1)i+q-1}\}$ with $0 \le i \le n - 1$. Let $y_1, ..., y_n$ be

n inputs each taking on values in D. Define the polynomials mentioned in [BS] (though not written down explicitly),

$$u_j(y) = 1 - \prod_{l=1}^{q-1-j} (1 - \frac{1}{q} \sum_{i=0}^{q-1} \zeta^{il} y^i),$$

for $y \in D$ and $1 \leq j \leq q - 1$. Writing $y = \zeta^s$, with $1 \leq s \leq q$, it is easy to verify that $u_j(y) = 0$ if $j \geq s$ and $u_j(y) = 1$ if $j < s$. Thus $u_1(y)u_2(y)...u_{q-1}(y)$, regarded as a string of bits, is $1^{s-1}0^{q-s}$. Restricting the input settings appropriately, we can then encode y_i as the string $x_{(q-1)i+1} x_{(q-1)i+2} \cdots x_{(q-1)i+q-1}$ by setting

$$x_{(q-1)i+j} = u_j(y_{i+1})$$

for $0 \leq i \leq n - 1$ and $1 \leq j \leq q - 1$.

Up to this point, the argument is exactly the same as that given in [BS]. However we must now remember that we are working in $\mathbf{Z}/m\mathbf{Z}$, while the polynomials u_j have coefficients which are not necessarily integers. Therefore instead of computing the polynomial $p(x_1, ..., x_N)$ mod $m\mathbf{Z}$, we compute it mod $m\Omega$. Since $p(x_1, ..., x_N) \equiv 0$ $(m\mathbf{Z})$ iff $p(x_1, ..., x_N) \equiv 0$ $(m\Omega)$, we lose no generality in doing this. Recall from the proof of Lemma 4 that q has an inverse in $\Omega/m\Omega$. Thus, working in $\Omega/m\Omega$, we regard u_j as a polynomial of degree at most $q - 1$ (and weight at most 1) with algebraic integer coefficients. Using the u_j's we can define a polynomial $t : D^n \to \mathbf{Z}$ with coefficients in Ω which agrees with p when the x_i's encode y_i's according to the above scheme:

$$t(y_1, ..., y_n) \equiv p(u_1(y_1), ..., u_{q-1}(y_1), ..., u_1(y_n), ..., u_{q-1}(y_n)) \ (m\Omega).$$

It is easy to see that the *weight* of any monomial in t is at most d, the degree of p. Note that $d < \lfloor \frac{N}{2(q-1)} \rfloor = \lfloor \frac{n}{2} \rfloor$ and hence $d < \frac{n}{2}$. Thus t fulfills the requirements of Lemma 4. We solve for the coefficients c_e of t by that lemma:

$$c_e \equiv \langle \prod_{i \in S_e} y_i^{e_i}, t(y_1, ..., y_n) \rangle_r \ (m\Omega).$$

By the hypothesis of the theorem, every term on the right hand side is zero. Hence for any e, $c_e \equiv 0$ $(m\Omega)$, from which we conclude that for any $y_1, ..., y_n \in D$, $t(y_1, ..., y_n) \equiv 0$ $(m\Omega)$ and therefore, since $t(y_1, ..., y_n)$ is an integer, $t(y_1, ..., y_n) \equiv 0$ $(m\mathbf{Z})$. This immediately implies that $p(x_1, ..., x_N) \equiv 0$ (m) for those q^n input settings of the x_i's that encode y_i's. By re-labelling the x_i's and repeating the argument for each re-labelling we conclude that $p(x_1, ..., x_N) \equiv 0$ (m) for all 2^N settings of the x_i's. ∎

Corollary 6. [Tsai] *Suppose m is fixed and is not a prime power, and let q_{max}^e be the largest prime power dividing m. Then any polynomial which m-represents $\neg\text{Mod}_m$ must have degree at least $\lfloor \frac{n}{2q_{max}^e} \rfloor$.*

Proof. Let p be a polynomial of degree less than $\lfloor \frac{n}{2q^e_{max}} \rfloor$ which m-represents $\neg \text{Mod}_m$. For any prime factor s of m, let $e(s) = ord_s(m)$, i.e., $e(s)$ is the greatest integer such that $s^{e(s)}$ divides m. Let r, s be two distinct prime factors of m. Since $\sum_{i=1}^n x_i \not\equiv 0 \ (m) \Longrightarrow p(x_1, ..., x_n) \equiv 0 \ (m)$, it follows that,

$$\sum_{i=1}^n x_i \not\equiv 0 \ (s^{e(s)}) \Longrightarrow p(x_1, ..., x_n) \equiv 0 \ (r^{e(r)}).$$

Since the degree of p is less than $\lfloor \frac{n}{2s^{e(s)}} \rfloor$, it follows from Theorem 5 that p is the zero function mod $r^{e(r)}$. As this holds for any prime divisor r of m, we conclude that p is identically zero mod m, which is a contradiction. ∎

3 Simulations and Lower Bounds for Equals-of-Mod$_p^+$ Circuits

Let p be a prime. The main result of this section is that the negation of any equals-of-Mod$_p^+$ circuit of size 2^{n^ϵ} (with $\epsilon < 1$) can be p^s-represented, for some $s \in \mathbf{N}$, by a polynomial of sub-linear degree. By Theorem 1, such a polynomial cannot p^s-represent $\text{Mod}_{q,r}$ or $\neg\text{Mod}_{q,r}$ if q is a prime $\neq p$. Hence equals-of-Mod$_p^+$ circuits of size 2^{n^ϵ} cannot compute these functions.

Theorem 7. *Fix any real number $\epsilon < 1$. Let $\{C_n\}$ be a family of equals-of-Mod$_p^+$ circuits of size less than 2^{n^ϵ}. There exist an $\epsilon' < 1$ and an integer n_0 such that for any $n > n_0$, for some $s \in \mathbf{N}$, $\neg C_n$ can be p^s-represented by a polynomial of degree $O(n^{\epsilon'})$.*

Proof. (Sketch): We follow the proof of the second part of Toda's theorem, as applied to circuits as in (e.g.) [BT] or [GKRST]. Suppose the fan-in of the AND's in the Mod$_p^+$ circuits is bounded by $(\log n)^c$. Choose $\epsilon < \epsilon' < 1$ and n_0 sufficiently large that $\epsilon + c\frac{\log \log n_0}{\log n_0} < \epsilon'$. Let $n > n_0$. Apply the degree $O(n^\epsilon)$ "Toda polynomial" Q_{n^ϵ} (see [BT]) to the Mod$_p^+$ subcircuits (it is here we use the primality of p). This amplifies the polynomials computing the Mod$_p^+$ functions sufficiently that we can write down a polynomial of degree $O(n^{\epsilon'})$ which p^{n^ϵ}-represents $\neg C_n$. ∎

Corollary 8. *Let p, q be distinct primes and $\epsilon < 1$. No family of equals-of-Mod$_p^+$ circuits of size 2^{n^ϵ} can compute the functions $\text{Mod}_{q,r}$ or $\neg\text{Mod}_{q,r}$.*

We also make an easy observation here that was mentioned in the introduction.

Proposition 9. *The MOD-degree of the AND function is n.*

Proof. This is immediate from a result of Tarui [Ta] (viz. proposition 1 in that reference). ∎

Applying Theorem 7, it follows that,

Corollary 10. *For any prime p and $\epsilon < 1$, no family of equals-of-Mod_p^+ circuits of size 2^{n^ϵ} can compute the OR function.*

4 The Classes $\mathrm{M}_{=}\mathrm{P}_q$ and Oracle Separations of $\mathrm{C}_{=}\mathrm{P}^{\mathrm{Mod}_q\mathrm{P}}$

In [GKRST], the "Middle-Bit" class MP was defined. One way of defining it is as follows.

Definition 11. A language L is in MP if there exists a #P function f and a polynomial g such that for all x, $x \in L \Leftrightarrow f(x) \bmod 2^{g(|x|)} \geq 2^{g(|x|)-1}$.

One way of varying the definition, of course, is to formulate it in other bases: Replacing the "2" in the definition with a prime "p", we thus obtain a family of classes MP_p (so $\mathrm{MP}=\mathrm{MP}_2$). The question of whether MP is robust under such changes of base, i.e., whether $\mathrm{MP}=\mathrm{MP}_p$ for all prime p relative to all oracles, may be very difficult. If it isn't robust in this sense, to prove it one would need lower bounds for ACC, by the results of [GKRST]. If we weaken the definition by replacing the "$\geq$" with an "$=$", we obtain a family of complexity classes which, in certain ways, is probably much weaker than MP, but is nevertheless polynomial-time Turing-equivalent to it. For these classes, using the results of this paper, we *can* show that, relative to some oracle, the definition is not robust under changes of base.

Definition 12. A language L is in $\mathrm{M}_{=}\mathrm{P}_p$, where p is prime, if there exists a GapP [FFK] function f and a polynomial g such that for all x, $x \in L \Leftrightarrow f(x) \equiv 0 \ (p^{g(|x|)})$.

Note that the definitions of $\mathrm{M}_{=}\mathrm{P}_p$ and MP bear the same relation that that of $\mathrm{C}_{=}\mathrm{P}$ bears to that of PP. However, although $\mathrm{C}_{=}\mathrm{P}$ and PP are not polynomial-time Turing equivalent relative to all oracles ([Gre 93],[Ta]), $\mathrm{M}_{=}\mathrm{P}_p$ and MP (and PP) are.

Proposition 13. $\mathrm{P}^{\mathrm{MP}} = \mathrm{P}^{\mathrm{PP}} = \mathrm{P}^{\mathrm{M}_{=}\mathrm{P}_p}$ *for any prime p.*

Proof. The value of a #P function f can be computed in polynomial time with queries to an $\mathrm{M}_{=}\mathrm{P}_p$ set. For any x, the digits of $f(x)$ in base p are computed adaptively, from right to left. ∎

Note that one hint of the weakness of $\mathrm{M}_{=}\mathrm{P}_p$ lies in the fact that the value of a #P function is computable with *non-adaptive* queries to MP [GKRST]. But since the bits are computed from right to left, $M_=P_2$ captures a kind of counting strategy which complements that of PP (which amounts to binary search, extracting the bits from left to right). Also, $M_=P_p$ and PP are probably incomparable for any p since trivially co-$Mod_pP \subseteq M_=P_p$. Moreover, by generalizing the Turing machine analogue of the proof of Theorem 7, we obtain,

Theorem 14. *For any prime p, Mod_pP is low for $M_=P_p$, that is, $M_=P_p^{Mod_pP} = M_=P_p$.*

Proof. Omitted. ∎

We can now obtain the oracle separations.

Theorem 15. *For any pair of distinct primes q, p, there is an oracle A such that $Mod_qP^A \not\subseteq M_=P_p^A$.*

Proof. (Sketch): We use a standard reduction of the oracle separation problem to a circuit problem. To construct the oracle it is sufficient that the Mod_q function cannot be p^s-represented for any s by a polynomial of small degree. But this follows from Theorem 1. ∎

Corollary 16. *For any pair of distinct primes q, p, there is an oracle A such that $Mod_qP^A \not\subseteq C_=P^{Mod_pP^A}$*

Proof. Obviously, relative to any oracle B, $C_=P^B \subseteq M_=P_p^B$. Hence, for any A, applying Theorem 14 (which relativizes), $C_=P^{Mod_pP^A} \subseteq M_=P_p^{Mod_pP^A} = M_=P_p^A$. Let A be the oracle of Theorem 15. One could also argue directly from Corollary 8. ∎

Finally, we remark that Toda's theorem $PH \subseteq PP^{\oplus P}$ cannot be improved to $PH \subseteq C_=P^{\oplus P}$ relative to all oracles.

Theorem 17. *There is an oracle A such that $NP^A \not\subseteq M_=P_p^A$, and hence $NP^A \not\subseteq C_=P^{Mod_pP^A}$, for all prime p.*

Proof. This follows via standard techniques (as in Theorem 15) and Corollary 10. ∎

References

[ABFR] J ASPNES, R. BEIGEL, M. FURST, AND S. RUDICH, The expressive power of voting polynomials. In *Proceedings of the 23rd Symposium on Theory of Computing*, (1991), 402-409.

[Al] E. ALLENDER, A note on the power of threshold circuits. In *Proceedings of the 30th Symposium on Foundations of Computer Science*, (1989), 580-584.

[Bar] D. BARRINGTON, Bounded-width polynomial-size branching programs recognize exactly those languages in NC^1, in *Journal of Computer and System Sciences* **38**, (1989), 150-164.

[BBR] D. M. BARRINGTON, R. BEIGEL, AND S. RUDICH, Representing Boolean functions as polynomials modulo composite numbers, *Proceedings of the 24th ACM Symposium on Theory of Computing* (1992) 455-461.

[Bei] R. BEIGEL, When do extra majority gates help? polylog(n) majority gates are equivalent to one, in *Proceedings of the 24th ACM Symposium on Theory of Computing* (1992) 450-454.

[BRS] R. BEIGEL, N. REINGOLD, AND D. SPIELMAN, PP is closed under intersection, in *Proceedings of the 23rd ACM Symposium on the Theory of Computation*, (1991), 1-11. A journal version is to appear in *Journal of Computer and System Sciences*.

[BS] D. M. BARRINGTON, H. STRAUBING, Complex polynomials and circuit lower bounds for modular counting, to appear in *Computational Complexity* (also see LATIN '92).

[BT] R. BEIGEL, J. TARUI, On ACC. In *Proceedings of the 32nd Symposium on Foundations of Computer Science*, (1991), 783-792.

[CGT] J.-Y. CAI, F. GREEN AND T. THIERAUF, On the correlation of symmetric functions, to appear in *Mathematical Systems Theory*.

[FFK] S. FENNER, L. FORTNOW AND S. KURTZ, Gap-definable counting classes, in *Proceedings of the Sixth Annual Conference on Structure in Complexity Theory*, IEEE Computer Society Press (1991) 30-42.

[GKRST] F. GREEN, J. KÖBLER, K. REGAN, T. SCHWENTICK, AND J. TORÁN, The power of the middle bit of a #P function, to appear in *Journal of Computer and System Sciences*. Preliminary versions appeared in *Proceedings of the 7th Structure in Complexity Theory Conference*, IEEE Computer Society Press, (1992), 111-117, and in *Proceedings of the Fourth Italian Conference on Theoretical Computer Science*, World-Scientific, Singapore, (1991), 317-329.

[Gre 91] F. GREEN, An oracle separating $\oplus$P from PP^{PH}, *Information Processing Letters* **37** (1991) 149-153.

[Gre 93] F. GREEN, On the power of deterministic reductions to $C_=P$, in *Mathematical Systems Theory* **26** (1993) 215-233.

[Has] J. HÅSTAD, Computational limitations of small-depth circuits, the MIT press, Cambridge, 1987.

[HMPST] A. HAJNAL, W. MAASS, P. PUDLÁK, M. SZEGEDY, AND G. TURÁN, Threshold circuits of bounded depth, in *Proceedings 28th Annual IEEE Symposium on Foundations of Computer Science*, IEEE Computer Society Press (1987) 99-110.

[IR] K. IRELAND AND M. ROSEN, A classical introduction to modern number theory, Second Edition, Springer-Verlag, New York, 1990.

[KP] M. KRAUSE AND P. PUDLÁK, On the computational power of depth 2 circuits with threshold and modulo gates, in *Proceedings of the Twenty-Sixth Annual ACM Symposium on the Theory of Computing*, ACM Press (1994) 48-57.

[Raz] A. A. RAZBOROV, Lower bounds on the size of bounded depth networks over a complete basis with logical addition, *Matematicheskie Zametki* **41** (1987) 598-607. English translation in *Mathematical Notes of the Academy of Sciences of the USSR* **41** (1987) 333-338.

[Sm] R. SMOLENSKY, Algebraic methods in the theory of lower bounds for Boolean circuit complexity, in *Proceedings of the 19th Annual ACM Symposium on Theory of Computing* (1987) 77-82.

[Ta] J. TARUI, Degree complexity of Boolean functions and its applications to relativized separations, in *Proceedings of the Sixth Annual Conference on Structure in Complexity Theory*, IEEE Computer Society Press (1991) 382-390.

[Tod] S. TODA. PP is as hard as the polynomial-time hierarchy. In *SIAM Journal on Computing* **20**, (1991) 865-877.

[Tsai] S.-C. TSAI, Lower bounds on representing Boolean functions as polynomials in Z_m, in *Proceedings of the Eighth Annual Conference on Structure in Complexity Theory*, IEEE Computer Society Press (1993) 96-101.

On Realizing Iterated Multiplication by Small Depth Threshold Circuits

Matthias Krause

Lehrstuhl Informatik II, Universität Dortmund, krause@daedalus.
informatik.uni-dortmund.de

Abstract. Using a lower bound argument based on probabilistic communication complexity it will be shown that iterated multiplication of n–bit numbers modulo $polylog(n)$–bit integers cannot be done efficiently by depth two threshold circuits. As a consequence we obtain that for iterated multiplication of n–bit numbers, in contrast to multiplication, powering, and division, decomposition via Chinese Remaindering does not yield efficient depth 3 threshold circuits.

1 Introduction

In the last years there has been proved a lot of interesting results on the power of small depth threshold circuits [A89,HMPST87,GHK92,Y90,BHKS92]. A main observation is that depth 3 threshold circuits are surprisingly powerful. So, it was shown by *Allender* [A89] that AC_0–functions can be realized by depth 3 threshold circuits of nearly polynomial size. This could still be improved by *Yao* who proved that this is true even for ACC–functions [Y90]. Another group of results concerns efficient small depth realizations of arithmetic operations. For example, *addition* and *comparison* of two n–bit numbers can be done by depth 2 threshold circuits with polynomially many edges [B90,AB91,BHKS92]. For other basic operations such as *multiple addition, sorting, multiplication, squaring, powering*, and *division* of n–bit numbers there are known depth 3 threshold circuits with polynomially many edges [BHKS92,H93]. A certain eyecatching exception is *iterated multiplication*, the multiplication of n n–bit numbers, for which the best known polynomial size threshold circuits have depth 4 [BHKS92].

This paper was initiated by several unsuccessful trials made at several places to construct more efficient threshold circuits for *iterated multiplication*. Is it really possible to construct depth 3 polynomial size circuits for this problem? We give a negative answer of the following type. The main and up to now only successful strategy for getting small depth realizations of arithmetic operations is to decompose the problem via Chinese Remaindering and handle the resulting subproblems in parallel [BHKS92,H93]. Using methods based on probabilistic communication complexity we show that in contrast to *multiple addition, multiplication* and *division* in the case of *iterated multiplication* this strategy does not lead to polynomial size depth 3 threshold circuits.

Observe that, unless there is a significant breakthrough in circuit lower bounds, an exhaustive negative answer cannot be expected because we don't know any method for proving even superlinear lower bounds on the size of depth 3 threshold circuits.

The paper is organized as follows. For making this article self–contained in section 2 we review the main techniques developed in [H93,BHKS92] for designing small depth threshold realizations, including the concepts of approximability and linear representations of Boolean functions. In section 3 we describe a connection between 1–approximability of multi–output functions and probabilistic communication complexity, which is the basis for our lower bound results presented in section 4.

Still one technical remark. For sake of shortness at many places in the text there will occur phrases like "Let $g : \{0,1\}^n \longrightarrow \{0,1\}$ be a Boolean function, where $C(g) \in n^{O(1)}$ ..." instead of "Let $g = (g_n : \{0,1\}^n \longrightarrow \{0,1\})_{n \in \mathbb{N}}$ be a sequence of Boolean functions, where $C(g_n) \in n^{O(1)}$ ...". Please do not get confused by this.

2 Preliminaries

2.1 Different notations of threshold realizations and approximability

The basic processing elements of threshold circuits are Boolean threshold gates, T_r^n, producing one if and only if at least r of the n input bits are one. The class $TC_{0,k}$, $k \geq 1$, contains all problems having depth k threshold circuits with polynomially many edges. As usual, we denote $TC_0 = \bigcup_{k \in \mathbb{N}} TC_{0,k}$. A Boolean function $t : \{0,1\}^n \longrightarrow \{0,1\}$ is called a threshold function if t can be realized by one single threshold gate.

Let $f : \{0,1\}^n \longrightarrow \{0,1\}$ be a Boolean function. Let G be a set of Boolean functions over $\{0,1\}^n$ which is closed with respect to negation and contains the constant functions.

Definition 2.1 *We say that f has a threshold representation over G if f can be realized by a depth two circuit consisting of gates performing functions from G at the bottom level and a threshold gate at the top. The number of edges is called the weight of the representation.*

Clearly, $f \in TC_{0,k}$ if and only if f has a polynomial weight threshold representation over $TC_{0,k-1}$. Sometimes it will be convenient to work with different (but equivalent) notations of threshold representations of f over G.

Lemma 1. (i) *The function f has a threshold representation over G if and only if there are functions $g_1, \ldots, g_s \in G$, real numbers $r, w_1, \ldots, w_s$ and a distance parameter $\delta > 0$ such that for all inputs x*

$$f(x) = 1 \implies \sum_{k=1}^{s} w_k g_k(x) \geq r + \delta$$

$$f(x) = 0 \implies \sum_{k=1}^{s} w_k g_k(x) \leq r - \delta.$$

(ii) *The function f has a threshold representation of polynomial weight over G if and only if there is a representation as in (i), and s, δ^{-1}, as well as $|r|, |w_1|, \ldots, |w_s|$ are polynomially bounded in n.* □

A further useful notation is given by the following

Lemma 2. *A threshold representation of f, given by functions $g_1, \ldots, g_s$ from G and reals $r, w_1, \ldots, w_s$, uniquely defines a probability distribution R on $0, 1, \ldots, s$ fulfilling*

$$Prob_{k \in R\{0,\ldots,s\}}[f(x) = g_k(x)] > \frac{1}{2}.$$

for all inputs x. In dependence of the threshold r, g_0 will be the constant 1 or the constant 0 function.

Proof: W.l.o.g suppose that $r, w_1, \ldots, w_s$ are positive. Otherwise, if $w_k < 0$, g_k has to be replaced by its negations according to the rule $w_k g_k(x) = (-w_k)(1 - g_k(x)) + w_k$ and the threshold r has to be modified correspondingly.

Define $w = \sum_{k=1}^{s} w_k$ and observe that $0 \leq r \leq w$. (Otherwise f would be constant.)

If $\frac{r}{w} > \frac{1}{2}$, define g_0 to be the constant 0 function and p_0 to be the uniquely defined number fulfilling $(1 - p_0)\frac{r}{w} = \frac{1}{2}$. If $\frac{r}{w} < \frac{1}{2}$, define g_0 to be the constant 1 function and p_0 to be the uniquely defined number fulfilling $p_0 + (1 - p_0)\frac{r}{w} = \frac{1}{2}$.

Let $R(0) = p_0$ and $R(k) = (1 - p_0)\frac{w_k}{w}$ for $k = 1, \ldots, s$. It is easy to check that R matches all our requirements. □

Definition 2.2 *Let f, G, g_k, w_k, R be defined as above. Then R is called associated to the fixed threshold representation of f over G. The maximal number $\epsilon > 0$ fulfilling*

$$Prob_{k \in R\{0,\ldots,s\}}[f(x) = g_k(x)] \geq \frac{1}{2} + \epsilon$$

for all inputs x is called the advantage of the representation.

The following useful lemmata can now easily be derived.

Lemma 3. *Let $w_1, \ldots, w_s \in \mathbb{R}$, $g_1, \ldots, g_s \in G$ define a threshold representation of f over G with distance parameter $\delta > 0$. Then the advantage of this representation is bounded from below by $\frac{\delta}{2\sum_{k=1}^{s}|w_k|}$.* □

Lemma 4. **(i)** *The function f has a threshold representation over G if and only if there are $g_1, \ldots, g_s \in G$, a number $\epsilon > 0$ and a probability distribution R on $\{1, \ldots, s\}$ fulfilling for all inputs x $Prob_{k \in R\{1,\ldots,s\}}[g_k(x) = f(x)] \geq \frac{1}{2} + \epsilon$.*
(ii) *The function f has a polynomial weight threshold representation over G if and only if there are g_k, R, ϵ, s as above, where additionally s and ϵ^{-1} are polynomially bounded in n.* □

For constructing small depth realizations of arithmetic operations it is important to consider the following special case of threshold representations of f over G.

Definition 2.3 *The function f is called G-approximable if for any $\epsilon > 0$ there are $g_1, \ldots, g_s \in G$, $w_1, \ldots, w_s \in \mathbb{R}$, where s and $w = \sum_{k=1}^{s} |w_k|$ are polynomially bounded in n and ϵ^{-1}, such that for all x $|f(x) - \sum_{k=1}^{s} w_k g_k(x)| \leq \epsilon$.*

It can easily be proved that the G-approximability of f provides a polynomial weight threshold representation of f over G. Our special interest is devoted to $TC_{0,k}$-approximability which we shortly denote by *k-approximability*.

In the next section we present some examples of 1-approximable problems. The main technique for obtaining small depth realizations of explicit problems is to decompose the problems into k-approximable subproblems for small constant k. In the next section we will demonstrate this method. The special effect of saving depth is due to the following basic property of G-approximability.

Lemma 5. *Suppose we are given G-approximable functions $h_1, \ldots, h_m$, where m is polynomially bounded in n. Further suppose that f has a polynomial weight threshold representation over $\{h_1, \ldots, h_m\}$. Then f has a polynomial weight threshold representation over G.*

Observe that the lemma provides a polynomial size depth three circuit for f consisting of a bottom level of G-gates, a middle level of threshold gates realizing the functions $h_1, \ldots, h_m$ and a threshold gate at the top. The lemma states that the middle level can be saved by getting a polynomial increase in size.

<u>Proof:</u> By definition there are $\delta > 0$ and reals $r, w_1', \ldots, w_m'$, where δ^{-1} and $w' = \sum_{l=1}^{m} |w_l'|$ are polynomially bounded in n such that for all inputs x

$$f(x) = 1 \implies \sum_{l=1}^{m} w_l' h_l(x) \geq r + \delta \quad \text{and} \quad f(x) = 0 \implies \sum_{l=1}^{m} w_l' h_l(x) \leq r - \delta.$$

Now, for each l, $1 \leq l \leq m$, take a polynomial weight threshold representation of h_l over G which approximates h_l with error $\frac{\delta}{2w'}$. Combining these approximators according to $w_1', \ldots, w_m'$ yields a polynomial weight threshold representation of f over G. $\square$

2.2 Linear representations of Boolean functions

We need the 1-approximability for Boolean functions of the following type.

Definition 2.4 *A function $\phi : \mathbb{R} \longrightarrow \{0,1\}$ and a linear mapping $l : \mathbb{R}^n \longrightarrow \mathbb{R}$ is called a linear representation of a given Boolean function $f : \{0,1\}^n \longrightarrow \{0,1\}$ if for all inputs $x = (x_1, \ldots, x_n)$*

$$f(x) = \phi(l(x)).$$

A set of pairwise disjoint intervals $[a_1, b_1], [a_2, b_2], \ldots, [a_q, b_q]$ of the real line is called a complete set of 1-intervals of the representation if for all inputs x

$$f(x) = 1 \quad \Longleftrightarrow \quad l(x) \in \bigcup_{j=1}^{q} [a_j, b_j].$$

Observe that the linear mapping $l(x_1, \ldots, x_n) = \sum_{i=1}^{n} 2^i x_i$ induces a linear representation for each Boolean function f. The function f is symmetric if and only if it has a linear representation with respect to $l(x_1, \ldots, x_n) = \sum_{i=1}^{n} x_i$. A threshold function is characterized by the property that it has at most one 1–interval. We will essentially make use of the following observation [BHKS92,H93].

Lemma 6. *If $f : \{0,1\}^n \longrightarrow \{0,1\}$ has a linear representation with a complete set of only polynomially many 1–intervals, then f is 1–approximable.*

Proof: Fix a linear representation ϕ, l of f and a related complete set of 1–intervals, say $[a_1, b_1], [a_2, b_2], \ldots [a_q, b_q]$, where $q \in n^{O(1)}$. Observe that f can be written as

$$f(x) = \sum_{i=1}^{q} (t_i(x) + t_i'(x)) - q,$$

where the unbounded weight threshold functions t_i and t_i' test whether $l(x) \geq a_i$ and $l(x) \leq b_i$, respectively. It has been shown in [GHR92] that arbitrary threshold functions are 1–approximable. In [GK93] there has been given an explicit construction of those approximators. Combining $\frac{\epsilon}{2q}$–approximators for all t_i, t_i' with the above exact representation gives an ϵ–approximator for f. Hence, f is 1–approximable. $\square$

Exhibiting the existence of linear representations with complete sets of polynomially many 1–intervals, one can prove 1–approximability for Boolean operations of the following types. From now on we identify natural numbers with their binary representation.

Definition 2.5 *Let $a_1, \ldots, a_n \in \mathbb{N}$ be arbitrarily fixed n–bit numbers and denote $\mathbf{a} = (a_1, \ldots, a_n)$. Let a_0 be a further arbitrarily fixed n–bit number.*

(i) *Let $T_\mathbf{a} : \{0,1\}^n \longrightarrow \{0,1\}^{n + \lceil \log n \rceil}$ defined by $T_\mathbf{a}(x_1, \ldots, x_n) = \sum_{i=1}^{n} a_i x_i$.*
(ii) *The operation $M_{a_0, \mathbf{a}} : (\{0,1\}^p)^n \longrightarrow \{0,1\}^n$, where the inputs are n p–bit numbers $x^1, \ldots, x^n$ is defined as $M_{a_0, \mathbf{a}}(x_1, \ldots, x_n) = \sum_{i=1}^{n} a_i x^i \bmod a_0$.*

Lemma 7. (i) *Each output bit of the operation $T_\mathbf{a}$ is 1–approximable.*

(ii) *If $p = O(\log n)$ and $\frac{\sum_{i=1}^{n} a_i}{a_0} \in n^{O(1)}$ then each output bit of the operation $M_{a_0, \mathbf{a}}$ is 1–approximable.*

The proof of (i) is quite straightforward and can be found in [BHKS92,H93]. Item (ii) can be obtained from (i) by replacing $x^i = \sum_{j=0}^{p-1} 2^j x_j^i$. $\square$

2.3 Realizing operations by Chinese Remaindering

Realizing an arithmetic operation $F : \{0,1\}^n \longrightarrow \{0,1\}^m$, where $m \in n^{O(1)}$ by Chinese Remaindering means the following. Fix p–bit numbers $q_1 \ldots, q_r$ and set $Q = \prod_{j=1}^{r} q_j$ such that $p \in O(\log(n))$, $Q \geq 2^m$, $\log(Q) \in n^{O(1)}$ and for all $i \neq$

$j \in \{1, \ldots, r\}$ the greatest common divisor of q_i and q_j is one. The corresponding Chinese Remaindering Transformation $CRT : \{0,1\}^m \longrightarrow (\{0,1\}^p)^r$ is defined

$$CRT(y) = (y \bmod q_1, \ldots, y \bmod qr).$$

Given $F, q_1 \ldots, q_r, Q$ as above let $F^{(j)}(x) = F(x) \bmod q_j$.

Lemma 8. *If for all $j = 1, \ldots, r$ each output bit of $F^{(j)}$ is k-approximable then all output bits of F are $(k+1)$-approximable.*

Proof: It is sufficient to show that $CRT^{-1} : (\{0,1\}^p)^r \longrightarrow \{0,1\}^m$, the inverse transformation of Chinese Remaindering, is 1–approximable. Observe that CRT^{-1} is given by

$$CRT^{-1}(y^1, \ldots, y^r) = \sum_{j=1}^{r} e_j y^j \bmod Q,$$

where $e_1, \ldots, e_r$ are fixed numbers from $\{1, \ldots, q-1\}$, the so–called orthogonal idempotents, characterized by the property $e_i \bmod q_j = \delta_{i,j}$. It is easy to check that CRT^{-1} matches all requirements of Lemma 7, thus all its output bits are 1–approximable. □

For the sake of illustration we present the proof of 2–approximability of the multiplication of two n bit numbers $mult_n : \{0,1\}^n \times \{0,1\}^n \longrightarrow \{0,1\}^{2n}$.

Lemma 9. *Let $n, m = 2n, Q, q_1, \ldots, q_r$ be defined as above. Then for all $j = 1, \ldots, r$ $mult_n^{(j)}$ is 1–approximable.*

Proof: For all n–bit numbers $x = (x_{n-1}, \ldots, x_0), y = (y_{n-1}, \ldots, y_0) \in \{0,1\}^n$ define

$$l(x,y) = \sum_{i=0}^{n-1} a_i x_i + nq_j \left(\sum_{i=0}^{n-1} a_i y_i \right),$$

where for all $i = 1, \ldots, n$, $a_i = 2^i \bmod q_j$. It can easily be checked that l induces a linear representation of $mult_n^{(j)}$. As $\max\{l(x,y), \ x, y \in \{0,1\}^n\} \in n^{O(1)}$ there exists a complete set of polynomially many 1–intervals for this representation. By Lemma 6, all output bits of $mult_n^{(j)}$ are 1–approximable. □

How is the situation for $it.mult_n : (\{0,1\}^n)^n \longrightarrow \{0,1\}^{n^2}$, the multiplication of n n–bit numbers? The best known realization of $it.mult_n(x^1, \ldots, x^n)$, which shows that $it.mult_n$ is 3–approximable, requires that $q_1, \ldots, q_r$ are prime numbers. Further we need in advance for each $j = 1 \ldots r$ a number u_j having multiplicative order $q_j - 1$ in $\mathbb{F}_{q_j}^*$. The first step is to compute in parallel $\log_{u_j} x^i$, $i = 1 \ldots n$, $j = 1 \ldots r$, this is 1–approximable. Computing from this $it.mult_n(x^1, \ldots, x^n) \bmod q_j$ via adding the discrete logarithms is also 1–approximable. We obtain 2–approximability of all $it.mult_n^{(j)}$ and 3–approximability of $it.mult_n$.

The main result of this paper is that for all p–bit numbers q, where $p \in O(\log(n))$, which have a prime factor not smaller than 5, $it.mult_n \bmod q$ is not 1–approximable, not depending on how the binary code of the output is chosen. Consequently, realizing $it.mult$ by Chinese Remaindering does not lead to polynomial size depth three circuits.

3   1–Approximability and Probabilistic Communication Complexity

This section is devoted to the proof of the following statement:

Theorem 10. *Let* $g : \{0,1\}^n \longrightarrow \{0,1\}^m$ *be a 1–approximable Boolean operation with* $m = O(\log(n))$. *Further let* $h : \{0,1\}^m \longrightarrow \{0,1\}$ *be arbitrarily fixed. Then the probabilistic communication complexity of* $f = h \circ g : \{0,1\}^n \longrightarrow \{0,1\}$ *with respect to an arbitrarily fixed partition of the set of input variables is at most* $O(m \log(n))$.

We will work with the following elementary notation of one–way probabilistic communication protocols, for more details see [HR88,K91]. Suppose we are given a Boolean function $f = f(x_1,\ldots,x_n,y_1,\ldots,y_n)$ in a fixed distributed form. Communication protocols for f refer to a pair (P_0,P_1) of processors of unbounded computational power which want to cooperate in computing $f(x,y)$ under the restriction that P_0 only knows the left input half x, and P_1 only knows the right input half y. A protocol Π of length k works as follows. In dependence of x and a private random string r, processor P_0 computes a message $M = M(x,r) \in \{0,1\}^k$ and sends it to P_1. Then processor P_1 decides in dependence of w and y deterministically whether to accept or to reject the input. Π computes the function f with advantage ϵ if for all inputs (x,y) it holds

$$f(x,y) = 1 \quad \Longrightarrow \quad \text{Prob}[\Pi \text{ accepts } (x,y)] \geq \frac{1}{2} + \epsilon.$$

$$f(x,y) = 0 \quad \Longrightarrow \quad \text{Prob}[\Pi \text{ accepts } (x,y)] \leq \frac{1}{2} - \epsilon.$$

Let us fix a number $\epsilon = \frac{1}{3}2^{-4m}$. By definition, there are numbers $s, w, W \in n^{O(1)}$, threshold functions $T_1,\ldots,T_s : \{0,1\}^n \times \{0,1\}^n \longrightarrow \{0,1\}$ of weight $\leq W$, and real functions $g'_j = \sum_{k=1}^s w_{j,k}T_k$, $j = 1,\ldots,m$, fulfilling for all j,k $|w_{j,k}| \leq w$, such that $\left|g_j(x,y) - g'_j(x,y)\right| \leq \epsilon$ for all inputs $x,y \in \{0,1\}^n$ and all j, $1 \leq j \leq m$.

Now consider the basis $\{x^\alpha : \{0,1\}^m \longrightarrow \{0,1\}, \ \alpha \in \{0,1\}^m\}$ of all monomials, resp. AND–functions, which are defined as follows. For $\alpha = (0,0,\ldots,0)$ set $x^\alpha = e_1$, the constant–1–function. Otherwise let $x^\alpha = \prod_{j,\alpha_j=1} x_j = \bigwedge_{j,\alpha_j=1} x_j$. It can easily be checked that $\{x^\alpha, \ \alpha \in \{0,1\}^m\}$ generates the whole set $\mathbb{R}^{\{0,1\}^m}$ as real linear vector space.

Consequently, h has a unique representation $h = \sum_{\alpha \in \{0,1\}^m} \lambda_\alpha x^\alpha$, where $\lambda_\alpha \in \mathbb{R}$ for all $\alpha \in \{0,1\}^m$. Using *Cramer*'s rule it can be derived that all coefficients λ_α are integers between -2^m and 2^m.

Denote by $h' = \sum_{\alpha \in \{0,1\}^m} \lambda_\alpha x^\alpha : \mathbf{R}^m \longrightarrow \mathbf{R}$ the unique multilinear extension of h and consider $f' : \{0,1\}^n \times \{0,1\}^n \longrightarrow \mathbf{R}$ defined by $f' = h' \circ g'$.

Observe that for all $x, y \in \{0,1\}^n$ $|f(x,y) - f'(x,y)| = |h'(z) - h'(z')|$, where $z = (g_1(x,y), \ldots, g_m(x,y))$ and $z' = (g'_1(x,y), \ldots, g'_m(x,y))$.

Consequently,

$$|f(x,y) - f'(x,y)| \le 2^{2m} \max_{\alpha \in \{0,1\}^m} |z^\alpha - z'^\alpha| \le$$

$$\le 2^{2m} \max\{2\epsilon, (1+\epsilon)^m - (1-\epsilon)^m\} \le 2^{2m} 2\epsilon m (1+\epsilon)^{m-1} \le \epsilon 2^{4m}.$$

By definition of ϵ we obtain that for all $x, y \in \{0,1\}^n$

$$|f(x,y) - f'(x,y)| \le \frac{1}{3}. \tag{1}$$

Applying the distributive law to $f' = h' \circ g'$ and simplifying the expression appropriately, the function f' can be written as

$$f' = \sum_{J \subseteq \{1,\ldots,s\}, |J| \le m} v_J U_J,$$

where $U_J : \{0,1\}^n \times \{0,1\}^n \longrightarrow \{0,1\}$ are defined as $U_J(x,y) = \bigwedge_{j \in J} T_j(x,y)$. Observe that for all $J \subseteq \{1, \ldots, s\}$ it holds that

$$|v_J| \in n^{O(m)}. \tag{2}$$

Further observe that by (1) f' defines a threshold representation of f. Denote by R the probability distribution on $U = \{U_J, J \subseteq \{1, \ldots, s\}, |J| \le m\}$ corresponding to this representation. (See Lemma 2, eventually some of the U_J have to be replaced by their negation.) We denote by ϵ^* the advantage of this representation. By Lemma 3, (1) and (2) it follows straightforwardly that $\epsilon^{*-1} \in n^{O(m)}$.

Now we are ready to define an efficient probabilistic communication protocol Π for f. Suppose that for all j, $1 \le j \le s$, the threshold function T_j is defined as

$$T_j(x,y) = 1 \iff \sum_{i=1}^n a_{i,j} x_i + \sum_{i=1}^n b_{i,j} y_i \ge c_j,$$

where $a_{i,j}, b_{i,j}, c_j$ are integers fulfilling $\sum_{i=1}^n |a_{i,j}| + \sum_{i=1}^n |b_{i,j}| + |c_j| \le W$.

Given the input x to player P_0 and y to player P_1, P_0 chooses randomly according to R a function $u \in U$, and sends the message $M(x,u)$ to P_1, where

$$M(x,u) = t' \# \sum_{i=1}^n a_{i,j_1} x_i \# \ldots \# \sum_{i=1}^n a_{i,j_l} x_i$$

and $T_{i_1}, \ldots, T_{i_l}$, $l \le m$, are the threshold functions u is concerned with.

Knowing $M(x,u)$, player P_1 can now compute $T_{i_1}(x,y), \ldots, T_{i_l}(x,y)$ and, consequently, $u(x,y)$. P_1 accepts if $u(x,y) = 1$ and rejects otherwise.

It can easily be checked that this protocol computes g with advantage ϵ^*. The length of the protocol is not larger than $\log(t) + m \log(W) \in O(m \log(n))$. $\square$

4 Iterated multiplication modulo small integers is not 1–approximable

This section is devoted to the proof of

Lemma 11. *Let $q \geq 5$ be an $O(\log(n))$–bit prime number. Then the problem $it.mult_n \bmod q$ is not 1–approximable.*

Using this lemma it is quite straightforward to show

Theorem 12. *Let r be an $O(\log(n))$–bit number having a prime factor not smaller than 5. Then the problem $it.mult_n \bmod r$ is not 1–approximable.*

Proof: Suppose there is a prime number $q \geq 5$, a natural number $r = r'q$ and an output representation

$$it.mult_n \bmod r : (\{0,1\}^n)^n \longrightarrow \{0,1\}^m,$$

$m = O(\log(n))$, for $it.mult_n \bmod r$ such that each output bit is 1–approximable. By Theorem 10, this 1–approximator can be used to construct a 1–approximator for each output bit of $it.mult_n \bmod q$. This contradicts Lemma 11. $\square$

We will prove Lemma 11 by using the following lower bound result from [HR88] on the probabilistic communication complexity of ip_n^2 defined by

$$ip_n^2(x_1, \ldots, x_n, y_1, \ldots, y_n) = x_1 y_1 \oplus \ldots \oplus x_n y_n.$$

Lemma 13. *For all $\epsilon > 0$ fulfilling $\epsilon^{-1} \in 2^{\log^{O(1)} n}$ it holds that the length of any probabilistic communication protocol computing ip_n^2 with advantage ϵ is $\Omega(n)$.* $\square$

An alternative proof of this result which extends to $MOD_m(x_1 y_1, \ldots, x_n y_n)$ for all $m \in \mathbb{N}$ can be found in [K91,KW91].

Consider now the function $f : (\{0,1\}^n)^n \longrightarrow \{0,1\}$, over n n–bit numbers $x^{(1)}, \ldots, x^{(n)}$ defined by

$$f(x^{(1)}, \ldots, x^{(n)}) = 1 \quad \Longleftrightarrow \quad \prod_{i=1}^n x^{(i)} \text{ is a quadratic non–residue mod } q.$$

We construct a partition of the n^2 input variables of f into subsets U and V such that for any $\epsilon > 0$, $\epsilon^{-1} \in 2^{\log^{O(1)} n}$ the length of any probabilistic communication protocol computing f with advantage ϵ is $\Omega(n)$. By Theorem 10 this proves Lemma 11.

We do that by defining a *rectangular reduction* of ip_n^2 to f, i.e. we define mappings $l : \{0,1\}^n \longrightarrow \{0,1\}^U$ and $r : \{0,1\}^n \longrightarrow \{0,1\}^V$ such that either $ip_n^2(x,y) = f(l(x), r(y))$ for all $x, y \in \{0,1\}^n$, or $ip_n^2(x,y) = \neg f(l(x), r(y))$ for all $x, y \in \{0,1\}^n$. This is sufficient as l and r translate each protocol for f into a protocol of the same length for ip_n^2. Before defining U, V, l, r observe the following facts.

Lemma 14. *For all primes $q \geq 5$ there is a natural number $a, 1 \leq a \leq q - 3$, fulfilling*

$$\left(\frac{a}{q}\right) = \left(\frac{a+1}{q}\right) \neq \left(\frac{a+2}{q}\right)$$

<u>Proof:</u> As usual, $\left(\frac{a}{q}\right)$ denotes the *Legendre* symbol defined as

$$\left(\frac{a}{q}\right) = \begin{cases} 0, & \text{if } q \text{ divides } a \\ 1, & \text{if } a \text{ is a quadratic residue modulo } p \\ -1, & \text{if } a \text{ is a quadratic non--residue modulo } p \end{cases}$$

The multiplicative group $\mathbf{F}_q^*$ can be written as $\{1, \omega, \omega^2, \ldots, \omega^{q-1}\}$ for some $\omega \in \mathbf{F}_q^*$. Clearly, $a' \in \mathbf{F}_q^*$ is a quadratic residue modulo p if and only if $\log_\omega a'$ is even.

Consequently, it is sufficient to prove the existence of a, $1 \leq a \leq q - 2$, such that $\left(\frac{a}{q}\right) = \left(\frac{a+1}{q}\right)$. But this follows straightforwardly from the fact that $\left(\frac{1}{q}\right) = \left(\frac{4}{q}\right) = 1$. $\square$

We get l, r by defining mappings $\bar{l} : \{0,1\} \longrightarrow \{0,1\}$ and $\bar{r} : \{0,1\} \longrightarrow \{0, 1, \ldots, 2^n - 1\}$ and setting

$$(l, r)(x_1, \ldots, x_n, y_1, \ldots, y_n) = (\bar{l}(x_1) + 2\bar{r}(y_1), \ldots, \bar{l}(x_n) + 2\bar{r}(y_n)).$$

The corresponding partition (U, V) is given by putting all last bits of the n--bit input numbers $x^{(1)}, \ldots, x^{(n)}$ into U and the remaining input bits into V.

The mapping $\bar{l}$ will be the identity, i.e., $\bar{l}(b) = b$ for $b \in \{0,1\}$, and $\bar{r}$ will be defined as $\bar{r}(0) = A$ and $\bar{r}(1) = A + 1$ for some appropriate number A, $1 \leq A \leq p - 1$.

Now observe that $f(x^{(1)}, \ldots, x^{(n)}) = 1$ if and only if there is no i, $1 \leq i \leq n$, such that q divides $x^{(i)}$ and the number of those i with $\left(\frac{x^{(i)}}{q}\right) = -1$ is odd.

Consequently, the mappings l and r will do their job if A has one of the following properties.

(a) It holds $\left(\frac{\bar{l}(0)+2\bar{r}(0)}{q}\right) = \left(\frac{\bar{l}(0)+2\bar{r}(1)}{q}\right) = \left(\frac{\bar{l}(1)+2\bar{r}(0)}{q}\right) = 1$ and $\left(\frac{\bar{l}(1)+2\bar{r}(1)}{q}\right) = -1$.
This is equivalent to $\left(\frac{2A}{q}\right) = \left(\frac{2A+1}{q}\right) = 1$ and $\left(\frac{2A+2}{q}\right) = -1$ and means that l, r reduces ip_n^2 to f.

(b) It holds $\left(\frac{\bar{l}(0)+2\bar{r}(0)}{q}\right) = \left(\frac{\bar{l}(0)+2\bar{r}(1)}{q}\right) = \left(\frac{\bar{l}(1)+2\bar{r}(0)}{q}\right) = -1$ and $\left(\frac{\bar{l}(1)+2\bar{r}(1)}{q}\right) = 1$.
This is equivalent to $\left(\frac{2A}{q}\right) = \left(\frac{2A+1}{q}\right) = -1$ and $\left(\frac{2A+2}{q}\right) = 1$ and means that l, r reduces ip_n^2 to f, if n is odd, or l, r reduces ip_n^2 to $\neg f$ if n is even.

By Lemma 14 there is some a, $1 \leq a \leq q - 3$, such that $\left(\frac{a}{q}\right) = \left(\frac{a+1}{q}\right) \neq \left(\frac{a+2}{q}\right)$. It is easy to check that $A = ca \bmod q$ where c denotes the multiplicative inverse of 2 in $\mathbf{F}_q^*$, matches all our requirements. $\square$

5 Concluding Remarks

Our results were concerned with the design of threshold circuits of very small depth by decomposing given problems into subproblems with bounded linear representations. Observe that there are still several critical points concerning the uniformity of the described circuits. Computing the orthogonal idempotents which are needed for the inversion of Chinese Remaindering is not known to be in NC. Another critical point are the approximators given in [GK93] for unbounded weight threshold functions occuring in all of the described circuits. Is it possible to find less complicated approximators for the particular threshold functions induced by arithmetic operations?

Another open question is to determine the complexity of $it.mult_n \mod q$ for integers q only divisible by 2 and 3. First investigations in this direction were made in [BHK94]. There it is shown that the last three bits of $it.mult$ corresponding to $q = 2, 4, 8$ are 1–approximable, while $it.mult \mod q$ for integers divisible by 9 or 16 is not 1–approximable. Further, it could be shown there that for numbers q not divisible by 2 or 3 $it.mult \mod q$ is not in $TC_{0,2}$. But for $q \in \{3, 6, 12, 24\}$, the situation is unclear.

Acknowledgment

I would like to thank Claudia Bertram, Thomas Hofmeister, Ingo Wegener, and Stephan Waack for helpful discussions.

References

[A89] Allender,E.: *A note on the power of threshold circuits*, Proceedings der 30. IEEE Symposium FOCS, 1989, 580–584.

[AB91] Alon,N.,J.Bruck: *Explicit constructions of depth–2 majority circuits for comparison and addition*, Technical Report RJ 8300 (75661) of the IBM Almaden Research Center, San Jose, 1991.

[B90] Bruck,J. *Harmonic analysis of polynomial threshold functions*, SIAM Journal of Discrete Mathematics, 3, Nr. 22, 1990, 168–177.

[BHK94] Bertram,C.,Hofmeister,Th.,Krause,M., *Multiple product mod small numbers* manuscript Dortmund 1994

[BHKS92] Bruck,J.,Th.Hofmeister,Th.Kailath,K.Y.Siu, *Depth efficient networks for division and related problems.* Technical Report 1992, to appear in IEEE Transactions on Information Theory.

[GHR92] Goldmann,M.,J.Håstad,A.A.Razborov: *Majority Gates versus general weighted threshold gates*, J. of Computational Complexity 2 (1992), 277–300.

[GK93] Goldmann,M.,M.Karpinski: *Simulating Threshold Circuits by Majority Circuits.* Proc. 25th ACM Conference STOC, 1993.

[HMPST87] Hajnal,A.,W.Maass, P.Pudlák, M.Szegedy, G.Turán: *Threshold circuits of bounded depth,* Proc. 28th IEEE Conf. FOCS, 1987, 99–110.

[HR88] Halstenberg,B.,R.Reischuk *Relations between communication complexity classes* Proc. of the 3. IEEE Structure in Complexity Theory Conference, 1988, 19–28.

[H93] Hofmeister, Th. *Depth–efficient threshold circuits for arithmetic functions* in: *Theoretical Advances in Neural Computation and Learning* eds. Roychowdhury et.al., Kluwer Academic Publishers, ISBN 0-7923-9478-X.

[HHK91] Hofmeister,Th.,W.Hohberg,S.Köhling: *Some notes on threshold circuits and multiplication in depth 4* IPL 39 (1991) 219–225.

[K91] Krause,M. *Geometric Arguments yield better bounds for threshold circuits and distributed computing* Proc. of the 6. IEEE Structure in Complexity Theory Conference, 314–322.

[KW91] Krause,M.,S.Waack, *Variation ranks of communication matrices and lower bounds for depth two circuits having symmetric gates with unbounded fan-in,* Proc. 32th IEEE Conference FOCS, 1991, 777–787.

[RT92] Reif,J.H.,S.R.Tate *On threshold circuits and polynomial computation* SIAM Journal of Computing, Vol.21,Nr.5,pp.896–908, 1992

[Y90] Yao,A.C.: *On ACC and Threshold Circuits,* Proc. 31th IEEE Conference FOCS, 1990, 619–628.

A Random NP-complete problem for inversion of 2D Cellular Automata*

Bruno Durand

LIP, ENS-Lyon CNRS, 46 Allée d'Italie, 69364 Lyon Cedex 07, France.

Abstract. In this paper, we prove the co-RNP-completeness (RNP= Random NP) of the following decision problem: "Given a 2-dimensional cellular automaton $\mathcal{A}$, is $\mathcal{A}$ reversible when restricted to finite configurations extending a given row?" In order to prove this result, we introduce a polynomial reduction from problems concerning finite tilings into problems concerning cellular automata. Then we add to tile sets and cellular automata two probability functions and we prove that these problems are not only co-NP-complete, but co-RNP-complete too.

Topics: computational complexity, automata and formal languages, computer systems theory, cryptography.

1 Introduction

Cellular automata (CA for short) have been intensively studied as model for parallel phenomena: a cellular automaton makes a large amount of very simple cell work together synchronously. Each cell is very rudimentary (modeled by a finite state automaton) but the whole system is capable of very complex evolutions. As soon as the notion of CA has been formalized, people tried to characterize their evolutions in terms of surjectivity or bijectivity. In 1962-63, Moore and Myhill proved the so-called "garden of Eden" theorem which states that *surjectivity* is equivalent to *injectivity on finite configurations* [17, 16]. In 1972, Richardson proved that if a CA realizes a bijective function, then there exists another CA called its *inverse* that realizes the inverse function [18]. The same year, Amoroso and Patt proved that the reversibility (or the surjectivity) of 1-dimensional CA is decidable [1].

Recently, Jarkko Kari proved that the reversibility of 2-dimensional CA fails to be decidable [13, 14] as well as their surjectivity (for which a more straightforward proof can be found in [7] and an improved version in [10]). An easy consequence of this result is that the inverse of a reversible 2D CA cannot be found by an algorithm: its size can be greater than any computable function of the size of the reversible CA. The proof of Kari's theorem consists in transforming the tiling problem of the plane which has been proved undecidable in

---

* This work was partially supported by the Esprit Basic Research Action "Algebraic and Syntactic Methods In Computer Science" and by the PRC "Mathématique et Informatique".

1966 by Berger [3, 19] into the reversibility problem on an adequate family of CA. Physicists have been very interested by this work since they use CA for modeling complex natural systems with local interactions (see [21] for a review of the domain).

Kari's work also revived the idea of using invertible CA for public key cryptography. This idea had been presented by Stephen Wolfram in the 80's using 1-dimensional CA. But it was not a success since the problem of inversion is too easy for 1D CA. For 2D CA, we prove that even if we use bounded CA (*i.e.* CA working on finite or periodic configurations) the problem of inversion is very difficult. We have proved in [6, 9, 8], that the problem of inversion when the CA are restricted to *finite* or *periodic* bounded configurations is co-NP-complete. But NP-completeness is not considered as a good characterization of intractability, hence is not a good argument for the security of a crypto-system: KNAPSACK is NP-complete, but crypto-systems based on this problem are not secure since most of the instance of the problem are very easy to solve even if the worst case is difficult. In this paper, we prove that a randomized version of the inversion problem is co-NP-complete *in average* (also called co-Random-NP-complete or co-RNP-complete). Our result also holds for k-dimensional CA where $k \geq 2$. But in the case of 1-dimensional CA, the reversibility problem can be solved in polynomial time in the size of the transition table (see [20] for another point of view on this problem).

The class RNP has been introduced by Levin in [15]. The idea is to add a probability function to the instances of the problem. Levin introduced what could be the notion of polynomial reduction between these probabilistic problems. There are two different kinds of reduction leading to a weak version and a strong version of RNP-completeness: *average polynomial* reductions and *strict polynomial* reductions. Very few RNP-complete problems are known, even in the weak model. Our problem is co-RNP-complete in the strong model: we present a strict polynomial reduction from Levin's tiling problem into ours.

In the following, we first present briefly usual definitions of CA and tilings and the problematic of RNP-completeness. We introduce farther the problem FINITE-TILING proved RNP-complete by Levin. In the following section, we present our problem, called CA-FINITE-INJECTIVE, dealing with finite configurations of 2D CA. We present in full details the reduction of FINITE-TILING into CA-FINITE-INJECTIVE.

2 Definitions and basic properties

2.1 Cellular automata

Cellular automata are formally defined as quadruplets (n, S, N, f). The integer n is the *dimension* of the space the CA will work on. $S = \{s_1, s_2, \ldots, s_k\}$ is a finite set called the set of *states*. The *neighborhood* N is a v-tuple of distinct vectors of $\mathbb{Z}^n$. For us, $N = (x_1, \ldots, x_v)$: the x_i's are the relative positions of the neighbor cells with respect to a given center cell. The states of these neighbors are used to compute the new state of the center cell. The *local function* of the cellular automaton $f : S^v \mapsto S$ gives the local transition rule.

A *configuration* is an application from $\mathbb{Z}^n$ to S. The set of configurations is $S^{\mathbb{Z}^n}$ on which the *global function* G of the cellular automaton is defined via f:

$$\forall c \in S^{\mathbb{Z}^n}, \forall i \in \mathbb{Z}^n, G(c)(i) = f(c(i + x_1), \ldots, c(i + x_v)).$$

Remark that cellular automata are characterized by S, N and f, but, even if two cellular automata are syntactically different, they may compute the same global function G. In the following, we consider mainly two-dimensional CA ($n = 2$).

Sometimes, a state q for which $f(q, q, \ldots, q) = q$ is distinguished in S and is called a *quiescent* state. A *finite configuration* is an almost everywhere quiescent configuration. If there exist two integers i and j such that all the non-quiescent cells of the configuration are located inside a rectangle of size $i \times j$, then, we say that the size of the finite configuration is smaller than (or equal to) $i \times j$.

In order to prove complexity results, it is very important to define precisely what are sizes of instances. We use the following convention:

Size: *The size necessary to code a cellular automaton is* $\mathcal{O}(s^v . \log s)$ *where s is its number of states and v the number of elements of its neighborhood.*

The size of the coding of a CA is exactly the sum of the size of its local transition function and of the size of its neighborhood. The local transition function is only a v-dimensional table, hence its size is $\mathcal{O}(s^v . \log s)$. The size of the neighborhood is the size of the coding of the coordinates of each neighbor cell. We assume in the following that this last size is lower than the size of the transition table, more precisely, that $\forall x \in N, |x| \leq Cs^v$ where $|x|$ denotes the length of the coding of x and C is a constant.

This hypothesis is natural because if it were not the case, the neighbors of a cell would be very far from it hence a single iteration of the CA would be intractable! If we refuse this hypothesis, the problems we present farther remain co-NP-*hard* (resp. co-RNP-hard) and may not be in co-NP (resp. in co-RNP).

2.2 Tilings

A tile is a square the sides of which are colored. Colors belong to a finite set C called the *color set*. A set of tiles τ is a subset of C^4. All tiles have the same (unit) size. A tiling of the plane is *valid* if and only if all pairs of adjacent sides have the same color. Notice that it is not allowed to turn tiles. The following well-known theorem is due to Berger [3] in 1966 and a simplified proof was given in 1971 by Robinson [19].

Theorem 1. *Given a tile set, it is undecidable whether this tile set can be used to tile the plane.*

We can also define *finite tilings*. We assume that the set of colors contains a special "blank" color and that the set of tiles contains a "blank" tile *i.e.* a tile whose sides are blank. A finite tiling is an *almost everywhere blank* tiling of the plane. If there exist two integers i and j such that all the non-blank tiles of the tiling are located inside a rectangle of size $i \times j$, then, we say that the size of the finite tiling is lower than $i \times j$. Notice that inside the $i \times j$ rectangle, there can be blank and non-blank tiles. If there is at least one non-blank tile, then the tiling is called *non-trivial*.

Another undecidability result can be proved simply by using a construction presented by Robinson in [19] which reduces the undecidability of the halting problem for Turing Machines into it:

Theorem 2. *Given a tile set with a blank tile, it is undecidable whether this tile set can be used to form a valid finite non-trivial tiling of the plane.*

3 Random NP-complete problems

We present below the complexity class "Random NP" (RNP for short) introduced by Leonid Levin in 1986 [15]. We also present the notion of reduction from a RNP problem to another which allowed Levin to present the first known RNP-complete problem in the same paper. These notions have been discussed in more details and some problems have been proved RNP-complete by Yuri Gurevich *et al.* in [11, 12, 4, 5]. We do not present *average* polynomial-time reductions between RNP problems since this notion is weaker than the notion of (strict) polynomial-time reductions that we use.

3.1 Motivations

After Cook and Levin's presentation of NP-completeness theory in 1971, many problems have been proved NP-complete. In order to cope with these problems, people use to look for algorithms that are not polynomial in the worst case, but run as polynomial algorithms in practical cases. This led to the notion of average-case polynomial algorithms (AP) where, to all inputs of the algorithm, is assigned a probability function μ in order to define the notion of polynomiality in average. Very soon, it seemed that, if for some NP-complete problems it was possible to find such average polynomial time algorithms (hence that these problems belong to AP), it was a very difficult task for others.

Levin proved in 1985 that there exists a problem complete for average case polynomial reductions. If this problem were in AP, then such would be all problems of RNP, hence RNP would be included in AP which is very unlikely. It would imply that problems solved in non-deterministic exponential time (NEXP) can be solved in deterministic exponential (DEXP) time which is very unlikely (see [12]). Furthermore, there exists a subclass of problems in RNP(called *flat* problems) that cannot be complete unless NEXP and DEXP are equal (see [2]). This class of problems includes most probabilistic graphs problems and many others, such as a probabilistic version of SAT. A problem is *flat* if $\mu(x) \leq 2^{-n^\varepsilon}$ ($\varepsilon > 0$) for all instances x of sufficiently large size n.

4 Definitions

Let us recall that a *decision problem* is a pair $D = (I, Q)$ where I is a set of *instances* and Q is a question concerning elements of I. More precisely, I is a subset of Σ^* (Σ is any finite alphabet) and the answer to Q is "yes" or "no". We are only interested in answering Q on elements of I. $Q : I \rightarrow \{$yes,no$\}$.

Definition 3. A *randomized decision problem* is a pair (D, μ) where D is a decision problem and μ a probability function on the instances of D.

In the following, we assume that μ is a positive probability function: if μ were negative on an instance, it would not correspond to a reasonable notion of a computation. We also assume that inputs are ordered (for instance they can be ordered by length and then lexicographically). For instance, μ can be the *standard probability* function on the set $A = \{1, 2, \ldots a\}^*$ (*i.e.* for a word x of length n, $\mu(x) = \frac{6}{\pi^2.(n+1)^2.a^n}$). Thus $\sum_{x \in A} \mu(x) = 1$. We shall denote by μ^* the distribution associated to the probability μ: $\mu^*(x) = \sum_{y < x} \mu(y)$.

We define below the notions of reduction from a randomized decision problem D_1 defined on A_1 with the probability μ_1 to another randomized decision problem D_2 defined on A_2 with the probability μ_2. Consider f being a function from A_1 to A_2.

Definition 4. Assume that $A_1 = A_2$ and that there exists a function p such that

$$\forall x \in A_1, \mu_2(x).p(|x|) > \mu_1(x).$$

- If p is polynomial, then we say that μ_2 *P-dominates* μ_1.
- f is said to *transform* μ_1 into μ_2 iff $\mu_2(y) = \sum_{f(x)=y} \mu_1(x)$.

Definition 5. Assume that f reduces the decision problem D_1 into the decision problem D_2, and that there exists a probability function μ which is f-transformed into μ_2. If f is P-time computable, and if μ P-dominates μ_1, then f is said to P-*time reduce* (D_1, μ_1) into (D_2, μ_2).

First of all, remark that this notion of reduction is closed under composition. It is the key point that permits to define the notions of completeness with respect to this reduction. A reduction between randomized problems should not diminish too much the probability of a given instance.

Definition 6. A randomized decision problem is *polynomial in average* iff the problem on the instance x is solved in time $T(|x|)$ such that

$$\exists k \in \mathbb{N}, \sum_{x \in A} \mu(x) \frac{T(|x|)^{1/k}}{|x|} \text{ converges.}$$

Remark that if T is a polynomial function, then k corresponds to its degree. If f P-time reduces (D_1, μ_1) into (D_2, μ_2), if (D_2, μ_2) is polynomial in average, then (D_1, μ_1) is polynomial in average too: the difference between the degrees of the polynomial average costs is bounded by the degree of the domination polynomial.

Lemma 7 Gurevich 87. *Assume that f reduces the decision problem D_1 into the decision problem D_2, and that f is P-time computable. If μ_2 P-dominates the image of the f-transformation of μ_1, then f P-times reduces (D_1, μ_1) to (D_2, μ_2).*

This Lemma is very convenient but its converse is not true.

Definition 8. A randomized decision problem (D, μ) is in RNP (for Randomized NP) if D is in NP and the probability distribution μ^* is P-time computable.

4.1 Method

Assume now that there exists a RNP-complete problem which will be proved in the next section. A sufficient construction to prove that a given problem is RNP-complete with respect to P-time reductions, consists in the following:

1. prove that your problem is in NP and that its probability distribution is P-time computable.
2. take a RNP-complete problem with a probability function μ_1.
3. consider this problem only as an NP-complete problem and reduce it polynomially to your problem: your problem is proved NP-complete. Call the reduction function f.
4. prove that the image by f of μ_1 is P-dominated by the probability function of your problem (see Lemma 7).

4.2 A few RNP-complete problems

The notion of RNP-completeness seems very interesting because if an RNP-complete problem is polynomial in average, then so are all the problems in RNP. We have explained at the beginning of the paper why it is very unlikely. We present below the first problem that has been proved RNP-complete; we shall use it further in our reductions.

Consider any reasonable P-time computable encoding of NDTM (Kleene's enumeration is suitable).

NDTM-TIME

Instance: A *Non-Deterministic* Turing Machine γ, a word ω over the alphabet $\{0, 1\}$, an integer n coded in unary, $n > |\omega|$ and $n > |\gamma|$ (*i.e.* the word $\gamma.\omega.1^n$).

Question: Is there a computation of γ beginning on ω and halting after at most n steps?

Probability: We take a probability function proportional to $\frac{1}{n^4.2^{|\omega|}.2^{|\gamma|}}$.

The previous probability function corresponds to the following natural experiment: "choose an integer n according to the standard probability function $\mu(n) = \frac{6}{\pi^2}\frac{1}{n^2}$. Then choose independently two integers m and k lower than n – your probability function is now proportional to $\frac{1}{n^4}$. Choose two words of length m and k representing respectively the coding of γ and ω". This experiment defines a function proportional to $\frac{1}{n^4.2^{|\omega|}.2^{|\gamma|}}$.

Theorem 9 Levin, Gurevich. NDTM-TIME *is* RNP-*complete with respect to* P-*time reductions.*

This theorem proves that there exists at least a complete problem for RNP-complete with respect to P-time reductions. Note that we could have imposed that n be greater than a fixed polynomial of the sizes $|\omega|$ and $|\gamma|$. We shall use this remark in the proof of Theorem 11. The following problem, FINITE-TILING, has been proved RNP-complete by Levin who implicitly reduced NDTM-TIME to it. We explain below the main ideas of the proof.

FINITE-TILING

Instance: A finite set C of colors ($|C| = c$) with a blank color, a collection $\tau \in C^4$ of tiles including a blank tile; a row R of non blank matching tiles, with blank sides above and on the sides of the row; an integer n coded in unary, $n > |\tau|$, $n > |R|$ (*i.e.* the word $\tau.R.1^n$).

Question: Is there an extension of the row R forming a finite non-trivial tiling of the plane of size at most $|R| \times n$?

Probability: Consider any reasonable P-time computable encoding of tile sets. We take a probability function corresponding to the following experiment: "choose n; choose a number of tiles lower than n, choose n tiles according to your favorite probability function; chose a length for the row lower than n, chose each tile one after another such that the current one matches the already chosen ones".

Theorem 10 Levin 1986. FINITE-TILING *is* RNP-*complete with respect to* P-*time reductions.*

5   Complexity results for 2D cellular automata

5.1   CA-FINITE-INJECTIVE is co-RNP-complete

A transformation between tilings and two-dimensional cellular automata was first presented by Jarkko Kari in [13] (a more complete proof can be found in [14]). The main idea of the transformation is to introduce a special set of tiles which has an ad hoc property called *finite plane filling property*. We introduce another set of tiles, simpler than Kari's, which satisfies a slightly more restrictive property. We shall refer to this tile set as δ. With the help of δ, for each tile set

τ, we construct a cellular automaton $\mathcal{A}_\tau$ in order to reduce FINITE-TILING to CA-FINITE-INJECTIVE.

CA-FINITE-INJECTIVE

Instance: A two-dimensional cellular automaton $\mathcal{A}$; a row R of potentially non-quiescent cells (see below) with quiescent sides above and on the sides of the row; an integer n coded in unary, $n > |\mathcal{A}|$, $n > |R|$ (*i.e.* the word $\mathcal{A}.R.1^n$).

Question: Is $\mathcal{A}$ injective restricted to all finite configurations extending the row R and smaller than $|R| \times n$?

Probability: Consider any reasonable P-time computable encoding of cellular automata. We take a probability function corresponding to the following experiment: "choose n; choose a cellular automaton of size lower than n according to your favorite probability function; chose a length for the row lower than n, chose each cell one after another such that the current one is potentially non-quiescent.

Being "potentially non-quiescent" correspond to the matching property for rows of tiles. More precisely, consider a cell x and assume that some of its neighbors are fixed cells, and some are not. x is *potentially non-quiescent* iff there exists a possible completion of its neighborhood such that the state of one of x's neighbors is *not* transformed into itself by the cellular automaton. In other terms, the state of a neighbor cell of x *may* change when the cellular automaton is applied (depending on the states of other neighbors).

Theorem 11. CA-FINITE-INJECTIVE *is co-RNP-complete.*

5.2 The reduction

We present below our reduction in order to prove Theorem 11. We transform any tile set τ into a cellular automaton $\mathcal{A}_\tau$, any row of τ into a row of $\mathcal{A}_\tau$, and we add 2 to the integer n. Before presenting the reduction, we introduce an auxiliary tile set (called δ) and its properties. This tile set does not depend on τ. The sides contain a color ("blank", "border", "odd", "even", or "the-end"), and possibly an arrow. With this set of tiles, a tiling is considered as valid if and only if all pairs of adjacent sides have the same color, and for each arrow of the plane, its head points out on the tail of an arrow in the adjacent cell. Tiles of δ can be found in Fig. 1.

In the rest of the section, we present a few Lemma without their proofs, which are not difficult but rather long and tedious. Then, we prove our theorem.

Definition 12. A *basic rectangle* of size $p \times q$ (see Fig. 2) is a finite valid tiling of the plane of size $p \times q$ with no side labeled "blank" inside the rectangle.

Lemma 13. *Using the tile set δ, for every integers p and q, both greater than 3, there exists a basic rectangle of size $p \times 2q$. Each valid finite tiling of the plane consists of a finite number of juxtaposed basic rectangles.*

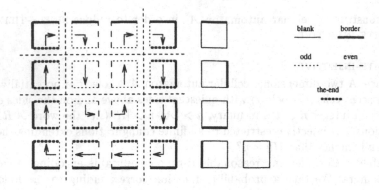

Fig. 1. Tiles of δ

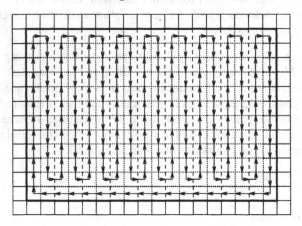

Fig. 2. A basic rectangle

Lemma 14. *Consider a basic rectangle. The path defined by the arrows of the cells forms a loop which visits one time each tile of the inside of the rectangle.*

Lemma 15. *Consider a finite tiling (valid or not). If the tiling is valid on each cell of a path, then this path forms a loop and visits every inside tile of a basic rectangle.*

We explain now our reduction. Consider a finite set C of colors with a blank color, and a collection $\tau \in C^4$ of tiles including a blank tile. We construct a cellular automaton $\mathcal{A}_\tau = (2, S, N, f_\tau)$ defined as follows:

— The *state* set S is included in $\delta \times \tau \times \{0, 1\}$.
  S contains all triplets (d, t, α) of $\delta \times \tau \times \{0, 1\}$ under the following restriction:
  - if d is the blank tile of δ, then t is the blank tile of τ.
  - if a side of d is "blank", then $\alpha = 0$.
— The *neighborhood* N is the von Neumann neighborhood iterated twice *i.e.* the radius 2 ball for $\| \cdot \|_1$.

– The *local rule* f_τ, applied on a cell the state of which is (d, t, α), may change only the bit component α. At each cell both the tilings δ and τ are checked. If there is a tiling error in the neighborhood, or if the tile d contains no arrow, then the state of the cell is not altered. Otherwise, there is no tiling error around the concerned cell and the cell contains an arrow; the bit component is changed by performing an "exclusive or" operation with the bit attached to the cell pointed by the direction of the δ-component.

The quiescent state of $\mathcal{A}_\tau$ is (blank, blank, 0).

Now, before proving our main theorem, we have just to explain how we transform the row of tiles into a row of cells. We keep the row of tiles as is, and add a blank tile at each side; we superimpose on this row a bottom row of a basic rectangle of same length, the bit component 0, and thus obtain a row of cells. It is very important to see that there are no other possible construction of a row for $\mathcal{A}$ τ than the kind of row described above: the τ component must be a correct row of τ-tiles because if there is a tiling error, then according to the local function, neighbor cells could *not* change and the cell would not be potentially non-quiescent. For the same reason, δ-tiles form a matching row with blank tiles above and on the sides, hence it is the bottom row of a basic rectangle. As cells of this bottom row contain blank tiles, by the restriction on the set of states, the bit component must be 0. These remarks prove the following very important Lemma:

Lemma 16. *If there are k choices for the i-th tile of a row of τ; then there are exactly k choices for the $i + 1$-th cell of the corresponding row of $\mathcal{A}_\tau$. This last row is 2 cells longer than the row of τ. There is only one possible choice for the two ending cells.*

One could remark that only instances of FINITE TILING with sufficiently great n are mapped onto CA-FINITE-INJECTIVE because the size of $\mathcal{A}_\tau$ is greater than the size of τ. But we remarked in the case of NDTM-TIME that we can start with greater n in the first problem provided that the increase of n is bounded by a polynomial – which is here obviously the case.

Proof of theorem 11. It is clear that CA-FINITE-INJECTIVE is in co-NP and that its probability distribution is P-time computable. Let us prove first that it is co-NP-complete.

Assume that $\mathcal{A}_\tau$ is not injective restricted to all finite configurations extending the row R and smaller than $|R| \times n$. Then, there exist two different finite configurations c and c' having the same image by $\mathcal{A}_\tau$. Remark that only the bits can be different in c and c' since $\mathcal{A}_\tau$ does not affect the tiles components: c and c' are different in at least one cell. On this cell, there is an arrow and the tilings are correct, otherwise the images of c and c' could not be the same. Thus c and c' differ in the cell pointed by the arrow because an "exclusive or" is performed by $\mathcal{A}_\tau$. By finite induction, by Lemma 15, the constructed path forms a loop and there exists a basic rectangle of δ on which the tiling of τ is correct. By Lemma 14, the borders of the rectangle are blank in the state component of τ, hence we can construct a finite tiling with τ. The tiling is not trivial because τ is not blank on the cells of R. The size of the tiling is at most $(|R| + 2) \times (n + 2)$.

Conversely, assume that there exists a finite non-trivial tiling of the plane by τ extending R, of size lower than $|R| \times n$. We put this tiling inside a $(|R| + 2) \times (n + 2)$ basic rectangle tiled by δ. We define two configurations c and c' of size $(|R| + 2) \times (n + 2)$: c is obtained by turning the bit component to 0 everywhere. For c', we keep the two tilings, and turn the bit component to 1 on the cells whose δ-component has an arrow, to 0 elsewhere. As both tilings are correct, $\mathcal{A}_\tau$ performs an "exclusive or" on the loop of the rectangle and both c and c' have the same image (which is in fact c). Hence $\mathcal{A}_\tau$ restricted to finite configurations of size lower than $(|R| + 2) \times (n + 2)$ is not injective.

Concerning probabilities, we use once more the trick of fixing the tile set τ. This tile set is in fact obtained by the transformation of the universal NDTM γ_u. Hence $\mathcal{A}_\tau$ is a fixed cellular automaton. The key point of the domination relation is Lemma 16: to each choice of tiles in the first row corresponds the same choice in the row of cells. Hence the row probability distributions are the same, and considering that the other parts of probabilities are polynomially bounded, the probability distribution of FINITE-TILING is dominated by the probability distribution of CA-FINITE-INJECTIVE.

6 Conclusion

We have proved in this paper that a problem of inversion of 2D CA is difficult in average. One can ask whether this problem is natural in cellular automata's theory. The problem of knowing whether a cellular automaton is injective on finite configurations of bounded length, or on periodic configurations of bounded period, is considered as important by many people including physicists. The problem here is that we work with a row of tile (or of cells) which is not very natural neither for tilings nor for cellular automata. But concerning tilings, people usually think that related problems are realy difficult among NPproblems. We think that it is also the case for inversion of 2D cellular automata. Furthermore, we think that RNP-complete problems can be considered as "generic" among NP-complete ones. NDTM-TIME, which represent the halting of a Nondeterministic Turing Machine, or the Bounded Post Correspondence Problem (see [12]) are RNP-complete too, and all these problems seem inherently more difficult that SAT or KNAPSACK.

Acknowledgments

I am very gratefull to Yury Gurevich who discussed average case completeness with me. He helped me to see more clearly in this complicated topic.

References

1. S. Amoroso and Y.N. Patt. Decision procedures for surjectivity and injectivity of parallel maps for tesselation structures. *J. Comp. Syst. Sci.*, 6:448–464, 1972.
2. S. Ben-David, B. Chor, O. Goldreich, and M. Luby. On the theory of average case complexity. In *STOC*, pages 204–216, 1989.
3. R. Berger. The undecidability of the domino problem. *Memoirs of the American Mathematical Society*, 66, 1966.
4. A. Blass and Y. Gurevich. Randomizing reductions of search problems. *SIAM Journal on Computing*, 22(5):949–975, 1993.
5. A. Blass and Y. Gurevich. Matrix transformation is complete for the average case. *SIAM Journal on computing*, (to appear).
6. B. Durand. Global properties of 2D cellular automata: some complexity results. In *MFCS'93*, Lecture Notes in Computer Science. Springer Verlag, September 1993.
7. B. Durand. Undecidability of the surjectivity problem for 2D cellular automata: A simplified proof. In *FCT'93*, Lecture Notes in Computer Science. Springer Verlag, August 1993.
8. B. Durand. *Automates cellulaires: réversibilité et complexité*. PhD thesis, Ecole Normale Supérieure de Lyon, 1994.
9. B. Durand. Inversion of 2d cellular automata: some complexity results. *Theoretical Computer Science*, (to appear).
10. B. Durand. The surjectivity problem for 2D cellular automata. *Journal of Computer and Systems Science*, (to appear).
11. Y. Gurevich. Complete and incomplete randomized NP problems. In *FOCS*, 1987.
12. Y. Gurevich. Average case completeness. *Journal of Computer and System Sciences*, 42:346–398, 1991.
13. J. Kari. Reversability of 2D cellular automata is undecidable. *Physica*, D 45:379–385, 1990.
14. J. Kari. Reversibility and surjectivity problems of cellular automata. *Journal of Computer and System Sciences*, 48:149–182, 1994.
15. L. Levin. Average case complete problems. *SIAM J. Comput*, 15(1):285–286, February 1986.
16. E.F. Moore. Machine models of self–reproduction. *Proc. Symp. Apl. Math.*, 14:13–33, 1962.
17. J. Myhill. The converse to Moore's garden-of-eden theorem. *Proc. Am. Math. Soc.*, 14:685–686, 1963.
18. D. Richardson. Tesselations with local transformations. *Journal of Computer and System Sciences*, 6:373–388, 1972.
19. R.M. Robinson. Undecidability and nonperiodicity for tilings of the plane. *Inventiones Mathematicae*, 12:177–209, 1971.
20. K. Sutner. De Bruijn graphs and linear cellular automata. *Complex Systems*, 5:19–30, 1991.
21. T. Toffoli and N. Margolus. Invertible cellular automata: a review. *Physica*, D 45:229–253, 1990.

On the subword equivalence problem for infinite words

Isabelle Fagnot

L.I.T.P. - I.B.P. Université Paris 6, 4, place Jussieu, 75252 Paris Cedex 05
Isabelle.Fagnot@litp.ibp.fr

Abstract. Two infinite words x and y are said to be *subword equivalent* if they have the same set of finite subwords (factors). The *subword equivalence problem* is the question whether two infinite words are subword equivalent. We show that, under mild hypotheses, the decidability of the subword equivalence problem implies the decidability of the ω-sequence equivalence problem, a problem which has been shown to be decidable by Čulik and Harju for morphic words (i.e. words generated by iterating a morphism).

We prove that the subword equivalence problem is decidable for two morphic words, provided the morphisms are primitive and have bounded delays. We also prove that the subword equivalence problem is decidable for any pair of morphic words in the case of a binary alphabet.

The subword equivalence problem is also shown to be decidable for two p-automatic words. We also prove a Cobham-like theorem: let p and q be two multiplicatively independent integers, and let x be a p-automatic word and let y be a q-automatic word, both with bounded gaps. If x and y are subword equivalent, then they are both ultimately periodic.

Our results hold in fact for a stronger version, namely for the subword inclusion problem.

1 Introduction

The problem we consider here is the subword equivalence problem, that is to say: given two infinite words, is it decidable whether their finite factors are the same?

This problem is of interest in several contexts. First, it is well-known that two infinite words generate the same discrete dynamical system if and only if they have the same set of subwords (see e.g. Queffelec [Qu]).

Next, it is easy to show that, under mild hypotheses, the decidability of the subword equivalence problem implies the decidability of the equality. This latter problem was open for a long time in the case of D0L-systems, and has been solved by Čulik and Harju [ČuHa].

In this paper, we consider the problem for *morphic* words, that is words obtained by iterating a morphism, and for *automatic* words, also called uniform tag sequences.

For morphic words x and y, we show that the subword equivalence problem is decidable if they are generated by primitive morphisms with bounded delays (theorem 3). As a matter of fact, the proof is by reducing the problem to the ω-sequence equivalence problem and to apply the theorem of Čulik and Harju. It appears that the decidability holds even for the subword inclusion problem.

In the case of a binary alphabet, both conditions on the morphisms can be overcome (theorem 4), using methods which are standard in the theory of D0L-systems (see e.g. Ehrenfeucht, Karhumaki and Rozenberg [EhKaRo]).

Automatic words, also called uniform tag sequences, have been widely considered, especially in connection with number theory. One of the most famous results is Cobham's base dependence theorem for which a new proof has been given recently by Hansel [Ha, Vi].

Consider two automatic words, x and y, such that x is k-automatic and y is ℓ-automatic. We prove the decidability of the subword inclusion when k and ℓ are multiplicatively dependent, that is to say when there exist two integers $n, m \geq 1$ such that $k^n = \ell^m$ (theorem 9). Next, when k and ℓ are multiplicatively independent, we prove, provided x has bounded gaps, that the subword equivalence of x and y implies that x and y are ultimately periodic (theorem 6). Therefore, we can decide the subword equivalence problem under the above-mentioned hypotheses (corollary 8). This latter result is a partial generalization of the theorem of Cobham [Co1].

2 The problem

Let A be a finite alphabet. The set of finite words is denoted by A^* and the set of infinite words by A^ω. Let f be an endomorphism on A^*. If there exists a letter $a \in A$ such that $f(a) \in aA^*$ and $\lim_{n \to \infty} |f^n(a)| = \infty$ then we can define the infinite word $x = f^\omega(a)$ as the unique infinite word which has $f^n(a)$ as prefix for any integer n. Then x is said to be *generated* by iterating f and f is said to be a *generator* of x. We say that an infinite word is *morphic* when it is generated by iterating a morphism (see [BeSe]).

Given two words u and v, we write $u < v$ to denote that u is a prefix of v. Given an infinite word x over A, the set of all the finite factors (subwords) of x is denoted by Fact(x).

An endomorphism f on A^* has *bounded delay* $p \geq 1$ *from left to right* if

$$\forall a_1, \ldots, a_p, b_1, \ldots, b_p \in A \quad f(a_1 \cdots a_p) < f(b_1 \cdots b_p) \Rightarrow a_1 = b_1.$$

An endomorphism f on A^* is called *primitive* if

$$\exists n \in \mathbb{N}, \ \forall \partial, \in \mathbb{A}, \ \partial \in \text{Fact}(\mho^\kappa()).$$

Let k be an integer. A morphism $f : A^* \to B^*$ is said to be k-*uniform* if for all letter $a \in A$, we have $|f(a)| = k$. A 1-uniform morphism is said to be *literal*. An infinite word x over A is k-*automatic* if there exist an alphabet B, a morphic word y over B generated by a k-uniform morphism and a literal morphism $\varphi : B^* \to A^*$ such that $x = \varphi(y)$.

Let x be an infinite word over A, $x = a_0 a_1 \cdots a_n \cdots$. For integers $i \leq j$, we define $x[i, j[= a_i a_{i+1} \cdots a_{j-1}$.

An infinite word x is said to have *bounded gaps* if for any word $u \in \text{Fact}(x)$, there exists an integer d such that for any integer i, the word u has an occurrence in $x[i, i + d[$. In the literature, instead of bounded gaps one can also find *almost periodic* (cf. [Co2]) and *uniformly recurrent* (cf. [Fu]).

Two integers k and ℓ are said to be *multiplicatively dependent* if there exist two integers $n, m \geq 1$ such that $k^n = \ell^m$. Otherwise, k and ℓ are said *multiplicatively independent*.

We consider the following:
Problems: Given two infinite words x and y, the *subword equivalence problem* is to decide whether they have the same finite factors, i.e. whether $\text{Fact}(x) = \text{Fact}(y)$. The *subword inclusion problem* is to decide whether $\text{Fact}(x) \subset \text{Fact}(y)$.

Example: Let A be the binary alphabet $\{0, 1\}$. Let f be the endomorphism over A^* defined by:

$$f : 0 \mapsto 01$$
$$1 \mapsto 10$$

This morphism generates two infinite words (called Thue-Morse words)

$$\mathbf{t} = f^\omega(0) = 0110100110010110\cdots$$

and

$$\mathbf{t}' = f^\omega(1) = 1001011001101001\cdots.$$

None of the words $\mathbf{t}$ and $\mathbf{t}'$ is a prefix of the other; they even have no common prefix. However, it is easily seen that they are subword equivalent. (The subwords are all overlap-free but there are overlap-free binary words that are not subwords, e.g. 100100.)

For morphic words and for automatic words, the subword equivalence problem is a generalization of the equality problem. Given an infinite word x and a letter S, let $\tau(x, S)$ be the infinite word obtained by replacing the first letter of x by S. With these notations, we have the following easy proposition:

Proposition 1 *Let $\mathcal{L}$ be a family of infinite words that are described in a finitary manner. Let us suppose that the two conditions above are verified*

1. *If $x \in \mathcal{L}$ and $S \notin \text{alph}(x)$, then $\tau(x, S) \in \mathcal{L}$;*
2. *The mapping $(x, S) \mapsto \tau(x, S)$ is effective.*

If the subword equivalence problem is decidable for $\mathcal{L}$ then the equality problem is decidable for $\mathcal{L}$.

Remark: The second condition in the proposition means that from the finitary definition of x, we can effectively deduce the finitary definition of $y = \tau(x, S)$. It is easy to see that the family of morphic words, as well as the family of automatic words, satisfies the above conditions.

3 Main results

We consider the subword equivalence problem and the subword inclusion problem in two cases, namely for morphic words and for automatic words. First, we consider the case of morphic words. Let us recall the following result of Čulik and Harju [ČuHa].

Theorem 2 ([ČuHa]) *Let* x *and* y *be two morphic words over* A^*. *Then the equality* x = y *is decidable.*

We have the following partial generalization of the above theorem. In fact, to prove it we reduce the subword equivalence problem to the equality problem, and then, we apply the theorem of Čulik and Harju.

Theorem 3 *Let* x *and* y *be two infinite words generated by primitive morphisms which have bounded delays. Then the inclusion* Fact(x) $\subset$ Fact(y) *is decidable.*

Remark : We do not know whether the above-mentioned hypotheses are necessary but until now, we have not succeeded in doing without. Nevertheless, the condition of primitiveness is a classical one (see e.g. [Mo]).

We have a more general result in the binary case :

Theorem 4 *Let* x *and* y *be two infinite morphic words over a binary alphabet. Then the inclusion* Fact(x) $\subset$ Fact(y) *is decidable.*

Next, let us consider the case of automatic words. We recall the well known theorem of Cobham.

Theorem 5 ([Co1]) *Let* $k, \ell \geq 2$ *be two multiplicatively independent integers. Let* x *be an infinite word which is* k *and* ℓ-*automatic. Then* x *is ultimately periodic.*

We have some partial generalization of this theorem the proof of which is similar to the proof of the theorem of Cobham due to Hansel [Ha, Pe] :

Theorem 6 *Let* $k, \ell \geq 2$ *be two multiplicatively independent integers. Let* x *be a* k-*automatic word with bounded gaps and* y *an* ℓ-*automatic word. If* Fact(x) $\subset$ Fact(y) *then* x *is ultimately periodic.*

Remark : we think that this theorem holds even if x has not bounded gaps but we have not been able to show it. From this theorem we can easily deduce :

Corollary 7 *Let* $k, \ell \geq 2$ *be two multiplicatively independent integers. Let* x *be a* k-*automatic word with bounded gaps and* y *an* ℓ-*automatic word. If* Fact(x) = Fact(y), *then one of the words* x *or* y *is suffix of the other.*

The above theorem leads to the following result of decidability :

Corollary 8 *Let* $k, \ell \geq 2$ *be two multiplicatively independent integers. Let* x *be a* k-*automatic word with bounded gaps and* y *an* ℓ-*automatic word. Then the equality* Fact(x) = Fact(y) *is decidable.*

If k and ℓ are multiplicatively dependent, we have also the following result.

Theorem 9 *Let $k, \ell \geq 2$ be two multiplicatively dependent integers. Let x be a k-automatic word and y an ℓ-automatic word. Then the inclusion* $\mathrm{Fact}(x) \subset \mathrm{Fact}(y)$ *is decidable.*

The main part of this article is devoted to a sketch of the proof of theorem 3. Through lack of place, the other proofs are omitted. They can be found in more details in [Fa1] and [Fa2]. Theorem 4 is obtained by using the proof of theorem 3 and by analyzing binary morphisms which have been widely studied (cf. [Se] and [EhKaRo]). The proof of theorem 6 employs the proof of the Cobham theorem due to Hansel [Ha, Pe] and the lemma 11 which will be stated later. The proof of theorem 9 is not really difficult but appears to be long if written carefully.

4 Sketch of proof of theorem 3

First we give the algorithm of decidability. But before, we recall a result of Harju and Linna.

Theorem 10 ([HaLi]) *Let z be an infinite word. It is decidable whether z is ultimately periodic. And if so, we can effectively compute a preperiod and a period, i.e. words u and v such that $z = uv^\omega$.* ∎

Algorithm

At first, we test whether x is ultimately periodic or not, which is possible in view of theorem 10.

1. If x is ultimately periodic, we test whether y is ultimately periodic.
   (a) If y is not ultimately periodic, then we cannot have $\mathrm{Fact}(x) \subset \mathrm{Fact}(y)$. Indeed, the morphism which generates y is primitive and so y cannot be strongly repetitive, i.e. there cannot exist a nonempty word u such that for all integer n, the word u^n is a factor of y.
   (b) Otherwise, if y is ultimately periodic : we can compute the period and the preperiod of x and y by means of theorem 10. Then we can easily decide whether $\mathrm{Fact}(x) \subset \mathrm{Fact}(y)$.
2. If x is not ultimately periodic, then
   (a) if y is ultimately periodic, then we cannot have $\mathrm{Fact}(x) \subset \mathrm{Fact}(y)$, because there would be much more factors in x than there would in y.
   (b) If neither x nor y are ultimately periodic, we effectively compute a finite set $\mathcal{C}$ of couples of morphic words which have the property :

   $$\mathrm{Fact}(x) \subset \mathrm{Fact}(y) \text{ if and only if } \exists (x', y') \in \mathcal{C} \text{ such that } x' = y',$$

   and we test the equalities $x' = y'$ by means of the theorem of Čulik and Harju [ČuHa].

This part is the difficult one and we will see it in more details. First, let us recall some additional definitions. Then, we state without proof three lemmas (lemmas 11, 12 and 13). Next, we sketch the proof of point 2-a of the algorithm. This heavily relies on lemma 14, the proof of which will be given separately.

A morphism f on A^* is said to be *everywhere growing* if

$$\forall a \in A, \quad |f(a)| \geq 2.$$

A morphism f on A^* is said to be *nonerasing* if

$$\forall a \in A, \quad |f(a)| \geq 1.$$

Given two words u and v on A, we say that u and v are *comparable*, denoted by $u \gtrless v$, if u is a prefix of v or v is a prefix of u.

We denote σ the *shift operator* over $A^* \cup A^\omega$, defined as follow : given a word u over A if $u = av$ where a is a letter and v a word over A then $\sigma(u) = v$, otherwise, $\sigma(1) = 1$.

Next, let us give some preliminary results. To begin with, we state a sort of "tiling" lemma:

Lemma 11 *Let A and B be two alphabets and* $x \in B^\omega$, $y \in A^\omega$. *Let g be a nonerasing morphism :* $A^* \to B^*$. *If* $\text{Fact}(x) \subset \text{Fact}(g(y))$, *then there exists* $z \in A^\omega$ *such that* x *is a suffix of* $g(z)$ *and* $\text{Fact}(z) \subset \text{Fact}(y)$. ∎

Remark : The proof of this lemma is not a constructive one, but we only need the existence of z.

Moreover, we need two technical lemmas about morphisms with bounded delays.

Lemma 12 *Let f be an everywhere growing endomorphism. If f has bounded delay p then for any integer n, the morphism f^n has bounded delay $2p - 1$.* ∎

We need to construct the following morphisms.
Definitions : For all integer m, we define the alphabet

$$B_m = \left\{ \begin{pmatrix} a_1 a_2 \cdots a_m \\ b_1 b_2 \cdots b_m \end{pmatrix} \in A^m \times A^m \mid \forall i, 1 \geq i \geq m, a_i, b_i \in A, a_1 \neq b_1 \right\}.$$

Given two words $u, v \in A^*$ and an integer m, we define the word $u/_m v$ as following: if there exist words $w, s, t \in A^*$ and letters $a_1, \ldots, a_m, b_1, \ldots, b_m, a_1 \neq b_1$ such that $u = wa_1 \cdots a_m s$ and $v = wb_1 \cdots b_m t$ then $u/_m v = \begin{pmatrix} a_1 \cdots a_m \\ b_1 \cdots b_m \end{pmatrix} s$, otherwise $u/_m v = 1$

Let f be an everywhere growing endomorphism over A^* which have bounded delay p. Let $q = 4p - 3$. We define the endomorphism $\varphi = T_q(f)$ over $(A \cup B_q)^*$ by

$$\varphi(a) = f(a) \quad (a \in A),$$

$$\varphi\binom{x}{y} = f(x)/_q f(y) \quad \left(\binom{x}{y} \in B_q\right).$$

The endomorphism φ has the following interesting property:

Lemma 13 *For all integer n, for all letter $\binom{x}{y} \in B_q$,*

$$\varphi^n\binom{x}{y} = f^n(x)/_q f^n(y) \ i.e. \ T_q(f^n) = (T_q(f))^n.$$

Remark: In the definition, as in the lemma, for all integer $n \neq 0$, the fact that f^n is everywhere growing and have bounded delay $2p - 1$ implies that for all letter $\binom{u}{v} \in B_q$,

$$f^n(u)/_q f^n(v) \neq 1.$$

This result can be illustrated by this figure:
(Here $p = 1$ i.e. f is prefix, $q = 1$.)

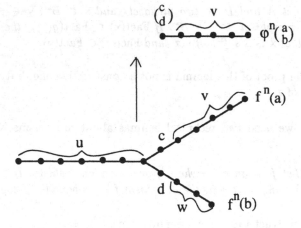

Example: For the morphism of bounded delay 2 (here $q = 5$)

$$f : a \mapsto ab$$
$$b \mapsto aba,$$

one has

$$f(aabba) = aba.babaa.baab,$$
$$f(bbaba) = aba.abaab.abaab.$$

So,

$$\varphi\begin{pmatrix} aabba \\ bbaba \end{pmatrix} = \begin{pmatrix} babaa \\ abaab \end{pmatrix} baab.$$

Moreover

$$f^2(aabba) = ababaababa.ababa.abababaababababa,$$
$$f^2(bbaba) = ababaababa.baaba.babaababaababababa,$$

and, indeed we have

$$\varphi^2\begin{pmatrix} aabba \\ bbaba \end{pmatrix} = \varphi\left(\begin{pmatrix} babaa \\ abaab \end{pmatrix} baab \right)$$

$$= \begin{pmatrix} ababa \\ baaba \end{pmatrix} abababaababababa$$

$$= f^2(aabba)/_q f^2(bbaba).$$

Proof of the step 2-a of the algorithm : Let f and g be two primitive morphisms with bounded delays generating respectively x and y. Since f and g are primitive there exists an integer n such that f^n and g^n are everywhere growing. Consequently, in the following, we will suppose that f and g are everywhere growing.

Let p be an integer such that f and g have bounded delay p. Let $q = 4p - 3$, $\varphi = T_q(f)$ and $\psi = T_q(g)$.

We define the set C as follows : whenever there exist $u, v, \binom{u}{v} \in B_q$, $a \in A$, $s, t \in A^*$ and an integer r such that

- $ua \in \text{Fact}(x)$,
- $\begin{cases} \varphi^r\left(\binom{u}{v}a \right) = \binom{u}{v}as \\ \psi^r\left(\binom{u}{v}a \right) = \binom{u}{v}at \end{cases}$
- r is minimal for these two latter properties.

Then, we define the endomorphisms φ' and ψ' over $(A \cup \{S\})^*$, where S is a new letter, by

$$\varphi' : S \mapsto Ss$$
$$x \mapsto \varphi^r(x) = f^r(x), \ \forall x \in A,$$

and

$$\psi' : S \mapsto St$$
$$x \mapsto \varphi^r(x) = f^r(x), \ \forall x \in A.$$

The set C will be the set of all couples $(\varphi'^\omega(S), \psi'^\omega(S))$.

It is not difficult to see that if there exist φ' and ψ' such that $\varphi'^\omega(S) = \psi'^\omega(S)$ then Fact(x) = Fact(y). Conversely, we are going to prove that if Fact(x) =

Fact(y), then there exist φ' and ψ' defined as above such that $(\varphi'^{\omega}(S), \psi'^{\omega}(S)) \in C$. Let us assume that we have proved the following lemma which we will prove later.

Lemma 14 *Under the above-mentioned hypotheses, if* Fact(x) $\subset$ Fact(y) *and neither* x *nor* y *are ultimately periodic then, for all* n, *there exist letters* $\binom{u_n}{v_n}$, $\binom{w_n}{t_n} \in B_q$ *and* $a_n, b_n \in A$ *such that* $u_n a_n, v_n a_n \in$ Fact(x), $w_n b_n, t_n b_n \in$ Fact(y) *and*

$$\varphi^n \left(\binom{u_n}{v_n} a_n \right) \not\asymp \psi^n \left(\binom{w_n}{t_n} b_n \right).$$

Then we can show that there exist $\binom{u}{v} \in B$, $a \in A$, $s, t \in A^*$ and an integer r such that $ua \in$ Fact(x),

$$\varphi^r \left(\binom{u}{v} a \right) = \binom{u}{v} as,$$

$$\psi^r \left(\binom{u}{v} a \right) = \binom{u}{v} at,$$

and

$$\varphi^{r\omega} \left(\binom{u}{v} a \right) = \psi^{r\omega} \left(\binom{u}{v} a \right).$$

Moreover, we can choose r minimal such that the first two relations are satisfied without changing the infinite words $\varphi^{r\omega}\left(\binom{u}{v}a\right)$ and $\psi^{r\omega}\left(\binom{u}{v}a\right)$.

Now, if we define φ' and ψ' as in the definition of C, we have

$$\varphi'^{\omega}(S) = \psi'^{\omega}(S).$$

Since $(\varphi'^{\omega}(S), \psi'^{\omega}(S)) \in C$, we have shown that there exists a couple $(x', y') \in C$ such that $x' = y'$.

q.e.d.

5 Proof of lemma 14

Let $x = x_0 x_1 \cdots x_p \cdots$ Let n be fixed. By the Lemma 11, we can "tile" x with $g^n(a)$, $a \in A$, that is to say:

$$\exists z = z_0 \cdots z_p \cdots, \exists r \in \mathbb{N} \text{ such that } x = \sigma^{\backsim}(\eth^{\times}(z)) \text{ and } \text{Fact}(z) \subset \text{Fact}(y)$$

$f^n(x_0)$		$f^n(x_1)$		$f^n(x_2)$	$\cdots$
$g^n(z_0)$		$g^n(z_1)$	$g^n(z_2)$	$\cdots$	

Let us introduce two additional definitions.

Definitions: A *configuration of order n* is a 7-tuple $c = (a, b, u, \varepsilon, v, w, \eta)$ where $a, b \in A, u, v, w \in A^*, \varepsilon, \eta \in \{0, 1\}$ such that

$$\begin{cases} f^n(a) = u^\varepsilon v w^\eta \\ g^n(b) = u^{1-\varepsilon} v w^{1-\eta} \\ |v| > 0. \end{cases}$$

Example: Here $\varepsilon = \eta = 0$

$f^n(a)$		
$g^n(b)$		
u	v	w

A configuration $c = (a, b, u, \varepsilon, v, w, \eta)$ has an *occurrence* at the point (i, j) if

$$\begin{cases} |f^n(\mathsf{x}[0, i-1])u^\varepsilon| = |\sigma^r g^n(\mathsf{x}[0, j-1])u^{1-\varepsilon}|, \\ x_i = a, \\ z_j = b. \end{cases}$$

Let us go back to the proof of the lemma. There is a finite number of possible configurations (with n, f and g fixed), so there exists a configuration $c = (\alpha, \beta, \delta, \varepsilon, \mu, \nu, \eta)$ which has two distinct occurrences (i, j) and (k, ℓ). So, we have

$$\delta^{1-\varepsilon} f^n(\mathsf{x}[i, +\infty[) = \delta^\varepsilon g^n(\mathsf{z}[j, +\infty[), \tag{1}$$
$$\delta^{1-\varepsilon} f^n(\mathsf{x}[k, +\infty[) = \delta^\varepsilon g^n(\mathsf{z}[\ell, +\infty[). \tag{2}$$

Furthermore, since x is not ultimately periodic, the sequences $x_i, x_{i+1}, \ldots$ and $x_k, x_{k+1}, \ldots$ cannot be equal, and it is the same for the sequences $z_j, z_{j+1}, \ldots$ and $z_\ell, z_{\ell+1}, \ldots$, that is to say: there exist integers r and s such that

$$\begin{cases} x_{i+r} \neq x_{k+r}, \\ z_{j+s} \neq z_{\ell+s}, \end{cases}$$

which are minimal for this property.

δ	$f^n(x_i)$	$f^n(x_{i+1})$	$\cdots$	$f^n(x_{i+r})$	$\cdots$
$g^n(z_j)$		$g^n(z_{j+1})$	$\cdots$	$g^n(z_{j+s})$	$\cdots$
=				$\neq$	
δ	$f^n(x_k)$	$f^n(x_{k+1})$	$\cdots$	$f^n(x_{k+r})$	$\cdots$
$g^n(z_\ell)$		$g^n(z_{\ell+1})$	$\cdots$	$g^n(z_{\ell+s})$	$\cdots$

Let $\pi = \delta^{1-\varepsilon} f^n(\mathsf{x}[i, i+r-1]) = \delta^{1-\varepsilon} f^n(\mathsf{x}[k, k+r-1])$ and $\rho = \delta^\varepsilon g^n(\mathsf{z}[j, j+s-1]) = \delta^\varepsilon g^n(\mathsf{z}[\ell, \ell+s-1])$.

Since f^n and g^n have bounded delay q, there exist letters $\binom{c}{d}, \binom{c'}{d'} \in B_q$ and words u, v, w, u', v', w' such that

$$f^n(\mathsf{x}[i+r, i+r+q-1]) = ucv,$$
$$f^n(\mathsf{x}[k+r, k+r+q-1]) = udw,$$

and

$$g^n(\mathsf{x}[j+s, j+s+q-1]) = u'c'v',$$
$$g^n(\mathsf{x}[\ell+s, \ell+s+q-1]) = u'd'w'.$$

The equalities (1) and (2) give

$$\pi ucv f^n(x_{i+r+q}) \asymp \rho u'c'v'g^n(z_{j+s+q}),$$
$$\pi udw f^n(x_{k+r+q}) \asymp \rho u'd'w'g^n(z_{\ell+s+q}).$$

Hence, we deduce that $\pi u = \rho u'$, $c = c'$, $d = d'$ and

$$cv f^n(x_{i+r+q}) \asymp c'v'g^n(z_{j+s+q}),$$
$$dw f^n(x_{k+r+q}) \asymp d'w'g^n(z_{\ell+s+q}),$$

which can also be written

$$f^n(\mathsf{x}[i+r, i+r+q])/_q f^n(\mathsf{x}[k+r, k+r+q]) = g^n(\mathsf{z}[j+s, j+s+q])/_q g^n(\mathsf{z}[\ell+s, \ell+s+q]).$$

So, by lemma 13

$$\varphi^n\left(\binom{\mathsf{x}[i+r, i+r+q-1]}{\mathsf{x}[k+r, k+r+q-1]} x_{i+r+q}\right) \asymp \psi^n\left(\binom{\mathsf{z}[j+s, j+s+q-1]}{\mathsf{z}[\ell+s, \ell+s+q-1]} z_{j+s+q}\right).$$

Now, let $u_n = \mathsf{x}[i+r, i+r+q-1]$, $v_n = \mathsf{x}[k+r, k+r+q-1]$
$w_n = \mathsf{z}[j+s, j+s+q-1]$, $t_n = \mathsf{z}[\ell+s, \ell+s+q-1]$,
$a_n = x_{i+r+q}$ and $b_n = z_{j+s+q}$.

We obtain the formula:

$$\varphi^n\left(\binom{u_n}{v_n} a_n\right) \asymp \psi^n\left(\binom{w_n}{t_n} b_n\right)$$

which completes the proof.

Acknowledgments: *I would like to thank J. Berstel who proposed this problem to me and for fruitful discussions and J. Cassaigne for suggesting me a generalization of a previous version of Lemma 11*

References

[BeSe] J. Berstel and P. Séébold, A remark on morphic Sturmian words, *Inform. Theor. Appl.* **28**, n° 3–4, (1994), p. 225–263.

[Co1] A. Cobham, On the base-dependence of sets of numbers recognizable by finite automata, *Math. Systems Theory* **3** (1969), p. 186–192.

[Co2] A. Cobham, Uniform tag sequences, *Math. Systems Theory* **6** (1972), p. 164–192.

[ČuFr] K. Čulik II and I. Fris, The decidability of the equivalence problem for D0L-systems, *Inform. Control* **35** (1977), p. 20–39.

[ČuHa] K. Čulik II and T. Harju, The ω-sequence equivalence problem for D0L-systems is decidable, *J. Assoc. Comput. Mach.*, **31** (1984), p. 282–298.

[EhKaRo] A. Ehrenfeucht, J. Karhumaki and G. Rozenberg, On binary equality sets and a solution to the test set conjecture in the binary case, *J. Algebra* **85** (1983), p. 76–85.

[EhRo] A. Ehrenfeucht and G. Rozenberg, Repetition of subwords in D0L languages, *Inform. and Control* **59** (1983), p. 13–35.

[Fa1] I. Fagnot, Sur le problème de l'égalité des facteurs dans les mots morphiques, *Technical report of L. I. T. P.*, **94/63**, (1994).

[Fa2] I. Fagnot, Sur les facteurs des mots automatiques, *Technical report of L. I. T. P.*, to appear.

[Fu] H. Furstenberg, *Recurrence in ergodic theory and combinatorial number theory*, Princeton Universty Press, Princeton (1981).

[Ha] G. Hansel, A propos d'un théorème de Cobham, in: *Actes de la fête des mots*, D. Perrin Ed., Greco de Programmation, CNRS, Rouen (1982)

[HaLi] T. Harju and M. Linna, On the periodicity of morphisms on free monoids, *Inform. Theor Appl.* **20**, n° 1, (1986), p. 47–54.

[Mo] B, Mossé, Puissance de mots et reconnaissabilité des points fixes d'une substitution, *Theoret. Comput. Sci.* **99** (1992), p. 327–334.

[Pe] D. Perrin, Finite automata, dans *Handbook of theoretical computer science*, Vol. B, J. Van Leeuwen Ed., Elsevier, Amsterdam (1990), p. 1–57.

[Qu] M. Queffelec, Substitution dynamical systems-Spectral analysis, *Lecture Notes in Math.* **1294** (1987), Springer-Verlag.

[Se] P. Séébold, An effective solution to the D0L periodicity problem in the binary case, *EATCS Bull.* **36** (1988), p. 137–151.

[Vi] R. Villemaire, joining k- and ℓ-recognizable sets of natural numbers, Proc. Stacs'92, *Lecture notes in Comput. Sci.* **577** (1992), p. 83–94.

On the separators on an infinite word generated by a morphism

Emmanuelle Garel

LITP 4, Place Jussieu, 75252 PARIS Cedex 05, France
emmanuelle.garel@litp.ibp.fr

Abstract. Let $\mathbf{x}$ be an infinite non periodic word on a finite alphabet A. For each position n, the *separator* of $\mathbf{x}$ at n is the smallest factor of $\mathbf{x}$ that starts at n and that does not appear before in $\mathbf{x}$. Denote by $S_{\mathbf{x}}(n)$ the length of the separator of $\mathbf{x}$ at n and $S_{\mathbf{x}}$ the corresponding function. We consider the problem of computing $S_{\mathbf{x}}$ in the case where $\mathbf{x}$ is generated by iterating some morphism $\sigma : A^* \to A^*$. We prove that if σ is q-uniform ($q \geq 2$) and $\mathbf{x}$ is circular then $S_{\mathbf{x}}$ is q-regular (in the sense of Allouche and Shallit [2], [23]), or, in other words that the corresponding formal power series that associates $S_{\mathbf{x}}(n)$ to the q-ary expression of n is rational (Salomaa, Soittola [22]).

Keywords : Combinatoric on infinite words, circularity, q-regularity.

1   Introduction

This paper deals with the computation of a function $S_{\mathbf{x}}$ that describes a particular subset of factors of an infinite word $\mathbf{x}$ called *separators*. These factors are defined as following : for each position n, the separator of $\mathbf{x}$ at n is the smallest factor of $\mathbf{x}$ that starts at n and that does not appear before in $\mathbf{x}$. We denote by $S_{\mathbf{x}}(n)$ its length and consider the corresponding function $S_{\mathbf{x}}$.

The motivations originate first in combinatorial theory. A classical approach for understanding the structure of finite or infinite words is to study the specific properties of their factors, for example the repartition in the word, their complexity. Our aim is to characterize the special subset of factors consisting of the separators defined above. If w is the separator of a word $\mathbf{x}$ at the index n, since w does not occur at any index $j \leq n - 1$, in a certain sense, w separates the indices n and j and moreover w is minimal. Thus we can derive pratical applications from the computation of $S_{\mathbf{x}}$ for instance the calculus of minimal automata. (for example see Blumer and al. [5] and [6], Crochemore [9] and [10])

Now, suppose $\mathbf{x}$ be an infinite word on an alphabet A that is obtained by iterating a morphism $\sigma : A^* \to A^*$. In this case, $\mathbf{x}$ is the prefix limit of a family $(\sigma^n(a))$, $a \in A$. The computation of particular examples shows that generally the separators at any n and their length $S_{\mathbf{x}}(n)$ satisfy recurrent formula in keeping with the sequence $(|\sigma^n(a)|)$ of the length of the images $\sigma^n(a)$. For example, consider the Fibonacci word $\mathbf{x} = \lim_n \sigma^n(a)$ where σ is the morphism $\sigma : \{0,1\}^* \to \{0,1\}^*$ defined by $\sigma(0) = 01$, $\sigma(1) = 0$. A prefix of $\mathbf{x}$ is :

$$\mathbf{x} = 01\ 0\ 01\ 01\ 0\ 01001\ 01001010\ 010 \cdots$$

Note by (u_n) the sequence of the Fibonacci integers $u_0 = 1$, $u_1 = 2$, $u_{n+2} = u_{n+1} + u_n$. For any n we have $|\sigma^n(0)| = u_n$. We can verify, for any index $m > 2$, $u_n \leq m < u_{n+1}$, that the separator of $\mathbf{x}$ at m is the product vwa where v is the suffix of $\sigma^{n-1}(0)$ whose length is $|v| = u_{n+1} - m$, w is the prefix of $\sigma^n(0)$ whose length is $|w| = u_{n-1} - 2$, $a = 0$ if n is even and $a = 1$ if n is odd. We obtain $S_{\mathbf{x}}(m) = u_{n+2} - m - 1$. The function $S_{\mathbf{x}}$ can be calculated by using a finite tranducer in the Fibonacci base.

In the case where σ is q-uniform, the formula depend on the sequence (q^n) and generally the set of separators can be calculated with finite tranducers in base q. The main result we prove is the following : if σ is a q-uniform morphism, if $\mathbf{x}$ is a circular word that is generated by iterating σ then $S_{\mathbf{x}}$ is q-regular.

The fundamental basic property used is circularity. This notion has been used in ergodic theory to study some dynamical systems. Later it was used in coding theory for characterizing a particular class of codes. In the case of DOL-systems Mignosi and Séébold in [18] defined a notion of circularity close to the one mentioned above. In the particular case where the language is the set of factors of an infinite word obtained by iterating a morphism σ, the formulation is simpler. In [20] Mossé introduced the term of bilatéralement reconnaissable. In this paper we adopt the point of view given in [18].

We also use the notion of q-regularity. The automatic sequences were introduced by Cobham [8] (uniform tag-systems) and later extended by Allouche and Shallit [2], [23]. They introduced the notion of q-regularity. About q-automaticity we adopt the point of view developped by Christol and al. in [7] and about q-regularity our references are Allouche and Shallit in [2].

Plan : In section 2 we present the fundamental concepts and give the main results. In section 3 we sketch the proofs, a complete version of full proofs will appear shortly as a LITP report.

2 Fundamental concepts, notations and results

2.1 Some notations

Let A be a finite alphabet, A^* be the set of finite words and A^ω be the set of infinite words over A. The empty word is denoted by ϵ. For every word $w \in A^*$, if the length of w is n then we note $n = |w|$.

A word v is a *factor* of u if there exist u' and $u'' \in A^*$ such that $u = u'vu''$. If $u' = \epsilon$ then v is a prefix of u. If $u'' = \epsilon$ then v is a suffix of u.

Consider a family (u_n) of words over A such that any u_n is a proper prefix of u_{n+1}. The infinite word $\mathbf{x} = \lim_n u_n$ is the unique one such that, for any n, u_n is a prefix of $\mathbf{x}$. Generally $\mathbf{x}$ is called the prefix limit of (u_n).

For any $\mathbf{x} \in A^\omega$ the set of the factors of $\mathbf{x}$ is denoted by $F(\mathbf{x})$.

A word $\mathbf{x} \in A^\omega$ is *ultimately periodic* if there exist u and $v \in A^*$, $|v| \geq 1$, such that $\mathbf{x} = \lim_n uv^n$.

A word $\mathbf{x} \in A^\omega$ is *generated by iterating a morphism* $\sigma : A \to A^*$ if there exists $a \in A$ such that $\mathbf{x} = \lim_n \sigma^n(a)$ ($\mathbf{x}$ is a fixed point of σ).

A q-*automaton* will be a deterministic and finite automaton labelled in $\{0, \cdots, q-1\}$ with an output function that is defined over the set of the states of the automaton (see Eilenberg [13] and Allouche [1] and [2]). A subset of N is said q-*recognizable* if its elements in base q are recognized by a q-automaton.

2.2 About q-regularity Our references are Allouche and Shallit in [2]. In the framework of our subjet we only consider sequences whose elements belong to N. Let $u = (u_n)$ a N-sequence. The q-*kernel* $K(u)$ of u is the Z-module that is generated by the set of sub-sequences $\{(u_{q^a n + b}), \text{ where } a \in N \text{ and } 0 \leq b < q^a\}$. The sequence u is q-*regular* if $K(u)$ is a finitely generated Z-module.

A function $\ell : N \to N$ is q-*regular* if the sequence $(\ell(n))$ of its values is q-*regular*. Let us give some examples that we will need later.

1) Fix n_0 an integer ≥ 2 and let $H = \{m \in N, q^k n_0 \leq m < q^k(n_0 + 1), k \in N\}$. Denote by $c = (c_n)$ the characteristic sequence that is associated to H :
$$c_n = \begin{cases} 1 & \text{if } n \in H \\ 0 & \text{else.} \end{cases}$$
Consider the following sequence $u = (u_n)$,

$$u_n = \begin{cases} n - q^k n_0 & \text{if } q^k n_0 \leq n < q^k(n_0 + 1) \\ 0 & n \notin H. \end{cases}$$

The sequence u is q-regular. For any $a \in N$, any $0 \leq b < q^a$, for any $n \geq n_0$ we have $u_{q^a n + b} = q^a u_n + b c_n$.

2) Fix an integer $n_0 \geq 2$ and let $H = \{q^k n_0, k \in N\}$. Note again by $c = (c_n)$ the characteristic sequence that is associated to H. Let $\{a_0, \cdots, a_{D-1}\}$ be a finite set of integers. Consider a reccurrent sequence $(l(n))$ defined as following :

$$\begin{cases} l(n_0) & \text{some integer. For any } n \in N, \\ l(q^{n+1} n_0) & = ql(q^n n_0) + a_{n+1 \bmod D} \\ l(m) = 0 & \text{if } m \notin H. \end{cases}$$

The sequence $(l(n))$ is q-regular.

3) Let $\alpha \in Z$ and let (u_n) and (v_n) be two q-regular N-sequences. Then $\alpha(u_n)$ and $(u_n) + (v_n)$ are also q-regular.

$\Diamond$

2.3 About circularity F. Mignosi and P. Séébold introduced in [18] the notion of circularity relatively to the DOL-systems. In the particular case where the language L is the set of the factors of an infinite word obtained by iterating a morphism $\sigma : A^* \to A^*$, if σ is injective and q-uniform then we obtain a refined characterization. That is the only that we will use from now and that is the following :

Proposition *Let σ be an injective and q-uniform morphism, let $\mathbf{x}$ a fixed point of σ. The word $\mathbf{x}$ is circular if and only if there exists a constant $C > 0$ such that, if n and m are the indices of two occurrences of some factor w, $|w| \geq C$, in $\mathbf{x}$ then*

If w factorizes at n as $w = u\sigma(\mathbf{x}[i \cdots j])v$, u a suffix of $\sigma(\mathbf{x}[i-1])$, v prefix of $\sigma(\mathbf{x}[j+1])$ and at m as $w = u'\sigma(\mathbf{x}[i' \cdots j'])v'$, u' suffix of $\sigma(\mathbf{x}[i'-1])$, v' prefix of $\sigma(\mathbf{x}[j'+1])$, all of u, u', v, v' are chosen $\neq \epsilon$, then $\mathbf{x}[i \cdots j] = \mathbf{x}[i' \cdots j']$, $u = u'$ and $v = v'$.

In particular $n \equiv m$ modulo q.

Now, let us give the main theorem and a few examples.

2.4 Theorem

Let A be a finite alphabet. Let $\mathbf{x}$ be an infinite, non ultimately periodic and circular word over A. If $\mathbf{x}$ is obtained by iterating some injective and q-uniform morphism $\sigma : A^* \to A^*$ ($q \geq 2$), then the application $S_{\mathbf{x}}$ that associates to any $n \in N$ the length of the separator of $\mathbf{x}$ at n is q-regular.

2.5 Examples

1) Let $A = \{0, 1, 2, 3\}$ and consider thre dragon sequence, (see [14] and [15]), defined over A and generated by the morphism $\eta : A^* \to A^*$ $\quad \eta(0) = 01$, $\eta(1) = 21$, $\eta(2) = 03$, $\eta(3) = 23$. Note $\mathbf{x} = \lim_n \eta^n(0)$.

$$\mathbf{x} = 0121\,0321\,0123\,0321\,0121\,0323 \cdots$$

Let $B = \{0, 1\}$. Consider the morphism $\pi : A^* \longrightarrow B^*$ defined by $\pi(0) = \pi(1) = 1$, $\pi(2) = \pi(3) = 0$. The infinite word $\mathbf{w} = \pi(\mathbf{x})$ is the word usually associated to the regular paperfolding sequence, (see [1] and [17]).

$$\mathbf{w} = 1101\,1001\,1100\,1001\,1101\,1000 \cdots$$

Note that $\mathbf{x}$ verifies the hypotheses of the theorem. The computation of $S_{\mathbf{x}}$ give the function :

$S_{\mathbf{x}}(0) = S_{\mathbf{x}}(1) = S_{\mathbf{x}}(2) = 1$ and for any integer $m \geq 3$

$$S_{\mathbf{x}}(m) = \begin{cases} 5 \times 2^k - m & \text{if } 3 \times 2^k \leq m < 4 \times 2^k \\ 6 \times 2^k - m & \text{if } 4 \times 2^k \leq m < 5 \times 2^k + 2^{k-1}, k \geq 2 \\ 6 \times 2^k + 2^{k-1} - m & \text{if } 5 \times 2^k + 2^{k-1} \leq m < 6 \times 2^k \end{cases}$$

Let $H = \{m \geq 3, 3 \times 2^k \leq m < 4 \times 2^k, k \in N\}$. Let $m \in N$, $m \neq 0$ we denote by $w(m)$ the word of the 2-adic decomposition of m (i.e. $w(m) \in \{0, 1\}^*$. If $w(m) = a_0 \cdots a_r$, $a_i \in A$, then $a_r = 1$ and $m = a_0 + a_1 2 + \cdots + a_r 2^r$. Let $m \in H$. The value $w(S_{\mathbf{x}}(m))$ is obtained by applying $A(H)$ to the word $w(m)^{\bullet(2)} = a_0 a_1 \cdots a_{r-2}$. The output function is the concatenation with 01 for the state 1, and the concatenation with 1 for any other state.

Examples : $m = 6$, $w(m) = 011$, $w(S_\mathbf{x}(m)) = 001$, $S_\mathbf{x}(m) = 4$ and the separator of x at 6 is 2101.

$m = 13$, $w(m) = 1011$, $w(S_\mathbf{x}(m)) = 111$, $S_\mathbf{x}(m) = 7$ and the separator of x at 13 is 3210121.

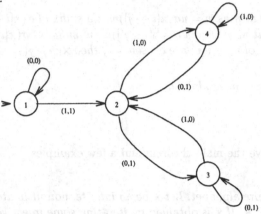

The automaton A(H) that computes $S_{\mathbf{x}H}$.

It can be easily verified that $S_\mathbf{w}(m) = S_\mathbf{x}(m)$ for every $m \geq 24$.

2) Let x be an infinite word over A. Consider the map $J : F(\mathbf{x}) \to N$ that associates to every factor $w \in F(\mathbf{x})$ the smallest index of N where w occurs. We have :

Proposition   *The map J is surjective if and only if x is not ultimately periodic.*

$\diamond$

We deduce than, if x is an infinite and ultimately periodic word then $S_\mathbf{x}$ is only defined over a finite subset of N and, if x is not ultimately periodic then $S_\mathbf{x}$ is defined over N.

3) Let $\sigma : A^* \to A^*$ be a morphism. If σ is q-uniform then, σ is injective if and only if the restriction map $\sigma : A \to A^*$ is injective.

Consider a non injective and q-uniform morphism $\sigma : A^* \to A^*$. Suppose there exists an infinite and non periodic word x such that $\mathbf{x} = \lim_n \sigma^n(a_0)$, for some $a_0 \in A$.

Denote by B the quotient set $B = A/ \sim$ where $\sim$ is the relation : for a, $b \in A$, $a \sim b$ if and only if $\sigma(a) = \sigma(b)$. Denote by π the canonical map $\pi : A^* \to B^*$, defined by setting $\pi(b) = \bar{b}$ where $\bar{b}$ is the equivalence class of $b \in A$. Let $\mathbf{y} = \pi(\mathbf{x})$ and let $\eta : B^* \to B^*$ be the morphism defined by $\eta(\bar{b}) = \pi(\sigma(b))$ for $\bar{b} \in B$. We have $\mathbf{y} = \lim_n \eta^n(\bar{a_0})$. Changing σ in σ^s and q in q^s where s is a suitable integer ≥ 1, we can suppose that η is injective.

Moreover if we suppose x circular and y is non ultimately periodic then y is also circular. Thus y satisfies the hypotheses of the theorem 2.4 and $S_\mathbf{y}$ is q-regular. Then we can deduce $S_\mathbf{x}$ from $S_\mathbf{y}$.

124

Finally the only case we have to consider is the case where the morphism σ is injective.

3 Sketch of proofs

Let $u \in A^*$. For convenience we denote by $u^\bullet$ the word u minus its last letter (resp. $^\bullet u$ is the word u minus its first letter). More generally, let $s \in N$, $u^{\bullet(s)}$ is the word u minus its suffix that length is s (resp. $^{\bullet(s)}u$ the word u minus its prefix that length is s).

Denote by ϑ the map $\vartheta : N \to F(\mathbf{x})$ that associates to any $n \in N$ the separator of $\mathbf{x}$ at n.

Denote by $J : F(\mathbf{x}) \to N$ the first occurrence map that associates to any $w \in F(\mathbf{x})$ the smallest index of $\mathbf{x}$ where w occurs. In particular we have $J(\vartheta(n)) = n$ for any $n \in N$.

We denote by $gcp(u,v)$ the greatest common prefix of two words u and v and $gcs(u,v)$ the greatest common suffix of u and v.

From now on, we suppose that $\mathbf{x}$ is an infinite, non ultimately periodic and circular word that is generated by iterating an injective and q-uniform morphism $\sigma : A^* \to A^*$ $(q \geq 2)$. We fix $C \geq 2$, a constant that is associated with the circular property given by proposition 2.3.

First we can remark that a direct consequence of the definition of ϑ is :

3.1 Proposition For any $n \in N$ we have $S_\mathbf{x}(n+1) \geq S_\mathbf{x}(n) - 1$ and $^\bullet\vartheta(n)$ is a prefix of $\vartheta(n+1)$. $\diamond$

So, to simplify we will say

- there exists a **step** between n and $n+1$ if $S_\mathbf{x}(n+1) \geq S_\mathbf{x}(n)$. In this case $^\bullet\vartheta(n)$ is a strict prefix of $\vartheta(n+1)^\bullet$,

- there exists **no step** between n and $n+1$ if $S_\mathbf{x}(n+1) = S_\mathbf{x}(n) - 1$. In this case $\vartheta(n+1) = ^\bullet\vartheta(n)$.

Note : if there exists no *step* between n and $n+d$ then $S_\mathbf{x}(n+d) = S_\mathbf{x}(n) - d$ and $\vartheta(n+d) = ^{\bullet(d)}\vartheta(n)$.

It is not difficult to establish the following propositions 3.2 and 3.3 :

3.2 Proposition Let $n \in N$ such that $S_\mathbf{x}(n) \geq C$. Note by a the last letter of $\vartheta(n)$. For any $k \in N$ we have $\vartheta(q^k n) = \sigma^k(\vartheta(n)^\bullet)z$ where z is a prefix of $\sigma^k(a)$, $z \neq \epsilon$, and we have $q^k S_\mathbf{x}(n) - q^k + 1 \leq S_\mathbf{x}(q^k n) \leq q^k S_\mathbf{x}(n)$. $\diamond$

3.3 Corollary We have the two following properties :

1) Let n be an integer such that $S_\mathbf{x}(n) \geq C$. If there exists a step between n and $n+1$ then there also exists a step between qn and $qn+q$ (at least).

2) If $S_{\mathbf{X}}(n) \geq C$ then $S_{\mathbf{X}}(m) \geq C$ for any $qn \leq m \leq qn + q - 1$.

$\diamond$

Let $m \in N$ be an integer and let $H = \{q^k m, \ k \in N\}$. First we prove that if m is large enough then the restriction mapping $S_{\mathbf{X}H}$ of $S_{\mathbf{X}}$ to H is q-regular. In order to do that, we associate to H a canonical family, denoted by $(I(k))$, of sets of indices $< m$. This sequence $(I(k))$ is ultimately periodic which allows us to obtain the values $S_{\mathbf{X}}(q^k m)$ with recurrent formula. Thus we can conclude that $S_{\mathbf{X}H}$ is q-regular. In more detail, we have :

3.4 Proposition *Let $m \in N$ be an index such that $S_{\mathbf{X}}(m) > C$ and let $H = \{q^k m, \ k \in N\}$. The restriction map $S_{\mathbf{X}H}$ of $S_{\mathbf{X}}$ to H is q-regular.*

Proof :

Fix $m \in N$ such that $S_{\mathbf{X}}(m) > C$ and let $H = \{q^k m, \ k \in N\}$. Note that H is q-recognizable. Define the sequence $(I(k))$ of the following subsets of N :

$$I = \{i < m, \text{ such that } \vartheta(m)^\bullet \text{ occurs at } i\} \text{ and}$$

$$I(k) = \{i \in I \text{ such that } \vartheta(q^k m)^\bullet \text{ occurs at } q^k i\}.$$

Applying the properties of injectivity of σ and of circularity, we can show that, for every $k \in N$, there exists a correspondance one to one between $I(k)$ and the set of indices $j < q^k m$ where $\vartheta(q^k m)^\bullet$ occurs. Moreover we have $I(k+1) \subset I(k)$. The sequence $(I(k))$ is a decreasing sequence of finite sets, not any $I(k)$ is empty. We conclude $(I(k))$ is stationary and its limit value is not an empty set.

Thus there exists an integer k_0 such that $(I(k))_{k \geq k_0}$ is a constant sequence. Denote by $E = \{i_1, \cdots, i_h\}$ its value. For any $k \in N$, for any $1 \leq j \leq h$, $q^k i_j$ determines the beginning of one occurrence of $\vartheta(q^k m)^\bullet$ such that $q^k i_j < q^k m$. Conversely if $l < q^k m$ is the index of one occurrence of $\vartheta(q^k m)^\bullet$ then $l = q^k i_j$ for some $j \in \{1, \cdots, h\}$.

Define a sequence $(d_n)_{n \geq k_0}$ in A^{h+1} by setting

- $d_n = (a_0^n, a_1^n, \cdots, a_h^n)$,

- a_0^n is the last letter of $\vartheta(q^n m)$,

- for any $1 \leq j \leq h$, a_j^n is the letter immediately after the factor $\vartheta(q^n m)^\bullet$ occurring at $q^n i_j$.

Note w_n the prefix of $\sigma(a_0^{n-1})$ $(n \geq 1)$ such that $\vartheta(q^n m) = \sigma(\vartheta(q^{n-1} m)^\bullet) w_n$, in particular $w_n \neq \epsilon$.

Lemma *The sequence $(d_n)_{n \geq k_0}$ is ultimately periodic.*

$\diamond$

Therefore, there exists an integer $k_1 \geq k_0$ such that $(d_n)_{n \geq k_1}$ is periodic. Fix and denote by D some period of (d_n). The set $\{w_n\}$ defined above is reduced to the finite set $\{w_1, \cdots, w_D\}$. Note $w_0 = w_D$. Since $\vartheta(q^{n+1} m) = \sigma(\vartheta(q^n m)^\bullet) w_{n+1}$, we have

$$S_{\mathbf{X}}(q^{n+1} m) = q(S_{\mathbf{X}}(q^n m) - 1) + |w_{n+1 \bmod D}|.$$

Thus $S_{\mathbf{X}}(q^n m)$, $n \geq k_1$ can be calculated by using a recurrence formula bearing up D terms and this proves the restriction map of $S_{\mathbf{X}}$ to H is q-regular.

$$\diamond \ \diamond$$

Now, using the description of ϑ and of $S_{\mathbf{X}}$ we can easily prove the following proposition :

3.5 Proposition

Let $n_0 \in N$ be an index such that $S_{\mathbf{X}}(n_0) > C$ and let $H = \{m \in N,\ q^k n_0 \leq m < q^k(n_0 + 1),\ k \in N\}$.

i) If, for any $k \in N$, there exists no step in the interval $[q^k n_0, q^k(n_0 + 1) - 1]$ then the restriction map of $S_{\mathbf{X}}$ to H is q-regular.

ii) If, for any $k \in N$, there exists a unique step in each interval $[q^k n_0, q^k(n_0 + 1) - 1]$, between the indices denoted by m_k and m_{k+1}, $q^k n_0 \leq m_k \leq q^k(n_0+1)-1$, then the set $\{m_k\}_{k \in N}$ is q-recognizable.

iii) Suppose there exists one and only one step, between the indices m_k and m_{k+1}, $q^k n_0 \leq m_k \leq q^k(n_0 + 1) - 1$, in each interval $[q^k n_0, q^k(n_0 + 1) - 1]$, then the restriction map of $S_{\mathbf{X}}$ to H is q-regular.

Proof

Proof of i) and iii) is omitted. Let us detail the proof of ii).

Suppose there exists a step between n_0 and $n_0 + 1$, and suppose there exists only one step in any interval $[q^k n_0, q^k(n_0 + 1)]$. Denote by m_k the index such that $q^k n_0 \leq m_k < m_k + 1 \leq q^k(n_0 + 1)$, there exists a step between m_k et $m_k + 1$ and nowhere else. First let us introduce some notations.

$\vartheta(n_0) = avb$, a and $b \in A$, $v \in A^*$, and $\vartheta(n_0 + 1) = vbw$. The existence of a step between n_0 and $n_0 + 1$ implies $|w| \geq 1$.

Let $I = \{i < n_0 + 1$ such that v occurrs at $i\}$, and for any $m \in H$, $m = q^k n_0 + m'$, $m' \leq q^k$ define
$I(m) = \{i \in I$ such that $\vartheta(m)^\bullet$ occurrs at $q^k(i - 1) + m'\}$.

<u>Remark</u> : There exists a correspondance one to one between $I(m)$, $m = q^k n_0 + m'$, $m' \leq q^k$, and the set of indices $q^k(i - 1) + m'\}$, $i \in I$ where $\vartheta(q^k m)^\bullet$ occurs.

The sequence $(I(q^k(n_0 + 1)))$ is stationary. Denote by E its limit value.

Let $a_0 = \mathbf{x}[n_0]$ and for any $i \in E$ let $a_i = \mathbf{x}[i - 1]$ be the letter of $\mathbf{x}$ just before the factor v occurring at i.

Let $w(k, i) = gcs(\sigma^k(a_i), \sigma^k(a_0))$ for any $i \in E$ and for any $k \in N$.

<u>Remark</u> : Let $j \in E$, let α be the letter just before $w(k, j)$ in $\sigma^k(a_0)$ and β be the letter just before $w(k, j)$ in $\sigma^k(a_j)$. We have $\alpha \neq \beta$ and the factorizations

$$\sigma^k(a_0) = u\alpha\, w(k, j),$$
$$\sigma^k(a_j) = u'\beta z = u'\beta\, w(k, j) \text{ for some suitable } u \text{ and } u' \in A^*.$$ By mapping σ we obtain $\sigma(\alpha) \neq \sigma(\beta)$.

Let $u_j = gcs(\sigma(\alpha), \sigma(\beta))$. We have

$$w(k+1, j) = gcs(\sigma^{k+1}(a_j), \sigma^{k+1}(a_0)) = u_j\, \sigma(w(k, j)).$$

Now consider the sequence $(I(m_k + 1))$. Applying the properties injectivity of σ and of circularity, and using the definition of ϑ, we can prove that

1) $i \in I(m_k + 1) \implies x[m_k + 1 \cdots q^k(n_0 + 1) - 1] = w(k, i)$,

2) $i \in I(m_k + 1) \iff w(k, i) = \sup_{j \in E} w(k, j)$. The sup means than $|w(k, i)| \geq |w(k, j)|$ for every $j \in E$,

3) $I(m_{k+1} + 1) \subset I(m_k + 1)$, for any $k \in N$.

We conclude from 1), 2) and 3) that $(I(m_k + 1))$ is a decreasing sequence of finite sets, any $I(m_k + 1)$ is not an empty set and $(I(m_k + 1))$ is stationary. Its limit value is not an empty set. We denote by $E' = \{i_1, \cdots, i_h\}$ this limit (in particular $E' \subset E$) and we choose k_0, an integer such that $I(m_k + 1) = E'$ for any $k \geq k_0$.

In a similar way to what we did in proposition 3.4, let us define a sequence $(p_n)_{n \geq k_0}$ in A^{h+1} by setting :

- $m_n = q^n n_0 + m'_n$ with $m'_n \leq q^n$,

- $p_n = (a_0^n, a_1^n, \cdots, a_h^n)$,

- $a_0^n = x[m_n]$ is the letter just before the factor $\vartheta(m_n + 1)$ occurring at $m_n + 1$,

- $a_j^n = x[q^n(i_j - 1) + m'_n]$ is the letter just before the factor $\vartheta(m_n + 1)^\bullet$ occurring at $q^n(i_j - 1) + m'_n + 1$. Note that this letter always exists because $i_j \in E'$.

Denote by z_n the common suffix $z_n = gcs(\sigma(a_j^{n-1}), \sigma(a_0^{n-1}))$, in particular since $\sigma(a_j^{n-1}) \neq \sigma(a_0^{n-1})$ we have $0 \leq |z_n| < q$.

Lemma *The sequence (p_n) is ultimately periodic.*

The proof is omitted.

$\diamond$

Now, choose an integer $k_1 \geq k_0$, such that the sequence $(p_k)_{k \geq k_1}$ is periodic and choose $D > 0$ some period. The set $\{z_k\}$ defined above is reduced to the finite set $\{z_1, \cdots, z_D\}$. Note $z_0 = z_D$. For any $j \in E'$, for any $k \geq k_1$ we have

$$w(k+1, j) = z_{k+1}\, \sigma(w(k, j)) = z_{k+1 \bmod D}\, \sigma(w(k, j)), \text{ that implies}$$

$$|w(k+1, j)| = |z_{k+1 \bmod D}| + q|w(k, j)|.$$

$$m_k + 1 = q^k(n_0 + 1) - |w(k, j)| \text{ and } m_{k+1} + 1 = q^{k+1}(n_0 + 1) - |w(k+1, j)|.$$

Finally we obtain $m_{k+1} = qm_k + q - 1 - |z_{k+1 \bmod D}|$ and that proves that the set $\{m_k, k \in N\}$ is q-recognizable.

We now extend our investigation to the subsets of N like $H(n_0) = \{m \in N, q^k n_0 \leq m < q^k(n_0 + 1), k \in N\}$. The set $H(n_0)$ can be decomposed in a disjoint and finite union of q-recognizable subsets such that the restriction of S_X to each of them is q-regular and then $S_{XH(n_0)}$ is q-regular. More precisely, we have the following proposition :

3.7 Proposition *Let $n_0 \in N$ be an index such that $S_X(n_0) > C$ and let $H = \{m \in N, q^k n_0 \leq m < q^k(n_0 + 1), k \in N\}$. The restriction map of S_X to H is q-regular.*

Proof For convenience note again

- $\vartheta(n_0) = avb$, a and $b \in A$, $v \in A^*$,

- $\vartheta(n_0 + 1) = vbw$, $w \in A^*$ (the existence of a step between n_0 and $n_0 + 1$ is equivalent to $|w| \geq 1$)

- $I = \{i < n_0 + 1 \text{ corresponding to a beginning of an occurrence of } v\}$.

Let $m \in H$ and let $m = q^k n_0 + m'$, $m' \leq q^k$ be its canonical decomposition. Note

- $I(m) = \{i \in I \text{ such that } \vartheta(m)^\bullet \text{ occurs at } q^k(i - 1) + m'\}$.

- (N_k) the sequence where N_k is the number of steps existing in the interval $[q^k n_0, q^k(n_0 + 1)]$, $k \in N$.

We can verify that

1) For any $m \in H$, $I(m) \neq \emptyset$.

2) Let $q^k n_0 \leq m_1 < m_2 \leq q^k(n_0 + 1)$ be two elements in H. If there exists no step between m_1 and m_2 then $I(m_1) \subset I(m_2)$. If there exists a step between m_1 and m_2 then $I(m_1) \cap I(m_2) = \emptyset$.

Let k be an integer and let $q^k n_0 \leq m_1 < \cdots < m_{N_k} < q^k(n_0 + 1)$ be the indices such that there exists a step between m_i and $m_i + 1$ and nowhere else. By the corollary 3.3, we know that there exists one step (at least) in every interval $[q m_i, q(m_i + 1)]$ and that implies $N_{k+1} \geq N_k$.

Note $r = N_k$ and $m_{r+1} = q^k(n_0 + 1)$. By the proposition 3.4, we have $I(m_j) \neq \emptyset$ for any $1 \leq j \leq r + 1$, $\cup_{1 \leq j \leq r+1} I(m_j) \subset I$ and $I(m_i) \cap I(m_j) = \emptyset$ for any $i \neq j$. We deduce $r \leq \text{Card}(I)$. Thus the increasing sequence (N_k) is bounded by $\text{Card}(I)$ and (N_k) is stationary.

Now, choose k_0 an integer such that $N_k = N_{k_0}$ for $k \geq k_0$. For every $n \in [q^{k_0} n_0, q^{k_0}(n_0 + 1)[$, denote by $H(n)$ the sets $H(n) = \{m \in N, q^k n \leq m < q^k(n + 1), k \in N\}$ and let $H' = H \setminus \cup_{n \in [q^{k_0} n_0, q^{k_0}(n_0+1)[} H(n)$.

By the proposition 3.5, the restriction maps $S_{XH(n)}$ of S_X to $H(n)$ respectively are q-regular and moreover H' is a finite set. We can conclude that the restriction of S_X to H is also q-regular.

◇

Finally, we prove that N is the disjoint union of in the one hand a finite set and on the other hand, a disjoint and finite union of sets like $H(n_0)$. Thus, it establishes the q-regularity of $S_\mathbf{x}$.

Proof of theorem 2.4

Suppose $\mathbf{x}$ is an infinite, circular and non ultimately periodic word over A that is generated by iterating an injective and q-uniform morphism $\sigma : A^* \to A^*$ ($q \geq 2$). Note again C a constant associated to the circularity of $\mathbf{x}$.

The hypothese $\mathbf{x}$ is not ultimately periodic implies that the applications ϑ and $S_\mathbf{x}$ exist over N. Fix $k_0 \in N$ such that $S_\mathbf{x}(m) > C$ for any $m \in [q^{k_0}, q^{k_0+1}]$. For any $n \in [q^{k_0}, q^{k_0+1}[$, denote by $H(n)$ the sets

$$H(n) = \{m \in N, \ q^k n \leq m < q^k(n+1), \ k \in N\} \text{ and note}$$

$H' = \{m \in N, \ m < q^{k_0}\}$. We obtain N as an union of disjoint sets

$$N = H' \cup \left(\cup_{q^{k_0} \leq n < q^{k_0+1}} H(n) \right)$$

H' is a finite set. The restriction mapping $S_{\mathbf{x}\,H(n)}$ is q-regular for any $n \in [q^{k_0}, q^{k_0+1}[$. We deduce that $S_\mathbf{x}$ is q-regular.

◇

4 Acknowledgment

I wish to thank Jean Berstel who introduced me to the surprising world of infinite words and suggested me this problem to me.

References

[1] J.P. Allouche. Automates Finis en Théorie des Nombres. *Expo. Math.*, 5:239–266, 1987.

[2] J.-P. Allouche and J. O. Shallit. The ring of k-regular sequences. *Theorical Computer Science*, 98:163–197, 1992.

[3] J. Berstel. Fonctions rationnelles et addition. *Actes de l'Ecole de Printemps de Théorie des Langages*, LITP:177–183, 1981.

[4] J. Berstel, C. Retenauer. *Les séries rationnelles et leurs langages*. Masson, 1984.

[5] A. Blumer, J. Blumer, A. Ehrenfeucht, D. Haussler, M.T. Chen and J. Seiferas. The smallest automaton recognizing the subwords of a text. *Theorical Computer Science*, 40:31–55, 1985.

[6] A. Blumer, J. Blumer, A. Ehrenfeucht, D. Haussler, M.T. Chen and J. Seiferas. Building the Minimal DFA for the Set of all Subwords of a Word One-line in Linear Time. *Proc. ICALP '84*, Springer Verlag, LNCS-172:109–118, 1984.

[7]   G. Christol, T. Kamae, M. Mendés-France and G. Rauzy. Suites algébriques, automates et substitutions. *Bull. Soc. Math. France*, 108:401–419, 1980.

[8]   A. Cobham. Uniform tag sequences. *Mathem. Syst. Theory*, 6:164–192, 1972.

[9]   M. Crochemore. Optimal factor transducers, in A. Apostolico and Z. Galil. *Combinatorics on words,*Springer, Berlin, 31–43, 1984.

[10]   M. Crochemore. Transducers and repetitions. *Theorical Computer Science*, 45:63–86, 1984.

[11]   C. Davis, D. E. Knuth. Number representations and dragon curves. *Journal of Recreational Mathematics*, 3:2, 1982, April :66–81, 1970, 3:3, 1982, on july :133–149, 1970.

[12]   M. Dekking, M. Mendés-France, A. van der Poorten. FOLDS. *Math. Intelligencer*, 4:130–138, 4:190–195, 1982, Errata in *Math. Intelligencer*, 5:5, 1983.

[13]   *Automata, Languages and Machines*. Academic Press, vol A, 1974.

[14]   M. Gardner. An optimal parallel Mathematical Games. *Sciences America*, july :115–120, 1967.

[15]   M. Mendès-France. Courbes du dragon par pliage. *The Mathematical Intelligencer*, 4:815–866, 1983.

[16]   M. Mendès-France and J.O. Shallit. Wire Bending. *Journal of Combinatorial Theory*, Srie A, 50:1–23, 1989.

[17]   M. Mendès-France and G. Tenenbaum. Dimension des courbes planes, papiers pliés et suites de Rudin-Shapiro. *Bulletin de la SMF*, 2, 109:143–268, 1981.

[18]   F. Mignosi and P. Séébold. If a DOL Language is k-Power Free then it is Circular. *Publications de l'université d'Amiens*.

[19]   B. Mossé. Puissances de mots et reconnaissabilité des points fixes d'une substitution. *Theorical Computer Science*, 2, 99:327–334, 1992.

[20]   B. Mossé. Notions de reconnaissabilité pour les points fixes substitutions et complexit des suites automatiques. *Publications du LMD*, Luminy, Marseille.

[21]   M. Queffélec. *Substitutions Dynamical Systems Spectral Analysis*. Springer Verlag, LNM- 1294, 1987.

[22]   A. Salomaa and M. Soittola. *Automata-Theoretic Aspects of Formal Power Series*. Springer Verlag, LNM-1294, 1987. Texts and monographs in computer science.

[23]   J. Shallit. A Generalisation of automatic sequences. *Theorical computer Science*, Springer Verlag, LNCS-61:1–16, 1988.

[24]   P. Séébold. Morphismes itérés, Mot de Morse et Mot de Fibonacci. *C.R.Acad.Sc.Paris*, 295, 1982.

[25]   T. Tapsoba. *Complexité des suites automatiques*, Thesis, Université d'Aix-Marseille II, 1987.

Systolic Tree ω-Languages

Angelo Monti[1] and Adriano Peron[2]

[1] Dipartimento Scienze dell'Informazione, Università di Roma (La Sapienza), 00198,
Via Salaria 113, Italy, E-mail: monti@dsi.uniroma1.it
[2] Dipartimento di Matematica e Informatica, Università di Udine, 33100,
Via Zanon 6, Italy, E-mail: peron@dimi.uniud.it

Abstract. The class of ω-languages recognized by systolic tree automata is introduced. That class extends the class of Büchi ω-languages and is closed under boolean operations. The emptiness problem for systolic tree automata on infinite sequences is decidable. A characterization of systolic tree ω-languages in terms of a (suitable) concatenation of (finitary) systolic tree languages is also provided.

1 Introduction

The subject of automata accepting infinite sequences was established in the sixties by Büchi, McNaughton and Rabin (for a survey, see [1]). Their work opened connections between automata theory and fields of logic and set-theoretic topology. The early papers were motivated by decision problems in mathematical logic (e.g., see [2]). One motivation for considering automata on infinite sequences (Büchi automata) was the analysis of the "sequential calculus", a system of monadic second-order logic for the formalization of properties of sequences. Büchi showed that any condition on sequences that it is written in this calculus can be reformulated as a statement about acceptance of sequences by a Büchi automaton. The resulted theory is fundamental for those areas in computer science where nonterminating computations are studied (e.g. modal logics of programs and in specification and verification of concurrent programs).

Systolic tree automata were introduced in the eighties by Culik II, Salomaa and Wood (see [4]) as a tool for studying computational power and properties of systolic systems. From a formal language viewpoint, the main interest of systolic tree automata is that the class of (finitary) languages they recognize strictly includes the class of regular languages and it preserves decidability and closure (w.r.t. operations on languages) properties of regular languages. Systolic automata as recognizers of finitary languages have been largely investigated (e.g., see [3]), but, as far as we know, they have never been considered as acceptors of infinite sequences. This work is a first step towards this investigation.

We show that, as the class of systolic tree languages is a meaningful extension of the class of regular languages, so the class of systolic tree ω-languages is a proper extension of the class of Büchi ω-languages. We prove also that systolic tree ω-languages enjoy the same nice properties of Büchi ω-languages, namely, the emptiness problem for systolic tree automata on infinite sequences is decidable and the class of recognized ω-languages is closed under boolean operations.

Moreover, as Büchi ω-languages can be characterized in terms of concatenations of regular sets, so systolic tree ω-languages can be characterized in terms of (suitable) concatenations of systolic tree (finitary) languages.

This work could be extended naturally by investigating a correspondence (analogous to that stated between Büchi ω-languages and the sequential calculus) between systolic tree ω-languages and a suitable decidable extension of the sequential calculus.

2 Preliminaries

Throughout this paper Σ denotes an alphabet and Σ^* (resp.: Σ^ω) denotes the set of finite words (resp.: $\omega - words$) on Σ. Finite words are indicated by $u, v, w, \ldots$ and sets of finite words by $U, V, W \ldots$. Letters $\alpha, \beta \ldots$ are used for ω-words and $L, L', \ldots$ for sets of ω-words. For an ω-word α, $\alpha(i)$, with $i \in \mathbb{N}$, denotes the i-th element of α; $\alpha(m, n)$ denotes the segment $\alpha(m) \ldots \alpha(n)$.

For a set of finite words $W \subseteq \Sigma^*$, let $\overrightarrow{W} \overset{def}{=} \{\alpha \in \Sigma^\omega : \alpha(0, n) \in W$ for infinitely many $n \in \mathbb{N}\}$ and $\widetilde{W} \overset{def}{=} \{\alpha \in \Sigma^\omega : \alpha(0, 2^n - 1) \in W$ for infinitely many $n \in \mathbb{N}\}$.

Definition 1. A *Büchi automaton* is a tuple $\mathcal{B} = (\Sigma, \mathcal{Q}, q_0, \Delta, \mathcal{F})$, where

- Σ is the finite *input alphabet*;
- $\mathcal{Q}$ is the finite set of *states*;
- q_0 is the *initial state*;
- $\Delta \subseteq \mathcal{Q} \times \Sigma \times \mathcal{Q}$ is the *transition relation*;
- $\mathcal{F} \subseteq \mathcal{Q}$ is the set of *final states*.

Automaton $\mathcal{B}$ is *deterministic* iff $(q, a, q'), (q, a, q'') \in \mathcal{Q}$ implies $q' = q''$. A *run* of $\mathcal{B}$ on an ω-word $\alpha \in \Sigma^\omega$ is a ω-word $\sigma \in \mathcal{Q}^\omega$ such that $\sigma(0) = q_0$ and $(\sigma(i), \alpha(i), \sigma(i+1)) \in \Delta$, for $i \geq 0$. Run σ is *successful* iff some state of $\mathcal{F}$ occurs infinitely often in it. Automaton $\mathcal{B}$ *accepts* α iff there is a successful run σ on α. Let $\mathcal{L}(\mathcal{B}) \overset{def}{=} \{\alpha \in \Sigma^\omega : \mathcal{B}$ accepts $\alpha\}$ be the ω-language accepted by $\mathcal{B}$. An ω-language L is *regular*, iff there exists a Büchi automaton $\mathcal{B}$ such that $\mathcal{L}(\mathcal{B}) = L$. The class of regular ω-languages is denoted by $\mathcal{L}(BA)$. The class of ω-languages recognized by deterministic Büchi automata is denoted by $\mathcal{L}(DBA)$.

We recall some results about regular ω-languages (see [1]):

1. $\mathcal{L}(BA)$ is (effectively) closed under union, intersection and complementation;
2. $L \in \mathcal{L}(DBA)$ iff $L = \overrightarrow{W}$, for some regular set $W \subseteq \Sigma^*$;
3. $L \in \mathcal{L}(BA)$ iff L is the finite union of sets of ω-words having the form $U.V^\omega$, where $V, U \subseteq \Sigma^*$ are regular sets (. denotes concatenation on strings);
4. the emptiness problem for Büchi automata is decidable.

Systolic languages are sets of words accepted by systolic automata ([4]). In the following we give an informal description of *systolic binary tree automata* (shortly $SBTA$). A systolic automaton consists of an infinite number of nodes which can

133

be interpreted as memoryless processors. Nodes are linked among them and the resulting structure is an (infinite) leafless perfectly balanced binary tree. In order to process a word w, the first level m of the tree is chosen which has at least $|w|$ nodes. Now, the automaton is fed in such a way that adjacent processors at level m are fed with adjacent symbols of w, and that the rightmost processor is fed with the last symbol of w. If the number of processors is greater than the word length, then exceeding processors (i.e., each i-th processor, for $1 \leq i < 2^m - |w|$) are fed with a special symbol #. In Fig.1 an example is given for an input word of length five. Now, all the processors at level m synchronously output, accordingly with an *input relation*, a symbol belonging to a *state alphabet* Q. Each processor at the level $m-1$ receives the couple of states outputed by its pair of sons and it synchronously (w.r.t. processors at the same level) outputs a symbol belonging to Q accordingly with a *transition relation*. Therefore, information flows bottom-up, in parallel and synchronously, level by level. The word is accepted whenever the root of the tree outputs a symbol belonging to a given set of *final states*.

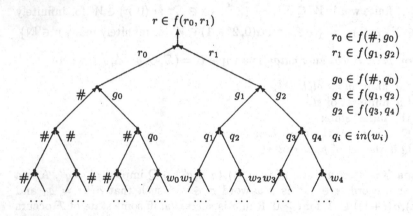

Fig. 1. A computation of a SBTA fed with $w_0.w_1.w_2.w_3.w_4$

Definition 2. A *systolic automaton* is a tuple $\mathcal{A} = (\Sigma, Q, in, f, F)$ where

- Σ is the finite *input alphabet*;
- Q is the finite set of *states*;
- $in \subseteq (\Sigma \cup \{\#\}) \times (Q \cup \{\#\})$ is the *input relation* such that $(x, \#) \in in$ iff $x = \#$;
- $f \subseteq (Q \cup \{\#\}) \times (Q \cup \{\#\}) \times (Q \cup \{\#\})$ is the *transition relation* such that $(p, q, \#) \in f$ iff $p = q = \#$;
- $F \subseteq Q \cup \{\#\}$ is the set of *final states*.

Abusing notation, we shall write $y \in in(x)$ (resp.: $z \in f(x,y)$) instead of $(x,y) \in in$ (resp.: $(x,y,z) \in f$); we shall write $y = in(x)$ (resp.: $z = f(x,y)$) if in (resp.: f) is a function. Automaton $\mathcal{A}$ is *deterministic* if in and f are total functions. Relation $O_{\mathcal{A}} \subseteq (\Sigma \cup \{\#\})^* \times Q$ is recursively defined as follows:

- if $|w| = 1$, then $(w, q) \in O_{\mathcal{A}}$ iff $q \in in(w)$;
- if $2^{m-1} < |w| \le 2^m$, with $m > 0$, then $(w, q) \in O_{\mathcal{A}}$ iff $q \in f(q_1, q_2)$ and q_1, q_2 are such that $(w_1, q_1), (w_2, q_2) \in O_{\mathcal{A}}$ with $|w_1| = |w_2| = 2^{m-1}$ and $w_1.w_2 = \#^{2^m - |w|}.w$.

Let $\mathcal{L}_{fin}(\mathcal{A}) \overset{def}{=} \{w \in \Sigma^* : (w, q) \in O_{\mathcal{A}}, q \in F\}$ be the *language (of finite words)* recognized by $\mathcal{A}$. The class of languages recognized by SBTA (resp.: by deterministic SBTA) is denoted by $\mathcal{L}_{fin}(SBTA)$ (resp.: $\mathcal{L}_{fin}(DSBTA)$).

A remark. The given definition of systolic tree automaton differs from the standard definition of [4] in the way processors are fed with an input word. In the standard definition adjacent processors at the input level are fed with adjacent symbols of the input word, but the leftmost processor is fed with the first symbol of the word. The class of systolic binary tree languages recognized by automata defined as in [4] and the class $\mathcal{L}_{fin}(SBTA)$ are uncomparable. However, $\mathcal{L}_{fin}(SBTA)$ and the standard class of systolic binary tree languages enjoy analogous properties. In particular, proofs of properties of $\mathcal{L}_{fin}(SBTA)$ can be obtained by slightly modifying those given in literature for the corresponding properties of the standard class. For this reason, we shall argue a property of $\mathcal{L}_{fin}(SBTA)$ by referring to the proof of the corresponding property in the standard case. We modify the standard notion of systolic automaton only for technical reasons, i.e., for achieving a more elegant characterization of the class of systolic ω-languages in terms of finitary systolic languages.
We recall some properties of $\mathcal{L}_{fin}(SBTA)$ (see [1]):

1. $\mathcal{L}_{fin}(SBTA)$ is (effectively) closed under union, intersection and complementation;
2. the class of regular languages is a proper subclass of $\mathcal{L}_{fin}(SBTA)$;
3. the emptiness problem for systolic tree automata is decidable;
4. $\mathcal{L}_{fin}(DSBTA) = \mathcal{L}_{fin}(SBTA)$.

3 Systolic Tree ω-Languages

We endow SBTA with an acceptance condition for ω-words. Then, we prove the decidability of emptiness problem for SBTA on infinite sequences and we compare their expressive power to that of Büchi automata.

Definition 3. For a systolic automaton $\mathcal{A} = (\Sigma, Q, in, f, F)$, a *systolic run* of $\mathcal{A}$ on an ω-word $\alpha \in \Sigma^\omega$ (see Fig.2), is a ω-word $\sigma \in Q^\omega$ such that

- $\sigma(0) \in in(\alpha(0))$;
- $\sigma(i) \in f(\sigma(i-1), q)$, with $(\alpha(2^{i-1}, 2^i - 1), q) \in O_{\mathcal{A}}$.

A systolic run σ is *successful* iff some state of F occurs infinitely often in σ.
Automaton $\mathcal{A}$ *accepts* α iff there is a successful systolic run on α.
Let $\mathcal{L}_\omega(\mathcal{A}) \overset{def}{=} \{\alpha \in \Sigma^\omega : \mathcal{A} \text{ accepts } \alpha\}$ be the ω-language recognized by $\mathcal{A}$.

The class of ω-languages recognized by systolic (resp.: by deterministic systolic) automata is denoted by $\mathcal{L}_\omega(SBTA)$ (resp.: $\mathcal{L}_\omega(DSBTA)$).

Let $\mathcal{SR}(A) \stackrel{def}{=} \{\sigma \in Q^\omega : \sigma$ is a successful systolic run on α, for some $\alpha \in \Sigma^\omega\}$ be the ω-language of successful runs of A.

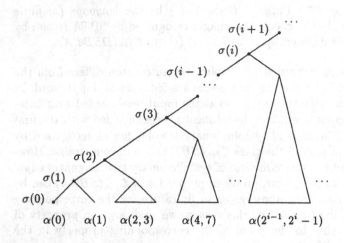

Fig. 2. A systolic run σ on α

Example 1. Let us consider the ω-language $L = \{a^{2^i}.\{b\}^\omega : i \geq 0\}$.

L is clearly non regular and it is recognized by the deterministic systolic tree automaton $A = (\Sigma, Q, in, f, F)$ defined as follows:

$\Sigma = \{a, b\}$; $Q = \{q_1, q_2, q_3, E\}$; $F = \{q_3\}$; $q_1 = in(a)$, $q_2 = in(b)$ and $\# = in(\#)$; $q_1 = f(q_1, q_1)$, $q_2 = f(q_2, q_2)$, $q_3 = f(q_1, q_2) = f(q_3, q_2)$, $\# = f(\#, \#)$ and $E = f(x, y)$ in all the remaining cases.

$L' = \{b.a^{2^1-1}.b.a^{2^2-1}.b\dots b.a^{2^i-1}.b.\dots\}$ is another example of non regular ω-language. Language $L' \in \mathcal{L}_\omega(DSTBA)$ is recognized by $A = (\Sigma, Q, in, f, F)$, with: $\Sigma = \{a, b\}$; $Q = \{q_1, q_2, q_3, q_4, q_5, E\}$; $F = \{q_5\}$; $q_1 = in(a)$ and $q_2 = in(b)$; $q_1 = f(q_1, q_1)$, $q_3 = f(q_2, q_1)$, $q_4 = f(q_1, q_3) = f(q_1, q_4)$, $q_5 = f(q_5, q_4)$, $\# = f(\#, \#)$ and $E = f(x, y)$ in all the remaining cases.

The emptiness problem for SBTA on ω-words is decidable, since the language of successful runs of a SBTA A is a regular ω-language.

Theorem 4. *For any systolic automaton A, $\mathcal{SR}(A)$ is a regular ω-language.*

Proof. Let $A = (\Sigma, Q, in, f, F)$ be a systolic automaton, we define a Büchi automaton $B = (Q, \mathcal{Q}, q_0, \Delta, \mathcal{F})$ such that $\mathcal{L}(B) = \mathcal{SR}(A)$ (notice that alphabet of B is the set of states of A). Let $\Xi : \mathbb{N} \to 2^Q$ be the function defined as follows:

- $\Xi(0) = \{q : q \in in(x), x \in \Sigma\}$;

$- \; \varXi(i) = \{q : q \in f(q_1, q_2), \text{ with } q_1, q_2 \in \varXi(i-1)\}.$

It is immediate to see that $q \in \varXi(i)$ iff there is a word $w \in \Sigma^*$, with $|w| = 2^i$ and $(w, q) \in O_A$. That Σ and Q are finite, implies $\varXi$ is ultimately periodic. Let n and m be the natural numbers representing the length of the preperiod and the period (respectively) of $\varXi$ and $k \stackrel{def}{=} n + m + 1$.

There are finitely many systolic runs $\sigma_1 \ldots \sigma_p$ on $\mathcal{A}$ such that $\sigma_i(0, k-1) \neq \sigma_j(0, k-1)$, for all $1 \leq i, j \leq p$ with $i \neq j$ and such that, for any systolic run σ' there exists $1 \leq i \leq p$ with $\sigma_i(0, k-1) = \sigma'(0, k-1)$. Each word $\sigma_j(0, k-1)$ naturally induces a strictly sequential automaton (see Fig.3), having states $V_j \stackrel{def}{=}$ $\{[q_o]\} \cup \{[j, i] : 1 \leq i \leq k\}$ and having transitions $E_j \stackrel{def}{=} \{([j, i], \sigma_j(i), [j, i+1]) :$ $1 \leq i \leq k-1\} \cup \{([q_o], \sigma_j(0), [j, 1])\}$. A path leading from $[q_o]$ to $[j, i+1]$ represents the fact that $(\alpha(0, 2^i - 1), \sigma_j(i)) \in O_A$, for some $\alpha \in \Sigma^\omega$ such that σ_j is a systolic run on α. Due to ultimately periodicity of $\varXi$ the set of states $\bigcup_{1 \leq j \leq p} V_j$ is enough for defining automaton $\mathcal{B}$. Consider now $K_j \stackrel{def}{=} \{([j, k], q, [l, n+2]) :$ $([l, n+1], q, [l, n+2]) \in E_l,$ and $\sigma_j(0, k-1).q = \sigma'(0, k)$ for some systolic run $\sigma'\}$. Namely, the state reached by a transition departing from $[j, k]$ leads a node reachable from state $[q_o]$ by a path of length $n+2$ whose last step is labelled by q. Finally, $\mathcal{B}$ is as follows: $Q \stackrel{def}{=} \bigcup_{1 \leq j \leq p} V_j; \; \Delta \stackrel{def}{=} \bigcup_{1 \leq j \leq p} E_j \cup K_j; \; \mathcal{F} \stackrel{def}{=} \{x : x \in Q,$ there exists $(y, q, x) \in \Delta,$ and $q \in F\}$.

It is easy to verify that automaton $\mathcal{B}$ satisfies the following property: a path from $[q_o]$ leads to a state $[j, u]$ iff the length of the path is $u + (h \times m)$, for some $h \geq 0$ and with $0 \leq u \leq k$.

We start with showing that if σ is a systolic run of $\mathcal{A}$ on some $\alpha \in \Sigma^\omega$, then there exists a path on $\mathcal{B}$ starting form $[q_o]$ and labelled by $\sigma(0, n + h \times m)$, for any $h \geq 1$. The proof is by induction on h. If $h = 1$, then by construction there exists a sequential automaton whose path is labelled $\sigma(0, k-1)$. Assume, by inductive hypothesis, that there exists a path labelled by $\sigma(0, n + h \times m)$. The length of the path is $k + (h-1) \times m$ and so the path leads to a state $[j, k]$ for some $1 \leq j \leq p$. Let us consider the word $\sigma(k + (h-1) \times m, k-1 + h \times m)$, then by periodicity of $\varXi$ there must be l with $1 \leq l \leq p$ such that $\sigma(k + (h-1) \times m, k-1 + h \times m)$ $= \sigma_l(n+1, k-1)$. Thus, transition $([j, k], \sigma(k + (h-1) \times m), [l, n+2])$ belongs to V_j and there exists a path from $[q_o]$ to $[l, k]$ labelled by $\sigma(0, k-1 + h \times m)$ (notice $k - 1 + h \times m = n + (h+1) \times m$).

We prove now that if there exists an infinite path in $\mathcal{B}$ from $[q_o]$ labelled by the ω-word β, then there exists a systolic run σ such that $\sigma(0, i) = \beta(0, i)$, for all $i \geq 0$. The proof is by induction on i. The property is guaranteed by construction of $\mathcal{B}$, for $0 \leq i \leq k-1$. Let us assume that $i \geq k$ and that the property holds for i, namely there exists a systolic run σ such that $\sigma(0, i) = \beta(0, i)$. The length of the path is $i + 1$ and so the reached state is $[j, u]$ for some $n + 1 < u \leq k$ such that $i + 1 = u + (h \times m)$. Now, assume that $\beta(i+1) = q$ (i.e., there is a transition from $[j, u]$ labelled by q). This implies, by construction of $\mathcal{B}$, that there exists $q' \in \varXi(u-1)$ such that $q \in f(\sigma(i), q')$. But $\varXi(u-1) = \varXi(u-1 + h \times m) = \varXi(i)$ and then there exists a systolic run σ' such that $\sigma'(0, i+1) = \sigma(0, i).q = \beta(0, i+1)$.

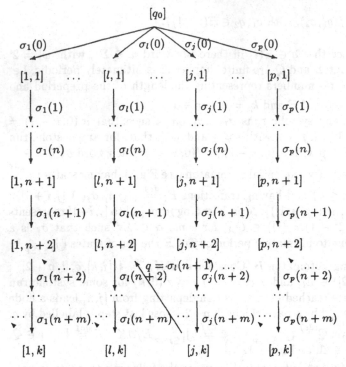

Fig. 3. A Büchi automaton B recognizing $SR(A)$

It remains to show that β as above is accepted by B iff it is a successful systolic run of A. If β is accepted by B, then there exists $[j, u] \in \mathcal{F}$, for some $0 \leq j \leq p$ and for some $n + 2 \leq u \leq k$, to which the path leads infinitely often. By construction, each state $[j, i] \in Q$ is such that if $([l, s], q, [j, i]), ([l', s'], q', [j, i]) \in \Delta$, then it must be $q = q'$. If q is the label of transitions leading to $[j, u]$, then q occurs infinitely often in β and $q \in F$ since $[j, u] \in \mathcal{F}$, thus proving that β is a successful systolic run of A. Conversely, assume that β is a successful systolic run of A and that $q \in F$ occurs infinitely often in β. Then, β is the sequence of labels occurring in an infinite path of B and all of the states reached by a transition labelled by q are final states. States are finitely many, and then there is a a final state which is reached by a transition labelled by q infinitely often. $\square$

Corollary 5. *The emptiness, inclusion and equivalence problems for SBTA on ω-words are decidable.*

Proof. As concerns emptiness, decidability follows from Th.4 and the decidability of emptiness of regular ω-languages (see [2]). By Th.15 and Th.21, $\mathcal{L}_\omega(SBTA)$ is effectively closed under union, intersection and complement. Hence the inclusion and equivalence problems reduce to the emptiness problem. $\square$

We investigate now the relationship between systolic tree ω-languages and regular ω-languages. In particular, we prove that the class of systolic ω-languages properly contains that of regular ω-languages and that the class of deterministic systolic ω-languages properly contains that of deterministic regular ω-languages.

Lemma 6. *If U is a regular set, then $\overrightarrow{U} \in \mathcal{L}_\omega(DSBTA)$.*

Proof. Let $\mathcal{A} = (\Sigma, Q, in, f, F)$ be a deterministic systolic automaton such that $\mathcal{L}_{fin}(\mathcal{A}) = U$. Assume without loss of generality that $\mathcal{A}$ is a weakly superstable automaton (i.e., $(w, q) \in O_\mathcal{A}$ and $q \in F$ iff, for each i, j with $2^i - |w| - j \geq 0$, there exists $q' \in F$ such that $(\#^j.w.\#^{2^i - |w| - j}, q') \in O_\mathcal{A})$ (see [3])). Consider the deterministic automaton $\mathcal{A}' = (\Sigma, Q', in', f', F')$, where:

- $Q' = 2^{Q \times Q \times \{L, R\}}$;
- $F' \subseteq 2^{Q \times Q \times \{R\}}$ s.t. $X \in F'$ implies there is $(q, q', R) \in X$ with $q \in F$;
- $in'(a) = \{(p, p, R) : p \in in(a)\}$, for all $a \in \Sigma$;
- for all $X, Y \in Q'$, $f'(X, Y) = \{(q_1, q_3, R), (q_2, q_3, S) : q_1 \in f(p_2, p_3), q_2 \in f(p_1, \#), q_3 \in f(p_2, p_4), \text{ and } (p_1, p_2, z) \in X, (p_3, p_4, z') \in Y, \text{ with } \{z, z'\} \in \{L, R\}\}$.

By construction of $\mathcal{A}'$, for each $w \in \Sigma^*$ with $|w| = 2^i$, $i \geq 0$ it holds $(w, q) \in O_{\mathcal{A}'}$ iff $q = \{(q_1, q_2, z) : (w(0, j-1).\#^{2^i - j}, q_1) \in O_\mathcal{A}, (w, q_2) \in O_\mathcal{A}, 0 \leq j < |w|, \text{ and } z = L \text{ if } j < 2^{i-1}, z = R \text{ otherwise}\}$. Hence, $w \in \mathcal{L}(\mathcal{A}')$ iff there exists j, with $2^{i-1} < j \leq 2^i$ such that $(w(0, j-1).\#^{2^i - j}, q) \in O_\mathcal{A}$ and $q \in F$. Automaton $\mathcal{A}$ is weakly superstable and then $w \in \mathcal{L}(\mathcal{A}')$ iff there exists $k > \frac{|w|}{2}$ such that $w(0, k) \in U$ and then by Prop.8 we have $\mathcal{L}_\omega(\mathcal{A}') = \overrightarrow{U}$. $\square$

Theorem 7. *Relations $\mathcal{L}(DBA) \subset \mathcal{L}_\omega(DSBTA)$, $\mathcal{L}(BA) \subset \mathcal{L}_\omega(SBTA)$ and $\mathcal{L}_\omega(DSBTA) \subset \mathcal{L}_\omega(SBTA)$ hold.*

Proof. $(\mathcal{L}(DBA) \subset \mathcal{L}_\omega(DSBTA).)$ As stated in [2], $L \in \mathcal{L}(DBA)$ iff there is a regular set $V \in \Sigma^*$ such that $L = \overrightarrow{V}$. Now, $V \in \mathcal{L}_{fin}(DBSTA)$ and by lemma 6 we have that $L \in \mathcal{L}_\omega(DSBTA)$. Ex.1 shows that the inclusion is proper.
$(\mathcal{L}(BA) \subset \mathcal{L}_\omega(SBTA).)$ As stated in [2] L is a regular ω-language iff L is the finite union of sets having the form $\overrightarrow{W} \cap \neg \overrightarrow{W'}$ with regular $W, W' \subseteq \Sigma^*$. Given a regular language $V \subseteq \Sigma^*$, there exists a systolic automaton $\mathcal{A}$ such that $\mathcal{L}_{fin}(\mathcal{A}) = V$ (see [3]) and by lemma 6 we have that $\overrightarrow{W}, \overrightarrow{W'} \in \mathcal{L}_\omega(DSBTA)$. The thesis follows since, by theorems 15 and 21, the class $\mathcal{L}_\omega(SBTA)$ is closed under intersection and complement. Ex.1 shows that the inclusion is proper.
$(\mathcal{L}_\omega(DSBTA) \subset \mathcal{L}_\omega(SBTA).)$ (Sketched) Relation $\mathcal{L}_\omega(DSBTA) \subseteq \mathcal{L}_\omega(SBTA)$ holds by definition. Now, it can be shown that the ω-language $L = (a + b)^*.b^\omega$ belongs to $\mathcal{L}(BA)$ and that $L \notin \mathcal{L}_\omega(DSBTA)$. The inclusion is proper by the previous point. $\square$

4 A Characterization of Systolic Tree ω-Languages

In this section a characterization of systolic ω-languages is provided. In [2], it has been shown that any regular ω-language can be expressed as the finite union of languages having the form $U.V^\omega$, where U and V are regular sets. Systolic ω-languages allows a similar characterization, namely, they can be expressed as the finite union of languages having the form $U \diamond V^{\diamond\omega}$, where U and V are systolic languages and $\diamond$ is a suitable refinement of concatenation on strings.

For a deterministic systolic automaton $\mathcal{A}$, the characterization is straightforward. In fact, if σ is a systolic run on α, $(\alpha(0, 2^{i+1}-1), q) \in O_{\mathcal{A}}$ iff $q = f(\sigma(i), q')$ with $(\alpha(2^i, 2^{i+1}-1), q') \in O_{\mathcal{A}}$. So, the ω-language recognized by $\mathcal{A}$ can be easily characterized in terms of $\mathcal{L}_{fin}(\mathcal{A})$.

Proposition 8. *For any deterministic systolic automaton* $\mathcal{A}$, $\mathcal{L}_\omega(\mathcal{A}) = \overrightarrow{\mathcal{L}_{fin}(\mathcal{A})}$.

Notations. Throughout this section $2^{[m,n]}$ (for $m \leq n$) represents $\sum_{j=m}^{n} 2^j$, $\Pi \stackrel{def}{=} \{2^{[m,n]} : m, n \in \mathbb{N}\}$ and $\Sigma^\Pi \stackrel{def}{=} \{w \in \Sigma^* : |w| \in \Pi\}$.

Definition 9. The binary operation $\diamond$ on Σ^Π is defined for $w, w' \in \Sigma^\Pi$ iff $|w| = 2^m$ and $|w'| = 2^{[m,n]}$, for some $m, n \geq 0$, and in this case $w \diamond w' \stackrel{def}{=} w.w'$. For $U, V \subseteq \Sigma^\Pi$:

1. $U \diamond V \stackrel{def}{=} \{w \diamond w' : w \in U, w' \in V\}$;
2. $U^{\diamond\omega} \stackrel{def}{=} \{w_1 \diamond w_2 \diamond w_3 \diamond \ldots : w_i \in U, \text{ for } i \geq 1\}$;
3. $U \diamond V^{\diamond\omega} \stackrel{def}{=} \{w_1 \diamond w_2 \diamond w_3 \diamond \ldots : w_1 \in U \text{ and } w_i \in V, \text{ for } i \geq 2\}$;

A remark. The operation $\diamond$ is not associative. So, when we write $w_1 \diamond w_2 \diamond w_3 \diamond \ldots$, we actually mean $((w_1 \diamond w_2) \diamond w_3) \diamond \ldots$.

Lemma 10. *For any* $U, V \in \mathcal{L}_{fin}(SBTA)$, $U \diamond V^{\diamond\omega} \in \mathcal{L}_\omega(SBTA)$.

Proof. Let $\mathcal{A}_i = (\Sigma, Q_i, in_i, f_i, F_i)$, $i \in \{1, 2\}$, be two SBTA such that $\mathcal{L}_{fin}(\mathcal{A}_1) = U$ and $\mathcal{L}_{fin}(\mathcal{A}_2) = V$. Assume without loss of generality that $\mathcal{A}_2$ is a stable automaton (i.e., $(w, q) \in O_{\mathcal{A}_2}$ and $q \in F$ iff for each $i \in \mathbb{N}$ with $2^i \geq |w|$, there exists $q' \in F$ such that $(\#^{2^i - |w|}.w, q') \in O_{\mathcal{A}_2}$) (see [3]). Assume also that Q_1, Q_2, $\overline{Q_2} \stackrel{def}{=} \{\overline{q} : q \in Q_2\}$ and $F_2 \stackrel{def}{=} \{q : q \in F_2\}$ are pairwise disjoint sets which do not contain symbol E. Consider the automaton $\mathcal{A} = (\Sigma, Q, in, f, F)$, where:

- $Q = Q_1 \cup Q_2 \cup \overline{Q_2} \cup F_2 \cup \{E\}$;
- $F = F_2$;
- $r \in in(x)$ iff either $r \in in_1(x)$ or $r \in in_2(x)$, for $x \in \Sigma$;
- if $p, p', s \in Q_1$ and $q, q', r \in Q_2$, then
  $s \in f(p, p')$ iff $s \in f_1(p, p')$; $p \in F_1$, then $\overline{r} \in f(p, q)$ iff $r \in f(\#, q)$;
  if $p \in F_1$, then $r \in f(p, q)$ iff $r \in f(\#, q)$ and $r \in F_2$;
  $r \in f(q, q')$ iff $r \in f_2(q, q')$; $\overline{r} \in f(\overline{q}, q')$ iff $r \in f_2(q, q')$;
  $r \in f(\overline{q}, q')$ iff $r \in f_2(q, q')$ and $r \in F_2$; $\overline{r} \in f(q, q')$ iff $r \in f_2(\#, q')$;
  $r \in f(q, q')$ iff $r \in f_2(\#, q')$ and $E \in f(q, q')$, for all $q, q' \in Q$.

We prove that $\mathcal{L}_\omega(\mathcal{A}) = U \diamond V^{\diamond \omega}$.

($\subseteq$) If $\alpha \in \mathcal{L}_\omega(\mathcal{A})$, then there exists a successful run σ such that $\sigma(i) \neq E$. Let $m_1, m_2, \ldots$ be the infinite sequence of integers such that $\sigma(m_i) \in F$, for $i \geq 1$ and such that $\sigma(k) \in F$ implies $k = m_j$, for some j. We prove by induction on $i \in \mathbb{N}$ that $\alpha(0, 2^{m_i} - 1) = u \diamond v_1 \diamond \ldots \diamond v_i$, for some $u \in U$ and $v_i \in V$. By construction of $\mathcal{A}$, if $\sigma(m_1) \in F$, then there must be $k < m_1$ such that $(\alpha(0, 2_1^k), q') \in O_{\mathcal{A}_1}$ with $q' \in F_1$ (i.e., $\alpha(0, 2_1^k) \in U$) and $(\#^{2^k}.\alpha(2^k, 2^{m_1} - 1), q'') \in O_{\mathcal{A}_2}$ with $q'' \in F_2$ (i.e., $\alpha(2^k, 2^{m_1} - 1) \in V$ by stability of $\mathcal{A}_2$). Assume that $\alpha(0, 2^{m_i} - 1) = u \diamond v_1 \diamond \ldots \diamond v_i$, with $u \in U$, $v_j \in V$, $1 \leq j \leq i$. We have that $\alpha(0, 2^{m_{i+1}} - 1) = u \diamond v_1 \diamond \ldots \diamond v_i \diamond \alpha(2^{m_i}, 2^{m_{i+1}} - 1)$. Now, we have that $\sigma(m_i), \sigma(m_{i+1}) \in F$ and $\sigma(k) \notin F$, for all $m_i < k < m_{i+1}$ and then $(\#^{2^{m_i}}.\alpha(2^{m_i}, 2^{m_{i+1}} - 1), q) \in O_{\mathcal{A}_2}$, for some $q \in F_2$ (in particular, $q = \sigma(m_{i+1})$) and then $\alpha(2^{m_i}, 2^{m_{i+1}} - 1) \in V$ by stability of $\mathcal{A}_2$.

($\supseteq$) Let $\alpha = u \diamond v_1 \diamond v_2 \diamond \ldots$, $u \in U$, $v_i \in V$, $i \geq 1$. Consider the infinite sequence of integers $m_1, \ldots, m_i \ldots$ such that $|u.v_1.v_2 \ldots v_i| = 2^{m_i}$, $i \geq 1$. We prove, by induction on i, that there exists a run σ on α such that $\sigma(m_j) \in F$, $1 \leq j \leq i$. That $u \in U$ implies $(u, q) \in O_{\mathcal{A}_1}$ for some $q \in F_1$; $v_1 \in V$ implies $(v_1, q') \in O_{\mathcal{A}_2}$ for some $q' \in F_2$ and, by stability of $\mathcal{A}_2$, $(\#^{|u|}.v_1, p) \in O_{\mathcal{A}_2}$ for some $p \in F_2$. Now, by construction of $\mathcal{A}$, there exists a run σ such that $\sigma(k) = q$, with $2^k = |w|$, and $\sigma(m_1) = p$. Assume that there exists a run σ such that $\sigma(m_j) \in F$, for $1 \leq j \leq i$. By inductive hypothesis, we have that $\sigma(m_i) \in F$. Now, $v_{i+1} \in V$ implies $(v_{i+1}, q) \in O_{\mathcal{A}_2}$ for some $q \in F_2$ and, by stability, $(\#^{m_i}.v_{i+1}, p) \in O_{\mathcal{A}_2}$ for some $p \in F_2$. Then, by construction, there is a run σ' such that $\sigma'(j) = \sigma(j)$, for $0 \leq j \leq m_i$ and such that $\sigma'(m_{i+1}) = p$. $\qquad\square$

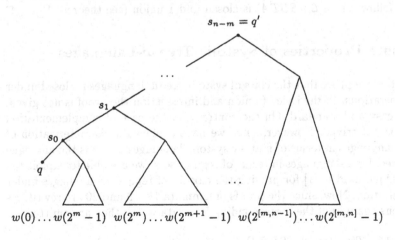

$$s_{n-m} = q'$$

$$w(0) \ldots w(2^m - 1) \quad w(2^m) \ldots w(2^{m+1} - 1) \quad w(2^{[m,n-1]}) \ldots w(2^{[m,n]} - 1)$$

Fig. 4. $(q, w, q') \in \Gamma_{\mathcal{A}}$

Definition 11. For a systolic automaton $\mathcal{A} = (\Sigma, Q, in, f, F)$, relation $\Gamma_{\mathcal{A}} \subseteq Q \times \Sigma^{\Pi} \times Q$ is such that $(q, w, q') \in \Gamma_{\mathcal{A}}$, with $|w| = 2^{[m,n]}$, iff there exists a sequence $s_0 \ldots s_{n-m}$ (see Fig.4), where $s_{n-m} = q'$ and

1. $s_0 \in f(q, q_0)$, with $(w(0, 2^m - 1), q_0) \in O_{\mathcal{A}}$;
2. $s_j \in f(s_{j-1}, q_j)$, with $(w(2^{[m,m+j-1]}, 2^{[m,m+j]} - 1), q_j) \in O_{\mathcal{A}}$, with $1 \leq j \leq n - m$.

Let $\Gamma_{\mathcal{A}}^F \subseteq \Gamma_{\mathcal{A}}$ be the relation such that $(q, w, q') \in \Gamma_{\mathcal{A}}^F$ iff there exists a sequence $s_0 \ldots s_{n-m}$ as above such that $s_j \in F$, for some $0 \leq j \leq m - n$.

For $q, q' \in Q$, let $W_{q,q'}^{\mathcal{A}} \overset{def}{=} \{w : (q, w, q') \in \Gamma_{\mathcal{A}}\}$, $W_{q,q'}^{\mathcal{A}F} \overset{def}{=} \{w : (q, w, q') \in \Gamma_{\mathcal{A}}^F\}$ and $W_q^{\mathcal{A}} \overset{def}{=} \{w : |w| = 2^i, \text{ with } (w, q) \in O_{\mathcal{A}}\}$.

The proofs of the two following lemmata are easy but tedious and then are omitted (the former one is by simulation and the latter is by induction).

Lemma 12. *For any systolic automaton* $\mathcal{A} = (\Sigma, Q, in, f, F)$, $W_{q,q'}^{\mathcal{A}}$, $W_{q,q'}^{\mathcal{A}F}$ *and* $W_q^{\mathcal{A}}$ *belong to* $\mathcal{L}_{fin}(SBTA)$, *for any* $q, q' \in Q$.

Lemma 13. *For any* $\mathcal{A} = (\Sigma, Q, in, f, F)$, $\mathcal{L}_\omega(\mathcal{A}) = \bigcup_{q \in F} W_q^{\mathcal{A}} \diamond (W_{q,q}^{\mathcal{A}})^{\diamond\omega}$.

Theorem 14. *An* ω-*language* L *belongs to* $\mathcal{L}_\omega(SBTA)$ *iff* L *is the finite union of sets having the form* $U \diamond V^{\diamond\omega}$ *with* $U, V \in \mathcal{L}_{fin}(SBTA)$.

Proof. ($\Longrightarrow$) If $L \in \mathcal{L}_\omega(SBTA)$, then $L = \bigcup_{q \in F} W_q^{\mathcal{A}} \diamond W_{q,q}^{\mathcal{A}\omega}$, for some systolic automaton $\mathcal{A} = (\Sigma, Q, in, f, F)$ (see lemma 13). By lemma 12, $W_q^{\mathcal{A}}$ and $W_{q,q}^{\mathcal{A}}$ belong to $\mathcal{L}_{fin}(SBTA)$, for any $q \in F$.
($\Longleftarrow$) If $U, V \in \mathcal{L}_{fin}(SBTA)$, then $U \diamond V^{\diamond\omega} \in \mathcal{L}_\omega(SBTA)$ (see lemma 10). Thus, the thesis follows since $\mathcal{L}_\omega(SBTA)$ is closed under union (see theorem 15). $\square$

5 Closure Properties of Systolic Tree ω-Languages

In this section we prove that the class of systolic tree ω-languages is closed under boolean operations. In the case of union and intersection the proof is not given, since it is easy and standard. On the contrary, in the case of complementation the proof is not trivial. However, since we have achieved a characterization of systolic ω-languages in terms of finitary systolic languages which is the analogue of that of regular ω-languages in terms of regular sets, we are able to exploit the same technique used in [1] for proving the closure of regular ω-languages under complementation. Now, since the proofs of lemmata 18, 19 and 20 are rewritings with obvious changes of the corresponding lemmata in [1], they are omitted.

Theorem 15. *The class* $\mathcal{L}_\omega(SBTA)$ *is (effectively) closed under union and intersection.*

Definition 16. Relation $\sim_{\mathcal{A}} \subseteq \Sigma^\Pi \times \Sigma^\Pi$ is s.t. $u \sim_{\mathcal{A}} v$ iff for each $q, q' \in Q$:

1. $(q, u, q') \in \Gamma_{\mathcal{A}}$ iff $(q, u, q') \in \Gamma_{\mathcal{A}}$;
2. $(q, u, q') \in \Gamma_{\mathcal{A}}^F$ iff $(q, u, q') \in \Gamma_{\mathcal{A}}^F$.

Relation $\approx_A \subseteq \Sigma^{\Pi} \times \Sigma^{\Pi}$ is such that $u \approx_A v$ iff $|u| = 2^m$ and $|v| = 2^n$, for some $n, m \geq 0$ and, for each $q \in Q$, $(u, q) \in O_A$ iff $(v, q) \in O_A$.

Proposition 17. *For any systolic automaton A, relation $\sim_A$ is a finite index equivalence relation on Σ^{Π} which weakly preserves $\diamond$ (i.e., if $u \sim_A u'$, $v \sim_A v'$, and $u \diamond v$ and $u' \diamond v'$ are defined then $u \diamond v \sim_A u' \diamond v'$).*

Lemma 18. *For any $w \in \Sigma^{\Pi}$ and any automaton A, the equivalence class (with respect to $\sim_A$) containing w (written as $[w]_A$) belongs to $\mathcal{L}_{fin}(SBTA)$.*

Lemma 19. *For each equivalence class U of $\approx_A$ and each equivalence class V of $\sim_A$, if $U \diamond V^{\diamond \omega} \cap \mathcal{L}_\omega(A) \neq \emptyset$, then $U \diamond V^{\diamond \omega} \subseteq \mathcal{L}_\omega(A)$.*

Lemma 20. *For any ω-word $\alpha \in \Sigma^\omega$ and any systolic automaton A, there exists an equivalence class U for $\approx_A$ and an equivalence class V for $\sim_A$ such that $\alpha \in U \diamond V^{\diamond \omega}$.*

Theorem 21. *The class $\mathcal{L}_\omega(SBTA)$ is (effectively) closed under complement.*

Proof. Let $L = \mathcal{L}_\omega(A)$, for some systolic automaton A and let $\overline{L}$ be the union of sets having the form $U \diamond V^{\diamond \omega}$ with U an equivalence class of $\approx_A$, V an equivalence class of $\sim_A$ and $U \diamond V^{\diamond \omega} \cap L = \emptyset$. As a consequence of lemma 19 we have that $\overline{L} \subseteq \neg L$. The opposite inclusion is a consequence of lemma 20 and thus $\overline{L} = \neg L$. That $\overline{L} \in \mathcal{L}_\omega(SBTA)$ is a consequence of the following facts: equivalence classes of $\sim_A$ and $\approx_A$ belong to $\mathcal{L}_{fin}(SBTA)$ (see lemma 18); each set $U \diamond V^{\diamond \omega}$ defined as above belongs to $\mathcal{L}_\omega(SBTA)$ (see lemma 10); there are finitely many $U \diamond V^{\diamond \omega}$ defined as above which are disjoint with respect to L ($\approx_A$ and $\sim_A$ have finitely many equivalence classes); class $\mathcal{L}_\omega(SBTA)$ is closed under union (see Th.15). It remains to show that $\overline{L}$ can be effectively constructed. It is immediate to see that equivalence classes of $\approx_A$ and $\sim_A$ can be effectively constructed, and that sets having the form $U \diamond V^{\diamond \omega}$ also can be. Intersection of languages in $\mathcal{L}_\omega(SBTA)$ is effective (see Th.15) and emptiness is decidable (see Th.5) and thus the condition $U \diamond V^{\diamond \omega} \cap L$ can be effectively checked. Finally, that union of languages in $\mathcal{L}_\omega(BTSA)$ is effective (see Th.15), leads to the thesis. $\square$

Acknowledgements. We like to thank Alberto Policriti for discussions which inspired this work and for suggestions about the contents of this paper.

References

1. Thomas, W.: Automata on Infinite Objects, Handbook of Theoretical Computer Science, Elsevier (1990), Vol. B, pp. 133–191.
2. Büchi, J.R.: On a Decision Method in Restricted Second Order Arithmetic, Proceedings International Congress on Logic, Methodology and Philosophy of Science, Stanford Univ. Press (1960), pp. 1–11.
3. Gruska, J.: Synthesis, Structure and Power of Systolic Computations, Theoretical Computer Science **71** (1990), pp. 47–78.
4. Culik II, K., Salomaa, A., Wood, D., Systolic Tree Acceptors, R.A.I.R.O Informatique Théorique **18** (1984), pp. 53–69.

Structural Complexity of ω-automata

Sriram C. Krishnan *, Anuj Puri**, Robert K. Brayton
Email: {krishnan,anuj,brayton}@eecs.berkeley.edu

Department of EECS, University of California, Berkeley, CA-94720

Abstract. In this paper we relate expressiveness of ω-automata to their complexity. Expressiveness is related to the different subclasses of the ω-regular languages that are accepted by automata that arise by restrictions on the acceptance conditions used. For example, different subclasses of the ω-regular languages arise from identifying the ω-languages with different classes and levels in the Borel hierarchy. Within the class of ω-regular languages, Wagner and Kaminski identified a strict hierarchy of languages induced by restricting the number of pairs allowed in a deterministic Rabin automaton (DRA).

Complexity relates to the smallest size automaton required to realize an ω-regular language. Safra shows that there are ω-regular languages for which deterministic Streett automata (DSA) are exponentially smaller than nondeterministic Buchi automata; in contrast, we show that for every DSA or DRA whose language is in class G_δ, there exists a DBA of size linear in the original automaton. We show in particular that the language of a DRA is in class G_δ if and only if the language can be realized as a DBA on the same transition structure as the DRA. We present a simple construction to transform a DRA with h pairs and n states to an equivalent DRA with $O(n.h^k)$ states and k pairs (i.e. $DR(n,h) \to DR(n.h^k,k)$), where k is the Rabin Index (RI) of the language—the minimum number of pairs required to realize the language as a DRA. We also present a construction to translate a DSA into a minimum-pair DRA, achieving a transformation $DS(n,h) \to DR(n.h^k,r)$, where k is the Streett index (SI), and r the RI of the language.

We prove that it is NP-hard to determine the RI (SI) of a language specified by a DRA (DSA). However, for a DRA (DSA) with h pairs, determining whether the RI (SI) is h, or any constant c, is in polynomial time.

1 Introduction

Two important distinguishing characteristics of the different ω-automata are their expressiveness and complexity. Expressiveness is the attribute referring to the subset of the class of ω-regular languages that an automaton can realize. It is known that deterministic Rabin (DRA), Streett (DSA), and Muller automata

---

* supported by California MICRO program grant 93-026, DEC, and Intel
** supported by NSF grant ECS 9111907 and California PATH program

[12] can realize any ω-regular language. Deterministic Buchi automata (DBA) however can only express a strict subset of the ω-regular languages.

Complexity on the other hand refers to the size of the minimal automaton required to realize an ω-regular language. Safra in [10] studied some problems relating to the relative complexity of different ω-automata. He showed that for some ω-regular languages, DSA are exponentially more compact than *nondeterministic* Buchi automata. From this it follows that for some ω-regular languages, DSA are exponentially more compact than DRA, and for some others DRA are exponentially more compact than DSA.

In this paper we study the complexity of automata vis-a-vis expressiveness. We relate the two by considering subclasses of the ω-regular languages and study the complexity of automata within each subclass. We also study the complexity of the problem of deciding if a language lies within a subclass. We restrict our attention to complete deterministic automata.

Expressiveness is related to topological and structural properties of the languages. In the Cantor Topology [12], the ω-regular languages have been identified with certain levels in the Borel hierarchy—wherein, the Safety languages [2, 12] correspond to the class F of closed sets, the ω-regular languages in the class G_δ are exactly those accepted by DBA, and all the ω-regular languages are contained within the class $G_{\delta\sigma} \cap F_{\sigma\delta}$ [12, 13, 11]. Within the class of ω-regular languages, there is an infinite hierarchy of languages induced by restricting the number of pairs allowed in a DRA. Wagner [13] and independently Kaminski [5] showed that this hierarchy is strict, i.e. for every n there exists a language that cannot be realized by a DRA with fewer than n pairs. The minimum number of pairs required to realize a language as a DRA is called the Rabin index (RI) of the language.

For the ω-regular languages in the class G_δ, we show that DBA are linearly as compact as DRA or DSA. In particular, we show that the language of a DRA lies in G_δ (i.e. is DBA-realizable) if and only if it can be realized as a DBA on the same transition structure as the DRA. In contrast, there exists DSA whose languages lie in G_δ but cannot be realized as DBA on the same transition structure [6]; nevertheless we show that for every DSA whose language is in G_δ there exists a DBA whose size is linear in the size of the original DSA.

We offer a simple construction to translate a DRA with h pairs to a DRA with a minimum number of pairs. We achieve a transformation $DR(n, h) \rightarrow DR(n.h^k, k)$, i.e. from an n-state h-pair DRA to a DRA with $O(n.h^k)$ states and k pairs, where k is the Rabin index (RI) of the language. It follows that for the class of languages realizable by DRA with a constant number of pairs (i.e. within a constant level in the Wagner/Kaminski hierarchy), the minimum pair automaton is polynomially related in size to any arbitrary equivalent deterministic automaton in this class. In [1] is an algorithm to yield a minimum-pair DRA with $O(n^h 4^{2h^2})$ number of states—significantly worse than ours.

We also provide a construction to translate DSA to minimum-pair DRA, achieving a transformation $DS(n, h) \rightarrow DR(n.h^k, r)$, where k is the Streett index (SI) of the language, and r is the RI of the language; r is either k or

$k + 1$. Safra's construction for translating DSA to DRA achieves a transformation $DS(n, h) \to DR(n.h^h, h + 1)$; ours is superior to Safra's in general (when $k < h$), and matches his in the worst case.

We also consider decision problems relating to locating languages specified as a DRA or DSA at the lowest level in the Wagner/Kaminski hierarchy. Wagner and Kaminski showed that for any deterministic automaton realizing a language of RI k, there is no chain of alternating accepting and rejecting strongly connected sets of length greater than k. We prove that it is NP-hard to determine the Rabin (Streett) index of a language specified by a DRA (DSA). However, for a DRA (DSA) with h pairs, determining whether the RI (SI) is h, or c, for any constant c, is in polynomial time. Our resolution of the complexity of determining the R/S Index of a language settles an open problem posed by Manna and Pnueli in [8] (page 383).

Finally, we also provide a method for obtaining results similar to Wagner and Kaminski for other subclasses of ω-regular languages. In particular, we show that the star-free ω-regular sets also form an infinite hierarchy within the Wagner/Kaminski hierarchy.

Section 2 presents our notation. In introducing ω-automata, we attempt to unify the different acceptance criteria that are used by specifying acceptance conditions using Boolean formulae. We also discuss the complexity of various problems when acceptance conditions are specified with Boolean formulae. In Section 2.1 we describe the Wagner/Kaminski hierarchy. In Section 3.1, we present our basic constructions for converting a DRA (DSA) with language in class G_δ to an equivalent DBA whose size is linear in size of the original automaton. In Section 3.2 we extend our basic constructions to transform a DSA into an equivalent minimum-pair DSA or DRA. In Section 4, we discuss the complexity of deciding the Rabin Index. In Section 5 we consider extensions to acceptance conditions and their relationship with the Wagner/Kaminski hierarchy of Section 2.1.

2 Preliminaries

An ω-automaton [12, 7] over a finite alphabet, Σ, is $\mathcal{A} = \langle T, \phi \rangle$, where T is a transition structure and ϕ is the acceptance condition. The transition structure is $T = \langle Q, q_0, \Sigma, \delta \rangle$ where Q is a finite set of states, $q_0 \in Q$ is the initial state, and $\delta : Q \times \Sigma \to Q$ is the transition function. In this paper we restrict our attention to complete deterministic ω-automata (DOA), i.e. δ is a *total* function.

Definition 1. A word $\sigma \in \Sigma^\omega$ has the run $r_\sigma \in Q^\omega$, where $r_\sigma(0) = q_0$ and $\delta(r_\sigma(i), \sigma(i)) = r_\sigma(i + 1)$.

The infinity set of the run r_σ, denoted $inf(r_\sigma)$, is the set of states that are visited infinitely often in r_σ. The acceptance condition ϕ is a Boolean formula, where the Boolean variables are the states $Q = \{q_1, \ldots, q_n\}$.

Definition 2. A Boolean formula is generated by the following rules
1) $q_i \in Q$ is a Boolean formula

2) If ϕ_1, ϕ_2 are Boolean formulae, then $\neg\phi_1$, $\phi_1 \vee \phi_2$, and $\phi_1 \wedge \phi_2$ are Boolean formulae.

The truth of $q_i \in Q$ is determined by the run r_σ. For $C \subseteq Q$ define the assignment $q_i = true$ provided $q_i \in C$. Let $\phi[C]$ denote the truth value of ϕ under this assignment.

Definition 3. The language generated by the ω-automaton $A = \langle T, \phi \rangle$, denoted $\mathcal{L}(A)$, is $\{\sigma | \sigma \in \Sigma^\omega \text{ and } \phi[inf(r_\sigma)] = true\}$.

Definition 4. For $Q = Q_1 \times Q_2$ and $q = (q_1, q_2) \in Q$, define $\pi_{Q_i}(q) = q_i$, for $i \in \{1, 2\}$.

Definition 5. We define various types of Boolean formulae [10] which are used to define acceptance criteria :
1) A disjunctive formula (DF) is a disjunction of Boolean variables, i.e., $\phi = q_{i_1} \vee \ldots \vee q_{i_k}$.
2) A Rabin formula is $\phi = \vee_{i=1}^{n}(L_i \wedge \neg(\overline{U_i}))$ where $L_i, U_i, 1 \leq i \leq n$ are DF.
3) A Streett formula is $\phi = \wedge_{i=1}^{n}(L_i \vee \neg(\overline{U_i}))$ where $L_i, U_i, 1 \leq i \leq n$ are DF.
4) A positive Boolean formula (PBF) is a Boolean formula with no negations.
5) A negative Boolean formula (NBF) is $\neg\phi$ where ϕ is a PBF.

A Buchi automaton (DBA) is $A = \langle T, \phi \rangle$, where ϕ is a DF. A Rabin automaton (DRA) is defined by a Rabin formula and a Streett automaton (DSA) with a Streett formula. Since each DF identifies a set of states the Buchi condition is often called the final states. The Rabin and Streett acceptance conditions are also referred to as a set of **pairs** (L_i, U_i) of subsets of states. Informally, a run r_σ in a DRA is accepting if for some pair, $inf(r_\sigma)$ "touches" L_i and is contained in U_i. A DRA may be complemented to yield a DSA (and vice-versa) on the same transition structure and the same number of pairs, by replacing each pair (L_i, U_i) by $(\overline{U_i}, \overline{L_i})$. Thus DSA and DRA are syntactic complements of each other.

Definition 6. Given an ω-automaton $A = \langle T, \phi \rangle$ with states Q, a *strongly connected set* (SCS) $C \subseteq Q$, is said to be an **accepting** SCS provided $\phi[C] = true$. Otherwise C is termed a **rejecting** SCS.

Definition 7. Given an ω-automaton $A = \langle T = (Q, q_0, \Sigma, \delta), \phi \rangle$, a state $q \in Q$ is termed **final** provided every SCS C containing q is accepting. An accepting SCS C is said to be **superset closed** provided every SCS C', such that $C \subseteq C'$ is accepting. Let SCC(q) denote the largest SCS containing q.

The terminology, final state, comes from BA where every SCS containing a final state is accepting. An ω-regular language is any language accepted by a DSA or DRA; in this paper we use language synonymously with ω-regular language. The languages accepted by DBA form a strict subset of the class of ω-regular languages, and are contained in the Borel class G_δ.

Theorem 8 (Landweber). *[12] Given a deterministic ω-automaton A, $L(A)$ is in G_δ if and only if every accepting SCS C is superset closed.*

It is known that the language-emptiness problem for Buchi and Rabin automata is logspace complete for NLOGSPACE [12]. Also quadratic time algorithms are known for checking emptiness of Streett automata [3]. We address the complexity of the emptiness problem for automata with Boolean formulae.

Theorem 9. *For $A = \langle T, \phi \rangle$, where ϕ is a PBF, checking $\mathcal{L}(A) = \emptyset$ is logspace complete for NLOGSPACE.*

It can be shown that if ϕ is a PBF, the language is in G_δ. In contrast, the emptiness problem for automata with negative Boolean formulae is NP-complete (the proof is similar to that of Theorem 4.7 in [3] and is omitted for space).

Theorem 10. *For $A = \langle T, \psi \rangle$ where ψ is a NBF, checking $\mathcal{L}(A) = \emptyset$ is NP-complete.*

2.1 The Wagner/Kaminski Hierarchy

From McNaughton's theorem [12], it follows that every ω-regular language is recognized by a deterministic Muller automaton (DMA). Using this it can be shown that an ω-regular language $\mathcal{L} = \cup_{i=1}^{h}(D_i \cap C_i)$ where $D_i \in G_\delta$ and $C_i \in F_\sigma$, are ω-regular and $F_\sigma = \overline{G_\delta}$. Wagner [13] and Kaminski [5] showed that:

Lemma 11. $\mathcal{L} = \cup_{i=1}^{h}(D_i \cap C_i), D_i \in G_\delta, C_i \in F_\sigma \Leftrightarrow \mathcal{L}$ *is accepted by a DRA with h pairs*

Definition 12. Let $Rn(k)$ be the set of all languages which are accepted by DRA with k or less pairs. For every ω-regular language $\mathcal{L}$, the least k such that $\mathcal{L} \in Rn(k)$ is called the **Rabin Index** (*RI*) of the language.

Clearly $Rn(k-1) \subseteq Rn(k)$. Wagner [13] and Kaminski [5] proved that:

Theorem 13. *For each $k \geq 2$, $Rn(k-1) \subset Rn(k)$, i.e. $Rn(k) \setminus Rn(k-1)$ is non-empty.*

Wagner and Kaminski also gave a structural characterization of languages in $Rn(k)$ by extending Landweber's characterization of DBA. This characterization is in terms of the longest chain of alternating accepting and rejecting SCS.

Definition 14. Given an automaton $A = \langle T, \phi \rangle$, a **positive** chain of length k is $G_1 \subset B_1 \subset \ldots \subset G_k (\subset B_k)$ where G_i are accepting SCS and B_i rejecting SCS.

Theorem 15 (Wagner & Kaminski). *$\mathcal{L} \in Rn(k) \Leftrightarrow$ for any deterministic automaton accepting $\mathcal{L}$, the longest positive chain is of length at most k*

Since DRA and DSA are complementary, an analogous development follows for DSA as well. We can define $St(k)$, the **Streett Index** (SI), and formulate a structural invariant on deterministic automata accepting languages in $St(k)$: namely, there is no **negative chain** of length $> k$, where a negative chain starts with a rejecting SCS. Clearly $Rn(k) = \overline{St(k)}$. It can also be shown that $St(k) \subseteq Rn(k+1)$; we offer a simple constructive proof of this in Section 3.2. Due to the complementary relationship between DSA and DRA, any construction to transform a DSA into another DSA or a DRA also immediately yields a construction to transform a DRA into another DRA or a DSA.

3 Compactness of Deterministic Automata

3.1 Languages realizable as DBA

In this section, we introduce our basic constructions and convert DRA and DSA whose language is in G_δ to equivalent DBA. We formulate two basic constructions. The first is an exclusion construction that transforms a deterministic automaton $\mathcal{A} = \langle T, \phi \rangle$ to a deterministic automaton $\mathcal{A}' = \langle T', \phi' \rangle$ and identifies a subset of states $S \subseteq Q'$ with the following properties: 1) $L(\mathcal{A}') = L(\mathcal{A}) \setminus L_B$, where $L_B = \{\sigma | \sigma \in L(\mathcal{A}) \text{ and } inf(r_\sigma) \text{ is superset closed}\}$, and 2) $L(\langle T', S \rangle) = L_B$ where $\langle T', S \rangle$ denotes the DBA on transition structure T' with final states S. Intuitively, L_B is the largest language in G_δ that is a subset of $L(\mathcal{A})$, and $L(\mathcal{A}')$ is $L(\mathcal{A})$ with L_B excluded. To check that the language of a deterministic automaton is in G_δ we apply the exclusion construction and test if the resulting automaton has empty language.

The other useful construction we need is a restoration construction: Given a DOA $\mathcal{A} = \langle T, \phi \rangle$ and a subset of its states S, it returns a DOA $\mathcal{A}' = \langle T, \phi' \rangle$ such that the accepting SCS of $\mathcal{A}'$ are the union of those of $\mathcal{A}$ and any SCS C such that $C \cap S \neq \emptyset$. Basically, $L(\mathcal{A}') = L(\mathcal{A}) \cup L(\langle T, S \rangle)$, where $\langle T, S \rangle$ is the DBA on T with final state set S.

Rabin automata

We defined the notion of a final state in Section 2. We showed in [6] how to determine in polynomial time if a state in a RA is final.

Lemma 16. *Given a DRA $\mathcal{A}$, an accepting SCS C is superset closed if and only if $C \cap F \neq \emptyset$, where F is the set of final states of the DRA.*

Proof. If $C \cap F \neq \emptyset$ then C is clearly superset closed.

Assume $C \cap F = \emptyset$, and delete F. C is still a SCS. Consider the strongly connected component, S, that C is contained in. Since C is superset closed, S is accepting. Therefore $S \subseteq U_i$ and $S \cap L_i \neq \emptyset$ for (say) the ith pair. Any $q \in (S \cap L_i)$ has to be final, a contradiction. $\qquad\square$

From Landweber's theorem and Lemma 16 it follows that:

Theorem 17. *Given a DRA $\mathcal{A} = \langle T, \phi \rangle$, $L(\mathcal{A}) \in G_\delta$ if and only if for the DBA $\mathcal{A}' = \langle T, F \rangle$, $L(\mathcal{A}) = L(\mathcal{A}')$, where F is the set of final states of the DRA $\mathcal{A}$.*

RABIN EXCLUSION CONSTRUCTION (*RabExcl*)
INPUT: DRA $\mathcal{A} = \langle T = (Q, q_0, \Sigma, \delta), \phi \rangle$ where ϕ consists of h pairs (L_i, U_i).
OUTPUT: DRA $\mathcal{A}' = \langle T, \phi' \rangle$ where ϕ' consists of h pairs, $(L_i', U_i') = (L_i \setminus F, U_i \setminus F)$, and F the final states of $\mathcal{A}$.

Theorem 18. *RabExcl has the property that $L(\mathcal{A}') = L(\mathcal{A}) \setminus L(\mathcal{A}_B)$, where $\mathcal{A}_B = \langle T, F \rangle$ denotes the DBA with F as the set of final states.*

We also define a Rabin Restoration Construction that we use later in translating DSA to DRA.

RABIN RESTORATION CONSTRUCTION (*RabRest*)

INPUT: DRA $\mathcal{A} = \langle T = (Q, q_0, \Sigma, \delta), \phi \rangle$ where ϕ consists of h pairs (L_i, U_i), and $S \subseteq Q$

OUTPUT: DRA $\mathcal{A}' = \langle T, \phi' \rangle$ where ϕ' consists of $h + 1$ pairs: $(L_i', U_i') = (L_i, U_i)$, for $1 \leq i \leq h$, and $(L_{h+1}', U_{h+1}') = (S, Q)$.

It can be easily shown that:

Lemma 19. *The Rabin restoration construction gives DRA $\mathcal{A}'$ such that $L(\mathcal{A}') = L(\mathcal{A}) \cup L(\mathcal{A}_B)$, where $\mathcal{A}_B = \langle T, S \rangle$ denotes the DBA with S as final states.*

Streett Automata

Consider a DSA $\mathcal{A} = \langle T, \phi \rangle$ with h pairs. Without loss of generality we can assume $L_i \cap U_i = \emptyset$. Let $\mathcal{A}_i = \langle T, \phi_i \rangle$ denote the DSA with a single pair: the ith pair, (L_i, U_i), of ϕ.

Lemma 20. *For DSA $\mathcal{A}_i$, an accepting SCS C is superset closed if and only if $C \cap F_i \neq \emptyset$, where F_i is the set of final states of $\mathcal{A}_i$.*

Proof. Note that $q \in F_i$ provided either $q \in L_i$ or after deleting L_i, $SCC(q) \subseteq U_i$.

Consider a superset closed accepting SCS C. Assume $C \cap L_i = \emptyset$. Therefore $C \subseteq U_i$. Since C is superset closed, $SCC(C) \subseteq U_i$, and therefore every state $s \in C$ is final. Thus $C \cap F_i \neq \emptyset$. ◻

Theorem 21. *For a DSA $\mathcal{A}$, an accepting SCS C is superset closed if and only if $C \cap F_i \neq \emptyset$ for each i, where F_i is the set of final states of $\mathcal{A}_i$.*

Proof. If for each i, $C \cap F_i \neq \emptyset$, then C is superset closed in $\mathcal{A}$ since C is superset closed for each pair.

Conversely, assume C is superset closed. Since $L(\mathcal{A}) = \cap_i L(\mathcal{A}_i)$, considering each pair (L_i, U_i), C is superset closed. By Lemma 20, $C \cap F_i \neq \emptyset$ for each i. ◻

The Streett exclusion construction is given below. The basic idea is to make h copies of the transition structure and direct the transitions from the states in F_i in the ith copy to the corresponding states in the $(i + 1)^{st}$ copy.

STREETT EXCLUSION CONSTRUCTION (*StrExcl*)

INPUT: DSA $\mathcal{A} = \langle T = (Q, q_0, \Sigma, \delta), \phi \rangle$ where ϕ consists of h pairs (L_i, U_i).

OUTPUT: DSA $\mathcal{A}' = \langle T' = (Q', q_0', \Sigma, \delta'), \phi' \rangle$ and $S \subseteq Q'$

Let F_i denote the final states for the DSA $\mathcal{A}_i$

$Q' = Q \times \{1, \ldots, h\}$, $\quad q_0' = (q_0, 1)$

$$\delta'((q, j), a) = \begin{cases} (\delta(q, a), j) & \text{if } q \notin F_j \\ (\delta(q, a), j + 1) & \text{if } q \in F_j \text{ and } j < h \\ (\delta(q, a), 1) & \text{if } q \in F_h \end{cases}$$

$S = \{(q, h) | q \in F_h\}$, $\quad \phi'$ consists of $h + 1$ pairs (L_i', U_i'), where

$L_i' = \{(q,j)|q \in L_i \text{ and } 1 \leq j \leq h\}$,
$U_i' = \{(q,j)|q \in U_i \text{ and } 1 \leq j \leq h\}$, and $(L_{h+1}', U_{h+1}') = (\emptyset, \overline{S})$.
From Theorem 21 it follows that:

Theorem 22. *StrExcl has the property that $L(\mathcal{A}') = L(\mathcal{A})\backslash L(\mathcal{A}_B)$, where $\mathcal{A}_B = \langle T', S \rangle$ denotes the DBA with S as the set of final states. Furthermore $\sigma \in L(\mathcal{A}_B)$ if and only if $\sigma \in L(\mathcal{A})$ and $inf(r_\sigma)$ is superset closed, where r_σ denotes the run of σ in $\mathcal{A}$.*

Theorem 23. *For a DSA $\mathcal{A}$ such that $L(\mathcal{A}) \in G_\delta$, $\mathcal{A}_B = \langle T', S \rangle$ obtained from StrExcl is an equivalent DBA with $n.h$ states, where n is the number of states of $\mathcal{A}$ and h is the number of pairs.*

STREETT RESTORATION CONSTRUCTION (*StrRest*)
INPUT: DSA $\mathcal{A} = \langle T = (Q, q_0, \Sigma, \delta), \phi \rangle$ where ϕ consists of h pairs (L_i, U_i), and $S \subseteq Q$
OUTPUT: DSA $\mathcal{A}' = \langle T, \phi' \rangle$ where ϕ' consists of h pairs:
$(L_i', U_i') = (L_i \cup S, U_i)$.

Lemma 24. *The Streett restoration construction gives DSA $\mathcal{A}'$ such that $L(\mathcal{A}') = L(\mathcal{A}) \cup L(\mathcal{A}_B)$, where $\mathcal{A}_B = \langle T, S \rangle$ denotes the DBA with S as final states.*

3.2 Equivalent Minimum-pair Automaton

In this section we give the construction to realize the equivalent minimum-pair DSA or DRA, for a given DSA.

Assume a DSA $\mathcal{A}$ with h pairs such that $L(\mathcal{A})$ has Streett index k. Therefore the longest negative chain is of length k, i.e. there is no negative chain longer than $B_1 \subset G_1 \subset \ldots \subset B_k(\subset G_k)$.

The idea behind the construction of the equivalent minimum-pairs DSA or DRA is to use the basic constructions of the previous section to exactly isolate superset closed (accepting) SCS and to successively "peel" off these superset closed SCS. Given a DSA, we can apply *StrExcl*, complement, apply *RabExcl*, and complement again to yield a DSA with SI value one less than before. The construction is recursive. The means of restoring the peeled off SCS (using the restoration constructions) differs according as an equivalent DSA or DRA is desired; this step distinguishes the two constructions *MinPairStr* (Fig. 2) and *MinPairRabin* (Fig. 1).

The *MinPairRabin* construction to convert a DSA into a minimum-pair DRA is given in Figure 1. The RI of a language of SI k, can be k or $k+1$. If the language has RI k, the longest positive chain is: $G_1' \subset B_1' \subset \ldots \subset G_k'(\subset B_k')$; furthermore there is no rejecting SCS contained in G_1' and no accepting SCS contained in B_1 of the longest negative chain. To detect the case of the language with RI k we first peel off the "superset closed" *rejecting* SCS of the DSA $\mathcal{A}$ to yield $\mathcal{B}$. The construction is explained in greater detail via its proof of correctness.

$MinPairRabin(\mathcal{A} = \langle T = (Q, q_0, \Sigma, \delta), \phi \rangle)$
INPUT: DSA $\mathcal{A}$ with h pairs; OUTPUT: DRA with RI pairs.
$\mathcal{D} = \overline{\mathcal{A}}$. Let F_0 denote the final states of DRA $\mathcal{D}$
$\mathcal{B} = StrRest(\mathcal{A}, F_0)$; EqualStrRabInd = 0;
$\mathcal{A}' = \langle T' = (Q', q', \Sigma, \delta') , \phi' \rangle \leftarrow MinStrToRabin(\mathcal{A}, \mathcal{B})$ {
1) $(\mathcal{A}_1 = \langle T_1 = (Q_1, q_{0_1}, \Sigma, \delta_1), \phi_1 \rangle, R_1) = StrExcl(\mathcal{A})$;
$(\mathcal{B}_1 = \langle T'_1 = (Q'_1, q'_{0_1}, \Sigma, \delta'_1), \phi'_1 \rangle, S_1) = StrExcl(\mathcal{B})$;
If $L(\mathcal{B}_1) = \emptyset$, EqualStrRabInd = 1
   return DRA $\langle T'_1, \phi' \rangle$, where ϕ' consists of 1 pair: $\{S_1, Q'_1\}$
2) $\mathcal{A}_2 = \overline{\mathcal{A}_1}$; $\mathcal{B}_2 = \overline{\mathcal{B}_1}$;
3) $(\mathcal{A}_3 = \langle T_1, \phi_3 \rangle, R_3) = RabExcl(\mathcal{A}_2)$; $(\mathcal{B}_3 = \langle T'_1, \phi'_3 \rangle, S_3) = RabExcl(\mathcal{B}_2)$;
If $L(\mathcal{A}_3) = \emptyset$
4) return DRA $\langle T_1, \phi' \rangle$, where ϕ' consists of 2 pairs: $\{(Q_1, Q_1 \setminus R_3), (R_1, Q_1)\}$
Else
5) $\mathcal{A}_4 = \overline{\mathcal{A}_3}$; $\mathcal{B}_4 = \overline{\mathcal{B}_3}$;
6) $\mathcal{A}_5 = \langle T_2 = (Q_2, q_{0_2}, \Sigma, \delta_2), \phi_6 \rangle = MinStrToRabin(\mathcal{A}_4, \mathcal{B}_4)$
If (EqualStrRabInd) then $F_1 = S_1$; $F_3 = S_3$; $P_1 = Q'_1$;
   Else $F_1 = R_1$; $F_3 = R_3$; $P_1 = Q_1$;
7) $\mathcal{A}_6 = \overline{\mathcal{A}_5}$; 8) Let $F_8 = \{q | q \in Q_2 \text{ and } \pi_{P_1}(q) \in F_3\}$, $\mathcal{A}_7 = StrRest(\mathcal{A}_6, F_8)$
9) $\mathcal{A}_8 = \overline{\mathcal{A}_7}$; 10) Return $RabRest(\mathcal{A}_8, \{q | q \in Q_2 \text{ and } \pi_{P_1}(q) \in F_1\})$
} /* End of $MinStrToRabin$ */
If EqualStrRabInd then
   Let $M = \{q | q \in Q' \text{ and } \pi_Q(q) \in F_0\}$
   $\mathcal{B}' = \langle T', \phi'' \rangle$, where $\phi'' = \{(L_i \setminus M, U_i \setminus M) | (L_i, U_i) \in \phi' \}$;   Return $\mathcal{B}'$
Else Return $\mathcal{A}'$

Fig. 1. DSA to minimum-pair DRA construction

Theorem 25. *Given a DSA $\mathcal{A}$ such that $L(\mathcal{A})$ has SI k the construction of Fig. 1 correctly computes an equivalent DRA with RI pairs and $O(n.h^k)$ states, where n is the number of states, and h is the number of pairs of $\mathcal{A}$.*

Proof Sketch. The proof is by induction on k, the SI of the language.

Base case:$(k = 1)$. The longest negative chain is of the form: $B_1(\subset G_1)$. G_1 is superset closed SCS. By Theorem 22, $StrExcl$ exactly excludes the superset closed SCS and returns the states that capture these SCS. The number of states of $\mathcal{A}_1$ and $\mathcal{B}_1$ is $n.h$. If the RI is 2, then after complementing in step 2, in DRA $\mathcal{A}_2$ the longest positive chain is of the form G''_1, i.e. all accepting SCS are superset closed; when we exclude the superset closed SCS from $\mathcal{A}_2$, the resulting $L(\mathcal{A}_3)$ is empty. The language of $\mathcal{A}_2$ (being in G_δ) by Lemma 19 can be realized by restoring the superset closed SCS via a Streett pair $(F_3, \emptyset)$, which on complementation yields a Rabin pair $(Q_1, Q_1 \setminus F_3)$. To realize the language of $\mathcal{A}$ we restore the superset closed SCS of $\mathcal{A}$ by adding a Rabin pair (F_1, Q_1). Thus we have a 2-pair DRA in case RI is 2; if the RI is 1, one pair suffices to realize $L(\mathcal{B})$ as a DRA, and for removing the superset closed rejecting SCS that were added to $\mathcal{A}$ to yield $\mathcal{B}$.

Assume the hypothesis holds for $k = l$. Consider the case $k = l + 1$. Let the RI of the language be r. As a result of applying steps 1-3 we can argue that

$\mathcal{A}_4$ and $\mathcal{B}_4$ have SI (RI) one less, i.e. l ($r \leq l + 1$). Therefore from step 6 we get an $(r - 1)$-pair DRA, $\mathcal{A}_5$, realizing the language of $\mathcal{A}_4$ or $\mathcal{B}_4$ according as the RI is greater or equal to the SI. Complement $\mathcal{A}_5$ to yield a DSA $\mathcal{A}_6$, and $L(\mathcal{A}_6) = L(\mathcal{A}_3)$ (or $\mathcal{B}_3$). In the construction we expand the transition structure in step 1 only. From the definition of the Streett exclusion construction it follows that $Q_2 = Q_1 \times Q'$ for some set Q' and so $\pi_{Q_1}(q)$ for $q \in Q_2$ is well defined (π is defined in Section 2). It can be argued that for $\sigma \in \Sigma^\omega$, if $q \in inf(r_\sigma^2)$, for $q \in Q_2$, then $\pi_{Q_1}(q) \in inf(r_\sigma^1)$, and if for $q_1 \in Q_1$, $q_1 \in inf(r_\sigma^1)$, then there exists $q_2 \in Q_2$ such that $q_2 \in inf(r_\sigma^2)$ and $\pi_{Q_1}(q_2) = q_1$, where r_σ^i is the run of σ on the automaton with state set Q_i. The correctness of steps 8-10, involving restoration of superset closed SCS, then follows from Lemma 19 and Lemma 24.

At each iteration of the construction in step 1, we expand the transition structure h fold and add a pair also. Therefore in k iterations the transition structure has size: $nh(h + 1)(h + 2) \ldots (h + k - 1) = O(n.h^k)$. $\qquad\square$

Our transformation from DSA to DRA has complexity $DS(n, h) \rightarrow DR(n.h^k, r)$, where k is the SI, and $r \leq (k+1)$ is the RI of the language, an improvement over Safra's construction (as observed in Section 1). Also, Safra's exponential lower bound (Lemma 2.3 in [10]) for translating DSA to NBA, precludes the existence of a polynomial-transformation from DS to DR, since there is a simple linear transformation from DR to NB.

Figure 2 is the construction, *MinPairStr*, to convert a DSA to a minimum-pair DSA. The basic idea is that since the isolation of superset closed SCS is by means of identifying a subset of states as being final (if necessary by expanding the transition structure in the case of *StrExcl*), we retain the flexibility of restoring them either in Rabin or Streett form. *MinPairStr* differs from *MinPairRabin* in steps 4-10, the base case and the restoration steps.

```
A' = ⟨T', φ'⟩ ← MinPairStr(A = ⟨T, φ⟩)
INPUT: DSA A with h pairs; OUTPUT: DSA A' with SI number of pairs.
1) (A₁ = ⟨T₁ = (Q₁, q₀₁, Σ, δ₁), φ₁⟩, F₁) = StrExcl(A);
2) A₂ = Ā₁; 3) (A₃ = ⟨T₁, φ₃⟩, F₃) = RabExcl(A₂);
If L(A₃) = ∅
4) return DSA ⟨T₁, {(F₁, Q₁ \ F₃)}⟩
Else
5) A₄ = Ā₃; 6) A₅ = ⟨T₂ = (Q₂, q₀₂, Σ, δ₂), φ₆⟩ = MinPairStr(A₄); 7) A₆ = Ā₅
8) Let F₈ = {q|q ∈ Q₂ and π_Q₁(q) ∈ F₃}, A₇ = RabRest(A₆, F₈)
9) A₈ = Ā₇; 10) A' = StrRest(A₈, {q|q ∈ Q₂ and π_Q₁(q) ∈ F₁}), return A'
```

Fig. 2. DSA to minimum-pair DSA construction

Theorem 26. *Given a DSA $\mathcal{A}$ such that $L(\mathcal{A})$ has SI k the construction of Fig. 2 correctly computes an equivalent DSA with k pairs with state set of size $O(n.h^k)$, where n is the number of states, and h the number of pairs of $\mathcal{A}$.*

The constructions presented are also a simple constructive proof that if the longest negative chain in a DSA is of length k, then there is a k-pair DSA to realize the language, as well as a $(k+1)$-pair DRA. Furthermore, it follows from the complexity of the constructions in this section, that for the class of languages in $St(c)$, for c a constant, the minimum-pair equivalent DSA is polynomially related to any equivalent DOA.

4 Determining the Streett/Rabin Index

Given a DSA with h pairs, we first show that determining if the SI is h, or c (for c a constant), is in polynomial time and prove in Section 4.1 that it is NP-hard to determine the index in general.

The construction of Fig. 2 yields a polynomial time algorithm to check if a DSA is of SI c, for c a constant. The depth of the recursion when $L(\mathcal{A}_3) = \emptyset$, is the SI of the language. If the depth of the recursion is c, the automaton $\mathcal{A}_3$ will have $O(n.h^c)$ states and $h + c$ pairs, and since RA language-emptiness is in polynomial time [3], a polynomial time algorithm follows.

The language of a DSA has SI h if there exists a negative chain of length h. That is, we need to construct a chain of SCS, $(G_0 \subset)B_1 \subset G_1 \subset \ldots \subset B_h(\subset G_h)$, where B_i is a rejecting SCS and G_i an accepting SCS. This is equivalent to stating that there is a sequence $J_0 \subset J_1 \subset \ldots \subset J_h$ with $J_i \subseteq \{1, \ldots, h\}$ and $|J_{i+1}| = |J_i| + 1$, with the property that: For the accepting SCS G_i, $G_i \not\subseteq U_j$ and $G_i \cap L_j \neq \emptyset$ for $j \in J_i$, and $G_i \subset U_k$ and $G_i \cap L_k = \emptyset$ for $k \notin J_i$. The rejecting SCS B_{i+1} is obtained by augmenting G_i such that $B_{i+1} \not\subset U_j$ and $B_{i+1} \cap L_j = \emptyset$ for $j \in J_{i+1} \setminus J_i$.

Algorithm to check if a DSA has SI h

Choose J_0 so that it satisfies the property above.

Let $J_{i+1} = J_i \cup \{k\}$ where $k \notin J_i$ and J_{i+1} satisfies the property.

Theorem 27. *Given a DSA $\mathcal{A}$, the above algorithm will construct a sequence $J_0 \subset J_1 \subset \ldots \subset J_h$ which satisfies the property defined above if and only if the SI of $L(\mathcal{A})$ is h.*

Proof. Suppose the Streett index is h and the sequence $J_0^* \subset J_1^* \subset \ldots \subset J_h^*$ satisfies the property defined above of the J-sequence. Suppose our algorithm produces the sequence $J_0 \subset J_1 \subset \ldots \subset J_k$ where $k < h$. Then let i be the smallest index such that $w \in J_i^*$ but $w \notin J_k$ for some w. Define $J_{k+1} = J_k \cup \{w\}$. It is clear the J_{k+1} satisfies the J-sequence property. Therefore our algorithm produces a sequence $J_0 \subset J_1 \subset \ldots \subset J_h$. $\qquad\square$

4.1 Determining the Streett/Rabin Index is NP-hard

A given DSA has SI k if the longest negative chain is of length k; it will be sufficient to prove that the following decision problem is NP-complete.

MIN STREETT INDEX (MSI)

INSTANCE A DSA $\mathcal{A}$ whose transition structure is strongly connected and a

positive integer $k < h$, where h is the number of pairs in the DSA.
QUESTION Does there exist a negative chain of length $\geq k$?

Theorem 28. *MSI is NP-complete.*

Proof Sketch. MSI is clearly in NP. To show it is NP-hard we will transform the problem MCC, which we define first and then show to be NP-complete.

MAX CONTAINED CYCLE (MCC)

INSTANCE A strongly connected directed graph $G = (V, E)$,
subsets $U_1, \ldots, U_m$ of V, and a positive integer $k' \leq m$.
QUESTION Does there exist a strongly connected subset of the vertices C,
such that $|\{j | C \subseteq U_j\}| \geq k'$, i.e. is C contained in at least k' of the U sets?

Lemma 29. *MCC is NP-complete.*

Proof of the lemma. MCC is clearly in NP. To show that MCC is NP-hard we transform MIN COVER [4] to it. The construction is due to McMillan [9].

MIN COVER (MC)

INSTANCE A set $\sigma = \{1, \ldots, l\}$, and a set $S = \{S_1, \ldots, S_n\}$ of subsets of σ,
and a positive integer k.
QUESTION Does there exist a subset of S of size $\leq k$ whose union is σ?

Given an instance of MC the corresponding instance of MCC is: a directed graph $G = (V, E)$ with l "layers" of vertices. $V = \{(i, j) | i \in S_j \text{ and } 1 \leq i \leq l\}$. $E = \{((i, j), (i', j')) | i' = i + 1 \text{ or } i = l \text{ and } i' = 1\}$. Create n subsets $U_1, \ldots, U_n$, where $U_j = \overline{R_j}$, and $R_j = \{(i, j) | 1 \leq i \leq l \wedge (i, j) \in E\}$. $k' = n - k$.

Note that the graph G created is strongly connected and there are no self-loops and hence no cycles involving single vertices. Furthermore any strongly connected set has to involve at least one vertex from each layer.

Assume there is an SCS C contained in $\geq k'$ U's. If $(i, j) \in C$, then $C \not\subseteq U_j$. Since $k' = n - k$, there are at most k distinct j such that $(i, j) \in C$ for any i, i.e. $|\{j | (i, j) \in C, 1 \leq i \leq l\}| \leq k$. Hence, S_j for such j form a cover of size $\leq k$ for σ.

The converse can be argued similarly. $\qquad\Box$

We now transform MCC to MSI. The transition structure of the DSA for the MSI instance will augment the graph G of MCC. Create a pair $(V \setminus \{s_i\}, \emptyset)$ for each $s_i \in V$. For each set U_i of MCC construct a pair (L'_i, U'_i). Start with $L'_i = \emptyset$ and $U'_i = U_i$. The next part of the construction involves adding states to the pairs (L'_i, U'_i) and adding states/edges to the transition structure.

For each state $s_i \in V$ such that $|\{j | s_i \in U_j\}| \geq k'$:
1. For each j s.t. $s_i \notin U_j$ create a state s_{ijl} and add edges $(s_i, s_{ijl}), (s_{ijl}, s_i)$. Add s_{ijl} to L'_j and to U'_q for every q s.t. $s_i \in U'_q$.
2. For each j s.t. $s_i \in U_j$ create two states s_{ij1} and s_{ij2}.
Add edges $(s_i, s_{ij1}), (s_{ij1}, s_i), (s_i, s_{ij2})$, and (s_{ij2}, s_i). Add s_{ij1} and s_{ij2} to all U'_q s.t. $s_i \in U'_q$ and $q \neq j$. Also add S_{ij2} to L'_j.
Mark any state of V as initial state. Augment the alphabet suitably to result in a deterministic structure. k for the MSI instance is $(k' + 1)$.

The transformation is clearly in polynomial time. We prove next that the MCC instance has a SCS that is contained in $\geq k'$ U's iff the DSA created has a negative chain of length $\geq (k' + 1)$.

Assume a SCS C and $C \subseteq U_j$ for at least k' distinct j. Since C cannot be a singleton $C \cap \overline{s_i} \neq \emptyset$ for each $s_i \in V$. Also C cannot be contained in all the subsets U since the NP-hard instance of MC has to have at least one set in the cover. Thus $C \not\subseteq U'_j$ for some j, and therefore C is a rejecting SCS (call it B_1). For each j such that $C \not\subseteq U_j$, $\exists s_q \in C$ such that $s_q \notin U_j$. Use states s_{qjl} to construct accepting SCS G_1. Now every state $s_q \in C$ is in $\geq k'$ U's. Use s_{qj1} and s_{qj2} states for j such that $s_q \in U_j$ to alternately create rejecting and accepting sets to increase the chain length by k'.

For the other direction: first note that in any negative chain, G_1 has to have at least two states from V. Furthermore by virtue of all additional states in the MSI instance being added as "loops" on states of V it follows that any accepting SCS of the DSA projected to V is strongly connected in V as well. Therefore G_1 projected to V, call it C', is strongly connected and since the length of the chain is $\geq (k' + 1)$ it follows that $C \subseteq U'_i$ for at least k' such U's. But since $C' \subseteq V$ and $C' \subseteq U'_i$, it follows that $C' \subseteq U_i$ for k' such U_i's. $\quad\Box$

Remark. Although, in the transformation above, the alphabet is a function of the MCC instance, we can modify it to result in an MSI instance with an alphabet of size 2, still resulting in a polynomial transformation.

5 Extension of Acceptance Conditions

Previously we had used Boolean formulae to specify acceptance conditions. Alternately, the acceptance conditions can be specified by using a temporal logic such as Propositional Linear Temporal Logic, *PLTL* [8]. *PLTL* is expressively equivalent to the star-free ω-regular sets. For example, the condition that q_i is visited infinitely often could be stated with the formula $\psi = \Box\Diamond q_i$. We define a run r_σ to be accepting provided $r_\sigma \models \psi$ and $\mathcal{L}(\mathcal{A}) = \{\sigma | r_\sigma \models \psi\}$.

More abstractly, we think of an ω-automaton $\mathcal{A} = \langle T, \mathcal{L}_Q \rangle$ where $\mathcal{L}_Q \subset Q^\omega$ is the set of acceptable runs and $\mathcal{L}(A) = \{\sigma \in \Sigma^\omega | r_\sigma \in \mathcal{L}_Q\}$. We discuss the relationship between $\mathcal{L}_Q$ and the language $\mathcal{L}(A)$.

Lemma 30. *If $\mathcal{A} = \langle T, \mathcal{L}_Q \rangle$ and $\mathcal{L}_Q$ is ω-regular, then $\mathcal{L}(A)$ is ω-regular.*

Lemma 31. *If $\mathcal{A} = \langle T, \mathcal{L}(\mathcal{F}) \rangle$ and $\mathcal{L}(\mathcal{F}) \in Rn(n)$, then $\mathcal{L}(A) \in Rn(n)$.*

We use these results to discuss where*PLTL* [8] lies in the Wagner/Kaminski hierarchy. For a PLTL formula ψ, we define $\mathcal{L}(\psi) = \{\sigma | \sigma \models \psi\}$.

Theorem 32. *For each n, there is a PLTL formula ψ such that $\mathcal{L}(\psi) \in Rn(n) \setminus Rn(n-1)$.*

Proof. Since $Rn(n) \setminus Rn(n-1)$ is non-empty, let $\mathcal{L} \in Rn(n) \setminus Rn(n-1)$. Then the Rabin automaton accepting $\mathcal{L}$ is (T, ϕ) where ϕ has n pairs. We obtain the PLTL formula ψ from ϕ by replacing q_i with $\Box\Diamond q_i$. Clearly $\mathcal{L} = (T, \mathcal{L}(\psi))$. From Lemma 31, it follows that $\mathcal{L}(\psi) \in Rn(n) \setminus Rn(n-1)$. $\quad\Box$

156

6 Conclusion

We related the expressiveness of ω-automata to their complexity. In contrast to Safra's result that there are ω-regular languages for which DSA are exponentially smaller than nondeterministic Buchi automata, we showed that within class G_δ DSA and DRA are linearly related to DBA. We presented simple constructions to transform a DRA with n states and h pairs to either a minimum-pair DRA or DSA, each with $O(n.h^k)$ states, where k is the Rabin Index of the language.

We proved that it is NP-hard to determine the Rabin (Streett) index of a language specified as a DRA (DSA). However, it is decidable in polynomial time whether an h-pair DRA (DSA) has RI (SI) h or any constant c.

Since it is NP-hard to determine the Rabin Index of a language, it is almost certain that even if there is a polynomial relation between an arbitrary h-pair DRA and the minimum-pair DRA, it is unlikely (unless $P = NP$) that a polynomial time construction to effect this translation exists. Nevertheless, the complexity question remains open (it is however known that an exponential translation from a DRA to DSA is unavoidable).

References

1. O. Carton. Chain Automata. In *IFIP 13th World Computer Congress*, pages 451–458, August 1994.
2. E. S. Chang, Z. Manna, and A. Pnueli. The Safety-Progress Classification. In F. L. Bauer, W. Bauer, and H. Schwichtenberg, editors, *Logic and Algebra of Specification*, pages 143–202, 1993.
3. E. A. Emerson and C. L. Lei. Modalities for Model Checking: Branching Time Logic Strikes Back. *Science of Computer Programming*, 8(3):275–306, June 1987.
4. M. R. Garey and D. S. Johnson. *Computers and Intractability: A Guide to the Theory of NP-Completeness*. W. H. Freeman and Company, New York, 1979.
5. M. Kaminski. A Classification of ω-regular languages. *Theoretical Computer Science*, 36:217–229, 1985.
6. S. C. Krishnan, A. Puri, and R. K. Brayton. Deterministic ω-automata vis-a-vis Deterministic Buchi Automata. In *Algorithms and Computation*, volume 834 of *LNCS*, pages 378–386. Springer-Verlag, 1994.
7. R. P. Kurshan. *Automata-Theoretic Verification of Coordinating Processes* Princeton University Press, 1994. To appear.
8. Z. Manna and A. Pnueli. *The Temporal Logic of Reactive and Concurrent Systems*. Springer Verlag, 1992.
9. Kenneth L. McMillan. Personal communication, August 1994.
10. Shmuel Safra. *Complexity of Automata on Infinite Objects*. PhD thesis, The Weizmann Institute of Science, Rehovot, Israel, March 1989.
11. L. Staiger. Research in the theory of ω-languages. *Journal of Information Processing and Cybernetics*, 23:415–439, 1987.
12. W. Thomas. Automata on Infinite Objects. In J. van Leeuwen, editor, *Formal Models and Semantics*, volume B of *Handbook of Theoretical Computer Science*, pages 133–191. Elsevier Science, 1990.
13. K. Wagner. On ω-Regular Sets. *Information and Control*, 43:123–177, 1979.

Algorithms Explained by Symmetries

Torsten Minkwitz*

Institut für Algorithmen und Kognitive Systeme, Universität Karlsruhe,
minkwitz@ira.uka.de

Abstract. Many of the linear transforms that are used in digital sig-
nalprocessing and other areas have a lot of symmetry properties. This
makes the development of fast algorithms for them possible. The usual
quadratic cost of multiplying with the matrix is reduced, in some cases to
an almost linear complexity. Salient examples are the Fourier transform,
the Cosine transform, linear maps with Toepliz matrices or convolutions.
The article gives an exact definition of the notion of symmetry that leads
to fast algorithms and presents a method to construct those algorithms
automatically in the case of an existing symmetry with a soluble group.
The results may serve to speed up the multiplication with a transform
matrix and also to solve a linear system of equations with symmetry.
Even though the construction is done at the level of abstract algebra,
the derived algorithms for many linear transforms compare well with the
best found in the literature [CoTu65, ElRa82, Ra68, RaYi90]. In most
cases, where the new method was applicable, even the manually optimized algorithms [Nu81] were not better, while nothing more than the
transform matrix and its symmetry were provided here to optain the
results.

1 Introduction

The multiplication with a previously known matrix is a reoccurring problem in
many areas. This is especially true for digital signal processing. The quadratic
number of scalar operations is often too costly to achieve realtime speed. Therefore, general methods to reduce the cost are of great importance. The derivation of fast algorithms for linear transforms has been attempted many times
[Ba88, Be84, Be89, Cl88, Cl89a, Cl89b, Ka77]. The most important mathematical tool has usually been the representation theory of finite groups. This will
continue to be so in this article. The difference to earlier approaches is a reversed
view on the problem. The traditional way had been to define a linear transform
for any finite symmetry group, then to be concerned with fast algorithms for
its application and finally hope that some practically relevant transform has
been produced. Now, first a symmetry group and a representation is optained
(if possible) for a given transform matrix, then the algorithmics are solved for
that symmetry and in the end a fast algorithm for the application of the actual

* Research sponsored by DFG through the Graduiertenkolleg "Beherrschbarkeit kom-
plexer Systeme"

transform matrix one is interested in is optained. Also, the old approach was restricted to so called regular representations of groups. This is no longer the case and this way, many other transforms, such as the Cosine-, Sine- or Hartley-transforms could be treated. With the support of computer algebra systems such as GAP, which was written by the team around J. Neubüser and M. Schönert at the RWTH in Aachen, the generation of algorithms has been automized.

Any finite linear system can be described by its system matrix A. A factorization of the system matrix A into few sparse factors yields a fast algorithm for multiplying with A. This paper is concerned with a certain type of sparse matrices.

Definition 1. A matrix A is called blockpermuted, if there are permutation matrices P and Q, such that PAQ is a matrix with blocks on the diagonal and zeros everywhere else. Entries that are in a common block of PAQ comprise a block of A.

The objective will be to find a factorization of A with few factors that are blockpermuted with small blocks.

2   The Structure of Linear Systems

Consider now a finite linear system given by a matrix A over a ring R. Hence the matrix A describes an R-module homomorphism. The computational problem is to multiply with A. To get a better idea of the approach chosen here, a further notion is needed.

Definition 2. Let A be a matrix over a ring R. A pair of matrices P and Q with $AP = QA$ is called a pair of adjuncts for A.

Assume that there exists a pair of adjuncts P and Q for A, to which invertible matrices T_P and T_Q belong, such that $P' = T_P P T_P^{-1} = T_Q Q T_Q^{-1}$ hold for some sparse, blockpermuted canonical form P'. The matrices P and Q must be invertible. Further assume that fast algorithms for multiplying with T_P, T_Q and their inverses are known. This means that P and Q are chosen from a set of matrices for which we already know how to perform a fast base change for the construction of some sparse canonical form P'. That situation is displayed in figure 1.

Instead of multiplying with A directly, the computational path along the outer dotted line of the diagram in figure 1 is chosen. This yields the factorization $A = T_Q^{-1} P'^{-1} E P' T_P$ with $E := T_Q A T_P^{-1}$. It was assumed that fast algorithms for multiplying with T_Q^{-1} and T_P exist and that P' is a sparse matrix. So, the only question left concerns the structure of E. To answer it, the fact that the matrices describe R-module homomorphisms is utilized. The system matrix A defines a homomorphism $f_A : \mathcal{M} \to \mathcal{N}$ with R-modules $\mathcal{M}$ and $\mathcal{N}$. T_P and P describe endomorphisms for $\mathcal{M}$ and T_Q and Q for $\mathcal{N}$, while P' describes endomorphisms for both $\mathcal{M}$ and $\mathcal{N}$. From the R-modules one can construct $R[P']$-modules in

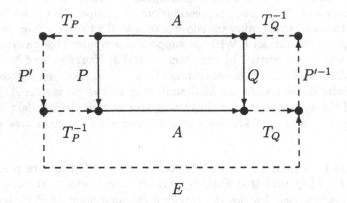

Fig. 1. Factorization through Pairs of Adjuncts.

the usual way. The multiplication of the new scalars from the polynomial ring $R[P']$ with elements of the module is defined by the following equation:

$$(c_0 + c_1 P' + c_2 P'^2 + \cdots + c_n P'^n)m = c_0 m + c_1(P'm) + c_2(P'^2 m) + \cdots + c_n(P'^n m),$$

where the c_i are coefficients from the ring R and m is an element of the original R-module. From the factorization of A and the definition of E one can deduce the equation $P'E = EP'$. This accounts to the fact that the matrix E defines a homomorphism from $\mathcal{M}$ as an $R[P']$-module to $\mathcal{N}$ as an $R[P']$-module. To learn about the structure of E, the following lemma on module homomorphisms is needed.

Lemma 3. *Let $\mathcal{M}$ and $\mathcal{N}$ be completely reducible modules and $f : \mathcal{M} \to \mathcal{N}$ a homomorphism. Furthermore, let $\{\mathcal{M}_i\}_{i \in I}$ be a system of representatives of classes of isomorphic, irreducible submodules of $\mathcal{M}$ and $\{\mathcal{N}_j\}_{j \in J}$ one of $\mathcal{N}$. Then*

$$H_i^{\mathcal{M}} = \bigoplus_{\mathcal{M}' \cong \overline{\mathcal{M}_i}, \mathcal{M}' \subseteq \mathcal{M}} \mathcal{M}' \quad and \quad H_j^{\mathcal{N}} = \bigoplus_{\mathcal{N}' \cong \overline{\mathcal{N}_j}, \mathcal{N}' \subseteq \mathcal{N}} \mathcal{N}'$$

are called the homogeneous components of $\mathcal{M}$ and $\mathcal{N}$ respectively.

(i) It holds that

$$\mathcal{M} = \bigoplus_{i \in I} H_i^{\mathcal{M}} \quad and \quad \mathcal{N} = \bigoplus_{j \in J} H_j^{\mathcal{N}}.$$

So the modules decompose into their homogeneous components. This decomposition is unique.

(ii) There exists an injective, partial map $\pi : J \to I$, and homomorphisms $f_j : H_{\pi(j)}^{\mathcal{M}} \to H_j^{\mathcal{N}}, j \in J$ between the homogeneous components, such that for all $x \in \mathcal{M}$

$$f(x) = \bigoplus_{j \in J, \pi(j) \text{ is defined}} f_j(x_{\pi(j)}) \quad with \quad x_i \in H_i^{\mathcal{M}}$$

holds. So every module homomorphism decomposes with respect to the homogeneous components of $\mathcal{N}$.

Proof:

(i) See [CuRe81] p. 46 or [Ja80] p. 121.

(ii) Schur's lemma states that a homomorphism between irreducible modules is either 0 or an isomorphism. Since $\mathcal{M}$ and $\mathcal{N}$ are completely reducible, f vanishes on all restrictions to non-isomorphic components of $\mathcal{M}$ and $\mathcal{N}$ respectively. So, only the parts of f that map between homogeneous components of the same isomorphism class contribute to f (s. fig. 2). $\pi(j)$ is the index of the homogeneous components of $\mathcal{M}$ which is of the same isomorphism class as the the homogeneous component of $\mathcal{N}$ with index j. Sometimes no such component exists in $\mathcal{M}$ and π becomes partial. Since there can be only one homogeneous component from an isomorphism class in $\mathcal{M}$ and $\mathcal{N}$ respectively, π is injective.

□

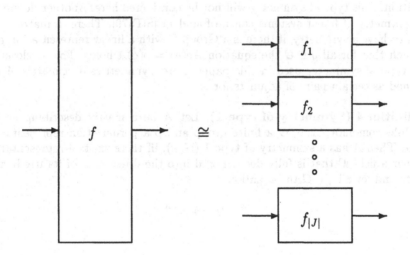

Fig. 2. Parallel Decomposition of Module Homomorphisms

Lemma 3 proves that the matrix E is blockpermuted, and the blocks are determined by the homogeneous components of the $R[P']$-modules $\mathcal{M}$ and $\mathcal{N}$. If $\mathcal{M}$ and $\mathcal{N}$ are not already completely reducible, then, if R is a domain, they can be made so by injecting into the respective module over the quotient field of R. Since P' is a canonical form, it is blockpermuted with each block corresponding to a term of the direct sum that comprises some homogeneous component of each $\mathcal{M}$ and $\mathcal{N}$ (as $R[P']$-modules). Therefore, if subblocks correspond to subsets of block-defining indices for rows and columns, P' is made up of subblocks of blocks of E. This blockstructure is invariant under matrix inversion. Hence, the invertible matrix P'^{-1} will have the same as P'. From this it follows that $E' := P'^{-1}EP'$ has the same blocks and therefore requires the same amount of scalar operations for multiplying with a vector as E. The final factorization of A is therefore

$$A = T_Q^{-1} E' T_P.$$

If the $R[P']$-modules $\mathcal{M}$ and $\mathcal{N}$ are decomposed into sufficiently many homogeneous components and the base changes described by T_P and T_Q^{-1} can be performed quickly, a fast algorithm for multiplying with A has been found. The next section will describe a suitable class of matrices from which the pairs of adjuncts P, Q can be chosen. Thereafter a method for constructing the necessary fast base changes for matrices from this class is presented.

3 Symmetry

Traditionally, a matrix is called symmetric, if it is invariant with respect to transposition. This type of symmetry will not be considered here. Another definition of symmetry of linear systems can be found in [StFa79]. There, a matrix A is said to have a symmetry, if there is a Group G with a linear representation ρ of G such that for all $g \in G$ the equation $A\rho(g) = \rho(g)A$ holds. This is closer to the type of symmetry used in this paper. Here, symmetries of a matrix A are defined as certain pairs of adjuncts for A.

Definition 4 (Symmetry of type 1). Let A be a matrix describing an R-module homomorphism, G a finite group and ρ a permutation representation of G. Then A has a symmetry of type 1 (G, ρ), iff there exists a representation φ over a field $\mathbb{F}$ that is fully decomposed into the direct sum of its irreducible parts and for all $g \in G$ the equation

$$A\rho(g) = \varphi(g)A$$

holds.

For this definition to make sense, R and $\mathbb{F}$ must be embeddable into a ring R'. The actual calculations are therefore done in R'.

Definition 5 (Symmetry of type 2). Let A be a matrix describing an R-module homomorphism, G a finite group and ρ a permutation representation of G. Then A has a symmetry of type 2 (G, ρ), iff for all $g \in G$ the equation

$$A\rho(g) = \rho(g)A$$

holds.

The equations in the definitions are similar to the equation $AP = QA$ used in the last section to factorize A. This was achieved through base changes from P and Q to a common canonical form P'. The number of scalar operations for multiplying with A could often be reduced. P and Q are now chosen from the set of representation matrices of permutation representations or fully decomposed representations of finite groups. One now has pairs of adjuncts of representation matrices.

Consider again the diagram of figure 1. For symmetries, the pair of adjuncts P, Q is replaced by certain representation matrices:

$$\forall g \in G: \quad A\rho(g) = \varphi(g)A.$$

The system matrix A is factorized: $A = T_Q^{-1}E'T_P$. To achieve a fast method to multiply with A, fast methods to multiply with these factors are needed. Lemma 3 determines the block structure of E'. However, instead of $R[P']$-modules, now $\mathbb{F}G$-modules are present if the pairs of adjuncts for all $g \in G$ are considered simultaneously. The matrices T_Q and T_P are base change matrices, which convert the representations ρ and φ resp. to a fully decomposed, blockpermuted form. Thus, such matrices must be factorized into sparse factors.

Definition 6. Let (G, ρ) be a symmetry. An invertible matrix T_ρ such that $\rho' : g \mapsto T_\rho\rho(g)T_\rho^{-1}$ is a fully decomposed representation with irreducible blocks is called a decomposition matrix for (G, ρ).

It should be noted that decomposition matrices only depend on the representation they decompose. Therefore, the factorization of these into sparse factors can be treated independently.

4 Generating Algorithms

Now the problem of factorizing decomposition matrices and thus of generating fast algorithms for multiplying with a system matrix having symmetries is tackled. The procedure is restricted to the subclass of symmetries with a soluble group. It does not work in general for non-soluble groups. However, it will also improve the algorithms for symmetry groups having a prime index normal subgroup.

Consider the problem of finding a decomposition matrix T_ρ of a symmetry (G, ρ). This can be done using the **projection formula**:

$$p_\varphi := \frac{n}{|G|} \sum_{g \in G} r_{i,i}(g^{-1})\rho(g),$$

where $r_{i,j}(g)$ are the coefficients of the matrix $\varphi(g)$ and φ is an irreducible representation of G contained in ρ. If one has computed the character table of G, then it can easily be determined through the orthogonality relations of characters, which irreducible parts ρ contains. The projection formula is then used to compute the needed transformation. However, this decomposition matrix is usually not sparse. To achieve that, another approach is needed. It is achieved through the procedure ALGOGEN:

ALGOGEN:

Input   : a symmetry (G, ρ)
Output : a factored decomposition matrix for (G, ρ)

Step 0: Since ρ is a permutation representation, G permutes a set Y. If $|Y| = 1$, nothing has to be done. Any 1×1-matrix ($\neq 0$) is a valid decomposition matrix. If $G = < 1 >$, then one is also through and any diagonal matrix with determinant $\neq 0$ is a decomposition matrix. If neither $|Y| = 1$ nor $G = < 1 >$, then move to step 1.

Step 1: If G acts transitively on Y, then go to step 2. Otherwise, the orbits already define a partial decomposition. The blocks of the matrices $\rho(g)$ belonging to the respective orbits can be decomposed separately. Therefore, ALGOGEN must only be called for $(G, \rho_{G(y)})$, where the $\rho_{G(y)}$ are the permutation representations defined by the action of G on the different orbits $G(y)$. The resulting factorized decomposition matrices are combined to decompose the different blocks of the $\rho(g)$ belonging to the respective orbits. This way a decomposition matrix for (G, ρ) has been constructed.

Step 2: If G is a direct product of G^1 and G^2, and ρ is a tensor product of representations ρ_1 of G^1 and ρ_2 of G^2, then a decomposition matrix can be found. ALGOGEN is called for (G^1, ρ_1) and (G^2, ρ_2) to computed the respective factorized decomposition matrices T_1 and T_2. Now the Kronecker product $T = T_1 \otimes T_2$ yields a decomposition matrix for (G, ρ). Since $\rho = \rho_1 \otimes \rho_2$ and since tensor products of irreducible representations are again irreducibles for the direct product group, the identities

$$T \rho T^{-1} = (T_1 \otimes T_2)(\rho_1 \otimes \rho_2)(T_1^{-1} \otimes T_2^{-1}) = (T_1 \rho_1 T_1^{-1}) \otimes (T_2 \rho_2 T_2^{-1})$$

show that T is indeed a decomposition matrix for (G, ρ). The factorizations of T_1 and T_2 respectively are preserved, because

$$T = T_1 \otimes T_2 = (T_1 \otimes id)(id \otimes T_2),$$

$$T_1 \otimes id = (T_{11} \cdots T_{1k}) \otimes id = (T_{11} \otimes id) \cdots (T_{1k} \otimes id) \text{ and}$$

$$id \otimes T_2 = id \otimes (T_{21} \cdots T_{2l}) = (id \otimes T_{21}) \cdots (id \otimes T_{2l}).$$

If (G, ρ) does not have such a product property, then move to step 3.

Step 3: Since G now acts transitively on Y, it holds that G is isomorphic to its action on the cosets of any stabilizer G_y with $y \in Y$. This also means that for any $y \in Y$, the permutation representation ρ is isomorphic to an induced representation [Se77]:

$$\rho \cong Ind_{G_y}^G (1),$$

where 1 denotes the trivial representation in a 1-dimensional representation space. Assume now that G has a normal subgroup K containing
G_y and with a prime order factor G/K. If no such normal subgroup
exists, then go to step 4. From the transitivity of the induction operator
[Se77] it now holds that:

$$\rho \cong Ind_{G_y}^G(1) \cong Ind_K^G(Ind_{G_y}^K(1)).$$

To explain how decomposition matrices are found in this case, consider the definition of induced representations as given in [CuRe81]: If
$\varphi := Ind_{G_y}^K(1)$ is a representation of K, then the induced representation
$Ind_K^G(\varphi)$ is:

$$\rho(g) = Ind_K^G(\varphi)(g) := \begin{pmatrix} \hat{\varphi}(g_1^{-1}gg_1) & \cdots & \hat{\varphi}(g_1^{-1}gg_{|G/K|}) \\ \vdots & \ddots & \vdots \\ \hat{\varphi}(g_{|G/K|}^{-1}gg_1) & \cdots & \hat{\varphi}(g_{|G/K|}^{-1}gg_{|G/K|}) \end{pmatrix}, \quad g \in G,$$

where $\hat{\varphi}(g)$ is $\varphi(g)$ if $g \in K$ and the zero matrix otherwise. The set
$\{g_i\}_{1 \le i \le |G/K|}$ is any transversal of representatives from the cosets of K
in G. It can easily be proved that in every row and column only one of
the $\hat{\varphi}(g_igg_j)$ is non-zero. Assume now that ALGOGEN has been used
to compute a factorized decomposition matrix T_φ for φ. Then for all
$g \in G$ the product $\rho_1(g) := (id \otimes T_\varphi)\rho(g)(id \otimes T_\varphi)^{-1}$ is:

$$\rho_1(g) = \begin{pmatrix} T_\varphi\hat{\varphi}(g_1^{-1}gg_1)T_\varphi^{-1} & \cdots & T_\varphi\hat{\varphi}(g_1^{-1}gg_{|G/K|})T_\varphi^{-1} \\ \vdots & \ddots & \vdots \\ T_\varphi\hat{\varphi}(g_{|G/K|}^{-1}gg_1)T_\varphi^{-1} & \cdots & T_\varphi\hat{\varphi}(g_{|G/K|}^{-1}gg_{|G/K|})T_\varphi^{-1} \end{pmatrix}.$$

Since T_φ is a decomposition matrix for φ, the non-zero boxes of ρ_1 are
all comprised of blocks of irreducible representations for K on their diagonals. As K has prime index, Clifford theory (s. [ClBa93]) states that
for those irreducibles either their induction to G yields an irreducible
of G (induction case) or else they are the restriction of an irreducible of
G (restriction case). Let ϕ be equal to $T_\varphi\varphi T_\varphi^{-1}$, except that it is set to
identity on the blocks belonging to the induction case. The induction
case blocks must not be treated further, because their blocks in ρ_1 are
already irreducibles of G by definition. For them $(id \otimes T_\varphi)$ is already a
decomposition matrix. Now let $\bar{\phi}$ be the representation of G such that
its restriction to K is ϕ. If T is the matrix with $\bar{\phi}(g_1)$ to $\bar{\phi}(g_{|G/H|})$ on
the diagonal and zeros everywhere else, then $\rho_2 := T\rho_1 T^{-1}$ is decom-
posed into already irreducible blocks (induction case) and blocks with
equal restriction case parts of $\hat{\phi}$, because $\bar{\phi}(g_i)\hat{\phi}(g_i^{-1}gg_j)\bar{\phi}(g_j)^{-1} = \hat{\phi}(g)$
(restriction case). Again $\hat{\phi}(g)$ is $\phi(g)$ for $g \in K$ and the zero matrix oth-
erwise. The only problem left now is the fact that the non-zero $\hat{\phi}$ are not
all on the diagonal and are therefore not really independant blocks. G
permutes the representation spaces of the $|G/K|$ versions of ϕ through

its action by ρ_2. Since K is a normal subgroup, this permutation action is isomorphic to G/K and using ALGOGEN, a decomposition matrix T_{fact} for the so-defined permutation representation can be found. Together $T_\rho := (T_{fact} \otimes id)T(id \otimes T_\varphi)$ is a factorized decomposition matrix for ρ. The blocks of the restriction case become irreducible, because G/K is abelian, its irreducibles are therefore 1-dimensional and so the degrees of the blocks stay that of the irreducible blocks of ϕ.

Step 4: If G is a composite order soluble group, then it will now contain a normal subgroup K', such that $K'G_y = G$. This holds, because if K' is chosen maximal, then it has prime index and no group lies between it and G. Since $K' < K'G_y < G$ and step 3 had not been successfull, G_y is not in K' and $K'G_y$ must be G. For such a K', Mackey's subgroup theorem [Se77] reduces to

$$Res_{K'}(Ind_{G_y}^G(1)) \cong Ind_H^{K'}(1) \quad with \quad H = G_y \cap K'.$$

If ALGOGEN is called for $(K', Ind_H^{K'}(1))$, then from the factorized decomposition matrix T' optained that way, a decomposition matrix T_ρ for ρ can be constructed. Let T_ρ' be any decomposition matrix for ρ. Then the restriction of $T_\rho'\rho(T_\rho')^{-1}$ to K' will not necessarily be fully decomposed. Some blocks might have become reducible. These can be further reduced through a base change matrix C. Note that the product CT_ρ' is also a decomposition matrix for ρ, because C only maps within irreducible blocks of ρ. Now $\varphi_1 := Res_{K'}(CT_\rho'\rho(T_\rho')^{-1}C^{-1})$ is a fully decomposed representation of K'. The same holds true for $\varphi_2 := T'Ind_H^{K'}(1)T'^{-1}$ by definition. Both φ_1 and φ_2 define $\mathbb{F}K'$-Modules. They are isomorphic because of the reduced form of Mackey's subgroup theorem. Lemma 3 states that any isomorphism between them decomposes with respect to the homogeneous components. Let D be transform matrix of such an isomorphism. It is blockdecomposed with respect to the homogeneous components of φ_i. This way $T_\rho = CT_\rho' = DT'$ becomes a decomposition matrix for ρ. It should be noted that D can be set to identity on all blocks of irreducible homogeneous components without DT' loosing its property of being a decomposition matrix.

Step 5: At this point G is either not soluble, or an abelian group of prime order. In the latter case, any fast algorithm of computing fast Fourier transforms of prime length can be used, because those Fourier matrices are decomposition matrices for such symmetries, which is easily proved through the translation property of the discrete Fourier transform.

5 Conclusion

The work of Karpovsky, Trachtenberg, Beth, Clausen and Baum [Ba88, Be84, Be89, Cl88, Cl89a, Cl89b, Ka77, KaTr77] has been extended to include group representations beyond the regular representation. Also the engineering process has been reversed. Instead of constructing transforms and their fast algorithms for a number of groups and then afterwards looking for an application of these transforms, now, a given transform or another linear system is examined and if symmetries are found, algorithms are automatically generated. However, the method presented here can also be utilized to generate numerous new transforms and filters from finite groups and their permutation representations, while the restriction to regular representations is no longer valid.

The work presented here has become part of the IDEAS system that was written at the IAKS in Karlsruhe. That system is a tool to derive realizations for mathematically well structured problems on many implementation technologies such as C-programs for general purpose processors or VLSI layouts. I wish to thank my advisor T. Beth and my colleague A. Nückel for their support and comments.

References

[Ba88]   BAUM, U.: *Schnelle Algorithmen zur Spektraltransformation endlicher Gruppen*. Diplomthesis, University of Karlsruhe, August (1988)

[Be84]   BETH, Th.: *Verfahren der schnellen Fourier-Transformation*. B. G. Teubner: Stuttgart (1984)

[Be89]   BETH, Th.: *Generating fast Hartley transforms - another application of the algebraic discrete Fourier transform*. URSI-ISSSE'89, Erlangen (1989), pp. 688-692

[Cl88]   CLAUSEN, M.: *Contributions to the design of fast spectral transforms*. Habilitation, University of Karlsruhe (1988)

[Cl89a]   CLAUSEN, M.: *Fast Fourier transforms for metabelian groups*. SIAM J. Comput. **18** (1989) No. 3, pp. 584-593

[Cl89b]   CLAUSEN, M.: *Fast generalized Fourier transforms*. Theoret. Comp. Science **67** (1989), pp. 55-63

[ClBa93] CLAUSEN, M. - BAUM, U. *Fast Fourier Transforms*. BI-Wissenschaftsverlag (1993)

[CoTu65] COOLEY, J. W. - TUKEY, J. W.: *An algorithm for the machine calculation of complex Fourier series*. Math. Comp. **19** (1965), pp. 297-301

[CuRe81] CURTIS, C. W. - REINER, I. : *Methods of Representation theory I*. Wiley-Interscience Publ. (1981)

[ElRa82] ELLIOT, D. F. - RAO, K. R. : *Fast Transforms: Algorithms, Analyses, Applications*. Academic Press Inc. (1982)

[StFa79] STIEFEL, E. - FÄSSLER, A. : *Gruppentheoretische Methoden und ihre Anwendungen*. B. G. Teubner: Stuttgart (1979)

[Ja80]   JACOBSON, N.: *Basic Algebra II*. W. H. Freeman and Company: New York (1980)

[Ka77]   KARPOVSKY, M. G.: *Fast Fourier transforms on finite non-abelian groups*. IEEE Trans. Comput. **C-26** (1977), pp. 1028-1030

[KaTr77] KARPOVSKY, M. G. - TRACHTENBERG, E. A.: *Some optimization problems for convolution systems over finite groups*. Information and Control **34** (1977), pp. 227-247

[KaTr79] KARPOVSKY, M. G. - TRACHTENBERG, E. A.: *Fourier transform over finite groups for error detection and error correction in computation channels*. Information and Control **40** (1979), pp. 335-358

[MiCr92] MINKWITZ, T. - CREUTZBURG, R. : *A New Fast Algebraic Convolution Algorithm*. Proceedings of EUSIPCO **6** (1992), pp. 933-936

[Mi93] MINKWITZ, T. : *Algorithmensynthese für lineare Systeme mit Symmetrie*. Doctoral Thesis, University of Karlsruhe (1993)

[Nu81] NUSSBAUMER, H. J. : *Fast Fourier Transforms and Convolution Algoithms*. Springer: Berlin (1981)

[Ra68] RADER, C. M.: *Discrete Fourier transforms when the number of data samples is prime*. Proc. IEEE **56** (1968), pp. 1107-1108

[RaYi90] RAO, K. R. - YIP, P. : *Discrete Cosine Transform: Algorithms, Advantages, Applications*. Academic Press Inc. (1990)

[Se77] SERRE, J.-P. : *Linear Representations of Finite Groups*. Graduate Texts in Mathematics **42**, Springer-Verlag (1977)

Generalized Scans and Tri-Diagonal Systems

Paul F. Fischer*
Franco P. Preparata**
John E. Savage**

Brown University
Providence, Rhode Island 02912

Abstract. The classical problem of solving tridiagonal linear systems of equations is reconsidered. An extremely simple factorization of the system's matrix – implied by but not explicit in the known techniques – is identified and shown to belong to a class of transformations termed **generalized scans**. This class has an associative property which is the key to the complete parallelization of the technique. Due to the very weak constraints upon which it is based, the method extends naturally to arbitrary banded systems.

1 Introduction

A number of work-efficient methods that exploit parallelism have been developed to solve tridiagonal linear systems. They include Stone's "scan-based" (or "recursive doubling") algorithm [S73], "cyclic reduction" [H64] [Swa74] [Swe74] [Swe77], and "partitioning" [J87]. In this paper we identify an extremely simple factorization of the system's matrix – implied but not explicit in these techniques – that is the key to the efficient solution of the problem. The resulting technique can be generalized to a class of length-preserving transformations, which we call **generalized scans**. Generalized scans, which contain ordinary prefix computations [LF80] as a special case, possess an interesting associative structure. Our approach is particularly simple, is fully parallelizable, uses the same work as the best-known serial algorithm, and generalizes to banded systems.

Stone's algorithm [S73] solves a tridiagonal system with coefficient matrix B by inverting the diagonal matrix D arising from the LDU decomposition of B using a prefix computation (hereafter referred to as "scan" for brevity). Because the scan operation can be fully parallelized, Stone's method is very attractive computationally. However, it requires multiplicative commutativity of the entries of B and is therefore not applicable to rings lacking this property. Thus, it does

* Division of Applied Mathematics. (*pff@cfm.brown.edu*) Supported in part by NSF Grant ACS-9405403 and AFOSR grant F49620-93-1-0090.

** Department of Computer Science. The research of F.P. Preparata (*franco@cs.brown.-edu*) and J.E. Savage (*jes@cs.brown.edu*) was supported in part by the Office of Naval Research under contract N00014-91-J-4052, ARPA Order 8225. In addition F.P. Preparata and J.E. Savage were supported in part by NSF Grants CCR-9400232 and MIP-902570, respectively.

not apply to block tridiagonal systems (i.e., general banded systems), except – as can be readily shown – in the case in which either all upper or all lower off-diagonal blocks are invertible.

Cyclic (or even-odd) reduction of a tridiagonal system successively eliminates and renumbers the even- or odd-numbered variables. After a single elimination step, the resultant system is again tridiagonal in the remaining variables and can be renumbered to yield a new system of half the original size. The elimination and renumbering of variables can proceed in parallel because the odd- (or even-) numbered equations are only indirectly coupled. Block cyclic-reduction (BCR) has also been studied as a means of extending this approach to banded systems [J85].

Partitioning, or substructuring, algorithms [W81] [DS84] [M85] [J87] are designed to exploit parallelism in the solution of banded matrices. When a system of n equations of bandwidth $2s + 1$ is to be solved on a p-processor parallel computer, the diagonal band of the coefficient matrix is partitioned as a block-tridiagonal system of order $2p - 1$. The block matrices on the diagonal are of two sizes: p large blocks, or "substructures," of size $m = \lceil ((n - s(p - 1))/p \rceil$ alternate with $p - 1$ blocks of size s called "separators." Because they are coupled only via the separators, the system associated with each substructure can be factored simultaneously to eliminate blocks directly above and below the substructures. Updates to the separator elements during this inital phase are additive and therefore may be asynchronous. The substructure elimination leads to a remaining small block-tridiagonal system of order $(p - 1)$, with blocks of order s, which must be solved, for example, by BCR. Thus substructuring is equivalent to BCR if one takes the substructure size equal to the separator size, which for the tridiagonal case, implies $m = s = 1$.

The cyclic elimination and substructuring methods can be viewed as standard LU factorizations of a symmetric permutation of the original tridiagonal system matrix, $\tilde{A} = PAP^T$, for a particular choice of P. Numerical stability of these solution methods follows directly in the case where A is either diagonally dominant or positive definite, as these properties are inherited by the permuted system. In the succeeding discussion, it will be clear that these are particular instances of nearly arbitrary elimination sequences (or permutations) which one could choose in developing a parallel solver for tri-diagonal or banded systems.

This paper is organized as follows: The connection between tridiagonal systems and scan operations is made in the next section. In Section 3 we present the factorization of a tridiagonal matrix forming the basis for our approach to solving tridiagonal systems; multiple factorizations of this kind are used in all three prior approaches to solving such systems. In Section 4 we introduce the class of length-preserving transformations called generalized scans and show that the conventional scan operation and tridiagonal solver are in this class. In Section 5 we apply our factorization method to the development of parallel, work-efficient algorithms for this problem. We conclude with the extension of the method to general banded systems.

2   Tridiagonal Systems and Scans

A tridiagonal system of equations in the unknown y_1, y_2, ..., y_n is described by the following:

$$a_j y_{j-1} + b_j y_j + c_{j+1} y_{j+1} = d_j$$

for $1 \leq j \leq n$ where it is assumed that coefficients with indices outside of this range are zero. (The reason for the choice of this notation will become apparent shortly.)

This set of equations is described by a tridiagonal matrix of coefficients, as illustrated below:

$$B = \begin{bmatrix} b_1 & c_2 & & & & & \\ a_2 & b_2 & c_3 & & & & \\ & a_3 & b_3 & & & & \\ & & & \ddots & c_j & & \\ & & & a_j & b_j & & \\ & & & & & \ddots & c_n \\ & & & & & a_n & b_n \end{bmatrix}$$

Let the system of equations associated with the matrix B be

$$B\underline{y} = \underline{d} \tag{1}$$

(where, of course, $\underline{y}$ and $\underline{d}$ are column vectors). We are interested in solving such systems when the matrix B is **positive definite**. This restriction involves no loss of generality since the method is readily applicable to block tridiagonal systems (i.e., banded systems). If the matrix B is not positive definite, as is well-known, the system $B^T B \underline{y} = B^T \underline{d}$ has the same solution as (1) and the matrix $B^T B$ is (symmetric) positive definite (although its bandwidth is twice as large).

The data for this system (1) is conveniently characterized by the following set of n four-tuples (**lambda notation**):

$$\underline{\lambda}_i = \begin{cases} (0, b_0, 0, d_0) & i = 1 \\ (a_i, b_i, c_i, d_i) & 2 \leq i \leq n \end{cases} \tag{2}$$

We digress to review scan computations. Given a sequence $\underline{d} = (d_1, d_2, \ldots, d_n)$ of elements over a semigroup $\mathcal{S} = (S, \otimes)$, where $\otimes$ is an associative operator over S, a **scan** function provides the result vector $(y_1, y_2, \ldots, y_n)$ where $y_1 = d_1$ and for $2 \leq i \leq n$

$$y_i = d_1 \otimes d_2 \otimes \ldots \otimes d_i$$

If we interpret $\otimes$ as an "additive" operator and adjoin to S a "multiplicative" identity 1, then a scan can be viewed as the following matrix-vector multiplication:

$$y = \begin{bmatrix} 1 & & & & \\ 1 & 1 & & & \\ 1 & 1 & 1 & & \\ & & & \ddots & \\ 1 & 1 & 1 & 1 & 1 \end{bmatrix} \underline{d}$$

Over a ring that includes the multiplicative identity and additive inverses, the inverse of the preceding matrix is the **lower bi-diagonal matrix** P given below.

$$P = \begin{bmatrix} 1 & & & & \\ -1 & 1 & & & \\ & -1 & 1 & & \\ & & & \ddots & \\ & & & -1 & 1 \end{bmatrix} \tag{3}$$

Although the semigroup S may not contain additive inverses, we shall see that they are not needed. With this formulation, the scan computation corresponds to solving the system

$$P\underline{y} = \underline{d}$$

Since the matrix P is a special case of a tridiagonal matrix, we see that solving such a system will provide a solution to the scan problem if we can insure that we do not use additive inverses.

3 Solving Tridiagonal Systems

We give a method for factoring a tridiagonal matrix that leads to a recursive solution to a tridiagonal system. This factorization is not only parallelizable (see Section 5) but leads to algorithms that use a number of operations linear in the size of the problem. We begin by factoring a submatrix of the matrix B.

For $2 \leq j \leq n-1$ let T_j be the 3×3 submatrix of the matrix B shown below.

$$T_j = \begin{bmatrix} b_{j-1} & c_j & \\ a_j & b_j & c_{j+1} \\ & a_{j+1} & b_{j+1} \end{bmatrix}$$

This matrix can be factored into the product $T_j = U_j V_j W_j$ where U_j, V_j, and W_j are given below. Here we denote with b_j^{-1} the multiplicative inverse of b_j, and do not assume that the ring of the entries of T_j is multiplicatively commutative.

$$U_j = \begin{bmatrix} 1 & c_j b_j^{-1} & \\ & 1 & \\ & a_{j+1} b_j^{-1} & 1 \end{bmatrix}, W_j = \begin{bmatrix} 1 & & \\ b_j^{-1} a_j & 1 & b_j^{-1} c_{j+1} \\ & & 1 \end{bmatrix}$$

$$V_j = \begin{bmatrix} b_{j-1} - c_j b_j^{-1} a_j & & -c_j b_j^{-1} c_{j+1} \\ & b_j & \\ -a_{j+1} b_j^{-1} a_j & & b_{j+1} - a_{j+1} b_j^{-1} c_{j+1} \end{bmatrix}$$

The inverses of U_j and W_j can be obtained by replacing off-diagonal entries by their additive inverses.

We use the matrices U_j, V_j, and W_j as components of the matrices L_j, B_j, R_j, given below, to factor the matrix B as $B = L_j B_j R_j$. Here B_j is obtained by replacing the submatrix T_j by the submatrix V_j. Also, I_k is a $k \times k$ identity matrix.

$$L_j = \begin{bmatrix} I_{j-2} & & \\ & U_j & \\ & & I_{n-j-1} \end{bmatrix}, R_j = \begin{bmatrix} I_{j-2} & & \\ & W_j & \\ & & I_{n-j-1} \end{bmatrix}$$

$$B_j = \begin{bmatrix} b_1 & c_2 & & & & & & \\ a_2 & \ddots & & & & & & \\ & & b_{j-2} & c_{j-1} & & & & \\ & & a_{j-1} & & & & & \\ & & & & V_j & & & \\ & & & & & c_{j+2} & & \\ & & & & a_{j+2} & b_{j+2} & & \\ & & & & & & \ddots & c_n \\ & & & & & & a_n & b_n \end{bmatrix}$$

We say that B has been **factored on the jth row and column**.

The solution to the system of equations (1) defined by B can be obtained by inverting B, as suggested below.

$$\underline{y} = R_j^{-1} B_j^{-1} L_j^{-1} \underline{d}$$

The inverses of L_j and R_j are

$$L_j^{-1} = \begin{bmatrix} I_{j-2} & & \\ & U_j^{-1} & \\ & & I_{n-j-1} \end{bmatrix}, R_j^{-1} = \begin{bmatrix} I_{j-2} & & \\ & W_j^{-1} & \\ & & I_{n-j-1} \end{bmatrix}$$

where the inverses of U_j and W_j are obtained by changing the sign of their off-diagonal entries, as mentioned above.

It follows that to solve for $\underline{y}$ it suffices to compute

$$\hat{\underline{d}} = L_j^{-1} \underline{d}, \tag{4}$$

solve the system

$$B_j \underline{z} = \hat{\underline{d}} \tag{5}$$

for $\underline{z}$, and then compute the mapping

$$\underline{y} = R_j^{-1} \underline{z} \tag{6}$$

From (4) we have

$$\hat{d}_i = \begin{cases} d_{j-1} - c_j b_j^{-1} d_j & i = j - 1 \\ d_j & i = j \\ d_{j+1} - a_{j+1} b_j^{-1} d_j & i = j + 1 \\ d_i & \text{otherwise} \end{cases} \tag{7}$$

By consulting the definitions of V_j and B_j it is clear that the system (5) is solved by computing z_j from $z_j = b_j^{-1} d_j$ and deleting the jth row and column of B_j to reduce it to a tridiagonal matrix on one fewer row and column. The information needed to compute z_j as well as solve the reduced system is captured by the following lambda notation:

$$\hat{\lambda}_i = \begin{cases} (a_{j-1}, b_{j-1} - c_j b_j^{-1} a_j, c_{j-1}, d_{j-1} - c_j b_j^{-1} d_j) & i = j - 1 \\ (a_j, b_j^{-1}, c_{j+1}, d_j) \text{ (special)} & i = j \\ (-a_{j+1} b_j^{-1} a_j, b_{j+1} - a_{j+1} b_j^{-1} c_{j+1}, & \\ \quad - c_j b_j^{-1} c_{j+1}, d_{j+1} - a_{j+1} b_j^{-1} d_j) & i = j + 1 \\ (a_i, b_i, c_i, d_i) & \text{otherwise} \end{cases} \tag{8}$$

The reduced system is solved by applying the same procedure to all but the jth four-tuple in the above set of four-tuples. The jth is a special four-tuple that contains the additional information needed to compute the jth component, y_j, of the solution.

The solution vector $\underline{y}$ is obtained from (6) where

$$y_i = \begin{cases} z_i & i \neq j \\ -b_j^{-1} a_j z_{j-1} + b_j^{-1} d_j - b_j^{-1} c_{j+1} z_{j+1} & i = j \end{cases} \tag{9}$$

This recursive process is illustrated by the network of Figure 1. It consists of three cascaded components: an initial one that reduces by one the dimension of the system, an intermediate one that recursively solves the reduced system, and a final component that computes an additional unknown.

Scanning Figure 1 from left-to-right illustrates the iterative execution of the described recursive schema. When, near the completion of the reduction process, the reduced system has dimension smaller than 3 (i.e., equal to 2), we directly solve it and transform a pair $(\lambda_1^*, \lambda_2^*)$ to a pair (z_1, z_2). After this step (bottom of the recursion, denoted by the hexagonal module of Figure 1) we apply transformation (9) according to a schedule which is the exact time-reversal of the reduction schedule.

The process just described is serial (it handles one index at a time). This is reflected in the network of Figure 1. As we shall see in Section 5, this schema lends itself to very effective parallelization.

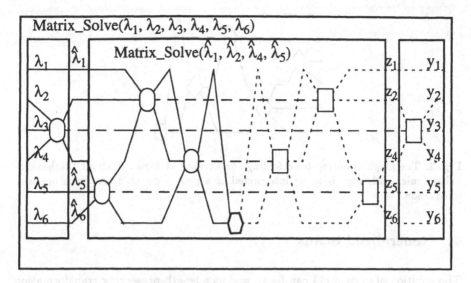

Fig. 1. Illustration of the recursive method. Oval boxes perform the transformation (8), rectangular boxes perform the transformation (9), and the hexagonal box handles the bottom of the recursion. Solid lines carry ordinary four-tuples, dashed lines carry "special" four-tuples, and dotted lines carry final solutions.

We now turn our attention to the conventional scan operation described in (3) by the matrix P. This corresponds to setting $B = P$. In this case the matrix T_j is lower bidiagonal. Its factors, U_j, V_j, and W_j, are given below.

$$U_j = \begin{bmatrix} 1 & & \\ & 1 & \\ & -1 & 1 \end{bmatrix}, V_j = \begin{bmatrix} 1 & & \\ & 1 & \\ & -1 & 1 \end{bmatrix}, W_j = \begin{bmatrix} 1 & & \\ -1 & 1 & \\ & & 1 \end{bmatrix}$$

The preceding algorithm uses inverses of U_j and W_j which are clearly obtained by simply changing the sign of off-diagonal terms. Therefore, U_j^{-1} and W_j^{-1} contain only unit elements. After deleting the jth row and column from B_j we obtain a bidiagonal matrix of the same type as P. This elimination process continues until we obtain the 2×2 matrix $\begin{bmatrix} 1 & \\ -1 & 1 \end{bmatrix}$ whose inverse is $\begin{bmatrix} 1 & \\ 1 & 1 \end{bmatrix}$. Thus, no additive inverses are ever used in the procedure, as stated at the conclusion of Section 2. We conclude that a scan computation is a special case of solving a tridiagonal linear system.

In the next section we show that the technique described above is an instance of a general class of computations based on associative operators that we call "generalized scans."

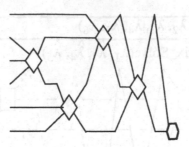

Fig. 2. The graph resulting from folding the network of Figure 1 about the hexagonal module. Each edge is to be interpreted as a pair of directed arcs with opposite orientation.

4 Generalized Scans

The solution of system (1) can be viewed as a length-preserving transformation of a sequence $\underline{\gamma} = (\underline{\lambda}_1, \underline{\lambda}_2, \ldots, \underline{\lambda}_n)$ of four-tuples (of type (2)) over a ring into a sequence $(y_1, y_2, \ldots, y_n)$ of single entries (of the same ring). If we fold the diagram of Figure 1 at the singular (hexagonal) module, we obtain the network shown in Figure 2, where each diamond-shaped module combines an oval and a rectangular module, as used in Figure 1. The lines are traversed from left-to-right in the first phase, and conversely in the second phase. Obviously each broken line of Figure 1 collapses within a module, reflecting the use of memory. Note that in the left-to-right sweep of Figure 2 each diamond-shaped module effectively suppresses one index that is restored in the right-to-left sweep. The transformation from $(\underline{\lambda}_1, \underline{\lambda}_2, \ldots, \underline{\lambda}_n)$ to $(y_1, y_2, \ldots, y_n)$ is a special case of the following class of computations.

A **generalized scan** is a length-preserving transformation of a sequence $\underline{\gamma}$ over a set S_{IN} to a sequence $\underline{y}$ over a set S_{OUT}. The transformation consists of three components: "reduction," "recursion," and "expansion." **Reduction** transforms $\underline{\gamma} \in S_{IN}^n$ to a sequence $\underline{\hat{\gamma}} \in S_{IN}^{n-1}$ and a term $\mu \in S_{IN}$ (to be retained); **recursion** transforms the sequence $\underline{\hat{\gamma}}$ to a sequence $\underline{z} \in S_{OUT}^{n-1}$; **expansion** transforms $\underline{z}$ together with μ to a sequence $\underline{y} \in S_{OUT}^n$. This process mirrors the structure shown in Figure 1.

The reduction operator maps $\underline{\gamma}$ to $\underline{\hat{\gamma}}$ and μ by replacing the substring $(\gamma_{j-\rho}, \ldots, \gamma_j, \ldots, \gamma_{j+\sigma})$ in $\underline{\hat{\gamma}}$ by $(\hat{\gamma}_{j-\rho}, \ldots, \hat{\gamma}_{j-1}, \hat{\gamma}_{j+1}, \ldots, \hat{\gamma}_{j+\sigma})$, that is, the jth index is suppressed.

The expansion operator maps $\underline{z}$ and μ to $\underline{y}$ by replacing the substring $(z_{j-\rho}, \ldots, z_{j-1}, z_{j+1}, \ldots, z_{j+\sigma})$ by $(y_{j-\rho}, \ldots, y_{j-1}, y_j, y_{j+1}, \ldots, y_{j+\sigma})$. In particular, jth index is added.

Clearly a generalized scan is completely specified by the reduction and expansion operators and by a termination operator acting at the bottom of the recursion.

Specifically we have for integers ρ and σ not simultaneously zero:

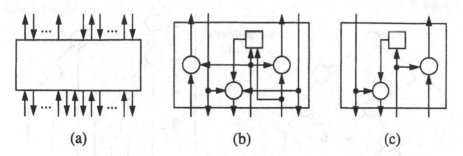

Fig. 3. Constructions used in generalized scan operations: (a) general form of combining node; (b) combining node for tridiagonal system; (c) combining node for scan.

1. **Reduction Operator.** It is specified by a set

$$\{\varphi_i : S_{IN}^{\rho+\sigma+1} \mapsto S_{IN} \,|\, i = 1, \ldots, \rho+\sigma\} \cup \{\mu : S_{IN}^{\rho+\sigma+1} \mapsto S_{IN}\}$$

of $(\rho+\sigma+1)$ functions of $(\rho+\sigma+1)$ arguments. Here $\hat{\gamma}_i = \varphi_{i-j+\rho+1} \, (\gamma_{j-\rho}, \ldots, \gamma_{j+\sigma})$ for $j - \rho \le i < j$, $\hat{\gamma}_i = \varphi_{i-j+\rho}(\gamma_{j-\rho}, \ldots, \gamma_{j+\sigma})$ for $j < i \le j + \sigma$, and $\mu_j = \mu(\gamma_{j-\rho}, \ldots, \gamma_{j+\sigma})$.

2. **Expansion Operator.** It is specified by a set

$$\{\psi_i : S_{OUT}^{\rho+\sigma} \cup S_{IN} \mapsto S_{OUT} \,|\, i = 1, \ldots, \rho+\sigma+1\}$$

of $(\rho+\sigma+1)$ functions of $(\rho+\sigma+1)$ arguments. Here $y_i = \psi_{i-j+\rho+1} \, (z_{j-\rho}, \ldots, z_{j-1}, \mu_j, z_{j+1}, \ldots, z_{j+\sigma})$ for $j - \rho \le i \le j + \sigma$ and $y_i = z_i$ otherwise.

3. **Termination operator.** When the sequence over S_{IN} consists of $\nu < (\rho + \sigma + 1)$ terms, the *length-preserving transformation* described by the following functions is applied:

$$\{\chi_i : S_{IN}^{\nu} \mapsto S_{OUT} \,|\, i = 1, \ldots, \nu\}$$

We may combine the reduction and expansion operations into a single module (with memory), as is illustrated in Figure 3 (a). The $(\rho+1)$st index is the one suppressed or restored.

It is now immediate that this formulation specializes to the known cases of tridiagonal-system solution and prefix computation.

(a) tridiagonal systems. $\rho = \sigma = 1$ Letting $\lambda_i = (a_i, b_i, c_i, d_i)$, $i = 1, 2, 3$.

$$\begin{cases} \varphi_1(\lambda_1, \lambda_2, \lambda_3) = (a_1, \ b_1 - c_2 b_2^{-1} a_2, \ c_1, \ d_1 - c_2 b_2^{-1} d_2) \\ \varphi_2(\lambda_1, \lambda_2, \lambda_3) = (-a_3 b_2^{-1} a_2, \ b_3 - a_3 b_2^{-1} c_3, \ -c_2 b_2^{-1} c_3, \ d_3 - a_3 b_2^{-1} d_2) \\ \mu(\lambda_1, \lambda_2, \lambda_3) \ = (a_2, \ b_2^{-1}, \ c_3, \ d_2) \end{cases}$$

$$\begin{cases} \psi_1(z_1, \mu_2, z_3) = z_1 \\ \psi_2(z_1, \mu_2, z_3) = -b_2^{-1} a_2 z_1 + b_2^{-1} d_2 - b_2^{-1} c_3 z_3 \\ \psi_3(z_1, \mu_2, z_3) = z_3 \end{cases}$$

The structure of the corresponding module is shown in Figure 3 (b).

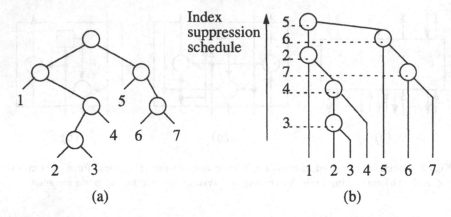

Fig. 4. (a) A tree schedule and (b) an isomorphic tree illustrating the index suppression schedule $(3,4,7,2,6,5)$.

(b) prefix computation over semigroup $(S, \otimes)$. $\rho = 0, \sigma = 1$

$$\begin{cases} \varphi_1(x_1, x_2) = x_1 \otimes x_2 \\ \mu(x_1, x_2) = x_2 \end{cases}$$

$$\begin{cases} \psi_1(z_1, x_2) = z_1 \\ \psi_2(z_1, x_2) = z_1 \otimes x_2 \end{cases}$$

The structure of the corresponding module is shown in Figure 3 (c).

It is worth pointing out that the operation involved in generalized scans enjoys a sort of associative property. Indeed, an application of the ordinary associative property of a semigroup S can be viewed as the selection of an arbitrary n-leaf binary tree T to specify the computation of an n-term product over S. This tree, in turn, is consistent with a number of "schedules" of index suppressions. This is synthetically illustrated in Figure 4, where we interpret the execution of $a_s \otimes a_t$ as the "suppression" of the rightmost index t.

It is immediately realized that the same freedom of choice of the index to be suppressed exists in generalized scans, i.e., in a string of $\nu > (\rho + \sigma + 1)$ terms **any** substring of $(\rho + \sigma + 1)$ terms can be selected for the suppression of the $(\rho + 1)$st index relative to this substring.

But even more revealing is the following observation. Although an arbitrary legal suppression sequence gives rise to a computation graph (dag) that is in general **not** a tree (see Figure 2), there are schedules that produce a tree computation. Specifically, consider a string of size $2(\rho + \sigma)$, and apply to this string any schedule of $(\rho + \sigma)$ reductions (each acting on a full support of $(\rho + \sigma + 1)$ arguments), yielding $(\rho + \sigma)$ outputs. If we interpret a string of $(\rho + \sigma)$ inputs as an element of a set Σ, then the described action is an operation on Σ (computing the "product" of two terms of Σ), which is trivially associative. This is illustrated in Figure 5 for the solution of a tridiagonal system $(\rho + \sigma = 2)$.

178

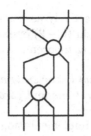

Fig. 5. An associative operator in a generalized scan (illustrated for a tridiagonal system solver).

5 Parallelization of the Method

Although the solution of a tridiagonal system illustrated in Sections 2 and 3 has been presented as a serial algorithm, the technique lends itself directly to parallelization.

We begin by observing that the factorization of B as $B = L_j B_j R_j$ involves rows/columns of indices $j-1$, j, and $j+1$ and eliminates index j. Therefore, it is evident that any other index i for which $|i-j| \geq 3$ can be concurrently eliminated since such an operation involves rows/columns disjoint from those with indices $\{j-1, j, j+1\}$. Thus, up to $\lfloor n/3 \rfloor$ such index eliminations can be performed in parallel, reducing in parallel the system's dimensions by a factor of at least $2/3$. Therefore, with about $\log_{3/2} n$ parallel steps the original system can be reduced to a directly solvable two-variable system. Approximately $\log_{3/2} n$ subsequent parallel (expansion) steps generate the entire solution. The same argument can be applied to generalized scans as discussed in Section 4; they can be executed in about $2 \log_\alpha n$ parallel steps, where $\alpha = 1 + 1/(\rho + \sigma)$.

This straightforward parallelization, however, can be improved upon in the case of tridiagonal systems due to the particular nature of the φ- and ψ-functions. Since

$$V_j = T_j - \begin{bmatrix} \cdot & c_j & \cdot \\ a_j & \cdot & c_{j+1} \\ \cdot & a_{j+1} & \cdot \end{bmatrix} + \begin{bmatrix} -c_j b_j^{-1} a_j & \cdot & -c_j b_j^{-1} c_{j+1} \\ \cdot & \cdot & \cdot \\ -a_{j+1} b_j^{-1} a_j & \cdot & -a_{j+1} b_j^{-1} c_{j+1} \end{bmatrix}$$

elimination of index j involves inverting b_j, *additively* updating b_{j-1} and b_{j+1}, introducing off-diagonal terms. It follows that any two indices can be simultaneously eliminated provided they are not adjacent, i.e., $|i - j| \geq 2$ rather than $|i - j| \geq 3$. As a consequence each reduction step decreases the system dimension by a factor of two, thereby yielding about $\log_2 n$ parallel reduction steps and the same number of expansion steps. Referring to (8) and (9), each reduction step uses one inversion, nine multiplications, and four additions/subtractions of matrix entries, whereas each expansion step uses two multiplications and two additions/subtractions. Assuming that over the basic ring each of these operations is executable in constant time, each parallel step is also executable in constant time. Moreover, each index is bijectively associated with a reduction/expansion operation pair, globally resulting in $(n-2)$ operations of each type. We summarize this discussion in the following theorem.

Theorem 1. *An $n \times n$ tridiagonal linear system of equations can be solved with an algorithm that uses $O(n)$ operations and parallel time $O(\log n)$.*

It is of interest to analyze implementations of this method on so-called "coarse-grained" parallel systems, i.e., a suitable interconnection of p powerful uniprocessors, each equipped with a sizable private memory [DFR93]. Such a system configuration is the most plausible model for today's parallel computers. The only hypothesis we make about the p-processor interconnection is that it contain a Hamiltonian path, a property exhibited by linear arrays, meshes, and hypercubic networks. The performance analysis is particularly interesting when $p \ll n$. In such situations each processor is assigned an interval of about n/p indices upon which it acts serially until there are just two surviving indices (**serial phase**). Adjacent intervals of indices are assigned to adjacent processors on this Hamiltonian path. It may be necessary for processors to exchange information with neighbors during the serial phase. At the completion of this phase, execution of the algorithm is continued on the p-processor network (**parallel phase**).

We contrast two typical coarse-grained parallel implementations of this strategy corresponding to two distinct elimination schedules, which obviously perform the same number of operations. For simplicity let $n = 2^k$ and consider only the reduction process (expansion being analogous).

The first schedule, denoted $\mathcal{A}_1$, eliminates all even indices in a first subphase, eliminates all even indices of those remaining in the second subphase, etc., and terminates with 2 remaining indices. It has therefore $k - 1 = \log n - 1$ subphases. Of these, the first $\log(n/p)$ are executed in the serial phase, and the rest in the parallel phase. During the serial phase, each processor works on its assigned set of n/p indices, sharing information with its neighbors as necessary.

The second schedule, denoted $\mathcal{A}_2$, eliminates two out of every four indices according to the scheme specified in Figure 5 in a first subphase, and so on in each of the following subphases. This schedule also has $k - 1$ subphases. Of these, the first $\log(n/p) - 1$ are executed by the serial phase (which terminates with $2p$ remaining indices), and the residual ones by the parallel phase.

If communication occurs strictly on the Hamiltonian path, and K denotes the ratio of running times of interprocessor communication and execution of a reduction operation, then it is easily realized that the parallel phase runs in time approximately $Kp \log p$ and $K2p \log p$ for $\mathcal{A}_1$ and $\mathcal{A}_2$, respectively (time is normalized, the unit being the time to eliminate an index).

The serial phase is where the two schedules differ most markedly. Indeed, in schedule $\mathcal{A}_1$, when a processor suppresses the rightmost index of its current set it must communicate with its right neighbor, i.e., it must communicate altogether $\log(n/p)$ times, whereas, in schedule $\mathcal{A}_2$ no processor ever communicates with its neighbors during the serial phase. Since the serial phase runs in time $\approx n/p$

for both schedules, we have the following normalized times for these schedules:

$$\mathcal{A}_1 : T_1 \le n/p + K(\log n/p + p \log p)$$
$$\mathcal{A}_2 : \qquad T_2 \le n/p + K(2p \log p)$$

This discussion suggests that as long as $p \ll \sqrt{n/K \log n}$ the two schedules are basically equivalent and optimal parallel speed-up is achievable.

6 Banded Systems

The algorithms given above to solve a tridiagonal system apply directly to banded positive definite systems by covering the non-zero entries in the coefficient matrix with block tridiagonal matrices. Positive definiteness implies that the diagonal blocks in this covering are non-singular and that this property is inherited by the reduced matrices. We conclude

Theorem 2. *An $n \times n$ banded linear system of bandwidth b can be solved with $O(nW(b)/b)$ work and $O(T(b) \log n)$ parallel time where $W(b)$ and $T(b)$ are respectively the work and parallel time to invert a $b \times b$ non-singular matrix.*

References

[DFR93] F. Dehne, A. Fabri, and A. Rau-Chaplin, Scalable Parallel Geometric Algorithms for Coarse Grained Multicomputers. *Proceedings of the 2nd Annual ACM Symposium on Computational Geometry*, 298-307, 1993.

[DS84] J.J. Dongarra and A.H. Sameh. On Some Parallel Banded System Solvers. *Parallel Computing*, 1:223–235, 1984.

[H64] R.W. Hockney. A Fast Direct Solution of Poisson's Equation Using Fourier Analysis. *JACM*, 12:95–113, 1965.

[J85] S.L. Johnsson. Solving Narrow Banded Systems on Ensemble Architectures. Research Report YALEU/DCS/RR-418 Dept. of Computer Science, Yale University New Haven, CT, August 1985.

[J87] S.L. Johnsson. Solving Tridiagonal Systems on Ensemble Architectures *SIAM J. of. Sci. Statist. Comput.*, 8:354–392, 1987.

[LF80] R. E. Ladner and M. J. Fischer. Parallel Prefix Computation. *JACM*, 27:831–838, Oct. 1980.

[M85] U. Meier. A Parallel Partition Method for Solving Banded Systems of Linear Equations. *Parallel Computing*, 2:33–43, 1985.

[S73] H.S. Stone. An Efficient Parallel Algorithm for the Solution of a Tridiagonal Linear System of Equations. *JACM*, 20:27–38, Jan. 1973.

[Swa74] P.N. Swarztrauber. A Direct Method for the Discrete Solution of Separable Elliptic Equations. *SIAM J. of Num. Anal.*, 11:1136–1150, 1974.

[Swe74] R.A. Sweet. A Generalized Cyclic-Reduction Algorithm. *SIAM J. of Num. Anal.*, 11:506–520, 1974.

[Swe77] R.A. Sweet. A Cyclic-Reduction Algorithm for Solving Block Tridiagonal Systems of Arbitrary Dimension. *SIAM J. of. Num. Anal.*, 14:706–720, 1977.

[W81] H.H. Wang. A Parallel Method for Tridiagonal Equations. *ACM Trans. Math. Software*, 7:170–183, 1981.

Two-Dimensional Pattern Matching in Linear Time and Small Space

(EXTENDED ABSTRACT)

Maxime Crochemore[1]   Leszek Gąsieniec[2] *   Wojciech Plandowski[2] *
Wojciech Rytter[2] *

[1] Institut Gaspard Monge, Université de Marne la Vallée, Noisy le Grand,
mac@litp.ibp.fr

[2] Instytut Informatki, Uniwersytet Warszawski, Warszawa,
{lechu,wojtekpl,rytter}@mimuw.edu.pl

Abstract. We present the first known (alphabet independent) algorithm for two-dimensional pattern matching which works in linear time
and small space simultaneously. The searching phase of our algorithm
works in $O(1)$ space and is followed by pattern preprocessing performed
in $O(\log m)$ space. Up to now there was not known even any efficient
sublinear space algorithm for this problem. The main tools in our algorithm are several 2-dimensional variations of deterministic sampling,
originally used in parallel pattern matching: *small*, *frame* and *wide* samples. Another novel idea used in our algorithm is the technique of *zooming
sequences*: the sequences of nonperiodic decreasing parts of the pattern
(samples) of similar regular shapes. Their regularity allows to encode the
zooming sequences in small memory (logarithmic number of bits) while
nonperiodicity allows to make shifts (*kill* positions as candidates for a
match) in a way amortizing the work. The preprocessing phase is recursive, its structure is similar to the linear time algorithm for the selection
problem. The stack of the recursion consists of logarithmic number of
integers. Our algorithm is rather complicated, but all known alphabet-
independent linear time algorithms (even with unrestricted space) for
2d-matching are quite complicated, too.

1 Introduction

The problem of *two dimensional pattern matching* (2d-matching, in short) is to
find all occurrences of a two dimensional pattern array P in a text array T. The
sides of P are of length m and sides of T are of length n. The total size of T is
$N = n^2$ and the total size of P is $M = m^2$. Assume $m < n$. The total size of
the entire problem is equal to N. The space is measured as a number of integers
with logarithmic number of bits. The pattern and the text are given as *read only*
tables and by the *space* we mean additional auxiliary memory cells.

There are known several (complicated) algorithms for 1-dimensional *string-
matching* in linear time and small space, see [7, 8, 12]. However 1-dimensional

---

* Supported by the Grant KBN 2-1190-91-01

algorithms are hardly extendible to the 2-dimensional case. Up to now there was not known any 2d-matching algorithm working in linear time and small space for all patterns. Some partial results were obtained before in [9] for a class of patterns. The pattern-matching usually consists of two quite independent parts: the preprocessing and the searching phase. The alphabet-independent linear time algorithms for searching and preprocessing phase were constructed in [2] and [11], see also [10]. Our main result is the following theorem.

Theorem 1. (Main Result)
Two-dimensional text searching can be done in $O(N)$ time and $O(1)$ space (using constant number of logarithmic bits registers), after the $O(M)$-time preprocessing performed in $O(\log M)$ space. □

Properties of 2-dimensional periodicities are theoretical basis of algorithms for 2d-matching. The periods of a 2-dimensional pattern are 2-dimensional vectors with integers components. The size of a 2d-vector $\alpha = (\alpha_1, \alpha_2)$ is $|\alpha| = \max(|\alpha_1|, |\alpha_2|)$. Only (potential periods) vectors of size at most $c \cdot m$ are considered, where $c = 1/8$. We call such vectors *short*. We also consider subpatterns which are rectangles, in this case we define the *short* vectors as vectors whose each coordinate (horizontal, vertical) has absolute value not exceeding c times the corresponding side of the rectangle. The vector α is a *period* of P iff $P[x] = P[x + \alpha]$ for each position x in P such that both sides of the equation correspond to positions in the pattern. We say that the pattern P is *periodic* iff it has a *short* period.

A *sample* is a set S of some positions in the pattern P. By an *S-occurrence* of the pattern P at position x in text T (this means we place P with its left upper corner at x in T) we mean a partial occurrence of P such that all positions in S match corresponding positions in T. Denote by $PartialMatch(x, S)$ the corresponding predicate. A *full match* or an *occurrence* of P in a text T is a position x in T such that left upper corner of P is aligned with x and P match proper subarray of T completely. The full match corresponds to an *S-occurrence* with $S = P$. If $PartialMatch(x, S)$ then one of the rectangles, such that all positions in it, except the position x, are *killed* as candidates for *full matches*, is distinguished and called the *field of fire* of S. The position of x relative to the field of fire $\mathcal{F}$ of S is called the *handle* of S. $\mathcal{F}$ is a rectangle placed on the plane, and the handle is a distinguished position on the plane, not necessarily in $\mathcal{F}$. Assume the rectangle $\mathcal{F}$ is placed on T in such a way that the handle is placed on a position x in T. Denote by $CoveredBy(T, \mathcal{F}, x)$ all positions in T covered by $\mathcal{F}$ excluding the position x. The *field of fire* $\mathcal{F}$ of S satisfies for each text array T the following condition: if $PartialMatch(x, S)$ then there is no (full) occurrence of P in $CoveredBy(T, \mathcal{F}, x)$. Assume the pattern or its subpattern is of shape $m' \times m''$. Two basic types of *samples* considered in the paper are listed below.

Small sample S consists of two pattern positions (with associated symbols) and *field of fire* $\mathcal{F}$ is an $c \cdot m' \times c \cdot m''$ rectangle with the *handle* not necessarily in the middle of the *field of fire*.

Frame sample is identified by a pair of numbers (e, i). The sample is the $e \times e$ square subarray of T with the $(i - 1) \times (i - 1)$ central subarray removed (the removed part is called the *hole*). We call it a *frame* with boundaries (e, i), and denote it by $\Theta(e, i)$. The *thickness* of the *frame sample* is $\phi(\Theta) = e - i + 1$. The *field of fire* $\mathcal{F}$ is a square of the shape $c \cdot \phi(\Theta) \times c \cdot \phi(\Theta)$. The *handle* of *frame sample* is in the center of its field of fire $\mathcal{F}$. Such position of the *handle* is of great advantage.

The cost of (work needed to check) an S-occurrence of the sample is its size (the total number of positions in S). The efficiency corresponds to the area of the *field of fire*. In this sense the most efficient is the *small sample*. However it is inefficient with respect to the position of its *handle*. On the other hand *frame samples* are inefficient since the area of such a *sample* can be quadratic with respect to the area of the *field of fire*. Notice that in the 1-dimensional string-matching problem the position of the *handle* with respect to the field of fire has essentially no importance while in the 2-dimensional case it is crucial.

2 Searching for Nonperiodic 2D-Patterns

In this section we assume, to simplify the presentation, that P is a square array. However the results can be extended to the case of rectangular P. We consider first the patterns having small samples. Assume that P is nonperiodic and has a small sample S. If the handle of S is not in the center of $\mathcal{F}$ then we can assume that it is in the corner of $\mathcal{F}$, by taking a suitable square part of $\mathcal{F}$ containing the *handle* in the corner. We can assume later (without loss of generality) that in the case of *small* samples the handle is one position to the right of the lower right corner of the *field of fire*. Hence the *small* sample *kills* a square of candidates positioned in the columns strictly to the left of x and rows (simultaneously) above or at the same level as x. The crucial role in the searching play special sequences of subpatterns. A *zooming sequence* is a sequence of similar *regular* objects of decreasing size. The similarity and regularity means that the next object can be computed from the previous one in a constant time and space. We explain the idea of zooming by the example of 1-dimensional matching. a given 1-dimensional pattern p is nonperiodic (a given word w is periodic iff its shortest period is $\leq \frac{|w|}{4}$). Then the prefix or the suffix of p of length $\frac{2}{3}|p|$ is nonperiodic. Denote it by $next(p)$. Then the sequence $zoomseq = (p, next(p), next(next(p)), \dots)$ is the *zooming sequence* of nonperiodic subpatterns of p. It ends with a subpattern of a constant size. When we search for p in a 1-dimensional text t then we start to match consecutive subpatterns of the sequence $zoomseq$, extending $next^{(i+1)}(p)$ to $next^{(i)}(p)$, starting from the shortest constant size one. Whenever the whole p is found we report a *full match*. The shift, caused by some mismatch, is proportional to the last matched subpattern in the sequence $zoomseq$. Since each element of the zooming sequence, is nonperiodic all shifts amortize the total work efficiently. The sequence $zoomseq$ can be stored using logarithmic number of bits (each bit indicates whether we choose the prefix or the suffix), so constant space in the sense of small integers. This gives probably a simplest algorithm for

1-dimensional *string-matching* in linear time and constant space, see [13].

Unfortunately, this approach does not work for 2d-patterns directly. It is possible that the whole pattern P is nonperiodic but all its proper rectangular subpatterns are periodic. However, a similar approach works if rectangles are replaced by frames (rectangles with rectangular holes inside). Recall, that we defined the *frame sample* $\Theta(e, i)$ as a central $e \times e$ subarray of P with its central $i - 1 \times i - 1$ subarray removed and by the thickness of the *frame sample* we mean the number $\phi(\Theta) = e - i + 1$. Let $\Theta = \Theta(e, i)$ be a *frame* of thickness $t = \phi(\Theta)$. Denote by $Outer(\Theta)$, $Inner(\Theta)$ and $Center(\Theta)$ the *subframes* $\Theta(e, i + 2c \cdot t)$, $\Theta(e - 2c \cdot t, i)$, and $\Theta((e+i)/2 - c \cdot t, (e+i)/2 + c \cdot t)$, respectively. They are called *outer*, *inner* and *central* subframes of Θ. The *inner* and *outer* subframes play the same role in the defined below zooming sequence $\mathcal{Z}$ as the suffix and prefix of the 1d-pattern in the sequence *zoomseq*. Assume, that the whole pattern is its *subframe* with the *empty hole*. By a *zooming sequence* $\mathcal{Z} = ZoomSeq(P)$ of frame samples we mean the sequence of *nonperiodic* (in the sense defined below) subframes $\mathcal{Z} = (\Theta_1, \ldots, \Theta_k)$ where $\Theta_1 = P$, Θ_k has thickness $\phi(\Theta_k)$ of a constant size. And for each $1 \leq i < k$ $\Theta_{i+1} = Outer(\Theta_i)$ or $\Theta_{i+1} = Inner(\Theta_i)$.

The sequence $\mathcal{Z}$ can be stored using constant space, i.e. one integer with logarithmic number of bits. We have only to store for each $1 \leq i < k$ whether $\Theta_{i+1} = Outer(\Theta_i)$ or $\Theta_{i+1} = Inner(\Theta_i)$. The area (cost) of the frame sample of thickness $t = \phi(\Theta)$ is $O(m \cdot t)$.

The concept of a *period* can be defined for the frames in a similar way as for the rectangular text arrays, however we make a subtle difference. We say that two points $x, y \in \Theta$ are *line-connected* in Θ iff all integer points between x and y lying on the line connecting x and y are in Θ. In a frame with the empty hole each two points are line-connected. The vector α is a *period* of a frame Θ iff $P[x] = P[x + \alpha]$ for each position x in P, whenever points x, $x + \alpha$ are *line-connected* in Θ. We say that the frame Θ is periodic iff it has a *period* of size at most $c \cdot \phi(\Theta)$.

If the frame Θ is nonperiodic then it is a sample with the $c \cdot \phi(\Theta) \times c \cdot \phi(\Theta)$ *field of fire* $\mathcal{F}$ with the *handle* in the center of $\mathcal{F}$.

Lemma 2.

(1) *Assume $Inner(\Theta)$ is periodic and two points $x, y \in \Theta$ are line-connected in $Inner(\Theta)$, where $x - y$ is a short vector with respect to Θ. Then there are two line-connected points $x', y' \in Center(\Theta)$ such that $P[x] = P[x']$, $P[y] = P[y']$ and $x - y = x' - y'$.*

(2) *If the frame Θ is nonperiodic then at least one of its $Inner(\Theta)$ or $Outer(\Theta)$ subframes is nonperiodic.*

Proof.

add (1) Assume there is a small period π of the subframe $\Theta' = Inner(\Theta)$. Let L be the line which contains the pair of points x, y. Consider the case that π is not parallel to L. We can assume that if we go in direction π from L then we do not enter the *hole* of the frame Θ. Transpose the pair x, y by multiple applications of the vector π as far as it is possible inside Θ'. Then the pair x, y

is shifted to the destination points x', y'. The case that π is parallel to L can be handled analogously.

add (2) If the inner subframe is nonperiodic we are done. Otherwise, assume that both the inner and outer subframes are periodic. Hence $\Theta' = Inner(\Theta)$ has a small period π and a small vector α is a period of $\Theta'' = Outer(\Theta)$. Due to nonperiodicity of the whole frame Θ there should be a pair (x, y) of line-connected positions inside Θ which "kills" this vector: i.e. $x - y = \alpha$ and $P[x] \neq P[y]$. It could happen that $x, y \in \Theta''$, however in this case x, y should be not line-connected in Θ'', and this implies they are close to the internal border of Θ'' and they are in Θ' due to large overlap of both subframes. Hence in each case we can assume that x, y are in the inner subframe. Due to case (1) the positions x and y can be shifted to some other positions $(x', y') \in Center(\Theta)$ such that $P[x'] = P[x]$ and $P[y'] = P[y]$. Notice that $Center(\Theta) \subseteq \Theta''$. The pair (x', y') breaks periodicity α in the outer frame if both points are *line-connected* in the outer frame. The crucial point is that each two positions inside $Center(\Theta)$ are always *line-connected* with respect to Θ'', since all points in $Center(\Theta)$ are far enough from the internal border (hole) of $Outer(\Theta)$. Hence $x', x' + \alpha \in \Theta''$, x' and $x' + \alpha$ are *line-connected* in $Outer(\Theta)$ and $P[x'] \neq P[x' + \alpha]$. This contradicts our assumption that α is a period of $Outer(\Theta)$. The contradiction proves that the inner and outer subframes cannot be both periodic, so one of them is nonperiodic. This completes the proof.

As a consequence of Lemma 2 we know that for each nonperiodic 2d-pattern P there exists a zooming sequence of frame samples which can be stored in $O(\log m)$ bits (or using one small integer). Assume that we have already computed:

a *small sample* S and a *zooming sequence* Z of *frame samples* for P.

Recall, that $PartialMatch(x, \Psi)$ is the boolean predicate which is satisfied iff the text array T agrees with the subset Ψ of positions of the pattern placed at x. We have different types of samples and Ψ we mean any of them. Recall that samples differ with respect to the field of fire. Divide the text array T into disjoint *windows*. Each *window* is a $\frac{c}{2} \cdot m \times \frac{c}{2} \cdot m$ square subarray of T. Due to nonperiodicity of P there is at most one occurrence of P in one *window*. It is enough to show how to find an occurrence (at most one) of the pattern P in a fixed *window* W. We assume (without loss of generality) that the *handle* of the *field of fire* F of the small sample S is at the bottom-right corner of F.

Remark. Assume P is nonperiodic and $x \in W$. If $PartialMatch(x, S)$ then all points in columns to the left of x and (simultaneously) in rows above x can be eliminated (we know they are not full occurrences).

We construct an algorithm which scans a given window W and searches for the pattern. In every moment the window W is partitioned into the area of "nonactive" positions and the area A of "active" positions. We know (due to information we have at the moment) that there is no occurrence at any "nonactive" position, all "active" positions are candidates for a full match. Initially all positions of the window are *active* and $\mathcal{A} = \mathcal{W}$. We have only small memory to categorize positions. The set $\mathcal{A}$ should be simple enough to remember it easily. Let $x \in \mathcal{W}$ and $r \geq 0$, then $\Gamma(x, r)$ denotes the area consisting of all points $z \in \mathcal{W}$ which are in the same column as x or to the right of this column and in the rows not below x and which satisfy $dist(x, z) > r$, where $dist((x_1, x_2), (y_1, y_2)) = \max\{|x_1 - y_1|, |x_2 - y_2|\}$. If a *field of fire* is a $f \times f$ square then by its *radius* we mean the number $\max\{\lfloor \frac{f}{2} \rfloor, 1\}$. $\Gamma(x, r)$ has the following property. Assume that we know there is no full match below the row containing x and we found at position x the partial match (sample) S and the frame sample Θ_i whose *field of fire* has *radius* r. Then we know that the set of active (possible candidates for a full match) positions is contained in $\Gamma(x, r)$.

The algorithm scans (inspects) positions of $\mathcal{W}$ for an occurrence of P in a systematic way, due to limited memory the scanning order is quite important. Define the *linear order* $\prec$ of points of $\mathcal{A}$ as follows. The points of $\mathcal{W}$ are ordered from bottom to upper rows and right-to-left in each row. Hence the first point in $\mathcal{W}$ is its bottom-right corner. Denote by $Next(x, \mathcal{A})$ the point following x in $\mathcal{A}$ according to the order defined above. If there is no such point or $\mathcal{A} = \emptyset$ then $Next(x, \mathcal{A}) = nil$.

Algorithm *Sampling-Zooming*
{searching for pattern P in a given window $\mathcal{W}$,
P is nonperiodic and has a small sample S }

1: $\mathcal{A} = \mathcal{W}$; $x :=$ bottom-right corner of $\mathcal{W}$;
2: **while** $x \neq nil$ **do**
    begin {main iteration}
        if $PartialMatch(x, S)$ **then**
        begin
            $j := \min\{i \geq 1 : PartialMatch(x, \Theta_i)\}$;
            if $j = 1$ **then**
                report *full match* at x and STOP;
            $r :=$ the *radius* of *field of fire* of Θ_j;
            $\mathcal{A} := \Gamma(x, r)$; $x := Next(x, \mathcal{A})$;
        end ;
    end {main iteration}

Lemma 3. *The algorithm Sampling-Zooming finds an occurrence of P, if there is any, in $O(N)$ time and $O(1)$ space.*

Proof. Note first, that since the size of S is constant, the total cost of all executed operations $PartialMatch(S)$ is linear with respect to the size of the window. The most expensive part is the computation of the values of j, see algorithm *Sampling-Zooming*. It can be realized by testing partial match at x

of $\Theta_k, \Theta_{k-1}, \ldots, \Theta_j$ successively. The zooming sequence is kept in (and recovered from) a logarithmic sequence of bits, and can be stored in a single integer. Hence the space needed to compute j is constant. The successive partial matches for Θ_i are tested *naively*. Their sizes grow geometrically and their total cost is proportional to the size of Θ_j which is $O(\phi(\Theta_j) \cdot m)$. In the same time $\phi(\Theta_j)$ is proportional to the *radius* r of the *field of fire* of Θ_j. Notice that the value $j = \min\{i \geq 1 : PartialMatch(x, \Theta_i)\}$ can be computed in constant space and $O(r \cdot m)$ time, where r is the *radius* of the field of fire of Θ_j. In the course of the algorithm there is processed a sequence $x_1, x_2, \ldots, x_p$ and $r_1, r_2, \ldots, r_p$ of values of x and r, respectively. Hence, the total time of the algorithm is proportional to $\sum_{i=1}^{p} r_i \cdot m$. Notice that each point x_i is right and up to the previous one and $dist(x_i, x_{i+1}) \geq r_i$. Hence the sum of all r_i's is at most m. This implies that the sum above is bounded by m^2, in other words it is linear with respect to the total size of the pattern. There are $O(\frac{n^2}{m^2})$ windows $\mathcal{W}$ and they can be processed systematically in time $O(|\mathcal{W}|)$ each. Hence total time is linear with respect to the total size of the text array T.

We consider now general nonperiodc patterns, so we drop the assumption that P has a small sample.

Denote by $truncate(P)$ the subarray of P of shape $(1 - c) \cdot m \times m$ which consists of the bottom $(1 - c) \cdot m$ rows of P. *Wide samples* are nonperiodic subpatterns resulting from P by cutting off some consecutive top rows. They are *wide* in the sense that they have m columns.

Lemma 4. *Assume P is nonperiodic and $truncate(P)$ is periodic. Then P has a small sample S which consists of two positions.*

We construct the *zooming sequence* $\mathcal{Z}$ of *wide* samples as the sequence of nonperiodic subpatterns $P = P_0, P_1, \ldots, P_k$, where $P_{i+1} = truncate(P_i)$, for $1 \leq i < j$, and P_k has a small sample. We take P_k such that $truncate(P_j)$ is periodic or P_k is of a constant size.

We show how to search in a *window* $\mathcal{W}$ of the shape $\frac{c}{2} \cdot m \times \frac{c}{2} \cdot m$. The crucial point is that wide samples P_i are *wide* enough to guarantee that their field of fire has a width (number of columns) equal to $\frac{c}{2} \cdot m$. This implies that the *active area* (set of candidates for a *match*) has now much simpler shape and consists of a small number of topmost consecutive rows of $\mathcal{W}$. We use the linear ordering $\prec$ of points (right-left, bottom-up) in the window $\mathcal{W}$ defined in the preceding section. Let $FindNext(x, P', \mathcal{W})$ be the function which returns the first occurrence of some subpattern P', for $P' \in \{P = P_0, P_1, \ldots, P_k\}$ in $\mathcal{W}$ following a given point x (including x) with respect to the defined linear order $\prec$. The returned value is *nil* if there is no occurrence. Denote by $ShiftUp(x, s, \mathcal{W})$ the function which returns the first point in the row which is s rows higher than x in $\mathcal{W}$. If there is no such point (we go outside $\mathcal{W}$) then the returned value is *nil*. The work performed in one iteration is proportional to the *shift* (the total size of *skipped* rows) in the operation $ShiftUp$. Hence the time in a given window is proportional to its size. Finally we have shown that searching for nonperiodic patterns can be done in linear time and constant space, in case it is followed by pattern preprocessing.

Algorithm *Searching_General_Nonperiodic*
$x :=$ bottom-right corner of $\mathcal{W}$;
while $x \neq nil$ **do**
begin {main iteration}
  compute $x := FindNext(x, P_k, \mathcal{W})$ using
  algorithm *Sampling-Zooming*;
  $j := \min\{i \geq 1 : PartialMatch(x, P_i)\}$;
  if $j = 1$ **then** report *full match* at x and STOP;
  $h :=$ the *height* of P_j ; $x := ShiftUp(x, \frac{c \cdot h}{2}, \mathcal{W})$;
end {main iteration}

---

3 The Searching for Periodic 2D-Patterns

We have to deal with three categories of 2-dimensional periodic patterns: *lattice-periodic*, *radiant-periodic* and *line-periodic* patterns, see [1, 11].

Lemma 5. *Text searching for periodic 2d-patterns can be done in $O(N)$ time and $O(1)$ space.*

Proof. We present the proof only for the line-periodic case, which is the hardest case. We can reduce this case to other (simpler) cases: nonperiodic, lattice-periodic and radiant-periodic.

Assume the pattern is line-periodic. Let π be the *shortest* period of P, its direction is the ratio $\alpha(\pi) = \frac{x}{y}$. Assume $|\alpha(\pi)| \geq 1$. A *horizontal stripe* of height h is an $h \times m$ subrectangle of P. Let $P1, P2$ be the upper and the lower stripes of height $h = 3|\pi|$. It is not difficult to prove that $P1, P2$ are *together nonperiodic*. This means that every nonzero vector $v = (x, y)$ such that $|x| \leq c \cdot h$ and $|y| \leq c \cdot m$ and which is not a period of P is *killed* by one of $P1, P2$. Denote by D the pair $P1, P2$. It can be treated as a *double pattern*. D can be also treated as a *sample* of the whole pattern P. In this sense it has the rectangular *field of fire* of shape $c \cdot h \times c \cdot m$ and the *handle* in the center. An algorithm for searching for such *together nonperiodic* double patterns D is essentially the same as the one for searching for nonperiodic ordinary patterns.

The algorithm for searching line-periodic patterns goes as follows. Divide text T into $c \cdot \frac{m}{2} \times c \cdot \frac{m}{2}$-size windows. Now every window is divided in $c \cdot \frac{h}{2} \times c \cdot \frac{m}{2}$-size subwindows. Since the field of fire of D is a rectangle of shape $c \cdot h \times c \cdot m$ there is at most one occurrence of D in one subwindow. Starting from the lowest subwindow of the window we search for D. Suppose we have found an occurrence of D in i-th subwindow starting from the bottom of the window. If there was an occurrence of the pattern in the window then we check if the direction of the line which contains the position of the last occurrence of the pattern and the current position is the direction of periods of P. If it is not, we continue searching for D starting from the $(i+1)$-th subwindow. Otherwise, we find the most thick possible outer frame of P which matches the text at the found position. We start by checking naively if the frame of thickness h matches the text T. If it does not match then we continue searching for D starting from the $(i+1)$-th subwindow. If the frame matches properly then we find the most thick possible matching frame of P avoiding comparisons of symbols belonging to the last occurrence of P. If there was any occurrence of P before then we know that the symbols from the last occurrence of P match. Assume the thickness of this frame is r. If tested position is not the occurrence of the pattern we omit $t = max(0, \frac{r-h}{\pi})$ subwindows and continue searching for D from the $(i+t+1)$-th subwindow. If the position is the occurrence of P we report the occurrence and store the position as the last found occurrence of the pattern. The linear time complexity of the algorithm follows from two facts. The first one is that comparisons involved in searching of D occurrences (but not P) are amortized by proportional shifts over subwindows. The second one is that each symbol of the text is tested at most constant number of times after we enter the phase when full occurrences of the pattern P are checked. We omit the details.

As a direct implication we get the following theorem.

Theorem 6. *The searching for 2d-patterns, followed by the pattern preprocessing, can be performed in linear time and constant space.* □

4 Preprocessing of Two-Dimensional Patterns

The crucial operation in the preprocessing is the computation of the shortest period in a given direction α, to simplify its computation the notion of the 2d-period is slightly redefined. For a given vector π define $LINES(\pi)$ as the set of lines in the pattern which are parallel to π. For example set $LINES(1,1)$ consists of all lines parallel to the one of the diagonals. A line $\mathcal{L}$ is *long with respect to* π iff its length is at least $c' \cdot |\pi|$, for some fixed constant $c' > 0$. , that a vector is *short* iff its size is at most $c \cdot m$. A vector π is a *weak period* of P iff $|\pi|$ is a period of each line $\mathcal{L} \in LINES(\pi)$ and is long with respect to π. The pattern is *strongly nonperiodic* (*weakly periodic*) iff it has no (it has a) *short* weak period. Each strongly nonperiodic pattern is nonperiodic in the standard periodicity meaning. We say, that a vector π is in a direction α iff it is parallel to π. Denote by $LinePeriod(\alpha, P)$ the shortest period in direction α in P. Define analogously $LinePeriod(\alpha, \Theta)$ for a frame Θ. In later presentation we replace standard *periods* by *weak periods* in the definition of samples and zooming sequences used in the searching phase. Define $m \times m$ square to be radiant periodic if after removing $2c \cdot m \times 2c \cdot m$ opposite corner squares it is a lattice. Then the searching phase works essentially in the same way as before.

Remark. Assume the pattern P is weakly periodic in a direction α. Then all weak periods of P in the direction α are multiples of $LinePeriod(\alpha, P)$.

We omit later the words *weak* and *strong* and assume that periodicity means *weak* periodicity. We can compute periods of each line in a given direction in the decreasing order with respect to the lengths of these lines, using 1-dimensional string-matching on each line.

Lemma 7. *Vectors $LinePeriod(\alpha, P)$ and $LinePeriod(\alpha, \Theta)$ can be computed in linear time and constant space, for a given direction α,* $\quad\square$

The *preprocessing data* for nonperiodic patterns consists of the following objects:
   (1) A sequence $\mathcal{T} = P_1, \cdots, P_k$ of *wide* samples;
   (2) A *small sample* S of P_k;
   (3) A *zooming sequence* $\mathcal{Z}$ of *frame samples* for P_k.
If P is periodic then the preprocessing consists of computing the *periodicity* of P. This means that we have to recognize pattern periodicity type among line-periodic, radiant-periodic and lattice-periodic ones. Moreover, if P is line-periodic then we compute the shortest weak period of the pattern and if it is radiant periodic or lattice periodic we compute a pair of basis vectors defining the lattice inside the pattern, see [1].
   Denote by P_{center} the central subsquare of the shape $c'' \cdot m \times c'' \cdot m$ of the pattern P where $c'' = 4c$. In the case of *frames* with nonempty holes we define P_{center} as the central subarray of the top rectangle of the frame. In the discussion below we assume that we deal with subpatterns without *holes*, the frame case can be considered similarly.

Lemma 8. $T_{center}(M) = O(M)$, *where $T_{center}(M)$ is the time to compute the periodicity of the pattern P of total size M in constant space under the assumption that the P_{center} has been preprocessed.*

Proof. Let $\mathcal{W}$ be a window in P of shape $2c \cdot m \times 2c \cdot m$ whose center is left upper corner of the square P_{center} in P. Notice that if π is a short weak period of the pattern P and x is a position of the left upper corner of P_{center} in P then the square P_{center} occurs in P at position $x + \pi$ inside $\mathcal{W}$ and π is a period (not necessarily short) of P_{center}. We use the linear time algorithm from the previous section to search P_{center} inside the pattern P in the window $\mathcal{W}$ (this can be done since P_{center} has been already processed). If there is no occurrence of P_{center} in $\mathcal{W}$ then P is nonperiodic. If all occurrences lie on one line then the pattern is either nonperiodic or line periodic and the direction of the periods is the direction of the line. In that case, by Lemma 7, the periodicity of P can be computed in linear time and constant space. If not all occurrences of the square lie on one line then the square P_{center} has two (not necessarily short with respect to P_{center}) periods in different directions and therefore the central part of it is a part of a lattice. Starting from the center of P (which is also the center of P_{center}) we check how far this lattice can be extended in P. If it extends to the whole pattern then the pattern is lattice periodic. Let a *defect* be a point which "breaks" lattice periodicity of the center of P_{center}. If there are no defects outside opposite $2c \cdot m \times 2c \cdot m$ square corners of the pattern then the pattern is radiant periodic.

Otherwise, the pattern is either line periodic in a direction α or nonperiodic. We describe briefly how to find a potential direction α. Once we find it, we use Lemma 7. Consider a quadrant of P containing two defects one of them lying outside its corner square, if there is no such quadrant then P is nonperiodic. Assume it is the left upper quadrant of P. Consider its $\frac{m}{2} \times \frac{m}{2}$ frame Θ of thickness $c \cdot m$. Denote by A, B left upper and right bottom $c \cdot m \times c \cdot m$ corner squares of the quadrant. Denote by C, D connected parts of Θ that result from Θ after removing parts A, B. If there are no defects inside Θ then P is nonperiodic.

If any defect from outside of A lies in C then we divide Θ into two parts, C with B, and D with A, otherwise we divide it in parts, C with A, and D with B. Denote these parts by C', D'. If one of them contains no defects then P is nonperiodic. Otherwise, we say that a line $\mathcal{L}$ is a *defect line* (*d_line* for short) iff it contains defects in C' and D'. Denote by D_LINES the set of all *d_lines*. Notice that there is exactly one line $\mathcal{L} \in D\_LINES$ such that all defects in Θ lie on the same side of $\mathcal{L}$ (as the left upper corner of Θ). Denote it by $d\_line(\Theta)$. This line is a tangent to the convex hulls of defects from each part of Θ.

Claim 9 *If the pattern is line periodic in a direction α then α is parallel to $d\_line(\Theta)$.*

Proof. Denote by P_LINES the set of lines crossing Θ and containing defects whose direction is the direction of periods. If $\mathcal{L} \in P\_LINES$ then there are defects on $\mathcal{L}$ which are inside Θ. Let $\mathcal{L}$ be the closest line to the center of the pattern among lines in P_LINES. Then $\mathcal{L}$ is a *d_line* and $\mathcal{L} = d\_line(\Theta)$. This completes the proof of the claim.

A line $d\_line(\Theta)$ can be found in $O(M)$ time and constant space by an algorithm which finds its successive approximations. We omit the details. Having the direction we check if the pattern is line periodic in this direction, applying algorithm used in Lemma 7. This completes the proof.

Theorem 10. *The pattern preprocessing can be done in linear time and logarithmic space.*

Proof. In the preprocessing we have first to find a *nonperiodic part* P' of P. If P is a nonperiodic pattern or a frame then *nonperiodic part* means *truncate*(P) or nonperiodic subframe (if P is a frame). If P is periodic then nonperiodic part consists of two nonperiodic corners (in radiant-periodic case), central nonperiodic part (in lattice-periodic case) or a double pattern D which contains two stripes (in line-periodic case). The computation has a recursive structure and informally can be described as follows.

- Preprocess recursively the central subpattern P_{center};
- Compute the *periodicity* of P in time $O(T_{center}(M))$;

- Find the *nonperiodic part* P' of P;
- Preprocess recursively P'.

The total size of P' is bounded by $c'' \cdot M$ and the total size of P_{center} is bounded by $c' \cdot M$. Hence the time complexity $T_{pre}(M)$ to preprocess an object of total size M satisfies the following inequality:

$$T_{pre}(M) \leq T_{pre}(c' \cdot M) + T_{pre}(c'' \cdot M) + T_{center}(M) + O(M);$$

We choose c', c'' such that $c' + c'' < 1$, $T_{center}(M) = O(M)$. This implies that $T_{pre}(M) = O(M)$. The stack of the recursion is of logarithmic size, so the additional memory is $O(\log m)$. The details are omitted.

References

1. A. Amir and G. Benson, Two dimensional periodicity and its applications, *Proc. 3rd ACM-SIAM SODA'92*, p.440-452.
2. A. Amir, G. Benson and M. Farach, Alphabet independent two dimensional matching, *Proc. 24th ACM STOC'92*, p.59-68.
3. A. Amir, G. Benson and M.Farach, Optimal parallel two dimensional pattern matching, *Proc. 5th ACM SPAA'93*, p.79-85.
4. T. J. Baker, A technique for extending rapid exact-match string matching to arrays of more than one dimension, *SIAM J. Comp.* 7 (1978), p.533-541.
5. R. S. Bird, Two dimensional pattern matching, *Inf. Proc. Letters* 6, (1977) p.168-170.
6. R. Cole, M. Crochemore, Z. Galil, L. Gąsieniec, R. Hariharan, S. Muthukrishnan, K. Park and W. Rytter, Optimally fast parallel algorithms for preprocessing and pattern matching in one and two dimensions, *Proc. 34th IEEE FOCS'93*, p.248-258.
7. M. Crochemore, String matching for ordered alphabets, *TCS* 92 (1992), p.225-251.
8. M. Crochemore and D. Perrin, Two-way string matching, *JACM* 38:3 (1991), p.651-675.
9. M. Crochemore, L. Gąsieniec and W. Rytter, Two-dimensional pattern matching by sampling, *IPL* 46 (1993), p.159-162.
10. M. Crochemore and W. Rytter, A version of Galil-Park two-dimensional matching, *Report IGM* 94-05, Universite Marne la Valle (1994).
11. Z. Galil and K. Park, Truly alphabet independent two dimensional matching, *Proc. 33th IEEE FOCS'92*, (1992) p.247-256.
12. Z. Galil and J. Seiferas, Time-space optimal string matching, *J. Comp. Syst. Sc.* 26 (1983), p.280-294.
13. L. Gąsieniec, W. Plandowski and W. Rytter, The zooming method: a recursive approach to time-space efficient string-matching, *TCS*, to appear.
14. U. Vishkin, Deterministic sampling - a new technique for fast pattern matching, *SIAM J. Comput.* 20 (1991), p. 22-40.

On-line and Dynamic Algorithms for Shortest Path Problems *

Hristo N. Djidjev[1], Grammati E. Pantziou[2] and Christos D. Zaroliagis[3]

[1] Computer Science Dept, Rice University, P.O. Box 1892, Houston, TX 77251, USA
[2] Computer Science Dept, University of Central Florida, Orlando FL 82816, USA
[3] Max-Planck Institut für Informatik, Im Stadtwald, 66123 Saarbrücken, Germany

Abstract. We describe algorithms for finding shortest paths and distances in a planar digraph which exploit the particular topology of the input graph. An important feature of our algorithms is that they can work in a dynamic environment, where the cost of any edge can be changed or the edge can be deleted. Our data structures can be updated after any such change in only polylogarithmic time, while a single-pair query is answered in sublinear time. We also describe the first parallel algorithms for solving the dynamic version of the shortest path problem.

1 Introduction

There has been a growing interest in dynamic graph problems in the recent years [1, 9, 17, 24, 28]. The goal is to design efficient data structures that not only allow one to give fast answers to a series of queries, but that can also be easily updated after a modification of the input data. Such an approach has immediate applications to a variety of problems (see e.g. [3, 31, 32]).

Let G be an n-vertex digraph with real valued edge costs but no negative cycles. The *length* of a path p in G is the sum of the costs of all edges of p and the *distance* between two vertices v and w of G is the minimum length of a path between v and w. The path of minimum length is called a *shortest path* between v and w. Finding shortest path information in graphs is an important and intensively studied problem with many applications. Recent papers [4, 6, 11, 12, 13, 16, 21, 25, 27] investigate the problem for different classes of input graphs and models of computation. All of the above-mentioned results, however, relate to the static version of the problem, i.e. the graph and the costs on its edges do not change over time. In contrast, we consider here a *dynamic environment*, where edges can be deleted and their costs can be modified. More precisely, we investigate the following *on-line and dynamic shortest path problem*: given G (as above), build a data structure that will enable fast on-line shortest path or distance queries. In case of edge deletion or edge cost modification of G, update the data structure in an appropriately short time.

The dynamic version of the shortest paths problem has a lot of applications. A dynamic algorithm for the shortest path problem can be used to dynamically maintain

---

* This work was partially supported by the EC ESPRIT Basic Research Action No. 7141 (ALCOM II), by the EC Cooperative Action IC-1000 (project AL-TEC) and by the NSF grants No. CDA-9211155 and No. CCR-9409191. Email: hristo@cs.rice.edu, pantziou@cs.ucf.edu, zaro@mpi-sb.mpg.de.

a maximum st-flow in a planar network [19], a feasible flow between multiple sources and sinks, as well as a bipartite perfect matching in planar graphs [26]. Dynamic algorithms for shortest paths appear also to be fundamental procedures in incremental computations for data flow analysis and interactive systems design [29, 32].

There are a few previously known algorithms for the dynamic shortest path problem. For general digraphs, the best previous algorithms in the case of updating the data structure after edge insertions/deletions were due to [8] and require $O(n^2)$ update time after an edge insertion and $O(n^2 \log n)$ update time after an edge deletion. Some improvements of these algorithms have been achieved in [1] with respect to the amortized cost of a sequence of edge insertions, if the edge costs are integers. Also the recent results of [23] for single-source shortest paths in planar digraphs (along with other techniques) lead to dynamic algorithms for shortest paths in planar digraphs with integral edge costs. However, the preprocessing as well as the update and query time bounds are superlinear. For example, the time for a query or an update operation is $O(n^{9/7} \log n)$. In the case of planar digraphs with real edge costs the best dynamic algorithms are due to [10]. The preprocessing time and space is $O(n \log n)$ ($O(n)$ space can be achieved, if the computation is restricted to finding distances only.) A single-pair query can be answered in $O(n)$ time, while a single-source query takes $O(n\sqrt{\log \log n})$ time. An update operation to this data structure, after an edge cost modification or deletion, can be performed in $O(\log^3 n)$ time. In parallel (NC) computation we are not aware of any previous results related to dynamic structures for maintaining shortest path information in the case of edge cost updates. On the other hand, efficient data structures for answering very fast on-line shortest path or distance queries for the sequential and the parallel models of computation have been proposed in [6, 14], but they do not support dynamization.

In this paper, we give efficient algorithms for solving the on-line and dynamic shortest path problem in planar digraphs which are parameterized in terms of a topological measure q of the input digraph. Our main result is the following (Section 4): *Given an n-vertex planar digraph G with real-valued edge costs but no negative cycles, there exists an algorithm for the on-line and dynamic shortest path problem on G that supports edge cost modification and edge deletion with the following performance characteristics: (i) preprocessing time and space $O(n + q \log q)$; (ii) single-pair distance query time $O(q + \log n)$; (iii) single-pair shortest path query time $O(L + q + \log n)$ (where L is the number of edges of the path); (iv) single-source shortest path tree query time $O(n + q\sqrt{\log \log q})$; (v) update time (after an edge cost modification or edge deletion) $O(\log n + \log^3 q)$. In the case where the computation is restricted to finding distances only the space can be reduced to $O(n)$.*

Here q is a topological measure of the input planar digraph G introduced by Frederickson in [12, 13] which is proportional to the cardinality of a minimum number of faces covering all vertices of G (among all embeddings of G in the plane). Note that q can be as small as 1 and is always strictly smaller than n in the worst-case. Hence, our results are improvements over the best previous ones in all cases where $q = o(n)$, i.e. in all cases where G has nice topological properties. As an example, consider outerplanar digraphs ($q = 1$), or planar digraphs which satisfy the k-interval property ($k \ll n$ and $q = k$) as they are defined in [15]. Another class of graphs with important applications are the graphs describing global area networks. Typically such graphs can be represented as a tree plus a small number of non-tree edges and thus have a small value of q. In the case where G is outerplanar our preprocessing time and space are optimal (linear) and the distance query and the update time are logarithmic. (Similar results have been achieved independently in [2].) Our algorithms provide a simple direct solution compared with the algorithms in [13, 14] which are not dynamic and were based on manipulations with compact routing tables.

Our solution is based on the following ideas: (a) The input planar digraph is decomposed into a number, $O(q)$, of outerplanar subgraphs (called *hammocks*) satisfying certain separator conditions [13, 27]. (b) A decomposition strategy based on graph separators is employed for the efficient solution of the problem for the case of *outerplanar* digraphs (Section 2). (c) A data structure is constructed during the decomposition of the outerplanar digraph and is updated after each edge cost modification or edge deletion (Section 3). This data structure contains information about the shortest paths between properly chosen $\Theta(n)$ pairs of vertices. It also has the property that the shortest path between any pair of vertices is a composition of $O(\log n)$ of the predefined paths and that any edge of the graph belongs to $O(\log n)$ of those paths (n is the size of the outerplanar digraph).

Our algorithms can detect a negative cycle, either if it exists in the initial digraph, or if it is created after an edge cost modification. Although our algorithms do not directly support edge insertion, they are so fast that even if the preprocessing algorithm is run from scratch after any edge insertion, they still provide better performance compared with [8]. Moreover, our algorithms can support a special kind of edge insertion, called edge *re-insertion*. That is, we can insert any edge that has previously been deleted within the resource bounds of the update operation. An efficient parallelization, as well as other extensions of our results are discussed in Section 5. Due to lack of space some proofs are omitted, but can be found in the full paper [7].

2 Preliminaries

Let $G = (V(G), E(G))$ be a connected planar n-vertex digraph with real edge costs but no negative cycles. A *separation pair* is a pair (x, y) of vertices whose removal divides G into two disjoint subgraphs G_1 and G_2. We add the vertices x, y and the edges $\langle x, y \rangle$ and $\langle y, x \rangle$ to both G_1 and G_2. Let $0 < \alpha < 1$ be a constant. An α-*separator* S of G is a pair of sets $(V(S), D(S))$, where $D(S)$ is a set of separation pairs and $V(S)$ is the set of the vertices of $D(S)$, such that the removal of $V(S)$ leaves no connected component of more than αn vertices. We will call the separation vertices (pairs) of S that belong to any such resulting component H and separate it from the rest of the graph separation vertices (pairs) *attached to* H. It is well known that if G is outerplanar then there exists a 2/3-separator of G which is a single separation pair. Also, given an n-vertex outerplanar digraph G_{op} and a set M of vertices of G_{op}, *compressing* G_{op} *with respect to* M means constructing a new outerplanar digraph of $O(|M|)$ size that contains M and such that the distance between any pair of vertices of M in the resulting graph is the same as the distance between the same vertices in G_{op} [13]. (In our algorithms the size of M will be $O(1)$.)

Definition 1. Let G_{op} be an outerplanar digraph and S be an α-separator of G_{op} that divides G_{op} into connected components one of which is G. Let $p = (p_1, p_2)$ be a separation pair of G. Construct a graph $SR(G)$ as follows: divide G into two subgraphs by using p as a separation pair, compress each resulting subgraph K with respect to $(V(S) \cup \{p_1, p_2\}) \cap V(K)$, and join the resulting graphs at vertices p_1, p_2. We call $SR(G)$ the *sparse representative* of G.

A *hammock decomposition* of G is a decomposition of G into certain outerplanar digraphs called *hammocks*. This decomposition is defined with respect to a given set of faces that cover all vertices of G. Let q be the minimum number of such faces (among all embeddings of G). It has been proved in [13, 27] that a planar digraph G can be decomposed into $O(q)$ hammocks either in $O(n)$ sequential time, or in $O(\log n \log^* n)$ parallel time and $O(n \log n \log^* n)$ work on a CREW PRAM. Also, by [12, 21], we have that an embedding of G does not need to be provided by the input in order to compute a hammock decomposition of $O(q)$ hammocks. Hammocks satisfy the following properties: (i) each hammock has at most *four* vertices in common with any other hammock (and therefore with the rest of the graph) called *attachment vertices*; (ii) the hammock decomposition spans all the edges of G, i.e. each edge belongs to exactly one hammock; and (iii) the number of hammocks produced is the minimum possible (within a constant factor) among all possible decompositions.

In the sequel, we can assume w.l.o.g. that G_{op} is a biconnected n-vertex outerplanar digraph. Note that if G_{op} is not biconnected we can add an appropriate number of additional edges of very large costs in order to convert it into a biconnected outerplanar digraph (see [13, 27]).

2.1 Constructing a separator decomposition

We describe an algorithm that generates a decomposition of G_{op} (by finding successive separators in a recursive way) that will be used in the construction of a suitable data structure for maintaining shortest path information in G_{op}. Our goal will be that, at each level of recursion, (i) the sizes of the connected components resulting after the deletion of the previously found separator vertices are appropriately small, and (ii) the number of separation vertices attached to each resulting component is $O(1)$. The following algorithm finds such a partitioning and constructs the associated *separator tree*, $ST(G_{op})$, used to support binary search in G_{op}. Let in the algorithm below G denote a subgraph of G_{op} (initially $G := G_{op}$).

ALGORITHM Sep_Tree($G, ST(G)$)

   1. If $|V(G)| \leq 4$, then halt. Else let S denote the set of separation pairs in G_{op} found during all previous iterations. (Initially $S = \emptyset$.) Let n_{sep} denote the number of separation pairs of S attached to G.

   1.1. If $n_{sep} \leq 3$, then let $p = \{p_1, p_2\}$ be a separation pair of G that divides G into two subgraphs G_1 and G_2 with no more than $2n/3$ vertices each.

   1.2. Otherwise ($n_{sep} > 3$), let $p = \{p_1, p_2\}$ be a separation pair that separates G into subgraphs G_1 and G_2 each containing no more than $2/3$ of the number of separation pairs attached to G.

   2. Add p to S and run this algorithm recursively on G_i for $i = 1, 2$. Create a separator tree $ST(G)$ rooted at a new node v associated with p and G, and whose children are the roots of $ST(G_1)$ and $ST(G_2)$.

Observe that the nodes of $ST(G_{op})$ are associated with subgraphs of G_{op} which we will call *descendant subgraphs* of G_{op}. With each descendant subgraph a distinct separation pair is associated. From the description of the algorithm, it follows that:

Lemma 2. *Any descendant subgraph G of G_{op} at level i in $ST(G_{op})$ has no more than 4 separation pairs attached to it and the number of its vertices is no more than $(2/3)^i n$.*

Algorithm Sep_Tree can be easily implemented to run in $O(n \log n)$ time and $O(n)$ space. Using the dynamic tree data structure of [30] and working on the dual graph of G_{op} (which is a tree), we can show the following [7]:

Lemma 3. *Algorithm Sep_Tree(G_{op}, $ST(G_{op})$) can be implemented to run in $O(n)$ time and space. The depth of the resulting separator tree $ST(G_{op})$ is $O(\log n)$.*

3 Dynamic Algorithms for Outerplanar Digraphs

In this section we will give algorithms for solving the on-line and dynamic shortest path problem for the special case of outerplanar digraphs. We will use these algorithms in Section 4 for solving shortest path problems for general planar digraphs. Throughout this section we denote by G_{op} an n-vertex biconnected outerplanar digraph.

3.1 The data structures and the preprocessing algorithm

The data structures used by our algorithms are the following:

(I) The separator tree $ST(G_{op})$. Each node of $ST(G_{op})$ is associated with a descendant subgraph G of G_{op} along with its separation pair as determined by algorithm Sep_Tree and also contains a pointer to the sparse representative $SR(G)$ of G.

(II) The sparse representative $SR(G)$ for all graphs G of $ST(G_{op})$. According to Definition 1, $SR(G)$ consists of the union of the compressed versions of G_1 and G_2 with respect to the separation pairs attached to G plus the separation pair dividing G, where G_1 and G_2 are the children of G in $ST(G_{op})$. Therefore the size of $SR(G)$ is $O(1)$. Note also that: (a) since the size of $SR(G)$ is $O(1)$, we can compute the distances between the vertices of $SR(G)$ in constant time; (b) for each leaf of $ST(G_{op})$ we have that $SR(G) \equiv G$, since in this case G is of $O(1)$ size.

In the following sections we will use the properties of the separator decomposition to show that the shortest path information encoded in the sparse representatives of the descendant subgraphs of G_{op} is sufficient to compute the distance between any 2 vertices of G_{op} in $O(\log n)$ time and that all sparse representatives can be updated after any edge cost modification also in $O(\log n)$ time. We next give an algorithm that constructs the above data structures in linear time.

ALGORITHM Pre_Outerplanar(G_{op})
1. Construct a separator tree $ST(G_{op})$ using algorithm Sep_Tree(G_{op}, $ST(G_{op})$).
2. Compute the sparse representative $SR(G_{op})$ of G_{op} as follows.
   for each child G of G_{op} in $ST(G_{op})$ **do**
(a) **if** G is a leaf of $ST(G_{op})$ **then** $SR(G) = G$
   else find $SR(G)$ by running Step 2 recursively on G.
(b) Construct the sparse representative of G_{op} as described in Definition 1 by using the sparse representatives of the children of G_{op}.

Lemma 4. *Algorithm Pre_Outerplanar(G_{op}) runs in $O(n)$ time and uses $O(n)$ space.*

Proof. Step 1 needs $O(n)$ time and space by Lemma 3. Let $P(n)$ be the maximum time required by Step 2. Then $P(n)$ satisfies the recurrence $P(n) \leq \max\{P(n_1) + P(n_2) \mid n_1 + n_2 = n, \ n_1, n_2 \leq 2n/3\} + O(1), \ n > 1$, which has a solution $P(n) = O(n)$. The space required is proportional to the size of $ST(G_{op})$ since each sparse representative has $O(1)$ size. Therefore the space needed for the above data structures is $O(|ST(G_{op})|) = O(n)$. The bounds follow. $\qquad\square$

3.2 The single-pair query algorithm

We will first briefly describe the idea of the query algorithm for finding the distance between any two vertices v and z of G_{op}. The algorithm proceeds as follows. First search $ST(G_{op})$ to find a descendant subgraph G of G_{op} such that the separation pair $p = (p_1, p_2)$ associated with G separates v from z. Let $d(v, z)$ denote the distance between v and z. Then obviously

$$d(v, z) = \min\{d(v, p_1) + d(p_1, z), d(v, p_2) + d(p_2, z)\}. \tag{1}$$

Hence, it suffices to compute the distances $d(v, p_1)$, $d(p_1, z)$, $d(v, p_2)$ and $d(p_2, z)$. In order to do this we will need the shortest path information encoded in the sparse representatives.

Now we will analyze how one can use the information the sparse representatives provide. Let $s = (s_1, s_2)$ be any separation pair attached to G. Let s divide some descendant subgraph H of G_{op} into subgraphs H_1 and H_2 where H_1 has no other common vertices with G except for s_1 and s_2. If H is an ancestor of G in $ST(G_{op})$, we call s an *ancestor* separation pair of G and if H is a parent of G, we call s a *parent* separation pair of G. The distance from s_1 to s_2 in $SR(G)$ is, by the preprocessing algorithm, equal to the distance between s_1 and s_2 in G. However, the distance from s_1 to s_2 in G might be different from the distance between these vertices in G_{op}, if s is an ancestor separation pair. (If s is not an ancestor separation pair the distances are the same.) Note that G can have more than one ancestor separation pair, but only one parent separation pair (if $G \neq G_{op}$).

Assume that $G \neq G_{op}$. Denote by $M(G)$ the set of the parent separation pairs of all descendant subgraphs of G_{op} that are ancestors of G in $ST(G_{op})$ (including G). Then $M(G)$ contains all ancestor separation pairs of G. Let $D(G)$ be the set of all distances $d(x_1, x_2)$ and $d(x_2, x_1)$ in G_{op}, where (x_1, x_2) is a separation pair in $M(G)$. Then $D(G)$ can be found by the following algorithm.

ALGORITHM Parent_Pairs(G)
1. Let G' be the parent of G in $ST(G_{op})$. If $G' = G_{op}$ then $D(G') := \emptyset$; otherwise compute recursively $D(G')$ by this algorithm.
2. Find $d(s_1', s_2')$ and $d(s_2', s_1')$ in G_{op} by using $SR(G')$ and the information in $D(G')$, where (s_1', s_2') is the separation pair associated with G'. Set $D(G) := D(G') \cup \{d(s_1', s_2'), d(s_2', s_1')\}$.

Note that by the above discussion $D(G)$ contains the distances in G_{op} between the vertices of all ancestor separation pairs attached to G. The time complexity of Algorithm Parent_Pairs is clearly $O(\log n)$. Thus Algorithm Parent_Pairs can be used to compute in $O(\log n)$ time the distances in G_{op} between the pairs of vertices of all ancestor separation pairs attached to G so that one can ignore the rest of G_{op} when computing distances in G.

Next we describe the query algorithm. Let v' be a vertex that belongs to the same descendant subgraph of G_{op} that is a leaf of $ST(G_{op})$ and that contains v. Let $p(v)$ be the pair of vertices v, v'. Similarly define a pair of vertices $p(z)$ that contains z and a vertex z' which belongs to the leaf of $ST(G_{op})$ containing z. For any two pairs p' and p'' of vertices, let $D(p', p'')$ denote the set of all four distances in a vertex from p' to a vertex in p''. Then (1) shows that $D(p(v), p(z))$ can be found in constant time, given $D(p(v), p)$ and $D(p, p(z))$. The following recursive algorithm is based on the above fact.

ALGORITHM Dist_Query_Outerplanar(G_{op}, v, z)

1. Search $ST(G_{op})$ (starting from the root) to find pairs of vertices $p(v)$ and $p(z)$ as defined above.

2. Search $ST(G_{op})$ (starting from the root) to find a descendant subgraph G of G_{op} such that the separation pair p associated with G separates $p(v)$ and $p(z)$ in G.

3. Find the distances between the vertices of the ancestor separation pairs of G by Algorithm Parent_Pairs (if G has an ancestor separation pair).

4. Find $D(p(v), p)$ as follows:

4.1. Search $ST(G_{op})$ (starting from G) to find a descendant subgraph G' of G such that the separation pair p' associated with G' separates $p(v)$ and p in G'.

4.2. If G' is a leaf of $ST(G_{op})$, then determine $D(p(v), p')$ directly in constant time.

4.3. If G' is not a leaf then find $D(p(v), p')$ by executing Step 4 recursively with $p := p'$, $G := G'$, and then find $D(p(v), p)$ by using (1). Note that $D(p', p)$ can be taken from $SR(G')$.

5. Find $D(p, p(z))$ as in Step 4.

6. Use $D(p(v), p)$, $D(p, p(z))$, and (1) to determine $D(p(v), p(z))$.

Lemma 5. *Algorithm Dist_Query_Outerplanar(G_{op}, v, z) finds the distance   between any two vertices v and z of an n-vertex outerplanar digraph G_{op} in $O(\log n)$ time.*

Proof. The correctness follows from the description of the algorithm. Searching the tree $ST(G_{op})$ in Steps 1 and 2 takes in total $O(\log n)$ time by Lemma 3. Step 3 takes $O(\log n)$ time by the above analysis. Let $Q(l)$ be the maximum time necessary to compute $D(p(v), p)$, where l is the level of G in $ST(G_{op})$ and l_{max} is the maximum level of $ST(G_{op})$. Then from the description of the algorithm $Q(l) \leq Q(l+1) + O(1)$ for $l < l_{max}$, which gives $Q(l) = O(l) = O(\log n)$. Similarly, the time necessary for Step 5 is $O(\log n)$. Thus the total time needed by the algorithm is $O(\log n)$. $\quad\square$

Algorithm Dist_Query_Outerplanar can be modified in order to answer path queries. The additional work (compared with the case of distances) involves uncompressing the shortest paths corresponding to edges of the sparse representatives of the graphs from $ST(G_{op})$. Uncompressing an edge from a graph $SR(G)$ involves a traversal of a subtree of $ST(G_{op})$, where at each step an edge is replaced by two new edges each possibly corresponding to a compressed path. Obviously this subtree will have no more than L leaves, where L is the number of the edges of the output path. Then the traversal time can not exceed the number of the vertices of a binary tree with L leaves in which each internal node has exactly 2 children. Any such tree has $2L - 1$ vertices. Hence:

Lemma 6. *The shortest path between any two vertices v and z of an n-vertex outerplanar digraph G_{op} can be found in $O(\log n + L)$ time, where L is the number of edges of the path.*

3.3   The update algorithm

In the sequel, we will show how we can update our data structures for answering on-line shortest path and distance queries in outerplanar digraphs, in the case where an edge cost is modified. (Note that updating after an edge deletion is equivalent to the updating of the cost of the particular edge with a very large cost, such that this edge will not be used by any shortest path.) The algorithm for updating the cost of an edge e in an n-vertex outerplanar digraph G_{op} is based on the following idea: the edge will belong to at most $O(\log n)$ subgraphs of G_{op}, as they are determined by the Sep-Tree algorithm. Therefore, it suffices to update (in a bottom-up fashion) the sparse representatives of those subgraphs that are on the path from the subgraph G containing e (where G is a leaf of $ST(G_{op})$) to the root of $ST(G_{op})$. Let $parent(G)$ denote the parent of a node G in $ST(G_{op})$, and $\hat{G}$ denote the sibling of a node G in a $ST(G_{op})$. Note that $G \cup \hat{G} = parent(G)$ and $SR(G) \cup SR(\hat{G}) \supset SR(parent(G))$. The algorithm for the update operation is the following.

ALGORITHM Update_Outerplanar($G_{op}, e, w(e)$)
1. Find a leaf G of $ST(G_{op})$ for which $e \in E(G)$.
2. Update the cost of e in G with the new cost $w(e)$.
3. If e belongs also to $\hat{G}$ then update the cost of e in $\hat{G}$.
4. **While** $G \neq G_{op}$ **do**
      (a) Update $SR(parent(G))$ using the new versions of $SR(G)$ and $SR(\hat{G})$.
      (b) $G := parent(G)$.

Lemma 7. *Algorithm Update_Outerplanar updates after an edge cost modification the data structures created by the preprocessing algorithm in $O(\log n)$ time.*

3.4 Handling of negative cycles and summary of the results

The initial digraph G_{op} can be tested for existence of a negative cycle in $O(n)$ time by [21]. Assume now that G_{op} does not contain a negative cycle and that the cost $c(v, w)$ of an edge $\langle v, w \rangle$ in G_{op} has to be changed to $c'(v, w)$. We must check if this change does not create a negative cycle. We modify our algorithms in the following way. Before running the Update_Outerplanar algorithm, run the algorithm Dist_Query_Outerplanar to find the distance $d(w, v)$. If $d(w, v) + c'(v, w) < 0$, then halt and announce non-acceptance of this edge cost modification. Otherwise, continue with the original update algorithms. Clearly, the above procedures for testing the initial digraph and testing the acceptance of the edge cost modification do not affect the resource bounds of our preprocessing or of our update algorithm, respectively. Our results, in the case of outerplanar digraphs, can be summarized in the following theorem.

Theorem 8. *Given an n-vertex outerplanar digraph G_{op} with real-valued edge costs but no negative cycles, there exists an algorithm for the on-line and dynamic shortest path problem on G that supports edge cost modification and edge deletion with the following performance characteristics: (i) preprocessing time and space $O(n)$; (ii) single-pair distance query time $O(\log n)$; (iii) single-pair shortest path query time $O(L+\log n)$ (where L is the number of edges of the path); (iv) update time (after an edge cost modification or edge deletion) $O(\log n)$.*

4 Dynamic Algorithms for Planar Digraphs

The algorithms for maintaining all pairs shortest paths information in a planar digraph G are based on the hammock decomposition idea and on the algorithms of the previous section. Let q be the minimum cardinality of a hammock decomposition of G. The preprocessing algorithm for G is the following: (1) Find a hammock decomposition of G into $O(q)$ hammocks. (2) Run the algorithm Pre_Outerplanar(H) in each hammock H. (3) Compress each hammock H with respect to its attachment vertices. This results into a planar digraph G_q, which is of size $O(q)$. (4) Run the preprocessing algorithm of [10] in G_q. Let us call the above algorithm *Pre-Planar*. From the results in [10, 13], the discussion in Section 2 and Theorem 8, we have that algorithm Pre-Planar takes $O(n + q \log q)$ time and space.

The update algorithm is straightforward. Let e be the edge whose cost has been modified. There are two data structures that should be updated. The first one concerns the hammock H where e belongs to. This can be done by the algorithm Update-Outerplanar in $O(\log n)$ time. Note that this algorithm provides G_q with a new updated sparse representative of H, from which the compressed version of H (with respect to its attachment vertices) can be constructed in $O(1)$ time. The second data structure is that of the digraph G_q and can be updated in $O(\log^3 q)$ time by [10]. Therefore, the data structures created by algorithm Pre-Planar can be updated in $O(\log n + \log^3 q)$ time.

A single-pair query between any two vertices v and z can be answered as follows (using the above data structures). If v and z do not belong to the same hammock, then their distance $d(v, z) = \min_{i,j}\{d(v, a_i) + d(a_i, a'_j) + d(a'_j, z)\}$ where a_i and a'_j respectively are the attachment vertices of the hammocks in which v and z belong to. If both v and z belong to the same hammock H, then note that the shortest path between them does not necessarily have to stay in H. Hence, first compute (using algorithm Dist-Query-Outerplanar) their distance $d_H(v, z)$ inside H. After that compute $d_{ij}(v, z) = \min_{i,j}\{d(v, a_i) + d(a_i, a_j) + d(a_j, z)\}$. Clearly, $d(v, z) = \min\{d_H(v, z), d_{ij}(v, z)\}$. Since querying in G_q's data structure takes $O(q)$ time by [10] and querying in each hammock takes $O(\log n)$ time, we have that distance query takes $O(q + \log n)$ time in total. (A shortest path query can be computed similarly.)

The case of negative edge costs is handled in a similar way with that of outerplanar digraphs. Therefore, we have:

Theorem 9. *Let G be an n-vertex planar digraph with real-valued edge costs but no negative cycles and let q be the minimum cardinality of a hammock decomposition of G. There exists an algorithm for the on-line and dynamic shortest path problem on G that supports edge cost modification and edge deletion with the following performance characteristics: (i) preprocessing time and space $O(n + q \log q)$; (ii) single-pair distance query time $O(q + \log n)$; (iii) single-pair shortest path query time $O(L + q + \log n)$ (where L is the number of edges of the path); (iv) update time (after an edge cost modification or edge deletion) $O(\log n + \log^3 q)$. In the case where the computation is restricted to finding distances only, the space can be reduced to $O(n)$.*

5   Further Results

In this section we give other results following from our approach to the dynamic shortest path problem. We shall first discuss the parallel implementation of our algorithms on the CREW PRAM model of computation.

Using the dual graph of G_{op} (which is a tree) and standard techniques for computing functions in a tree (see e.g. [20], Chapter 3), we can implement the data structure from Theorem 8 in $O(\log n)$ time and $O(n \log n)$ work. The sequential distance query and the update algorithms for outerplanar digraphs are logarithmic, but the shortest path sequential query algorithm requires $O(L + \log n)$ time, where L is the number of edges of the path. We can find an optimal logarithmic-time parallel implementation of the shortest path query algorithm by the following observations. Algorithm

Dist_Query_Outerplanar determines in $O(\log n)$ time a subtree of $ST(G_{op})$ consisting of the descendant subgraphs of G_{op} that contain the path. This subtree has at most L leaves and size $O(L)$. Thus we can output the path in $O(\log n)$ time and $O(L)$ work.

In the case of planar digraphs we need a parallel algorithm to build the data structures in G_q (recall Section 4). We will make use of the following recent result of Cohen [4]: *In any q-vertex planar digraph J the shortest paths from s sources can be computed in $O(\log^2 q)$ time and $O(sq)$ work. A preprocessing phase is needed which takes $O(\log^3 q)$ time and $O(q^{1.5})$ work.* Note that J should be provided by a separator decomposition (i.e. a recursive decomposition of J using 2/3-separators of size $O(\sqrt{q})$), for the algorithm of [4] to be applied. Using the result of [18], such a decomposition for J is constructed in $O(\log^5 q)$ time using $O(q^{1+\epsilon})$ work, for any arbitrarily small $(1/2) > \epsilon > 0$. Furthermore, finding a hammock decomposition (Step 1 of algorithm Pre_Planar) takes $O(\log n \log^* n)$ time and $O(n \log n \log^* n)$ work by [27]. Combining these results with the ones discussed above for outerplanar digraphs and using the construction from Section 4 we have the following.

Theorem 10. *Let G be an n-vertex planar digraph with real-valued edge costs but no negative cycles and let q be the minimum cardinality of a hammock decomposition of G. There exists a CREW PRAM algorithm for the on-line and dynamic shortest path problem on G that supports edge cost modification and edge deletion with the following performance characteristics: (i) preprocessing time $O(\log n \log^* n + \log^5 q)$ and $O(n \log n \log^* n + q^{1.5})$ work, using $O(n + q^{1.5})$ space; (ii) distance query time $O(\log n + \log^2 q)$ and $O(\log n + q)$ work; (iii) shortest path query time $O(\log n + \log^2 q)$ and $O(\log n + q + L)$ work; and (iv) update time (after an edge cost modification or edge deletion) $O(\log n + \log^3 q)$ and $O(\log n + q^{1.5})$ work.*

Observe that we can cut the additive factors depending on q in both preprocessing and update bounds, at the expense of an additive factor of $O(q^{1.5})$ in the query work.

Another well-known version of the shortest path problem is to find a single-source shortest path tree rooted at a vertex v of a digraph G, i.e. find shortest paths between v and all other vertices in G. This problem can be solved by the same data structure and by using similar techniques with the ones described in Sections 3 and 4. We will first present the solution for the outerplanar case.

Let G_{op} be an outerplanar digraph. Let $U \subset V$ be a subset of $O(1)$ vertices of G_{op} with a weight $d_0(u)$ on any $u \in U$. For any vertex v of G_{op} the weighted distance $d(U, v)$ is defined by $d(U, v) = \min\{d_o(u) + d(u, v) | u \in U\}$. We assume that $d(U, v) = d_0(v)$ for every $v \in U$. The following algorithm computes $d(U, v), \forall v \in G_{op}$.

ALGORITHM Single_Source_Query_Outerplanar(G_{op}, U)

1. Let S be the 2/3-separator associated with the root G_{op} of $ST(G_{op})$. Compute $d(u, s)$ for all vertices $u \in U$ and $s \in S$ by using algorithm Dist_Query_Outerplanar.

2. For any $s \in S$ define $d_0(s) = \min\{d(u, s) | u \in U\} = d(U, s)$.

3. Run recursively Single_Source_Query_Outerplanar($G, (S \cup U) \cap G$), on each child subgraph G of G_{op} which is not a leaf of $ST(G_{op})$. (If G is a leaf, then distances are computed easily since the associated subgraph is of $O(1)$ size.)

The correctness of the algorithm follows easily from its description. Let $D(n)$ be the running time of the algorithm. Then, $D(n) \leq \max\{D(n_1) + D(n_2) \mid n_1 + n_2 = n, \ n_1, n_2 \leq 2n/3\} + O(|S| \cdot |U| \cdot \log n) = \max\{D(n_1) + D(n_2) \mid n_1 + n_2 = n, \ n_1, n_2 \leq 2n/3\} + O(\log n)$, which gives $D(n) = O(n)$.

Let v be any vertex of G_{op}. By running Single_Source_Query_Outerplanar($G_{op}, \{v\}$) with $d_0(v) = 0$, we can compute, in $O(n)$ time, all distances from v to every other vertex in G_{op}. Having the distances, it is not difficult to compute the single-source shortest path tree rooted at v in $O(n)$ time.

Using the above result and the methodology of Section 4, our data structures for planar digraphs can answer single-source shortest path tree queries, in $O(n + q\sqrt{\log\log q})$ time. It is not difficult to see that algorithm Single_Source_Query_Outerplanar can be implemented to run in $O(\log^2 n)$ time and $O(n)$ work on a CREW PRAM. Within the same resource bounds the shortest path tree can be also constructed.

The hammock decomposition technique can be extended to n-vertex digraphs G of genus $\gamma = o(n)$. We make use of the fact [12] that the minimum number q of hammocks is at most a constant factor times $\gamma + q'$, where q' is the minimum number of faces of any embedding of G on a surface of genus γ that cover all vertices of G. Note that the methods of [12, 21] do not require such an embedding to be provided by the input in order to produce the hammock decomposition in $O(q)$ hammocks. The decomposition can be found in $O(n + m)$ sequential time [12], or in $O(\log n \log \log n)$ parallel time and $O((n + m) \log n \log \log n)$ work on a CREW PRAM [21], where m is the number of the edges of G. The only other property of planar graphs that is relevant to our shortest path algorithms (as well as to the algorithms in [10]) is the existence of a 2/3-separator of size $O(\sqrt{n})$ for any planar n-vertex graph. For any n-vertex graph of genus $\gamma > 0$, a 2/3-separator of size $O(\sqrt{\gamma n})$ exists and such a separator can be found in linear time [5]. Furthermore, an embedding of G does not need to be provided by the input. (For the CREW PRAM implementation, such a separator should be provided with the input [4].) Thus the statement of Theorem 9 as well as its extensions discussed in this section, hold for the class of graphs of genus $\gamma = o(n)$.

References

1. G. Ausiello, G.F. Italiano, A.M. Spaccamela, U. Nanni, "Incremental algorithms for minimal length paths", *J. of Algorithms*, 12 (1991), pp.615-638.

2. H. Bondlaender, "Dynamic Algorithms for Graphs with Treewidth 2", *Proc. 19th WG'93*, LNCS 790, pp.112-124, Springer-Verlag, 1994.

3. M. Carroll and B. Ryder, "Incremental Data Flow Analysis via Dominator and Attribute Grammars", *Proc. 15th Ann. ACM POPL*, 1988.

4. E. Cohen, "Efficient Parallel Shortest-paths in Digraphs with a Separator Decomposition", *Proc. 5th ACM SPAA*, 1993, pp.57-67.

5. H. Djidjev, "A Linear Algorithm for Partitioning Graphs of Fixed Genus", SERDICA, Vol.11, 1985, pp.369-387.

6. H. Djidjev, G. Pantziou and C. Zaroliagis, "Computing Shortest Paths and Distances in Planar Graphs", *Proc. 18th ICALP'91*, LNCS 510, pp.327-339, Springer-Verlag.

7. H. Djidjev, G. Pantziou and C. Zaroliagis, "On-line and Dynamic Algorithms for Shortest Path Problems", Tech. Rep. MPI-I-94-114, Max-Planck-Institut für Informatik, April 1994.

8. S. Even and H. Gazit, "Updating distances in dynamic graphs", *Methods of Operations Research*, Vol.49, 1985, pp.371-387.

9. D. Eppstein, Z. Galil, G. Italiano and A. Nissenzweig, "Sparsification - A Technique for Speeding Up Dynamic Graph Algorithms", *Proc. 33rd FOCS*, 1992, pp.60-69.

10. E. Feuerstein and A.M. Spaccamela, "Dynamic Algorithms for Shortest Paths in Planar Graphs", *Theor. Computer Science*, 116 (1993), pp.359-371.

11. G.N. Frederickson, "Fast algorithms for shortest paths in planar graphs, with applications", *SIAM J. on Computing*, 16 (1987), pp.1004-1022.
12. G.N. Frederickson, "Using Cellular Graph Embeddings in Solving All Pairs Shortest Path Problems", *Proc. 30th IEEE Symp. on FOCS*, 1989, pp.448-453.
13. G.N. Frederickson, "Planar Graph Decomposition and All Pairs Shortest Paths", *J. ACM*, Vol.38, No.1, January 1991, pp.162-204.
14. G.N. Frederickson, "Searching among Intervals and Compact Routing Tables", *Proc. 20th ICALP'93*, LNCS 700, pp.28-39, Springer-Verlag.
15. G.N. Frederickson and R. Janardan, "Designing Networks with Compact Routing Tables", *Algorithmica*, 3(1988), pp.171-190.
16. M. Fredman and R. Tarjan, "Fibonacci heaps and their uses in improved network optimization algorithms", *JACM*, 34(1987), pp. 596-615.
17. Z. Galil and G. Italiano, "Fully Dynamic Algorithms for Edge-connectivity Problems", *Proc. 23rd ACM STOC*, 1991, pp.317-327.
18. H. Gazit and G. Miller, "A Parallel Algorithm for finding a Separator in Planar Graphs", *Proc. 28th IEEE Symp. on FOCS*, 1987, pp.238-248.
19. R. Hassin, "Maximum flow in (s, t)-planar networks", *IPL*, 13(1981), p.107.
20. J. JáJá, "An Introduction to Parallel Algorithms", Addison-Wesley, 1992.
21. D. Kavvadias, G. Pantziou, P. Spirakis and C. Zaroliagis, "Hammock-on-Ears Decomposition: A Technique for the Efficient Parallel Solution of Shortest Paths and Other Problems", *Proc. 19th MFCS'94*, LNCS 841, pp.462-472, Springer-Verlag.
22. D. Kavvadias, G. Pantziou, P. Spirakis and C. Zaroliagis, "Efficient Sequential and Parallel Algorithms for the Negative Cycle Problem", *Proc. 5th ISAAC'94*, LNCS 834, pp.270-278, Springer-Verlag.
23. P. Klein, S. Rao, M. Rauch and S. Subramanian, "Faster shortest-path algorithms for planar graphs", *Proc. 26th ACM STOC*, 1994, pp.27-37.
24. J.A. La Poutré, "Alpha-Algorithms for Incremental Planarity Testing", *Proc. 26th ACM STOC*, 1994, pp.706-715.
25. A. Lingas, "Efficient Parallel Algorithms for Path Problems in Planar Directed Graphs", *Proc. SIGAL'90*, LNCS 450, pp.447-457, 1990, Springer-Verlag.
26. G. Miller and J. Naor, "Flows in planar graphs with multiple sources and sinks", *Proc. 30th IEEE Symp. on FOCS*, 1991, pp.112-117.
27. G. Pantziou, P. Spirakis and C. Zaroliagis, "Efficient Parallel Algorithms for Shortest Paths in Planar Digraphs", *BIT* 32 (1992), pp.215-236.
28. M. Rauch, "Fully Dynamic Biconnectivity in Graphs", *Proc. 33rd IEEE Symp. on FOCS*, 1992, pp.50-59.
29. G. Ramalingan and T. Reps, "On the Computational Complexity of Incremental Algorithms", Technical Report, University of Wisconsin-Madison, 1991.
30. D. Sleator and R. Tarjan, "A Data Structure for Dynamic Trees", *Journal Comput. System Sci.* 26 (1983), pp. 362–391.
31. M. Yannakakis, "Graph Theoretic Methods in Database Theory", *Proc. ACM conference on Principles of Database Systems*, 1990.
32. D. Yellin and R. Strom, "INC: A language for incremental computations", *ACM Trans. Prog. Lang. Systems*, 13 (2), pp.211-236, April 1991.

On Compact Representations of Propositional Circumscription*

Marco Cadoli and Francesco M. Donini and Marco Schaerf

Dipartimento di Informatica e Sistemistica,
Università di Roma "La Sapienza",
Via Salaria 113, I-00198 Roma, Italy,
email: <lastname>@dis.uniroma1.it

Abstract. We prove that – unless the polynomial hierarchy collapses at the second level – the size of a purely propositional representation of the circumscription $CIRC(T)$ of a propositional formula T grows faster than any polynomial as the size of T increases. We then analyze the significance of this result in the related field of closed-world reasoning.

1 Introduction

Reasoning with selected (or intended) models of a logical formula is a common reasoning technique used in Databases, Logic Programming, Knowledge Representation and Artificial Intelligence (AI). One of the most popular criteria for selecting intended models is *minimality* wrt the set of true atoms. The idea behind minimality is to assume that a fact is false whenever possible. Such a criterion allows one to represent only true statements of a theory, saving the explicit representation of all false ones. For propositional theories, the explicit (and finite) representation is always possible; but how large is its size, compared with the size of the implicit representation?

In this paper we address the following problem:

Is it the case that for each propositional formula T, there is a "compact" propositional formula T' which represents exactly the minimal models of T? By compact we mean polynomially-sized wrt the size of T, for some fixed polynomial.

We are able give a negative answer to this problem.

1.1 Motivation

A well-established formalization of minimality is *circumscription*, which has been introduced in the AI literature [11] for capturing some important aspects of common-sense reasoning, and was shown to be strictly related to closed-world

---

* This work has been supported by the ESPRIT Basic Research Action N.6810 (COMPULOG 2) and by the *Progetto Finalizzato Sistemi Informatici e Calcolo Parallelo* of the CNR (Italian Research Council), *LdR "Ibridi"*.

reasoning in Databases. From the formal point of view, circumscription is a fragment of second-order logic, as circumscription of a first-order formula yields a second-order universal formula. The propositional version has also been defined: Circumscription of a propositional formula yields a universally quantified boolean formula.

Several studies about computational properties of circumscription appeared in the literature. Several aspects, such as time complexity of inference, model checking and model finding have been studied. Noticeably, those studies proved that reasoning with circumscriptive formulae is harder than reasoning with formulae of classical logic. As an example, inference in propositional circumscription is Π_2^p-complete [2], while the same problem is coNP-complete in classical propositional logic.

Another interesting computational aspect that has been addressed is *collapsibility*. The question can be stated as follows: Given a first-order formula T, is its circumscription $CIRC(T)$ – which is a second-order formula – equivalent to some first-order formula? The answer in general is no [7, 8], but there are syntactically restricted classes of formulae in which this is true [7, 10, 14].

As for the propositional case, collapsibility is not a problem at all: Given a propositional formula T we can easily write a propositional formula T' that is equivalent to $CIRC(T)$. A trivial way to do that is to make a disjunction of all the minimal models of T, as they are exactly the models of $CIRC(T)$. It's easy to see that such a process may generate an exponentially-sized representation of $CIRC(T)$, as T can have exponentially many minimal models. A smarter method would be to compute the *extended generalized closed world assumption* $EGCWA(T)$ of T, which is equivalent to $CIRC(T)$ [3, 15]. Syntactically, $EGCWA(T)$ is T plus a set of clauses, which constrain the models exactly to the minimal ones. Nevertheless the size of $EGCWA(T)$ may be exponential, as discussed in Section 4.

In this paper we prove that, unless the polynomial hierarchy collapses at the second level, as the size of T increases, the size of the explicit representation of $CIRC(T)$ grows faster than any polynomial. This result has several consequences. Suppose you have a knowledge base T and you want to pose it several different queries under circumscription. An (apparently) reasonable approach is to rewrite (off-line) the knowledge base into a propositional one T', equivalent to $CIRC(T)$, and then query (on-line) T'. This approach seems to move the complexity from on-line to off-line. Our result shows that, in general, this approach is not feasible and it does not make on-line reasoning any quicker, due to the super-polynomial increase in the size of the knowledge base.

While this is a negative result on circumscription, it has a positive side. In fact, our result also implies that circumscription is able to represent information in a very compact fashion: Imagine you have a certain amount of propositional knowledge to be represented; you may go for classical semantics or for circumscriptive semantics. Let A and B be the formulae you obtain, respectively (obviously $A \equiv CIRC(B)$ must hold). There are chances that the size of A is significantly bigger than the size of B.

1.2 Related work

The problem of compactability of the (collapsible) circumscription of first-order formulae has already been studied. It is noted in [7] that computing the first-order sentence equivalent to the circumscription of a first-order existential formula T is possible, but may increase the size of T exponentially. The question whether this is inherent to existential first-order formulae is left as an open problem.

Related work appears also in AI: A popular idea in this field is that of preprocessing a logical formula T to obtain a data structure in which fast algorithms for answering $T \models Q$ can be used. In general, one wants a *vivid* form of knowledge where reasoning is polynomially tractable [9]. An example of this kind is reported by Moses & Tennenholtz in [13]. In the paper they analyze the possibility of speeding up query answering in propositional logic (i.e. , checking whether $T \models Q$ holds) through a previous off-line transformation of the theory T. Abstractly, they want to transform a coNP-complete problem into a polynomial one (obviously not in polynomial time).

In the same spirit, our problem can be seen as an attempt at transforming a reasoning problem into a simpler one via off-line reasoning. In fact, if we are able to construct a polynomially-sized T' equivalent to $CIRC(T)$ then inference under circumscription (which is Π_2^p-complete [2]) is transformed into inference in propositional logic (which is coNP-complete). Similarly, model checking in circumscription (i.e. given a propositional theory T and an interpretation M decide whether $M \models CIRC(T)$, a coNP-complete problem [1]), is transformed into model checking in propositional logic (which is solvable in polynomial time). Therefore it is unlikely that the transformation from T to T' can be accomplished in polynomial time. In fact in this paper we do not impose any restriction on the time needed for the construction of T', which could even be a non-recursive process.

1.3 Main result

Corollary 8 of our main theorem is that – unless the polynomial hierarchy collapses at the second level – the size of a purely propositional representation of $CIRC(T)$ grows faster than any polynomial as the size of T increases. The major tools we use are: (1) the notion of *non-uniform* computation [4]; (2) a result proving that model checking in propositional circumscription is coNP-complete [1]; (3) a result proving that if NP is included in the class of problems solvable in non-uniform polynomial time, then the polynomial hierarchy collapses [5].

2 Preliminaries

The *alphabet* of a propositional formula is the set of all propositional atoms occurring in it. An *interpretation* of a formula is a truth assignment to the atoms of its alphabet. A *model* M of a formula T is an interpretation that satisfies T

(written $M \models T$). Interpretations and models of propositional formulae will be denoted as sets of atoms (those which are mapped into 1). Given a propositional formula T, we denote with $\mathcal{M}(T)$ the set of its models. Following Lifschitz [10], we define:

Definition 1. Let $M \in \mathcal{M}(T)$. M is called a *minimal* model of T if there is no model N of T such that $N \subset M$ (i.e., $N \not\equiv M$ and $N \subseteq M$.)

Definition 2. Let T be a propositional formula and $X = \{x_1, \ldots, x_n\}$ its alphabet. The *circumscription* $CIRC(T)$ is the following quantified boolean formula

$$T \wedge (\forall Y.T[Y] \rightarrow \neg(Y < X)) \tag{1}$$

where $Y = \{y_1, \ldots, y_n\}$ is a list of atoms disjoint from X, $T[Y]$ is T with all the occurrences of atoms of X substituted by the corresponding ones in Y. The meaning of $Y < X$ is defined in terms of the relation $\leq$. In particular $Y < X$ is $(Y \leq X) \wedge \neg(X \leq Y)$, and $Y \leq X$ stands for the conjunction of the formulae

$$y_i \rightarrow x_i \ (1 \leq i \leq n).$$

Proposition 3. (Lifschitz [10, Proposition 1]) *A model M of T is minimal iff it is a model of $CIRC(T)$, i.e. iff $M \models CIRC(T)$.*

More sophisticated definitions of minimal models and circumscription have been defined (e.g., not all atoms are minimized [3, Definition 3.1]). As such definitions are extensions of basic circumscription, the results we present in this paper hold for them.

Throughout this paper, the symbol $|x|$ denotes the size of x. As already pointed out, our proof uses the notion of non-uniform computations. We now briefly introduce the non-uniform classes needed in the sequel. Following Johnson [4] we define:

Definition 4. An *advice-taking Turing machine* is a Turing machine that has associated with it a special "advice oracle" A, one that is a (not necessarily recursive) function. On input x, a special "advice tape" is automatically loaded with $A(|x|)$ and from then on the computation proceeds as normal, based on the two inputs, x and $A(|x|)$.

Definition 5. An advice-taking Turing machine uses *polynomial* advice if its advice oracle A satisfies $|A(n)| \leq p(n)$ for some fixed polynomial p and all nonnegative integers n.

Definition 6. If C is a class of languages defined in terms of resource-bounded Turing machines, then C/poly is the class of languages defined by Turing machines with the same resource bounds but augmented by polynomial advice.

Any class C/poly is also known as non-uniform C. Non-uniformity is due to the presence of the advice. Notice that the advice is only function of the size of the input, not of the input itself. Throughout the paper, we will be interested in the class P/poly. Relations between non-uniform and uniform complexity classes, were studied in the literature, cf. e.g. [5, 16].

3 Main Result

In this section we prove that, unless the polynomial hierarchy collapses at the second level, there is no polynomial p such that for each propositional formula T, the shortest propositional formula representing exactly the minimal models of T has size less than $p(|T|)$. In order to achieve this result we first prove a stronger one based on the following idea:

Let p be a fixed polynomial; by doing some off-line computation, for any propositional formula T we want to find a data structure D_T with the following characteristics:

1. $|D_T| < p(|T|)$;
2. there exists a relation $ASK(\cdot, \cdot)$, such that given any interpretation M of T, $ASK(D_T, M)$ is true iff $M \not\models CIRC(T)$ (i.e. ASK computes the complement of model checking);
3. deciding the relation $ASK(\cdot, \cdot)$ is a problem in P, where the inputs are its arguments.

Intuitively, this means that we are trying to "compile" $CIRC(T)$ in such a way that the NP-complete problem of deciding $M \not\models CIRC(T)$ becomes a problem in P. One way to do that would be to rewrite $CIRC(T)$ into an equivalent propositional formula T' of size bounded by $p(|T|)$, where ASK corresponds to the complement of classical model checking, i.e. $ASK(T', M) = true$ iff $M \not\models T'$ (which can be checked in time polynomial wrt the size of M and T').

We are able to show that it is very unlikely that such a polynomial p and data structure D_T may exist. As a consequence, T' does not exist either. In order to prove it, we resort on the notion of non-uniform computation. In what follows a relation R such that deciding R is a problem in P will be called P-relation.

Theorem 7 (Main Theorem). *Let p be any polynomial. If for each CNF formula T there are a data structure D_T such that $|D_T| < p(|T|)$ and P-relation $ASK(\cdot, \cdot)$ such that given any interpretation M, $M \not\models CIRC(T)$ if and only if $ASK(D_T, M)$ is true, then $NP \subseteq P/poly$.*

Proof. Since the proof is rather long, we first give an outline to improve its readability. The proof consists of the following steps:

1. Choice of an NP-complete problem π;
2. Showing that for any integer n there exists a CNF formula T_n (depending only on n and of size polynomial wrt n) and for any instance F of π, with $|F| = n$, there exists an interpretation M_F such that $M_F \not\models CIRC(T_n)$ iff F is a "yes" instance of π;
3. Showing that if for each T_n there exists a D_{T_n} and a P-relation ASK with the required properties, then NP is contained in P/poly.

Step 1: We consider the standard NP-complete problem 3-SATISFIABILITY: Given an alphabet $X = \{x_1, \ldots, x_k, \ldots\}$, and a 3CNF formula F, of size n, containing literals from X, decide if F is satisfiable. Without loss of generality, we can assume that F contains, at most, the first n atoms $\{x_1, \ldots, x_n\}$.

Step 2: We show that for any integer n, there exists a 5CNF propositional formula T_n, depending only on n and of size polynomial wrt n, such that given any 3CNF formula F on alphabet $X = \{x_1, \ldots, x_n\}$, there exists an interpretation M_F such that F is satisfiable iff $M_F \not\models CIRC(T_n)$.

The proof uses a reduction showing that checking whether an interpretation is a minimal model of a propositional formula is coNP-complete. The key point is that we need to code every possible 3CNF formula on an alphabet of n atoms in a single formula T_n.

Let C be a set of new atoms, one for each three-literals clause over X, i.e., $C = \{c_i \mid \gamma_i$ is a three-literals clause of $X\}$. Moreover, let D be a set of new atoms in one-to-one correspondence with atoms of C. Finally, let the alphabet of T_n (denoted by L) be the set $X \cup C \cup D \cup \{u\}$, where u is a distinguished new atom. Notice that $|L| \in O(n^3)$.

We want to impose non-equivalence between atoms in C and their correspondent in D. The formula Σ_n is defined as:

$$\Sigma_n = \bigwedge_{c_i \in C} (c_i \vee d_i) \wedge (\neg c_i \vee \neg d_i).$$

Note that Σ_n is a 2CNF formula and that it contains $O(n^3)$ clauses.

Now we want to code every possible 3CNF formula over X, using the atoms in C as "enabling gates". The formula Γ_n is defined as:

$$\Gamma_n = \bigwedge_{c_i \in C} \gamma_i \vee \neg c_i.$$

Γ_n is a 4CNF formula and it contains $O(n^3)$ clauses.

We define T_n as:

$$T_n = \Sigma_n \wedge [(\Gamma_n \wedge \neg u) \vee (x_1 \wedge \cdots \wedge x_n \wedge u)] \tag{2}$$

Note that the size of T_n is $O(n^3)$, and T_n can be rewritten as an equivalent 5CNF formula. Moreover, T_n does not depend on a specific 3CNF formula F, but only on the size n of its alphabet.

Given a 3CNF formula F, we denote

$$C_F = \{c_i \in C \mid \gamma_i \text{ is a clause of } F\}$$

and similarly for D_F. Moreover, $\overline{C_F} = C - C_F$, and $\overline{D_F} = D - D_F$. We define the interpretation M_F as:

$$M_F = \{u\} \cup X \cup \{c \mid c \in C_F\} \cup \{d \mid d \in \overline{D_F}\}.$$

Note that $M_F \models T_n$, as $M_F \models \Sigma_n \wedge (x_1 \wedge \cdots \wedge x_n \wedge u)$. We prove our point by showing that F is satisfiable iff $M_F \not\models CIRC(T_n)$.

If part. We assume that $M_F \not\models CIRC(T_n)$, i.e. , there is a model $N \in \mathcal{M}(T_n)$ such that $N \subset M_F$. This implies that there is at least one atom $l \in L$ such that $l \in M_F$ and $l \notin N$. Since both M_F and N are models of Σ_n, it holds that $M_F \cap (C \cup D) \equiv N \cap (C \cup D)$. As a consequence, $l \notin C \cup D$ and $l \in \{u\} \cup X$, which in turn implies that $N \not\models (x_1 \wedge \cdots \wedge x_n \wedge u)$ and $N \models \Sigma_n \wedge (\Gamma_n \wedge \neg u)$. N must satisfy each clause $\gamma_i \vee \neg c_i$ of Γ_n. Let Φ be the set of clauses in Γ_n such that $c_i \in C_F$. As $N \models \Phi$ and $N \models c_i$ for each $c_i \in C_F$, it must be the case that $N \models \gamma_i$ for each clause $\gamma_i \vee \neg c_i$ of Φ, i.e. , $N \models F$. This concludes the proof that F is satisfiable, $N \cap X$ being one of its models.

Only if part. We assume that F is satisfiable. Let P be one of its models, i.e. , $P \subseteq X$ and $P \models F$. We define the interpretation N of T_n as:

$$N \equiv P \cup \{c \mid c \in C_F\} \cup \{d \mid d \in \overline{D_F}\}.$$

Note that $N \subset M_F$ and that $N \models F$. We now prove that N is a model of T_n, thus showing that $M_F \not\models CIRC(T_n)$. By definition $N \models \Sigma_n \wedge \neg u$, therefore it suffices to show that $N \models \Gamma_n$. Let Φ be the set of clauses $\gamma_i \vee \neg c_i$ of Γ_n such that $c_i \in C_F$. Let $\overline{\Phi}$ be the set of clauses $\gamma_i \vee \neg c_i$ of Γ_n such that $c_i \in \overline{C_F}$. As $N \models F$, it follows that $N \models \Phi$. As $N \models \neg c_i$ for each $c_i \in \overline{C_F}$, it follows that $N \models \overline{\Phi}$. Therefore $N \models \Gamma_n$ and the proof is concluded.

Step 3: Let us assume that there exists a polynomial p with the properties claimed in the statement of Theorem 7. Then, for each T_n there exists a data structure D_{T_n}, with $|D_{T_n}| < p(|T_n|)$, and a P-relation $ASK(\cdot, \cdot)$ such that given any interpretation M of T_n, $ASK(D_{T_n}, M)$ is true iff $M \not\models CIRC(T_n)$. We can define an advice-taking Turing machine solving satisfiability of 3CNF formulae in this way: given a generic 3CNF formula F, with $|F| = n$, the machine loads the advice D_{T_n}, computes M_F, and then decides $ASK(D_n, M_F)$ in polynomial time. Since $|T_n| = O(n^3)$, the advice D_{T_n} has polynomial size wrt n, hence we have shown that deciding satisfiability of 3CNF formulae is in non-uniform P. Therefore, an NP-complete problem belongs to P/poly, which implies that NP $\subseteq$ P/poly. $\square$

A proof with a similar structure was exhibited in [6]. The above theorem shows the unfeasibility, under certain conditions, of compiling the original circumscription so that the compiled version is more effective when performing model checking. Notice that no bound is imposed on the time spent in the compilation process. The result is conditioned on NP not being included in P/poly. As a matter of fact, if NP $\subseteq$ P/poly then Σ_2^p = PH, i.e. the polynomial hierarchy collapses at the second level [5, Theorem 6.1].

An immediate consequence of this result is the following corollary:

Corollary 8. *Let p be any polynomial. If for each propositional formula T over the alphabet L there is a formula T' over the same alphabet L, which is equivalent to $CIRC(T)$ and whose size is bounded by $p(|T|)$, then Σ_2^p = PH.*

The above corollary states that the size of any formula T' such that $T' \equiv CIRC(T)$ grows faster than any polynomial as the size of T increases. What happens if we give up logical equivalence "≡" and go for the weaker "query equivalence"? I.e., consider formulae T' over an extended alphabet such that $\{q \mid T' \models q\} = \{q \mid CIRC(T) \models q\}$ where q is any formula over the alphabet of T. Using a similar technique, we are able to prove that under slightly more restricted conditions (i.e. unless $\Sigma_4^p = \mathrm{PH}$) such a T' cannot have polynomial size.

Theorem 9. *Let p be any polynomial. If for each propositional formula T over the alphabet L there is a formula T' over an extended alphabet, whose size is bounded by $p(|T|)$, such that $\{q \mid T' \models q\} = \{q \mid CIRC(T) \models q\}$ where q is any formula over the alphabet L, then $\Sigma_4^p = \mathrm{PH}$.*

4 Analysis of the Result

In this section we analyze the impact of our result on a topic strictly related to circumscription, namely *closed-world reasoning*. Closed-world reasoning is a collection of ideas and definitions developed in the Database field for addressing the issue of reasoning using *lack* of information. Motivations for closed-world reasoning are very close in spirit to those behind circumscription. The main difference is that, while the circumscription of a propositional formula T is defined as a second-order formula (cf. (1)), making the closure of T amounts to add to T new propositional formulae according to some criterion (cf. (3)). Despite these syntactical differences, the two approaches are strictly related at the semantic level.

We first recall two different proposals of Closed-World Assumption (CWA): Generalized CWA (GCWA) and Extended Generalized CWA (EGCWA). Then we show how the proof of our main theorem can be used to define theories whose closure under EGCWA has super-polynomial size. Finally, we discuss the generality of our technique ("is it always possible to exploit intractability results to show incompressibility?") and take GCWA as an example of a closure which is compressible. The reason why compressibility of GCWA is interesting is that the two closures have similar time complexity: if T, q are propositional formulae and M is an interpretation, both testing $GCWA(T) \models q$ and $EGCWA(T) \models q$ are Π_2^p-hard problems, and both testing $M \models GCWA(T)$ and $M \models EGCWA(T)$ are coNP-hard problems.

4.1 Closed-World Reasoning

Generalized Closed World Assumption $GCWA(T)$ of a propositional formula T [12] is defined as follows (K is an atom and B is a clause – possibly empty – in which only positive literals occur):

$$T \cup \{\neg K \mid \forall B.\ T \not\models B \Rightarrow T \not\models B \vee K\}. \tag{3}$$

All models of $CIRC(T)$ are models of $GCWA(T)$, but not the other way around [12, Theorem 2].

A semantically more clear formalism for treatment of incomplete information is *Extended Generalized Closed World Assumption EGCWA(T)* [15]. Its definition is like (3), except that K is now an arbitrary conjunction of atoms. Such conjunctions are called "free-for-negation" for T. Observe that in a reasonable representation of $EGCWA(T)$, only minimal conjunctions of atoms need to be added to T, where a free-for-negation conjunction K is minimal iff any subconjunction of K is not free-for-negation. The models of $EGCWA(T)$ are exactly the models of $CIRC(T)$ [15], therefore Corollary 8 says that the size of $EGCWA(T)$ is likely not to be polynomial in $|T|$.

It is worth noting that $EGCWA(T)$ might be a much smarter representation of $CIRC(T)$ than listing all minimal models of T. As an example, let $a_1, \ldots, a_n, b_1, \ldots, b_n$ be distinct atoms and T be $(a_1 \vee b_1) \wedge \cdots \wedge (a_n \vee b_n)$. $EGCWA(T)$ is $T \wedge (\neg a_1 \vee \neg b_1) \wedge \cdots \wedge (\neg a_n \vee \neg b_n)$. The simple-minded representation of $CIRC(T)$ is the disjunction of all possible conjunctions $x_1 \wedge \cdots \wedge x_n \wedge \neg y_1 \wedge \cdots \wedge \neg y_n$, where for all i ($1 \leq i \leq n$), x_i is a member of $\{a_i, b_i\}$, and y_i is the other member. The latter representation has clearly exponential size.

4.2 Large Instances of EGCWA

We now see an infinite set of T where – even considering minimal free-for-negation conjunctions – the size of $EGCWA(T)$ is superpolynomial. Such a T is inspired by the one built in the proof of Theorem 7. This is, to the best of our knowledge, the first example proving that such a smart technique for representing propositional circumscription outputs, in the worst case, a theory of superpolynomial size.

We use the alphabets of atoms $X = \{x_1, \ldots, x_n\}$, $C = \{c_1^+, c_1^-, \ldots, c_n^+, c_n^-\}$, $D = \{d_1^+, d_1^-, \ldots, d_n^+, d_n^-\}$ and a new distinct atom u. We define a propositional formula T_n over these alphabets, with the help of two formulae Γ_n, Σ_n, which are analogous to Γ_n, Σ_n of Theorem 7. Let

$$\Gamma_n = \bigwedge\{x_i \vee \neg c_i^+ | 1 \leq i \leq n\} \wedge \bigwedge\{\neg x_i \vee \neg c_i^- | 1 \leq i \leq n\}$$

$$\Sigma_n = \bigwedge\{c_i^+ \neq d_i^+ | 1 \leq i \leq n\} \wedge \bigwedge\{c_i^- \neq d_i^- | 1 \leq i \leq n\}$$

$$T_n = \Sigma_n \wedge [(u \wedge x_1 \wedge \cdots \wedge x_n) \vee \Gamma_n]$$

Notice that the size of $X \cup C \cup D$ is $5n$, and the size of T_n is $O(n)$. Given a subset E of X, we define $C_E = \{c_i^+ | x_i \in E\} \cup \{c_i^- | x_i \notin E\}$, and similarly $D_E = \{d_i^+ | x_i \in E\} \cup \{d_i^- | x_i \notin E\}$. Moreover, let $\overline{D_E} = D - D_E = \{d_i^+ | c_i^+ \notin C_E\} \cup \{d_i^- | c_i^- \notin C_E\}$.

Proposition 10. *Let T_n be as above, and for any $E \subseteq X$ let $M_E = E \cup C_E \cup \overline{D_E}$. M_E is a minimal model of T_n.*

Proof. Since $M_E \cup C_E$ satisfies Γ_n, and $C_E \cup \overline{D_E}$ satisfies Σ_n, M_E is a model of T_n. Suppose $M \subset M_E$ is also a model of T_n, and let $M_C = M \cap C$, $M_D = M \cap D$, and $M_X = M \cap X$. Since M satisfies Σ_n, if $M_C \subset C_E$ then $M_D \supset D_E$, and vice versa if $M_D \subset D_E$ then $M_C \supset C_E$. Hence, $M_C = C_E$ and $M_D = D_E$. Therefore, it should be $M_X \subset E$, so let $x_i \in E - M_X$. By definition of C_E, $c_i^+ \in C_E$, hence the clause $x_i \vee \neg c_i^+$ is not satisfied by M, hence Γ_n is not satisfied. Since also the conjunction $u \wedge x_1 \wedge \cdots \wedge x_n$ is not satisfied, we conclude that any such M is not a model of T_n, therefore M_E is minimal. □

We exploit the previous property in the proof of our next theorem. To simplify notation, we denote with $\overline{D_E} \wedge u$ the formula obtained as a conjunction of all atoms in the set $\overline{D_E}$ and u.

Theorem 11. *Let E be any subset of X; then $\overline{D_E} \wedge u$ is a minimal free-for-negation formula for T_n.*

Proof. First of all, we show by contradiction that $\overline{D_E} \wedge u$ is free-for-negation: Assume there exists a minimal model M of T_n satisfying $\overline{D_E} \wedge u$. Now M must also satisfy $x_1, \ldots, x_n$, because otherwise M satisfies Γ_n, and $M - \{u\}$ would be a model, contradicting minimality of M. Therefore $M \supseteq \overline{D_E} \cup \{x_1, \ldots, x_n\} \cup \{u\}$.

Let $M_C = M \cap C$, $M_D = M \cap D$, so M can be partitioned as $M_C \cup M_D \cup \{x_1, \ldots, x_n\} \cup \{u\}$. Since M satisfies $\overline{D_E} \wedge u$, then $M_D \supseteq \overline{D_E}$. Then $M_C \subseteq C_E$, since M satisfies also Σ_n. Now let $N = E \cup M_C \cup M_D$. We show that N satisfies T_n. First, N satisfies Σ_n because it gives the same interpretation of M to literals in C and D. We now show that N satisfies each clause of Γ_n.

1. Let $x_i \in E$. Then the clause $x_i \vee \neg c_i^+$ is satisfied by N. By definition of C_E, $c_i^- \notin C_E$. Since $M_C \subseteq C_E$, also $c_i^- \notin M_C$. Hence the clause $\neg x_i \vee \neg c_i^-$ is satisfied too.
2. Let $x_i \notin E$. Then the clause $\neg x_i \vee \neg c_i^-$ is satisfied. By definition of C_E, this time $c_i^+ \notin C_E$, so $c_i^+ \notin M_C$. Hence the clause $x_i \vee \neg c_i^+$ is satisfied.

Since $N \subset M$, M is not minimal, contradicting the hypothesis. We conlude that $\overline{D_E} \wedge u$ is free-for-negation.

We now show that if we remove one conjunct from $\overline{D_E} \wedge u$, the resulting formula is not free-for-negation, thus showing that $\overline{D_E} \wedge u$ is a minimal free-for-negation formula.

First observe that if we remove u, then $\overline{D_E}$ (considered as a conjunction) is not free-for-negation because M_E satisfies it, and by Proposition 10 M_E is a minimal model. Secondly, we prove that if we take out a literal $d_i^- \in D$ from $\overline{D_E} \wedge u$ the resulting formula is not free-for-negation. In fact, let $M = (\overline{D_E} - \{d_i^-\}) \cup C_E \cup \{c_i^-\} \cup \{u\} \cup X$ be an interpretation satisfying the smaller conjunction. It holds that M satisfies Σ_n, hence M is also a model of T_n because it satisfies $u \wedge x_1 \wedge \cdots \wedge x_n$. We now show that M is also a minimal model of T_n, by proving that for any model N such that $N \subseteq M$, it results $N = M$. Since N satisfies Σ_n, if $N \cap C \subset M \cap C$ then $N \cap D \supset M \cap D$. Hence to be $N \subseteq M$, it must be $N \cap C = M \cap C$, and also $N \cap D = M \cap D$. Therefore N and M can differ at most on $X \cup \{u\}$. But notice that both c_i^+ and c_i^- belong to M, hence they belong to N too. Observe that Γ_n contains the two clauses $x_i \vee \neg c_i^+$ and $\neg x_i \vee \neg c_i^-$, which cannot be satisfied by N, for any possible interpretation of x_i. Hence N

cannot satisfy Γ_n. Therefore to satisfy T_n, N must satisfy $u \wedge x_1 \wedge \cdots \wedge x_n$. But this implies $N = M$. □

Since there are exponentially many subsets of X, there are also exponentially many distinct free-for-negation conjuncts. So $EGCWA(T_n)$ contains at least 2^n clauses $\neg K$, each clause having $n + 1$ disjuncts. Therefore $|EGCWA(T_n)|$ is $\Omega(n2^n)$, while $|T_n|$ is $O(n)$. Observe also that T_n could be rewritten as a 3CNF-formula (by distributing the conjunction $u \wedge x_1 \wedge \cdots \wedge x_n$ over Γ_n) having $O(n^2)$ clauses. Hence, even when T_n is in 3CNF, the above line of reasoning yields a super-polynomial lower bound for the size of $EGCWA(T_n)$.

4.3 Generality of Main Result

In Theorem 7 we used the reduction of an NP-hard problem – deciding whether $M \not\models CIRC(T)$ or not – to show that a polynomially-sized representation of $CIRC(T)$ is unlikely to exist, regardless of the effort we spend for doing the "compilation" of $CIRC(T)$. The technique employed readily applies to a much wider spectrum of reasoning problems in knowledge bases. In fact, we were able to extend our result to the explicit representations of disjunctive databases under the stable or well-founded semantics as extended by Przymusinski, skeptical reasoning in default logic and most operators of belief revision. However, the technique is not applicable to all reductions of NP-hard problems in knowledge representation. As an example, we now show that model checking under GCWA is coNP-hard, but the closure of a theory under GCWA has always a representation of polynomial size.

The reduction for GCWA rephrases the one showing that $M \not\models CIRC(T)$ is NP-hard. Given any formula F on alphabet $X = \{x_1, \ldots, x_n\}$, and another atom $u \notin X$, define $T = (F \wedge \neg u) \vee (u \wedge x_1 \wedge \cdots \wedge x_n)$. Let $M = \{u\} \cup X$. We can show that F is satisfiable iff $M \not\models GCWA(T)$. Hence model checking under GCWA is coNP-hard.

Nevertheless, there exists a simple polynomially-sized explicit representation of $GCWA(T)$: for every atom K, simply decide if $\neg K$ must be added or not to T, and if so add it. Hence, if T is fixed then $GCWA(T)$ can be "compiled", once and for all. Observe that this does not prove NP $\subseteq$ P/poly, since the compilation of $GCWA(T)$ depends on T itself, and not only on its size.

5 Conclusions and open problems

In this paper we have proven that, unless the polynomial hierarchy collapses at the second level, the size of the explicit representation of $CIRC(T)$ grows faster than any polynomial. This result has a negative side: It is unfeasible to (off-line) compile a knowledge base so that (on-line) reasoning under circumscription becomes easier. On the other side, our result implies that circumscription allows more compact representation of knowledge.

Some questions are left open by the above results:

1. whether it holds the converse of Theorem 7, i.e., that if NP $\subseteq$ P/poly then there is a compact representation of $CIRC(T)$ for all T's;
2. what happens if we take into account infinite alphabets?
3. why formalisms with similar time complexity (e.g., GCWA and EGCWA) have different compactability properties?

Acknowledgements The authors are grateful to Pierluigi Crescenzi for an interesting discussion on the non-uniform polynomial hierarchy.

References

1. M. Cadoli. The complexity of model checking for circumscriptive formulae. *Information Processing Letters*, 44:113–118, 1992.
2. T. Eiter and G. Gottlob. Propositional circumscription and extended closed world reasoning are Π_2^p-complete. *Theoretical Computer Science*, pages 231–245, 1993.
3. M. Gelfond, H. Przymusinska, and T. Przymusinsky. On the relationship between circumscription and negation as failure. *Artificial Intelligence Journal*, 38:49–73, 1989.
4. D. S. Johnson. A catalog of complexity classes. In J. van Leeuwen, editor, *Handbook of Theoretical Computer Science*, volume A, chapter 2. Elsevier Science Publishers (North-Holland), Amsterdam, 1990.
5. R. M. Karp and R. J. Lipton. Some connections between non-uniform and uniform complexity classes. In *Proc. of the 12th ACM Sym. on Theory of Computing (STOC-80)*, pages 302–309, 1980.
6. H. A. Kautz and B. Selman. Forming concepts for fast inference. In *Proc. of the 10th Nat. Conf. on Artificial Intelligence (AAAI-92)*, pages 786–793, 1992.
7. P. G. Kolaitis and C. H. Papadimitriou. Some computational aspects of circumscription. *Journal of the ACM*, 37(1):1–14, 1990.
8. T. Krishnaprasad. On the computability of circumscription. *Information Processing Letters*, 27:237–243, 1988.
9. H. J. Levesque. Making believers out of computers. *Artificial Intelligence Journal*, 30:81–108, 1986.
10. V. Lifschitz. Computing circumscription. In *Proc. of the 9th Int. Joint Conf. on Artificial Intelligence (IJCAI-85)*, pages 121–127, 1985.
11. J. McCarthy. Circumscription - A form of non-monotonic reasoning. *Artificial Intelligence Journal*, 13:27–39, 1980.
12. J. Minker. On indefinite databases and the closed world assumption. In *Proc. of the 6th Conf. on Automated Deduction (CADE-82)*, pages 292–308, 1982.
13. Y. Moses and M. Tennenholtz. Off-line reasoning for on-line efficiency. In *Proc. of the 13th Int. Joint Conf. on Artificial Intelligence (IJCAI-93)*, pages 490–495, 1993.
14. A. Rabinov. A generalization of collapsible cases of circumscription. *Artificial Intelligence Journal*, 38:111–117, 1989.
15. A. Yahya and L. J. Henschen. Deduction in non-Horn databases. *Journal of Automated Reasoning*, 1:141–160, 1985.
16. C. K. Yap. Some consequences of non-uniform conditions on uniform classes. *Theoretical Computer Science*, 26:287–300, 1983.

A set-theoretic translation method for (poly)modal logics*

Giovanna D'Agostino[1], Angelo Montanari[1,2], and Alberto Policriti[1]

[1] Dipartimento di Matematica e Informatica, Università di Udine
Via Zanon, 6 - 33100 Udine, Italy.
[2] ILLC, Universiteit van Amsterdam
Plantage Muidergracht, 24, 1018 TV Amsterdam, The Netherlands.

Abstract. The paper presents a *set-theoretic translation method* for polymodal logics that reduces the derivability problem of a large class of propositional polymodal logics to the derivability problem of a very weak first-order set theory Ω. Unlike most existing translation methods, the one we propose applies to any normal complete finitely-axiomatizable polymodal logic, regardless if it is first-order complete. Moreover, the finite axiomatizability of Ω makes it possible to implement mechanical proof search procedures via the deduction theorem or more specialized and efficient techniques. In the last part of the paper, we briefly discuss the application of *set T-resolution* to support automated derivability in (a suitable extension of) Ω.

1 Introduction

The paper deals with derivability in modal logic. Most inference systems for modal logic are defined in the style of sequent or tableaux calculi, e.g. [8]. As an alternative, a number of translation methods for modal logic into classical first-order logic have been proposed in the literature (for an up-to-date survey see [10]); such methods allow the use of Predicate Calculus mechanical theorem provers to implement modal theorem provers. Compared with the direct approach of finding a proof algorithm for a particular modal logic, the translation methods have the advantage of being *independent* from the modal logic under consideration: a single theorem prover may be used for any translatable modal logic.

In the simplest approach the first-order language L into which the translation is carried out contains a constant τ denoting the initial world in the frame, a binary relation $R(x, y)$ denoting the accessibility relation, and a denumerable amount of unary predicates $P_1(x), \ldots, P_n(x), \ldots$. The translation function π is defined by induction on the structure of the modal formula as follows:

$\pi(P_j, x) \equiv P_j(x)$; $\pi(-, x)$ commutes with the boolean connective;
$\pi(\Box\psi, x) \equiv \forall y(xRy \to \pi(\psi, y))$; $\pi(\Diamond\psi, x) \equiv \exists y(xRy \land \pi(\psi, y))$.

* This work has been supported by funds MURST 40% and 60%. The second author was supported by a grant from the Italian Consiglio Nazionale delle Ricerche (CNR).

Let H be a normal modal logic. H is *first-order complete* if there exists a first-order sentence Ax_H of L, involving only a binary relational symbol $R(x,y)$ and the equality symbol, such that a modal formula ϕ is derivable from H if and only if the formula ϕ is true in the initial world τ of all generated frames satisfying Ax_H. For these logics, $\vdash_H \phi$ if and only if $\vdash Ax_H \rightarrow \pi(\phi, \tau)$, where $\vdash$ stands for derivability in classical Predicate Calculus. Therefore, as long as we have Ax_H, at least in principle, a classical theorem prover can be used as a theorem prover for H.

Efficiency concerns have motivated further investigations on the above (relational) translation method. Such studies suggested a "functional" semantics for modal logic and resulted in a family of more efficient and general translation methods. For a normal modal logic H with a first-order semantics Ax_H, this method guarantees a sound and complete correspondence between satisfiability with respect to H and satisfiability with respect to first-order structures satisfying Ax_H. From the computational point of view, the functional translation may still cause some problems when using a first-order theorem prover, due to the presence of equalities in Ax_H. A way to limit the complexity induced by the introduction of equality using a mixed relational/functional translation [10].

A common feature of all the mentioned methods is that, in order to be applied directly, the underlying modal logic must have a first-order semantics. Up to our knowledge any attempt to deal with logics not having a first-order semantics requires ad-hoc techniques. Moreover, if the logic has a first-order semantics, but it is implicitly specified with Hilbert axioms only, a preliminary step is necessary to find the corresponding first-order axioms. The question of automatically solving this last problem has been extensively studied and algorithms have been proposed, e.g. [2, 9].

The main motivation of the present work is to find a translation applicable to all complete modal logics, regardless of the first-order axiomatizability of their semantics. The set-theoretic translation we propose works for all normal complete finitely-axiomatizable modal logics, possibly specified with Hilbert axioms only. The basic idea behind our translation is to represent any Kripke frame as a set, with the accessibility relation modeled using the membership relation $\in$. Moreover, in order to achieve a computationally valid result, we want to refer to a *finitely* (first-order) axiomatizable set theory. We succeeded in carrying out our translation in a very weak[3] set theory called Ω. Given a modal formula $\phi(P_1, ..., P_n)$ we define as its translation the *set-theoretic term*, with variables $x, x_1, ..., x_n$, denoted by $\phi^*(x, x_1, ..., x_n)$ and built using $\cup, \backslash, Pow$. Intuitively the term $\phi^*(x, x_1, ..., x_n)$ represents the set of those worlds in which the formula ϕ holds.

We prove that for any normal modal logic $H = K + \psi(\alpha_{j_1}, .., \alpha_{j_m})$, where $\psi(\alpha_{j_1}, .., \alpha_{j_m})$ is an axiom schema, the following holds:

$$\vdash_H \phi \quad \Rightarrow \quad \Omega \vdash \forall x(Trans(x) \wedge Ax_H(x) \rightarrow \forall x_1...\forall x_n(x \subseteq \phi^*(x, x_1, ...x_n))),$$

---

[3] Compare this theory with more classical finite axiomatizations of Set Theory, such as NBG.

$$\Omega \vdash \forall x (Trans(x) \wedge Ax_H(x) \rightarrow \forall x_1 ... \forall x_n (x \subseteq \phi^*(x, x_1, ... x_n))) \quad \Rightarrow \quad \psi \models \phi,$$

where $Trans(x)$ and $Ax_H(x)$ stand for $\forall y \, (y \in x \rightarrow y \subseteq x)$ and $\forall x_{j_1}, .., \forall x_{j_m} (x \subseteq \psi^*(x, x_{j_1}, .., x_{j_m}))$, respectively, and $\models$ represents frame logical consequence. In case H is complete the notions of $\vdash_H$ and $\psi \models$ coincide and modal derivability from H of a given formula is equivalent to first order derivability from Ω of the translated formula.

Instead of translating Hilbert axioms, one may use a set-theoretic semantics for H when such a semantics is available. We will study the case of G as an example of such an approach. The proposed set-theoretic translation method is then generalized to polymodal logics. Such a generalization involves the revision of the definition of the translation function to cope with a set of different modal operators instead of a single one.

In the last part of the paper, we consider the application of set-theory resolution techniques to support derivability in Ω. In order to apply such techniques, it is necessary to guarantee the decidability, with respect to Ω, of the class of ground formulae written in any language which extends the one in which the axioms of Ω are written with skolem functions. We succeeded in providing such a decidability result, and the main steps of the proof are outlined [5] (the details can be found in [7]).

The paper is organized as follows. In section 2, we introduce the proposed set-theoretic translation method by showing its application to the modal logic G, providing an example of how the method applies to a logic with a non-first-order semantics. In section 3, we consider the general case and we exploit the possibility of translating the Hilbert axioms of the logic. In section 4, we generalize the proposed method to polymodal logics. Finally, in section 5, we briefly discuss the application of set-theory resolution techniques to support derivability in Ω.

2   A set-theoretic translation of G

We first consider the case of the propositional modal logic G obtained by adding the Löb axiom schema $\Box(\Box\alpha \rightarrow \alpha) \rightarrow \Box\alpha$ to K. Our goal is to find a translation of G formulae into the language of Set Theory and a finitely axiomatizable theory Ω such that, for any modal formula ϕ, $\vdash_G \phi$ if and only if Ω proves the translation of ϕ.

We consider the theory Ω specified by the following axioms in the language with relational symbols $\in, \subseteq$, and functional symbols $\cup, \backslash, Pow$:

$x \in y \cup z \leftrightarrow x \in y \vee x \in z;$ $x \in y \backslash z \leftrightarrow x \in y \wedge x \notin z;$

$x \subseteq y \leftrightarrow \forall z (z \in x \rightarrow z \in y);$ $x \in Pow(y) \leftrightarrow x \subseteq y.$

Notice that neither the extensionality axiom nor the axiom of foundation are in Ω. In the next section we will make essential use of the latter fact since we will model the accessibility relation with the membership relation. In order to do this we will be forced to work in universes containing non-well-founded sets. However, we will see that in the case of G a standard set theory suffices to carry out the proofs.

Given a modal formula $\phi(P_1, ..., P_n)$, its translation is the *set-theoretic term* $\phi^*(x, x_1, ..., x_n)$, with variables $x, x_1, ..., x_n$, inductively defined as follows:

$$P_i^* \equiv x_i; \qquad\qquad\qquad (\phi \vee \psi)^* \equiv \phi^* \cup \psi^*;$$
$$(\phi \wedge \psi)^* \equiv \phi^* \cap \psi^*; \qquad\qquad (\neg\phi)^* \equiv x \setminus \phi^*;$$
$$(\phi \rightarrow \psi)^* \equiv (x \setminus \phi^*) \cup \psi^*; \qquad (\Box\phi)^* \equiv Pow(\phi^*).$$

where x is a syntactically unique variable, i.e., it differs from x_i for $i = 1, .., n$, $\phi^* \cap \psi^*$ stands for $\phi^* \setminus (\phi^* \setminus \psi^*)$, and $\diamond$ is translated as $\neg\Box\neg$. We will show that:

$$\vdash_G \phi \text{ iff } \Omega \vdash \forall x(Trans(x) \wedge Ax_G(x) \rightarrow \forall x_1...\forall x_n(x \subseteq \phi^*(x, x_1, ..., x_n)))$$

where $Trans(x)$ stands for $\forall y(y \in x \rightarrow y \subseteq x)$ (x is transitive), and $Ax_G(x)$ represents the conjunction of $\forall y(y \subseteq x \wedge \exists z(z \in y) \rightarrow \exists s(s \in y \wedge \forall v(v \notin s \cap y)))$ and $\forall z \forall w \forall y(z \in x \wedge w \in x \wedge y \in x \wedge z \in w \wedge w \in y \rightarrow z \in y)$ (x is well-founded and $\in$ restricted to x is transitive, respectively).

We prove that the proposed translation is complete and sound. The proof of completeness is straightforward; the proof of soundness relies on the characterization of G by the class of all finite trees.

Theorem 1. (Completeness of the translation method) *For each formula* ϕ *of G involving n propositional variables* $P_1, .., P_n$

$$\vdash_G \phi \text{ implies } \Omega \vdash \forall x(Trans(x) \wedge Ax_G(x) \rightarrow \forall x_1...\forall x_n(x \subseteq \phi^*(x, x_1, ..., x_n)))$$

Proof. The proof, which is by induction on the derivation $\vdash_G \phi(P_1, ..., P_n)$, is rather straightforward, except for the addition of some intermediate steps to cope with the lack of extensionality in Ω.

The cases of tautologies, K axiom schema, closure under modus ponens, and closure under necessitation are not too difficult, and thus they are omitted (a proof can be found in [5]). We explicitly prove the thesis for Löb's axiom schema only. We show that if $P_1, .., P_n$ are the n variables occurring in ϕ, then

$$\Omega \vdash \forall x(Trans(x) \wedge Ax_G(x) \rightarrow \forall x_1...\forall x_n(x \subseteq (\Box(\Box\phi \rightarrow \phi) \rightarrow \Box\phi)^*))$$

The proof is nothing but the formalization in Ω of the proof of the validity of the Löb's axiom schema in any well-founded transitive frame (cfr, e.g., [12]).

By definition, $(\Box(\Box\phi \rightarrow \phi) \rightarrow \Box\phi)^* \equiv (x \setminus t) \cup Pow(\phi^*)$, where t stands for the term $Pow((x \setminus Pow(\phi^*)) \cup \phi^*)$. We want to prove that if x satisfies $Trans(x) \wedge Ax_G(x)$, then $\forall s(s \in x \wedge s \in t \rightarrow s \in Pow(\phi^*))$. This is equivalent to showing that there exists no set belonging to the subset y of x with $y = x \cap t \setminus Pow(\phi^*)$. We consider the formula:

$$\forall y(\forall s(s \in y \rightarrow \exists v(v \in s \cap y)) \rightarrow (y \subseteq x \rightarrow \forall z(z \notin y)))$$

which can be derived from the axiom stating the well-foundedness of x, and show that for $y = x \cap t \setminus Pow(\phi^*)$ the formula $\forall s(s \in y \rightarrow \exists v(v \in s \cap y))$ holds. Since $y \subseteq x$, this proves the thesis.

If $s \in y$ then $s \in x$, $s \in t = Pow((x \setminus Pow(\phi^*)) \cup \phi^*)$, and $s \notin Pow(\phi^*)$. From the last conjunct, we derive that $\exists v(v \in s \wedge v \notin \phi^*)$. Since x satisfies $Trans(x)$ and $Ax_G(x)$ (in particular, the transitivity of $\in$ with respect to x holds), and $s \in x$, from $v \in s$ it follows that $v \subseteq s$. Now, from $s \in Pow((x \setminus Pow(\phi^*)) \cup \phi^*)$ and $v \subseteq s$, it follows that $v \in Pow((x \setminus Pow(\phi^*)) \cup \phi^*)$, that is, $v \in t$. Finally, from $v \in s$, $s \subseteq (x \setminus Pow(\phi^*)) \cup \phi^*$, and $v \notin \phi^*$ it follows that $v \in x \setminus Pow(\phi^*)$, and then $v \notin Pow(\phi^*)$. From $v \in x$, $v \in t$, and $v \notin Pow(\phi^*)$ we can conclude that $v \in x \cap t \setminus Pow(\phi^*) = y$ that proves the thesis.

(T1) ∎

The only feature of the previous result is the fact that all the set theoretic principles involved in the proof are the extremely elementar axioms of Ω.

The converse of the above theorem exploit the characterization of the frames in which G holds. The Completeness Theorem says that $\vdash_G \phi$ iff ϕ is valid in every finite tree, where by a finite tree is meant a frame (W, R, r) in which W is a finite set containing the element r (the root), R is transitive and asymmetric and the set of R−predecessors of any element contains r and is linearly ordered by R (see [12] for details).

Theorem 2. (Soundness of the translation method) *For each formula ϕ of G involving n propositional variables $P_1, ..., P_n$*

$$\Omega \vdash \forall x(Trans(x) \wedge Ax_G(x) \rightarrow \forall x_1...\forall x_n(x \subseteq \phi^*(x, x_1, ..., x_n))) \text{ implies } \vdash_G \phi.$$

Proof.

Let HF^A be the structure for the language of Ω consisting of all hereditarily finite sets built from atoms in $A = \{a_0, a_1, ...\}$, with the natural set-theoretic interpretation of the relational and functional symbols $\in, \subseteq, \cap, \cup, \setminus, Pow$. HF^A is a model for Ω^4. Then, for every term $t(x_0, ..., x_n)$ and for every $h_0, ..., h_n$ in HF^A, we may consider the element $t^{HF^A}(h_0, ..., h_n)$ in HF^A; in particular, if $\phi(P_1, ..., P_n)$ is a modal formula, the term $\phi^*(x, x_1, ..., x_n)$ may be evaluated in the elements $h_0, ..., h_n$ giving an element of HF^A.

We will proceed as follows. Given a finite tree (W, R, r), we find an element W^* of HF^A such that (i) $Trans(W^*) \wedge Ax_G(W^*)$ holds in the model HF^A, and (ii) given a modal formula $\phi(P_1, ..., P_n)$, if $\forall x_1...\forall x_n(W^* \subseteq \phi^*(W^*, x_1, ..., x_n))$ holds in HF^A, then $\phi(P_1, ..., P_n)$ is valid in (W, R, r).

Fix an injection π from the leaves of W (i.e. nodes without any successor) to A. We define W^* in HF^A as follows. For every node $w \in W$ let

$$w^* = \begin{cases} \pi(w) & \text{if } w \text{ is a leaf of } W \\ \{v^* : wRv\} & \text{otherwise.} \end{cases}$$

Define W^* as r^*. First, notice that $w^* \in HF^A$ for every $w \in W$. Moreover, it is not difficult to see that $HF^A \models Trans(W^*) \wedge Ax_G(W^*)$.

---

[4] Actually, HF^A is also a model for the extensionality axiom for all non-atomic elements, even though we do not require such an axiom in Ω.

Let $\models$ be a valuation of the propositional variables $P_1, ..., P_n$ on W. Consider the elements $P_1^*, ..., P_n^*$ given by $P_i^* = \{w^* \in W^* : w \models P_i\}$. Since W is finite, we have that $P_1^*, ..., P_n^*$ belong to HF^A.

Notice that if the elements w^* and v^* are equal in HF^A, then $w = v$ (by induction on the height $h(w)$ of the node w in the tree (W, R, r)), a fact that will useful in proving the following Lemma.

Lemma 3. *For all $w \in W$ and for all formula $\phi(P_1, ..., P_n)$,*

$$w \models \phi(P_1, ..., P_n) \text{ iff } w^* \in \phi^*(W^*, P_1^*, ..., P_n^*) \text{ holds in } HF^A$$

Proof. By induction on the structure of the formula $\phi(P_1, ..., P_n)$.

If $\phi(P_1, ..., P_n) \equiv P_i$ and $w \models P_i$ then by definition of P_i^* one has $w^* \in P_i^*$. Viceversa, if $w^* \in P_i^*$ then $w^* = z^*$ for some $z \in W$ with $z \models P_i$. But in this case we proved that $w = z$ and so $w \models P_i$. The proof for boolean connectives is straightforward [5]. Consider now the formula $\Box\phi(P_1, ..., P_n)$: $w \models \Box\phi(P_1, ..., P_n)$ iff, for all $z \in W$, wRz implies $z \models \phi(P_1, ..., P_n)$ iff, for all $z \in W$, wRz implies $z^* \in \phi^*(W^*, P_1^*, ..., P_n^*)$ iff $\{z^* : wRz\} \subseteq \phi^*(W^*, P_1^*, ..., P_n^*)$ iff (by definition of w^*), $w^* \subseteq \phi^*(W^*, P_1^*, ..., P_n^*)$ iff $w^* \in Pow^*(\phi^*(W^*, P_1^*, ..., P_n^*))$ iff $w^* \in (\Box\phi)^*(W^*, P_1^*, ..., P_n^*)$.

$$(L3) \ \blacksquare$$

On the basis of Lemma (3), we can conclude that $\phi(P_1, ..., P_n)$ is valid in the model $(W, R, \models)$ if and only if the corresponding set W^* in HF^A is a subset of $\phi^*(W^*, P_1^*, ..., P_n^*)$.

To conclude the proof of Theorem (2), suppose that

$$\Omega \vdash \forall x(Trans(x) \wedge Ax_G(x) \to \forall x_1...\forall x_n(x \subseteq \phi^*(x, x_1, .., x_n)))$$

If (W, R, r) is a finite tree, then the corresponding set W^* in HF^A satisfies $Trans(W^*) \wedge Ax_G(W^*)$. Therefore, from $\Omega \vdash \forall x(Trans(x) \wedge Ax_G(x) \to \forall x_1...\forall x_n(x \subseteq \phi^*))$, it follows that, for all elements $h_1, ..., h_n$ in HF^A, we have $W^* \subseteq \phi^*(W^*, h_1, ..., h_n)$. In particular, for all valuations $\models$ of the propositional variables $P_1, ..., P_n$ on W, this is true for the sets $P_1^*, ..., P_n^*$ defined as in Lemma (3). From the same lemma one deduces that $\phi(P_1, ..., P_n)$ is valid in the model $(W, R, \models)$, and from the finite tree Completeness Theorem it follows $\vdash_G \phi$.

$$(T2) \ \blacksquare$$

3 The set-theoretic translation method

In this section we generalize the proposed translation method to any normal finitely-axiomatizable modal logic, possibly specified by Hilbert axioms only.

Let $\psi(\alpha_{j_1}, ..., \alpha_{j_m})$ be an axiom schema and let H be the modal logic obtained by adding $\psi(\alpha_{j_1}, ..., \alpha_{j_m})$ to K. The completeness of the translation will be shown with respect to derivabiltity from H, while soundness holds, in general, with respect to logical consequence.

We shall prove that for any formula ϕ involving n propositional variables $P_1, .., P_n$

$$\vdash_H \phi \quad \Rightarrow \quad \Omega \vdash \forall x(Trans(x) \wedge Ax_H(x) \rightarrow \forall x_1...\forall x_n(x \subseteq \phi^*(x, x_1, ...x_n))),$$

$$\Omega \vdash \forall x(Trans(x) \wedge Ax_H(x) \rightarrow \forall x_1...\forall x_n(x \subseteq \phi^*(x, x_1, ...x_n))) \quad \Rightarrow \quad \psi \models \phi,$$

where $Trans(x)$ is the formula $\forall y\ (y \in x \rightarrow y \subseteq x)$ and $Ax_H(x)$ is the formula $\forall x_{j_1}, .., \forall x_{j_m}(x \subseteq \psi^*(x, x_{j_1}, .., x_{j_m}))$.

In case H is complete the notions of $\vdash_H$ and $\psi \models$ coincide and modal derivability from H of a given formula is equivalent to first order derivability from Ω of the translated formula.

As in the case of G, the proof of completeness is much easier than the proof of soundness; it can be found in [5].

Theorem 4. (Soundness of the translation method) *For each formula ϕ of H involving n propositional variables $P_1, .., P_n$*

$$\Omega \vdash \forall x(Trans(x) \wedge Ax_H(x) \rightarrow \forall x_1...\forall x_n(x \subseteq \phi^*(x, x_1, .., x_n)))\ implies\ \psi \models \phi$$

Proof. Hereinafter, let $\mathcal{U}$ denote a universe of hypersets satisfying all the axioms of ZF^- (ZF except foundation) and AFA, namely a universe in which, for any graph (W, R), there is a (unique) function d such that, for every $w \in W$, the following holds:

$$d(w) = \{d(v)|v \in W \wedge wRv\}$$

(see [1] for details). Actually, it can be seen that the use of AFA it is not essential for this proof and a model falsifying foundation "whenever needed" could be used instead. However, as we will see, the use of AFA will simplify the argument making our construction more uniform.

Lemma 5. *Let α be an ordinal, V_α be the set of all well-founded sets of rank less than α, and $\mathcal{U} \setminus V_\alpha$ be the universe of all hypersets not belonging to V_α. The structure for the language of Ω with support (domain) $\mathcal{U} \setminus V_\alpha$, and interpretation function $\_'$ defined as follows[5]:*

$$x \in' y\ iff\ x \in y;\ x \cup' y = x \cup y;\ x \subseteq' y\ iff\ x \setminus V_\alpha \subseteq y;$$

$$x \setminus' y = \begin{cases} x \setminus y & if\ x \setminus y \notin V_\alpha \\ V_\alpha & otherwise \end{cases};\ Pow'(y) = \{x : x \setminus V_\alpha \subseteq y\}.$$

is a model of Ω.

The proof is accomplished in two steps. First, we show that the functions $\cup', \setminus'$, and Pow' are well-defined over $\mathcal{U} \setminus V_\alpha$; then, we show that the proposed interpretation verifies the Ω-axioms. The details are given in [5].

Given a frame (W, R), we want to interpret it in the universe $\mathcal{U} \setminus V_\alpha$, for a suitable ordinal α depending on $|W|$. Let us associate a set $a \downarrow$ in $\mathcal{U}$ with each

---

[5] We denote the defined interpretation of symbols $\in, \cup, \setminus, \subseteq, Pow$ in $\mathcal{U} \setminus V_\alpha$ by $\in'$ $, \cup', \setminus', \subseteq', Pow'$, and the standard interpretation in $\mathcal{U}$ simply by $\in, \cup, \setminus, \subseteq, Pow$.

world $a \in W$. From the axiom AFA it follows that, for each $a \in W$, there exists a unique labeled decoration * such that $a^* = \{b^* : aRb\} \cup a \downarrow$ [1]. Moreover, it is possible to define $a \downarrow$ in such a way that, for every a, b in W, $a^* \notin b \downarrow$ and $a \neq b$ in W implies $a^* \neq b^*$. For this purpose, let us consider a set $\tilde{W}$ in $\mathcal{U}$, whose elements are well-founded sets of the same rank α, and such that there exists a biunivocal correspondence between $\tilde{W}$ and W. For each $a \in W$, we denote the image of a in $\tilde{W}$ with $\tilde{a}$, and define $a \downarrow = \{\tilde{a}\}$. The following lemma can be easily proved.

Lemma 6. *For each a, b in W, $a^* \notin b \downarrow$. Furthermore, from $a \neq b$ in W it follows that $a^* \neq b^*$. Finally, for each $a \in W$, $a^* \notin V_{\alpha+1}$ and $a^* \setminus V_{\alpha+1} = \{b^* : aRb\}$.*

Proof. If $a^* \in b \downarrow$, then $b \downarrow = \{\tilde{b}\}$ implies that $a^* = \tilde{b}$. Since $\tilde{a} \in a \downarrow$ and $a \downarrow \subseteq a^*$, it follows that $\tilde{a} \in \tilde{b}$, but this is impossible because $\tilde{a}$ and $\tilde{b}$ have the same rank α. Let us show now that if $a \neq b$ in W then $a^* \neq b^*$. Suppose that $a^* = b^*$. From such an assumption it follows that $\tilde{a} \in b^*$, with $b^* = \{c^* : bRc\} \cup b \downarrow$. If $\tilde{a} \in b \downarrow$ then $\tilde{a} = \tilde{b}$, contradicting $a \neq b$. If $\tilde{a} = c^*$, for a given c such that bRc, then $\tilde{c} \in \tilde{a}$ (contradiction). The remaining part of the proof easily follows.

(L6) ∎

Consider now a valuation $\models$ of the propositional variables $P_1, ..., P_n$ over the frame (W, R), and let W^* be equal to $\{a^* : a \in W\}$, where * is the previously introduced labeled decoration. W^* does not belong to $V_{\alpha+1}$ because $V_{\alpha+1}$ is transitive and, for each $a \in W$, $a^* \notin V_{\alpha+1}$. Furthermore, let P_i^* be equal to $\{a^* \in W^* : a \models P_i\}$ if such a set is not empty, and to $V_{\alpha+1}$ otherwise. It is possible to prove the following lemma.

Lemma 7. *For each $a \in W$ and each formula $\phi(P_1, ..., P_n)$*

$$a \models \phi(P_1, ..., P_n) \text{ iff } a^* \in' \phi^*(W^*, P_1^*, ..., P_n^*) \text{ in the universe } \mathcal{U} \setminus V_{\alpha+1}.$$

Proof. By induction on the structure of the formula $\phi(P_1, ..., P_n)$ [5]. The cases of propositional variables and boolean combinations of formulae are left to the reader. In the case of a formula of the form $\Box \phi(P_1, ..., P_n)$, we have that:
$a \models \Box\phi(P_1, ..., P_n)$ iff for all $b \in W$, aRb implies $b \models \phi(P_1, ..., P_n)$ iff for all $b \in W$, aRb implies $b^* \in' \phi^*(W^*, P_1^*, ..., P_n^*)$ iff $a^* \setminus V_{\alpha+1} \subseteq \phi^*(W^*, P_1^*, ..., P_n^*)$ iff $a^* \in' Pow'(\phi^*(W^*, P_1^*, ..., P_n^*))$ iff $a^* \in' (\Box \phi)^*(W^*, P_1^*, ..., P_n^*)$.

(L7) ∎

On the basis of Lemma (7), we can conclude that a formula $\phi(P_1, ..., P_n)$ is valid in a model $(W, R, \models)$ if and only if $W^* \subseteq \phi^*(W^*, P_1^*, ..., P_n^*)$ in the model $\mathcal{U} \setminus V_{\alpha+1}$. This result can be generalized to frames.

Lemma 8. *A formula $\phi(P_1, ..., P_n)$ is valid in the frame (W, R) if and only if for the corresponding hyperset W^* $\forall x_1, ..., x_n W^* \subseteq' \phi^*(W^*, x_1, ..., x_n)$ holds in $\mathcal{U} \setminus V_{\alpha+1}$.*

Proof. For each $a \in W$ and $x_1, .., x_n \in \mathcal{U} \setminus V_{\alpha+1}$, it is easy to prove that $a^* \in' \phi^*(W^*, x_1, ..., x_n)$ if and only if $a^* \in' \phi^*(W^*, x_1 \cap' W^*, ..., x_n \cap' W^*)$. The proof is by induction on the structure of the formula ϕ [5]. We only report the proof of the inductive step for $\phi \equiv \Box\beta$:

$a^* \in' (\Box\beta)^*(W^*, x_1, ..., x_n)$ iff $a^* \in' Pow'(\beta^*(W^*, x_1, ..., x_n))$ iff $a^* \setminus V_{\alpha+1} \subseteq \beta^*(W^*, x_1, ..., x_n)$ iff for all $b \in W$, if aRb then $b^* \in' \beta^*(W^*, x_1, ..., x_n)$ iff for all $b \in W$, if aRb then $b^* \in' \beta^*(W^*, x_1 \cap' W^*, ..., x_n \cap' W^*)$ iff $a^* \setminus V_{\alpha+1} \subseteq \beta^*(W^*, x_1 \cap' W^*, ..., x_n \cap' W^*)$ iff $a^* \in' (\Box\beta)^*(W^*, x_1 \cap' W^*, ..., x_n \cap' W^*)$.

Given n hypersets $x_1, ..., x_n$ belonging to $\mathcal{U} \setminus V_{\alpha+1}$, we define a valuation $\models$ of the propositional variables $P_1, ..., P_n$ such that, for each $a \in W$, $a \models P_i$ if and only if $a^* \in' x_i \cap' W^*$. It is straightforward to see that, if $P_1^*, .., P_n^*$ are the hypersets defined in Lemma (7) on the basis of the valuation $\models$, then P_i^* and $x_i \cap' W^*$ have the same elements in the model $\mathcal{U} \setminus V_{\alpha+1}$. From this, it is easy to verify by induction on ϕ that $\phi^*(W^*, P_1^*, .., P_n^*)$ and $\phi^*(W^*, x_1 \cap' W^*, ..., x_n \cap' W^*)$ have the same elements. Suppose now that a formula ϕ is valid in the frame (W, R); then it is also valid in the model $(W, R, \models)$, and from Lemma (7) it follows that, for all $a \in W$, $a^* \in' \phi^*(W^*, x_1 \cap' W^*, ..., x_n \cap' W^*)$. This allows us to conclude that $a^* \in' \phi^*(W^*, x_1, ..., x_n)$, and, therefore, for all hypersets $x_1, ..., x_n$ in $\mathcal{U} \setminus V_{\alpha+1}$, $W^* \subseteq' \phi^*(W^*, x_1, ..., x_n)$.

The vice versa can be easily proved by associating the hypersets $P_1^*, .., P_n^*$ (where P_i^* is equal to $\{a^* \in' W^* : a \models P_i\}$ if such a set is not empty, and to $V_{\alpha+1}$ otherwise) with each valuation $\models$ of the propositional variables $P_1, ..., P_n$.

$$(L8) \quad \blacksquare$$

To conclude the proof of Theorem (4), let us suppose that

$$\Omega \vdash \forall x(Trans(x) \wedge Ax_H(x) \rightarrow \forall x_1...\forall x_n(x \subseteq \phi^*(x, x_1, .., x_n))).$$

Let (W, R) be a frame in which the the formula $\psi(P_{j_1}, ..., P_{j_m})$ is valid; from Lemma (8), it follows that the formula $\forall x_{j_1}, ..., \forall x_{j_m} W^* \subseteq' \psi^*(W^*, x_{j_1}, ..., x_{j_m})$ is true in the universe $\mathcal{U} \setminus V_{\alpha+1}$. Furthermore, it is easy to prove that $Trans(W^*)$ holds as well. Since $\mathcal{U} \setminus V_{\alpha+1}$ is an Ω model, from the hypotheses it follows that the formula $\forall x_1...\forall x_n (W^* \subseteq' \phi^*(W^*, x_1, .., x_n))$ is true in $\mathcal{U} \setminus V_{\alpha+1}$, and then, again from Lemma (8), that the formula ϕ is valid in (W, R).

$$(T4) \quad \blacksquare$$

4 The generalization to polymodal logics

Let us now generalize the proposed set-theoretic translation method to poly-modal logics. For the sake of simplicity, we describe its generalization to bimodal logics. The extension of the resulting translation method for bimodal logics to polymodal ones is straightforward. Complete details can be found in [6].

In order to deal with bimodal (polymodal) logics, the translation function $(.)^*$ must be changed to take into account 2 (n) different modalities $\Box_1$ and $\Box_2$. Given a bimodal formula $\phi(P_1, .., P_n)$, its translation is a term $\phi^*(x, y_1, y_2, x_1, .., x_n)$, where y_1 and y_2 are new variables, inductively defined as follows:

- *propositional variables and boolean connectives: as in the monomodal case;*
- $(\Box_1\phi)^* \equiv Pow(((x \cup y_2) \setminus y_1) \cup Pow(\phi^*))$;
- $(\Box_2\phi)^* \equiv Pow(((x \cup y_1) \setminus y_2) \cup Pow(\phi^*))$.

Given a bi-frame $(U, \lhd_1, \lhd_2)$, we first trasform it in a mono-frame (W, R), and then we interpret it as a set W^*, in a particular model of Ω, in such a way that a formula ϕ is valid in $(U, \lhd_1, \lhd_2)$ if and only if $\forall x_1, ... \forall x_n U^* \subseteq \phi^*(U^*, U_1^*, U_2^*, x_1, ..., x_n)$, for suitable elements U^*, U_1^*, U_2^* of the model such that $W^* = U^* \cup U_1^* \cup U_2^*$.

The first transformation is done by considering two disjoint copies U_1, U_2 of U (we indicate the biunivocal correspondences between U and U_1, respectively U_2, by $u \mapsto u_1$, respectively $u \mapsto u_2$). The mono-frame (W, R) is defined as follows:

$$W = U \cup U_1 \cup U_2; \quad u_1 R v \text{ iff } u \lhd_1 v; \quad u_2 R v \text{ iff } u \lhd_2 v; \quad u R u_1 \text{ and } u R u_2.$$

By applying Lemma (6) to (W, R), it is possible to determine an ordinal α, an element W^* of $\mathcal{U} \setminus V_{\alpha+1}$ and a mappping * from W to W^* such that, from $a \neq b$ in W, it follows that $a^* \neq b^*$, and, for each $a \in W$, $a^* \notin V_{\alpha+1}$ and $a^* \setminus V_{\alpha+1} = \{b^* : aRb\}$. Then, let us define U^*, U_1^* and U_2^* as the sets $\{u^* : u \in U\}$, $\{u_1^* : u_1 \in U_1\}$ and $\{u_2^* : u_2 \in U_2\}$, respectively. It is possible to show that they do not belong to $V_{\alpha+1}$, and thus that they are elements of the model $\mathcal{U} \setminus V_{\alpha+1}$ of Lemma (6). Finally, consider a valuation $\models$ of the propositional variables $P_1, ..., P_n$ over the frame $(U, \lhd_1, \lhd_2)$, and let P_i^* be equal to $\{u^* \in U^* : u \models P_i\}$ if such a set is not empty, and to $V_{\alpha+1}$ otherwise.

The following lemma generalizes Lemma (7) to bimodal logics:

Lemma 9. *For each $u \in U$ and each bimodal formula $\phi(P_1, ..., P_n)$*

$$u \models \phi(P_1, ..., P_n) \text{ iff } u^* \in' \phi^*(U^*, U_1^*, U_2^*, P_1^*, ..., P_n^*) \text{ in the universe } \mathcal{U} \setminus V_{\alpha+1}.$$

Proof.
By induction on the structure of the formula $\phi(P_1, ..., P_n)$. The cases of propositional variables and of boolean connectives are the same as in Lemma (7). We consider the case of the formula $\Box_1\phi(P_1, .., P_n)$:

$u \models \Box_1\phi(P_1, ..., P_n)$ iff $\forall t(u \lhd_1 t \rightarrow t \models \phi(P_1, ..., P_n))$ iff $\forall v(uRv \wedge v \in U_1 \rightarrow \forall t(vRt \rightarrow t \models \phi(P_1, ..., P_n)))$ iff $\forall v(v^* \in' u^* \wedge v^* \in' U_1^* \rightarrow \forall t(t^* \in' v^* \rightarrow t^* \in' \phi^*(U^*, U_1^*, U_2^*, P_1^*, ..., P_n^*)))$ iff $u^* \cap U_1^* \subseteq' Pow(\phi^*)$ iff $u^* \subseteq' ((U^* \cup U_2^*) \setminus U_1^*) \cup Pow(\phi^*)$ iff $u^* \in' Pow(((U^* \cup U_2^*) \setminus U_1^*) \cup P(\phi^*))$ iff $u^* \in' (\Box_1\phi)^*(U^*, U_1^*, U_2^*, P_1^*, ..., P_n^*)$.

The case of of the formula $\Box_2\phi(P_1, .., P_n)$ is perfectly symmetric, and thus omitted.

$$(L9) \blacksquare$$

On the basis of Lemma (9), we can conclude that a formula $\phi(P_1, ..., P_n)$ is valid in a model $(U, \lhd_1, \lhd_2, \models)$ if and only if the corresponding hyperset U^* is a subset of $\phi^*(U^*, U_1^*, U_2^*, P_1^*, ..., P_n^*)$ in the model $\mathcal{U} \setminus V_{\alpha+1}$. This result can be generalized to frames as shown by Lemma (8) in the case of monomodal logics.

Finally notice that, in the model $\mathcal{U} \setminus V_{\alpha+1}$, U^* has the following property:

$Trans^2(U^*) \equiv \forall x \forall y\ (x \in y \wedge y \in U^* \rightarrow x \subseteq U^*)$, that is, $U^* \subseteq Pow(Pow(U^*))$.

Putting all these results together we can prove the soundness of the extended translation method for bimodal logics (the proof is basically the same as in the monomodal case, and thus it is omitted):

Theorem 10. (Soundness of the translation method for polymodal logics) *Let H be a bimodal logic extending $K \bigotimes K$ by means of the axiom schema $\psi(\alpha_{j_1}, .., \alpha_{j_m})$. If H is complete, then for each bimodal formula ϕ involving n propositional variables $P_1, .., P_n$, $\Omega \vdash \forall x \forall y_1 \forall y_2 (Trans^2(x) \wedge Ax_H(x, y_1, y_2) \rightarrow \forall x_1.\forall x_n(x \subseteq \phi^*(x, y_1, y_2, x_1, .., x_n)))$ implies $\vdash_H \phi$, where $Ax_H(x, y_1, y_2)$ is $\forall x_1...\forall x_m(x \subseteq \psi^*(x, y_1, y_2, x_1, .., x_m))$.*

Finally, the completeness of the extended translation can be proved by induction on the derivation $\vdash_H \phi$ as in the case of monomodal logics (the details are given in [6]).

5 On the application of set-theory resolution

Let us briefly consider the problem of applying set-theory resolution techniques to our translation method. In order to exploit them, it is necessary to be able to guarantee the decidability, with respect to Ω, of the class of ground formulae written in any language which extends the one in which the axioms of Ω are written with skolem functions. The language of Ω ($\mathcal{L}_\Omega$ from now on) consists of the symbols $\emptyset, \cup, \setminus, \subseteq, \in, Pow$. In [11], it has been shown that the satisfiability problem with respect to any theory T of ground formulae on a given language $\mathcal{L}$ obtained from $\mathcal{L}_T$ adding an arbitrary amount of functional and constant symbols, is equivalent to the T-satisfiability of the class of purely existential formulae written in $\mathcal{L}_T$. Therefore we are interested to this last problem in the case of Ω.

First of all, notice that decidability results for classes very similar to the one we want to deal with have already been proved by Cantone, Schwartz, and Ferro [4]. Unfortunately, the mentioned results cannot be applied to our context, the problem being the background set theory upon which they rest. Our theory Ω is very weak, while it can be easily checked that the proofs in [4] make an essential use of assumptions such as regularity, existence of the transitive closure of sets, extensionality, etc., which are certainly not derivable from Ω.

We succeeded in providing a proof of the decidability result we need in a theory Ω' slightly stronger than Ω that assumes some simple consequences of Cantor's theorem on the number of subsets of a given set, not derivable from Ω [5]. Moreover, since the difference between Ω and Ω' lies only in the presence of axioms that (practically) do not introduce new function symbols, but only give more *structure* to the possible models of Ω, the decidability result we obtained with respect to Ω' is sufficient to show also the ground decidability of Ω'.

An extended discussion of the above result can be found in [5]; complete details will appear in [7].

Conclusions

In the paper we proposed a new translation method mapping polymodal formulae into set-theoretic terms of the very week set theory Ω. The method can be used for any normal complete finitely-axiomatizable polymodal logic, possibly specified with Hilbert axioms only, and applies to a large class of theories extending Ω. Moreover, it can be generalized to incomplete logics adapting the translation to represent general frames, but maintaining the base theory Ω unchanged, as shown in [3].

A possible line for further investigations is the generalization of the proposed method to first-order (poly)modal logics. We are also investigating the possibility of exploiting our translation method to reduce undecidable decision problems for particular propositional polymodal logics to the derivability problem with respect to Ω of formulae of type $\forall^*\exists$, thereby showing the undecidability of the latter problem.

References

1. P. Aczel, *Non-well-founded sets*, CSLI, Lecture Notes No. 14, 1988.
2. J. van Benthem, *Modal Logic and Classical Logic*; Bibliopolis, Napoli and Atlantic Heights (N.J.), 1985.
3. J. van Benthem, G. D'Agostino, A. Montanari, A. Policriti, *Modal Deduction in Second-Order Logic and Set Theory* (in preparation).
4. D. Cantone, A. Ferro, and E.G Omodeo, *Computable Set Theory. Vol. 1*; Oxford University Press, Int. Series of Monographs on Computer Science, 1989.
5. G. D'Agostino, A. Montanari, A. Policriti, *Translating modal formulae as set-theoretic terms*; Research Report 10/94, Dipartimento di Matematica e Informatica, Università di Udine, May 1994 (an abstract will appear in the Proc. of Logic Colloquium '94, Journal of Symbolic Logic).
6. G. D'Agostino, A. Montanari, A. Policriti, *A set-theoretic translation method for polymodal logics*; The ILLC Prepublication Series, ML-94-09, University of Amsterdam, October 1994.
7. G. D'Agostino, A. Montanari, A. Policriti, *Decidability results for modal theorem proving* (in preparation).
8. M. Fitting, *Proofs Methods for Modal and Intuitionistic Logics*; D. Reidel Pub. Comp., Dordrecht, Boston, and Lancaster, 1983.
9. D. M. Gabbay, H. J. Ohlbach, *Quantifier elimination in second-order predicate logic*; in Proc. KR'92, Morgan Kaufmann, 1992, 425-436.
10. H. J. Ohlbach, Translation Methods for Non-Classical Logics: An Overview; *Bull. of the IGLP*, 1 (1): 69–89, 1993.
11. A. Policriti, J. T. Schwartz, *T Theorem Proving I*; Research Report 08/92, Università di Udine, July 1992 (submitted for publication).
12. C. Smoryński, *Self-Reference and Modal Logic*; Springer Verlag, New York, 1985.

On the Synthesis of Discrete Controllers for Timed Systems*
(An Extended Abstract)

Oded Maler[1] Amir Pnueli[2] Joseph Sifakis[1]

[1] SPECTRE – VERIMAG, Miniparc-ZIRST, 38330 Montbonnot, France,
Oded.Maler@imag.fr
[2] Dept. of Computer Science, Weizmann Inst. Rehovot 76100, Israel,
amir@wisdom.weizmann.ac.il

Abstract. This paper presents algorithms for the automatic synthesis of real-time controllers by finding a winning strategy for certain games defined by the timed-automata of Alur and Dill. In such games, the outcome depends on the players' actions as well as on their *timing*. We believe that these results will pave the way for the application of program synthesis techniques to the construction of real-time embedded systems from their specifications.

1 Introduction

Consider a dynamical system P whose presentation describes all its possible behaviors. This system can be viewed as a plant to be controlled. A subset of the plant's behaviors, satisfying some criterion is defined as good (or acceptable). If the plant is, e.g., an airplane, this subset might consist of all behaviors which start at the departure point and end in the destination within some temporal interval (and with the number of living passengers kept constant). A controller C is another system which can interact with P in a certain manner by observing the state of P and by issuing control actions that influence the behavior of P, hopefully restricting it to be included in the subset of good behaviors. Carrying on with the airplane example, the controller might be in charge for turning the engines on and off, increasing the fuel consumption, etc. The synthesis problem is then, to find out whether, for a given P, there exists a realizable controller C such that their interaction will produce only good behaviors.

There are many variants of the formulation of this problem, differing from each other in the kind of dynamics considered and in the way the system and the goodness criteria are specified. The two most extreme examples are *reactive program synthesis* and *classical control theory*. In the former, the models are based

---
* This research was supported in part by the France-Israel project for cooperation in Computer Science and by the European Community ESPRIT Basic Research Action Projects REACT (6021). VERIMAG is a joint laboratory of CNRS, INPG, UJF and VERILOG SA. SPECTRE is a project of INRIA.

on discrete transition-systems (automata). The plant P represents a combination of the environment actions and the specification of the desired interaction between the synthesized program C and the environment. The dynamics for this case is defined by a non-deterministic automaton, whose acceptance condition distinguishes good behaviors (interactions) from bad ones. The program has control over some of the transitions, and the problem is to find a strategy, that is, an effective rule for selecting at each state one among the possible transitions, such that bad behaviors are excluded. In classical control theory, the plant is a continuous dynamical system defined by a non-autonomous (that is, with input) differential equation. The input serves to express both the non-determinism of the environment (disturbances) and the effect of the controller actions. The controller synthesis problem in this context is to define a *feed-back law*, which *continuously* determines the controller's input to the plant, such that behavioral specification are met.

In this paper we are concerned with *real-time systems* where discrete state-transitions interact with the continuous passage of time. In this setting we model the plant as a *timed automaton*, that is, an automaton equipped with clocks that grow continuously in time while the automaton is in any of its states. The values of the clocks may interfere with the transitions by appearing in *guards*, which are the enabling conditions of the transitions. Thus, a transition may take place, for example, only if some clock value has passed a certain threshold. Transitions may as well reset clocks.

We show that the control synthesis problem is solvable when the plant specification is given by a timed automaton. This means that another timed automaton can be synthesized (when possible) such that its interaction with the environment will introduce only good timed traces. We arrive to these results by providing at first a simple and intuitive (if not new) solution to the discrete version of the problem and then adapt it to timed automata defined over a *dense* time domains. Technically, the solution is obtained by solving fixed-point equations involving both discrete transition relations and linear inequalities.

The rest of the paper is organized as follows: in section 2 we give a motivating toy example of a real-time controller synthesis problem. In section 3 we treat the discrete case and the real-time case is solved in section 4. The last section discusses some relevant past and future work.

2 An Example of a Real-time Control Synthesis problem

Consider the following game depicted in figure 1. Player P_1 starts running from the initial position marked by a circle at the left of the figure. It takes her e_1 seconds to reach the junction. At the junction she can either wait and do nothing or choose to run – either to the left or to the right. After having run in the chosen direction for e_2 seconds she reaches the corresponding bridge, and if the latter is not blocked (see below) she can run and reach the end position within e_3 seconds. If this final position is reached within less than c seconds since the game started, Player P_1 wins. The other player P_2 starts the game located between the two bridges and within d seconds she *must* choose between blocking the left or the right bridge (which she does immediately upon making the decision). The whole

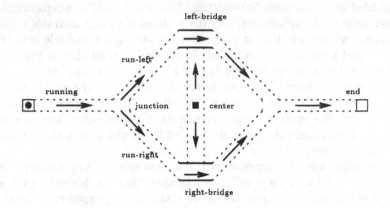

Fig. 1. A pursuit game.

system can be described as a product of two timed-automata having two clocks. The first clock x measures the amount of time elapsed since the beginning of the game. The second clock, y is used to impose velocity constraints on the behavior of P_1. These two automata are depicted[3] in figure 2. The product of these two automata is the timed-automaton of figure 3. One can see that there is a strategy to win from state AJ iff $\max(d, e_1) + e_2 + e_3 < c$. If this inequality holds, the strategy for Player P_1 is to stay at BJ until $x = \max(d, e_1)$. Then, after Player P_2 takes the system to either BI or BK, Player P_1 takes the transition to CI or DK, respectively and reaches the goal on time.

3 The Discrete Case

Definition 1 (Plant). *A plant automaton is a tuple* $\mathcal{P} = (Q, \Sigma_c, \delta, q_0)$*, where* Q *is a finite set of states,* Σ_c *is a set of controller commands,* $\delta : Q \times \Sigma_c \mapsto 2^Q$ *is the transition function and* $q_0 \in Q$ *is an initial state.*

For each controller command $\sigma \in \Sigma_c$ at some state $q \in Q$ there are several possible consequences denoted by $\delta(q, \sigma)$. This set indicates the possible reactions

---

[3] In order to economize the use of arrows we employ a Statechart-like notation, i.e., an arrow originating from a super-state (dashed rectangle) represents identical arrows coming out of all the states contained in that super-state. We write transition guards above the arrows, clock resettings below and invariants inside states (as in state J of the first automaton). Note that the right automaton "observes" both clocks as well as the state of the left automaton.

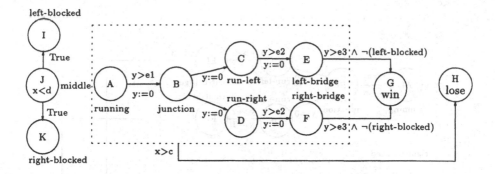

Fig. 2. The game as two interacting timed-automata.

of the plant to the controller's command, some of which may reflect a possible interference by the environment.[4] Choosing a command $\sigma \in \Sigma_c$ is what the controller can do at every stage of the game. A good choice is supposed to work for all possible continuations indicated by $\delta(q, \sigma)$.

Definition 2 (Controllers). *A controller (strategy) for a plant specified by $\mathcal{P} = (Q, \Sigma_c, \delta, q_0)$ is a function $C : Q^+ \mapsto \Sigma_c$. A simple controller is a controller that can be written[5] as a function $C : Q \mapsto \Sigma_c$.*

According to this definition, a general controller may base its selection of the next command upon the complete history of states visited up to this point. This general definition does not impose any bound on the amount of memory the controller might need in order to implement the strategy. We are interested in the simpler cases of controllers that base their decisions on a finite memory, a special case of which is the simple controller where the decision is based on the last visited automaton state. Such controllers need only observe the current state of the plant.

For an infinite sequence of states $\alpha : q[0], q[1], \ldots$ and a natural number n, we denote by $\alpha[0..n]$ the finite sequence $q[0], q[1], \ldots, q[n]$.

Definition 3 (Trajectories). *Let $\mathcal{P}$ be a plant and let $C : Q^+ \mapsto \Sigma_c$ be a controller. An infinite sequence of states $\alpha : q[0], q[1], \ldots$ such that $q[0] = q_0$ is called a trajectory of $\mathcal{P}$ if*

$$q[i + 1] \in \bigcup_{\sigma \in \Sigma_c} \delta(q[i], \sigma)$$

---

[4] Unlike other formulation of 2-person games where there is an explicit description of the transition function of both players, here we represent the response of the second player (the environment) as a non-deterministic choice among the transitions labeled by the same σ.

[5] Which means that for every $q \in Q, w, w' \in Q^*$, $C(wq) = C(w'q)$.

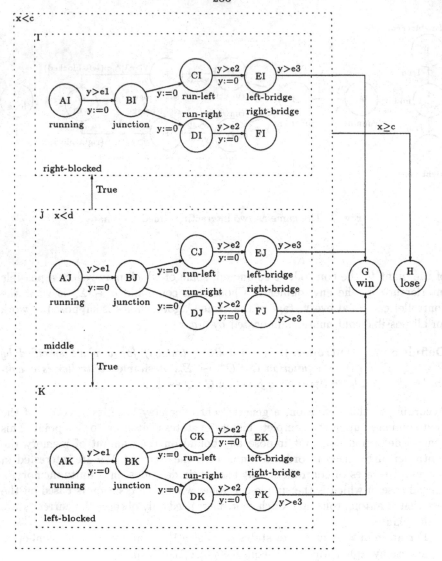

Fig. 3. The game described globally.

and a C-trajectory if $q[i+1] \in \delta(q[i], C(\alpha[0..i]))$ for every $i \geq 0$. The corresponding sets of trajectories are denoted by $L(\mathcal{P})$ and $L_C(\mathcal{P})$.

Clearly, every C-trajectory is a trajectory and $L_C(\mathcal{P}) \subseteq L(\mathcal{P})$. What remains is to define acceptance conditions, that is, a criterion to classify trajectories as good or bad. For every infinite trajectory $\alpha \in L(\mathcal{P})$, we let $Vis(\alpha)$ denote the set of all states appearing in α and let $Inf(\alpha)$ denote the set of all states appearing in α infinitely many times.

Definition 4 (Acceptance Condition). *Let* $\mathcal{P} = (Q, \Sigma_c, \delta, q_0)$ *be a plant. An acceptance condition for $\mathcal{P}$ is*

$$\Omega \in \{(F, \Diamond), (F, \Box), (F, \Diamond\Box), (F, \Box\Diamond), (\mathcal{F}, \mathcal{R}_n)\}$$

where $\mathcal{F} = \{(F_i, G_i)\}_{i=1}^n$ (Rabin condition) and F, F_i and G_i are certain subsets of Q referred as the good states. *The set of sequences of $\mathcal{P}$ that are accepted according to Ω is defined as follows:*

$L(\mathcal{P}, F, \Box)$	$\{\alpha \in L(\mathcal{P}) : Vis(\alpha) \subseteq F\}$	α always remains in F
$L(\mathcal{P}, F, \Diamond)$	$\{\alpha \in L(\mathcal{P}) : Vis(\alpha) \cap F \neq \emptyset\}$	α eventually visits F
$L(\mathcal{P}, F, \Diamond\Box)$	$\{\alpha \in L(\mathcal{P}) : Inf(\alpha) \subseteq F\}$	α eventually remains in F
$L(\mathcal{P}, F, \Box\Diamond)$	$\{\alpha \in L(\mathcal{P}) : Inf(\alpha) \cap F \neq \emptyset\}$	α visits F infinitely often
$L(\mathcal{P}, \mathcal{F}, \mathcal{R}_n)$	$\{\alpha \in L(\mathcal{P}) : \exists i.$ $\alpha \in L(\mathcal{P}, F_i, \Box\Diamond) \cap L(\mathcal{P}, G_i, \Diamond\Box)\}$	α visits F_i infinitely often and eventually stays in G_i

Definition 5 (Controller Synthesis Problem). *For a plant $\mathcal{P}$ and an acceptance condition Ω, the problem* **Synth**$(\mathcal{P}, \Omega)$ *is: Find a controller C such that $L_C(\mathcal{P}) \subseteq L(\mathcal{P}, \Omega)$ or otherwise show that such a controller does not exist.*

In case the answer is positive we say that $(\mathcal{P}, \Omega)$ is controllable.

Definition 6 (Controllable Predecessors). *Let $\mathcal{P} = (Q, \Sigma_c, \delta, q_0)$ be a plant. We define a function $\pi : 2^Q \mapsto 2^Q$, mapping a set of states $P \subseteq Q$ into the set of its* controllable predecessors, *i.e., the set of states from which the controller can "force" the plant into P in one step:*

$$\pi(P) = \{q \ : \ \exists \sigma \in \Sigma_c \cdot \delta(q, \sigma) \subseteq P\}$$

Theorem 1. *For every $\Omega \in \{(F, \Diamond), (F, \Box), (F, \Diamond\Box), (F, \Box\Diamond), (\mathcal{F}, \mathcal{R}_1)\}$ the problem* **Synth**$(\mathcal{P}, \Omega)$ *is solvable. Moreover, if $(\mathcal{P}, \Omega)$ is controllable then it is controllable by a simple controller.*[6]

Sketch of Proof: Let us denote by W the set of *winning* states, namely, the set of states from which a controller can enforce good behaviors (according to criterion Ω). They can be characterized by the following fixed-point expressions:

---

[6] A first variant of this theorem has been proved by Büchi and Landweber in [BL69] with respect to the more general Muller acceptance condition. In that case the controller is finite-state but not necessarily simple. The fact that games defined by Rabin condition can be won using a simple (memory-less) strategies is implicit in various papers on decision problems for tree-automata [V94]. In a more extensive version of the paper, we hope to present an alternative and more systematic treatment of winning strategies with respect to Boolean combinations of acceptance conditions as well as a fixed-point characterization of $\mathcal{R}_n$ for a general n. Impatient or pessimistic readers may look at such a characterization in [TW94a].

$$\square : \nu W \Big(F \cap \pi(W) \Big) \tag{1}$$

$$\lozenge : \mu W \Big(F \cup \pi(W) \Big) \tag{2}$$

$$\lozenge\square : \mu W \nu H \Big(\pi(H) \cap (F \cup \pi(W)) \Big) \tag{3}$$

$$\square\lozenge : \nu W \mu H \Big(\pi(H) \cup (F \cap \pi(W)) \Big) \tag{4}$$

$$\mathcal{R}_1 : \mu W \Big\{ \pi(W) \ \cup \ \nu Y \mu H . W \cup G \cap \Big(\pi(H) \cup (F \cap \pi(Y)) \Big) \Big\} \tag{5}$$

The plant is controllable iff $q_0 \in W$.

For a given plant and the induced controllable predecessor function π, it is straightforward to calculate the sets W defined by the fixed-point expressions (1)–(5) and check whether $q_0 \in W$. However, it may be illuminating to review the iterative process by which these sets are calculated.

Consider the cases $\lozenge$ and $\square$: the iteration processes can be described, respectively, by the following schemes:

$\lozenge$:
$W_0 := \emptyset$
for $i = 0, 1, \ldots$, **repeat**
$\quad W_{i+1} := F \cup \pi(W_i)$
until $W_{i+1} = W_i$

$\square$:
$W_0 := Q$
for $i = 0, 1, \ldots$, **repeat**
$\quad W_{i+1} := F \cap \pi(W_i)$
until $W_{i+1} = W_i$

For the $\lozenge$-case, each W_i contains the states from which a visit to F can be enforced after at most i steps and in the $\square$-case, it consists of the states from which the plant can be kept in F for at least i steps. The sequences $\{W_i\}$ are monotone over a finite domain and hence convergence is guaranteed.

This procedure is constructive in the following sense: in the process of calculating W_{i+1}, whenever we add a state q to W_i (or do not remove it from W_i in the $\square$-case) there must be at least one action $\sigma \in \Sigma_c$ such that $\delta(q, \sigma) \subseteq W_i$. So we define the controller at q as $C(q) = \sigma$. When the process terminates the controller is synthesized for all the winning states. It can be seen that if the process fails, that is, $q_0 \notin W$, then for every controller command there is a possibly bad consequence that will put the system outside F, and no controller, even an infinite-state one, can prevent this.

Consider now the case $\square\lozenge$: this case calls for nested iterations; an external major iteration varying the values of the set W, and a nested minor iteration varying the values of the set H. This double iteration is described by the following scheme:

$$W_0 := Q$$
$$\textbf{for } i = 0, 1, \ldots, \textbf{ repeat}$$
$$\begin{bmatrix} H_0 := \emptyset \\ \textbf{for } j = 0, 1, \ldots, \textbf{ repeat} \\ \quad H_{j+1} := \pi(H_j) \cup (F \cap \pi(W_i)) \\ \textbf{until } H_{j+1} = H_j \\ W_{i+1} := H_j \end{bmatrix}$$
$$\textbf{until } W_{i+1} = W_i$$

The major iteration starts with $W_0 = Q$. For that value of W, we iterate on H to compute the set of states from which a single visit to F can be enforced. For the next major iteration, we take W_1 to be this set. We now recompute H with respect to W_1 which yields the set of states from which one can enforce a visit to F followed by a visit to W_1 (and hence two visits to F). This process constructs a decreasing sequence $W_0, W_1, \ldots$, where each W_i is the set of states from which i visits to F can be enforced. This sequence converges to the set of states from which the plant can be driven to F infinitely many times. The strategy is extracted within the last execution of the inner loop as in the $\Diamond$-case. Formulation of the iterative processes for $\Diamond \Box$ and $\mathcal{R}_1$ is left as an exercise. ∎

4 The Real Time Case

Timed automata ([AD94]) are automata equipped with clocks whose values grow continuously. The clocks interact with the transitions by participating in pre-conditions (guards) for certain transitions and they are possibly reset when some transitions are taken. We let T denote $I\!\!R^+$ (the non-negative reals) and let $X = T^d$ (the clock space). We write elements of X as $\mathbf{x} = (x_1, \ldots, x_d)$ and denote the d-dimensional unit vector by $\mathbf{1} = \underbrace{(1, \ldots, 1)}_{d}$. Since X is infinite and non-countable, we need a language to express certain subsets of X as well as operations on these subsets.

Definition 7 (k-polyhedral sets). *Let k be a positive integer constant. We associate with k three subsets of 2^X:*

- *$\mathcal{H}_k$ – the set of half-spaces consisting of all sets having one of the following forms: X, $\emptyset$, $\{\mathbf{x} \in I\!\!R^+ : x_i \# c\}$, $\{\mathbf{x} \in I\!\!R^+ : x_i - x_j \# c\}$, for some $\# \in \{<, \leq , >, \geq\}$, $c \in \{0, \ldots, k\}$.*
- *$\mathcal{H}_k^\cap$ – the set of convex sets consisting of intersections of elements of $\mathcal{H}_k$.*
- *$\mathcal{H}_k^*$ – the set of k-polyhedral sets containing all sets obtained ¿from $\mathcal{H}_k$ via union, intersection and complementation.*

Clearly, for every k, $\mathcal{H}_k^*$ has a finite number of elements, each of which can be written as a finite union of convex sets. Some authors call the elements of $\mathcal{H}_k^*$ *regions*.

Definition 8 (Reset Functions). *Let $F(X)$ denote the class of functions f : $X \mapsto X$ that can be written in the form $f(x_1, \ldots, x_d) = (f_1, \ldots f_d)$ where each f_i is either x_i or 0.*

Definition 9 (Timed Automata). *A timed automaton is a tuple $\mathcal{T} = (Q, X, \Sigma, I, R, q_0)$ consisting of Q, a finite set of discrete states,[7] a clock domain $X = (\mathbb{R}^+)^d$ for some $d > 0$, an input alphabet Σ ($\Sigma = \Sigma_c \cup \{e\}$ including the controller actions Σ_c and a single environment action e), $I : Q \mapsto \mathcal{H}_k^\cap$ is the state invariance function (we denote $I(q)$ by I_q) and $R \subseteq Q \times \Sigma \times \mathcal{H}_k^\cap \times F(X) \times Q$ is a set of transition relations, each of the form $\langle q, \sigma, g, f, q' \rangle$, where $q, q' \in Q$, $\sigma \in \Sigma$, $g \in \mathcal{H}_k^\cap$, and $f \in F(X)$, $q_0 \in Q$ is the initial state of $\mathcal{T}$.*

A *configuration* of $\mathcal{T}$ is a pair $(q, \mathbf{x}) \in Q \times X$ denoting a discrete state and the values of the clocks. When in a configuration $(q, \mathbf{x})$ such that $\mathbf{x} \in I_q$, the automaton can "let" time progress, i.e., remain in q and let the values of the clocks increase uniformly as long as $\mathbf{x}$ is still in I_q. Whenever $\mathcal{T}$ is in $(q, \mathbf{x})$ such that for some $r = \langle q, \sigma, g, f, q' \rangle \in R$, $\mathbf{x} \in g$ (the "guard" of r is satisfied), the automaton can respond to a σ input and move to $(q', f(\mathbf{x}))$. Sometimes $I_q \cap g \neq \emptyset$ and both options are possible, namely at some configurations we can either stay in q and let $\mathbf{x}$ increase with time or take a transition.

Without loss of generality, we assume that for every $q \in Q$ and every $\mathbf{x} \in X$, there exists some $t \in T$ such that $\mathbf{x} + 1t \notin I_q$. That is, the automaton cannot stay in any of its discrete states forever.

Definition 10 (Steps and Trajectories). *A step of $\mathcal{T}$ is a pair of configurations $((q, \mathbf{x}), (q', \mathbf{x}'))$ such that either:*

1. *$q = q'$ and for some $t \in T$, $\mathbf{x}' = \mathbf{x} + 1t$, $\mathbf{x} \in I_q$ and $\mathbf{x}' \in I_q$. In this case we say that $(q', \mathbf{x}')$ is a t-successor of $(q, \mathbf{x})$ and that $((q, \mathbf{x}), (q', \mathbf{x}'))$ is a t-step.*
2. *There is some $r = \langle q, \sigma, g, f, q' \rangle \in R$ such that $\mathbf{x} \in g$ and $\mathbf{x}' = f(\mathbf{x})$. In this case we say that $(q', \mathbf{x}')$ is a σ-successor of $(q, \mathbf{x})$ and that $((q, \mathbf{x}), (q', \mathbf{x}'))$ is a σ-step.*

A trajectory of $\mathcal{T}$ is a sequence $\beta = (q[0], \mathbf{x}[0]), (q[1], \mathbf{x}[1]), \ldots$ of configurations such that for every i, $((q[i], \mathbf{x}[i]), (q[i+1], \mathbf{x}[i+1]))$ is a step.

A trajectory is *non-Zeno* if it has infinitely many t-steps and the sum of the corresponding t's diverges. We denote the set of all non-Zeno trajectories that $\mathcal{T}$ can generate by $L(\mathcal{T})$. Given a trajectory β we can define $Vis(\beta)$ and $Inf(\beta)$ as in the discrete case by referring to the projection of β on Q and use $L(\mathcal{T}, \Omega)$ to denote acceptable trajectories as in definition 4.

Definition 11 (Real-time Controllers). *A simple real-time controller is a function $C : Q \times X \mapsto \Sigma_c \cup \{\bot\}$.*

---

[7] Called "locations" by some authors, in order to distinguish them from global states that include the clock values – we will use "configurations" for the latter.

According to this function the controller chooses at any configuration $(q, \mathbf{x})$ whether to issue some enabled transition σ or to do nothing and let time go by. We denote by $\Sigma_c^\perp$ the range of controller commands $\Sigma_c \cup \{\perp\}$. We also require that the controller is k-polyhedral, i.e, for every $\sigma \in \Sigma_c^\perp$, $C^{-1}(\sigma)$ is a k-polyhedral set.

Definition 12 (Controlled Trajectories). *Given a simple controller C, a pair $((q, \mathbf{x}), (q', \mathbf{x}'))$ of configurations is a C-step if it is either*

1. *an e-step, or*
2. *a σ-step such that $C(q, \mathbf{x}) = \sigma \in \Sigma_c$ or*
3. *a t-step for some $t \in T$ such that for every t', $t' \in [0, t)$, $C(q, \mathbf{x} + \mathbf{1}t') = \perp$.*

A C-trajectory is a trajectory consisting of C-steps. We denote the set of C-trajectories of T by $L_C(T)$.

Definition 13 (Real-Time Controller Synthesis). *Given a timed automaton T and an acceptance condition Ω, the problem $\mathbf{RT\text{-}Synth}(T, \Omega)$ is: Construct a real-time controller C such that $L_C(T) \subseteq L(T, \Omega)$.*

In order to tackle the real-time controller synthesis problem we introduce the following definitions. For $t \in T$ and $\sigma \in \Sigma$, the configuration $(q', \mathbf{x}')$ is defined to be a (t, σ)-*successor* of the configuration $(q, \mathbf{x})$ if there exists an intermediate configuration $(\hat{q}, \hat{\mathbf{x}})$, such that $(\hat{q}, \hat{\mathbf{x}})$ is a t-successor of $(q, \mathbf{x})$ and $(q', \mathbf{x}')$ is a σ-successor of $(\hat{q}, \hat{\mathbf{x}})$.[8] Then we define function $\delta : (Q \times X) \times (T \times \Sigma_c^\perp) \mapsto 2^{Q \times X}$, where $\delta((q, \mathbf{x}), (t, \sigma))$ stands for all the possible consequences of the controller attempting to issue the command $\sigma \in \Sigma_c^\perp$ after waiting t time units starting at configuration $(q, \mathbf{x})$.

Definition 14 (Extended Transition Function). *For every $t \in T$ and $\sigma \in \Sigma_c$, the set $\delta((q, \mathbf{x}), (t, \sigma))$ consists of all the configurations $(q', \mathbf{x}')$ such that either*

1. *$(q', \mathbf{x}')$ is a (t, σ)-successor of $(q, \mathbf{x})$, or*
2. *$(q', \mathbf{x}')$ is a (t', e)-successor of $(q, \mathbf{x})$ for some $t' \in [0, t]$.*

This definition covers successor configurations that are obtained in one of two possible ways. Some configurations result from the plant waiting patiently at state q for t time units, and then taking a σ-labeled transition according to the controller recommendation. The second possibility is of configurations obtained by taking an environment transition at any time $t' \leq t$. *This is in fact the crucial new feature of real-time games – there are no "turns" and the adversary need not wait for the player's next move.*

As in the discrete case, we define a predecessor function that indicates the configurations from which the controller can force the automaton into a given set of configurations.

---

[8] Note that this covers the case of $(q', \mathbf{x}')$ being simply a σ-successor of $(q, \mathbf{x})$ by viewing it as a $(0, \sigma)$-successor of $(q, \mathbf{x})$.

Definition 15 (Controllable Predecessors). *The controllable predecessor function* $\pi : 2^Q \times 2^X \mapsto 2^Q \times 2^X$ *is defined for every* $K \subseteq Q \times X$ *by*

$$\pi(K) = \{(q, \mathbf{x}) : \exists t \in T . \exists \sigma \in \Sigma_c . \delta((q, \mathbf{x}), (t, \sigma)) \subseteq K\}$$

As in the discrete case, the sets of winning configurations can be characterized by a fixed-point expressions similar to (1)-(5) over $2^Q \times 2^X$. Unlike the discrete case, the iteration is not over a finite domain, yet some nice properties of timed-automata (see [AD94], [ACD93], [HNSY94] for more detailed proofs) guarantee convergence. Assume that $Q = \{q_0, \dots, q_m\}$. Clearly, any set of configurations can be written as $K = \{q_0\} \times P_0 \cup \dots \cup \{q_m\} \times P_m$, where $P_0, \dots, P_m$ are subsets of X. Thus, the set K can be uniquely represented by a *set tuple* $\mathcal{K} = \langle P_0, \dots, P_m \rangle$ and we can view π as a transformation on set tuples.

A set tuple $\mathcal{K}$ is called k-*polyhedral* if each component P_i, $i = 0, \dots, m$, belongs to $\mathcal{H}_k^*$. We will show that the function π always maps a k-polyhedral set tuple to another k-polyhedral set tuple. As a first step, we will represent the function π in terms of its action on components. Without loss of generality, we assume that for every $q \in Q$, $\sigma \in \Sigma_c$ there is at most one $r = \langle q, \sigma, g, f, q' \rangle \in R$. Let $\langle P_0', \dots, P_m' \rangle = \pi(\langle P_0, \dots, P_m \rangle)$. Then, for each $i = 0, \dots, m$, the set P_i' can be expressed as

$$P_i' = \bigcup_{\langle q_i, \sigma, g, f, q_j \rangle \in R} \{\mathbf{x} : \exists t \in T . \begin{pmatrix} \mathbf{x} \in I_{q_i} \wedge \mathbf{x} + \mathbf{1}t \in I_{q_i} \wedge \\ \mathbf{x} + \mathbf{1}t \in g \wedge f(\mathbf{x} + \mathbf{1}t) \in P_j \wedge \\ (\forall t' \leq t) \qquad\qquad \bigwedge_{\langle q_i, e, g', f', q_k \rangle \in R} \\ (\mathbf{x} + \mathbf{1}t' \in g' \rightarrow f(\mathbf{x} + \mathbf{1}t') \in P_k) \end{pmatrix} \} \quad (6)$$

This ugly-looking formula just states that $\mathbf{x}$ is in P_i' iff for some j, σ and t we can stay in q_i for t time units and then make a transition to some configuration in $\{q_j\} \times P_j$, while all other environment transitions that might be enabled between 0 and t will lead us to a configurations which are in some $\{p_k\} \times P_k$.

Claim 2 (Closure of $\mathcal{H}_k^*$ under π). *If* $\mathcal{K} = \langle P_0, \dots, P_m \rangle$ *is k-polyhedral so is* $\pi(\mathcal{K}) = \langle P_0', \dots, P_m' \rangle$.

Sketch of Proof: It can be verified that every P_i' can be written as a Boolean combinations of sets of the form:

$$I_{q_i} \cap \{\mathbf{x} : \exists t . \mathbf{x} + \mathbf{1}t \in I_{q_i} \cap g \cap f^{-1}(P_j) \wedge \forall t' \leq t . \mathbf{x} + \mathbf{1}t' \in \overline{g'} \cup f'^{-1}(P_k)\}$$

for some guards g, g' and reset functions f, f', where we use $f^{-1}(P)$ to denote $\{\mathbf{x} : f(\mathbf{x}) \in P\}$. Since timed reachability is distributive over union, i.e.,

$$\{\mathbf{x} : \exists t . \mathbf{x} + \mathbf{1}t \in S_1 \cup S_2\} = \{\mathbf{x} : \exists t . \mathbf{x} + \mathbf{1}t \in S_1\} \cup \{\mathbf{x} : \exists t . \mathbf{x} + \mathbf{1}t \in S_2\}$$

it is sufficient to prove the claim assuming k-convex polyhedral sets. Clearly, when f is a reset function $f^{-1}(S) = \{\mathbf{x} : f(\mathbf{x}) \in S\}$ is k-convex whenever S is. So what remains to show is that for any two k-convex sets S_1 and S_2, the set

$\pi_{t',t}(S_1, S_2)$, denoting all the points in S_1 from which we can reach S_2 (via time progress) without leaving S_1, and defined as

$$\pi_{t',t}(S_1, S_2) = \{\mathbf{x} : \exists t \,.\, \mathbf{x} + \mathbf{1}t \in S_2 \wedge \forall t' \leq t \,.\, \mathbf{x} + \mathbf{1}t' \in S_1\}$$

is also k-convex. Based on elementary linear algebra it can be shown that $\pi_{t',t}(S_1, S_2)$ is an intersection of some of the half-spaces defining S_1 and S_2, together with half-spaces of the form $x_i \geq 0$, and half-spaces of the form $\{\mathbf{x} : x_i - x_j \# c\}$ where c is an integer constant not larger than the maximal constant in the definitions of S_1 and S_2 (see figure 4 for intuition). ∎

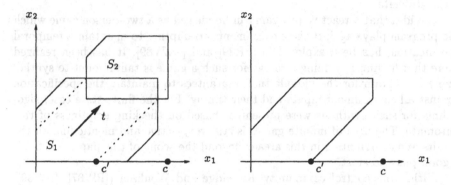

Fig. 4. The set $\pi_{t',t}(S_1, S_2)$ for the sets S_1, S_2 appearing in the right hand side appears in the left. One can see that the the integer constant c' in the new inequality $x_1 - x_2 < c'$ is an integer and is smaller than the constant c in the S_2 inequality $x_1 \leq c$.

Theorem 3 (Control Synthesis for Timed Systems). *Given a timed automaton T and an acceptance condition*

$$\Omega \in \{(F, \Diamond), (F, \Box), (F, \Diamond\Box), (F, \Box\Diamond), (\mathcal{F}, \mathcal{R}_1)\},$$

the problem **RT-Synth**(T, Ω) *is solvable.*

Sketch of Proof: We have just shown that $2^Q \times \mathcal{H}_k^*$ is closed under π. Any of the iterative processes for the fixed-point equations (1)–(5) starts with an element of $2^Q \times \mathcal{H}_k^*$. For example, the iteration for $\Diamond$ starts with $W_0 = Q \times F$. Each iteration consists of applying Boolean set-theoretic operations and the predecessor operation, which implies that every W_i is also an element of $2^Q \times \mathcal{H}_k^*$ – a finite set. Thus, by monotonicity, a fixed-point is eventually reached. ∎

The strategy is extracted in a similar manner as in the discrete case. Whenever a configuration $(q, \mathbf{x})$ is added to W, it is due to one or more pairs of the form $([t_1, t_2], \sigma)$ indicating that within any t, $t_1 < t < t_2$, issuing σ after waiting t will lead to a winning position. Hence by letting $C(q, \mathbf{x}) = \bot$ when $t_1 > 0$ and $C(q, \mathbf{x}) = \sigma$ when $t_1 = 0$ we obtain a k-polyhedral controller.

5   Relation to Other Work

The problem of finding a winning strategy for finite and infinite games has a long history, and it lies in the intersection of Logic, Game Theory, Descriptive Set Theory and Program Synthesis. The pioneering constructive result in this area is due to Büchi and Landweber (see [BL69], [TB73] [R72]) where the winning strategy is extracted from the description of the game, in the case when the game is ω-regular. These games can be viewed as a special case of a more general type of games expressed using Rabin's *tree automata*, introduced by Gurevich and Harrington ([GH82]). Emerson and Jutla [EJ91] used fixed-point equations (over a richer language) to characterize winning states for games associated with such automata.

The idea that a reactive program can be viewed as a two-person game which the program plays against the environment, attempting to maintain a temporal specification, has been explored in [PR89] and [ALW89]. It has been realized there that finding a winning strategy for such a game is tantamount to synthesizing a program for the module that guarantees to maintain the specification against all environment inputs and their timing. For the finite-state case, algorithms for such synthesis were presented, based on checking emptiness of tree automata. The area of infinite games is still very active and mentioning all the results and contribution in this area is beyond the scope of this paper – [T94] is a good place to start.

Within the control community, Ramadge and Wonham ([RW87], [RW89]) have built an extensive automata-theoretic framework (RW) for defining and solving control synthesis problems for discrete-event systems. Thistle and Wonham [TW94a] have proposed a fixed-point characterization for the winning states in an automaton game, and their approach is very close to ours in what concerns the discrete part. A similar characterization of controllability has been suggested by Le Borgne [LB93] in the context of dynamical systems over finite fields.

As for real-time games, an extension of the RW framework for *discrete* timed systems has been proposed in [BW93]. Unlike this approach, we work in the timed automaton framework (suggested by Alur and Dill [AD94] and studied extensively by, e.g., [HNSY94], [ACD93]), where Time is a continuous entity, whose passage interacts with discrete transitions.

The only work within the RW framework on timed automata that we are aware of is that of Wong-Toi and Hoffman [WTH92]. Our work differs from theirs in the following aspects: They adhere to the language-oriented approach of [RW89], while we prefer to develop a state-oriented model, which we believe to be more adequate for real-time and hybrid systems because timed languages are not easy objects to work with. Secondly, they solve the control problem by completely "discretizing" the timed-automaton into a finite-state automaton (the "region graph") and then solve the discrete synthesis problem. This procedure can introduce an unnecessary blow-up in the size of the system. Our method, working *directly* on the timed automaton, makes only the discretizations necessary to solve the control problem.

The approach we have outlined can be extended immediately to treat *hybrid automata* – a generalization of timed automata where the continuous variables can grow in different rates, and where the guards and invariants can be constructed from arbitrary linear inequalities. As in the the corresponding *analysis* problems for such systems, the fixed-point iteration might not converge, and thus we have only a semi-decision procedure.

Another interesting and important problem is that of partial observation: We assumed that the controller can precisely observe the the whole configuration of the plant, including the values of *all* the relevant clocks. In realistic situations the plant can be observed only up to some equivalence relation on its states, and the controller has to operate under some uncertainty.

References

[AD94] R. Alur and D.L. Dill, A Theory of Timed Automata, *Theoretical Computer Science* 126, 183–235, 1994.

[ACD93] R. Alur, C. Courcoubetis, and D.L. Dill, Model Checking in Dense Real Time, Information and Computation 104, 2–34, 1993.

[ALW89] M. Abadi, L. Lamport, and P. Wolper, Realizable and Unrealizable Concurrent Program Specifications. In *Proc. 16th Int. Colloq. Aut. Lang. Prog.*, volume 372 of *Lect. Notes in Comp. Sci.*, pages 1–17. Springer-Verlag, 1989.

[BW93] B.A. Brandin and W.M. Wonham, Supervisory Control of Timed Discrete-event Systems, *IEEE Transactions on Automatic Control*, 39, 329-342, 1994.

[BL69] J.R. Büchi and L.H. Landweber, Solving Sequential Conditions by Finite-state Operators, *Trans. of the AMS* 138, 295-311, 1969.

[EJ91] E.A. Emerson and C.J. Jutla, Tree Automata, μ-calculus and Determinacy, *Proc. 32nd FOCS*, 1991.

[GH82] Y. Gurevich and L. Harrington, Trees, Automata and Games, *Proc. 14th STOC*, 1982.

[HNSY94] T. Henzinger, X. Nicollin, J. Sifakis, and S. Yovine, Symbolic Model-checking for Real-time Systems, *Information and Computation* 111, 193–244, 1994.

[LB93] M. Le Borgne, *Dynamical Systems over Finite Fields*, Ph.D. thesis, Univ. Rennes 1, 1993 (In French).

[PR89] A. Pnueli and R. Rosner. On the Synthesis of a Reactive Module, In *Proc. 16th ACM Symp. Princ. of Prog. Lang.*, pages 179–190, 1989.

[R72] M.O. Rabin, Automata on Infinite Objects and Church's Problem, AMS, 1972.

[RW87] P.J. Ramadge and W.M. Wonham, Supervisory Control of a Class of Discrete Event Processes, *SIAM J. of Control and Optimization* 25, 206-230, 1987.

[RW89] P.J. Ramadge and W.M. Wonham, The Control of Discrete Event Systems, *Proc. of the IEEE* 77, 81-98, 1989.

[TW94a] J.G. Thistle and W.M. Wonham, Control of Infinite Behavior of Finite Automata, *SIAM J. of Control and Optimization* 32, 1075-1097, 1994.

[T94] W. Thomas, On the Synthesis of Strategies in Infinite Games, *These proceedings*.

[TB73] B.A. Trakhtenbrot and Y.M. Barzdin, *Finite Automata: Behavior and Synthesis*, North-Holland, Amsterdam, 1973.

[V94] M.Y. Vardi, Personal communication.

[WTH92] H. Wong-Toi and G. Hoffmann, The Control of Dense Real-Time Discrete Event Systems, Technical report STAN-CS-92-1411, Stanford University, 1992.

A fully abstract semantics
for causality in the π-calculus

Michele Boreale[1] and Davide Sangiorgi[2]

[1] Università di Roma "La Sapienza"
[2] University of Edinburgh

Abstract. We examine the meaning of causality in calculi for mobile processes like the π-calculus, and we investigate the relationship between interleaving and causal semantics for such calculi.
We separate two forms of causal dependencies on actions of π-calculus processes, called *subject* and *object* dependencies: The former originate from the nesting of prefixes and are propagated through interactions among processes; the latter originate from the binding mechanisms on names. We develop a notion of causal bisimulation which distinguishes processes which differ for the subject or for the object dependencies. We show that this *causal* equivalence can be reconducted to, or implemented into, the ordinary *interleaving* observation equivalence. This allows us to exploit the simpler theory of the interleaving semantics to reason about the causal one.

1 Introduction

Lately, there has been a growth of interest for *name-passing* process algebras, in which the possibility of communicating *names* (a synonymous for 'channels') permits the modeling of systems with dynamic linkage reconfigurations. The best known of these calculi is the *π-calculus* [MPW92]. Most theoretical research on the π-calculus has dealt with interleaving semantics [MPW92, San92, Wal94]; a major concern has been investigation of its expressiveness. The non-interleaving side remains largely unexplored.

The main goal of this paper is to investigate the the relationship between interleaving and causal semantics for the π-calculus. We focus on the interleaving *observation equivalence* ≈ [Mil89, MPW92], and on the non-interleaving *causal bisimulation* ≈$_c$ [DDM88, DD89, GG89, Kie91]; these are among the most studied behavioural equivalences in the respective groups. W.r.t. observation equivalence, causal bisimulation makes additional distinctions on processes on the basis of the causal dependencies for their actions. Our major result shows that causal bisimulation can be reconducted to observation equivalence. This is an expressiveness result for the π-calculus — it shows that the causality relation among actions can be faithfully implemented. The result also allows us to use the simpler theory of the interleaving semantics to reason about the causal one.

Known descriptions of causal bisimulation over CCS-like languages [DDM88, GG89, RT88] are based on operational transition rules more complex than the standard interleaving ones [Mil89], because they carry information about causal dependencies, in form of pointer-like objects among actions. This extra structure also has to be lifted at the syntactic level, forcing an extension of the basic language; existing algebraic theories and proof systems of causal bisimulation [DD89, Kie93] heavily rely on the added causal operators. A motivation for trying to implement causal bisimulation at the interleaving level is to seek ways for avoiding the introduction of this extra structure.

Another goal of this paper is to investigate the meaning of causality in calculi for mobile processes. We have individuated two forms of dependencies between actions, which we have called *subject* and *object* dependencies. Subject dependencies originate from the nesting of prefixes and are propagated through internal communications of processes. For example, the processes $a.b.0 + b.a.0$ can perform actions a and b in either order. In either case, there is a dependency between the two actions — the firing of the first enables the firing of the second. The propagation of subject dependencies through interactions is shown in $\nu c\,(a.c.0\,|\,\overline{c}.b.0)$ (we use the π-calculus notation $\nu\,a\,P$ for the restriction of name a in process P). In this process, the interaction at c creates a dependency of b from a; indeed, it holds that $\nu c\,(a.c.0\,|\,\overline{c}.b.0)$ is causally equivalent with $a.b.0$. In CCS-like languages, i.e., languages in which actions represent pure synchronisation, subject dependencies are the only form of causal dependencies. Subject dependencies cannot be detected at the interleaving level. For example, one cannot detect the dependency between the actions a and b of the process $a.b.0 + b.a.0$. Hence, in an interleaving semantics this process is equated to the process $a.0\,|\,b.0$; this equality is rejected in a causal semantics because in $a.0\,|\,b.0$ actions a and b are independent.

The other form of dependencies, namely the object dependencies, are determined by π-calculus binding mechanisms on actions; therefore they do not exist in CCS. Approximately, an action λ is object dependent from a previous action μ if μ acts as binder for some name of λ; as such, μ can be thought of as supplying some names to λ. There are two binding actions in the π-calculus, namely input and bound output — the latter denoting the output of a restricted, i.e., private, name.

By contrast with subject dependencies, the possible object dependencies in a process can be detected at the interleaving level, simply revealed by the occurrences of names in actions. For instance, consider the bound output transition $P_1 \xrightarrow{(\nu\,b)\overline{a}\langle b\rangle} P_2$, which says that P_1 can perform the output at a of the private name b and become P_2 in doing so; the object dependencies from the action $(\nu\,b)\overline{a}\langle b\rangle$ are given by those actions in the successive behaviour of P_2 in which b occurs free. A similar consideration can be made for input transitions $P_1 \xrightarrow{a\langle b\rangle} P_2$ — which says that P_1 can perform the input at a of b so becoming P_2 — if name b is not already present in P_1. In other words, observationally equivalent processes show the same object dependencies.

In most of the cases, an object dependency is also a subject dependency (for instance, this is always the case for the object dependencies arising from input actions). There are, however, exceptions. For instance, the process $P \overset{def}{=}$

$\nu\, b\, (\overline{a}\langle b\rangle.\, \mathbf{0} \mid \overline{b}\langle y\rangle.\, \mathbf{0})$ can perform the output at a of the restricted name b and then an output at b; the former action enables the latter, because it "opens" the restriction at b. There is an object dependency of the action at b from the action at a, but no subject dependency.

In this paper, we have chosen to separate subject dependencies from object dependencies, because they represent logically different forms of causality and because the resulting equivalence is easier to formalise and encode. Thus we shall distinguish processes which differ for the subject or for the object dependencies. For instance, we shall discriminate between the process P above and the process $Q \stackrel{def}{=} \nu\, b\, (\overline{a}\langle b\rangle.\, \overline{b}\langle y\rangle.\, \mathbf{0})$. Both processes can perform an action at a and then an action at b. However, in Q there is a double causal dependency between the two actions: One given by a prefix-nesting (i.e., a subject dependency), and the other given by a name-binding (i.e., an object dependency). By contrast, in P there is a single dependency between the two actions, given by name-binding.

To define a causal bisimulation which reflects these discriminations on processes, we add explicit causal informations into π-calculus syntax and and operational semantics. We then show that the sophisticated observational machinery of causal bisimulation ($\approx_c$) can be represented from within the interleaving observation equivalence ($\approx$). We define a compositional encoding $[\![.]\!]$ from the enriched calculus to the basic one, and we prove that it is fully abstract w.r.t. $\approx_c$ and $\approx$; i.e., for each pair of terms A and B in the enriched calculus we have:

$$A \approx_c B \text{ if and only if } [\![A]\!] \approx [\![B]\!].$$

Through various examples, we show how this result and the algebraic theory of $\approx$ can be used to prove properties about $\approx_c$. When restricted to the sublanguage with no object dependencies, that is CCS, our encoding yields a characterisation of the classic causal bisimulation of [DD89, Kie91] in terms of the observation equivalence of the monadic π-calculus.

In the definition of encoding, we exploit an important feature of the π-calculus: The calculus naturally permits the description of *data structures* which can be created and combined at run time. We use data structures called *wires* to encode the observability of the explicit causes used in the definition of causal bisimulation. A wire receives names at an *entrance-point* and retransmit them at a bunch of *end-points*. Several wires can be connected together, connection representing union of causes. Reachability among wires, i.e. if an end-point of a wire can be reached from the entrance-point of another wire, encodes the subject dependencies between actions. Transmission of causes across a parallel composition, a distinguishing feature of causal bisimulation, is rendered as an exchange of a private name, by which two previously separated wires get connected. The proof of our full abstraction theorem exploits a few properties of concatenation of wires that permit symbolic manipulations of these structures.

The paper mainly relates to [San94]. There, a programme similar to that of the present paper is carried out for *location bisimulation* [BCHK91], one of the most convincing spatial-sensitive non-interleaving semantics. An encoding from an enriched π-calculus of *located processes* to the standard π-calculus is given and proved to be fully abstract w.r.t. location bisimulation and observation equivalence. The treatment of causes in communications is what distinguishes causal bisimulation from location bisimulation: In the former, the causes of the interacting actions must be appropriately merged, whereas in the latter they remain separate. This explains the difference between the data structures (the wires) used in the encoding of the two equivalences, here and in [San94]. In the case of causal bisimulation, the connections among wires, established as the computation proceeds, may create *branching* chains; by contrast, in the case of location bisimulation connections among wires may only create *linear* chains. The difference also shows up in the proofs: Although the overall structure of the proofs of full abstraction is similar in the two papers, the technical details are quite different, sometimes strikingly so.

Due to lack of space, details of the proofs have been confined to [BS94].

2 The polyadic π-calculus and observation equivalence

Definition 1 Standard processes. Consider an infinite countable set $\mathcal{N}$ of names s.t. $\mathcal{N} \cap \{\tau\} = \emptyset$. The class of the *polyadic standard processes over names* $\mathcal{N}$, written $\mathcal{P}(\mathcal{N})$, is built from the operators of inaction, input prefix, output prefix, silent prefix, sum, parallel composition, restriction, and replication:

$$P := \mathbf{0} \mid a(\widetilde{b}).P \mid \overline{a}\langle\widetilde{b}\rangle.P \mid \tau.P \mid P_1 + P_2 \mid P_1 \mid P_2 \mid \nu a P \mid !P.$$

In the sequel, $a, b, \ldots, x, y, \ldots$ range over names, and P, Q, R over standard processes. A tilde denotes a tuple. When the tilde is empty, the surrounding brackets () and $\langle\rangle$ will be omitted. We refer to [Mil91] for detailed discussions on the operators of the language. We write $\Pi_{i \in I} P_i$ as an abbreviation for $P_{i_1} \mid \ldots \mid P_{i_n}$, $I = \{i_1, \ldots, i_n\}$. We assign parallel composition and sum the lowest precedence among the operators.

Following Milner [Mil91], we only admit *well-sorted agents*, that is agents which obey a predefined *sorting* discipline in their manipulation of names. The sorting prevents arity mismatching in communications, like in $\overline{a}\langle b, c\rangle.P \mid a(x).Q$. We do not present the sorting system because it is not essential to understand the contents of this paper.

We omit the definition of the standard transition system of π-calculus (for this, see for instance [San94]). We only recall that a π-calculus process has three possible forms of action: A *silent action* $P \xrightarrow{\tau} P'$ represents interaction, i.e. an internal activity in P. *Input* and *output actions* are, respectively, of the form $P \xrightarrow{a(\widetilde{b})} P'$ and $P \xrightarrow{(\nu \widetilde{b'})\overline{a}\langle\widetilde{b}\rangle} P'$. In both cases, the action occurs at a. In the input action, $\widetilde{b}$ is the tuple of names which are received. In the output action, $\widetilde{b}$ is the tuple of names which are emitted, and $\widetilde{b'} \subseteq \widetilde{b}$ are private names which are carried out from their current scope. We use μ to represent the label of a generic action (not to be confused with α, which represents prefixes). Bound names, free names and names of ana action μ are written bn(μ), fn(μ) and n(μ), respectively. We identify alpha convertible processes.

As usual, the 'weak' arrow $\Longrightarrow$ is the reflexive and transitive closure of $\xrightarrow{\tau}$, and $\overset{\mu}{\Longrightarrow}$ is $\Longrightarrow\xrightarrow{\mu}\Longrightarrow$. We write $P \overset{\widehat{\mu}}{\Longrightarrow} Q$ to mean $P \overset{\mu}{\Longrightarrow} Q$, if $\mu \neq \tau$, and $P \Longrightarrow Q$, if $\mu = \tau$.

Definition 2 observation equivalence. *Observation equivalence* is the largest symmetric relation $\approx\, \subseteq\, \mathcal{P}(\mathcal{N}) \times \mathcal{P}(\mathcal{N})$ s.t. $P \approx Q$ and $P \overset{\mu}{\Longrightarrow} P'$ imply that there exists Q' s.t. $Q \overset{\widehat{\mu}}{\Longrightarrow} Q'$ and $P' \approx Q'$.

Observation equivalence is preserved by all operators but input prefix and sum.

3 Causal bisimulation

In Section 1 we observed that in the π-calculus there are two forms of causal dependencies, which we called *object dependencies* and *subject dependencies*, and that the object dependencies can be detected within the standard (i.e., interleaving) transition system. To capture the subject dependencies we follow Kiehn [Kie91] and we add explicit causal information to the standard syntax and operational semantics of the calculus. For the extra causal information, we use an auxiliary set $\mathcal{K}$ of *causes*. In the enriched system, visible transitions are of the form $A \xrightarrow[K;\,k]{\mu} A'$. The visible action μ is associated with a unique cause $k \in \mathcal{K}$. The set of actions from which μ is causally related is revealed by means of the set $K \subseteq_{\mathsf{fin}} \mathcal{K}$ of their associated causes. We call K the *cause-set* for μ. If a successive action μ' is caused by μ, then μ' will have k (i.e., the cause associated with μ) in its cause-set. In the term syntax, the explicit use of causes is accompanied by the introduction of a causal prefix $K :: A$, for $K \subseteq_{\mathsf{fin}} \mathcal{K}$, which says that the cause-set of any action of the process A must contain K.

By contrast, silent actions are not observable and do not exhibit causes. However, causes do play an important role in the communication rule, for the causes of two interacting actions must be appropriately merged. Consider the sequence of transitions

$$\nu b\big(a.\,b.\,c.\,\mathbf{0} \,|\, d.\,\overline{b}.\,\mathbf{0}\big) \xrightarrow[\emptyset;\,k_1]{a} \nu b\big(\{k_1\} :: b.\,c.\,\mathbf{0} \,|\, d.\,\overline{b}.\,\mathbf{0}\big) \xrightarrow[\emptyset;\,k_2]{d}$$
$$\nu b\big(\{k_1\} :: b.\,c.\,\mathbf{0} \,|\, \{k_2\} :: \overline{b}.\,\mathbf{0}\big) \xrightarrow{\tau} \nu b\big(\{k_1, k_2\} :: c.\,\mathbf{0} \,|\, \{k_1, k_2\} :: \mathbf{0}\big) \xrightarrow[\{k_1,k_2\};\,k_3]{c}$$
$$\nu b\big(\{k_1, k_2\} :: \{k_3\} :: \mathbf{0} \,|\, \{k_1, k_2\} :: \mathbf{0}\big).$$

They show that the actions at a and d have no cause; and that the action at c is causally dependent on a and d. The latter makes sense: c could fire only because both a and d fired. Note that in the τ-transition, the cause-sets $\{k_1\}$ and $\{k_2\}$ of the consumed actions are merged.

We let k and h range over causes (i.e., elements of $\mathcal{K}$), K and H over finite subsets of $\mathcal{K}$, and A and B over causal processes. To improve readability, in the syntax of our terms and of our operational rules we abbreviate a union of sets of causes $K \cup K'$ as K, K' and we write a singleton set $\{k\}$ simply as k. Thus, $A \xrightarrow[K,K';\,k]{\mu} A'$ stands for $A \xrightarrow[K \cup K';\,k]{\mu} A'$, and $k :: A$ stands for $\{k\} :: A$.

Definition 3 causal processes. Consider an infinite countable set $\mathcal{N}$ of names, and an infinite countable set $\mathcal{K}$ of *causes* with $\mathcal{K}$, $\mathcal{N}$ and $\{\tau\}$ pairwise disjoint. The language of *polyadic causal processes over causes $\mathcal{K}$ and names $\mathcal{N}$*, written $\mathcal{P}_c(\mathcal{N}, \mathcal{K})$, is given by the following grammar:

$$A := K :: A \mid A \mid A \mid \nu a A \mid P$$

where P is a $\mathcal{P}(\mathcal{N})$ term (i.e., a standard term) and $K \subseteq_{\text{fin}} \mathcal{K}$.

We do not allow the presence of causes underneath dynamic operators (prefixes, sums and replications), because we are only interested in derivatives of standard processes, for which these cases may never arise. This is clear from the transition rules for causal terms, in Table 1. Rule Com implements the cause exchange discussed at the beginning of this section. In the rule, the notation $A[k \rightsquigarrow K]$ indicates the replacement of k with the elements of K, in any set of causes in A. For instance, $(\{k_1, k_2\} :: \alpha.0)[k_2 \rightsquigarrow \{k_3, k_4\}]$ is $\{k_1, k_3, k_4\} :: \alpha.0$. Weak causal transitions are defined in the usual manner, therefore $A \overset{\mu}{\underset{K;k}{\Longrightarrow}} A'$ is $A \Longrightarrow \overset{\mu}{\underset{K;k}{\longrightarrow}} \Longrightarrow A'$.

Definition 4. *Causal bisimulation* is the largest symmetric relation $\approx_c \subseteq \mathcal{P}_c(\mathcal{N}, \mathcal{K}) \times \mathcal{P}_c(\mathcal{N}, \mathcal{K})$ s.t. $A \mathcal{R} B$ implies:

1. whenever $A \Longrightarrow A'$ there exists B s.t. $B \Longrightarrow B'$ and $A' \approx_c B'$;
2. whenever $A \overset{\mu}{\underset{K;k}{\Longrightarrow}} A'$ and k does not appear in A or B, there exists B' s.t. $B \overset{\mu}{\underset{K;k}{\Longrightarrow}} B'$ and $A' \approx_c B'$. $\qquad\qquad\square$

4 The Encoding

We use two new sorts $\mathcal{C}$ and $\mathcal{T}$ of names, 'new' meaning that these names do not appear in the source causal terms. Therefore in the sequel, unless otherwise specified, all causal and standard processes considered are from $\mathcal{P}_c(\mathcal{N}, \mathcal{K})$ and from $\mathcal{P}(\mathcal{N} \cup \mathcal{C} \cup \mathcal{T})$, respectively. There will be a one-to-one correspondence between causes — i.e. elements of the set $\mathcal{K}$ — in a causal process, and names of sort $\mathcal{C}$ in the standard process encoding it. Hence, for notational convenience, we identify the sets $\mathcal{C}$ and $\mathcal{K}$. Names in $\mathcal{C}$ carry names of sort $\mathcal{T}$. We sometimes call a name in $\mathcal{T}$ a *token*.

The intuition underlying the encoding is as follows. Causes in a causal term A are encoded in the standard term $[\![A]\!]$ as standard processes called *wires*. A wire $k \rhd K$ is so defined: $\qquad k \rhd K \overset{def}{=} \, !k(v). \, \Pi_{k' \in K} \, !\overline{k'}\langle v \rangle$.

It takes a token in input at the *entrance point* k and emits it, as an output, at each *end-point* $k' \in K$. The outermost replication in the definition of $k \rhd K$ is to make the wire persistent, so that it can be used an arbitrary number of times. The innermost replications ensures that a token which has reached an end-point will be transmitted to all unboundedly many wires connected with it. Two wires are connected when an end-point of the first is the entrance-point of the other;

Rules for visible transitions:

$$\textbf{Out}: \quad \overline{a}\langle\widetilde{b}\rangle.A \xrightarrow[\emptyset\,;\,k]{\overline{a}\langle\widetilde{b}\rangle} k :: A \qquad\qquad \textbf{Inp}: \quad a\langle\widetilde{b}\rangle.A \xrightarrow[\emptyset\,;\,k]{a\langle\widetilde{c}\rangle} k :: A\{\widetilde{c}/\widetilde{b}\}$$

$$\textbf{Cau}: \quad \frac{A \xrightarrow[K\,;\,k]{\mu} A'}{K' :: A \xrightarrow[K,\overline{K'}\,;\,k]{\mu} K' :: A'} \qquad \textbf{Par}: \quad \frac{A_1 \xrightarrow[K\,;\,k]{\mu} A_1'}{A_1 \mid A_2 \xrightarrow[K\,;\,k]{\mu} A_1' \mid A_2}\ \ \mathrm{bn}(\mu)\cap\mathrm{fn}(A_2)=\emptyset$$

$$\textbf{Res}: \quad \frac{A \xrightarrow[K\,;\,k]{\mu} A'}{\nu c A \xrightarrow[K\,;\,k]{\mu} \nu c A'},\, c\notin\mathrm{n}(\mu) \quad \textbf{Open}: \quad \frac{A \xrightarrow[K\,;\,k]{(\nu\,\widetilde{b'})\overline{a}\langle\widetilde{b}\rangle} A'}{\nu c A \xrightarrow[K\,;\,k]{(\nu\,\widetilde{b'}c)\overline{a}\langle\widetilde{b}\rangle} \nu c A'},\, c\neq a, c\in\widetilde{b}-\widetilde{b'}$$

$$\textbf{Sum}: \quad \frac{A_1 \xrightarrow[K\,;\,k]{\mu} A_1'}{A_1+A_2 \xrightarrow[K\,;\,k]{\mu} A_1'} \qquad\qquad \textbf{Rep}: \quad \frac{A\mid !A \xrightarrow[K\,;\,k]{\mu} A'}{!A \xrightarrow[K\,;\,k]{\mu} A'}$$

Rules for silent transitions:

$$\textbf{T-pre}: \quad \tau.A \xrightarrow{\tau} A \qquad\qquad \textbf{T-sum}: \quad \frac{A_1 \xrightarrow{\tau} A_1'}{A_1+A_2 \xrightarrow{\tau} A_1'}$$

$$\textbf{T-par}: \quad \frac{A_1 \xrightarrow{\tau} A_1'}{A_1\mid A_2 \xrightarrow{\tau} A_1'\mid A_2} \qquad \textbf{T-res}: \quad \frac{A \xrightarrow{\tau} A'}{\nu c A \xrightarrow{\tau} \nu c A'}$$

$$\textbf{Com}: \quad \frac{A_1 \xrightarrow[K_1\,;\,k]{(\nu\,\widetilde{b'})\overline{a}\langle\widetilde{b}\rangle} A_1' \quad A_2 \xrightarrow[K_2\,;\,k]{a\langle\widetilde{b}\rangle} A_2'}{A_1\mid A_2 \xrightarrow{\tau} \nu\,\widetilde{b'}\,(A_1'[k\rightsquigarrow K_2]\mid A_2'[k\rightsquigarrow K_1])}\ \ \widetilde{b'}\cap\mathrm{fn}(A_2)=\emptyset,\, k\notin\mathcal{K}(A_1,A_2)$$

$$\textbf{T-cau}: \quad \frac{A \xrightarrow{\tau} A'}{K :: A \xrightarrow{\tau} K :: A'} \qquad\qquad \textbf{T-rep}: \quad \frac{A\mid !A \xrightarrow{\tau} A'}{!A \xrightarrow{\tau} A'}$$

Table 1. SOS of causal terms

this connection represents union of causes. When $[\![A]\!]$ performs a visible action, a name k is emitted and a wire with entrance-point k is created. Intuitively, k represents the unique cause associated to that transition, whose cause-set is represented by all end-points of all wires reachable from k. An observer that receives k can determine this cause-set by sending a token at k and and observing *where* (i.e., at which end-points) the token can be retrieved.

As an example, the encoding of the causal process $K :: a.b.0$ will have the following transitions:

$$[\![K :: a.b.0]\!] \xrightarrow{a\langle k\rangle} k \triangleright K \mid [\![k :: b.0]\!] \xrightarrow{b\langle h\rangle} k \triangleright K \mid h \triangleright k \mid [\![h :: 0]\!].$$

(This shows how *linear* chains are generated.) A crucial point is the modeling of silent transitions. The "merging of causes" discussed at the beginning of Section 3 is implemented as an exchange of a bound name, by which the appropriate wires get connected. As an example, we have:

$$[K :: a.P \mid H :: \bar{a}.Q] \xrightarrow{\tau} \nu k\, (\, k \rhd K \mid k \rhd H \mid [k :: P \mid k :: Q])$$

(This shows how *branching* chains arise.) After the communication, P and Q have a common cause-set $K \cup H$, referred to by k. Indeed, the derivative of the above transition will turn out to be observationally equivalent to $[K \cup H :: P \mid K \cup H :: Q]$.

The encoding is presented in Table 2. It acts as a homomorphism everywhere but on prefixes. The encoding adds adds extra components (the wires) into processes, thus increasing the number of their states. The problem, however, is strongly alleviated by Lemmata 6 and 7 and the Cancellation Lemma 8, in Section 5, which allow us to get rid of wires when they appear at the outermost level of processes.

To ease the notation, we abbreviate $k \rhd (K \cup H)$ as $k \rhd (K, H)$, and $k \rhd (\{k'\}, K)$ as $k \rhd (k', K)$. Similarly, we abbreviate $[A](K \cup K')$ as $[A](K, K')$ and $[A](\{k\}, K')$ as $[A](k, K')$. Note that when the source term are 0-adic terms (i.e., CCS terms), Table 2 gives us an encoding of the classical causal bisimulation of CCS [DD89, Kie91] into the observation equivalence of the monadic π-calculus.

We assume $k : C$, $K \subseteq_{\mathrm{fin}} C$ and $v : T$; we set $[A] \stackrel{def}{=} [A]\emptyset$, where $[A]K$ is defined by induction on the structure of A as follows:

$$[a(\tilde{b}).A]K \stackrel{def}{=} a(\tilde{b}k).(\, k \rhd K \mid [A]\{k\}),\ k \in \mathcal{K} - K$$
$$[\bar{a}(\tilde{b}).A]K \stackrel{def}{=} \nu k\, \bar{a}(\tilde{b}k).(\, k \rhd K \mid [A]\{k\}),\ k \in \mathcal{K} - K$$
$$[K' :: A]K \stackrel{def}{=} [A](K', K) \qquad\qquad [\tau.A]K \stackrel{def}{=} \tau.[A]K$$
$$[A_1 \mid A_2]K \stackrel{def}{=} [A_1]K \mid [A_2]K \quad [A_1 + A_2]K \stackrel{def}{=} [A_1]K + [A_2]K$$
$$[\nu a\, A]K \stackrel{def}{=} \nu a\, [A]K \qquad\qquad [0]K \stackrel{def}{=} 0$$
$$[!\, A]K \stackrel{def}{=} ![A]K$$

Table 2. The encoding of causal terms

---

5 Correctness of the encoding

The analysis of the correctness of the encoding, in particular the proof of its full abstraction, absorbs a substantial part of the full paper [BS94]. An important role is played by various lemmata which establish properties of wire processes $k \rhd K$. Here, due to lack of space, we can only state a few of the main results.

Lemma 5 shows that a wires which is private to a composition of processes can be made private to each of the processes in the composition.

Lemma 5.

1. $\nu k ([A_1] | [A_2] | k \triangleright K) \approx \nu k ([A_1] | k \triangleright K) | \nu k ([A_2] | k \triangleright K)$

2. $\nu k (! [A] | k \triangleright K) \approx ! \nu k ([A] | k \triangleright K)$ □

Lemma 6 and Lemma 7 deal with properties of compositions of wires. Lemma 6 shows that two wires $k' \triangleright (k, K')$ and $k \triangleright K$, in which the entrance point of the second is among the end-points of the first, are, so to speak, 'connected': Hence the end-points K of the second can be added to the end-points K' of the first. Lemma 7 show that if, in addition to the above hypothesis, we assume that the common extreme k of the two wires is inaccessible, then their composition yields a single wire $k' \triangleright (K, K')$, whose end-points include all end-points of the given wires, except the inaccessible k.

Lemma 6. $k' \triangleright (k, K') | k \triangleright K \approx k' \triangleright (k, K', K) | k \triangleright K$. □

Lemma 7. *If* $k \notin (\{k'\} \cup K' \cup K)$*, then*
$\nu k (k' \triangleright (K', k) | k \triangleright K) \approx k' \triangleright (K', K)$ □

Lemma 8 shows a cancellation property which is very useful to reason about the processes returned by the encoding.

Lemma 8 Cancellation Lemma. *Suppose that* $A \xrightarrow[K;k]{\mu} A'$ *and* $B \xrightarrow[K';k]{\mu} B'$, *and* k *does not occur in* A *and* B. *Then* $k \triangleright K | [A'] \approx k \triangleright K' | [B']$ *implies* $K = K'$ *and* $[A'] \approx [B']$. □

There is a close correspondence between the actions of a causal process A and those of the encoding standard process $[A]$. Proposition 9 shows the correspondence on visible actions, and Proposition 10 on silent actions. Both propositions are proved by transition induction. In the cases of the input, output and communication rules, Lemmata 5-7 are used, to record the effect of a wire onto a process in parallel with the wire itself: This accounts for the occurrences of $\approx$ in the two propositions.

Proposition 9 correspondence on visible transitions.

1. (a) If $A \xrightarrow[H;k]{a\widetilde{(b)}} A'$ *then* $[A]K \xrightarrow{a\widetilde{(bk)}} \approx k \triangleright (H, K) | [A']K$.

   (b) If $A \xrightarrow[H;k]{\nu \widetilde{b'} \, \overline{a}\widetilde{(b)}} A'$ *then* $[A]K \xrightarrow{(\nu \widetilde{b'} k)\overline{a}\widetilde{(bk)}} \approx k \triangleright (H, K) | [A']K$.

2. The converse of (1), on the actions from $[A]K$:

   (a) If $[A]K \xrightarrow{a\widetilde{(bk)}} P$ *then there exist* A', H *s.t.* $A \xrightarrow[H;k]{a\widetilde{(b)}} A'$ *and* $P \approx k \triangleright (H, K) | [A']K$.

   (b) If $[A]K \xrightarrow{(\nu \widetilde{b'} k)\overline{a}\widetilde{(bk)}} P$ *then there exist* A', H *s.t.* $A \xrightarrow[H;k]{\nu \widetilde{b'} \, \overline{a}\widetilde{(b)}} A'$ *and* $P \approx k \triangleright (H, K) | [A']K$. □

Proposition 10 correspondence on silent transitions.

1. *If* $A \xrightarrow{\tau} A'$, *then* $[A]K \xrightarrow{\tau} \approx [A']K$.
2. *If* $[A]K \xrightarrow{\tau} P$, *then there exists* A' *such that* $A \xrightarrow{\tau} A'$ *and* $P \approx [A']K$. $\square$

Theorem 11 full abstraction of the encoding. *For all causal terms* A *and* B, *it holds that* $A \approx_c B$ *iff* $[A] \approx [B]$. $\qquad\qquad\qquad\square$

6 Examples of applications

Some simple laws for causal bisimulation follow directly from the definition of the encoding; for example:

$$K :: (A \mid B) \approx_c (K :: A) \mid (K :: B),$$
$$K :: H :: A \approx_c K \cup H :: A,$$
$$\emptyset :: A \approx_c A.$$

As an easy corollary of the definition of our encoding and its full abstraction, we can derive the congruence of $\approx_c$ w.r.t. the causal prefix $K :: -$ and all operators which preserve $\approx$. For instance, the following sequence of implications, that holds for any causal processes A, B and C, provides the argument for parallel composition:

$$A \approx_c B \qquad \text{implies} \qquad [A] \approx [B]$$
$$\text{which implies} \quad [A \mid C] = [A] \mid [C] \approx [B] \mid [C] = [B \mid C],$$
$$\text{which implies} \quad A \mid C \approx_c B \mid C.$$

Similarly, we can use the encoding to check that $\approx_c$ is not preserved by sum, basing the argument on the analogous failure for $\approx$. Thus, the only congruence property for $\approx_c$ remained is the one for the input prefix operator $a(\tilde{b}). -$. This is a non-trivial issue; discussion on this is postponed to Section 7.

More complex laws can be proved by taking advantage of the well-understood algebraic theory of $\approx$. For instance, consider $P \stackrel{def}{=} \nu b (a.b.c \mid \bar{b}.d)$ and $Q \stackrel{def}{=} \nu b (a.b.d \mid \bar{b}.c)$. Processes P and Q differ only because c and d are placed at different locations. However, in both cases c and d have the same cause, namely a. Indeed, it holds that $P \approx_c Q$. We can prove this fact by algebraic manipulations of the encoding processes $[P]$ and $[Q]$, with which $[P] \approx [Q]$ is derived. If $R \stackrel{def}{=} h \triangleright \emptyset \mid [d]h$, then

$$[P] = \nu b \big(a(k). (k \triangleright \emptyset \mid [b.c]k) \mid \nu h \bar{b}\langle h \rangle. R \big).$$

Using the expansion law and simple laws for restriction we obtain

$$[P] \approx a(k). (k \triangleright \emptyset \mid \nu b ([b.c]k \mid \nu h \bar{b}\langle h \rangle. R)). \qquad (1)$$

By definition, $[b.c]k = b(h). (h \triangleright k \mid [c]h)$. Using the same laws as above, and the definitions of $[b.c]k$ and of R, we can derive

$$\nu b ([b.c]k \mid \nu h \bar{b}\langle h \rangle. R) \approx \tau.\nu h (h \triangleright k \mid [c]h \mid h \triangleright \emptyset \mid [d]h)$$

from which, using the definition of the encoding and Lemmata 5 and 7, we can derive

$$\nu\, b\, ([\![b.c]\!]k \mid \nu\, h\, \overline{b}\langle h\rangle.\, R) \approx \tau.\nu\, h\, \big(\, h \rhd k \mid h \rhd \emptyset \;\; [\![c \mid d]\!]\big) \approx \tau.[\![c \mid d]\!]k\,. \qquad (2)$$

This relation holds for any cause k. By the congruence properties of $\approx$, from (1) and (2) we get

$$[\![P]\!] \approx a(k).\big(\, k \rhd \emptyset \;\mid \tau.[\![c \mid d]\!]k\,\big). \qquad (3)$$

In a symmetric way — exchanging the roles of c and d — one proves that

$$[\![Q]\!] \approx a(k).\big(\, k \rhd \emptyset \;\mid \tau.[\![d \mid c]\!]k\,\big). \qquad (4)$$

Now, $[\![P]\!] \approx [\![Q]\!]$ follows from (3) and (4) using the definition of the encoding and the commutativity of parallel composition. Note that in the above sequence of transformations, Lemma 5 and Lemma 7 avoid us having to unfold the definition of wire processes, and hence having to explicitly deal with the replication operator. A proof of $P \approx_c Q$ is also possible utilising a proof system for $\approx_c$ on CCS, like Kiehn's [Kie93]. The advantage of using $\approx$ is that it has simpler laws, which and do not require the introduction of extra operators. Kiehn's system, besides the causal prefix $K :: -$, uses the *left merge* and the *communication merge* operators, to express an appropriate form of expansion law for causal bisimulation. Moreover, Kiehn's system is not purely equational — it includes non-trivial inference rules.

7 Future work

An interesting issue is the study of the congruence properties for the input-prefix operator in causal-sensitive behavioural equivalences. Intuitively, a relation over π-calculus processes is preserved by input prefix if it is preserved by name substitutions. This property usually fails if the *matching* operator is present, as for the calculus in [MPW92]. A matching $[a = b]P$ represents an **if-then** construct with guard "$a = b$". With the matching operator observation equivalence, location bisimulation and causal bisimulation are all not preserved by substitutions[San94]. However, in many situations matching can be avoided or simulated. Hence one might wish to consider a matching-free calculus, as we did in the present paper. On such a language, the congruence for substitutions still fails for observation equivalence and location bisimulation [San94], but we conjecture that it holds for causal bisimulation.

We have individuated two forms of causal dependency between π-calculus actions, which we called subject and object dependencies. The former originate from prefix-nesting and are propagated through interactions within processes, the latter originate from the name-binding mechanisms. Our formulation of causal bisimulation distinguishes between processes which differ for the subject or for the object dependencies. Thus we discriminate between $P \overset{def}{=} \nu\, b\,(\overline{a}\langle b\rangle.\, 0 \mid \overline{b}\langle y\rangle.\, 0)$ and $Q \overset{def}{=} \nu\, b\,(\overline{a}\langle b\rangle.\, \overline{b}\langle y\rangle.\, 0)$, because in P there is both a subject and an object dependency between the actions at a and at b, whereas in Q there is only an object dependency. We would like to compare this notion of causal bisimulation with one in which subject and object dependencies are still taken into account but not separated, so to equate P and Q. One possibility is to carry out this analysis using our encoding or variations of it.

Acknowledgments. We are most grateful to Rocco De Nicola for comments and discussions on the topic of the paper. Michele Boreale has been partially supported by the HCM Network "EXPRESS". Davide Sangiorgi's research has been supported by the ESPRIT BRA project 6454 "CONFER".

References

[BCHK91] G. Boudol, I. Castellani, M. Hennessy, and A. Kiehn. A theory of processes with localities. To appear in *Formal Aspects of Computing*.

[BS94] M. Boreale and D. Sangiorgi. Full version of this paper. Technical Report, ECS–LFCS–94–297, University of Edinburgh, 1994.

[DD89] P. Degano and P. Darondeau. Causal trees. In *15th ICALP*, LNCS 372, pages 234–248. Springer Verlag, 1989.

[DDM88] P. Degano , R. De Nicola and U. Montanari. Partial Ordering Descriptions and Observations of Concurrent Processes. LNCS 354, Springer-Verlag, 1988.

[GG89] R.J. van Glabbeek and U. Goltz. Equivalence notions for concurrent systems and refinement of actions. In *Proc. MFCS'89*, LNCS 379. Springer Verlag, 1989.

[Kie91] A. Kiehn. Local and global causes. Technical Report Report 342/23/91, Technische Universität München, 1991.

[Kie93] A. Kiehn. Proof systems for cause based equivalences. In *Proc. MFCS 93*, LNCS 711. Springer Verlag, 1993.

[Mil89] R. Milner. *Communication and Concurrency*. Prentice Hall, 1989.

[Mil91] R. Milner. The polyadic π-calculus: a tutorial. In *Logic and Algebra of Specification*, Springer Verlag, 1993.

[MPW92] R. Milner, J. Parrow, and D. Walker. A calculus of mobile processes, (Parts I and II). *Information and Computation*, 100:1–77, 1992.

[RT88] A. Rabinovich and B.A. Trakhetenbrot. Behaviour structures and nets. *Fundamenta Informaticae*, XI(4):357–404, 1988.

[San92] D. Sangiorgi. *Expressing Mobility in Process Algebras: First-Order and Higher-Order Paradigms*. PhD thesis CST–99–93, Department of Computer Science, University of Edinburgh, 1992.

[San94] D. Sangiorgi. Locality and non-interleaving semantics in calculi for mobile processes. In *Proc. TACS '94*, LNCS 789, Springer Verlag.

[Wal94] D. Walker. Objects in the π-calculus. *Information and Computation*, 1994. To appear.

On the Sizes of Permutation Networks and Consequences for Efficient Simulation of Hypercube Algorithms on Bounded-Degree Networks [*]

(Extended Abstract)

J. Hromkovič [1],[**], K. Loryś [2],[***], P. Kanarek [2],[***], R. Klasing [3], W. Unger [3], H. Wagener [3],[†]

[1] Institut für Informatik und Praktische Mathematik, Universität zu Kiel, D-24098 Kiel, Germany, E-Mail: jhr@informatik.uni-kiel.d400.de
[2] University of Wrocław, Institute of Computer Science, PL-51-151 Wrocław, Poland, E-Mail: lorys,pka@ii.uni.wroc.pl
[3] Fachbereich Mathematik/Informatik, Universität-GH Paderborn, D-33095 Paderborn, Germany, E-Mail: klasing@uni-paderborn.de

Classification: theory of parallel and distributed computation, parallel algorithms.

Abstract. The sizes of permutation networks for special sets of permutations are investigated. The study of the planar realization and the search for small but hard sets of permutations are also included. Several asymptotically optimal estimations for distinct subsets of the set of all permutations are established here.

The two main results are:

  (i) an asymptotically optimal permutation network of size $6 \cdot N \cdot \log \log N$ for shifts of power 2.
  (ii) an asymptotically optimal planar permutation network of size $\Theta(N^2 \cdot (\log \log N / \log N)^2)$ for shifts of power 2.

A consequence of our results is a construction of a 4-degree network which can simulate each communication step of any hypercube algorithm using edges from at most a constant number of different dimensions in one step in $O(\log \log N)$ communication steps. A new sorting network as well as an essential improvement of gossiping in vertex-disjoint path mode in bounded-degree networks follow.

---

[*] This work was partially supported by grants Mo 285/9-1 and Me 872/6-1 (Leibniz Award) of the German Research Association (DFG), and by the ESPRIT Basic Research Action No. 7141 (ALCOM II).
[**] Supported by SAV Grant 2/1138/94 and by EC Cooperation Action IC 1000 ALTEC
[***] Supported by Polish Government grants KBN 2 1197 91 01, KBN 8 S503 002 07, KBN 2 P301 034 07 & Volkswagen Stiftung (Joint project of Wrocław University and Heinz–Nixdorf–Institut, University of Paderborn).
[†] This author was supported by the Ministerium für Wissenschaft und Forschung des Landes Nordrhein-Westfalen.

1 Introduction and Definition

The study and the comparison of the computational power of distinct interconnection networks as candidates for the use as parallel architectures for existing parallel computers is an intensively investigated research branch of current computation theory. One of the fundamental approaches helping to search for the best (most effective) structures of interconnection networks is the study of the communication facilities of networks (i.e., of the complexity (effectivity) of solving fundamental communication tasks). The basic communication tasks are routing (for an extensive survey see [Le92]), broadcasting, and gossiping. Our paper is devoted to the search for effective, realistic 1-to-1 routing (permutation) networks. The effectivity in our paper is mainly interpreted as the minimal size of a network realizing a given subset of permutations (one-to-one routing tasks). By realistic we mean that we consider only networks with bounded degree (usually with degree 4).

Our study of the sizes of permutation networks for distinct subclasses of permutations has been motivated not only by searching for efficient bounded-degree networks for special routing tasks, but mainly by looking for realistic networks in the class of bounded-degree networks with very high (or even with the highest possible) communication facilities supporting different fundamental computing and communicational tasks. For instance, the study of permutation networks for shifts 2^i is well-motivated by the simulation of hypercube algorithms in networks of bounded degree, and, in our case, especially by sorting and gossiping.

This paper is organized as follows. In this section we give the basic definitions and the overview of the achieved results. Section 2 contains the exact formulation of the results. In this extended abstract, we give some proof ideas only for theorems which do not have long technical proofs, and we completely omit the proof of theorems requiring too many technical details.

Section 2 is divided into three subsections. Section 2.1 is devoted to permutation networks for all permutations of N elements, all shifts, shifts of power two, and shifts by Fibonacci numbers. The main results of this subsection are the constructions of 4-degree permutation networks of size $6 \cdot N \cdot \log \log N$ for the shifts 2^i for $i = 1, 2, \ldots, \log_2 N$, and the construction of 4-degree permutation networks of size $O\left(N \cdot 2^{2\sqrt{\log \log N}}\right)$ for Fibonacci shifts. The results for shifts of power of two is asymptotically optimal.

Subsection 2.2 is devoted to planar permutation networks. Here one needs to distinguish between vertex-disjoint and edge-disjoint permutation networks. For instance, for the vertex-disjoint path mode one needs networks of size $\Theta(N^3)$ to realize all permutations [KL92], but we show that the size $O(N^2)$ is necessary and sufficient for the realization in the edge-disjoint path mode. Moreover, five random permutations are as hard as the set of all permutations for planar realization in the edge-disjoint path mode. Finally, the main result of this subsection shows that the optimal planar permutation network for shifts of power two has the size in $\Theta(N^2 \cdot (\log \log N / \log N)^2)$.

The last Subsection 2.3 shows various applications of the results of the previous subsections. The smallest delay to simulate hypercubes of N nodes on bounded-degree networks is $\log_2 N$. A constant delay is possible if the communication steps of the hypercube algorithm consist only of communication via edges of one dimension and additionally any two consecutive communication steps correspond to communication in two consecutive dimensions [Ul84]. Here, using the permutation networks for shifts 2^i, we obtain the delay $6d \cdot \log\log N$ for the simulation of hypercube algorithms communicating via edges of d dimensions in one communication step. As a consequence of this, we obtain a sorting network of size $6 \cdot N \log\log N$ which sorts N elements in time $O(\log N \cdot (\log\log N)^3)$. Our network is neither the best in time (the Ajtai et al. network [AKS83] works in $O(\log_2 N)$ time), nor in hardware (Plaxton [CP93] and Kutyłowski [KLOW94] have quick networks using $O(N)$ hardware). But our network is an intermediate case from the periodic sorting point of view. The network of Kutyłowski et al. [KLOW94] has depth 5 and the data periodically flows $O((\log_2 N)^2)$ times via the 5 levels of the network to sort. The network of Ajtai et al. [AKS83] can be viewed as a periodic network of depth $O(\log_2 N)$ (of size $N \cdot \log N$) with only one flow of data via the $O(\log N)$ levels of the network. Our network has depth $O(\log\log N)$ and the number of repetitions is $O(\log N \cdot (\log\log N)^2)$. Another consequence are quick gossip algorithms for bounded-degree networks in vertex-disjoint path mode. This is an essential improvement of the results established in [HKS93, HKSW93, HKUW94, Kl94] for gossiping in disjoint-path modes.

Now, we give the fundamental definitions. Let Π_N denote the set of all permutations of N elements. For any set A, $|A|$ denotes the cardinality of A. $F(i)$ denotes the i-th Fibonacci number of any positive integer i.

Definition 1. Let A be a subset of Π_N, and k be a positive integer. We say that a graph $G = (V, E)$ is a **vertex-disjoint (edge-disjoint) k-permutation network for A** if the following conditions hold:

  (i) the degree of G is bounded by k,
  (ii) V contains $2N$ special vertices $x_1, x_2, \ldots, x_N, y_1, y_2, \ldots, y_N$,
      $(x_1, x_2, \ldots, x_N$ are called **inputs**, $y_1, y_2, \ldots, y_N$ are called **outputs** of G)
  (iii) for every permutation $\pi = (i_1, i_2, \ldots, i_N) \in A$ there exist N vertex-disjoint (edge-disjoint) paths $x_1, \ldots, y_{i_1}; x_2, \ldots, y_{i_2}; \ldots; x_N, \ldots, y_{i_N}$ in G.

The size of G, denoted $s(G)$, is $|V|$. The depth of G (according to A), denoted **depth(G)**, is $\max\{\min\{$ length of $P \mid P$ is a path from x_i to $y_j\} \mid i,j \in \{1, \ldots, N\}, \pi(i) = j$ for some $\pi \in A\}$. A k-permutation network $G = (V, E)$ is **leveled** if V can be partitioned into $r = $ depth$(G) + 1$ nonempty subsets $V_1, \ldots, V_r$ such that

  (a) $V_1 = \{x_1, \ldots, x_N\}$, $V_r = \{y_1, \ldots, y_N\}$;
  (b) $V_i \cap V_j = \emptyset$ for $i \neq j$, $i, j \in 1, \ldots, r\}$;
  (c) for every edge $e \in E$, there exists $i \in \{1, \ldots, r-1\}$ such that e connects one vertex from V_i with one vertex from V_{i+1}. $\qquad\qquad\square$

Note that almost all permutation networks constructed here are leveled and of degree at most 4. Moreover, we use the edges only in the direction from the

i-th level to the $(i + 1)$-st level. On the other hand, the lower bound proofs are general, i.e, they work for any constant-degree network and the property to be leveled is not needed.

Definition 2. Let A be a subset of Π_N, and k be a positive integer. We define

> **Size-vd$_k$(A)** $= \min\{s(G) \mid G$ is a
> > vertex-disjoint k-permutation network for $A\}$,
>
> **Size-ed$_k$(A)** $= \min\{s(G) \mid G$ is an
> > edge-disjoint k-permutation network for $A\}$,
>
> **Plsize-vd$_k$(A)** $= \min\{s(G) \mid G$ is planar and G is a
> > vertex-disjoint k-permutation network for $A\}$,
>
> **Plsize-ed$_k$(A)** $= \min\{s(G) \mid G$ is planar and G is an
> > edge-disjoint k-permutation network for $A\}$.

□

In what follows we use the following notation.

$S_N \subseteq \Pi_N$ ... the set of all shifts,

$\text{Pow}\,2_N \subseteq S_N$ ... the set of all shifts of the power of 2 $((1 + 2^i) \bmod N, (2 + 2^i) \bmod N, \ldots, (N + 2^i) \bmod N)$ for $i = 1, 2, \ldots, \log_2 N$,

$\text{Fib}_N \subseteq S_N$ ... the set of all shifts $((1 + F(i)) \bmod N, (2 + F(i)) \bmod N, \ldots, (N + F(i)) \bmod N)$ for all Fibonacci numbers $F(1)$, $F(2), \ldots, F(k)$, where k is the largest integer with the property $F(k) \le N$.

Definition 3. Let N be a positive integer, and A be a subset of Π_N. We say that B is a **kernel** of A if $B \subseteq A$ and Size-ed$_k(B) = \Omega(\text{Size-ed}_k(A))$ for any constant $k \ge 4$. We say that B is a **planar e-kernel [v-kernel]** of A if $B \subseteq A$ and for any constant $k \ge 4$ Plsize-ed$_k(B) = \Omega(\text{Plsize-ed}_k(A))$ [Plsize-vd$_k(B) = \Omega(\text{Plsize-vd}_k(A))$]. A kernel (planar e-kernel, planar v-kernel) B of A is called **(asymptotically) minimal** if, for every kernel (planer e-kernel, planar v-kernel) C of A, $|B| = \Omega(|C|)$.

□

2 Results

2.1 On the Sizes of Permutation Networks for Special Subclasses of Permutations

Since there is no asymptotical difference between Size-vd$_k(A)$ and Size-ed$_k(A)$ for any permutation set A we shall consider only the edge-disjoint path mode in this subsection. It is well-known that

$$\text{Size-ed}_k(\Pi_N) = \Theta(N \log N) = \text{Size-ed}_k(S_N).$$

To see the upper bound Size-ed$_k$ $(\Pi_N) = O(N \log N)$ it is sufficient to take the well-known permutation network [Be64, Be65, Wa68]. To see the lower bound Size-ed$_k(S_N) = \Omega(N \log N)$ one has to apply the following lower bound method of [PV76] to S_N.

Lemma 4 [PV76], Theorem 2.2.1. *Let A be any subset of Π_N. If A fulfils the following property*

(i) *Each input is assigned to $|A|$ different outputs by the $|A|$ permutations.*

then Size-ed$_k(A) = \Omega(N \cdot \log_2 |A|)$. $\qquad\qquad\qquad\qquad\qquad\qquad$ □

Thus, we obtain that S_N is a kernel of Π_N. But S_N is not the minimal kernel of Π_N because a random set A with $|A| \leq \log_2 N$ has Size-ed$_k(A) = \Omega(N \cdot |A|)$ with probability tending to 1 with growing N and $|A|$ [We94]. Obviously each $A \subseteq \Pi_N$ has Size-ed$_4(A) = O(N \cdot |A|)$, and so the random sets of $\log_2 N$ permutations are **minimal kernels** of Π_N.

In [HKS93] it has been conjectured that Pow2_N and Fib$_N$ are kernels of S_N. We now show that this is not the case.

Theorem 5. *Size-ed$_4(Pow\,2_N) \leq 6 \cdot N \cdot \log\log N + 3$.*

Idea of the Proof. The construction of the permutation network can be described in a recursive way. Assume we have a permutation network of $M = 2^{i/2}$ inputs for shifts $2^0, 2^1, ..., 2^{i/2}$ and one wants to construct a network for shifts $2^0, 2^1, ..., 2^i$. The idea is to put $M = 2^{i/2}$ networks for shifts $2^0, 2^1, ..., 2^{i/2}$ next to each other in the same levels and to add a few (constant) further levels to connect them. These new levels are created in such a way that they are able to establish the following two distinct kinds of connections:

(i) If one wants to realize "small" shifts of size $z \in \{2^0, 2^1, ..., 2^{i/2}\}$ for $N = 2^i$ inputs, the first levels copy the inputs to the inputs of M "small" networks (of M inputs). Then the "small" networks realize the local shifts of size z. To get the right output of the whole network, the last level shifts the outputs of the small networks which are not at the right positions because of the local mod z shifts realization.

(ii) If one wants to realize "big" shifts of size $z \in \{2^{i/2+1}, 2^{i/2+2}, ..., 2^i\}$ for $N = 2^i$ inputs, the first levels shuffle the inputs to the inputs of the small networks in such a way that the M small networks realize exactly the large shifts.

If this works and the number of additional levels is in $O(1)$, then one obtains the following recurrence for the depth of the permutation network with N inputs: $depth(N) \leq depth(\sqrt{N}) + O(1)$. Obviously, the solution is $depth(N) \leq O(\log\log N)$. Some additional technicalities are necessary to get the constant small (i.e. $depth(N) \leq 6 \cdot \log\log N + O(1)$). $\qquad\qquad$ □

Theorem 6. *Size-ed$_4(Fib_N) \leq 13 \cdot N \cdot 2^{2\sqrt{\log\log N}}$.*

Proof. The proof is omitted in this extended abstract. $\qquad\square$

Corollary 7. $Size\text{-}ed_k(Pow\,2_N) = \Theta(N \cdot \log\log N)$ *for any constant k independent of N.*

Proof. The upper bound is in Theorem 5 and the lower bound follows from the fact that $Pow\,2_N$ fulfils Property (i) of Lemma 4. $\qquad\square$

Note that especially Theorem 5 brings a crucial contribution for the simulation of hypercube algorithms in bounded-degree networks of degree 4 for several fundamental computing problems. More about this can be found in Subsection 2.3.

2.2 On the Sizes of Planar Permutation Networks

It is well-known that $Plsize\text{-}vd_k(\Pi_N) = \Theta(N^3)$ [CS78, KL92]. Our first result shows that there is an essential difference between edge-disjoint paths mode and vertex-disjoint paths mode for planar permutation networks.

Theorem 8. *For any constant $k \geq 4$ independent of N*

$$Plsize\text{-}ed_k(\Pi_N) = \Theta(N^2) = Plsize\text{-}ed_k(S_N).$$

Outline of the Proof. We start with the upper bound. Consider the following network $PE_N = (V, E)$ defined by $V = \{ v_{i,j} \, ; 1 \leq i < N \, , \, 1 \leq j \leq N \} \cup \{ x_i, y_i \, ; 1 \leq i \leq N \}$ and $\{v_{i,j}, v_{k,l}\} \in E$ iff $(i+1 = k$ and $j = l)$ or $(i = k$ and $j \bmod N = l-1)$. Furthermore $\{x_i, v_{1,i}\} \in E$ for $1 \leq i \leq N$ and $\{v_{N-1,i}, y_i\} \in E$ for $1 \leq i \leq N$. Observe that PE_N is planar (see Figure 1).

Furthermore, it is well-known that any permutation from Π_N can be built from $N-1$ transpositions. On each of the rows $(v_{i,1}, v_{i,2}, v_{i,3}, ..., v_{i,N})$ $(1 \leq i < N)$ one of these transpositions can be carried out. This is also shown in Figure 1: The nodes marked by a circle send the messages from the top edge to the right hand side edge and the message from the left hand side to the bottom edge. The other nodes send the messages from the top edge to the bottom edge and the message from the left hand side to the right hand side edge. In Figure 1 the permutation $(5, 4, 1, 3, 2)$ is carried out. Thus we conclude $Plsize\text{-}ed_4(\Pi_N) \leq N \cdot (N + 1)$.

The lower bound proof is based on the planar separator theorem of Lipton and Tarjan [LT79]. Let, for any subset of permutations $A \subseteq \Pi_N$, $G(A) = (V, E)$, where $V = \{x_1, \ldots, x_N, y_1, \ldots, y_N\}$ and, for every $\pi = (i_1, i_2, \ldots, i_N) \in A$, E contains the edges $(x_1, y_{i_1}), \ldots, (x_N, y_{i_N})$. Let (V_1, V_2), $V_1 \cup V_2 = V$, $|V_1| = |V_2| = N$, be a bisection of $G(A)$. The bisection width of $G(A)$ according to (V_1, V_2) and π, $bw(G(A), (V_1, V_2), \pi)$, is the number of edges defined by π and leading between V_1 and V_2. $\overline{bw(G(A), (V_1, V_2))} = \max\{bw(G(A), (V_1, V_2), \pi) \mid \pi \in A\}$. The balanced bisection width of $\overline{G(A)}$ is $bw(G(A)) = \min\{bw(G(A), (V_1, V_2)) \mid (V_1, \overline{V_2})$ is a bisection of $G(A)\}$. We observe that each permutation network realizing A must have bisection width at least $bw(G(A))$. Since $bw(S_N) \geq \lceil N/2 \rceil$

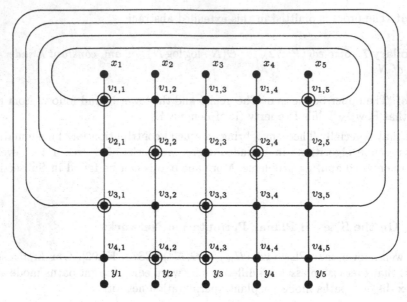

Fig. 1. PE_5

and each planar graph of m nodes has an $O(\sqrt{m})$ separator [LT79], we obtain Plsize-ed$_k(S_N) = \Omega(N^2)$. □

Again, we see that S_N is a planar e-kernel of Π_N. But the next result showing that S_N is no planar v-kernel of Π_N underlines the difference between these two communication modes.

Theorem 9. $Plsize\text{-}vd_4(S_N) \le N \cdot (N+2)$.

Outline of the Proof. We define the network $PS_N = (V, E)$ by $V = \{v_{i,j} \,;\, 0 \le i, j < N\} \cup \{x_i, y_i \,;\, 1 \le i \le N\}$ and $\{v_{i,j}, v_{k,l}\} \in E$ iff $i + 1 = k$ and $l \in \{j, (j+1) \bmod N\}$. Furthermore $\{x_i, v_{0,i-1}\} \in E$ for $1 \le i \le N$ and $\{v_{N-1,i-1}, y_i\} \in E$ for $1 \le i \le N$. Observe that PS_N is planar (see Figure 2). The messages from the nodes $\{x_i \,;\, 1 \le i \le N\}$ are shifted to the nodes $\{y_i \,;\, 1 \le i \le N\}$. The $i-th$ message $(1 \le i \le N)$ uses the path P_i^s when a shift by s $(0 \le s < N)$ is carried out, where $P_i^s = (x_i, v_{0,i-1}, v_{1,(i+\min(1,s)-1)\bmod N}, \dots,$ $v_{2,(i+\min(2,s)-1)\bmod N}, \dots, v_{j,(i+\min(j,s)-1)\bmod N}, \dots, v_{N-1,(i+\min(N-1,s)-1)\bmod N},$ $y_{(i+s-1)\bmod N+1})$. Again it is easy to observe that these paths are vertex-disjoint (see Figure 2). □

Corollary 10. *For any constant $k \ge 4$ independent of N*

$$Plsize\text{-}vd_k(S_N) = \Theta(N^2).$$

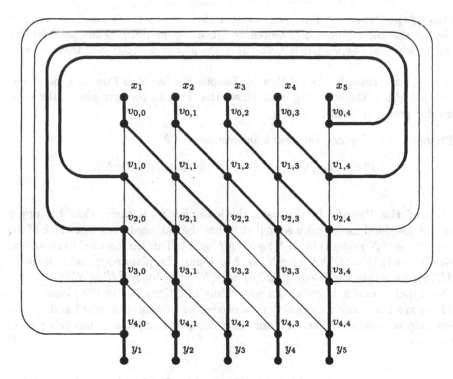

Fig. 2. a shift by 2 realized by PS_5

Proof. The result is a direct consequence of Theorem 8 and Theorem 9. □

Again, as in the general case (Subsection 2.1), S_N is no minimal e-kernel of Π_N. In the following we show that there are e-kernels of Π_N of size 5.

Theorem 11. *Let $N = m^2$, $A_m = \{0, 1, \ldots, m-1\} \times \{0, 1, \ldots, m-1\}$, and let $B_N = \{\pi_1, \pi_2, \pi_3, \pi_4, \pi_5\} \subseteq \Pi_N$ be the following permutations on A_m:*

$$\pi_1(x,y) = (x,y),$$
$$\pi_2(x,y) = (x, x+y),$$
$$\pi_3(x,y) = (x, x+y+1),$$
$$\pi_4(x,y) = (x+y, y),$$
$$\pi_5(x,y) = (x+y+1, y),$$

where the $+$ is modulo m. Then, for any constant k independent of N,

$$Plsize\text{-}ed_k(B_N) = \Theta(N^2).$$

Theorem 12. *Let R_N be a set of 5 random permutations from Π_N. Then, with probability tending to 1 with growing N*

$$Plsize\text{-}ed_k(R_N) = \Theta(N^2),$$

for any constant k independent of N.

Idea of the Proofs of Theorem 11 and 12. The proofs are based on the same idea as the lower bound of Theorem 8. Since B_N and R_N define permutation graphs which are expanders [GG81, Pi77], the planar realization of them is hard. □

Finally, let us consider the set $\text{Pow} \, 2_N$. Despite the fact that $\text{Pow} \, 2_N$ is no planar e-kernel of Π_N, the following result shows that $\text{Pow} \, 2_N$ requires almost the same size for planar realization as Π_N.

Theorem 13. *For any constant k independent of N*

$$Plsize\text{-}ed_k(\text{Pow} \, 2_N) = \Theta(N^2 \cdot (\log \log N)^2 / (\log N)^2)$$

Idea of the Proof. In this case, the lower bound is easier than the upper bound. Leighton has mentioned in [Le92] that the balanced bisection width of the hypercube of N nodes is in $\Omega(N \log \log N / \log N)$. This can be used to show that $bw(G(\text{Pow} \, 2_N)) = \Omega(N \log \log N / \log N)$. Using the planar separator theorem [LT79], we obtain $Plsize\text{-}ed_k(\text{Pow} \, 2_N) = \Omega(N^2 \cdot (\log \log N)^2 / (\log N)^2)$.

The upper bound is based on an embedding of $G(\text{Pow} \, 2_N)$ in the planar grids. There are too many technical details needed to present this proof and it does not help to show only part of them. Therefore, we completely omit this part of the proof. □

2.3 Application of Permutation Networks for Sorting and Gossiping

The aim of this subsection is to show the consequences of Theorem 5 and 6 for other tasks than routing of messages. The main idea of the use of Theorem 5 is in the simulation of hypercube algorithms in degree-bounded networks. Here, we consider the hypercube algorithms as synchronized parallel algorithms executing alternatively communication steps and computing steps. In each computing step each processor of the hypercube executes some computation on its local data. In each communication step one processor can exchange some message with one neighbour via an adjacent edge. Each processor may communicate with at most one neighbour in one communication step. We distinguish three classes of hypercube algorithms:

(1) **general hypercube algorithms,** as described above
(2) **leveled hypercube algorithms** [Le92, Wi92], which communicate in every communication step via edges of one fixed dimension of the hypercube
(3) **normal hypercube algorithms** [Ul84] are leveled ones with the additional condition that two consecutive communication steps use two consecutive dimensions of the hypercube.

Additionally, we define **d-leveled hypercube algorithms** as hypercube algorithms using edges of at most d different dimensions in each communication step. Any communication step of a normal hypercube algorithm running on a hypercube of size N can be simulated by two communication steps by the Shuffle-Exchange network of size N. For general algorithms, the best simulation of one communication step of the hypercube by bounded-degree networks uses $\log_2 N$ steps. Using the network from Theorem 5 we can construct a 4-degree network simulating one communication step of any leveled hypercube algorithm in $6 \cdot \log_2 \log_2 N$ steps.

Theorem 14. *There is a 4-degree network of size $6 \cdot N \cdot \log \log N$ which can simulate any communication step of any d-leveled hypercube algorithm on a hypercube of N nodes in $6 \cdot d \cdot \log \log N$ communication steps.*

Because almost all common hypercube algorithms are leveled, we obtain several efficient parallel algorithms running on bounded-degree networks as a consequence of Theorem 14. Note that our simulation beats the previous ones in the delay. All the previous simulations of the general and the d-leveled hypercube algorithms by degree-bounded networks had delay $O(\log N)$ [Le92], while we have delay $O(\log \log N)$. Another positive property of our network is its size $6 \cdot N \log \log N$, i.e. we do not need to pay too much with the increase of the size for this small delay.

We omit the formulation of all possible consequences of Theorem 14 in this extended abstract. We only present some results for sorting and gossiping.

Theorem 15. *For every $N = 2^n, n \in I\!N$, there is a leveled network $\overline{G}_N$ of size $6 \cdot N \log \log N$ sorting N elements in $O(\log N \cdot (\log \log N)^3)$ steps. This network has depth $6 \cdot \log \log N$ and the sorting algorithm periodically uses the network $O(\log N \cdot (\log \log N)^2)$ times.*

Our network is neither the best in time (the Ajtai et al. network [AKS83] works in $O(\log_2 N)$ time), nor in hardware (Cypher and Plaxton [CP93] and Kutyłowski et al. [KLOW94] have quick networks using $O(N)$ hardware). But our network is an intermediate case from the periodic sorting point of view. The network of Kutyłowski et al. [KLOW94] has depth 5 and the data periodically flows $O((\log_2 N)^2)$ times via the 5 levels of the network to sort. The network of Ajtai et al. [AKS83] can be viewed as a periodic network of depth $O(\log_2 N)$ (of size $N \cdot \log N$) with only one flow of data via the $O(\log N)$ levels of the network. Our network has depth $O(\log \log N)$ and the number of repetitions is $O(\log N \cdot (\log \log N)^2)$. If one considers the complexity measure $(\text{Depth})^2 \cdot$ (the number of repetitions) for periodic sorting networks [note that this measure is reasonable because the depth of the network influences both important parameters of the network – the size of the hardware and the time complexity], our network is even better than the networks from [AKS83, KLOW94] because we have $(\text{Depth})^2 \cdot$ (the number of repetitions) $= O(\log N \cdot (\log \log N)^4)$ and both previous networks [AKS83, KLOW94] have $(\text{Depth})^2 \cdot$ (the number of repetitions) $= O((\log N)^2)$.

Another application of the previous theorems is related to gossiping (all to all broadcasting) in edge-disjoint (vertex-disjoint) paths mode. Let C_N denote the complete graph of N nodes. In [HKS93] it is shown that there are bounded-degree networks of size N whose

(i) two-way vertex-disjoint gossip complexity is $r_2(C_N) + O(\log \log N)$, where $r_2(C_N) = \log_2 N$ is the two-way gossip complexity of the complete graph C_N on N nodes, and

(ii) one-way vertex-disjoint gossip complexity is $r_1(C_N) + O(\log \log N)$, where $r_1(C_N) \approx 1.44 \ldots \log_2 N$ is the one-way gossip complexity of C_N.

Thus, one can gossip in bounded-degree networks almost as quickly as in complete graphs using the vertex-disjoint paths mode. In [HKS93] it has been conjectured that the additional $\log \log N$ steps are necessary to gossip in bounded-degree networks. Theorems 5 and 6 surprisingly provide networks which can gossip even faster.

Theorem 16. *There is a 4-degree network of size $M = 6 \cdot N \cdot \log \log N$ for any positive integer $N \geq 16$ with two-way vertex-disjoint paths gossip complexity smaller than $r_2(C_M) + \log \log \log M + const$.*

Theorem 17. *There is a 4-degree network of size $M = O\left(N \cdot 2^{2\sqrt{\log \log N}}\right)$ for every positive integer $N \geq 16$ with one-way vertex-disjoint paths gossip complexity smaller than $r_1(C_M) + 1.12 \ldots \sqrt{\log \log M} + const$.*

Idea of the Proofs of Theorems 16 and 17. To see the connection between Theorems 5 and 6 and gossiping in the two-way mode and one-way mode resp. one has to take a look at the concept of three-phase gossip algorithms in [HKS93, HKSW93]. □

3 Conclusion

In this paper, we presented asymptotically optimal planar and non-planar permutation networks for shifts of power 2. A new sorting network as well as an essential improvement of gossiping in two-way vertex-disjoint paths mode in bounded-degree networks follow. For the set of Fibonacci shifts, Fib_N, which are crucial for the design of efficient gossip algorithms in one-way vertex-disjoint paths mode, we were not able to prove the optimality of our constructions. Thus, the main open problem left is to determine Size-ed$_k(Fib_N)$ and Plsize-ed$_k(Fib_N)$ exactly.

References

[AKS83]   M. Ajtai, J. Komlós, E. Szemerédi, An $O(n \log n)$ sorting network. *Proc. 15th ACM Symposium on Theory of Computing*, pp. 1-9, 1983.

[Be64]   V. Beneš, "Permutation groups, complexes, and rearrangeable multistage connecting networks", *Bell System Technical Journal*, vol. 43, pp. 1619-1640, 1964.

[Be65]   V. Beneš, "Mathematical Theory of Connecting Networks and Telephone Traffic", *Academic Press*, New York, NY, 1965.

[CP93]   R. Cypher, C.G. Plaxton: Deterministic Sorting in Nearly Logarithmic Time on the Hypercube and Related Computers. *Journal of Computer and System Sciences*, No. 47, 1993, pp. 501-548.

[CS78]   M. Cutler, Y. Shiloach: Permutation layout. *Networks*, vol. 8 (1978) 253-278.

[GG81]   O. Gabber, Z. Galil: Explicit Construction of Linear-Sized Superconcentrators. *Journal of Computer and System Sciences*, No. 22, 1981, pp. 407-420.

[HKS93]   J. Hromkovič, R. Klasing, E.A. Stöhr, "Gossiping in Vertex-Disjoint Paths Mode in Interconnection Networks", Proc. of the 19th Int. Workshop on Graph-Theoretic Concepts in Computer Science (*WG'93*), Springer LNCS 790, pp. 288-300.

[HKSW93] J. Hromkovič, R. Klasing, E.A. Stöhr, H. Wagener, "Gossiping in Vertex-Disjoint Paths Mode in d-Dimensional Grids and Planar Graphs", Proc. of the First Annual European Symposium on Algorithms (*ESA'93*), Springer LNCS 726, pp. 200-211.

[HKUW94] J. Hromkovič, R. Klasing, W. Unger, H. Wagener, "Optimal Algorithms for Broadcast and Gossip in the Edge-Disjoint Path Modes", Proc. of the 4th Scandinavian Workshop on Algorithm Theory (*SWAT'94*), Springer LNCS 824, pp. 219-230.

[Kl94]   R. Klasing, "The Relationship Between Gossiping in Vertex-Disjoint Paths Mode and Bisection Width", Proc. of the 19th International Symposium on Mathematical Foundations of Computer Science (MFCS'94), Springer LNCS 841, pp. 473-483.

[KL92]   M. Klawe, T. Leighton: A tight lower bound on the size of planar permutation networks. *SIAM J. Disc. Math.*, Vol. 5, No. 4, pp. 558-563, November 1992.

[KLOW94] M. Kutyłowski, K. Loryś, B. Oesterdiekhoff, R. Wanka: Fast and feasible periodic sorting networks of constant depth; Proc. 35th Annual Symposium on Foundations of Computer Science (*FOCS '94*), to appear.

[Le92]   F.T. Leighton: Introduction to parallel algorithms and architectures: Arrays, Trees, Hypercubes. *Morgan Kaufmann Publisher* (1992).

[LT79]   R.J. Lipton, R.E. Tarjan, "A separator theorem for planar graphs", *SIAM J. Appl. Math.* 36(2), 1979, pp. 177-189.

[Pi77]   N. Pippenger: Superconcentrators. *SIAM Journal of Computing*, No. 6, 1977, pp. 298-304.

[PV76]   N. Pippenger, L. Valiant: Shifting graphs and their applications. *Journal of the ACM*, Vol. 23, No. 3, July 1976, pp. 423-432.

[Ul84]   Ullman, J.D., Computational Aspects of VLSI *Computer Science Press*, Rockville, MD, 1984, 495 p.

[Wa68]   A. Waksman, "A permutation network", *Journal of the ACM*, vol. 15, no. 1, pp. 159-163, January 1968.

[We94]   R. Werchner, personal communication.

[Wi92]   D.B. Wilson: Embedding leveled hypercube algorithms into hypercubes. Proc. 4th ACM Symposium on Parallel Algorithms and Architectures (*SPAA '92*), pp. 264-270.

Exploiting Storage Redundancy to Speed Up Randomized Shared Memory Simulations

(Extended Abstract)

Friedhelm Meyer auf der Heide*, Christian Scheideler**, Volker Stemann***

Department of Mathematics and Computer Science
and Heinz Nixdorf Institute, University of Paderborn
33095 Paderborn, Germany

Abstract. This paper presents and analyses efficient implementations of a so-called *direct* process on distributed memory machines (DMMs) that yields

- a simulation of an n-processor PRAM on an n-processor *optical crossbar* DMM with delay $O(\log \log n)$,
- a simulation of an n-processor PRAM on an n-processor *arbitrary* DMM with delay $O(\frac{\log \log n}{\log \log \log n})$,
- an implementation of a static dictionary on an n-processor *arbitrary* DMM with parallel access time of $O(\log^* n)$.

We further prove a lower bound for executing the above process, showing that our implementations are optimal.

1 Introduction

Parallel machines that communicate via a shared memory, so-called *parallel random access machines* (PRAMs), represent an idealization of a parallel computation model. The user does not have to worry about synchronization, locality of data, communication capacity, delay effects or memory contention.

On the other hand, PRAMs are very unrealistic from a technological point of view; large machines with shared memory can only be built at the cost of very slow shared memory access. A more realistic model is the *distributed memory machine* (DMM), where the memory is partitioned into modules, one per processor. In this case a parallel memory access is restricted in so far as only one access to each module can be performed per parallel step. Thus memory contention occurs if a PRAM algorithm is run on a DMM; parallel accesses to cells stored in one module have to be sequentialized.

Many authors have already investigated methods for simulating PRAMs on DMMs. If one focuses on a complete network between processors and modules, the main problem is the distribution of the shared memory cells over the modules to allow fast accesses. A standard method is to use universal hashing for distributing the shared

* email: fmadh@uni-paderborn.de. Supported in part by DFG-Forschergruppe "Effiziente Nutzung massiv paralleler Systeme, Teilprojekt 4", by Volkswagen Foundation and by the Esprit Basic Research Action Nr 7141 (ALCOM II)

** email: chrsch@uni-paderborn.de. Supported by the DFG-grant Me 872/6-1 (Leibniz Preis)

*** email: vost@hni.uni-paderborn.de. Supported by the DFG-Graduiertenkolleg "Parallele Rechnernetzwerke in der Produktionstechnik", ME 872/4-1 memory among the memory modules of the DMM. In this paper we consider both simulations of PRAMs and implementations of parallel static dictionaries on DMMs, based on distributing the shared memory cells among the modules using not only one but several hash functions.

1.1 Computation Models

A *parallel random access machine* (PRAM) consists of processors $P_1, \ldots, P_n$ and a shared memory with cells $U = \{1, \ldots, p\}$, each capable of storing one integer. The processors work synchronously and have random access to the shared memory cells. In this paper we will only consider the exclusive-read exclusive-write PRAM (EREW PRAM) model, that is, no two processors are allowed to access the same shared memory cell at the same time during a read or write step.

A *distributed memory machine* (DMM) consists of n processors $Q_1, \ldots, Q_n$ and n memory modules $M_1, \ldots, M_n$. Each processor has a link to each module. A basic communication step of such a DMM consists of the processors sending read or write requests to the memory modules, at most one request per processor. Each module processes some of the requests directed to it and sends an acknowledgement to each processor whose request was chosen to be processed.

We distinguish between the following rules for choosing requests for processing. ($c \geq 1$ is a fixed integer. For a discussion of the models see [DM93] or [M92].)

- *arbitrary DMM* : In this case, one arbitrarily chosen request out of all requests arriving at one module is processed per step. The answer given by a module is accessible by all processors accessing the module.
- *c-collision DMM* : In this case, all requests arriving at one module are processed in one step, as long as there are at most c of them; otherwise none is processed. An answer is only accessible by the issuing processor. (Note : For $c = 1$ this model corresponds to a communication mechanism based on optical crossbars (compare [AM88], [GT92] and [V90]). c-collision DMMs can easily be simulated on arbitrary DMMs with delay $O(c)$.)

1.2 Dictionaries and Shared Memory Simulations

Shared memory simulations on a DMM based on hashing begin with a preprocessing phase. In this phase each processor P_i of the PRAM is mapped to processor Q_i of the DMM and the shared memory cells (we say *keys* for short) of the PRAM are distributed among the modules of the DMM via $a \geq 1$ randomly and independently chosen hash functions from some suitable universal class of hash functions (see below), i.e. each shared memory cell has a copies. This *redundant storage representation* needs space $a \cdot |U|$.

In this paper we will only deal with $a \geq 2$. The basic access distribution phase (we say *basic process* for short) will be organized in such a way that each processor P_i that wants to get access to a key $x_i \in U$ tries to send requests to the modules containing copies of x_i until it got access to at least b of the a copies of x_i, $b < a$. To resolve conflicts arising from colliding requests the modules will work according to the c-collision rule or the arbitrary rule. This process is *direct* in a sense introduced by Goldberg et al. [GJL93]. A process for distributing the requests of the processors to the modules is called *direct* if it runs in rounds and in each round the only messages allowed are requests of an arbitrary number of copies of each key.

If we choose, for example, $b > \frac{a}{2}$ then the basic process yields a simulation of an n-processor EREW PRAM on an n-processor DMM using the trick introduced in [UW87], which we will call the *majority trick* :
If each shared memory cell possesses $a > 2$ copies distributed among the memory

modules of the DMM then it suffices to access arbitrary $\lfloor \frac{a}{2} \rfloor + 1$ out of these a copies to guarantee a correct simulation of both a read and a write step.

To clarify how this trick works suppose that an update of a copy of a key contains a time stamp indicating the update time. If $b > \frac{a}{2}$ copies of a key x are up-to-date then it suffices to access arbitrary b copies of x. This guarantees that at least one up-to-date copy is accessed. It can be recognized by its time stamp.

The read and write accesses to the shared memory can be looked upon as the lookup and update operations of a *parallel dynamic dictionary*, i.e. a data structure that supports the above operations on the given set U of keys. In case we only want to support lookups, we are allowed to execute some preprocessing such that afterwards parallel lookups can be supported efficiently. We refer to such a data structure as a *parallel static dictionary*. In our framework, the static version is easier to handle as all the copies are up-to-date all the time. Thus choosing $b = 1$ is good enough. Furthermore, we can afford a larger storage overhead because we do not have to execute updates.

Our runtime bounds only hold with a certain probability (w.r.t. the choices of the hash functions). By *'with high probability'* (w.h.p.) we mean a probability of at least $1 - \frac{1}{n^\alpha}$ for a fixed $\alpha > 0$.

For our analysis it will be sufficient to assume that the hash functions $h_1, \ldots, h_a$ are randomly and independently drawn from a $\log^3 n$-universal* class of hash functions, that is, for any set $\{x_1, \ldots, x_k\} \subset U$ of keys and locations $l_1, \ldots, l_k \in \{1, \ldots, n\}$ it holds for all $k \le \log^3 n$:

$$Pr(h_i(x_1) = l_1 \wedge \ldots \wedge h_i(x_k) = l_k) \le \frac{1}{n^k}.$$

Such classes can be found in [S89]. The advantage of these hash functions is that they can be generated and evaluated in constant time on an n-processor DMM.

1.3 Previous Results

Shared memory simulations and static dictionaries that use only one hash function to distribute the shared memory cells over the modules of the DMM have an inherent delay of $\Theta(\log n / \log \log n)$ even if the hash function behaves like a random function (see [DM90]). Faster static dictionaries are only known for PRAMs, see [GMV91] and [BH91]. On such machines constant access time can be achieved using linear space.

Karp et al. [KLM92] were the first to consider shared memory simulations using two hash functions. They also present a fast implementation of write steps. The simulation runs on an arbitrary DMM with delay $O(\log \log n)$ and can be made time-processor optimal. Dietzfelbinger and Meyer auf der Heide [DM93] achieve the same delay with a very simple scheme using the majority trick (see section 1.2) with three hash functions. The scheme can be executed on the weaker c-collision DMM with $c \ge 3$. For a survey of shared memory simulations see [M92].

Recently, MacKenzie et al. [MPR94] showed that an EREW PRAM can even be simulated on a 1-collision DMM with storage overhead of at least 5. This result was finally extended to a time-processor optimal simulation of an $n \log \log n$-processor EREW PRAM on an n-processor 1-collision DMM by Goldberg et al. [GMR94]. Their simulation uses only three hash functions.

1.4 New Results

In this paper we focus on the analysis and the implementation of a simple process for shared memory simulations, that generalizes the processes and simulations from

---

* In this paper log denotes the logarithm with base 2, $\log^k n$ denotes $(\log n)^k$.

[KLM92], [DM93] and [MPR94] mentioned above. We show how to simulate an n-processor PRAM on an n-processor optical crossbar DMM with delay $O(\log \log n)$ or on an arbitrary DMM with delay $O(\log \log n / \log \log \log n)$ and implement a static dictionary on an arbitrary DMM with parallel access time $O(\log^* n)$.

Finally, we ask whether we can find faster implementations of direct processes than ours. More precisely, we consider a wide class of direct processes for shared memory simulations and allow each processor to access several copies of a key in parallel. We prove a lower bound for executing processes within this class, showing that our implementations are optimal.

1.5 Organization of the Paper

In Section 2 we introduce the basic process for our simulations and analyse it. Section 3 shows implementations of the process on c-collision and arbitrary DMMs. Section 4 finally contains the lower bound.

In this extended abstract we omit or only scetch most of the proofs because of space limitations. A full version is about to appear as a Technical Report.

2 The Basic Process

In order to get a clean description of our process we assume a DMM with n processors and $a \cdot n$ memory modules $M_{j,k}$, $j \in \{1, \ldots, a\}$, $k \in \{1, \ldots, n\}$. Suppose that a hash functions $h_1, \ldots, h_a : U \rightarrow \{1, \ldots, n\}$ distribute the keys from U among the modules, so each key x has a copies, stored in $M_{1,h_1(x)}, \ldots, M_{a,h_a(x)}$. Let $x_1, \ldots, x_{\epsilon n} \in U$, $\epsilon \leq 1$, be some keys for which we want to get access to at least b out of a copies. Let $I_i \subseteq \{1, \ldots, a\}$, $i \in \{1, \ldots, \epsilon n\}$, be the set of all copies of x_i for which we have already been successful. The following process forms the basis of our algorithms to implement static dictionaries and shared memory simulations.

(n, ϵ, a, b, c)-**process** :

initially : active keys $x_1, \ldots, x_{\epsilon n}$, $I_1 = \ldots = I_{\epsilon n} = \emptyset$
execute the following round until all keys are inactive :
    for each $j \in \{1, \ldots, a\}$:
        for each active key x_i with $j \notin I_i$:
            x_i tries to access $M_{j,h_j(x_i)}$
            { Each module $M_{j,l}$ works according to the c-collision rule }
            if x_i's access is accepted **then** $I_i := I_i \cup \{j\}$
            if $|I_i| \geq b$ **then** x_i becomes inactive

The following holds for the number of rounds needed by our process.

Main Theorem: Let $h_1, \ldots, h_a : U \rightarrow \{1, \ldots, n\}$ be randomly and independently chosen from a $\log^3 n$-universal class of hash functions. Let $0 < \epsilon \leq 1$, $2 \leq a \leq \sqrt[3]{\log n}$, $b < a$ and constant c be chosen such that

$$\frac{c^2(a-b)}{c+1} > 1 \quad and \quad \epsilon \cdot \binom{a-1}{a-b}\left(\frac{1}{c!}\right)^{a-b} \leq \frac{1}{2}.$$

(a) Then, for each t, $4 \leq t \leq \frac{\log \log n}{\log(c(a-b))} + 1$, at most $n / 2^{(c(a-b))^{t-2}}$ keys are still active after t rounds of the (n, ϵ, a, b, c)-process, w.h.p..

(b) In particular, the (n, ϵ, a, b, c)-process finishes within $\frac{\log \log n}{\log(c(a-b))} + 3$ rounds, w.h.p..

We want to give a short outline of the proof for the Main Theorem. A module is called *blocked* at round t of the (n, ϵ, a, b, c)-process if it gets more than c requests at round t. Note that a module will be blocked consecutively until it gets at most c requests for the first time. In this round it answers all of them. Afterwards, it gets no requests any more.

We view the distribution of the requests among the modules as a graph, the *access graph* $G = (V_K, V_M, E)$. $V_K = \{1, \ldots, \epsilon n\}$ represents the keys $x_1, \ldots, x_{\epsilon n}$ and $V_M = \{(j, k) \mid j \in \{1, \ldots, a\}, k \in \{1, \ldots, n\}\}$ the modules $M_{1,1}, \ldots, M_{a,n}$. Node $i \in V_K$ is connected with $(j, k) \in V_M$ in G if $h_j(x_i) = k$, that is, $M_{j,k}$ possesses the j-th copy of the key x_i. Thus $E = \{\{i, (j, k)\} \mid i \in V_K, (j, k) \in V_M, h_j(x_i) = k\}$.

It is easy to easy that if a module $M_{j,k}$ is still blocked after t rounds of the (n, ϵ, a, b, c)-process, the following tree can be embedded into G, such that its root is embedded in the V_M-node (j, k), V_{TM}-nodes are mapped to V_M-nodes and V_{TK}-nodes are mapped to V_K-nodes.

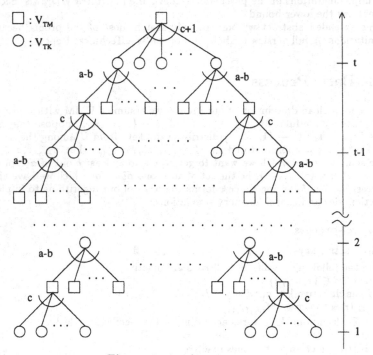

Figure 1: A witness tree

Let us call this tree $T_t = (V_{TK}, V_{TM}, E_T)$ a *witness tree* of depth t. Note that, if two V_{TK}-nodes v and w are embedded into the same V_K-node, then we can *identically* embed modules and keys into nodes of T_t below v and w in a way we just described above. The following definition formalizes what kind of embeddings of T_t into G we only have to consider.

Definition 1. An embedding ϕ of T_t into G is called *valid* if

(1) for each $v \in V_{TM}$, all neighbours v' of v are embedded into different V_K-nodes,
(2) for each $v \in V_{TK}$, all neighbours v' of v are embedded into V_M-nodes (j, k) with different j,
(3) for each $\{u, v\} \in E_T$ we have $\{\phi(u), \phi(v)\} \in E$,

(4) for each $v, w \in V_{TK}$ let T_v, T_w be the subtrees of T_t rooted in v and w, resp., $d = depth(T_v) \leq depth(T_w)$. If v and w are embedded identically then T_v is embedded identical to the top part of T_w of depth d (compare figure 2).

The following lemma is a direct result of our discussion above.

Lemma 2. *If module $M_{j,k}$ is still blocked after round t of the (n, ϵ, a, b, c)-process then there is a valid embedding ϕ of T_t into G.* □

The above lemma implies that it suffices to find a bound for the probability (w.r.t. random choices of h_i's as indicated in the Main Theorem) that T_t has a valid embedding into G in order to prove part (b) of the Main Theorem. From the above definition of valid embeddings one can conclude that a valid embedding of T_t into G is already completely described by a small (at most size $\epsilon|V_{TK}|$) subtree $\tilde{T}$ of T_t with the same root as T_t and a set of V_{TK}-nodes mapped injectively to V_K, except for the leaves of $\tilde{T}$. The following figure will give an example for such a subtree for $a = 7$, $b = 6$ and $c = 2$.

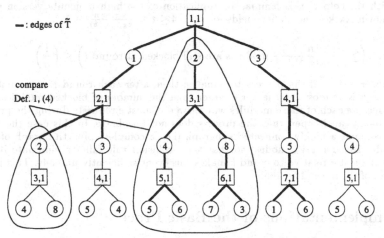

Figure 2: A valid embedding of a witness tree

These observations allow us to use an (involved) counting argument to show the following probability bounds. The proof is omitted in this extended abstract.

Lemma 3. *Let $h_1, \ldots, h_a$, ϵ, a, b and c be chosen as in the Main Theorem. Consider a module $M_{j,k}$. Then it holds :*

Prob(There is a valid embedding of T_t in G with root embedding $M_{j,k}$) $\leq$

$$\leq \begin{cases} \left(\frac{1}{2}\right)^{\sum_{j=1}^{t-2}(c(a-b))^j} & : \quad 2 \leq t \leq \frac{\log \log n}{\log(c(a-b))} + 2 \\ (\log n)^2 \cdot \left(\frac{1}{n}\right)^{\frac{c^2(a-b)}{c+1}} & : \quad t \geq \frac{\log \log n}{\log(c(a-b))} + 3 \end{cases}$$

□

Part (b) of the Main Theorem follows directly from the above two lemmas. For the proof of part (a) of the Main Theorem we first observe that, by Lemma 3, the expected number of modules still blocked after t rounds, $2 \leq t \leq \frac{\log \log n}{\log(c(a-b))} + 1$, is at most $n/2^{\sum_{j=1}^{t-2}(c(a-b))^j}$. Thus part (a) of the Main Theorem would easily follow by the well-known Chernoff bound if the events "There is a valid embedding of T_t in G with root embedding $M_{j,k}$" were independent for different (j,k). This is not true because the embeddings may overlap. On the other hand, we can show that an overlap of more than one node is very unlikely, as long as we only consider up to $\log n$ many (j,k). Formally we prove:

Lemma 4. *For any* $\{(j_1, k_1), \ldots, (j_s, k_s)\} \subseteq \{1, \ldots, a\} \times \{1, \ldots, n\}$, $s \leq \log n$, *it holds for all* t, $2 \leq t \leq \frac{\log \log n}{\log(c(a-b))} + 1$:

$$Prob(M_{j_1, k_1}, \ldots, M_{j_s, k_s} \text{ are blocked at round } t) \leq \left[\left(\frac{1}{2}\right)^{\sum_{j=1}^{t-2}(c(a-b))^j} + \frac{1}{n} \right]^s$$

$\square$

With the help of this lemma, an application of the high moments version of the well-known Markov inequality yields for all t, $4 \leq t \leq \frac{\log \log n}{\log(c(a-b))} + 1$:

$$\text{Prob}\left(\geq \frac{n}{c \cdot 2^{(c(a-b))^{t-2}}} \text{ modules are still blocked at round } t\right) \leq \left(\frac{1}{n}\right)^{\frac{1}{2}\log n - 1}$$

Now observe that, if the process terminates, then, after each round t, the number of active keys is at most by a factor c larger than the number of blocked modules. This holds because each of these modules will answer at most c requests during the process. Note that it can happen that the process does not terminate. In this case the access graph contains a highly connected subgraph (i.e., a complete bipartite graph of $c + 1$ V_K-nodes and $c + 1$ V_M-nodes) so that the c-collision rule fails to eliminate it. The choice of ϵ and c relative to a and b makes this event sufficiently unlikely. This proves part (a) of the Main Theorem.

3 Implementations of the Basic Process

3.1 Implementations on a c-collision DMM

Suppose we have an n-processor c-collision DMM, where U, the set of shared memory cells, is distributed among the modules with hash functions $h_1, \ldots, h_a : U \to \{1, \ldots, n\}$. So for every $i \in \{1, \ldots, a\}$ and $x \in U$, $M_{h_i(x)}$ contains the i-th copy of x. Each processor of the DMM knows at most one active key and the hash functions $h_1, \ldots, h_a$. Such a processor is called *active*. Then the (n, ϵ, a, b, c)-process can be implemented in such a way that every active processor tries to get access to all a copies of its key sequentially until it got access to at least b. Because of the c-collision rule, after each trial, the active processors have to wait c time steps to know whether their request was successful or not. Thus a round takes time $c \cdot a$. Now we can derive the following Theorem from part (b) of the Main Theorem:

Theorem 5. *Let* $h_1, \ldots, h_a$, ϵ, a, b *and* c *be chosen as in the Main Theorem. Then the above implementation of the* (n, ϵ, a, b, c)-*process on a* c-*collision DMM needs at most time* $c \cdot a \cdot \left(\frac{\log \log n}{\log(c(a-b))} + 3\right)$, *w.h.p..*

$\square$

It is easy to see that the above theorem yields simulations of a static dictionary with access time $O(\log \log n)$, w.h.p., for example for $\epsilon = 1$, $a = 2$ and $b = 1$ on a 2-collision DMM or for $\epsilon = \frac{1}{2}$, $a = 4$ and $b = 1$ on a 1-collision DMM.

With the help of the majority trick, that is $b > \frac{a}{2}$, the above theorem also yields simulations of shared memory, for instance for $\epsilon = \frac{1}{2}$ and $a = 3$ on a 2-collision DMM (a similar result is shown in [DM93], but with $\epsilon = 1/3$ and $c = 3$) or for $\epsilon = \frac{1}{40}$ and $a = 7$ on a 1-collision DMM. Thus Theorem 5 shows that an EREW PRAM can be simulated on an optical crossbar DMM with delay not exceeding $O(\log \log n)$, w.h.p..

3.2 Implementations on an arbitrary DMM

We want to find a way to execute a round of (a still direct variant of) our $(n, 1, a, b, c)$-process on an n-processor arbitrary DMM much faster than on a c-collision DMM. For this purpose we partition the arbitrary DMM into a groups $A_1, \ldots, A_a$ of $\frac{n}{a}$ processors, each, and a groups $B_1, \ldots, B_a$ of $\frac{n}{a}$ modules, each. Each function h_j, $j \in \{1, \ldots, a\}$, now maps U to modules in B_j only, i.e. has a range of size $\frac{n}{a}$ instead of n.

Let us first assume that we only have $\frac{n}{a}$ keys $x_1, \ldots, x_{n/a}$, where x_i is known to the i-th processor of each A_j, $j \in \{1, \ldots, a\}$. Then all requests of a round of the $(\frac{n}{a}, 1, a, b, c)$-process can be sent to the modules in time c. But it is not yet possible to check in constant time whether x_i got at least b answers after that round, because we have to compute whether a 0-1 vector of length a has at least b 1's, i.e. we have to compute a threshold function on a bits with threshold b.

Assume now that we only have $n/(a \cdot 2^a)$ keys, each known by $a \cdot 2^a$ processors. These processors can easily compute the above threshold function in constant time on an arbitrary DMM. Thus a round of the $(\frac{n}{a}, \frac{1}{2^a}, a, b, c)$-process can be run in such a way that it only needs constant time.

It remains to show how to reduce the set of keys from n to $\frac{n}{a2^a}$. Let us first consider the more difficult case that $b \leq \frac{a}{2}$. Then the implementation consists of the following three steps.

Initial reduction step: Assume there are n active keys $x_1, \ldots, x_n \in U$ at the beginning, where x_i is only known by processor Q_i. Each group A_j of processors chooses $a_0 := 2b$ hash functions to distribute its requests. The task of this step is to reduce the number of active keys from n to at most $n/2^{a_0}$. Let $m := \frac{n}{a}$. If 4 rounds of the $(m, 1, a_0, b, c)$-process are run on each of the a groups A_j of processors such that requests from different A_j never collide, we can use part (a) of the Main Theorem independently for each group A_j to obtain that it only takes $O(a_0) = O(b)$ time to reduce the number of active keys from n to $n/2^{a_0^2}$, w.h.p..

Final reduction step: We now want to reduce the remaining $n/2^{a_0}$ keys to at most $n/2^{a^2}$ active keys. Let a_0 be chosen as above and $a_i := \min\{2^{a_{i-1}}, a\}$ for all $i \geq 1$. For $s \geq 0$ let $m_s := a_s m$ and $A_i^s := \bigcup_{j=(i-1)a_s+1}^{i \cdot a_s} A_j$, $i \in \{1, \ldots, \frac{a}{a_s}\}$, be subsets of the set of processors with $|A_i^s| = m_s$. The A_i^s are chosen in such a way that all the remaining keys in A_i^s can send requests via a_s hash functions in parallel without colliding with keys from other groups $A_{i'}^s$. For the rest of this chapter the ϵ in the (m, ϵ, a, b, c)-process will mean that our process is started with at most ϵm active keys. Run the following scheme for $s = 1, 2, \ldots, \log^* a - \log^* b + 1$, i.e. until $a_s = a$.

simultaneously for each A_i^s, $i \in \{1, \ldots, \frac{a}{a_s}\}$:

(1) allocate a_s processors $Q_1^j, \ldots, Q_{a_s}^j$ for each active key x_j

(2) run 4 rounds of the $(m, \frac{1}{a_s}, a_s, b, c)$-process on all active keys of A_i^s

It is not difficult to prove by induction on s that, after s iterations, at most $m_s/(2^{a_s})^2$ keys are still active in each group A_i^s, w.h.p.. Furthermore, it can be proved with the help of the Main Theorem and [BH91] that each iteration takes only time $O(b)$, w.h.p.. (Some problems occur in the analysis of the last iteration. The details can be found in our Technical Report.) So altogether the final reduction step needs at most time $O(b(\log^* a - \log^* b + 1))$, w.h.p., to reduce the actve keys from at most $n/2^{a_0^2}$ to at most $n/(2^a)^2$.

Elimination step: We now try to get rid of all the remaining $n/(2^a)^2$ keys. According to [BH91] it takes at most time $O(\log^* n)$ w.h.p. to allocate $a \cdot 2^a$ processors for each active key. We can show the following lemma. It is not directly implied by the Main Theorem because, in contrast to the reduction steps, we now allow collisions among keys from different groups A_j w.r.t. hash functions we have already used in the reduction steps. The proof is omitted in this extended abstract.

Lemma 6. *Let $h_1, \ldots, h_a$, ϵ, a, b and c be chosen as in the Main Theorem. If in addition it holds that $a \geq 4$, $b < a - 1$ and $c \geq \frac{a}{a-b}$ then the elimination step finishes within $\frac{\log \log n}{\log(c(a-b))} + 3$ rounds, w.h.p..* □

As noted above, each round of this process can be executed in constant time. It follows that the whole implementation needs time $O(b(\log^* a - \log^* b + 1) + \log^* n + \frac{\log \log n}{\log(c(a-b))})$, w.h.p., for $b \leq \frac{a}{2}$.

For the case $b > \frac{a}{2}$ the implementation is similar to that for the case $b \leq \frac{a}{2}$, except that we set $a_0 := a$ and thus can omit the final reduction step. So altogether we get:

Theorem 7. *Let $h_1, \ldots, h_a$, ϵ, a, b and c be chosen as in Lemma 6. Then the above implementation of the $(\frac{n}{a}, a, a, b, c)$-process on an arbitrary DMM needs time*

$$O\left(b(log^* a - \log^* b + 1) + \log^* n + \frac{\log \log n}{\log(c(a-b))} \right),$$

w.h.p.. □

This theorem yields a shared memory simulation with delay $O(\frac{\log \log n}{\log \log \log n})$ if we use $\sqrt{\log \log n}$ hash functions, and a simulation of a static dictionary with access time $O(\log^* n)$ using $a = (\log n)^{1/\log^* n}$ hash functions.

4 The Lower Bound

In this section we ask whether there exist faster implementations of direct processes than ours. More precisely, we assume that the keys are distributed among the modules of an arbitrary DMM using a independent, truly random hash functions. We demand that, given n keys, one copy of each of them has to be accessed. We allow the processors to try to access several copies in parallel and to communicate with other processors. We restrict this communication to the oblivious mode, i.e. the communication is independent of the input keys. Based on the information gathered about the topology of the access graph by such oblivious communication and results of previous requests to copies of keys, a processor may decide on which copies to request in the next round. To formalize this we need the following definitions:

Definition 8. A configuration of the access-structure in round t of the processor P_l for $1 \leq l \leq n$ is the set $I_l^t = \{A_l^t, D_l^t, E_l^t, G_l^t\}$, where

A_l^t = {indices of active keys the processor P_l knows at the end of round t}

D_l^t = {indices of inactive keys the processor P_l knows at the end of round t}

E_l^t = {accesses P_l knows, i.e. pairs $(i, (j, k))$ with $i \in A_l^t \cup D_l^t$, $h_j(x_i) = k$,

      $j \in \{1, \ldots, a\}$, $k \in \{1, \ldots, n\}\}$

G_l^t is called the *collision graph*. It is a subgraph of the access graph G defined in

       section 2. The vertices are restricted to $\{A_l^t\} \cup \{D_l^t\}$ and the edges are

       restricted to $\{E_l^t\}$.

The lower bound we want to prove holds for a class of direct schemes as described below. Let us call this class of algorithms *simple schemes*.

Suppose there are a independent random hash functions with disjoint ranges, i.e. we duplicate the number of modules a times. In the initial configuration I_l^0 of processor P_l it knows one active key and the destinations of this key w.r.t. all a hash functions. We consider now the configuration I_l^t of processor P_l after some round t. In round $t+1$, a processor P_l can do the following:

(1) *Access step:* P_l requests all copies of all keys in A_l^t. We assume that requests w.r.t. different hash functions never collide, i.e. we assume that each module exists in a copies. An access for x_i, $i \in A_l^t$, w.r.t. a hash function h_j is stated as follows: The processor sends the key x_i to the module $M_{h_j(x_i)}$ accompanied by its complete information I_l^t. If a module gets k requests, it decides in the best way, based on the topology of the union of the incoming $G_{l'}^t$'s, which of the accesses it is going to answer. If $M_{h_j(x_i)}$ answers request y, y becomes inactive and is added to $D_{l'}^t$ for each asking processor $P_{l'}$. (This modified access step is at least as strong as the one stated in the informal description of the generalized direct scheme above. The main difference is that we do not let the processor decide whether it wants to make an access $h_j(x_i)$ or not. Instead, we let the module decide which request it wants to answer in a friendly way, based on the knowledge of the topology of the collisiongraphs of all processors that try to access it.)

(2) *Communication step:* Every processor P_l can communicate in one round with at most one other processor $P_{l'}$, in the oblivious mode, i.e., independent of the input keys. In this case P_l gets the information $I_{l'}^t$.

In the proof of the lower bound we assume that we can change w.l.o.g. an active key to an inactive one, i.e. with this operation we do not prejudice any simulation. Further we use mainly two techniques. The first one has been stated in [V75] and allows to restrict the number of active keys one processor knows to at most one. The second one keeps the decisions of the modules which key to answer independent. This idea is given formally in the following invariant, which must hold in each round t.

Lemma 9. *At the end of round t, $1 \leq t \leq \log\log n$, with probability $1 - O(\frac{1}{\log n})$ the following properties are satisfied if at most $n - \frac{n}{3\log^2 n} - \log^{10} n$ keys are changed from active to inactive:*

(i) *Every processor $P_l, 1 \leq l \leq n$, knows at most one active key, i.e. $|A_l^t| \leq 1$.*

(ii) *Every active module has answered exactly t requests.*

(iii) *Consider a module M_m which k processors $P_1, \ldots, P_k$ want to access. The structure of the unified collisiongraph $\bigcup_{l=1}^{k} G_l^t$ can be divided in two parts:*

    (1) A symmetric tree component: Each active index (processor) is connected to M_m and the root of a complete tree of depth 2 with $t(a-1)$ leaves denoting

keys (processors) that have been successful at the other modules where copies
of the keys are stored. All these subtrees are disjoint.
(2) The remaining structure is disjoint to (1).

Proof (Sketch): For $t = 0$ (i.e., before the scheme starts) the lemma obviously holds.
The access step does not affect statement (i), because a processor learns about keys
that become inactive in round t. Hence, we only have to consider the communication
steps. Since they are oblivious we can perform the at most $\log\log n$ communication
steps in advance. Define the communication graph $\tilde{G} = (A, E)$, where A is the set of all
keys. There is an edge $\{i, j\} \in E$ if some processor with active key $x_i \in A$ communicates
with some processor with active key $x_j \in A$ during a round t, for $1 \le t \le \log\log n$. For
t in the stated bounds we can bound the number of edges in the graph by $n \log^2 n$. If
we restrict the set of active keys to a maximum independent set by setting the others
inactive, we will satisfy (i). Using Turans Theorem it is easy to compute that we are
left with at least $\frac{n}{3\log^2 n}$ active keys.
In each round each active module receives at least one request and decides to answer
exactly one because of fact (i). If a module does not get a request in some round, it
will never get one later, so (ii) holds.
As $t \le \log\log n$ simple counting yields that each processor P_l can only collect
$O(a\log^2 n)$ keys using communication and access steps. Standard probability theory
yields that, with probability $1 - O(\frac{1}{\log n})$, $O(\log^{10} n)$ keys lie in the intersections of
the symmetric components (iii.1) and the remaining components (iii.2). If we change
$O(\log^{10} n)$ keys from active to inactive in each round, we fulfill (iii.2) with probability
at least $1 - O(\frac{1}{\log n})$. (iii.1) follows directly from (i), (ii) and the fact, that we have no
cycles of length smaller than six in our access-graph, w.h.p.. $\quad\square$

The lemma is used to show the independece of the decisions of the modules which
key to answer in each round.

Claim: Let $0 \le t \le \log\log n$. All decisions in a round t made by the active modules to
answer an access are independent.

Informally, the proof is based on the following basic observation. Decisions of a
module M are only based on the topological structure of the part of the access graph
it knows. As this structure is symmetric around M (see iii.1) and the remaining part
M knows disjoint from this symmetric part (see iii.2) this decision is random.

Lemma 10. Let the number of active keys be at least $\frac{n}{k}$, $k \le n^{\frac{1}{4a+2}}$, $a \le \log n$, and all
modules indepently answer one key in an access step. After performing t access steps
at least $\frac{n}{k(5a)^t}$ active keys are left, for $1 \le t \le \frac{\log\log n - \log\log k}{2\log(5a)}$, w.h.p.. $\quad\square$

The proof is omitted in this extended abstract.
If we deactivate in advance enough keys to satisfy the assumptions in Lemma 9,
Lemma 10 together with the claim immediately imply the following theorem:

Theorem 11. Any simple scheme based on a random, independent hash functions to
distribute the shared memory needs time $\Omega(\frac{\log\log n}{\log a})$ with probability $1 - O(\frac{1}{\log n})$. $\quad\square$

For shared memory simulations, also a, the number of hash functions used, is a
lower bound, because at least $\frac{a}{2}$ copies have to be updated.

Corollary 12. Any shared memory simulation within the class of simple schemes based
on a independent, truly random hash functions to distribute the shared memory has

delay $\Omega(a + \frac{\log\log n}{\log a})$. Thus any choice of a can only yield simulations with delay $\Omega(\frac{\log\log n}{\log\log\log n})$, i.e. the result from Theorem 7 is optimal. $\square$

References

[AM88]   R.J. Anderson and G.L. Miller. Optical Communication for Pointer Based Algorithms, Technical Report CRI 88-14, Computer Science Department, University of Southern Carolina, Los Angeles, CA 90089-0782 USA, 1988.

[BH91]   H. Bast and T. Hagerup. Fast and reliable parallel hashing. In *Proc. of the 3rd Ann. ACM Symp. on Parallel Algorithms and Architectures*, pp. 50-61, 1991.

[DM90]   M. Dietzfelbinger, F. Meyer auf der Heide. How to distribute a hash table in a complete network. In *Proc. of the 22nd Ann. ACM Symp. on Theory of Computing*, pp. 117-127, 1990.

[DM93]   M. Dietzfelbinger and F. Meyer auf der Heide. Simple efficient shared memory simulations. In *Proceedings of the 5th Ann. ACM Symposium on Parallel Algorithms and Architectures*, pp. 110-119, 1993.

[GT92]   M. Geréb-Graus and T. Tsantilas. Efficient Optical Communication in Parallel Computers. In *Proceedings of the 4th ACM Symposium on Parallel Algorithms and Architectures*, pp. 41-48, 1992.

[GJL93] L. A. Goldberg and M. Jerrum and T. Leighton. A doubly logarithmic communication algorithm for the completely connected optical communication parallel computer. In *Proceedings of the 5th Ann. ACM Symposium on Parallel Algorithms and Architectures*, pp. 300-309, 1993.

[GMR94] L.A. Goldberg, Y. Matias, S. Rao. An optical simulation of shared memory. Technical Report, 1994.

[GMV91] J. Gil, Y. Matias, U. Vishkin. Towards a theory of nearly constant time parallel algorithms. In *Proc. of the 32nd Ann. IEEE Symp. on Foundations of Computer Science*, pp. 698-710, 1991.

[KLM92] R. Karp, M. Luby and F. Meyer auf der Heide. Efficient PRAM simulation on distributed memory machine. In *Proc. of the 24th Ann. ACM Symp. on Theory of Computing*, pp. 318-326, 1992.

[M92]   F. Meyer auf der Heide. Hashing strategies for simulating shared memory on distributed memory machines. In *Proc. of the 1st Heinz Nixdorf Symposium "Parallel Architectures and Their Efficient Use"*, F. Meyer auf der Heide, B. Monien, A.L. Rosenberg, eds., pp. 20-29, 1992.

[MPR94] P.D. MacKenzie, C.G. Plaxton, R. Rajamaran. On contention resolution protocols and associated phenomena. University of Texas at Austin, Technical Report 94-06, 1994.

[S89]   A. Siegel. On universal classes of fast high performance hash functions, their time-space tradeoff, and their applications. In *Proc. of the 30th IEEE Ann. Symp. on Foundations of Computer Science*, pp. 20-25, 1989.

[UW87]   E. Upfal, A. Wigderson. How to share memory in a distributed system. *J. Assoc. Comput. Mach.* 34, pp. 116-127, 1987.

[V75]   L. Valiant. Parallelism in comparison problems. In *SIAM J. Comp. 4(3)*, pp. 348-355, 1975.

[V90]   L. Valiant. General Purpose Parallel Architectures, Chapter 18 of Handbook of Theoretical Computer Science. Edited by J. van Leeuwen, Elsevier 1990.

Interval Routing Schemes [*]

Michele Flammini[1,3], Giorgio Gambosi[2], Sandro Salomone[3]

[1] Dipartimento di Informatica e Sistemistica, University of Rome "La Sapienza", via Salaria 113, I-00198 Rome, Italy
[2] Dipartimento di Matematica, University of Rome "Tor Vergata", via della Ricerca Scientifica, I-00133 Rome, Italy
[3] Dipartimento di Matematica Pura ed Applicata, University of L'Aquila, via Vetoio loc. Coppito, I-67010 l'Aquila, Italy. E-mail: flammini@vxscaq.aquila.infn.it

Abstract. In this paper, the problem of routing messages along shortest paths in a distributed network without using complete routing tables is considered. In particular, the complexity of designing minimum (in terms of number of intervals) Interval Routing Schemes is analyzed under different requirements. For all the considered cases NP-hardness proofs are given, while some approximability results are provided. Moreover, relations among the different considered cases are studied.

Topics: computational complexity, theory of parallel and distributed computing.

1 Introduction

Routing messages between pairs of processors is a fundamental task in a distributed network. A network of processors is modeled as an (undirected) connected graph $G = (V, E)$, where V is a set of n processors and E is a set of pairwise communication links. Assuming some cost function on the network edges exists, it is important to route each message along a shortest path from its source to the destination.

This can be trivially accomplished by referring, at each node v, to a complete routing table which specifies, for each destination u, the set of links incident to v which are on shortest paths between u and v. Such a table has $\Theta(n) \lceil \log d \rceil$-bits entries [4] ($d$-bits if all shortest paths between each pair of processors have to be represented), where d is the node degree.

Research activities focused on identifying classes of network topologies where the shortest path information at each node can be succinctly stored, assuming that suitably "short" labels can be assigned to nodes and links at preprocessing time. Such labels are used to encode useful information about the network structure, with special regard to shortest paths.

---

[*] Work supported by the EEC ESPRIT II Basic Research Action Program under contract No.7141 "Algorithms and Complexity II", by the EEC "Human Capital and Mobility" MAP project and by the Italian MURST 40% project "Algoritmi, Modelli di Calcolo e Strutture Informative".
[4] In the following, all logarithms will be assumed with base 2.

In the ILS (*Interval Labeling Scheme*) routing scheme ([10], [11], [12]) node labels belong to the set $\{1, \ldots, n\}$, assumed cyclically ordered, while link labels are pairs of node labels representing disjoint intervals on $\{1, \ldots, n\}$.

To transmit a message m from node v_i to node v_j, m is broadcast by v_i on the (unique) link $e = (v_i, v_k)$ such that the label of v_j belongs to the interval associated to e. With this approach, one always obtains an optimal memory occupation, while the problem is to choose node and link labels in such a way that messages are routed along shortest paths.

In [10], [11], [12] it is shown how the ILS approach can be applied to optimally route on particular network topologies, such as trees, rings, etc. The ILS approach has also been used in other papers as a basic building block for routing schemes based on network decomposition and clustering ([1], [2], [4], [5], [6], [9]).

In [11], the approach has been extended to allow that more than 1 interval is associated to each node (K-ILS routing scheme); in particular, a 2-ILS scheme - that is a scheme associating at most 2 intervals for each edge - is proposed for two dimensional doubly wrapped grids.

However, both the ILS scheme and its extension to multiple intervals aim to represent, for any pair of nodes u, v, one shortest path between u and v.

In this paper, we are interested in schemes which represent more than one shortest path between pairs of nodes. Such an approach seems particularly interesting if the necessity of dealing also with problems of faults and traffic distribution is taken into account. In such a framework, we will consider different types of schemes, according to the set of shortest paths to be represented for each pair of nodes and to the particular memory occupation measure considered. Moreover, we study the case where it is possible to include a node label inside intervals associated to its outgoing links.

We first analyze the relations between such schemes. Next, we prove that, given a graph $G = (V, E)$, for all such schemes it is NP-hard to devise an interval routing scheme with a minimum memory occupation. We also show that a good approximation can be derived in particular cases.

The paper is organized as follows: in section 2 we give some preliminary definitions; in section 3 we study the relations between the various interval schemes; in section 4 we prove the NP-hardness of finding optimal schemes with respect to the various factors, and finally in section 5 we present some approximation results for specific cases.

2 Definitions

Let us first provide some preliminary definitions. Let $G = (V, E)$ ($|V| = n$) be a graph with weighted edges. Given a node $v \in V$, we will denote as $I(v) \subseteq E$ the set of edges incident to v. For each node u and each edge $e \in I(u)$, let us denote as $s(u, e)$ the set of nodes v optimally reachable from u through that edge (i.e. such that e belongs to some shortest path from u to v). We denote by *path representation* a function $d : V \times E \mapsto 2^V$ such that:

- if $e \in I(u)$ then $d(u, e) \subseteq s(u, e)$;
- if $e \notin I(u)$ then $d(u, e) =undefined$;
- for each $u \in V$, $\bigcup_{e \in I(u)} d(u, e) = V - \{u\}$.

Definition 1. A path representation is *Overall* if $\forall u \in V$ $d(u, e) = s(u, e)$. That is, all shortest paths are represented.

Definition 2. A path representation is *Multiple(p)* if $\forall u, v \in V, u \neq v$
$|\{e \in I(u) \mid v \in d(u, e)\}| = Min(|\{e \in I(u) \mid v \in s(u, e)\}|, p)$. That is, for any pair $u, v \in V$, at most p shortest paths between u and v are represented.

Definition 3. A path representation is *Single* if $\forall u, v \in V, u \neq v$
$|\{e \in I(u) \mid v \in d(u, e)\}| = 1$. That is, if exactly one shortest path is represented for any pair of nodes.

Note that in the Single case, for each $u \in V$, sets $d(u, e)$ $(e \in I(u))$ partition set $V - \{u\}$.

The path representations defined above merely correspond to our informal definitions of the various schemes. They are defined in order to emphasize in all cases the paths that are represented, as each set $d(u, e)$ is the subset of $s(u, e)$ for which the link e is activated.

Given a 1-1 function $f : V \to \{1, \ldots, n\}$ and a path representation d, we will also denote as $\mathcal{N}(f, d, u, e)$ the minimum number of disjoint subintervals of $\{1, \ldots, n\}$ (assumed cyclically ordered) such that their union is equal to $\{f(v) \mid v \in d(u, e)\}$.

Given a network, if we are interested to minimize the overall number of intervals to represent the shortest paths, then, according to the above path representations, we can identify the following problems:

Definition 4. Global Overall Interval Labeling Problem ([7]):

- INSTANCE: A weighted graph $G = (V, E)$ and an integer $K > 0$.
- QUESTION: Is there a K-Global Overall interval scheme, i.e. a 1-1 function $f : V \to \{1, \ldots, |V|\}$ and an Overall path representation d such that $\sum_{u \in V} \sum_{e \in I(u)} \mathcal{N}(f, d, u, e) \leq K$?

Definition 5. Global Multiple Interval Labeling Problem:

- INSTANCE: A weighted graph $G = (V, E)$ and integers $K > 0$ and $p > 0$.
- QUESTION: Is there a K-Global Multiple(p) interval scheme, i.e. a 1-1 function $f : V \to \{1, \ldots, |V|\}$ and a Multiple(p) path representation d such that $\sum_{u \in V} \sum_{e \in I(u)} \mathcal{N}(f, d, u, e) \leq K$?

Definition 6. Global Single Interval Labeling Problem:

- INSTANCE: A weighted graph $G = (V, E)$ and an integer $K > 0$.
- QUESTION: Is there a K-Global Single interval scheme, i.e. a 1-1 function $f : V \to \{1, \ldots, |V|\}$ and a Single path representation d such that $\sum_{u \in V} \sum_{e \in I(u)} \mathcal{N}(f, d, u, e) \leq K$?

Similar problems can be defined for the corresponding Balanced cases by considering the condition

$max_{u \in V} max_{e \in I(u)} \mathcal{N}(f, d, u, e) \leq K$ instead of $\sum_{u \in V} \sum_{e \in I(u)} \mathcal{N}(f, d, u, e) \leq K$.

Clearly, f corresponds to a labeling of the nodes of the graph, and $\mathcal{N}(f, d, u, e)$ can be also interpreted as the minimum number of intervals necessary to represent set $d(u, e)$, with elements labeled according to f, for a certain link e.

Hence, the corresponding global scheme requires an overall $O(\sum_{u \in V} \sum_{e \in I(u)} \mathcal{N}(f, d, u, e) \cdot \log n)$ bits of information to optimally route messages, and the corresponding balanced scheme requires $O(max_{u \in V} max_{e \in I(u)} \mathcal{N}(f, d, u, e) \cdot \log n)$ bits for each $u \in V$ and $e \in I(u)$.

In order to reduce the number of intervals, in the classical Interval Labeling Scheme nodes are allowed to have their labels inside intervals associated to their outgoing links. Thus, to have a complete classification of the Interval schemes we have to consider this *Inner* case:

Definition 7. A path representation is *Inner* if $\forall u \in V$, $d(u, e) \subseteq s(u, e) \cup \{u\}$.

All definitions and considerations above trivially extend to Inner path representations.

Note that the *ILS*-Scheme corresponds to the Single Balanced one in the Inner case.

3 Relations between Schemes

In this section we analyze, both in the balanced and in the global case, the relations between the various schemes with respect to the shortest paths that are represented.

It is possible to see that the design of routing schemes can be easily reduced to the problem of permuting the rows of a suitable boolean matrix M in such a way to minimize the number of consecutive blocks of 1's occurring in the columns. Informally speaking, given a graph $G = (V, E)$, such a matrix can be obtained by associating a row to each $v \in V$ and a column to each pair $v \in V$, $e \in I(v)$. For each entry, $M[u, (v, e)] = 1$ if and only if $u \in d(v, e)$, i.e. if u can be optimally reached from node v through link e. We denote M as *matrix path representation* of the path representation d.

In order to prove relations between the above defined schemes we use the following lemma.

Lemma 8. *Given an $m \times n$ boolean matrix M and an integer $p \leq n$ it is possible, by turning a suitable set of entries from 1 to 0, to derive a matrix M' such that:*
- for each row M with more than p 1's, the corresponding row of M' has precisely p 1's;
- all other rows are the same in M and M';
- for each column of M the number of (maximal) blocks of consecutive 1's is not less than the number of (maximal) blocks of 1's in the corresponding column of M'.

Proof. Given an entry $M[i,j] = 1$, let us call it a *k-order entry* if and only if there exist $(k-1)$ entries equal to 1 preceding it in its row.

The transformation is obtained as follows: let us consider the first column j in which there is at least one $(p+1)$-order entry. Let $B = \{M[i,j], \ldots, M[i+s,j]\}$ be a (maximal) block of consecutive 1's in the column: if entries $M[i,j], \ldots, M[i+k_1,j]$ ($k_1 \leq s$) are $(p+1)$-order entries then we delete them (by turning their values to 0). The same is applied to entries $M[i+k_2,j], \ldots, M[i+s,j]$ ($k_2 > k_1, k_2 < s$).

If some entry has not been turned to 0 (that is, at least one entry in B was not a $(p+1)$-order entry), let us consider any maximal subblock $B' = \{M[i+r,j], \ldots, M[i+t,j]\}$ ($r > k_1, t < k_2$) of B with only $(p+1)$-order entries. Then, there must exist some column $k < j$ containing a block $B'' = \{M[i+r,k], \ldots, M[i+q,k]\}$ with $M[i+q+1,k] = 0$. If $q \geq t$ then let us now delete entries $M[i+r,k], \ldots, M[i+t,k]$; otherwise, we may apply the same considerations to block $M[i+q+1,j], \ldots, M[i+t,j]$. This results in transforming all the $((p+1)$-order) entries of B' in p-order entries. The same procedure can be applied for all the other maximal blocks in B', thus eliminating all $(p+1)$-order entries in column j.

By iterating the same procedure starting from the next column with at least one $(p+1)$-order entry, we finally obtain a new matrix M' containing only j-order entries for $j \leq p$. Note that each row in M with a number of 1's greater than or equal to p has p entries equal to 1 in M', while other rows remain unchanged. Moreover, it is immediate that the above procedure never increases the number of blocks in any column.

From such a lemma, the following theorem can be proved:

Theorem 9. *Given a graph $G = (V, E)$ and $K > 0$, if there exists a K-Global Overall scheme on G, then there also exists a K-Global Multiple(p) scheme (for every $p > 0$) on G. Moreover, given $G = (V, E)$ and $p, K > 0$, if there exists a K-Global Multiple(p) scheme on G then there exists a K-Global Single scheme on G.*

Proof. First of all let us observe that the Overall case corresponds to the Multiple$(n-1)$ case, while Single corresponds to Multiple(1). It will then suffice to prove that if a Multiple(p) scheme exists than there also exists a Multiple(p') for any $p' < p$.

Let us consider the matrix path representation of a K-Global Multiple(p) scheme. Given a node u consider such a matrix restricted to u, that is the submatrix obtained by considering only the columns associated to u and all its incident links. Given $p' < p$ if we apply to this matrix the transformation in Lemma 8 we obtain a matrix in which at node u we represent exactly p' shortest paths to every other node. By repeating the transformation over all the nodes we obtain a Multiple(p') path representation.

Since the same proof technique can be applied to the balanced case, the following theorem holds:

Theorem 10. *K-Balanced Overall scheme $\Rightarrow$ K-Balanced Multiple(p) scheme $\Rightarrow$ K-Balanced Single scheme (for every $K, p > 0$).*

It is easy to see that the converse of theorems 9 and 10 does not hold, that is Single $\not\Rightarrow$ Multiple(p) $\not\Rightarrow$ Overall.

Since each path representation is also an Inner path representation $(d(u, e) \subseteq s(u, e) \subseteq s(u, e) \cup \{u\})$, given a graph $G = (V, E)$, if there exists a K-Global Overall (resp. Multiple(p), Single) scheme on G, then there exists a K-Global Overall (resp. Multiple(p), Single) Inner scheme. Moreover, if there exists a K-Balanced Overall (resp. Multiple(p), Single) scheme on G, then there exists a K-Balanced Overall (resp. Multiple(p), Single) Inner scheme.

The converse in general is not true, as shown in the counterexample in figure 1. In the considered graph there exists a unique shortest path between each pair of nodes. This implies that in the normal case all path representation coincide. It is easy to verify that, in the considered graph, it is not possible to associate a unique interval to each node-edge pair in the normal case. On the contrary, in the Inner case it is possible to associate a unique interval to each node-edge pair.

$$w(v_2, v_4) = 1 + \varepsilon$$
$$w(v_2, v_5) = 1 - \varepsilon$$
$$w(v_4, v_5) = 1 - \varepsilon$$
$$w(v_5, v_6) = 1 + \varepsilon$$
$$w(v_3, v_6) = 1 + \varepsilon$$

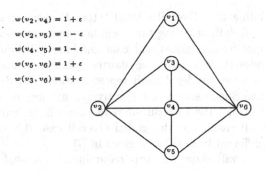

Fig. 1. Counterexample

Given an Inner scheme, at each edge the label of the starting node can only be included in one interval. By removing such a label, we can increase the number of intervals associated to that edge by at most one, thus deriving the following theorem:

Theorem 11. *Given a graph $G = (V, E)$, if G admits a K-Balanced Overall (Multiple(p), Single) Inner scheme, then G admits a $(K + 1)$-Balanced Overall (Multiple(p), Single) scheme.*

For the Global case, the following holds:

Theorem 12. *Given a graph $G = (V, E)$, if G admits a K-Global Multiple(p) Inner scheme $(p > 0)$, then G admits a K'-Global Multiple(p) scheme, where $K' = (K + min(2 \cdot \mid E \mid, np))$.*

Proof. Given an Inner scheme for G, a normal (not Inner) scheme can be obtained by removing, for each node v_i, its label l_i from the intervals associated to its outgoing links. As stated in the Balanced case, this increases the number of intervals for each node-link pair by at most one, thus $K' \leq K + 2 \mid E \mid$.

For any node u_i, the two labels adjacent to l_i may appear together in at most p intervals (one per edge) associated to the outgoing links of u_i. Thus, by removing l_i, the number of intervals can increase by at most p. By summing up over all nodes $u \in V$, it results $K' \leq K + np$, and the theorem holds.

The following corollary derives immediately.

Corollary 13. *If $G = (V, E)$ admits a K-Global Single Inner scheme, then it also admits a $(K + n)$-Global Single scheme.*

Notice that the K-Balanced Single scheme in the Inner case just corresponds to the K-ILS scheme.

4 Hardness results

The problem of finding a K-Overall Global Interval scheme has been proved NP-Hard in [7]. By carefully selecting the possible reductions we will obtain two transformation graphs for the global and balanced cases. Within these graphs, for each pair of nodes there is only one shortest path connecting them. This means that in both cases the legal path representations d_P, d_F, d_S, (for the Overall, Multiple and Single schemes, respectively), are unique and coincident ($d_P = d_F = d_S$). Thus, the introduced reduction will actually represent a hardness proof for all cases. For the global Overall case this can be seen as an hardness proof different from the one given in [7].

In the sequel, we will show the two reductions for global and balanced schemes.

For the sake of brevity, given $U \subseteq V$ we will denote by $\mathcal{N}(f, U)$ the minimum number of disjoint intervals such that their union is equal to $\{f(v) \mid v \in U\}$.

4.1 Global case

In order to prove the hardness result we provide a polynomial transformation from the Hamiltonian Path Problem ([8]).

Let $G' = (V', E')$ be an instance of the Hamiltonian Path problem. Let us denote by v_i' and by e_j' respectively a generic node and a generic edge of G'. Starting from G', we derive a weighted graph $G = (V, E)$ (see figure 2) with weight function $W : V \rightarrow \Re$, where $V = V_1 \cup V_2 \cup V_3 \cup V_4 \cup V_5$, with:

$V_1 = \{u_i \mid i = 1, ..., |V'|\}$, $V_2 = \{v_j \mid j = 1, ..., |E'|\}$, $V_3 = \{w_j \mid j = 1, ..., |E'|\}$,

$V_4 = \{v\}$, $V_5 = \{z_i \mid i = 1, ..., |V'| + 4|E'| + 1\}$ and

$E = V \times V - E_1 - E_2 - \{(u, u) \mid u \in V\}$, where

$E_1 = \{(w_i, u_{i_1}) \mid e_i' = (v_{i_1}', v_{i_2}') \in E'\} \bigcup \{(w_i, u_{i_2}) \mid e_i' = (v_{i_1}', v_{i_2}') \in E'\}$,

$E_2 = V_1 \times V_5$. For what regards weights we assume $W(e) = (1+\varepsilon)$ if $e \in E_3 \cup E_4$, where: $E_3 = V_2 \times V_5$, $E_4 = \{(w_i, u) \mid u \in V\} \bigcap E - \{(w_i, v_i)\}$. Otherwise, we assume $W(e) = 1$.

Thus we have $n = |V| = 2 \cdot |V'| + 6 \cdot |E'| + 2$ and
$$m = |E| = \frac{|V| \cdot (|V|-1)}{2} - |E_1| - |E_2| =$$
$$= |V'|^2 + 18 \cdot |E'|^2 + 8 \cdot |V'| \cdot |E'| + 2 \cdot |V'| + 7 \cdot |E'| + 1.$$

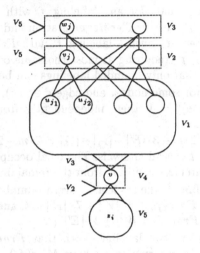

Fig. 2. The Transformation Graph (global case)

Informally, we associate to each $v_i' \in V'$ a node $u_i \in V_1$, to each edge $e_k' = (v_i', v_j') \in E'$ an edge component of two nodes w_k, v_k configured in such a way that w_k is adjacent to all nodes except u_i and u_j and is connected to u_i and u_j by a shortest path through v_k. We call u_i and u_j the *endpoints* of the edge component. Since all edges incident to w_k have weight $1 + \varepsilon$ but (w_k, v_k), there is only one shortest path between w_k and u_i (the one including v_k), and the same holds for u_j. Furthermore, each node in V_5 is not connected to any node in V_1 and all its incident edges have weight $1+\varepsilon$, except the one to $v \in V_4$. Thus, for each $u \in V_1$ and $z \in V_5$ the (unique) shortest path between u and z includes node v. This constraining component forces the optimal solution to be such that the labels associated to nodes in V_1 are in a single interval.

All pairs of nodes not mentioned before are linked directly. Notice that between every two nodes there is only one shortest path and that, by the considerations at the beginning of this section, all schemes collapse.

For the sake of brevity, when introducing a labeling f we will denote it as *bounded* if, recalling that labels are assumed cyclically ordered, it assigns a unique interval of labels to nodes in V_1, a unique interval of labels to nodes in V_5 and both such intervals are adjacent to the label of v. We will denote a scheme as bounded if the corresponding labeling is bounded.

The only paths of length 2 are between pairs of nodes in V_1 and V_5 and between each w_k and the two endpoints u_i and u_j of the corresponding edge component. Thus, it is easy to see that, given any labeling f, the labeling f' obtained by compacting all labels of nodes in V_5 in a unique interval and leaving unchanged the relative order of all other nodes yields a scheme requiring an overall number of intervals at most equal to the scheme corresponding to the use of f. Hence, in the following we restrict our attention only to such labelings.

Let us define the *fragmentation* of a labeling f as $Frag(f) = \mathcal{N}(f, V_1 \cup V_4)$. Let us then show that, for any labeling f with $Frag(f) > 1$, there exists another labeling f' with smaller fragmentation and with a lower overall number of intervals. Moreover, given a labeling f' with $Frag(f') = 1$ we can obtain a bounded labeling f'' requiring at most the same overall number of intervals of f'. This implies that only bounded labelings can be considered.

Note that if for some node u and edge $e \in I(u)$, given a path representation d, we have $|d(u, e)| = 1$, then, independently from the labeling f, it results $\mathcal{N}(f, d, u, e) = 1$.
As there are $t = 2 \cdot m - 3 \cdot |E'| - |V_1| - |V_5| = 2 \cdot m - 2 \cdot |V'| - 7 \cdot |E'| - 1$ node-edge pairs, they yield t overall intervals. The total occupation is then equal to t plus the number of intervals resulting from the remaining (node, edge) pairs.

Given a labeling f, the associated overall number of intervals is at most $Max(f) = |V_5| \cdot Frag(f) + 2 \cdot |V'| + 7 \cdot |E'| + t$, and at least $Min(f) = |V_5| \cdot Frag(f) + |V'| + 3 \cdot |E'| + t$.

If f_1 and f_2 are two labelings such that $Frag(f_1) < Frag(f_2)$ then, by plugging in the above formulae, we have $Max(f_1) < Min(f_2)$.

Let us now consider a labeling f with $Frag(f) = 1$. By hypothesis, labels of u_i-s and v are in a unique interval. If the label of v is not an endpoint of this interval, then the labeling of the other nodes obtained by compacting the labels of the nodes u_i-s (leaving unchanged the relative order) and putting the label of v to one endpoint yields at most the same overall number of intervals, since the fragmentation is unchanged and node v is connected to each node w_k.

Finally, by similar considerations it derives that if we put the interval of labels of V_5 adjacent to the label of v then we can only improve memory occupation, obtaining a bounded labeling.

Let us now consider an edge component. Clearly, if we assign adjacent labels to nodes w_k and v_k, which is always possible for bounded labelings, we may only reduce the space occupation. Furthermore, we can put only one node v_k adjacent to nodes u_i. Hence, if a is the maximum number of edge components such that the endpoints u_i and u_j receive adjacent labels, the best scheme requires an overall number of intervals equal to
$$t + |V_5| + |V'| + 2 \cdot |E'| + 3 \cdot (|E'| - a) + 2 \cdot a - 1 = t + 2 \cdot |V'| + 9 \cdot |E'| - a \geq K,$$
where $K = t + |V'| + 9 \cdot |E'| + 1$.

Clearly a is at most $|V'| - 1$ and the equality holds if and only if G' has an Hamiltonian path. Thus, the scheme globally requires at most K intervals if and only if G' has an Hamiltonian path.

By the above, by the polynomiality of the reduction and by the unicity of the paths representation, the following theorems derive:

Theorem 14. *[7] The problem of finding a Global Overall scheme with a minimum overall number of intervals is NP-hard.*

Theorem 15. *The problem of finding a Global Multiple(p) scheme with a minimum overall number of intervals is NP-hard.*

Theorem 16. *The problem of finding a Global Single scheme with a minimum overall number of intervals is NP-hard.*

4.2 Balanced case

The following result will be useful to prove the NP-hardness of designing routing schemes in the balanced cases.

Definition 17. Balanced Column Consecutive Blocks Minimization:

- INSTANCE: An $m \times n$ boolean matrix A and an integer $K > 0$.
- QUESTION: Is there a permutation of the rows of A such that for each column the number of blocks of consecutive 1's is at most K?

Theorem 18. *The Balanced Column Consecutive Blocks Minimization problem is NP-complete.*

Proof. Such a problem can be proved NP-complete by a reduction from the Consecutive Blocks Minimization Problem ([8]), that is the corresponding problem in which we take into account the sum of the blocks over all columns. The proof will appear in the full paper.

By a polynomial reduction from the *Balanced Column Consecutive Blocks Minimization* problem, it is possible to prove the following theorems:

Theorem 19. *The problem of finding a Balanced Overall scheme having a minimum overall number of intervals is NP-hard.*

Theorem 20. *The problem of finding a Balanced Multiple(p) scheme having a minimum overall number of intervals is NP-hard.*

Theorem 21. *The problem of finding a Balanced Single scheme having a minimum overall number of intervals is NP-hard.*

We summarize the proven results in the table 3.

It is easy to see that in both the two reduction graphs for the global and the balanced case, it is not possible to save intervals using the Inner facility, so the results in table 3 remain true in the Inner case.

289

	Single	Multiple(p)	Overall
Global	NP-Hard	NP-Hard	NP-Hard [7]
Balanced	NP-Hard	NP-Hard	NP-Hard

Fig. 3. Hardness results

4.3 Approximation of Global Overall Schemes

Given a minimization problem P and an instance I, we denote by $OPT_P(I)$ the value of the optimal solution.

In [7] an efficient approximation algorithm is given for the GO problem (Global Overall Interval Labeling). In particular, the following theorem is proved.

Theorem 22. *[7] There exists a polynomial algorithm which, for any instance G of the GO problem (Global Overall Interval Labeling problem), returns a solution with an overall number of intervals $\leq 1.5 \cdot OPT_{GO}(G)$, where $OPT_{GO}(G)$ is the overall number of intervals of the optimum solution.*

In the GO_{Inner} problem, that is the GO problem in the Inner case, for each node u it is possible to decide, in order to reduce the number of intervals, whether or not to include u's label in the intervals associated to each incident edge. It follows that in the matrix path representation, given the row associated to u and in correspondence to all columns associated to pairs (u, e) such that $e \in I(u)$, entries can be suitably set to 0 or 1 in order to reduce the overall number of blocks. We call such entries δ-*entries* and for the sake of brevity we denote their value as δ.

This means that theorem 22 cannot be applied in the Inner case if a particular assignment of the δ-entries is not selected, and if we set the δ values to 0 or 1 arbitrarily, the algorithm in [7] does not return an 1.5 approximate solution, because only one of the possibly exponentially many assignments is considered.

However, it is possible to prove the following theorem:

Theorem 23. *For any instance G of the GO_{Inner} problem, the above algorithm returns, in polynomial time, a solution with an overall number of intervals $\leq 3 \cdot OPT_{GO_{Inner}}(G)$, where $OPT_{GO_{Inner}}(G)$ is the overall number of intervals of the optimum solution.*

Proof. Given an optimal solution for the Inner case, by removing at each node u its label from the intervals associated to its incident edges, the number of intervals assigned to each edge can be increased at most by 1, thus globally increasing the overall number of intervals by at most $2 \mid E \mid$.

Hence,

$$OPT_{GO}(G) \leq OPT_{GO_{Inner}}(G) + 2 \mid E \mid),$$

and since each Global Inner scheme requires at least $2 \mid E \mid$ intervals,

$$OPT_{GO_{Inner}}(G) \geq 2 \mid E \mid .$$

Thus, if s is the number of intervals of the solution returned by the algorithm, it results

$$s \leq 1.5 \cdot OPT_{GO}(G) \leq 1.5 \cdot (OPT_{GO_{Inner}}(G) + 2 \cdot \mid E \mid)) \leq 3 \cdot OPT_{GO_{Inner}}(G).$$

References

1. B. Awerbuch, A. Bar-Noy, N. Linial, D. Peleg. *Compact distributed data structures for adaptive routing*. Proc. 21st ACM Symp. on Theory of Computing, pp. 479-489, **1989**.
2. B. Awerbuch, A. Bar-Noy, N. Linial, D. Peleg. *Improved routing strategies with succinct tables*. Journal of Algorithms, 11, pp. 307-341, **1990**.
3. N. Christofides. *Worst case analysis of a new heuristic for the travelling salesman problem*. Report No. 388, GSIA, Carnegie–Mellon University, Pittsburgh, PA, **1976**.
4. G.N. Frederickson, R. Janardan. *Designing networks with compact routing tables*. Algorithmica, 3, pp. 171-190, **1988**.
5. G.N. Frederickson, R. Janardan. *Efficient message routing in planar networks*. SIAM Journal on Computing, 18, pp. 843-857, **1989**.
6. G.N. Frederickson, R. Janardan. *Space efficient message routing in c-decomposable networks*. SIAM Journal on Computing, 19, pp. 164-181, **1990**.
7. M. Flammini, G. Gambosi, S. Salomone. *Boolean Routing*. Proc. 7th Int. Workshop on Distributed Algorithms (WDAG), Lecture Notes in Computer Science n. 725, Springer Verlag, pp. 219-233, **1993**.
8. M.R. Garey, D.S. Johnson. *Computers and Intractability. A guide to the theory of NP-completeness*. W.H. Freeman, San Francisco, **1979**.
9. D. Peleg, E. Upfal. *A trade-off between space and efficiency for routing tables*. Journal of the ACM, 36, 3, pp. 510-530, **1989**.
10. M. Santoro, R. Khatib. *Labelling and implicit routing in networks*. The Computer Journal, 28, pp. 5-8, **1985**.
11. J. van Leeuwen, R.B. Tan. *Routing with compact routing tables*. In "The book of L", G.Rozemberg and A.Salomaa eds., Springer Verlag, pp. 259-273, **1986**.
12. J. van Leeuwen, R.B. Tan. *Interval routing*. The Computer Journal, 30, pp. 298-307, **1987**.

A Packet Routing Protocol for Arbitrary Networks*

Friedhelm Meyer auf der Heide and Berthold Vöcking

Department for Mathematics and Computer Science
and Heinz Nixdorf Institute, University of Paderborn,
33098 Paderborn, Germany

Abstract. In this paper, we introduce an on-line protocol which routes any set of packets along shortest paths through an arbitrary N-node network in $O(\text{congestion} + \text{diameter} + \log N)$ rounds, with high probability. This time bound is optimal up to the additive $\log N$, and it was previously only reached for bounded-degree levelled networks.

Further, we prove bounds on the congestion of random routing problems for Cayley networks and general node symmetric networks based on the construction of shortest paths systems. In particular, we give construction schemes for shortest paths systems and show that if every processor sends p packets to random destinations along the paths described in the paths system, then the congestion is bounded by $O(p \cdot \text{diameter} + \log N)$, with high probability.

Finally, we prove an (apparently suboptimal) congestion bound for random routing problems on randomly chosen regular networks.

1 Introduction

Communication among the processors of a parallel computer usually requires a large portion of runtime of a parallel algorithm. These computers are often realized as relatively sparse networks of a large number of processors such that each processor can communicate directly only with a few neighbours. Thus, most of the communication must proceed through intermediate processors. One of the basic problems in this context is to route simultanously many *packets* through the network. Most previous theoretical research on packet routing concentrates on special classes of networks. We are interested in packet routing problems on networks with arbitrary topology.

Assume that we are given an arbitrary network with N nodes (processors) and with directed edges (channels). A *packet routing problem* on this network is defined by a set of packets. Each of the packets is assigned a destination and a source node, and the goal is to route each packet from its source to its destination. A routing problem in which every node is the source of p packets

* Supported in part by the DFG Forschergruppe 'Effiziente Nutzung massiv paralleler Systeme, Teilprojekt 4', by the Esprit Basic Research Action No. 7141 (ALCOM II), and by the Volkswagen Foundation.

and the destination of p packets is called a *p-to-p-routing problem*, and a routing problem in which every node sends p packets to random destinations chosen independently and uniformly from the set of nodes is called a *random p-routing problem*.

Our investigations are based on the *store-and-forward* model. In this model, the packets are viewed as atomic objects, and it is assumed that the routing proceeds in synchronized rounds such that each edge can transmit only one packet in each round. At the beginning of the first round, a packet is stored in an *initial queue* at its source node. During the routing it moves forward step by step, and at each node, it is stored in a *packet buffer* until it is allowed to move forward to the next node. Arriving at its destination the packet is inserted into a *final queue*. The path traversed by the packet from its source to its destination is called the *routing path* of the packet.

A *routing protocol* describes the rules for moving the packets to their destinations. We aim to construct routing protocols that minimize the total number of rounds required to deliver all packets. A further goal is to minimize the size of the buffers for the packets in transit. We break this problem into two parts: the problem of selecting the routing paths and the problem of scheduling the movements of the packets along these paths.

First, we turn to the second problem. A *scheduling protocol* describes the rules for moving forward packets along preset routing paths. In particular, it specifies for each node, which packets are allowed to move forward in a round and which have to wait. If the schedule is produced while the packets are routed through the network, this is called *on-line* routing. If we allow a global controller to precompute the schedule, we talk about *off-line* routing. We are interested in the construction of on-line scheduling protocols.

Of course, the following parameters greatly influence the routing time for a set of packets with preset routing paths: the *congestion* C, i.e. the maximum number of routing paths that pass through the same edge, and the *dilation* D, i.e. the maximum length of the packet's routing paths. Clearly, if packets only have to wait at an edge since another packet moves forward along this edge, then each packet waits at most $C-1$ rounds at each edge on its path. Thus, it arrives at its destination in at most $C \cdot D$ rounds. On the other hand $\max(\{C, D\}) = \Omega(C+D)$ is a lower bound, since at least one edge is traversed by C packets, and at least one packet has to traverse D edges.

The path selection problem is defined as follows. We are given the sources and the destinations of the packets, and we have to determine the routing paths. This we do by a *shortest paths system* W which is a set of N^2 shortest paths through the network. It includes a path $w(u, v) = (u \rightarrow \cdots \rightarrow v)$ for every pair u and v of nodes. For every packet with source u and destination v we choose the path $w(u, v)$ as its routing path.

In the following, we represent the underlying processor network by a digraph $\mathcal{G} = (V, E)$, where V is the set of nodes or processors, and $E \subseteq V \times V$ is the set of directed edges or channels. Of course, any network description which is based on undirected graphs can be represented in the digraph model just by replacing each undirected edge by two directed edges in opposite direction. We call a network an *undirected network*, if there is an opposite edge (v, u) for every edge (u, v).

1.1 Known Results

Leighton, Maggs, and Rao [LMR88, LMR94] show that for any set of packets whose paths have congestion C and dilation D there exists a schedule that delivers all packets in $O(C + D)$ rounds using constant-size packet buffers at each edge, thereby achieving the naive lower bound for scheduling on arbitrary networks. The proposed protocol is off-line, and the best known sequential algorithm [LM94] for computing the schedule takes time $O((PM)^{1+\epsilon})$ for any fixed constant ϵ, where P is the number of packets and M the number of edges in the network.

Further, Leighton, Maggs, and Rao [LMR94] present a probabilistic on-line scheduling protocol for routing on arbitrary networks. The protocol completes the routing of P packets along arbitrary preset paths with congestion C and dilation D in $O(C + D \log(DP))$ rounds[2] using packet buffers of size $O(\log(DP))$ at every node. This is the best known result for on-line routing on arbitrary networks.

Much better results are known for the class of bounded-degree levelled networks. In a *levelled network of depth L*, the nodes can be partitioned into levels $0, \ldots, L$ such that each edge in the network leads from some node on level i to some node on level $i + 1$ for $0 \le i \le L - 1$.

Ranade [Ran91] proposes a probabilistic on-line routing protocol for butterfly networks which is based on techniques developed by Valiant [Val82] and Upfal [Up84]. It can be easily extended to the class of bounded-degree levelled networks [Lei92] [LMRR94]. Ranade's protocol uses packet buffers of constant size at each edge. The protocol completes the routing of any set of packets along preset routing paths in $O(C + L + \log N)$ rounds, w.h.p.[3], where C is the congestion of the routing paths, L the depth of the network, and N the size of the network. Moreover, several standard networks can emulate a levelled network, e.g. the hypercube and the shuffle-exchange networks [LMRR94]. As a result, the above protocol routes with optimal delay on these networks using constant-size packet buffers.

Leighton [Lei92] introduces a simple probabilistic protocol for butterfly networks. It is called the *random-rank protocol*. This protocol is a simple version of Ranade's protocol. Initially, each packet is assigned a random rank. The ranks determine which packets move forward and which have to wait in a round. As Ranade's protocol, the random-rank protocol can easily be extended to the class of bounded-degree levelled networks. It routes any set of packets along preset paths in $O(C + L + \log N)$ rounds, w.h.p., using buffers of size C at each edge,

---

[2] Throughout this paper $\log N$ denotes $\log_2 N$ and $\log^2 N$ denotes $(\log N)^2$.
[3] Throughout this paper *w.h.p.* (with high probability) means with probability at least $1 - N^{-\alpha}$ for any fixed constant α, where N is the size of the network.

where C is the congestion of the paths, L the depth of the network, and N the size of the network.

1.2 Overview — New Results

In Section 2, we introduce a new probabilistic on-line scheduling protocol which we call *growing-rank protocol*. We show that the growing-rank protocol routes any set of packets along shortest paths with congestion C and dilation $D \leq D^*$ on an arbitrary N-node network in $O(C + D^* + \log N)$ rounds, w.h.p., where D^* is an upper bound on the dilation which is known by every node. D^* e.g. can be chosen to be the diameter of the network. Thus, we obtain the same bound for arbitrary networks as previously known only for bounded-degree levelled networks.

The protocol requires buffers of size C at each edge. If the size is bounded, then the possibility of *deadlock* arises. Suppose there are k nodes $v_0, \ldots, v_{k-1}$ with full packet buffers, and every node v_i is trying to move forward a packet to node $v_{(i+1) \bmod k}$ for $0 \leq i \leq k - 1$. Then each node is blocked, i.e. a deadlock occurs. The deadlock problem does not occur on levelled networks even with constant-size buffers, since the packets move forward only in the direction of increasing levels. Avoiding deadlocks seems to be the major problem to be solved in order to generalize our results to networks with bounded buffers.

Whereas the diameter of the network is a good bound for the dilation, the congestion heavily depends on the routing problem. In Section 3, we study the congestion of random p-routing problems on node symmetric and on randomly chosen regular networks.

For node symmetric networks, we construct shortest paths systems such that the congestion of random p-routing problems is $O(p \cdot diam + \log N)$, w.h.p.. Combining this bound and the runtime bound of our growing-rank protocol, we achieve routing time $O(p \cdot diam + \log N)$ for random p-routing problems on node symmetric networks. Applying Valiant's paradigm *first routing to a random destination*, the above bounds for random p-routing problems hold for any p-to-p-routing problem as well.

Finally, we show that the congestion of random p-routing problems (w.r.t. shortest paths) on random regular networks is bounded by $O(p \cdot \log^2 N)$ with probability $1 - o(1)$. We do not believe that this result is optimal, but that $O(p \cdot \log n)$ is the truth. Getting a better result for shortest paths systems seems to be a hard problem.

2   The New Protocol

In this section, we introduce the growing-rank protocol. Suppose $\mathcal{G}$ is an arbitrary network of size N, and fix a set of packets with preset routing paths which are shortest paths in $\mathcal{G}$. We denote the congestion of the routing paths by C, the dilation of these paths by D, and we assume that each node knows upper bounds of C and D denoted by C^* and D^*. For example, we can use the total number of packets for C^* and the diameter of the network for D^*. (Better congestion bounds which depend on the underlying paths systems are given in Section 3.) Further, we assume that each packet p has a unique *ident-number*, denoted by $\mathrm{id}(p)$. For example, the ith packet in the initial queue of the jth node has the ident-number $i \cdot N + j$ for $i \geq 0$ and $0 \leq j \leq N - 1$. The maximum ident-number of all packets we denote by $\mathrm{id}_{\max}$.

2.1 Description of the Growing-Rank Protocol

During the routing, a node stores all packets that wait for moving forward along an outgoing edge a in an edge buffer $\mathcal{Q}_a$. At the beginning of each round, each node examines all its edge buffers and selects one packet from each non-empty buffer. The selected packets are forwarded along their routing paths. The other packets have to wait for moving forward in a later round. Thus, a node moves forward at the most one packet over each outgoing edge in a round.

The selection of the packets is determined by random ranks. Initially, each packet is assigned an integer rank chosen randomly, independently, and uniformly from the range $[0, R - 1]$. R is a multiple of D^* with $R \geq 12eC^* + 2D^* + (\alpha + 2)\log N$ for α specified later. The rank of a packet is increased by $\frac{R}{D^*}$ whenever the packet traverses an edge. If two or more packets in a buffer $\mathcal{Q}_a$ are contending to move forward along the edge a in a round, then one of those with minimum rank is chosen. Thus, for each outgoing edge a, a round looks like this:

1. choose a packet $p \in \mathcal{Q}_a$ with minimum rank,
2. increase the rank of p by $\frac{R}{D^*}$,
3. move p forward along the edge a, and finally,
4. insert all arriving packets that must move along a into $\mathcal{Q}_a$.

In order to break ties, if there are multiple packets with the same minimum rank, the one with smallest ident-number is chosen.

Remark 1. The major difference between the growing-rank protocol and the random-rank protocol is that the rank of a packet is increased whenever the packet traverses an edge. As a result, packets that are often delayed have a tendency to be preferred. In levelled networks, the increase of the ranks has only slight effect. In particular, if all packets start at level 0, then there is no effect at all, since every packet that passes level i has moved forward along i edges on its path, and thus the ranks of all packets that arrive at a node are increased by the same value.

In the following, we denote the rank of a packet p while waiting at a node v by $\mathrm{rank}^v(p)$. Further, we define the *ident-rank* of p at v as $\mathrm{rank}^v(p) + \frac{\mathrm{id}(p)}{\mathrm{id}_{\max}+1}$ and denote it by $\mathrm{id\text{-}rank}^v(p)$. Note that, in each round, the ident-ranks of all packets are distinct. The protocol ensures that whenever a packet p delays a packet p' at a node v it is $\mathrm{id\text{-}rank}^v(p) < \mathrm{id\text{-}rank}^v(p')$. The following lemma shows that none of the ranks becomes greater than $2R - 1$.

Lemma 2. *Suppose p is a packet which is stored at a node v in some round. Then $\mathrm{rank}^v(p) \leq 2R - 1$.*

Proof. Initially, the rank of p is at most $R - 1$. Since the length of the routing path of p is at most D, the rank of p is increased by $\frac{R}{D^*}$ for at most D times. Thus, $\mathrm{rank}^v(p) \leq R - 1 + D \cdot \frac{R}{D^*} \leq 2R - 1$. $\qquad\qquad\square$

2.2 Analysis of the Protocol

We will show that the growing-rank protocol completes the routing along arbitrary shortest paths in $O(C + D^* + \log N)$ rounds, w.h.p.. Our analysis is based on a delay sequence argument similar to that in [Lei92], [LMRR94] and [Ran91].

Definition 3 ((s, ℓ)-delay sequence). An (s, ℓ)-delay sequence consists of

1. $s + 1$ not necessarily distinct *collision nodes* $v_0, v_1, \ldots, v_s$;
2. s *delay packets* $p_1, p_2, \ldots, p_s$ such that the routing path of p_i crosses the node v_i and the node v_{i-1} in that order for $1 \leq i \leq s$, and the path of p_i leaves the node v_{i-1} along the same edge as the path of p_{i-1} for $2 \leq i \leq s$;
3. s integers $\ell_1, \ell_2, \ldots, \ell_s$ such that ℓ_i is the number of edges on the routing path of packet p_i from node v_i to node v_{i-1} for $1 \leq i \leq s$, and $\sum_{i=1}^{s} \ell_i \leq \ell$; and
4. s integer keys $r_1, r_2, \ldots, r_s$ such that $0 \leq r_s \leq \cdots \leq r_2 \leq r_1 \leq 2R - 1$.

We call s the *length* of the delay sequence, and we say a delay sequence is *active*, if $\mathrm{rank}^{v_i}(p_i) = r_i$ for $1 \leq i \leq s$.

Lemma 4. *Suppose the routing takes $T \geq 2D^*$ or more rounds. Then a $(T - 2D^*, 2D^*)$-delay sequence is active.*

Proof. First, we give a construction scheme for a delay sequence. Let p_1 be a packet that moves forward in round T to a node v_0. We follow p_1's routing path backwards to the last node on this path where it was delayed. This node we call v_1. Let p_2 be the packet that caused the delay, since it was preferred against p_1. We now follow the path of p_2 backwards until we reach a node v_2 at which p_2 was forced to wait, because the packet p_3 was preferred. We change the packet again and follow the path of p_3 backwards. We can continue this construction until we reach round 1. Here it ends with a packet p_s starting at its source v_s.

The path from v_s to v_0 recorded by this process in reversed order is called *delay path*. It consists of contiguous parts of routing paths. In particular, the part of the delay path from node v_i to node v_{i-1} is a subpath of the routing path of packet p_i; we define ℓ_i to be the length of this subpath for $1 \leq i \leq s$. Further, p_i leaves the node v_{i-1} along the same edge as p_{i-1}, since p_i delays p_{i-1} at this node for $2 \leq i \leq s$. Figure 1 illustrates the situation.

We set $r_i := \mathrm{rank}^{v_i}(p_i)$ for $1 \leq i \leq s$. Because of the rules of the protocol we have $r_1 \geq r_2 \geq \cdots \geq r_s \geq 0$. Further, Lemma 2 yields that $2R - 1 \geq r_1$. Thus, we have constructed an active (s, ℓ)-delay sequence for every $\ell \geq \sum_{i=1}^{s} \ell_i$.

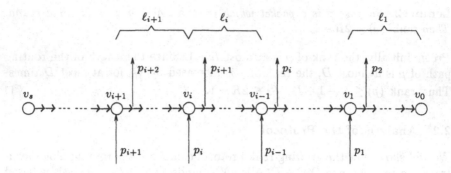

Fig. 1. The components of the delay-path.

Our next goal is to to bound the sum of the ℓ_i's. In addition to the ranks $r_1, \ldots, r_s$, we denote by r_0 the rank of p_1 in v_0. It follows immediately from the protocol that $r_i + \ell_i \cdot \frac{R}{D^*} \leq r_{i-1}$ for $1 \leq i \leq s$. As a consequence,

$$\sum_{i=1}^{s} \ell_i \cdot \frac{R}{D^*} \leq r_0 \overset{\text{Lemma 2}}{\Longrightarrow} \sum_{i=1}^{s} \ell_i \leq (2R-1) \cdot \frac{D^*}{R} \leq 2D^* . \tag{1}$$

Since the delay sequence covers up T rounds and consists of $\sum_{i=1}^{s} \ell_i$ moves and $s-1$ delays, we have $T = \sum_{i=1}^{s} \ell_i + s - 1$. It follows that

$$s = T - \sum_{i=1}^{s} \ell_i + 1 \overset{(1)}{\geq} T - 2D^* + 1 .$$

Consequently, if we stop the above construction at packet p_{T-2D^*}, we have found an active $(T - 2D^*, 2D^*)$-delay sequence. $\qquad\square$

Lemma 5. *If the routing paths of the packets are shortest paths, then the delay packets in the above construction are pairwise distinct.*

Proof. Suppose, in contrast to our claim, that there is some packet p appearing twice in the delay sequence. Then there exist i and j with $1 \leq i < j \leq s$ and $p = p_i = p_j$. Thus, the routing path of p crosses the delay path at the collision nodes v_j and v_i in that order.

Let m denote the distance from the node v_j to the node v_i. If the routing paths are shortest paths, then the rank of p is increased m times while moving from v_j to v_i, and hence,

$$\text{id-rank}^{v_i}(p) = \text{id-rank}^{v_j}(p) + m \cdot \frac{R}{D^*} . \tag{2}$$

On the other hand, each packet p_{k+1} delays the packet p_k at node v_k, and consequently, $\text{id-rank}^{v_k}(p_k) > \text{id-rank}^{v_k}(p_{k+1})$ for $1 \leq k \leq s-1$. Further, the length of the routing path of packet p_{k+1} from v_{k+1} to v_k is ℓ_{k+1}, and thus the rank of p_{k+1} is increased by $\ell_{k+1} \cdot \frac{R}{D^*}$ on its path from v_{k+1} to v_k for $1 \leq k \leq s-1$. It follows that id-rank$^{v_k}(p_k) >$ id-rank$^{v_{k+1}}(p_{k+1}) + \ell_{k+1} \cdot \frac{R}{D^*}$ for $1 \leq k \leq s-1$. This yields

$$\text{id-rank}^{v_i}(p) > \text{id-rank}^{v_j}(p) + \sum_{k=i}^{j-1} \ell_{k+1} \cdot \frac{R}{D^*} \geq \text{id-rank}^{v_j}(p) + m \cdot \frac{R}{D^*} \ . \quad (3)$$

Since (3) contradicts (2), there is no packet that appears twice in the delay sequence. □

Lemma 6. *The number of different active (s, ℓ)-delay sequences is at most*

$$N^2 2^\ell \left(\frac{2eC(s+2R)}{s} \right)^s .$$

Proof. We count the number of possible choices for each component:

- Since $\sum_{i=1}^s \ell_i \leq \ell$, there are $\binom{s+\ell}{s}$ ways to choose the ℓ_i's.
- Once the ℓ_i's are chosen, there are at most $N^2 C^s$ choices for the delay packets and the collision nodes. This is because there are at most N possibilities to determine the node v_0, and if v_0 is fixed, there are at most $N \cdot C$ choices for the packet p_1, since v_0 has at most N incoming edges. Furthermore, if v_0, p_1 and ℓ_1 are fixed, then v_1 is fixed, since v_1 is the node on the routing path of p_1 with distance ℓ_1 to v_0.
  Now, suppose v_{i-1}, p_{i-1} and ℓ_i are fixed for $2 \leq i \leq s$. From the definition of the delay sequence, we know that p_i leaves the node v_{i-1} along the same edge as p_{i-1}. Thus, we have at most C choices for p_i. Moreover, if v_{i-1}, p_i and ℓ_i are determined, then v_i is determined as well, since it is the node on the routing path of p_i with distance ℓ_i to v_{i-1}.
- Finally, there are $\binom{s+2R-1}{s} \leq \binom{s+2R}{s}$ possibilities to choose the r_i's such that $2R - 1 \geq r_1 \geq r_2 \geq \cdots \geq r_s \geq 0$.

Altogether, we find that the number of active (s, ℓ)-delay sequences is at most

$$N^2 C^s \binom{s+\ell}{s} \binom{s+2R}{s} .$$

Applying the inequalities $\binom{a}{b} \leq 2^a$ and $\binom{a}{b} \leq \left(\frac{ea}{b} \right)^b$, the desired upper bound is

$$N^2 C^s 2^{s+\ell} \left(\frac{e(s+2R)}{s} \right)^s \leq N^2 2^\ell \left(\frac{2eC(s+2R)}{s} \right)^s .$$

□

Theorem 7. *Let $\mathcal{G}$ be an arbitrary network of size N. Then the growing-rank protocol completes the routing of any set of packets whose routing paths are shortest paths in $\mathcal{G}$ with congestion $C \leq C^*$ and dilation $D \leq D^*$ in $O(C + D^*) + (\alpha + 2) \log N$ rounds using buffers of size C at each edge with probability $1 - N^{-\alpha}$ for every α.*

Remark 8. The above time bound depends on the dilation bound D^*, but not on the congestion bound C^*. The bound C^* only influences the range of the ranks.

Remark 9. The shortest paths condition is necessary to show that packets can not appear twice in the delay sequence. This condition can be slightly weakened: A set of paths on a network $\mathcal{G} = (V, E)$ is said to be *shortcut-free*, if there is a subnetwork $\mathcal{G}' = (V, E')$ with $E' \subseteq E$ such that the paths in the set are shortest path in $\mathcal{G}'$. Of course, every set of shortest paths is shortcut-free. It is easy to check that Lemma 5, holds also for shortcut-free paths. Hence, the growing-rank protocol routes any set of packets whose routing paths are shortcut-free and have congestion $C \le C^*$ and dilation $D \le D^*$ in $O(C + D^* + \log N)$ rounds, w.h.p..

Proof of Theorem 7. The probability that a particular delay sequence with s distinct packets is active is R^{-s}. This is because a sequence with s distinct packets determines s ranks. As a consequence,

$$\text{Prob(the routing takes } T = s - 2D^* \text{ or more rounds)}$$

$$\overset{\text{Lemma}}{\underset{4 + 5}{\le}} \text{Prob} \left(\begin{array}{c} \text{an } (s, 2D^*)\text{-delay sequence with} \\ \text{distinct delay packets is active} \end{array} \right)$$

$$\le N^2 2^{2D^*} \left(\frac{2eC(s + 2R)}{s} \right)^s \cdot R^{-s} .$$

We choose $T = 12eC + 4D^* + (\alpha + 2) \log N$. This yields

$$s \ge 12eC , \tag{4}$$
$$s \ge (\alpha + 2) \log N + 2D^* , \text{ and} \tag{5}$$
$$R \ge s , \tag{6}$$

because $R \ge 12eC^* + 2D^* + (\alpha + 2) \log N$. As a consequence,

$$\text{Prob(the routing takes } T = s - 2D^* \text{ or more rounds)}$$

$$\overset{(6)}{\le} N^2 2^{2D^*} \left(\frac{6eC}{s} \right)^s \overset{(4)+(5)}{\le} N^2 2^{2D^*} \left(\frac{1}{2} \right)^{(\alpha+2) \log N + 2D^*} = N^{-\alpha} .$$

$\square$

3 Congestion Bounds

The congestion is an upper bound for the running time of oblivious routing protocols. It depends on the network, on the path system, and on the routing problem. The following lemma is a simple application of a Chernoff bound. It relates the expected individual congestions of the edges to the congestion of the network, and gives a tail estimate.

Lemma 10. *Let $\mathcal{G} = (V, E)$ be an arbitrary strongly connected network of size N. Suppose the packets of a random routing problem move forward along the paths of a paths system W on $\mathcal{G}$. Let $E(C_a)$ denote the expected congestion of edge $a \in E$, i.e. the expected number of routing paths that pass through the edge a. Then the congestion of the routing paths is $O(\max(\{E(C_a) \mid a \in E\}) + \log N)$, w.h.p..*

Proof. Fix an edge $a \in E$ arbitrarily. We define $X_{v,i}$ to be 0-1-random variables such that $X_{v,i} = 1$, iff the path of the ith packet of node v traverses a for $v \in V$ and $0 \leq i \leq p - 1$. Then $C_a = \sum_{v \in V} \sum_{i=0}^{p-1} X_{v,i}$. Since the random variables $X_{v,i}$ are pairwise independent, we can apply the following Chernoff bound.

$$\text{Prob}(C_a \geq 2eE(C_a) + (\alpha + 2)\log N) \leq 2^{-(2eE(C_a) + (\alpha+2)\log N)} \leq N^{-\alpha+2}$$

for any α (cf. [HR90]). Up to now we have bounded the congestion of the edge a. Taking into account all edges, we can bound the congestion C as follows.

$$\text{Prob}(C \geq 2eE(C_a) + (\alpha + 2)\log N) \leq |E| \cdot N^{-\alpha+2} \leq N^{-\alpha}$$

for any α. $\qquad\qquad\qquad\qquad\qquad\qquad\qquad\qquad\qquad\qquad\qquad\qquad\qquad\Box$

3.1 Node Symmetric Networks

An *automorphism* of a network $\mathcal{G} = (V, E)$ is a permutation $\phi : V \longrightarrow V$ with the property that $(u, v) \in E \Leftrightarrow (\phi(u), \phi(v)) \in E$. The automorphisms of $\mathcal{G}$ form an algebraic group under the operation of composition. This group is denoted by $Aut(\mathcal{G})$. An automorphism group $U \subseteq Aut(\mathcal{G})$ is said to be *transitive* on $\mathcal{G}$, if given any two nodes u and v there is an automorphism $\phi \in U$ such that $\phi(u) = v$, and a network $\mathcal{G}$ is called *node symmetric*, if $Aut(\mathcal{G})$ is transitive on it. Intuitively, a node symmetric network looks the same, if viewed from any node of the network. We use this property to construct paths systems for which the number of paths that pass through a node is similar for all nodes.

Cayley Networks. The class of Cayley networks is an important subclass of node symmetric networks. Many standard networks belong to this class, for instance the multidimensional arrays (generalized hypercubes), the cube-connected-cycles, the wrapped butterflies, the bubble-sort networks, and the star networks.

Definition 11 (Cayley network). Let Γ be a finite algebraic group with identity 1, and suppose Σ is a set of generators of Γ with $1 \notin \Sigma$. Then the Cayley network $\mathcal{G}_{\Gamma,\Sigma} = (V, E)$ is defined by

$$V = \Gamma \quad \text{and} \quad E = \{(a, b) \mid a^{-1}b \in \Sigma\} .$$

Definition 12 (symmetric paths system). Let W be a paths system on a network $\mathcal{G} = (V, E)$. Then we call W symmetric, if given any two nodes u und v of $\mathcal{G}$ there is a permutation $\psi : V \longrightarrow V$ such that for every path $(w_0 \to w_1 \to \cdots \to w_\ell) \in W$ with $w_i = u$ there is a path $(\psi(w_0) \to \psi(w_1) \to \cdots \to \psi(w_\ell)) \in W$ with $\psi(w_i) = v$ for $0 \le i \le \ell$.

Roughly speaking, a *symmetric paths system* has the property that it looks the same viewed from any node of the network.

Lemma 13. *For every Cayley network, there is a symmetric shortest paths system.*

Proof. Let $\mathcal{G}_{\Gamma,\Sigma} = (V, E)$ be a Cayley network. Then there is a transitive automorphism group U of size $|V|$ [Biggs93]. We denote by ϕ_u^v the automorphism of U which maps the node u onto the node v for $u, v \in V$. Thus, $U = \{\phi_u^v \mid v \in V\}$ for any $u \in V$.

Suppose $w = (w_0 \to w_1 \to \cdots \to w_\ell)$ is a path in $\mathcal{G}$ and ϕ is an automorphism of $\mathcal{G}$. Then we define $\phi(w) := (\phi(w_0) \to \phi(w_1) \to \cdots \to \phi(w_\ell))$. Since ϕ is an automorphism, $\phi(w)$ is a shortest path in $\mathcal{G}$ iff w is a shortest path in $\mathcal{G}$.

We construct a symmetric shortest paths system in two steps. (For simplicity of notation, we assume $V = \{0, 1 \ldots, N - 1\}$.)

Step 1: choose arbitrarily a shortest path $w(0, v)$ from the node 0 to every node $v \in V$.

Step 2: for every $u \in V \setminus \{0\}$ and every $v \in V$, define the path $w(u, v)$ from u to v by $w(u, v) := \phi_0^u(w(0, \phi_u^0(v)))$.

In the first step we have chosen N *prototype paths* (inclusive the trivial one from 0 to 0). In the second step we have made $N - 1$ copies of each prototype path. Thus, every automorphism of U, except for the identity, has been used once for copying each prototype path. In a full version of this paper, we show that this paths system is symmetric. $\qquad\square$

The following theorem can be concluded using Lemmata 10 and 13.

Theorem 14. *Let $\mathcal{G}_{\Gamma,\Sigma} = (V, E)$ be a Cayley network of size N. Let W be a symmetric shortest paths system. Then the congestion of a random p-routing problem is bounded by $O(p \cdot \mathrm{diam}(\mathcal{G}_{\Gamma,\Sigma}) + \log N)$, w.h.p..*

Node Symmetric Non-Cayley Networks. For bounding the congestion in Theorem 14 we used a symmetric paths system. As seen, this can be easily constructed for Cayley networks. For non-Cayley node symmetric networks, like for example the Petersen graph [Yap86], the construction in the proof of Lemma 13 fails. In a full version of this paper, we show how to reach the same congestion bound as in Theorem 14 for general node symmetric networks.

3.2 Random Regular Networks

An undirected network is called Δ-regular if the degree of each node is Δ. Define

$$G(N, \Delta) := \left\{ \mathcal{G} = (V, E) \;\middle|\; \begin{array}{l} \mathcal{G} \text{ is a } \Delta\text{-regular undirected network} \\ \text{with } V = \{0, 1, \ldots, N - 1\} \end{array} \right\}.$$

Bollobás and de la Vega [BV81] show that the diameter of a network which is chosen randomly from $G(N, \Delta)$ is at most $\log_{\Delta-1} N + \log_{\Delta-1} \ln N + 5$ with probability $1 - o(1)$. In a full paper, we use this bound to show the following theorem.

Theorem 15. *Choose $\mathcal{G} = (V, E)$ randomly from $G(n, \Delta)$, where Δ is a fixed constant. Suppose W is an arbitrary shortest path system on $\mathcal{G}$. Then the congestion of a random p-routing problem is $O(p \cdot \log^2 N)$ with probability $1 - o(1)$.*

References

[Biggs93] N.L. Biggs, *Algebraic graph theory*, Second Edition, Cambridge University Press (Cambridge 1993).

[BV81] B. Bollobás and W. Fernandez de la Vega, The diameter of random regular graphs, *Combinatorica* 2 (2) (1982) pp. 125–134.

[HR90] T. Hagerup and C. Rüb, A guided tour of Chernoff bounds, *Information Processing Letters* 33/6 (1989/90) pp. 305–308.

[Lei92] F.T. Leighton, *Introduction to parallel algorithms and architectures: arrays · trees · hypercubes*, Morgan Kaufmann Publishers (San Mateo, CA 1992).

[LM94] F.T. Leighton and B.M. Maggs, Fast algorithms for finding O(congestion + dilation) packet routing schedules, Unpublished Manuscript (1994).

[LMR88] F.T. Leighton, B.M. Maggs, and S.B. Rao, Universal packet routing algorithms (Extended Abstract), *Proceedings of the 29th Annual Symposium on Foundations of Computer Science*, IEEE (White Plains, NY 1988) pp. 256–271.

[LMR94] F.T. Leighton, B.M. Maggs, and S.B. Rao, Packet routing and job-shop scheduling in O(congestion + dilation) steps, *Combinatorica* 14 (2) (1994) pp. 167-186.

[LMRR94] F.T. Leighton, B.M. Maggs, A.G. Ranade, and S.B. Rao, Randomized routing and sorting on fixed-connection networks, *Journal of Algorithms* 17 (1994) pp. 157–205.

[Ran91] A.G. Ranade, How to emulate shared memory, *Journal of Computer and System Sciences* 42 (1991) pp. 307–326.

[Up84] E. Upfal, Efficient schemes for parallel communication, *Journal of the Association for Computing Machinery* Vol. 31, No. 3 (July 1984) pp. 507–517.

[Val82] L.G. Valiant, A scheme for fast parallel communication, *SIAM Journal on Computing* 11/2 (1982) pp. 350–361.

[Yap86] H.P. Yap, *Some topics in graph theory*, Cambridge University Press (Cambridge 1986).

A Family of Tag Systems for Paperfolding Sequences
(preliminary version)

Christiane Bercoff

I.U.T. de Soissons, les Terrasses du Mail, 02880 Cuffies, France
LAMIFA, 33 rue Saint Leu, 80039 Amiens Cedex, France
e-mail : bercoff @ crihan.fr
fax : 33-23 59 34 13

Abstract. If one folds in two parts a strip of paper several times on itself (all folds being parallel) one obtains after unfolding a sequence of "valley" and "ridge" folds. If one codes these folds over a two-letter alphabet, one obtains a paperfolding word associated to the sequence of folding instructions. A paperfolding sequence is an infinite paperfolding word.

This paper is devoted to the effective construction of 2-uniform tag systems which generate every paperfolding sequences associated to ultimately periodic sequences of (un)folding instructions.

Topics: automata and formal languages
combinatorics on words

1 - Introduction

If one folds in two parts a strip of paper several times on itself (all folds being parallel) one obtains after unfolding a sequence of "valley" and "ridge" folds. In particular, if one represents the "valley" folds (resp. the "ridge" folds) by moving left (resp. right), one obtains the classic "dragon curves" (see [11,12,14]). If one codes these folds over a two-letter alphabet, one obtains a paperfolding word associated to the sequence of folding instructions. A paperfolding sequence is an infinite paperfolding word. These words had been widely studied both in the beginning of the 80's (see for example, [12,19,21]) and very recently [2,3,4,5,20,25,31]. More generally, they are related to well-known problems in number theory, combinatorics on words and other domains in mathematics or computer science(see, for example, [1,16,18,22,23,24,28, 29,30]). Moreover, we will see that they closely related to the notion of morphism which is a particular case of DOL-system (see, for example, [7,10,13,17,18,26]).

It is well known that ultimately periodic (ie periodic from some rank) sequences can be automatically generated. A. Cobham in [9] characterizes the class of sequences which, though they are not ultimately periodic, can be automatically generated by uniform tag system (see also [8]). From the paper of M. Mendès-France and J. Shallit [20], using the results of [9], the characterization of A. Cobham can be translated by : *a paperfolding sequence is 2-automatic* (ie generated by a 2-uniform tag system) *if and only if the sequence of unfolding instructions* (to which it is associated) *is ultimately periodic* (see also [2,21]).

The regular paperfolding sequences are the sequences whose foldings are all realized on the same way : either "positive" or "negative". Up to now, the only 2-uniform tag system generating a paperfolding sequence has been described by J.-P. Allouche [2] and M. Dekking, M. Mendès-France, A. J. van der Poorten [12]. This tag system is the following : let θ be the morphism defined by $\theta(0) = 0\ 1$, $\theta(1) = 2\ 1$, $\theta(2) = 0\ 3$, $\theta(3) = 2\ 3$ and σ be the literal morphism defined by $\sigma(0) = \sigma(1) = +$ and $\sigma(2) = \sigma(3) = -$, then $\theta^{\omega}(0) = \lim_{n \to \infty} \theta^n(0)$ is an infinite word defined over $\{0, 1, 2, 3\}$ and $\sigma[\theta^{\omega}(0)]$ is the "positive" regular paperfolding sequence (defined over $\{+,-\}$). Exchanging $+$ with $-$, one obtains the "negative" regular paperfolding sequence.

Thus, up to now, the only known 2-uniform tag system generating a paperfolding sequence is the one for the regular paperfolding sequence.

In this paper, at first, we show that can obtain **all** the paperfolding sequences by applying a coding to the Toeplitz word which is defined on an infinite "alphabet". After that, we explain how to restrict to finite alphabets in order to obtain tag systems for **all** the 2-automatic paperfolding sequences.

This construction of uniform tag systems for 2-automatic paperfolding sequences is effective and solves entirely the problem of generating paperfolding sequences in such a way.

2 - Definitions and notations

Most of the notions are classical in formal language theory (see [15] or [27]) and we just recall what is a tag system.

Let A be a finite or infinite set of letters. A morphism $\theta : A^* \to A^*$ (ie a mapping such that $\forall u,v \in A^*$, $\theta(uv) = \theta(u)\ \theta(v)$) is *expansive on* $a \in A$ if $\exists\ w \in A^+$ such that $\theta(a) = a\ w$. A morphism $\theta : A^* \to A^*$ is *nonerasing* if $\forall\ a \in A\ \ \theta(a) \neq \varepsilon$. A morphism $\theta : A^* \to A^*$ is *k-uniform* $(k \in N \setminus \{0\})$ if $\forall\ a \in A\ \ |\theta(a)| = k$. If $k = 1$, θ is called a *literal morphism*.

Remark 1 A k-uniform morphism is nonerasing.

$\forall\ n \in N$, we note $\theta^n = \begin{cases} \text{the identity if } n = 0 \\ \theta^{n-1} \circ \theta \quad \text{if } n \geq 1 \end{cases}$

Now, if θ is a nonerasing morphism and expansive on $a \in A$ then, $\forall\ n \in N$, $\theta^n(a)$ is a proper prefix of $\theta^{n+1}(a)$. In this case, $\exists\ \underline{x} \in A^{\omega}$ defined by " $\underline{x}[k] = \theta^n(a)$ for $k = |\theta^n(a)|$ and $n \in N$ " and such that $\underline{x} = \lim_{n \to \infty} \theta^n(a) = \theta^{\omega}(a)$.

We say that $\underline{x}$ is *generic (resp. k-generic) of base* θ (resp. if θ is k-uniform).

It is not always possible to generate a given infinite word by iterating a morphism (see [6] for an example of such a word). But for the study of infinite words, it is often useful to be able to generate them automatically. Such an automatic process to generate infinite words has been developed by A. Cobham in [9] : let A, B be alphabets, $\theta : A^* \to A^*$ a morphism (resp. k-uniform morphism) expansive on $a \in A$ and $\eta : A^* \to B^*$ a literal morphism. Then $\mathfrak{I} = <$ A, a, θ, B, $\eta >$ is called a *tag system* (resp. *k-uniform tag system*). $\mathfrak{I}$ generates the word $\eta \circ \theta^{\omega}(a)$ which is an infinite word if θ is nonerasing. If $\mathfrak{I}$ is a k-uniform tag system, then the infinite word $\theta^{\omega}(a)$ is k-generic and the infinite word $\eta \circ \theta^{\omega}(a)$ is said to be *k-automatic*.

Now, we introduce some useful notations.

With every integer n we associate two letters denoted by n and $\overline{n}$ (by abusive notation). This allows us to build an infinite "alphabet" $\Sigma \cup \overline{\Sigma}$ defined by $\Sigma = \{n, n \in N\}$ and $\overline{\Sigma} = \{\overline{n}, n \in N\}$.

Again by abusive notation, we shall denote $\forall r \in \Sigma \cup \overline{\Sigma}$

$$r+1 = \begin{cases} t+1 \in \Sigma & \text{if } r = t \in \Sigma \\ \overline{t+1} \in \overline{\Sigma} & \text{if } r = \overline{t} \in \overline{\Sigma} \end{cases}$$

In particular, if $r = \overline{i} \in \overline{\Sigma}$ we shall write either $r+1$ or $\overline{i+1}$.

Let $\tau : (\Sigma \cup \overline{\Sigma})^* \to (\Sigma \cup \overline{\Sigma})^*$ be the morphism defined by

$$\begin{cases} \tau(\varepsilon) = \varepsilon \\ \tau(r) = \begin{cases} \overline{i} \in \overline{\Sigma} & \text{if } r = i \in \Sigma \\ i \in \Sigma & \text{if } r = \overline{i} \in \overline{\Sigma} \end{cases} \end{cases}$$

Let $\mu : (\Sigma \cup \overline{\Sigma})^* \to (\Sigma \cup \overline{\Sigma})^*$ be the morphism defined by

$$\begin{cases} \mu(\varepsilon) = \varepsilon \\ \mu(ur) = r\mu(u) \quad \forall u \in (\Sigma \cup \overline{\Sigma})^* \text{ and } \forall r \in \Sigma \cup \overline{\Sigma} \end{cases}$$

For all $u \in (\Sigma \cup \overline{\Sigma})^*$ $\tau \circ \mu(u) = \mu \circ \tau(u)$ is called *video-reversal word of u*.

Simplifying the writing, we denote $\begin{cases} \overline{u} & \text{instead of } \tau(u) \\ \tilde{u} & \text{instead of } \mu(u) \\ \hat{u} \text{ or } (u)^\wedge & \text{instead of } \tau \circ \mu(u) \end{cases}$

The following properties easily result from the definitions :

Fact 1 For all $u \in (\Sigma \cup \overline{\Sigma})^*$ (1) if $|u| = 1$ then $\hat{u} = \overline{u}$

                           (2) $(\hat{u})^\wedge = u$

                           (3) $(uv)^\wedge = \hat{v}\,\hat{u}$

3 - Paperfolding sequences and Toeplitz word

3.1 Paperfolding technique

1) Folding and coding sequences of folding instructions (see [14,19,21])

A *sequence of folding instructions* $\pi = \pi(1)\pi(2) \cdots \pi(n)$ (resp. an infinite sequence $\pi = (\pi(n))_{n \geq 1}$) is any word (resp. any infinite word) over the alphabet $\{+,-\}$.

Given a strip of paper fixed in some point Ω, one can fold it according to π in the following manner :

- At the first step, one folds it in two parts, putting up the right part :
  - over the left part if $\pi(1) = +$
  - under the left part if $\pi(1) = -$

$(+)$ $(-)$

- At the second step, one folds again the strip as above, the new folds being parallel to the first one. For the second folding there are also two possible cases depending on $\pi(2) = +$ or $-$.
- And so on, until the nth step $(n \geq 1)$.

Remark 2 For every n, the 2^n sequences of folding instructions are all different.

2) Unfolding and coding paperfolding words

- The first folding according to instruction π (1) induces one fold.
Unfold the strip of paper such that the fold forms an angle :

$\Bigl\{ \begin{array}{l} \text{if } \pi(1) = +, \text{this fold yields a "}\vee\text{" called "valley" and coded by } + \\ \text{if } \pi(1) = -, \text{this fold yields a "}\wedge\text{" called "ridge" and coded by } - \end{array}$

- The second folding according to instruction $\pi(2)$ induces 2 new folds.
The unfolding (as above) yields 3 folds. By coding as above this 3 folds, we obtain a word of length 3 over the alphabet $\{+,-\}$.

- The nth folding according to instruction $\pi(n)$ induces (2^{n-1}) new folds.

The unfolding (as above) yields (2^n-1) folds. By coding as above this (2^n-1) folds, we obtain a word of length (2^n-1) over the alphabet $\{+,-\}$ denoted by w_π and called *paperfolding word of order n associated to the sequence of folding instructions* $\pi = \pi(1)\,\pi(2)\cdots\pi(n)$.

Remark 3 The 2^n sequences of folding instructions $\pi = \pi(1)\,\pi(2)\cdots\pi(n)$ give 2^n different paperfolding words of order n.

Example 1

if $\pi = +$	$w_\pi = +$	if $\pi = -$	$w_\pi = -$
if $\pi = ++$	$w_\pi = ++-$	if $\pi = --$	$w_\pi = --+$
if $\pi = -+$	$w_\pi = +--$	if $\pi = +-$	$w_\pi = -++$
if $\pi = +++$	$w_\pi = ++-++-$	if $\pi = ---$	$w_\pi = --+--++$
if $\pi = -++$	$w_\pi = ++--+--$	if $\pi = +--$	$w_\pi = --++-++$
if $\pi = +-+$	$w_\pi = +--+++-$	if $\pi = -+-$	$w_\pi = -++---+$
if $\pi = --+$	$w_\pi = +---++-$	if $\pi = +--$	$w_\pi = -+++--+$

3.2 Paperfolding sequences

Let $w_\pi = (w_\pi(r))_{1 \le r \le 2^n-1}$ be the paperfolding word of order n $(n \ge 1)$ associated to the sequence of folding instructions $\pi = \pi(1)\,\pi(2)\cdots\pi(n)$. If we remark that for $1 \le i \le n$, the folds coming from the ith step are alternatively "valley" after "ridge" if $\pi(i) = +$(resp. "ridge" after "valley" if $\pi(i) = -$), we may give a definition of w_π in terms of its folding instructions $\pi(1), \pi(2), \cdots, \pi(n)$. This definition is based on the fact that all nonzero integers have an unique decomposition as follows : $\forall r \in N \setminus \{0\}$ $\exists! s \in N$ $\exists! j \in N$ such that $r = 2^s(2j+1)$.

Definition 1 [31]

w_π is the *paperfolding word of order n associated to π* if $\forall r,j \in N$

$$w_\pi(2^s(2j+1)) = \begin{cases} \pi(n-s) & \text{if } j \text{ is even} \\ \overline{\pi(n-s)} & \text{if } j \text{ is odd} \end{cases}$$

Remark 4 The first letter of w_π is obtained when $s = j = 0$. Thus it is $\pi(n)$. The second letter is $\pi(n-1)$, the third letter is $\overline{\pi(n)}$, the fourth letter is $\pi(n-2)$ and so on. In fact, the order in which the letters of π appear in w_π is the inverse of the order in π. That's why the useful notion is that of unfolding instructions which corresponds to $\tilde{\pi}$ (see section 4 below).

Now if $\underline{w} = (w(r))_{r \ge 1}$ denotes the infinite word such that $\underline{w}\,[2^n-1] = w_\pi$, we obtain the classic recursive definition of paperfolding sequences :

Definition 2 [3,5,12,20,21]

The sequence $\underline{w} = (w(r))_{r \geq 1}$ is a *paperfolding sequence* if

$$\begin{cases} w(2j+1) = \begin{cases} + \ (resp. -) & \text{if } j \text{ is even} \\ - \ (resp. +) & \text{if } j \text{ is odd} \end{cases} \\ (w(2r))_{r \geq 1} \quad \text{is a paperfolding sequence} \end{cases}$$

That is, any paperfolding sequence is entirely determined by the subsequence $(w(2^s))_{s \geq 0}$.

3.3 The Toeplitz word $\underline{T}$

An alternative way to define paperfolding sequences is to use the notion of Toeplitz word :
Let $(t_n)_{n \geq 1}$ be the sequence over $\Sigma \cup \overline{\Sigma}$ defined by

$$\begin{cases} t_1 = 0 \\ t_{n+1} = t_n \, n \, \hat{t}_n \quad \text{for } n \geq 2 \end{cases}$$

The first terms of $(t_n)_{n \geq 1}$ are listed below :

n	t_n
1	0
2	$01\overline{0}$
3	$01\overline{0}20\overline{1}\overline{0}$
4	$01\overline{0}20\overline{1}\overline{0}301\overline{0}\overline{2}0\overline{1}\overline{0}$
5	$01\overline{0}20\overline{1}\overline{0}301\overline{0}20\overline{1}\overline{0}401\overline{0}20\overline{1}\overline{0}301\overline{0}\overline{2}0\overline{1}\overline{0}$

The infinite word $\underline{T} = \lim_{n \to \infty} t_n$ is called *Toeplitz word*.

The Toeplitz word $\underline{T}$ has the following characterization which will be useful later. This property is, as for the paperfolding words, based on the fact that all nonzero integers have an unique decomposition as follows : $\forall r \in N \setminus \{0\} \ \exists! \, s \in N \ \exists! \, j \in N$ such that $r = 2^s (2j+1)$.

Proposition 1 (see also [5,20])

Let $\underline{T} = (T(r))_{r \geq 1}$. Then $\forall s, j \in N$, $T(2^s(2j+1)) = \begin{cases} s & \text{if } j \text{ is even} \\ \overline{s} & \text{if } j \text{ is odd} \end{cases}$

The proof by induction is omitted here.

The utility of defining $\underline{T}$ is the correspondence between paperfolding sequences and the Toeplitz word $\underline{T}$. This correspondence is given by the following first important result which need a new definition :

Given any infinite word $\underline{f} = (f(n))_{n \geq 1}$ over $\{+,-\}$, we define the literal morphism

$$\sigma_f : \left(\Sigma \cup \overline{\Sigma} \right)^* \to \{+,-\}^* \quad by \quad \begin{cases} \sigma_f(n) = f(n) \\ \sigma_f(\overline{n}) = \overline{f(n)} \end{cases}$$

Proposition 2 Let $\underline{w}$ be an infinite word over $\{+,-\}$. The two following assertions are equivalent : (i) $\underline{w}$ is a paperfolding sequence

(ii) there exits a morphism σ_f such that $\underline{w} = \sigma_f(\underline{T})$

The proof of this proposition, omitted here, is based on the similarity between definition 1 and proposition 1.

4 - Main results

We are now ready to establish the main result of this paper which is the construction of a family of tag systems which generate all the 2-automatic paperfolding sequences. This result is based on the following fact that the Toeplitz word $\underline{T}$ can be generated by a morphism.

4.1 The genericity of $\underline{T}$

Let $h:(\Sigma\cup\overline{\Sigma})^* \to (\Sigma\cup\overline{\Sigma})^*$ be the 2-uniform and expansive on 0 morphism defined by

$$\begin{cases} h(0)=01 \quad h(\overline{0})=0\,\overline{1} \\ h(r)=\overline{0}\,(r+1) \quad \forall r\in(\Sigma\cup\overline{\Sigma}) \quad \{0,\overline{0}\} \end{cases}$$

Lemma 1 $\forall n\in N\setminus\{0\}$ $t_{n+1}=h(t_n)\,\overline{0}$ and $\hat{t}_{n+1}=h(\hat{t}_n)\,\overline{0}$

Lemma 2 $\forall n\in N\setminus\{0\}$ $h^n(0)=t_n\,n$

The proofs of these two lemmas, easily done by induction, are omitted here.

From this, we deduce our first fundamental result :

Proposition 3 The Toeplitz word $\underline{T}$ is 2-generic of base h.

Proof. We have $h^\omega(0)=\lim_{n\to\infty}h^n(0)=\lim_{n\to\infty}(t_n\,n)=\lim_{n\to\infty}(t_n)=\underline{T}$. ◆

An immediate consequence of propositions 2 and 3 is that each paperfolding sequence (they are an uncountable infinite number) is the image by a literal morphism of a 2-generic word of base h. However this does not imply that the paperfolding sequences are all 2-automatic because this process of generation is not a tag system since the morphism h is defined over an infinite "alphabet". In fact, it is already known [2,20] that only the paperfolding sequences associated to ultimately periodic sequences of unfolding instructions are 2-automatic. Therefore, we will only consider the class of paperfolding sequences associated to ultimately periodic sequences of unfolding instructions $\underline{f}_{p,q}=f(0)\,f(1)\,...\,f(p)\,(f(p+1)\,...\,f(p+q))^\omega$

where $p,q\in N\times N\setminus\{0\}$.

4.2 The paperfolding sequences associated to $\underline{f}_{p,q}$

In the sequel, we will denote (by abusive notation) $\forall r\in\Sigma\cup\overline{\Sigma}$,
$s\le r\le t$ instead of $r\in\{s,s+1,\cdots,t\}\cup\{\overline{s},\overline{s+1},\cdots,\overline{t}\}$ and
$r>t$ instead of $r\in\{t+1,t+2,\cdots\}\cup\{\overline{t+1},\overline{t+2},\cdots\}$.

Let $\underline{f}_{p,q}=(f_{p,q}(n))_{n\ge0}$ for (p,q) given in $N\times N\setminus\{0\}$.

Fact 2 For $p+1\le\alpha\le p+q$ and $k>0$, $f_{p,q}(\alpha+kq)=f_{p,q}(\alpha)$, $\sigma_{p,q}(\alpha+kq)=\sigma_{p,q}(\alpha)$ (where $\sigma_{p,q}$ denotes $\sigma_{f_{p,q}}$) and $\sigma_{p,q}(T(2^{\alpha+kq}(2j+1)))=\sigma_{p,q}(T(2^\alpha(2j+1)))$ $\forall j\in N$.

Thus, $\underline{f}_{p,q}$ defines the morphism $\rho:(\Sigma\cup\overline{\Sigma})^* \to (\{0,1,...,p+q\}\cup\{\overline{0},\overline{1},...,\overline{p+q}\})^*$ such that

$$\begin{cases} \rho(r)=r \quad if\ r\le p+q \\ \rho(r)=\alpha \quad if\ r=\alpha+kq\ with\ p+1\le\alpha\le p+q,\ k\in N\ \{0\} \end{cases}$$

Fact 3 $\rho\circ h^\omega(0)=\rho(\underline{T})=(\rho(T(r))_{r\ge1}$ is the infinite word defined $\forall s,j\in N$, by

$$\rho(T(2^s(2j+1)))=\begin{cases} \rho(s) \quad if\ j\ is\ even \\ \rho(\overline{s}) \quad if\ j\ is\ odd \end{cases}$$

and for (p,q) given in $N\times N\setminus\{0\}$, $\sigma_{p,q}(\rho(\underline{T}))$ is the paperfolding sequence associated to $\underline{f}_{p,q}$.

In other words, the sequence $\underline{w} = ((w(r))_{r \geq 1}$ is associated to $\underline{f}_{p,q}$ if it is entirely determined by the $(p+q)$ subsequences $(f(s))_{0 \leq s \leq p+q-1} = (w(2^s))_{0 \leq s \leq p+q-1}$. So for a given pair of integers (p,q), the word $\sigma_{p,q}(\rho(\underline{T}))$ generates $2^{(p+q)}$ different paperfolding sequences.

Now, we are going to describe the tag system which generate $\sigma_{p,q}(\rho(\underline{T}))$.

At first, we define the "restriction" of h on the alphabet $\{0,1,...,p+q\} \cup \{\overline{0},\overline{1},...,\overline{p+q}\}$:

let $h_{p,q} : (\{0,1,...,p+q\} \cup \{\overline{0},\overline{1},...,\overline{p+q}\})^* \rightarrow (\{0,1,...,p+q\} \cup \{\overline{0},\overline{1},...,\overline{p+q}\})^*$ such that

$$\begin{cases} h_{p,q}(r) = h(r) & \text{for } r \leq p+q-1 \\ h_{p,q}(p+q) = \overline{0}\,(p+1) \end{cases}$$

Fact 4 (i) $\forall p,q \in N \times N \setminus \{0\}$, $h_{p,q}(0) = h(0) = 0\,1$, $h_{p,q}(\overline{0}) = h(\overline{0}) = 0\,\overline{1}$.

(ii) $h_{p,q}(p+q) = h(p)$ iff $p \neq 0$.

(iii) $\forall q \in N \setminus \{0\}$, $h_{0,q}(0+q) = \overline{0}\,1$, $h_{0,q}(\overline{0+q}) = \overline{0}\,\overline{1}$.

Secondly, we establish that $\rho(\underline{T})$ is 2-generic of base $h_{p,q}$ by virtue of the following relations between the morphisms h and $h_{p,q}$:

Lemma 3 (i) $\forall r \in \Sigma \cup \overline{\Sigma}$ $h_{p,q} \circ \rho(r) = \rho \circ h(r)$

(ii) $\forall n \in N \times N \setminus \{0\}$ $h_{p,q}^{n}(0) = \rho[h^{n}(0)]$

Proof.
(i) - if $r \leq p+q-1$, then $h_{p,q} \circ \rho(r) = h_{p,q}(r) = h(r) = \rho \circ h(r)$, since $h(r) = \overline{0}\,(p+q)$

- if $r = p+q$, then $h_{p,q} \circ \rho(p+q) = h_{p,q}(p+q) = \overline{0}\,(p+1)$

and $\rho \circ h(p+q) = \rho(\overline{0}\,(p+q+1)) = \overline{0}\,(p+1)$

- if $r \geq p+q+1$, write $r = \alpha + kq$ with $p+1 \leq \alpha \leq p+q$ and $k \in N \setminus \{0\}$

then $h_{p,q} \circ \rho(r) = h_{p,q}(\alpha) = \begin{cases} h(\alpha) & \text{if } \alpha \leq p+q-1 \\ \overline{0}\,(p+1) & \text{if } \alpha = p+q \end{cases}$

and $\rho \circ h(r) = \rho(\overline{0}\,(r+1)) = \begin{cases} \overline{0}\,(\alpha+1) = h(\alpha) & \text{if } \alpha \leq p+q-1 \\ \overline{0}\,(p+1) & \text{if } \alpha = p+q \end{cases}$

so, in every case, $h_{p,q} \circ \rho(r) = \rho \circ h(r)$

(ii) will be shown by induction on n. Since $p+q \geq 1$, we have $h_{p,q}(0) = h(0) = \rho \circ h(0)$.

Suppose that $h_{p,q}^{n}(0) = \rho[h^{n}(0)]$ for $n \geq 1$

then $h_{p,q}^{n+1}(0) = h_{p,q} \circ \rho[h^{n}(0)] = \rho \circ h[h^{n}(0)] = \rho[h^{n+1}(0)]$. ◆

From this, we deduce that :

Lemma 4 $h_{p,q}^{\omega}(0) = \rho[h^{\omega}(0)]$.

In other words, the word $h_{p,q}^{\omega}(0)$ is obtained from the word $h^{\omega}(0)$ replacing :

$$\begin{cases} p+q+1,\, p+2q+1,\cdots,\, p+kq+1,\cdots & \text{by} \quad p+1 \\ p+q+2,\, p+2q+2,\cdots,\, p+kq+2,\cdots & \text{by} \quad p+2 \\ \quad\cdots \\ p+2q,\quad p+3q,\quad\cdots,\, p+(k+1)q,\cdots & \text{by} \quad p+q \end{cases}$$

Example 2

$h^5(0)$	01$\overline{0}$ 2 0$\overline{1}$0 3 01$\overline{0}$ $\overline{2}$ 0$\overline{1}$0 4 01$\overline{0}$ 2 0$\overline{1}$0 $\overline{3}$ 01$\overline{0}$ $\overline{2}$ 0$\overline{1}$0 5
$h^5_{0,1}(0)$	01$\overline{0}$ 1 0$\overline{1}$0 1 01$\overline{0}$ $\overline{1}$ 0$\overline{1}$0 1 01$\overline{0}$ 1 0$\overline{1}$0 $\overline{1}$ 01$\overline{0}$ $\overline{1}$ 0$\overline{1}$0 1
$h^5_{0,2}(0)$	01$\overline{0}$ 2 0$\overline{1}$0 1 01$\overline{0}$ $\overline{2}$ 0$\overline{1}$0 2 01$\overline{0}$ 2 0$\overline{1}$0 $\overline{1}$ 01$\overline{0}$ $\overline{2}$ 0$\overline{1}$0 1
$h^5_{1,1}(0)$	01$\overline{0}$ 2 0$\overline{1}$0 2 01$\overline{0}$ $\overline{2}$ 0$\overline{1}$0 2 01$\overline{0}$ 2 0$\overline{1}$0 $\overline{2}$ 01$\overline{0}$ $\overline{2}$ 0$\overline{1}$0 2
$h^5_{0,3}(0)$	01$\overline{0}$ 2 0$\overline{1}$0 3 01$\overline{0}$ $\overline{2}$ 0$\overline{1}$0 1 01$\overline{0}$ 2 0$\overline{1}$0 3 01$\overline{0}$ $\overline{2}$ 0$\overline{1}$0 2
$h^5_{1,2}(0)$	01$\overline{0}$ 2 0$\overline{1}$0 3 01$\overline{0}$ $\overline{2}$ 0$\overline{1}$0 2 01$\overline{0}$ 2 0$\overline{1}$0 3 01$\overline{0}$ $\overline{2}$ 0$\overline{1}$0 3
$h^5_{2,1}(0)$	01$\overline{0}$ 2 0$\overline{1}$0 3 01$\overline{0}$ $\overline{2}$ 0$\overline{1}$0 3 01$\overline{0}$ 2 0$\overline{1}$0 3 01$\overline{0}$ $\overline{2}$ 0$\overline{1}$0 3

We are now ready to prove the main result :

Theorem *For each pair of integers (p,q) given in $N \times N \setminus \{0\}$, the 2-uniform tag system $S_{p,q}(\underline{f}) = <\{0,1,...,p+q\} \cup \{\overline{0},\overline{1},...,\overline{p+q}\},\ 0,\ h_{p,q},\ \{+,-\},\ \sigma_{p,q} >$ generates the paperfolding sequence associated to the ultimately periodic sequence of unfolding instructions $\underline{f}_{p,q} = f(0)f(1) \ldots f(p) \,(f(p+1) \ldots f(p+q))^{\omega}$. Conversely, every 2-automatic paperfolding sequence is generated by such a tag system.*

Proof. The first part is clear by vertue of the foregoing : for each (p,q) given in $N \times N \setminus \{0\}$, we have $\sigma_{p,q}(\rho(\underline{T})) = \sigma_{p,q}(h^{\omega}_{p,q}(0))$ i.e. the paperfolding sequence $\sigma_{p,q}(\rho(\underline{T}))$ associated to $\underline{f}_{p,q}$ (see above fact in 3.3) is 2-automatic (because $h_{p,q}$ is a 2-uniform and expansive on 0 morphism since h is, and $\sigma_{p,q}$ is a literal morphism since σ_f is).

The converse part is deduced of the three following arguments :
- a paperfolding sequence is 2-automatic if and only if its associated sequence of unfolding instructions is ultimately periodic (see [2,20,21]).
- each pair (p,q) given in $N \times N \setminus \{0\}$ determines an ulmitately periodic sequence $\underline{f}_{p,q}$, so we obtain all the ulmitately periodic sequences if we consider all the pairs (p,q) of $N \times N \setminus \{0\}$.
- each different sequence $\underline{f}_{p,q}$ determines a different 2-uniform tag system $S_{p,q}(\underline{f})$. ♦

5 - Conclusion

The 2-uniform tag systems defined in this paper are very simple which allowed us to make an implementation of a new algorithm to generate the dragon curves (in sense of [11]). These 2-uniform tag systems notably complete the published family which, up to now, was only containing the regular case [2,12].
Another automatique process is build by M. Mendès-France and J. Shallit in [20] : it generates the wire-bending sequence in alternate planes which is the generalization, in three dimensions,

of the alternate sequence. Also, these authors prove that any sequence of turns is 2-automatic iff the associated sequence of unbending instructions is ultimately periodic. To show the necessary condition, they build an automaton which accepts the unbending instructions. But it doesn't seem that the tag systems associated to sequences in two dimensions could be easily obtained from this automaton.

On the other hand, one can fold paper other than "in half ", for instance in p parts (p≥2) : one says, in this case, of p-paperfolding sequences (see [11,12,25]). Does there exist a similar family of p-uniform tag systems to generate all the p-paperfolding sequences associated to ultimately periodic sequences of unfolding instructions ? The answer to this question will be the subject of my next work.

Acknowledgement

I wish to express my gratitude to Pr. Patrice Séébold for his many hints and helpful comments.

References

[1] S. I. ADIAN, The Burnside Problem and Identities in Groups, *Springer-Verlag, 1979.*

[2] J.-P. ALLOUCHE, Automates finis en théorie des nombres, *Expo. Math. 5, (1987) 239-266.*

[3] J.-P. ALLOUCHE, The number of factors in a paperfolding sequences, *Bull. Austral. Math. Soc. 46 (1992) 23-32.*

[4] J.-P. ALLOUCHE, R. BACHER, Toeplitz sequences, paperfolding, towers of Hanoi and progression-free sequences of integers, *Ens. Math. 38 (1992) 315-327.*

[5] J.-P. ALLOUCHE, M. BOUSQUET-MÉLOU, Canonical positions for the factors in the paperfolding sequences, *(1993) to appear in Theor. Comp. Sci.*

[6] J. BERSTEL, Mots sans carrés et morphismes itérés, *Discrete Math. 29 (1980) 235-244.*

[7] J. BERSTEL, Every iterated morphism yields a co-CFL, *Inform. Proc. Lett. 22 (1986) 7-9.*

[8] G. CHRISTOL, T. KAMAE, M. MENDÈS-FRANCE, G. RAUZY, Suites algébriques, automates et substitutions, *Bull. Soc. math. France 108 (1980) 401-419.*

[9] A. COBHAM, Uniform Tag Sequences, *Math. Systems Theory 6 (1972) 164-192.*

[10] K. CULIK I I, I. FRIS, The decidability of the Equivalence Problem for DOL-Systems, *Inform. Control 35 (1977) 20-39.*

[11] C. DAVIS, D. E. KNUTH, Number representations and dragon curves, *J. Recreational Math. t.3 (1970) 66-81 and 133-149.*

[12] M. DEKKING, M. MENDÈS-FRANCE, A. J. VAN DER POORTEN, Folds ! *Math. Intell. 4 (1983) n° 3 : 130-138, n° 4 : 173-181 and 190-195.*

[13] A. EHRENFEUCHT, G. ROZENBERG, Elementary homomorphisms and a solution to the DOL sequence equivalence problem, *Theor. Comp. Sci. 7 (1978) 169-187.*

[14] M. GARDNER, Mathematical games, *Scientific American (1967) 216 : 118-125, 217 : 115.*

[15] M. HARRISON, Introduction to formal language theory, *Addison-Wesley, Read. Mass, 1978*

[16] S. ISTRAIL, On irreducible languages and nonrational numbers, *Bull. Math. Soc. Sci. Math. R.S. Roumanie 21 (1977) 301-308.*

[17] J. KARHUMÄKI, On the Equivalence Problem for Binary DOL Systems, *Inform. Control 50 (1981) 276-284.*

[18] M. LOTHAIRE, Combinatorics on words, *Addison-Wesley, Reading, Mass., 1983.*

[19] M. MENDÈS-FRANCE, Principe de la symétrie pertubée, *Séminaire de théorie des nombres Paris 1980, in Séminaire Delange-Pisot (1981) 77-98.*

[20] M. MENDÈS-FRANCE, J. SHALLIT, Wire Bending, *J. Comb. Theory, SerieA 50(1989) 1-23.*

[21] M. MENDÈS-FRANCE, A. J. VAN DER POORTEN, Arithmetic and analytic properties of paper sequences, *Bull. Austral. Math. Soc. 24 (1981) 123-131.*

[22] M. MORSE, Recurrent geodesics on a surface of negative curvature, *Trans. Amer. Math. Soc. 22 (1921) 84-100.*

[23] M. MORSE, G. A. HEDLUND, Symbolic dynamics, *Amer. J. Math. 60 (1938) 815-866.*

[24] M. MORSE, G. A. HEDLUND, Symbolic dynamics II-Sturmian trajectories, *Amer. J. Math. 62 (1940) 1-42.*

[25] D. RAZAFY ANDRIAMAMPIANINA, Le p-pliage de papier, *Ann. fac. Sci. Toulouse Math. vol X n° 1 (1989) 401-414.*

[26] G. ROZENBERG, A. SALOMAA, The Mathematical Theory of L Systems, *Acad. Press, 1980.*

[27] A. SALOMAA, Formal languages, *Academic Press, London, 1973.*

[28] M. P. SCHÜTZENBERGER, On a special class of recurrent events, *Annals Math. Stat. 322 (1961) 1201-1213.*

[29] A. THUE, Über unendliche Zeichenreihen, *Christiania Vid. Selsk. Skr. I. Mat.-Nat. Kl. 7, (1906) 1-22.*

[30] A. THUE, Über die gegenseitige Lage gleicher Teile gewisser Zeichenreihen, *Vidensk. Skr. I. Mat.-Naturv. Kl. 1, Kristiania (1912) 1-67.*

[31] A. J. VAN DER POORTEN, J. SHALLIT, Folded continued fractions, *J. Number Theory 40 (1992) 237-250.*

Growing Context-Sensitive Languages and Church-Rosser Languages

Gerhard Buntrock[1] and Friedrich Otto[2]

[1] Institut für Informatik, Universität, Würzburg,
bunt@informatik.uni-wuerzburg.de
[2] Fachbereich Mathematik/Informatik, Universität-GH, Kassel,
otto@theory.informatik.uni-kassel.de

Abstract. The growing context-sensitive languages (GCSL) are characterized by a nondeterministic machine model, the so-called shrinking two-pushdown automaton (sTPDA). Then the deterministic version of this automaton (sDTPDA) is shown to characterize the class of generalized Church-Rosser languages (GCRL). Finally, we prove that each growing context-sensitive language is accepted in polynomial time by some one-way auxiliary pushdown automaton with a logarithmic space bound (OW-auxPDA[log,poly]). As a consequence the class of (generalized) Church-Rosser languages and the class of context-free languages are incomparable under set inclusion, which verifies a conjecture of McNaughton et al [MNO88].

1 Introduction

It is well-known that the class of context-sensitive languages (CSL) coincides with the nondeterministic space complexity class NSPACE(n), and that there exist context-sensitive languages for which the membership problem is PSPACE-complete. Thus, in their full generality these languages are too powerful for practical applications. On the other hand, context-free languages (CFL) are not powerful enough to completely describe all the syntactical aspects of a programming language like PASCAL, since some of them are inherently context dependent. There are various alternatives to define classes of languages that are strictly in between CFL and CSL. One approach is based on making the context-free grammars more powerful by adding certain attributes that must be evaluated in order to decide whether a sentence derived from that grammar is considered to be 'valid' [Knu68]. Another approach is based on restricting the power of context-sensitive grammars. For example, Gladkij considers context-sensitive grammars with an additional bound on the length of derivations ([Gla64], see also [Boo69]). With a linear time-bound these grammars generate the languages in the class CSL_{lin}, which, however, still contains NP-complete languages [Boo78]. Also these restrictions seem to be rather artificial.

Dahlhaus and Warmuth [DW86] consider 'growing context-sensitive grammars', that is, context-sensitive grammars for which each production rule is strictly length-increasing. Obviously, for such a grammar the length of a derivation is bounded from above by the length of the sentence derived. Dahlhaus and

Warmuth prove that all growing context-sensitive languages (GCSL), that is, the languages that are generated by growing context-sensitive grammars, have membership problems that are solvable in polynomial time. In fact, GCSL is contained in the class LOGCFL of languages that are logspace-reducible to context-free languages. In addition, GCSL is contained in the uniform circuit complexity class AC^1, and hence, for each growing context-sensitive language there exists an efficient parallel algorithm for deciding membership in that language [Ruz80]. In particular, the class GCSL is strictly in between the classes CFL and CSL.

From the definition it might appear that GCSL is not an interesting class of languages, but as shown by Buntrock and Loryś, GCSL is an abstract family of languages [BL92], that is, this class of languages is closed under union, concatenation, iteration, intersection with regular languages, ϵ-free homomorphisms and inverse homomorphisms. Exploiting these closure properties Buntrock and Loryś have characterized the class GCSL by various other classes of grammars that are less restricted [BL92].

Using these grammars we characterize the class GCSL by a nondeterministic machine model. The basis of this model is the nondeterministic pushdown automaton with two pushdown stores (TPDA). Several variants of this machine model have been investigated [Wal70, GH68, Boo82]. We have found that the variant, where the input is provided as the initial contents of one of the pushdown stores, is most appropriate for our purposes. Since in full generality this model is equivalent to the Turing machine, we place an additional restriction on it. We assign a positive weight to each tape symbol and each internal state symbol of the machine. By adding up the weights this gives a weight for each configuration. Now we require that the weight of the actual configuration strictly decreases with each step of the TPDA. In this way we obtain the so-called shrinking TPDA. Our first main result states that a language is growing context-sensitive if and only if it is accepted by some shrinking TPDA.

Since the TPDA is a nondeterministic device, it is only natural to ask what class of languages is characterized by the deterministic variant of the shrinking TPDA. The languages accepted by them could be called 'deterministic growing context-sensitive languages', but we have chosen a different name based on another characterization for this class of languages. In [MNO88] McNaughton, Narendran and Otto define the concept of a Church-Rosser language (CRL). Essentially, a language is a Church-Rosser language if it consists of all the ancestors of a special symbol with respect to a finite, length-reducing, and confluent string-rewriting system (see Section 4 for the exact definitions). String-rewriting systems are a classical means for investigating formal languages and congruence relations over finite alphabets. Of particular interest are those string-rewriting systems that are noetherian and confluent. Here a system is called noetherian if it does not admit infinite sequences of reductions. Examples are systems that are length-reducing or weight-reducing. It is called confluent if it satisfies the confluence property for all strings (see Section 4). Systems that are both noetherian and confluent are of interest, since they define unique normal forms for all their congruence classes (see [BO93] for a thorough discussion of these topics). In [Boo82] a deterministic TPDA is presented that, on input string w, computes the irreducible descendant (that is, the normal form) of w with respect to a noetherian and confluent string-rewriting system. In general, this deterministic TPDA is not shrinking, but if the underlying string-rewriting system is length-reducing, then it is. Based on this observation we prove that each CRL is accepted by a shrinking deterministic TPDA. Unfortunately, it is not at all clear whether all the languages accepted by these machines are indeed Church-Rosser languages. However, by admitting finite, weight-reducing, and confluent string-rewriting systems we arrive at the concept of a generalized Church-Rosser language (GCRL), and our second main result states that a language is accepted by a shrinking deterministic TPDA if and only if it is a GCRL. This establishes an unexpectedly close relationship between the growing context-sensitive languages and the (generalized) Church-Rosser languages.

Finally, we improve upon a result of Dahlhaus and Warmuth mentioned before by showing that each growing context-sensitive language belongs to the class OW-LOGCFL, that is, it is reducible to a context-free language by a one-way logspace reduction. Based on this result we then conclude that the classes of languages GCRL and CFL, and therewith CRL and CFL, are incomparable under set inclusion, thus confirming a conjecture of [MNO88]. This also proves that GCRL is a proper subclass of GCSL, which means that the nondeterministic variant of the shrinking TPDA is strictly more powerful than its deterministic counter part. The paper closes with a short discussion of open problems concerning our results and the language classes considered.

2 Shrinking Two-Pushdown Automata

A function $f : \Sigma \to \mathbf{N}_+$ is called a *weight-function for* Σ. The obvious extension of f to Σ^* will also be denoted by f. Now we present the machine model that is central to our investigations.

Definition 1. (a) A *two-pushdown automaton* (TPDA) is a nondeterministic automaton with two pushdown stores. Formally, it is defined as a 7-tuple $M = (Q, \Sigma, \Gamma, \delta, q_0, \perp, F)$, where

- Q is the finite set of states,
- Σ is the finite input alphabet,
- Γ is the finite tape alphabet with $\Gamma \supset \Sigma$ and $\Gamma \cap Q = \emptyset$,
- $q_0 \in Q$ is the initial state,
- $\perp \in \Gamma \setminus \Sigma$ is the bottom marker of the pushdown stores,
- $F \subseteq Q$ is the set of final (or accepting) states, and
- $\delta : Q \times \Gamma \times \Gamma \to 2^{Q \times \Gamma^* \times \Gamma^*}$ is the transition relation, where $\delta(q, a, b)$ is a finite set for each triple $(q, a, b) \in Q \times \Gamma \times \Gamma$.

M is a *deterministic two-pushdown automaton* (DTPDA), if δ is a (partial) function from $Q \times \Gamma \times \Gamma$ into $Q \times \Gamma^* \times \Gamma^*$.

(b) A *configuration* of a TPDA M is described as uqv with $q \in Q$ and $u, v \in \Gamma^*$, where u is the contents of the first pushdown store with the first letter of u at the bottom and the last letter of u at the top, q is the current state, and v is the contents of the second pushdown store with the last letter of v at the bottom and the first letter of v at the top. M induces a *computation* *relation* $\vdash_M^*$ on the set of configurations. For an input string $w \in \Sigma^*$, the corresponding *initial configuration* is $\bot q_0 w \bot$. M can accept either by empty pushdown stores or by final state:

$$N(M) := \{w \in \Sigma^* \mid \exists q \in Q : \bot q_0 w \bot \vdash_M^* q\},$$
$$L(M) := \{w \in \Sigma^* \mid \exists q \in F \, \exists \alpha \in \Gamma^* : \bot q_0 w \bot \vdash_M^* \alpha q\}.$$

(c) A (D)TPDA M is called *shrinking* if there exists a weight-function $\varphi :$ $Q \cup \Gamma \rightarrow \mathbf{N}_+$ such that, for all configurations $u_1 q_1 v_1$ and $u_2 q_2 v_2$ of M, if $u_1 q_1 v_1 \vdash_M u_2 q_2 v_2$, then $\varphi(u_1 q_1 v_1) > \varphi(u_2 q_2 v_2)$. By sTPDA and sDTPDA we denote the corresponding classes of automata.

Observe that even when accepting by final state, a TPDA is forced to consume the input completely. Using standard techniques from automata theory it can be shown that we may require the following property for a (shrinking) (D)TPDA $M = (Q, \Sigma, \Gamma, \delta, q_0, \bot, F)$:
Whenever a pushdown store of M is nonempty, then its contents is of the form $u\bot$ with $u \in (\Gamma \setminus \{\bot\})^*$, where $\bot$ is at the bottom, that is, the special symbol $\bot$ can only occur at the bottom of a pushdown store, and no other symbol can occur at that place.

From the definition of the transition relation δ we see that M halts immediately whenever one of its pushdown stores is emptied. Because of the above property this happens if and only if a transition of the form $\delta(q, a, \bot) \mapsto (q', \alpha, \varepsilon)$ or $\delta(q, \bot, b) \mapsto (q', \varepsilon, \beta)$ is performed. Thus, it suffices to have a single accepting state q_f for M. Further, we have the following result, which is easily proved based on the above remarks.

Proposition 2. *(a) Let M be a TPDA (sTPDA, DTPDA, sDTPDA). Then there exists an automaton M' of the same type such that $N(M) = L(M')$.*
(b) Let M be a TPDA (sTPDA, DTPDA, sDTPDA). Then there exists an automaton M'' of the same type such that $L(M) = N(M'')$.

Thus, in the following we can always take the notion of acceptance that is most convenient. If we require that the transition relation δ is a mapping from $Q \times \Gamma \times \Gamma$ to finite subsets of $Q \times \Gamma^* \times (\Gamma \cup \{\varepsilon\})$, then we get a variant of the pushdown automaton. Thus, with this additional restriction the TPDA characterizes the context-free languages. In particular, the corresponding version of the DTPDA characterizes the class of deterministic context-free languages. However, due to the extra symbol on the 'input tape' this version of the DTPDA is more powerful with respect to the acceptance by empty pushdown than the deterministic pushdown automaton.

3 Growing Context-Sensitive Languages

The class of growing context-sensitive languages (GCSL) is defined by a syntactical restriction on context-sensitive grammars [DW86]. Here we give a characterization of this class in terms of the sTPDA.

Definition 3. A grammar is a quadruple $G = (N, T, S, P)$, where N and T are the finite disjoint alphabets of nonterminal and terminal symbols, respectively, $S \in N$ is the start symbol, and P is a finite set of productions of the form $\alpha \rightarrow \beta$ with $\alpha, \beta \in (N \cup T)^*$, where α contains at least one nonterminal symbol.

(a) If $|\alpha| \le |\beta|$ holds for all $(\alpha \to \beta) \in P$, then G is called a *context-sensitive grammar* (CSG).

(b) The grammar G is a *growing context-sensitive grammar* (GCSG), if the start symbol S does not appear on the right-hand side of any production of G, and if $|\alpha| < |\beta|$ holds for all productions $(\alpha \to \beta) \in P$ satisfying $\alpha \ne S$.

(c) The grammar G is a *quasi-growing grammar* (QGG) if there exists a weight-function $\varphi : N \cup T \to \mathbf{N}_+$ such that $\varphi(\alpha) < \varphi(\beta)$ for all $(\alpha \to \beta) \in P$.

(d) The grammar G is a *quasi-growing context-sensitive grammar* (QGCSG), if it is quasi-growing and context-sensitive.

(e) A language L is called *context-sensitive* (*growing context-sensitive*), if it is generated by some context-sensitive (growing context-sensitive) grammar. These language classes will be denoted by CSL and GCSL, respectively.

The quasi-growing grammars were introduced by Buntrock and Loryś [BL92], who also derived the following result.

Proposition 4. [BL92].
A language is growing context-sensitive if and only if it is generated by a QGG, respectively a QGCSG.

Now we come to the first part of our intended characterization theorem.

Theorem 5. *If a language L is accepted by some shrinking TPDA, then L is a growing context-sensitive language.*

Proof. Let $M = (Q, \Sigma, \Gamma, \delta, q_0, \perp, \{q_a\})$ be a TPDA such that $N(M) = L$, and let $\varphi : Q \cup \Gamma \to \mathbf{N}_+$ be a weight-function such that M is shrinking with respect to φ. From M we construct a grammar $G = (N, T, S, P)$ as follows:

- $N := (Q \setminus \{q_0\}) \cup (\Gamma \setminus (\Sigma \cup \{\perp\})) \cup \{S\}$, where S is a new symbol,
- $T := \Sigma \cup \{q_0, \perp\}$, and
- P consists of the following rules:

$$
\begin{aligned}
S &\to \perp q \perp && \text{if} & (q', \varepsilon, \varepsilon) &\in \delta(q, \perp, \perp) \\
\alpha q' \beta &\to aqb && \text{if} & (q', \alpha, \beta) &\in \delta(q, a, b)
\end{aligned}
$$

for all $q \in Q$ and $a, b \in \Gamma$. Recall that we assume that $Q \cap \Gamma = \emptyset$.

By induction on the number n of steps in a computation it can now be shown that $\perp q_0 w \perp \vdash_M^{(n)} \alpha q \beta$ if and only if $\alpha q \beta \Rightarrow_G^{(n)} \perp q_0 w \perp$. Hence, for all $w \in \Sigma^*$, $w \in L = N(M)$ if and only if $\perp q_0 w \perp \vdash_M^* q'$ for some $q' \in Q$ if and only if $S \Rightarrow_G^* \perp q_0 w \perp$ if and only if $\perp q_0 w \perp \in L(G)$.

Define a weight-function ψ for G by extending φ to $N \cup T$ by taking $\psi(S) := 1$. Then $\psi(\alpha) < \psi(\beta)$ for each production $(\alpha \to \beta) \in P$, and so we see that G is a QGG. Thus, the language $\{\perp q_0\} \cdot L \cdot \{\perp\}$ is growing context-sensitive. Since the class GCSL is closed under bounded homomorphisms [Bun93], this implies that L is in GCSL. $\qquad\Box$

To establish the converse result we need the technical notion of connectivity. A grammar is called *connected* if each proper derivation is connected, that is, for every two consecutive steps in a proper derivation at least one of the symbols that are replaced in the later step was produced by the former. Gladkij has shown that each context-sensitive grammar can be transformed into an equivalent context-sensitive grammar that is connected [Gla64]. Based on Book's proof for Gladkij's result [Boo69] the following technical result can be derived.

Theorem 6. *For each quasi-growing context-sensitive grammar G, there exists an equivalent quasi-growing context-sensitive grammar G_0 that is connected, and that produces every string $w \in L(G_0)$ strictly from right to left.*

Now we are prepared to establish the following converse of Theorem 5.

Theorem 7. *Every GCSL is accepted by some sTPDA.*

Proof. Let L be a GCSL. By Proposition 4 there exist a QGCSG $G = (N, T, S, P)$ and a weight-function $\varphi : N \cup T \to \mathbb{N}_+$ such that $L(G) = L$, and $\varphi(\ell) < \varphi(r)$ holds for all $(\ell \to r) \in P$. By Theorem 6 we may assume that the grammar G is connected, and that it produces every terminal string $w \in L$ strictly from right to left. We can even assume that $N = N' \cup \hat{N}$, where $N' \cap \hat{N} = \emptyset$, and that each sentential form contains a single symbol from $\hat{N}$.

Based on this particular grammar, a TPDA M with a single state q can be constructed that, when given a string $w \in T^*$ as input, tries to simulate a connected derivation $\hat{S} \Rightarrow^* w$ in the reverse order. Hence, for all $w \in T^*$, $\hat{S} \Rightarrow^* w$ if and only if $\perp qw\perp \vdash_M^* \perp q\perp \vdash_M q$. Thus, $L = N(M)$. By taking $\varphi(\perp) := \varphi(q) := 1$, φ is extended to a weight function for M. □

We can summarize the results of this section as follows.

Corollary 8. *A language is growing context-sensitive if and only if it is accepted by some sTPDA.*

It is immediate from the definition that each sTPDA is linearly time-bounded, and it accepts a language from P. In Definition 3, if we only require that the weight of the actual configuration does not increase in any step, then we obtain the so-called *non-strictly shrinking* TPDA. Such an automaton will in general not be linearly time-bounded. However, with an additional linear time-bound this type of automaton characterizes Gladkij's class CSL_{lin} [Gla64], which contains NP-complete languages [Boo78]. It is an open problem whether the linearly time-bounded TPDA that are not required to be non-strictly shrinking accept the same class of languages [Boo69]. Observe that all these classes are proper subclasses of Q, the set of languages accepted by non-deterministic Turing machines in linear time [Boo69, WW86].

4 Generalized Church-Rosser Languages

Now we consider the class of languages that is characterized by the shrinking deterministic TPDA. We give a characterization of this class in terms of certain restricted string-rewriting systems leading to the notion of generalized Church-Rosser languages.

String-rewriting systems form a special class of term-rewriting systems, and as such they have been investigated extensively. Here we just restate a few basic facts that we need in this paper. As our main reference on string-rewriting systems we use the monograph by Book and Otto [BO93], where the various aspects of string-rewriting systems are discussed in detail, and where references to the original literature can be found.

Definition 9. Let $R \subseteq \Sigma^* \times \Sigma^*$ be a finite string-rewriting system. By $\to_R$ we denote the *single-step reduction relation* on Σ^* that is induced by R. The reflexive transitive closure $\to_R^*$ of $\to_R$ is the corresponding *reduction relation*, and the reflexive, symmetric, and transitive closure $\leftrightarrow_R^*$ is the *Thue congruence* generated by R. The system R is called

- *length-reducing* if $|\ell| > |r|$ holds for each rule $(\ell \to r) \in R$,
- *weight-reducing* if there exists a weight-function $f : \Sigma \to \mathbf{N}_+$ such that $f(\ell) > f(r)$ holds for each rule $(\ell \to r) \in R$,
- *confluent* if $u \to_R^* v$ and $u \to_R^* w$ imply that $v \to_R^* z$ and $w \to_R^* z$ for some $z \in \Sigma^*$,
- *normalized* if $r \in IRR(R)$ and $\ell \in IRR(R \setminus \{\ell \to r\})$ hold for each rule $(\ell \to r) \in R$, where $IRR(R)$ denotes the set of strings that are *irreducible* with respect to R, that is, $w \in IRR(R)$ if and only if w does not contain the left-hand side ℓ of any rule $(\ell \to r) \in R$ as a factor.

If R is a finite string-rewriting system, then $IRR(R)$ is a regular language, and from R a deterministic finite-state acceptor (DFA) can be constructed in polynomial time for the set $IRR(R)$.

If a string-rewriting system R is weight-reducing and confluent, then each congruence class $[u]_R := \{w \in \Sigma^* \mid u \leftrightarrow_R^* w\}$ contains a unique irreducible string u_0, which can then serve as a normal form for this class. For each $w \in [u]_R$, $w \to_R^* u_0$, and given a string $u \in \Sigma^*$, its normal form u_0 can be determined in linear time.

Finally, if R is a length-reducing or a weight-reducing string-rewriting system that is also confluent, then one can construct a confluent system R_0 that is length-reducing or weight-reducing, respectively, in polynomial time from R such that R and R_0 are equivalent, that is, $\leftrightarrow_R^* = \leftrightarrow_{R_0}^*$, and, in addition, R_0 is normalized. Thus, in the following we will restrict our attention to length-reducing, respectively weight-reducing, confluent systems that are normalized.

In [MNO88] the notion of Church-Rosser languages is introduced.

Definition 10. A language $L \subseteq \Sigma^*$ is a *Church-Rosser language* (CRL), respectively a *generalized Church-Rosser language* (GCRL), if there exist an alphabet $\Gamma \supset \Sigma$, a finite length-reducing, respectively weight-reducing, confluent string-rewriting system R on Γ, two strings $t_1, t_2 \in (\Gamma \setminus \Sigma)^* \cap IRR(R)$ and a letter $Y \in (\Gamma \setminus \Sigma) \cap IRR(R)$ such that, for all $w \in \Sigma^*$, $t_1 w t_2 \to_R^* Y$ if and only if $w \in L$.

We claim that the class of generalized Church-Rosser languages coincides with the class of languages that are accepted by sDTPDA. The first half of this result is easily established.

Theorem 11. *If a language L is accepted by some sDTPDA, then L is a GCRL.*

Proof. Let L be accepted by the sDTPDA $M = (Q, \Sigma, \Gamma, \delta, q_0, \perp, \{q_f\})$ with weight-function g, that is, $L = L(M)$. We claim that L is a GCRL.

Let $\Delta := Q \cup \Gamma \cup \bar{\Gamma}$, where $\bar{\Gamma}$ is a new alphabet in 1-to-1 correspondence with Γ. We assume that the three sets Q, Γ, and $\bar{\Gamma}$ are pairwise disjoint. The weight-function g is extended to Δ by taking $g(\bar{a}) := g(a)$ for all $a \in \Gamma$. Further, define $t_1 := \bar{\bot}q_0$ and $t_2 := \bot$. It remains to define a finite string-rewriting system R on Δ. Let R be the system that contains the following rules:

$$\bar{a}qb \to \bar{u}q'v \quad \text{if } \delta(q, a, b) = (q', u, v), \ q \in Q, \ a, b \in \Gamma,$$
$$\bar{a}q_f \to q_f \quad \text{for all } \bar{a} \in \bar{\Gamma}.$$

Here $^{-} : \Gamma^* \to \bar{\Gamma}^*$ denotes the obvious isomorphism.

It is immediate that R is a weight-reducing system. Since M is deterministic, there are no overlaps between left-hand sides of rules of R, and so R is confluent. Also t_1, t_2, and q_f are irreducible with respect to R. Since, for all $w \in \Sigma^*$, $w \in L$ if and only if $t_1 w t_2 = \bar{\bot}q_0 w \bot \to_R^* \bar{\bot}\bar{a}q_f \to_R^* q_f$, R, t_1, t_2 and q_f witness the fact that L is a GCRL. $\qquad\qquad\square$

To show the converse result we need some preparations.

Definition 12. Let R be a string-rewriting system on Σ. A reduction $w \to_R z$ is called *leftmost*, denoted $w \ _L\!\to_R z$, if the following condition is satisfied: if $w = x_1 \ell_1 y_1$, $z = x_1 r_1 y_1$, and $(\ell_1 \to r_1) \in R$, and also $w = x_2 \ell_2 y_2$ for some rule $(\ell_2 \to r_2) \in R$, then $x_1 \ell_1$ is a proper prefix of $x_2 \ell_2$, or $x_1 \ell_1 = x_2 \ell_2$ and x_1 is a proper prefix of x_2, or $x_1 = x_2$ and $\ell_1 = \ell_2$. Let $_L\!\to_R^*$ denote the reflexive transitive closure of $_L\!\to_R$. For every $w, z \in \Sigma^*$, a sequence of reductions that begins with w and ends with z such that every step is leftmost is called a *leftmost reduction* from w to z.

If the system R is normalized, then, for each $w \notin IRR(R)$, there exists a unique $z \in \Sigma^*$ such that $w \ _L\!\to_R z$. Hence, for normalized systems the process of leftmost reduction is deterministic. In particular, if R is normalized and confluent, then for each $w \notin IRR(R)$, there is a unique leftmost reduction from w to its normal form $w_0 \in IRR(R)$.

In [Boo82] a DTPDA is described that, given a string $w \in \Sigma^*$ as input, computes a leftmost reduction from w to $w_0 \in IRR(R)$. By modifying this DTPDA appropriately, and by choosing a suitable weight-function the following technical result can be established.

Theorem 13. *Let R be a finite string-rewriting system that is normalized and weight-reducing. For $w \in \Sigma^*$, let $w_0 \in IRR(R)$ denote the unique irreducible descendant of w with respect to leftmost reductions. Then a shrinking DTPDA $M(R) = (Q, \Sigma, \Gamma, \delta, q_0, \bot, \{q_f\})$ can be constructed such that, for each $w \in \Sigma^*$, $\bot q_0 w \bot \vdash_{M(R)}^* \bot \varphi_2(w_0) q_f$. Here $\Sigma_2 \subseteq \Gamma \setminus \Sigma$ is an alphabet in 1-to-1 correspondence to Σ, and $\varphi_2 : \Sigma^* \to \Sigma_2^*$ is the corresponding isomorphism.*

Let R be a string-rewriting system on Σ, and let $w \in IRR(R)$. Then $\nabla_R^L(w) := \{u \in \Sigma^* \mid u \ _L\!\to_R^* w\}$ is the set of all *leftmost ancestors* of w. For $S \subseteq IRR(R)$, $\nabla_R^L(S) := \bigcup_{w \in S} \nabla_R^L(w)$.

Theorem 14. *Let R be a normalized and weight-reducing string-rewriting system on Σ, and let $S \subseteq IRR(R)$ be a regular language. Then the set $\nabla_R^L(S)$ is accepted by some sDTPDA.*

Proof. Since $S \subseteq IRR(R)$ is a regular language, there exists a DFA B on Σ_2 such that $L(B) = \{(\varphi_2(w))^R \mid w \in S\}$. Here Σ_2 is a new alphabet in 1-to-1 correspondence to Σ, $\varphi_2 : \Sigma^* \to \Sigma_2^*$ is the corresponding isomorphism, and u^R denotes the reversal of u.

From Theorem 13 we get an sDTPDA $M(R) := (Q, \Sigma, \Gamma, \delta, q_0, \perp, \{q_f\})$ such that, for each $w \in \Sigma^*$, $\perp q_0 w \perp \vdash^*_{M(R)} \perp \varphi_2(w_0) q_f$, where $w_0 \in IRR(R)$ is the unique irreducible string satisfying $w \; _L\!\to^*_R w_0$.

Now the DFA B and the sDTPDA $M(R)$ are combined as follows. Given $w \in \Sigma^*$ as input, the combined DTPDA M first simulates $M(R)$. However, when the string $\varphi_2(w_0)$ has been computed, then, instead of erasing the bottom marker from the second pushdown store, M simulates the DFA B using its first pushdown store as input tape. Hence, M accepts the set $\nabla_R^L(S)$, and it is easily seen that the weight-function f of $M(R)$ can be extended such that M is shrinking with respect to f. $\qquad\qquad\square$

Actually, Theorem 14 can be extended to all languages $S \subseteq IRR(R)$ that are accepted by shrinking DTPDAs.

If R is a finite weight-reducing string-rewriting system that is normalized and confluent, then $[w]_R = \nabla_R^L(w)$ for each string $w \in IRR(R)$. Thus, Theorem 14 implies that in this situation, $[S]_R := \bigcup_{w \in S} [w]_R$ is accepted by some shrinking DTPDA for each regular set S contained in $IRR(R)$. Based on this observation we can now prove the intended converse of Theorem 11.

Theorem 15. *Each generalized Church-Rosser language is accepted by some shrinking DTPDA.*

Proof. Let $S \subseteq \Sigma^*$ be a GCRL. Then there are some alphabet $\Gamma \supset \Sigma$, a finite, weight-reducing, confluent string-rewriting system R on Γ, strings $t_1, t_2 \in (\Gamma \setminus \Sigma)^* \cap IRR(R)$ and a letter $Y \in (\Gamma \setminus \Sigma) \cap IRR(R)$ such that, for all $w \in \Sigma^*$, $t_1 w t_2 \to^*_R Y$ if and only if $w \in S$. Without loss of generality we can assume that the system R is normalized. Hence, by Theorem 14 there is an sDTPDA M_1 that accepts the language $\nabla_R^L(Y) = [Y]_R$. This sDTPDA M_1 is now transformed into a shrinking DTPDA M_2 that accepts the language S. M_2 executes the following three steps.

(i) Before reading any input M_2 writes $\varphi_2(t_1)$ onto its first pushdown store. By assigning a sufficiently large weight to the initial state symbol, this step can be made weight-reducing.

(ii) Then M_2 simulates the DTPDA M_1, that is, it computes a left-most reduction with respect to R. M_2 continues with this simulation until it encounters the bottom marker $\perp$ on its second pushdown store.

(iii) When the bottom marker $\perp$ is encountered on the second pushdown store, then M_2 pushes the string t_2 onto the second pushdown store. Thereafter, it continues with the simulation of M_1. Since this intermediate step occurs only once, it can be made weight-reducing by introducing a second set of states in 1-to-1 correspondence to the states of M_1.

Thus, M_2 accepts on input $w \in \Sigma^*$ if and only if $t_1 w t_2 \; _L\!\to^*_R Y$ if and only if $w \in S$. Since M_2 is an sDTPDA, this proves our result. $\qquad\square$

Combining Theorem 11 and Theorem 15 we obtain the following characterization.

Corollary 16. *A language is accepted by some* sDTPDA *if and only if it is a* GCRL.

5 Separation Results

As is well-known GCSL is a proper subclass of CSL, since, for example, the Gladkij language $\{w \phi w^R \phi w \mid w \in \{a, b\}^*\}$ belongs to CSL\GCSL [Gla64, Boo69]. On the other hand, CFL is a proper subclass of GCSL, since already CRL contains the non-context-free language $\{a^{2^n} \mid n \geq 0\}$ [MNO88], while it is easily seen that each CFL is generated by some quasi-growing grammar. Finally, DCFL is properly contained in CFL as well as in CRL [MNO88]. Thus, the situation can be depicted as follows, where arrows indicate set inclusions, while dashed arrows indicate proper inclusions:

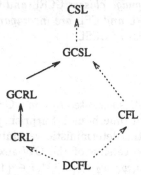

In addition, we know that CRL is not contained in CFL. In [MNO88] it has been conjectured that CFL is not contained in CRL, either. Here we will finally settle this conjecture in the affirmative. In fact, we will prove that CFL is not even contained in GCRL, which then implies that GCRL is strictly contained in GCSL. Thus, the shrinking TPDA is strictly more powerful than its deterministic variant.

Recall that an *auxiliary pushdown automaton* (auxPDA) with *space bound* s is a non-deterministic Turing machine M with a read-only input tape, a pushdown tape, and an auxiliary work tape which is initialized to have exactly $s(n)$ squares, limited by end markers, if M is started on an input of length n. It is a *one-way auxiliary pushdown automaton* (OW-auxPDA) with space bound s, if it is limited to a one-way input tape. The closure of the class CFL of context-free languages under log-space reductions is denoted by LOGCFL, and OW-LOGCFL denotes the closure of the class CFL under one-way log-space reductions. It is known that LOGCFL coincides with the class of languages that are accepted by auxPDAs with logarithmic space bound and polynomial time bound [Sud78], and OW-LOGCFL coincides with the class of languages that are accepted by OW-auxPDAs with logarithmic space bound and polynomial time bound [Lau88].

For more details about auxPDAs see [HU79], for OW-auxPDAs see [Bra77, Chy77], and for one-way reductions see [HIM78].

Dahlhaus and Warmuth [DW86] have shown that the class GCSL is contained in LOGCFL. Using their technique actually the following stronger result can be obtained.

Theorem 17. *Each growing context-sensitive language is accepted by some OW-auxPDA with logarithmic space bound and polynomial time bound, that is, GCSL is contained in* OW-LOGCFL.

Based on this theorem we now derive the announced result. Let L_0 denote the language $L_0 := \{ww \mid w \in \{a, b\}^*\}$. Then L_0 is not context-free, while its complement $L_0^c := \{a, b\}^* \setminus L_0$ is a context-free language. However, it is known that L_0 does not belong to OW-LOGCFL [Chy76, Lau88], and hence, by Theorem 17 L_0 is not a growing context-sensitive language. Since the class GCRL is closed under complementation, this implies that L_0^c is not a generalized Church-Rosser language. Thus, we have the following consequences.

Corollary 18. *(a) The language classes* GCRL *and* CFL *are incomparable.*
(b) The language classes CRL *and* CFL *are incomparable.*
(c) GCRL *is a proper subclass of* GCSL.

6 Conclusion

We have seen that each GCSL is accepted by some OW-auxPDA with logarithmic space bound and polynomial time bound. Surprisingly the generalized Church-Rosser languages, that is, the deterministic variants of the GCSL, are not accepted by the deterministic version of the OW-auxPDA, as witnessed by the language $\{w \# w_1 \# w_2 \# i \mid w, w_1, w_2 \in \{0, 1\}^*, i \in \{1, 2\}, w = w_i^R\}$. However, a lot of open questions remain unanswered at this time.

First of all the generalized Church-Rosser languages are obtained from the Church-Rosser languages by admitting string-rewriting systems in the definition that are less severely restricted. Hence, CRL is contained in GCRL, but we don't know yet whether this inclusion is a proper one. In [MNO88] it was not only conjectured that CFL $\not\subset$ CRL, but in fact it was conjectured more specifically that the linear language $L := \{ww^R \mid w \in \{a, b\}^*\}$ is not a Church-Rosser language. Actually, we expect that L is not even a generalized Church-Rosser language, but we have no proof for this yet.

Also it has not yet been determined under which operations and mappings the classes GCRL and CRL are closed. It is easily seen that the class GCRL is closed under complement, reversal and intersection with regular sets. On the other hand, GCRL is neither closed under union nor under intersection. Nor is GCRL closed under alphabetic morphisms. Concerning the class CRL even less is known. It is closed under reversal, and under left and right quotient with a single string [MNO88], but for example, it is not even known whether it is closed under complement. If CRL is closed under inverse homomorphisms, then the classes CRL and GCRL coincide.

Finally, the classes CRL and GCRL should be compared to the various subclasses of the class CSL that Jančar, Mráz and Plátek define based on their machine model of a forgetting automaton [JMP93].

References

[BL92]   G. Buntrock and K. Loryś. On growing context-sensitive languages. In *Proc. of 19th ICALP, LNCS*, 623:77–88, Springer, 1992.

[Boo69]   R. V. Book. *Grammars with Time Functions*. PhD Diss., Harvard University, Cambridge, MA, 1969.

[Boo78]   R. V. Book. On the complexity of formal grammars. *Acta Informatica*, 9:171–181, 1978.

[Boo82]   R. V. Book. Confluent and other types of Thue systems. *Journal of the ACM*, 29:171–182, 1982.

[BO93]   R. V. Book and F. Otto. *String-Rewriting Systems*. Springer, 1993.

[Bra77]   F.J. Brandenburg. On one-way auxiliary pushdown automata. In *Proc. of 3rd GI-Conference on Theoretical Computer Science, LNCS*, 48:132–144, Springer, 1977.

[Bun93]   G. Buntrock. Growing context-sensitive languages and automata. *Preprint, Nr. 69*. Institut für Informatik, Universität Würzburg, November 1993.

[Chy76]   M. Chytil. Analysis of the non-context-free component of formal languages. In *Proc. of 5th MFCS, LNCS*, 45:230–236, Springer, 1976.

[Chy77]   M. Chytil. Comparison of the active visiting and the crossing complexities. In *Proc. of 6th MFCS, LNCS*, 53:272–281, Springer, 1977.

[DW86]   E. Dahlhaus and M. K. Warmuth. Membership for growing context-sensitive grammars is polynomial. *Journal of Computer and System Sciences*, 33:456–472, 1986.

[GH68]   S. Ginsburg and M. A. Harrison. One-way nondeterministic real-time list-storage languages. *Journal of the ACM*, 15:428–447, 1968.

[Gla64]   A. W. Gladkij. On the complexity of derivations for context-sensitive grammars. *Algebri i Logika Sem.*, 3:29–44, 1964. In Russian.

[HIM78]   J. Hartmanis, N. Immerman, and S. R. Mahaney. One-way log-tape reductions. In *Proc. of 19th FOCS*, 1978, 65–71.

[HU79]   J. E. Hopcroft and J. D. Ullman. *Introduction to Automata Theory, Languages and Computation*. Addison-Wesley, 1979.

[JMP93]   P. Jančar, F. Mráz, and M. Plátek. A taxonomy of forgetting automata. In *Proc. of 18th MFCS, LNCS*, 711:527–536, Springer, 1993.

[Knu68]   D. E. Knuth. Semantics of context-free languages. *Mathematical Systems Theory*, 2:127–145, 1968.

[Lau88]   C. Lautemann. One pushdown and a small tape. In K. Wagner, ed., *Dirk Siefkes zum 50. Geburtstag*, pages 42–47. Technische Universität Berlin and Universität Augsburg, 1988.

[MNO88]   R. McNaughton, P. Narendran, and F. Otto. Church-Rosser Thue systems and formal languages. *Journal of the ACM*, 35(2):324–344, 1988.

[Ruz80]   W. L. Ruzzo. Tree-size bounded alternation. *Journal of Computer and System Sciences*, 21:218–235, 1980.

[Sud78]   I. H. Sudborough. On the tape complexity of deterministic context-free languages. *Journal of the ACM*, 25(3):405–414, 1978.

[Wal70]   D. A. Walters. Deterministic context-sensitive languages: Part II. *Information and Control*, 17:41–61, 1970.

[WW86]   K. Wagner and G. Wechsung. *Computational Complexity*. VEB Deutscher Verlag der Wissenschaften and Reidel Verlag, Dordrecht, 1986.

Deterministic Generalized Automata *

Dora Giammarresi** and Rosa Montalbano

Dipartimento di Matematica ed Applicazioni, Università di Palermo
via Archirafi, 34 - 90123 Palermo - ITALY
e-mail: {dora,rosalba}@altair.math.unipa.it

Abstract. A generalized automaton (GA) is a finite automaton where the single transitions are defined on words rather than on single letters. Generalized automata were considered by K. Hashiguchi who proved that the problem of calculating the size of a minimal GA is decidable.
We define the model of deterministic generalized automaton (DGA) and study the problem of its minimization. A DGA has the restriction that, for each state, the sets of words corresponding to the transitions of that state are prefix sets. We solve the problem of calculating the number of states of a minimal DGA for a given language, by giving a procedure that effectively constructs it starting from the minimal (conventional) deterministic automaton.

1 Introduction

Generalized automata (GA) are a model of representation for regular languages that extends the notion of finite automata by allowing the single transitions to be defined on words rather than on single letters. Intuitively, a generalized automaton can be obtained from a conventional one by shrinking long paths of the graph in a unique edge with a "long" label. Therefore, generalized automata are usually more concise than conventional ones representing the same event.

In the past decades, several efforts have been devoted to compute the complexity of representation of a given language inside different models of representation (deterministic, non-deterministic, unambiguous, two-way, alternating, probabilistic, pebbles automata, regular expressions, logical formalisms and so on). The complexity of a language in a given model is generally understood as the size of the minimal representation of the language in that model. For example, a classical measure of the complexity of a finite automaton is its number of states and the complexity of a language in this model is the number of states of a minimal (with respect to the number of states) automaton recognizing it.

In this context, Hashiguchi in 1991 investigated the problem of computing the size of the minimal representation of a given regular language in the model

* Work partially supported by the ESPRIT II Basic Research Actions Program of the EC under Project ASMICS 2 (contract No. 6317) and in part by MURST under project 40% *Algoritmi, Modelli di Calcolo, Strutture Informative*.
** Partially supported by a research fellowship by *(INdAM)*.

of generalized automata (see [H91]). In particular, he proved that the problem of calculating the number of states of a minimal GA is actually decidable.

A strictly related problem consists of effectively computing a minimal representation of a given language in a model. In the case of conventional deterministic finite automata, it can be proved that the minimal automaton is unique and an algorithm to calculate it starting from any equivalent deterministic automaton can be obtained using the Myhill-Nerode's theorem (see, for example, [HU79]). For non-deterministic automata there are only partial results stating that there is no unique minimal automaton but there are no constructive procedures for computing it, excepting the one that lists all possible automata. In [JR91] the computational complexity of different problems concerning minimization is studied in a general setting for non-deterministic automata and it is proved that all these problems are computationally hard.

In this paper we introduce the model of *deterministic generalized automata* (DGA) and deal with the minimization problem for this model. In order to preserve all properties implied by the notion of determinism in the case of conventional automata, DGA have the restriction that the sets of words corresponding to the transitions of each state are prefix sets. We solve the problem of computing the number of states of a minimal DGA by giving a procedure to construct a minimal DGA for a given language starting from the minimal (conventional) deterministic one. We introduce two operations that allow one to reduce the number of states of a DGA: the first, called $\mathcal{I}$-*reduction*, contracts states that are "indistinguishable" and the second, called S-*reduction*, suppresses states that are "superfluous". Then we give the conditions under which such operations can be performed. We show that there can be deterministic GA that are irreducible (with respect to the above operations) but not minimal and give necessary and sufficient conditions to reduce a deterministic GA to get a minimal one. Moreover, we show that, differently from the case of conventional deterministic automata, the minimal deterministic GA is not unique.

The size of the minimal representation of a language in a given model (which measures the complexity of the language) plays a primary role also in comparing different models according to their intrinsic succinctness. Much work has been devoted to studying succinctness of representation when transducers are considered (see, for example [WK94]). In the case of finite automata, very recently, Harel et al. studied exponential discrepancies in the succinctness of finite automata when augmented by combinations of various additional mechanisms like alternation (i.e. both universal and existential branching), concurrency, "two-wayness" and pebbles (see [GH94]). We conclude the paper by discussing problems of discrepancy in succinctness between non-deterministic and deterministic versions of generalized automata and give some open problems.

2 Preliminaries

We denote by Σ a finite alphabet and by Σ^* the free monoid generated by Σ. The elements of Σ are called letters, those of Σ^* are called words; the subsets of Σ^* (i.e. the sets of words) are called languages over Σ. The length of a word w is denoted by $|w|$. Given two words v and w, we say that v is a *prefix* of w if there exists a word u such that $w = vu$. Given a set of words X, we say that X is a *prefix set* if no word in X is prefix of some other word in X. Given two sets of words X and Y, the *concatenation of X and Y*, indicated as $X \cdot Y$ contains all words xy with $x \in X$ and $y \in Y$.

A *finite (non deterministic) automaton* is a quintuple $\mathcal{A} = (\Sigma, Q, I, F, E)$ where Q is a finite set of *states*, $I, F \subseteq Q$ are the sets of *initial* and of *final states* respectively and $E \subseteq Q \times \Sigma \times Q$ is a set of labeled *edges*. We denote an edge of $\mathcal{A}$ by $e = (r, a, s)$, where $r, s \in Q$ and $a \in \Sigma$ is the label of e. A *path of length* n in $\mathcal{A}$ is a sequence of edges $e_i = (r_i, a_i, r_{i+1}) \in E$, for $i = 1, \ldots n$, that we denote by $[r_1, a_1 \ldots a_n, r_{n+1}]$. The word $w = a_1 \ldots a_n$ is called the label of the path $e_1, \ldots, e_n$. If $r_1 \in I$ and $r_{n+1} \in F$ then $e_1, \ldots, e_n$ is called *accepting path* and word w is said *accepted by* (or *recognized by*) $\mathcal{A}$. The language accepted (or recognized) by the automaton $\mathcal{A}$ is the set of all accepted words. A language L over Σ is *recognizable* if L is the language accepted by some finite automaton.

Two finite automata are *equivalent* if they accept the same language. A *minimal* automaton for a language L is an automaton with the minimum number of states among all equivalent automata accepting L. An automaton $\mathcal{A} = (\Sigma, Q, I, F, E)$ is *deterministic* if $|I| = 1$, and for any state $q \in Q$ and any letter $a \in \Sigma$, there exists at most one state $p \in Q$ such that edge $(q, a, p) \in E$. It can be proved (see [HU79]) that for any (non-deterministic) automaton there exists an equivalent deterministic automaton. However, in general, the non-deterministic automaton has a minor number of states than the corresponding deterministic one. The *minimal deterministic automaton* for a given language L is the automaton with minimal number of states among all equivalent deterministic automata accepting L. It can be proved that there is a unique minimal deterministic automaton equivalent to a given deterministic automaton $\mathcal{A} = (\Sigma, Q, i, F, E)$. It can be to obtained as follows (see [HU79] or [P90] for more details). We define an equivalence relation in the set of states Q called *indistinguishability*: two states $p, q \in Q$ are *indistinguishable* if for any word $w \in \Sigma^*$, there exists a path $[p, w, f]$ with $f \in F$ if and only if there exists a path $[q, w, f']$ with $f' \in F$. The minimal deterministic automaton equivalent to $\mathcal{A}$ can be obtained by contracting indistinguishable states of $\mathcal{A}$.

Since an automaton is actually a directed labeled graph, in the following we will need further notations on graphs. Given an edge $e = (p, a, q)$, we call p the beginning and q the end, respectively, of e. An edge e is said *incident* to a state q if it begins or ends in q. An edge $e = (p, a, q)$ is a *self-loop* if $p = q$. A path $e_1, e_2, \ldots, e_n$, where $e_i = (r_i, a_i, r_{i+1})$, is a *cycle* if $r_1 = r_{n+1}$. Notice that, a self-loop is a cycle of length one. A graph is *acyclic* if it does not contain cycles.

Let $G = (Q, E)$ be a directed graph where Q is the set of vertices and E is the set of edges. If $S \subseteq Q$, the subgraph of G induced by S is the graph $G_S = (S, E')$ such that $E' \subseteq E$ is the set of all edges whose beginnings and ends are in S. We say that S induces a *maximal acyclic subgraph* if G_S is an acyclic subgraph of G that is not a subgraph of any other acyclic subgraph of G.

3 Generalized automata

In this section we consider a generalization of the conventional model of automaton described above. Differently from that model, the labels of the edges are words over the alphabet Σ (i.e. not only single letters).

Definition 1. A *generalized (non-deterministic) automaton* (GA) is a quintuple $\mathcal{A} = (\Sigma, Q, I, F, E)$ where Q is a finite set of *states*, $I, F \subseteq Q$ are the sets of *initial* and *final* states and $E \subseteq Q \times \Sigma^* \times Q$ is a *finite* set of labeled *edges*.

Notice that the finiteness of the set E is now necessary to get a finite device: without this restriction we could have as many edges as the words in Σ^*.

The notion of recognizability for a language by generalized automata is the same as by conventional automata, i.e. a word is accepted if it is the label of an accepting path. More precisely, a word $w \in \Sigma^*$ is recognized by a generalized automaton $\mathcal{A}$ if there exist words $w_1, w_2, \ldots, w_n \in \Sigma^*$ and edges $e_1, e_2, \ldots, e_n \in E$ such that w_i is the label of e_i for $i = 1, \ldots, n$, the sequence $e_1, e_2, \ldots, e_n$ is an accepting path and $w_1 w_2 \ldots w_n = w$.

Observe that, in this case, the fact that a word w is accepted by a generalized automaton does not imply that all factors of w are labels of some path in the automaton. Consider, for example, the generalized automaton below recognizing the language $L = (ab + a^2)^* ba^2$ over $\Sigma = \{a, b\}$. Notice that the prefix ab^2 of the accepted word $ab^2 a^2$ does not correspond to any path in the graph.

In general, by allowing the labels of the edges to be words of any length, a generalized automaton gives a representation of a language by means of a graph that is possibly much smaller than the corresponding representation by conventional automaton. For example, any finite language can be represented by a GA with only two states, despite of the length of its words.

Generalized automata were considered by Hashiguchi in [H91]. He studied the problem of calculating the number of states of a minimal generalized automaton for a given language and proved that this problem is decidable.

If $\mathcal{A}$ is a GA, denote by $D(\mathcal{A})$ the maximal length of the labels of the edges in $\mathcal{A}$. The decidability is a consequence of the following theorem.

Theorem 2. [K. Hashiguchi 1991] *Let L be a recognizable language and m the cardinality of the syntactic monoid for L. There exists a minimal generalized automaton $\mathcal{A}$ recognizing L such that $D(\mathcal{A}) \leq 2m(m + 2)(4m(m + 2) + 3)$.*

We observe that the number $D(\mathcal{A})$ in the statement of the theorem is actually a very huge number. This because the cardinality of the syntactic monoid of a language is of the order of n^n where n is the number of states of the minimal deterministic (conventional) automaton for L (see [P90]).

4 Deterministic generalized automata

We now define and study the model of generalized automaton in the deterministic case. We start with a remark. In the case of deterministic conventional automata, the "local" condition that, given any state q, for any letter a there is at most one edge beginning in q with label a implies the "global" condition that also for any word w there is at most one path beginning in q with label w. The same does not hold in the case of GA's as shown by following example.

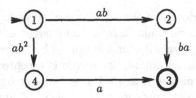

Notice that there exist two paths in $\mathcal{A}$ beginning in state 1 with label ab^2a and this despite $\mathcal{A}$ is deterministic in the "classical" sense (i.e. despite for any state q and any word w there is at most one edge beginning in q with label w).

To capture the "global" property of the conventional notion of determinism we need a stronger condition on the set of edges. Given a GA $\mathcal{A} = (\Sigma, Q, I, F, E)$, for any state $q \in Q$, we define the set $W(q) = \{w \in \Sigma^* \,|\, (q, w, r) \in E, r \in Q\}$. In other words, $W(q)$ contains the labels of all edges beginning in q in $\mathcal{A}$.

Definition 3. Let $\mathcal{A} = (\Sigma, Q, I, F, E)$ be a generalized automaton. We say that $\mathcal{A}$ is *deterministic* if $|I| = 1$ and for any state $q \in Q$, the set $W(q)$ is a prefix set.

Notice that the condition that $W(q)$ is a prefix set effectively guarantees that for any state q and for any word w there is at most one path beginning in q with label w. Moreover conventional deterministic automata satisfy the above definition because the $W(q)$'s are subsets of the alphabet that is a prefix set.

We now focus on the problem of reducing (with respect to the number of states) a given DGA. We will define two operations that transform a DGA into a smaller equivalent one. The first operation contracts indistinguishable states similarly to the minimization operation for conventional deterministic automata. The second operation reduces the number of states by shrinking long paths in a unique edge with a "long" label.

Given a DGA $\mathcal{A} = (\Sigma, Q, i, F, E)$, for any $q \in Q$, we denote by L_{qF} the set of words corresponding to paths from state q to a final state. Two states $p, q \in Q$ are *indistinguishable* if $L_{pF} = L_{qF}$.

Notice that the above definition of indistinguishability among states is an extension to generalized automata of the corresponding definition for conventional automata (cf. [HU79]). The indistinguishability is an equivalence relation over the set of states that we indicate by $\sim$. Therefore we can construct a reduced DGA $\mathcal{A}'$ by contracting all states belonging to the same equivalence class. The edges of $\mathcal{A}'$ can be defined as follows. If $[q]$ denotes the equivalence class of state

q, we define $W([q])$ as the prefix set of the shortest words in $\bigcup_{p \sim q} W(p)$. Observe that, for any $w \in W([q])$ there exists at least a state $p \sim q$ such that $w \in W(p)$. Then, for any (p, w, p') in $\mathcal{A}$ there is edge $([q], w, [p'])$ in $\mathcal{A}'$. We omit the proof that the DGA $\mathcal{A}'$ is equivalent to $\mathcal{A}$. We say that an automaton is $\mathcal{I}$-*irreducible* if it has no indistinguishable states.

Now we give a definition for a transformation S corresponding to the second operation mentioned above. Let $\mathcal{A}$ be a DGA and r, s be two states of $\mathcal{A}$. We denote by L_{rs} the set of words over Σ that are labels of all paths from r to s in $\mathcal{A}$. We define transformation S that suppresses states in $\mathcal{A}$ preserving sets L_{rs} for any pair of states r, s not suppressed.

Given a state q of $\mathcal{A}$, transformation S computes a smaller DGA $S(\mathcal{A}, q)$ from $\mathcal{A}$ by suppressing the state q and redefining all the edges that were incident in q. More precisely, S suppresses state q together with all its incident edges and, for any pair of edges (r, u, q) and (q, v, s) that were in $\mathcal{A}$, S defines a new edge (r, uv, s). Observe that, in order to preserve sets L_{rs} without compromising the finiteness of automaton $S(\mathcal{A}, q)$, state q must not have self-loops. Since our final goal is to minimize a DGA, we are actually interested in transformations that reduce a DGA preserving the recognized language (i.e. preserving all sets L_{if} where i is the initial state and f is any final state): therefore we do not apply S both to i and to any final state. We give the following definition.

Definition 4. Given a DGA $\mathcal{A} = (\Sigma, Q, i, F, E)$. A state $q \in Q$ is a *superfluous state* for $\mathcal{A}$ if q is neither an initial nor a final state and it has no self-loops.

The set of all superfluous states for $\mathcal{A}$ will be denoted by $Super(Q)$. We now formally define transformation S.

Definition 5. Let $\mathcal{A} = (\Sigma, Q, i, F, E)$ be a DGA and $q \in Q$ be a superfluous state. Then $S(\mathcal{A}, q) = (\Sigma, Q_q, i, F, E_q)$ is a (generalized) automaton where $Q_q = Q - \{q\}$ and $(r, u, s) \in E_q$ if either $(r, u, s) \in E$ or there exist $(r, u_1, q), (q, u_2, s) \in E$ such that $u_1 u_2 = u$.

For each $r \in Q_q$, the set $W_q(r)$ of words associated to r in the transformed automaton can be calculated starting from the sets $W(r)$ and $W(q)$ as follows. We split the set $W(r)$ in two disjoint subsets $W(r) = X(r, q) \cup \overline{X}(r, q)$ such that $X(r, q)$ contains the words that are labels of edges ending in state q and $\overline{X}(r, q)$ is its complement in $W(r)$. Then, we have: $W_q(r) = X(r, q) \cdot W(q) \cup \overline{X}(r, q)$.

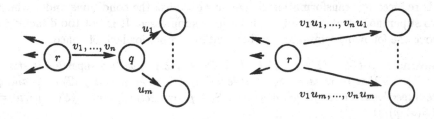

Lemma 6. *Let A be a DGA and let q be a superfluous state for A. The transformed automaton $S(A, q)$ is a DGA equivalent to A.*

Proof. Let $A_q = S(A, q) = (\Sigma, Q_q, i, F, E_q)$ be as in the Definition 5. The set $W_q(r)$ is a prefix set for any $r \in Q_q$ (see also Proposition 4.1 in [BP85]).

We now have to prove that A and A_q recognize the same language. Notice that, by construction, each edge (r, u, s) in A_q corresponds in A either to the same edge or to the path $\{(r, u_1, q), (q, u_2, s)\}$ where $u_1 u_2 = u$. Then, for any word $v \in \Sigma^*$, v is the label of an accepting path in A_q if and only if it is a label of an accepting path in A. □

We say that an automaton without superfluous states is S-*irreducible*.

Definition 7. A DGA is *irreducible* if it is both $\mathcal{I}$-irreducible and S-irreducible.

We remark that irreducibility does not imply minimality. In fact the following DGA over the alphabet $\Sigma = \{a, b\}$ admits two equivalent DGA that are both irreducible but have a different number of states.

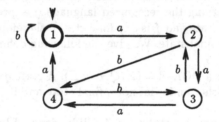

By suppressing state 3, we get an irreducible DGA that is is not minimal because a smaller irreducible DGA can be obtained by orderly suppressing states 2 and 4 from the initial automaton.

5 Irreducible DGA

In this section we consider the problem of calculating an irreducible DGA equivalent to a given one. In particular we will find conditions to apply transformation S to a given DGA in order to "suppress" as many as possible superfluous states.

Notice that, if p and q are both superfluous states of a given DGA A then p is not necessarily still a superfluous state for the transformed automaton $S(A, q)$. In other words, in general, the set of superfluous states of a DGA changes when it is reduced by transformation S. We now establish the conditions under which two superfluous states p and q can both be suppressed. It is not too difficult to prove the following lemma, given here without proof for lack of space.

Lemma 8. *Let $A = (\Sigma, Q, i, F, E)$ be a DGA and p, q be two superfluous states for A such that there is no cycle of length two between p and q. Then p and q are superfluous states for $S(A, q)$ and $S(A, p)$ respectively and $S(S(A, q), p) = S(S(A, p), q)$.*

Lemma 8 allows us to adopt the notation $S(S(\mathcal{A}, q), p) = S(S(\mathcal{A}, p), q) = S(\mathcal{A}, \{p, q\})$. We now want to investigate under which conditions this notation can be extended to any set $S = \{s_1, s_2, \ldots, s_h\} \subseteq Q$.

We indicate by $\mathcal{A}_i$ the DGA obtained from $\mathcal{A}$ by suppressing in order states $s_1, s_2, \ldots, s_i$ for $i = 1, \ldots, h$. Notice that the transformation

$$S((\ldots S(S(\mathcal{A}, s_1), s_2) \ldots), s_h) \tag{1}$$

can be realized only if, for any $i = 1, \ldots, h - 1$, state s_{i+1} is an superfluous state for $\mathcal{A}_i$. We use the notation $S(\mathcal{A}, \{s_1, \ldots, s_h\}) = S(\mathcal{A}, S)$ to refer to expression (1): this will be justified later.

We recall that $Super(Q)$ denotes the set of all superfluous states of $\mathcal{A}$. The following lemma characterizes those sets $S \subseteq Q$ for which $S(\mathcal{A}, S)$ can be calculated. The proof is in a short form for lack of space.

Lemma 9. *Let $\mathcal{A} = (\Sigma, Q, i, F, E)$ be a DGA and $S \subseteq Q$. Then $S(\mathcal{A}, S)$ can be calculated if and only if $S \subseteq Super(Q)$ and it induces an acyclic subgraph in $\mathcal{A}$.*

Proof. Observe that, given automata $\mathcal{A}$ and $S(\mathcal{A}, q)$, there is a cycle containing two states $r, s \neq q$ in $\mathcal{A}$ if and only if there is a cycle containing r and s in $S(\mathcal{A}, q)$. Then we can apply induction on the cardinality of S. The base of the induction is given by Lemma 8. □

Lemma 8 guaranties that the computation of DGA $S(\mathcal{A}, S)$ is independent of the order in which the states s_i's are suppressed from $\mathcal{A}$ and justifies this notation. As immediate consequence of Lemma 9 we get the following theorem. We recall that a DGA is irreducible if the set of its superfluous states $Super(Q) = \emptyset$. We refer to the subgraph induced by $Super(Q)$ as $\mathcal{A}_{Super(Q)}$.

Theorem 10. *Let $\mathcal{A} = (\Sigma, Q, i, F, E)$ be a DGA and $S \subseteq Super(Q)$. The DGA $S(\mathcal{A}, S)$ is S-irreducible if and only if S induces a maximal acyclic subgraph in $\mathcal{A}_{Super(Q)}$.*

Observe that, given an automaton $\mathcal{A}$, finding the set of states S of the above theorem is an NP-complete problem since it is strictly related to the problem "Given a direct graph, find the minimum number of states to be deleted so that resulting subgraph is acyclic" that is NP-complete (see [LY80]).

6 Minimal DGA

In this section we study the problem of finding a minimal DGA recognizing a given language. We recall that a minimal DGA does not have either indistinguishable or superfluous states. We start by remarking that, given a DGA, the procedure consisting of an S-reduction followed by an $\mathcal{I}$-reduction in not equivalent to the procedure that inverts these two operations. This can be seen from the following example.

Consider the DGA $\mathcal{A}$ over the alphabet $\Sigma = \{a, b\}$ given below.

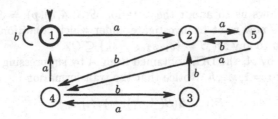

Observe that the subset $S = \{3,5\}$ induces in $\mathcal{A}$ a maximal acyclic subgraph so that $\mathcal{A}_1 = \mathcal{S}(\mathcal{A}, S)$ is an S-irreducible DGA. $\mathcal{A}_1$ is represented below.

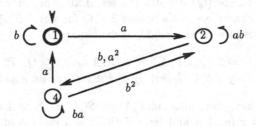

Since in $\mathcal{A}_1$ there are no indistinguishable states we conclude that $\mathcal{I}(\mathcal{A}_1) = \mathcal{A}_1$ is both an S-irreducible and an $\mathcal{I}$-irreducible DGA equivalent to $\mathcal{A}$. Now observe, that states 3 and 5 are indistinguishable in $\mathcal{A}$ so that we can contract them in a unique state called 3. We obtain the $\mathcal{I}$-irreducible automaton $\mathcal{A}_2 = \mathcal{I}(\mathcal{A})$ given below on the left. Then the set of states $S' = \{2,4\}$ induces a maximal acyclic graph in $\mathcal{A}_2$ so that $\mathcal{A}_2' = \mathcal{S}(\mathcal{A}_2, S')$ is an S-irreducible DGA. $\mathcal{A}_2'$ is represented by the graph given below on the right.

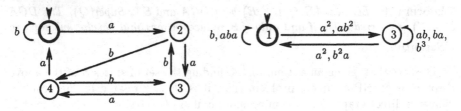

Notice that the two resulting DGA , $\mathcal{A}_1$ and $\mathcal{A}_2'$, are both S- and $\mathcal{I}$-irreducible but they have a different number of states.

Theorem 11. *Let L be a regular language and let $\mathcal{N}$ be a minimal DGA recognizing L. If $\mathcal{M}$ is the equivalent minimal conventional deterministic automaton then there exists a set S of states of $\mathcal{M}$ such that $\mathcal{N} = \mathcal{S}(\mathcal{M}, S)$.*

Proof. Let $\mathcal{N} = (Q_\mathcal{N}, i_\mathcal{N}, F_\mathcal{N}, E_\mathcal{N})$ and $\mathcal{M} = (Q_\mathcal{M}, i_\mathcal{M}, F_\mathcal{M}, E_\mathcal{M})$. We prove that there exists a set $S \subseteq Q_\mathcal{M}$ such that $\mathcal{N} = \mathcal{S}(\mathcal{M}, S)$ by defining a mapping $\varphi : Q_\mathcal{N} \to Q_\mathcal{M}$ and showing that states in $Q_\mathcal{M}$ that have no counterimage in $Q_\mathcal{N}$ are superfluous states for $\mathcal{M}$.

The mapping φ is defined as follows: $i_\mathcal{M} = \varphi(i_\mathcal{N})$ and if $q_\mathcal{N} \in Q_\mathcal{N}$ and $q_\mathcal{M} \in Q_\mathcal{M}$ then $\varphi(q_\mathcal{N}) = q_\mathcal{M}$ if and only if there exists a word $w \in L_{i_\mathcal{N} q_\mathcal{N}} \cap L_{i_\mathcal{M} q_\mathcal{M}}$.

We first show that φ is actually a function over $Q_\mathcal{N}$. Since automata $\mathcal{N}$ and $\mathcal{M}$ are equivalent then, given $q_\mathcal{N} \in Q_\mathcal{N}$ there exists $q_\mathcal{M} \in Q_\mathcal{M}$ such that $\varphi(q_\mathcal{N}) = q_\mathcal{M}$. Such state $q_\mathcal{M}$ is unique. Suppose that there exists also $p_\mathcal{M} \in Q_\mathcal{M}$ such that $\varphi(q_\mathcal{N}) = p_\mathcal{M}$: then, by the definition of φ, there exist two words u, v such that paths $[i_\mathcal{N}, u, q_\mathcal{N}]$ and $[i_\mathcal{N}, v, q_\mathcal{N}]$ are in $\mathcal{N}$ and paths $[i_\mathcal{M}, u, q_\mathcal{M}]$ and $[i_\mathcal{M}, v, p_\mathcal{M}]$ are in $\mathcal{M}$. But the equivalence of $\mathcal{N}$ and $\mathcal{M}$ implies that $q_\mathcal{M}$ and $p_\mathcal{M}$ are indistinguishable and this contradicts the hypothesis that $\mathcal{M}$ is minimal.

Then we can define a set $S = Q_\mathcal{M} - \varphi(Q_\mathcal{N})$. Notice that S contains all states of $\mathcal{M}$ that do not correspond to any state of $\mathcal{N}$. We now prove that $\mathcal{M}' = S(\mathcal{M}, S)$ is defined, that is it satisfies the conditions of Lemma 9, and that $\mathcal{N} = \mathcal{M}'$. Let us first observe that $F_\mathcal{M} \subseteq \varphi(Q_\mathcal{N})$: therefore the set S does not contains both the initial state $i_\mathcal{M}$ and the set of final states of $\mathcal{M}$. We now show that S induces an acyclic subgraph in $\mathcal{M}$.

Suppose that in $\mathcal{M}$ there is a cycle $[s, u, s]$ whose states are all in S. Let v, w be two words such that the paths $[i_\mathcal{M}, v, s], [s, w, f_\mathcal{M}]$ are in $\mathcal{M}$ where $f_\mathcal{M} \in F_\mathcal{M}$. The words $vu^n w \in L$ for all integers $n \geq 0$: therefore in $\mathcal{N}$ for any n there exists a path $[i_\mathcal{N}, vu^n w, f_\mathcal{N}]$, where $f_\mathcal{N} \in F_\mathcal{N}$. Since $Q_\mathcal{N}$ is a finite set, there exist infinite values of n for which path $[i_\mathcal{N}, uv^n w, f_\mathcal{N}]$ in $\mathcal{N}$ contains a cycle and it can be split as paths $[i_\mathcal{N}, x, r], [r, y, r], [r, y, r], \ldots, [r, y, r], [r, z, f_\mathcal{N}]$ that is $vu^n w = xy^k z$ for a suitable value of k.

Therefore we can choose k, h in a way that $k \geq h$, $|xy^h| \geq |v|$ and $|y^{k-h} z| \geq |w|$ while $xy^k z = vu^n w$. We observe that $|xy^h| \leq |vu^n|$ otherwise $|xy^k z| = |xy^h| + |y^{k-h} z| > |vu^n w|$ contradicting the hypothesis. Since the word xy^h is a prefix of $vu^n w$ (that belongs to L) then there exists a state s' in $\mathcal{M}$ such that the path $[i_\mathcal{M}, xy^h, s']$ is in $\mathcal{M}$. From the definition of φ we have: $s' = \varphi(r)$ that is $s' \in \varphi(Q_\mathcal{N})$ (and therefore s' does not belongs to S). Moreover, notice that since $|v| \leq |xy^h| \leq |vu^n|$, then the state s' is a state in the cycle $[s, u, s]$ in $\mathcal{M}$. But this implies that $s' \in S$ contradicting what we stated before.

It remains to show that $\mathcal{N} = \mathcal{M}'$. We already know that $\mathcal{N}$ and $\mathcal{M}'$ are equivalent, $i_{\mathcal{M}'} = i_\mathcal{M} = \varphi(i_\mathcal{N})$ and that map φ is defined onto the set of states $Q_{\mathcal{M}'}$ of $\mathcal{M}'$ that is $Q_{\mathcal{M}'} = Q_\mathcal{M} - S = \varphi(Q_\mathcal{N})$. Mapping φ is actually a bijection from $Q_\mathcal{N}$ in $Q_{\mathcal{M}'}$. In fact if there exist two states $p, q \in Q_\mathcal{N}$ such that $\varphi(p) = \varphi(q)$ then $|Q_{\mathcal{M}'}| < |Q_\mathcal{N}|$ and this contradicts the hypothesis of $\mathcal{N}$ minimal DGA. $\square$

From this theorem we get a procedure to compute the size n of a minimal DGA recognizing a given language L: we calculate the minimal conventional deterministic automaton $\mathcal{M}$ for L and then calculate a maximal set of states S of $\mathcal{M}$ that induces a maximal acyclic subgraph. Then $n = |Q_\mathcal{M}| - |S|$. This solves the corresponding problem studied by Hashiguchi in [H91] for the deterministic setting. Notice that, the maximal length of the labels in the edges of a minimal DGA $\mathcal{N}$ (referred as $D(\mathcal{N})$ by Hashigushi in [H91]), is equal, at most, to the number of states suppressed in $\mathcal{M}$ plus 1, that is at most n, where n is the number of states of the minimal deterministic automaton recognizing L. Differently from the case of conventional deterministic automata, it holds the following.

Theorem 12. *Given a language L, there is not a unique minimal DGA recognizing L.*

The proof is given by the following example. Let L be the language recognized by the minimal deterministic automaton $\mathcal{A}$ represented below.

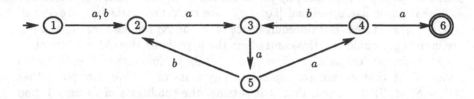

In $\mathcal{A}$ there are two maximal superfluous sets, $S_1 = \{2,3,4\}$ and $S_2 = \{2,4,5\}$. By suppressing S_1 in $\mathcal{A}$ we obtain the minimal DGA for L given below on the left. In the same way, by suppressing S_2 in $\mathcal{A}$ we obtain another minimal DGA for L different from the previous one that is given below on the right.

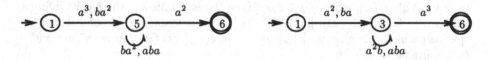

As immediate consequence of Theorems 10 and 11, we obtain a procedure to find all minimal DGA equivalent to a given deterministic automaton $\mathcal{A}$. We take the minimal (conventional) deterministic automaton $\mathcal{M}$ equivalent to $\mathcal{A}$ and compute all maximal sets among all superfluous sets that induce maximal acyclic subgraphs in $\mathcal{M}_{Super(Q_{\mathcal{M}})}$. All minimal DGA equivalent to $\mathcal{A}$ can be computed by applying an S-reduction to $\mathcal{M}$ with respect to such sets.

We finish the section by remarking that the inverse operation of transformation S (that is breaking edges with "long" labels and create a sequence of edges with "shorter" labels) is easy to define. Given the edge $(p, w_1 w_2 \ldots w_n, q)$ we can insert states $r_1, r_2, \ldots, r_{n-1}$ and edges $(p, w_1; r_1), (r_1, w_2, r_2), \ldots, (r_{n-1}, w_n, q)$. Therefore, to solve the problem of minimizing a given DGA $\mathcal{A}$, we apply this inverse operation to $\mathcal{A}$ until we obtain a conventional deterministic automaton $\mathcal{A}'$ and then we minimize $\mathcal{A}'$. Finally we apply Theorem 11.

7 Final discussions and further work

It is well known that, in the case of conventional automata there is an exponential gap in the complexity of representation between the non-deterministic and deterministic versions. In fact, consider the language $L_n = (a+b)^* a(a+b)^{n-1}$, for any integer n: the minimal deterministic automaton for L_n has exactly 2^n states while the corresponding non-deterministic one has $n + 1$ states. We notice that such discrepancy in succinctness between non-deterministic and deterministic versions still holds inside the model of GA. In fact, the minimal (conventional) deterministic automaton for L_n has exactly 2^{n-1} final states (therefore not superfluous) that will be necessarily also in any minimal DGA. On the other hand the minimal (non-deterministic) GA has only two states for any n.

The above example suggests that, if the minimal conventional deterministic automaton has "too many" final states, then the corresponding GA cannot be reduced too much. A further direction for this work is then to investigate about the succinctness in the case of automata with only one final state. This is related with the decomposition of a regular language in unitary components ([E74]).

As final observation, notice that the transformation S can be defined as well for non-deterministic GA. It still gives an equivalent GA but in general we do not know whether there exists a procedure that compute a minimal non-deterministic (generalized) automaton.

Acknowledgments

We are deeply grateful to Antonio Restivo for several discussions that inspired this paper and for his helpful comments and hearty encouragements. We also thank Pino Italiano and Sergio Salemi for some useful suggestions and an anonymous referee for his careful reading.

References

[AHU] A. Aho, J. E. Hopcroft and J. D. Ullman. *The Design and the Analysis of Computer Algorithm.* Addison-Wesley, Reading, MA 1974.

[BP85] J. Berstel and D. Perrin *Theory of Codes* Academic Press, 1985.

[E74] S. Eilenberg. *Automata, Languages and Machines* Vol.A, Academic Press,1974.

[GH94] N. Globerman and D. Harel. Complexity results for multi-pebble automata and their logics. In Proc. *(ICALP'94).* S. Abiteboul and E. Shamir Eds. Springer-Verlag, n.820, pp. 73–82 (1994).

[H91] K. Hashigushi. Algorithms for determining the smallest number of nonterminals (states) sufficient for generating (accepting) a regular language. In Proc. *(ICALP'91).* J.Leach Albert *et al.* Eds. Springer-Verlag, n.510, pp. 641–648 (1991).

[HU79] J. E. Hopcroft and J. D. Ullman. *Introduction to Automata Theory, Languages and Computation.* Addison-Wesley, Reading, MA 1979.

[JR91] Tao Jiang and B. Ravikumar. Minimal NFA problems are hard. In Proc. *(ICALP'91).* J.Leach Albert *et al.* Eds. Springer-Verlag, n.510, pp. 629–640 (1991).

[LY80] J. M. Lewis and M. Yannakakis. The node-deletion problem for hereditary properties is NP-complete. *Journal of Comp. and System Science,* 20, pp. 219–230 (1980).

[P90] D. Perrin. Finite Automata. In *Handbook of Theoretical Computer Science.* J. Van Leeuwen ed. Elsevier, Vol.B, pp. 1–57, 1990.

[WK94] A. Weber and R. Klemm. Economy of description for single-valued transducers. In Proc. *(STACS'94).* P. Enjalbert *et al.* Eds. Springer-Verlag, n.775, pp. 607–618 (1994).

Optimal simulation of automata by neural nets

P. Indyk

Instytut Informatyki, Uniwersytet Warszawski, Banacha 2, 02-097 Warszawa, Poland.
indyk@zaa.mimuw.edu.pl

Abstract. The problem of simulation of automata by neural networks is investigated. In the case of discrete networks with polynomially bounded weights, the optimal lower and upper bounds for the number of neurons necessary to simulate any finite automata of size n are presented. For the analog case we prove the 15-neuron upper bound for any finite automaton. By extending this construction we show that a 25-neuron network may simulate any Turing machine, and hence its behavior is undecidable.

1 Introduction

Recurrent neural networks are a model of parallel computation. They have been applied successfully to problems of pattern recognition and associative memory [7]. Recurrent networks can also perform more general computations (see [15, 12] for instance). In this paper we address the task of comparing the computational power of recurrent networks to more traditional models of computation, such as finite automata and counter machines [6].

This research is along the lines of the recent interest in complexity issues of both discrete [4, 1, 12] and analog [11, 15, 10, 8, 2] neural networks. For a general introduction to neural computation, see the textbook [3]; for some aspects of recurrent networks, see [7]; and for computational complexity issues, see the survey papers [13] and [14].

The specific problems that we study concern the upper and lower bounds for a minimal number of neurons needed to simulate any automaton of n states. When we restrict the state of a neuron to be 0 or 1, we improve the result of [1] by showing that $O(n^{\frac{1}{2}})$ neurons suffice, as opposed to $O(n^{\frac{3}{4}})$ in [1]. Moreover we show that if the weights of the network are polynomial with respect to the size of the network (such networks known as threshold circuits are very common, see [13] for more information), then most of finite automata require $\Omega(n^{\frac{1}{2}})$ neurons. The proof of this fact involves an analysis of several properties of random finite automata.

In the general case, when the state of the neuron may be a rational number from the interval $[0, 1]$, we show that any finite automaton can be simulated by a neural network with 15 neurons. This disproves the conjecture, stated in [1], that more complicated neural network models are incapable to reduce the lower bounds given in [1]. Moreover, by extending the construction slightly, we obtain a network with 25 units capable to simulate any 2-counter machine and hence any Turing machine [6]. This improves significantly the results given in [15] (1058 neurons) and in [2] (at least 114 neurons when the network is built according to the authors' instruction in the proof of Theorem 2) and shows that even the recurrent networks used in practice are inherently unpredictable (see also [9]), where recurrent neural networks of size up to 29 units are used for financial market prediction).

2 Preliminaries

In this section we introduce some definitions and basic notions used later.

2.1 Finite automata

We work with the finite automata in which the alphabet set is $\{0,1\}$, the state set is $\{1 \ldots n\}$ and the initial state is 1. Formally, a (deterministic) *finite automaton* is a pair (δ, F), where elements of $F \subset \{1 \ldots n\}$ are called *accepting states* and $\delta : \{1 \ldots n\} \times \{0,1\} \to \{1 \ldots n\}$ is called a *transition function*. Sometimes we use the notation $\delta_b(q)$ to denote $\delta(q, b)$. Any pair $< q, \delta(q, b) >$, for $q \in \{1 \ldots n\}$ and $b \in \{0,1\}$, is called an *edge*. For any $q_1, q_2 \in \{1 \ldots n\}$, if either both of them belong or neither belongs to F, then they are said to have the same *acceptance mode*. The set of all finite automata with n states is denoted as $\mathcal{A}_n$ (or $\mathcal{A}$ when n is fixed). It is easy to see that $|\mathcal{A}_n| = 2^n n^{2n}$. Let A be a subset of $\mathcal{A}_n$. The *rate* of A is defined as

$$\mathcal{P}_n(A) = \frac{|A|}{2^n n^{2n}}$$

(we also write $\mathcal{P}(A)$ when n is fixed). The language recognized by an automaton a is denoted as $\mathcal{L}(a)$, similarly, for a set of automata A, the set of languages recognized by the elements of A is denoted by $\mathcal{L}(A)$. For $a \in \mathcal{A}$, the notation $\mathcal{R}(a)$ means the set of states q such that for some input w the automaton a stops in q. The states from $\mathcal{R}(a)$ are called *reachable* .

Recall the well known [6] equivalence relation $r(a)$ on states of the automaton a : state q_1 is in relation with state q_2 iff for any input word w the execution of the automaton on w starting from q_1 leads to a state with the same acceptance mode as the state which is the result of execution of the automaton on w starting from q_2. Let $[q]$ denote an equivalence class of this relation. The automaton a is *k-minimal* if $\max_q |[q]| = k$. The automaton a is said to be $\geq$ *k-minimal* ($\leq$ *k-minimal*, resp.), if it is k'-minimal for some $k' \geq k$ ($k' \leq k$, resp.). It is well known [6] that for every automaton a there exists a 1-minimal automaton a' which recognizes the same language as a. To obtain such an automaton, for every state q of a redirect all the edges leading to states in $[q]$ to one specific state from $[q]$, say, with the lowest number. Then eliminate all the unreachable states, and renumber the remaining ones with numbers from $\{1 \ldots \#(a)\}$ ($\#(a)$ denotes the number of classes of abstraction of $r(a)$), say by numbering the i-th maximal state with i. This procedure is referred to as the *minimization* of a.

2.2 Neural networks

We consider two types of neural networks, namely *discrete* and *analog* ones. The variants are similar, hence we give one definition, pointing to the differences if necessary.

The *neural network* is a 6-tuple (U, I, E, W, T, s_0) where U is called the set of *units* (or *neurons*) of cardinality m, $I \subset U$ is the set of *input* units, (the units from $U - I$ are called *internal*), $E \subset U \times U$ is the set of *edges* (or *connections*), $W : E \rightarrow Z$ is the *weight* function. Here Z is the set of integers in the case of discrete network, and the set of rational numbers in the case of analog networks. The function $T : U \rightarrow Z$ is the *threshold* function (with Z defined as above), and s_0 is the *initial* state of the network. The *state* of a network is a function $s : U \rightarrow V$, where $V = \{0, 1\}$ (for the discrete network) or V is a set of rational numbers from the $[0, 1]$ interval (for the analog network). We often write $u = b$ or that neuron u is set to b instead of the formal notation $s_t(u) = b$.

At each time step t, the network computes its new state s_t from its old state s_{t-1} according to the formula:

$$s_t(u) = f \left(\sum_{<v,u> \in E} W(< v, u >) s_{t-1}(v) + T(u) \right)$$

where $u \in U - I$ and f is defined depending on the type of the network:

- discrete network: $f(x) = \begin{cases} 0 \ if \ x < 0 \\ 1 \ if \ x \geq 0 \end{cases}$

- analog network: $f(x) = \begin{cases} 0 \ if \ x < 0 \\ x \ if \ 0 \leq x < 1 \\ 1 \ if \ x \geq 1 \end{cases}$

The state of the input units may be set arbitrarily by the environment. Throughout this paper we assume that there exists a constant z such that, for all edges e, the weight $W(e)$ satisfies $-m^z \leq W(e) \leq m^z$.

2.3 Neural network as a finite automaton

We would like to be able to consider neural networks as acceptors of languages over the alphabet $\{0,1\}$. Assume that the neural network has exactly one input unit u_{in} and two special internal units u_{out} and u_{sign}. The language recognition is defined as follows. Let w be any word with symbols from $\{0,1\}$. We take the first digit b of w and set u_{in} to b. Then perform the computation steps of the network until eventually u_{sign} becomes equal to 1. If this happens, set u_{in} to the next digit of w (if there is any left) and then proceed with the computations. When there is no digit left then the value of u_{out} indicates if the word w is recognized by the network (1 if yes, otherwise no). If u_{sign} is never set to 1, after having read a prefix of the word w in the manner indicated, then the word w is not recognized.

This definition is similar to that given by [1]. The only difference is the existence of the u_{signal} unit, which enables the network to respond in irregular periods of time. This possibility is used in the case of analog networks only and helps to save a few neurons in construction given in Section 5. The discrete network given in Section 4 gives the answer every equal (and constant) period of time.

2.4 Mathematical facts

Suppose that the random variables $X_1 \ldots X_d$ have a binomial distribution with $\Pr(X_k = 1) = p$ and $\Pr(X_k = 0) = 1-p$. Let $Y = \sum_{k=1}^{d} X_k$. Then $EY = d \cdot p = \mu$ and the following inequality, known as the Chernoff bound holds (see [5]):

$$\Pr(|Y - \mu| \geq \epsilon \cdot \mu) < \exp(-\epsilon^2 \mu / 3)$$

for $0 < \epsilon \leq 1$.

We also use the following well known bound

$$\binom{n}{k} \leq \left(\frac{ne}{k}\right)^k$$

on the binomial coefficients.

3 Lower bound for discrete networks

In this section we show the lower bound $\Omega(n^{\frac{1}{2}})$ for the numbers of units such that any finite automaton of size n may be simulated by discrete neural network of this size. In fact we show much more, i.e. that a finite automaton randomly chosen from the set of all automata of size n requires $\Omega(n^{\frac{1}{2}})$ size neural network to be simulated with a high probability. We start with some lemmas.

Lemma 1. *There exists a constant d_3 such that the probability that a randomly chosen automaton with n states is ≥ 3-minimal is less than $\frac{d_3}{n}$.*

Proof. Let $[q_1]$ denote the class of maximal cardinality. The probability of $\|[q_1]\| \geq 3$, denoted by $\mathcal{P}(\|[q_1]\| \geq 3)$, is equal to

$$\sum_{i=3}^{n} \mathcal{P}(\|[q_1]\| = i) = \sum_{i=3}^{(1+\epsilon)\frac{n}{2}} \mathcal{P}(\|[q_1]\| = i) + \mathcal{P}\left(\|[q_1]\| > (1+\epsilon)\frac{n}{2}\right)$$

The second term may be bounded by the probability of $\max(|F|, n - |F|) > (1 + \epsilon)\frac{n}{2}$, which by Chernoff bound is less than $e^{-\frac{\epsilon^2}{3}\frac{n}{2}}$. The first one is bounded by (the number of possible sets of cardinality not greater than $(1 + \epsilon)\frac{n}{2}$ chosen as $[q_1]$) times (the probability of $\delta(q, j) \in [\delta(q_1, j)]$ for all $j = 0, 1$ and $q \in [q_1]$)

times (the probability of all states from $[q_1]$ having the same acceptance mode), which is equal to :

$$\sum_{i=3}^{(1+\epsilon)\frac{n}{2}} \binom{n}{i}\left(\frac{i}{n}\right)^{2(i-1)} 2^{-(i-1)} = \binom{n}{3}\left(\frac{3}{n}\right)^4 2^{-2} + \sum_{i=4}^{c\log n} \binom{n}{i}\left(\frac{i}{n}\right)^{2(i-1)} 2^{-(i-1)}$$

$$+ \sum_{i=c\log n+1}^{(1+\epsilon)\frac{n}{2}} \binom{n}{i}\left(\frac{i}{n}\right)^{2(i-1)} 2^{-(i-1)} \le \frac{27}{8n} + S_1 + S_2$$

where

$$S_1 \le \sum_{i=4}^{c\log n} \left(\frac{ne}{i}\right)^i \left(\frac{i}{n}\right)^{2i-2} = \sum_{i=4}^{c\log n} e^i \left(\frac{i}{n}\right)^{i-2} \le \sum_{i=4}^{c\log n} e^i \left(\frac{c\log n}{n}\right)^{i-2} \le$$

$$\le \frac{(\frac{c\log n}{n})^2 e^4}{1 - \frac{ec\log n}{n}} = \frac{1}{n} \cdot \frac{(c\log n)^2 e^4}{n(1 - \frac{ec\log n}{n})}$$

and

$$S_2 \le \sum_{i=c\log n+1}^{(1+\epsilon)\frac{n}{2}} e^i \left(\frac{i}{n}\right)^{i-2} 2^{-(i-1)} \le \sum_{i=c\log n+1}^{(1+\epsilon)\frac{n}{2}} \frac{e^i(\frac{1+\epsilon}{2})^{i-2}}{2^{i-1}} \le \frac{\frac{e^2}{2}(\frac{e(1+\epsilon)}{4})^{c\log n-1}}{1 - \frac{e(1+\epsilon)}{4}}$$

For $e(1+\epsilon) < 4$ and c large enough it is possible to find d_3 such that $e^{-\frac{\epsilon^2}{3}\frac{n}{2}} + \frac{27}{8n} + S_1 + S_2 < \frac{d_3}{n}$.

Lemma 2. *There exist constants β and d_2 such that for a randomly chosen automaton a with n states the probability of $|\mathcal{R}(a)| < \beta n$ is less that $\frac{d_2}{n}$.*

Proof. The probability that less than βn states are reachable is bounded by the probability of existence of some set of states containing state 1 with cardinality less than βn such that all edges starting from this set also ends in this set. This may be bounded by

$$\sum_{i=1}^{\beta n-2} \binom{n}{i-1}\left(\frac{i}{n}\right)^{2i} \le \sum_{i=1}^{\beta n-2} \left(\frac{ne}{i-1}\right)^{i-1}\left(\frac{i}{n}\right)^{2i} = \sum_{i=1}^{\beta n-2} \left(\frac{i}{i-1}\right)^{i-1} \frac{i^{i+1}e^{i-1}}{n^{i+1}} \le$$

$$\le \sum_{i=1}^{\beta n-2} \frac{i^{i+1}}{n^{i+1}} e^i \le \sum_{i=1}^{c\log n} \left(\frac{c\log n}{n}\right)^{i+1} e^i + \sum_{i=c\log n+1}^{\beta n-2} \left(\frac{\beta n}{n}\right)^{i+1} e^i \le$$

$$\le \frac{(\frac{c\log n}{n})^2 e}{1 - \frac{c\log n}{n}e} + \frac{\beta^{c\log n+2} e^{c\log n+1}}{1 - \beta e}$$

By setting $\beta = \frac{1}{2e}$ we may bound this by

$$\frac{1}{n} \cdot \frac{e(c\log n)^2}{n(1 - \frac{ce\log n}{n})} + \frac{1}{e} \cdot \frac{1}{2^{c\log n}} < \frac{d_2}{n}$$

for some c and d_2.

Lemma 3. *There are at most $2^{O(m^2 \log m)}$ different languages recognizable by all discrete neural networks with m neurons.*

Proof. There exist at most m^2 connections and m thresholds in neural network with m neurons. The number of values of a given weight is bounded by $2m^z + 1$ for some constant z. Moreover there are only 2^m different initial states. Hence the number of different neural networks is $2^m(2m^z + 1)^{m^2+m} = 2^{O(m^2 \log m)}$. The number of different languages recognized by those networks cannot be greater.

Theorem 4. *There exist constants b and d such that for any set $A \subset A_n$ if any automata from A may be simulated by a discrete neural network of size less than $bn^{\frac{1}{2}}$ then $\mathcal{P}(A) < \frac{d}{n}$.*

Proof. . From Lemma 3 it is sufficient to show that there exist constants b_2 and d such that for any $A \subset A_n$ if $|\mathcal{L}(A)| < 2^{b_2 n \log n}$ then $\mathcal{P}(A) < \frac{d}{n}$ (or equivalently, if $\mathcal{P}(A) \geq \frac{d}{n}$ then $|\mathcal{L}(A)| \geq 2^{b_2 n \log n}$).

Let B denote the set of automata $a \in A_n$ such that $|\mathcal{R}(a)| < \beta n$ and C the set of ≥ 3 -minimal automata from A_n. From the Lemmas 1 and 2 it follows that $\mathcal{P}(B) < \frac{d_2}{n}$ and $\mathcal{P}(C) < \frac{d_3}{n}$. Hence $\mathcal{P}(A - B - C) > \frac{d-d_2-d_3}{n} = \frac{d_1}{n}$.

Let A_{REACH} be the set of automata obtained by eliminating unreachable states in automata from $A - B - C$ and numbering their states by consecutive numbers. Of course, all automata from A_{REACH} are $\leq$ 2-minimal. Then, for some n_1 such that $\beta n \leq n_1 \leq n$, $P_{n_1}(A_{REACH} \cap A_{n_1}) > \frac{d_1}{n}$. Let $A' = A_{REACH} \cap A_{n_1}$. It is easy to see that for one minimal automaton a' with $n_2 < n_1$ states the number of 2-minimal automata a with n_1 states such that the minimization of a results in a' is bounded by (the number of choosing n_2 numbers from $\{1 \dots n_1\}$ which labels the states of a' in a) times (the number of possible assigments of remaining $n_1 - n_2$ states of a) times (the number of possible destinations of edges due to addition of new states). This may be bounded by

$$\binom{n_1}{n_2} n_1^{n_1-n_2} 2^{2n_1} \leq 2^{3n_1} n_1^{\frac{n_1}{2}}$$

because $n_2 \geq \frac{n_1}{2}$. Hence if A_M denotes the set of automata obtained by minimization of automata from A', then

$$|A_M| \geq \frac{|A'|}{2^{3n_1} n_1^{\frac{n_1}{2}}}$$

Moreover for every automaton from A_M there exist no more than $n_1!$ automata isomorphic to it. Hence if A_U denotes the maximal subset of A_M not containing any pair of isomorphic automata, then

$$|A_U| \geq \frac{|A'|}{2^{3n_1} n_1^{\frac{n_1}{2}} n_1!} \geq \frac{d_1 2^{n_1} n_1^{2n_1}}{n 2^{3n_1} n_1^{\frac{n_1}{2}} n_1!} \geq \frac{d_1 n_1^{\frac{n_1}{2}}}{n 2^{2n_1}} \geq 2^{b_2 n \log n}$$

for some b_2. This completes the proof, since different automata from A_U recognize different languages.

Concerning Lemma 3, one can show also the corresponding lower bound, i.e. that there are $2^{\Omega(m^2 \log m)}$ different languages recognizable by neural networks of size m. This will be proved in the full version of this paper.

4 Upper bound for discrete networks

In this section we show $O(n^{\frac{1}{2}})$ upper bound for the number of neurons such that any n-state finite automaton may be simulated by a network of this size. This is an improvement of the bound from [1].

Theorem 5. *Every n-state automaton may be simulated by a neural network with $O(n^{\frac{1}{2}})$ units.*

Proof. First notice that by using one neuron it is possible to compute functions AND and OR (denoted as $\wedge$ and $\vee$) of many literals, each of them possibly a negation of the input. We assume the existence of one input unit u_{inp}. We also assume for simplicity that $n = r^4$, for some natural number r.

Let π be a permutation of the set $\{1 \ldots n\}$. Let assign a quadruple (l_1, l_2, l_3, l_4) to each state i, due to the formula $F_4(i) = (l_1, l_2, l_3, l_4)$, where $l_j = \lfloor \frac{\pi(i)}{r^{j-1}} \rfloor \mod r$, for $j = 1 \ldots 4$. The idea is that each state corresponds to a point in 4-dimensional cube with side length r. Moreover, let us denote by $(l, *, *, *)$ the set of all (l_1, l_2, l_3, l_4) such that $l_1 = l$. Take $4r$ units denoted as u_l^j, for $j = 1 \ldots 4$ and $l = 0 \ldots r - 1$. At any time and for any j, exactly one of u_l^j is set to 1, the others to 0. When $u_{l_1}^1, u_{l_2}^2, u_{l_3}^3, u_{l_4}^4$ are set to 1, the simulated automaton is in the state corresponding to (l_1, l_2, l_3, l_4). Now for each unit u_l^j we build a network which takes all u_l^j-s and u_{inp} as inputs, and computes the new value of u_l^j. For simplicity, assume $j = 1$ and $l = 0$. For the purpose of computing a new value for u_0^1 it is sufficient to create two networks with neurons u_b for $b = 0, 1$ such that u_b is set to 1 iff there is an edge labeled with b from the state $F_4^{-1}(l_1, l_2, l_3, l_4)$ to any state from $F_4^{-1}(0, *, *, *)$ (formally $(l_1, l_2, l_3, l_4) \in F_4(\delta_b^{-1}(F_4^{-1}(0, *, *, *)))$). Then, having two such networks, for $b = 0$ and $b = 1$, we may compute $u_0^1 = (u_0 \wedge \neg u_{inp}) \vee (u_1 \wedge u_{inp})$.

Now we show how to build the needed network for the set A defined as $F_4(\delta_0^{-1}(F_4^{-1}(0, *, *, *)))$ First, we transform quadruples into pairs, i.e create the units v_k^j for $j = 1, 2$ and $k = 0 \ldots r^2 - 1$ which compute the function $v_{rl_1 + l_2}^j = u_{l_1}^{2j-1} \wedge u_{l_2}^{2j}$. Let F_2 denote the function that transforms (l_1, l_2, l_3, l_4) into $(rl_1 + l_2, rl_3 + l_4)$. Let $(*, k)$ be the set of all pairs (k_1, k_2) such that $k_2 = k$. Let c be the minimal value such that for every k the inequality $|F_2(A) \cap (*, k)| \leq c$ holds. For simplicity, assume that $|F_2(A) \cap (*, k)| = c$ for every k. Let $f_i, i = 1 \ldots c$ be the functions such that $(f_i(k), k) \in F_2(A)$ and $f_i(k) \neq f_{i'}(k)$ for every k and $i \neq i'$. For each f_i we build a network as follows (see [1]). Assume that $f_i(k)$ is non-decreasing (otherwise we may permute the edges leading from the units v_k^j in the construction given below). Split the domain of f_i into consecutive intervals such that the value of f_i is different for each interval and constant on each interval. Let k belong to the j-th interval. Then set $w_k = j$ and $w'_{f(k)} = r^2 - j + 1$. The

w'_p-s not defined in this way are set to 0. It is easy to see that for any k_1, k_2, the equality $k_1 = f_i(k_2)$ holds iff $w_{k_2} + w'_{k_1} = r^2 + 1$. It is easy to build a 3-node network that tests this equality. By OR-ing the networks constructed for each f_i-s we obtain the network for A.

The efficiency of the construction depends on the value c. We may bound it using the following lemma :

Lemma 6. *Let π be a permutation randomly chosen from the set of all $n!$ permutations of $\{1\ldots n\}$. Then, for any k and with the probability at least $1 - \frac{d}{n}$, the following inequality holds*

$$|F_2(A) \cap (*,k)| \leq \max(\beta \frac{|F_2(A)|}{r^2}, \beta \log n)$$

for some d and β.

Proof. (Sketch). We may assume, that random π is obtained by choosing F_4 at random in the following way. First, we choose randomly the set $F_4^{-1}(0,*,*,*)$. In this way we fix A. Split A into $A' = A \cap (0,*,*,*)$ and $A'' = A - A'$. By placing states from $F_4^{-1}(0,*,*,*)$ (respectively from $F_4^{-1}((*,*,*,*) - (0,*,*,*))$) on the random positions in $(0,*,*,*)$ (respectively in $(*,*,*,*) - (0,*,*,*)$) we obtain random π. Consider A' (for A'' we proceed in the same way). Set $S = F_4^{-1}(0,*,*,*)$, $L = F_4^{-1}(A')$ and $Z = F_4^{-1}((0,*,*,*) \cap F_2^{-1}(*,k))$. The sets S and L are fixed, and Z is chosen randomly from S. The probability that $Y = |Z \cap L| = |F_4^{-1}(A') \cap F_4^{-1}((0,*,*,*) \cap F_2^{-1}(*,k))| = |A' \cap F_2^{-1}(*,k)| = |F_2(A') \cap (*,k)|$ is greater or equal to y is less than the probability that in Z trials, each with the $\frac{|L|}{|S|-|Z|}$ chance of success, the number of successes Y' is greater or equal to y. The latter probability may be bounded using Chernoff bound, with

$$EY' = \frac{|L|}{|S| - |Z|}|Z| = \frac{|F_4^{-1}(A')|}{r^3 - r}r = \frac{|F_2(A')|}{r^2 - 1}$$

By summing up the probabilities we obtain that the probability of choosing π which satisfies the thesis of Lemma 6 for all k,j,l,b is at least $1 - \frac{8dn^{\frac{3}{4}}}{n}$, which means that such a permutation exists.

The construction given above enables the network to change the simulated state according to the transition function. Let $F_4(1) = (l_1, l_2, l_3, l_4)$. By setting $u^1_{l_1}, u^2_{l_2}, u^3_{l_3}, u^4_{l_4}$ to 1 in the beginning of the computations we obtain that the network is always in the state corresponding to the proper state of the simulated automaton. As the network for state transition goes from state to state in 5 steps, it is sufficient to set u_{signal} unit to 1 every 5 steps. This may be easily performed by a 5-node cyclically joint network.

The only point left is to build a network which computes the proper value of the output unit. It may be constructed using units v^j_k as inputs, again for the cases $b = 0$ and $b = 1$ depending on the input. Let the unit x_k compute the function $x_k = v^1_k \wedge (v^2_{k_1} \vee v^2_{k_2} \ldots)$ for all k_i such that the state corresponding to (k, k_i) has the output edge labeled by b leading to the accepting state. Then it is sufficient to OR all x_k-s and compare b with the input, in order to compute the value of the output unit.

This completes the description of the construction. Now consider its size. The number of the v_k^j-s is $O(n^{\frac{1}{2}})$ and this part is the same for all the networks designed for A-s. Let A_{ljb} denote the set A for specific l,j and b, and let $p_{ljb} = |F_2(A_{ljb})|$. Then the number of units in networks for A-s is proportional to the sum

$$\sum_{b=0}^{1}\sum_{j=1}^{4}\sum_{l=0}^{n^{\frac{1}{4}}-1} \max(\beta\frac{p_{ljb}}{r^2}, \beta\log n) \leq \sum_{b=0}^{1}\sum_{j=1}^{4}\sum_{l=0}^{n^{\frac{1}{4}}-1} \beta\frac{p_{ljb}}{r^2} + 8\sum_{l=0}^{n^{\frac{1}{4}}-1} \beta\log n =$$

$$= 8\beta\left(\frac{n}{n^{\frac{1}{2}}} + n^{\frac{1}{4}}\log n\right) = O(n^{\frac{1}{2}})$$

as for each j and b the sum $\sum_{l=0}^{n^{\frac{1}{4}}-1} p_{ljb}$ is equal to n. The size of the network computing the output is $O(n^{\frac{1}{2}})$. Hence the whole network has the size $O(n^{\frac{1}{2}})$.

5   Analog networks

In this section we show how to build a 15-neuron network that simulates a given finite automaton. Then we show how to extend this simulation to obtain a 25-neuron network simulating any 2-counter machine and hence (see [6]) simulating any Turing machine. The main idea of both constructions is to put all the information about transition function in one rational number. To simulate the step of the automaton, the network reviews the information stored in that number and changes its state according to the information found.

5.1   Simulation of finite automata

We prove the following theorem :

Theorem 7. *For every finite automaton* $a = (\delta, F)$ *with* n *states there exists a 15-unit neural network simulating* a.

Proof. The neural network is defined as on the Figure 1, where $B = 4n + 10$, the *state weight* is equal to

$$w_s = \sum_{q\in\{1...n\},b\in\{0,1\}} \frac{2\delta(q,b)+2}{(2n+5)^{2q+b-1}}$$

and the *output weight* is equal to

$$w_o = \sum_{q\in\{1...n\},b\in\{0,1\}} \frac{2(|\{\delta(q,b)\}\cap F|)+1}{4^{2q+b-1}}$$

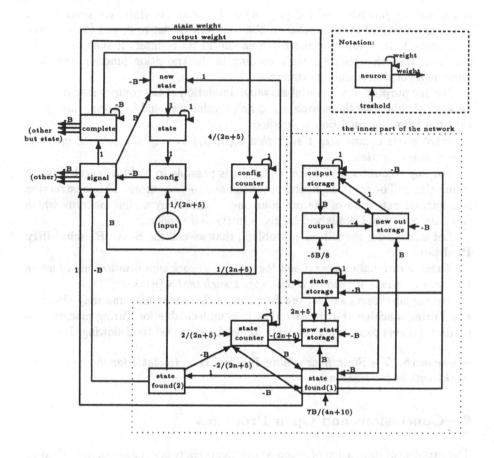

Fig. 1. The neural network simulating finite automata

The initial state of the network is defined as follows : the *config counter* and the *state* are set to $\frac{4}{2n+5}$, the *state storage* is set to w_s, the *output storage* is set to w_o, other units are set to 0.

The correctness of this construction will be proved in the full version of this paper.

5.2 Simulation of the 2-counter machine

First, we recall the definition of the automaton with counters. A k-counter machine with n states is a pair (δ, f), where

$$\delta : \{empty, nonempty\}^k \times \{1 \ldots n\} \to \{+, -\}^k \times \{1 \ldots n\}$$

is a *transition function* and $f \in \{1 \ldots n\}$ is the *accepting state*. We assume that in the beginning of the computation the counters are set to 0, and the machine is in state 1. In every step the machine checks its counters if they are set to 0 or not, then changes its state according to the transition function and then increments or decrements its counters.

For the purpose of the neural-network simulation of the counter machine, the network should have the neuron u_{state} and a value v should be prespecified such that the following condition is satisfied:

there exists a time step t such that $s_t(u_{state}) = v$ iff the counter machine ever reaches the state f.

For any k-counter machine $a = (\delta, f)$ it is possible to build a neural network simulating a. The resulting neural network has $11 + 7k$ neurons. The construction is a natural extension of the previous one, obtained by adding neurons which simulate counters. Details will be given in the full version.

Let us consider the following problem, that we call the **State Reachability Problem**:

Given a rational number v and the neural network with n units, one of which is a unit u, decide if there is a time step t such that $s_t(u) = v$

By the discussion above, the fact that a 2-counter machine may simulate any Turing machine and the fact that it is undecidable for Turing machines to predict if it ever reaches a given state [6], we have proved the following theorem :

Theorem 8. *The State Reachability Problem is undecidable for the neural networks with at least 25 units.*

6 Conclusions and Open Problems

The problem of simulation of automata by neural networks has been investigated. For discrete networks with polynomially bounded weights, provably optimal upper and lower bounds were given. In the case of analog networks, we gave a 15-neuron upper bound and applied this result to prove that the behavior of a 25-neuron network is undecidable.

Our research still leaves many interesting questions open. The most natural is to ask if the upper bound may be improved for the neural networks with unbounded weights. Or oppositely, does there exist any other natural subclasses of neural networks for which optimal results may be shown?

In the proof of the lower bound we investigated several properties of the random automata. It would be interesting to investigate other properties of random automata as well as the properties of random neural networks. For example, it is easy to see that some neural networks with m neurons simulate a 2^m-state minimal finite automata. Can one show that this behavior is typical (i.e. with high probability holds for a randomly chosen neural network)? Or maybe the typical neural network simulates a polynomial size automaton?

Other open problems are related to the analog case. How many units must the network have in order to simulate any finite automaton or to be undecidable?

In both cases it is easy to show the lower bound $n \geq 2$. May this simple bound be improved?

The construction from the Section 5 has the nonconstant delay between two consecutive time steps when u_{signal} is set to 1. It may even reach $O(n^2)$ time steps. Can the duration of the delay be reduced? We conjecture that for any possible simulation one may find a family of finite automata which cannot be simulated in constant time. There may even exist a tradeoff between the time of simulation and the number of neurons.

Acknowledgment: I would like to thank Bogdan Chlebus for his comments on the preliminary version of this paper and to the referees for their remarks.

References

1. N. Alon, A.K. Dewdney, T.J. Ott, Efficient simulation of finite automata by neural nets, Journal of ACM, vol. 38 (1991), 495-514.
2. M. Cosnard, M. Garzon, P. Koiran, Computability properties of low-dimensional dynamical systems, Proc. 10th Symp. on Theoretical Aspects of Computer Science (1993), LNCS 665, 365-373.
3. J. Hertz, A. Krogh, R. G. Palmer, Introduction to the theory of Neural Computation, Addison Wesley, Redwood City, CA (1991).
4. A. Hajnal, W. Maass, P. Pudlak, M. Szegedy anf G. Turan, Threshold circuits of bounded depth, Proc. 28th Annual IEEE Symp. on Foundations of Computer Science (1987), 99-110.
5. T. Hagerup and Ch. Rüb, A guided tour of Chernoff bounds, Inf. Proc. Letters 33 (1989/90), 305-308.
6. J. E. Hopcroft, J. D. Ullman, Introduction to automata theory, languages and computation, Addison-Wesley (1979).
7. Y. Kamp, M. Hasler, Recursive neural networks for Associative Memory, John Wiley & Sons, Chichester (1990).
8. W. Maass, Bounds for the computational power and learning complexity of analog neural nets, Proc. 25th ACM symposium on Theory of Computing (1993), 335-344.
9. M. C. Mozer, Neural net architecture for temporal sequence processing (1993), to appear in A. Weigend, N. Gershenfeld (eds.), Predicting the future and understanding the past, Addison Wesley, Redwood City, CA.
10. A. Macintyre, E. D. Sontag, Finiteness results for Sigmoidal "Neural" Networks, Proc. 25th ACM Symp. on Theory of Computing (1993), 325-334.
11. W. Maass, G. Schnitger, E.D. Sontag, On the computational power of sigmoid versus boolean threshold circuits, Proc. 32nd Annual IEEE Symp. on Foundation of Computer Science (1991), 767-776.
12. P. Orponen, On the computational power of discrete Hopfield nets, Proc. 20th International Colloquium on Automata, Languages and Programming (1993).
13. P. Orponen, Neural Networks and Complexity Theory, Proc. 17th Symp. on Mathemathical Foundations of Computer Science (1992), 50-61.
14. I. Parberry, A primer on the complexity theory of neural networks, In :Formal techniques in artificial intelligence :A sourcebook (ed. R. B. Banerji), Elsevier - North-Holland, Amsterdam (1990), 217-268.
15. H.T. Siegelmann, E. D. Sontag, On the computational power of neural nets, Proc. Fifth ACM Workshop on Computational Learning Theory (1992), 440-449.

Concurrent Process Equivalences:
Some Decision Problems
(Invited Talk)

Albert R. Meyer

Hitachi America Professor of Engineering
MIT Lab. for Computer Science

Abstract. My favorite example of a simple, "interesting" identity between regular expressions is

$$(X^*.Y^*)^* = (X + Y)^*$$

This identity is true for ALL formal languages X, Y. An easy "folk" theorem shows that this can be verified by instantiating the language variables X, Y as single letters a,b and verifying that $(a^*.b^*)^* = (a + b)^*$. Checking this second, variable-free, identity is a routine matter of checking equivalence of finite automata.

In the "algebraic" approach to concurrent process theory pioneered by Milner and Hoare, the original Kleene operators of language union, concatenation and star are enriched with various renaming and parallel combination operators. The simplest of these is the NONcommunicating parallel connective, $\|$, corresponding to the shuffle or merge product of languages. Even this operator creates some interesting complications: the "interleaving identity"

$$a\|b = a.b + b.a$$

is certainly true for single letters a,b, but the version with language variables

$$X\|Y = X.Y + Y.X$$

is not true for all X,Y (let $X = a$, $Y = bc$).

In this talk, I survey some of the results and open problems concerning language identities motivated by concurrent process theory. For example, Rabinovitch and I have shown that the validity problem for regular identities with shuffle is exponential space complete.

Optimal Lower Bounds on the
Multiparty Communication Complexity*

Pavol Ďuriš[1] and José D. P. Rolim[2]

[1] Department of Computer Science, Comenius University, Mlynská dolina, 842 15
Bratislava, Slovakia, duris@dcs.fmph.uniba.sk
[2] Centre Universitaire d'Informatique, Université de Genève, 24 rue Général Dufour,
CH 1211 Genève 4, Switzerland, rolim@cui.unige.ch

Abstract. In this paper, we derive optimal lower and upper bounds on
the multiparty communication complexity of boolean functions. We generalize the two-party method based on a crossing sequence argument
introduced in [Y79] for the multiparty communication model. Lower
bounds for the multiparty model have been a challenge since [DF89],
where only the an upper bound on the number of bits exchanged by a
deterministic algorithm computing a boolean function $f(x_1, \ldots, x_n)$ was
derived; namely of the order $(k_0 C_0)(k_1 C_1)^2$, up to logarithmic factors,
where k_1 and C_1 are the number of processors accessed and the bits exchanged in a nondeterministic algorithm for f, and k_0 and C_0 are the
analogous parameters for the complementary function $1 - f$.
In our paper, we show that $C_0 \leq n(1 + 2^{C_1})$ and $D \leq n(1 + 2^{C_1})$,
where D is the number of bits exchanged by a deterministic algorithm
computing f. We investigate also the power of a restricted multiparty
communication model in which the coordinator is allowed to send at
most one message to each party. We show that all the upper and lower
bounds are optimal.

1 Introduction

In the two-party communication model, each of two processors has a part (half)
of the input, and the goal is to compute a given boolean function on the input
minimizing the amount of communication. The multiparty model generalizes
the two-party model in such a way that the input $(x_1, \ldots, x_n)$ is distributed
among n processors (parties), where party i knows x_i and the goal is the same:
to compute a given boolean function $f(x_1, \ldots, x_n)$ on the input minimizing the
total amount of communication. It is assumed that there is a coordinator that
is allowed to communicate to each party, but the parties are not allowed to
communicate (directly) among them.

The study of two-party communication was inspired by VLSI complexity.
The relative power of determinism, nondeterminism and randomization were

* This work was supported in part by the Swiss National Science Foundation grant
number 20-40354-94

the main studied issues [AUY83, DGS87, F87, MS82, PS82, Y79]. Two-party communication with limited number of exchanged messages have been studied in [DGS87, PS82].

Our paper was motivated by a challenge stated in [DF89] to obtain lower bounds for the multiparty model. For two-party communication, Yao [Y79] has introduced a method based on a crossing sequence argument (or on a fooling set argument) to bound the amount of information that needs to be exchanged. We generalize the Yao's method for multiparty communication model as follows. A fooling set for party i is any subset M of inputs such that for each $x = (x_1, \ldots, x_i, \ldots, x_n)$ in the subset M of inputs there exists $x'_i \neq x_i$ such that $x' = (x_1, \ldots, x_{i-1}, x'_i, x_{i+1}, \ldots, x_n)$ belongs to M but $f(x') \neq f(x)$. Given function f we will try to find a (as big as possible) subset Y of inputs and a (as small as possible) number d_i for each party i such that each subset M of Y with cardinality exceeding d_i is a fooling set for party i. Then, knowing the numbers d_i's and a lower bound on the cardinality of Y, we will be able (using a counting argument) to establish a lower bound on the total amount of information that needs to be communicate to compute f. Note that our method is suitable for the deterministic as well as for the nondeterministic communication model, and also to bound the amount of information that needs to be exchanged between the coordinator and a particular party i.

In our paper we use the generalized proof method to derive (roughly) optimal lower and upper bounds on the multiparty communication complexity of some simple particular boolean functions. Dolev and Feder [DF89] have derived an upper bound on the number of bits exchanged by a deterministic algorithm computing a boolean function $f(x_1, \ldots, x_n)$ of the order $(k_0 C_0)(k_1 C_1)^2$, up to logarithmic factors, where k_1 and C_1 are the number of processors accessed and the bits exchanged in a nondeterministic algorithm for f, and k_0 and C_0 are the analogous parameters for the complementary function $1 - f$. (Note that for the two-party communication model (i.e. for $n = 2$), the corresponding upper bound is at most $O(C_0 C_1)$, see for example [AUY83].) In our paper we show that $C_0 \leq n(1 + 2^{C_1})$ and $D \leq n(1 + 2^{C_1})$, where D is the number of bits exchanged by a deterministic algorithm computing f. Finally we investigate also power of a restricted multiparty communication model in which the coordinator is allowed to send at most one message to each party, and we present some other results. We will see that all the upper and the lower bounds are (roughly) optimal.

2 Definitions

To state our result more precisely, we first give several definitions. Let ϵ be the empty string and let $w = w_1 \$ w_2 \$ \ldots \$ w_l$, $l \geq 1$, $w_i \in \{0,1\}^+$ for every i. We define: $h(\epsilon) = \epsilon$ and $h(w) = w_1 w_2 \ldots w_l$. Let $r = (r_1, r_2, \ldots, r_t)$, $t \geq 1$, where ether $r_i = r_i^1 \$ r_i^2 \$ \ldots \$ r_i^{j_i}$, $r_{j_i}^l \in \{0,1\}^+$, $j_i \geq 1$, or $r_i = \epsilon$. We define: $h(r) = h(r_1) h(r_2) \ldots h(r_t)$. We denote the length of a string w (the cardinality of a set S) by $|w|$ (by $|S|$).

Suppose a coordinator wishes to evaluate a function $f(x_1, x_2, \ldots, x_n)$. The input vector $x = (x_1, x_2, \ldots, x_n)$ is distributed among n parties, with x_i is known only to party i, where x_i is chosen from $\{0,1\}^m$ for every i. Suppose there is a nondeterministic algorithm $\mathcal{N}$ that accepts the language defined by f (when the value of f is 1). (In such a case we will say that $\mathcal{N}$ computes f). Generally, the computation of $\mathcal{N}$ consists of several phases, where one phase is as follows: The coordinator sends some messages (nonempty binary strings) to some parties (not necessary to all parties) and then, each party that got a message, sends a message back to the coordinator. The communication behaviour of $\mathcal{N}$ can be described by a communication vector $s = (s_1, s_2, \ldots, s_n)$, where either $s_i = s_i^1 \$ s_i^2 \$ \ldots \$ s_i^{j_i}$, $j_i \geq 2$, $s_i^l \in \{0,1\}^+$, or $s_i = \epsilon$; s_i is a communication sequence between the coordinator and the party i (if there is no communication then $s_i = \epsilon$). Note that j_i is an even number (each party must response after obtaining any nonempty message), and s_i^{2l-1} [s_i^{2l}] is not necessary the message sent [received] by the coordinator in the phase l (since the coordinator may have sent no message to the party i in some previous phase $k < l$). We will also say "communication sequence on the link i" instead of "communication sequence between the coordinator and the party i".

We require that the nonempty communication sequences on each link are *self-delimiting*, i.e. if $s_i = s_i^1 \$ s_i^2 \$ \ldots \$ s_i^{j_i}$ and $r_i = r_i^1 \$ r_i^2 \$ \ldots \$ r_i^{l_i}$ are any two different nonempty communication sequences on the link i under $\mathcal{N}$, and if $s_i^1 = r_i^1, \ldots, s_i^q = r_i^q$ for some $q \geq 0$, then $q < \min\{j_i, l_i\}$ and s_i^{q+1} is not any proper prefix of r_i^{q+1}, or vice versa. (Note that one can easy show that then $h(s_i) \neq h(r_i)$ and $h(s_i)$ is not any proper prefix of $h(r_i)$, or vice versa.) Each possible run of $\mathcal{N}$ has a corresponding communication vector $s = (s_1, s_2, \ldots, s_n)$. A communication vector is a 1-*certificate* if the algorithm $\mathcal{N}$ accepts the input when the communication with n parties under $\mathcal{N}$ is given by s.

Let $J = \{i_1, i_2, \ldots, i_p\} \subseteq \{1, 2, \ldots, n\}$, and let R be a set of the communication vectors under $\mathcal{N}$. Let $s = (s_1, s_2, \ldots, s_n) \in R$. We denote the p-tuple $(s_{i_1}, s_{i_2}, \ldots, s_{i_p})$ and the sets $\{s/J | s \in R\}$, $\{h(s) | s \in R\}$, and $\{h(s/J) | s \in R\}$ by s/J, R/J, $h(R)$, and $h(R/J)$, respectively. Let S be the set of all 1-certificates under $\mathcal{N}$. By $C(f)$ [by $C(f/J)$] we denote the maximum over all $s \in S$ of $|h(s)|$ [of $|h(s/J)|$] minimized over all the nondeterministic algorithms accepting the language defined by f. By $C_k(f)$ we denote an analogy of $C(f)$ for the nondeterministic algorithms accepting the language defined by f in at most k phases.

One can also define the appropriate terminology for the deterministic algorithm $\mathcal{D}$ accepting the language defined by f. Note that the set S above is in the deterministic case the set of all communication vectors under $\mathcal{D}$. An analogy of $C(f)$, $C(f/J)$, $C_k(f)$ for the deterministic algorithms is denoted by $DC(f)$, $DC(f/J)$, and $DC_k(f)$, respectively.

Let $f(x_1, \ldots, x_n)$ be any boolean function with $x_i \in \{0,1\}^m$ for $1 \leq i \leq n$. Let Y be any nonempty subset of $f^{-1}(1)$. We say that j, $1 \leq j \leq n$, is *important for f with respect to Y*, if for every $y = (y_1, \ldots, y_n) \in Y$ there is $y_j' \in \{0,1\}^m$ such that $f(y_1, \ldots, y_{j-1}, y_j', y_{j+1}, \ldots, y_n) = 0$.

Let $x = (x_1, x_2, \ldots, x_n)$ and $x' = (x_1', x_2', \ldots, x_n')$ be any two input vectors and let J be any nonempty subset of $\{1, 2, \ldots, n\}$. By $[x : x']/J$ we denote the vector $(y_1, y_2, \ldots, y_n)$, where $y_i = x_i$ if $i \in J$ and $y_i = x'_i$ if $i \notin J$.

All the logarithms are of base two through this paper.

3 Results

Our first result (Theorem 1 below) is an useful tool for deriving the lower bounds on the nondeterministic (and hence also on the deterministic) communication complexity of some functions including the lower bounds on the communication complexity on the particular links. We will use Theorem 1 to prove several results below. For example, we will show by using it that nm bits are necessary to communicate (nondeterministically) in order to compute the simple functions f_1, f_2 and f_3 mentioned in Corollary 1 below. On the other hand, one can easy observe that $n(m + 1)$ bits are enough to communicate (even deterministically and in one phase) in order to compute any function $f(x_1, \ldots, x_n)$ with $x_i \in \{0, 1\}^m$ for every i.

Theorem 1. Let $f(x_1, x_2, \ldots, x_n)$ be a boolean function. Let Y be any subset nonempty of $f^{-1}(1)$, let $J_1, J_2, \ldots, J_r$, $r \leq n$, be any nonempty pairwise disjoint subsets of $\{1, 2, \ldots, n\}$, let every $j \in \bigcup_{i=1}^{r} J_i$ be the important index for f with respect to Y, and let $d_1, d_2, \ldots, d_r$ be any integers with $1 \leq d_i \leq |Y|$ for every $i = 1, 2, \ldots, r$. If there is no set $M_i \subseteq Y$ with $|M_i| > d_i$ such that if $x, x' \in M_i$ then $f(x) = f(x') = f([x : x']/J_i) = f([x' : x]/J_i) = 1$, for any i, $1 \leq i \leq r$, then

$$C(f) \geq \sum_{i=1}^{r} \lceil \log(|Y|/d_i) \rceil \text{ and } C(f/J_i) \geq \lceil (\log(|Y|/d_i) \rceil$$

for every $i = 1, 2, \ldots, r$.

Let b be a nonempty string. We denote by $v(b)$ the integer represented by b.

Corollary 1. Let $f_1(x_1, \ldots, x_n) = 1$ iff $x_1 = \cdots = x_n$, $f_2(x_1, \ldots, x_n) = 1$ iff $x_1 \ldots x_{n/2} = x_{n/2+1} \ldots x_n$, and $f_3(x_1, \ldots, x_n) = 1$ iff $v(x_1 \ldots x_{n/2}) \leq v(x_{n/2+1} \ldots x_n)$, where $x_i \in \{0, 1\}^m$ for every $i = 1, 2, \ldots, n$. Then $nm \leq C(f_j)$ for $j = 1, 2, 3$, and $nm - 2 \leq C(1 - f_3)$.

The next Corollary tell us that given numbers $t_1, \ldots, t_n$ (satisfying a simple condition) there is a function f with communication complexity roughly $\sum_i t_i$ and with communication complexity on the i-th link roughly t_i.

Corollary 2. Let $t_1, t_2, \ldots, t_n$, $n \geq 2$, be any positive integers such that $t_l \leq m$, $\sum_{i=1}^{n} t_i$ is an even number, and $2t_l \leq \sum_{i=1}^{n} t_i$ for every $l = 1, 2, \ldots, n$. Then there is a boolean function $f(x_1, x_2, \ldots, x_n)$, where $x_i \in \{0, 1\}^m$ for every i, such that

$C(f) \geq \sum_{i=1}^{n} t_i$, $DC(f) \leq \sum_{i=1}^{n} (t_i + 1)$, $C(f/\{i\}) \geq t_i$ and $DC(f/\{i\}) \leq t_i + 1$ for every $i = 1, 2, \ldots, n$.

It is interesting to see that if a function f is product of k nonconstant functions $f_1, \ldots, f_k$ with different variables then $C(f) = \sum_{i=1}^{n} C(f_i)$, (Theorem 2 below). Unfortunately, we were not able to prove any similar result for the deterministic complexity.

Theorem 2. Let $0 = n_1 < n_2 < \cdots < n_{k+1} = n$, $k \geq 1$, be any integers with $n_i + 2 \leq n_{i+1}$ and let f_i be an $(n_{i+1} - n_i)$-ary boolean function with $C(f_i) > 0$ for $i = 1, 2, \ldots, n$. Let

$$f(x_1, x_2, \ldots, x_n) = \prod_{i=1}^{k} f_i(x_{n_i+1}, x_{n_i+2}, \ldots, x_{n_{i+1}}).$$

Then

$$C(f) = \sum_{i=1}^{k} C(f_i).$$

The following result relates the deterministic and the nondeterministic communication complexity of the functions and their complementary functions.

Theorem 3. Let $f(x_1, \ldots, x_n)$ be any boolean function and let J be any subset nonempty of $\{1, 2, \ldots, n\}$. Then $DC(f/J) = DC((1-f)/J)$, $DC_1(f/J) \leq |J|(1 + 2^{C(f/J)})$ and $C(f/J) \leq |J|(1 + 2^{C((1-f)/J)})$.

To show that the upper bounds of Theorem 3 are not too weak, we state the following Theorem.

Theorem 4. Let $f(x_1, \ldots, x_n) = 1$ iff $x_1 = \cdots = x_n$, where $x_i \in \{0,1\}^m$ for every i. Then (a), (b) and (c) hold.

(a) $nm \leq C(f) \leq n(m+1)$ and $m \leq C(f/\{i\}) \leq m+1$ for $i = 1, 2, \ldots, n$,
(b) $\lfloor \log(m-1) \rfloor \leq C(1-f) \leq 2\lfloor \log m \rfloor + 2$ and
    $\lfloor \log(m-1) \rfloor \leq C((1-f)/\{i\}) \leq \lfloor \log m \rfloor + 1$ for $i = 1, 2, \ldots, n$, and
(c) $nm \leq DC(f) = DC(1-f) \leq n(m+1)$.

We have shown in Corollary 1 that both the functions f_3 and $1 - f_3$ have high (and roughly the same) nondeterministic communication complexity. But this is not true for the function f of Theorem 4. Moreover, $C(1-f)$ does not depend on n and it is close to $C((1-f)/\{i\})$. Since $DC(1-f) \geq nm$ and $C(f) \geq nm$, the gap between $C(1-f)$ and $DC(1-f)$, as well as, between $C(f)$ and $C(1-f)$ may be as big as we wish (choosing n large enough).

The last Theorem is an analogy of the known results for the two-party model relating 1-phase and the multiphase protocols.

Theorem 5. $C_1(f) = C(f)$ and $DC_1(f) \le DC(f)2^{DC(f)+1}$ for each boolean function $f(x_1, \ldots, x_n)$.

Using Theorem 2 of [DGS87] it is easy to see that for every k and infinitely many m with $k \le m/(1000 \log m)$ there is a boolean function $f_{k,m}(x_1, x_2)$ with $x_1, x_2 \in \{0,1\}^m$ such that $DC_{k+1}(f_{k,m}) \le (2 + 40k \log m)$ and $DC_{k-1}(f_{k,m}) \ge m/20k$. Hence the upper bound on $DC_1(f)$ in Theorem 5 must be exponential in $DC(f)$.

4 The proofs

Proof of Theorem 1. Let $\mathcal{N}$ be any nondeterministic algorithm accepting the language defined by f. To prove Theorem 1, we need the following Claim and Lemma.

Claim 1. Let J be any nonempty subset of $\{1, 2, \ldots, n\}$ and let s, s' be any 1-certificates under $\mathcal{N}$ for the inputs x and x', respectively. If $s/J = s'/J$ then $f([x : x']/J) = f(x) = 1 = f(x') = f([x' : x]/J)$.

Proof. Apply a standard crossing sequence argument to the links with indices in J. □

Lemma 1. Let p and q be any two positive integers with $q \le p$ and let $b_1, b_2, \ldots, b_p$ be any sequence of nonempty binary strings such that no element of this sequence occurs in it more than q times. Then $\sum_{i=1}^{p} |b_i| \ge p \log \lceil p/q \rceil$.

Proof. For $i = 1, 2, \ldots, q$, let Q_i be the set containing each element of the sequence $b_1, \ldots, b_p$ that occurs in this sequence at least i times. Hence $\sum_{i=1}^{q} |Q_i| = p$. Let q' be the number of all nonempty Q_i's. For each nonempty set Q_i there is a corresponding binary tree such that the elements of Q_i encode the pathes from a root to the leaves of the tree. Let G be the forest corresponding to the nonempty Q_i's. Let $T(H)$ denote the total sum of the depths of all the leaves of a forest H. Clearly, $T(G) = \sum_{i=1}^{q} \sum_{b \in Q_i} |b| = \sum_{i=1}^{p} |b_i|$, and G has p leaves. Now repeat the following procedure on G as many times as possible. If there is a vertex v with exactly one son then delete it, and if v is not any root then add the edge connecting the son of v with the father of v. After finishing this process, each vertex (excluding the leaves) has exactly two sons. Now repeat an other procedure as many times as possible. Let v_1 and v_2 be any two leaves such that there is no leaf with the depth greater than $depth(v_1)$ or smaller than $depth(v_2)$. Suppose $depth(v_1) \ge depth(v_2) + 2$. (If there are no such v_1 and v_2 we have done.) Let v [v'] be the father [the second son] of v_1. Then delete the edges (v, v_1) and (v, v'), and add the edges (v_2, v_1) and (v_2, v'). One can easy observe that after finishing this process, the resulting forest (denote it by G') has p leaves, consists of q' binary trees, $T(G') \le T(G)$, each vertex of G' (excluding the leaves) has two sons, and there is a nonnegative integer t such that each leaf of G' has the depth either t or $t+1$. Thus $q'2^t \leq p < q'2^{t+1}$ and $T(G') \geq pt$. Hence $\sum_{i=1}^{p} |b_i| = T(G) \geq T(G') \geq pt = p\lceil \log p/q' \rceil \geq p\lceil \log p/q \rceil$, see above. $\square$

Now we are ready to complete the proof of Theorem 1. let $z_1, z_2, \ldots, z_{|Y|}$ be all the inputs from Y and let $s_{z_1}, s_{z_2}, \ldots, s_{z_{|Y|}}$ be the corresponding 1-certificates under $\mathcal{N}$ on these inputs. Fix any k, $1 \leq k \leq r$. Let u denote the sequence $s_{z_1}/J_k, s_{z_2}/J_k, \ldots, s_{z_{|Y|}}/J_k$. Since $\mathcal{N}$ accepts the language defined by f, it follows from the definition of the important index for f with respect to Y above, that there is no 1-certificate under $\mathcal{N}$ for any input with an empty computation on any important index. (Note that 1-certificate with an empty computation on the j-th link is not able to detect any change of the input belonging to the party j and thus there is no y'_j with the desired property, see the definition of the important index.) It means, together with the fact that the computations on each link are self-delimiting, that if s_{z_i}/J_k and s_{z_j}/J_k are different then also the binary strings $h(s_{z_i}/J_k)$ and $h(s_{z_j}/J_k)$ are different. Therefore if no element of the sequence u occurs in it more than d_k times, the same must hold also for the sequence $v = h(s_{z_1}/J_k), \ldots, h(s_{z_{|Y|}}/J_k)$. But, in fact, no element occurs in u more than d_k times; (otherwise the corresponding inputs should form a set M_k with $M_k > d_k$ such that if $x, x' \in M_k$ then $f([x : x']/J_k) = f(x) = 1 = f(x') = f([x' : x]/J_k)$, by Claim 1, but it would contradict an assumption of Theorem 1). Hence we can apply Lemma 1 to the sequence v and we have

$$\sum_{i=1}^{|Y|} |h(s_{z_i}/J_k)| \geq |Y|\lceil \log |Y|/d_k \rceil.$$

Therefore $C(f/J_k) \geq \lceil \log |Y|/d_k \rceil$, since

$$|Y|C(f/J_k) \geq \sum_{i=1}^{|Y|} |h(s_{z_i}/J_k)|.$$

Similarly,

$$|Y|C(f) \geq \sum_{i=1}^{|Y|} |h(s_{z_i})| = \sum_{k=1}^{r} \sum_{i=1}^{|Y|} |h(s_{z_i}/J_k)| \geq \sum_{k=1}^{r} |Y|\lceil \log(|Y|/d_k) \rceil,$$

thus, $C(f) \geq \sum_{k=1}^{r} \lceil \log |Y|/d_k \rceil$. $\square$

Proof of Corollary 1. We set $r = n$, $J_i = \{i\}$, $d_i = 1$ for $i = 1, 2, \ldots, n$, and $Y = \{(x_1, \ldots, x_n)|x_1 = \cdots = x_n\}$ for f_1. By Theorem 1, $C(f_1) \geq nm$. We set $r = 2$, $J_1 = \{1, 2, \ldots, n/2\}$, $J_2 = \{n/2 + 1, n/2 + 2, \ldots, n\}$, $d_1 = d_2 = 1$ and $Y = \{(x_1, \ldots, x_n)|x_1 \ldots x_{n/2} = x_{n/2+1} \ldots x_n\}$ for f_2 and f_3; the values r, J_1, J_2, d_1, d_2 are the same, and $Y = \{(x_1, \ldots, x_n)|v(x_1 \ldots x_{n/2}) = v(x_{n/2+1} \ldots x_n) + 1\}$ for $1 - f_3$. By Theorem 1, $C(f_2) \geq nm$, $C(f_3) \geq nm$ and $C(1 - f_3) \geq nm - 2$. $\square$

Proof of Corollary 2. Since $\sum_{i=1}^{n} t_i$ is an even number and $2t_l \leq \sum_{i=1}^{n} t_i$ for every l, there is an index j such that $t'_j + \sum_{i=1}^{j-1} t_i = t''_j + \sum_{i=j+1}^{n} t_i$, where

$t_j = t'_j + t''_j$, $t'_j, t''_j \geq 0$. Let

$$Y = \{(x_1, \ldots, x_n) | x_i = y_i z_i, \ y_i \in \{0,1\}^{t_i}, \ z_i \in \{0,1\}^{m-t_i} \text{ for every } i,$$
$$y_j = y'_j y''_j, y'_j, y''_j \in \{0,1\}^{t'_j}, y''_j \in \{0,1\}^{t''_j} \text{ and}$$
$$y_1 \ldots y_{j-1} y'_j = y''_j y_{j+1} \ldots y_n\}.$$

Let $f(x_1, \ldots, x_n) = 1$ iff $(x_1, \ldots, x_n) \in Y$. In order to apply Theorem 1, we set $r = n$, $J_i = \{i\}$ and $d_i = |Y|/2^{t_i}$ for $i = 1, 2, \ldots, n$. Now it is enough to show that for each $M_i \subseteq Y$, $1 \leq i \leq n$, such that if $x, x' \in M_i$ then

$$f(x) = f(x') = f([x : x']/\{i\}) = f([x' : x]/\{i\}) = 1,$$

it holds $|M_i| \leq d_i$.

To do so, fix any i and choose any M_i with the property mentioned above. For each $x = (y_1 z_1, \ldots, y_n z_n)$ with $|y_i| = t_i$ and $|z_i| = m - t_i$ for each i, let $y(x)$, $z(x)$ denote the string $y_1 \ldots y_n$, and $z_1 \ldots z_n$, respectively. Choose any two inputs $\bar{x} = (\bar{y}_1 \bar{z}_1, \ldots, \bar{y}_i \bar{z}_i, \ldots, \bar{y}_n \bar{z}_n)$ and $\tilde{x} = (\tilde{y}_1 \tilde{z}_1, \ldots, \tilde{y}_i \tilde{z}_i, \ldots, \tilde{y}_n \tilde{z}_n)$ from M_i. Thus $f([\bar{x} : \tilde{x}]/\{i\}) = 1$. Hence $[\bar{x} : \tilde{x}]/\{i\} \in Y$. It means that the left and the right half of the string $y([\bar{x} : \tilde{x}]/\{i\})$ must be the same (see the definition of Y above). But this property cannot be satisfied if $\tilde{y}_i \neq \bar{y}_i$, since the left and the right half of the string $\bar{y}_1 \ldots \bar{y}_i \ldots \bar{y}_n$ are the same (recall $\bar{x} \in M_i \subseteq Y$), $y([\bar{x} : \tilde{x}]/\{i\}) = \bar{y}_1 \ldots \bar{y}_{i-1} \tilde{y}_i \bar{y}_{i+1} \ldots \bar{y}_n$, and $\tilde{y}_i$ is too short (note that $|\tilde{y}_i| = t_i < (\sum_{p=1}^n t_p)/2 + 1 = |\bar{y}_1 \ldots \bar{y}_i \ldots \bar{y}_n|/2 + 1$, see the assumption of Corollary 2) to overlap the l-th bit of the left and also of the right half of $\bar{y}_1 \ldots \bar{y}_i \ldots \bar{y}_n$ for any l. Therefore all the inputs in M_i must agree on the prefix $\bar{y}_i$ in the entry i.

Now let us bound the cardinality of M_i. Each input $x \in M_i$ is uniquely described by the string $y(x)z(x)$ satisfying the following property. The left and the right half of $y(x)$ must be the same (since x is also in Y), and $y(x) = u\bar{y}_i v$ for some u, v with $|u| = \sum_{p=1}^{i-1} t_p$ (since the inputs in M_i agree on the prefix $\bar{y}_i$ in the entry i). The number of all possible descriptions of the inputs in M_i is at most $2^{|y(x)|/2 - t_i + |z(x)|}$, since $\bar{y}_i$ determines $t_i = |\bar{y}_i|$ bits of $y(x)$, and the left and the right half of $y(x)$ are the same. Hence $|M_i| \leq 2^{|y(x)|/2 - t_i + |z(x)|}$. Now the desired result, $|M_i| \leq |Y|/2^{t_i} = d_i$, follows from the easy observable fact that $|Y| = 2^{|y(x)|/2 + |z(x)|}$.

Thus, by Theorem 1, $C(f) \geq \sum_{i=1}^n t_i$ and $C(f/\{i\}) \geq t_i$ for $i = 1, 2, \ldots, n$. On the other hand, it is easy to see that $DC(f) \leq \sum_{i=1}^n (t_i + 1)$ and $DC(f/\{i\}) \geq t_i + 1$ for $i = 1, 2, \ldots, n$. $\square$

Proof of Theorem 2. Fist we prove the following Lemma.

Lemma 2. Let $f(x_1, \ldots, x_p, \ldots, x_n) = f_1(x_1, \ldots, x_p) \cdot f_2(x_p, \ldots, x_n)$. If $C(f_1) > 0$ and $C(f_2) > 0$ then $C(f) = C(f_1) + C(f_2)$.

Proof. Let $\mathcal{N}$ be any nondeterministic algorithm accepting the language defined by f with the complexity $C(f)$. For every input $y \in f_1^{-1}(1) \times f_2^{-1}(1)$ choose any 1-certificate under $\mathcal{N}$ and denote it by s_y. Note that $f_1^{-1}(1) \neq \emptyset$ and $f_2^{-1}(1) \neq \emptyset$, since $C(f_1) > 0$ and $C(f_2) > 0$. Let $f_1^{-1}(1) = \{u_1, \ldots, u_t\}$ for some t. The inequality $C(f) \leq C(f_1) + C(f_2)$ is obvious. To prove the symmetric inequality it is enough to show that there is $y \in f_1^{-1}(1) \times f_2^{-1}(1)$ such that $|s_y/J_1| \geq C(f_1)$ and $|s_y/J_2| \geq C(f_2)$, where $J_1 = \{1, \ldots, p\}$ and $J_2 = \{p+1, \ldots, n\}$. It is easy to see that for every $i = 1, 2, \ldots, t$ there is an input $v_i \in \{u_i\} \times f_2^{-1}(1)$ such that $|s_{v_i}/J_2| \geq C(f_2)$, because otherwise there would be $i, 1 \leq i \leq t$, such that the set $f_2^{-1}(1)$ would be accepted by the 1-certificates s_y/J_2, $y \in \{u_i\} \times f_2^{-1}(1)$, which would be shorter than $C(f_2)$, a contradiction. Therefore there is an input v_j such that $|s_{v_j}/J_1| \geq C(f_1)$, because otherwise the set $f_1^{-1}(1)$ would be accepted by the 1-certificates s_{v_i}/J_1, $i = 1, 2, \ldots, t$, which would be shorter than $C(f_1)$, a contradiction. This completes the proof of Lemma 2. $\square$

Now one can show by induction on i that $C(f) = \sum_{i=1}^{n} C(f_i)$. $\square$

Proof of Theorem 3. The equality $DC(f/J) = DC((1 - f)/J)$ is obvious.

Now let us prove that $DC_1(f/J) \leq |J|(1 + 2^{C(f/J)})$. Let $\mathcal{N}$ be any nondeterministic algorithm accepting the language defined by f with the complexity $C(f/J)$ on the links with indices in J. Let d_i, $i = 1, 2, \ldots, n$, denote the number of all different nonempty communications on the link i counted over all the different 1-certificates under $\mathcal{N}$. One can easy observe that $d_i \leq 2^{C(f/J)}$ for each $i \in J$, since the nonempty communications on each link are self-delimiting, and $|h(s/\{i\})| \leq |h(s/J)| \leq C(f(/J)$ for each 1-certificate s under $\mathcal{N}$ and for each $i \in J$. Our 1-phase deterministic algorithm simulates $\mathcal{N}$ as follows. Let the party i own an input x_i, $i = 1, 2, \ldots, n$. The coordinator sends one bit (say 1) to each party i with $d_i > 0$ and it sends nothing to the other parties. Then each party i with $d_i > 0$ responds a binary string of length d_i of which the j-th bit is 1 iff the j-th nonempty communication on the link i may be an accepting one from the point of view of the party i with respect to x_i. Then the coordinator has enough information to decide whether to accept the input or not.

The first two results of Theorem 3 yield that $C(f/J) \leq DC(f/J) = DC((1 - f)/J) \leq DC^1((1 - f)/J) \leq |J|(1 + 2^{C((1-f)/J)})$. $\square$

Proof of Theorem 4. All the upper bounds are obvious. By Corollary 1, $nm \leq C(f)$, and thus, by Theorem 3, $nm \leq C(f) \leq DC(f) = DC(1 - f)$. One can easy observe using Theorem 1 that $m \leq C(f/\{i\})$. Therefore, by Theorem 3, $\lceil \log(m - 1) \rceil \leq C((1 - f)/\{i\})$. Hence, $\lceil \log(m - 1) \rceil \leq C(1 - f)$, too. $\square$

Proof of Theorem 5. The inequality $C(f) \leq C_1(f)$ is obvious. Let f be any boolean function and let $\mathcal{N}$ be any nondeterministic algorithm accepting the language defined by f. We can simulate $\mathcal{N}$ by an 1-phase nondeterministic algorithm as follows. The coordinator sends the same messages that it may send in the first phase under $\mathcal{N}$. Let s_i^1 be any such message sent to the party i. Then the party i (owning an input x_i) responds any message z of the form $s_i^2 s_i^3 \ldots s_i^{t_i}$, where $s_i^1 \$ s_i^2 \$ \ldots \$ s_i^{t_i}$ is any possible communication on the link i under $\mathcal{N}$ from the point of view of the party i with respect to x_i. Then the coordinator has enough information to decide whether to accept the input or not. (Note that the coordinator is able to restore the string $s_i^2\$\ldots\$s_i^{t_i}$ from z, because the nonempty communications are self-delimiting on each link.)

To prove the desired inequality for the deterministic algorithms, we need the following Claim.

Claim 2. *Let $\mathcal{D}$ be any deterministic t-phase algorithm. Let $u_{i,j}$ $[v_{i,j}]$ be the message (if there is any) sent [received] by the coordinator at the phase i through the link j under $\mathcal{D}$ on an input $(x_1,\ldots,x_n)$; if there is no such message then $u_{i,j}$ $[v_{i,j}]$ is the empty string ϵ. Let $u'_{i,j}$ $[v'_{i,j}]$ be the analogy of $u_{i,j}$ $[v_{i,j}]$ for an input $(x'_1,\ldots,x'_n)$. Let $y_1 z_1 \ldots y_t z_t = y'_1 z'_1 \ldots y'_t z'_t w$ for some $w \in \{0,1\}^*$, where $y_i = u_{i,1}\ldots u_{i,n}$, $z_i = v_{i,1}\ldots v_{i,n}$, $y'_i = u'_{i,1}\ldots u'_{i,n}$, and $z'_i = v'_{i,1}\ldots v'_{i,n}$, for $i = 1,2,\ldots,t$, $j = 1,2,\ldots,n$. Then $u_{i,j} = u'_{i,j}$ and $v_{i,j} = v'_{i,j}$ for $i = 1,2,\ldots,t$ and $j = 1,2,\ldots,n$.*

Proof of Claim 2. Assume to the contrary that l is the minimum index with $u_{l,j} \neq u'_{l,j}$ or $v_{l,j} \neq v'_{l,j}$ for some j. One can observe (by the minimality of l) that $u_{l,j} = u'_{l,j}$ for $j = 1,2,\ldots,n$, since all the strings $u_{l,j}$ $[u'_{l,j}]$ sent by the coordinator are fully determined only by the strings $u_{i,j}$ and $v_{i,j}$ [only by the strings $u'_{i,j}$ and $v'_{i,j}$] for $i = 1,2,\ldots,l-1$ and $j = 1,2,\ldots,n$. Hence $v_{l,j} \neq v'_{l,j}$ for some j. Let k be minimum index such that $v_{l,k} \neq v'_{l,k}$. Since $u_{l,k} = u'_{l,k}$ (see above), both the strings $u_{l,k}$ and $u'_{l,k}$ are empty or both are nonempty. Suppose $u_{l,k} = u'_{l,k} = \epsilon$. In such a case, the party k cannot respond anything in the phase l (for both the inputs $(x_1,\ldots,x_n)$ and $(x'_1\ldots,x'_n)$) and hence $v_{l,k} = v'_{l,k} = \epsilon$. But it contradicts our assumption $v_{l,k} \neq v'_{l,k}$ above. Therefore both $u_{l,k}$ and $u'_{l,k}$ must be nonempty. In such a case, the party k must respond a nonempty string (for both the inputs $(x_1\ldots,x_n)$ and $(x'_1\ldots,x'_n)$), i.e. both $v_{l,k}$ and $v'_{l,k}$ are nonempty. The equelity $y_1 z_1 \ldots y_n z_n = y'_1 z'_1 \ldots y'_n z'_n$ of Claim 2, the minimality of k and l, and the facts that $v_{l,k}$ and $v'_{l,k}$ are nonempty and different (see above) yield that $v_{l,k}$ is a proper prefix of $v'_{l,k}$ or vice versa. But it contradicts the self-delimiting property of the communications on the link k. This completes the proof of Claim 2. $\square$

Now we are ready to complete the proof of Theorem 5. Let $\mathcal{D}$ be any deterministic algorithm computing f with the complexity $DC(f)$ and let $d_i \geq 0$ be the number of all different nonempty communications on the link i under $\mathcal{D}$. Let $\mathcal{D}'$ be an 1-phase deterministic algorithm simulating $\mathcal{D}$ as follows. For every i with $d_i > 0$, the coordinator sends one bit (say 1) to the party i and then the party i (owning an input x_i) responds a binary string of the length d_i of which the j-th bit is 1 (for $j = 1,2,\ldots,d_i$) iff the j-th computation on the link i may be an accepting one from the point of view of the party i with respect to x_i. If $d_i = 0$ then the coordinator does not send any message to the party i. After obtaining the messages, the coordinator has enough information to decide whether to accept the input or not. By Claim 2, the number of all different nonempty computations under $\mathcal{D}$ is not greater than the number of all binary strings of the length $DC(f)$, i.e. $2^{DC(f)}$. Hence $\sum_{i=1}^{n} d_i \leq DC(f)2^{DC(f)}$, since any d_i cannot exceed the number of all bits exchanged on the link i over all different computations under $\mathcal{D}$, and the number of all bits exchanged over all links over all different computations under $\mathcal{D}$ is at most $DC(f)2^{DC(f)}$ Therefore the number of all bits sent by coordinator to the parties during each computation under $\mathcal{D}'$ is at most $DC(f)2^{DC(f)}$. The desired result follows now from the fact that $\sum_{i=1}^{n} d_i$ is the the total length of all the messages sent by the parties to the coordinator during each computation under $\mathcal{D}'$. $\square$

References

[AUY83] Aho, A., V., Ullman, J., D. and Yanakakis, M., Y.: On notion of information transfer in VLSI. In: *Proc. 15th ACM STOC*, 1983, 133-139.

[DF89] Dolev, D. and Feder, T.: Multiparty communication complexity. In: *Proc. 30th IEEE FOCS*, 1989, 428-433.

[DGS87] Ďuriš, P., Galil, Z. and Schitger, G.: Lower bounds on communication complexity. *Information and Computation*, **73** (1987), 1-22.

[F87] Fürer, M.: The power of randomness in communication complexity. In: *Proc. 19th ACM STOC*, 1987, 178-181.

[MS82] Melhorn, K. and Schmidt, E., M.: Las Vegas is better in VLSI and distributed computing. *Proc. 14th ACM STOC*, 1982, 330-337.

[PS82] Papadimitriou C., H. and Sipser, M.: Communication complexity. In: *Proc. 14th ACM STOC*, 1982, 196-200.

[Y79] Yao, A.: Some complexity questions related to distributive computing. In: *Proc. 11th ACM STOC*, 1979, 209-213.

Simultaneous Messages vs. Communication

László Babai*
Peter G. Kimmel**
Satyanarayana V. Lokam ***

Department of Computer Science
The University of Chicago
1100 East 58th Street
Chicago, Illinois 60637

Abstract. In the multiparty communication game introduced by Chandra, Furst, and Lipton [CFL] (1983), k players wish to evaluate collaboratively a function $f(x_0, \ldots, x_{k-1})$ for which player i sees all inputs except x_i. The players have unlimited computational power. The objective is to minimize the amount of communication.

We consider a restricted version of the multiparty communication game which we call the *simultaneous messages* model. The difference is that in this model, each of the k players simultaneously sends a message to a referee, who sees none of the input. The referee then announces the function value.

We show demonstrate an exponential gap between the Simultaneous Messages and the Communication models for up to $(\log n)^{1-\epsilon}$ players, for any $\epsilon > 0$. The separation is obtained by comparing the respective complexities of the *generalized addressing function*, $\mathrm{GAF}_{n,k}$, in each model. This work is motivated by an approach suggested by the results of Håstad & Goldmann (1991), Yao (1990), and Beigel & Tarui (1991) to separate ACC from complexity classes containing it.

1 Introduction

Chandra, Furst, and Lipton [CFL] introduced the following multiparty communication game: Let f be a boolean function of k arguments, each of fixed length $\leq n$ bits. k parties wish to evaluate collaboratively $f(x_0, \ldots, x_{k-1})$. The ith party knows each input argument except x_i, and each party has unlimited computational power. They share a blackboard, viewed by all parties, where they can exchange messages. The objective is to minimize the number of bits written on the board.

Definition: The *cost* of a protocol is the number of bits written on the board for the worst case input. The *multiparty communication complexity* of f, denoted $C(f)$, is the minimum cost of a protocol computing f.

---

* Email: laci@cs.uchicago.edu. Partially supported by NSF Grant CCR-9014562.
** Email: kimmel@cs.uchicago.edu. Partially supported by an NDSEG fellowship.
*** Email: satya@cs.uchicago.edu.

Fairly strong multiparty communication complexity lower bounds of the form n/c^k were obtained by Babai, Nisan, and Szegedy [BNS] for families of explicit functions. However, it seems that those methods do not extend to logarithmic number of players and beyond.

Håstad and Goldmann [HG] found a curious application of the [BNS] bounds to lower bounds for small depth threshold circuits. Subsequent work by Yao [Y] and Beigel and Tarui [BT] reduces ACC circuits (bounded depth, polynomial size circuits with Boolean and MOD m gates) to small depth circuits similar to those considered by [HG]. These results imply that a super-polylogarithmic lower bound for the communication complexity of a class of explicit functions with super-polylogarithmic number of players would separate ACC from whatever class we take the target functions from.

In fact, this separation would already follow from similar lower bounds in a weaker model which we call the *simultaneous messages* model (SM) (see definition below). This connection was pointed out to us by Avi Wigderson.

Although we are unable to prove SM lower bounds for $\geq \log n$ players, we do show that the SM model is exponentially weaker than the general multiparty communication model for up to $(\log n)^{1-\epsilon}$ players. So, this result supports the hope that it might be easier to obtain stronger lower bounds in the SM model.

The paper is organized as follows. In Section 2, we introduce the SM model. In Section 3, we derive the lower bound for the *generalized addressing function*, $\text{GAF}_{n,k}$. In Section 4, we show that this lower bound holds even for the distributional version of this model (average case input). We give a nontrivial upper bound on the SM complexity of $\text{GAF}_{n,k}$ in Section 5. In Section 6, we generalize the $\text{GAF}_{n,k}$ lower bounds to addressing in finite groups. Section 7 concludes the paper with some open problems.

2 Simultaneous Messages Complexity

As above, let f be a boolean function of k arguments, each of fixed length $\leq n$. k players and one referee wish to evaluate collaboratively $f(x_0, \ldots, x_{k-1})$. For $0 \leq i \leq k-1$, the ith player knows each input argument except x_i. The referee sees none of the input. Each player p_i simultaneously passes a message of fixed length ℓ_i to the referee, after which the referee announces the function value. Each player (including the referee) is a function of the arguments it "knows".

Definition: A *protocol P for f* is a set of players along with a referee that correctly computes f on all inputs. The *cost* of a protocol for f is $\ell_0 + \cdots + \ell_{k-1}$. The *simultaneous messages complexity* of f, denoted $C_0(f)$, is the minimum cost of a protocol computing f.

Note: This model appears to have first been considered by Nisan and Wigderson for $k = 3$ [NW].

Definition: Let x_0 be an n-bit string, and let $x_1, \ldots, x_{k-1}$ be $\lfloor \log n \rfloor$-bit strings. Let '$\oplus$' be bitwise sum mod 2, and $x_0[a]$ be the ath bit of x_0. Define the *generalized addressing function* for k players as follows:

$$\text{GAF}_{n,k}(x_0, \ldots, x_{k-1}) := x_0[x_1 \oplus \cdots \oplus x_{k-1}].$$

Observation 1 $C(\text{GAF}_{n,k}) \leq \log n$.

Proof: Player p_0 writes $a = x_1 \oplus \cdots \oplus x_{k-1}$; then p_1 announces $x_0[a]$. $\quad\square$

Note: A special case of the communication model is *one-way communication*, in which each player may write on the blackboard only once, and they proceed in order $(p_0, p_1, \ldots, p_{k-1})$. Let $C_1(f)$ denote the *one-way communication complexity of f*. Clearly $nk \geq C_0(f) \geq C_1(f) \geq C(f)$, for any function f. For $\text{GAF}_{n,k}$, the above proof implies the following:

Corollary 2. $C_1(\text{GAF}_{n,k}) \leq \log n$.

In the next section, we demonstrate an exponential separation between $C_0(\text{GAF}_{n,k})$ and $C_1(\text{GAF}_{n,k})$ for $k \leq (\log n)^{1-\epsilon}$. It should be noted, however, that $\text{GAF}_{n,k}$ is in ACC and therefore cannot be used to separate ACC from other classes. In Section 6, we give generalizations of $\text{GAF}_{n,k}$, some of which do not seem to lie in ACC.

We note that by Yao [Y], Beigel-Tarui [BT], and Håstad-Goldmann [HG], to any function $f \in$ ACC there exist constants c and d such that no matter how we split the variables between $k \geq (\log n)^c$ players, $C_0(f) \leq (\log n)^d$. This in particular applies to $\text{GAF}_{n,k}$. An explicit protocol to accomplish this follows in Section 5. See the remark after Theorem 12.

3 Generalized Addressing Function: A Lower Bound

Theorem 3. $C_0(\text{GAF}_{n,k}) \geq \dfrac{n^{1/(k-1)}}{8(k-1)} - \log n$.

Remark: For $k = 3$, this result gives an $\Omega(\sqrt{n})$ lower bound. Nisan and Wigderson [NW] give an $\Omega(\sqrt{n})$ lower bound for a different function, based on hash functions [MNT]. They actually show this lower bound for one-way complexity, establishing an exponential gap between $C_1(f)$ and $C(f)$ for $k = 3$.

Proof of Theorem 3: We actually show that this is a lower bound even on the length of the longest message sent by a player.

Let P be any protocol computing $\text{GAF}_{n,k}$. Let m_i denote p_i's message in P. Let P' be the protocol in which p_0 sends nothing, p_i sends x_{i+1} concatenated with m_i for $1 \leq i \leq k-2$, and p_{k-1} sends x_1 concatenated with m_{k-1}. Any message sent by p_0 in P can be computed by the referee in P', therefore the referee of P' is able to compute $\text{GAF}_{n,k}$.

Let ℓ be the length of the longest message sent in P'. We show that $\ell \geq n^{1/(k-1)}/8(k-1)$. This implies the lower bound stated in the theorem since $\ell = \max\{|m_i| : 1 \leq i \leq k-1\} + \log n$.

For $1 \leq i \leq k-1$, let $\hat{x}_i$ denote $(x_1, \ldots, x_{i-1}, x_{i+1}, \ldots, x_{k-1})$. For $1 \leq i \leq k-1$, player p_i of P' is a function $p_i(x_0, \hat{x}_i) : \{0,1\}^{n+(k-2)\log n} \to \{0,1\}^\ell$. The referee is a function $r(u_1, \ldots, u_{k-1}) : \{0,1\}^{(k-1)\ell} \longrightarrow \{0,1\}$. The correctness of P' is described by the equation

$$r(p_1(x_0, \hat{x}_1), \ldots, p_{k-1}(x_0, \hat{x}_{k-1})) = \text{GAF}_{n,k}(x_0, \ldots, x_{k-1}).$$

Let $t = \lfloor \log n \rfloor$. Let $n' = 2^t \geq n/2$. Decompose the vector space $GF(2)^t$ into a direct sum of $k-1$ subspaces: $GF(2)^t = H_1 \oplus \cdots \oplus H_{k-1}$, where each H_i has dimension $\geq \lfloor t/(k-1) \rfloor$ and hence size $\geq 2^{-1+t/(k-1)}$. Let $\hat{H}_i = \prod_{j \neq i} H_j$ (Cartesian product). The size of $\hat{H}_i$ is

$$|\hat{H}_i| = \frac{n}{|H_i|} \leq \frac{2n}{2^{t/(k-1)}} \leq \frac{2n}{(n/2)^{1/(k-1)}} = 2^{k/(k-1)} n^{(k-2)/(k-1)} \leq 4n^{(k-2)/(k-1)}.$$

Let $N = \sum_{i=1}^{k-1} |\hat{H}_i| \leq 4(k-1)n^{(k-2)/(k-1)}$. We construct a function $F :$ $\{0,1\}^{\ell N} \longrightarrow \{0,1\}^{n'}$ as follows: An input y to F is segmented into N strings of length ℓ. The segments are labeled by pairs $(i, \hat{x}_i)$, where $1 \leq i \leq k-1$, and $\hat{x}_i \in \hat{H}_i$. That is, the ℓ-tuples of y are labeled by elements in $\hat{H}_1 \dot{\cup} \cdots \dot{\cup} \hat{H}_{k-1}$. For $1 \leq j \leq n'$, we define the jth coordinate of $F(y)$ as follows:

$$F(y)[j] := r(y(1, \hat{x}_1), \ldots, y(k-1, \hat{x}_{k-1})),$$

where $x_1, \ldots, x_{k-1}$ are defined by the unique decomposition $j' = x_1 + \cdots + x_{k-1} \in H_1 \oplus \cdots \oplus H_{k-1} = GF(2)^t$, where j' is the binary representation of j.

Claim 4 *F is onto.*

Proof of Claim 4: Let $x_0 \in \{0,1\}^{n'}$. Define $y \in \{0,1\}^{\ell N}$ as follows: For $1 \leq i \leq k-1$ and $\hat{x}_i \in \hat{H}_i$, let $y(i, \hat{x}_i) := p_i(x_0, \hat{x}_i)$. For $0 \leq j \leq n'-1$, this yields:

$$F(y)[j] = r(y(1, \hat{x}_1), \ldots, y(k-1, \hat{x}_{k-1})) = r(p_1(x_0, \hat{x}_1), \ldots, p_{k-1}(x_0, \hat{x}_{k-1})),$$

where $x_1, \ldots, x_{k-1}$ are the unique elements in $H_1, \ldots, H_{k-1}$ whose bitwise sum mod 2 is the binary expansion of j. The correctness of protocol P' means

$$r(p_1(x_0, \hat{x}_1), \ldots, p_{k-1}(x_0, \hat{x}_{k-1})) = \text{GAF}_{n,k}(x_0, \ldots, x_{k-1}) = x_0[j].$$

Therefore, $F(y) = x_0$, and hence F is onto. $\qquad \square$ Claim 4

By the Claim and the definition of F, we have

$$4\ell(k-1)n^{(k-2)/(k-1)} \geq \ell N = \log|\text{Domain}(F)| \geq \log|\text{Image}(F)| = n' \geq n/2.$$

The proof is completed by solving for ℓ. $\qquad \square$ Theorem 3.

4 Distributional Simultaneous Messages Complexity

Definition: Let P be a Simultaneous Messages protocol. The *bias* P achieves on a function f, denoted $B(P, f)$, is defined to be

$$B(P, f) = |\Pr[P(x) = f(x)] - \Pr[P(x) \neq f(x)]|,$$

where $x = (x_0, \ldots, x_{k-1})$ is chosen uniformly over all k-tuples of n-bit strings. Equivalently, a protocol P achieves bias ϵ on f if it computes f correctly on at least a $(1 + \epsilon)/2$ fraction of the inputs. Note that $0 \leq B(P, f) \leq 1$ for all P and f, and P computes f correctly if and only if $B(P, f) = 1$.

Definition: The ϵ-*distributional simultaneous messages complexity* of f, denoted $C_0^\epsilon(f)$, is the minimum cost of a protocol which achieves a bias of at least ϵ on f.

Note: Yao's reduction [Y] for the separation of ACC would require a distributional complexity lower bound for super-polylogarithmic number of players in the simultaneous messages model. The strengthening of Yao's result by Beigel and Tarui [BT] eliminates the need for distributional complexity lower bounds for this problem.

As we shall see, the extension of our lower bounds to distributional complexity requires little extra effort.

Theorem 5. *For* $.98 \leq \epsilon < 1$, $C_0^\epsilon(\mathrm{GAF}_{n,k}) \geq \dfrac{n^{1/(k-1)}}{16(k-1)} - \log n - 2.$

Remark: By standard arguments, for any fixed $\epsilon > 0$, the lower bound for $C_0^\epsilon(f)$ is also a lower bound, up to a positive constant factor, on the *randomized simultaneous messages complexity* of f, where in a randomized protocol, everyone randomizes, and for all inputs x, the probability that the protocol gives the correct value $f(x)$ is at least $(1 + \delta)/2$ where δ is another positive constant. The factor of proportionality depends on ϵ and δ; it is 1 if $\epsilon = \delta$.

Proof of Theorem 5: As in the proof of Theorem 3, let $t = \lfloor \log n \rfloor$. (Recall $n = |x_0|$, and $|x_i| = t$, $1 \leq i \leq k - 1$.) Let $n' = 2^t \geq n/2$.

Let P be a protocol which achieves bias $\epsilon \geq .98$ on $\mathrm{GAF}_{n,k}$. Let P' be the protocol obtained from P as in the proof of Theorem 3. Let ℓ be the length of the longest message sent in P'.

Recall that an *affine subspace* of a vector space is a *translate* of a linear subspace.

Lemma 6. *There exist affine subspaces* $H_1, \ldots, H_{k-1}$ *of* $GF(2)^t$ *s.t.*
  (1) $GF(2)^t = H_1 \oplus \cdots \oplus H_{k-1}$, *where* H_i *has dimension* $\geq \lfloor t/(k-1) \rfloor$, *and*
  (2) $P' = \mathrm{GAF}_{n,k}$ *on at least a* $(1+\epsilon)/2$ *fraction of the inputs from* $\{0,1\}^n \times H_1 \times \cdots \times H_{k-1}$.

Proof of Lemma 6: As in the proof of Theorem 3, decompose the vector space $GF(2)^t$ into a direct sum of $k - 1$ linear subspaces: $GF(2)^t = V_1 \oplus \cdots \oplus V_{k-1}$, where each V_i has dimension $\geq \lfloor t/(k-1) \rfloor$.

For any $v \in GF(2)^t$, we have $GF(2)^t = GF(2)^t + v$, so for any $u_1, \ldots, u_{k-1} \in GF(2)^t$ we have $GF(2)^t = GF(2)^t + u_1 + \cdots + u_{k-1} = (V_1 + u_1) \oplus \cdots \oplus (V_{k-1} + u_{k-1})$.

Let $\alpha(u_1, \ldots, u_{k-1})$ denote the fraction of inputs $(x_0, x_1, \ldots, x_{k-1})$ from $\{0,1\}^n \times (V_1 + u_1) \times \cdots \times (V_{k-1} + u_{k-1})$ on which P' computes $\mathrm{GAF}_{n,k}$ correctly. Clearly, the average of this quantity over all choices of $(u_1, \ldots, u_{k-1})$ is the corresponding fraction over the entire space; hence, it is $\geq (1 + \epsilon)/2$. Pick $u_1, \ldots, u_{k-1} \in GF(2)^t$ such that $\alpha(u_1, \ldots, u_{k-1}) \geq (1 + \epsilon)/2$. Letting $H_i = V_i + u_i$ concludes the proof. $\qquad\square$ Lemma 6.

Choose $H_1, \ldots, H_{k-1}$ to fit the properties in Lemma 6, and let $\hat{H}_i = \prod_{j \neq i} H_j$ (Cartesian product).

Let $r : \{0,1\}^{(k-1)\ell} \to \{0,1\}$ denote the referee function.

Let $N = \sum_{i=1}^{k-1} |\hat{H}_i| \leq 4(k-1)n^{(k-2)/(k-1)}$, as in the proof of Theorem 3.

Define $F : \{0,1\}^{\ell N} \longrightarrow \{0,1\}^{n'}$ also as in the proof of Theorem 3.

Claim 7 $|\text{Image}(F)| \geq 2^{n'/2-2}$.

Note: Claim 7 implies $4\ell(k-1)n^{(k-2)/(k-1)} \geq \ell N = \log |\text{Domain}(F)|$
$\geq \log |\text{Image}(F)| \geq n'/2 - 2 \geq n/4 - 2$.

This implies $\ell \geq n^{1/(k-1)}/16(k-1) - 2$. The theorem will follow, since $\ell = \max\{|m_i| : 1 \leq i \leq k-1\} + \log n$, where as before m_i denotes p_i's message in P.

Proof of Claim 7: Since P' computes f correctly on at least a $(1+\epsilon)/2$ fraction of inputs $(x_0, \ldots, x_{k-1}) \in \{0,1\}^{n+t(k-1)}$, there exists a $w \in \{0,1\}^{n-n'}$ such that P' computes f correctly on at least a $(1+\epsilon)/2$ fraction of inputs from the set

$$\{(x_0, \ldots, x_{k-1}) \mid x_0 = x'_0 \circ w, \; x'_0 \in \{0,1\}^{n'}, \; x_1, \ldots, x_{k-1} \in \{0,1\}^t \},$$

where 'o' stands for concatenation.

Let M be a matrix whose rows are labeled by inputs $x'_0 \in \{0,1\}^{n'}$ and whose columns are labeled by inputs $(x_1, \ldots, x_{k-1})$ from $H_1 \times \cdots \times H_{k-1}$. Let $M(x'_0, (x_1, \ldots, x_{k-1})) = 1$ if $P'(x'_0 \circ w, x_1, \ldots, x_{k-1}) = \text{GAF}_{n,k}(x'_0 \circ w, x_1, \ldots, x_{k-1})$, and 0 otherwise.

Note that M has at least a $(1+\epsilon)/2$ fraction of ones, by our choice of w.

The fraction of rows of M with greater than a $\sqrt{(1-\epsilon)/2}$ fraction of zeroes is less than $\sqrt{(1-\epsilon)/2}$; otherwise M would have more than a $(1-\epsilon)/2$ fraction of zeroes.

Let $s = \sqrt{(1-\epsilon)/2}$. Let S be a set of $2^{n'}(1-s)$ rows each with at most an s fraction of zeroes. For every row $x'_0 \in S$, define $y_{x'_0} \in \{0,1\}^{\ell N}$ as in the proof of Claim 4. Let $Y = \{y_{x'_0} : x'_0 \in S\} \subseteq \text{domain}(F)$.

If row x'_0 consisted of all 1's, then $P'(x'_0 \circ w, x_1, \ldots, x_{k-1}) = \text{GAF}_{n,k}(x'_0 \circ w, x_1, \ldots, x_{k-1})$ for all $(x_1, \ldots, x_{k-1}) \in H_1 \times \cdots \times H_{k-1}$. Then we would have $F(y_{x'_0}) = x'_0$ as in Claim 4. However, row x'_0 may have up to sn' zeroes (s is the fraction of zeroes in each row, n' is the number of columns in each row), and thus $F(y_{x'_0})$ may differ from x'_0 in up to sn' coordinates.

Notation: Let x and $y \in GF(2)^m$, where m is a positive integer. The *Hamming distance* between x and y, denoted $\Delta(x,y)$, is the number of coordinates in which x and y differ. The *Hamming ball of radius b about x*, denoted $N(x,b)$, is the set $\{y : \Delta(x,y) \leq b\}$. The *neighborhood of radius b of $A \subseteq GF(2)^m$*, denoted $N(A,b)$ is $\bigcup_{x \in A} N(x,b)$. Let $\Lambda(m,b)$ denote $\sum_{j=0}^b \binom{m}{j}$. Note that for a given $x \in GF(2)^m$, we have $|N(x,b)| = \Lambda(m,b)$.

Fact 8 *If $A, B \subseteq GF(2)^m$ and $B \subseteq N(A,b)$, then $|A| \geq |B|/\Lambda(m,b)$.* □

Using this notation, we see $\Delta(x'_0, F(y_{x'_0})) \leq sn'$ and $F(Y) \subseteq N(S, sn')$. Setting $m = n', A = F(Y), B = S, b = sn'$ in Fact 8, we obtain the following inequalities. (Recall that $s = \sqrt{(1-\epsilon)/2}$, so for $.98 \leq \epsilon \leq 1$, we have $s \leq .1$. The third inequality uses the fact that for $b \leq m/3$, $\Lambda(m, b) \leq 2\binom{m}{b}$.)

$$|\text{Image}(F)| \geq |F(Y)| \geq \frac{|S|}{\Lambda(n', sn')} \geq \frac{2^{n'}(1-s)}{2\binom{n'}{sn'}} > \frac{2^{n'-2}}{\binom{n'}{sn'}} > \frac{2^{n'-2}}{(\frac{en'}{sn'})^{sn'}} = \frac{2^{n'-2}}{[(\frac{e}{s})^{s}]^{n'}}$$

$$> \frac{2^{n'-2}}{2^{n'/2}} = 2^{n'/2-2}. \qquad\qquad \Box \text{ Claim 7 and Theorem 5.}$$

5 A Simultaneous Messages Protocol for GAF$_{n,k}$

In this section, we give a nontrivial protocol for GAF$_{n,k}$ which yields an upper bound of about $n^{(\log k)/k}$ (see Theorem 12). We will think of the n-bit string A (previously denoted x_0) held by p_0 as a boolean function on $t := \log n$ variables $z_1, \ldots, z_t$, i.e., $A : \{0,1\}^t \longrightarrow \{0,1\}$. For $1 \leq i \leq k-1$, let $x_i := (x_{i,1}, \ldots, x_{i,t})$ be the t-bit string held by player p_i. Then we have

$$\text{GAF}_{n,k}(A, x_1, \ldots, x_{k-1}) = A(x_1 + \cdots + x_{k-1})$$

where here and in what follows $+$ denotes addition in $GF(2)^t$.

5.1 Three Players

We will first describe the protocol for three players. The idea naturally extends to the general case. For simplicity of notation let p_1 hold x and p_2 hold y. At the cost of $2t$ bits, p_0 sends the strings x and y to the referee. Since this communication will be insignificant, we can henceforth ignore p_0 and assume that the referee knows x and y. Then we want to minimize the number of bits sent by p_1 and p_2 that will enable the referee to compute $A(x + y)$.

The protocol will be based on the fact that the boolean function A can be represented as a multilinear polynomial of (total) degree at most t. In fact, the following lemma is the crucial observation in the protocol. Recall the notation

$$\Lambda(m, b) = \sum_{j=0}^{b} \binom{m}{j}.$$

Lemma 9. *Let A be a boolean function of t variables that can be represented as a multilinear polynomial of degree d over $GF(2)$. Then, GAF$_{n,3}(A, x, y)$ has an SM- protocol that uses at most $2\Lambda(t, \lfloor d/2 \rfloor) + 2t$ bits of communication.*

Proof of Lemma 9: Let A be given by $A(z) = \sum\limits_{S \subseteq [t], |S| \leq d} a_S Z_S$ where Z_S denotes the monomial $\prod_{i \in S} z_i$. Thus,

$$A(x + y) = \sum_{|S| \leq d} a_S \prod_{i \in S}(x_i + y_i) = \sum_{|S| \leq d} a_S \sum_{T_1 \dot{\cup} T_2 = S} X_{T_1} Y_{T_2}.$$

For $T_1, T_2 \subseteq [t]$, let us define a_{T_1,T_2} by

$$a_{T_1,T_2} = \begin{cases} a_{T_1 \dot\cup T_2} & \text{if } T_1 \cap T_2 = \emptyset \\ 0 & \text{otherwise} \end{cases}$$

Then, we can rewrite the above as $A(x+y) = \displaystyle\sum_{|T_1|+|T_2| \le d} a_{T_1,T_2} X_{T_1} Y_{T_2}$

$$= \sum_{|T_1| \le \lfloor d/2 \rfloor} \left(\sum_{|T_2| \le d - |T_1|} a_{T_1,T_2} Y_{T_2} \right) X_{T_1} + \sum_{|T_2| \le \lfloor d/2 \rfloor} \left(\sum_{|T_1| \le d - |T_2|} a_{T_1,T_2} X_{T_1} \right) Y_{T_2}$$

where we assume w.l.o.g. that terms $a_{T_1,T_2} X_{T_1} Y_{T_2}$ with both $|T_1|$ and $|T_2|$ less than or equal to $\lfloor d/2 \rfloor$ are placed in the first sum.

We now observe that the first sum in the last equation is a polynomial in x whose coefficients (they depend only on $a_{T_1,T_2} Y_{T_2}$) are known to p_1 and similarly the second sum is a polynomial whose coefficients are known to p_2. The degree of both polynomials is bounded by $\lfloor d/2 \rfloor$. Hence using at most $\Lambda(t, \lfloor d/2 \rfloor)$ bits each, the players can communicate their corresponding halves to the referee. Since the referee already knows x and y, he can evaluate the two polynomials and add them up to announce the value of $A(x+y)$. Noting that p_0 has used $2t$ bits to send x and y to the referee at the beginning of the protocol concludes the proof of the lemma. $\hfill\square$ Lemma 9

Remark: For small enough d the protocol is a quadratic improvement over the trivial one where the entire polynomial is communicated to the referee.

Suppose now that A is an arbitrary boolean function. We will use Lemma 9 on the low-degree part of A and the trivial protocol on the high-degree part. Since there are not too many high-degree terms, we will be able to keep the communication within n^c for some $c < 1$.

Theorem 10. *Let A be a t-variable boolean function with $n = 2^t$. Then there is an SM-protocol for $\mathrm{GAF}_{n,3}(A, x, y)$ that uses $o(n^{0.92})$ bits.*

Proof of Theorem 10: Let $A(z) = \sum_{S \subseteq [t]} a_S Z_S$. Define A' be the part of A corresponding to degree less than or equal to $2t/3$ and let A'' be the remaining part of A. That is,

$$A(z) = \sum_{|S| \le 2t/3} a_S Z_S + \sum_{|S| > 2t/3} a_S Z_S = A'(z) + A''(z)$$

Players p_1 and p_2 use the protocol of Lemma 9 on A'. They just send the high degree terms a_S for $|S| > 2t/3$ directly to the referee. The number of bits used by p_1 and p_2 is at most $2\Lambda(t, t/3) + \displaystyle\sum_{j > 2t/3} \binom{t}{j} \le 3\Lambda(t, t/3) \le O(2^{t\,H(1/3)}/\sqrt{t})$,

where $H(\theta) := -\theta \log \theta - (1-\theta) \log(1-\theta)$ is the binary entropy function. Adding the $2t$ bits sent by p_0, we see that the protocol has communication complexity at most

$$O(n^{H(1/3)}/\sqrt{\log n}) + 2 \log n$$

bits. Since $H(1/3) = 0.91829...$ the theorem follows. $\hfill\square$ Theorem 10

5.2 k Players

We generalize the idea from the preceding section to k players. An extension of Lemma 9 follows:

Lemma 11. *Let A be a t-variable boolean function of degree d over $GF(2)$. Then $\mathrm{GAF}_{n,k}(A, x_1, \ldots, x_{k-1})$ has an SM-protocol of complexity at most*

$$k\, \Lambda(t, \lfloor \frac{d}{k-1} \rfloor) + (k-1)\, t \ .$$

Proof of Lemma 11: Letting $A(z) = \sum_{S \subseteq [t], |S| \leq d} a_S\, Z_S.$, we have,

$$A(x_1 + \cdots + x_{k-1}) = \sum_{|S| \leq d} a_S \prod_{i \in S} (x_{1,i} + \cdots + x_{k-1,i})$$

$$= \sum_{|S| \leq d} a_S \sum_{T_1 \dot\cup \cdots \dot\cup T_k} X_{1,T_1} \cdots X_{k-1,T_{k-1}}$$

Let us consider a monomial $a_S\, Z_S$. Since the T_i are disjoint, $\sum_{i=1}^{k} |T_i| = |S| \leq d$, and hence the smallest T_i is of size at most $\lfloor d/(k-1) \rfloor$. Thus in the expansion,

$$\sum_{T_1 \dot\cup \cdots \dot\cup T_k} a_S\, X_{1,T_1} \cdots X_{k-1,T_{k-1}},$$

each term can be "owned" by a player p_i such that T_i is the smallest set in that term. (In case of ties, take the smallest such i.) As a result, the value of this monomial on $x_1 + \cdots + x_k$ can be distributed among the k players by giving them each a polynomial of degree at most $\lfloor |S|/(k-1) \rfloor$.

The proof follows by linearity and proceeds similarly to that of Lemma 9. We conclude that each player needs to send at most $\Lambda(t, \lfloor d/(k-1) \rfloor)$ bits.

$\square$ Lemma 11

Theorem 12. *There is an SM-protocol for $\mathrm{GAF}_{n,k}$ of complexity at most*

$$k\, \Lambda(t, \lfloor t/k \rfloor) + (k-1)t$$

where $t := \lceil \log n \rceil$. In particular, player p_0 sends $(k-1)t$ bits, and,

- *if $3 \leq k \leq \log n$, each player $p_i, 1 \leq i \leq k-1$ sends at most $O(n^{H(1/k)}/\sqrt{(\log n)/k})$ bits, and,*
- *if $k > \log n$, then each $p_i, 1 \leq i \leq k-1$ sends at most two bits (in fact, only one bit if $k > \log n + 1$).*

Proof of Theorem 12: Similar to the proof of Theorem 10 by separating the low-degree and high-degree parts of A around $t(1-1/k)$. Thus, for $1 \leq i \leq (k-1)$, p_i needs to send at most $2\Lambda(t, \lfloor t/k \rfloor)$ bits (by dividing the high-degree coefficients among themselves equally).

$\square$

Remark: For $k \geq 3$, $H(1/k) \leq \log(ek)/k$. Thus, if $k \geq c \log n$ for any constant $c > 0$, then each player sends at most *polylog(n)* bits to the referee.

6 Addressing by a Finite Group

Consider the following generalization of $\text{GAF}_{n,k}$: Given a group G of order n, we shall associate the n possible addresses with the elements of G. Now x_0 is a function $x_0 : G \to \{0,1\}$, and $x_i \in G$ for $i = 1,\ldots,k-1$. The goal is to compute $x_0[x_1 \cdot \ldots \cdot x_{k-1}]$, where $\cdot$ denotes the group operation in G.

Notation: We will denote the above function by $\text{GAF}_{G,k}$.

The lower bound technique of Section 3 can be generalized to addressing by any finite group. In the proof of Theorem 3, we wrote $GF(2)^t$ as a direct sum: $GF(2)^t = H_1 \oplus \ldots \oplus H_{k-1}$. We then obtained an upper bound for the size of $\hat{H}_i$, the Cartesian product of all H_j except the ith. For general finite groups, we define the following function, which will play the role of $|\hat{H}_i|$.

Definition: Let

$$\rho(G,u) = \min\{\rho : \exists H_i, i = 1,\ldots,u, \text{ s.t. } G = H_1 \cdot \ldots \cdot H_u \text{ and } \forall i, |\hat{H}_i| \leq \rho\},$$

where $\hat{H}_i$ is the product of all H_j except the ith.

The arguments in the proof of Theorem 3 along with this new definition imply the following.

Theorem 13. $C_0(\text{GAF}_{G,k}) \geq \Omega\left(\dfrac{n}{(k-1)\,\rho(G,k-1)}\right).$ □

Notice that $\rho(\mathbf{Z}_2^t, u) \leq n^{1-1/u}$, where $n = |\mathbf{Z}_2^t| = 2^t$. Letting $u = k-1$ in Theorem 13 gives Theorem 3 for the case when n is a power of 2. A similar argument shows $\rho(\mathbf{Z}_n, u) \leq 4n^{1-1/u}$ using the binary digits in the role of the coordinates in the proof of Theorem 3.

Corollary 14. $C_0(\text{GAF}_{\mathbf{Z}_n,k}) \geq \dfrac{n^{1/(k-1)}}{8(k-1)}.$ □

For general finite groups, the following lemma implies an upper bound on $\rho(G,u)$.

Lemma 15. *([BE]) Any group G of finite order can be written as a product of two-element sets, $G = \{1,a_1\} \cdot \ldots \cdot \{1,a_m\}$, where $m \leq \log_2 |G| + \log_2 \ln |G| + 2$.* □

Corollary 16. $C_0(\text{GAF}_{G,k}) \geq \dfrac{n^{1/(k-1)}}{(k-1)} \cdot \dfrac{1}{(8\ln n)^{1-1/(k-1)}}.$

Proof: Partition the two-element sets of Lemma 15 into $k-1$ classes of size at most $\lceil m/(k-1) \rceil$. Let H_i be the product of the sets in the ith class. Clearly $G = H_1 \cdot \ldots \cdot H_{k-1}$, and for each i we have

$$|H_i| \leq 2^{\lceil m/(k-1) \rceil} \leq 2^{(\log_2 |G| + \log_2 \ln |G| + 3)/(k-1)} \leq (8 \cdot |G| \cdot \ln |G|)^{1/k-1}$$

This implies $\rho(G,k-1) \leq (8n \ln n)^{1-1/(k-1)}$. By Theorem 13, we are done.
□

Remark: Using the classification of finite simple groups, one can prove that for every group G, $\rho(G, u) \leq c^{u-1} \cdot n^{(u-1)/u}$, for some constant c. This yields

$$C_0(\text{GAF}_{G,k}) \geq \frac{n^{1/(k-1)}}{(k-1) \cdot c^{k-2}}.$$

7 Open Problems

1. The main open problem remains to find a nontrivial lower bound for some explicit function for more than $\log n$ players. Some candidate functions are:

   (a) Majority of Majorities $\text{MM}_{n,k}$ defined as follows. Assume $k|n$. Divide the n inputs into n/k groups, each of size k. $\text{MM}_{n,k}$ takes the majority of each group, then the majority of the n/k answers. We have k players, and to each player, we assign n/k variables, one from each group. Beigel and Tarui suggest that for $k = \sqrt{n}$, the function $\text{MM}_{n,k}$ is a good candidate to be outside ACC. [BT]

   (b) Let F be a finite field of order q. Give each player a $t \times t$ matrix over F. Let M be the product (in a given order) of these matrices. Estimate the SM complexity of decision problems associated with M, such as, "Is trace(M) a quadratic residue in F?" (for odd q). Here $n \approx q^{t^2}$. The case $t = 2$ is of particular interest.

   (c) Quadratic Character of the Sum of the coordinates, defined as follows. Let p be an n-bit prime, x_i is an n-bit integer, $1 \leq i \leq k$ (x_i is the ith player's input). $\text{QCS}_{p,k}(x_1, \ldots, x_k) = 1$ iff $x_1 + \ldots + x_k$ is a quadratic residue mod p. Babai, Nisan, and Szegedy [BNS] show $C(\text{QCS}_{p,k}) \geq \Omega(n/2^k)$.

2. Though we know that functions in ACC have efficient SM protocols for polylog and greater number of players, it would still be interesting to give explicit nontrivial lower or upper bounds in the case where $k \geq 3$ for even the simplest of functions. One example is the "OR of ANDs" function: An $n \times k$, 0-1 matrix M is given. For $1 \leq i \leq k$, player i is given column i as its input. The function value is 1 iff M has a row consisting entirely of 1's. Note that if we replace the OR by PARITY (i.e., $f(M) = 1$ iff M has an odd number of all-1 rows), we obtain the Generalized Inner Product function (GIP_k), for which [BNS] show a lower bound of $\Omega(n/(4^k))$ for the communication complexity and Grolmusz gives a communication protocol which uses $(2k - 1)\lceil n/(2^{k-1} - 1) \rceil$ bits [G]. Grolmusz's protocol is "almost" an SM protocol in the sense that player 0 makes an announcement of $(k-1)\lceil n/(2^{k-1} - 1) \rceil$ bits, and then an SM protocol ensues, in which each player sends $\lceil n/(2^{k-1} - 1) \rceil$ bits to the referee.

3. Obtain an $n^{1-\epsilon}$ upper bound for $\text{GAF}_{G,k}$ for the case where G is a cyclic group. The best known upper bound is $O(n \log \log n / \log n)$ [PRS, Theorem 4.2]. The upper bound technique given in Section 5 seems to work only for elementary abelian p-groups (vector spaces) for small primes p.

4. Find a function f for which $C_1(f)$ is exponentially larger than $C(f)$, for $k \geq 4$ players. Such a gap is known for $k = 3$ [NW], cf. the remark after Theorem 3. We note that lower bounds for C_1 complexity have been applied in [BNS] to time-space tradeoffs, branching programs, and formula size lower bounds.

Acknowledgments

We are grateful to Avi Wigderson for suggesting to us the SM model and pointing out the connection of ACC with the model considered in this paper. In October of 1994, P. Pudlák kindly sent us the manuscript [PRS] by P. Pudlák, V. Rödl, and J. Sgall. Among many other things, that paper introduces SM complexity under the name "Oblivious Communication Complexity" and deduces the $GAF_{G,k}$ lower bound for cyclic groups by essentially the same methods as ours [PRS, Proposition 2.3].

References

[BE]   L. Babai, P. Erdős. *Representation of Group Elements as Short Products*. J. Turgeon, A. Rosa, G. Sabidussi, editor. Theory and Practice of Combinatorics, number 12, *in* Ann. Discr. Math., North-Holland, 1982, pp. 21-26.

[BNS]   L. Babai, N. Nisan, M. Szegedy. *Multiparty Protocols, Pseudorandom Generators for Logspace and Time-Space Trade-offs*. Journal of Computer and System Sciences 45 (1992), pp. 204-232.

[BT]   R. Beigel, J. Tarui, *On ACC*. Proc. of the 32nd IEEE FOCS, 1991, pp. 783-792.

[CFL]   A.K. Chandra, M.L. Furst, R.J. Lipton, *Multiparty protocols*. Proc. of the 15th ACM STOC, 1983, pp. 94-99.

[G]   V. Grolmusz, *The BNS Lower Bound for Multi-Party Protocols is Nearly Optimal*. Information and Computation, **112** (1994), pp. 51-54.

[HG]   J. Håstad, M. Goldmann, *On the Power of Small-Depth Threshold Circuits*. Computational Complexity, **1** (1991), pp. 113-129.

[MNT]   Y. Mansour, N. Nisan, P. Tiwari, *The Computational Complexity of Universal Hashing*. Theoretical Computer Science, **107** (1993), pp. 121-133.

[NW]   N. Nisan, A. Wigderson, *Rounds in Communication Complexity Revisited*. SIAM Journal on Computing, **22** (1993), pp. 211-219.

[PRS]   P. Pudlák, V. Rödl, J. Sgall. *Boolean circuits, tensor ranks and communication complexity*. manuscript, March 11, 1994.

[Y]   A. C-C. Yao, *On ACC and Threshold Circuits*. Proc. of the 31st IEEE FOCS, 1990, pp. 619-627.

Coding and Strong Coding in Trace Monoids[*]

Véronique Bruyère[1] and Clelia De Felice[2]

[1] Université de Mons-Hainaut, 15 Avenue Maistriau, B-7000 Mons, Belgium.
vero@sun1.umh.ac.be
[2] Dipartimento di Informatica ed Applicazioni, Università di Salerno, I-84081
Baronissi (SA), Italy. defelice@udsab.dia.unisa.it

Abstract. We compare two notions of coding on traces, called coding
and strong coding, in relation with the decision problem of the existence
of a coding between two given trace monoids. We positively solve this
problem if the first monoid is either a direct product of free monoids, or
a free product of free commutative monoids. We show how the situation
differs in the case of strong codings.

1 Introduction

Traces monoids were introduced by Cartier and Foata in [CF69]. They were
intensively studied, in particular as they are a possible model for parallel processing [Ma77]. The theory of traces is now well developed, in connection with
several fields of theoretical computer science. One aspect of this theory is the
extension of classical results of the free monoid theory, for which we refer to the
surveys [Ch86, Di90b, Du86a, Pe89].

We are here interested in *coding* in trace monoids. This notion was first
considered by Chrobak and Rytter in [CR87] and by Ochmański in [Oc88], in
relation with decision problems. A coding is defined as an injective morphism
from a trace monoid into another one. This is a natural way to generalize the
classical codings in free monoids to trace monoids [BP85]. On the other hand,
in [BDG94a], another concept of coding, called *strong coding*, is defined, which
is restrictive but more adapted to the interpretation of traces as concurrent
processes.

In this paper, we study the decision problem of the *existence of a coding
between two given trace monoids* [Oc88, Di90a]. In the case of strong coding, it
has been solved in [BDG94a, BDG94b] for two large families of trace monoids;
the general solution has been recently found by Diekert, Muscholl and Reinhardt
(see these Proceedings). We here partially solve this decision problem in the case
of (not strong) coding. We also compare coding and strong coding and we show
how the two situations differ.

More precisely we prove that the existence of a coding from a trace monoid
into another one is decidable, if the first monoid is a *direct product of free*

---

[*] This work was partially supported by ESPRIT-BRA Working Group 6317 *ASMICS*,
by Project 40% MURST *Algoritmi, Modelli di Calcolo e Strutture Informative* and
by Project 60% MURST.

monoids, or if it is a *free product of free commutative monoids*. Equivalently, this means that the dependence relation, or the independence relation of the first monoid is *transitive*. It is remarkable that the transitivity condition plays such central role in the theory of traces, especially in decision problems (see [AH89, Sa92] for a list of references). We also compare coding and strong coding in these cases and we show how the two situations differ. The techniques used in our proofs are based on the classical theory of codes and on properties of systems of linear equations.

This paper is organised in the following way. Section 2 announces the two main results and it recalls some basic definitions and properties on trace monoids. Sections 3 and 4 indicate useful properties of codings between trace monoids, where the first monoid is either a free commutative monoid $A^{\oplus}$ or a free product $A^{\oplus} * \{b\}^{\oplus}$. The last section contains the proofs of the results.

2 Results

Let A be a finite alphabet and $I \subseteq A \times A$ a symmetric irreflexive relation, called *independence relation*. The *dependence relation* D is the complement of I. The *trace monoid* $M(A, D)$ is the quotient of A^* by the congruence generated by the set of pairs $\{(ab, ba) \mid (a, b) \in I\}$. The elements of $M(A, D)$ are called *traces*. In particular, if $I = \emptyset$, then $M(A, D)$ is the free monoid A^* and if $I = (A \times A) \backslash \{(a, a) \mid a \in A\}$, then $M(A, D)$ is the free commutative monoid $A^{\oplus}$.

It is usual to associate with $M(A, D)$ an undirected graph (A, D), called the *dependence relation graph*, whose vertices are the letters of A and edges are drawn between pairs of distinct dependent letters. In the same way we can associate the *independence relation graph* (A, I).

Trace monoids with *transitive* independence (or dependence) relations I (or D) play an important role in the theory of traces, especially in decision problems. The independence relation I is transitive if and only if the connected components of the graph (A, I) are complete. Equivalently, one can see $M(A, D)$ as a *free product of free commutative monoids* $B_1^{\oplus} * \cdots * B_s^{\oplus}$. We recall that the free product $M_1 * \cdots * M_s$ of s monoids $M_1, \ldots, M_s$ satisfying $M_r \cap M_{r'} = 1$ for any $r, r' \in \{1, \ldots, s\}$, $r \neq r'$, is the monoid whose elements are all finite sequences $(u_1, \ldots, u_n)$ of elements of $\bigcup_{r \in \{1, \ldots, s\}} (M_r \backslash 1)$ such that

$$\forall m \in \{1, \ldots, n-1\} \quad u_m \in M_r \Rightarrow u_{m+1} \notin M_r.$$

In a symmetrical way, the dependence relation D is transitive if and only if the connected components of the graph (A, D) are complete. In this case, $M(A, D)$ is a *direct product of free monoids* $B_1^* \times \cdots \times B_s^*$; and any trace $u \in M(A, D)$ is in correspondence with the s-tuple $(\pi_{B_1}(u), \ldots, \pi_{B_s}(u))$. Here, we denote π_B the projection morphism of $M(A, D)$ onto $M(B, D \cap (B \times B))$ defined by $\pi_B(a) = a$ if $a \in B$ and $\pi_B(a) = 1$ if $a \in A \backslash B$.

Coding in trace monoids was considered for the first time by Chrobak and Rytter in [CR87]. Ochmański then introduced *coding morphisms* as injective morphisms $F : M_1 \to M_2$ [Oc88], generalizing in a natural way coding morphisms between free monoids (see [BP85]). He also proposed the following problem [Oc88, Di90a].

Problem 1. Given two trace monoids $M_1 = M(A_1, D_1)$ and $M_2 = M(A_2, D_2)$, is the existence of a coding morphism $F : M_1 \to M_2$ decidable ?

This problem is easily solved if M_1 and M_2 are free monoids or if they are free commutative monoids. In the general case, this problem is still open and it seems difficult to solve it. In this paper we give a positive answer if the dependence or the independence relation of M_1 is transitive.

Theorem 2. *Let M_1 and M_2 be two trace monoids such that $M_1 = B_1^* \times \cdots \times B_s^*$. Then the existence of a coding morphism $F : M_1 \to M_2$ is decidable.*

Theorem 3. *Let M_1 and M_2 be two trace monoids such that $M_1 = B_1^\oplus * \cdots * B_s^\oplus$. Then the existence of a coding morphism $F : M_1 \to M_2$ is decidable.*

In [BDG94a], another notion of coding was introduced, the *coding strong morphisms*. For this new concept of coding, Problem 1 has been partially solved in [BDG94a, BDG94b]; recently, it has been completely solved by Diekert, Muscholl and Reinhardt (see these Proceedings).

Coding strong morphisms are injective strong morphisms. The difference between morphisms and strong morphisms is the following one. Recall [Ch86] that a morphism from M_1 into M_2 is a monoid morphism induced by a map $F : A_1 \to M_2$ such that

$$\forall a, b \in A_1 \quad aI_1 b \Rightarrow F(a)F(b) = F(b)F(a).$$

This morphism is *strong* if

$$\forall a, b \in A_1 \quad aI_1 b \Rightarrow F(a)I_2 F(b)$$

which means that $alphF(a)I_2alphF(b)$, with $alph(u)$ denoting the set of letters appearing in the trace u. This new concept of strong morphism is restrictive, but it is more suitable considering its interpretation in terms of semantics of concurrent processes [BDG94a].

As an example of coding strong morphisms, one can consider the following class of maps introduced in [BDG94a].

Proposition 4. *Let $F : M_1 \to M_2$ be a trace morphism such that there exist a clique-covering of (A_1, D_1) by n cliques $(C_m)_{m=1,\ldots,n}$, a set of n cliques $(C'_m)_{m=1,\ldots,n}$ of (A_2, D_2), and n injective morphisms $F_m : C_m^* \to C_m'^*$ between free monoids such that $alphF(A_1) \subseteq \cup_{m=1,\ldots,n} C'_m$ and*

$$\forall m \in \{1, \ldots, n\}, \forall a \in A_1, \quad \pi_{C'_m} F(a) = F_m \pi_{C_m} a.$$

Then F is a coding strong morphism.

We recall that $C \subseteq A$ is a *clique* of the graph (A, D) if the subgraph induced by C is complete. A family of cliques $(C_m)_{m=1,\ldots,n}$ is a *clique-covering* of the graph (A, D) if for any $a, b \in A$

$$aDb \quad \Rightarrow \quad \exists m \in \{1, \ldots, n\} \ \ a, b \in C_m.$$

Theorems 2 and 3 allow some comparison between coding morphisms and coding strong morphisms with respect to Problem 1. If M_1 is a direct product of free monoids, then Problem 1 has also a positive answer if strong morphisms are considered [BDG94a]. Moreover, we will prove

Proposition 5. *Let $M_1 = B_1^* \times \cdots \times B_s^*$. There exists a coding morphism $F : M_1 \to M_2$ if and only if there exists a coding strong morphism $F : M_1 \to M_2$.*

However, if M_1 is a free product of free commutative monoids, a coding morphism can exist when no coding strong morphism exists. The simplest example of this situation is the following one.

Example 1. Let M_1, M_2 be with dependence relation graphs:

(A_1, D_1) a —— c , b —— d (with crossing edges) (A_2, D_2) α —— γ , β —— δ

The function F induced by $F(a) = \alpha\beta$, $F(b) = \alpha\beta^2$, $F(c) = \gamma\delta$, $F(d) = \gamma\delta^2$, is a coding morphism from M_1 into M_2 (see proof of Theorem 13). However, no coding strong morphism exists between them (see [BDG94a]).

We end this section with some notations, definitions and known results needed in the next sections.

Trace monoids are cancellative and the equality of two traces can be checked thanks to the following result [CP85, Du86a].

Proposition 6. *Let $M(A, D)$ be a trace monoid and $(C_m)_{m=1,\ldots,n}$ be a clique-covering of the graph (A, D). Let $u, v \in M(A, D)$. Then $u = v$ if and only if $\pi_{C_m} u = \pi_{C_m} v$ for all $m \in \{1, \ldots, n\}$.* $\qquad\qquad\square$

In the sequel, we will often use this result with the clique-covering of (A, D) by the cliques of size 1 and 2.

A trace $u \in M(A, D)$ is *connected* if the subgraph G_u of (A, D) induced by $alph(u)$ is connected. Thus, for any trace u, the connected components of G_u induce a canonical decomposition of u into a product of connected traces, called the *components* of u. Duboc proved the following combinatorial properties of traces [Du86a, Du86b].

Proposition 7. *Let $x, y \in M(A, D) \backslash 1$.*
1) If $xy = yx$, then for any components u of x and v of y, we have $uv = vu$.
2) If $xy = yx$ and x, y are connected traces, then either xIy or $x = t^i$, $y = t^j$, with $t \in M(A, D)$, $i, j \geq 1$.
3) If $x^n = y^m$, with $n, m \geq 1$, then there exist $t \in M(A, D)$ and $i, j \geq 1$ such that $x = t^i$ and $y = t^j$.

This third property shows that any trace x has a unique *root* t such that $x = t^i$, $i \geq 1$, i maximum.

Finally, we recall the classical concept of code. A subset X of A^+ is a *code* if any word in X^* has a unique factorization into words of X, i.e. for any $n, n' \geq 1$ and $x_1, \ldots, x_n, x'_1, \ldots, x'_{n'} \in X$,

$$x_1 \cdots x_n = x'_1 \cdots x'_{n'} \quad \Rightarrow \quad n = n' \quad \text{and} \quad x_m = x'_m \quad \text{for } m \in \{1, \ldots, n\}.$$

A simple example of code is any set whose words have the same length, as for instance the set $u \sqcup\!\!\!\sqcup v$, with $u, v \in A^+$. We recall that the *shuffle* $u \sqcup\!\!\!\sqcup v$ is defined by:

$$u \sqcup\!\!\!\sqcup v = \{u_1 v_1 u_2 v_2 \cdots u_n v_n \mid n > 0, u_m, v_m \in A^*, u = u_1 \cdots u_n, v = v_1 \cdots v_n\}.$$

3 Free Commutative Monoids

In this section, we describe properties of coding morphisms F between M_1 and M_2, where the first monoid M_1 is free commutative. In particular, we prove that if such coding exists, then M_2 contains a submonoid isomorphic to M_1 such that the isomorphism is alphabetic (Corollary 9). The next proposition was partially proved in [Oc88].

Proposition 8. *Let $A_1 = \{a_1, \ldots, a_k\}$ and $M_1 = A_1^{\oplus}$ be a free commutative monoid. Let $F : M_1 \to M_2$ be a coding morphism. Then, there exist n pairwise independent connected traces $t_m \in M_2 \backslash 1$, $m \in \{1, \ldots, n\}$, such that for all $l \in \{1, \ldots, k\}$,*

$$F(a_l) = \prod_{m \in \{1, \ldots, n\}} t_m^{p_{m,l}} \qquad p_{m,l} \geq 0.$$

Moreover, the rank of the matrix $(p_{m,l})$ is equal to k. In particular, $n \geq \text{card}(A_1)$.

Proof. First notice that for any $a, b \in A_1$, since $a I_1 b$, we have $F(a)F(b) = F(b)F(a)$. Then by Proposition 7, if u, v are components of $F(a)$ and $F(b)$ respectively, then either u, v are independent or they have the same root. Let T_l be the set of roots of the components of $F(a_l)$, $l \in \{1, \ldots, k\}$. Thus $\cup_{l \in \{1, \ldots, k\}} T_l$ is a set of n independent traces t_m such that for all $l \in \{1, \ldots, k\}$

$$F(a_l) = \prod_{m \in \{1, \ldots, n\}} t_m^{p_{m,l}} \qquad p_{m,l} \geq 0.$$

Now, let $u, v \in M_1$ such that $F(u) = F(v)$. We get

$$F(u) = F(v) = \prod_{m \in \{1, \ldots, n\}} t_m^{q_m} \qquad q_m \geq 0.$$

Equivalently, $(x_1 - y_1, x_2 - y_2, \ldots, x_k - y_k)$ is a solution of the homogeneous system of linear equations

$$\begin{cases} p_{1,1}z_1 + \cdots + p_{1,k}z_k = 0 \\ \quad\vdots \qquad\qquad\quad \vdots \\ p_{n,1}z_1 + \cdots + p_{n,k}z_k = 0 \end{cases}$$

where x_l (respectively y_l), denotes the number of occurrences of the letter a_l in the trace u (respectively v).

Assume that $rank(p_{m,l}) < k$. Thus, this system has an infinite number of solutions in $\mathbf{Z}^k$, since the coefficients $p_{m,l}$ are all in $\mathbf{Z}$. In particular, there exists a non trivial solution $(x_1 - y_1, x_2 - y_2, \ldots, x_k - y_k)$. This is impossible as F is a coding. □

The traces t_m, $m \in \{1, \ldots, n\}$, described in the previous proposition, are called the *independent roots* of the morphism $F : A_1^{\oplus} \to M_2$.

Corollary 9. *If $F : A_1^{\oplus} \to M_2$ is a coding morphism, then M_2 has a submonoid $C^{\oplus}$ isomorphic to $A_1^{\oplus}$, such that $C \subseteq A_2$, and $\alpha \in alphF(a)$, where $\alpha \in C$ is associated with $a \in A_1$.*

Proof. By Proposition 8, the matrix $(p_{m,l})$ has rank $k = card(A_1)$. In other words, one can extract a square $k \times k$ matrix $(p_{m',l})_{m',l\in\{1,\ldots,k\}}$ with a non null determinant. By definition,

$$\det(p_{m',l}) = \sum_{\sigma} sg(\sigma)p_{\sigma(1),1} \cdots p_{\sigma(k),k}$$

where the sum is over all the permutations σ of $\{1, \ldots, k\}$. As $\det(p_{m',l}) \neq 0$, there exists a permutation σ such that

$$p_{\sigma(1),1} \cdots p_{\sigma(k),k} \neq 0.$$

This permutation associates with any $a_l \in A_1$, a distinct independent root $t_{\sigma(l)}$, appearing in $F(a_l)$ with a non null exponent $p_{\sigma(l),l}$. To conclude, just pick a letter α_l in $alph(t_{\sigma(l)})$. The α_l's are independent as the traces $t_{\sigma(l)}$'s are independent. □

4 Free Products $A^{\oplus} * \{b\}^{\oplus}$

In this section, we study coding morphisms $F : M_1 \to M_2$ such that the first monoid M_1 has the form $A^{\oplus} * \{b\}^{\oplus}$. Under this condition, Proposition 11 states strong dependencies in the second monoid M_2. Its proof needs the next lemma.

Lemma 10. *Let $F : M_1 \to M_2$ be a coding morphism and $a, b \in A_1$, with aD_1b, $a \neq b$. Then, there exist $\alpha \in alphF(a)$, $\beta \in alphF(b)$, $\alpha \neq \beta$, such that $\alpha D_2\beta$. Moreover, for any $c \in A_1$, $cI_1\{a, b\}$, we have $alphF(c)I_2\{\alpha, \beta\}$.*

Proof. First, let us prove that the pair $\alpha D_2 \beta$ exists, with the additional property that $\pi_{\alpha,\beta} F(a)$ and $\pi_{\alpha,\beta} F(b)$ have distinct roots.

As $a D_1 b$, then $F(ab) \neq F(ba)$. By Proposition 6, there exist $\alpha \neq \beta$ in A_2, $\alpha D_2 \beta$, such that $\pi_{\alpha,\beta} F(ab) \neq \pi_{\alpha,\beta} F(ba)$ and $\alpha \in alphF(a)$, $\beta \in alphF(b)$.

Assume that $\pi_{\alpha,\beta} F(a) = t^i$ and $\pi_{\alpha,\beta} F(b) = t^j$, with $t \in \{\alpha, \beta\}^+$ and $i, j \geq 1$. We obtain $\pi_{\alpha,\beta} F(ab) = t^{i+j} = \pi_{\alpha,\beta} F(ba)$, which is impossible.

Now, let $c \in A_1$, with $c I_1 \{a, b\}$. Then $F(a)F(c) = F(c)F(a)$ and $F(b)F(c) = F(c)F(b)$. By contradiction, assume that $\gamma D_2 \alpha$, for some $\gamma \in alphF(c)$. We denote by u (v, w respectively) the component of $F(a)$ ($F(b), F(c)$ respectively) containing α (β, γ respectively).

Since $\alpha D_2 \gamma$, then $u D_2 w$. So, Proposition 7 applied to $F(a)F(c) = F(c)F(a)$ states that u and w have the same root. In particular, $\alpha \in alph(w)$. Then, by $\alpha D_2 \beta$, we get $w D_2 v$. Again by Proposition 7 applied to $F(b)F(c) = F(c)F(b)$, v and w have the same root. It follows that u, v have the same root (Proposition 7) and that

$$\pi_{\alpha,\beta} F(a) = \pi_{\alpha,\beta} u = t^i, \quad \pi_{\alpha,\beta} F(b) = \pi_{\alpha,\beta} v = t^j.$$

with $t \in \{\alpha, \beta\}^+$, $i, j \geq 1$. This is in contradiction with the properties of the pair $\alpha D_2 \beta$. □

Proposition 11. *Let $M_1 = \{a_1, \ldots, a_k\}^{\oplus} * \{b\}^{\oplus}$ and $F : M_1 \to M_2$ be a coding morphism. Then, there exist k pairs $\alpha_l D_2 \beta_l$, with $\alpha_l \neq \beta_l$, such that the α_l's appear in distinct independent roots of the restriction of F to $\{a_1, \ldots, a_k\}$, and each β_l belongs to $alphF(b)$.*

Proof. The restriction of F to $\{a_1, \ldots, a_k\}^{\oplus}$ is still a coding morphism. By Proposition 8, there are $n \geq k$ independent roots $t_m \in M_2 \backslash 1$, $m \in \{1, \ldots n\}$, such that for all $l \in \{1, \ldots, k\}$

$$F(a_l) = \prod_{m \in \{1, \ldots, n\}} t_m^{p_{m,l}} \qquad p_{m,l} \geq 0. \qquad (1)$$

Let us suppose that the set

$$T = \{t_m \mid t_m F(b) \neq F(b) t_m\}$$

has cardinality $< k$. We consider the morphism $F' : \{a_1, \ldots, a_k\}^{\oplus} \to M_2$, obtained from F by deleting traces $t_m \notin T$:

$$F'(a_l) = \prod_{t_m \in T} t_m^{p_{m,l}} \qquad l \in \{1, \ldots, k\}.$$

As $card(T) < k$, by Proposition 8, F' is not a coding morphism and there exist $u, v \in \{a_1, \ldots, a_k\}^{\oplus}$, $u \neq v$, such that $F'(u) = F'(v)$.

Let us prove that $F(ubv) = F(vbu)$. First, we have $F(u) = F'(u)x = xF'(u)$ and $F(v) = F'(v)y = yF'(v)$, where x, y are some products of traces $t_m \notin T$.

Second, we have $xF(b)y = yF(b)x$, by definition of T. Finally, by $F'(u) = F'(v)$, we get

$$F(ubv) = F'(u)xF(b)yF'(v)$$
$$= F'(u)yF(b)xF'(v)$$
$$= F'(v)yF(b)xF'(u)$$
$$= F(vbu).$$

But F is a coding morphism, it follows that $ubv = vbu$ in the free product $\{a_1, \ldots, a_k\}^{\oplus} * \{b\}^{\oplus}$. Recall that $u, v \in \{a_1, \ldots, a_k\}^{\oplus}$. By definition of the free product, it follows that $u = v$. This is impossible.

So $card(T) \geq k$. For any $t_m \in T$, by Proposition 6, there exist $\alpha_m \in alph(t_m)$, $\beta_m \in alphF(b)$ such that $\alpha_m D_2 \beta_m$ and $\alpha_m \neq \beta_m$. This concludes the proof. $\square$

5 Proofs of the Main Results

We prove in this section the main results that we enunciated in Section 2 (Theorems 2, 3 and Proposition 5). We first study the case where M_1 is a direct product of free monoids. Theorem 2 is a corollary of the next result.

Theorem 12. Let $M_1 = B_1^* \times \cdots \times B_s^*$. There exists a coding morphism from $F : M_1 \to M_2$ if and only if M_2 has a submonoid $C_1^* \times \cdots \times C_s^*$ such that for any $r \in \{1, \ldots, s\}$, $C_r \subseteq A_2$, $card(C_r) = 2$ if $card(B_r) \geq 2$ and $card(C_r) = 1$ if $card(B_r) = 1$.

Proof of Theorem 2. It is easy to verify on its dependence relation graph that a trace monoid M is a direct product of free monoids: the connected components of this graph are all complete graphs. Therefore, M_2 has a submonoid of the form $C_1^* \times \cdots \times C_s^*$, as described in Theorem 12, if and only if its dependence relation graph has an induced subgraph whose connected components are either isolated vertices or edges, and there is the right number of each of them. This property is decidable. $\square$

Proof of Theorem 12. Suppose that there exists a coding morphism $F : M_1 \to M_2$. The direct product of all the B_r^*'s, with $card(B_r) = 1$, is a free commutative monoid $B^{\oplus}$. By Corollary 9, there are $card(B)$ independent letters $\gamma \in A_2$, such that with any $b \in B$ is associated a distinct $\gamma \in alphF(b)$. For every B_r with $card(B_r) \geq 2$, we apply Lemma 10 on two distinct letters $a, b \in B_r$. This gives rise to some pairs $\alpha D_2 \beta$ in A_2.

The second part of Lemma 10 shows that these pairs $\{\alpha, \beta\}$ and the latter letters γ are pairwise independent. This ends the first part of the proof.

Suppose now that M_2 has a submonoid $C_1^* \times \cdots \times C_s^*$ such that $card(C_r) = 2$ if $card(B_r) \geq 2$ and $card(C_r) = 1$ if $card(B_r) = 1$, $r \in \{1, \ldots, s\}$. It is easy to construct a coding morphism $F : M_1 \to M_2$.
If $B_r = \{c\}$ and $C_r = \{\gamma\}$, we define the coding morphism:

$$F_r : B_r^* \to C_r^*, \quad F_r(c) = \gamma.$$

If $B_r = \{a_1, \ldots, a_k\}$ and $C_r = \{\alpha, \beta\}$, we define the coding morphism:

$$F_r : B_r^* \to C_r^*, \quad F_r(a_l) = \alpha^l \beta, \quad l \in \{1, \ldots, k\}.$$

Let us define $F : M_1 \to M_2$, by setting $F(a) = F_r(a)$, for any $a \in B_r$ and $r \in \{1, \ldots, s\}$. It is a coding (strong) morphism by Proposition 4. □

Notice that Proposition 5 is implied by the previous proof.

We now turn to the case where M_1 is a free product of free commutative monoids. Theorem 3 follows from the next result.

Theorem 13. *Let* $M_1 = B_1^\oplus * \cdots * B_s^\oplus$. *There exists a coding morphism* $F :$ $M_1 \to M_2$ *if and only if for all* $r \in \{1, \ldots, s\}$, *there exists* $C_r \subseteq A_2$ *such that*
1)

$$C_r = \cup_{l \in \{1, \ldots, k_r\}} C_{r,l}$$

where k_r *equals* $\mathrm{card}(B_r)$ *and the* $C_{r,l}$'s *are pairwise independent alphabets,*
2) for any $r' \neq r$, $r' \in \{1, \ldots, s\}$, *there are* k_r *pairs*

$$\alpha_{r,r',l} D_2 \beta_{r,r',l} \qquad l \in \{1, \ldots, k_r\}$$

with $\alpha_{r,r',l} \in C_{r,l}$, $\beta_{r,r',l} \in C_{r'}$, $\alpha_{r,r',l} \neq \beta_{r,r',l}$.

Proof of Theorem 3. The property required in Theorem 13 can be checked on the dependence relation graph of M_2 (see also Example 1). □

Proof of Theorem 13. Let $F : M_1 \to M_2$ be a coding morphism. For any $r \in \{1, \ldots, s\}$, let $C_{r,l}$ be the alphabets of the independent roots t_l of the restriction of F to $B_r^\oplus$. The first part of the statement holds, by appling Proposition 11 to the free product $B_r^\oplus * b^\oplus$, for any $r, r' \in \{1, \ldots, s\}$, $r' \neq r$, and for some $b \in B_{r'}$.

For the converse, we first define a map F on A_1, we then prove that it is a morphism, and finally we show that this is a coding morphism.

Consider one particular pair $\alpha D_2 \beta$. For any alphabet C_r, one of the following four cases can occur: $\alpha, \beta \in C_r$, $\alpha \in C_r, \beta \notin C_r$ (or the contrary), $\alpha, \beta \notin C_r$. Notice that, if $C_r \cap \{\alpha, \beta\} \neq \emptyset$, there could exist other alphabets $C_{r'}$, $r' \neq r$, such that $C_{r'} \cap \{\alpha, \beta\} \neq \emptyset$. Moreover, since the alphabets $C_{r,l}$, $l \in \{1, \ldots, k_r\}$, are pairwise independent, if α or β belong to C_r, then they belong to only one $C_{r,l} \subseteq C_r$.

Then, there exists a sufficiently large $p \in N$, such that we can construct traces $t_{r,l}$ over the alphabet $C_{r,l}$, $r \in \{1, \ldots, s\}$, $l \in \{1, \ldots, k_r\}$, in a way that for any pair $\alpha D_2 \beta$, the following conditions are verified [(*)]:
1) if $\alpha, \beta \in C_{r,l}$

$$\pi_{\alpha,\beta} t_{r,l} \in \alpha^p \sqcup\!\sqcup \beta^p \setminus \{\alpha^p \beta^p, \beta^p \alpha^p\}$$

and if $\alpha, \beta \in C_{r',l'}$, with $r' \neq r$, the words $\pi_{\alpha,\beta} t_{r,l}$ and $\pi_{\alpha,\beta} t_{r',l'}$ are not equal,
2) if $\alpha \in C_{r,l}$ and $\beta \notin C_{r,l}$ (or the contrary)

$$\pi_{\alpha,\beta} t_{r,l} = \alpha^p \quad \text{(or } \beta^p\text{)},$$

3) if $\alpha, \beta \notin C_{r,l}$

$$\pi_{\alpha,\beta} t_{r,l} = 1$$

It follows that the set

$$X_{\alpha,\beta} = \{\pi_{\alpha,\beta} t_{r,l} \mid r \in \{1,\ldots,s\}, \, l \in \{1,\ldots,k_r\}\} \backslash 1$$

is a code. Remember that $X_{\alpha,\beta}$ associates a distinct word with any $C_{r,l} \supseteq \{\alpha, \beta\}$. However, it could associate the same word α^p with two distinct alphabets $C_{r,l}$, $C_{r',l'}$ (whenever $C_{r,l} \cap \{\alpha, \beta\} = C_{r',l'} \cap \{\alpha, \gamma\} = \{\alpha\}$, with $\alpha D_2 \gamma$ another pair).

For any $r \in \{1,\ldots,s\}$, let $B_r = \{a_{r,1}, a_{r,2}, \ldots, a_{r,k_r}\}$. We define F on A_1 as follows:

$$F(a_{r,1}) = \prod_{l \in \{1,\ldots,k_r\}} t_{r,l} \qquad F(a_{r,l}) = F(a_{r,1}) t_{r,l} \quad l \in \{2,\ldots,k_r\}.$$

This map is a morphism. Indeed, for any fixed r, the traces $t_{r,l}, \, l \in \{1,\ldots,k_r\}$ are independent, as $alph(t_{r,l}) \subseteq C_{r,l}$. Then the images $F(a)$, $F(b)$ commute, for any $a, b \in B_r$.

Suppose now that $F(u) = F(u')$, for some $u, u' \in M_1$. Suppose also that their decompositions in the free product $B_1^{\oplus} * \cdots * B_r^{\oplus}$ are respectively

$$u = u_1 \cdots u_n, \quad u' = u_1' \cdots u_{n'}', \quad n, n' \geq 0.$$

Then, for any pair $\alpha D_2 \beta$, we have

$$\pi_{\alpha\beta} F(u_1) \pi_{\alpha\beta} F(u_2 \cdots u_n) = \pi_{\alpha\beta} F(u_1') \pi_{\alpha\beta} F(u_2' \cdots u_{n'}') \in X_{\alpha,\beta}^*. \qquad (2)$$

First, we are going to prove that $n = n'$, and that for any $m \in \{1,\ldots,n\}$, there exists $r \in \{1,\ldots,s\}$ such that $u_m, u_m' \in B_r^{\oplus}$ and $F(u_m) = F(u_m')$. After, we will show that $u_m = u_m'$, $m \in \{1,\ldots,n\}$. This will prove that F is a coding morphism.

The first part of the proof is by induction on $\min\{n, n'\}$. If $\min\{n, n'\} = 0$, then $n = n' = 0$ and $u = u' = 1$. Suppose that $\min\{n, n'\} > 1$.

By contradiction, suppose that $u_1 \in B_r^{\oplus}$, $u_1' \in B_{r'}^{\oplus}$, with $r \neq r'$. By hypothesis, we can choose a pair $\alpha D_2 \beta$ such that $\alpha \in C_r$ and $\beta \in C_{r'}$. In particular, $\alpha \in C_{r,l}$, $\beta \in C_{r',l'}$. By (2), as $X_{\alpha,\beta}$ is a code, we have

$$\pi_{\alpha\beta} t_{r,l} = \pi_{\alpha\beta} t_{r',l'} \in X_{\alpha,\beta}^+,$$

and $\alpha, \beta \in C_{r,l} \cap C_{r',l'}$. This is in contradiction with [*].

Hence, $u_1, u_1' \in B_r^{\oplus}$, for some $r \in \{1,\ldots,s\}$; and $F(u_1), F(u_1')$ are both products of traces $t_{r,l}, \, l \in \{1,\ldots,k_r\}$ (by definition of F). Assume that $F(u_1) \neq F(u_1')$, i.e. some trace $t_{r,l}$ occurs with power q in $F(u_1)$, when it occurs with power $q' > q$ in $F(u_1')$. Then $n \geq 2$ and $u_2 \in B_{r'}^{\oplus}$, with $r' \neq r$. By hypothesis, we can choose a pair $\alpha D_2 \beta$ with $\alpha \in C_{r,l}$, $\beta \in C_{r'}$. By (2), we get

$$\pi_{\alpha\beta} F(u_1) = \pi_{\alpha\beta} t_{r,l}^q \neq \pi_{\alpha\beta} t_{r,l}^{q'} = \pi_{\alpha\beta} F(u_1').$$

But $X_{\alpha,\beta}$ is a code and $q' > q$, it follows that $\pi_{\alpha\beta}F(u_2 \cdots u_n)$ has the word $\pi_{\alpha\beta}t_{r,l}^{q'-q}$ as prefix. This is impossible (use $^{(*)}$ as above, with $\pi_{\alpha\beta}t_{r,l}^{q'-q}$ and $\pi_{\alpha,\beta}F(u_2)$ with $u_2 \in B_{r'}^{\oplus}$, $r' \neq r$).

Then, $F(u_1) = F(u_1')$, and $F(u_2 \cdots u_n) = F(u_2' \cdots u_{n'}')$, as trace monoids are cancellative. By induction hypothesis, $n = n'$, and for any $m \in \{1, \ldots, n\}$, there exists $r \in \{1, \ldots, s\}$ such that $u_m, u_m' \in B_r^{\oplus}$ and $F(u_m) = F(u_m')$.

It remains to prove that $u_m = u_m'$, $m \in \{1, \ldots, n\}$. By definition of F, for $r \in \{1, \ldots, s\}$ such that $u_m, u_m' \in B_r^{\oplus}$, we have:

$$F(u_m) = \prod_{l \in \{1, \ldots, k_r\}} t_{r,l}^{q_l} \qquad q_l \geq 1$$

and

$$\begin{cases} x_1 + x_2 + \quad \cdots + x_{k_r} = q_1 \\ x_1 + 2x_2 + \quad \cdots + x_{k_r} = q_2 \\ x_1 + x_2 + 2x_3 + \cdots + x_{k_r} = q_3 \\ \vdots \qquad\qquad\qquad \vdots \\ x_1 + x_2 + \quad \cdots + 2x_{k_r} = q_{k_r} \end{cases}$$

where x_l is the number of occurrences of the letter $a_{r,l} \in B_r = \{a_{r,1}, \ldots, a_{r,k_r}\}$ inside u_m. The previous system has exactly one solution since the determinant

$$\begin{vmatrix} 1 & 1 & 1 & \cdots & 1 \\ 1 & 2 & 1 & \cdots & 1 \\ 1 & 1 & 2 & \cdots & 1 \\ \vdots & & \vdots & & \\ 1 & 1 & 1 & \cdots & 2 \end{vmatrix}$$

equals 1. It follows that $u_m = u_{m'}$. This ends the proof. $\qquad\qquad\square$

Acknowledgments

We are grateful to G. Guaiana, P. Mammone, A. Muscholl and J. Sakarovitch for fruitful discussions. We also thank one of the referees for useful comments.

References

[AH89]   I.J. Aalbersberg, H.J. Hoogeboom, Characterizations of the decidability of some problems for regular trace languages, *Math. Systems Theory* **22** (1989) 1–19.

[BP85]   J. Berstel, D. Perrin, *Theory of Codes*, Academic Press, New York, 1985.

[BDG94a] V. Bruyère, C. De Felice, G. Guaiana, Coding with Traces, Proc. STACS'94, *Lecture Notes Comput. Sci.* **775** (1994) 353–364.

[BDG94b] V. Bruyère, C. De Felice, G. Guaiana, Decidability for coding between trace monoids, submitted (1994).

[CF69]   P. Cartier, D. Foata, *Problèmes combinatoires de commutation et réarrange-ments*, Lecture Notes in Mathematics **85**, Springer, Berlin Heidelberg New-York (1969).

[Ch86]   C. Choffrut, Free partially commutative monoids, *Technical report* **86-20**, LITP, Université Paris 7 (1986).

[CR87]   M. Chrobak, W. Rytter, Unique decipherability for partially commutative alphabets, *Fundamenta Informaticae* **10** (1987) 323–336.

[CP85]   R. Cori, D. Perrin, Automates et commutations partielles, *RAIRO, Inform. Théor.* **19** (1985) 21–32.

[Di90a]   V. Diekert, Research topics in the theory of free partially commutative monoids, *Bulletin of EATCS* **40** (1990) 479–491.

[Di90b]   V. Diekert, *Combinatorics on traces*, Lecture Notes in Comput. Sci. **454**, Springer, Berlin Heidelberg New-York (1990).

[Du86a]   C. Duboc, *Commutations dans les monoïdes libres: un cadre théorique pour l'étude du parallélisme*, thèse, Université de Rouen (1986).

[Du86b]   C. Duboc, On some equations in free partially commutative monoids, *Theoret. Comput. Sci.* **46** (1986) 159–174.

[Ma77]   A. Mazurkiewicz, *Concurrent program schemes and their interpretations*, DAIMI Rep. PB 78, Aarhus University, Aarhus (1977).

[Oc88]   E. Ochmański, On morphisms of trace monoids, Proc. STACS 88, *Lecture Notes Comput. Sci.* **294** (1988) 346–355.

[Pe89]   D. Perrin, Partial commutations, *Lecture Notes Comput. Sci.* **372** (1989) 637–651.

[Sa92]   J. Sakarovitch, The "last" decision problem for rational trace languages, Proc. Latin'92, *Lecture Notes Comput. Sci.* **583** (1992) 460–473.

On Codings of Traces

Extended Abstract [*]

Volker Diekert   Anca Muscholl   Klaus Reinhardt

Institut für Informatik, Universität Stuttgart
Breitwiesenstr. 20-22, D-70565 Stuttgart
e-mail: {diekert,muscholl,reinhard}@informatik.uni-stuttgart.de

Abstract. The paper solves the main open problem of [BFG94]. We show that given two dependence alphabets (Σ, D) and (Σ', D'), it is decidable whether there exists a strong coding $h : M(\Sigma, D) \longrightarrow M(\Sigma', D')$ between the associated trace monoids. In fact, we show that the problem is NP-complete. (A coding is an injective homomorphism, it is strong if independent letters are mapped to independent traces.) We exhibit an example of trace monoids where a coding between them exists, but no strong coding. The decidability of codings remains open, in general. We have a lower and an upper bound, which show both to be strict. We further discuss encodings of free products of trace monoids and give almost optimal constructions.

In the final section, we state that the coding property is undecidable in a naturally arising class of homomorphisms.

Topics: Formal languages, concurrency.

1 Introduction

The theory of traces has been recognized as an important tool for investigations about concurrent systems, see [DR95]. The origins of the theory go back to the work of Mazurkiewicz (trace theory), Karp/Miller, Keller (parallel program schemata), and Cartier/Foata (combinatorics), see [Maz87, Kel73, CF69].

Traces are of particular interest for a description of concurrent processes, since for many algorithms one can obtain complexity bounds, which are close to the corresponding algorithms on words, e.g. test of equality [AG91], pattern matching [HY92], or word problems [Die89, Die90]. A convenient data structure for these algorithms is a representation of traces as a tuple of words. This is nothing but a coding of a trace monoid in a direct product of free monoids and leads to the general problem to find codings between trace monoids. This question has been raised by Ochmański in [Och88] and reconsidered recently by Bruyère et al. in [BFG94] (see also [BF95] in this volume). A natural class of codings of trace monoids is given by strong codings. These are injective homomorphisms

---

[*] This research has been supported by the ESPRIT Basic Research Action No. 6317 ASMICS 2, *Algebraic and Syntactic Methods In Computer Science*.

such that independent letters are mapped to independent traces (similar to a refinement of actions in a concurrent system). The main result of [BFG94] is the decidability of the existence of a strong coding for two large families of trace monoids, but the authors left open the general problem: given two trace monoids $M(\Sigma, D)$ and $M(\Sigma', D')$, is it decidable whether there exists a strong coding of one into the other. The main result of the present paper solves this problem. We give a graph theoretical criterion for the existence of a strong coding thereby showing its NP-completeness, see Thm. 9.

The paper contains several other results. As mentioned above, from the viewpoint of applications, the most important codings are those into a direct product of free monoids. Again, there is a characterization for strong codings, which is directly related to a covering by cliques and which shows the NP-completeness of this restricted problem, too. Much less is known if we consider codings (i.e., injective homomorphisms), instead of strong codings. For certain dependence alphabets we are able to compute the least k for the existence of an encoding of the trace monoid into a k-fold direct product (e.g., the path and the cycle of n vertices). We show that if the dependence alphabet is a cycle of four vertices, then the associated trace monoid has a coding into a direct product of free monoids with two components, whereas at least four are needed for a strong coding. The existence of a coding between trace monoids is NP-hard, but we even do not know its decidability in the restricted case where the second monoid is a direct product of free monoids. We have a lower bound for the minimal number of components we need by the size of a maximal independent set and an upper bound by the number of cliques which are needed to cover all vertices and edges. The exact value remains unknown.

We give an example of a dependence alphabet (which is in fact a cograph), where both the lower and the upper bounds are strict. Finally, we give almost optimal constructions for encoding free products of trace monoids into direct products of free monoids. The results can be used for encoding efficiently trace monoids with a cograph dependence alphabet.

In the final section we reconsider the well-known result on the undecidability of whether a given homomorphism of trace monoids is a coding. The proof [HC72, CR87] uses a reduction of the Post correspondence problem, and it does not apply to restricted classes of homomorphisms. In this paper we start with a so-called strict morphism between independence alphabets. These morphisms induce in a canonical way homomorphisms between the associated trace monoids. (The homomorphism of the Projection Lemma is of this kind.) Thm. 22 states that the coding property for this natural class of homomorphisms is undecidable.

2   Notations and Preliminaries

A dependence alphabet is a pair (Σ, D), where Σ is a finite alphabet and $D \subseteq \Sigma \times \Sigma$ is a reflexive and symmetric relation, called dependence relation. The complement $I = (\Sigma \times \Sigma) \setminus D$ is called independence relation; it is irreflexive and symmetric. The pair (Σ, I) is denoted independence alphabet. We view both (Σ, D) and (Σ, I) as undirected graphs. The difference is that (Σ, D) has self-loops (which however will be omitted in pictures). An undirected graph is simply a pair (V, E), where $E \subseteq V \times V$ is a symmetric relation. We use the following basic operations on graphs: complementation $\overline{(V, E)} = (V, (V \times V) \setminus E)$, disjoint union $(V_1, E_1) \dot\cup (V_2, E_2) = (V_1 \dot\cup V_2, E_1 \dot\cup E_2)$, and complex product $(V_1, E_1) * (V_2, E_2) = (V_1 \dot\cup V_2, E_1 \dot\cup E_2 \dot\cup (V_1 \times V_2) \dot\cup (V_2 \times V_1))$. (The smallest family of graphs containing the one-point graphs which is closed under these operations is the family of cographs, see e.g. [CLB81, CPS85].)

Given a dependence alphabet (Σ, D) (or an independence alphabet (Σ, I) resp.) we associate the trace monoid $M(\Sigma, D)$. This is the quotient monoid $\Sigma^* / \{ab = ba \mid (a, b) \in I\}$; an element $t \in M(\Sigma, D)$ is called a trace, the length $|t|$ of a trace t is given by the length of any representing word. By $\mathrm{alph}(t)$ we denote the alphabet of a trace t, which is the set of letters occurring in t. The initial alphabet of t is the set $\mathrm{in}(t) = \{x \in \Sigma \mid \exists t' : t = xt'\}$. By 1 we denote both the empty word and the empty trace. Traces $s, t \in M(\Sigma, D)$ are called independent, if $\mathrm{alph}(s) \times \mathrm{alph}(t) \subseteq I$. We simply write $(s, t) \in I$ in this case. A trace $t \neq 1$ is called a *root*, if $t = u^n$ implies $n = 1$, for every u. A trace t is called connected, if $\mathrm{alph}(t)$ induces a connected subgraph of the dependence alphabet (Σ, D).

The constructions disjoint union and complex product resp., on dependence alphabets correspond to the direct product and the free product (= direct sum in the category of monoids) resp., for the associated trace monoids. Thus, we have $M((\Sigma_1, D_1) \dot\cup (\Sigma_2, D_2)) = M(\Sigma_1, D_1) \times M(\Sigma_2, D_2)$ and $M((\Sigma_1, D_1) * (\Sigma_2, D_2)) = M(\Sigma_1, D_1) * M(\Sigma_2, D_2)$. The situation for independence alphabets is dual.

Let $\Sigma' \subseteq \Sigma$ be a subalphabet and $D' = (\Sigma' \times \Sigma') \cap D$ the induced dependence relation. The canonical projection $\pi_{\Sigma'} : M(\Sigma, D) \to M(\Sigma', D')$ is induced by $\pi_{\Sigma'}(a) = a$, if $a \in \Sigma'$ and $\pi_{\Sigma'}(a) = 1$ otherwise. Consider (Σ, D) written as a union of cliques, i.e., $(\Sigma, D) = (\bigcup_{i=1}^{k} \Sigma_i, \bigcup_{i=1}^{k} \Sigma_i \times \Sigma_i)$. Then we have the following well-known Projection Lemma:

Proposition 1 [CL85, CP85]. *Let* $(\Sigma, D) = (\bigcup_{i=1}^{k} \Sigma_i, \bigcup_{i=1}^{k} \Sigma_i \times \Sigma_i)$. *Then the canonical homomorphism*

$$\pi : M(\Sigma, D) \to \prod_{i=1}^{k} \Sigma_i^*, \qquad t \mapsto (\pi_{\Sigma_i}(t))_{1 \leq i \leq k}$$

is injective.

In the following a homomorphism $h : M(\Sigma, D) \to M(\Sigma', D')$ is called a *coding*, if it is injective. It is called a *strong* homomorphism, if independent letters are mapped to independent traces, i.e., if $(a, b) \in I$ implies $(h(a), h(b)) \in I'$ for all $a, b \in \Sigma$. Of particular interest are strong codings, a notion which has been introduced in [BFG94].

The next proposition belongs probably to folklore:

Proposition 2. *Let* (Σ, D) *be a dependence alphabet and* $k \geq 1$. *The following assertions are equivalent:*

1. *The dependence alphabet (Σ, D) contains an independent set of size k.*
2. *There exists a strong coding $h : \mathbf{N}^k \to M(\Sigma, D)$.*
3. *There exists a coding $h : \mathbf{N}^k \to M(\Sigma, D)$.*

Proof. Since the implications 1) $\Rightarrow$ 2) $\Rightarrow$ 3) are obvious, we show 3) $\Rightarrow$ 1). Let $\{a_1, \ldots, a_k\}$ be a set of generators of $\mathbf{N}^k$ and let $t_i = h(a_i)$, $1 \leq i \leq k$. By a result of Duboc [Dub86] the equations $t_i t_j = t_j t_i$ $(1 \leq i \neq j \leq k)$ yield the existence of pairwise independent, connected roots $x_1, \ldots, x_l$, together with nonnegative integers n_{ij} $(1 \leq i \leq k, 1 \leq j \leq l)$ such that $t_i = x_1^{n_{i1}} \cdots x_l^{n_{il}}$ for $1 \leq i \leq k$. The set of roots $\{x_1, \ldots, x_l\}$ generates a commutative submonoid of $M(\Sigma, D)$, and the coding factorizes as $h : \mathbf{N}^k \to \mathbf{N}^l \to M(\Sigma, D)$. With h being injective we have $k \leq l$ by linear algebra. Finally, it suffices to choose some letter $b_i \in \mathrm{alph}(x_i)$, $1 \leq i \leq l$, in order to establish the result.

Corollary 3. *It is NP-complete to decide whether there exists a (strong) coding of $\mathbf{N}^k$ into $M(\Sigma, D)$. Therefore, the problem whether there exists a (strong) coding between two given trace monoids is (at least) NP-hard.*

3 Characterization of the existence of strong codings

Strong codings between trace monoids are closely related to morphisms of (in-) dependence alphabets.

Definition 4. Let (V, E) and (V', E') be undirected graphs. A *morphism* $H : (V, E) \to (V', E')$ is a relation between vertices $H \subseteq V \times V'$ such that $(a, b) \in E$ implies $H(a) \times H(b) \subseteq E'$ for all $a, b \in V$. (By $H(a)$ we mean the set $\{\alpha \in V' \mid (a, \alpha) \in H\}$ for $a \in V$.)

Obviously, undirected graphs with these morphisms form a category. For $H \subseteq V \times V'$ we denote by H^{-1} the inverse relation $H^{-1} = \{(\alpha, a) \in V' \times V \mid (a, \alpha) \in H\}$. A relation $H \subseteq V \times V'$ is a morphism $H : (V, E) \to (V', E')$ if and only if $H^{-1} : \overline{(V', E')} \to \overline{(V, E)}$ is a morphism on the complement graphs in the opposite direction. Hence, complementation yields a duality of the category.

The basic relation between strong homomorphisms of trace monoids and morphisms of undirected graphs is given by the next lemma, which follows directly from the above definitions.

Lemma 5. *Let $h : M(\Sigma, D) \to M(\Sigma', D')$ be a homomorphism of trace monoids. Define $H \subseteq \Sigma \times \Sigma'$ as*

$$H = \{(a, \alpha) \in \Sigma \times \Sigma' \mid \alpha \in \mathrm{alph}(h(a))\}.$$

The following assertions are equivalent:

1. *$h : M(\Sigma, D) \to M(\Sigma', D')$ is a strong homomorphism.*
2. *$H : (\Sigma, I) \to (\Sigma', I')$ is a morphism of independence alphabets.*
3. *$H^{-1} : (\Sigma', D') \to (\Sigma, D)$ is a morphism of dependence alphabets.*

Definition 6. A morphism $G : (\Sigma', D') \to (\Sigma, D)$ of dependence alphabets is called *covering*, if for all $a \in \Sigma$ there exists $\alpha \in \Sigma'$ with $a \in G(\alpha)$ and if for all $(a, b) \in D$, $a \neq b$ there exists $(\alpha, \beta) \in D'$, $\alpha \neq \beta$ with $(a, b) \in G(\alpha) \times G(\beta)$.

The following lemma is stated with a different notation in [BFG94].

Lemma 7. *Let* $h : M(\Sigma, D) \to M(\Sigma', D')$ *be a strong coding. Define* $H = \{(a, \alpha) \in \Sigma \times \Sigma' \mid \alpha \in \mathrm{alph}(h(a))\}$. *Then* $H^{-1} : (\Sigma', D') \to (\Sigma, D)$ *is a covering of dependence alphabets.*

Proof. By Lem. 5 the relation H^{-1} is a morphism. Let $a \in \Sigma$, then $h(a) \neq 1$, since h is a coding. Hence $a \in H^{-1}(\alpha)$ for some $\alpha \in \Sigma'$. Now, let $(a, b) \in D$, $a \neq b$. Since $h(ab) \neq h(ba)$ we find by Prop. 1 a pair $(\alpha, \beta) \in D'$, $\alpha \neq \beta$ such that $\pi_{\alpha,\beta} h(ab) \neq \pi_{\alpha,\beta} h(ba)$. Thus, either $(a, b) \in H^{-1}(\alpha) \times H^{-1}(\beta)$ or $(a, b) \in H^{-1}(\beta) \times H^{-1}(\alpha)$ holds. In any case H^{-1} is a covering.

Lemma 8. *Let* $H \subseteq \Sigma \times \Sigma'$ *be a relation such that* $H^{-1} : (\Sigma', D') \to (\Sigma, D)$ *is a covering of dependence alphabets.*
Then there exists a strong coding $h : M(\Sigma, D) \to M(\Sigma', D')$ *such that* $H = \{(a, \alpha) \in \Sigma \times \Sigma' \mid \alpha \in \mathrm{alph}(h(a))\}$.

Proof. Let $\Sigma = \{a_1, a_2, ...\}$ and $\Sigma' = \{\alpha_1, \alpha_2, ...\}$. For each i define $\overrightarrow{H(a_i)} = \alpha_{i_1} \cdots \alpha_{i_k}$ and $\overleftarrow{H(a_i)} = \alpha_{i_k} \cdots \alpha_{i_1}$, where $H(a_i) = \{\alpha_{i_1}, ..., \alpha_{i_k}\}$ and $i_1 < \cdots < i_k$. For $i = 1, 2, ...$ let

$$h(a_i) = (\overrightarrow{H(a_i)})^i \, \overleftarrow{H(a_i)}.$$

Lem. 5 states that h is a strong homomorphism. We have to show that h is injective, only. First note that $h(a) \neq 1$ for all $a \in \Sigma$. Assume by contradiction that $h(x) = h(y)$ for some $x \neq y$. Let x be of minimal length with this property. Then $x = ax'$ for some $a \in \Sigma$, $x' \in M(\Sigma, D)$. Since h is strong and $h(x) = h(y)$, there is some $b \in \mathrm{alph}(y)$ with $(a, b) \in D$. Hence we can write $y = zby'$ for some $b \in \Sigma, y', z \in M(\Sigma, D)$ such that $(a, z) \in I$ and $(a, b) \in D$.
We have $a \neq b$ since x is of minimal length. Since H^{-1} is a covering, we find $(\alpha, \beta) \in D'$, $\alpha \neq \beta$ such that $\alpha \in \mathrm{alph}(h(a))$ and $\beta \in \mathrm{alph}(h(b))$. For the contradiction it is enough to show $\pi_{\alpha,\beta} h(x) \neq \pi_{\alpha,\beta} h(y)$. Since h is strong, we have $\pi_{\alpha,\beta} h(z) = 1$. We may assume that α comes before β in Σ'. Let $a = a_i$ and $b = a_j$ $(i \neq j)$. We have $\pi_{\alpha,\beta} h(a) = (\alpha \beta^\epsilon)^i (\beta^\epsilon \alpha)$ and $\pi_{\alpha,\beta} h(b) = (\alpha^\delta \beta)^j (\beta \alpha^\delta)$ for some $\delta, \epsilon \in \{0, 1\}$. It follows that neither $\pi_{\alpha,\beta} h(a)$ is a prefix of $\pi_{\alpha,\beta} h(y)$ nor $\pi_{\alpha,\beta} h(zb)$ is a prefix of $\pi_{\alpha,\beta} h(x)$. Hence $h(x) = h(y)$ is impossible.

The following result solves the main open problem of [BFG94]. It follows by the conjunction of Lem. 7 and Lem. 8.

Theorem 9. *Let* (Σ, D) *and* (Σ', D') *be dependence alphabets. The following assertions are equivalent:*

1. *There exists a strong coding* $h : M(\Sigma, D) \to M(\Sigma', D')$.

2. *There exists a covering $G : (\Sigma', D') \to (\Sigma, D)$ of dependence alphabets.*

Furthermore there are effective constructions between h and G such that $G = H^{-1}$ and $H = \{(a, \alpha) \in \Sigma \times \Sigma' \mid \alpha \in alph(h(a))\}$.

Corollary 10. *The following problem is NP-complete:*
Input: Dependence alphabets (Σ, D), (Σ', D').
Question: Does there exist a strong coding from $M(\Sigma, D)$ into $M(\Sigma', D')$?

4 Codings into direct products of free monoids

In this section we investigate codings of a trace monoid into a k-fold direct product of free monoids. We are interested in the smallest possible value of k. For strong codings the situation is clear, as stated in Prop. 12 below. (This result follows also from [BFG94].)

Lemma 11. *Let $h : M(\Sigma, D) \to \prod_{i=1}^{k} \Sigma_i^*$ be a strong coding into a k-fold direct product of free monoids. Let $\pi_i = \pi_{\Sigma_i}$ denote the canonical projection onto the i-th component and $C_i = \{a \in \Sigma \mid \pi_i h(a) \neq 1\}$, $i = 1, \ldots, k$. Then C_i is a (dependence) clique for all $i = 1, \ldots, k$ and $(\Sigma, D) = (\bigcup_{i=1}^{k} C_i, \bigcup_{i=1}^{k} C_i \times C_i)$.*

Proof. Since h is injective, each $(a, b) \in D$ is contained in some $C_i \times C_i$. The set C_i is a clique, $i = 1, \ldots, k$, since h is strong.

Proposition 12. *Let (Σ, D) be a dependence alphabet and $|\Sigma_i| \geq 2$ for $i = 1, \ldots, k$. Then there exists a strong coding $h : M(\Sigma, D) \to \prod_{i=1}^{k} \Sigma_i^*$ if and only if (Σ, D) allows a covering by k cliques. In particular, deciding the existence of strong codings into k-fold direct product of free monoids is NP-complete.*

Proof. One direction is Lem. 11, the other follows from the Projection Lemma, Prop. 1. The question, whether the vertices *and* edges of a given graph can be covered by k cliques, is NP-complete, see [GJ78] for details.

4.1 A lower bound

We now turn to the problem of codings into direct products *without* the property of being a strong homomorphism. The following example shows a dependence alphabet where the existence of a coding into a k-fold direct product of free monoids also requires a covering by k cliques. Hence, in the example, the bound of Prop. 12 is optimal for codings, too.

Example 1. Let $(\Sigma, D) = P_n$ be the path of length $n \geq 1$, i.e., $\Sigma = \{a_1, \ldots, a_n\}$ with $D = \{(a_p, a_q) \mid 1 \leq p, q \leq n, |p - q| \leq 1\}$. Suppose $h : M(\Sigma, D) \to \prod_{i=1}^{k} \Sigma_i^*$ is a coding. Then we have $k \geq n - 1$.

Proof. Assume by contradiction that there is an embedding h into a k-fold direct product, $k \leq n - 2$. For $1 \leq m < n$ let $A_m = \{i \mid 1 \leq i \leq k, h_i(a_m a_{m+1}) \neq$

$h_i(a_{m+1}a_m)\}$, with $h_i = \pi_i h$. Clearly, $A_m \neq \emptyset$ and $|\bigcup_{m=1}^{n-1} A_m| \leq n-2$. Moreover, for every $1 \leq l < m < n$ with $m \geq l+2$ we have $A_m \cap A_l = \emptyset$ (since $\{a_{m+1}\} \times \{a_l, a_{l+1}\} \subseteq I$ and thus $h_i(a_{m+1}) = 1$ for $i \in A_l$).

Now, let $1 \leq p < q \leq n$ with $q - p$ minimal such that $|\bigcup_{m=p}^{q-1} A_m| \leq q - p - 1$. Then $A_m \cap A_{m+1} \neq \emptyset$ for every $p \leq m < q - 1$ follows by the minimality of $q - p$, together with the above observation. Furthermore, we have $|A_m \cup A_{m+1}| \geq 2$ (otherwise, it is easy to see that nonnegative integers $r, s \geq 1$ exist, such that $h(a_m^r a_{m+1} a_{m+2}^s) = h(a_{m+2}^s a_{m+1} a_m^r))$. We can now deduce that after renumbering we have $A_p = \{p\}$, $A_m = \{m-1, m\}$ ($p < m < q - 1$) and $A_{q-1} = \{q-2\}$.

The final step is to show the existence of integers $k_i \geq 1$ ($p \leq i \leq q$) with $h(a_p^{k_p} \cdots a_q^{k_q}) = h(a_q^{k_q} \cdots a_p^{k_p})$ (note $q > p$), which yields the contradiction. For this, write $h_m(a_m) = r_m^{s_m}$ and $h_m(a_{m+2}) = r_m^{t_m}$, for some words r_m and integers $s_m, t_m \geq 1$, $p \leq m \leq q - 2$. The claimed k_i, $p \leq i \leq q$, are now chosen as a (positive) solution of the system of $(q - p - 2)$ equations $s_m \cdot k_m = t_m \cdot k_{m+2}$.

Remark. It is interesting to note that if (Σ, D) corresponds to C_n (the cycle of length n) and $n \geq 5$, then the optimal k for encoding $M(\Sigma, D)$ into a k-fold direct product of free monoids is again $k = n - 1$. The lower bound can be seen using the above result on $|\bigcup_{m=1}^{n-1} A_m|$. For C_4 we can do better, see Ex. 2 below.

In the following we denote by $\alpha(\Sigma, D)$ the size of a maximal independent set of (Σ, D). Lem. 11 yields the following obvious lower bound.

Proposition 13. *Let* $h : M(\Sigma, D) \to \prod_{i=1}^k \Sigma_i^*$ *be a coding. Then we have* $\alpha(\Sigma, D) \leq k$.

Proof. $\mathbb{N}^{\alpha(\Sigma, D)}$ is a submonoid of $M(\Sigma, D)$.

4.2 Inductive methods

The following example (also used in [BF95]) provides two observations: For some codings we can achieve the lower bound $\alpha(\Sigma, D)$ of Prop. 13, and we may find a coding into a k-fold direct product, where no strong coding exists.

Example 2. Let (Σ, D) be a C_4, i.e., a cycle with four letters.

$$(\Sigma, D) = \begin{array}{c} a - d \\ | \quad | \\ b - c \end{array}$$

Then there is a coding $h : M(\Sigma, D) \to \{a, b\}^* \times \{c, d\}^*$. Thus for a coding a 2-fold ($2 = \alpha(\Sigma, D)$) direct product of free monoids is enough, whereas for a strong coding we need four components by Prop. 12.

Proof. Choose any nonnegative integers $m_1, m_2, n_1, n_2 > 0$ such that the matrix $\begin{pmatrix} m_1 & n_1 \\ m_2 & n_2 \end{pmatrix}$ is non-singular. Define $h : M(\Sigma, D) \to \{a, b\}^* \times \{c, d\}^*$ by

$$h(a) = (a^{m_1}, c^{n_1}), \quad h(b) = (b^{m_1}, d^{n_1}), \quad h(c) = (a^{m_2}, c^{n_2}), \quad h(d) = (b^{m_2}, d^{n_2}).$$

It is easily seen that h is injective. The basic observation is that $M(\Sigma, D)$ has the algebraic structure of a free product of $\mathbf{N}^2$ by $\mathbf{N}^2$.

In fact, Ex. 2 reveals a more general principle.

Proposition 14. *Let* $h_j : M(\Sigma_j, D_j) \to \prod_{i=1}^k \Gamma_i^*$ *be codings such that* $|\Gamma_i| \geq 2$ *and* $\pi_i h_j(a) \neq 1$ *for all* $a \in \Sigma_j$, $i = 1, \ldots, k$, $j = 1, \ldots, m$. *Then there exists a coding* $h : \overset{m}{\underset{j=1}{*}} M(\Sigma_j, D_j) \to \prod_{i=1}^k \Gamma_i^*$, *where* $\overset{m}{\underset{j=1}{*}} M(\Sigma_j, D_j)$ *denotes the m-fold free product. Furthermore, we find* h *such that* $\pi_i h(a) \neq 1$ *for all* $a \in \bigcup_{j=1}^m \Sigma_j$ *and* $i = 1, \ldots, k$.

Proof. (Sketch) For each j replace Γ_i by some Γ_{ij} such that the alphabets become disjoint for different j. The codings h_j define a canonical homomorphism $\overline{h} : \overset{m}{\underset{j=1}{*}} M(\Sigma_j, D_j) \to \prod_{i=1}^k (\bigcup_{j=1}^m \Gamma_{ij})^*$. Since $\pi_i h_j(a) \neq 1$ it is easy to see that $\overline{h}$ is a coding. Furthermore, we have $\pi_i \overline{h}(a) \neq 1$ for all $a \in \bigcup_{j=1}^m \Sigma_j$. Finally, since $|\Gamma_i| \geq 2$ for all $i = 1, \ldots, k$, we can code $(\bigcup_{j=1}^m \Gamma_{ij})^*$ into Γ_i^*.

Corollary 15. *Let* $k, m \geq 1$ *and* a, b *different letters,* $a \neq b$. *Then there exists a coding* $h : \overset{m}{\underset{i=1}{*}} \mathbf{N}^k \to \prod_{i=1}^k \{a, b\}^*$.

Unfortunately, the hypothesis $\pi_i h_j(a) \neq 1$ of Prop. 14 is very strong. As soon as (Σ, D) contains three letters a, b, c such that $(a, b) \in D$, $(a, c) \in I$, and $(b, c) \in I$ it cannot be satisfied anymore. Even for cographs (Σ, D) the number $k = \alpha(\Sigma, D)$ is, in general, not large enough in order to allow a coding of $M(\Sigma, D)$ into a k-fold direct product of free monoids. We have the following example showing the strictness of our lower and upper bounds:

Example 3. Let the dependence alphabet be the following cograph:

$$(\Sigma, D) = \quad , \text{ i.e., } (\Sigma, I) = \quad$$

Then we have $\alpha(\Sigma, D) = 2$ and $M(\Sigma, D) = (\{a, b\}^* \times \{c, d\}^*) * (\{p, q\}^* \times \{r, s\}^*)$. The least k such that a coding $h : M(\Sigma, D) \to \prod_{1 \leq i \leq k} \Sigma_i^*$ exists is $k = 3$.

Proof. (Sketch) First assume $h : M(\Sigma, D) \to \Sigma_1^* \times \Sigma_2^*$ would be a coding. A combinatorial argument yields the existence of letters $x \in \{a, b, c, d\}$ and

$y \in \{p,q,r,s\}$ such that $h(x) = (u,1)$, $h(y) = (1,v)$ for some $u \in \Sigma_1^*$, $v \in \Sigma_2^*$. Then $h(xy) = h(yx) = (u,v)$ contradicting $xy \neq yx$.

Finally, consider the homomorphism $h : M(\Sigma, D) \to \{a,b,p,q\}^* \times \{r,s,e\}^* \times \{c,d,f\}^*$ given by the following table (where the columns give $h(x)$, $x \in \Sigma$):

h	a	b	c	d	p	q	r	s
$\{a,b,p,q\}$	a	b	1	1	p	q	1	1
$\{r,s,e\}$	e	e	e	e	1	1	r	s
$\{c,d,f\}$	1	1	c	d	f	f	f	f

To check injectivity, note that for $t \in M(\Sigma, D)$, $h(t)$ allows to decode the initial alphabet of t: if the 2nd (resp. 3rd) component starts in $\{r,s\}$ (resp. in $\{c,d\}$) then the corresponding letter belongs to $in(t)$. Otherwise we have e and f in the last two components, which restricts $in(t)$ to the set $\{a,b,p,q\}$, which in turn is identified by the first component of the encoding.

The next results concern the special case of embedding trace monoids with co-graph dependence alphabets into direct products of free monoids. Consider two codings $h_1 : M_1 = M(\Sigma_1, D_1) \to \prod_{i=1}^{k} \Sigma_i^*$ and $h_2 : M_2 = M(\Sigma_2, D_2) \to \prod_{j=1}^{l} \Gamma_j^*$. Whereas the direct product $M_1 \times M_2$ can be embedded into a $(k+l)$-fold direct product (a tight bound), we are able to obtain a better upper bound for the free product $M_1 * M_2$. The next lemma presents an inductive method for embedding free products.

Lemma 16. *Let* $M_1 = M(\Sigma_1, D_1)$, $M_2 = M(\Sigma_2, D_2)$ *be given trace monoids. Let* Σ_1, Σ_2 *be pairwise disjoint, let* Γ *be an alphabet and* $x \notin \Gamma$ *a new letter. Then there exists a coding* $h : M_1 * (M_2 \times \Gamma^*) \to (M_1 * M_2) \times (\Gamma \cup \{x\})^*$.

Proof. Consider the homomorphism $h : M_1 * (M_2 \times \Gamma^*) \to (M_1 * M_2) \times (\Gamma \cup \{x\})^*$ given by

$$h(a) = \begin{cases} (a, x) & \text{for } a \in \Sigma_1 \\ (a, 1) & \text{for } a \in \Sigma_2 \\ (1, a) & \text{for } a \in \Gamma \end{cases}$$

Note that h allows the decoding of initial alphabets as follows. The 2nd component of an encoded trace $h(z)$, $\pi_{\Gamma \cup \{x\}} h(z)$, starts by $a \in \Gamma$ if and only if a belongs to the initial alphabet of z, $in(z)$. Otherwise, a letter $b \in (\Sigma_1 \cup \Sigma_2) \cap in(z)$ can be determined using $\pi_{\Sigma_1 \cup \Sigma_2} h(z) = \pi_{\Sigma_1 \cup \Sigma_2} z$.

Theorem 17. *Let* $h_1 : M(\Sigma_1, D_1) \to \prod_{i=1}^{k} \Sigma_i^*$ *and* $h_2 : M(\Sigma_2, D_2) \to \prod_{j=1}^{l} \Gamma_j^*$ *be codings,* $k, l \geq 1$. *Then there exists a coding of* $M(\Sigma_1, D_1) * M(\Sigma_2, D_2)$ *into a* $(k+l-1)$-*fold direct product of free monoids. Moreover, this bound is optimal, in general.*

Proof. Clearly, for trace monoids M_i, N_i such that M_i can be embedded into N_i ($i = 1, 2$), we can embed $M_1 * M_2$ canonically into $N_1 * N_2$. Thus, assume that $M_1 = M(\Sigma_1, D_1) = \prod_{i=1}^{k} \Sigma_i^*$ and $M_2 = M(\Sigma_2, D_2) = \prod_{j=1}^{l} \Gamma_j^*$ holds and let w.l.o.g. $l \geq 2$. By Lem. 16 we can embed $(\prod_{i=1}^{k} \Sigma_i^*) * ((\prod_{j=1}^{l-1} \Gamma_j^*) \times \Gamma_l^*)$ into the monoid $((\prod_{i=1}^{k} \Sigma_i^*) * (\prod_{j=1}^{l-1} \Gamma_j^*)) \times (\Gamma_l \cup \{x\})^*$. By induction, the left operand of the outer direct product can be embedded into a $(k + l - 2)$-fold direct product, which yields the result.

The lower bound of this construction is obtained by generalizing Ex. 3 to the monoid $(\prod_{i=1}^{k} \{a, b\}^*) * (\prod_{j=1}^{l} \{p, q\}^*)$.

We consider in Thm. 19 below a nearly optimal method (with regard to the number of components) of encoding m-fold free products, $m \geq 3$, into direct products of free monoids. Let us start with a technical

Lemma 18. *Let $k, m \geq 2$ and let Σ_{ij} be pairwise disjoint alphabets, $i = 1, \ldots, k$, $j = 1, \ldots, m$. Then there exists a coding* $h : \overset{m}{\underset{j=1}{*}} (\prod_{i=1}^{k} \Sigma_{ij}^*) \to (\bigcup_{j=1}^{m} \Sigma_{1,j})^* \times (\overset{m}{\underset{j=1}{*}} (\mathbf{N} \times \prod_{i=2}^{k} \Sigma_{ij}^*))$.

Proof. Let x_j, $j = 1, \ldots, m$, be new letters. We identify $\{x_j\}^* \times \prod_{i=2}^{k} \Sigma_{ij}^*$ with $\mathbf{N} \times \prod_{i=2}^{k} \Sigma_{ij}^*$. The following homomorphism h is easily seen to be injective:

$$h(a) = \begin{cases} (a, (x_j, 1)) & \text{if } a \in \Sigma_{1j} \text{ for some } 1 \leq j \leq m \\ (1, (1, a)) & \text{if } a \notin \bigcup_{j=1}^{m} \Sigma_{1j} \end{cases}$$

The theorem below can be applied in conjunction with Lem. 16 in order to encode m-fold free products efficiently for $m \geq 3$. (Lem. 16 is used for reducing the number of components.)

Theorem 19. *Let $h_j : M(\Sigma_j, D_j) \to \prod_{i=1}^{k} \Gamma_{ij}^*$ be codings, $j = 1, \ldots, m$, and $a \neq b$. Then there exists a coding* $h : \overset{m}{\underset{j=1}{*}} M(\Sigma_j, D_j) \to \prod_{i=1}^{2k} \{a, b\}^*$.

Proof. Assume Γ_{ij} to be pairwise disjoint. By repeated application of Lem. 18 we obtain a coding $h' : \overset{m}{\underset{j=1}{*}} (\prod_{i=1}^{k} \Gamma_{ij}^*) \to \prod_{i=1}^{k} \Theta_i^* \times (\overset{m}{\underset{j=1}{*}} \mathbf{N}^k)$, with $\Theta_i = \bigcup_{j=1}^{m} \Gamma_{ij}$ for $i = 1, \ldots, k$. By standard methods we encode Θ_i^* into $\{a, b\}^*$ and, by Cor. 15, $\overset{m}{\underset{j=1}{*}} \mathbf{N}^k$ into $\prod_{i=k+1}^{2k} \{a, b\}^*$. The result follows by composition with the coding of $\overset{m}{\underset{j=1}{*}} M(\Sigma_j, D_j)$ into $\overset{m}{\underset{j=1}{*}} (\prod_{i=1}^{k} \Gamma_{ij}^*)$.

Remark. Note that already for $m = 2$ the lower bound for Thm. 19 is by Thm. 17 the value $2k - 1$. Hence, Thm. 19 gives an almost optimal construction.

5 Clique-preserving morphisms

Throughout this section the notion of clique is meant w.r.t. independence alphabets.

Definition 20. A clique-preserving morphism of independence alphabets H : $(\Sigma, I) \to (\Sigma', I')$ is a relation $H \subseteq \Sigma \times \Sigma'$ such that $H(A) = \{\alpha \in \Sigma' \mid (a, \alpha) \in H, a \in A\}$ is a clique of (Σ', I') whenever $A \subseteq \Sigma$ is a clique of (Σ, I).

A clique-preserving morphism $H \subseteq \Sigma \times \Sigma'$ yields in a natural way a homomorphism $h : M(\Sigma, D) \to M(\Sigma', D')$ by letting $h(a) = \prod_{\alpha \in H(a)} \alpha$ for $a \in \Sigma$. Note that the product is well-defined since $H(a)$ is (by definition) a clique, i.e., a set of commuting elements. (In fact, our construction is a faithful covariant functor from independence alphabets to trace monoids.)

The most prominent homomorphism of trace monoids arising this way is the coding used in the Projection Lemma, Prop. 1. Write $(\Sigma, D) = (\bigcup_{i=1}^{k} \Sigma_i, \bigcup_{i=1}^{k} \Sigma_i \times \Sigma_i)$ and let $\Sigma' = \dot{\bigcup}_{i=1}^{k} \Sigma_i$ be the disjoint union. The identity relations $id_{\Sigma_i} \subseteq \Sigma_i \times \Sigma_i$ induce in a natural way a relation $H \subseteq \Sigma \times \Sigma'$ which by abuse of language can be written as $H = \bigcup_{i=1}^{k} id_{\Sigma_i} \subseteq \Sigma \times \Sigma'$. The associated homomorphism h is exactly the strong coding of Prop. 1, $h : M(\Sigma, D) \to \prod_{i=1}^{k} \Sigma_i^*$.

Remark. Note that a clique-preserving morphism is not a morphism of undirected graphs as defined in Sect. 3, in general. The reason is that for $(a, b) \in I$ we may have $H(a) \cap H(b) \neq \emptyset$. Therefore the induced homomorphisms of trace monoids are not strong, in general.

The following proposition is in major contrast to the final result of Thm. 22 below.

Proposition 21. *Let* $H \subseteq \Sigma \times \Sigma'$ *be a relation such that* $H(a)$ *is a clique of* (Σ', I') *for all* $a \in \Sigma$. *Then the induced homomorphism* $h : \Sigma^* \to M(\Sigma', D')$ *with* $h(a) = \prod_{\alpha \in H(a)} \alpha$ *is injective if and only if for all* $a, b \in \Sigma$, $a \neq b$ *there exists some* $(\alpha, \beta) \in D'$, $\alpha \neq \beta$ *with* $\alpha \in H(a), \beta \in H(b)$.

It is well-known that it is undecidable whether a homomorphism of trace monoids is injective, see [HC72, CR87]. The following theorem sharpens this result in the sense that we show the undecidability for a more natural class of homomorphism.

Theorem 22. *Given a clique-preserving morphism of independence alphabets* $H : (\Sigma, I) \to (\Sigma', I')$, *it is undecidable whether the associated homomorphism* $h : M(\Sigma, D) \to M(\Sigma', D')$, $h(a) = \prod_{\alpha \in H(a)} \alpha$ *for* $a \in \Sigma$, *is a coding.*

The proof of Thm. 22 is a technical and involved reduction of the halting problem of a two-counter machine. For lack of space we omit the details and refer to the full version of this paper.

6 Conclusion and open problems

In this paper we have solved the problem of the existence of strong codings for trace monoids by giving a NP-complete graph criterion. Whether or not the existence of codings is decidable remains an interesting open question. For strong codings into a k-fold direct product of free monoids we know the smallest possible value of k. For codings, we know a lower and an upper bound for k, only. It is still possible that the smallest k is uncomputable.

We have extended a well-known undecidability result to a very natural class of homomorphism. The proof (not included in the present extended abstract) is very complicated. It would be interesting to find a simple direct proof.

References

[AG91]   C. Àlvarez and J. Gabarró. The parallel complexity of two problems on concurrency. *Information Processing Letters*, 38:61–70, 1991.

[BF95]   V. Bruyère and C. De Felice. Coding and Strong Coding in Trace Monoids. *This volume.*

[BFG94] V. Bruyère, C. De Felice, and G. Guaiana. Coding with traces. In *Proc. of STACS'94*, LNCS 775, pp. 353–364. Springer, 1994.

[CF69]   P. Cartier and D. Foata. *Problèmes combinatoires de commutation et réarrangements.* Lecture Notes in Mathematics 85. Springer, 1969.

[CL85]   M. Clerbout and M. Latteux. Partial commutations and faithful rational transductions. *Theoretical Computer Science*, 35:241–254, 1985.

[CLB81] D. G. Corneil, H. Lerchs, and L. Stewart Burlingham. Complement reducible graphs. *Discrete Appl. Math.*, 3:163–174, 1981.

[CP85]   R. Cori and D. Perrin. Automates et commutations partielles. *R.A.I.R.O. — Informatique Théorique et Applications*, 19:21–32, 1985.

[CPS85] D. G. Corneil, Y. Pearl, and L. K. Stewart. A linear recognition algorithm for cographs. *SIAM Journal of Computing*, 14:926–934, 1985.

[CR87]   M. Chrobak and W. Rytter. Unique decipherability for partially commutative alphabets. *Fundamenta Informaticae*, X:323–336, 1987.

[Die89] V. Diekert. Word problems over traces which are solvable in linear time. *Theoretical Computer Science*, 74:3–18, 1990.

[Die90] V. Diekert. *Combinatorics on Traces.* LNCS 454. Springer, 1990.

[DR95]   V. Diekert and G. Rozenberg, eds. *The Book of Traces.* World Scientific, Singapore, 1995. To appear.

[Dub86] C. Duboc. On some equations in free partially commutative monoids. *Theoretical Computer Science*, 46:159–174, 1986.

[GJ78]   M. Garey and D. Johnson. *Computers and Intractability: A Guide to the Theory of NP-completeness.* Freeman, San Francisco, 1978.

[HC72]   G. Hotz and V. Claus. *Automatentheorie und Formale Sprachen, Band III.* Bibliographisches Institut, Mannheim, 1972.

[HY92]   K. Hashiguchi and K. Yamada. String matching problems over free partially commutative monoids. *Information and Computation*, 101:131–149, 1992.

[Kel73] R. Keller. Parallel program schemata and maximal parallelism I. Fundamental results. *Journal of the ACM*, 20:514–537, 1973.

[Maz87] A. Mazurkiewicz. Trace theory. In *Petri Nets, Applications and Relationship to other Models of Concurrency*, LNCS 255. Springer, 1987.

[Och88] E. Ochmański. On morphisms of trace monoids. In *Proc. of STACS'88*, LNCS 294, pp. 346–355. Springer, 1988.

Finding Largest Common Embeddable Subtrees

Arvind Gupta* and Naomi Nishimura**

Abstract. We consider the problem of determining the largest tree embeddable in two labeled trees T and T', where the embedding relation is one of subgraph isomorphism or topological embedding. This problem is a generalization of classical tree pattern matching where the problem is to determine if one labeled tree is isomorphic to a subgraph of another. In this paper, we present a general framework for the variations on the problem, for the two embedding relations and for different assumptions about labeling of nodes in the trees. Our general paradigm provides sequential and parallel algorithms for the various subproblems, many of which have no other known solutions.

1 Introduction

Trees and their generalizations are among the most common and best studied of all combinatorial structures arising in computer science, due in large part to the number of areas of research in which they are applicable. For example, in data structure design, trees are the primary vehicle for storing data; many efficient data structures are tree-based. Trees have also been used in such diverse areas as compiler design [PN91, Alb89], structured text databases [Kil92, KM92], and the theory of natural languages [MSH85, Fri81]. More recently, labeled trees have been used in phylogeny and molecular biology, where many of the underlying structures can be modeled with trees [FG85, KKM92, SW, FT94]. Due to the large number of application areas, often the same or similar problems are studied under different terminology. It is our goal to unify a particular class of tree problems into a common framework and to present general sequential and parallel algorithms for problems in the framework.

Over the years, researchers have developed a systematic theory through the study of the algorithmic aspects of trees. Recently, there has been a renewed focus on their combinatorial aspects. In part this is due to the central role of trees in the work by Robertson and Seymour on graph minors [RS84, RS86]. Their far-ranging work on general graphs begins with a treatment of trees as a base case. Variations of the following problem arise in this work.

* School of Computing Science, Simon Fraser University, Burnaby, BC, Canada, V5A 1S6. email: arvind@cs.sfu.ca, FAX (604) 291-3045. Research supported by the Natural Sciences and Engineering Research Council of Canada, the Center for System Sciences and the Advanced Systems Institute.

** Department of Computer Science, University of Waterloo, Waterloo, Ontario, Canada, N2L 3G1. email: nishi@plg.uwaterloo.ca, FAX (519) 885-1208. Research supported by the Natural Sciences and Engineering Research Council of Canada and the Information Technology Research Centre.

Embeddable Tree Problem: Given two trees T and T', determine whether or not T is embeddable in T'.

Some natural embeddings for which this problem has been studied include *subgraph isomorphism*, *topological embedding*, and *minor containment*; there has been considerable work done on the sequential and parallel complexities of these problems in the case where T and T' are unlabeled [Mat78, Chu87, LK89, GKMS90, GN92]. Further discussion of embedding problems and their formal definitions can be found in Section 2.

A more general problem is that of finding the largest tree common to both T and T'.

Largest Common Embeddable Tree Problem: Given two trees T and T', determine the largest tree S such that S is embeddable in both T and T'.

Here, the size of the subtree S refers to the number of labeled nodes in the tree. For the three embedding relations mentioned above, the *Embeddable Tree Problem* reduces to the *Largest Common Embeddable Tree Problem* since T is embeddable in T' if and only if T is the largest common embeddable tree.

Determining the largest common embeddable tree is a problem of interest in its own right, even when T is not embeddable in T'. Quantifying the similarity between two trees, or more generally between a given tree and each tree in a fixed set of templates, is a natural problem arising in many application areas; the size of the largest common embeddable tree is one such measure. In addition, identifying the largest common embeddable tree may make it possible to merge two or more trees representing slightly differing views of the same set of data. For example, for T and T' general trees with distinct leaf labels, the largest embeddable tree problem has applications in phylogeny when the embedding relation is topological embedding. Given two evolutionary trees derived using different methods, the largest subtree is a more robust evolutionary tree. This phylogeny problem and its variations have been studied extensively [FG85, KKM92, SW, FT94].

In this paper we study the sequential and parallel complexity of the *Largest Common Embeddable Tree Problem*, for four different sets of assumptions about T and T'. In particular, we consider the following possible restrictions on the node labels.

Unlabeled No labels appear on the nodes. This is equivalent to all nodes having the same label.

Leaf Labels Only leaves of T and T' are labeled.

Distinct Leaf Labels Only leaves of T and T' are labeled. Moreover, a particular label can appear at most once in T and at most once in T'.

Arbitrary Labels The nodes of T and T' can have any labels.

The definitions of the embedding problems vary slightly with the different restrictions. In particular, for problems with leaf labels, we will often be concerned with finding a common tree whose leaves map to the leaves of T and T'.

After introducing notation and some basic results in Section 2, we give a general outline of the technique used to solve the various *Largest Common Embeddable Tree Problems*. In particular, in Section 3 we compare the sequential algorithm for subgraph isomorphism on unlabeled trees to the technique used to solve the *Embeddable Tree Problem*, and outline how this can be extended to parallel algorithms and algorithms for different labelings. Next we discuss how this basic idea can be extended to solve topological embedding problems (Section 4). Finally, in Section 5 we present some directions for further research.

2 Preliminaries

2.1 Trees

For all the problems in this paper, we consider trees (graphs with no cycles) which are finite and have one distinguished node, the root. We denote the node and edge sets of a tree T by $V(T)$ and $E(T)$, respectively. The size of T, $|V(T)|$, is denoted by $|T|$ and the root of T is denoted by $\text{root}(T)$. For v a node of T, $d(v)$ will denote the number of children of v. Similarly, for $e = (p_e, c_e)$ an edge of T, where p_e is the parent and c_e is the child, $d(e)$ will denote $d(c_e)$. In several variants of the basic problem, we will consider trees which have labels on some or all of the nodes; a node v has label $\ell(v)$.

As part of our algorithms, we will make use of several types of trees other than the original input trees. One such tree, the *Brent tree* (defined in Section 2.3), is used in our parallel algorithms. For clarity, we will refer to *nodes* of a tree T and *vertices* of a Brent tree. We associate with each vertex in a Brent tree a *level number*, where the root of the tree is at level 1 and the child of a vertex at level t is at level $t + 1$.

In processing a tree T, we will distinguish between an arbitrary connected *subgraph* of T, and a *subtree* of T consisting of a node in $V(T)$ and all its descendants, where T_v denotes the subtree of T rooted at v. In the course of our algorithms, we will often be concerned with subgraphs that arise from removing one subtree from another. For S a subtree of T and $v \in V(S)$, $S \backslash S_v$ denotes the subgraph obtained by removing from S all proper descendants of v. In particular, this means that the node v is in the set $S \backslash S_v$. We say that $S \backslash S_v$ is a *node-scarred subtree* of T, where v is a *node-scar*, and that $S \backslash S_v$ is *node-scarred at* v.

At times we will instead decompose a tree into subgraphs based on edges. For an edge $e = (p_e, c_e) \in E(T)$ we define T_e to be the subgraph of T induced by the nodes $T_{c_e} \bigcup \{p_e\}$. Analogous to the definitions above, for a subtree S of T and an edge $f = (p_f, c_f)$ of S, we define $S \backslash S_f$ to be the subgraph of S obtained by removing all nodes in the graph S_{c_f}, except c_f itself. We then say that $S \backslash S_f$ is an *edge-scarred subtree* of T, where f is an *edge-scar*, and S is *edge-scarred at* f. The subgraphs $S \backslash S_f$ and $S \backslash S_{c_f}$ are not equivalent unless c_f is the only child of p_f.

In this context, we will say that an edge e is the *parent* of an edge f if $c_e = p_f$ and that an edge e is an *ancestor* of an edge g if c_e is an ancestor of p_g. Similarly,

f is a *child* of e if $p_f = c_e$ and g is a *descendant* of e if p_g is a descendant of c_e. Edges e and f are *siblings* if $p_e = p_f$.

2.2 Topological Embedding

We present the definition of topological embedding in terms of unlabeled trees; the definition for labeled trees can be derived by adding the further condition that the image of each node be a node with the same label.

Topological embedding can be seen as a generalization of subgraph isomorphism, that is, the problem of determining whether or not one tree is a subgraph of another.

Definition 1. A tree S is *topologically embeddable* in a tree T, $S \leq_e T$, if there is a one-to-one function $\phi : V(S) \to V(T)$ such that for any $v, w, x \in V(S)$ the following properties hold. If w is a child of v, then $\phi(w)$ is a descendant of $\phi(v)$. If w and x are distinct children of v, then the path from $\phi(v)$ to $\phi(w)$ and the path from $\phi(v)$ to $\phi(x)$ have exactly the node $\phi(v)$ in common. Equivalently, we will say that there is a *topological embedding* of S in T. The topological embedding is a *root-to-root topological embedding* if $\phi(\text{root}(S)) = \text{root}(T)$.

Intuitively, $S \leq_e T$ if we can map each node in S to a node in T such that the edges map to node-disjoint paths. For convenience, we may refer to a function ψ which maps edges in S to paths in T, and describe an edge in the path $\psi(e)$ as an edge in the image of ψ. In the remainder of the paper, we distinguish between topological embedding, as defined above, and embedding, referring to the class of problems containing subgraph isomorphism and topological embedding.

2.3 Brent Restructuring

To solve our tree problems in parallel, we apply results of Brent [Bre74] to divide a tree into a number of subgraphs, each a fixed fraction smaller than the original tree. We can obtain a recursive solution by solving the problem on the subgraphs, with the depth of recursion at most $O(\log n)$. This technique has been applied in a number of papers [Gup85, CGR86, GN92, GN94]; we refer the reader to [GN92] for a detailed discussion.

The method used by Brent in performing the division forms two different types of subgraphs of the original tree T, namely unscarred and scarred subtrees of T. The lemmas below, slight generalizations of results of Brent, contain the essential components of the division for the first case (Lemma 2) and the second case (Lemma 3). Proofs of these lemmas can be found in an earlier paper [GN92].

Lemma 2. *Let T be a tree with at least two nodes. Then there is a unique node v of T with children $c_0, \ldots, c_{k-1}$ such that:*

1. $|T \backslash T_v| \leq \frac{|T|}{2}$, (or equivalently $|T_v| > \frac{|T|}{2}$); and
2. $|T_{c_i}| \leq \frac{|T|}{2}$, for all $0 \leq i \leq k$.

Lemma 3. *Let T be a tree, $|T| > 2$, and l be a leaf of T. Then there is a unique ancestor v of l such that if c is the child of v for which $l \in T_c$ then:*

1. $|T \backslash T_v| \leq \frac{|T|}{2}$, *(or equivalently $|T_v| > \frac{|T|}{2}$); and*
2. $|T_c| \leq \frac{|T|}{2}$.

We obtain a division of the tree into subgraphs by starting with a tree T and recursively applying the two lemmas depending on whether or not a subgraph has a scar. In practice, we will view the applications of both Lemma 2 and Lemma 3 as two-step operations: first T is split into subgraphs $T \backslash T_v$ and T_v (a *Brent break*) and then T_v is split into subtrees $T_{c_0}, \ldots, T_{c_{k-1}}$ where $c_0, \ldots, c_{k-1}$ are the children of v (a *child break*). By applying a Brent break and then a child break to a graph (also known as *Brent restructuring*), we obtain subgraphs containing disjoint sets of the nodes. After $O(\log n)$ recursive applications of the lemmas, the resulting subgraphs will be of constant size.

In our parallel algorithms, we store all subgraphs arising from the Brent restructurings in a representation tree. For the tree T, this tree, denoted $\mathcal{B}_T$, is called the *Brent tree* of T [CGR86, GN92]. In $\mathcal{B}_T$, a vertex will correspond to a subgraph of the original tree and an edge between two vertices will indicate that the child is derived from the parent by a restructuring step. We can form $\mathcal{B}_T$ in $O(\log |T|)$ time using an $O(|T|^4)$-processor CREW PRAM [GN92].

3   Basic paradigm

3.1   The Embeddable Tree Problem

We begin by reviewing the basic paradigm for solving the *Embeddable Tree Problem*. This paradigm follows from early work of Matula [Mat78] who studied the sequential complexity of the subgraph isomorphism problem. The approach uses dynamic programming to work up from the leaves of T', in turn labeling each node $v' \in V(T')$ with the set of nodes $v \in V(T)$ such that each T_v is a subgraph of $T'_{v'}$. Given all such information about children of v and v', it is possible to determine whether or not a T_v is a subgraph of $T'_{v'}$, by determining whether or not there is a matching on a graph representing this information. We construct a bipartite graph $G_{(v,v')}(X, Y, E)$, where X corresponds to the children of v, Y corresponds to the children of v', and there is an edge from child w of v to child w' of v' if and only if T_w is a subgraph of $T'_{w'}$. The matching must include every node in X. Since bipartite matching is in $O(n^{2.5})$, this step will dominate and the total running time is in $O(n^{2.5})$.

To obtain parallel algorithms, the Brent tree of T, $\mathcal{B}_T$, is used to decompose our original problem into subproblems. We process $\mathcal{B}_T$ level by level from the bottom up; when a level has been completely processed, we will have determined all the possible locations of T' in which we can embed those subgraphs of T that correspond to vertices at that level in $\mathcal{B}_T$. Since each level of $\mathcal{B}_T$ corresponding to child breaks divides the nodes of T into disjoint subsets, the subgraphs to be embedded are disjoint; processing a level constitutes solving in parallel a number of independent problems, one associated with each vertex of $\mathcal{B}_T$.

To determine the time complexity of such an algorithm, we consider the time to process one level of the Brent tree and multiply it by the number of levels. The processing is dominated by the cost of bipartite matching. Since bipartite matching can be accomplished in time $O(\log^2 n)$ on a randomized CREW PRAM and since the Brent tree has height $O(\log n)$, the total running time for the algorithm is in $O(\log^3 n)$. The total number of processors required is in $O(n^{6.5})$.

Details of both the sequential and the parallel algorithms with their complexities can be found in earlier work [GN92].

3.2 The Largest Common Embeddable Tree Problem

For the *Largest Common Embeddable Tree Problem*, we also use a dynamic programming approach. In this case, for each node v in T and v' in T', we determine the size of the largest tree embeddable in T_v and in $T_{v'}$. For some of the problems, we instead focus on edges. As in the case of the *Embeddable Tree Problem*, this information can often be computed by examining the information obtained for children.

For subgraph isomorphism, with unlabeled nodes, Matula's algorithm can be adapted in the following simple way. The largest tree that is a subgraph of T_v and $T'_{v'}$ can also be seen as the largest subgraph of T_v that is a subgraph of $T'_{v'}$. Consequently, it is sufficient to work from the leaves to the root in T', at each node v' determining for each v the largest subgraph of T_v that is a subgraph of $T'_{v'}$, and such that v and v' are included in the mapping. The information thus acquired can be stored in an array A, where $A[v, v']$ contains the size of the largest common subtree associated with T_v and $T'_{v'}$.

To compute $A[v, v']$, it is sufficient to determine the maximum weighted matching on a graph representing the relations between the children of v and the children of v'. More formally, we construct a bipartite graph $G_{(v,v')}(X, Y, E)$, where X corresponds to the children of v, Y corresponds to the children of v', and the edge from child w of v to child w' of v' has weight $A[w, w']$. Then $A[v, v']$ is the size of the matching plus one (to count the mapping of v and v').

The size of the array A is $|T| \cdot |T'|$. Each entry in this array is computed by setting up a weighted bipartite matching. Since the weights are in $O(n)$, the complexity of weighted bipartite matching is in $O(n^{2.5} \log n)$ [GT89]. Now, a careful analysis yields a time complexity of $O(n^{2.5} \log n)$ for the whole algorithm.

This algorithm can be parallelized using Brent restructuring and other previously used techniques [GN92], and extended to labeled inputs. Since bipartite matching with unary edge weights can also be solved in $O(\log^2 n)$ time and $O(n^{4.5})$ processors [KUW86], we once again obtain an $O(\log^3 n)$-time $O(n^{6.5})$-processor parallel algorithm. To handle different labeling conditions, we add further restrictions on the array A. In the case of arbitrary labels, the entry for $A[v, v']$ is nonzero only if $\ell(v) = \ell(v')$. For leaf labels and distinct leaf labels, all leaves of S must be labeled. Consequently, we are identifying a subtree (as opposed to a subgraph) of T' which is isomorphic to a subtree of T. This can be accomplished by altering the base case to allow nonzero entries only for mappings of leaves to leaves.

4 Topological embedding

4.1 Sequential algorithm

As in the previous algorithms, in order to determine the size of the largest subgraph that can be topologically embedded in both T and T', we first solve the problem on subgraphs of T and T'. Unlike in the isomorphism algorithm, scarring will now take place at edges instead of nodes (this is a consequence of the fact that the mappings in the topological embedding relation are mappings of the edges). Therefore, in order to allow us to deal with all of T (respectively, T') uniformly, we begin by adding to each of T and T' an edge from the original root to a new node (which becomes the root of the new tree), forming trees $\hat{T}$ and $\hat{T}'$. In particular, for each $e \in \hat{T}$ and $e' \in \hat{T}'$, we determine the size of the largest tree $\hat{S}$ such that $\hat{S} \leq_e \hat{T}_e$, $\hat{S} \leq_e \hat{T}'_{e'}$, and e and e' are in the image of the same edge of $\hat{S}$ with respect to the mapping ψ. For convenience, we will say that such an $\hat{S}$ is *embeddable at e and e'*. More formally, we maintain an integer array A of size $|E(\hat{T})| \times |E(\hat{T}')|$, where $A[e, e']$ is the number of edges in the largest tree $\hat{S}$ that is embeddable at e and e'.

Although finding the maximum entry in A will tell us the size of $\hat{S}$, to find the graph itself we maintain an additional array B of the same size. The entries in B store information on how the values in A were obtained. The structure of $\hat{S}$ can be found by determining the maximum over all entries in array A, and then tracing down through selected entries of B in the appropriate order. Finally, we extract S from $\hat{S}$. The root has a single child, v (as shown in Lemma 4); we set S to be $\hat{S}_v$.

Lemma 4. $\hat{S}$ has exactly one child.

Proof (outline): We prove the lemma by contradiction. Suppose that $\hat{S}$ has more than child, and let R be formed by adding to $\hat{S}$ a new root and an edge from the new root to the old root. We now consider the topological embedding of $\hat{S}$ in $\hat{T}$. The root of $\hat{T}$ will not be in the image of the embedding since $d(root(\hat{S})) > d(root(\hat{T}))$; consequently, $R \leq_e \hat{T}$. By a similar argument we can show that $R \leq_e \hat{T}'$, contradicting the maximality of $\hat{S}$. ∎

This argument can be modified to show that the unique edge from the root of $\hat{S}$ exactly maps to the unique edge from the root of $\hat{T}$ and the unique edge from the root of $\hat{T}'$, respectively (since otherwise another edge could be added to the root of $\hat{S}$). Therefore, S can be obtained from $\hat{S}$ by deleting the root of $\hat{S}$.

When a tree $\hat{S}$ is embeddable at f and f', it is also embeddable at any e and e' such that e is an ancestor of f and e' is an ancestor of f'. To see this, consider the edge in $\hat{S}$ in whose image both f and f' lie. We can extend this image in $\hat{T}$

to contain edges on the path to and including the edge e, and similarly we can extend the image in $\hat{T}'$ to contain all edges on the path to and including the edge e'. Viewed from the point of view of the ancestors, $A[e, e']$ is at least as big as $A[f, f']$ for any descendants f of e and f' of e'.

We fill in the entries of A by working up from the leaves to the root in $\hat{T}'$. Consider the processing of a particular entry $A[e, e']$. There are three possible cases concerning the edge e_s of $\hat{S}$ in whose image both e and e' lie:

1. No descendant of e or f is in the image of e_s.
2. A descendant f of e is the image of e_s.
3. A descendant f' of e' is in the image of e_s.

The last two cases can be considered by examining previously filled entries in A; it will be sufficient to examine children of e and e' to determine the values. The first case is equivalent to stating that the topological embedding function f maps c_{e_s} to c_e in $\hat{T}$ and to $c_{e'}$ in $\hat{T}'$. In this case, we can determine the size of S by determining the sum of the sizes of the largest trees embeddable at the children of e and e' and adding one for e_s itself.

In order to handle the first case, we construct an instance of maximum weight bipartite matching in the following way. We construct a bipartite graph $G_{(e,e')} = (X, Y, E)$, where the sets X and Y correspond to the edges f in $\hat{T}$ with $p_f = c_e$ and, respectively, the edges f' in $\hat{T}'$ with $p_{f'} = c_{e'}$. The edge from a given f to f' will have weight $A[f, f']$. The weight of the resultant matching is compared to values obtained by the last two cases, and the result is stored in $A[e, e']$. The entry $B[e, e']$ is updated to indicate which of the three cases resulted in the largest number, and if it is the first case, which children are matched to which.

The algorithm can be summarized as follows:

```
For all e' ∈ E(T̂') such that c_e' is a leaf
    For all e ∈ E(T̂)
        Set A[e, e'] = 1
        Set B[e, e'] to contain an edge
For all other e' ∈ E(T̂') in topological order up to root
    For all e ∈ E(T̂) in topological order up to the root
        Let value1 = WBM(G_(e,e')) + 1
        Let value2 = max{A[e, f']|f' a child of e'}
        Let value3 = max{A[f, e']|f a child of e}
        Set A[e, e'] to max{value1, value2, value3}
        Set B[e, e'] to store f' (resp. f) if value2 (resp. value3) is
            the maximum, and to store the maximum matching otherwise.
Determine the maximum entry in A.
Reconstruct Ŝ from B by starting at the corresponding maximum
    entry in B and working downwards using results in B.
Extract S from Ŝ.
```

Note that in the above algorithm, WBM refers to weighted bipartite matching. To compute the running time of the algorithm, we first note that the time for the matching step dominates the complexity of the inner-most loop. Without loss of generality we can assume that $|T| = |T'| = n$. For a particular $e \in E(\hat{T})$ and $e' \in E(\hat{T}')$, $WBM(G_{(e,e')})$ can be computed in $O(\sqrt{n}d(e')d(e)\log n)$ [GT89]. Therefore the total running time is:

$$O(\sum_{e' \in E(\hat{T}')} \sum_{e \in E(\hat{T})} \sqrt{n}d(e')d(e)\log n) = O(\sqrt{n}\log n \sum_{e' \in E(\hat{T}')} d(e') \sum_{e \in E(\hat{T})} d(e))$$

$$= O(n^{2.5}\log n)$$

The following lemma shows that the algorithm is correct.

Lemma 5. *Let e and e' be edges in $\hat{T}$ and $\hat{T}'$, respectively. Then, S is the largest tree topologically embeddable in both $\hat{T}_e$ and $\hat{T}'_{e'}$ if and only if $A[e, e'] = |S|$.*

Proof (outline): It is clear from the construction that if $A[e, e'] = k$, then there is a tree of size k which topologically embeds in $\hat{T}_e$ and in $\hat{T}'_{e'}$.

To prove the converse, we show by induction that if S is the largest tree that embeds in $\hat{T}_e$ and in $\hat{T}'_{e'}$, then $A[e, e'] \geq |S|$. We work up from the leaves to the root of T' and then T. If there is a child f' of e' such that S embeds in $\hat{T}'_{f'}$, then $A[e, f'] \geq |S|$ and therefore $A[e, e'] \geq |S|$. Similarly, if there is a child f of e such that S embeds in $\hat{T}_f$, then $A[f, e'] \geq |S|$ and therefore $A[e, e'] \geq |S|$.

Now suppose that neither of these two cases holds. Then, by a maximality argument similar to that used in Lemma 4, S must consist of a root with a unique edge (say g) adjacent to this root. It is not hard to see that every topological embedding of S in $\hat{T}_e$ and $\hat{T}'_{e'}$ would map g to e and e', respectively.

Let $e_1, \ldots, e_j$, $e'_1, \ldots, e'_l$, and $g_1, \ldots, g_r$ be the children of e, e', and g, respectively. Without loss of generality, we can assume that the edges are numbered in such a way that S_{g_i} topologically embeds in $\hat{T}_{e_i}$ and in $\hat{T}'_{e'_i}$. By induction, we can conclude that for every i, $A[e_i, e'_i] \geq |S_{g_i}|$. Since $\{(e_i, e'_i) | 1 \leq i \leq r\}$ is a matching in $G_{(e,e')}$, it follows that $A[e, e'] \geq (\sum_{i=1}^{r} A[e_i, e'_i]) + 1 \geq |S|$. ∎

4.2 Parallel Algorithm

A naive parallel algorithm might process $\hat{T}'$ from leaves to root, resulting in a running time at least as great as the depth of $\hat{T}'$, which could be linear in the worst case. We instead make use of Brent restructuring to allow us to decompose $\hat{T}'$ into constant size pieces which can then be reassembled in $O(\log n)$ stages. The two main difficulties that result are that of making sure the matching problem deals properly with scars and of passing information up from descendants to ancestors without incurring a cost of at least linear time.

We generalize the arrays A and B to handle the case that a tree is scarred. It is not difficult to see that Lemmas 2 and 3 can be modified to handle edge-scars instead of node-scars. Because the break nodes in Lemmas 2 and 3 are unique, the scar g of $\hat{T}_e$ can be determined by knowing which level of the Brent tree is being processed. The unscarred trees are handled just as in the sequential case: for all $e \in \hat{T}$ and all $e' \in \hat{T}'$, $A[e, e', \epsilon]$ is defined to be the size of the largest tree S that is embeddable at e and e'. For all possible scars $g' \in \hat{T}'$, we let $A[e, e', g']$ be the size of the largest tree S that is embeddable at e and e' such that the scar g of $\hat{T}_e$ and the edge $g' \in \hat{T}'$ are in the image of the same edge of S with respect to the mapping ψ. We will say such an S is *embeddable at e and e' with scars g and g'*. B is defined analogously.

The parallel algorithm proceeds much like the sequential algorithm, except that information is propagated from descendants to all ancestors in one step rather than from children to parents. In this case, the bipartite graph $G = (X, Y, E)$ set up for each e, e', potential scars g, g', and child f of e (mapping to the scarred subtree), is defined as follows. The set X consists of all unscarred children of e and the set Y consists of all children of e' except f, the child of e that is the ancestor of scar g; the edge between $x \in X$ and $y \in Y$ is assigned weight $A[x, y, g']$.

To process a level of child breaks of the Brent tree is similar to a computation in the sequential algorithm, except that instead of computing the values to compare, we make use of information stored in A. In particular, for a subgraph $\hat{T}'_{e'} \backslash \hat{T}'_{g'}$, for each $e \in \hat{T}$ and for each descendant g of e, and for each child f' of e', we set up a matching using information in A and compare its weight to the size of $A[e, e', g']$. We update A and B with the current maxima by passing up information. Handling a level of Brent breaks is similar, but simpler, in that no matchings need to be computed. Finally, we observe that the complexity of the algorithm is identical to that given in Section 3, namely $O(\log^3 n)$ time and $O(n^{6.5})$ processors on a CREW PRAM.

The algorithm can easily be extended to handle trees with distinct leaf labels. Such problems are of particular importance in computational biology, as an evolutionary tree is a tree in which the leaf labels correspond to distinct species. A variant of the topological embedding problem has been studied in this context under the names *Unrooted Maximum Agreement Subtree Problem* and the *Rooted Maximum Agreement Subtree Problem* [FG85, KKM92, SW, FT94]; the goal of these problems is to to compare different evolutionary trees devised for the same species set. The best known sequential algorithms for these problems, due to Farach and Thorup [FT94], run in time $O(n^{2+o(1)})$ and $O(n^2)$, respectively, constituting an improvement over the basic algorithm given in Section 4.1. The key behind the improved running times is the concept of a κ-*core tree*, the use of which depends on the facts that leaves have unique labels and that the leaves of the largest embeddable tree must map to leaves in T and T'. The number and size of weighted bipartite matching problems solved in the dynamic programming solution are reduced by making use of properties of κ-core trees and potential solutions. Although the work of Gabow and Tarjan [GT89] on faster matching algorithms applies to problems of this type, the lack of a similar result in the parallel setting suggests that such techniques are not obviously parallelizable.

5 Conclusions and directions for further research

In this paper we have presented a basic paradigm for sequential and parallel algorithms for the *Largest Common Embeddable Tree Problem* for the subgraph isomorphism and topological embedding relations where the underlying trees can have a number of different types of labelings. For the problem of subgraph isomorphism, we have presented modifications of the basic dynamic-programming algorithms to yield a $O(n^{2.5} \log n)$-time sequential algorithm and an $O(\log^3 n)$-time, $O(n^{6.5})$-time processor CREW parallel algorithm.

Our topological embedding algorithm is novel in its use of edge breaks, unlike previous algorithms in which all breaks are performed at nodes. For this problem, we obtain a sequential algorithm with a running time of $O(n^{2.5} \log n)$ and a parallel algorithm with a running time of $O(\log^3 n)$ with $O(n^{6.5})$ processors. The parallel algorithm matches the best known complexity for the *Embeddable Tree Problem* under topological embedding; it is an interesting open problem to determine whether edge partitions can improve the running time in parallel.

It remains to be seen whether or not the basic paradigm can be further modified to hone running times and processor counts for special cases, for embeddings and labelings listed here and potentially for others as well, for both ordered and unordered trees. Further progress on the problem of weighted bipartite matching in parallel could have a serious impact on the possibility of such improvements.

Acknowledgements

We are grateful to Ernst Mayr for pointers to references on weighted bipartite matching and to Prabhakar Ragde for many useful suggestions which greatly improved the manuscript.

References

[ABG92] A. Apostolico, S. Browne and C. Guerra, Fast linear-space computations of longest common subsequence, *Theoretical Computer Science* **92** (1992), pp. 3–17.

[Alb89] H. Alblas, Iteration of transformation passes over attributed program trees, *Acta-Informatica* **27** (1989), pp. 1–40.

[Bre74] R. Brent, The parallel evaluation of general arithmetic expressions, *Journal of the ACM* **21**, 2 (1974), pp. 201–206.

[Chu87] M. J. Chung, $O(n^{2.5})$ time algorithms for the subgraph homeomorphism problem on trees, *Journal of Algorithms* **8**, (1987), pp. 106–112.

[CGR86] S. Cook, A. Gupta, and V. Ramachandran, A fast parallel algorithm for formula evaluation, unpublished manuscript, October 1986.

[FT94] M. Farach and M. Thorup, Fast Comparison of evolutionary trees, *Proceedings of the Fifth Annual ACM-SIAM Symposium on Discrete Algorithms*, pp. 481–488, 1984.

[FG85] C.R. Finden and A.D. Gordon, Obtaining common pruned trees, *Journal of Classification* **2**, (1985), pp. 255–276.

408

[Fri81]   J. Friedman, Expressing logical formulas in natural language. *Formal methods in the study of language, Part I*, Math. Centrum, Amsterdam, 1981, pp. 113–130.

[GT89]   H. Gabow and R. Tarjan, Faster scaling algorithms for network problems, *SIAM Journal on Computing* **18**, 5 (1989), pp. 1013–1036.

[GKMS90]   P. Gibbons, R. Karp, G. Miller, AND D. Soroker, Subtree isomorphism is in random NC, *Discrete Applied Mathematics* **29** (1990), pp. 35–62.

[Gup85]   A. Gupta, A fast parallel algorithm for recognition of parenthesis languages, Master's thesis, University of Toronto, 1985.

[GN92]   A. Gupta and N. Nishimura, The parallel complexity of tree embedding problems, *to appear in Journal of Algorithms*. A preliminary version has appeared in *Proceedings of the Ninth Annual Symposium on Theoretical Aspects of Computer Science*, pp. 21–32, 1992.

[GN94]   A. Gupta and N. Nishimura, Sequential and parallel algorithms for embedding problems on classes of partial k-trees, *Proceedings of the Fourth Scandinavian Workshop on Algorithm Theory*, pp. 172–182, 1994.

[KUW86]   R. Karp, E. Upfal, and A. Wigderson, Constructing a perfect matching is in random NC, *Combinatorica* **6**, 1, pp. 35–48, 1986.

[Kil92]   P. Kilpelainen, Tree matching problems with applications to structured text databases, Ph.D. thesis, University of Helsinki, Department of Computer Science, November 1992.

[KM92]   P. Kilpelainen and H. Mannila, Grammatical tree matching, *Combinatorial Pattern Matching*, 1992.

[KKM92]   E. Kubicka, G. Kubicki, and F.R. McMorris, On agreement subtrees of 2 binary trees, *Congressus-Numerantium* **88** (1992), pp. 217–224.

[LK89]   A. Lingas and M. Karpinski, Subtree isomorphism is NC reducible to bipartite perfect matching, *Information Processing Letters* **30** (1989), pp. 27–32.

[MSH85]   P. Materna, P. Sgall and Z. Hajicova, Linguistic constructions in transparent intensional logic, *Prague-Bulletin on Mathematical Linguistics* **43** (1985), pp. 5–24.

[Mat78]   D. Matula, Subtree isomorphism in $O(n^{5/2})$, *Annals of Discrete Mathematics* **2** (1978), pp. 91–106.

[PN91]   Complexity of optimal vector code generation, *Theoretical Computer Science* **80** (1991), pp. 105–115.

[RS84]   N. Robertson and P. Seymour, Graph Minors III. Planar tree-width, *Journal of Combinatorial Theory (Ser. B)* **36** (1984), pp. 49–64.

[RS86]   N. Robertson and P. Seymour, Graph Minors II. Algorithm aspects of tree-width, *Journal of Algorithms* **7** (1986), pp. 309–322.

[SW]   M. Steel and T. Warnow, Kaikoura tree theorems: Computing the maximum agreement subtrees. Submitted for publication.

The χ_t-Coloring Problem *

Damon Kaller, Arvind Gupta and Tom Shermer

School of Computing Science
Simon Fraser University
Burnaby, B.C., Canada, V5A 1S6
{kaller, arvind, shermer}@cs.sfu.ca

Abstract. Motivated by a problem in Scheduling Theory, we introduce the χ_t-*coloring problem*, a generalization of the chromatic number problem that places a bound of t on the size of any color class. For fixed t, we show that the *perfect* χ_t-coloring problem (in which each color class must have cardinality exactly t) can be expressed in the counting monadic second-order logic and, hence, has a linear-time algorithm over the class of graphs G of bounded treewidth: A solution is a partition of G into induced subgraphs, each isomorphic to a fixed graph consisting of t isolated vertices. The logical formalism generalizes to allow these t vertices to be t isomorphic connected components. The linear-time algorithm so derived for the perfect χ_t-coloring problem is used to design a linear-time algorithm for the optimization version of the general χ_t-coloring problem (for fixed t) on graphs of bounded treewidth. We also show that this problem has a polynomial-time algorithm on bipartite graphs.

1 Introduction

The following problem arises naturally in Scheduling Theory: There are n jobs that must be completed in the minimum time by t equivalent processors. A processor can handle only one job at a time, and each job requires one unit of time for completion. The scheduling is complicated by the fact that there are additional resources (*e.g.* I/O devices, communication links) required by some, but not all, of the jobs. Assume that a job can only be scheduled onto a processor in a given time unit after it has an exclusive lock on all of the resources that are required. Problems of this nature have been studied in the Operations Research literature; for example, Lotfi and Sarin [LS86] consider graph coloring heuristics for scheduling.

A similar problem arises in constructing a school course timetable: Here, the jobs correspond to courses, and the processors to classrooms; the teachers are an example of an additional resource. A more complex version of course timetable scheduling was studied by Kitagawa and Ikeda [KI88], who note that their problem includes graph coloring, as well as network flow, as special cases.

* Research supported by the Natural Sciences and Engineering Research Council of Canada.

In a more general form, these problems can be stated in terms of scheduling t equivalent machines to perform n jobs, where each job requires one time unit, and each machine can handle only one job at a time. Furthermore, there are pairwise *conflicts* between certain jobs—when jobs u and v conflict, they cannot be performed simultaneously. As many as t jobs may be active in the same time unit. Because of the conflicts, however, it be necessary to leave some of the machines idle in any given time unit, thus scheduling fewer than t jobs. An optimal schedule is one in which all jobs are completed within the minimum number of time units.

The scheduling problem can be solved by creating a graph G with a vertex for each of the n jobs, and an edge between every pair of conflicting jobs. Now, in each time unit we can perform any subset $C \subseteq V(G)$ of the jobs for which $|C| \leq t$ and C is an independent set in G. A minimum-length schedule corresponds to a partition of $V(G)$ into the fewest such independent sets (also known as *color classes*). This graph-theoretic problem will be called the χ_t-coloring problem.

The χ_t-coloring problem generalizes the chromatic number problem (GT4 of [GJ79]) by placing a bound of t on the size of each color class. An instance of the problem consists of a graph G and a class size t. A solution is a partition of the vertex set $V(G)$ into the minimum number of color classes, each of cardinality at most t. We will denote by $\chi_t(G)$ the minimum number of color classes required; the chromatic number of G can be written as $\chi_n(G)$, where $|V(G)| = n$. This paper will only be concerned with χ_t-coloring for fixed (constant) t. A χ_t-coloring of a graph G will be said to be *optimal* if it uses $\chi_t(G)$ color classes. A color class $C \subseteq V(G)$ will be called *full* whenever $|C| = t$; and will be called *partially full* whenever $1 \leq |C| < t$.

Notice that a χ_2-coloring of a graph G is a maximum matching in the complement graph $\overline{G}$. A maximum matching in $\overline{G}$ is called a *perfect* matching if it consists of $\frac{n}{2}$ pairwise disjoint edges, where $n = |V(G)| = |V(\overline{G})|$ is even. By analogy, we will say that a χ_t-coloring of G is *perfect* if t divides n and $\frac{n}{t}$ color classes are used.

The decision version of the χ_t-coloring problem is NP-complete for general graphs whenever $t \geq 3$. This follows from a trivial transformation from partition into isomorphic subgraphs (problem GT12 of [GJ79]). Here, we are given graphs G and H such that $|V(G)| = r|V(H)|$ (for some $r \in \mathbf{Z}^+$) and wish to partition $V(G)$ into $C_1, C_2, \ldots, C_r$ such that the subgraph of G induced by each C_i is isomorphic to H. Kirkpatrick and Hell [KH78] have shown this problem to be NP-complete for any fixed H with 3 or more vertices. In particular, we are interested in the graph H with $|V(H)| = t$ and $E(H) = \emptyset$. For this H, the yes-instances correspond to those G for which $\chi_t = \frac{|V(G)|}{t}$. From the equivalence of χ_2-coloring and matching on the complement graph (as noted above), it follows that χ_2-coloring can be solved in polynomial time.

Other generalizations of the chromatic number problem include *list coloring* [BH85], in which each vertex has a list of candidates from which its color must be chosen; and *equitable coloring* [Mey73], which requires that no two color classes differ in size by more than 1. See [JT95] for a comprehensive survey of other variants of graph coloring.

This paper begins a study of the χ_t-coloring problem. Since the problem is NP-complete in general, we restrict our attention to two classes of graphs—partial k-trees and bipartite graphs—for which the problem is tractable. In Section 2, we review partial k-trees and the counting monadic second-order (CMS) logic. In Section 3, we show that the *perfect χ_t-coloring* problem is expressible in CMS logic and hence, by a result of Courcelle [Cou90], has a linear time solution over the class of partial k-trees. The general χ_t-coloring problem, however, does not appear to be directly expressible in CMS logic. In Section 4, we show that a constant number of calls to the linear-time algorithm for perfect χ_t-coloring can be used to solve the general problem. In Section 5, we show that there is a polynomial-time algorithm for χ_t-coloring on bipartite graphs. We discuss further directions for research in Section 6.

2 Preliminaries

All graphs in this paper are finite, simple, loop-free and undirected. For a graph G, we denote its vertex set by $V(G)$, and its edge set by $E(G)$.

2.1 Partial k-Trees and Tree Decompositions

The class of *k-trees* is defined inductively as the smallest class that includes

- the clique on k vertices, and
- any graph obtained by adding, to a k-tree G, a vertex $v \notin V(G)$ and edges $\{v, u_i\}$ (for $i = 1, 2, \ldots, k$) where $u_1, u_2, \ldots, u_k \in V(G)$ are k distinct vertices that induce a clique in G.

A *partial k-tree* is any graph that can be obtained from a k-tree by deleting zero or more edges. For example, the class of partial 0-trees is equivalent to the class of edge-free graphs, and the class of partial 1-trees is equivalent to the class of forests. Series-parallel graphs and outerplanar graphs are subclasses of the partial 2-trees; Halin graphs form a subclass of the partial 3-trees.

A *tree decomposition* [RS86] of a graph G is a pair $(T, \mathcal{X})$ where T is a tree and $\mathcal{X} = \{X_a\}_{a \in V(T)}$ is a collection of subsets of $V(G)$, indexed by the vertices of T, for which

- $\bigcup_{a \in V(T)} X_a = V(G)$
- each edge $e \in E(G)$ has both its endpoints in some X_a (for $a \in V(T)$)
- for each vertex $v \in V(G)$, the subgraph of T induced by $\{a \in V(T) | v \in X_a\}$ is connected

The subset X_a is called the *bag* corresponding to node $a \in V(T)$. The *treewidth* of a tree decomposition is $\max\{|X_a| - 1 : a \in V(T)\}$.

It is well-known that the class of graphs having treewidth at most k is equivalent to the class of partial k-trees. Given a graph G, there is a linear-time algorithm [Bod93] to recognize whether it is a partial k-tree and, if so, to find a tree decomposition of width k.

2.2 Counting Monadic Second-Order Logic

The *counting monadic second-order* (CMS) language [Cou90] for graphs contains individual variables (used to represent vertices and/or edges), set variables (for sets of vertices and/or edges), the equality ($=$) and membership ($\in$) symbols, existential ($\exists$) and universal ($\forall$) quantifiers and the logic connectives: $\wedge$ ("and"), $\vee$ ("or"), $\neg$ ("not"), $\Rightarrow$ ("implies") and $\Leftrightarrow$ ("if and only if"). It also includes predicates of the form $\mathbf{card}_{\ell,t}(S)$, for constants $\ell < t \in \mathbf{N}$, which evaluates to true whenever S, an edge-subset or vertex-subset, has cardinality $\ell(\bmod t)$. Quantification is allowed over sets, and the graph structure can be accessed with the adjacency relation Adj. For a graph G and $u, v \in V(G)$, $Adj(u,v)$ is true if and only if $\{u,v\} \in E(G)$.

Given a graph G and an CMS formula Φ, we write $G \models \Phi$ to indicate that G satisfies the CMS formula Φ. A graph decision problem is said to be a CMS property over a class $\mathcal{K}$ of graphs whenever there exists an CMS formula Φ such that for each G in $\mathcal{K}$: G satisfies the property if and only if $G \models \Phi$. Courcelle [Cou90] has shown that any graph property that can be expressed in CMS logic has a linear-time recognition algorithm over the class of partial k-trees. Furthermore, once a CMS formula is known, a linear-time recognition algorithm can be generated automatically. Such an algorithm uses dynamic programming, and can be modeled as a tree automaton [GS84] which executes the tree decomposition of a partial k-tree. Arnborg, Lagergren and Seese [ALS91] obtained similar results, but their formalism does not include the $\mathbf{card}_{\ell,t}()$ predicates.

By identifying graph properties with graph/subgraph pairs, rather than with logical formulae, a characterization of linear-time solvable properties was formulated in terms of "regularity" and "locality" by Bern, Lawler and Wong [BLW87] and by Mahajan and Peters [MP87]. Such a characterization is well-defined in the sense that properties can be shown to be non-regular by invoking a pumping lemma. In this way, it can be shown that our χ_t-coloring problem (and also the "perfect" variant of the problem) is non-regular. In Section 3, we solve the perfect χ_t-coloring (formula (1)) problem by showing its decision version is equivalent to a CMS problem (formula (2)); the latter can be shown to satisfy the notion of regularity.

In other related work, Borie, Parker and Tovie [BPT92] used the framework of regularity to obtain results similar to those of Courcelle.

3   Perfect χ_t-Coloring of Partial k-trees

In this section, we consider the problem of whether the vertex set of a partial k-tree can be partitioned into independent sets of size t. That is, we are interested in finding a χ_t-coloring such that each color class is full. The yes-instances for this problem are those partial k-trees G for which t divides $n = |V(G)|$ and $\chi_t(G) = \frac{n}{t}$. This, the *perfect χ_t-coloring* problem, can be stated formally as follows:

$$\exists C_1, C_2, \ldots, C_r : \ (\{C_i\}_{i=1}^r \text{ forms a partition of } V(G)) \ \wedge$$
$$\bigwedge_{i=1}^r (C_i \text{ is independent} \wedge |C_i| = t) \tag{1}$$

This formula does not allow us to conclude that perfect χ_t-coloring is a CMS property over the class of partial k-trees, since its length depends upon the size of G: that is $r = \frac{n}{t}$. We will show that when G is a partial k-tree with sufficiently many vertices, then it is possible to gather some of the C_i together into a larger independent set. If the vertices of G have been partitioned into the C_i carefully, then the C_i can be divided into $2k+1$ groups, such that the union of vertices over each group is an independent set. In other words, we claim that the following CMS formula encodes the perfect χ_t-coloring problem for partial k-trees (provided G is big enough).

$$\exists D_1, D_2, \ldots, D_{2k+1} : \ (\{D_i\}_{i=1}^{2k+1} \text{ forms a partition of } V(G)) \ \wedge$$
$$\bigwedge_{i=1}^{2k+1} (D_i \text{ is independent} \wedge \mathbf{card}_{0,t}(D_i)) \tag{2}$$

It is clear that there is a perfect χ_t-coloring of G if formula (2) is satisfied: The satisfying assignment of $D_1, D_2, \ldots, D_{2k+1}$ can be converted into an assignment of $C_1, C_2, \ldots, C_r$ (to satisfy formula (1)) by breaking each D_i into $\frac{|D_i|}{t}$ sets of t vertices (this is possible because $|D_i| \equiv 0 \pmod{t}$). We now state Lemma 1, which shows the converse (provided G is big enough).

Lemma 1. *If a partial k-tree G has a perfect χ_t-coloring, then CMS formula (2) is satisfied, provided $|V(G)| \geq (5k+1)t$.*

We will prove Lemma 1 first under a simplifying restriction (Claim 4). Following this, we will sketch the technical details needed for the general result. We will need the following proposition:

Proposition 2. *Given a partial k-tree G, there exists a partition*

$$\mathcal{I}(G) = \{I_1, I_2, \ldots I_{k+1}\}$$

of $V(G)$ such that each $I_i \subseteq V(G)$ is an independent set, and the union of any $\ell + 1$ distinct members of $\mathcal{I}(G)$ induces a partial ℓ-tree (for $0 \leq \ell \leq k$). We will refer to such a partition $\mathcal{I}$ as a standard partition of $V(G)$.

Proof. Let $(T, \mathcal{X})$ be a width k tree decomposition of G. Let the vertices of G be distributed into the sets I_i such that, for every $a \in V(T)$, no two vertices of the corresponding bag X_a are in the same set. This is possible since $|X_a| \leq k+1$. It follows from the definition of a tree decomposition that each I_i is independent (as required).

Suppose G' is the subgraph of G induced by any $\ell + 1$ of the independent sets. Then $(T, \mathcal{X}')$ is a tree decomposition of G', where

$$\mathcal{X}' = \{X_a' = X_a \cap V(G') | X_a \in \mathcal{X}\}$$

Each bag of $\mathcal{X}'$ has, at most, $\ell + 1$ vertices. Therefore G' is a partial ℓ-tree. $\square$

Corollary 3. *If* $\mathcal{I}(G) = \{I_1, I_2, \ldots I_{k+1}\}$ *is a standard partition of the vertex set of a partial k-tree G, then the subgraph of G induced by* $I_i \cup I_j$ *(for* $1 \leq i < j \leq k + 1$*) is acyclic.*

Proof. By Proposition 2, the subgraph is a partial 1-tree, which is a forest. $\square$

We now restrict our attention to those partial k-trees G, on at least $3(k+1)t$ vertices, for which some standard partition of $|V(G)|$ has at least t vertices in each of its independent sets.

Claim 4. *If G is a partial k-tree with* $|V(G)| \equiv 0 \pmod{t}$*, for which there exists a standard partition of* $V(G)$ *with at least t vertices in each independent set, then CMS formula (2) is satisfied, provided* $|V(G)| \geq 3(k+1)t$.

Proof. Let $\mathcal{I}(G) = \{I_1, I_2, \ldots I_{k+1}\}$ be a standard partition of $V(G)$, with $|I_i| \geq t$ (for $i = 1, 2, \ldots, k + 1$). A satisfying assignment of $D_1, D_2, \ldots, D_{2k+1}$ (in formula (2)) is found by the algorithm below. We will say that a vertex is "colored" after it is assigned to some set D_i. Initially, no vertex of G is colored.

1. Repeat for $\ell = 1, 2, \ldots, k$:
   (a) Fix i such that I_i contains the minimum nonzero number of uncolored vertices.
   (b) Fix $j \neq i$ such that I_j contains the maximum number of uncolored vertices.
   (c) Create 2 sets, $D_{2\ell-1}$ and $D_{2\ell}$ (each of cardinality 0 (mod t)), using all of the vertices of I_i, and at most $t - 1$ of the vertices of I_j.
2. Assign the remaining uncolored vertices to D_{2k+1}.

It is clear that $D_{2k+1} \subseteq I_x$ for some $1 \leq x \leq k + 1$; hence D_{2k+1} is independent. We need only show that it is possible to form two independent sets $D_{2\ell-1}$ and $D_{2\ell}$ as specified in step (1c).

By induction on ℓ, we can show the following to be an invariant before each iteration of step (1c): I_j contains at least $2t$ uncolored vertices, and I_i contains at least t uncolored vertices.

Let F be the subgraph of G that is induced by the uncolored vertices of $I_i \cup I_j$. F is a forest, by Proposition 2. From the invariant, it follows that we can select $t - 1$ vertices of I_j whose removal from F produces a forest F', such that F' has at least t trees each containing one or more vertices of I_i, and F' contains at least t vertices of I_j. To see that this is possible, we remove the vertices $v \in I_j$ with maximum degree $\delta(v)$. If $\delta(v) \geq 2$ then the removal of v increases the number of trees which contain a vertex of I_i. Otherwise, every vertex of I_j in the forest has degree 0 or 1; hence, no two vertices of I_i are in the same tree.

Let $T_1, T_2, \ldots$ be the trees in F', numbered such that T_x ($x \geq 1$) contains at least as many vertices of I_j as does T_{x+1}. Suppose there are r uncolored vertices of I_i. We let $D_{2\ell-1}$ consist of $r - (r \pmod{t})$ of these vertices, chosen from the lowest-indexed trees. We form $D_{2\ell}$ with the remaining $r \pmod{t}$ uncolored vertices of I_i (from the highest-indexed trees) and enough vertices of I_j (chosen from the lowest-indexed trees) so that this set contains exactly t (or 0) vertices. When vertices are selected in this way, no tree may contribute both a vertex of I_i and a vertex of I_j to $D_{2\ell}$; so it is independent. $\qquad\square$

From Claim 4, it follows that a (large enough) partial k-tree G, for which t divides $|V(G)|$, can fail to have a perfect χ_t-coloring only if every standard partition of $V(G)$ contains at least one small independent set. We now give the general proof of Lemma 1, without the restriction used in Claim 4.

Proof Sketch of Lemma 1. Let G be a partial k-tree, having at least $(5k+1)t$ vertices, for which there exists a perfect χ_t-coloring. Let $\mathcal{I}(G) = \{I_1, I_2, \ldots I_{k+1}\}$ be a standard partition of $V(G)$. For $1 \le i \le k+1$, select $v_i \in I_i$ with maximum degree.

Let $\{C_1, C_2, \ldots, C_r\}$ be a perfect χ_t-coloring of G, which satisfies formula (1). Without loss of generality, we can assume the following for some $\ell \le k$, after possibly renumbering the sets I_i $(1 \le i \le k+1)$ and C_j $(1 \le j \le r)$.

- for $1 \le i \le \ell$, the following criteria are satisfied:
  C1 $v_i \in C_i \cap I_i$
  C2 v_i has degree at least $3kt$
  C3 $|I_i \cap (V(G) - C_1 - C_2 - \ldots - C_\ell)| < t$
- for $\ell + 1 \le i \le k+1$: if both C2 and C3 are satisfied, then $v_i \in C_1 \cup \ldots \cup C_\ell$

At this point, we consider the vertices of $C_1 \cup C_2 \cup \ldots \cup C_\ell$ to be "colored". Without loss of generality assume that C3 is satisfied for indices $1, 2, \ldots m \ge \ell$. So, for $\ell + 1 \le i \le m$, either I_i has no vertex of high degree (*i.e.* C2 is not satisfied) or $v_i \in I_i$ is a high-degree vertex that is colored with one of $C_1, C_2, \ldots, C_\ell$. Since $|V(G)| \ge (5k+1)t$, it follows that $m \le k$. Notice that when each I_i has sufficiently many vertices, C3 is never satisfied, and $\ell = m = 0$; in this case, the proof of Claim 4 carries through. Now, we will describe how the other cases are handled, using at most $2k + 1 - \ell$ color classes. As in the proof of Claim 4, we say that a vertex is colored after it has been assigned to one of the (cardinality 0 (mod t)) independent sets.

We work through $I_1, I_2, \ldots, I_{k+1}$, in that order. At the ith step, we color all uncolored vertices of I_i. There are several cases to consider. We prove **Case 1** in detail, and sketch the proofs of the other cases.

Case 1: $1 \le i \le \ell$

Before this iteration, we have colored at most $(\ell + i - 1)t$ vertices. The sets $I_{i+1}, \ldots, I_m$ satisfy C3 and, hence, their union contains at most $(m - i)(t - 1)$ uncolored vertices. Recall that we have colored a vertex $v_i \in I_i$ that has at least $3kt$ neighbors. Using the facts $m \ge \ell$ and $1 \le i \le m \le k$, and using the pigeonhole principle (PHP), v_i must have at least

$$\frac{3kt - (\ell + i - 1)t - (m - i)(t - 1)}{k - m + 1} \ge 2t$$

uncolored neighbors in some I_j $(m+1 \le j \le k+1)$. By Corollary 3, each vertex of $I_i - \{v_i\}$ can be adjacent to at most one of those $2t$ neighbors of v_i. This implies that we can form an independent set of size t (or 0) that contains all of the uncolored vertices of I_i and at most $t - 1$ of the $2t$ neighbors of v_i. Furthermore, I_j will still have at least t uncolored vertices after this iteration—which is helpful for proving the later cases.

Case 2: $\ell + 1 \leq i \leq m$

When **C2** is satisfied, $v_i \in I_i$ has already been colored with one of $C_1, \ldots, C_\ell$; we can handle I_i as in **Case 1**, using only 1 color class.

When **C2** is not satisfied, we can use the PHP to show that for some j, j' $(m + 1 \leq j, j' \leq k + 1$, possibly $j = j')$: I_j has at least $5t$ uncolored vertices, and $I_{j'}$ has at least $2t$ uncolored vertices that are *not* adjacent to an arbitrarily-chosen $v \in I_i$. If some $v \in I_i$ has t or more uncolored neighbors in I_j, then there is an independent set of size t which includes all uncolored vertices of $I_i - \{v\}$ and some of these neighbors of v; a second independent set can be formed from v and $t - 1$ of the uncolored vertices of $I_{j'}$ that are not adjacent to v. Otherwise (if each uncolored $v \in I_i$ has fewer than t uncolored neighbors in I_j) we can form 2 independent sets from the uncolored vertices of $I_i \cup I_j$ such that all uncolored vertices of I_i are contained in their union.

Case 3: $m + 1 \leq i \leq k$

Using the PHP, we can show that there are at least $2t$ uncolored vertices in some I_j $(i + 1 \leq j \leq k + 1)$. I_i contains at least t uncolored vertices, and can be handled, as in the proof of Claim 4, using 2 independent sets.

Case 4: $i = k + 1$

All uncolored vertices belong to some I_x and, hence, can be assigned to one independent set. □

Theorem 5. *The perfect χ_t-coloring problem, over the class of graphs having treewidth at most k, is encoded by the following CMS formula:*

$$\exists D_1, D_2, \ldots, D_{5k} : (\{D_i\}_{i=1}^{5k} \text{ forms a partition of } V(G)) \wedge$$
$$\bigwedge_{i=1}^{5k} (D_i \text{ is independent} \wedge \mathbf{card}_{0,t}(D_i))$$

Proof. A graph G has a perfect χ_t-coloring only if $|V(G)| \equiv 0 \pmod{t}$. In the case that $|V(G)| \leq 5kt$, a separate color class D_i is available for each of the cardinality t independent sets. Otherwise if $|V(G)| \geq (5k + 1)t$, Lemma 1 shows that only $2k + 1$ of the color classes are required. □

In passing, we note that Theorem 5 can be generalized to partitioning a partial k-tree G into (induced) isomorphic subgraphs H, where H consists of t pairwise isomorphic components. In the case of Theorem 5 these isomorphic components were isolated vertices. Let $G' \sqsubseteq G$ denote that G' is a subgraph of G; this relation is easy to express in the CMS language. The proof of Theorem 6 is a straightforward generalization of the proof of Theorem 5.

Theorem 6. *Given a fixed graph H consisting of t components each isomorphic to a connected graph H': the problem partition (of partial k-trees) into isomorphic* *subgraphs H is encoded by the following CMS formula:*

$$\exists G_1, G_2, \ldots, G_{5k} \sqsubseteq G, \quad \exists W_1, W_2, \ldots, W_{5k} \subseteq V(G) : \bigwedge_{i=1}^{5k} ($$
"G_i *is an induced subgraph of G*" $\wedge$
"*each maximal connected component (MCC) of* G_i *is isomorphic to H'* " $\wedge$
"W_i *contains exactly one vertex from each MCC of* G_i " $\wedge \mathbf{card}_{0,t}(W_i))$

4 A Linear Algorithm For χ_t-Coloring of Partial k-trees

In this section, we consider the optimization version of the χ_t-coloring problem. That is, we are interested in the minimum number of color classes required in a χ_t-coloring of a partial k-tree. This version of the problem does not appear to be directly expressible in CMS. However, after augmenting the graph with enough isolated vertices to fill all color classes, we can use the algorithm $\mathcal{A}$ for perfect χ_t-coloring in order to solve the general problem. A careful analysis of the proof of Lemma 1 shows that, by removing the requirement that the coloring be perfect, the only color classes that need be partially full (assuming $|V(G)| \geq (5k+1)t$) are $C_1, \ldots C_\ell$ (where $\ell \leq k$) and the last color class to be filled: that is, at most $k+1$ partially full color classes. It follows that, for big enough graphs, $k+1$ calls to $\mathcal{A}$ would suffice. When $|V(G)| < (5k+1)t$, we have a trivial bound of $O(k)$ calls to $\mathcal{A}$.

We present the following lemma which not only gives the tightest possible bound, but is also an interesting result on its own.

Lemma 7. *For a partial k-tree G, there exists an optimal χ_t-coloring of G in which at most $k+1$ color classes are partially full.*

Proof. Suppose G is a partial k-tree for which every optimal χ_t-coloring has more than $k+1$ partially full color classes. Let $C_1, C_2, \ldots, C_r$ be an optimal χ_t-coloring of G, chosen according to the following criteria:

C1 as many color classes as possible are full. Without loss of generality, assume
   C_i is not full (*i.e.* $|C_i| < t$) for $1 \leq i \leq k+2$
C2 $|C_{k+2}|$ is minimized among all χ_t-colorings that satisfy criterion **C1**

Let G' be the subgraph of G induced by the vertices of $C_1 \cup C_2 \cup \ldots \cup C_{k+2}$, and let H be any connected component of G' that contains at least one vertex of color class C_{k+2}. Let $(T, \mathcal{X})$ be a width k tree decomposition of H, where $\mathcal{X} = \{X_a | a \in V(T)\}$. Let $r \in V(T)$ be chosen arbitrarily as the root, and for $a \in V(T) - \{r\}$, denote by p_a the parent of a. For convenience, define $X_{p_r} = \emptyset$ for the root r. We will denote by T_a the subtree rooted at $a \in V(T)$, and

$$X_{T_a} = \bigcup_{b \in V(T_a)} X_b$$

Notice that we may recolor the vertices of H, using only the color classes $C_1, C_2, \ldots, C_{k+2}$, without regard to the vertices of $V(G) - V(H)$.

Claim. For $a \in V(T)$, the vertices of X_{T_a} can be colored with $C_1, C_2, \ldots, C_{k+2}$ in such a way that

1. every vertex of $X_{T_a} - X_{p_a}$ is colored with one of the classes $C_1, C_2, \ldots, C_{k+1}$, and

2. if a vertex of $X_{T_a} \cap X_{p_a}$ has color class C_{k+2}, then there is a C_j $(1 \leq j \leq k+1)$ that is not used for any vertex of X_b, for all those $b \in V(T_a)$ such that X_b contains a vertex of color C_{k+2}.

The proof of the claim (omitted in this version of the paper) operates by recoloring the vertices in $V(H) \cap X_{T_a}$ (for $a \in V(T)$) inductively, starting with the leaves a of T. The proof relies on the suppositions that we cannot have any C_j $(1 \leq j \leq k+2)$ filled nor empty, nor may $|C_{k+2} \cap V(H)|$ become reduced.

Since the root of T satisfies our claim, no vertex of H has color class C_{k+2} (a contradiction). □

It is easy to see that the upper bound of $k+1$ partially full color classes (given by Lemma 7) is tight whenever $t > 1$. Consider the clique on $k+1$ vertices. This is a partial k-tree, and no two vertices may share the same color class.

We obtain the following corollary to Lemma 7:

Corollary 8. *A partial k-tree G, with $|V(G)| = n$ has $\lceil \frac{n}{t} \rceil \leq \chi_t(G) \leq \lceil \frac{n}{t} \rceil + k$*

Given a partial k-tree G, let G^0 be the graph obtained by adding enough $(t-1$ or fewer$)$ isolated vertices to G so that t divides $|V(G^0)|$; for $i \leq i \leq k$, let G^i be constructed by adding ti isolated vertices to G^0. Corollary 8 can be restated as

Corollary 9. $\chi_t(G) = \min\{\lceil \frac{n}{t} \rceil + i \mid G^i$ *has a perfect χ_t-coloring* $, 0 \leq i \leq k\}$

From Corollary 9, Theorem 5 and Courcelle's result [Cou90] that any CMS property is linear-time solvable on the class of graphs of bounded treewidth, we obtain

Theorem 10. *The χ_t-coloring problem can be solved in linear time over the class of graphs of bounded treewidth.*

5   Bipartite Graphs

In this section, we show that the χ_t-coloring problem can be solved in polynomial time over the class of bipartite graphs. A bipartite graph G has its vertex set partitioned as $V(G) = X \cup Y$, such that each edge of $E(G)$ has one endpoint in X and the other endpoint in Y. Let $r_X \equiv |X| \pmod{t}$ and $r_Y \equiv |Y| \pmod{t}$.

A bipartite graph G can be χ_t-colored using either $\lceil \frac{n}{t} \rceil$ or $\lceil \frac{n}{t} \rceil + 1$ color classes (where $n = |V(G)|$). Since X and Y are independent sets, we can fill $\lfloor \frac{|X|}{t} \rfloor$ color classes as subsets of X, and $\lfloor \frac{|Y|}{t} \rfloor$ color classes as subsets of Y. The remaining "residue" vertices can be placed in (at most) two additional nonempty color classes $C_X \subseteq X$ and $C_Y \subseteq Y$, where $|C_X| = r_X$ and $|C_Y| = r_Y$. The following lemma is easy to see.

Lemma 11. *This straightforward approach gives an optimal χ_t-coloring if $r_X + r_Y > t$, or if t divides X, or if t divides Y.*

Otherwise, $r_X + r_Y \leq t$ and $1 \leq r_X, r_Y \leq t-1$. In this case, the straightforward approach uses $\lceil \frac{n}{t} \rceil + 1$ color classes, which may not be optimal. That is, it may be possible to use only $\lceil \frac{n}{t} \rceil$ color classes, by constructing some "mixed" classes, containing both elements of X and elements of Y.

Observation 12. *When $r_X + r_Y \leq t$ and $1 \leq r_X, r_Y \leq t-1$: the χ_t-coloring problem reduces to finding some number s (dependent only on t) of independent sets $C_1, C_2, \ldots, C_s$ such that:*

$$|X \cap (C_1 \cup C_2 \cup \ldots \cup C_s)| \equiv r_X \ (mod\ t)$$
$$|Y \cap (C_1 \cup C_2 \cup \ldots \cup C_s)| \equiv r_Y \ (mod\ t)$$
$$|C_1 \cup C_2 \cup \ldots \cup C_s| = t(s-1) + r_X + r_Y$$

If a solution can be found, then $\chi_t(G) = \lceil \frac{n}{t} \rceil$: A solution consists of these s independent sets, and $\lceil \frac{n}{t} \rceil - s$ full color classes—each a subset either of X or of Y—formed from the vertices of $V(G) - C_1 - C_2 - \ldots - C_s$. If a solution cannot be found, then $\chi_t(G) = \lceil \frac{n}{t} \rceil + 1$.

For fixed t, there are only a constant number of distinguishable (under isomorphism) solutions, and each solution consists of a constant number s of fixed-size independent sets. For example, when $t = 2, r_X = r_Y = 1$, we are simply looking for an edge in the complement graph $\overline{G}$. When $t = 3, r_X = 2, r_Y = 1$, there are two possible solutions:

1. a triangle in $\overline{G}$ with one vertex in Y and two vertices in X, or
2. two triangles in $\overline{G}$, each with one vertex in X and two vertices in Y

In all cases, we are looking for a fixed-size collection of bounded-size cliques in the complement graph $\overline{G}$. This problem can be solved in polynomial time.

This can be formalized in the following theorem:

Theorem 13. *The χ_t-coloring problem can be solved in polynomial time over the class of bipartite graphs.*

6   Conclusion

We have defined the χ_t-coloring problem—a natural problem arising in Scheduling Theory. While this problem is NP-complete for general graphs, we have shown that it has a linear-time algorithm for graphs of bounded treewidth, and a polynomial-time algorithm for bipartite graphs.

These results raise the following interesting question: If a problem P can be solved in $O(n)$ time on partial k-trees (with n vertices), then can P be solved in $O(n)$ time on the complements of partial k-trees? Equivalently, we could ask if the "complement problem"—obtained from a CMS formula encoding P by replacing each occurrence of $Adj(u, v)$ with $\neg Adj(u, v)$ (and vice-versa)—can be solved in $O(n)$ time on partial k-trees. Note that the complement of a partial k-tree has $O(n^2)$ edges, whereas a partial k-tree has only $O(n)$ edges. We have shown that this question can be answered in the affirmative for the problem of partition into t-cliques, whose complement is the χ_t-coloring problem; partition into t-cliques is well known to have a linear time algorithm on partial k-trees [ALS91, BLW87, BPT92, Cou90, MP87]. We note that there are problems (e.g. independent set) that are well-known to be solvable in linear-time on partial k-trees, and whose complement problems (viz. clique) are also known to have linear-time algorithms on partial k-trees. The general question remains open.

Acknowledgement. The authors wish to thank Sanjeev Mahajan for helpful discussions on the content of this paper.

References

[ALS91] S. Arnborg, J. Lagergren, and D. Seese. Easy problems for tree decomposable graphs. *J. Algorithms*, 12:308–340, 1991.

[BH85] B. Bollobás and A.J. Harris. List-colourings of graphs. *Graphs and Combinatorics*, 1:115–127, 1985.

[BLW87] M.W. Bern, E.L. Lawler, and A.L. Wong. Linear-time computation of optimal subgraphs of decomposable graphs. *J. Algorithms*, 8:216–235, 1987.

[Bod93] H.L. Bodlaender. A linear time algorithm for finding tree-decompositions of small treewidth. In *Proc. 25th STOC*, pages 226–234, 1993.

[BPT92] R.B. Borie, R.G. Parker, and C.A. Tovey. Automatic generation of linear-time algorithms from predicate calculus descriptions of problems on recursively constructed graph families. *Algorithmica*, 7:555–581, 1992.

[Cou90] B. Courcelle. The monadic second-order logic of graphs. I. recognizable sets of finite graphs. *Information and Computation*, 85:12–75, 1990.

[GJ79] M.R. Garey and D.S. Johnson. *Computers and Intractability: A Guide to the Theory of NP-Completeness*. W.H. Freeman and Company, New York, 1979.

[GS84] F. Gécseg and M. Steinby. *Tree Automata*. Akadémiai Kiadó, Budapest, 1984.

[JT95] T.R. Jensen and B. Toft. *Graph Coloring Problems*. Wiley Interscience, 1995.

[KH78] D.G. Kirkpatrick and P. Hell. On the complexity of a generalized matching problem. In *Proc. 10th STOC*, pages 240–245, 1978.

[KI88] F. Kitagawa and H. Ikeda. An existential problem of a weight-controlled subset and its application to school timetable construction. *Discrete Mathematics*, 72:195–211, 1988.

[LS86] V. Lotfi and S. Sarin. A graph coloring algorithm for large scale scheduling problems. *Comput. & Ops. Res.*, 13:27–32, 1986.

[Mey73] W. Meyer. Equitable coloring. *Amer. Math. Monthly*, 80:920–922, 1973.

[MP87] S. Mahajan and J.G. Peters. Algorithms for regular properties in recursive graphs. In *Proc. 25th Ann. Allerton Conf. Communication, Control, Comput.*, pages 14–23, 1987.

[RS86] N. Robertson and P.D. Seymour. Graph minors. II. Algorithmic aspects of tree-width. *J. Algorithms*, 7:309–322, 1986.

Expander properties in random regular graphs with edge faults *

Sotiris E. Nikoletseas[1] and Paul G. Spirakis[2]

[1] Computer Technology Institute, Patras, Greece, nikole@cti.gr
[2] Computer Technology Institute, Patras, Greece, spirakis@cti.gr

Abstract. Let H be an undirected graph. A random graph of type$-H$ is obtained by selecting edges of H independently and with probability p. We can thus represent a *communication network* H in which the links *fail independently* and with probability $f = 1 - p$. A fundamental type of H is the clique of n nodes (leading to the well-known random graph $G_{n,p}$). Another fundamental type of H is a *random member* of the set G_n^d of all regular graphs of degree d (leading to a new type of random graphs, of the class $G_{n,p}^d$). Note that $G_{n,p} = G_{n,p}^{n-1}$. The $G_{n,p}^d$ model was introduced in ([11]).
Information about the remaining (with high probability) structure of type$-H$ random graphs is of interest to applications in reliable network computing. For example, it is well known that any member of G_n^d is almost surely an *efficient certifiable expander*. Expanders are widely used in Computer Science. We have shown in ([11]) that $G_{n,p}^d$ has a *giant component of small diameter* even when $d = O(1)$. We wish to determine the *minimum* value of p for which the giant component of $G_{n,p}^d$ remains a certifiable expander with high probability. In this paper we show that the second eigenvalue of the adjacency matrix of the giant component of $G_{n,p}^d$ is concentrated in an interval of small width around its mean, and that its mean is $O((dp)^{3/4})$, provided that $dp > 256$. Thus, the giant component of a random member of $G_{n,p}^d$ remains, with high probability, a *certifiable efficient expander*, despite the link faults, provided that $dp > 256$.

1 Introduction

Modern multiprocessor architectures and communication networks compute over structured, regular interconnection graphs. In such environments, several applications may share the same network while executing concurrently. This may lead to unavailability of links for certain cases. Similarly, faults may cause non-availability of links or nodes.

When computing in the presence of faults one cannot assume that the actual structure of the computing environment is known. Either because of the network operating system actions or, in distributed computing where only local

* Work supported in part by the ESPRIT III Basic Research Programme of the EC under contract No. 9072 (Project GEPPCOM) and contract No. 7141 (Project AL-COM II)

connectivity information is available, one may assume computing over a *randomly assigned subnetwork*. This subnetwork in addition may suffer from link or node faults. Our work here addresses this interesting issue i.e. analyzing the average case taken over a set of topologies, in the presence of faults. Since random regular graphs are known to be *expanders*, we investigate whether *their partially destroyed due to faults* counterparts have still expander properties that can be efficiently verified. See also our previous works for multiconnectivity issues of faulty random regular graphs ([11], [8]) and the works on fault analysis for specific well-structured networks or PRAMS ([4],[6], [7], [14], [12], [16]).

2 Definitions, state of the art and our results

Let $G(V, E)$ be a graph of n vertices. We allow self-loops and multiple edges. Let A be its adjacency matrix. Its entries, $a_{i,j}$, are positive integers and count the number of edges from i to j (self-loops are counted twice). A is a $n \times n$ symmetric matrix.

The graph G is d−regular if $\sum_j a_{i,j} = d$, for $1 \leq i \leq n$.

Let $\lambda_1 \geq \lambda_2 \geq \cdots \geq \lambda_n$ the eigenvalues of the graph $G(V, E)$. For any d−regular graph, $\lambda_1 = d$. The subdominant eigenvalues λ_2 and λ_n provide important information about expansion properties of G. For d−regular graphs, one wants the size of $\rho = max\{d^{-1}|\lambda_2|, d^{-1}|\lambda_n|\}$ to be as small as possible.

For the graph G it is sometimes useful to consider the matrix P with entries $p_{i,j} = \frac{1}{d_i} a_{i,j}$ where d_i is the degree of vertex i. The matrix P can be viewed as the *transition matrix* of the Markov chain of n states, associated with a random walk on the graph G.

If G is not connected, then the Markov Chain is separated into a number of aperiodic and irreducible chains, one per connected component.

There is considerable recent interest in Markov chains that are "rapidly mixing" i.e. they get close (in terms of the variance distance) to the limit distribution after a polylog number of steps where the polylog is a function of the total number of states of the chain (see e.g. [15]). It is known that if G is an expander then the Markov chain associated with P is rapidly mixing.

Definition 1. A graph $G(V, E)$ is a c−expander if for every $X \subseteq V, |X| \leq n/2$ implies that $|N(X) - X| \geq c|X|$ where $N(X) = \{y|(x,y) \in E$ and $x \in X\}$ (i.e. $N(X)$ is the set of neighbours of X). The constant c is called the expansion constant.

Expanders are the building blocks of optimal networks and algorithms for many purposes such as sorting, routing, superconcentrators etc (see [13]). For d−regular graphs it is true that $c \geq \alpha(1 - \lambda_2/d)$ where $\alpha > 0$ is a constant.

Random d−regular graphs were shown to be almost surely very powerful expanders. Broder and Shamir ([2]) have shown that for most d−regular graphs, $|\lambda| \leq cd^{3/4}$ where $\lambda = max\{|\lambda_2|, |\lambda_n|\}$ and $c > 0$ a constant. Slightly better estimates were produced by ([3]). The above result leads to a quick randomised algorithm for generating *certified* efficient expanders:

Repeat
Construct a random member G of G_n^d ;
Evaluate its λ_2 ;
until a G is found with $\lambda_2 \leq cd^{3/4}$

By the result of ([2]), the expected number of repetitions is bounded.

Let now G be a random member of $G_{n,p}^d$. Let now λ_i be the eigenvalues of the adjacency matrix of *the giant component* of G. How does p affect λ_2? In fact, if the giant component of $G_{n,p}^d$ remains a certifiable efficient expander, despite edge faults, then this would lead to an efficient construction of *robust* fat-trees and other universal networks (see e.g. [10]). In this paper we prove that *for almost any member of* $G_{n,p}^d$, $|\lambda| \leq c(dp)^{3/4}$ for a constant $c > 0$. In fact $c^2 \leq \sqrt{256}$, provided $dp > 256$. Thus the efficient certifiable construction of robust expanders despite faults is indeed possible, when p is such that $dp > 256$.

3 The model and the general framework

We closely follow but judisiously modify and extend the framework of ([2]).

We construct an undirected random $2d$-regular graph G_n^{2d} by choosing independently d permutations uniformly randomly among all possible permutations of the n vertices. For each of the chosen permutations π and for each vertex i ($1 \leq i \leq n$) we add to the graph the edge $(i, \pi(i))$ *with probability* p, independently. Then an outcome of $G_{n,p}^{2d}$ is produced where each vertex i has a degree $d_i \leq 2d$.

In ([11]) we have shown that:

Fact 2. $G_{n,p}^d$ *is d-connected except for $O(1)$ vertices w.h.p. for all failure probabilities $f = 1 - p \leq n^{-\epsilon}$ ($\epsilon > 0$ fixed).*

Fact 3. *When $G_{n,p}^d$ is disconnected, it still has a giant (i.e. $\Theta(n)$-sized) connected component of $\Theta(\log n)$ diameter for any $f < 1 - \frac{32}{d}$, w.h.p. , for any $d \geq 64$.*

These facts are proved for the (different) d-regular graph model of ([1]) by first showing the results in the *configuration space* with edge faults. A configuration H is a collection of n labelled groups (supervertices) each group having d labelled (small) vertices and a partition of the set of nd vertices into pairs called edges. We then remove each edge independently with probability p.

One can translate the proofs of Facts 2, 3 to the permutation model by simply replacing k-th edge of the partition by k-th permutation. Furthermore, all the theorems proved in this paper for the permutation space hold also for the configuration space with the same mapping working in the opposite direction.

Let A be the incidence matrix of the giant component, C, of G (an outcome of $G_{n,p}^{2d}$) and P its Markov Chain matrix (irreducible, aperiodic) as before. Let C have $n' = \Theta(n)$ vertices. In the case where the graph G is connected, we simply take as C the graph G itself and $n' = n$.

Let the eigenvalues of P be $\rho_1, \ldots, \rho_{n'}$ where we consider them sorted: $\rho_1 = 1 \geq \rho_2 \geq \cdots \geq \rho_{n'}$. Let $\rho = max\{\rho_2, |\rho_{n'}|\}$. P has real eigenvalues, because the Markov Chain it defines is *reversible* (see [15]).

Lemma 4. *The Markov Chain defined by P (i.e. a random walk on the giant component C of G) is (time) reversible.*

Proof (sketch): It is enough to show that for all $i, j \in \{1, \ldots, n'\}$, $p_{ij}\pi_i = p_{ji}\pi_j$ where $\{1, \ldots, n'\}$ are the vertices of C, π_i is the (steady state) probability of state i and $p_{i,j} = \frac{\alpha_{ij}}{d_i}$ is the probability of walking in one step from state i to state j. It is well known (see [16]) that $\pi_i = \frac{d_i}{2e}$ where e is the number of edges of C. Thus $p_{ij}\pi_i = \frac{\alpha_{ij}}{2e} = \frac{\alpha_{ji}}{2e} = p_{ji}\pi_j$ (because C is undirected and A is symmetric). $\qquad\square$

Thus, the eigenvalues of P are also those of a *similar symmetric* matrix (see [15]) and so are all real.

Since

$$trace\left(P^{2k}\right) = \sum_i \rho_i^{2k}$$

and since P has real eigenvalues we get:

$$\rho^{2k} \leq trace\left(P^{2k}\right) - 1$$

for $k \geq 1$. Thus, by taking expectations:

$$E(\rho) \leq \left(E\left(\rho^{2k}\right)\right)^{1/2k} \leq \left[E\left(trace(P^{2k})\right) - 1\right]^{1/2k}$$

by Jensen's inequality.

Let $P_{ii}^{(2k)}$ be, for the graph C, the probability that a particle starting at vertex i and moving by following the random walk defined by P, is again at vertex i after $2k$ steps. Note that the probability $P_{ii}^{(2k)}$ is a random variable, since it depends on the (randomly produced) graph. Clearly $E(P_{ii}^{(2k)})$ does not depend on i when C is taken over $G_{n,p}^{2d}$, due to uniformity. Thus

$$E\left(trace\left(P^{(2k)}\right)\right) = n' E\left(P_{11}^{(2k)}\right) = \Theta(n) E\left(P_{11}^{(2k)}\right)$$

where the expectation is over all graphs $G \in G_{n,p}^{2d}$, and for their giant components C.

We view G as produced in two steps: First we choose a random member $G_{reg} \in G_n^{2d}$. Then we construct G by selecting each edge of G_{reg} with probability p. Fix a G_{reg}.

In order to study P_{11}, first we formally represent the particle motion on the C of G produced from the G_{reg} by a sequence of moves $S = \sigma_1 \sigma_2 \cdots \sigma_{2k}$. Each S is a word of length $2k$ in the free monoid M generated by the alphabet $A = \{f_1, f_1^{-1}, \ldots, f_d, f_d^{-1}\}$. Here the mapping f_i is "what remains" from $\pi(i)$ (out of which G_{reg} was constructed) after applying edge faults to edges of G_{reg} to get G. In fact f_i are "partial permutations" since some edges have been removed.

Second, we assign to each f_i a partial permutation by choosing, for each vertex v in G, equiprobably one of its (remaining) neighbours. The sequence S then determines, for each vertex x, a *trajectory* starting at x: $T = (x, x_1, x_2, \ldots, x_{2k})$ where $x_1 = f_1(x), \ldots, x_i = f_i(x_{i-1})$.

In the *free group* F generated by the letters $\{f_1, \ldots, f_d\}$ S is just an element. Let 1_F (e.g. equal to $f_1 f_1^{-1}$) be the identity element of F.

Definition 5. S is an identity sequence if $S \equiv 1_F$.

Definition 6. Given S, let $R(S)$ be the unique sequence of minimum length equivalent to S obtained by removing from S all identity subsequences. $R(S)$ is called the reduction of S.

Definition 7. Given S, if $S = R(S)$ then S is irreducible. If S^2 is irreducible, we call S strongly irreducible.

Then for G:

Remark. $P_{11}^{(2k)} = \Pr($ the particle starting at vertex 1 either returns to 1 after $2k$ steps because S is an identity sequence *or* it does so because S reduces to some non-empty irreducible sequence S' having a trajectory $T(S')$ with $x'_{2s} = 1$, where $2s$ is the length of S').

The above events are exclusive (the second event implies that S *is not an identity sequence*), thus $P_{11}^{(2k)}$ *is the sum* of their corresponding probabilities. We now bound from above these probabilities.

4 Estimation of $E(P_{11}^{(2k)})$ and of the mean of the second largest eigenvalue

In the sequel, we consider vertex 1 belonging to the giant component C of G.

Lemma 8. *Let S be a random word of length $2k$ in M. Then, assuming $k = \Theta(\log n)$, Prob(S is an identity sequence) $\leq 2 \left(\frac{256}{dp} \right)^{k/4}$.*

Proof: A balanced string of parentheses is equivalent to an identity sequence (just assign σ to every left parenthesis and σ^{-1} to the corresponding right and vice-versa). The number of balanced strings of parentheses is the Catalan number: $\frac{1}{2k+1} \binom{2k+1}{k}$. Let d_i be the degree of vertex x_i in G, for each vertex x_i in the trajectory $T(S)$. Consider first G_{reg} fixed and let G be an outcome of the experiment of sampling edges out of G_{reg}.

Let $X_v(k)$ be the number of paths of length k starting from vertex v in the giant component C of G. The fraction, y, of the number of all identity sequences of lenght $2k$ over the number of all paths of length $2k$ in G, will be bounded by

$$y \leq \frac{1}{2k+1} \binom{2k+1}{k} \frac{X_1(k)}{X_1(2k)}$$

Let $c_1(k)$ be the number of all cycles of length k starting (and returning) to vertex 1 of C. Then, clearly

$$X_1(2k) \geq c_1(k) X_1(k)$$

Thus

$$y \leq \frac{1}{2k+1} \binom{2k+1}{k} \frac{1}{c_1(k)}$$

In order to estimate a lower bound on $c_1(k)$, we must consider the degrees of the vertices of C. Let $d_1, d_2, \ldots, d_k$ the degrees in a cycle including vertex 1. From the experiment in G_{reg} we have $E(d_i) = 2dp$ for each vertex separately, because the edges are sampled in independently (of course there are dependencies among neighbours). For a particular vertex i, then

$$\Pr\{d_i > E(d_i)(1-\beta)\} \geq 1 - \exp\left(-\frac{\beta^2}{3} E(d_i)\right)$$

by Chernoff bounds in the Bernoulli of $2d$ experiments with success probability p. Fix a $\beta \in (0,1)$ and let $\gamma = 1 - \exp\left(-\frac{\beta^2}{3} 2dp\right)$ $(0 < \gamma < 1)$. Now, for each of the $\Theta(n)$ vertices of C, there are $\frac{\Theta(n)}{2d}$ such *independent* Bernoulli experiments (they are vertices which are not immediate neighbours and they do not share an edge). Let $N = \frac{\Theta(n)}{2d}$. We shall call a "success" in each of these N experiments the outcome "$d_i > 2dp(1-\beta)$" for the corresponding vertex i. The probability of success is γ and the N experiments are independent.

Fix a cycle in C of length k and let $k = 2\alpha \log n$ ($\alpha > 1$ to be determined). Consider on the cycle the $\frac{k}{2} = \alpha \log n$ vertices which are not neighbours. Then $c_1(k) \geq$ the number of cycles in the subgraph of C where all vertices have degree ≥ 1 except for the vertices i where a success happened, and they have degree $\geq 2dp(1-\beta)$. The number of such successes in a single cycle is at least $g(k) \geq \frac{k}{2} \gamma (1 - \beta')$ (where $\beta' \in (0,1)$) with probability at least $1 - \exp\left(-\frac{\beta'^2}{3} \frac{k}{2}\right)$ by Chernoff bounds. So, we have, per cycle, at least $g(k) = \alpha \log n \, \gamma(1-\beta')$ vertices of degree $d_i \geq 2dp(1-\beta)$ with probability at least $1-n^{-\alpha\frac{\beta'^2}{3}}$. Thus, conditioning on $g(k)$ successes, $c_1(k) \geq [2dp(1-\beta)]^{g(k)}$ i.e. $c_1(k) \geq [2dp(1-\beta)]^{\frac{k}{2}\gamma(1-\beta')}$. For $\beta = 0.1$ and $dp > 200$, we get $\gamma > \frac{2}{3}$ and for $\beta' = 0.1$, we get at least $\frac{k}{4}$ successes with probability at least $1-n^{-\alpha\frac{\beta'^2}{3}}$. Choose $\alpha > 600$ to get $1-n^{-\alpha\frac{\beta'^2}{3}} \geq 1-n^{-2}$. Let $\mathcal{E}$ be the event of "at least $\frac{k}{4}$ successes". We then have

$$\Pr[S \equiv 1_F | \mathcal{E}] \leq \frac{1}{2k+1} \binom{2k+1}{k} \frac{1}{(1.8dp)^{k/4}} \leq \frac{2^{2k}}{(1.8)^{k/4}} \frac{1}{(dp)^{k/4}}$$

But $(1-\beta)^{k/4} \geq 2^{k/8}$. Thus

$$\Pr[S \equiv 1_F | \mathcal{E}] \leq \frac{2^{2k-k/8}}{(dp)^{k/4}} \leq \left(\frac{2^{15}}{(dp)^2}\right)^{k/8}$$

When $dp > 2^8 = 256$ we get

$$\Pr\left[S \equiv 1_F | \mathcal{E}\right] \leq \left(\frac{1}{2}\right)^{k/8}$$

and since $k = 600 \log n$ we get

$$\Pr\left[S \equiv 1_F | \mathcal{E}\right] \leq n^{-75}$$

Hence

$$\Pr\left[S \equiv 1_F\right] \leq 2\left(n^{-75}\right)\left(1 - n^{-2}\right)$$

for $dp > 256$, for each G_{reg}, and by summing over all the G_{reg} (their total probability is 1) we get

$$\Pr\left[S \equiv 1_F\right] \leq 2\left(\frac{2^{15}}{(dp)^2}\right)^{k/8} \leq 2\left(\frac{2^{7.5}}{dp}\right)^{k/4} \leq 2\left(\frac{256}{dp}\right)^{k/4}$$

□

Let now S be a fixed sequence and let its trajectory be $T(S) = (1, x_1, \ldots, x_s)$. Clearly $x_1, \ldots, x_s$ are random variables depending on G and the assignment made to $f_1, \ldots, f_d$. We can view $x_1, \ldots, x_s$ constructed iteratively as follows: $\sigma_1(1)$ is chosen uniformly randomly in $\{1, \ldots, n\}$. (This *does not depend on d or p* since, if vertex 1 is connected to some vertex this could be any vertex in $\{1, \ldots, n\}$ equiprobably). For $i \geq 2$, if $\sigma_i(x_{i-1})$ is already *fixed* in S then $x_i \leftarrow \sigma_i(x_{i-1})$ else x_i is randomly chosen, etc. We call the former situation a *forced choice*, else a *free choice*.

Lemma 9. *Given any sequence S of length s, the probability that its $T(S)$ induces a subgraph of more than one loop is $O(\frac{s^4}{n^2})$, provided $dp \geq 2$.*

Proof: Same as in ([2]) since the trajectory $T(S)$ induces a subgraph of K_n being the set of all edges traversed by $T(S)$, and this *does not depend* on either d or p, provided $dp \geq 2$.
□
By a similar argument we get:

Lemma 10. *Given any irreducible sequense S of length s, the probability that its trajectory starting at 1 returns to 1 by traversing a single loop once is $\frac{1}{n} + O(\frac{s}{n^2})$.*

Lemma 11. *Let S be a sequence of length $2k$ chosen uniformly randomly. The probability that the reduction of S, $R(S)$, has length $2s$ is at most $\frac{2s+1}{2k+1}\binom{2k+1}{k-s}\frac{f(k-s)}{X_1(2k)}$, where $f(k-s)$ is the number of all sequences of length $2k$ with $2s$ unmatched left moves (parentheses) in C and the vertices corresponding to the $k-s$ matched left parentheses are randomly selected.*

Proof: Let $Y(2k, 2s)$ be the number of strings of parentheses of length $2k$ such that the number of right parentheses never exceeds the number of left parentheses counting from left to right and such that there are $2s$ more left than right parentheses. The number Y is the ballot number ([9]):

$$Y(2k, 2s) = \frac{2s+1}{2k+1} \binom{2k+1}{k-s}$$

If in the trajectory of S the degrees encountered are $d_1, \ldots, d_{2k}$, let the positions (vertices) $i_1, \ldots, i_{k-s+1} \in \{1, \ldots 2k\}$ correspond to each of the $k - s$ matched left parenthesis in $Y(2k, 2s)$. Let $j_1, \ldots, j_{2s-1}$ the remaining vertices. Then

$$f(k - s) = d_{i_1} d_{i_2} \cdots d_{i_{k-s+1}} (d_{j_1} - 1) d_{j_2} - 1) \cdots (d_{j_{2s-1}} - 1)$$

But the number of sequences of length $2k$ is the number of paths $X_1(2k) = \Theta(d_1 d_2 \cdots d_{2k})$ and the lemma follows because the desired probability is upper bounded by

$$\frac{Y(2k, 2s) d_{i_1} d_{i_2} \cdots d_{i_{k-s+1}} (d_{j_1} - 1) d_{j_2} - 1) \cdots (d_{j_{2s-1}} - 1)}{\Theta(d_1 d_2 \cdots d_{2k})}$$

$$\leq Y(2k, 2s) \Theta \left[\frac{1}{d_{\lambda_1} \cdots d_{\lambda_{k-s}}} \left(1 - \frac{1}{d_{j_1}}\right) \cdots \left(1 - \frac{1}{d_{j_{2s-1}}}\right) \right]$$

$\square$

By noticing that $E(d_{\lambda_i}) = 2dp$ and by the geometric dependence of the length reduction of S on the $d_{\lambda_i}^{-1}$, we conclude that if induced loops are traversed at least twice then the contribution to the probability (given that $R(S)$ is an identity) cannot be more than $\frac{k}{n} + O(\frac{k^2}{n^2})$ (due to Lemmas 9, 10). Thus we get

Lemma 12. *Let S be a sequence of length $2k$ chosen uniformly and randomly. The probability that S:*

1. *is not an identity and*
2. *the trajectory of S, $T(S)$ induces a subgraph of exactly one loop and*
3. *$T(S)$ returns to 1 by traversing the loop at least twice is*

$$O\left(2\frac{k}{n} \left(\frac{256}{dp}\right)^{k/4}\right)$$

Theorem 13. *If $k = \alpha \log n$, $\alpha \geq 600$ then*

$$E\left(P_{11}^{(2k)}\right) \leq 2 \left(\frac{256}{dp}\right)^{k/4} + \frac{1}{n} + O\left(\frac{k^4}{n^2}\right) + O\left(2\frac{k}{n} \left(\frac{256}{dp}\right)^{k/4}\right)$$

Now, from

$$E(\rho) \le E\left(trace(P^{2k}) - 1\right)^{1/(2k)}$$

and

$$E\left(trace(P^{2k})\right) = nE(P_{11}^{2k})$$

we get

$$E(\rho) \le \left[2n\left(\frac{256}{dp}\right)^{k/4} + O\left(\frac{k^4}{n}\right) + O\left(2k\left(\frac{256}{dp}\right)^{k/4}\right)\right]^{1/(2k)}$$

$$\le \left[2n\left(\frac{256}{dp}\right)^{k/4}(1 + o(1))\right]^{1/(2k)}$$

and by using $k = (4(2 - \epsilon)\log n)/\log(\frac{dp}{256})$ we get

$$E(\rho) \le \left(\frac{1}{n^{1-\epsilon}}\right)^{\frac{1}{8(2-\epsilon)\log n/\log(\frac{dp}{256})}}(1 + o(1))$$

and by using a suitable ϵ

$$E(\rho) \le \left(\frac{256}{dp}\right)^{1/4}(1 + o(1))$$

Thus we have:

Corollary 14. *Let P be the Markov chain probability matrix of a random member of $G_{n,p}^{2d}$. Then the second largest eigenvalue of the adjacency matrix of the giant component satisfies*

$$E(\rho) \le \left(\frac{256}{dp}\right)^{1/4}(1 + o(1))$$

Corollary 15. *The second largest eigenvalue, λ, of the adjacency matrix of $G_{n,p}^{2d}$ satisfies:*

$$E(|\lambda|) \le (256)^{1/4}(dp)^{3/4}(1 + o(1))$$

provided that $dp > 256$.

Note that in the proof of Lemma 8 we required paths of length $2k$, $k \ge 600\log n$. Since $k < n$, our result is asymptotic and holds for $n > k \ge 600\log n$ i.e. $\frac{n}{\log n} \ge 600$.

5 Concentration around the mean

A $G \in G_{n,p}^{2d}$ is determined by the choice of d permutations $\pi_1, \ldots, \pi_d$ and by the independent edge experiments. For $G, G' \in G_{n,p}^{2d}$ we define the equivalence relation: $G \sim_j G'$ iff ($\pi_i = \pi_i'$ for $1 \leq i \leq j$ and all edge choices in G, G' for π_i, π_i' ($1 \leq i \leq j$) coincide). Clearly $\sim_0$ is universal, $\sim_d$ is the identity. Any function h on $G_{n,p}^{2d}$ induces a stochastic process, Π, $(h_0, h_1, \ldots, h_d)$ where

$$h_j(G) = E(h(H)|H \sim_j G)$$

(H represents the graphs produced by the equivalence relation $\sim$ from G). Due to random selection of the rest of permutations and edges, it is easy to verify that

$$E(h_{j+1}|h_j) = h_j$$

i.e. Π is a martingale. Then if $\alpha > 0$ is such that

$$|h_{j+1} - h_j| \leq \alpha \text{ for } 0 \leq j \leq d$$

then

$$Prob(|h - E(h)| \geq \gamma \alpha \sqrt{d}) \leq exp\left(-\frac{\gamma^2}{2}\right)$$

The theorem follows:

Theorem 16. *For the second largest eigenvalue λ_2 of the giant component C of $G \in G_{n,p}^{2d}$ we have, if λ_2 is viewed as a function $\lambda_2(G)$, that*

$$|\lambda_2(G)_{j+1} - \lambda_2(G)_j| \leq 2p$$

Proof (sketch): Let A be the adjacency matrix of C. If f are the eigenfunctions of A (they are orthogonal when they correspond to distinct eigenvalues, thus for $v \in V$, $\sum_{v \in V} f(v) = 0$) then

$$\lambda_2 = \sup_{\sum f(v)=0} \frac{(Af, f)}{(f, f)}$$

when we vary just one permutation and one edge selection, thus we can easily prove $\frac{(Af,f)}{(f,f)} \leq 2p$ □

6 Conclusion and current work

In this paper we have shown that the random regular graphs with independent edge faults have (certifiably) expander properties (in their giant connected component), provided that $dp > 256$, where d is the degree and p the survival probability. We, in fact, have shown that the second largest eigenvalue of the giant component is bounded by $O((dp)^{3/4})$. This was shown for a particular model of random regular graphs, namely the permutation model, also used in ([2]).

In this paper we have shown the translation between the permutation and configuration spaces. Note that to tranlate from configuration space to regular graphs a sufficient condition is that either $2d = \Theta(\log n)$ or $2d \leq \frac{1}{2}\sqrt{\log n}$ (see [1], [11]). We leave open the interval in between.

Similar questions about the reliability properties of other random graphs of type$-H$ (e.g. motivated by interconnection networks of multiprocessors) are targets of future work.

Acknowledgement: We wish to thank D. Knuth and M. Yung for the encouragement we got from them in order to further investigate the $G_{n,p}^d$ model of random graphs and Friedhelm Meyer auf der Heide for his insightful remarks on a previous version of the paper,

References

1. B. Bollobas, "Random Graphs", Academic Press, 1985.
2. A. Broder and E. Shamir, "On the second eigenvalue of random regular graphs", Proc. 19st ACM Symp. on Theory of Computing, pp. 286–294, 1987.
3. J. Friedman, J. Kahn and E. Szemeredi, "On the second eigenvalue of random regular graphs", Proc. 21st ACM Symp. on Theory of Computing, pp. 286–294, 1989.
4. J. Hastad, T. Leighton and M. Newman, "Fast Computation Using Faulty Hypercubes", Proc. 21st ACM Symp. on Theory of Computing, pp. 251–263, 1989.
5. S. Janson, D. Knuth, T.Luczak, B. Pittel, "The birth of the giant component", Random Structures and Algorithms, vol. 4, pp. 232–355, 1993.
6. Z. Kedem, K. Palem, and P. Spirakis, "Efficient Robust Parallel Computations", Proc. 22nd ACM Symp. on Theory of Computing, pp. 138–148, 1990.
7. Z. Kedem, K. Palem, A. Raghunathan and P. Spirakis, "Combining Tentative and Definite Executions for Very Fast Dependable Parallel Computing", Proc. 23nd ACM Symp. on Theory of Computing, 1991.
8. Z. Kedem, K. Palem, P. Spirakis and M. Yung, "Faulty Random Graphs: reliable efficient-on-the-average network computing" , Computer Technology Institute (Patras, Greece) Technical Report, 1993.
9. D. E. Knuth, "The Art of Computer Programming", vol. 1, 2nd edition, Addison Wesley, 1973.
10. C. Leiserson, "Fat-trees: Universal networks for hardware-efficient supercomputing", IEEE Transactions on Computers, C-34 (10), pp. 892 – 900, October 1985.
11. S. Nikoletseas, K. Palem, P. Spirakis and M. Yung, "Short Vertex Disjoint Paths and Multiconnectivity in Random Graphs: Reliable Network Computing" , 21st International Colloquium on Automata, Languages and Programming (ICALP), pp. 508 – 519, 1994.
12. D. Peleg and E. Upfal, "Constructing Disjoint Paths on Expander Graphs", Proc. 19th ACM Symp. on Theory of Computing, pp. 264–273, 1987.
13. N. Pippenger, "Telephone switching networks", The Mathematics of Networks, AMS, Providence, 1982.
14. M. Rabin, "Efficient Dispersal of Information for Security, Load Balancing and Fault Tolerance", JACM, vol. 36, no. 2, pp. 335–348, 1989.
15. A. Sinclair, "Algorithms for random generation and Counting", ed. Birkhauser, 1992.

16. L. Valiant, "A Bridging Model for Parallel Computation", CACM, vol. 33, no. 8, pp. 103–111, 1990.

Dynamic analysis of the sizes of relations

Danièle Gardy[1] and Guy Louchard[2]

[1] Laboratoire PRISM, Université de Versailles Saint-Quentin / CNRS,
78035 Versailles Cedex (France) `Daniele.Gardy@prism.uvsq.fr`
[2] Département d'Informatique, Université Libre de Bruxelles, Bruxelles (Belgique)
`louchard@ulb.ac.be`

Abstract. We present a dynamic modelization of a database when submitted to a sequence of queries and updates, that allows us to study the evolution of the sizes of relations. While the problem of estimating the sizes of derived relations at a given time ("static" case) has been the subject of several studies, to the best of our knowledge the evolution of the relation sizes under queries and updates ("dynamic" cases) has not been studied so far. We consider the size of a relation as a random variable, and we study its probability distribution when the database is submitted to a sequence of insertions, deletions and queries. We show that it behaves asymptotically as a Gaussian process, whose expectation and covariance are proportional to the time. This approach also allows us to analyze the maximum of the size of the derived relation.

1 Introduction

Among the parameters that can be defined on relational databases, the sizes of the relations, either present in the database or computed by application of a relational operator ("derived relations") have long been recognized as important parameters in query optimization, i.e. in the search for an efficient way of answering users' queries, and many models have been proposed for their evaluation (see [20] for a survey). So-called *parametric models* are based on *a priori* assumptions on the probability distributions of the objects modelled in the database (relations, attributes...); they compute the mean, and sometime further moments, of the distribution of a derived relation size. Such models are used to estimate the size of a relation obtained by a selection, a projection or a join [2, 11, 24]. *Non-parametric models* use the values present in the database at a given time to obtain empirical information on the underlying probability distributions. This information is summed up in histograms that are then used to compute estimations of the sizes of derived relations [21], see also [22] for a related approach. An approach popular in recent years is based on *sampling;* again it uses information present in the database to compute estimates of derived relation sizes [12, 17, 23]. All these approaches consider a *static* database, the only exception being the recognized necessity of maintaining some parameters necessary to the sampling process [16].

Our work presents a *parametric model for dynamic databases:* We study the probabilistic behaviour of (initial and derived) relation sizes under assumptions

434

on the values that can be assumed by the database elements, and on the type
of operations allowed on the database. As such, it is in close relation to studies
on the dynamic behaviour of data structures (see for example [5, 6, 15, 18, 19]).

We gave in former papers [7, 8] conditions which ensure that, in the static
case (i.e. at a given time), the size of a derived relation, obtained by a projection, an equijoin or a semijoin, follows a normal limiting distribution. Our goal
here is to extend these results to *dynamic databases*, i.e. databases that can be
queried and updated. To this effect, we consider the size of a relation as a random
variable (r.v.) X, and we study its behaviour when the database is submitted
to a sequence of insertions, deletions and queries. We show that knowing the
initial and final sizes of a relation, the constraints on the relation (existence of a
functional dependency, sizes of attribute domains...), and the type of operations
(queries or updates, with specific probabilities of choosing a given operation at
a given time) allows us to completely characterize the r.v. X, and that, asymptotically (i.e. for a large number of operations), the size of an initial relation
behaves as a Markovian Gaussian process, and the size of a derived relation as a
(possibly non-Markovian) Gaussian process. In both cases, the expectation and
covariance are proportional to the time nt, and the process has a deterministic
part of order n on which is superimposed a random part of order $\sqrt{n}$ (see Fig. 1).
Such a characterization also allows us to analyze the maximum of the size of the
derived relation.

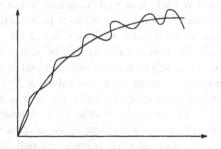

Fig. 1. Process describing a relation size

The rest of this paper is organized as follows. We recall in Section 2 the
database parameters that we shall study, and give a modelization in terms of
urn models; then we introduce the operations that may be considered. Section 3
presents the basic processes (number of tuples in a relation) corresponding to
different update models and to constraints on the initial objects (relations); for
many natural assumptions on the database, we obtain Gaussian Markovian processes. Section 4 then gives a characterization of the sizes of projections and joins
as Gaussian non-Markovian processes, and the distribution of their maximum.
Finally, Section 5 shows on some examples how these general results can be specified to obtain the behaviour of a derived relation according to constraints on
the type of initial relations and to specific update operations on the database.

2 Databases and urn models

The definitions relative to relational databases can be found in any text on database theory, and are not recalled here. Among the operators of the relational algebra, we shall consider the projection and the joins: the equijoin and the semijoin. We use the terms *initial relation* for the relation to which we apply a projection or a join, and *derived relation* for the relation resulting from the operation.

We presented in [7, 8] a modelization of relational operators in terms and urns and balls, that allows us to study the conditional distribution of the sizes of the derived relations obtained by a projection or by a join, assuming that the sizes of the initial relations are known. Now we want to study the influence of a sequence of updates and queries on the sizes of both the initial and derived relations. In the next subsections, we recall our urn models, then present the sequences of operations we shall study.

2.1 Urn models for relational operations

Model for the projection:

We consider a relation R with two attributes X and Y, and its projection on X, $\pi_X(R)$. Let d be the number of distinct possible values for the attribute X; we assume that, although it may become large, d is finite. We can modelize the projection of the relation R with urns and balls and relate the evaluation of its size to a well-known occupancy problem of discrete probability theory, as follows.

We consider a sequence of d urns, each urn being labelled with a distinct value of the attribute X. We have a finite supply of balls, and we allocate them at random among the d urns, each trial being independent of the others. Each ball corresponds to a tuple of the relation R, whose value on X is the label of the urn the ball falls into. After allocating all the balls, some urns are empty and some contain at least one ball. The number of urns with at least one ball is exactly the number of tuples in the projection of the relation R on the attribute X.

If, instead of the number of urns with at least one ball, we consider the number of empty urns, and if we assume that each urn can receive an unbounded number of balls, then we have a classical occupancy problem presented for example in [13]. Assuming that the urn size is infinite corresponds, in terms of relational databases, to a relation with a *key* on the attribute suppressed in the projection. As we shall also want to study relations without keys, we shall have to extend the classical model to the case where *the urns have a finite capacity:* There are δ places for balls (see [7] for a justification).

Models for the equijoin and for the semijoin:

The size of a relation obtained by an equijoin or a semijoin can likewise be expressed in the general framework of urn models, and we have presented two models to this effect in [8], which we briefly recall below.

Let us start with a sequence of d urns and with two kinds of balls, say blue and red; the balls of a given color are thrown into the urns independently of each other and of the balls of the other color. After throwing specified numbers of red and blue balls, we assign to the urns a certain number of balls of a third color, say green, according to one of the two sets of rules below. The red balls are associated with the relation R, the blue balls with the relation S, and the green balls with their equijoin $R \bowtie S$ or semijoin $R \rhd S$. The rules for allocating the green balls are as follows:

- For each urn, let i be the number of red balls and j the number of blue balls it has received.
- If we consider the *equijoin*, we put ij green balls in the urn.
- If we consider the *semijoin*, and if there is at least one blue ball ($j \geq 1$), we put as many green balls as there are red balls, i.e. i green balls.
- In both cases, the urns without balls or with balls of only one color do not receive any green ball.
- We now count the total number of green balls. The numbers r and s of red and blue balls are respectively the sizes of the relations R and S, and the final number of green balls is the size of their join.

In the rest of the paper, we shall use indifferently the terms *initial relation size* and *number of tuples*, or *number of balls*.

2.2 Database assumptions

We shall make the following assumptions in the present work, which cover a reasonable number of situations while keeping the computations manageable. We shall assume that *each urn is equally likely*, and that, when the urns have a finite capacity, *each place in an urn is equally likely*. In terms of relational databases, these assumptions mean that the possible values for the projection or join attribute X are uniformly distributed, and that, when the attribute Y or Z, suppressed by the projection or not participating in the join, is not a key of the relation, the possible values of Y or Z are also uniformly distributed . We point out that, when the attribute Y or Z is a key, the (possibly very skewed) probability distribution of the values has no influence on the size of the result, as long as we study the distribution of the relation size *conditioned by the initial size*.

We also assume that the relations satisfy standard independence assumptions: The coordinates of a tuple are independent, the tuples of a given relation are independent, and, for the join of two relations R and S, their values are independent (but see [3] for a discussion about these assumptions).

2.3 Dynamic models

We now introduce a modelization that allows us to consider the evolution of a relation subjected to a sequence of updates (insertions and deletions) and queries (searches, i.e. operations that do not modify the database). We shall denote by $\mathcal{I}$, $\mathcal{D}$ and $\mathcal{Q}$ an insertion, a deletion and a query, and by $p_{\mathcal{I}}$, $p_{\mathcal{D}}$ and $p_{\mathcal{Q}}$ the corresponding probabilities (of course, $p_{\mathcal{I}} + p_{\mathcal{D}} + p_{\mathcal{Q}} = 1$). If these probabilities vary according to the time t, we shall use the notations $p_{\mathcal{I}}(t)$, $p_{\mathcal{D}}(t)$ and $p_{\mathcal{Q}}(t)$. There are several constraints on the relations, which can be combined together;

we present them below.

- Unless indicated otherwise, we assume that, at the beginning, the relation is empty.
- At the end, the relation may be empty, or not. It the relation is not empty and if its size is known, we assume that it is proportional to the time.
- There are three possible operations at each step: insertion, deletion and query (search). We always assume that $p_I(t) \geq p_D(t)$.[3]
- If we choose to do a deletion, the conditional probability of deleting a given tuple, or ball, is $1/number\ of\ tuples\ at\ this\ time$.
- If we choose to do an insertion, the conditional probability of inserting a tuple with a given value on the projection or join attribute X, i.e. a ball into a given urn, depends on the constraints on the relation. *For a relation with a key, i.e. in the infinite urn model*, each urn has the same probability of receiving the new ball. *For a relation without key, i.e. if the urns are bounded*, each empty cell, whatever the urn it belongs to, has the same probability of receiving the ball once we have chosen to do an insertion.

3   The process $\mathcal{P}$ related to the initial relation size

Let n be some scaling parameter related to the time ($n \rightarrow +\infty$ later on), and let W be the number of balls at some time. We might choose the current number of steps (number of queries or updates) as a measure for the time, which would then belong to the intervall $[0, 2n]$. However, we shall study the asymptotic behaviour of W when the time goes to infinity, and it is interesting to change the time scale by choosing a time nt for $t \in [0, 2]$, and to normalize the r.v. W. For all the "natural" models, the number of tuples W has an expectation and a variance of order n: Assuming that we start from an empty structure at time 0, the expectation of the process $W([nt])$ is asymptotically equal to $nf_1(t)$, for a suitable function f_1 depending on the process, and [4]

$$\frac{W([nt]) - nf_1(t)}{\sqrt{n}} \Rightarrow X(t),\ 0 \leq t \leq 2,$$

where $X(t)$ is a Markovian Gaussian process whose covariance is denoted $f_2(s, t)$, $s \leq t$. As a consequence, for any r.v. ξ_1 and ξ_2, and with n_1 and n_2 the number of tuples of the relation, i.e. the total number of balls, at the times t_1 and t_2, the expectation $E[e^{i(\xi_1 n_1 + \xi_2 n_2)}]$ is asymptotically equal to $exp(nA(t_1, t_2))$, with

$$A(t_1, t_2) = i\left[\xi_1 f_1(t_1) + \xi_2 f_1(t_2)\right] - \frac{1}{2}\left[\xi_1^2 f_2(t_1, t_1) + 2\xi_1\xi_2 f_2(t_1, t_2) + \xi_2^2 f_2(t_2, t_2)\right]$$

---

[3] If this is not the case, the relation is either empty or has very few elements, which is of little interest.

[4] We note by $\Rightarrow$ the weak convergence of random functions in the space of all right-continuous functions having left limits and endowed with the Skorohod metric (see Billingsley [1]). All convergences with be defined for $n \rightarrow +\infty$.

We now turn to the presentation of the models we shall study (given below for probabilities independent of the time). The models **P1** and **P2** are relative to the projection, and the models **P3** and **P4** are relative to joins.

P1 : $\mathcal{I} + \mathcal{D} + \mathcal{Q}$ with arrival at a structure of size $2\bar{x}n + a\sqrt{n}$ (asymptotically proportional to the time). The mean and variance corresponding to one step are $\bar{x} = p_{\mathcal{I}} - p_{\mathcal{D}}$ and $\sigma^2 = p_{\mathcal{I}} + p_{\mathcal{D}} - \bar{x}^2$, and $(W([nt]) - n\bar{x}t)/\sqrt{n} \Rightarrow \sigma BB(t) + at/2$: We get a Brownian Bridge with mean and covariance

$$f_1(t) = \bar{x}t + \frac{at}{2\sqrt{n}}, \quad f_2(s, t) = \sigma^2 s \, \frac{2 - t}{2}, \quad s \le t.$$

P2 : with the *finite urn* case, let $\Delta = d\delta = \beta n$, with $\beta = \alpha\delta$: Δ is the maximal number of balls that we can allocate to the urns. Assume that each position taken at random among the Δ possible positions changes from status (full $\rightarrow$ empty, empty $\rightarrow$ full). This is equivalent to the Ehrenfest urn model ($\mathcal{I} + \mathcal{D}$). From Karlin and Taylor [14, p. 171], we know that, if $\Delta = 2N$, then

$$\frac{W([Nt]) - N}{\sqrt{N}} \Rightarrow OU(t) \quad \text{with} \quad OU(0) = 0 \text{ if } W(0) = N,$$

where OU is the classical Ornstein-Uhlenbeck process, with mean 0 and covariance $\frac{1}{2}[e^{-(t-s)} - e^{-(t+s)}]$, $s \le t$. Here $\Delta = 2N = \beta n$ so $N = \beta n/2$, $f_1(t) = \beta/2$ and $p_{\mathcal{I}}(t) = p_{\mathcal{D}}(t) = 1/2$. Hence, starting from $W(0) = \beta n/2$,

$$\frac{W([nt]) - \beta n/2}{\sqrt{n}} \Rightarrow \sqrt{\frac{\beta}{2}} \, OU\left(\frac{2t}{\beta}\right),$$

with covariance $f_2(s, t) = (\beta/4)\left[e^{-2(t-s)/\beta} - e^{-2(t+s)/\beta}\right]$.

If we start with $W(0) = 0$, then it is easily checked that $f_1(t) = (\beta/2)(1 - e^{-2t/\beta})$ and

$$\frac{W([nt]) - \beta n/2}{\sqrt{n}} + \frac{\beta}{2}\sqrt{n}e^{-2t/\beta} \Rightarrow \sqrt{\frac{\beta}{2}} \, OU\left(\frac{2t}{\beta}\right).$$

P3 : Here we have red (R) balls and blue (B) balls with probabilities $p_{\mathcal{I}}^R$, $p_{\mathcal{D}}^R$, $p_{\mathcal{I}}^B$, $p_{\mathcal{D}}^B$, $p_{\mathcal{Q}}$; at a given step, we throw, or delete, either a red ball or a blue ball; we are not allowed to modify the number of red balls and the number of blue balls at the same time. The mean and variance corresponding to one step, $\bar{x}_R, \sigma_R^2, \bar{x}_B, \sigma_B^2$, are given by formulæ similar to the ones for **P1**, and the covariance matrix of the 2-dimensional BM is easily written as

$$
\begin{array}{cc}
& \begin{array}{cccc} R_s & R_t & B_s & B_t \end{array} \\
\begin{array}{c} R_s \\ R_t \\ B_s \\ B_t \end{array} &
\left(
\begin{array}{cccc}
\sigma_R^2 s & \sigma_R^2 s & -\bar{x}_B\bar{x}_R s & -\bar{x}_B\bar{x}_R s \\
\sigma_R^2 s & \sigma_R^2 t & -\bar{x}_B\bar{x}_R s & -\bar{x}_B\bar{x}_R t \\
-\bar{x}_B\bar{x}_R s & -\bar{x}_B\bar{x}_R s & \sigma_B^2 s & \sigma_B^2 s \\
-\bar{x}_B\bar{x}_R s & -\bar{x}_B\bar{x}_R s & \sigma_B^2 s & \sigma_B^2 t
\end{array}
\right)
\end{array}
\quad s \le t. \qquad (1)
$$

So $f_1^R(t) = \bar{x}_R t$, $f_1^B(t) = \bar{x}_B t$ and $f_2^{\cdot\cdot}(s,t)$ is immediately written down from (1).

P4 : In this model, red balls and blue balls are thrown independently of each other: At a given step, we either throw only a red ball, or only a blue ball, or a red ball *and* a blue ball. Let p_{II}^{RB} be the probability that, at some step, we insert both a red ball and a blue ball, and similarly p_{ID}^{RB}, p_{DI}^{RB} and p_{DD}^{RB}. Let $\pi_I^R = p_I^R + p_{II}^{RB} + p_{ID}^{RB}$ and similarly for π_D^R, π_I^B and π_D^B. The mean and variance at one step are given for the red balls by $\bar{x}_R = \pi_I^R - \pi_D^R$, $\sigma_R^2 = \pi_I^R + \pi_D^R - \bar{x}_R^2$, and similarly for blue balls. The expectations are $f_1^R(t) = \bar{x}_R t$ and $f_1^B(t) = \bar{x}_B t$, and the covariance matrix is given by

$$
\begin{array}{cccc}
 & R_s & R_t & B_s & B_t
\end{array}
$$

$$
\begin{array}{c}
R_s \\ R_t \\ B_s \\ B_t
\end{array}
\left(
\begin{array}{cccc}
\sigma_R^2 s & \sigma_R^2 s & f_2^{RB}(s,s) & f_2^{RB}(s,t) \\
\sigma_R^2 s & \sigma_R^2 t & f_2^{RB}(s,t) & f_2^{RB}(t,t) \\
f_2^{RB}(s,s) & f_2^{RB}(s,t) & \sigma_B^2 s & \sigma_B^2 s \\
f_2^{RB}(s,t) & f_2^{RB}(t,t) & \sigma_B^2 s & \sigma_B^2 t
\end{array}
\right)
\quad s \le t.
$$

Hence $f_2^{R,B}(s,t) = f^{RB}(min(s,t))$ and $f^{RB}(t) = (p_{II}^{RB} + p_{DD}^{RB} - p_{ID}^{RB} - p_{DI}^{RB})t - \bar{x}_R \bar{x}_S t$.

The processes that we have just presented can be extended to relations that are conditioned to be empty at the time $2n$, to time-varying probabilities or to weighted structures (which, however, are more interesting when we consider only insertion and deletion than when queries are allowed): see [9, 10] for more examples of processes.

4 The process $\mathcal{Q}$ related to the derived relation size

4.1 Gaussian behaviour of $\mathcal{Q}$

Our goal here is to study the variation of the size of a derived relation under a sequence of queries and updates. We shall do this during a time interval of length $2n$ for large n. We consider several related stochastic processes, describing respectively the number of balls, denoted by $\mathcal{P}$ (or $\mathcal{P}^R$ and $\mathcal{P}^S$ for a join), and the size of the derived relation, denoted by $\mathcal{Q}$. We have shown in Section 3 that $\mathcal{P}$ has a deterministic component of order n, and a random component of order $\sqrt{n}$; now we prove that $\mathcal{Q}$ has the same property. In the two following theorems, the functions f_1 and f_2 are the expectation and the covariance of the process(es) $\mathcal{P}$ (or $\mathcal{P}^R$ and $\mathcal{P}^S$) describing the size(s) of the initial relation(s), and were given in Section 3 for the processes **P1** to **P4**.

Theorem 1. *The size $S[nt]$ of a projection at the time nt is asymptotically a (possibly non-Markovian) Gaussian process such that, with a relative error in the density of order $O(1/\sqrt{n})$:*

$$
E[S([nt])] \sim nG(t), \qquad VAR[S([nt])] \sim n\Phi(t),
$$

$$COV[S([nt_1]), S([nt_2])] \sim n\Psi_R(t_1, t_2),$$

with $G(t) := F(f_1(t))$, $\Phi(t) := \Psi_{NR}(t,t) + \gamma^2(t)f_2(t,t)$ and

$$\Psi_R(t_1, t_2) := \Psi_{NR}(t_1, t_2) + f_2(t_1, t_2)\gamma(t_1)\gamma(t_2).$$

The functions F and Ψ_{NR} depend on the constraints on the relation, i.e. on the type of the urn, and are presented below. The function γ is defined as $\gamma(t) := F'(f_1(t))$.

- For a relation with a key, i.e. infinite urns, let $ps_{1,2}$ be the probability of survival of one ball between t_1 and t_2; $ps_{1,2}$ can be computed from f_1 and p_D:

$$ps_{1,2} = ps_{1,2}(t_1, t_2) = exp\left[-\int_{t_1}^{t_2} \frac{p_D(s)}{f_1(s)}ds\right] \quad (= 1 \text{ if } t_1 = t_2).$$

Let $f_3(t_1, t_2) = \int_{t_1}^{t_2} p_I(u)\, ps_{1,2}(u, t_2)du$, and define $\alpha = n/d$. We get

$$F(x) = \alpha(1 - e^{-x/\alpha}); \quad \gamma(t) = e^{-f_1(t)/\alpha};$$
$$\Psi_{NR}(t_1, t_2) = \alpha e^{-f_1(t_1)/\alpha}(e^{-f_3(t_1,t_2)/\alpha} - e^{-f_1(t_2)/\alpha}) - f_1(t_1)ps_{1,2}e^{(f_1(t_1)+f_1(t_2))/\alpha}$$

- For a relation without a key, i.e. bounded urns, we recall that δ is the number of cells in an urn, and that $\alpha = n/d$ and $\beta = d\delta/n$. Let $p(t_1, t_2)$ be the probability that a place empty at t_1 is still empty at t_2, and $f_6(t_1, t_2) = exp(-\int_{t_1}^{t_2}(f_4(t) + f_5(t))dt)$, with $f_4(t) = p_I(t)/(\alpha\delta - f_1(t))$ and $f_5(t) = p_D(t)/f_1(t)$; we have that

$$p(t_1, t_2) = f_6(t_1, t_2) + \int_{t_1}^{t_2} f_5(u)f_6(u, t_2)du,$$

and again these functions can be computed from f_1, p_I and p_D:

$$F(x) = \alpha(1 - (1 - x/\beta)^\delta); \quad \gamma(t) = (1 - f_1(t)/\beta)^{\delta-1};$$

and $\Psi_{NR}(t_1, t_2) = (1 - \frac{f_1(t_1)}{\beta})^\delta \phi(t_1, t_2)$, with

$$\phi(t_1, t_2) = \alpha\, p(t_1, t_2)^\delta - (1 - \frac{f_1(t_2)}{\beta})^{\delta-1}(\alpha\, p(t_1, t_2) + (1 - \frac{1}{\delta})f_1(t_1)f_6(t_1, t_2)).$$

Theorem 2. *The size $S([nt])$ of an equijoin or a semijoin at the time nt is asymptotically a (possibly non-Markovian) Gaussian process such that, with a relative error of order $O(1/\sqrt{n})$ in the density:*

$$E[S([nt])] \sim nG(t); \quad VAR[S([nt])] \sim n\Phi(t);$$
$$COV[S([nt_1]), S([nt_2])] \sim n\Psi_R(t_1, t_2);$$

with

$$G(t) := F[f_1^R(t), f_1^B(t)];$$

$$\Psi_R(t_1, t_2) := \Psi_{NR}(t_1, t_2) + \gamma^R(t_1)\gamma^R(t_2)f_2^{R,R}(t_1, t_2) + \gamma^R(t_1)\gamma^B(t_2)f_2^{R,B}(t_1, t_2)$$

$$+\gamma^B(t_1)\gamma^R(t_2)f_2^{B,R}(t_1, t_2) + \gamma^B(t_1)\gamma^B(t_2)f_2^{B,B}(t_1, t_2);$$

$$\Phi(t) := \Psi_{NR}(t,t) + \gamma^R(t)^2 f_2^{R,R}(t,t) + 2\gamma^R(t)\gamma^B(t)f_2^{R,B}(t,t) + \gamma^B(t)^2 f_2^{B,B}(t,t)$$

The functions F, γ^R, γ^B and Ψ_{NR} depend on the type of the urns (bounded or infinite) and (as was the case for the projections) can be computed explicitly; see [10] for detailed expressions.

Using these two theorems, and a result due to Daniels on the maximum of a Gaussian process [4], we obtain the distribution of the maximum of a derived relation, and the time at which this maximum is attained.

Theorem 3. *The maximum size of a derived relation (projection or join) $M :=$* $\max_{[0,2]} S([nt])$ *is such that $M \sim n\bar{G}+\sqrt{nm}+O(n^{1/6})$, where $\bar{G}$ is the maximum value of $G(t)$ for $t \in [0,2]$, which we assume to be unique and attained for $t < 2$, and where m is a r.v. which can be precisely characterized.*

4.2 Sketch of the proofs

Due to space constraints, we give here a sketch of the proofs; the detailed computations can be found in [9, 10]. The presentation below is given for Theorem 4.1 (projection size); the ideas for Theorem 4.2 (join size) are the same, except that we are dealing with two-dimensional processes.

We start from the process $\mathcal{P}$ describing the number of tuples in the initial relation (see Section 3). To fully describe $\mathcal{P}$, we have to know the probabilities for insertion, deletion and query, and to give the initial and final sizes of the relation. In the cases we are interested in, $\mathcal{P}$ happens to be a Gaussian process with a deterministic part $\mathcal{P}_0$, on which is superimposed a random part $\mathcal{P}_1$:

$$\mathcal{P} = \mathcal{P}_0 + \mathcal{P}_1.$$

The process $\mathcal{P}_0$ follows a deterministic curve $nf_1(t)$; the function f_1 is the expectation of the number of balls, or number of tuples in the initial relation, and the process $\mathcal{P}_1$ is a Markovian Gaussian process of order $\sqrt{n}$.

The process $\mathcal{P}$: *number of tuples* determines another process $\mathcal{Q}$: *size of the projection*. Before considering $\mathcal{Q}$, we study another process $\mathcal{Q}_0$, defined as the size of the projection obtained when the size of the initial relation is given by the process $\mathcal{P}_0$, which is a first-order approximation of $\mathcal{P}$. To this effect, we define two random variables, say Y_1 and Y_2, which are simply the size of the derived relation at different times t_1 and t_2. We know from previous work [7] the conditional expectation and variance of the projection size, for a given size of the initial relation, and that the conditional distribution of the projection size follows asymptotically a normal distribution. Knowing the covariance $COV(Y_1, Y_2)$ allows us to characterize $\mathcal{Q}_0$ as a process composed of a deterministic part $nG(t)$ and a random part $\sqrt{n}\, V(t)$. The computation of $COV(Y_1, Y_2)$ depends on the stochastic behaviour of the number of balls in any one urn. For any combination of the hypotheses presented in Sections 2 and 3, it is possible to find a common form giving the covariance in terms of f_1, p_I and p_D:

$$COV(Y_1, Y_2) \sim n\Psi_{NR}(t_1, t_2).$$

We then consider the process $\mathcal{P}$ obtained by superimposing $\mathcal{P}_1$ on $\mathcal{P}_0$. We can again define two random variables *size of the projection* at the times t_1 and t_2;

let us call them S_1 and S_2. As we have done for Y_1 and Y_2, we compute their covariance. But the S_i are obtained from the Y_i by introducing a further degree of randomness, and it is possible to write their covariance as

$$Cov(S_1, S_2) = Cov(Y_1, Y_2) + \gamma(t_1)\,\gamma(t_2)\,f_2(t_1, t_2)$$

for a suitable function $\gamma(t)$, and for $f_2(t_1, t_2)$ related to the covariance of the process $\mathcal{P}_1$ taken at different times t_1 and t_2. The covariance of Y_1 and Y_2 thus characterizes the "static" part, and the term added to it to get the covariance of S_1 and S_2 comes from the fact that the number of tuples of the initial relation is not known exactly, but is itself a Gaussian process.

Once we have the covariance of S_1 and S_2, we prove that Q is asymptotically a Gaussian process, with a part Q_0 of order n coming from $\mathcal{P}_0$, on which is added a random part Q_1 of order $\sqrt{n}$ coming from $\mathcal{P}_0$ and from $\mathcal{P}_1$:

$$Q = Q_0 + Q_1.$$

5 Examples

The results presented in Section 4 can be further detailed when we know the combination of assumptions on relations and of queries and updates allowed. Although we cannot envision to treat all the possible cases, we shall illustrate our technique and results with two examples.

Projection/ P1/ unbounded urns

We study a sequence of insertions, deletions and queries, starting from an empty structure and arriving at a structure of size $2\bar{x}n + a\sqrt{n}$; we also assume that the urns have an infinite capacity, i.e. that the initial relation has a key on the attribute removed by the projection. The functions f_1 and f_2 are those of Section 3; $ps_{1,2}$ and f_3 are as follows ($\bar{x} = p_I - p_D$):

$$ps_{1,2}(t_1, t_2) = \left(\frac{t_1}{t_2}\right)^{p_D/\bar{x}} ; \quad f_3(t_1, t_2) = \bar{x}\left(t_2 - t_1\left(\frac{t_1}{t_2}\right)^{p_D/\bar{x}}\right).$$

Then $E[S([nt])] \sim n\alpha\left(1 - e^{-\bar{x}t/\alpha}\right) + \sqrt{n}\,at\,e^{-\bar{x}t/\alpha}$ and

$$COV(S([nt_1]), S([nt_2])) \sim ne^{-\bar{x}(t_1+t_2)/\alpha}\psi(t_1, t_2),$$

with

$$\psi(t_1, t_2) = \alpha\left(e^{\bar{x}t_1(t_1/t_2)^{p_D/\bar{x}}/\alpha} - 1\right) - \bar{x}t_1\left(\frac{t_1}{t_2}\right)^{p_D/\bar{x}} + \sigma^2\frac{t_1(2 - t_2)}{2}.$$

Equijoin/ P3/unbounded urns

We now study the equijoin when the urns for both relations are unbounded and when, at each step, either we throw a ball, or we delete a ball, or we make a search. The survival probability for red balls is here $ps_{1,2}^R = (t_1/t_2)^{\pi_D^R/\bar{x}_R}$; $ps_{1,2}^B$ is defined in the same way. After some algebra we obtain the expectation of the process *size of equijoin*: $E[S([nt])] \sim n\frac{\bar{x}_R\bar{x}_B t^2}{\alpha}$. The covariance is given by Theorem 4.2, with $\Psi_{NR} \sim \bar{x}_R\bar{x}_B t_1^2 ps_{1,2}^R ps_{1,2}^B/\alpha$, $\gamma^R(t) = f_1^B(t)/\alpha$, $\gamma^B(t) = f_1^R(t)/\alpha$, and the $f_2^{\cdot\cdot}$ are given by the covariance matrix (1).

6 Conclusion

We have presented in this paper a methodology for the dynamic analysis of some parameters of relational databases (relation sizes), and shown that these parameters behave asymptotically as Gaussian processes, with relatively simple expectation and covariance. Although we do not cover all possible cases, we believe that our results already treat many common situations. A user wishing to compute the exact values of the expectation and covariance, under specified assumptions on the relations and on the queries or updates, might find it helpful to use a standard computer algebra system (CAS) such as Maple. A possible extension of the work presented here would be the implementation of a "toolbox" that, given the relational algebra operator, the type of urn, and the constraints on the processes (operations allowed, with their probabilities, and relations at times 0 and $2n$), would compute automatically the parameters of the process describing the dynamic behaviour of the derived relation.

Another direction for further work would be to extend the assumptions on the relations, for example to allow for non-uniform probability distributions on all the attributes. We must then distinguish between the projection or join attribute and the attributes not participating in the projection or join. For the projection or join attribute, a non-uniformity assumption means that we must be able to deal with urns having different probabilities, which could possibly lead to quite intricate computations. For the other attributes, however, the situation is simpler: For one thing, we know that, if these attributes include a key, the distribution does not influence the (conditional) relation size. If not, then we have to consider bounded, equiprobable, urns; however, in each urn the cells are not uniformly distributed. Although this may lead to lengthy computations in some cases, again the final result should still be easily doable with the help of a CAS.

References

1. P. BILLINGSLEY. *Convergence of Probability Measures.* 1968, Wiley.
2. S. CHRISTODOULAKIS. Estimating block transfers and join sizes. *ACM SIGMOD:* 40-54, 1983.
3. S. CHRISTODOULAKIS. Implications of certains assumptions in database performance evaluation. *ACM Transactions on Database Systems,* 9(2): 165-186, 1984.
4. H.E. DANIELS. The maximum of a Gaussian process whose mean path has a maximum, with an application to the strength of bundles of fibres. *Adv. Appl. Prob.,* 21: 315-333, 1989.
5. P. FLAJOLET and J. FRANÇON and J. VUILLEMIN. Sequence of operations analysis for dynamic data structures. *Journal of Algorithms:* 111-141, 1980.
6. J. FRANÇON and C. PUECH. Histoires de files de priorité avec fusions. 1984, 9th Colloquium on Trees in Algebra and Programming, Bordeaux (France), *B. Courcelle Ed.:* 119-138, Cambridge University Press, 1984.
7. D. GARDY. Normal limiting distributions for projection and semijoin sizes. *SIAM Journal on Discrete Mathematics,* 5(2): 219-248, 1992.

8. D. GARDY. Join sizes, urn models and normal limiting distributions. *Theoretical Computer Science (A)*, 131: 375-414, 1994.

9. D. GARDY and G. LOUCHARD. Dynamic analysis of some relational data base parameters I: projections. Technical report, Lab. Prism, University of Versailles, No. 94-6, 1994.

10. D. GARDY and G. LOUCHARD. Dynamic analysis of some relational data base parameters II: equijoins and semijoins.. Technical report, Lab. Prism, University of Versailles, No. 94-7, 1994.

11. A. Van GELDER,. Multiple join size estimation by virtual domain. *Principles of Database Systems*, Washington (USA): 180-189, 1993.

12. W.-C. HOU and G. OZSOYOGLU. Statistical estimators for aggregate relational algebra queries. *ACM Transactions On Database Systems*, 16(4): 600-654, 1991.

13. N.L. JOHNSON and S. KOTZ. *Urn models and their application*. Wiley & Sons, 1977.

14. S. KARLIN and H.M. TAYLOR. *A second Course in Stochastic Processes*. Academic Press, 1981.

15. C.M. KENYON-MATHIEU and J.S. VITTER. General methods for the analysis of the maximum size of dynamic data structures. 16th *International Colloquium on Automata, Languages and Programming*, Springer-Verlag LNCS No. 372: 473-487, Stresa (Italy), 1989.

16. Y. LING and W. SUN. A supplement to sampling-based methods for query size estimation in a database system. *SIGMOD Record*, 21 (4), 1992.

17. R.L. LIPTON and J.F. NAUGHTON and D.A. SCHNEIDER and S. SESHADRI. Efficient sampling strategies for relational database operations. *Theoretical Computer Science*, 116 (1): 195-226, 1993.

18. G. LOUCHARD. Trie size in a dynamic list structure. *TAPSOFT'93, M.-C. Gaudel and J.-P. Jouannaud Eds.*, Springer Verlag LNCS No. 668: 719-731, 1993.

19. R.S. MAIER. A path integral approach to data structure evolution. *Journal of Complexity*: 232-260, 1991.

20. M. V. MANNINO and P. CHU and T. SAGER. Statistical profile estimation in database systems. *ACM Computing Surveys*, 20 (3): 191-221, 1988.

21. T.H. MERRETT and E. OTOO. Distribution models of relations. 5th Conference on Very Large Data Bases, (Rio de Janeiro), 418-425, 1979.

22. J. K. MULLIN. Estimating the size of a relational join. *Information Systems*, 18(3): 189-196, 1993.

23. B. MUTHUSWAMY and L. KERSCHBERG. A detailed statistical model for relational query optimization. Annual Conference of the ACM, Denver, Colorado (USA): 439-448, 1985.

24. W. SUN and Y. LING and N. RISHE and Y. DENG. An instant and accurate size estimation method for joins and selection in a retrieval-intensive environment. *ACM SIGMOD International Conference*, Washington, D.C. (USA): 79-88, 1993.

On Slender Context-free Languages

Danny Raz

The Weizmann Institute of Science, Rehovot, ISRAEL,
danny@wisdom.weizmann.ac.il

(preliminary version)

Abstract. In this paper we study slender context-free languages, i.e., those containing at most a constant number of words of each length. Recently, Ilie proved that every such language can be described by a finite union of terms of the form $uv^i wx^i y$ [I]. We provide a completely different proof of this, using constructive methods. This enables us to prove that thinness and slenderness are decidable. Our proofs are based upon a novel characterization of languages in terms of the structure of the infinite paths in their prefix closure. This characterization seems to be interesting in itself, and can be expanded to more general families of languages.

Key words. formal languages, context-free grammars, decidability

1 Introduction

Length considerations are an important part of language theory. In a recent series of papers [PS1, PS2, PS3], Păun and Salomaa investigated the family of slender languages. A language L is associated with the infinite sequence $\{l_n\}$, where l_n is the number of words in L of length n. Slender languages are ones for which l_n is bounded by a constant. A language L is termed k-thin if $l_n \leq k$ for all n, and a 1-thin language is termed *thin*. It turns out that these languages are not only interesting from the theoretical point of view, but they also have important applications in cryptography [ADPS].

In [PS1], regular and context-free slender languages are studied. A very simple characterization of the slender regular languages is provided, and it is proven that the relevant decision problems are all decidable, including the slenderness problem itself. In the context-free case, however, things become more complicated. A similar characterization result is only conjectured in [PS1], and the decidability of the slenderness problem is left open.

A language L is said to be a *union of paired loops* (UPL) iff there exists a constant $k \geq 1$ and words u_i, v_i, w_i, x_i, y_i, for $1 \leq i \leq k$, such that $L = \cup_{i=1}^k \{u_i v_i^n w_i x_i^n y_i | n \geq 0\}$. It is proven in [PS1] that every UPL has a representation in which all the sets are disjoint; hence every UPL is unambiguous. Păun and Salomaa conjectured in [PS1] that every slender context-free language is a UPL, so that the slender context-free languages form a family of unambiguous, but not necessarily deterministic, context-free languages. This was proved by Ilei in [I]. Another issue studied in [PS1] is the decidability of the thinness and slenderness problems. In [ADPS] these are shown to be decidable for unambiguous context-free languages, but the general question was left unanswered.

In this paper we provide a different proof of the fact that every slender context-free language is a UPL. The constructive nature of our arguments enables us to prove that the thinness and slenderness problems are decidable for general context-free languages.

For a start, a language over $\Sigma = \{a_1, \ldots, a_k\}$ is viewed in terms of a marking of the full k-tree. We associate with the node $i_1 i_2 \ldots i_l$ the word $a_{i_1} a_{i_2} \ldots a_{i_l}$. For a language L, mark all the nodes that have infinitely many descendants in L. Note that if L is infinite then (i) the root of the tree is marked, and (ii) if a node is marked then at least one of its offsprings is marked. Hence, if the language is infinite there exists at least one infinite path, all the nodes of which are marked. Call these paths ∞-paths. Our results follow from a close study of ∞-paths.

It turns out that every slender context-free language has only finitely many ∞-paths. The converse of this statement is true in the regular case, i.e., a regular language that has only finitely many ∞-paths is slender. In the context-free case some additional requirements are added in order to obtain a full characterization of Slenderness. Specificly, our result states that a context-free language L is slender if and only if it has a finite number of ∞-paths and there exists a constant k such that every word w that does not belong to an ∞-path is a prefix of at most k words in L. Nevertheless, studying the context-free languages that have finitely many ∞-paths enables us to prove that every slender context-free language is a UPL and to prove that slenderness is decidable.

This kind of approach to the study of formal languages seems to be useful in other settings too. Indeed, in the forthcoming contribution [R] we establish, among other things, a connection between bounded languages and the finiteness of the set of ∞-paths.

In the next section we describe the results of [PS1] in more detail, and give the basic definitions and terminology. The main results are stated and proven in Section 3. We then briefly discuss the results, and point out some interesting directions for further study.

2 Definitions and Previous Results

We assume that the reader is familiar with the basic notions of context-free languages and only present some of the important definitions. For further reading the reader is referred to [HA]. A *context-free grammar* is a tuple $G = \langle Y, \Sigma, P, S \rangle$, where Y is a set of *variables* distinct from the set of *terminals* Σ, and $V = Y \cup \Sigma$. The *initial variable* is $S \in Y$, and P is a finite set of *production rules*, each rule being a pair $v \to \gamma$, where $v \in Y$ and $\gamma \in V^*$.

If $v \to \gamma \in P$ and $\alpha, \beta \in V^*$, then $\alpha v \beta \Rightarrow \alpha \gamma \beta$. We use $\overset{*}{\Rightarrow}$ for the reflexive transitive closure of $\Rightarrow$. The language generated by a variable $X \in V$ is $L_X =$

$\{w \in \Sigma^* : X \stackrel{*}{\Rightarrow} w\}$, and the language generated by the grammar G is L_S.

Whenever $\alpha \stackrel{*}{\Rightarrow} \beta$, there exists a sequence of words $\alpha = \delta_1, \delta_2, \ldots, \delta_k = \beta$ such that $\delta_1 \Rightarrow \delta_2 \ldots \delta_{k-1} \Rightarrow \delta_k$. The sequence $\delta_1, \delta_2, \ldots, \delta_k$ is refered to as a *derivation* of β from α. Since the order in which the production rules are applied to create a derivation is not significant, we deal with derivation trees.

A tree from the alphabet $\Sigma = \{a_1, \ldots, a_k\}$ over a set D is a labeling of Σ^* by the elements of D. The empty word λ denotes the root of the tree. A language is represented by a tree over the set $\{0, 1\}$ where a word from Σ^* is labeled by 1 iff it is in the language. A tree can also represent the multiplicities of words in a language, in this case D would be the set of the non-negative integers N. A word over Σ, which is an element of Σ^* is a node in our tree. If w is a node then wa is a child of w for every $a \in \Sigma$. The descendants of a node w are all the words w', such that w is a proper prefix of w'. A word w is an ancestor of w' if w is a proper prefix of w'. A path is an infinite set of words $w_0, w_1, \ldots$ such that $w_0 = \lambda$, and for every i w_{i+1} is a child of w_i.

Consider a language L over the alphabet Σ. Denote by l_n the number of words of length n in L, that is

$$l_n = card\{w \in L \mid |w| = n\}.$$

The language L is called k-thin iff for some n_0

$$l_n \le k \text{ whenever } n \ge n_0.$$

A language is termed slender iff it is k-thin for some k, and is termed thin iff it is 1-thin. Thus, in our terminology a language is slender iff there exists a constant k such that the number of marked words in the tree at any fixed depth is bounded by k.

In [PS1] the notion of a union of single loops, or USL for short, is defined. A language L is said to be a USL iff there exists a constant $k \ge 1$ and words $u_i, v_i, w_i, 1 \le i \le k$, such that $L = \cup_{i=1}^k u_i v_i^* w_i$.

In a similar way, a language L is said to be a union of paired loops, or UPL for short, iff there exists a constant $k \ge 1$ and words $u_i, v_i, w_i, x_i, y_i, 1 \le i \le k$, such that $L = \cup_{i=1}^k \{u_i v_i{}^n w_i x_i{}^n y_i | n \ge 0\}$. A UPL is said to be a *disjoint union of paired loops*, or DUPL for short, iff the sets in the union are disjoint.

The following are two of the main results of [PS1]:

1. A regular language is slender if and only if it is USL.
2. Every UPL language is DUPL, hence it is slender, linear and unambiguous.

For a word w, define the set of extensions of w, $ex(w)$, to be the set of all the descendants of w. Let $e_L(w)$ be the cardinality of the set of descendants of w that are in L, that is $e_L(w) = card\{w' \in ex(w) \text{ and } w' \in L\}$. For a language L, define T to be a tree from Σ over $\{0, 1\}$, such that $T(w) = 1$ iff $e_L(w) = \infty$. In other words, we mark (label by 1) all the nodes that have infinitely many descendants in L. If L is infinite then λ is marked; if a word is marked then at least one of its offsprings is marked. Hence, if L is infinite then there exists at least one path that contains only marked nodes. Such a path is called an ∞-path.

Figure 1 shows an example of a marked tree for $L = \{a^i b^i | i \geq 1\}$. In this figure the marked nodes are represented by $\oplus$, and the words of L are emphasized.

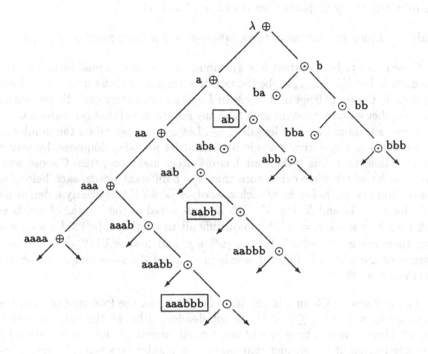

Fig. 1.

Our results follow from a close study of ∞-paths. We are interested in the number of these paths, which is a characteristic of the language. In Σ^*, for example, there are infinitely many ∞-paths, because every path in its tree is an ∞-path. It is not difficult to see that for any k, there exists a regular language L_k with exactly k different ∞-paths. As we shall prove in the next section, slender context-free languages have only finitely many ∞-paths.

3 Main Results

First, we would like to prove that every slender context-free language has a finite number of ∞-paths. Note that this claim is not true for general slender languages. For example, the language $L_1 = \{w\#1^i | i > 0 \text{ and } w \in \{0,1\}^* \text{ is a binary representation of } i\}$ is a slender context-sensitive language with infinitely many ∞-paths. For context-free languages this claim holds. The proof is a delicate combination of some well known facts about context-free languages. Recall that for every context-free language L, the set $\{i|\text{there exists a word } w \in L \text{ with } |w| = i\}$ is an ultimately periodic set. In particular, if L is infinite then this set contains a linear subset of N. Using this fact we will show that if a context-free language has infinitely many ∞-paths then it can not be slender.

Claim 1 *Every slender context-free language has a finite number of ∞-paths.*

Proof: Let G be a context-free grammar in Greibach normal form for some language L. Let $V_1, V_2, \ldots, V_m$ be the non-terminals of G such that L_{V_i} is infinite. For each V_i the set of lengths of words in L_{V_i} is an ultimately periodic set, with a period v_i. Let k_G be a constant such that any non-terminal that generates a word, generates a terminal word of length $< k_G$. Let c_G be a bound on the number of the variables in any derivation rule of G, and let $p = \Pi v_i$. Suppose, by way of contradiction, that L is k-thin but has infinitely many ∞-paths. Choose some length n, for which there exist more than $k \times p$ different words, each belonging to a different ∞-path. Let w be such a word. $S \overset{*}{\Rightarrow} wXV_iY$ is clearly a derivation in G, for some V_i and $X, Y \in V^*$. We are interested in the lengths of words w' such that $S \overset{*}{\Rightarrow} wXV_iY \overset{*}{\Rightarrow} w'$. It is not difficult to see that if $|w'| > k_G \times c_G \times n$, then there exists a word w'', $|w''| = |w'| + p$, and $S \overset{*}{\Rightarrow} wXV_iY \overset{*}{\Rightarrow} w''$. Hence, there exist more than k different words in L, all of the same length, which is a contradiction. $\blacksquare$

The converse of Claim 1 is not true. For example, the following context-free language $L_2 = \{a^i b^j \mid i \leq j \leq 2i\}$ is not slender, although the only ∞-path in it is a^*. Hence, we will have to add some requirements in order to achieve a full characterization of the slender languages. For regular languages, however, this is a full characterization.

Claim 2 *A regular language is slender if and only if it has a finite number of ∞-paths.*

This claim can be obtained from the results of section 3 in [PS1]. We will give a direct proof which will indicate the techniques that will be used later on when handling the much more complicated proof of the context-free case.

Proof: By Claim 1 every slender regular language has a finite number of ∞-paths. Let L be a regular language that has no more than k ∞-paths, and let M be a deterministic finite automaton with n states that accepts L. Let w be any word on an ∞-path in L, and assume that wa is not on an ∞-path, for some letter a. We claim that if $waw' \in L$ then $|w'| < n$ otherwise wa must be on some ∞-path. Hence, the number of words in L of the same length is bounded by $k \cdot n \cdot |\Sigma|^n$. $\blacksquare$

As we mentioned, the context-free case is more complicated. We start with the following fact.

Claim 3 *Let L be a context-free language. If $L \subset uv^*v'$, where v' is a prefix of v, then L is regular.*

Proof: Clearly, it suffices to prove that $L' = \{v^i \,|uv^iv' \in L\}$ is regular. Let $I = \{i \,|uv^iv' \in L\}$ and let $L_I = \{x^i \,|i \in I\}$, where x is a new letter. Define a homomorphism $\psi : \{x\}^* \to \Sigma^*$ by $\psi(x) = v$. Since $L_I = \psi^{-1}(L')$, and since context-free languages are closed under inverse homomorphism, L_I is context-free. L_I is defined on a one letter alphabet, hence by Parikh's theorem it is regular. However $L' = \psi(L_I)$, and regular languages are closed under homomorphism, hence L' is also regular. ∎

An infinite sequence of words $\{w_1, w_2, \ldots\}$ *describes* an ∞-path if for each i, $|w_{i+1}| > |w_i|$ and w_i lies on the path. The following is a basic observation.

Claim 4 *Let w be a word in L, and let $w = uvxyz$ be any partition such that $uv^ixy^iz \in L$. Then uv^i describes an ∞-path in L.*

We will now investigate the structure of context-free languages that have a finite number of ∞-paths. Let G be a context-free grammar in Chomsky normal form (Cnf) for such a language L, and let n be the number of variables in G. We start by characterizing the ∞-paths of L

Claim 5 *Every ∞-path in L can be described by uv^i, where $|u|, |v| < 2^n$, and v is primitive.*

Proof: Since the number of ∞-paths in L is finite, there exists an integer m, such that every word of length $> m$ that lies on some ∞-path determines the path, i.e., all the words in $ex(w)$ that lie on an ∞-path must lie on the same ∞-path.

Choose some word w' on some ∞-path in L such that $|w'| > m$, $|w'| > 2^n$ and let $w \in L$ be some word in $ex(w')$. Consider a derivation tree T for w in G; it must contain a path with more that n variables. Hence, there exists a variable X in V_G such that $S \overset{*}{\Rightarrow} uXz \overset{*}{\Rightarrow} uvXyz \overset{*}{\Rightarrow} uvxyz = w$. Clearly $uv^ixy^iz \in L$ for every i. Now consider the left most path in T that contains more than n variables, and let Y be the first variable that occurs twice on that path. Again $S \overset{*}{\Rightarrow} u'Yz' \overset{*}{\Rightarrow} u'v'Yy'z' \overset{*}{\Rightarrow} u'v'x'y'z' = w$ is in G, where $|u'|, |v'| < 2^n$. By Claim 4 both uv^i and $u'v'^i$ describe an ∞-path, we claim that it is the *same* path. Indeed, if uv^i and $u'v'^i$ describe different ∞-paths then one can find a word of length $> m$ such that in $ex(w)$ there are words on more than one ∞-path, which is a contradiction. ∎

Note that if a language L is slender, so is its reverse, L^r. Since both L and L^r have only a finite number of ∞-paths, and each of these paths can be described by uv^i, where $|u|, |v| < 2^n$, we may conclude the following.

Claim 6 *Every word w in a slender context-free language L can be written as $w = uv^iw_0v'^ju'$, for some words u, v, w_0, u', v', all of length bounded by 2^n.*

This last claim looks very similar to the conjecture we want to prove, i.e., that every slender context-free language is a UPL, but here i may be different from j. Some additional work is needed in order to achieve the full proof.

A variable $X \in V_G$ is *infinite* if the language L_X is infinite, otherwise, X is *finite*. A variable $X \in V_G$ is a *left concurrent* of a variable Y if they both appear in the same derivation tree, X is neither an ancestor nor a descendant of Y, and X appears in the tree to the left of Y.

Claim 7 *If X is a left concurrent of some infinite variable Y, then L_X is regular.*

Proof: Since Y is infinite, there are words w and w' such that $wL_X w'$ lies on some ∞-path. By Claim 5, every ∞-path can be described by uv^i, so L_X must be contained in $u'v^*v'$. Hence, by Claim 3, L_X is regular. ∎

An infinite variable X is termed *regular* if L_X is regular. Hence the variables of G are either finite or regular, or infinite but non-regular. Let S_r and S_{cf} be two new variables. We add the rules $S_r \to XY$ iff $S \to XY$ is in G, and at least one of X, Y is regular. We also add the rules $S_{cf} \to XY$ iff $S \to XY$ is in G, and at least one of X, Y is infinite but non-regular.

Claim 8 *If $L(G)$ is a slender context-free language, then:*

1. $L(S_r)$ *is a slender regular language.*
2. $L(S_{cf})$ *is a slender linear language.*
3. $L(S_r) \cup L(S_{cf}) = L(G)$.

Proof: As mentioned above, $L(G)$ is slender iff $L(G)^r$ is slender. Recall that a Cnf grammar for $L(G)^r$ can be obtained simply by changing the order of all the productions of G. Hence, by Claim 7, if $S \to XY$ is in G and at least one of X, Y is regular, then both X and Y must be regular. Now, since both X and Y are regular, their concatenation XY is also regular. S_r is a finite union of such terms, and hence it is regular too. Clearly, by the definition of S_r we have $L(S_r) \subset L(G)$, and hence $L(S_r)$ must be slender. Now, if $Z \to XY$ is in G and at least one of X, Y is infinite but non-regular, the other variable must be finite (otherwise they are both regular). Hence, $L(S_{cf})$ is a slender linear language. ∎

Every slender context-free language consists of two parts: one, the regular part, and the other, the (more interesting) context-free part. It is sufficient to show that $L(S_{cf})$ is a UPL. For this purpose we need some additional information about the structure of the linear grammar that produces a slender language. Lemma 9 addresses this. First we prove that such a grammar preserves a certain symmetry. Recall that a derivation tree in any linear grammar contains only one path with variables. We will show that there is a constant ratio between the lengths of the derived word from both sides of that path. Using this fact we are able to prove that there are only finitely many (and bounded globally) continuations to every word that does not lie on an ∞-path. This will enable us to show that such a language can be represented as a finite union of terms of the form $uv^i wx^i y$.

Let T be a *finite* tree over some finite alphabet Σ. A tree T' is a *reduction* of T if it can be obtained from T by replacing the subtree rooted at some node in it, with the subtree rooted at some descendant of that node which has the same label. The set $red(T)$ contains the trees that can be obtained from T by a finite number of reductions. A tree is *irreducible* if it cannot be reduced, i.e., all the labels on any path in it are distinct. Clearly, the number of irreducible trees is bounded by $k^{|\Sigma|}$, where k is the arity of the tree. Two trees, T_1 and T_2, are called *relatives*, if $red(T_1) \cap red(T_2)$ is non-empty. Therefore, if $\mathcal{T}$ is a set of trees with $|\mathcal{T}| > k^{|\Sigma|}$, then $\mathcal{T}$ must contain two relatives.

Lemma 9. *Let G be a linear context-free grammar for a non-regular language L, such that $L \subset v_1 v_2^* v_3 v_2'^* v_1'$, where $|v_1|, |v_2|, |v_3|, |v_2'|, |v_1'| \leq 2^n$, and v_2 and v_2' are primitive. Then the following conditions are equivalent:*

1. *L is slender.*
2. *Let X and Y be variables such that $X \overset{*}{\Rightarrow} xXx'$, $Y \overset{*}{\Rightarrow} yYy'$, $X \overset{*}{\Rightarrow} uYv$, $S \overset{*}{\Rightarrow} u'Xv'$, and $Y \overset{*}{\Rightarrow} w_0$ are derivations in G for some words x, y, u, v, u', v', w_0 and some non-empty words x', y'. Then $\frac{|x|}{|x'|} = \frac{|y|}{|y'|}$.*
3. *There exists a constant k such that for every i there are no more than k different words of $v_1 v_2^i v_3 v_2'^* v_1'$ in L.*
4. *L can be represented by a finite union of terms of the form $uv^i wx^i y$.*

Proof: $1 \Rightarrow 2$: Suppose, by way of contradiction, that $\frac{|x|}{|x'|} \neq \frac{|y|}{|y'|}$. We will show that L is not slender. More precisely, we will show that for an arbitrary large k, one can find at least k words in L, all of the same length. Note that $v_2 v_3 v_2'$ is not a subword of $v_1 v_2^*$ otherwise by Claim 3, L would be regular. Also note that $u'x^i u y^j w_0 y'^j v x'^i v' \in L$ for all i, j, hence $u'x^i u y^j$ lies on the ∞-path described by $v_1 v_2^*$. In a similar way we can look at the ∞-path of L^r and conclude that $y w_0 y'$ is not a subword of $u'x^i u y^j$ for any i, j.

Assume that $|x| = |y| = m$ and that $|x'| = l < n = |y'|$. Define

$$w_i = u'x^{(n+m)(k-i)} u y^{(m+l)i} w_0 y'^{(m+l)i} v x'^{(n+m)(k-i)} v'$$

for $1 \leq i \leq k$; obviously, $w_i \in L$. The length of each word w_i is given by

$$|w_i| = |u'v'w_0 vu| + k(m+l)(n+m) + i[(m+n)(m+l) - (m+l)(m+n)] =$$

$$= |u'v'w_0 vu| + k(m+l)(n+m)$$

which is independent of i, hence all the words w_i have the same length. It remains to prove that the k words are distinct. We already showed that $y w_0 y'$ is not a subword of $u'x^i u y^j$, hence since $|u'x^{(n+m)(k-i)} u y^{(m+l)i} w_0| = |u'uw_0| + m(k(n+m) + i(l-n))$ and $l - n > 0$ these words are indeed distinct.

$2 \Rightarrow 3$: Let T_1 and T_2 be two derivation trees in G for $v_1 v_2^i v_3 w_1$ and $v_1 v_2^i v_3 w_2$ respectively. Since $v_1 v_2^i v_3 w_1 \in L$ we know that $w_1 = v_2'^m v_1'$ for some m, and for the same reason $w_2 = v_2'^{m'} v_1'$ for some m'. We claim that if T_1 and T_2 are relatives then $w_1 = w_2$ (or $m' = m$), which implies clause 3, since if a set of trees is big enough it must contain two relatives. Note that if T is a derivation tree for some word w in G, then all the trees in $red(T)$ are also derivation trees in G. Let T be a derivation tree for a word w in G, such that $T \in red(T_1) \cap red(T_2)$. w is a word in L hence $w = v_1 v_2^{i-j} v_3 v_2'^{j} v_1'$ for some j. But $\frac{|v_2^{i-j}|}{|v_2'^{m-j'}|} = \frac{|v_2^{i-j}|}{|v_2'^{m'-j'}|} = \frac{|x|}{|x'|}$, hence $m = m'$.

$3 \Rightarrow 2$: Suppose, by way of contradiction, that $\frac{|x|}{|x'|} \neq \frac{|y|}{|y'|}$. We will show that for arbitrary large l, one can find more than l different words of $v_1 v_2^i v_3 v_2'^* v_1'$ in L. Assume that $|x| = |y| = m$ and that $|x'| \neq |y'|$. Define

$$ w_j = u'x^j u y^{l-j} w_0 y'^{l-j} v x'^j v' $$

Obviously, $w_j \in L$. All the w_js are also in $v_1 v_2^i v_3 v_2'^* v_1'$ for some fixed i. Since $|w_j| = |u'uw_0vv'| + l|x| + j|x'| + (l-j)|y'|$ each such word has a different length, hence they are all distinct.

$2 \Rightarrow 4$: Assume that L is infinite and let X and Y be any two variables like those of clause 2. Note that since v_2 and v_2' are primitive it must be the case that $x = \tilde{v}_2^{i_x}$, $y = \tilde{v}_2^{i_y}$, $x' = \tilde{v}_2'^{j_x}$, and $y' = \tilde{v}_2'^{j_y}$. Now since 2 holds $\frac{|x|}{|x'|} = \frac{|y|}{|y'|}$, hence we have that $\frac{i_x}{j_x} = \frac{i_y}{j_y} = r$. Define $L_R = \{v_1 v_2^i v_3 | v_1 v_2^i v_3 v_2'^{j} v_1' \in L\}$. L_R is a slender regular language hence, by [PS1] it can be represented by a finite union of terms of the form uv^iw. Clearly v must be a cyclic variant of v_2^j for some j. We get from clause 2 that $v_1(v_2^j)^i v_3 (v_2'^{j/r})^i v_1'$ is a representation of L in the desired form.

$4 \Rightarrow 1$: Clearly every UPL is slender. ∎

Now we can prove our main results:

Theorem 10. *Every slender context-free language is a UPL.*

Proof: Let G be a context-free grammar in Cnf for a language L. It is sufficient to prove that $L(G_{cf})$ is a UPL. We know from Claim 6 that every word in $L(G_{cf})$ can be written as $w = uv^iw_0v'^{j}u'$, where $|u|, |v|, |w_0|, |v'|, |u'| \leq 2^n$. Hence, it is sufficient to prove that $L' = L(G_{cf}) \cap uv^iw_0v'^{j}u'$ is a UPL. If L' is regular, then it is a regular slender language, and by [PS1] we are done. Otherwise, L' is a linear context-free language, such that $L' \subset uv^iw_0v'^{j}u'$, and L' is not regular. Hence by Lemma 9 it is a UPL. ∎

We also have now a full characterization of slender context-free languages:

Corollary 11. *A context-free language L is slender if and only if it has a finite number of ∞-paths and there exists a constant k such that every word w that does not belong to an ∞-path is a prefix of at most k words in L.*

Proof: Again, it is sufficient to prove the corollary for $L' = L(G_{cf}) \cap uv^iw_0v'^{j}u'$, and the proof is a direct consequence of clause 2 of Lemma 9. ∎

Using our previous results, it is not too difficult to prove that the slenderness problem is decidable.

Theorem 12. *It is decidable whether a language generated by a given context-free grammar is slender.*

Proof: Let G be a context-free grammar for a language L. Construct from G a Cnf grammar G' for L, and let n be the number of variables in G'. Let R be a union of all the sets of the form $uv^*w_0v'^*u'$ where $|u|, |v|, |w_0|, |u'|, |v'| \leq 2^n$. By Claim 6 if L is slender then $L \subset R$, and if $L \subset R$ then we can use Lemma 9 and check whether the conditions of clause 2 are satisfied. ∎

4 Discussion

This paper investigated the structure of slender context-free languages. We showed that every such language is a UPL, and proved that the slenderness problem is decidable for that family.

Slender languages can be generalized in various ways. One of them is to consider a family of languages in which l_n is bounded by a function of n rather than by a constant. Clearly, for any language $l_n \leq |\Sigma|^n$, but context-free languages with $l_n \leq log(n)$, for example, remains to be investigated.

The newly defined notion of ∞-path played an essential part in proving the results of this paper. This line of research may be useful when investigating other families of languages. Indeed, in a forthcoming contribution [R], we use an extended version of this concept to define a new family of languages which carries out some of the nice properties of the bounded languages.

Acknowledgment

I would like to thank my advisor, D. Harel, whose enlightened remarks, encouragement and support made this research possible.

References

[ADPS] M. Andrasiu, J. Dassow, Gh. Păun and A. Salomaa, "Language-theoretic problems arising from Richelieu cryptosystems", *Theoretical Computer Science* 116 (1993), 339–357.

[G] S. Ginsburg, *The Mathematical Theory of Context-Free Languages*, McGraw-Hill Book Company, 1966.

[HA] M. A. Harrison, *Introduction to Formal Language Theory*, Addison-Wesley Publishing Company, 1978, pp. 312–326.

[I] L. Ilie, "On a conjecture about slender context-free languages", *Theoretical Computer Science* 132 (1994), 427–434.

[PS1] G. Păun and A. Salomaa, "Thin and Slender Languages", *Discrete Applied Mathematics*, to appear.

[PS2] G. Păun and A. Salomaa, "Closure Properties of Slender Languages", *Theoretical Computer Science* 120 (1993), 293-301.

[PS3] G. Păun and A. Salomaa, "Decision Problems Concerning the Thinness of DOL Languages", *Bulletin of the EATCS* **46** (1992), 171–181.

[R] D. Raz "Recurrence in Formal Languages", in preparation.

Partial Derivatives of Regular Expressions and Finite Automata Constructions

Valentin Antimirov

CRIN (CNRS) & INRIA-Lorraine,
BP 239, F54506, Vandœuvre-lès-Nancy Cedex, FRANCE
e-mail: `Valentin.Antimirov@loria.fr`

Abstract. We introduce a notion of a *partial derivative* of a regular expression. It is a generalization to the non-deterministic case of the known notion of a *derivative* invented by Brzozowski. We give a constructive definition of partial derivatives, study their properties, and employ them to develop a new algorithm for turning regular expressions into relatively small NFA and to provide certain improvements to Brzozowski's algorithm constructing DFA. We report on a prototype implementation of our algorithm constructing NFA and present some examples.

Introduction

In 1964 Janusz Brzozowski introduced *word derivatives* of regular expressions and suggested an elegant algorithm turning a regular expression r into a deterministic finite automata (DFA); the main point of the algorithm is that the word derivatives of r serve as states of the resulting DFA [5].

In the following years derivatives were recognized as a quite useful and productive tool. Conway [8] uses derivatives to present various computational procedures in the algebra of regular expressions and to investigate some logical properties of this algebra. Krob [12] extends this differential calculus to a more general algebra of K-rational expressions. Brzozowski and Leiss [6] employ the idea of derivatives to ascertain relations between regular expressions, finite automata and boolean networks. Berry and Sethi [4] give a solid theoretical background for McNaughton and Yamada's algorithm [14] through the notion of *continuation* which is a particular kind of derivative. Ginzburg [9] uses derivatives to develop a procedure for proving equivalence of regular expressions; further development of this procedure is provided by Mizoguchi *et al* [15]. Yet another procedure for proving equivalence of extended regular expressions is suggested by the present author and Mosses [2, 3] and is also based on some constructions closely related to derivatives.

In the present paper we come up with a new notion of a *partial derivative* which is, in a sense, a non-deterministic generalization of the notion of derivative: likewise derivatives are related to DFA, partial derivatives are in the same natural way related to non-deterministic finite automata (NFA).

In Sect.2 we introduce partial derivatives which are regular expressions appearing as components of so-called *non-deterministic linear forms*. We give a set of recursive equations for computing linear forms and partial derivatives. Some basic properties of partial derivatives are established.

In Sect.3 we present two theorems which are the main theoretical results of the paper. These show that the set of all syntactically distinct partial derivatives of any regular expression r is finite[1] and its cardinality is quite small – less than or equal to one plus the number of occurrences of alphabet letters appearing in r; moreover, each partial derivative (and so the set of them) can be represented quite compactly.

Sect.4 is devoted to an application of the above theoretical results to finite automata constructions. First, we present a new top-down algorithm for turning a regular expression r into an NFA; the set of partial derivatives of r forms the set of states of the NFA. This implies that the above upper bound for the cardinality of the set of partial derivatives holds as an upper bound for the number of states of NFA produced by our algorithm. This upper bound coincides with the number of states of NFA produced by McNaughton and Yamada's algorithm [14] and by its improvement due to Berry and Sethi [4]. However, in many cases our NFA have actually fewer states than this upper bound. Moreover, there are examples when our NFA turn out to be smaller than those produced by a tricky Chang and Paige's algorithm [7] (which involves several non-trivial optimizations of the representation of NFA). The second procedure in this section provides several improvements to Brzozowski's algorithm [5] due to the use of partial derivatives.

We have implemented our algorithm turning regular expressions into NFA as an algebraic program in OBJ3 (see [11] for a description of the language). In Sect.5 we present several examples of NFA constructed by our program.

In this version of the paper we omit all the proofs as well as some auxiliary propositions and examples; see [1] for a more complete presentation.

1 Preliminaries

Given a set X, we denote its cardinality by $|X|$, its powerset (the set of all subsets of X) by $\mathcal{P}(X)$, and the set of all finite subsets of X by $\mathbf{Set}[X]$.

An *idempotent semiring* is an algebra on the signature including constants $\emptyset$ (called zero), λ (unit) and binary operations $\_ + \_$ (union or join) and $\_ \cdot \_$ (concatenation) such that these satisfy the following equational axioms:

$$a + (b + c) = (a + b) + c \qquad (1)$$
$$a + b = b + a \qquad (2)$$
$$a + a = a \qquad (3)$$
$$a + \emptyset = a \qquad (4)$$
$$(a \cdot b) \cdot c = a \cdot (b \cdot c) \qquad (5)$$
$$a \cdot \lambda = \lambda \cdot a = a \qquad (6)$$

---

[1] Note that derivatives do not enjoy this property.

$$a \cdot \emptyset = \emptyset \cdot a = \emptyset \tag{7}$$
$$a \cdot (b + c) = a \cdot b + a \cdot c \tag{8}$$
$$(a + b) \cdot c = a \cdot c + b \cdot c \tag{9}$$

Thus, the algebra is simultaneously an *upper semilattice with the bottom* (w.r.t. $\emptyset$ and $+$) and a monoid (w.r.t. λ and $\cdot$). We shall refer to the set of the equations (1–9) as to *SR-axioms*; the least congruence generated by these (on some appropriate algebra) will be called the *SR-congruence* and denoted by $\mathcal{E}(SR)$. Similarly, the set of equations (1–4) is called *ACIZ-axioms* and its subset (1–3) is called *ACI-axioms*; corresponding least congruences are denoted by $\mathcal{E}(ACIZ)$ and $\mathcal{E}(ACI)$. Note that the set $\mathbf{Set}[X]$ forms an upper semilattice with the join $\cup$ and the empty set $\emptyset$ as the bottom.

Given an alphabet (a finite set of letters) $\mathcal{A}$, let $\mathcal{A}^*$ be the set (and the free monoid) of words on $\mathcal{A}$, $\mathbf{Reg}[\mathcal{A}]$ be the set (and the algebra) of *regular* (or *rational*) languages on the alphabet $\mathcal{A}$ with the standard operations – concatenation $L_1 \cdot L_2$, union $L_1 \cup L_2$, and iteration L^*. Let $\mathbf{Reg1}[\mathcal{A}]$ be the subset of $\mathbf{Reg}[\mathcal{A}]$ consisting of all the regular languages containing the empty word λ; the complement of this subset is denoted by $\mathbf{Reg0}[\mathcal{A}]$. Let $\mathcal{A}^+ = \mathcal{A} \cdot \mathcal{A}^*$.

Given a regular language L, a *left quotient of L w.r.t. a word w*, written $w \setminus L$, is the language $\{\, u \in \mathcal{A}^* \mid w \cdot u \in L \,\}$. Note that the membership $w \in L$ is equivalent to $\lambda \in w \setminus L$ and that $(w \cdot x) \setminus L = x \setminus (w \setminus L)$.

We consider a *(non-deterministic) finite automaton* $\mathbf{M}$ on $\mathcal{A}$ as a quadruple $\langle M, \tau, \mu_0, F \rangle$ where M is a set of states, $\tau : M \times \mathcal{A} \to \mathbf{Set}[M]$ is a transition function (which can also be represented as a relation $\tau \subset M \times \mathcal{A} \times M$), $\mu_0 \in M$ is an initial state, and $F \subset M$ is a set of final states.[2] The automaton is *deterministic* if $|\tau(\mu, x)| \leq 1$ for all $\mu \in M$, $x \in \mathcal{A}$; in this case the transition function is represented as a partial one, $\tau : M \times \mathcal{A} \dashrightarrow M$, returning a state or nothing. The function can always be completed to a total one by adding one "sink" state $\emptyset$ to M such that $\tau(\emptyset, x) = \emptyset$ for all $x \in \mathcal{A}$. In any of the above cases, the extension $\tau(\mu, w)$ of the transition function to words $w \in \mathcal{A}^*$ is defined in the usual way. A word $w \in \mathcal{A}^*$ is said to be *accepted* by a state $\mu \in M$ if $\tau(\mu, w) \cap F \neq \emptyset$. The set of all words accepted by μ_0 is the language *recognized* by $\mathbf{M}$. Two automata are *equivalent* if they recognize the same language.

Regular (or *rational*) expressions are terms on the signature of the regular algebra $\mathbf{Reg}[\mathcal{A}]$. Actually, there exist different ways to choose the signature and to formalize the algebra. In this paper we follow the idea of [2] that $\mathbf{Reg}[\mathcal{A}]$ should be regarded as an *order-sorted* algebra [10] having a sort $\mathcal{A}$ for an alphabet which is a subsort of a sort *Reg* for all the regular expressions. Here we also introduce two further subsorts of *Reg*, namely *Reg0* and *Reg1*, to distinguish regular expressions denoting elements of $\mathbf{Reg0}[\mathcal{A}]$ and $\mathbf{Reg1}[\mathcal{A}]$ correspondingly. To sum up, the order-sorted signature *REG* on the alphabet $\mathcal{A} = \{\alpha_1, \alpha_2, \ldots, \alpha_k\}$ consists of the following components:[3]

---

[2] This is obviously not the most general definition, but we shall need just this particular kind of NFA.

[3] Argument places of operations are indicated by the underbar character "_".

sorts	$\mathcal{A}$, Reg, $Reg0$, $Reg1$.	
subsorts	$\mathcal{A} \le Reg0 \le Reg$, $Reg1 \le Reg$.	
constants	$\emptyset : Reg0$; $\lambda : Reg1$; $\alpha_1, \alpha_2, \ldots, \alpha_k : \mathcal{A}$.	
operations	$\_ + \_ : Reg\ Reg \to Reg$	$\_ \cdot \_ : Reg\ Reg \to Reg$
	$\_ + \_ : Reg1\ Reg \to Reg1$	$\_ \cdot \_ : Reg0\ Reg \to Reg0$
	$\_ + \_ : Reg\ Reg1 \to Reg1$	$\_ \cdot \_ : Reg\ Reg0 \to Reg0$
	$\_ + \_ : Reg0\ Reg0 \to Reg0$	$\_ \cdot \_ : Reg1\ Reg1 \to Reg1$
	$\_^* : Reg \to Reg1$.	

Sets of ground terms on the signature REG of the sorts Reg, $Reg0$, and $Reg1$ are defined in the usual way and denoted by $\mathcal{T}_{Reg}$, $\mathcal{T}_{Reg0}$, and $\mathcal{T}_{Reg1}$ correspondingly. In what follows we call the elements of $\mathcal{T}_{Reg}$ *regular terms*.

Given a regular term t, let $\|t\|$ denote its *alphabetic width* – the number of all the occurrences of letters from the alphabet $\mathcal{A}$ appearing in t.

A regular term t denotes a regular language $\mathcal{L}(t)$; this interpretation is determined by the homomorphism $\mathcal{L}(\_)$ from the absolutely free algebra of regular terms $\mathcal{T}_{Reg}$ to $\mathbf{Reg}[\mathcal{A}]$. Let $\mathcal{E}(\mathbf{Reg})$ be the kernel of this homomorphism, i.e. the congruence on $\mathcal{T}_{Reg}$ consisting of all the pairs $\langle t_1, t_2 \rangle$ such that $\mathcal{L}(t_1) = \mathcal{L}(t_2)$.

Recall that $\mathbf{Reg}[\mathcal{A}]$ is an idempotent semiring, i.e. satisfies the SR-axioms (1–9). There are further axioms concerning Kleene star (see e.g. [8] or [16]).

Thus, we have the following chain of quotients of $\mathcal{T}_{Reg}$ related by surjective homomorphisms:

$$\mathcal{T}_{Reg} \to \mathcal{T}_{Reg}/\mathcal{E}(ACI) \to \mathcal{T}_{Reg}/\mathcal{E}(ACIZ) \to \mathcal{T}_{Reg}/\mathcal{E}(SR) \to \mathcal{T}_{Reg}/\mathcal{E}(\mathbf{Reg}) \qquad (10)$$

where the last quotient is isomorphic to $\mathbf{Reg}[\mathcal{A}]$.

A *constant part* of a regular term t is equal to $o(t)$ where the function $o(\_)$ is defined on $\mathcal{T}_{Reg}$ as follows: $o(t) = $ if $t \in \mathcal{T}_{Reg1}$ then λ else $\emptyset$ fi.

Definition 1. (Derivatives) For any letter $x \in \mathcal{A}$ and word $w \in \mathcal{A}^*$ the functions $x^{-1}(\_)$ and $w^{-1}(\_)$ on $\mathcal{T}_{Reg}$ computing *(word) derivatives* of regular terms are defined recursively by the following equations for all $y \in \mathcal{A}$, $a, b \in \mathcal{T}_{Reg}$ [5]:

$$x^{-1}\emptyset = x^{-1}\lambda = \emptyset, \qquad\qquad\qquad x^{-1}(a^*) = (x^{-1}a) \cdot a^*,$$
$$x^{-1}y = \text{if } x = y \text{ then } \lambda \text{ else } \emptyset \text{ fi}, \qquad \lambda^{-1}a = a,$$
$$x^{-1}(a + b) = x^{-1}a + x^{-1}b, \qquad\qquad (w \cdot x)^{-1}a = x^{-1}(w^{-1}a).$$
$$x^{-1}(a \cdot b) = (x^{-1}a) \cdot b + o(a) \cdot x^{-1}b, \qquad\qquad\qquad\qquad \square$$

These equations are stable w.r.t. the congruences on $\mathcal{T}_{Reg}$ mentioned in (10), therefore $x^{-1}(\_)$ and $w^{-1}(\_)$ are correctly defined on the corresponding quotients of $\mathcal{T}_{Reg}$. It is known that $\mathcal{L}(w^{-1}r) = w \setminus \mathcal{L}(r)$.

Given a set of equations E on the signature REG, two derivatives are said to be E-*similar* if they are equivalent modulo E. The set $\mathcal{D}_E(t)$ of all E-*dissimilar* word derivatives of a regular term t is obtained as a set of representatives of the equivalence classes modulo E of terms $w^{-1}t$ for all $w \in \mathcal{A}^*$. It was proved in [5] that the set $\mathcal{D}_E(t)$ may be infinite for some regular term t when $E = \emptyset$, but it becomes finite (for all t) as soon as E includes the ACI-axioms (1–3). In the latter case the following fact holds which presents Brzozowski's method for constructing DFA:

Proposition 2. *Given a regular term t, consider the DFA $\mathbf{M}$ with the set of states $M = \mathcal{D}_E(t)$, the initial state $\mu_0 = t$, the transition function defined by $\tau(r, x) = x^{-1}r$ for all $x \in \mathcal{A}$, $r \in M$, and the set of final states $F = \{\, r \in M \mid o(r) = \lambda \,\}$. Then $\mathbf{M}$ recognizes the language $\mathcal{L}(t)$.*

Note that to practically implement this construction, one needs to compute the set $\mathcal{D}_E(t)$ that involves testing equivalence of regular expressions modulo E. Another technical problem is that for some t the cardinality of $\mathcal{D}_E(t)$ is an exponent in the size of t.

2 Introducing Partial Derivatives

It is a folk knowledge that any regular expression r on an alphabet $\mathcal{A} = \{x_1, \ldots, x_n\}$ can be represented in the following "linear" form:

$$r = o(r) + x_1 \cdot r_1 + \cdots + x_n \cdot r_n \qquad (11)$$

where all the r_i are some regular expressions (see [5, 18, 8]). In particular, one can take each r_i to be the derivative $x_i{}^{-1}r$. We are going to generalize this linear factorization in several ways to make it *non-deterministic* in a sense; this will lead us to partial derivatives. First we need to introduce some auxiliary notions.

Definition 3. Let $\mathbf{SetReg}$ be the upper semilattice $\mathbf{Set}[\mathcal{T}_{Reg}\setminus\{\emptyset\}]$ of finite sets of non-zero regular terms. We define a function $\rho : \mathcal{T}_{Reg} \to \mathbf{SetReg}$ which satisfies the conditions $\rho(\emptyset) = \emptyset$, $\rho(t_1 + t_2) = \rho(t_1) \cup \rho(t_2)$ for all t_1, $t_2 \in \mathcal{T}_{Reg}$, and maps any other regular term t to the singleton $\{t\}$. We call $\rho(t)$ a *set representation* of t. Two regular terms t_1, t_2 are said to be *weakly similar* if $\rho(t_1) = \rho(t_2)$. We denote this equivalence relation (which is a kernel of ρ) by $\sim_{ws}$. Finally, let $\mathcal{L}(R) = \bigcup_{r \in R} \mathcal{L}(r)$ for any $R \subset \mathcal{T}_{Reg}$. $\qquad\square$

The idea behind this construction is that it allows to take into account the ACIZ-properties of only those occurrences of "+" in regular terms which appear at the very upper level. E.g., the term $a + (b + c)^* + \emptyset$ is weakly similar to $(b + c)^* + a$, but not to $a + (c + b)^*$. Note that the equivalence relation $\sim_{ws}$ is weaker than $\mathcal{E}(ACIZ)$ on $\mathcal{T}_{Reg}$; and on the subset of regular terms not having occurrences of $\emptyset$ it is also weaker than $\mathcal{E}(ACI)$.

To relate finite sets of regular terms with corresponding regular terms modulo $\sim_{ws}$, we introduce the function $\sum\text{-} : \mathbf{SetReg} \to \mathcal{T}_{Reg}/\!\sim_{ws}$ which maps any singleton $\{t\}$ to the (equivalence class of the) regular term t and satisfies the conditions

$$\sum\emptyset = \emptyset, \quad \sum(R_1 \cup R_2) = \sum R_1 + \sum R_2$$

for all $R_1, R_2 \in \mathbf{SetReg}$. Note that $\mathcal{L}(\sum R) = \mathcal{L}(R)$ for any $R \in \mathbf{SetReg}$.

We shall also need an extension of the concatenation operation defined by the following equations for all $t \in \mathcal{T}_{Reg} \setminus \{\emptyset, \lambda\}$, $R \in \mathbf{SetReg}$:

$R \cdot \emptyset = \emptyset, \; R \cdot \lambda = R,$

$R \cdot t = \mathbf{if}\ \lambda \in R\ \mathbf{then}\ \{t\} \cup \{\, r \cdot t \mid r \in R \setminus \{\lambda\} \,\}\ \mathbf{else}\ \{\, r \cdot t \mid r \in R \,\}\ \mathbf{fi}.$

Definition 4. (Linear forms) Given a letter $x \in \mathcal{A}$ and a term $t \in \mathcal{T}_{Reg}$, we call the pair $\langle x, t \rangle$ a *monomial*. A *(non-deterministic) linear form* is a finite set of monomials. Let **Lin** denote the semilattice $\mathbf{Set}[\mathcal{A} \times \mathcal{T}_{Reg}]$ of linear forms. The function $lf(\_) : \mathcal{T}_{Reg} \to \mathbf{Lin}$, returning a linear form of its argument, is defined recursively by the following equations:

$$
\begin{aligned}
&lf(\emptyset) = \emptyset, &&lf(a^*) = lf(a) \odot a^*, \\
&lf(\lambda) = \emptyset, &&lf(a_0 \cdot b) = lf(a_0) \odot b, \\
&lf(x) = \{\langle x, \lambda \rangle\}, &&lf(a_1 \cdot b) = lf(a_1) \odot b \cup lf(b) \\
&lf(a + b) = lf(a) \cup lf(b),
\end{aligned}
$$

for all $x \in \mathcal{A}$, $a, b \in \mathcal{T}_{Reg}$, $a_0 \in \mathcal{T}_{Reg0}$, $a_1 \in \mathcal{T}_{Reg1}$. These equations involve an extension of concatenation, $\odot : \mathbf{Lin} \times \mathcal{T}_{Reg} \to \mathbf{Lin}$, defined as follows:

$$
\begin{aligned}
l \odot t = \ &\mathbf{if}\ t = \emptyset\ \mathbf{then}\ \emptyset \\
&\mathbf{else\ if}\ t = \lambda\ \mathbf{then}\ l \\
&\quad\ \mathbf{else}\ \{\ \langle x, p \cdot t \rangle \mid \langle x, p \rangle \in l \wedge p \neq \lambda\ \} \cup \{\ \langle x, t \rangle \mid \langle x, \lambda \rangle \in l\ \} \\
&\mathbf{fi\ fi}.
\end{aligned}
$$

for all $l \in \mathbf{Lin}$, $t \in \mathcal{T}_{Reg}$. $\qquad\qquad\qquad\qquad\qquad\qquad\qquad\qquad\qquad\qquad\square$

Regarding a monomial $\langle x, t \rangle$ as representing a regular term $x \cdot t$, the algebra **Lin** is isomorphic to a subalgebra of **SetReg**. This allows to apply the function $\sum\_$ defined above to translate a linear form l into a regular term $\sum l$ modulo weak similarity. The following proposition ensures that the function $lf(\_)$ provides a correct linear factorization of regular terms.

Proposition 5. *For any term $t \in \mathcal{T}_{Reg}$ the following equation holds in the algebra* **Reg**$[\mathcal{A}]$:

$$
t = o(t) + \sum lf(t). \tag{12}
$$

Remark. In general, a regular term t may have several linear forms which are distinct modulo $\mathcal{E}(SR)$, but all satisfy (12). Thus, the function $lf(t)$ returns a *particular* linear form of t. Note that it can be computed by one pass over t. The definition of lf can be extended by further equations which provide more compact linear forms for some terms (e.g., $lf(a_1 \cdot a_1) = lf(a_1) \cdot a_1$), but make computations more expensive (cf. [1]). $\qquad\square$

Now we come to the central definition of this paper.

Definition 6. (Partial derivatives) Given a regular term t and a letter $x \in \mathcal{A}$, a regular term p is called a *partial derivative of t w.r.t. x* if the linear form $lf(t)$ contains a monomial $\langle x, p \rangle$. We define a function $\partial_x : \mathcal{T}_{Reg} \to \mathbf{SetReg}$, which returns a set of all non-zero partial derivatives of its argument w.r.t. x, as follows:

$$
\partial_x(t) = \{\ p \in \mathcal{T}_{Reg} \setminus \{\emptyset\} \mid \langle x, p \rangle \in lf(t)\ \} \tag{13}
$$

The following equations extend this function allowing any word $w \in \mathcal{A}^*$ and set of words $W \subset \mathcal{A}^*$ at the place of x and any set of regular terms $R \subset T_{Reg}$ at the place of t:

$$\partial_\lambda(\emptyset) = \emptyset, \qquad\qquad \partial_w(R) = \bigcup_{r \in R} \partial_w(r),$$
$$\partial_\lambda(t) = \{t\} \text{ if } t \neq \emptyset,$$
$$\partial_{w \cdot x}(t) = \partial_x(\partial_w(t)), \qquad\qquad \partial_W(t) = \bigcup_{w \in W} \partial_w(t).$$

An element of the set $\partial_w(t)$ is called a *partial (word) derivative of* t w.r.t. w. $\square$

Example 1. Let's compute partial derivatives of the term $t = x^* \cdot (x \cdot x + y)^*$. Let r stand for $(x \cdot x + y)^*$. Using Def. 4, we obtain:

$$lf(t) = \{\langle x, t \rangle, \langle x, x \cdot r \rangle, \langle y, r \rangle\}, \quad lf(x \cdot r) = \{\langle x, r \rangle\}, \quad lf(r) = \{\langle x, x \cdot r \rangle, \langle y, r \rangle\},$$

hence

$$\partial_x(t) = \{t, x \cdot r\}, \qquad\qquad \partial_y(t) = \{r\},$$
$$\partial_{xx}(t) = \partial_x(\{t, x \cdot r\}) = \{t, x \cdot r, r\}, \qquad \partial_{yx}(t) = \partial_x(\{r\}) = \{x \cdot r\},$$
$$\partial_{xy}(t) = \partial_y(\{t, x \cdot r\}) = \{r\}, \qquad \partial_{yy}(t) = \partial_y(\{r\}) = \{r\},$$

etc. $\square$

The following facts explain semantics of partial derivatives and relate them to derivatives.

Proposition 7. $\mathcal{L}(\partial_w(t)) = w \setminus \mathcal{L}(t)$ *for any* $t \in T_{Reg}$, $w \in \mathcal{A}^*$. *In particular, any partial derivative* $p \in \partial_w(t)$ *denotes a subset of the left quotient* $w \setminus \mathcal{L}(t)$.

Corollary 8. *For any* $t \in T_{Reg}$, $w \in \mathcal{A}^*$ *the equation* $w^{-1}t = \sum \partial_w(t)$ *holds in the algebra* **Reg**$[\mathcal{A}]$. $\square$

Thus, partial derivatives in $\partial_w(t)$ represents "parts" of the derivative $w^{-1}t$ (that justifies their name).

3 Properties of Partial Derivatives

Let $\mathcal{PD}(t)$ stand for the set $\partial_{\mathcal{A}^*}(t)$ of all (syntactically distinct) partial word derivatives of t. The next two theorems present important properties of $\mathcal{PD}(t)$.

The first theorem shows that $\mathcal{PD}(t)$ is finite and gives a nice upper bound for its cardinality.

Theorem 9. $|\partial_{\mathcal{A}^+}(t)| \leq \|t\|$ *and* $|\mathcal{PD}(t)| \leq \|t\| + 1$ *hold for any* $t \in T_{Reg}$.

Corollary 10. $|\partial_W(t)| \leq \|t\| + 1$ *holds for any* $W \subset \mathcal{A}^*$. $\square$

Remark. It follows from Def. 6 and Prop. 7 that the term $\sum \partial_W(t)$ represents an *event derivative of* t w.r.t. W (cf. [8]). Thus, Corollary 10 implies Theorem 3 from [8, chapt.5] (which proves a half of Kleene's main theorem). $\square$

Example 2. In notation of Example 1, we have $\|t\| = 4$ and $\mathcal{PD}(t) = \{t,\ x \cdot r,\ r\}$. □

The second theorem clarifies the internal structure of partial derivatives.

Theorem 11. *Given a regular term* $t \in \mathcal{T}_{Reg}$, *any partial derivative of* t *is either* λ, *or a subterm of* t, *or a concatenation* $t_1 \cdot t_2 \cdot \ldots \cdot t_n$ *of several such subterms where* n *is not more than the number of occurrences of concatenation and Kleene star appearing in* t. □

It follows that the set $\mathcal{PD}(t)$ can be represented by a data structure of a relatively small size: each partial derivative of t is just a (possibly empty) list of references to subterms of t and there are not more than $\|t\| + 1$ such lists. In the next section it will be made clear that this data structure is virtually a set of states of an NFA recognizing the language $\mathcal{L}(t)$ and that it can also serve as a basis for compact representation of the set of all $\sim_{ws}$-dissimilar derivatives of t.

4 Finite Automata Constructions Using Partial Derivatives

In this section we apply partial derivatives to a classical problem of turning regular expressions into finite automata. There are several well-known algorithms performing this task [14, 19, 4]. Nevertheless, new algorithms, aimed at reducing sizes of resulting automata, improving their performance, etc., keep appearing (see e.g. a survey [20]). Using partial derivatives, we get yet another new algorithms.

4.1 From regular expressions to small NFA

In this subsection we describe a new algorithm turning a regular term t into an NFA having not more than $\|t\| + 1$ states. The following theorem presents our construction.

Theorem 12. *Given a regular term* t *on an alphabet* $\mathcal{A}$, *let an automaton* **M** *on* $\mathcal{A}$ *have the set of states* $M = \mathcal{PD}(t)$, *the initial state* $\mu_0 = t$, *the transition function* τ *defined by* $\tau(p,\ x) = \partial_x(p)$ *for all* $p \in \mathcal{PD}(t)$, $x \in \mathcal{A}$, *and the set of final states* $F = \{\ p \in \mathcal{PD}(t) \mid o(p) = \lambda\ \}$. *Then* **M** *recognizes* $\mathcal{L}(t)$. □

To practically implement this construction, one needs to compute the set $\mathcal{PD}(t)$ and the function τ (the set F can be obtained in the obvious way). This can be done through the following iterative process

$$\langle \mathcal{PD}_0,\ \Delta_0,\ \tau_0 \rangle := \langle \varnothing,\ \{t\},\ \varnothing \rangle \tag{14}$$

$$\mathcal{PD}_{i+1} := \mathcal{PD}_i \cup \Delta_i \tag{15}$$

$$\Delta_{i+1} := \bigcup_{p \in \Delta_i} \{\ q \mid \langle x,\ q \rangle \in \mathit{lf}(p) \wedge q \notin \mathcal{PD}_{i+1}\ \} \tag{16}$$

$$\tau_{i+1} := \tau_i \cup \{\ \langle p,\ x,\ q \rangle \mid p \in \Delta_i \wedge \langle x,\ q \rangle \in \mathit{lf}(p)\ \} \tag{17}$$

for $i = 0, 1, \ldots$ Here τ is represented as a finite subset of $M \times \mathcal{A} \times M$ (i.e., a transition relation). The set Δ_i accumulates new partial derivatives appearing at each step. In not more than $\|t\|$ steps Δ_i becomes empty – then $\mathcal{PD}_i$ and τ_i contain the needed results. All the basic operations involved into this construction can be computed in time between $O(n)$ and $O(n^2)$, hence it can be implemented as a respectably efficient program.

4.2 From regular expressions to DFA: improvements to Brzozowski's algorithm

Our construction of NFA presented in Theorem 12 can easily be modified into a procedure constructing DFA: the set $\mathcal{DD}(t) = \{ \partial_w(t) \mid w \in \mathcal{A}^* \}$ is to be taken as the set of states of the DFA, the initial state is the singleton $\{t\}$, the transition function is defined by $\tau(P, x) = \partial_x(P)$ for all $P \in \mathcal{DD}(t)$, $x \in \mathcal{A}$, and the set of final states is $F = \{ P \in \mathcal{DD}(t) \mid o(\sum P) = \lambda \}$.

Proposition 13. *The automaton* $\langle \mathcal{DD}(t), \tau, \{t\}, F \rangle$ *presented above recognizes the language* $\mathcal{L}(t)$. □

The relation between the sets $\partial_w(t)$ and the derivatives $w^{-1}t$ given by Prop.7 readily demonstrates that this construction is just a modification of Brzozowski's algorithm where each derivative $w^{-1}t$ is substituted by a corresponding set $\partial_w(t)$ of partial derivatives. However, the use of partial derivatives leads to several advantages:

1. Rather than to compute separately and to keep in memory all ACI-dissimilar derivatives of t, one can compute $\mathcal{PD}(t)$ and represent each deterministic state $\partial_w(t)$ as a set of *references* to corresponding elements in $\mathcal{PD}(t)$. Thus, $\mathcal{PD}(t)$ serves as a relatively small *basis* for the set $\mathcal{DD}(t)$ (and so for the set of all derivatives of t).

2. Computing the set $\mathcal{DD}(t)$ represented as suggested above, one compares its elements just as sets of references (that can be performed in $O(n \log n)$ time), rather than checks equivalence of derivatives modulo $\mathcal{E}(ACI)$, or any other non-trivial congruence.

3. Components of the transition function τ can be computed through the function $lf(\_)$ which gives a whole tuple of transitions $\{ \langle x, \partial_x(P) \rangle \mid x \in \mathcal{A} \}$ by one pass over P. This is more efficient than to compute separately each derivative w.r.t. $x \in \mathcal{A}$ (that requires one pass for each x). The bigger the alphabet, the more one gains from this optimization.

These improvements to the original algorithm by Brzozowski provide a more efficient programming implementation.[4]

Remark. The automata constructions presented above demonstrate that the relation between partial derivatives and derivatives is similar to the well known relation between

---

[4] Of course, one should bear in mind that the output of this procedure can have an exponential size.

NFA and DFA provided by the classical subset construction [17]. Really, suppose a regular term t is turned into an NFA as described in Theorem 12. This NFA can be transformed into an equivalent DFA by the subset construction; the states of the DFA will be represented by sets of states of the original NFA, i.e. by subsets of $\mathcal{PD}(t)$. On the other hand, the same DFA – with the set of states $\mathcal{DD}(t)$ – can be obtained directly from t as described in Prop. 13. Note that this gives a new algebraic interpretation of the subset construction. Also, taking into account Theorem 11, we come to an interesting conclusion that *states of a DFA recognizing $\mathcal{L}(t)$ are virtually finite sets of certain lists of subterms of t.*

5 Implementation and Examples

We have used the algebraic programming language OBJ3 [11] to develop a prototype implementation of the algorithms for computing partial derivatives of regular expressions and constructing NFA.

Recall that a finite automaton $\mathbf{M} = \langle M, \tau, \mu_0, F \rangle$ can be represented by a finite system of *state equations* of the form

$$\mu := o(\mu) + x_1 \cdot \mu_1 + \ldots + x_k \cdot \mu_k \tag{18}$$

for each state $\mu \in M$ where $x_i \in \mathcal{A}$ and $\mu_i \in \tau(\mu, x_i)$, $i = 1 \ldots k$ (see e.g. [6]). Here $o(\mu)$ is λ if $\mu \in F$, or $\emptyset$ otherwise – in the latter case it is omitted from the sum. The components $x_i \cdot \emptyset$ (if any) can also be omitted from the right-hand sides of (18), so that the resulting set of equations represents in general a non-complete NFA – without the sink state $\emptyset$.

Our program consists of several order-sorted term-rewriting systems implementing, in particular, Def.4 and the iterative process defined by the equations (14–17). It takes a regular term as an input and rewrites it into a set of state equations representing a corresponding NFA, and a set of partial derivatives corresponding to the states of the automaton. Below we present some examples obtained with the help of this program. We consider regular terms on the alphabet $\mathcal{A} = \{a, b, c, \ldots\}$. The concatenation sign is omitted from the terms.

Example 3. This is a working example from [7]: the regular expression

$$t = (a + b)^* abb.$$

Our algorithm turns it into the following NFA with 4 states and 5 edges:

State equations	Partial derivatives
$S_1 := a \cdot S_1 + b \cdot S_1 + a \cdot S_2$	$(a + b)^* abb$
$S_2 := b \cdot S_3$	bb
$S_3 := b \cdot S_4$	b
$S_4 := \lambda$	λ

In [7] the expression was first turned into an NFA with 6 states and 11 edges by Berry and Sethi's algorithm. Then this NFA was transformed into a so-called *compressed normalized NFA* with 5 states and 6 edges through several non-trivial optimizations. It is remarkable that our algorithm gives a smaller NFA without any additional optimization. □

Example 4. Given a natural constant $n \geq 2$, consider the following regular expression:[5]

$$t_n = (\lambda + a + a^2 + \ldots + a^{n-1})(a^n)^*.$$

One can see that $\|t_n\| = n(n+1)/2$. However, our algorithm turns t_n into an NFA with only $n + 1$ states. E.g., for $n = 4$ the NFA is as follows:

State equations	Partial derivatives
$S_1 := \lambda + a \cdot S_2 + a \cdot S_3 + a \cdot S_4 + a \cdot S_5$	$(\lambda + a + aa + aaa)(aaaa)^*$
$S_2 := \lambda + a \cdot S_5$	$(aaaa)^*$
$S_3 := a \cdot S_2$	$a(aaaa)^*$
$S_4 := a \cdot S_3$	$aa(aaaa)^*$
$S_5 := a \cdot S_4$	$aaa(aaaa)^*$

This demonstrates that in some cases our NFA can be an order of magnitude smaller than McNaughton and Yamada's or Berry and Sethi's ones. □

Example 5. This example is due to Gregory Kucherov: he proposed us to construct an automaton for the following regular expression (which is an example of those appearing in the study of word-rewriting systems with variables [13]):

$$t = (a + b)^*(babab(a + b)^*bab + bba(a + b)^*bab)(a + b)^*.$$

Our algorithm turns this expression into the following NFA with 11 states:

State equations	Partial derivatives
$S_1 := a \cdot S_1 + b \cdot S_1 + b \cdot S_2 + b \cdot S_3$	t
$S_2 := a \cdot S_4$	$abab(a + b)^*bab(a + b)^*$
$S_3 := b \cdot S_5$	$ba(a + b)^*bab(a + b)^*$
$S_4 := b \cdot S_6$	$bab(a + b)^*bab(a + b)^*$
$S_5 := a \cdot S_7$	$a(a + b)^*bab(a + b)^*$
$S_6 := a \cdot S_8$	$ab(a + b)^*bab(a + b)^*$
$S_7 := a \cdot S_7 + b \cdot S_7 + b \cdot S_9$	$(a + b)^*bab(a + b)^*$
$S_8 := b \cdot S_7$	$b(a + b)^*bab(a + b)^*$
$S_9 := a \cdot S_{10}$	$ab(a + b)^*$
$S_{10} := b \cdot S_{11}$	$b(a + b)^*$
$S_{11} := \lambda + a \cdot S_{11} + b \cdot S_{11}$	$(a + b)^*$

Note that $\|t\| = 22$, so McNaughton and Yamada's or Berry and Sethi's algorithms would turn this expression into an NFA with 23 states. □

Acknowledgements. The author thanks Pierre Lescanne and Gregory Kucherov for helpful discussions and comments on a draft version of this paper.

---

[5] Which comes from so-called *cyclic identities*, see e.g. [8].

References

1. V. M. Antimirov. Partial derivatives of regular expressions and finite automata constructions. Technical report, CRIN, 1994. (Forthcoming).
2. V. M. Antimirov and P. D. Mosses. Rewriting extended regular expressions (short version). In G. Rozenberg and A. Salomaa, editors, *Developments in Language Theory - At the Crossroads of Mathematics, Computer Science and Biology*, pages 195–209. World Scientific, Singapore, 1994.
3. V. M. Antimirov and P. D. Mosses. Rewriting extended regular expressions. *Theoretical Comput. Sci.*, 141, 1995. (To appear).
4. G. Berry and R. Sethi. From regular expressions to deterministic automata. *Theoretical Comput. Sci.*, 48:117–126, 1986.
5. J. A. Brzozowski. Derivatives of regular expressions. *J. ACM*, 11:481–494, 1964.
6. J. A. Brzozowski and E. L. Leiss. On equations for regular languages, finite automata, and sequential networks. *Theoretical Comput. Sci.*, 10:19–35, 1980.
7. C.-H. Chang and R. Paige. From regular expressions to DFA's using compressed NFA's. In A. Apostolico, M. Crochemore, Z. Galil, and U. Manber, editors, *Combinatorial Pattern Matching. Proceedings.*, volume 644 of *Lecture Notes in Computer Science*, pages 88–108. Springer-Verlag, 1992.
8. J. H. Conway. *Regular Algebra and Finite Machines*. Chapman and Hall, 1971.
9. A. Ginzburg. A procedure for checking equality of regular expressions. *J. ACM*, 14(2):355–362, 1967.
10. J. A. Goguen and J. Meseguer. Order-sorted algebra I: Equational deduction for multiple inheritance, overloading, exceptions and partial operations. *Theoretical Comput. Sci.*, 105:217–273, 1992.
11. J. A. Goguen and T. Winkler. Introducing OBJ3. Technical Report SRI-CSL-88-9, Computer Science Lab., SRI International, 1988.
12. D. Krob. Differentiation of K-rational expressions. *International Journal of Algebra and Computation*, 2(1):57–87, 1992.
13. G. Kucherov and M. Rusinowitch. On Ground-Reducibility Problem for Word Rewriting Systems with Variables. In E. Deaton and R. Wilkerson, editors, *Proceedings 1994 ACM/SIGAPP Symposium on Applied Computing*, Phoenix (USA), Mar. 1994. ACM-Press.
14. R. McNaughton and H. Yamada. Regular expressions and state graphs for automata. *IEEE Trans. on Electronic Computers*, 9(1):39–47, 1960.
15. Y. Mizoguchi, H. Ohtsuka, and Y. Kawahara. A symbolic calculus of regular expressions. *Bulletin of Informatics and Cybernetics*, 22(3–4):165–170, 1987.
16. D. Perrin. Finite automata. In J. van Leeuwen, A. Meyer, M. Nivat, M. Paterson, and D. Perrin, editors, *Handbook of Theoretical Computer Science*, volume B, chapter 1. Elsevier Science Publishers, Amsterdam; and MIT Press, 1990.
17. M. O. Rabin and D. Scott. Finite automata and their decision problems. *IBM Journal of Research and Development*, 3(2):114–125, Apr. 1959.
18. A. Salomaa. *Theory of Automata*. Pergamon, 1969.
19. K. Thompson. Regular expression search algorithms. *Communication ACM*, 11(6):419–422, 1968.
20. B. W. Watson. A taxonomy of finite automata construction algorithms. Computing Science Note 93/43, Eindhoven University of Technology, The Netherlands, 1993.

Dependence Orders for Computations of Concurrent Automata

Felipe Bracho[1], Manfred Droste[2]* and Dietrich Kuske[2]*

[1] IIMAS, Universidad Nacional Autónoma de México, 01000 México D.F.
[2] Abteilung Mathematik, Technische Universität Dresden, D–01062 Dresden, Germany, e-mail: {droste,kuske}@nalw01.math.tu-dresden.de

Abstract. An automaton with concurrency relations $\mathcal{A}$ is a labeled transition system with a collection of binary relations indicating when two events in a given state of the automaton can happen independently from each other. The concurrency relations induce a natural equivalence relation for finite computation sequences. We investigate two graph–theoretic representations of the equivalence classes of computation sequences and obtain that under suitable assumptions on $\mathcal{A}$ they are isomorphic. Furthermore, the graphs are shown to carry a monoid operation reflecting precisely the composition of computations. This generalizes fundamental graph–theoretical representation results due to Mazurkiewicz in trace theory.

1 Introduction

In the theory of concurrency, many different models have been investigated intensively including, e.g., Petri nets, CCS and CSP. The behaviour of Petri nets led Mazurkiewicz ([Ma77, Ma85]) to the investigation of trace alphabets and their associated trace monoids, a mathematical model for the sequential behaviour of a parallel system in which the order of two independent actions is regarded as irrelevant. *Trace theory* has now a well–developed mathematical theory, see [AR88, Di90] for surveys. One of its foundational results ([Ma85]), used in many difficult applications (*cf.* [Oc85, Di90]) is that each element of the (algebraically defined) trace monoid has a graph–theoretical representation. It is the aim of this paper to generalize this result and related versions of it to the context of automata with concurrency relations.

Let us recall basic notions of trace theory and of automata with concurrency relations. As introduced by Mazurkiewicz [Ma85], trace alphabets are pairs (E, D) consisting of a set E of unlabeled actions or events and a reflexive symmetric binary relation D in E indicating when two actions are dependent. Two sequences ab and ba are declared equivalent if $(a, b) \notin D$. This generates a congruence $\sim$ on the free monoid E^* of all words over E, and the quotient $M(E, D) := E^*/\sim$ is called the *trace monoid* (or free partially commutative monoid) over (E, D).

---

* Research supported by the German Research Foundation (DFG)

In trace alphabets, a single binary relation on E is used to represent the concurrency relation for all pairs of actions. Here, we will consider a more general model of labeled transition systems in which the concurrency relation depends not only on the two arriving actions, but also on the present state of the system. An *automaton with concurrency relations* is a tuple $\mathcal{A} = (Q, \mathcal{E}, \mathcal{T}, \|)$ where Q is the set of states, E as before the set of events or actions, $T \subseteq Q \times E \times Q$ the transition relation (assumed deterministic), and $\| = (\|_q)_{q \in Q}$ is a collection of concurrency relations $\|_q$ for E, indexed by the possible states $q \in Q$. Let $CS(\mathcal{A})$ comprise all finite computation sequences of $\mathcal{A}$, with concatenation as (partially defined) monoid operation. We declare two sequences $(p, a, q)(q, b, r)$ and $(p, b, q')(q', a, r)$ equivalent, if $a \|_p b$. As before, this induces a congruence $\sim$ on $CS(\mathcal{A})$; thus intuitively, two computation sequences are equivalent, if they represent "interleaved views" of a single computation. The quotient $M(\mathcal{A}) = CS(\mathcal{A}) / {\sim} \cup \{0\}$ (formally supplemented with 0 to obtain an everywhere defined monoid operation) is called the *concurrency monoid associated with $\mathcal{A}$*.

Automata with concurrency relations were introduced and studied in [Dr90, Dr92, BD93, BD94]. Their domains of computation sequences are closely related with event domains and dI–domains arising in denotational semantics of programming languages. These automata also generalize asynchronous transition systems ([Be87, WN94]). For applications of related structures we refer the reader to [Le78, BC88, PSS90, KP90]. Very recently, a formalization using several independence relations of the operational semantics of Occam was given in [BR94].

It seems that many results of the literature for trace monoids $M(E, D)$ can be generalized, under suitable assumptions, to concurrency monoids $M(\mathcal{A})$. An adjunction between automata with concurrency relations and place/transition–systems generalizing the one between asynchronous transition systems and Petri-nets (*cf.* [NRT92, WN94]) was given in [DS93]. The results of [Oc85, GRS92] on recognizable and on aperiodic languages in trace theory could be generalized to concurrency monoids in [Dr94a, Dr94b]. Now by a fundamental result in trace theory, mentioned before, the elements of a trace monoid can be represented pictorially nicely by certain labeled graphs, or even labeled partially ordered sets. There is even a multiplication of (isomorphism classes of) such graphs, yielding a monoid which turns out to be isomorphic to the trace monoid $M(E, D)$.

These results we wish to generalize here to concurrency monoids $M(\mathcal{A})$. For this, a useful (and almost necessary) assumption is that $\mathcal{A}$ is stably concurrent (see Def. 4 for a precise formulation). This means that the concurrency relations of $\mathcal{A}$ depend locally (but not globally) of each other. As shown in [Ku94b], stably concurrent automata generate precisely the class of dI–domains, and these distributivity properties will be crucial here.

We now give a summary of our results. Let $\mathcal{A}$ be a fixed stably concurrent automaton and γ a computation sequence of $\mathcal{A}$. First we define two labeled partial orders $DO(\gamma)$ and $PR(\gamma)$ associated with γ as follows. We let $DO(\gamma)$ comprise all enumerated occurrences (a, i) of actions $a \in E$ within the computation sequence γ. We put $(a, i) \sqsubseteq (b, j)$, if in each computation sequence δ equivalent with γ the i–th occurrence of a precedes the j–th occurrence of b. Finally, we label the element (a, i) with a. This provides a straightforward generalization of the dependence or occurrence orders (see [Ma85]) known in trace theory.

Then we define a labeled partial order $\mathrm{PR}(\gamma)$ as follows. For any $x, y \in \mathrm{M}(\mathcal{A})$ put $x \leq y$ if x divides y, i.e. there is $z \in \mathrm{M}(\mathcal{A})$ with $x \cdot z = y$. This partial order is known as the prefix ordering in trace theory (see [Ma85]). Given a computation sequence γ with equivalence class $[\gamma]$ in $\mathrm{M}(\mathcal{A})$, we may associate with it the partially ordered set $(\mathrm{Pr}(\gamma), \leq)$ of all prime elements of the distributive lattice $([\gamma]{\downarrow}, \leq)$ (see [Ku94b]). This procedure is standard in lattice theory ([Bi73]) and also known from the theory of stable event structures ([Wi87]). This poset $(\mathrm{Pr}(\gamma), \leq)$ carries a natural labeling function taking values in E, which completes the definition of $\mathrm{PR}(\gamma)$. One of our main results is that, although defined quite differently, the labeled partial orders $\mathrm{DO}(\gamma)$ and $\mathrm{PR}(\gamma)$ are isomorphic. This result provides the basis for our further investigation of the dependence order $\mathrm{DO}(\gamma)$. We show that the linear extensions of the partial order $\mathrm{DO}(\gamma)$ precisely give rise to the computation sequences δ equivalent to γ. In particular, two computation sequences γ and δ are equivalent if (and, clearly, only if) their dependence orders $\mathrm{DO}(\gamma)$ and $\mathrm{DO}(\delta)$ coincide. In [BDK94] we characterize for an arbitrary labeled poset when it is isomorphic to a dependence order $\mathrm{DO}(\gamma)$, for some computation sequence γ (for lack of place, we cannot present this result here). Finally, we define a multiplication on the set of (isomorphism classes of) dependence orders $\mathrm{DO}(\gamma)$ and show that we obtain a monoid isomorphic to the concurrency monoid $\mathrm{M}(\mathcal{A})$. This generalizes classical results of Mazurkiewicz ([Ma85, Di90]).

From the present work the question arises which further results of trace theory resting on the representation of traces by graphs can now be transferred into the more general context of concurrent automata. This has recently been achieved for logical definability of recognizable and aperiodic languages. Also, a more detailed investigation of the connection implicitly arisen here between computations in stably concurrent automata and stable event structures (via prime elements in distributive lattices) might be fruitful.

2 Concurrent computations

In this section we will introduce the automata with concurrency relations, our concept of concurrent computation, and a first graph–theoretic representation.

Definition 1. An *automaton with concurrency relations* is a quadruple $\mathcal{A} = (\mathcal{Q}, \mathcal{E}, \mathcal{T}, \|)$ such that

1. Q and E are sets of *states* and *events* or *actions*, respectively.
2. $T \subseteq Q \times E \times Q$ is a set of *transitions* such that whenever $(p, a, q), (p, a, r) \in T$, then $q = r$.
3. $\| = (\|_q)_{q \in Q}$ is a collection of irreflexive, symmetric binary relations on E; it is required that whenever $a \|_p b$, then there exist transitions (p, a, q), (p, b, q'), (q, b, r) and (q', a, r) in T.

Intuitively, a transition $\tau = (p, a, q)$ represents a potential computation step in which event a happens in state p of $\mathcal{A}$ and $\mathcal{A}$ changes from state p to state q. We write $\mathrm{ev}(\tau) = a$, the event of τ. The concurrency relations $\|_p$ describe the concurrency information for pairs of events at state p. The last requirement can be seen as in the diagram:

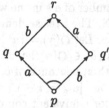

The angle at p indicates that $a \|_p b$ holds.

A *computation sequence* in $\mathcal{A}$ is either empty (denoted by ϵ), or a finite sequence $\gamma = \sigma_1 \ldots \sigma_n$ of transitions σ_i of the form $\sigma_i = (q_{i-1}, a_i, q_i)$ for $i = 1 \ldots n$; it can be depicted as

$$q_0 \xrightarrow{a_1} q_1 \xrightarrow{a_2} \cdots \xrightarrow{a_n} q_n.$$

We call q_0 the *domain* of γ, denoted by $\mathrm{dom}\,\gamma$, q_n the *codomain*, denoted by $\mathrm{cod}\,\gamma$, and n the length $|\gamma|$ of γ. The sequence $a_1 a_2 \ldots a_n$ is called *event sequence of* γ, denoted by $\mathrm{evs}\,\gamma$. To simplify the notation, we consider each state of Q as domain and as codomain of ϵ. We let $\mathrm{CS}(\mathcal{A})$ denote the set of all computation sequences of $\mathcal{A}$. The *composition* $\gamma\delta$ is defined in the natural way by concatenating γ and δ if $\mathrm{cod}\,\gamma = \mathrm{dom}\,\delta$. Formally we put $\gamma\epsilon = \epsilon\gamma = \gamma$.

Now we want the concurrency relations of $\mathcal{A}$ to induce an equivalence relation on $\mathrm{CS}(\mathcal{A})$ so that equivalent computation sequences are not differentiated by the order in which concurrent events appear. For this, we let $\sim$ be the smallest congruence with respect to composition on $\mathrm{CS}(\mathcal{A})$ making all sequences $p \xrightarrow{a} q \xrightarrow{b} r$ and $p \xrightarrow{b} q' \xrightarrow{a} r$ with $a \|_p b$ equivalent. We let $[\gamma]$ denote the equivalence class of γ with respect to $\sim$. Also, we let $1 := [\epsilon]$. It easily follows that any two equivalent computation sequences have the same length, domain and codomain. We now obtain the *monoid* $\mathrm{M}(\mathcal{A})$ *of computations associated with* $\mathcal{A}$ by letting $\mathrm{M}(\mathcal{A}) = \mathrm{CS}(\mathcal{A})/\!\sim \cup\, \{0\}$, where 0 is an additional symbol. That is, for $\gamma, \delta \in \mathrm{CS}(\mathcal{A})$ we have $[\gamma] \cdot [\delta] = [\gamma\delta]$ if $\mathrm{cod}\,\gamma = \mathrm{dom}\,\delta$ and $[\gamma] \cdot [\delta] = 0$ otherwise. Also, $x \cdot 0 = 0 \cdot x = 0$ and $x \cdot 1 = 1 \cdot x = x$ for any $x \in \mathrm{M}(\mathcal{A})$. Clearly, with this operation $\mathrm{M}(\mathcal{A})$ is a monoid with 1 as unit (and with 0 as zero).

Next we show why these automata and their monoids provide a generalization of trace alphabets and trace monoids. Let (E, D) be a trace alphabet. Then $\mathcal{A} = (Q, \mathcal{E}, \mathcal{T}, \|)$ with $Q = \{q\}$, $T = Q \times E \times Q$ and $\|_q = (E \times E) \setminus D$ is an automaton with concurrency relations. This automaton will be called *automaton induced by* (E, D). Obviously, $\mathrm{evs} : \mathrm{CS}(\mathcal{A}) \longrightarrow E^*$ is a bijection. Moreover, for $\gamma, \delta \in \mathrm{CS}(\mathcal{A})$ we have $\gamma \sim \delta$ iff $\mathrm{evs}\,\gamma \sim \mathrm{evs}\,\delta$ with respect to (E, D). Hence, evs induces a monoid–isomorphism between $\mathrm{M}(\mathcal{A}) \setminus \{0\}$ and $M(E, D)$. Thus, automata with concurrency relations generalize trace alphabets.

Now let $\mathcal{A}$ be an automaton with concurrency relations, and let $\gamma \in \mathrm{CS}(\mathcal{A})$. Analogously to trace theory we define a dependence order on those events that appear in γ. This order should reflect that a smaller event has to appear before a larger one, i.e. the smaller event is a necessary condition for the larger one. If two events are incomparable they can appear in any order or even in parallel. Since an event a can appear several times in γ we have to distinguish between the first, the second, ... appearance of a. For $a \in E$ let $|\gamma|_a$ denote the number of transitions σ in γ with ev $\sigma = a$, i.e. the number of a's in the word evs $\gamma \in E^*$. We abbreviate $a^i = (a, i)$ for $a \in E$ and $i \in \mathbb{N}$. The precise definition of the dependence order of γ can now be given as follows. Let $O(\gamma) = \{a^i \mid a \in \text{ev}\, \gamma,\ 1 \le i \le |\gamma|_a\}$. Then, obviously, $|O(\gamma)| = |\gamma|$. For $a^i, b^j \in O(\gamma)$ let $a^i \sqsubseteq_\gamma b^j$ iff the i-th appearance of a in γ occurs before the j-th appearance of b, i.e., formally, there are words $u, v, w \in E^*$ with evs $\gamma = uavbw$, $|u|_a = i - 1$ and $|uav|_b = j - 1$. Then $\sqsubseteq_\gamma$ is a linear order on $O(\gamma)$. Since for equivalent computation sequences γ and δ we always have $O(\gamma) = O(\delta)$, a partial order on $O(\gamma)$ can be defined by:

$$\sqsubseteq := \bigcap \{\sqsubseteq_\delta \mid \delta \sim \gamma\}.$$

Here $a^i \sqsubseteq b^j$ if and only if the i-th a appears before the j-th b in *any* computation sequence equivalent with γ. Let $l : O(\gamma) \longrightarrow E$ be the function defined by $l(a^i) = a$. Then the quadruple $DO(\gamma) = (O(\gamma), \sqsubseteq, l, \text{dom}\,\gamma)$ will be called the *dependence order associated with* γ.

Let $\mathcal{A}$ be the automaton induced by the trace alphabet (E, D) and $\gamma \in CS(\mathcal{A})$. Then the dependence order $DO(\gamma)$ coincides with the wellknown dependence or occurrence order of the trace evs(γ) (appart from the last component of the quadruple $DO(\gamma)$ since in such automata with concurrency relations it always equals q). Thus, we have a direct generalization of the dependence orders of traces to the computations of automata with concurrency relations.

The dependence orders introduced above motivate the following definition:

Definition 2. Let $\mathcal{A} = (Q, \mathcal{E}, \mathcal{T}, \|)$ be an automaton with concurrency relations. A quadruple $\mathbb{P} = (\mathbb{P}, \le, \lessdot, \shortparallel)$ is called a *labeled partial order over* $\mathcal{A}$ or *lpo* if $(P, \le)$ is a finite partially ordered set, $l : P \longrightarrow E$ is a function and $q \in Q$.

A sequence $A = (p_1, p_2, \ldots, p_n)$ is an *order–preserving enumeration* of $\mathbb{P}$ if A is an enumeration of P and $p_i \le p_j$ implies $i \le j$. Then a computation sequence δ is called the *linearisation of* $\mathbb{P}$ *induced by* A if dom $\delta = q$ and evs $\delta = l(p_1) l(p_2) \ldots l(p_n)$. We say that δ is a *linearisation* of $\mathbb{P}$, if it is a linearisation induced by some order–preserving enumeration.

Let $\text{Lin}(\mathbb{P})$ denote the set of all linearisations of $\mathbb{P}$.

Since any computation sequence is completely determined by its domain and event sequence, an order–preserving enumeration A of $\mathbb{P}$ induces at most one linearisation.

Lemma 3. *Let* $\mathcal{A}$ *be an automaton with concurrency relations and* $\gamma \in CS(\mathcal{A})$. *Then* $[\gamma] \subseteq \text{Lin}(DO(\gamma))$.

Proof: Let $\delta \in [\gamma]$, and let A be the sequence of enumerated occurences (a, i) of actions in evs(δ). Clearly, A is an order–preserving enumeration of $DO(\delta)$

(since $\sqsubseteq \subseteq \sqsubseteq_\delta$) and induces δ. Now $\gamma \sim \delta$ implies $DO(\gamma) = DO(\delta)$. Thus, δ is a linearisation of $DO(\gamma)$, i.e. $|\gamma| \subseteq \mathrm{Lin}(DO(\gamma))$. □

In trace theory this lemma even holds with equality. Moreover, any order–preserving enumeration of $DO(\gamma)$ induces a linearisation in this case (see [Ma85, p. 318]. The following example shows that this is not true for the case of automata with concurrency relations.

Example 1. Let $\mathcal{A}_\infty$ and $\mathcal{A}_\in$ be the two automata with concurrency relations depicted below.

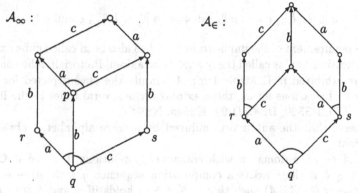

Consider the computation sequences $\gamma_1 \in CS(\mathcal{A}_\infty)$ with $\dom \gamma_1 = q$ and $evs \gamma_1 = abc$. Then the elements of $O(\gamma_1) = \{a^1, b^1, c^1\}$ are pairwise incomparable with respect to $\sqsubseteq$. Hence $A = (a^1, c^1, b^1)$ is an order–preserving enumeration of $(O(\gamma_1), \sqsubseteq)$. But A does not induce a linearisation. If we add the following transitions to the set T_1 then there exists a linearisation induced by A, but it is not equivalent with γ_1:

In fact, it can be checked that if such a linearisation $\delta \in CS(\mathcal{A}_\infty)$ induced by A equivalent with γ_1 exists, then $b \parallel_r c$ or $(a \parallel_s b$ and $a \parallel_q c)$ in $\mathcal{A}_\infty$. More generally, if any order–preserving enumeration induces a linearisation $\delta \in CS(\mathcal{A}_\infty)$ with $\gamma_1 \sim \delta$, then at least two of the following three statements are satisfied in $\mathcal{A}_\infty$: $b \parallel_r c$, $a \parallel_s b$ and $a \parallel_q c$. An automaton with concurrency relations satisfying all these statements is said to satisfy the cube axiom (see below).

Similar observations for $\gamma_2 \in CS(\mathcal{A}_\in)$ with $\dom \gamma_2 = q$ and $evs \gamma_2 = abc$ yield the following: Supposing that any order–preserving enumeration of $DO(\gamma_2)$ induces a linearisation δ with $\gamma_2 \sim \delta$ we obtain that at least two of the following three conditions are satisfied in $\mathcal{A}_\in$: $a \parallel_q b$, $b \parallel_q c$ and $a \parallel_p c$ where p is the uniquely determined state with $(q, b, p) \in T_2$ (by $a \parallel_q b$ or $b \parallel_q c$). An automaton with concurrency relations that satisfies all three statements is said to satisfy the inverse cube axiom (see below).

These two examples motivate the definition of stably concurrent automata. But first we have to define a (partial) transition function on $\mathcal{A}$ that describes the change of the state of an automaton in response to a finite sequence of events. Let $. : Q \times E^* \longrightarrow Q$ be the partial mapping defined by $p.w = q$ if there exists $\gamma \in CS(\mathcal{A})$ with $\dom \gamma = p$, $\operatorname{evs} \gamma = w$ and $\cod \gamma = q$. We write $p.w = \bot$ otherwise. To simplify the notation, we assume $\|_\bot = \emptyset$. Thus, for instance, $a \|_{q.b} c$ holds iff there exists a transition $(q, b, r) \in T$ with $a \|_r c$.

Definition 4. Let $\mathcal{A} = (Q, \mathcal{E}, T, \|)$ be an automaton with concurrency relations. $\mathcal{A}$ is called *stably concurrent*, if for all $q \in Q$ and all $a, b, c \in E$ the following equivalence holds:

$$a \|_q b, \ b \|_q c \text{ and } a \|_{q.b} c \iff a \|_q c, \ b \|_{q.a} c \text{ and } a \|_{q.c} b$$

The requirement of the implication " $\Rightarrow$ " has also been called cube axiom, and the implication " $\Leftarrow$ " is called the inverse cube axiom. Pictorially, the concurrency relations exhibited in Example 1 for $\mathcal{A}_\infty$ imply the ones depicted for $\mathcal{A}_\in$, and conversely. In various forms, these axioms arose several times in the literature, see *e.g.* [S89, PSS90, Dr90, Dr92, Ku94a, Ku94b].

Observe that the automaton induced by a trace alphabet is always stably concurrent.

Let $\mathcal{A}$ be an automaton with concurrency relations. For $\gamma, \delta \in CS(\mathcal{A})$ we define $\gamma \lesssim \delta$ if there exists a computation sequence η with $\gamma\eta \sim \delta$. Then $\lesssim$ is a preorder on $CS(\mathcal{A})$ such that $\gamma \lesssim \delta \lesssim \gamma$ holds iff γ and δ are equivalent. Therefore this preorder defines a partial order on $M(\mathcal{A})$ in the natural way: $[\gamma] \leq [\delta] :\iff \gamma \lesssim \delta$.

Proposition 5 [Ku94b]. *Let $\mathcal{A}$ be a stably concurrent automaton and $x \in M(\mathcal{A})$. Then $(\{y \in M(\mathcal{A}) \mid y \leq x\}, \leq)$ is a finite distributive lattice.*

Let $\mathcal{A}$ be an automaton with concurrency relations where for any computation sequence γ any order–preserving enumeration of the dependence order $DO(\gamma)$ induces a linearisation δ with $\gamma \sim \delta$. Example 1 implies that $\mathcal{A}$ is "almost" stably concurrent. Later we will see that any stably concurrent automaton has this property. By Prop. 5 we see that stably concurrent automata are closely related with finite distributive lattices. Therefore the following section is a short excursion into the field of finite distributive lattices.

3 Finite distributive lattices

In this section we recall, for the convenience of the reader, some basic definitions and results on partially ordered sets and on finite distributive lattices, *cf.* [Bi73] for proofs and further explanations.

Let $(P, \leq)$ be a partially ordered set (poset). Two elements x and y of P are *incomparable* (denoted by $x \| y$) if neither $x \leq y$ nor $y \leq x$ holds. For $x, y \in P$, we call y a *direct cover* of x (denoted $x \prec y$) if $x < y$ and there are no elements between x and y. The pair $\langle x, y \rangle$ is called a *prime interval*. Let $\langle x, y \rangle$ and $\langle x', y' \rangle$ be prime intervals. We say that $\langle x', y' \rangle$ is a *direct cover* of $\langle x, y \rangle$ iff

$x\!-\!\!<\!x'$, $y\!-\!\!<\!y'$ and $x' \neq y$. Let $>\!\!-\!\!<$ denote the smallest equivalence relation on the set of all prime intervals that contains $-\!\!<$.

For $x \in P$ let $x{\downarrow} := \{y \in P \mid y \leq x\}$ and $x{\uparrow} := \{y \in P \mid x \leq y\}$. A subset A of P is *downward closed* if $a{\downarrow} \subseteq A$ for any $a \in A$. Furthermore, x is the *supremum* (denoted $\bigvee A$) of A if it is the smallest upper bound. Dually, the infimum of A (denoted by $\bigwedge A$) is the largest lower bound.

$(P, \leq)$ is a *lattice* if the supremum and the infimum of any two elements exist and *distributive* if furthermore $x \vee (y \wedge z) = (x \vee y) \wedge (x \vee z)$ for any $x, y, z \in P$. Then $x \wedge (y \vee z) = (x \wedge y) \vee (x \wedge z)$, too.

Let $(L, \leq)$ be a finite lattice and $x \in L$. Let the *height of x* be the maximal cardinality of all totally ordered sets $C \leq x$. The *height* of $(L, \leq)$ is defined to be the height of the largest element of L. The element x is called *join-irreducible* if $\perp \neq x$ and if for all $a, b \in L$ the following implication holds:

$$x = a \vee b \implies x = a \text{ or } x = b.$$

Equivalently, there exists exactly one element $y \in L$ such that x is a direct cover of y. If $(L, \leq)$ is distributive, x is join–irreducible iff it is a complete prime (i.e. $\forall a, b \in L : x \leq a \vee b \implies x \leq a$ or $x \leq b$). The set of all join–irreducible elements of L is denoted by $\mathcal{J}(\mathcal{L}, \leq)$.

The following proposition describes the key properties of finite distributive lattices that will be used in our investigations frequently.

Proposition 6. *Let $(L, \leq)$ be a finite distributive lattice. Then for all $x \in L$, $x = \bigvee(x{\downarrow} \cap \mathcal{J}(\mathcal{L}, \leq))$ and x has height $|x{\downarrow} \cap \mathcal{J}(\mathcal{L}, \leq)|$. Indeed, if $M \subseteq \mathcal{J}(\mathcal{L}, \leq)$ is a downward closed set, then $\bigvee M$ has height $|M|$. In particular, the height of $(L, \leq)$ equals $|\mathcal{J}(\mathcal{L}, \leq)|$.*

4 Dependence orders

For all of this section, we assume that $\mathcal{A} = (\mathcal{Q}, \mathcal{E}, \mathcal{T}, \|)$ is a stably concurrent automaton.
In this section, we will introduce for $\gamma \in \mathrm{CS}(\mathcal{A})$ a labeled partial order $\mathrm{PR}(\gamma)$ and investigate its relationship with the labeled partial dependence order $\mathrm{DO}(\gamma)$ defined in Sect. 2.

Now we give the definition of $\mathrm{PR}(\gamma)$. By Prop. 5, $([\gamma]{\downarrow}, \leq)$ is a finite distributive lattice. Let $\Pr(\gamma) := \mathcal{J}([\gamma]{\downarrow}, \leq)$ be the set of all join–irreducible elements (or equivalently, all complete primes) of this lattice. For $x \in \Pr(\gamma)$ there exists a unique element $y \in \mathrm{M}(\mathcal{A})$ such that $y\!-\!\!<\!x$. Hence, we find a unique transition σ with $x = y \cdot [\sigma]$. Let $l_\gamma : \Pr(\gamma) \longrightarrow E$ be the function with $l_\gamma(x) := \mathrm{ev}\,\sigma$. Then $\mathrm{PR}(\gamma) := (\Pr(\gamma), \leq, l_\gamma, \mathrm{dom}\,\gamma)$ is a labeled partial order.

At first sight, this lpo $\mathrm{PR}(\gamma)$ has nothing to do with the lpo $\mathrm{DO}(\gamma)$. At the end of this section we will see that they are isomorphic in the following natural sense: We call two lpo's $(P_1, \leq_1, l_1, q_1)$ and $(P_2, \leq_2, l_2, q_2)$ *isomorphic*, if $q_1 = q_2$ and there is an order isomorphism $f : (P_1, \leq) \longrightarrow (P_2, \leq)$ such that $l_2(f(x)) = l_1(x)$ for any $x \in P_1$.

Theorem 7. *Let $\gamma \in \mathrm{CS}(\mathcal{A})$. Then $[\gamma] = \mathrm{Lin}(PR(\gamma))$. Furthermore, any order–preserving enumeration of $(\mathrm{Pr}(\gamma), \leq)$ induces a linearisation δ.*

Proof: We only prove the final statement and "$\supseteq$". Suppose that $A = (x_1, x_2, \ldots, x_n)$ is an order–preserving enumeration of $PR(\gamma)$. Since $x_i \in \mathrm{Pr}(\gamma)$ we find uniquely determined elements $x_i^- \in M(\mathcal{A})$ and transitions τ_i with $x_i = x_i^- \cdot [\tau_i]$ for $i = 1, 2, \ldots, n$. By definition, $l_\gamma(x_i) = \mathrm{ev}\, \tau_i$. Furthermore, let $y_i := \bigvee \{x_1, x_2, \ldots, x_i\} \in M(\mathcal{A})$ for $i = 1, 2, \ldots, n$. Also, put $y_0 := 1$. Let $i \in \{1, \ldots, n\}$. Since the sets $\{x_j \mid j \leq i - 1\}$ and $\{x_j \mid j \leq i\}$ are downward closed in $\mathrm{Pr}(\gamma)$ and differ in exactly one element, we have $y_{i-1} \prec y_i$ in $([\gamma]\!\downarrow, \leq)$. Thus, there exists a uniquely determined transition σ_i with $y_i = y_{i-1} \cdot [\sigma_i]$. Then $y_{i-1} \prec y_i = y_{i-1} \vee x_i$. Since $([\gamma]\!\downarrow, \leq)$ is distributive, this implies $y_{i-1} \wedge x_i \prec x_i$. Hence, $y_{i-1} \wedge x_i = x_i^-$, since x_i is join–irreducible. Thus we get $\langle y_{i-1}, y_i \rangle \succ\!\!\prec \langle x_i^-, x_i \rangle$. This implies $\mathrm{ev}\, \sigma_i = \mathrm{ev}\, \tau_i$.

Let $q_0 := \mathrm{dom}\, \gamma$ and $q_i = \mathrm{cod}\, \sigma_i$ for $1 \leq i \leq n$. For $i = 1$ we obtain $\sigma_1 = (q_0, \mathrm{ev}\, \tau_1, \mathrm{cod}\, \sigma_1) = (q_0, l_\gamma(x_1), q_1)$. For $i \in \{2, \ldots, n\}$ we get $\sigma_i = (\mathrm{cod}\, \sigma_{i-1}, \mathrm{ev}\, \tau_i, \mathrm{cod}\, \sigma_i) = (q_{i-1}, l_\gamma(x_i), q_i)$. Hence, $\delta := \sigma_1 \sigma_2 \ldots \sigma_n$ is a computation sequence with $\mathrm{dom}\, \delta = \mathrm{dom}\, \gamma$ and $\mathrm{evs}\, \delta = l_\gamma(x_1) l_\gamma(x_2) \ldots l_\gamma(x_n)$, i.e. δ is the linearisation of $PR(\gamma)$ induced by A. Since $y_i = y_{i-1}[\sigma_i]$ for $i = 1, 2, \ldots, n$, we obtain $[\delta] = [\sigma_1 \sigma_2 \ldots \sigma_n] = y_n = \bigvee_{i \leq n} x_i = [\gamma]$ and so $\gamma \sim \delta$. $\quad\Box$

While the dependence order $DO(\gamma)$ is computed using the set $\mathrm{evs}([\gamma])$, we defined $PR(\gamma)$ in terms of the finite distributive lattice $([\gamma]\!\downarrow, \leq)$. The following theorem shows that these two labeled partial orders are isomorphic.

Theorem 8. *Let $\gamma \in \mathrm{CS}(\mathcal{A})$. Then $DO(\gamma) \cong PR(\gamma)$.*

Proof: One can show that for any $a \in E$, the elements x of $\mathrm{Pr}(\gamma)$ with $l_\gamma(x) = a$ form a chain in $\mathrm{Pr}(\gamma)$. Let $x \in \mathrm{Pr}(\gamma)$. Define $n_\gamma(x) := |\{y \in \mathrm{Pr}(\gamma) \mid y \leq x, l_\gamma(x) = l_\gamma(y)\}|$, i.e. x is the $n_\gamma(x)$–th element of this chain. Obviously, $l_\gamma(x) = l_\gamma(y)$ and $n_\gamma(x) = n_\gamma(y)$ imply $x = y$. Thus, the mapping

$$f : \mathrm{Pr}(\gamma) \longrightarrow E \times \mathbb{N}$$
$$x \longmapsto l_\gamma(x)^{n_\gamma(x)}$$

is injective. Since (by Thm. 7) γ is a linearisation of $PR(\gamma)$, $|\{x \in \mathrm{Pr}(\gamma) \mid l_\gamma(x) = a\}| = |\gamma|_a$ for any $a \in E$. Hence we have $f(x) \in O(\gamma)$ for any $x \in \mathrm{Pr}(\gamma)$. Since $|O(\gamma)| = |\gamma| = |\mathrm{Pr}(\gamma)|$, f is a bijective mapping from $\mathrm{Pr}(\gamma)$ onto $O(\gamma)$ with $l_\gamma(x) = l(f(x))$. It remains to show that f is even an order–isomorphism.

Let $x, y \in \mathrm{Pr}(\gamma)$ with $x < y$. Let $\delta \in \mathrm{CS}(\mathcal{A})$ with $\gamma \sim \delta$. By Thm. 7 there exists an order–preserving enumeration $A = (x_1, x_2, \ldots, x_n)$ of $(\mathrm{Pr}(\gamma), \leq)$ that induces δ. Then $x = x_i$ and $y = x_j$ for some $i < j$, showing $l_\gamma(x)^{n_\gamma(x)} \sqsubseteq_\delta l_\gamma(y)^{n_\gamma(y)}$. Hence $f(x) \sqsubseteq f(y)$, i.e. f is order–preserving.

Assume conversely $f(x) \sqsubset f(y)$. Suppose $x \not< y$. Then there exists an order–preserving enumeration $A = (x_1, x_2, \ldots, x_n)$ with $x_i = x$ and $x_j = y$ and $j < i$. Let δ be the linearisation induced by A. Then $l_\gamma(y)^{n_\gamma(y)} \sqsubseteq_\delta l_\gamma(x)^{n_\gamma(x)}$, a contradiction to $f(x) \sqsubset f(y)$. Hence f is an order–isomorphism. $\quad\Box$

The following corollary summarizes the main results of this section.

Corollary 9. *Let* $\gamma, \delta \in \mathrm{CS}(\mathcal{A})$. *Then:*

$$\mathrm{DO}(\gamma) \cong \mathrm{DO}(\delta) \iff \gamma \sim \delta \iff \delta \in \mathrm{Lin}(\mathrm{DO}(\gamma)).$$

Considering automata induced by trace alphabets we obtain that the first equivalence in the corollary above generalizes [Ma85, Theorem 2.3.5]. The second equivalence generalizes [Ma85, Theorem 2.3.3].

5 Multiplication of lpo's

The aim of this section is to define a binary operation $\cdot$ such that $\mathrm{DO}(\gamma) \cdot \mathrm{DO}(\delta) \cong \mathrm{DO}(\gamma\delta)$ for $\gamma, \delta \in \mathrm{CS}(\mathcal{A})$ with $\mathrm{cod}\,\gamma = \mathrm{dom}\,\delta$. But first, we need the following definition.

Definition 10. Let $(P, \leq, l, q)$ be a lpo, A an order–preserving enumeration and $M \subseteq P$. Then $w_A(l, M) = l(z_1)l(z_2)\ldots l(z_m)$ where $(z_1, z_2, \ldots, z_m)$ is the subsequence of A with $M = \{z_1, z_2, \ldots, z_m\}$.

For $\gamma \in \mathrm{CS}(\mathcal{A})$ we have $\mathrm{cod}\,\gamma = (\mathrm{dom}\,\gamma).\mathrm{evs}\,\gamma$. Thus let A be any order–preserving enumeration of $\mathrm{DO}(\gamma)$. Then $\mathrm{cod}\,\gamma = \mathrm{dom}\,\delta$ iff $\mathrm{dom}\,\gamma.w_A(l_\gamma, O(\gamma)) = \mathrm{dom}\,\delta$.

Now let $\mathbb{P}_\sqsupset = (\mathbb{P}_\sqsupset, \sqsubseteq, <_\sqsupset, \|_\sqsupset)$ with $\mathbb{P}_{\not\nvdash} = \mathrm{DO}(\gamma)$ and $\mathbb{P}_{\not\vdash} = \mathrm{DO}(\delta)$ and A (B) an order–preserving enumeration of $\mathbb{P}_{\not\nvdash}$ $(\mathbb{P}_{\not\vdash})$. If $q_1.w_A(l_1, P_1) \neq q_2$ define $\mathbb{P}_{\not\nvdash} \cdot \mathbb{P}_{\not\vdash} := \not\vdash$. Now we consider the case $q_1.w_A(l_1, P_1) = q_2$. For $x \in P_1$ and $z \in P_2$ define $w(x, z) := w_A(l_1, P_1 \setminus x\!\uparrow)w_B(l_2, z\!\downarrow \setminus \{z\})$. Let

$$x \prec z \text{ iff not } l_1(x) \|_{q_1.w(x,z)} l_2(z).$$

On $P_1 \cup P_2$ we define $\sqsubseteq$ as the smallest partial order containing $\sqsubseteq_1$, $\sqsubseteq_2$ and $\prec$, i.e. $\sqsubseteq := (\sqsubseteq_1 \cup \prec \cup \sqsubseteq_2)^*$. Since $\prec$ is a subset of $P_1 \times P_2$ this equals $\sqsubseteq_1 \cup \sqsubseteq_2 \cup (\sqsubseteq_1 \circ \prec \circ \sqsubseteq_2)$.

Now we define the product of $\mathbb{P}_{\not\nvdash}$ and $\mathbb{P}_{\not\vdash}$ by putting

$$\mathbb{P}_{\not\nvdash} \cdot \mathbb{P}_{\not\vdash} := (\mathbb{P}_{\not\nvdash} \cup \mathbb{P}_{\not\vdash}, \sqsubseteq, <_{\not\nvdash} \cup <_{\not\vdash}, \|_{\not\nvdash}).$$

If $\mathcal{A}$ is the automaton induced by a trace alphabet, then we obviously have $x \prec z$ iff $(l_1(x), l_2(z)) \in D$. Hence our construction generalizes the construction known in trace theory (*cf.* [Ma85, p. 302]). Now we show:

Theorem 11. *Let $\mathcal{A}$ be a stably concurrent automaton and $\gamma, \delta \in \mathrm{CS}(\mathcal{A})$. Then $\mathrm{DO}(\gamma) \cdot \mathrm{DO}(\delta) \cong \mathrm{DO}(\gamma \cdot \delta)$.*

Proof: By Theorem 8, we have to show $\mathrm{PR}(\gamma) \cdot \mathrm{PR}(\delta) \cong \mathrm{PR}(\gamma \cdot \delta)$. If $\gamma\delta = 0$ we obtain $\mathrm{DO}(\gamma) \cdot \mathrm{DO}(\delta) = 0$ since $(\mathrm{dom}\,\gamma).w_A(l_\gamma, \mathrm{Pr}(\gamma)) = \mathrm{cod}\,\gamma \neq \mathrm{dom}\,\delta$ for any order–preserving enumeration A of $\mathrm{PR}(\gamma)$. Now suppose $\gamma\delta \neq 0$, i.e. $\mathrm{cod}\,\gamma = \mathrm{dom}\,\delta$.

Let $[\gamma] \leq x \leq [\gamma\delta]$. Since $M(\mathcal{A})$ is left–cancellative ([Dr92]), there exists a unique element $y \in M(\mathcal{A})$ with $[\gamma]y = x$. This computation y will be denoted by

$x \uparrow [\gamma]$ and called *residuum of x after* $[\gamma]$. As is easy to see, the map $\lambda x.x \uparrow [\gamma]$ is an order–isomorphism from $([[\gamma], [\gamma\delta]], \leq)$ to $([\delta]{\downarrow}, \leq)$. Then one can show that the function

$$f : \mathrm{Pr}(\gamma\delta) \longrightarrow \mathrm{Pr}(\gamma) \cup \mathrm{Pr}(\delta)$$

$$x \longmapsto \begin{cases} x & \text{if } x \leq [\gamma] \\ (x \vee [\gamma]) \uparrow [\gamma] & \text{else} \end{cases}$$

is the isomorphism searched for. □

In [BDK94] we give a characterization of all lpo's $\mathbb{P}$ over $\mathcal{A}$ such that there exists a computation sequence $\gamma \in \mathrm{CS}(\mathcal{A})$ with $\mathbb{P} \cong \mathrm{DO}(\gamma)$. We call these lpo's *nice lpo's*. This characterization enables us to show that DO is a monoid-isomorphism:

Theorem 12. *Let $\mathcal{A}$ be a stably concurrent automaton. Then* DO *and* PR *are isomorphisms (up to isomorphism between lpo's) from the monoid* $(\mathrm{M}(\mathcal{A}), \cdot)$ *to the monoid of all nice lpo's over $\mathcal{A}$ with the multiplication constructed above.*

Let $\mathcal{A}$ be the automaton induced by the trace alphabet (E, D). Then an lpo over $\mathcal{A}$ is nice iff it is the reflexive and transitive closure of a dependence graph over (E, D). Hence this theorem is a direct generalization of [Ma85, Theorem 2.3.6].

Finally we just note that several results of [Dr94a], *e.g.* a generalization of Levy's lemma, can now be proved pictorially using the previous results and graph–theoretic representations.

References

[AR88]   AALBERSBERG, I.J. and G. ROZENBERG: *Theory of traces.* Theor. Comp. Science 60 (1988), 1-82.

[Be87]   BEDNARCZYK, M.: *Categories of asynchronous systems.* Ph.D. thesis, University of Sussex, 1987.

[BC88]   BOUDOL, G. and I. CASTELLANI: *A non–interleaving semantics for CCS based on proved transitions.* Fundam. Inform. 11 (1988), 433–452.

[BR94]   BÖRGER, E. and D. ROSENZWEIG: *Occam: Specification and compiler correctness. Part I: Simple mathematical interpreters.* To appear.

[BD93]   BRACHO, F. and M. DROSTE: *From domains to automata with concurrency.* In: 20th ICALP, LNCS 700, Springer, 1993, pp. 669–681.

[BD94]   BRACHO, F. and M. DROSTE: *Labelled domains and automata with concurrency.* Theor. Comp. Science, in press.

[BDK94] BRACHO, F., M. DROSTE and D. KUSKE: *Representation of computations in concurrent automata by dependence orders.* Internal report of TU Dresden, MATH-AL-3-1994.

[Bi73]   BIRKHOFF, G.: *Lattice Theory.* AMS, Providence, 1973.

[Di90]   DIEKERT, V.: *Combinatorics on Traces.* LNCS 454, Springer, 1990.

[Dr90]   DROSTE, M.: *Concurrency, automata and domains.* In: *17th ICALP*, LNCS 443, Springer, 1990, pp. 195–208.

[Dr92]   DROSTE, M.: *Concurrent automata and domains.* Intern. J. of Found. of Comp. Science 3 (1992), 389–418.

478

[Dr94a] DROSTE, M.: *A Kleene theorem for recognizable languages over concurrency monoids.* In: 21st ICALP, LNCS 820, Springer 1994, pp. 388–399. (Full version to appear in Theor. Comp. Science)

[Dr94b] DROSTE, M.: *Aperiodic languages over concurrency monoids.* To appear.

[DS93] DROSTE, M. and R.M. SHORTT: *Petri nets and automata with concurrency relations – an adjunction.* In: *Semantics of Programming Languages and Model Theory* (M. Droste, Y. Gurevich, eds.), Gordon and Breach Science Publ., OPA (Amsterdam), 1993, 69–87.

[GRS92] GUAIANA, G., A. RESTIVO and S. SALEMI: *Star-free trace languages.* Theor. Comp. Science 97 (1992), 301–311.

[KP90] KATZ, S. and D. PELED: *Defining conditional independence using collapses.* In: *Semantics for Concurrency* (M.Z. Kwiatowska, M.W. Shields, R.M. Thomas, eds.), Proc. of the Int. BCS–FACS Workshop at Leicester, 1990, Springer, 262–280.

[Ku94a] KUSKE, D.: *Modelle nebenläufiger Prozesse – Monoide, Residuensysteme und Automaten.* Dissertation, Universität GHS Essen, 1994.

[Ku94b] KUSKE, D.: *Nondeterministic automata with concurrency relations.* Colloquium on Trees in Algebra and Programming, LNCS 787, Springer, 1994, 202–217.

[Le78] LEVY, J.J.: *Réductions correctes et optimales dans le λ-calcul.* Ph.D. Thesis, Université Paris VII, 1978.

[Ma77] MAZURKIEWICZ, A.: *Concurrent program schemes and their interpretation.* DAIMI Report PB–78, Aarhus University, Aarhus, 1977.

[Ma85] MAZURKIEWICZ, A.: *Trace theory.* In: *Advanced Course on Petri Nets*, LNCS 188, Springer, 1985, pp. 279–324.

[NRT92] NIELSEN, M., G. ROSENBERG and P.S. THIAGARAJAN: *Elementary transition systems.* Theor. Comp. Science 96 (1992), 3–33.

[Oc85] OCHMANSKI, E.: *Regular behaviour of concurrent systems*, Bull. Europ. Assoc. for Theoretical Computer Science 27 (1985), 56–67.

[PSS90] PANANGADEN, P., V. SHANBHOGUE and E.W. STARK: *Stability and sequentiability in dataflow networks.* In: *17th ICALP*, LNCS 443, Springer, 1990, pp. 308–321.

[S89] STARK, E.W.: *Connections between a concrete and an abstract model of concurrent systems.* In: *Proceedings of the 5th Conf. on the Mathematical Foundations of Programming Semantics*, LNCS 389, Springer, 1989, pp. 52–74.

[Wi87] WINSKEL, G.: *Event structures.* In: *Petri Nets: Applications and Relationships to Other Models of Concurrency* (W. Brauer, W. Reisig, G. Rozenberg, eds.), LNCS 255, Springer, 1987, pp. 325–392.

[WN94] WINSKEL, G. and M. NIELSEN: *Models for concurrency.* In: *Handbook of Logic in Computer Science* (S. Abramsky, D.M. Gabbay, T.S.E. Maibaum, eds.), to appear.

On the undecidability of deadlock detection in families of nets

Anne-Cécile Fabret[1] and Antoine Petit[2]

[1] Université Paris Sud, LRI, URA CNRS 410, Bât. 490, F-91405 Orsay Cedex,
fabret@lri.fr
[2] ENS Cachan, LIFAC, 61 av. Président Wilson, F-94235 Cachan Cedex,
petit@lifac.ens-cachan.fr

Abstract. In this paper, we are interested in modelization of some aspects of massively parallel computers built by connecting together copies of a unique given pattern. Thus, a natural and important question arises. Is it possible to verify that a property holds, not for one given configuration, but for all the configurations that can be constructed? Of course, the difficulty comes from the fact that the number of distinct configurations is infinite. We focus in this paper on the deadlock problem: can we verify that any net, constructed by connecting an arbitrary number of copies of the pattern, is deadlock free? As in a great number of models, the semantics of the pattern and thus the semantics of a net are given by finite transition systems. The main result of this paper proves that the deadlock problem is surprisingly undecidable.

1 Introduction

In this paper, we are interested in the modelization of some aspects of so-called massively parallel computers. These computers use a great number of processors connected together by a communication network. A large class of such machines, for instance Transputer based computers, are built in a modular way by connecting some cards together. Hence, an infinite number of configurations can be obtained from copies of a unique card. These configurations differ from the number of (copies of) cards that are used and from the topology under which these copies are connected.

Of course, such modular machines do not require, in general, distinct processes to be implemented on distinct cards. In contrary, in most cases, the same process is implemented on each card, containing communications or synchronizations with processes on adjacent cards (Specific programs can also require a bounded number of distinct processes to be implemented on the cards, depending for instance on the number of neighbours of the considered card). In the sequel, we will called pattern a card together with a process implemented on it. With such programming techniques, a larger number of patterns do not really change the underlying algorithm but rather the size of the possible data, the speed of the computation or the precision of the result.

Therefore a natural and important question arises. Assume that a pattern is given. If a configuration, built from this pattern, verifies some property, is it true that other (bigger) configurations, built from the same pattern, verify also this property. In other words, is it possible to verify that a property holds, not for one given configuration, but for all the configurations that can be constructed? Of course, the difficulty comes from the fact that the number of distinct configurations is infinite (and even not countable). Several papers consider this kind of problems, [CG87] and [SG87] deal with a very restricted class of network topologies, [BR85] study networks of communicating processes, [SG90] construct networks from graph grammars and consider properties described by temporal logic formulas. Note that, more generally, this idea to find a property which is verified for all the objects generated by some finite mechanism is current in computer science.

We focus in this paper on the deadlock problem: can we verify that any net, constructed by connecting an arbitrary number of patterns, is deadlock free? As in a great number of models, the semantics of the pattern is given by a finite transition system. The synchronizations between adjacent patterns are modelized by performing simultaneously the same action. Thus, the semantics of a given net can be constructed as a (big) finite transition system. A deadlock appears if there exists a state, reachable from an initial one, without outgoing transition. Therefore, the deadlock freeness of a given configuration can be detected. As we explained above, this procedure does not give any solution to verify that any configuration is deadlock free.

In [BCPVN91], the authors consider the particular case where the semantics of the pattern is a product of deterministic one-letter transition systems and they propose an algorithm to decide if any configuration built from such a pattern is deadlock-free. This decidability result depends closely on the very particular structure of the considered patterns.

Indeed, the main result of this paper proves that the deadlock problem is undecidable in general. Note that the undecidability does not come from exotic topology since this result remains true if we restrict ourselves to rectangular topologies. At least to our opinion, this result is quite surprising since all the parameters of the problem are very simple and regular: a unique pattern is considered and its semantics is given by a finite transition system.

The principle of the proof can be roughly described as follows. First, we show how the undecidability of the deadlock problem for nets built from several distinct patterns induces the undecidability of the deadlock problem for nets built from a unique pattern. For technical reasons, it is easier to prove first the undecidability in the case of several patterns. Then we consider a Turing machine and we construct a finite set of patterns associated with this machine. These patterns are built in such a way that there exists a net, constructed from these patterns, with deadlock if and only if there exists a successful computation in the Turing machine.

The remaining of the paper is organized as follows. Section 2 descibes the model we use and the notations. The deadlock problem is introduced in Section 3 where the main result and the principle of the proof are given. Section 4 presents a first coding by tiles, very closed from the one proposed in [Bea91], of a successful

481

computation of a Turing machine. The core of the proof is the construction of the patterns associated with each tile (Section 5) and the proof that there exists a net with deadlock if and only if there exists a successful computation in the Turing machine (Section 6). For length reasons, this draft does not contain proofs which can be found in the technical report [FP94].

2 The model

The nets that we consider in this paper are all built on the two dimension grid. Each point of this grid is defined by the pair $(x, y) \in \mathbb{Z} \times \mathbb{Z}$ of its coordinates (where $\mathbb{Z}$ is the set of negative and positive integers). The set of the four directions N, E, W, S is denoted by $\mathcal{D}ir$, furthermore we have $-N = S, -S = N,$ $-E = W$ and $-W = E$. Each point (x, y) of the grid has thus four neighbours, one in each direction. For any direction $d \in \mathcal{D}ir$, the notation $(x, y) + d$ denotes the coordinates of the neighbour in direction d of the point (x, y). For instance, the N-neighbour of a point (x, y) has $(x, y) + N = (x, y + 1)$ for coordinates. In this paper, we are mainly interested in nets constructed from a unique pattern. For technical reasons, we need to introduce a larger family of nets, those which are constructed from a finite set of patterns $\mathcal{P}at$. Precisely, a net n is just a mapping from a finite subset of $Z \times Z$, called the support of the net and denoted by $\text{supp}(n)$, into $\mathcal{P}at$. Since there is an infinite number of supports, an infinite family of nets $\mathcal{N}(\mathcal{P}at)$ can be constructed from a given finite set of patterns $\mathcal{P}at$. We are looking in this paper to the possibility or the unpossibility to derive, from the set $\mathcal{P}at$, the property that any net of the family $\mathcal{N}(\mathcal{P}at)$ is deadlock free. To define formally the notion of deadlock, we introduce now the semantics of the patterns and of a net.

We consider in the sequel a set of patterns $\mathcal{P}at = \{P_1, \ldots, P_h\}$. For any $i \in \{1, \ldots, h\}$, Int_i is the set of internal actions of P_i. For any $i, j \in \{1, \ldots, h\}$ $i \neq j$, $\text{Com}_{\{i,j\}}$ is the set of communication actions between P_i and P_j. We assume that the union of the sets Int_i is disjoint from the union of the sets $\text{Com}_{\{i,j\}}$. The semantics of each pattern P_i of $\mathcal{P}at$ is given by a finite transition system $(\Sigma_i, Q_i, \delta_i, I_i)$. The set Σ_i is the disjoint union of Int_i and of a set Synchro_i. This set Synchro_i is a subset of $\cup_j(\text{Com}_{\{i,j\}} \times \mathcal{D}ir)$ such that for any action $a \in \text{Com}_{\{i,j\}}$ and any direction $d \in \mathcal{D}ir$, if $(a, d) \in \text{Synchro}_i$ then $(a, -d) \in \text{Synchro}_j$. As usual, the set Q_i is the finite set of states, $I_i \subseteq Q_i$ is the subset of initial states and δ_i is the (non-deterministic) transition function from $\Sigma_i \times Q_i$ into the set of subsets of Q_i.

We can now present the semantics $\text{sem}(n)$ of a net $n : \text{supp}(n) \longrightarrow \mathcal{P}at$. Once again, the semantics is given by a transition system. For the sake of simplicity, any state s will be considered as a mapping from $\text{supp}(n)$ into $Q = \cup_{i \in \{1, \ldots, h\}} Q_i$ such that, for any $(x, y) \in \text{supp}(n)$, $s(x, y) \in Q_i$ if $n(x, y) = P_i$. The initial states are of course all the states of the form $s_0 : \text{supp}(n) \longrightarrow Q$ defined by, for any $(x, y) \in \text{supp}(n)$, $s_0(x, y) = q_0$ with $q_0 \in I_i$ and $n(x, y) = P_i$. The set of actions of the transition system is $\bigcup_{i \in \{1, \ldots, h\}} \text{Int}_i \cup \bigcup_{i, j \in \{1, \ldots, h\}} \text{Com}_{\{i,j\}}$. There exists a transition $s \xrightarrow{a} s'$ if and only if one of the two following situations holds.

1. A process of one pattern performs an internal action i.e. $\exists i \in \{1,\ldots,h\}$, $\exists (x,y) \in \text{supp}(n)$ such that $a \in \text{Int}_i$, $n(x,y) = P_i$ and $\delta_i(s(x,y),a) \neq \emptyset$. Therefore
   - $s'(x',y') = s(x,y)$ for any $(x',y') \in \text{supp}(n)$ with $(x',y') \neq (x,y)$
   - $s'(x,y) \in \delta_i(s(x,y),a)$

2. Two processes on neighbouring patterns execute a synchronization i.e. $\exists i,j \in \{1,\ldots,h\}$, $\exists(x,y) \in \text{supp}(n)$, $\exists d \in \mathcal{D}ir$ such that $(a,d) \in \text{Synchro}_i$, $n(x,y) = P_i$, $\delta_i(s(x,y),(a,d)) \neq \emptyset$, $n((x,y)+d) = P_j$ and $\delta_j(s((x,y)+d),(a,-d)) \neq \emptyset$ (note that, from the hypothesis on the sets Synchro, it holds thus $(a,-d) \in \text{Synchro}_j$).
   - $s'(x',y') = s(x,y)$ for any $(x',y') \in \text{supp}(n)$ with $(x',y') \neq (x,y)$ and $(x',y') \neq (x,y)+d$
   - $s'(x,y) \in \delta_i(s(x,y),(a,d))$
   - $s'((x,y)+d) \in \delta_j(s((x,y)+d),(a,-d))$

As usual, a network n is said to be deadlock-free if its semantics sem(n) does not contain a state, reachable from an initial one, without outgoing transition.

3 The result

Let $\mathcal{P}at$ be a finite set of patterns. For any given net n of $\mathcal{N}(\mathcal{P}at)$, it is of course possible to construct the semantics sem(n) from the semantics of the different patterns of $\mathcal{P}at$ and then to verify whether n is deadlock-free or not. But such a method can not be used for an infinite family of nets. In particular,

The deadlock problem: Given a pattern P, is any net of $\mathcal{N}(\{P\})$ deadlock-free?

remains open. In [BCPVN91], the authors studied the particular case where the semantics of the pattern is a product of deterministic single letter transition systems. They proved that in this particular case, it is decidable to know whether the family $\mathcal{N}(\{P\})$ contains a net with deadlock or not. The main result of this paper shows that this decidability depends closely on the structure of the pattern used. Namely, we claim:

Theorem 1. *The deadlock problem is undecidable.*

To prove this result, we will first show that the deadlock problem generalized to nets constructed from a finite set of patterns $\mathcal{P}at$ is undecidable. Then we obtain Theorem 1 using the next lemma.

Lemma 2. *If the deadlock problem generalized to nets constructed from a finite set of patterns $\mathcal{P}at$ is undecidable, then the deadlock problem is undecidable.*

The remaining of the paper is devoted to the proof that the deadlock problem generalized to nets constructed from a finite set of patterns $\mathcal{P}at$ is undecidable. The undecidability result is obtained by reducing the existence of a successful computation of a Turing machine to the existence of a non deadlock-free net. To this purpose, we use the coding of a successful computation of the Turing machine by an appropriate rectangle of symbols proposed in [Bea91]. Then we cover this rectangle with tiles of size 2×3. Conversely, we give a necessary and sufficient condition in order that a rectangle of tiles can be considered as a successful computation. Then we construct the patterns associated with each tile and we prove that there exists a net with deadlock if and only if the corresponding tiles form a successful computation of the Turing machine.

4 Coding of a successful computation

We recall that a Turing machine $\mathcal{M}$ is a 7-tuple $(Q, \Sigma, \Gamma, \delta, q_0, \flat, F)$ where

Q is a finite set of *states*,
Γ is the finite set of allowable *tape symbols* ; with $Q \cap \Gamma = \emptyset$,
$\flat \in \Gamma$ is the special *blank character*,
Σ, a subset of Γ not including $\flat$, is the set of *input symbols*,
δ is a finite *set of transitions* ; $\delta \subseteq Q \times \Gamma \times Q \times \Gamma \times \{L, R\}$ where symbols L, R (for left, right) denote the possible moves of the tape head,
$q_0 \in Q$ is the *initial state*,
$F \subseteq Q$, is the set of *final states*.

A *configuration* of $\mathcal{M}$ is a word $\alpha q \beta$ where $q \in Q$ is the current state of $\mathcal{M}$, $\alpha\beta \in \Gamma^*$ is the current content of the tape and the reading head points on the first symbol of β. A *successful computation* of $\mathcal{M}$ is a sequence $(c_1, \cdots, c_n)$ of words where c_i is the ith configuration of $\mathcal{M}$, the initial configuration c_1 is in $q_0 \Sigma^*$, the final configuration c_n is of the form $\alpha q_f \beta$ with $q_f \in F$ and we can pass from the configuration c_i, $i \in \{1, \cdots, n-1\}$, to the configuration c_{i+1} by a transition of δ.

We first recall the coding of a successful computation proposed in [Bea91]. Let $C = (c_1, \cdots, c_n)$ be a successful computation of $\mathcal{M}$ where $c_i = \alpha_i q_i \beta_i$ with $q_i \in Q$ for any $i \in \{1, \ldots, n\}$. We write the configurations one under the other in such a way that if in c_i, q_i has position j then, in c_{i+1}, q_{i+1} has position $j-1$ ($j+1$ resp.) if the move of the reading head in the transition from c_i to c_{i+1}, is L, (R resp.). Then, we complete each c_i with blank characters in order to obtain words of same length. At last, we board all the words with 2 blank characters on each side and a special new character $\# \notin Q \cup \Gamma$. The figure below represents the general form of the coding $\mathcal{C}od(C)$ of a successful computation C of $\mathcal{M}$.

$$
\begin{array}{cccccccccccccc}
\# & \# & \# & \# & \cdots & \# & \cdots & \# & \# & \cdots & \# & \# & \# & \# \\
\# & \flat & \flat & \flat & & & & q_0 & a_1 & \cdots & a_p & \flat & \flat & \# \\
\# & \flat & \flat & b_{2,1} & & & & q & \cdots & b_{2,m} & \flat & \flat & \# \\
& & & & \cdots & & & & & & & & & \\
\# & \flat & \flat & b_{n,1} & \cdots & q_f & & & & b_{n,m} & \flat & \flat & \# \\
\# & \# & \# & \# & \# & \# & \# & \# & \# & \# & \# & \# & \# & \#
\end{array}
$$

4.1 Covering by tiles

Let C be a successful computation of $\mathcal{M}$ and let $Cod(C)$ of size $(n+2) \times (m+6)$ be its coding as defined above. We scan $Cod(C)$ with a window of size 2×3. We start with the two first rows of $Cod(C)$ and we move the window from left to right of one position at each step. We thus obtain a sequence of $m + 4$ tiles. Then we repeat the operation with rows 2 and 3 and so on. Therefore we get $n + 1$ sequences. To summarize, the coding $Cod(C)$ is covered with a rectangle $\mathcal{R}_{Cod(C)} = (T_{i,j})_{1 \leq i \leq n+1, 1 \leq j \leq m+4}$ of tiles.

Let us remark that any pair $(T_{i,j}, T_{i,j+1})$ of adjacent tiles in a row of $\mathcal{R}_{Cod(C)}$ is *line compatible* i.e. the middle column of $T_{i,j}$ (the right column resp.) is equal to the left column (the middle column resp.) of $T_{i,j+1}$. In the same way, any pair $(T_{i,j}, T_{i+1,j})$ of adjacent tiles in a column is *column compatible* i.e. the second row of $T_{i,j}$ is equal to the first row of $T_{i+1,j}$.

$$
T_{i,j} \begin{array}{|c|c|c|}\hline a & b & c \\\hline d & e & f \\\hline\end{array}
\qquad
T_{i,j+1} \begin{array}{|c|c|c|}\hline b & c & d \\\hline e & f & k \\\hline\end{array}
$$

$$
T_{i+1,j} \begin{array}{|c|c|c|}\hline d & e & f \\\hline g & h & i \\\hline\end{array}
\qquad
T_{i+1,j+1} \begin{array}{|c|c|c|}\hline e & f & k \\\hline h & i & l \\\hline\end{array}
$$

Since the sets Q and Γ are finite, only a finite number of distinct tiles can appear in the covering of (the coding of) any successful computation of $\mathcal{M}$. We denote this set by $\mathcal{T}_\mathcal{M}$. It can be partitioned in three subsets F, M, L. The subset F (resp. L) contains the tiles that may appear during the scanning of the first row (resp. the last row) and M contains the remaining tiles. The set F can be split in 12 pairly disjoint subsets, the elements of each of these subsets are described below.

$$
F_{init} \begin{array}{|c|c|c|}\hline \# & \# & \# \\\hline \# & b & b \\\hline\end{array}
\quad
F_b \begin{array}{|c|c|c|}\hline \# & \# & \# \\\hline b & b & b \\\hline\end{array}
\quad
F_q \begin{array}{|c|c|c|}\hline \# & \# & \# \\\hline b & b & q_0 \\\hline\end{array}
\quad
F_{1,1} \begin{array}{|c|c|c|}\hline \# & \# & \# \\\hline b & q_0 & b \\\hline\end{array}
$$

$$
F_{1,2} \begin{array}{|c|c|c|}\hline \# & \# & \# \\\hline q_0 & b & b \\\hline\end{array}
\quad
F_{2,1} \begin{array}{|c|c|c|}\hline \# & \# & \# \\\hline b & q_0 & a \\\hline\end{array}
\quad
F_{2,2} \begin{array}{|c|c|c|}\hline \# & \# & \# \\\hline q_0 & a & b \\\hline\end{array}
\quad
F_4 \begin{array}{|c|c|c|}\hline \# & \# & \# \\\hline a & b & b \\\hline\end{array}
$$

$$
F_{3,1} \begin{array}{|c|c|c|}\hline \# & \# & \# \\\hline q_0 & a & b \\\hline\end{array}
\quad
F_{3,3} \begin{array}{|c|c|c|}\hline \# & \# & \# \\\hline a & b & b \\\hline\end{array}
\quad
F_{3,2} \begin{array}{|c|c|c|}\hline \# & \# & \# \\\hline a & b & c \\\hline\end{array}
\quad
F_{end} \begin{array}{|c|c|c|}\hline \# & \# & \# \\\hline b & b & \# \\\hline\end{array}
$$

where $a, b, c \in \Sigma$. Let us denote $F_{oth} = F \setminus (F_{init} \cup F_b \cup F_q \cup F_{end})$. In the same way, the set M can be split in the following 12 subsets.

$$
M_{3,11} \begin{array}{|c|c|c|}\hline a & b & p \\\hline a & b & c \\\hline\end{array}
\quad
M_{3,12} \begin{array}{|c|c|c|}\hline a & p & b \\\hline a & c & q \\\hline\end{array}
\quad
M_{q,13} \begin{array}{|c|c|c|}\hline p & b & c \\\hline a & q & c \\\hline\end{array}
\quad
M_{3,14} \begin{array}{|c|c|c|}\hline a & b & c \\\hline q & b & c \\\hline\end{array}
$$

$$
M_{3,21} \begin{array}{|c|c|c|}\hline a & b & c \\\hline a & b & q \\\hline\end{array}
\quad
M_{3,22} \begin{array}{|c|c|c|}\hline a & b & p \\\hline a & q & b \\\hline\end{array}
\quad
M_{q,23} \begin{array}{|c|c|c|}\hline a & p & b \\\hline q & a & c \\\hline\end{array}
\quad
M_{3,24} \begin{array}{|c|c|c|}\hline p & b & d \\\hline a & c & d \\\hline\end{array}
$$

$$
M_{3,3} \begin{array}{|c|c|c|}\hline a & c & d \\\hline b & c & d \\\hline\end{array}
\quad
M_2 \begin{array}{|c|c|c|}\hline a & b & c \\\hline a & b & c \\\hline\end{array}
\quad
M_{init} \begin{array}{|c|c|c|}\hline \# & b & b \\\hline \# & b & b \\\hline\end{array}
\quad
M_{end} \begin{array}{|c|c|c|}\hline b & b & \# \\\hline b & b & \# \\\hline\end{array}
$$

where $a, b, c, d \in \Gamma$ et $p, q \in Q$. Moreover any tile in $M_{q,13}$ and $M_{q,23}$ has to be compatible with the transitions of $\mathcal{M}$. More precisely, $\begin{array}{|c|c|c|}\hline p & c & a \\\hline b & q & a \\\hline\end{array} \in M_{q,13}$ iff $(p, c, q, b, R) \in \delta$ and $\begin{array}{|c|c|c|}\hline a & p & b \\\hline q & a & c \\\hline\end{array} \in M_{q,23}$ iff $(p, b, q, c, L) \in \delta$ with $a, b, c \in \Gamma$ et $p, q \in Q$.

Let us denote $M_q = M_{q,13} \cup M_{q,23}$ and $M_{oth} = M \setminus (M_{init} \cup M_q \cup M_{end})$.

At last, the set L is split in 6 subsets.

$$L_{init} \quad \begin{array}{|c|c|c|} \hline \# & b & b \\ \hline \# & \# & \# \\ \hline \end{array} \qquad L_{3,1} \quad \begin{array}{|c|c|c|} \hline a & b & q_f \\ \hline \# & \# & \# \\ \hline \end{array} \qquad L_q \quad \begin{array}{|c|c|c|} \hline q_f & a & b \\ \hline \# & \# & \# \\ \hline \end{array}$$

$$L_2 \quad \begin{array}{|c|c|c|} \hline a & b & c \\ \hline \# & \# & \# \\ \hline \end{array} \qquad L_{3,2} \quad \begin{array}{|c|c|c|} \hline a & q_f & b \\ \hline \# & \# & \# \\ \hline \end{array} \qquad L_{end} \quad \begin{array}{|c|c|c|} \hline b & b & \# \\ \hline \# & \# & \# \\ \hline \end{array}$$

where $a, b, c \in \Gamma$ and $q_f \in F$. Let us denote $L_{oth} = L_2 \cup L_{3,1} \cup L_{3,2}$.

A rectangle $\mathcal{R}$ of tiles of $\mathcal{T}_{\mathcal{M}}$ is said *valid* if there exists some successful computation C of $\mathcal{M}$ such that $\mathcal{R}_{Cod(C)} = \mathcal{R}$. From the definition of the sets F, M and L, it is immediate to verify that a rectangle $\mathcal{R} = (T_{i,j})_{1 \leq i \leq n, 1 \leq j \leq m}$ of tiles is valid if and only if

1. Any pair $(T_{i,j}, T_{i+1,j})$ of adjacent tiles in a column is column compatible
2. Any pair $(T_{i,j}, T_{i,j+1})$ of adjacent tiles in a row of $\mathcal{R}$ is line compatible
3. The first row $(T_{1,j})_{1 \leq j \leq m}$ denotes a word of

$$F_{init} F_b^* F_q (F_{1,1} F_{1,2} + F_{2,1} F_{2,2} F_4 + F_{2,1} F_{3,2}^* F_{3,3} F_4) F_b^* F_{end}$$

4. The last row $(T_{n,j})_{1 \leq j \leq m}$ denotes a word of

$$L_{init} L_2^* L_{3,1} L_{3,2} L_q L_2^* L_{end}$$

5. Any middle row $(T_{i,j})_{1 \leq j \leq m, 2 \leq i \leq n-1}$ denotes a word of

$$M_{init} M_2^* (M_{3,11} M_{3,12} M_{q,13} M_{3,14} + M_{3,21} M_{3,22} M_{q,23} M_{3,24} M_{3,3}) M_2^* M_{end}$$

We will use in the sequel another characterization of valid rectangles given by the following lemma. Its proof can be obtained without difficulty from the first characterization.

Lemma 3. *Let $\mathcal{M}$ be a Turing machine, let $\mathcal{T}_{\mathcal{M}}$ be its set of associated tiles and let $\mathcal{R} = (T_{i,j})_{1 \leq i \leq n, 1 \leq j \leq m}$ be a rectangle of tiles. Then $\mathcal{R}$ is valid if and only if*

1. *Any pair $(T_{i,j}, T_{i+1,j})$ of adjacent tiles in a column is column compatible*
2. *Any pair $(T_{i,j}, T_{i,j+1})$ of adjacent tiles in a row of $\mathcal{R}$ is line compatible*
3. *The first row $(T_{1,j})_{1 \leq j \leq m}$ denotes a word of $F_{init} F_b^* F_q (F_b + F_{oth})^* F_{end}$*
4. *The last row $(T_{n,j})_{1 \leq j \leq m}$ contains a unique tile of L_q.*
5. *Any middle row $(T_{i,j})_{1 \leq j \leq m, 2 \leq i \leq n-1}$ contains a unique element of M_q.*

5 Patterns associated with tiles

This Section is the core of our paper. We will associate with any Turing machine $\mathcal{M}$, a set $\mathcal{P}at_\mathcal{M}$ of patterns in such a way that $\mathcal{M}$ admits a successful computation if and only if there is a net with deadlock in $\mathcal{N}(\mathcal{P}at_\mathcal{M})$. This set $\mathcal{P}at_\mathcal{M}$ is defined through the set of tiles $\mathcal{T}_\mathcal{M}$ introduced in the previous section : one or two patterns are associated with each tile. The synchronizations between patterns are built in such a way that a net of $\mathcal{N}(\mathcal{P}at_\mathcal{M})$ presents a deadlock only if the corresponding tiles verify conditions of Lemma 3 and thus form a valid rectangle.

Let us illustrate the principle of these synchronizations on a small example. Let T, T' be two tiles, let d be the second row of T and let u' be the first row of T'. In order to test whether (T, T') is column compatible, we construct the following net n. The support of n is $\{(0,0),(0,1)\}$ and $n(0,0) = P$, $n(0,1) = P'$ where the semantics of the patterns are given by the picture below. The action λ is internal.

Then the transitions (d, W) and (u', E) can be fired if and only if $d = u'$. Therefore, the state $(2, 2')$ is reachable from the initial state of $\text{sem}(n)$, and thus the net n presents a deadlock, if and only if the pair of tiles (T, T') is column compatible.

The above principle is general in our algorithm. The synchronizations will be possible if and only if the conditions of Lemma 3 are fulfilled. If a condition is not verified, then the only possible behavior of the pattern will be to go in its state *Internal* and to perform an internal action indefinitely (and thus this pattern will not be in deadlock). On the contrary, if all the conditions are verified then the patterns will all reach the state *Deadlock*.

We present now the patterns associated with the tiles. Explanations on the behavior of the patterns are proposed just after this technical description. Each pattern is an instance of one the 6 parametrized transition systems presented in Figures 1,2,3 and 4 below where the action λ is the unique internal action.

The instances of the transition systems will use the following notations. Let T be a tile $\begin{array}{|c|c|c|}\hline a & b & c \\\hline d & e & f \\\hline\end{array}$, we note u (d resp.), the first row $\begin{array}{|c|c|c|}\hline a & b & c \\\hline\end{array}$ (the second row $\begin{array}{|c|c|c|}\hline d & e & f \\\hline\end{array}$ resp.) of T and we note l (r resp.) the first two columns $\begin{array}{|c|c|}\hline a & b \\\hline d & e \\\hline\end{array}$ (the last two columns $\begin{array}{|c|c|}\hline b & c \\\hline e & f \\\hline\end{array}$ resp.) of T. In the sequel, doted or double doted letters denote copies of a given letter. For instance, r' and r'', are copies of r. The two letters q and $\bar{q}$ represent informations about the detection of patterns associated with tiles in F_q, M_q or L_q. The set of patterns $\mathcal{P}at_\mathcal{M}$ associated with the tiles of $\mathcal{T}_\mathcal{M}$ is formally defined as follows:

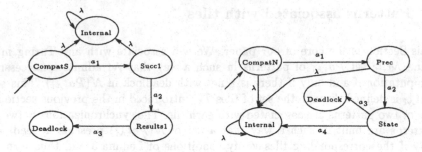

Fig. 1. Functions $f_1^{W \to E}(a_1, \cdots, a_3)$ and $f_4(a_1, \cdots, a_4)$

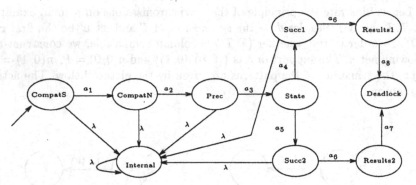

Fig. 2. Function $f_2^{W \to E}(a_1, \cdots, a_8)$

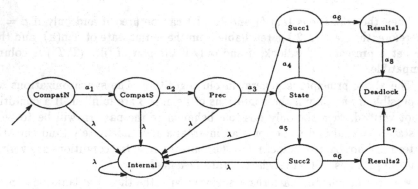

Fig. 3. Function $f_2^{E \to W}(a_1, \cdots, a_8)$

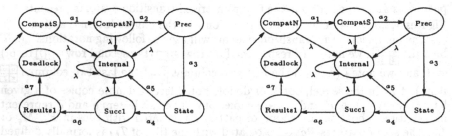

Fig. 4. Functions $f_3^{W \to E}(a_1, \cdots, a_7)$ and $f_3^{E \to W}(a_1, \cdots, a_7)$

$$T \in F_{init} \;\mapsto\; P^{W \to E} = f_1^{W \to E}((d,S),(r',E),(\overline{q},E))$$

$$T \in F_{\flat} \;\mapsto\; P^{W \to E} = f_2^{W \to E}((d,S),\lambda,(l',W),(q,W),(\overline{q},W),(r',E),(\overline{q},E),(q,E))$$

$$T \in F_q \;\mapsto\; P^{W \to E} = f_3^{W \to E}((d,S),\lambda,(l',W),(\overline{q},W),(q,W),(r',E),(q,E))$$

$$T \in F_{oth} \;\mapsto\; P^{W \to E} = f_3^{W \to E}((d,S),\lambda,(l',W),(q,W),(\overline{q},W),(r',E),(q,E))$$

$$T \in F_{end} \;\mapsto\; P^{W \to E} = f_3^{W \to E}((d,S),\lambda,(l',W),(q,W),(\overline{q},W),(d'',S),(\overline{q},S))$$

$$T \in M_{init} \;\mapsto\; \{P^{W \to E} = f_3^{W \to E}((d,S),(u,N),(u',N),(\overline{q},N),(q,N),(r',E),(\overline{q},E))$$
$$P^{E \to W} = f_3^{E \to W}((u,N),(d,S),(r'',E),(q,E),(\overline{q},E),(d',S),(\overline{q},S))\}$$

$$T \in M_{oth} \;\mapsto\; \{P^{W \to E} = f_2^{W \to E}((d,S),(u,N),(l',W),(q,W),(\overline{q},W),(r',E),(\overline{q},E),(q,E))$$
$$P^{E \to W} = f_2^{E \to W}((u,N),(d,S),(r'',E),(q,E),(\overline{q},E),(l'',W),(\overline{q},W),(q,W))\}$$

$$T \in M_q \;\mapsto\; \{P^{W \to E} = f_3^{W \to E}((d,S),(u,N),(l',W),(\overline{q},W),(q,W),(r',E),(q,E))$$
$$P^{E \to W} = f_3^{E \to W}((u,N),(d,S),(r'',E),(\overline{q},E),(q,E),(l'',W),(q,W))\}$$

$$T \in M_{end} \;\mapsto\; \{P^{W \to E} = f_3^{W \to E}((d,S),(u,N),(l',W),(q,W),(\overline{q},W),(d'',S),(\overline{q},S))$$
$$P^{E \to W} = f_3^{E \to W}((u,N),(d,S),(u'',N),(\overline{q},N),(q,N),(l'',W),(\overline{q},W))\}$$

$$T \in L_{init} \;\mapsto\; \{P^{W \to E} = f_3^{W \to E}(\lambda,(u,N),(u',N),(\overline{q},N),(q,N),(r',E),(\overline{q},E))$$
$$P^{E \to W} = f_4((u,N),(r'',E),(q,E),(\overline{q},E))\}$$

$$T \in L_{oth} \;\mapsto\; \{P^{W \to E} = f_2^{W \to E}(\lambda,(u,N),(l',W),(q,W),(\overline{q},W),(r',E),(\overline{q},E),(q,E))$$
$$P^{E \to W} = f_2^{E \to W}((u,N),\lambda,(r'',E),(q,E),(\overline{q},E),(l'',W),(\overline{q},W),(q,W))\}$$

$$T \in L_q \;\mapsto\; \{P^{W \to E} = f_3^{W \to E}(\lambda,(u,N),(l',W),(\overline{q},W),(q,W),(r',E),(q,E))$$
$$P^{E \to W} = f_3^{E \to W}((u,N),\lambda,(r'',E),(\overline{q},E),(q,E),(l'',W),(q,W))\}$$

$$T \in L_{end} \;\mapsto\; \{P^{W \to E} = f_4((u,N),(l',W),(q,W),(\overline{q},W))$$
$$P^{E \to W} = f_3^{E \to W}((u,N),\lambda,(u'',N),(\overline{q},N),(q,N),(l'',W),(\overline{q},W))\}$$

Given a net n with rectangular support $[x_1, x_2] \times [y_1, y_2]$, we define a total order between the points of the support in the following way. We scan row after row, alternatively from West to East and from East to West, beginning with row y_2 from West to East. With this order, each point of the support (excepted (x_1, y_2) and either (x_1, y_1) or (x_2, y_1)) has exactly one predecessor and one successor. We will illustrate the behaviors of the algorithm on the example of a pattern $P = P^{W \to E}$ associated with a tile of type M_{oth}.

1. The pattern P tests its compatibility with its south-neighbour and thus its north-neighbour by synchronizations from states *CompatS* and *CompatN*. This tests correspond to the verification of column compatibility. If one of these tests fail then the pattern reachs its state *Internal* and there is no deadlock.

2. The pattern P tests its compatibility with its predecessor by a synchronization from its state *Prec*. If this synchronisation is possible then the predecessor is necessarily in its state *Succ*1 or *Succ*2.

3. The pattern P tries to execute a synchronization with its predecessor from the state *State* to detect if some pattern with type M_q precedes it or not in the row. If a pattern M_q precedes it, the synchronization is made from the state *State* to the state *Succ*1 (and the predecessor goes from *Results*1 to *Deadlock*) otherwise, this synchronization is performed from *State* to *Succ*2 (and the predecessor goes from *Results*2 to *Deadlock*).

4. The pattern P synchronizes from its state *Succ*1 or *Succ*2 with its successor in the same way that its predecessor synchronizes with him in point 2. Once again if the test fails, the pattern reachs its state *Internal*.

5. The pattern P synchronizes once more with its successor to indicate to it if M_q precedes the successor in the row (this point in analogous to point 3).

6 Proof of the theorem

6.1 If $\mathcal{M}$ halts, then $\mathcal{N}(\mathcal{P}at_{\mathcal{M}})$ contains net with deadlock

Let C be a successful computation of $\mathcal{M}$. We construct a net of $\mathcal{N}(\mathcal{P}at_{\mathcal{M}})$ in the following way. We start from the valid rectangle $\mathcal{R}_{Cod(C)}$ and we associate with each tile T a pattern P as defined above (when necessary, $P^{W \to E}$ is choiced for tiles of odd rows whereas $P^{E \to W}$ for tiles of even rows). It can be verified without difficulty that the patterns succeed all their tests before being locked in their states *Deadlock*. Hence the net presents a global deadlock.

6.2 If $\mathcal{N}(\mathcal{P}at_{\mathcal{M}})$ contain a net with deadlock then $\mathcal{M}$ halts

We assume that a net n of $\mathcal{N}(\mathcal{P}at_{\mathcal{M}})$ is given and that this net presents a deadlock. By studying precisely their structures, it can be shown that the patterns can be locked only in their states *Deadlock*.

Assume now that all the patterns of n are in their *Deadlock* state. We show that necessarily the support of n is a rectangle and that the tiles associated with the patterns verify the conditions of Lemma 3 and thus correspond to a successful computation of $\mathcal{M}$.

First, note that, in this case, all the patterns have fired the transitions testing the row and column-compatibilities. It is also easy to verify that there must be a pattern associated with F_{init} in the net. Otherwise there is at least one pattern which has to reach its state *Internal*. For analogous reasons, all the patterns of the sides have to be present in the net. From this observations, it can be shown that the tiles associated with the net n form a rectangle which verifies Lemma 3. Thus the Turing machine $\mathcal{M}$ admits a successful computation.

In conclusion, the Turing machine $\mathcal{M}$ halts if and only if the family of nets $\mathcal{N}(\mathcal{P}at_{\mathcal{M}})$ contains a net with deadlock and, using Lemma 2, Theorem 1 is proved.

7 Conclusion

We have proved that the deadlock problem is undecidable in the case of networks built in a modular way from a unique pattern. We emphasize once more on the fact that this result is, at least to our opinion, very surprising since the semantics of the pattern that we consider is a finite transition system.

In this draft, we consider only the case of global deadlock. In the case of local deadlocks, the deadlock problem remains undecidable. The proof is very similar, it suffices to construct the semantics of the patterns in such a way that any local deadlock implies the existence of a (later) global deadlock. Roughly, we add to the transition systems that we consider in this draft some transitions to inform the predecessors of a process that a an error has been found in the computation (see [FP94] for more details).

As suggested by one of the referees, the dominoes problem (see e.g. [Ber66, LP81]) can also be used to prove our main result (Theorem 1). The proof in this new framework is easier to explain but requires some supplementary technical work that we did not yet achieve for lack of time. Therefore the reduction to the dominoes problem has not been included in these proceedings and will be presented in a full version to appear elsewhere.

References

[Bea91]   D. Beauquier. An undecidable problem about rational sets and contour words of polyominoes. *Information Processing Letters*, 37:257-263, 1991.

[BCPVN91] J.Beauquier, A. Choquet, A. Petit and G. Vidal-Naquet. Detection of deadlocks in an infinite family of nets. *Proceedings of STACS'91*, LNCS 480:334-347, 1991.

[LP81]   H.R.Lewis and C.H.Papadimitriou. Elements of the Theory of Computation. Prentice-Hall, 1981.

[Ber66]   R. Berger. The undecidability of the domino problem. *Memoirs of the American Mathematical Society*, 66, 1966.

[BR85]   Brookes and Roscoe. Deadlock analysis in networks of communicating process. *Logic and Models of Concurrent Systems*, NATO ASI series F, Vol. 13, 1985.

[CG87]   E. M. Clarke and O. Grumberg. Avoiding the State Explosion in Temporal Logic Model Checking Algorithms. *Proceedings of PODC'87*, ACM, 294-303, 1987.

[FP94]   A.-C. Fabret and A. Petit. On the undecidability of deadlock detection in families of nets. *Technical Report*, LIFAC, ENS Cachan, 1994.

[SG90]   Z. Shtadler and O. Grumberg. Networks Grammars, Communication Behaviors and Automatic Verification. *Proceedings of CAV'90*, LNCS-407:151-165, 1990.

[SG87]   A. P. Sistla and S. German. Reasoning with many processes. *Proceedings of LICS'87*, 1987.

On the Average Running Time of
Odd-Even Merge Sort

Christine Rüb[1]

Max-Planck-Institut für Informatik, Im Stadtwald, D-66123 Saarbrücken,
rueb@mpi-sb.mpg.de

Abstract. This paper is concerned with the average running time of
Batcher's odd-even merge sort when implemented on a collection of
processors. We consider the case where the size n of the input is an
arbitrary multiple of the number p of processors used. We show that
Batcher's odd-even merge (for two sorted lists of length m each) can be
implemented to run in time $O((m/p)(1 + \log(1 + p^2/m)))$ on the average, and that odd-even merge sort can be implemented to run in time
$O((n/p)(\log(n/p) + \log p(1 + \log(1 + p^2/n))))$ on the average. In the case
of merging (sorting) the average is taken over all possible outcomes of the
merging (all possible permutations of n elements). That means that odd-
even merge and odd-even merge sort have an optimal average running
time if $n \geq p^2$.

1 Introduction

This paper is concerned with a long-known parallel algorithm for sorting, namely
Batcher's odd-even merge sort. Originally this algorithm was described as a
comparator network of size $O(n \log^2 n)$ that sorts n elements in time $O(\log^2 n)$ [1,
11]. However, it can also be used as a sorting procedure on a parallel computer. In
this case there will, in general, be less processors than input elements. Odd-even
merge can then be implemented by substituting all comparisons (and exchanges)
between two elements by splits of two sorted lists at the median of their union (for
details see Section 2). If this is done in a straightforward way (that means, two
processors that have to communicate exchange all their elements), the running
time will be $\Theta((n/p)(\log(n/p) + \log^2 p))$, where p is the number of processors
used.

In practice, when comparing different sorting algorithms [4, 9, 6], odd-even
merge sort has not been used often. Instead, another sorting algorithm proposed
by Batcher [1], namely bitonic merge sort, has been used in the comparisons.
Because of its small constant factors, bitonic merge sort is quite efficient on
many parallel machines. One reason that has been mentioned for this preference
of bitonic merge sort is that odd-even merge sort is not as composable [3].

In this paper we will show, however, that odd-even merge sort can be implemented (by keeping the communication between processors at a minimum)
such that it performs on the average much better than bitonic merge sort. More
precisely, we will show that the average running time of odd-even merge sort can

be $O((n/p)(\log(n/p) + \log p(1 + \log(1 + p^2/n))))$ (with small constant factors), whereas the average running time of bitonic merge sort is $\Theta((n/p)(\log(n/p) + \log^2 p)$. (Here n is the size of the input and p is the number of processors used. The average is taken over all possible ways to store the input elements evenly distributed among the processors.) In particular, odd-even merge sort needs on the average much less communication than bitonic merge sort; this is important since communication is still relatively expensive on existing parallel machines. (Here we assume that all required connections between processors are present, e.g., that the processors from a completely connected graph. In Section 4 we will comment on this and present some implementation results.)

To my surprise, I could not find a reference to this result in the literature. (Perhaps this is the case because odd-even merge sort has not been used often in practice.) There do exist several papers about the average number of exchanged elements for the comparator network, i.e., for the case that $n = p$ [14, 8, 12]. In these papers it is shown that odd-even merge for two sorted lists of length m each needs $\Theta(m \log m)$ exchanges of elements. Another related result is presented in [2]. The authors consider an algorithm (called Gray Sort) for sorting n elements using p processors that consists of $\log p$ phases. Each phase consists of the first and the last step of (several instances of) odd-even merge on subsets of the processors. (The authors seem not to be aware of this; odd-even merge is not mentioned in the paper.) They show that this algorithm sorts with high probability if $n \geq cp^2 \log p$ for a constant $c > 18 * \ln(2)$.

This paper is organized as follows. In Section 2 we analyze the average running time of odd-even merge. These results are used to derive an upper bound for odd-even merge sort in Section 3. Section 4 contains implementation results and draws some conclusions.

2 The average running time of Odd-Even Merge

In this section we analyze the average running time of odd-even merge on a collection of processors. We consider the following machine model: Given are p processors, each with its own local memory. The processors communicate by exchanging messages. For ease of explanation, we assume in this and the following section that the processors form a complete graph, i.e., each pair of processors is connected (we will comment on this in Section 4). However, in one step, a processor may only communicate with one of its neighbours. At the beginning the elements are distributed evenly among the processors. We assume that every outcome of the merging is equally likely, and that p is a power of 2.

We use the following argument. Consider the odd-even merging network for two sorted lists of $p/2$ elements each. It consists of $\log p$ steps where elements are compared and rearranged. We can use this procedure to merge two sorted lists of length m each using p processors by substituting all comparisons (and exchanges) between two elements by splits of two sorted lists at the median of their union (for details see below). If this is done in a straightforward way (that means, two processors that have to communicate exchange all their elements), the running time will be $\Theta((m/p)\log p)$. However, the average running time of an implementation can be reduced considerably if the splitting of lists is done in a more efficient way, i.e., if the communication between processors is kept to a minimum. For example, if two processors have to communicate in a step, they first test whether they hold any elements that have to be exchanged. If this is the case for any pair of processors that communicate in a given step we say this step is *executed*. We will see that if m is large enough, with high probability only few of the $\log p$ steps of odd-even merge will be executed. More precisely, we show that the average number of steps executed by odd-even merge is $O(1 + \log(1 + p^2/m))$. From this follows that the average running time of this implementation of odd-even merge is $O((m/p)(1 + \log(1 + p^2/m)))$.

Odd-even merge works as follows:

Let $A = A_0, A_1, A_2, ..., A_{m-1}$ and $B = B_0, B_1, B_2, ..., B_{m-1}$ be the two sequences to be merged and denote by $E_0, ..., E_{2m-1}$ the outcome of the merging.

If $m = 1$, compare and exchange, if necessary, A_0 and B_0. Else merge recursively sublists of A and B containing only elements with even or with odd indexes. More precisely, merge $A_{\text{even}} = A_0, A_2, A_4, ...$ with $B_{\text{even}} = B_0, B_2, B_4, ...$ into $C = C_0, C_1, C_2, ...$ and $A_{\text{odd}} = A_1, A_3, ...$ with $B_{\text{odd}} = B_1, B_3, ...$ into $D = D_0, D_1, D_2, ...$ After this is done, compare and exchange, if necessary, D_i with C_{i+1} to form elements E_{2i+1} and E_{2i+2} of the output, $i \geq 0$.

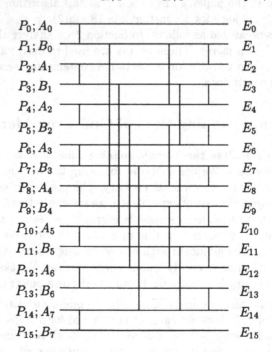

Fig. 1. Odd-even merge with 16 processors.

We want to use this procedure for merging using a collection of processors and have thus to determine where the elements are stored. (The average number of exchanged elements depends on how this is done; we will comment on this later.) As it turns out, the best way to do this is the way already proposed by Batcher. To begin with we assume that $2m$ processors are available. Thus we store the list $A_0, A_1, A_2, ...$ at processors $P_0, P_2, P_4, ...$, the list $B_0, B_1, B_2, ...$ at processors $P_1, P_3, P_5, ...$, and the list $E_0, E_1, E_2, E_3, ...$ at processors $P_0, P_1, P_2, P_3, ...$ (see Figure 1). By unfolding the recursion we get the following procedure (see, e.g., [14]). Let $p = 2m$.

procedure Odd_Even_Merge(p);
for all i, $0 \le i \le p/2$, **pardo**
   compare-exchange(P_{2i}, P_{2i+1});
for $i = \log p - 1$ **downto** 1 **do**
   for all $j, 1 \le j \le (p - 2^i)/2$, **pardo**
      compare-exchange(P_{2j-1}, P_{2j+2^i-2});

Compare-exchange(P_i, P_j) denotes a procedure where P_i gets the smaller one of the two elements stored at P_i and P_j and P_j gets the larger one.

This procedure can be generalized to the case where $p < 2m$, i.e., where each processor holds more than one element. We assume that p divides $2m$ and that the sequences A and B are stored at the processors such that the even indexed processors hold subsequences of A and the odd indexed processors hold subsequences of B. Then we can use the same procedure as above, where compare-exchange(P_i, P_j) now denotes a procedure where P_i gets the smallest $2m/p$ elements of all elements stored at P_i and P_j together and P_j gets the largest $2m/p$ elements of these. That this works can be shown as follows (in [11] it is shown that this can be done for all comparator sorting networks).

Definition 1. For $X \in \{A, B, C, D, E\}$, let $X^y = X_{y(2m/p)}, X_{y(2m/p)+1}, X_{y(2m/p)+2}, ..., X_{y(2m/p)+(2m/p)-1}$.

Lemma 2. *The procedure Odd_Even_Merge(p) merges two sorted lists of length m each (where p divides m) correctly.*

Proof. Let $N = 2m/p$, i.e., N is the number of elements per processor. We will show that the last step completes the merging of the two sequences. Let D_i be fixed and let $i = i_1 N + i_2$, $0 \le i_2 < N$. We will show that D_i either belongs to E^{2i_1+1} or to E^{2i_1+2}.

W.l.o.g. we assume that $D_i \in A_{odd}$. Let l be the number of elements in A_{odd} that are smaller than D_i, $l = l_1 N + l_2$, $l_2 < N$, and let k be the number of elements from B_{odd} that are smaller than D_i, $k = k_1 N + k_2$, $k_2 < N$. Then $i = l + k$. Since $D_i \in A_{odd}$, there are exactly $(l_1 + 1)N$ elements in A_{even} that are smaller than D_i, and between $k_1 N$ and $(k_1 + 1)N$ elements in B_{even} that are smaller than D_i. (Note that there are exactly $(k_1 + 1)N$ of the latter elements if $k_2 \ne 0$.) Thus $D_i = E_j$ where $(2l_1 + 2k_1 + 1)N + l_2 + k_2 \le j \le (2l_1 + 2k_2 + 2)N + l_2 + k_2$. We distinguish two cases. In the first case $i_1 = l_1 + k_1$. Then $(2i_1 + 1)N = (2l_1 + 2k_1 + 1)N \le (2l_1 + 2k_1 + 1)N + l_2 + k_2$ (the leftmost expression is the index of the smallest element in E^{2i_1+1}), and $(2i_1 + 3)N - 1 = (2l_1 + 2k_1 + 3)N - 1 \geq (2l_1 + 2k_2 + 2)N + l_2 + k_2$ (here the leftmost expression is the index of the largest element in E^{2i_1+2}). In the second case, $i_1 = l_1 + k_1 + 1$. Then $l_2 + k_2 > N$ and thus $k_2 \neq 0$. Thus $j = (2l_1 + 2k_2 + 2)N + l_2 + k_2$, and $(2i_1 + 1)N = (2l_1 + 2k_1 + 3)N \leq j$, and $(2i_1 + 3)N - 1 = (2l_1 + 2k_1 + 5)N - 1 \geq j$. From this the claim follows. $\qquad\square$

We still have to specify how to implement *compare-exchange*(P_i, P_j). We want to minimize the amount of communication (which is always relatively expensive). This can be done in the following way. Processor P_i sends its largest element to P_j and P_j sends its smallest element to P_i. This is repeated until the element sent by P_i is smaller than the element sent by P_j. Thus the number of elements exchanged here is at most two plus the number of elements that have to change the processor.

Note that if any elements have to be exchanged between P_i and P_j, both processors have to merge two sorted lists to get the sorted list of the elements now assigned to them.

To derive an upper bound for the average running time of odd-even merge, we will use the following argument. Assume that m is large compared with p. Consider the above iterative description of odd-even merge. In the first step corresponding subsequences of A and B are compared and rearranged. If we choose the input at random most of the elements in the subsequence of A (namely those lying in the middle of the subsequence) will be compared with their neighbours in B and vice versa. This is because on the average the rank of an element in A will not differ much from its rank in B if $(2m/p)$ is large enough. Moreover, the elements stored at processors P_{2i} and P_{2i+1} at the beginning, namely those with ranks in A (B, resp.,) between $i(2m/p)$ and $(i + 1)(2m/p) - 1$, are stored at the processors that will hold E^{2i} and E^{2i+1} at the end. However, the elements in $E^{2i} \cup E^{2i+1}$ are those with overall rank between $2i(2m/p)$ and $2(i+1)(2m/p) - 1$. Thus for most inputs most of the elements will be stored at the correct processors after the first step. (This observation shows why it is best to store the input and the output as suggested by Batcher and as done here.)

Next consider the for-loop of the algorithm. If there are many steps where elements are exchanged there has to be a large i where this happens. Assume the first (or largest) i where at least one element has to be exchanged between two processors is i_{max}. We will show that then there exists an elements x such that the difference between the rank of x in A and the rank of x in B is large – namely at least $(2^{i_{max}-1} - 1)(2m/p) + 1$. For example, if all $\log p - 1$ steps of the for-loop are executed, there exists at least one element with a difference of $m/2$ between its rank in A and its rank in B. However, there are not many inputs for merging with this property if m/p and i_{max} are large.

Next we will analyze this property more closely and then show what it means for the average running time of odd-even merge.

Lemma 3. *Assume that at least two elements are exchanged in the for-loop of* *the algorithm for a fixed i. Then there exists an element x in $A \cup B$ where the rank of x in A differs from the rank of x in B by at least $(2^{i-1} - 1)(2m/p) + 1$.*

Proof. Let $i_{max} = max\{i;$ at least two elements are exchanged in the for-loop$\}$. Thus, before the execution of the loop with $i = i_{max}$ processors P_{2j} and processors P_{2j+1} hold all elements in $A^j \cup B^j$, $0 \leq j < p/2$.

Let $\delta = 2^{i_{max}}$. Let P_k and $P_{k+\delta-1}$ be two processors that exchange elements in this step. Then one of them sends only elements from A and the other one only elements from B (this follows from the observation above.) W.l.o.g. assume that P_k sends only elements from A. Let $k = 2j + 1$. The largest element from A that P_k holds is $x = A_{(j+1)(2m/p)-1}$, and the smallest element from B that $P_{k+\delta-1}$ holds is $B_{(j+\delta/2)(2m/p)}$. Thus the rank of x in A differs from the rank of x in B by at least $(j + \delta/2)(2m/p) - ((j+1)(2m/p) - 1) = (\delta/2 - 1)(2m/p) + 1$. Since $i_{max} \geq i$, the claim follows. $\square$

Next we upper bound the probability that there exists an element $x \in A \cup B$ such that the rank of x in A differs from the rank of x in B by Δ.

Lemma 4. *Let A and B be two sorted sequences of length m each, and let each outcome of merging A and B be equally likely. Then the probability that there exists an element x in $A \cup B$ where the rank of x in A differs from the rank of x in B by Δ is at most*

$$2\binom{2m}{m + \Delta + 1} \Big/ \binom{2m}{m}.$$

Proof. This can be shown with the help of the reflection principle (see, e.g., [7], pp. 72–73) as follows. We can represent each input as a path from the point $(0,0)$ to the point $(2m, 0)$ (see Fig. 2).

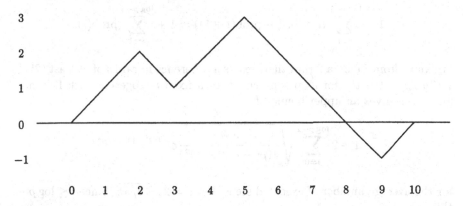

Fig. 2: $m = 5$. The path shown corresponds to the input where the outcome of the merging is $AABAABBBBA$.

We are interested in all paths that touch or cross the line $y = \Delta + 1$ or the line $y = -(\Delta + 1)$: these correspond to inputs where there exists a difference in ranks of at least Δ. According to the reflection principle, the number of paths that touch or cross the line $y = a$, $a > 0$, is equal to the number of paths from $(0,0)$ to $(2m, 2a)$. Thus the number of inputs with a difference in ranks of at least Δ is at most $2\binom{2m}{m+\Delta+1}$, and the probability that an input has this property is at most $2\binom{2m}{m+\Delta+1}/\binom{2m}{m}$. □

The following lemma gives an upper bound for $\binom{2m}{m+\Delta}/\binom{2m}{m}$.

Lemma 5.

$$\binom{2m}{m+\Delta}\bigg/\binom{2m}{m} \leq \sqrt{\frac{(2m)^2}{\pi(m+\Delta)(m-\Delta)}}\, e^{-(\frac{\Delta^2}{m}+\frac{\Delta^4}{6m^3}+\frac{\Delta^6}{15m^5})}.$$

Proof. This can be shown with the help of Stirling's approximation of $n!$ and Taylor series expansion of $\ln x$. □

Now we are ready to prove an upper bound on the average number of steps executed in odd-even merge.

Lemma 6. *The average number of steps executed in odd-even merge is bounded by $O(1 + \log(1 + p^2/m))$.*

Proof. Let $\mathrm{prob}(i)$ be the probability that the for-loop is executed for a fixed i. Remember that we say a step of odd-even merge is executed if at least two processors have to exchange elements. The average number of executed steps is bounded by

$$1 + \sum_{i=1}^{\log p - 1} i(\mathrm{prob}(i) - \mathrm{prob}(i+1)) = 1 + \sum_{i=1}^{\log p - 1} \mathrm{prob}(i).$$

We know from Lemma 2 that there exists a difference in ranks of at least $(2^{i-1} - 1)(2m/p) + 1$ if the for-loop is executed for a fixed i. Together with Lemmas 3 and 4 this gives an upper bound of

$$1 + 2 \sum_{i=0}^{\log p - 2} \sqrt{\frac{4p^2}{\pi(p^2 - 4(2^i - 1)^2)}}\, e^{-4(2^i-1)^2 m/p^2}$$

for the average number of executed steps. Let $c = 2\sqrt{16/3\pi}$. Since $i \leq \log p - 2$, this is

$$\leq 1 + c \left(\sum_{i=0}^{\lceil \log(1+\sqrt{1.1p^2/(4mx)}) \rceil - 1} 1 + \sum_{i=\lceil \log(1+\sqrt{1.1p^2/(4mx)}) \rceil}^{\log p - 2} e^{-4(2^i-1)^2 m/p^2} \right)$$

for any x, and this is

$$\leq 1 + c\left(\left\lceil \log\left(1 + \sqrt{1.1p^2/(4mx)}\right)\right\rceil + \sum_{i=1}^{\log p - 2 - \left\lceil \log\left(1 + \sqrt{1.1p^2/4mx}\right)\right\rceil} e^{-i^2/x}\right)$$

$$\leq 1 + c\left(\left\lceil \log\left(1 + \sqrt{1.1p^2/(4mx)}\right)\right\rceil + 0.5\int_{-\infty}^{+\infty} e^{-i^2/x}di\right)$$

$$\leq 1 + c\left(\left\lceil \log\left(1 + \sqrt{p^2/(4mx)}\right)\right\rceil + \sqrt{x\pi}/2\right).$$

If we choose $x = 1.27$, we get that the average number of steps executed in odd-even merge is bounded by

$$2 + 2.61\left\lceil \log\left(1 + \sqrt{p^2/(4.62m)}\right)\right\rceil.$$

$\square$

Since each step of odd-even merge can be executed in time $O(m/p)$, we get the following upper bound for the average running time of odd-even merge.

Lemma 7. *The average running time of odd-even merge is $O((n/p)(1 + \log(1 + p^2/n)))$, where p is the number of processors and n is the size of the input.*

3 The average running time of odd-even merge sort

Building on the results from Section 2 we can now derive an upper bound on the running time of odd-even merge sort. Odd-even merge sort works as follows. Let n be the size of the input, let p be the number of processors, let p divide n, and let the processors be numbered from 0 to $p - 1$. At the beginning each processor stores n/p of the elements. In the first step each processors sorts locally its portion of the input. In the following $\log p$ steps these sorted lists are merged together in the following way. In step i, $0 \leq i \leq \log p - 1$, the lists stored at processors $P_j, P_{j+\delta}, P_{j+2\delta}, \ldots$ and processors $P_{j+\delta/2}, P_{j+\delta/2+\delta}, P_{j+\delta/2+2\delta}, \ldots$ are merged, where $\delta = p/2^i$ and $0 \leq j < p/2^{i+1}$ (see Fig. 3). Note that this means that in each instant of odd-even merge the elements are stored as required in the previous section.

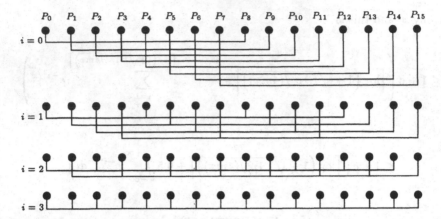

Fig. 3 The processors that work together in step i are shown connected.

Again we will derive an upper bound for the number of steps where elements have to be exchanged.

Lemma 8. *In the i-th call of odd-even merge, $0 \leq i \leq \log p - 1$, the average number of steps where elements are exchanged is bounded by $1 + \log(1 + \sqrt{\ln(p/2^{i+1}) \frac{p2^{i+1}}{2n}}) + \sqrt{\pi}$.*

Proof. In the i-th call of odd-even merge, $p/2^{i+1}$ independent mergings are performed, each with 2^{i+1} processors and $(n/p)2^{i+1}$ elements. Thus, the for-loop in odd-even merge consists of i steps. Let $c = 2\sqrt{16/3\pi}$. The probability that at least two elements are exchanged in the j-th execution of the for-loop for any of the $p/2^{i+1}$ mergings, is bounded by

$$\min\{1, p/2^{i+1} c e^{-2(2^{\log p - j} - 1)^2 n/(p2^{i+1})}\},$$

and the average number of steps with data exchanges is bounded by

$$1 + \sum_{j=0}^{i+1} \min\{1, p/2^{i+1} c e^{-2(2^j - 1)^2 n/(p2^{i+1})}\}$$

$$= 1 + \sum_{j=0}^{i+1} \min\{1, e^{-2(2^j - 1)^2 n/(p2^{i+1}) + \ln(cp/2^{i+1})}\}.$$

By splitting the sum we get as upper bound

$$1 + \left\lceil \log\left(1 + \sqrt{(1 + \ln(cp/2^{i+1})) \frac{1.1p2^{i+1}}{2n}}\right) \right\rceil$$

$$+ \sum_{j=\lceil \log(1 + \sqrt{(1 + \ln(cp/2^{i+1}))1.1p2^{i+1}/2n}) \rceil}^{j=i+1} e^{-2(2^j - 1)^2 n/(p2^{i+1}) + \ln(cp/2^{i+1})}$$

$$\leq 1 + \left\lceil \log \left(1 + \sqrt{(1 + \ln{(cp/2^{i+1})}) \, 1.1 p 2^{i+1}/(2n)} \right) \right\rceil + \sum_{j=1}^{j=\infty} e^{-i^2}$$

$$\leq 1 + \left\lceil \log \left(1 + \sqrt{(1 + \ln{(cp/2^{i+1})}) \, 1.1 p 2^{i+1}/(2n)} \right) \right\rceil + 0.5\sqrt{\pi}. \quad \square$$

Now we can derive an upper bound for the average number of steps with data exchanges in odd-even merge sort.

Lemma 9. *The average number of steps in odd-even merge sort where data are exchanged is $O(\log p (1 + \log(1 + \sqrt{p^2/n})))$, where n is the size of the input and p is the number of processors.*

Proof. Let $c = 2\sqrt{16/3\pi}$. According to Lemma 7, the average number of steps with data exchanges is

$$\sum_{i=0}^{\log p - 1} \left(1 + \left\lceil \log \left(1 + \sqrt{(1 + \ln{(cp/2^{i+1})}) \, 1.1 p 2^{i+1}/(2n)} \right) \right\rceil + 0.5\sqrt{\pi} \right)$$

$$\leq \log p \left(1 + 0.5\sqrt{\pi} + \left\lceil \log \left(1 + \sqrt{(1 + \ln{(c)}) \, 1.1 p^2/(2n)} \right) \right\rceil \right)$$

$$\leq \log p \left(1.89 + \left\lceil \log \left(1 + \sqrt{1.08 p^2/n} \right) \right\rceil \right). \square$$

Since each step in odd-even merge (except for the initial local sorting) can be executed in linear time, we arrive at the following lemma.

Lemma 10. *The average running time of odd-even merge sort is bounded by $O((n/p)(\log(n/p) + \log p(1 + \log(1 + p^2/n))))$ where n is the size of the input and p is the number of processors used.*

4 Implementation and comparison with other sorting algorithms

In the previous sections we assumed for the sake of simplicity that all processors that have to communicate in odd-even merge sort are connected. On existing parallel computers this is, in general, not the case. However, many existing parallel machines can be viewed as complete graphs as long as the number of processors is not too large [5]. Other machine models where the running time from Section 3 can be achieved are the hypercube (by using gray code [13]) and the hypercube with E-router [10]. A hypercube with E-router can perform shifts without conflicts; i.e., the running time for a shift operation will be $O(l)$ where l is the maximal length of a message sent, if $l \geq \log p$. (Intel's iPSC/860 and NCube's NCube are hypercubes with E-router.)

We have implemented the above algorithm to run on the iPSC/860 from Intel and the CM5 from Thinking Machines in the following way. If two processors have to communicate in a step, they first check whether they have to exchange any elements. If this is the case, they use binary search to determine which elements have to be exchanged. (This method was proposed in [15].) This is done in order to be able to send the data in larger blocks (on existing parallel computers this is, in general, much cheaper than sending the same data in small blocks). The elements at each processor are stored as a linear list; when new elements arrive, they are merged with the already present elements. If one of the two lists that have to be merged in a step is short, binary search is used to determine where the elements in the shorter list belong. Communication is done using asynchronous send and receive; on the iPSC/860 this allows to perform communication and local computation in parallel and to "hide" part of the communication time.

The speedups achieved for large inputs are quite high; e.g., the speedup on the iPSC/860 for 100000 longs per processor and using 16 processors is 12.3 or 77% of the maximal possible; for 1600000 long per processor it is 14.5 or 90.6% of the maximal possible. For small inputs the speedups are not as high as one could perhaps expect from the asymptotic upper bounds. E.g., for 300 longs per processor and 16 processors of the iPSC/860 the speedup is 1.5, that is, the parallel algorithm is only slightly faster than the sequential algorithm (for 5000 longs per processor it is already 55%). The reason for this is that the start-up time for messages is quite large; only if long messages are sent (much more than 300 longs), the full bandwidth of the communication links can be utilized. (All of the above listed speedups are for randomly generated input.)

How does this algorithm compare with other parallel sorting algorithms? We mentioned in the introduction that odd-even merge sort can, on the average, be faster than bitonic merge sort, the worst case running time being about the same. This is true if the elements are stored as in the original version of bitonic merge sort – i.e., if two lists that have to be merged are stored one after the other. However, also for bitonic merge sort the elements can be stored as proposed for odd-even merge sort. Then the average running time of bitonic merge sort will be similar to the average running time of odd-even merge sort.

Note that this way to store the elements in a parallel merge sort also make the sorting algorithm adaptive: if the input is nearly sorted in the sense that no element is stored far away from its position in the sorted list, this will be reflected by the running time.

We have also compared odd-even merge sort with the sorting algorithm proposed in [15]. In the first phase of this algorithm the input is "presorted" by a hypercubic descend algorithm; in the second phase the sorting is then finished by odd-even merge sort. The authors claim that this algorithm performs much better than odd-even merge sort alone; however, we cannot confirm this. According to our experiments, the running time is almost the same. (For large inputs, the algorithm with presorting executes less steps but sends more elements.)

For large inputs sample sort (see, e.g., [3]) will have a smaller running time. The idea of sample sort is as follows. First splitters are determined by sampling the input elements. These splitters are sorted and used to form buckets. The buckets are then distributed among the processors and each input element is sent to the processor responsible for the bucket that contains it. One advantage of this method is that each input element is moved only once. On the other hand, this method does not work well if the input is small or if there are many identical elements.

References

1. K.E.. Batcher. Sorting networks and their applications. *Proceedings, AFIPS Spring Joint Computer Conference*, 307–314, 1968.
2. D.T. Blackston, A. Ranade. SnakeSort: a family of simple optimal randomized sorting algorithms. *Proc., Int. Conf. on Parallel Processing*, Vol. III, 201–204, 1993.
3. G.E. Blelloch, L. Dagum, S.J. Smith, K. Thearling, M. Zagha. An evaluation of sorting as a supercomputer benchmark. Technical Report RNR-93-002, NAS Applied Research Branch, Jan. 1993.
4. G.E. Blelloch, C.E. Leiserson, B.M. Maggs, C.G. Plaxton, S.J. Smith, M. Zagha. A comparison of sorting algorithms for the Connection Machine CM-2. *Proc., Symp. on Parallel Algorithms and Architectures*, 3–16, 1991.
5. D. Culler, R. Karp, M. Patterson, A. Sahay, K.E. Schauser, E. Santos, R. Subramonian, T. von Eicken. LogP: Towards a Realistic Model of Parallel Computation. *ACM SIGPLAN Symposium on Principles & Practice of Parallel Programming: PPOPP*, 1993.
6. R. Diekmann, J. Gehring, R. Lülling, B. Monien, M. Nübel, R. Wanka. Sorting large data sets on a massively parallel system. Technical Report, Universität Paderborn.
7. W. Feller. An introduction to probability theory and its applications, Vol. 1. New Wiley series in probability and mathematical statistics, 1957, Wiley, New York.
8. R. Flajolet, L. Ramshaw. A note on gray code and odd-even merge. *SIAM J. Comput.*, Vol. 9, 142–158, 1980.
9. W.L. Hightower, J.F. Prins, J.H. Reif. Implementations of randomized sorting on large parallel machines. *Proc. Symp. on Parallel Processing*, 158–167, 1992.
10. K. Hwang. Advanced Computer Architecture : Parallelism, Scalability, Programmability. McGraw-Hill, New York, 1993.
11. D.E. Knuth. The art of computer programming : Vol. 3 / sorting and searching. Addison-Wesley series in computer science and information processing, 1973, Addison Wesley, Reading, Mass.
12. G. Larcher, R.F. Tichy. A note on gray code and odd-even merge. *Discrete Applied Mathematics 18*, 309–313, 1987.
13. D. Nassimi, Y.D. Tsai. An efficient implementation of Batcher's odd-even merge on a SIMD-hypercube. *J. Parallel and Distributed Computing*, Vol. 19, 58–63, 1993.
14. R. Sedgewick. Data movement in odd-even merging. *SIAM J. Comput.*, Vol. 7, 239–272, 1978.
15. A. Tridgell, R. Brent. An implementation of a general-purpose parallel sorting algorithm. Technical Report TR-CS-93-01, Computer Sciences Laboratory, Australian National University, 1993.

Optimal Average Case Sorting on Arrays*

Manfred Kunde[2], Rolf Niedermeier[1], Klaus Reinhardt[1], and Peter Rossmanith[2]

[1] Wilhelm-Schickard-Institut für Informatik, Universität Tübingen, Sand 13,
D-72076 Tübingen, Fed. Rep. of Germany
[2] Fakultät für Informatik, Technische Universität München, Arcisstr. 21,
D-80290 München, Fed. Rep. of Germany

Abstract. We present algorithms for sorting and routing on two-dimensional mesh-connected parallel architectures that are optimal on average. If one processor has many packets then we asymptotically halve the up to now best running times. For a load of one optimal algorithms are known for the mesh. We improve this to a load of eight without increasing the running time. For tori no optimal algorithms were known even for a load of one. Our algorithm is optimal for every load. Other architectures we consider include meshes with diagonals and reconfigurable meshes. Furthermore, the method applies to meshes of arbitrary higher dimensions and also enables optimal solutions for the routing problem.

1 Introduction

We present deterministic algorithms that sort and route on mesh-connected computers fast on average. For important, fundamental classes of problems (so called h–h relations) we completely solve the problem in that sense that our approach is optimal for all cases. (We present matching lower bounds.)

A two-dimensional mesh-connected computer is a processor array, where each processor has one bidirectional connection to each of its four neighbors. Meshes are a promising parallel architecture due to their scalability, their regular interconnection structure with its locality of communication, and since they need only linear space in the VLSI-model. We also consider meshes with wrap-around connections, also known as tori, meshes with additional diagonal connections, and reconfigurable meshes.

Average case analysis is in general more difficult than worst case analysis. This is the reason why there are much more results about the worst case behavior than about the average case for many parallel models. Often, however, the average case behavior is the more realistic one and an algorithm good in the average is usually superior to an algorithm whose good worst-case behavior is at its average case behavior's cost. A good example is Quicksort [9].

Our algorithms are based on the following simple principle: Let us for the moment assume that the input consists only of zeros and ones. We can assume

* This research was supported by the Deutsche Forschungsgemeinschaft, Sonderforschungsbereich 0342, TP A4 "KLARA."

that on average the input is very uniformly distributed over the whole mesh. If we divide the mesh into equal-sized blocks, the relative number of ones in each block will be about the same. Sorting the blocks leads to a situation where all blocks look like nearly the same. There are zeros, followed by ones. The point where the zeros end and the ones begin is about the same in each block.

Let us assume that there are k blocks and let us also divide each block into k bricks. Now the first bricks of all blocks will contain only zeros, the second bricks, too. The last bricks of all blocks will contain only ones. Around the, say, ith brick, however, zeros end and ones begin. In some blocks it might be the ith brick, in others the $i + 1$st, in others the $i - 1$st, but we can assume that in all blocks this happens somewhere near the ith brick. Next, we perform a so-called all-to-all mapping that sends the first bricks of all blocks into the first block, the second bricks of all blocks into the second block, and so on. Now the first block contains only zeros, the last block only ones. Only around the ith block, ones and zeros occur together. The input is therefore almost sorted.

To finish, we must sort some adjacent blocks and we are done. (Note that in this paper we will not describe the concrete realization of all-to-all mappings. For this purpose we just refer to the literature [10, 11].)

Of course, this does not work for all inputs, but it works for most inputs. We will see that the probability that it works is exponentially near to one.

When all-to-all mappings were introduced, for the first time an algorithm matching the trivial bisection bound came up [10]. This algorithm solves the h–h sorting problem optimally on meshes, where $h \geq 8$. That is, each processor has at most h data packets in the beginning and the end. The input is sorted according to an indexing, that is, an ordering of all places in the grid. The algorithms based on all-to-all mappings work for a lot of different indexing schemes. The bisection bound is based on the fact that in the worst case the upper half and the lower half of the mesh have to be swapped. Then $hn^2/2$ data packets must travel over n communication links, which obviously takes at least $hn/2$ steps.

In the average case the bisection bound does not hold. So we can improve upon algorithms that even match this lower bound. For a long time no algorithm came even close to the bisection bound and up to now algorithms matching the bisection bound asymptotically were state of the art. Now we improve upon these algorithms; actually we even halve their running times. For $h < 8$ also no optimal algorithm are known in general, but the 1–1 problem was solved by Chlebus [1] in asymptotically optimal $2n + o(n)$ steps on average. We show that up to $h = 8$ we can sort within the same time bound. Recently, Kaufmann, Sibeyn, and Suel [7] showed that the 1–1 problem can be solved within the same time bound even in the worst case. The good worst case behavior is, however, at the expense of big constants, especially a buffer size of the processors around 25. Chlebus' algorithm and ours are superior; they only need buffer size 1.

In the case of mesh-connected tori the best known algorithms with buffer size 1 solve the 1–1 sorting problem in $1.5n + o(n)$ steps for a blocked snake-like row major order, and in $2n + o(n)$ steps for a row major and a snake-like row major order [3]. Gu and Gu improved herein the previous results each by $0.5n$.

We improve their running times by another $0.5n$ to $n + o(n)$, $1.5n + o(n)$, and $1.5n + o(n)$, respectively. Instead of a blocked snake-like row major we may use other blocked indexing schemes, as well. We thereby also refute a conjecture of Gu and Gu: They conjectured that $n + o(n)$ steps cannot be reached for tori.

Our algorithm and its probabilistic analysis differs significantly from the algorithms and proofs given by Chlebus [1] and Gu and Gu [3].

Fast all-to-all mappings are also known for higher dimensional grids [10], grids with diagonals [11], and reconfigurable meshes [6]. Therefore, we also obtain optimal results for average case sorting on these models of parallel computation.

The following table summarizes the running times for all models considered in this paper. Our algorithms are optimal with respect to asymptotic running times and in most cases also with respect to buffer sizes.

Problem	Model	New Result		Old Result	
1–1 sorting	mesh	$2n$		$2n$	[1]
	torus	n		$1.5n$	[3]
h–h sorting	mesh	$2n$,	$h \leq 8$	$4n$	[10]
		$hn/4$,	$h > 8$	$hn/2$	[10]
	torus	n,	$h \leq 8$	$2n$	[10]
		$hn/8$,	$h > 8$	$hn/4$	[10]
	mesh with diagonals	n,	$h \leq 9$	$2n$	[11]
		n,	$h \leq 12$	$hn \cdot 2/9$	[11]
		$hn/12$,	$h > 12$	$hn \cdot 2/9$	[11]
	torus with diagonals	$n/2$,	$h \leq 10$	n	[11]
		$n/2$,	$h \leq 12$	$hn/9$	[11]
		$hn/24$,	$h > 12$	$hn/9$	[11]
	reconfigurable mesh	$hn/2$,	$h \geq 1$	hn	[6]

Additive low order terms in the running times are omitted.
For $h \geq 2$ no average case running times faster than for the worst-case were known.

In the next section we provide basic notation and some more facts about our models of computation. In the third section we present our algorithm for average case sorting. In the fourth section we analyze the average case behavior of our algorithm on independent random inputs from the unit interval and on random permutations of sets and multisets, and finally prove matching lower bounds. In the fifth section we explain the applications of our findings to tori, grids with diagonals, and reconfigurable meshes and also to the routing problem. We end with some conclusions and open questions in the sixth section.

506

2 Preliminaries

Leighton [12, 13] provides a general view of most of the topics we deal with. We assume familiarity with basic facts and concepts of elementary probability theory [2, 5].

A processor grid (or, equivalently, mesh) consists of n^2 processors arranged in a two-dimensional array. All processors work in parallel synchronously, and only nearest neighbors may exchange data. For h–h problems each processor contains at most h data elements in the beginning and at the end of the algorithm. Each element in a processor lies in one of h local places. A processor is said to have buffer size s if it can retain at most s elements during the whole computation. For h–h sorting problems we need an indexing scheme for the processor places. An index function numbers the places of the grid processors from 0 to $hn^2 - 1$. The ith smallest element will be transported to the place indexed $i - 1$. In one step a communication channel can transport at most one element (as an atomic unit) in each direction. For complexity considerations we only count communication steps; we ignore operations within a processor.

From the description of a grid we easily obtain several further parallel architectures to be considered in this paper. So we get processor tori simply by adding wrap-around connections to processor grids. Grids or tori with diagonals evolve if we add diagonal connections, replacing four-neighborhoods by eight-neighborhoods. Eventually, reconfigurable grids differ from conventional grids in that they have switches with reconnection capability. So they build a grid-shaped reconfigurable bus system, which is changeable by adjusting the local connections between ports within each processor. A communication through a bus is assumed to take unit time no matter how long the bus is. For details we refer to e.g. [6, 14].

In order to describe our algorithm, we introduce some more concepts concerning the partitioning of grids into subgrids and indexing schemes. We subdivide an $n \times n$ grid of processors into $k = n^{2/3-2\epsilon}$ subgrids of $b = n^{2/3+\epsilon} \times n^{2/3+\epsilon}$ processors, called *blocks*. Here ϵ is some real constant with $0 < \epsilon < 1/3$. Each block is subdivided into k *bricks* of $n^{1/3+2\epsilon} \times n^{1/3+2\epsilon}$ processors.

The algorithm will sort according to any indexing fulfilling the following requirements. If we number the blocks from 1 to k, then blocks i and $i + 1$ have to be neighbors and the indexing is chosen in such a way that all places in block i have smaller indices than places in block $i + 1$. That means the indexing is *continuous* with respect to blocks.

All-to-all mappings [10], as described in the introduction, are employed to exchange bricks between all pairs of blocks in the grid. As it will turn out in the next section, the time complexity of the all-to-all mapping dominates the overall complexity of our average case sorting algorithm. So, e.g., the existence of algorithms realizing all-to-all mappings for h–h relations with $h \leq 8$ on meshes in $2n$ steps [10] implies that our algorithm in this case needs time $2n + o(n)$.

3 The Algorithm

Our Algorithm A for average case sorting is based on the principle of sorting with *all-to-all mappings* [10, 11]. Roughly speaking, an all-to-all mapping performs a global distribution of data by sending a brick from each block to each other block of the grid. A quick and raw description of sorting with all-to-all mappings then looks as follows. First sort each block individually, then perform an all-to-all mapping, then again sort each block individually, then again perform an all-to-all mapping and finally sort all adjacent pairs of blocks (Algorithm B). Let us only mention in pass that the time complexity of that algorithm is clearly predominated by the complexity of the two all-to-all mappings. We omit any further details concerning the above algorithm and now immediately start with our algorithm for average case sorting.

In simplified terms, Algorithm A works as follows. It consists of mainly two parts. First, we use a cut version of Algorithm B with only *one* all-to-all mapping. Second, we apply a worst case linear time sorting algorithm, which, however, is only executed if the first part fails to sort the input. In the following section we will show that failure of the first part is extremely unlikely.

Before we sketch the details of our algorithm, note that in each individual sorting of a block we sort according to an indexing that again is continuous. Let us number the bricks of a block from 1 to k. Then the block local indexing is chosen in such a way that all places in brick i have smaller indices than all places in brick $i+1$. The ith brick of each block will be sent to the ith block of the grid by means of an all-to-all mapping. Algorithm A works for both grids and tori.

Algorithm A.
1.1. Sort each block.
1.2. All-to-all mapping.
1.3. Sort all adjacent pairs of blocks.
2.   If elements are out of order, sort again with some other linear time algorithm.

Algorithm B. [10]
1. Sort each block.
2. All-to-all mapping.
3. Sort each block.
4. All-to-all mapping.
5. Sort adjacent pairs of blocks.

Now we analyze the time complexity of Algorithm A. Steps 1.1 and 1.3 take time proportional to the side length of a block, i.e., $O(n^{2/3+\epsilon})$. Step 1.2 takes time $2n$ for $h \leq 8$ and it takes time $hn/4$ for $h > 8$. Step 2 takes linear time. Since we will show in the next section that it is extremely unlikely for randomly given inputs that step 2 will be executed, we can derive an average case running time of $2n + O(n^{2/3+\epsilon})$ for $h \leq 8$ and $hn/4 + O(n^{2/3+\epsilon})$ for $h > 8$ in the case of grids.

Let us end this section with a case of special interest: 1–1 sorting with buffer size 1. It is straightforward to see that for small, constant h our algorithm always works with small, constant buffer size. For 1–1 problems we even may perform the all-to-all mapping with buffer size 1, which implies an average case sorting algorithm on grids with buffer size 1 running in time $2n + O(n^{2/3+\epsilon})$. For the case of tori, where we get running time $n + O(n^{2/3+\epsilon})$ this is a direct consequence of the fact that the shift operations used in the original algorithm [10] can be implemented using cyclic shifts in rows and columns. We omit the details.

For the case of grids, the situation is a bit more delicate. The basic idea here is as follows. Partition the grid horizontally into two equally sized parts. We transport half of the elements of the lower part to the upper part and vice versa as follows. Subdivide the grids vertically into strips of width 2 and length n. Within the strips perform a rotary traffic of the elements in the natural way. It takes time $n/2$ to get half of the elements of the lower strip to the upper and vice versa. Next we perform the same idea for the exchange of half of the elements between the upper two quarters and between the lower two quarters of the grid each time. This again takes $n/2$ steps. Eventually we recursively perform the same method within each of the four quarters of the grid and so on. We defer the details to the full paper.

4 Analysis

In this section we provide the probabilistic analysis of Algorithm A. We proceed as follows. First, we show that the first part of Algorithm A correctly sorts independently chosen random numbers between 0 and 1 with overwhelming probability. Next, we prove that this also implies the same behavior when the input is a uniformly chosen permutation of a set or multiset of hn^2 fixed elements. Finally, we state our matching lower bounds for average case sorting on grids.

4.1 Sorting random numbers

Definition 1. An algorithm T-separates an input $x_1, \ldots, x_N$ if it permutes it into $y_1, \ldots, y_N$ such that $y_i < T$ and $y_j \geq T$ implies $i < j$.

To T-separate a set of data is a step forward to sorting the set. For example, Quicksort sorts by recursively T-separating for certain T's. Obviously, if $y_1, \ldots, y_N$ are simultaneously y_1-, y_2-,..., and y_N-separated, then they are sorted, since no pair is out of order. In the following, we show that the first part of Algorithm A sorts with high probability by proving that it T-separates for all T's with high probability.

Lemma 2. If $X_1, \ldots, X_N$ are independent random variables that are uniformly distributed over the unit interval, then the first part of Algorithm A with block size b and number of blocks k will T-separate the input $X_1, \ldots, X_N$ with probability at least $1 - 2ke^{-b/(4k^2)}$ for a fixed $T \in [0, 1]$.

Proof. We focus on the first block containing elements $X_1, \ldots, X_b$. After sorting the blocks, these elements are in order. Let us call a brick *dirty* if it contains both elements smaller than T and greater than or equal to T. There is at most one dirty brick because the indexing of places follows the numbering of bricks. Let Z be the number of elements in the block that are smaller than T. Since $Pr(X_i \leq T) = T$, the expected value of Z is Tb. We apply Chernoff-bounds in order to estimate the probability that Z deviates more than a half brick's size $b/(2k)$ from its expectation. We use inequalities (1) and (12) of Hagerup and Rüb [4]. Let $S := 1 - T$.

$$Pr(\, Z \geq (T + 1/(2k))\, b\,) \leq$$
$$\leq \left(\frac{Tb}{(T + 1/(2k))b} \right)^{(T+1/(2k))b} \left(\frac{Sb}{(S - 1/(2k))b} \right)^{(S-1/(2k))b}$$
$$= \left(1 + \frac{1}{(2kT)} \right)^{-(T+1/(2k))b} \left(1 - \frac{1}{(2kS)} \right)^{-(S-1/(2k))b}$$
$$\leq \exp(-\tfrac{1}{2kT}(T + 1/(2k))b) \cdot \exp(\tfrac{1}{2kS}(S - 1/(2k))b)$$
$$\leq e^{-b/(4k^2)}$$

Similarly,
$$Pr(\, Z \leq (T - 1/(2k))\, b\,) \leq e^{-b/(4k^2)}$$

follows. Together we have

$$Pr(\, |Z - Tb| \geq b/(2k)\,) \leq 2e^{-b/(4k^2)}. \qquad (*)$$

If $Tb - b/(2k) < Z < Tb + b/(2k)$, then the dirty brick is the ith brick, where $i = \lceil \frac{Z}{b/k} \rceil$, i.e.,

$$i \in \{ \lceil Tk - \tfrac{1}{2} \rceil, \lceil Tk + \tfrac{1}{2} \rceil \}. \qquad (**)$$

The exact position does not matter; it is only important that we can spot the dirty brick in a small region with high probability. For all other blocks, the probability that the dirty brick lies in one of the two positions is the same. Therefore, the probability that the dirty brick in *all* k blocks is in one of the two positions is at least $1 - 2ke^{-b/(4k^2)}$. If this is the case, then the positions of the *dirty blocks* after the all-to-all mapping are also restricted to $(**)$. Local sorting of adjacent blocks at the end of Algorithm A then "cleans" these dirty blocks. $\qquad \Box$

It remains to generalize Lemma 2 from some fixed T to all values of interest.

Lemma 3. *If $X_1, \ldots, X_N$ are independent random variables that are uniformly distributed over the unit interval, then the first part of Algorithm A will T-separate the input $X_1, \ldots, X_N$ with probability at least $1 - 2Nke^{-b/(4k^2)}$ simultaneously for all $T \in [0,1]$.*

Proof. If the algorithm X_1-, X_2-, $\ldots$, and X_N-separates the input, then it T-separates it for *all* $T \in [0,1]$. So by Lemma 2 the probability is at least $1 - 2Nke^{-b/(4k^2)}$. $\qquad \Box$

We summarize our findings in the following corollary, employing $N = hn^2$ and the given values for b and k.

Corollary 4. *The first part of Algorithm A sorts random inputs from the unit interval with probability at least $1 - 2hn^{8/3-2\epsilon}e^{-n^{1.5\epsilon}}$.*

4.2 Sorting permutations of sets and multisets

In the previous subsection we proved the correctness and efficiency of our algorithm on input elements that were given by independently chosen random numbers from the infinite probability space $[0,1]^{hn^2}$. As a direct consequence our algorithm is also suitable to sort hn^2 fixed elements that are in random order. We start with the case of hn^2 distinct elements and give a rigorous proof, though the consequence might seem obvious.

Theorem 5. *In the average, Algorithm A sorts a permutation of a set of hn^2 distinct elements on grids in $2n + O(n^{2/3+\epsilon})$ steps if $h \leq 8$ and in $hn/4 + O(n^{2/3+\epsilon})$ steps if $h > 8$.*

Proof. Let $N = hn^2$ and $x_1, \ldots, x_N \in [0,1]$. Let V be the set of all vectors $(x_1, \ldots, x_N) \in [0,1]^N$, where all x_i are pairwise distinct. The probability that a vector chosen randomly from $[0,1]^N$ lies in V is 1. The set V can now be partitioned into $N!$ disjoint sets by the surjective mapping $P : V \to S_N$, where S_N is the set of permutations of $\{1, \ldots, N\}$ and $P(x_1, \ldots, x_N) = \pi$ iff $x_{\pi(1)} < x_{\pi(2)} < \cdots < x_{\pi(N)}$. That is, $P^{-1}(\pi)$ is the set of those inputs $x_1, \ldots, x_N$ that are sorted by π. Since Algorithm A is comparison-based, we get immediately: If $P(x_1, \ldots, x_N) = P(y_1, \ldots, y_N)$ then the first part of Algorithm A sorts $x_1, \ldots, x_N$ correctly if and only if it sorts $y_1, \ldots, y_N$ correctly.

Now let $\rho \in S_N$ be an arbitrary permutation. The probability that a randomly chosen vector $x_1, \ldots, x_N$ from V lies in $P^{-1}(\rho)$ is $1/N!$ [8, page 64], i.e., $Pr((x_1, \ldots, x_N) \in P^{-1}(\rho)) = 1/N!$. Let I denote the set of "good" input vectors, i.e., the set of vectors from $[0,1]^N$ that are sorted correctly by the first part of Algorithm A and let G be the set of "good" permutations:

$$G := \{ P(x_1, \ldots, x_N) \mid (x_1, \ldots, x_N) \in I \cap V \}$$

Then

$$Pr(\mathbf{x} \in I \cap V) = Pr(\mathbf{x} \in \bigcup_{\pi \in G} P^{-1}(\pi))$$

$$= \sum_{\pi \in G} Pr(\mathbf{x} \in P^{-1}(\pi)) = |G|/N!$$

The probability that a uniformly chosen permutation is a good permutation is exactly $|G|/N!$. Since $Pr(\mathbf{x} \notin V) = 0$ and by Lemma 3 we conclude that $|G|/N! = Pr(\mathbf{x} \in I \cap V) = Pr(\mathbf{x} \in I) \geq 1 - 2Nke^{-b/(4k^2)}$. □

We continue with the case of multiset sorting, putting it down to the case of permutations on sets.

Theorem 6. *In the average, Algorithm A sorts a permutation of a multiset of hn^2 elements on grids in $2n + O(n^{2/3+\epsilon})$ steps if $h \leq 8$ and in $hn/4 + O(n^{2/3+\epsilon})$ steps if $h > 8$.*

Proof. Assume that the input consists of hn^2 not necessarily distinct elements. Replace each element x by a pair (x, z), where the first component is the original element and the second component is a random number z uniformly chosen from $[0, 1]$. Let us further define $(x_1, z_1) < (x_2, z_2)$ iff $x_1 < x_2$ or $x_1 = x_2$ and $z_1 < z_2$. Then all pairs are distinct from each other with probability 1 and we may follow exactly the same line of argumentation as in Theorem 5 to show that our algorithm sorts the pair elements according to the newly defined ordering $<$. Herein observe that since all permutations over the multiset are equally likely, the order of the pairs according to $<$ is also random.

It remains to be shown that sorting the pairs implies sorting the original input. It suffices to observe that pair elements with same first components will stand side by side after the above sorting and removing the second components of all pairs yields the multiset in sorted order. On the other hand, our choice of $<$ does at most affect the order of subsequences of equal elements.   □

4.3 Lower bounds

Chlebus [1] showed that the distance bound for grids is a lower bound also in the average case, by proving that with high probability an element near the upper left corner must travel near to the lower right corner. The lower bound holds also for h–h problems with $h > 1$. For $h \leq 8$ we have algorithms that sort in $2n + O(n^{3/4})$ steps; these algorithms are therefore asymptotically optimal.

For $h > 8$ our algorithms need asymptotically more than $2n$ steps. Still we show that even for $h > 8$ the algorithms remain optimal by proving a new lower bound that asymptotically matches the running time of our best algorithms.

Theorem 7. *Every algorithm that solves the h–h sorting problem on a grid for all $\delta > 0$ needs at least $hn/4 - O(n^{1/3+\delta})$ steps on average.*

Proof. Divide the grid horizontally into two halves and choose an indexing such that no block is divided and that only two neighboring blocks are divided. Figure 1 shows a blockwise snake-like ordering as an example. The first part of Algorithm A sorts correctly with very high probability and moves at least $hn^2/4 - O(n^{4/3+2\epsilon})$ packets from the upper half to the lower half, because an all-to-all mapping moves $hn^2/4$ packets in the respective other half and a local sort moves up to one block back.

Look again at the figure. Since only adjacent pairs of blocks are sorted after the all-to-all mapping took place, only the contents of block 33 might travel back into the upper half. That means that in total half of the contents of 32 blocks travelled from the upper into the lower half and then at most one block back into the upper half.

With very small probability the first part of Algorithm A does not sort correctly and the second part of Algorithm A moves up to $hn^2/2$ packets from the upper half to the lower half. Anyways, the expected value of packets that travel from the upper into the lower half remains $hn^2/4 - O(n^{4/3+2\epsilon})$. This amount of packets has to be transported through the dividing line that consists of only n

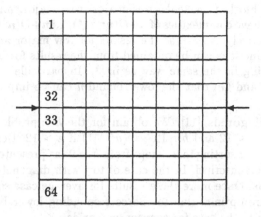

Fig. 1. The lower bounds argument

wires. So only n packets travel down in one step and thus $hn/4 - O(n^{1/3+2\epsilon})$ steps are necessary. This holds for *every* sorting algorithm, since every algorithm that sorts must perform the same transports if all input elements are distinct (though perhaps in a different sequence). □

Note that in the above proof we made indirect use of the upper bound provided by Algorithm A in order to prove the lower bound.

5 Applications

A closer look at our algorithm and its analysis reveals that the fundamental properties we used were the partitioning of the grid into blocks and bricks and the existence of an efficient all-to-all mapping. Thus we may apply our algorithmic idea together with its analysis to all cases where an efficient all-to-all mapping exists. With other words: We can replace Algorithm B by Algorithm A independently of the underlying parallel computer. In this way we get results for higher dimensional meshes and tori [10], meshes with additional diagonal connections [11], and reconfigurable meshes [6]. The table in the introduction provides a summary of all our results discussed in the following.

Tori. For tori (meshes with wraparound connections) we simply make use of the known fact that the all-to-all mapping can be implemented twice as fast as for conventional grids [10]. That yields a complexity of $n + O(n^{2/3+\epsilon})$ for h–h problems if $h \leq 8$ and $hn/8 + O(n^{2/3+\epsilon})$ if $h > 8$. These results are optimal for all h and improve results of Gu and Gu [3] in three aspects. First, we are in general faster than they are by an additive term of $0.5n$ for 1–1 sorting with buffer size 1, second, we deal optimally with h–h problems for general h, and, third, we allow for more general indexing schemes as they do. More precisely, for the three cases of indexing functions for 1–1 sorting with buffer size 1 considered by Gu and Gu—blocked snakelike row major, row major, and snakelike row major order—we have complexities of $n+O(n^{2/3+\epsilon})$, $1.5n+O(n^{2/3+\epsilon})$, and $1.5n+O(n^{2/3+\epsilon})$, respectively. Note that the results for row major and snakelike row major indexing functions can be obtained from the results for blocked snakelike row major indexing in the same way as in [3]. In particular, we disprove the conjecture of Gu and Gu that the lower bound n can be improved by showing that it is tight.

Meshes with diagonals [11]. We obtain for the h–h problem in this model $n + O(n^{2/3+\epsilon})$ if $h \le 12$ and $hn/12 + O(n^{2/3+\epsilon})$ if $h > 12$. Here we use recent improvements of h–h sorting in $2n$ steps from $h = 9$ (as presented in [11]) to $h = 12$ [unpublished manuscript]. In the case of tori with diagonals we again halve these time bounds. Once more these results for average case sorting on meshes with diagonals are optimal due to the corresponding lower bound derived in complete analogy to the case for conventional grids.

Reconfigurable meshes [6]. The bisection bound here is hn for $h \ge 1$ due to the model assumption that processor links only may be used unidirectionally at a time. For average case sorting we can show that $hn/2 - O(n^{2/3})$ is a lower bound. We match this lower bound up to the additive term $O(n^{2/3+\epsilon})$ noting that an all-to-all mapping here needs $hn/2$ steps. Let us only mention in pass that for $h > 4$ reconfigurable meshes show to be inferior to conventional meshes with respect to average case sorting.

Routing. Our results for sorting also imply the same optimal results for the corresponding routing problems simply by making use of routing by sorting.

Since all upper bounds in our paper have matching lower bounds, improvements will only be possible with respect to the low order term.

6   Conclusion

This paper solves the problem of average case h–h sorting on meshes and tori for all $h \ge 1$ in the sense that we give asymptotically matching upper and lower bounds.

A few questions remain open. One is whether it is possible to improve our algorithm for 1–1 sorting on tori for row major or snakelike row major indexing. We expect that it is possible to give a lower bound of $1.5n$, showing the optimality of our results also for these special cases of indexing functions. Another point is to study input distributions different from the uniform distribution as utilized here. For practical purposes it would be desirable to improve the additional low order terms.

514

References

1. B. S. Chlebus. Sorting within distance bound on a mesh-connected processor array. In H. Djidjev, editor, *Proc. of International Symposium on Optimal Algorithms*, number 401 in Lecture Notes in Computer Science, pages 232–238, Varna, Bulgaria, May/June 1989. Springer.
2. W. Feller. *An Introduction to Probability Theory and its Applications*, volume I. Wiley, 3d edition, 1968.
3. Q. P. Gu and J. Gu. Algorithms and average time bounds of sorting on a mesh-connected computer. *IEEE Transactions on Parallel and Distributed Systems*, 5(3):308–315, March 1994.
4. T. Hagerup and C. Rüb. A guided tour of Chernoff bounds. *Information Processing Letters*, 33:305–308, 1990.
5. M. Hofri. *Probabilistic analysis of algorithms*. Texts and Monographs in Computer Science. Springer-Verlag, 1987.
6. M. Kaufmann, H. Schröder, and J. F. Sibeyn. Routing and sorting on reconfigurable meshes. 1994. To appear in *Parallel Processing Letters*.
7. M. Kaufmann, J. F. Sibeyn, and T. Suel. Derandomizing algorithms for routing and sorting on meshes. In *Proceedings of the 5th ACM-SIAM Symposium on Discrete Algorithms*, pages 669–679, 1994.
8. D. E. Knuth. *Seminumerical Algorithms*, volume 2 of *The Art of Computer Programming*. Addison-Wesley, 2nd edition, 1969.
9. D. E. Knuth. *Sorting and Searching*, volume 3 of *The Art of Computer Programming*. Addison-Wesley, 1973.
10. M. Kunde. Block gossiping on grids and tori: Sorting and routing match the bisection bound deterministically. In T. Lengauer, editor, *Proceedings of the 1st European Symposium on Algorithms*, number 726 in Lecture Notes in Computer Science, pages 272–283, Bad Honnef, Federal Republic of Germany, September 1993. Springer.
11. M. Kunde, R. Niedermeier, and P. Rossmanith. Faster sorting and routing on grids with diagonals. In P. Enjalbert, E. W. Mayr, and K. W. Wagner, editors, *Proceedings of the 11th Symposium on Theoretical Aspects of Computer Science*, Lecture Notes in Computer Science, pages 225–236. Springer, 1994.
12. T. Leighton. *Introduction to Parallel Algorithms and Architectures: Arrays, Trees, Hypercubes*. Morgan Kaufmann, 1992.
13. T. Leighton. Methods for message routing in parallel machines. In *Proceedings of the 24th ACM Symposium on Theory of Computing*, pages 77–96, 1992.
14. R. Miller, V. K. Prasanna-Kumar, D. I. Reisis, and Q. F. Stout. Parallel computation on reconfigurable meshes. *IEEE Transactions on Computers*, 42(6):678–692, June 1993.

Normal Numbers and Sources for BPP*

Martin Strauss

Department of Mathematics, Rutgers University, New Brunswick, NJ 08903,
mstrauss@math.rutgers.edu

Abstract. In [L90], Lutz proposed a notion of *source*, a nonrandom sequence that can substitute in a certain way for the random bits used by bounded-error probabilistic machines. He showed that almost every sequence in DSPACE($2^{\text{polynomial}}$) is a source. We improve this abundance result to PSPACE, by first showing that the sources are exactly the classical normal numbers of Borel. We go on to show there are sources in AC^0. Unfortunately, this suggests that alternate notions of source should be explored.

1 Introduction

In [L90], Lutz examines a particular kind of pseudorandomness useful for simulating the bounded-error probabilistic machines. The pseudorandomness is not in the form of a generator, that expands a short truly random string, but instead is a single computable sequence, called a source, whose elements can substitute for random bits in a repeated simulation of every bounded-error machine. Thus a source is a particular sequence that is "random enough" in a quantifiable way.

Lutz's work captures two intuitive properties of sources. Intuitively, sources are *universal*, i.e., a single source should work for all machines and all inputs, and sources are *abundant*, i.e., almost all sequences should be sources. Universality is built in to the definition of source (see below), while abundance is at a particular level of resource boundedness – almost every sequence in E_2SPACE = DSPACE($2^{\text{polynomial}}$) is shown to be a source. Lutz also trades some universality for abundance, showing that for any one machine, almost all sequences in ESPACE = DSPACE(2^{linear}) are, for all inputs, sources.

While Lutz was primarily interested in the BPP machines, he notes that the results hold for all bounded error machines, i.e., almost every sequence in E_2SPACE can replace a random sequence for bounded-error machines of arbitrary complexity. This suggests that the complexity of a sequence S has little to do with the complexity of languages having machines for which S is a source. We show that if a sequence is known to be a source for the constant-time bounded-error machines, then it will be a source for arbitrary bounded-error machines, since these sequences are exactly the classical normal sequences (or normal numbers) of [Bor]. The condition of normality proves easier to work with than the

---

* Research supported by NSF grant CCR-9204874.

condition of being a source, and in this way we are able to improve the arguments of [L90], showing that almost all sequences in PSPACE are sources.

A third intuitive property of sources is *hardness*. There should be no sources in P unless P = BPP. There are, however, very simple normal numbers, and we go on to construct a normal number in AC^0. The existence of our AC^0 source does not make BPP languages any easier, and so the sources considered here are not hard by this criterion. Other definitions of source addressing this issue are explored in [AS].

2 Definitions

A *probabilistic machine* is a Turing machine with a usual input tape and another one-way, read-only input tape, called the random tape, each cell of which contains a 0 or a 1. For each input x and each sequence S on the random tape the machine halts. For each x we write $\Pr_M(x) = \sum 2^{-|s|}$, where the sum is over all strings s such that, in the course of deciding x with some (and therefore any) extension S of s on the random tape, M reads exactly the bits in s and then accepts x. A *bounded-error machine* is a probabilistic machine with the property that there's a real number $r > 0$ such that for each x, $|\Pr_M(x) - 1/2| \geq r$ (the maximum such r is the *reliability* of the machine). This machine is said to recognize the language $L(M)$ of words x such that $\Pr(x \in L) = \Pr_M(x) > 1/2$. The class of bounded-error machines will be denoted B.

We also consider a small class of machines, B1. A B1 machine ignores its input, flips some finite number of coins (the number of coins flipped may depend on the outcome of already-flipped coins, but is finite on all paths), and decides whether or not to accept its input (the 1 in B1 is supposed to stand for constant time: since a B1 machine ignores its input, it runs in constant time). We require the probability of acceptance to be bounded away from 1/2 (the probability will be exactly $a/2^b$, for some $a \neq 2^{b-1}$ and b equal to the maximum number of coins flipped). The class of languages accepted by such machines is $\{\emptyset, \{0,1\}^*\}$. Note that a B1 machine is a BPP machine, which in turn is a B machine, where BPP denotes the polynomial-time bounded-error *machines*.

For many of the machines in this paper, the input is either ignored or can be considered part of the machine. We are interested in how changes to the random tape affect the outcome of the computation. In these cases, it will be convenient to let "run M on s" mean "run M with s on the random tape."

We define source as in [L90].

Definition 1. A *source* is a sequence S such that for all bounded-error machines M of reliability r and all inputs x, if we run M on x repeatedly, using successive bits from S, then the lower density of correctly deciding runs is at least $(1/2 + r)$.

That is, for a bounded-error machine M of reliability r and input x, let M' be the machine that repeatedly runs M on x and outputs a sequence $\langle a_i(M, x, S) \rangle$ such that $a_i = 1$ if the ith run of M correctly decides x and $a_i = 0$ otherwise. The machine M' is a probabilistic transducer whose output depends the on coin flip outcomes, but M' uses randomness only to simulate M. A sequence S is a source if for all M and x we have $\liminf_n \frac{1}{n} \sum_{i=1}^{n} a_i(M, x, S) \geq \frac{1}{2} + r$.

We will let UB1, UBPP and UB denote the classes of B1, BPP and B machines, respectively, that, for each input x, always flip some number $m(x)$ random bits on each path of computation.

We turn now from machines to sequences.

For a sequence S, let S_N denote the first N bits of S. For a string s, let s_- denote the string formed by dropping the last bit of s, and let s' denote the string formed by changing the last bit of s. Finally, let $S[i..j]$ denote bits i through j of S.

A string is said to "appear at position i in a sequence S" if $S[i - |s| + j] = s[j]$ for $j = 1, 2, \ldots |s|$. The string appears k times if there are k different i such that the string appears at position i, so 00 appears three times in 0000. If a string s appears k times in a longer finite string $\tilde{s}$, we will say "the density of s on $\tilde{s}$ is $k/|\tilde{s}|$" (the empty string λ is deemed to appear $|\tilde{s}|$ times on $\tilde{s}$, so the density of λ is always 1). The density of s on the sequence S will be the limit of the density on S_n, when that exists, and the lower and upper densities are the liminf and limsup, respectively.

The following notation will be useful. The ratio of the number of appearances of s to the number of appearances of s_- in S_N will be denoted $s :_{S_N} s_-$ (when there's only one sequence under discussion, we will write $s :_N s_-$).

Definition 2. An r-ary sequence S is *normal* in the scale of r if each finite string s has density $2^{-|s|}$ on S.

Normal sequences were first mentioned in [Bor], where it is noted that all reals except on a set of measure zero are normal numbers, i.e., have binary expansions which are normal in the scale of 2. In [Ch], it is shown that the decimal version of the sequence 1 10 11 100 101 110 111 1000..., formed by concatenating the binary numbers, is normal.

A language L will be identified with its characteristic sequence χ_L: enumerate the strings, and set bit i of χ_L to 1 iff the ith string is in L. Following [L90], we have

Definition 3. $S \in C$ if the language $\{x :$ the xth bit of S is 1$\}$ is in C.

Finally, we briefly recall the formulation of resource-bounded measure. This is only used in section 4, which is self-contained.

The concept of resource-bounded measure on exponential and larger time and space classes was introduced by Lutz (see [L92]). Extending measure downward to PSPACE or P involves some subtleties, and is accomplished in [M2] and [AS]. We refer the reader to [M2] for the details of the measure on PSPACE used here (we'll use the notation $\Phi(\text{PSPACE})$ of [AS]). Briefly, a martingale is a function d from $\{0, 1\}^*$ to the nonnegative reals satisfying $d(\lambda) = 1$ and $d(w) = (d(w0) + d(w1))/2$. A set A of languages is said to have Lebesgue measure zero and is intuitively small if there's a martingale d such that for each $L \in A$ we have $\limsup_{n \to \infty} d(\chi_L[0..n]) = \infty$ ("d covers A"). In [M2] machines are

considered that are given the allowable workspace, read their input once from left
to right, and work in polylogspace (Φ(PSPACE) machines). If there's a d covering
$A \subseteq$ PSPACE computed by a Φ(PSPACE) machine then A is said to have
measure zero in PSPACE (or "A is Φ(PSPACE)-null"). If a single Φ(PSPACE)
machine $d_i(w) = d(i, w)$ is such that d_i covers A_i, then it is shown $\bigcup_i A_i$ is null.
Many intuitive properties of measure are proven about measure on PSPACE,
including the fact that DSPACE(n^k) is Φ(PSPACE)-null but PSPACE itself is
not. Also, if $d_i(w)$ is a Φ(PSPACE) machine and d_i covers A_i, then it is proven
that $\bigcup A_i$ is null. The complement of a measure zero set is said to have measure
one, and we say that almost every language in PSPACE is in the complement.

In the next section we will show that a sequence is a source for B or B1 iff it
is normal, thus characterizing the sources. In subsequent sections, we will show
that almost all PSPACE sequences are normal, and finally, that there's a normal
sequence in DLOGTIME-uniform AC^0, which implies there are uncountably
many normal sequences in nonuniform AC^0.

3   SOURCE(B1) = NORMAL = SOURCE(B)

We will show that B1 sources are normal, then that normal sequences are sources
for B. Since a B1 machine is a B machine, all sources for B are sources for B1.
In particular, this shows that a sequence is a source for B iff it is a source for
any class of bounded error machines between B1 and B, e.g., BPP.

Theorem 4. *Any source for* B1 *is normal.*

Proof. Suppose S is not normal. Then there's a string s with one-sided density
bounded away from $2^{-|s|}$. We may assume s is of minimal length; so in particular
s_- has density $2^{-|s|-1}$. Let $\epsilon \in (0, 1/2)$ be such that the relative frequency of s
to s_- is at least $1/2 + \epsilon$ infinitely often (or is at most $1/2 - \epsilon$, wlog assume the
former). We will construct a B1 machine M that detects this bias. That is, we
will construct an infinite set A of integers n, so that M on S_n accepts more than
half the time, while M as a probabilistic machine rejects.

First we consider the case $s_- \neq \lambda$. Choose $\eta > 0$ small enough that

$$(1 - \eta)(1/2 + \epsilon) > 1/2.$$

Next, choose N large enough that

$$\frac{|s_-|}{\eta N} < \frac{1}{2}2^{-|s_-|}.$$

Choose n' large enough that for all $n > n'$

$$\text{the density of } s_- \text{ is at least } \tfrac{1}{2}2^{-|s_-|} \text{ on } S_n, \tag{1}$$

and, finally, let A be the set of $n > \max(n', N)$ so that

$$(s :_{S_n} s_-) \geq (1/2 + \epsilon).$$

The machine M is defined by the following: Read random bits until either s or s' appears, but not more than N random bits. If s appears before s' accept, if s' appears before s reject (and read no more bits in these cases), and if neither s nor s' appears in N random bits reject (but read all N bits even if after reading $N - |s| + 1$ bits it is known that neither s nor s' will appear).

As a probabilistic machine, M accepts with probability strictly less than $1/2$, so M is a bounded-error machine accepting $\emptyset$. Also, note that M ignores its input. Thus M is a B1 machine. We will check the performance of M run on S, verifying that M behaves differently on S than on random strings. Fix $n \in A$. The main observation is that when M is run on S_n, at least $(1 - \eta)$ of the runs see s or s'. Otherwise, if out of T runs at least ηT runs see neither s nor s', then they use at least ηNT bits, so at least ηNT bits are used altogether. The string s_- appears at most once among bits seen by a run of M, and at most $(|s_-| - 1)$ times spanning two runs of M, altogether $|s_-|T$ times. This would make the density of s_- on S_n at most

$$\frac{|s_-|T}{\eta NT} < \frac{1}{2} 2^{-|s_-|},$$

contradicting (1). Finally, of the runs that see s_-, at least $(1/2 + \epsilon)$ see s, and so these $(1 - \eta)(1/2 + \epsilon) > 1/2$ runs accept, while fewer than $1/2$ of the runs reject. Thus for infinitely many n, the machine M accepts $\{0,1\}^*$ in at least $1/2$ of the runs on S_n. Therefore S is not a source.

If $s_- = \lambda$, then the density of 0 (wlog) is greater than $1/2 + \epsilon$ infinitely often. Pick N large enough that

$$(1 - 2^{-N})(1/2 + \epsilon) > 1/2.$$

By the pigeonhole principle, there is some $i \in [0, N]$ such that, for an infinite set A' of n's, the frequency of 0 in positions less than n and congruent to i mod $(N+1)$ is at least $1/2 + \epsilon$ (wlog $i = N$). Of the 2^N strings of length N, there is some string σ, so that for an infinite set $A \subseteq A'$ of n's, the frequency of σ appearing starting in positions congruent to 0 mod $(N + 1)$ is at most 2^{-N}. The machine M will read $N + 1$ random bits. If σ appears as the first N bits, positions 0 through $(N - 1)$, reject. Otherwise, if the bit in position N is 0 accept, and if the bit in position N is 1 reject (the machine M reads all $N + 1$ bits even if the outcome is determined earlier).

As a probabilistic machine, M accepts with probability

$$(1 - 2^{-N}) \cdot 1/2 = 1/2 - 2^{-(N+1)},$$

so M is a bounded error machine accepting $\emptyset$. On the other hand, for $n \in A$ and M run on S_n, the machine M accepts at least

$$(1 - 2^{-N})(1/2 + \epsilon) > 1/2$$

of the time. That is, for infinitely many n, M accepts $\{0,1\}^*$ more than half the time when run on S_n, so S is not a source.

To prove the next inclusion, we need some lemmas:

Lemma 5. *If $S = \langle b_0, b_1 \ldots \rangle$ is normal in the scale of 2, then for all m the sequence*

$$\langle b_0 b_1 \ldots b_{m-1}, b_m b_{m+1} \ldots b_{2m-1}, \ldots \rangle$$

is normal in the scale of 2^m.

Here we regard S as a sequence of digits in base 2^m by the natural grouping of bits.

Proof. See [NZ], or [K, Theorem C] for a "simplified" proof of a statement more general than the lemma.

The next corollary follows directly from lemma 5:

Corollary 6. *Any normal sequence S is a source for* UB.

The rest of this section is devoted to showing that normal numbers are sources for B machines.

Lemma 7. *For all machines M (with reliability r), all inputs x, and all $\eta > 0, \epsilon > 0$ there's an N such that if M is run repeatedly on x through at least N random bits, the probability is less than η that M will decide correctly on fewer than $(1/2 + r)(1 - \epsilon)$ of the runs.*

Proof. If we run M through N complete runs rather than through N random bits, the conclusion follows from the law of large numbers. A proof of the lemma is only slightly more subtle. See [F, equation 6.4].

Theorem 8. *Any normal sequence is a source for* B.

Proof. Fix a normal sequence S, an input x, a machine M of reliability $r > 0$, and suppose that M flips between m_1 and m_2 coins on any path of computation.

Since M flips a variable number of coins, we cannot apply lemma 5 directly as above. Instead we argue as follows: Let M' be a machine that repetitively performs as many complete runs of M as possible on at most $n \gg m_2$ random bits, and the ith run of M' outputs the fraction a_i of correct runs of M. Then the number of coins flipped by M' is very close (in ratio) to being the same on all paths, so we can apply an argument like the above and conclude that $\frac{1}{n} \sum_{i=1}^{n} a_i \to \frac{1}{2} + r$. It follows that $1/2 + r$ of the runs of M are correct.

We now give the argument more formally. Let $r' < r$; we will show that for large enough n, if M is repeatedly run on x using random bits from S_n, at least $(1/2 + r')$ of the runs will be correct. Put

$$R = \left(\frac{1/2 + r'}{1/2 + r} \right) < 1,$$

so it is sufficient to show at least $(1/2 + r)R$ runs succeed using bits of S. Pick ϵ, η small enough that

$$\begin{cases} (1 - \epsilon) & > R^{1/3} \\ (1 - 2\eta m_2^2) > R^{1/3} \\ 2\eta m_2^3/m_1 & < \frac{R^{-1/3}-1}{3} \end{cases}$$

Next, pick N large enough that

$$\frac{4\eta m_2^4 + m_1 m_2}{N m_1} < \frac{R^{-1/3} - 1}{3}$$

and, by lemma 7,

$$\Pr \begin{pmatrix} \text{on runs through at least } N \text{ random bits, less than} \\ \text{the fraction } (1/2 + r)(1 - \epsilon) \text{ of runs are correct} \end{pmatrix} < \eta. \qquad (2)$$

Finally, by lemma 5, pick n' large enough so that for $n > n'$ we have

$$\frac{m_2(N + 2m_2)^2}{Nn m_1} < \frac{R^{-1/3} - 1}{3}$$

and on S_n each (2^{N+2m_2})-digit occurs with density at most $2 \cdot 2^{-(N+2m_2)}$, i.e., at most

$$2 \cdot 2^{-(N+2m_2)} \frac{n}{N + 2m_2} \qquad (3)$$

times among the (2^{N+2m_2})-digits in S_n, of which there are $n/(N + 2m_2)$.

When M is run repeatedly on S_n, some runs of M span two consecutive (2^{N+2m_2})-digits of S_n, while others use bits entirely within a single (2^{N+2m_2})-digit. For any (2^{N+2m_2})-digit d in S_n, let the *interior* of d denote the maximal infix substring s of d such that some run of M on S_n starts on the first bit of s, and some later run of M on S_n ends on the last bit of s. Note that the interior of any (2^{N+2m_2})-digit is at least N bits long.

Call a string of length at least N "good" if it causes M to run correctly at least $(\frac{1}{2} + r)(1 - \epsilon)$ of the time, otherwise call it "bad." For each $i, j \in [0, m_2)$, there are by (2) at most $\eta 2^{N+2m_2}$ strings of length $N + 2m_2$ containing a bad string starting in position i and ending in position $N + 2m_2 - j$. Thus there are at most $m_2^2 \eta 2^{N+2m_2}$ strings of length $N + 2m_2$ containing bad strings starting in any position in $[0, m_2)$ and ending in any position $(N + m_2, N + 2m_2]$. By (3), each of these strings of length $N + 2m_2$ appears with density at most $2 \cdot 2^{-(N+2m_2)}$ among the (2^{N+2m_2})-digits of S_n, so at most $2\eta m_2^2 \frac{n}{N+2m_2}$ of the interiors of S_n are bad, the other $(1 - 2\eta m_2^2) \frac{n}{N+2m_2}$ are good.

The ratio of correct to total runs on the good interiors is at least $(\frac{1}{2} + r)(1 - \epsilon)$. The good interiors account for at least $(1 - 2\eta m_2^2) \frac{n}{N+2m_2} \frac{N}{a}$ runs of M, where $a \leq m_2$ is the average on the good interiors of the number of bits used per run. Besides these runs, there are at most $2\eta m_2^2 \frac{n}{N+2m_2} \frac{N+2m_2}{m_1}$ runs on the $2\eta m_2^2 \frac{n}{N+2m_2}$ bad interiors, at most $\frac{n}{N+2m_2}$ runs spanning boundaries of consecutive (2^{N+2m_2})-digits of S_n, and at most $\frac{N+2m_2}{m_1}$ runs on the final partial 2^{N+2m_2} digit.

The correct-to-total ratio on all S_n is the correct-to-total ratio on the good interiors times the ratio of runs on good interiors to total runs. That is, canceling $\frac{n}{N+2m_2}\frac{N}{a}$, and using $a \leq m_2$ in (4), the ratio of correct runs to total runs on S_n is at least

$$
\left(\frac{1}{2}+r\right)(1-\epsilon)\frac{(1-2\eta m_2^2)}{1+2\eta am_2^2\frac{N+2m_2}{Nm_1}+\frac{a}{N}+\frac{a(N+2m_2)^2}{Nnm_1}}
$$

$$
> \left(\frac{1}{2}+r\right)(1-\epsilon)\frac{(1-2\eta m_2^2)}{1+\frac{2\eta m_2^3}{m_1}+\frac{4\eta m_2^4+m_1 m_2}{Nm_1}+\frac{m_2(N+2m_2)^2}{Nnm_1}} \quad (4)
$$

$$
> \left(\frac{1}{2}+r\right)R^{1/3}\frac{R^{1/3}}{1+\frac{R^{-1/3}-1}{3}+\frac{R^{-1/3}-1}{3}+\frac{R^{-1/3}-1}{3}}
$$

$$
= \left(\frac{1}{2}+r\right)R
$$

$$
= \left(\frac{1}{2}+r'\right).
$$

Since a B1 machine is a B machine, we have, for any class B' with $B1 \subseteq B' \subseteq B$ (e.g., $B' = BPP$),

Corollary 9. *The following are equivalent:*

- *The sequence S is a source for* B.
- *The sequence S is a source for* B'.
- *The sequence S is normal.*

4 Abundance of Normal Numbers

It is easily shown that (in the sense of Lebesgue measure) almost every real number between 0 and 1 is normal, i.e., has a normal binary expansion (see [Bor]; the fact also follows from a proof that almost every sequence is normal in a resource-bounded sense). Lutz has shown [L90] that almost every E_2SPACE sequence is a source for B, (in the sense of measure defined there). We now show that almost every PSPACE sequence is normal (in the sense of measure in [M]), thereby concluding that almost every PSPACE sequence is a source.

We cover the abnormal sequences by writing them as a Φ(PSPACE)-union of more manageable pieces.

Definition 10. A sequence S is (s,ϵ)-*terminally-upper-seminormal* (or briefly (s,ϵ)-tusn) if s_- appears finitely often in S or for almost every N, we have $(s :_{S_N} s_-) \leq (\frac{1}{2}+\epsilon)$.

We regard the finite appearance condition as a technicality and the $(s :_N s_-)$ bound as the main condition that gives the term its name.

Lemma 11. *For each string s and each ε a power of 2, almost every PSPACE language is (s, ϵ)-tusn.*

Proof. We will define a martingale d covering the non-(s, ϵ)-tusn sequences, i.e., sequences where s_- appears infinitely often and for infinitely many N we have $(s :_N s_-) \geq (\frac{1}{2} + \epsilon)$. Define a martingale by $d(\lambda) = 1$ and

$$d(w) = \begin{cases} (1 + 2\epsilon)d(w_-); & s \text{ is a suffix of } w \\ (1 - 2\epsilon)d(w_-); & s' \text{ is a suffix of } w \\ d(w_-); & \text{otherwise.} \end{cases}$$

Suppose for some w we have $(s :_{|w|} s_-) > (\frac{1}{2} + \epsilon)$, and s_- appears j times on w. Then s appears $j(s :_{|w|} s_-)$ times on w and s' appears $j(s' :_{|w|} s_-)$ times on w. We have:

$$\begin{aligned} d(w) &= (1 + 2\epsilon)^{(s:_{|w|}s_-)j}(1 - 2\epsilon)^{(s':_{|w|}s_-)j} \\ &> (1 + 2\epsilon)^{(\frac{1}{2}+\epsilon)j}(1 - 2\epsilon)^{(\frac{1}{2}-\epsilon)j} \\ &= 2^{(1-h(\frac{1}{2}+\epsilon))j}, \end{aligned}$$

where $h(x) = -(x \log x + (1 - x) \log(1 - x))$ is the entropy function, strictly less than 1 for $x \neq \frac{1}{2}$. We show that d is unbounded on the appropriate languages: Fix arbitrary M, Find n so that s_- appears $j \geq \log(M)/(1 - h(\frac{1}{2} + \epsilon))$ times on S_n, and finally find w of length at least n so that $(s :_{|w|} s_-) > (\frac{1}{2} + \epsilon)$. For this w we have $d(w) \geq M$.

We have to show this density function is $\Phi(\text{PSPACE})$-computable. There are two issues: First, as the algorithm was given above we need $d(w_-)$ in order to compute $d(w)$, but a $\Phi(\text{PSPACE})$ algorithm must do this bottom-up. Also, we need to be able to do the necessary arithmetic in polylogspace.

As we scan the input w, having just read a prefix $z \sqsubseteq w$, keep track of three things: the number of occurrences of s and s', the last $|s| - 1$ bits of z, and $d(z)$. The number of occurrences of s and s' is at most $|w|$. Storing the last $|s| - 1$ bits of z takes $|s|$ space. We can record $d(z)$ by recording two exponents, a and b, such that $d(z) = (1 + 2\epsilon)^a(1 - 2\epsilon)^b$. Each of a and b is at most $|w|$, so we can store these in $\log |w|$ space.

Finally, we need to compute $d(w) = (1 + 2\epsilon)^a(1 - 2\epsilon)^b$ in polylog($|w|$) space, but only for the final a and b. Note $a, b \sim |w|$, so $d(w)$ will have about $|w|$ bits, too many to write down all at once, but the model of computation requires only that we spit out the output bits in order without seeing them again. Suppose $2\epsilon = 2^{-k}$. We can write

$$d(w) = \left(\sum_{i=0}^{a} \binom{a}{i} 2^{-ik} \right) \left(\sum_{i=0}^{b} \binom{b}{i} (-2)^{-ik} \right).$$

Perform the operations without storing intermediate results, but rather restarting the computation for each required bit in an intermediate result. Note that no intermediate result is bigger than $|w|!$, which has $\sim |w| \log |w|$ bits, and so needs less than $2 \log |w|$ space for a register.

Theorem 12. *Almost every PSPACE sequence is normal, and so a source.*

Proof. Let $X_{s,j,\pm} = \emptyset$ unless j is a power of 2. For j a power of 2, let $X_{s,j,+}$ denote the non-$(s, 1/j)$-tusn languages, and let $X_{s,j,-}$ denote the similarly-definded non-$(s, 1/j)$-terminally-lower-seminormal languages. It is straightforward to show that the abnormal sequences is a $\Phi(\text{PSPACE})$-union of the $X_{s,j,\pm}$.

5 An Easily-Computed Normal Sequence

In this section we construct a normal sequence in DLOGTIME-uniform AC^0.

Let s_r denote the concatenation of the strings of length r, so for example $s_2 = 00\,01\,10\,11$ (we will say that s_r is the concatenation of the padded numerals of length r). In [Ch] it is shown that the decimal version of the sequence

$$S = s_1 s_2 s_3 \ldots = 0\,1\,00\,01\,10\,11\,000\ldots,$$

formed by concatenating the numerals, is normal. While this sequence is easy to describe, we have no proof that it's in AC^0. Moreover, a straightforward way of computing it requires division by small numbers, and division by 3 is known not to be in AC^0 (see [BL]). Thus we use a variant, S', computed by the program in figure 1, and shown in part in figure 2. In figure 2 we put

$$g_r = \sum_{j=1}^{r} |s_j| = \sum_{j=1}^{r} j2^j = 2(r-1)2^r + 2,$$

so there are g_r bits in the listing of all numerals of length at most r.

Fig. 1. Program to compute S'

```
for j = 1 to ∞
    if j is a power of 2
        output sⱼ
    else
        {
            let j' be the largest power of 2 less than ʲ⁄₂
            for i = 1 to (j2ʲ)/(j'2ʲ')
                output sⱼ'
        }
```

Note that j' of the program is a power of 2 and $2^{j-j'} > j-j' > j'$, so j' divides $2^{j-j'}$. Thus, for example, in the 24 bits from bit $10 = g_2$ to bit $33 = g_3 - 1$, S lists

Fig. 2. Comparison of S and S'

Pos: 0	$2 = g_1$	$10 = g_2$	$34 = g_3$	$98 = g_4$

$$
\begin{array}{llll}
\downarrow\ \downarrow & \downarrow & \downarrow & \downarrow \\
S\ =0\ 1\,00\,01\,10\,11\,000001 & \ldots 111\ 0000 \ldots 1111\ 00000 & & 00001\ldots \\
\ =s_1\ s_2 \qquad\quad s_3 & \qquad\quad s_4 & s_5 s_6 647 s_7 s_8 \ldots \\
S'\ =0\ 1\,00\,01\,10\,11\,01\ 01\ 01 \ldots 1\ 01\ 0000 \ldots 1111\ 00\ 01\ 10\ 11\ 00\ldots \\
\ =s_1\ s_2 \qquad\quad s_1^{12} & \qquad\quad s_4 & s_2^{20} s_2^{48} s_2^{112} s_8 \ldots
\end{array}
$$

s_3, while S' lists s_1^{12} (1 is the greatest power of 2 less than 3/2). The numeral 0000 starts at bit $34 = g_3$ in both S and S'. In general, S' is a concatenation of numerals with lengths a power of 2, and, for r a power of 2, the string 0^r first appears as a single numeral at position g_{r-1} in both S and S'. Note that from position g_{4k} on, S' lists numerals longer than k.

To prove that S' is normal, we need the following lemma, proved (for base 10) in [Ch, lemma (ii)]. (Note the lemma follows immediately from the normality of Champernowne's number.)

Lemma 13. *Any string s appears $2^{-|s|}n + o(|s_r|)$ times in the first n digits of s_r.*

Here $r \to \infty$, and n can assume any value less than $|s_r| = r2^r$.

Proposition 14. *The sequence S' is normal.*

Proof. Let s be a finite string. First, only finitely-many of the s_r's in S' have $r < |s|$, so we may ignore these. For $r \geq |s|$, the density of s is perfect on any (complete) appearance of s_r, ignoring $o(|s_r|)$ appearances of s spanning the boundary of two consecutive numerals within s_r. Comparing the sequences S and S' we see there are at least $\Theta(r2^r)$ bits preceding any appearance of s_r, so by the lemma, the density of s is asymptotically correct on the last fragment of an s_r.

Proposition 15. *The sequence S' is in AC^0.*

Proof. The straightforward algorithm for S' involves finding the largest k with $g_{2^k-1} \leq x$, then dividing and remaindering by 2^{k-1} to find bit x in S'. Note that $k \sim \log\log x$ is truly small. In AC^0 we can perform addition (and therefore subtraction and comparison) of numbers of linear size, and shift left and right by a linear number of bits. Computation of $g_{2^k-1} = (2^k - 2)2^{2^k}$ involves nothing more than these operations. We can search all $k \leq \log\log x$ to find the maximal k with $g_{2^k-1} \leq x$. The divisions and remainders mentioned can all be done by bit shifts, as can the final test of a specified bit of a specified string, for bit positions up to $2^k \sim \log x$.

6 Conclusion

We've shown that the sources, as defined, are exactly the normal numbers, and so there's a source in AC^0. This result does not, however, make BPP problems easier, since we may need to run exponentially many simulations before the behavior becomes close to asymptotic. We consider this is a drawback in the definition of source. Intuitively, we feel that a notion of source should make the complexity of a source at least the complexity of the languages decidable using the source. [AS] explores other possible notions of source.

Acknowledgment

I gratefully acknowledge helpful discussions with Eric Allender.

References

[AS]   E. Allender and M. Strauss, "Measure on small complexity classes, with applications for bpp." *Proc. 35th Annual IEEE Symp. on Foundations of Computer Science*, (1994).

[BDG]   J. Balcázar, J. Díaz and J. Gabarró, *Structural complexity I*, Springer-Verlag EATCS Monographs on Theoretical Computer Science, (1988), New York, pp. 130-141.

[BL]   Ravi Boppana and Jeff Lagarias, "One-way functions and circuit complexity." *Information and Computation* **74**, (1987), pp. 226-240.

[Bor]   E. Borel, *Leçons sur la théorie des fonctions*, (1914), pp. 182-216.

[Ch]   D. G. Champernowne, "The construction of decimals normal in the scale of ten." *J. London Math Soc.*, **8** (1933), pp. 254-260.

[F]   W. Feller, *An Introduction to probability theory and its applications*, Wiley, (1968), New York, pp. 320-322.

[K]   D. Knuth, *The art of computer programming v. 2*, Addison-Wesley, (1981), Reading, Mass, pp. 149-151.

[L90]   J. Lutz, "Pseudorandom sources for BPP." *J. Computer and System Sciences*, **41** (1990), pp. 307-320.

[L92]   J. Lutz, "Almost everywhere high nonuniform complexity." *Journal of Computer and System Sciences* **44** (1992), pp. 220-258.

[M]   E. Mayordomo, *Contributions to the study of resource-bounded measure*. PhD Thesis, Universitat Politècnica de Catalunya, Barcelona, 1994. See also [M2], in which a preliminary version of the PSPACE measure appears.

[M2]   E. Mayordomo, "Measuring in PSPACE." to appear in *Proc. International Meeting of Young Computer Scientists '92*, Topics in Computer Science series, Gordon and Breach.

[NZ]   I. Niven and H. Zuckerman, "On the definition of normal numbers." *Pacific J. Math*, **1** (1951), pp. 103-109.

Lower Bounds on Learning Decision Lists and Trees
(*Extended Abstract*)[*]

Thomas Hancock[1] and Tao Jiang[2] and Ming Li[3] and John Tromp[4]

[1] Siemens Corporate Research, 755 College Road East, Princeton, NJ 08540,
hancock@scr.siemens.com
[2] Dept. of Comp. Sci., McMaster University, Hamilton, Ont. L8S 4K1, Canada,
jiang@maccs.mcmaster.ca
[3] Dept. of Comp. Sci., University of Waterloo, Waterloo, Ont. N3L 3G1, Canada,
mli@math.uwaterloo.ca
[4] Dept. of Comp. Sci., University of Waterloo, Waterloo, Ont. N3L 3G1, Canada,
tromp@math.uwaterloo.ca

Abstract. k-decision lists and decision trees play important roles in learning theory as well as in practical learning systems. k-decision lists generalize classes such as monomials, k-DNF, and k-CNF and like these subclasses is polynomially PAC-learnable [19]. This leaves open the question of whether k-decision lists can be learned as efficiently as k-DNF. We answer this question negatively in a certain sense, thus disproving a claim in a popular textbook [2]. Decision trees, on the other hand, are not even known to be polynomially PAC-learnable, despite their widespread practical application. We will show that decision trees are not likely to be efficiently PAC-learnable. We summarize our specific results.
The following problems cannot be approximated in polynomial time within a factor of $2^{\log^\delta n}$ for any $\delta < 1$, unless NP $\subset$ DTIME$[2^{\text{polylog } n}]$: a generalized set cover, k-decision lists, k-decision lists by monotone decision lists, and decision trees. Decision lists cannot be approximated in polynomial time within a factor of n^δ, for some constant $\delta > 0$, unless NP = P. Also, k-decision lists with l 0-1 alternations cannot be approximated within a factor $\log^l n$ unless NP $\subset$ DTIME$[n^{O(\log \log n)}]$ (providing an interesting comparison to the upper bound recently obtained in [1]).

1 Introduction

This paper proves lower bounds on the approximability of decision lists and trees. An instance of such a problem is a set of boolean n-vectors each labeled with a binary classification, true or false. The desired output is a decision list (or tree) over the n attributes that is consistent with the set of examples and whose size (according to some natural measure) is within a certain approximation factor of the minimum solution size.

[*] The research was supported by NSERC Research Grants OGP0046613 and OGP-0046506, an NSERC International Fellowship, and ITRC.

This is an important problem in learning theory, since the existence of a polynomial time approximation algorithm implies that the class is PAC learnable (given certain technical conditions [6]). Such algorithms, with a mere logarithmic approximation factor, exist for k-DNF and k-CNF, for example. Tighter approximation algorithms imply more efficient learning algorithms (in terms of sample complexity). Furthermore, the non-existence of such algorithms has negative implications for learnability. If there is no polynomial approximation algorithm that produces a representation within a certain factor of the minimum size, then there is no PAC learning algorithm whose hypothesis is within that factor of the minimum possible unless RP = NP [12]. Our main results will show that based on the assumption that NP is not contained in randomized pseudopolynomial time, size l k-decision lists (or trees) are not learnable by size $l2^{\log^{\delta} l}$ k-decision lists (trees, respectively) for any $\delta < 1$. Under the weaker condition that RP $\neq$ NP, it is hard to learn general decision lists by size $l^{1+\epsilon}$ decision lists for some $\epsilon > 0$.

Decision trees are the key concept in learning systems such as ID3 [15] and CART [7], and have found a use in many applications. There is an enormous amount of machine learning literature concerned with decision trees (see, for example, [14, 15, 16]). However, the PAC-learnability of decision trees remains as one of the most prominent open questions in learning theory. Other than many heuristic learning algorithms using principles such as minimum description length and maximum entropy, the theoretically best learning algorithm [8] PAC-learns a decision tree using $O(n^{\log n})$ samples. It is thus a very important question in learning theory (and learning practice) whether decision trees are polynomially PAC-learnable; that is, whether we can find the approximately smallest decision tree with high probability. We will provide a negative result in this direction, showing that decision trees cannot be efficiently approximated. One of the main motivations for the use of decision trees in empirical learning work is that small decision trees are believed to be a good output representation for human comprehensibility. Hence negative results regarding finding such a hypothesis are particularly relevant. Note that it was not even known if finding the smallest decision tree is NP-hard. What was known is that finding a decision tree with the minimum external path length is NP-hard [11, 9].

2 Learning Theory and Complexity of Approximation

This section introduces concepts and results in learning theory and complexity of approximation that are needed in this paper. We will consider the following classes of Boolean functions, with Boolean variables $\{x_1, \ldots, x_n\}$, defined on $\{0, 1\}$:

- M_n: all monomials defined on $\{0, 1\}^n$, where a *monomial* is a conjunction of zero or more literals.
- $M_{n,k}$: all monomials defined on $\{0, 1\}^n$ having at most k literals.

- DNF (Disjunctive Normal Form): set of formulas described as disjunctions of monomials defined on $\{0,1\}^n$. CNF (Conjunctive Normal Form) is a conjunction of disjunctions of literals.
- k-DNF: set of the DNF formulas with each monomial term in $M_{n,k}$. k-CNF is defined analogously.
- DL: class of decision lists. A *decision list* defined on $\{0,1\}^n$ is a list $L = (m_1, c_1)(m_2, c_2)\dots(m_l, c_l)$, where for each $i = 1, \dots, l$, $m_i \in M_n$ is a monomial and $c_i \in \{0,1\}$. For an input Boolean vector from $\{0,1\}^n$, the value of list L is c_i if i is the smallest integer such that m_i is satisfied, If no m_i is satisfied then $L = 0$.[5] *Monotone* decision lists are those not containing any negated variables.
- k-DL: class of k-decision lists. A k-*decision list* is a decision list in which each term belongs to $M_{n,k}$.
- DT: class of decision trees. A *decision tree* defined on $\{0,1\}^n$ is a binary tree T, each of whose non-leaf nodes is labeled with one of n variables $x_1, \dots, x_n$, and whose leaves are labeled 0 or 1. The value of T on an input vector is obtained as the label of the leaf reached from the root as follows: at each node go to the left or right child depending on whether the input bit corresponding the label is 0 or 1, respectively.

A PAC learning algorithm, for a hypothesis class H, solves the following problem:

Input: Constants $0 < \epsilon, \delta < 1$, and a source of random examples EX that, when queried, provides in unit time a pair $< x, c(x) >$ where x is drawn independently according to some unknown distribution D and c is some fixed unknown concept from H.

Output: A hypothesis $h \in H$.

Requirement: The input determines the probability of any hypothesis h being output by the learning algorithm. The essential requirement of PAC learning is that the probability of outputting a *bad* hypothesis (one for which $D(h(x) \neq c(x))\epsilon$) is bounded by δ.

The learner is allowed running time polynomial in $1/\epsilon$, $1/\delta$, and the size of the target concept c. For more details of Valiant's PAC-learning model, we refer the reader to [2]. The basic question in learning theory is to identify the polynomially learnable classes. Among the most prominent polynomially learnable classes are monomials, k-DNF, k-CNF, and k-DL. It is clear that monomials, k-DNF, and k-CNF are subclasses of k-DL.

An efficient learning algorithm that produces a hypothesis for a certain class can be converted into a randomized approximation algorithm for that class by a construction of [3] (the essence of the conversion is that approximation for a sample m can be obtained by the learner if the learner is trained with the uniform distribution on m and is forced to achieve accuracy close to $1/|m|$).

---

[5] Our definition follows [19]. In [2], the class of DL is defined as a more general class such that each term may be a Boolean function from some class K rather than just monomials.

Recently, there has been significant progress in the complexity theoretic aspects of approximation. Below we list the results that will be needed in this paper.

Theorem 1. *1. Unless* NP = P*:*

    (a) Graph Coloring cannot be approximated in polynomial time with ratio n^ϵ, for some $\epsilon > 0$ [13].

    (b) Set Covering cannot be approximated in polynomial time to within any constant [13].

    (c) Vertex Cover does not have a polynomial time approximation scheme [4].

2. Unless NP is contained in DTIME[$n^{O(\log \log n)}$]:

    (a) Set Covering cannot be approximated in polynomial time with a ratio of $c \log n$, for any $c < 1/8$ [5, 13].

Our hardness results for k-decision lists and decision trees start with a basic approximation preserving (linear) reduction from Set Covering to show that approximation within a constant factor is hard. Then we use a "squaring" process to in essence combine two problems into one in a way that amplifies approximation difficulty. For k-decision lists, this amplification is done using a new form of the set covering problem that we define, show to be difficult to approximate, and then reduce finding a consistent k-decision list to. For decision trees, we do the amplification on decision trees themselves to show how arbitrary approximability can be improved with additional computation. This allows us to achieve a greater lower bound on approximation than the constant implied by our reduction from Set Covering.

Our hardness results for generalized decision lists are based on an approximation preserving reduction from Graph Coloring.

3 Non-approximability of k-Decision Lists

Our results build upon the non-approximability of Set Covering (items 1b,2a above) and Vertex Cover (item 1c above), which can be viewed as a special case of Set Covering. Given a collection $S_1, S_2, \ldots, S_m \subset U = \{1, 2, \ldots, t\}$ of sets, we are to find a minimum-size subcollection that covers U. This lower bound translates to a lower bound on approximability of monomials, where, given a set of positive and negative examples, we are to find a shortest monomial consistent with those examples. The reduction from Set Covering to monomials is as follows. Given an instance of Set Covering, $S_1, S_2, \ldots, S_m \subset \{1, 2, \ldots, t\}$, create examples of length m bits, one bit for each set. For each element of U, create a negative example that has a 0 for all sets containing it and 1's elsewhere. Also create one positive example of all 1's. The latter prevents any negative literals from occurring in a consistent monomial. It is easy to see that a consistent monomial of k literals exists iff a size-k set cover exists. So, under assumption 2, the shortest consistent monomial cannot be approximated in polynomial time within ratio $c \log n$, for any $c < 1/8$.

For monomials (and k-DNF/k-CNF), this result is sharp, since a greedy algorithm finds a monomial that is at most logarithmically longer than the shortest one [10]. Decision lists, however, are of a different nature, since their individual components are ordered in an essential way. They correspond not to Set Covering, but to a generalization that we call (P, N) *Covering*: Given disjoint sets P, N and a collection $S_1, S_2, \ldots, S_m \subset P \cup N$, we are to find a shortest sequence $S_{i_1}, \ldots, S_{i_k}$ that covers P such that for each $1 \leq r \leq k$,

$$S'_{i_r} \stackrel{\text{def}}{=} S_{i_r} \setminus \bigcup j < r S_{i_j}$$

is a subset of either P or N. If S'_{i_r} is non-empty and $S'_{i_r} \subset X$, we say S_{i_r} *uncovers* X. Here, X can be P, N, or a subset of either.

3.1   Non-approximability of (P, N) Covering

We show how to amplify the non-approximability of Set Covering by a blow-up reduction from Set Covering to (P, N) Covering. The basis of this blow-up is formed by a construction that "multiplies" a Set Covering instance A with a (P, N) Covering instance B to obtain a (P, N) Covering instance C whose smallest solution has a size close to the product of those of A and B. Let instance A consist of covering sets $s_1, s_2, \ldots, s_m \subset U = \{1, 2, \ldots, t\}$. Let instance B consist of covering sets $r_1, \ldots r_l \subset P \cup N$. Instance C will consist of the following elements: a copy of U, m copies of P and N called $P_i, N_i, 1 \leq i \leq m$ and two extra elements x, y. These elements are partitioned into $P_C = U \cup \bigcup_i N_i \cup \{x\}$ and $N_C = \bigcup_i P_i \cup \{y\}$. Denote the copy of r_j in $P_i \cup N_i$ by $r_{i,j}$. The covering sets of C are

- $r_{i,j}$ for all $1 \leq i \leq m$ and $1 \leq j \leq l$.
- $s_i \cup P_i$, for all $1 \leq i \leq m$.
- $U \cup N_C$
- $P_C \cup N_C$

Claim 2 *If a and b are the sizes of minimum covers of A and B, then the minimum cover of C has size $a(b + 1) + 2$. Furthermore, for any c, d, given a covering of C of size at most $c(d + 1) + 2$, one can find either a cover of A of size at most c, or a cover of B of size at most d.*

Proof. Recall that a cover of C means a cover of set P_C. Since this contains an element x which occurs in covering set $P_C \cup N_C$ only, set N_C must be covered first. Since only $U \cup N_C$ can uncover $y \in N_C$, set U must be uncovered by the sets $s_i \cup P_i$, which takes exactly a of them. Each of those requires P_i to be covered first, which takes b of the $r_{i,j}$ sets. Thus, $a(b+1)$ sets are necessary and sufficient to cover U, after which the sets $U \cup N_C$ and $P_C \cup N_C$ suffice (and are needed) to complete the covering of P_C. For the second part one can use the induced covering of U or the smallest induced covering of P. Clearly, if the former is of size more than c and the latter of size more than d, then this contradicts the assumption.

We can now define "powers" $A^0, A^1, \ldots$ of a Set Cover instance A, where A^0 is an empty (P, N) Cover instance, and $A^{i+1} = AA^i$. Solving for size, we find that A^i has minimal size $(a^i - 1)\frac{a+2}{a-1}$. Furthermore, Claim 2 implies that, from a cover of A^i of size c, we can find a cover of A of size at most $\sqrt[i]{c\frac{a-1}{a+2} + 1}$.

This blow-up technique allows us to prove

Theorem 3. (P, N) *Covering cannot be approximated in polynomial time within a factor of $2^{\log^\delta n}$, for any $\delta < 1$, unless* NP *is contained in* DTIME$[2^{\text{polylog } n}]$.

Proof. Suppose, by way of contradiction, that it could. Let an arbitrary Set Covering instance A have a smallest solution of n. In $2^{\text{polylog } n}$ time, we form A^d where $d = \log^r n$ with $r = 2\delta/(1 - \delta)$. This (P, N) Covering instance has a smallest solution of size $(n^d - 1)\frac{n+2}{n-1}$. Then, using the (P, N) Covering approximation, we find a solution of size at most $(n^d - 1)\frac{n+2}{n-1} 2^{d^\delta \log^\delta n}$, from which we can find a solution to A of size approximately the dth root of that, which is

$$n 2^{d^{-(1-\delta)} \log^\delta n} = n 2^{\log^{\delta - r(1-\delta)} n} = O(n),$$

which contradicts the non-approximability of Set Covering (Theorem 1). □

3.2 A Variant of (P, N) Covering and k-decision Lists

Theorem 3 can be adapted to a slight variant of (P, N) Covering, called *Complementary (P, N) Covering*, where the collection of covering sets is closed under complementation. Given an instance A of (P, N) Covering, introduce three new elements x, y, z, let $P' = P \cup \{x\}$ and $N' = N \cup \{y, z\}$. Add for each covering set its complement (which includes x, y and z), and add the complementary covering sets $N \cup \{x, z\}$, $P \cup \{y\}$, $P \cup N \cup \{z\}$, and $\{x, y\}$. to get a new instance A'. None of $\{x, y, z\}$ can be covered until P is covered, so the complements of original sets are not useful, and once P is covered, it takes two additional sets to cover x and thereby P'. Note that covering N' also takes two additional sets, a fact that will be used later. Hence, A has a size-k solution if and only if A' has a solution of size $k + 2$. So, similarly to Theorem 3, we have

Corollary 4. *Complementary (P, N) Covering cannot be approximated in polynomial time within a factor of $2^{\log^\delta n}$, for any $\delta < 1$, unless* NP *is contained in* DTIME$[2^{\text{polylog } n}]$.

Using this result we prove the non-approximability of k-decision lists.

Theorem 5. k-*decision lists cannot be approximated in polynomial time by k-decision lists within a factor of $2^{\log^\delta n}$, for any $\delta < 1$, unless* NP *is contained in* DTIME$[2^{\text{polylog } n}]$.

Proof. We first show that 1-decision lists are as hard to approximate as Complementary (P, N) Covering, by a proper encoding.

Consider an instance A of Complementary (P, N) Covering with sets $S_1, \bar{S}_1, \ldots, S_m, \bar{S}_m \subseteq P \cup N$ (we'll assume A is derived as in Section 3.2). For each element s in $P \cup N$ we create a bit-vector e of length m. The ith bit of e is 1 if S_i contains element s, otherwise the ith bit of e is 0. The example e is labeled positive or negative depending on whether s is from P or N, respectively. The 1-decision list problem on these examples is isomorphic to problem A, since a decision list node with literal x_i or $\bar{x}_i$ selects covering set S_i or $\bar{S}_i$, and the constant of the node is then determined by whether this set uncovers P or N. Also, the part of N that remains not covered corresponds to the default 0 classification of examples in the decision list. Thus there is a 1-decision list of l terms iff there is a l set covering for the Complementary (P, N) Covering problem.

To extend the results to k-decision lists, for $k > 1$, we add two additional fields, called x and y, to the bit-vectors. Field x has length k and field y length $k - 1$. We create a k-decision list problem instance B as follows. Replace each old example e by $k2^k$ length $m + 2k - 1$ examples exy, consisting of

1. 2^k examples where x ranges over all k bit strings and $y = 1^{k-1}$, all classified the same as the old example.
2. $2^k(k - 1)$ examples where x ranges over all k bit strings and y consists of $k - 2$ ones and one 0, classified positive or negative as the parity of x is 1 or 0, respectively.

Intuitively, the purpose of these examples is to force $k - 1$ of the k literals in each decision-list node to be wasted on distinguishing the examples of type 1 from the examples of type 2, leaving only one literal to select a covering set as in the $k = 1$ case. After all the type 1 examples have been ccovered in this way, those of type 2 can be covered with 2^{k-1} (a constant) nodes each using all k literals to test x for parity 1.

The next claims (proofs ommitted) conclude the proof of the theorem.

Claim 6 *As long as both positive and negative type 1 examples remain uncovered, each node in L node must test all $k - 1$ y variables,*

Claim 7 *Complementary (P, N) Covering problem A has a size l covering iff there is a solution to the k-decision list problem B of size $l + c_k$, where c_k is a constant depending only on k.*

The following learning result follows from the standard technique mentioned in the introduction [12].

Corollary 8. *For no $\delta < 1$ does there exist a polynomial time PAC learning algorithm for k-decision lists whose hypothesis class is k-decision lists of size no more than $l2^{\log^\delta l}$, where l is the size of the target k-decision list, unless $NP \subset RTIME[2^{\text{polylog } n}]$.*

3.3 Non-approximability of k-decision Lists by Monotone Decision Lists

In learning theory, one often considers the problem of learning a class of concepts by a *broader* class of hypothesis. The freedom to formulate hypothesis from a richer class generally makes the leaningg task easier. Analogously, we can ask whether it is for instance easier to approximate a k decision list with a $2k$ decision list, or even an arbitrary decision list, with no bound on the length of the monomials. We provide an answer to a variation of the latter problem, where no negative literals are allowed in the monomials.

Theorem 9. *k-decision lists cannot be approximated in polynomial time by monotone decision lists within a factor of $2^{\log^\delta n}$, for any $\delta < 1$, unless NP is contained in DTIME$[2^{\text{polylog } n}]$.*

Proof. We present a variant on the multiplication of Section 3.1 to produce an instance of (P, N) Covering where the intersections of covering sets are of no use. This variant is based on the Vertex Cover problem, which can be regarded as a restricted form of Set Covering where each element appears in exactly 2 covering sets.

Again the basis of the blow-up is formed by a construction that multiplies a Vertex Covering instance A with a (P, N) Covering instance B to obtain a (P, N) Covering instance C whose smallest solution has a size close to the product of those of A and B. Let instance A consist of covering sets $s_1, s_2, \ldots, s_m \subset U = \{1, 2, \ldots, t\}$. Let instance B consist of covering sets $r_1, \ldots r_l \subset P \cup N$. Instance C will consist of the following elements: a copy of U, $m(m+1)/2$ copies of P and N indexed by an unordered pair of the m set indices ($P_{i,j} = P_{j,i}$ and $N_{i,j} = N_{j,i}$), and two extra elements x, y. We take $P_C = U \cup \bigcup_{1 \leq i,j \leq m} N_{i,j} \cup \{x\}$ and $N_C = \bigcup_{1 \leq i,j \leq m} P_{i,j} \cup \{y\}$. The copy of r_h in $P_{i,j} \cup N_{i,j}$ is referred to as $r_{i,j,h}$. We take the following covering sets:

- for each $1 \leq i \leq m, 1 \leq h \leq l$ a set $S_{i,h} = \bigcup_{1 \leq j \leq m} r_{i,j,h}$
- for each $1 \leq i \leq m$, a set $S_i = s_i \cup \bigcup 1 \leq j \leq m P_{i,j}$
- for each $1 \leq i,j \leq m$, a set $I_{i,j} = S_i \cap S_j = (s_i \cap s_j) \cup P_{i,j}$
- $U \cup N_C$
- $P_C \cup N_C$

Note that the collection of sets containing parts of both P_C and N_C is closed under intersections since for any i, $S_i \subset U \cup N_C \subset P_C \cup N_C$. Also, the intersection of 3 or more sets S_i is empty, because in the Vertex Cover problem, each element appears in only 2 covering sets. The sets $S_{i,a}$ are not closed under intersections, but such intersections are not helpful in a covering anyway.

Claim 10 *If a and b are the sizes of minimum covers of A and B, then the minimum cover of C has size $a(b+1) + 2$. Furthermore, for any c, d, given a covering of C of size at most $c(d+1) + 2$, one can find either a cover of A of size at most c, or a cover of B of size at most d.*

As before, we can define powers of a Vertex Cover instance A, and find that A^i has minimal size $(a^i - 1)\frac{a+2}{a-1}$.

Continuing the proof of Theorem 9, now we need the fact that Vertex Cover cannot be approximated within a factor of $1 + \epsilon$ for some $\epsilon > 0$ [4]. Suppose, by way of contradiction, that k-decision lists can be approximated by monotone decision lists within a factor of $2^{\log^\delta n}$ for some $\delta < 1$. Let an arbitrary Vertex Cover instance have a smallest solution of size n, and let ϵ be any positive number. Let $d = \log^r n$, where $r = 2\delta/(1 - \delta)$, and consider the dth power of the Vertex Cover problem. Because the collection of covering sets is closed under intersections, the reduction of Theorem 5 gives an equivalent monotone decision list problem. Hence the approximability implies we can find a solution to the blown-up Vertex Cover problem of size $n^d 2^{d^\delta \log^\delta n}$, from which we can find a Vertex Cover solution of size approximately the dth root of that, which is

$$n 2^{d^{-(1-\delta)} \log^\delta n} = n 2^{\log^{\delta - r(1-\delta)} n} \leq n 2^{\log^{-\delta} n} \leq n(1 + \epsilon),$$

for sufficiently large n. This contradicts the non-approximability of Vertex Cover. $\square$

4 Non-approximability of General Decision Lists

In this section, we will show that decision lists also cannot be efficiently approximated, unless NP = P. Notice that the non-approximability results for k-DL in the last section does not say anything about DL, and our bound in this section will be stronger than that of the previous section.

The result below on DNF easily follows from a reduction from the Graph Coloring problem to the approximation of the smallest consistent DNF given in [18] (see also [12]) and the n^ϵ non-approximability lower bound for Graph Coloring in [13].

Theorem 11. [Pitt-Valiant, Lund-Yannakakis] *DNF's cannot be approximated in polynomial time by DNF's within a factor of n^ϵ, for some $\epsilon > 0$, unless* NP = P.

We will prove the same non-approximability ratio for decision lists. Our result in fact strengthens Theorem 11 by showing that DNF's cannot be approximated by the richer class of decision lists within a ratio of n^ϵ.

Theorem 12. *Decision lists cannot be approximated in polynomial time by decision lists within a factor of n^ϵ, for some $\epsilon > 0$, unless* NP = P.

Proof. Similar to that of [18], which linearly reduces the Graph Coloring problem to DNF. Showing that a consistent decision list of k term can yields a k-coloring is however slightly more involved. We omit the details here.
$\square$

Corollary 13. *DNF's cannot be approximated in polynomial time by decision lists within a factor of n^ϵ, for some $\epsilon > 0$, unless* NP = P.

Corollary 14. *There exists an $\epsilon > 0$ such that there is no polynomial time PAC learning algorithm for decision lists (or DNF) that, when run on examples from a decision list (DNF, respectively) of size l, will on success (i.e. with probability exceeding $1 - \delta$) always output as a hypothesis a decision list of size at most $l^{1+\epsilon}$ unless* NP = RP.

5 Non-approximability of Decision Trees

We now consider the problem of finding a small decision tree consistent with a set M of examples. For notational convenience we measure the size of the tree as the number of leaves (*i.e.*, one more than the number of interior nodes in a binary tree).

Theorem 15. *Decision trees cannot be approximated in polynomial time by decision trees within a constant factor c, for some $c > 1$, unless* P = NP.

Proof. The argument is entirely similar to the one used in section 3 to show the hardness of approximating monomials. Decision trees are clearly at least as expressive as monomials. It remains to show that for the given boolean vectors (a negative one for each element of the universe and an all 1s positive one), they are not more expressive. To this end, observe that in a consistent decision tree, any node's 0 subtree can be safely replaced by a single lead labelled 0, the result being a degenerate tree that's equivalent to a monomial.

We now discuss how to amplify this result to show that an algorithm to approximate decision trees within a factor of $2^{\log^\delta n}$ could in fact be improved to approximate within an arbitrary constant factor in pseudo-polynomial time.

A key idea is that we can "square" a decision tree problem as described in the following construction. Let M be a set of m examples with n variables. Construct a set M' with m^2 examples over $2n$ variables by concatenating xy for each $x, y \in M$. If $f(x)$ is the classification of example x, let each example xy have the classification $f'(xy) = f(x) \oplus f(y)$ (i.e. f' is the exclusive OR of two copies of f over different variables).

The obvious way to build a decision tree for M' is to take a decision tree T for M on the first n attributes and place at each of its leaves a copy of T over the second set of n attributes. This converts a k-leaf tree for M into a k^2 leaf tree for M'. We show that this construction is optimal as a consequence of the following stronger lemma which shows how we can efficiently convert a tree for M' back to trees for M in a manner that has implications for approximation.

Lemma 16. *There is an efficient algorithm to convert a decision tree with k' leaves that is consistent with M' into a tree with no more than $\sqrt{k'}$ leaves that is consistent with M.*

Proof. To prove the lemma we first consider the simple case where T' is constructed such that every path in T' has all its tests of the first n attributes (variables $x_1, \ldots, x_n$) before it tests any of the second n attributes (variables $y_1, \ldots, y_n$). We describe such a tree as being in "standard form".

It is easy to show that both the top x part of T' and each of the y subtrees must have k or more leaves, so that T' has at least $k' = k^2$ leaves and also that we can derive from T' a $\sqrt{k'}$ leaf tree for M.

We now argue that if T' is not in standard form, then an efficient transformation can find another equivalent tree that is in standard form and has no more leaves than T'. From this the lemma follows.

The transformation process will process T' incrementally from the bottom up. After each node is processed, the following two properties will be true:

1. The subtree rooted at the node is in standard form.
2. All of the various $y_1, \ldots, y_n$ subtrees reachable from the node are identical (except possibly for having complementary leaf settings).

We omit the, rather straightforward, details of this transformation, but suffice to mention that it is easily done without increasing the size of the tree. □

The construction generalizes to an arbitrary depth d. I.e. by concatenating d copies of the original variables we get a sample $M^{(d)}$ of m^d examples over dn attributes for which the minimum decision tree has k^d nodes iff k is the minimum number of nodes for a decision tree over M. Entirely analogous to theorem 3, this blow-up technique gives us

Theorem 17. *Decision trees cannot be approximated in polynomial time by decision trees within a factor of $2^{\log^\delta n}$, for any $\delta < 1$, unless NP is contained in* DTIME$[2^{\text{polylog } n}]$.

Proof. Suppose, by way of contradiction, that it could. Let an arbitrary Set Covering instance A have a smallest solution of n. In $2^{\text{polylog } n}$ time, we form a tree decicion problem A^d where $d = \log^r n$ with $r = 2\delta/(1 - \delta)$. The smallest solution of A' has size n^d. Then, using the tree decision approximation, we find a solution of size at most $n^d 2^{d^\delta \log^\delta n}$, from which we can find a solution to A of size the dth root of that, which is

$$n 2^{d^{-(1-\delta)} \log^\delta n} = n 2^{\log^{\delta - r(1-\delta)} n} = O(n),$$

which contradicts the non-approximability of Set Covering (Theorem 1). □

Corollary 18. *For no $\delta < 1$ does there exist a polynomial time PAC learning algorithm for decision trees whose hypothesis class is decision trees with no more than $l^{2\log^\delta l}$ leaves, where l is the number of leaves in the target decision tree, unless* NP $\subset$ RTIME$[2^{\text{polylog } n}]$.

Acknowledgments. We thank Martin Anthony and Ron Rivest for information about decision lists. Also thanks to Lisa Hellerstein for pointing out an omission in our proofs.

538

References

1. Aditi Dhagat and Lisa Hellerstein. PAC learning with irrelevant attributes. To appear in *Proc. 35rd IEEE Symp. Found. Comp. Sci.*, 1994.
2. M. Anthony and N. Biggs. *Computational Learning Theory*. Cambridge University Press, 1992.
3. R. Board and L. Pitt, On the necessity of Occam Algorithms. 1990 *STOC*, pp. 54-63.
4. A. Arora, C. Lund, R. Motwani, M. Sudan, and M. Szegedy. Proof verification and hardness of approximation problems. *Proc. 33rd IEEE Symp. Found. Comp. Sci.*, 1992, 14–23.
5. M. Bellare, S. Goldwasser, C. Lund, and A. Russel. Efficient probabilistically checkable proofs and applications to approximation. *Proc. 25th ACM Symp. on Theory of Computing*, 1993, 294–304.
6. A. Blumer and A. Ehrenfeucht and D. Haussler and M. Warmuth. Learnability and the Vapnik-Chervonenkis dimension. *J. Assoc. Comput. Mach.*, 35(1989), 929-965.
7. L. Breiman, J. Friedman, R. Olshen and C. Stone. Classification and Regression Trees. Wadsworth International Group, Belmont, CA (1984).
8. A. Ehrenfeucht and D. Haussler. Learning decision trees from random examples. *COLT'88*.
9. M. Garey and D. Johnson. *Computers and Intractability*. Freeman, New York, 1979.
10. D. Haussler. Quantifying inductive bias: AI learning algorithms and Valiant's learning framework. *Artificial Intelligence* 36:2(1988), 177–222.
11. L. Hyafil and R. Rivest. Constructing optimal decision trees is NP-complete. *IPL*, 5:1(1976), 15-17.
12. M. Kearns, M. Li, L. Pitt, L. Valiant. On the learnability of Boolean functions. *Proc. 19th STOC*, 1987, New York, 285–295.
13. C. Lund and M. Yannakakis. On the hardness of approximating minimization problems. *Proc. 25th ACM Symp. on Theory of Computing*, 1993, 286–293.
14. J. Mingers. An empirical comparison of selection measures for decision-tree induction. *Machine Learning.* 3 (1989), 319–342.
15. J.R. Quinlan. Induction of decision trees. *Machine Learning.* 1 (1986), 81–106.
16. J.R. Quinlan and R. Rivest. Inferring decision trees using the minimum description length principle. *Inform. Computation*, 80(1989), 227–248.
17. C.H. Papadimitriou and M. Yannakakis. Optimization, approximation, and complexity classes. Extended abstract in *Proc. 20th ACM Symp. on Theory of Computing.* 1988, 229-234; full version in *Journal of Computer and System Sciences* 43, 1991, 425–440.
18. L. Pitt and L. Valiant. Computational limitations on learning from examples. *Journal of the ACM*, 35:4(1988), 965–984.
19. R. Rivest. Learning decision lists. *Machine Learning*, 2(1987), 229–246.
20. L. Valiant. A theory of the learnable. *Communications of the ACM.* 27(1984), 1134–1142.

Line segmentation of digital curves in parallel

Peter Damaschke

FernUniversität, Theoretische Informatik II
58084 Hagen, Germany
peter.damaschke@fernuni-hagen.de

Abstract. Partitioning digital curves into digital straight line segments (DLS) is important in several branches of image processing. We present a parallel algorithm for this task which runs in $O(\log n)$ time using $O(n \log^2 n)$ operations on a CREW PRAM. In contrast to earlier sequential algorithms it is not founded on number-theoretic properties of digital lines, instead we only use geometrical tools. The main observation for obtaining our complexity bounds is that the convex hull of a DLS of length n has $O(\log n)$ vertices. We also construct a sequence of DLS showing that this bound is tight.

1 Introduction

The segmentation of digital curves into straight line segments is of major interest in several branches of image processing, including shape recognition and image data compression. Much work has been done on digital lines, cf. the references. Linear time *sequential* algorithms for line segmentation have been given in [5] [4], after earlier approaches with worse behaviour. The incremental algorithm in [4] excels by naturalness and easy handling, reached by clever exploitation of (elementary but non-trivial) number-theoretic properties during the segment growing process.

In the present paper we turn to the *parallel* segmentation of digital curves into lines. Our algorithm runs in $O(\log n)$ time using $O(n \log^2 n)$ operations on a CREW PRAM. (We will not further mention that our computation model is the CREW PRAM.) It is purely based on the use of convex hulls of digital line segments, i.e. we do not rest on the connections to elementary number theory.

After recalling some basic properties, we show in Section 2 that the convex hull of a digital line segment of length n has $O(\log n)$ vertices. (In [1] the convex hull was already used for the linear time *recognition* of digital lines. The authors suspected there that the number of vertices may be large for long segments, but they did not follow up the question.)

Section 3 establishes the basic step of our algorithm: the concatenation of consecutive line segments, and the verification whether their union is still a line segment. This is done only with support of the convex hulls where we essentially use a result from [2].

After that, standard techniques suffice to develop the main program in Section 4. The complexity follows from the result of Section 2.

As a supplement we show in Section 5 that this $O(\log n)$ bound for the vertex number is tight, by presenting a sequence of examples. The proof works with an unusual representation of integers, namely with Fibonacci arithmetic. Recently we learned that our result could also be derived from considerations in [8] where modular inequalities are studied with help of a generalization of Euclid's algorithm, but our explicit construction manages without this number-theoretic background.

We start with giving the denotations and a precise definition of the problem. The elements of the grid Z^2 are often called *pixels*. They are written as (x, y).

A *digital curve* is a finite sequence of pixels (x_i, y_i), $1 \leq i \leq n$ such that $|x_{i+1} - x_i| \leq 1$ and $|y_{i+1} - y_i| \leq 1$, but not both 0, for all $i < n$. Here n is called the *length* of the curve. We will denote the subcurve with $l \leq i \leq r$ simply by $[l, r]$. Hence the entire curve is also denoted by $[1, n]$.

A *naive line* (denotation from [4]) is the set of all pixels (x, y) satisfying $y = \lfloor \frac{ax - \mu}{b} \rfloor$ where a, b, μ are fixed integers with $0 \leq a \leq b$, $0 < b$, and $\gcd(a, b) = 1$. The equation $y = \lfloor \frac{ax - \mu}{b} \rfloor$ is equivelent to:

$$\frac{ax - \mu}{b} - 1 < y \leq \frac{ax - \mu}{b}$$

$$\mu \leq ax - by < \mu + b$$

Since by is integer, the left upper inequality can be equivalently written as:

$$y \geq \frac{ax - \mu}{b} - 1 + \frac{1}{b}$$

The condition $\gcd(a, b) = 1$ is not a restriction: If a, b have a common divisor d then the middle term in

$$\frac{\mu}{d} \leq \frac{a}{d}x - \frac{b}{d}y < \frac{\mu}{d} + \frac{b}{d}$$

is integer, hence $\frac{\mu}{d}$ and $\frac{\mu}{d} + \frac{b}{d}$ can be replaced by $\lceil \frac{\mu}{d} \rceil$ and $\lceil \frac{\mu+b}{d} \rceil = \lceil \frac{\mu}{d} \rceil + \frac{b}{d}$, respectively, without altering the set of solutions (x, y).

A *digital line* is a set of pixels obtained from a naive line by $90°$ rotations and/or mirror reflections at the coordinate axes. Digital lines (naive lines) can be considered as digitalizations of of euclidean lines (with slope between 0 and 1).

A *digital line segment (DLS)* is a finite consecutive portion of a digital line.

A *line segmentation* of a digital curve (x_i, y_i), $1 \leq i \leq n$, is a partition of $[1, n]$ into segments $[l_1, r_1], \ldots, [l_k, r_k]$, all being DLS, such that $l_1 = 1$, $l_{j+1} = r_j + 1$, $r_k = n$. There is always a trivial segmentation into n DLS, so we are interested in partitions into DLS which are as long as possible.

The *greedy segmentation* is characterized by the property that for all j, r_j is the maximal r such that $[l_j, r]$ is still a DLS. [4] give an incremental algorithm for computing the greedy segmentation. The greedy segmentation guarantees the minimum number of segments, but its drawback is that it depends on the start pixel, i.e. the restriction of the greedy segmentation of $[1, n]$ to some $[j, n]$

can differ from the greedy segmentation of $[j, n]$ itself. Therefore we pose a more general problem: Given a digital curve S, find all (with respect to inclusion) maximal DLS within S. From this family of maximal DLS we can easily obtain also the greedy segmentation.

A digital curve is called *standard* if $x_{i+1} - x_i = 1$ and $0 \leq y_{i+1} - y_i \leq 1$ for all i. A standard curve can be considered as the graph of a monotone increasing function in an interval, growing by at most 1 in each step. Obviously, each DLS within a digital curve S is entirely contained in some standard subcurve of S (up to 90° rotations and reflections at the axes). Furthermore it is not difficult to partition S into maximal standard curves (possibly rotated or reversed) in a preprocessing which needs $O(\log n)$ time and $O(n)$ operations. (Note that the maximal standard curves may overlap, but at most 2 in each pixel.) So we can restrict attention to standard curves. From now we consider the following problem:

Given a standard curve S, find all maximal DLS (which are naive line segments then) within S.

2 The convex hull of a digital line segment

A *stripe* is a topologically closed part of the plane, bounded by two parallel euclidean lines with rational slope s, $0 \leq s \leq 1$. A single line is considered as a degenerated stripe. The *vertical breadth* of a stripe is the distance between the intersection points of the two boundary lines with an arbitrary vertical line. $H(S)$ denotes the convex hull of the point set S.

The first lemma summarizes some well-known properties. To make the paper more self-contained, we give the proof, too.

Lemma 1. *A standard curve S is a DLS iff S is contained in a stripe with vertical breadth properly less than 1. This stripe can be choosen in such a way that one line goes through an edge of $H(S)$ and the other line goes through an edge or a vertex of $H(S)$. (This will be called a leaning stripe.) Furthermore, any DLS of length n can be described by an equation $y = \lfloor \frac{ax-\mu}{b} \rfloor$ such that $0 < b < n$.*

Proof. Let S be a DLS with $\mu \leq ax - by < \mu + b$ for all $(x, y) \in S$. Then, due to the remark in Section 1, S lies in the stripe bounded by $y = \frac{a}{b}x - \frac{\mu}{b} - 1 + \frac{1}{b}$ and $y = \frac{a}{b}x - \frac{\mu}{b}$ with vertical breadth $1 - \frac{1}{b}$.

Conversely, let all pixels (x, y) of a standard curve S satisfy

$$\frac{a}{b}x - \nu - \beta \leq y \leq \frac{a}{b}x - \nu$$

where $0 \leq a \leq b$ are integers with $\gcd(a, b) = 1$, and ν, β are real numbers with $0 \leq \beta < 1$. Then we have:

$$b\nu \leq ax - by \leq b\nu + b\beta$$

Since $ax - by$ is integer and $\beta < 1$, this implies for $\mu := \lceil b\nu \rceil$ that

$$\mu \leq ax - by < \mu + b$$

for all $(x, y) \in S$. That means, S is subset of a digital line. Since S was supposed to be a standard curve, S is a DLS.

By vertical translations we can pull up the boundary lines of our stripe towards S, until the resulting parallel lines go through vertices of $H(S)$. Rotating the lines around these vertices by the same angle, we reach the situation that at least one of the lines even goes through an edge of $H(S)$. We have two possible directions for this rotation. Note that always in one of these directions the vertical breadth becomes smaller. So we obtain a leaning stripe whose vertical breadth is smaller than 1.

The second papragraph of our proof works particularly for leaning stripes and shows therefore that S has a description $y = \lfloor \frac{ax - \mu}{b} \rfloor$ where $\frac{a}{b}$ is the slope of the stripe. Since one of the boundary lines now goes through two points of S, we get immediately $b < n$.

The boundary of the convex hull of a finite point set M in the plane can be partitioned into the upper and lower envelope whose vertex sets are denoted $U(M)$ and $L(M)$, respectively. If there is a unique point with minimal (maximal) abscissa (e.g. in a standard curve) then it shall belong to both $U(M)$ and $L(M)$. The vertices and edges on the upper (lower) envelope are briefly called upper (lower) vertices and edges. If $U(M)$ is sorted by increasing abscissa then it consists of a sequence $I(M)$ of vertices with increasing ordinates, followed by a sequence with decreasing ordinates.

Note that a point $(x_0, y_0) \in M$ belongs to $L(M)$ iff all $(x_1, y_1) \in M$ and $(x_2, y_2) \in M$ with $x_1 < x_0 < x_2$ satisfy the condition

$$\frac{y_1 - y_0}{x_1 - x_0} < \frac{y_2 - y_0}{x_2 - x_0}.$$

A similar characterization holds for $U(M)$: just reverse the $<$ sign.

Lemma 2. *Let M be a pixel set of the form*

$$M = \{(x, (ax - \mu) \bmod b) : a, b, x \text{ integers}, 0 \leq a \leq b \leq n, l \leq x \leq r\}$$

where $n = r - l + 1$. Then the cardinality of $I(M)$ is $O(\log n)$.

Proof. Let $I(M)$ be the sequence $(x_1, y_1), \ldots, (x_c, y_c)$. By definition we have $x_1 < \ldots < x_c$ and $y_1 < \ldots < y_c$. Assume that $x_{k+1} - x_k \leq r - x_{k+1}$ and $y_{k+1} - y_k < b - y_k$ for some k, that is $2x_{k+1} - x_k \leq r$ and $2y_{k+1} - y_k < b$. Since $y_j = (ax_j - \mu) \bmod b$ we get:

$$
\begin{aligned}
(a(2x_{k+1} - x_k) - \mu) \bmod b &= (2ax_{k+1} - ax_k - 2\mu + \mu) \bmod b \\
&= (2(ax_{k+1} - \mu) - (ax_k - \mu)) \bmod b \\
&= (2y_{k+1} - y_k) \bmod b \\
&= 2y_{k+1} - y_k
\end{aligned}
$$

Hence (x_k, y_k), (x_{k+1}, y_{k+1}), and $(2x_{k+1} - x_k, 2y_{k+1} - y_k)$ are collinear points of M which contradicts $(x_{k+1}, y_{k+1}) \in I(M)$. Thus in each step $r - x_k$ or $b - y_k$ must be reduced by a factor at least 2. Together with $b < n$ this yields $c = O(\log n)$.

Corollary 3. *The convex hull of a set M as in Lemma 2 has $O(\log n)$ vertices.*

Proof. We can analogously conclude for the decreasing part of $U(M)$ and for $L(M)$. (Use $-x$ instead of x, $b-a$ instead of a, etc.)

Next we estimate the number of vertices of $H(S)$ when S is a DLS of length n. We reduce the problem to the above sets M, that means, we drop the linear part of the DLS and keep only the oscillations.

Theorem 4. *The convex hull of a DLS of length n has $O(\log n)$ vertices.*

Proof. Let S be the DLS with equation $y = \lfloor \frac{ax-\mu}{b} \rfloor$ for $l \leq x \leq r$, $n = r - l + 1$. By Lemma 1 we can w.l.o.g. suppose $b < n$. Let M be defined as in Lemma 2.
For a fixed x_0 let

$$h(x) = b \frac{\lfloor \frac{ax-\mu}{b} \rfloor - \lfloor \frac{ax_0-\mu}{b} \rfloor}{x - x_0}$$

and

$$m(x) = \frac{(ax - \mu) \bmod b - (ax_0 - \mu) \bmod b}{x - x_0}.$$

Then we have $\left(x_0, \lfloor \frac{ax_0-\mu}{b} \rfloor\right) \in L(S)$ iff $\forall x_1 < x_0 < x_2 : h(x_1) < h(x_2)$.
On the other hand,

$$h(x) = \frac{ax - \mu - (ax - \mu) \bmod b - (ax_0 - \mu) + (ax_0 - \mu) \bmod b}{x - x_0}$$

$$= a - \frac{(ax - \mu) \bmod b - (ax_0 - \mu) \bmod b}{x - x_0}.$$

Hence $h(x_1) < h(x_2)$ is equivalent to $m(x_1) > m(x_2)$ which means $(x_0, (ax_0 - \mu) \bmod b) \in U(M)$. We have a similar correspondence between $U(S)$ and $L(M)$. Now the result follows from Lemma 3.

Interestingly, this $O(\log n)$ bound is tight. Since we first want to give our segmentation algorithm, we postpone the proof until the end of our paper.

3 Concatenating two digital line segments

In our segmentation algorithm for standard curves $[1, n]$ we maintain the segments $S = [l, r] \subseteq [1, n]$ which are already recognized as DLS, together with their convex hulls $H(S)$, by a data structure $D(S)$ consisting of the following components:

- a doubly linked list of all upper vertices and edges in their natural ordering,
- a similar list for the lower envelope,
- a table for the function p defined as follows: for any upper (lower) vertex $v = (x, y)$ let $p(v)$ be that lower (upper) edge with end vertices (x_1, y_1) and (x_2, y_2) satisfying $x_1 < x < x_2$.

Note that $p(v)$ always exists, except for $x = l$ and $x = r$.

Lemma 5. *Let S be a DLS and $L \supset S$ a stripe such that one boundary goes through edge e and the other boundary line goes through vertex v of $H(S)$. L has minimal vertical breadth among all leaning stripes of S iff $p(v) = e$.*

Moreover, these L and e are uniquely determined, and there exists at most one further vertex u on the boundary of L with $p(u) = e$. In this case, vu is an edge of $H(S)$ with the same slope as e.

Proof. If $p(v) \neq e$ then we can rotate the lines of L around v resp. the end vertex of e being horizontally closer to v, thus obtaining a leaning stripe with smaller vertical breadth. This proves the "if" direction.

By a monotonicity argument we easily find that there exists only one stripe L whose boundary lines include e, v with $p(v) = e$. Since *every* leaning stripe with minimal vertical breadth must satisfy $p(v) = e$ (as we have seen above), this condition is already sufficient for minimality. So the equivalence is shown.

The last assertion is trivial.

Now we introduce the basic routine of our algorithm.

Lemma 6. *Let $S = [l, k]$ and $T = [k + 1, r]$ be consecutive DLS in a standard curve $[1, n]$. Assume $D(S)$ and $D(T)$ are already computed. Then we can construct $D(S \cup T)$ and decide whether $S \cup T$ is a DLS in $O(1)$ time using $O(\log m)$ operations, where $m = r - l + 1$ is the total length.*

Proof. Let c denote the number of vertices of $H(S)$ and $H(T)$. Given $H(S)$ and $H(T)$, one can compute $H(S \cup T)$ in $O(1)$ time using $O(c)$ operations by the refined algorithm of [2]. Actually this algorithm finds the common upper and lower tangent of $H(S)$ and $H(T)$. So the lists describing the upper and lower envelope of $H(S \cup T)$ can be obtained from the lists of $H(S)$ and $H(T)$ in $O(1)$ sequential time by cut-and-paste.

Let l_0 and r_0 be the abscissa of end vertices of the new upper edge of $H(S \cup T)$ (i.e. a portion of the common upper tangent). Then the function p can be updated for the lower vertices v of $H(S \cup T)$ as follows: If $p(v)$ has end vertices with abscissa l_1 and r_1 then the new $p(v)$ ends at abscissa $\min(l_0, l_1)$ and $\max(r_0, r_1)$. More simply said: If the old $p(v)$ is still an edge then it remains unchanged, otherwise $p(v)$ is the new upper edge. For the vertices v with abscissa k and $k + 1$ (if elements of $L(S \cup T)$), $p(v)$ is always the new upper edge. Analogously we proceed with the upper vertices. This can be done in $O(1)$ time using $O(c)$ operations.

Next we test for all vertices v in parallel whether some leaning stripe L of $S \cup T$ goes through v and $e = p(v)$, and in this case the vertical breadth of this L is computed. Obviously, such an L exists iff $s(f) \leq s(e) \leq s(g)$ where f, g are the edges incident with v, and s denotes the slope. Therefore the test needs $O(1)$ time. From Lemma 5 we know that the test is affirmative for only one vertex v or for two neighbored vertices v, u such that vu is an edge with slope $s(vu) = s(e)$. So we can easily manage that only one active processor writes the vertical breadth of L into some register reserved for the result. (Remember that we work on a CREW PRAM.) By Lemma 1, $S \cup T$ is a DLS iff this value is smaller than 1.

Altogether we need $O(1)$ time and $O(c)$ operations. Now the bounds follow from Theorem 4.

4 Line segmentation of a standard curve

Now we give the parallel algorithm which finds all maximal DLS in a given standard curve. Our "main program" does no longer refer to special properties of DLS; all geometry is already invested in the previous sections. It remains to apply standard techniques from parallel algorithmics. So the following considerations could also be done in a more abstract setting: On the integer interval $[1, n]$ we want to determine an unknown family F of subintervals which is closed under inclusion (here: the DLS). Because of this closure property it suffices to find the maximal intervals from F. For this, an oracle is available which says for consecutive members of F whether their union still belongs to F. However, we stay in the language of our special problem.

Let us given a standard curve $[1, n]$. First we determine all DLS in $[1, n]$ whose lenghts are powers of 2. These DLS are called *pieces* in the following.

Lemma 7. *All pieces can be found in $O(\log n)$ time using $O(n \log^2 n)$ operations.*

Proof. Find in stages $k = 0, 1, 2, \ldots, \lfloor \log_2 n \rfloor$ all DLS of length 2^k. Stage 0 is trivial: The pieces are all $[l, l]$, $1 \le l \le n$. In stage $k + 1$ we link in parallel all pairs of pieces $[l + 1, l + 2^k]$ and $[l + 2^k + 1, l + 2^{k+1}]$ from stage k and check $[l + 1, l + 2^{k+1}]$ for being DLS as in Lemma 6. The total number of pieces is $O(n \log n)$, thus the complexity bounds follow from Lemma 6.

Trivially, each DLS S is a concatenation of pieces with strongly decreasing lengths. (Consider the binary representation of the length of S.) This suggests the following procedure which is executed for all l ($1 \le l \le n$) in parallel.

```
begin
S(l) := ∅; r := l − 1;
for k := ⌈log₂ n⌉ downto 0 do
    if [r + 1, r + 2ᵏ] is a piece and S(l) ∪ [r + 1, r + 2ᵏ] is a DLS
    then begin S(l) := S(l) ∪ [r + 1, r + 2ᵏ]; r := r + 2ᵏ end
end.
```

Lemma 8. *Finally $S(l)$ is the largest DLS whose leftmost pixel has abscissa l. The procedure runs in $O(\log n)$ time using totally $O(n \log^2 n)$ operations.*

Proof. By easy induction we see that the procedure always adds the maximal possible piece to $S(l)$, thus the correctness is clear. Each test for a piece needs $O(1)$ sequential time, presumed that we have already computed the set of pieces due to Lemma 7. Each DLS test runs in $O(1)$ time using $O(\log n)$ operations, by Lemma 6. Since we have $O(\log n)$ tests, we altogether need $O(\log n)$ time and $O(\log^2 n)$ operations for each l.

For determining all maximal DLS it remains to find for each r the longest DLS (i.e. with minimal l) $S(l) = [l, r]$. For this we sort in parallel the $S(l)$ with respect to their right ends r and remove for each r the non-maximal candidates. This does not exceed our complexity bounds. Altogether we have shown:

Theorem 9. *All maximal DLS in a standard curve of length n can be found in $O(\log n)$ time using $O(n \log^2 n)$ operations.*

As a byproduct we get:

Corollary 10. *The greedy segmentation of a standard curve of length n can be found within the same bounds as in Theorem 9.*

Proof. Clearly the greedy segmentation only consists of segments $S(l)$ determined above. More precisely, if g is defined by $g(l) := r + 1$ for $S(l) = [l, r]$ then $S(l)$ is a member of the greedy segmentation iff $l = g^i(1)$ for some i. The iterations of g are computable within the asserted bounds by standard techniques.

5 Convex hulls of digital line segments can have logarithmically many vertices

For proving this, we will show that the lower envelope of

$$M_k = \{(i, y_i) : 1 \leq i \leq f_k, \ y_i = f_{k-1} i \bmod f_k\}$$

where f_k is the k-th Fibonacci number, has about $k/2 = \Omega(\log f_k)$ vertices. Inverting the transformation from Theorem 4, this gives a sequence of DLS with the claimed asymptotic complexity. Their slopes approximate the golden section.

First we recall some facts on Fibonacci numbers (briefly: F numbers). Let $f_1 = 1$, $f_2 = 2$, and $f_j = f_{j-1} + f_{j-2}$.

We consider a partition of an integer n into a sum of F numbers which are not necessarily distinct. In such a sum, every pair of summands $f_{j-1} + f_{j-2}$ can be replaced by f_j, thus reducing the number of summands. Every pair of summands $f_j + f_j$ ($j \geq 3$) can be replaced by $f_{j+1} + f_{j-2}$, thus reducing the product(!) of all summands. Further we can replace 1+1 by 2 and 2+2 by 3+1. Since these manipulations properly decrease parameters of the partition which are positive integers, these rules can be applied only finitely often. Thus we finally get a sum of F numbers where all indices of summands differ by at least 2. We call this partition an F representation of n.

A trivial induction shows $f_k - 1 = f_{k-1} + f_{k-3} + f_{k-5} + \ldots$ (the last summand is 2 or 1, depending on the parity of k). Hence the F representation of n with $f_{k-1} \leq n < f_k$ must contain the summand f_{k-1}, otherwise the remaining summands cannot give the sum n. Since this holds similarly for $n - f_{k-1} < f_{k-2}$, we conclude by induction that every positive integer has a unique F representation.

In the following let k be fixed. We write the F representation of n also as a string $e_{k-1} e_{k-2} \ldots e_2 e_1$ where $e_j = 1$ iff f_j is a summand, and $e_j = 0$ otherwise. Hence between any two 1's there must stand at least one 0. For a string w let w^p denote the concatenation of p copies of w.

As a further property of F numbers we need the identity $f_{k-1} f_j - f_k f_{j-1} = f_{k-j-1}$ for even j, which can be easily shown by induction. It follows

$$f_{k-1} f_j \bmod f_k = f_{k-j-1}$$

Hence we have $(f_j, f_{k-j-1}) \in M_k$ for even j. The edges joining the neighbored pixels of this form have properly increasing slopes, that is:

$$\frac{f_{k-j-3} - f_{k-j-1}}{f_{j+2} - f_j} < \frac{f_{k-j-5} - f_{k-j-3}}{f_{j+4} - f_{j+2}}$$

We claim that all these pixels are lower vertices of $H(M_k)$. It suffices to show that no pixel from M_k lies under some lower edge. There even holds a sharper assertion: $f_j < i < f_{j+2}$ (j even) implies $y_i > f_{k-j-1}$. This can conveniently be shown with help of the F representations of the $y_i = f_{k-1} i \bmod f_k$. In the following, r always denotes a suffix of suitable length (such that the F representation has length $k - 1$).

Lemma 11. $y_i = (10)^p 1000r$ implies $y_{i+1} = (01)^p 0010r$.
Similarly, $y_i = (10)^p 10010r$ implies $y_{i+1} = (01)^p 01000r$.

Proof. We prove the first assertion. We temporarily allow consecutive 1's and digits larger than 1 in the F representations.

Since $y_i + f_{k-1} > f_{k-1} + f_{k-1} > f_k$ we have:

$$y_{i+1} = y_i + f_{k-1} - f_k = y_i - f_{k-2} = y_i - f_{k-1} + f_{k-3} = 0020(10)^{p-2} 1000r$$

By induction on q we show $y_{i+1} = (01)^q 0020(10)^{p-q-2} 1000r$. For $q = 0$ this is already proved. In the induction step we get:

$$y_{i+1} = (01)^q 002010(10)^{p-q-3} 1000r$$
$$= (01)^q 001120(10)^{p-q-3} 1000r$$
$$= (01)^q 010020(10)^{p-q-3} 1000r$$
$$= (01)^{q+1} 0020(10)^{p-q-3} 1000r.$$

So we have finally:

$$y_{i+1} = (01)^{p-2}00201000r$$
$$= (01)^{p-2}00112000r$$
$$= (01)^{p-2}01001110r$$
$$= (01)^{p-2}01010010r$$
$$= (01)^p 0010r.$$

The second assertion is similarly verified. The only difference lies in the last computations:

$$y_{i+1} = (01)^{p-2}002010010r$$
$$= (01)^{p-2}001120010r$$
$$= (01)^{p-2}010011110r$$
$$= (01)^{p-2}010101000r$$
$$= (01)^p 01000r.$$

Lemma 12. *Assume that we start at some abscissa i, increase i step by step, and observe the behaviour of F representations of the y_i.*
(a) If $y_i = (00)^p 00r$ then we reach the string $(10)^p 10r$ without changing the suffix $0r$ in between.
(b) If $y_i = (01)^p 0r$ then we reach the string $(00)^p 0r$ without changing the suffix $0r$ in between.
Furthermore, in every intermediate step there stands at least one symbol 1 in the first $2p + 1$ positions.

Proof. by induction on p. The assertions are quite trivial for $p = 0$ and $p = 1$. Suppose the lemma holds for all exponents smaller than p.

(a) From $(00)^p 00r = (00)^{p-1}0000r$ we get (by increasing the abscissa) the ordinate $(10)^{p-1}1000r$ such that $000r$ has never been affected. The next step yields $(01)^{p-1}0010r$, by Lemma 11. Now apply (b) for $p-1$. We get $(00)^{p-1}0010r$ after some further steps. Note that the first 1 now stands at the $(2p + 1)$-th position. Applying (a) for $p - 1$ again, we reach $(10)^{p-1}1010r = (10)^p 10r$, and (a) is shown for p.

(b) From $(01)^p 0r = (01)^{p-1}010r$ we reach $(00)^{p-1}010r$ due to the induction hypothesis. Now (a), applied to $(00)^{p-2}00010r$, yields $(10)^{p-2}10010r$. By Lemma 11, the next step gives $(01)^{p-2}01000r = (01)^{p-1}000r$. From this we finally reach $(00)^{p-1}000r = (00)^p 0r$. The last assertion follows obviously from the induction hypothesis.

Now we apply the lemmata for starting position $i = f_j$ (j even). Note that $y_{f_j} = f_{k-j-1} = 0^{j-2}10^{k-j} = 0^{j-4}0010^{k-j}$. Since j is even, we can set $p = (j - 4)/2$, and by (a) we reach $(10)^{(j-4)/2}1010^{k-j} = (10)^{(j-2)/2}10^{k-j}$. By

549

Lemma 11 the next step gives $(01)^{(j-2)/2}0010^{k-j-2}$. Now we can apply (b) for $p = (j-2)/2$ and reach $0^j10^{k-j-2} = f_{k-j-3} = y_{f_{j+2}}$.

The climax is that in all intermediate steps the first $j-1$ positions of the F representations contain at least one symbol 1, which implies $y_i > f_{k-j-1}$ as we have claimed. This completes the proof of

Theorem 13. *There exists a sequence of DLS of unbounded length n whose convex hulls have $\Omega(\log n)$ vertices.*

6 Conclusions

We presented an efficient parallel algorithm for finding all digital line segments in a digital curve. Due to its bottom-up structure it works worst just in the case that the given curve is a DLS. (Then we have the maximum number of pieces.) On the other hand, a DLS can be *recognized* more efficiently than with $O(n\log^2 n)$ operations. This provokes the question whether the operation bound can be reduced by a more ingenious organization of concatenations and tests. Another open question is concerned with the optimal sequential time for finding all DLS.

References

1. T.A.Anderson, C.E.Kim: Representation of digital line segments and their preimages, *Comp. Vision, Graphics, and Image Proc.* 30 (1985), 279-288
2. M.J.Atallah, M.T. Goodrich: Parallel algorithms for some functions of two convex polygons, *Algorithmica* 3 (1988), 535-548
3. E.Creutzburg, A.Hübler, V.Wedler: Decomposition of digital arcs and contours into a minimal number of digital line segments (abstract), *Proc. 6th Int. Conf. on Pattern Recognition*, Munich 1982, 1218
4. I.Debled-Rennesson, J.P.Reveillès: A linear algorithm for segmentation of digital curves, *3rd Int. Workshop on Parallel Image Analysis*, College Park/MD 1994
5. L.Dorst, A.W.M.Smeulders: Decomposition of discrete curves into piecewise segments in linear time, *Contemporary Math.* 119 (1991), 169-195
6. V.A.Kovalesky: New definition and fast recognition of digital straight segments and arcs, *10th Int. Conf. on Pattern Recognition*, Atlantic City/NJ 1990
7. S.Pham: On the boundary of digital straight line segments, in: T.l.Kunii (ed.), *Advanced Computer Graphics, Proc. Computer Graphics, Tokyo 1986*, Springer, 79-109
8. J.P.Reveillès: Géométrie discrète, calcul en nombres entiers et algorithmique, Thèse d'Etat, Univ. Louis Pasteur, Strasbourg 1991
9. A.Rosenfeld: Digital straight line segments, *IEEE Trans. on Comp.* 23 (1974), 1264-1269
10. A.Trœsch: Interprétation géométrique de l'algorithme d'Euclide et reconnaissance des segments, *Theor. Computer Science* 115 (1993), 291-319
11. L.D.Wu: On the chain code of a line, *IEEE Trans. PAMI* 4 (1982), 347-353

Computability of Convex Sets
(Extended Abstract)

Martin Kummer and Marcus Schäfer

Institut für Logik, Komplexität und Deduktionssysteme, Universität Karlsruhe,
D-76128 Karlsruhe, Germany. {kummer; marcus}@ira.uka.de

Abstract. We investigate computability of convex sets restricted to rational inputs. Several quite different algorithmic characterizations are presented, like the existence of effective approximations by polygons or effective line intersection tests. We also consider approximate computations of the n-fold characteristic function for several natural classes of convex sets. This yields many different concrete examples of $(1, n)$-computable sets.

1 Introduction

Convex sets play a prominent role in mathematical programming, computational geometry, convex analysis, and many other areas. There is a large number of papers dealing with polynomial time computable convex sets, but the basic question "Which convex sets are computable?" was scarcely studied.

In this paper we characterize computable convex sets and show that several quite different approches lead to the same notion. We call a convex set A computable if there is an algorithm which computes the characteristc function of A for all rational inputs that do not belong to the boundary of A. It turns out that all other apparently weaker notions which have been proposed in the literature are equivalent to this definition. For instance, the existence of an algorithm for the "weak membership problem" of Grötschel, Lovász, and Schrijver [GLS88], or the property of being "Turing located" introduced by Ge and Nerode [GN94]. On the other hand, the apparently stronger requirement that there is a computable double sequence of rational polygons converging to A from inside and from outside, is also equivalent. Finally, if it is decidable which rational lines intersect the interior of A, then A is already computable.

In the second part we show that several natural classes of convex sets are "approximable", in the sense that for some fixed n and any rational numbers $x_1, \ldots, x_n$ we can effectively exclude one of the 2^n possibilities for the n-fold characteristic function $(\chi_A(x_1), \ldots, \chi_A(x_n))$. Approximable sets have previously been studied in recursion theory and complexity theory where such sets have been constructed by diagonalization. In contrast, we provide many natural and intuitive examples. Our results are established by effectivizing the concept of the Vapnik-Červonenkis-dimension.

In the following we will mostly deal with a special class of convex sets, namely, bounded convex sets which have an interior point. We will call these sets *convex regions*.

The following notations are used: we write xy for the line segment joining the points x and y. The line through these points is denoted by $l(x,y)$. As usual $S(x,r)$ is the closed circle (sphere) with radius r and center x. The interior, the closure, and the boundary of A are denoted by A°, $\overline{A}$, and ∂A, respectively. The complement of A is written as A^c. We use $d_H(A,B)$ to denote the Hausdorff distance between two subsets A and B of $\mathbb{R}^2$.

In section 2 we only present proof sketches, in section 3 we have to omit all proofs. For full details the reader is invited to consult [Sch94].

2   Computable Convex Sets

We are interested in establishing a suitable notion of computability for convex sets. For the sake of exposition we restrict ourselves to convex regions in $\mathbb{R}^2$, but with more technical and notational effort it is possible to generalize the definitions and results to higher dimensions.

As we have decided to use the rational model for our investigations the following definition might appear natural: a set A is called computable if we can effectively decide whether a rational point lies in A or not. Approaching convex sets in a geometric setting will show that this definition is not very helpful. Typically geometric operations depend on interior points and cannot distinguish two sets differing only on their boundary. Another problem is that the boundary of a set may turn out to be quite complicated (in the sense of computability) although the set itself and its complement are not: take for example the circle around the origin with radius 1. There are uncountably many sets that differ from this circle only in the rational points on the boundary, so most of them are not computable.

This motivates the following definition which will prove invariant to different approaches.

Definition 1. (Weak characteristic function) Let A be a subset of $\mathbb{R}^2$. The function

$$\omega_A : \mathbb{Q}^2 \to \{0,1\} : x \mapsto \begin{cases} 1 & x \in A^\circ \\ 0 & x \notin \overline{A} \\ \uparrow & \text{else} \end{cases}$$

is called the *weak characteristic function* of A.

The attribute "weak" is justified for convex regions as in this case the weak characteristic function is Turing reducible to the characteristic function (even uniformly). As we mentioned above, the converse is not true; one can even construct (by diagonalization) a convex *compact* set A such that ω_A is partial recursive but χ_A is not.

We will now list a couple of other natural algorithmic problems. First we consider two operations on sets which can be regarded as approximations (from a geometric viewpoint).

Definition 2. (Weak Membership Tests) For a set $A \subseteq \mathbb{R}^2$ every partial function $\alpha : \mathbb{Q}^2 \times \mathbb{Q}_+ \to \{0,1\}$ which for all $x \in \mathbb{Q}^2$ and $r \in \mathbb{Q}_+$ satisfies the conditions

- $S(x,r) \subseteq A^\circ \Rightarrow \alpha(x,r) = 1$
- $S(x,r) \subseteq (A^c)^\circ \Rightarrow \alpha(x,r) = 0$

is called a *Weak Membership Test (WMT)* for A. We will write α_A for a WMT for A.

The name WMT is explained by the observation that $\alpha_A(x,r) = 1$ implies $d(x,A) \leq r$, and $\alpha_A(x,r) = 0$ implies $d(x,A^c) \leq r$. Note, however, that we do not require α to be everywhere defined. Also, if $S(x,r)$ intersects both A and its complement then $\alpha_A(x,r)$ may give an arbitrary answer.

The following definition is due to Grötschel, Lovász, and Schrijver [GLS88].

Definition 3. (WMEM) For a set $A \subseteq \mathbb{R}^2$ we say that *the Weak Membership Problem (WMEM) is solvable* if there is a total recursive function β_A from $\mathbb{Q}^2 \times \mathbb{Q}_+$ to $\{0,1\}$ such that

- $\beta_A(x,r) = 1 \Rightarrow S(x,r) \cap \overline{A} \neq \emptyset$
- $\beta_A(x,r) = 0 \Rightarrow S(x,r) \cap (\overline{A})^c \neq \emptyset$

Analogically to WMTs we investigate another operation which is based on lines intersecting the set A.

Definition 4. (Line Intersection Tests) Given a set $A \subseteq \mathbb{R}^2$ every partial function $\gamma : \mathbb{Q}^2 \times \mathbb{Q}^2 \to \{0,1\}$ which satisfies the conditions

- $l(x,y) \cap A^\circ \neq \emptyset \Rightarrow \gamma(x,y) = 1$
- $l(x,y) \cap \overline{A} = \emptyset \Rightarrow \gamma(x,y) = 0$

is called a *Line Intersection Test (LIT)*. We will write γ_A for a LIT with respect to A.

With regard to LITs the following notion from convex geometry will prove helpful and can be used to establish another equivalent characterization:

Definition 5. (Extremal points) A point x of a set $A \subseteq \mathbb{R}^2$ is said to be *extremal (for A)* if it does not lie on a line strictly between two other points of A. The set of extremal points of A is denoted by $\text{ext}(A)$.

To define the next notion we need to recall a concept from recursive analysis [Ko91, PR89]. A real number $x \in \mathbb{R}^k$ is represented by a function $\phi : N \to \mathbb{Q}^k$ if $|f(n) - x| \leq 2^{-n}$ for all n. A real function $f : \mathbb{R}^k \to \mathbb{R}^m$ is computable if there is an oracle Turing machine M such that for every x and every representation ϕ of x, $\lambda n. \, M^\phi(n)$ is a representation of $f(x)$, i.e., M computes a representation of $f(x)$ if it is given a representation of x as an oracle.

Definition 6. (Turing located) A set $A \subset \mathbb{R}^2$ is called *Turing located* if the real function $x \mapsto d(x,A)$ is computable.

This definition was introduced by Ge and Nerode [GN94] who were looking for an effective version of the Krein-Milman theorem. They proved that a convex compact set A is Turing located iff the extreme points of A can be approximated in the following sense: There is a uniformly computable sequence of real numbers $\{y_i\}_{i \in N}$ such that their closure is the closure of the set of extreme points of A, and there is a computable function g such that $d_H(\text{conv}(y_1, \ldots, y_{g(n)}), A) \leq 2^{-n}$ for all n.

We can now state our main theorem which says that for convex regions all the above definitions are equivalent.

Theorem 7. *Let A be a convex region. Then the following are equivalent:*

(i) *ω_A is partial recursive.*
(ii) *There are computable sequences $(P_i)_{i \in N}$ and $(Q_i)_{i \in N}$ of rational polygons such that $P_i \subseteq A \subseteq Q_i$ and $d_H(P_i, Q_i) < 2^{-i}$ for all i.*
(iii) *There is a partial recursive WMT α_A.*
(iv) *There is a partial recursive LIT γ_A.*
(v) *The Weak Membership Problem for A is solvable.*
(vi) *A is Turing located.*

Sketch. For the proof we introduce the following variants of (iii) and (iv):

(iii′) The WMT $\qquad \alpha_A(x, r) := \begin{cases} 1 & S(x, r) \subseteq A^\circ \\ 0 & S(x, r) \subseteq (A^c)^\circ \qquad \text{is partial recursive.} \\ \uparrow & \text{else} \end{cases}$

(v′) The LIT $\qquad \gamma_A(x, y) := \begin{cases} 1 & l(x, y) \cap A^\circ \neq \emptyset \\ 0 & l(x, y) \cap \overline{A} = \emptyset \qquad \text{is partial recursive.} \\ \uparrow & \text{else} \end{cases}$

The proof has several parts:

(ii) $\Rightarrow$ (iii′) **and** (ii) $\Rightarrow$ (iv′) This is a direct construction: We search for an i such that $S(x, r) \subseteq (P_i)^\circ$ or $S(x, r) \cap Q_i = \emptyset$. The search terminates iff $(x, r) \in \text{dom}(\alpha_A)$. The argument for LITs is similar.

(iii′) $\Rightarrow$ (iii) **and** (iv′) $\Rightarrow$ (iv) Trivial.

(iii) $\Rightarrow$ (i) To prove this we need the following technical notion:

Definition 8. (Wedgeset) Call a set $A \subseteq \mathbb{R}^2$ a *wedgeset* if there is a triangle $\triangle$ such that for every $x \in A$ there is a congruent copy of $\triangle$ which is a subset of A and has x as a vertex.

Note that without loss of generality we may assume that the triangle is isosceles with vertex x.

Lemma 9. *Every convex region and its complement are wedgesets.*

The simple proof is omitted. Now, all we need is the following lemma.

Lemma 10. *Let $A \subseteq \mathbb{R}^2$ be a set for which A^c is a wedgeset and the WMT α_A is partial recursive. Then the rational points of A^o are recursively enumerable.*

The last two lemmas together directly yield the desired implication. We will only sketch the geometric idea behind the proof of the last lemma.

Sketch. The rather intuitive idea of the proof is that a point which is closely surrounded by a ring of discs which do not lie in the complement of A has to be an interior point. Naturally there have to be some conditions concerning the location of the discs to render this argument correct.

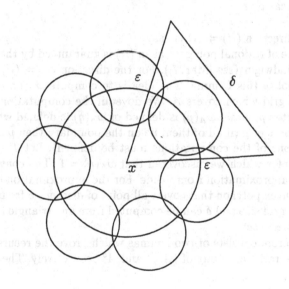

Fig. 1. Construction in Lemma 10

As A^c is a wedgeset there is a triangle $\triangle$ with legs of (rational) length ε and δ the (rational) length of the base. For a point x we search for a set of discs which fulfill the following conditions

(1) The centers of all discs have distance $r \in \mathbb{Q}_+$ from x with $r < \frac{\varepsilon}{2}$.
(2) The discs have radius $\frac{r}{4}\frac{\delta}{\varepsilon}$
(3) The discs cover the circle with radius r and center x.
(4) α_A is 1 for all discs in the set.

First of all, it is obvious that for each interior point x of A there is such a set of discs (choosing r small enough) and we are able to find it effectively by dovetailing the computations. The interesting part is to prove that whenever we find such a set of discs for a point x, this point is, in fact, an interior point. Granted we have found a set of discs satisfying (1) to (4), suppose for a contradiction that $x \notin A^\circ$, that is $x \in A^c$ or $x \in \partial A$.

If $x \in A^c$ we know that there is a triangle with vertex x which is a subset of A^c. We claim that one disc out of the set of discs wholly lies inside the triangle. Otherwise there is a point on the circle with radius r and center x, which is not covered by one disc out of the set of discs. Actually the point where the bisector of $\triangle$ in x intersects the circle has distance $> \frac{\delta}{\varepsilon}\frac{r}{2}$ from the nearest point on the boundary of $\triangle$. As the diameter of the discs is smaller than $\frac{\delta}{\varepsilon}\frac{r}{2}$ this point is not covered. Thus there is a disc which lies inside $\triangle$ and thereby in the interior of A^c which contradicts the fact that it was valued 1 by α_A. For $x \in \partial A$ we use the same argument for a point $x' \in A^c$ which is sufficiently near to x.

(i) $\Leftrightarrow$ (ii) The direction $(ii) \Rightarrow (i)$ is easy.

The existence of rational polygons as in (ii) is guaranteed by the well-known Lemma of Hadwiger (see [Mar77]). For the direction $(i) \Rightarrow (ii)$ we need an effective proof of this Lemma. The idea is to compute ω_A on a sufficiently fine rational grid which covers A. We dovetail the computation of ω_A until for every vertex p, either $\omega_A(p)$ is defined or $\omega_A(q)$ is defined where q is one of the neighbors of p (if all of them lie on the boundary then p is an interior point, thus one of the computations must be defined). Let T be the set of all vertices p for which we discovered that $\omega_A(p) = 1$. The convex hull of T gives us the approximation from inside. For the approximation from outside we take a convex polygon that covers all point of distance δ from T. Suitable values of the grid size and δ can be computed from any triangle $\triangle$ witnessing that A is a wedgeset.

(iv) $\Rightarrow$ (i) The proof consists of two lemmas which prove the recursive enumerability of the rational points of $(A^c)^\circ$ and A° respectively. The easy part is the following

Lemma 11. *Let A be a convex region which has a computable LIT γ_A. Then the rational points of $(A^c)^\circ$ are recursively enumerable.*

Sketch. Since $A^\circ \neq \emptyset$ there is a rational point $p \in A^\circ$. Then for all $x \in \mathbb{Q}^2$ (in fact for all $x \in \mathbb{R}^2$):

$$x \in (A^c)^\circ \Leftrightarrow (\exists y, z \in \mathbb{Q}^2)[x \notin l(y, z) \wedge \gamma_A(y, z) = 0 \wedge xp \cap l(y, z) \neq \emptyset] ,$$

i.e. there is a rational line $(l(y, z))$ which separates x and p without intersecting the interior of A. For the implication from left to right the boundedness of A is important as the example of a half plane with noncomputable slope shows.

We now show that the rational points in the interior of A are recursively enumerable. This is more complicated and requires the notion of extremal point as defined above.

The main theorem on extremal points is by Minkowski (later generalized as the famous Krein-Milman theorem of functional analysis):

Proposition 12 Minkowski [Min11, Jac71, Brø83]. *Let A be a convex and compact subset of $\mathbb{R}^2$ then A is the convex hull of its extremal points:*

$$A = \text{conv}(\text{ext}(A))$$

The following lemma proves an interesting fact about extremal points which makes it possible to approximate them:

Lemma 13. *Let A be a convex region, $x \in \text{ext}(\overline{A})$. Then for every $\delta > 0$ there are two rational points with distance less than δ from x which do not lie in $\overline{A}$ but the line segment joining the two points contains an interior point of A.*

We will omit the proof (it is by contradiction).

Lemma 14. *Let A be a convex region which has a partial recursive LIT γ_A. Then the rational points of $A°$ are recursively enumerable.*

Sketch. Let p be a rational interior point of A. Search for triplets (y, z, w) of rational points which satisfy

(1) $\gamma_A(y, w) = 0$ $(\Rightarrow l(y, w) \cap A° = \emptyset)$
(2) $\gamma_A(z, w) = 0$ $(\Rightarrow l(z, w) \cap A° = \emptyset)$
(3) $\gamma_A(y, z) = 1$ $(\Rightarrow l(y, z) \cap \overline{A} \neq \emptyset)$
(4) pw intersects yz.

The diagram shows the relative position of the points.

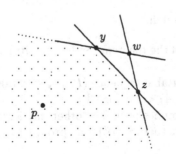

Fig. 2. Construction in Lemma 14

In this situation we know that the triangle $\triangle(w, y, z)$ contains a point of $\overline{A}$. On the other hand the preceding lemma guarantees that every extremal point of A can be approximated in this manner.

As every interior point of A lies in the interior of the convex hull of at most four extremal points of $\overline{A}$ and conversely, we have an algorithm at hand to detect whether $x \in \mathbb{Q}^2$ is an interior point: search for approximations of (three and four) extremal points as described above and check whether x is in the intersection of all convex hulls generated by vertices in the approximating triangles. If x is indeed an interior point there will be a sufficiently close approximation of extremal points (because of the preceding lemma) such that x is contained in all of these convex hulls. On the other hand only interior points will satisfy these conditions. The search can be done effectively by dovetailing.

(iii) $\Leftrightarrow$ (v) Let the WMEM problem be solvable by β_A. We claim that β_A is a WMT:

- $S(x, r) \subseteq A^\circ \Rightarrow S(x, r) \cap (\overline{A})^c = \emptyset \Rightarrow \beta_A(x, r) \neq 0 \Rightarrow \beta_A(x, r) = 1$
- $S(x, r) \subseteq (A^c)^\circ \Rightarrow S(x, r) \cap \overline{A} = \emptyset \Rightarrow \beta_A(x, r) \neq 1 \Rightarrow \beta_A(x, r) = 0$

On the other hand the existence of a partial recursive WMT implies (ii). So we can effectively approximate A by P_i and Q_i from inside and outside. To solve the Weak Membership Problem we wait until $S(x, r)$ intersects either P_i or Q_i^c (this computation terminates, because $d_H(P_i, Q_i) \to 0$). In the first case we let β_A be 1 and 0 else. It is easy to see that the resulting function solves WMEM.

(ii) $\Rightarrow$ (vi) This follows using the fact that if x is a computable real, then the distance from x to any given rational polygon is also (uniformly) computable.

(vi) $\Rightarrow$ (iii) To prove this implication it must be shown that a WMT is computable if A is Turing located. For a pair $(x, r) \in \mathbb{Q}^2 \times \mathbb{Q}_+$ compute $d \in \mathbb{Q}_+$ such that $|d(x, A) - d| < \frac{r}{3}$ (this is effectively possible since A is Turing located). Define $\alpha_A(x, r)$ to be 1 if $d < \frac{r}{2}$ and 0 else. We have to check that this is indeed a WMT:

- $S(x, r) \subseteq A^\circ \Rightarrow d(x, A) = 0 \Rightarrow d < \frac{r}{3} < \frac{r}{2} \Rightarrow \alpha_A(x, r) = 1$
- $S(x, r) \subseteq (A^c)^\circ \Rightarrow d(x, A) > r \Rightarrow d > \frac{2}{3}r > \frac{r}{2} \Rightarrow \alpha_A(x, r) = 0$

This finishes the proof sketch.

Remarks. (1) Item (ii) of the theorem can be substituted by a seemingly weaker variant:

  (ii') There is a computable sequence $(P_i)_{i \in \mathbb{N}}$ of rational polygons
    such that $d_H(P_i, A) < 2^{-i}$ for all i.

Now (ii) obviously implies (ii'). The other implication follows from $(ii') \Rightarrow$ (vi). The implication $(vi) \Rightarrow (ii')$ was proved by Ge and Nerode in their paper [GN94].

(2) We have the following, by no means obvious, result:
  A convex region is Turing located iff its complement is Turing located.

If the complement of a set is Turing located we can show as in the proof
of $(vi) \Rightarrow (iii)$ that a WMT is computable. On the other hand we have
$(vi) \Rightarrow (ii)$ and (ii) implies that the complement of a convex region is Turing
located as in $(ii) \Rightarrow (vi)$.

(3) Grötschel, Lovász and Schrijver in their book [GLS88] take WMEM as a
starting point to prove further equivalent variants (even preserving polynomial time computability) like optimization of linear functions, separation by
hyperplanes and others.

At this point the question of recursive enumerability of convex sets suggests
itself. Adhering to our concept (excluding the boundary) we call a set $A \subseteq \mathbb{R}^2$
recursively enumerable if the rational interior points of A are recursively enumerable. A list of results rather similar to those of the theorem can be obtained. For
example (using the same method as above) one easily proves that A is r.e. iff the
rational circles which intersect A are recursively enumerable. The same result
(although with a new proof) holds for intersecting lines. Furthermore A is r.e.
iff it can be approximated from within by rational polygons. The convergence
in this case will in general not be effective, because by the theorem this would
automatically imply that A is recursive. Analogically a weaker variant of the
concept Turing located can be used to give another equivalent characterization.

3 Approximable Convex Sets

In this section we do not require our geometric sets to be computable. Nevertheless, in many cases we can still compute certain types of approximations
which are currently intensively studied in recursion theory [BGGO93, Ga91] and
complexity theory [BKS94]. Natural examples of noncomputable sets which are
approximable in this sense were rare and so it came as a surprise that the well-
known convex figures dealt with in elementary geometry like circles and polygons
should prove quite resourceful in this respect. The results are established in terms
of an effective variant of the Vapnik-Červonenkis-dimension [Ass83, VC71] used
in probability theory ([Dud84]), learning theory ([BE89]) and computational
geometry ([HW87]).

Definition 15. (Approximable sets) A set $A \subseteq \mathbb{Q}^d$ is $(1,n)$-*computable* if there
is a recursive function f from $(\mathbb{Q}^d)^n$ into $\{0,1\}^n$ such that for all rational points
$x_1, \ldots, x_n$: $(\chi_A(x_1), \ldots, \chi_A(x_n)) \neq f(x_1, \ldots, x_n)$. A set is called *approximable* if
there is an n such that the set is $(1,n)$-computable. In this case the greatest n
such that the set is not $(1,n)$-computable is called the *effective Vapnik-Červonenkis-dimension of A* and is denoted by $VC_{eff}(A)$. The *effective Vapnik-Červonenkis-dimension of a concept class C* is defined to be the supremum of the
effective Vapnik-Červonenkis-dimension of its members (the *concepts*).

In other words, the effective Vapnik-Červonenkis-dimension of a concept class
is the smallest n such that for every concept from the class there is an algorithm
to exclude one of the 2^{n+1} possibilities of the $(n+1)$-fold characteristic function.

This is related to the original VC-dimension as follows: The VC-dimension of a concept class is the greatest n such that there is a set of n points which is *shattered* by the concept class (i.e. every subset of the n points can be written as the intersection of the set of n points with a concept). In other words, for any $n+1$ points $x_1, \ldots, x_{n+1}$ there is a vector $v \in \{0,1\}^{n+1}$ such that $v \neq (\chi_A(x_1), \ldots, \chi_A(x_{n+1}))$ for *all* $A \in C$. For all natural concept classes C, there is a *computable* function f such that $f(x_1, \ldots, x_{n+1}) = v$. So, every concept from the class is $(1, n+1)$-computable via the same f, in particular, $VC(C) \geq VC_{eff}(C)$. However, note that in the definition of VC_{eff}, f can depend on A, and therefore the inequality may be strict.

A lower bound for $VC(C)$ is shown by exhibiting a configuration of points which cannot be shattered by C. In contrast, a lower bound for $VC_{eff}(C)$ requires a more complicated construction. To show that $VC_{eff}(C) \geq n$, we construct a particular concept $A \in C$ such that A is not $(1, n)$-computable. A is constructed as the limit of concepts $A_0, A_1, \ldots$ such that A_i is not $(1, n)$-computable via the first i recursive functions. To this end we need to consider "local shatterings", i.e., we are given a concept $B \in C$ and any $\epsilon > 0$ and need a configuration of n points that is shattered by $\{C \in C : d_H(C, B) < \epsilon\}$. An example where this becomes quite involved is the class of all triangles.

The following table summarizes our results:

concept class C	$VC(C)$	$VC_{eff}(C)$
half spaces in $\mathbb{R}^d$	$d+1$	d
bounded intervals in $\mathbb{R}$	2	2
bounded intervals with rational length	2	1
triangles	7	7
convex n-gons	$2n+1$	probably $2n+1$
spheres in $\mathbb{R}^d$	$d+1$	$d+1$
discs with rational radius	3	3
spheres in $\mathbb{R}^d$ with rational center	$d+1$	1

The results concerning VC are well-known (see [WD81]). The results on VC_{eff} are new. Here is an example of how the VC_{eff} column should be read: an effective Vapnik-Červonenkis-dimension of 7 for triangles means that every triangle is $(1, 8)$-computable but there is a triangle which is not $(1, 7)$-computable.

The upper bounds of the above table can be stated in a stronger form: Beigel, Kummer and Stephan in [BKS94] introduced the concept of polynomially approximable sets, that is approximable sets which are approximable by polynomial time functions. All of the examples in the table are even polynomially approximable, thus we also obtain nontrivial examples in this context. Agrawal and Arvind [AgAr94] have recently shown that even infinite nonuniform families of half spaces share many properties of approximable sets in the resource-bounded setting.

The results of the table can be generalized.

Definition 16. A subset A of $\mathbb{Q}^d$ is *algebraic* if it is a Boolean combination (i.e. union, intersection, and complement) of sets of the form $\{x \in \mathbb{Q}^d : f(x) > 0\}$ where f is a real polynomial.

Algebraic sets comprise most of the sets usually dealt with in elementary geometry. This holds especially for convex sets like spheres, half spaces, conics.

Theorem 17. *Every algebraic set is approximable.*

This theorem is a direct consequence of some effective versions of results proved in [Dud84]. The effective versions appear in [Sch94]. The theorem yields another interesting conclusion: it is known that approximable sets (i.e. sets with $VC_{e\!f\!f}(A) < \infty$) are not m-complete (since the halting problem is not approximable, see e.g. [Ga91, Theorem 23]), so we have:

Corollary 18. *No algebraic set is m-complete.*

Acknowledgement: We would like to thank Frank Stephan for helpful discussions.

References

[AgAr94] Manindra Agrawal, V. Arvind. Geometric sets of low information content. School of Mathematics, SPIC Science Foundation, Internal Report TCS-94-5, Madras, June 1994.

[Ass83] Patrick Assouad. Densité et dimension. *Ann. Inst. Fourier, Grenoble*, 33,3:233–282, 1983.

[BGGO93] R. Beigel, W. I. Gasarch, J. Gill, J. C. Owings, Jr. Terse, superterse, and verbose sets. *Information and Computation*, 103:68–85, 1993.

[BKS94] Richard Beigel, Martin Kummer, Frank Stephan. Approximable sets. In: *Proceedings Structure in Complexity Theory. Ninth Annual Conference*, pp.12–23, IEEE Computer Society Press, 1994.

[BE89] Anselm Blumer, Andzej Ehrenfeucht, David Haussler, Manfred K. Warmuth. Learnability and the Vapnik-Chervonenkis dimension. *Journal of the Association for Computing Machinery*, 36,4: 929–965, 1989.

[Brø83] Arne Brøndsted. *An introduction to convex polytopes*. Springer-Verlag, New York, 1983.

[Dud84] Richard Mansfield Dudley. A course on empirical processes. In: *École d'Été de Probabilités de Saint-Flour XII - 1982*. Lecture Notes in Mathematics 1097, Springer-Verlag, Berlin, 2–142, 1984.

[Ga91] William I. Gasarch. Bounded queries in recursion theory: a survey. In: *Proceedings Structure in Complexity Theory. Sixth Annual Conference*, pp.62–78, IEEE Computer Society Press, 1991.

[GN94] Xiaolin Ge, Anil Nerode. On extreme points of convex compact Turing located sets. In: *Proceedings LFCS'94, St. Petersburg, Russia, July 1994*, pp. 114–128, Lecture Notes in Computer Science Vol. 813, Springer-Verlag, Berlin, 1994.

[GLS88] Martin Grötschel, László Lovász, Alexander Schrijver. *Geometric algorithms and combinatorial optimization*. Springer-Verlag, Berlin, Heidelberg, 1988.

[HW87] David Haussler, Emo Welzl. ϵ-nets and simplex range queries. *Discrete Comput. Geometry*, 2:127–151, 1987.

[Jac71] Konrad Jacobs. Extremalpunkte konvexer Mengen. In: *Selecta Mathematica III*, Springer-Verlag, Heidelberg, 1971.

[Ko91] Ker-I Ko. *Complexity theory of real functions*. Birkhäuser, Boston, 1991.

[Mar77] Jürg T. Marti. *Konvexe Analysis*. Birkhäuser, Basel, 1977.

[Min11] H. Minkowski. *Gesammelte Abhandlungen*, Bd. II. Teubner, Leipzig, 157–161, 1911.

[PR89] Marian Boykan Pour-El, Jonathan Ian Richards. *Computability in analysis and physics*. Springer-Verlag, Berlin, 1989.

[Sch94] Marcus Schäfer. *Anfragekomplexität geometrischer Mengen*. Diplomarbeit, Fakultät für Informatik, Universität Karlsruhe, January 1994.

[VC71] V. N. Vapnik, A. Ya. Červonenkis. On the uniform convergence of relative frequencies of events to their probabilities. *Theory Probab. Appl.*, 16:264–280, 1971.

[WD81] R. S. Wencour, R. M. Dudley. Some special Vapnik-Chervonenkis classes. *Discrete Mathematics*, 33:313–318, 1981.

Enumerating Extreme Points in Higher Dimensions*

Th. Ottmann and S. Schuierer and S. Soundaralakshmi

Universität Freiburg, Institut für Informatik, Am Flughafen 17, 79110 Freiburg, FRG. {ottmann,schuiere}@informatik.uni-freiburg.de, Fax: (0761) 203-8122

Abstract. We consider the problem of enumerating all extreme points of a given set P of n points in d dimensions. We present an algorithm with $O(n)$ space and $O(nm)$ time where m is the number of extreme points of P.
We also present an algorithm to compute the depth of each point of the given set of n points in d-dimensions. This algorithm has complexity $O(n^2)$ which significantly improves the $O(n^3)$ complexity of the previously best known deterministic algorithm. It also improves the best known randomized algorithm which has a expected running time of $O(n^{3-\frac{2}{1+\lfloor d/2 \rfloor}+\delta})$ (for any fixed $\delta > 0$).

Topics: Computational Geometry

1 Introduction

The convex hull of a set of points is the smallest convex set that contains the points. The construction of the convex hull is a central problem in computational geometry, with applications to pattern recognition, image processing, generation of Voronoi diagrams and a number of other problems, where the generation of the convex hull is often a preprocessing step for a main algorithm.

Given a set P of n points in d dimensions we say that point p in P is an *extreme point* of P if $conv(P) \neq conv(P \setminus \{p\})$ where $conv(P)$ denotes the convex hull of P. The set of extreme points of P can also be characterized as the minimal subset E of P with $conv(P) = conv(E)$. In particular, the extreme points of P are the vertices of the convex hull of P. In dimensions two and three the problem of determining the extreme points of a given set P can be solved in optimal time $O(n \log n)$ by computing the convex hull of P. The problem of finding the convex hull of a set of n points has been extensively studied and many elegant algorithms exist for its solution [2, 3, 11, 13, 14, 15, 16]. The method for identifying the points on the convex hull in two and three dimensions cannot be extended to dimensions greater than three since the number of facets of the convex hull of P has an exponential growth in higher dimensions, i.e., there can be up to $\Omega(n^{\lfloor d/2 \rfloor})$ facets [5].

* This research is supported by the DFG-Project "Diskrete Probleme", No. Ot 64/8-1.

Deciding whether a point in P is an extreme point or not can be formulated as a linear programming problem. There are many deterministic and randomized algorithms that solve a linear program with n constraints in time $O(n)$ [5, 8, 10, 18, 22, 23]. Unfortunately, the constants are exponential functions of d. The best known deterministic algorithm has a running time of $O(2^{O(d \log d)} n)$ [5] while one of the fastest randomized algorithms is a combination of the approach of Clarkson [8] and Sharir and Welzl [23] with a running time of $O(d^2 n + d^3 \sqrt{n} \log n + d^5 2^d \log n)$ [23].

Given one of the algorithms for linear programming, the extreme points can be determined if one linear program is solved for each of the n points of P and, therefore, the extreme points of P can be enumerated in $O(n^2)$ time.

Seidel and Welzl present a randomized algorithm which improves the time complexity to $O(n^{3/2} \log n)$ expected running time in dimension 4 and to expected time $O(n^{2-c_d})$ in any fixed dimension $d \geq 5$, where c_d is given by $1/c_d = O(\lfloor d/2 \rfloor!^2)$ [20]. They use a randomized divide and conquer approach to partition the problem into suitable smaller subproblems, which are then solved by linear programming. Their result is further improved by Matousek and Schwarzkopf [17]. They present a randomized algorithm that determines the extreme points of a set of n points in d dimensions in $O(n^{2-\frac{2}{1+\lfloor d/2 \rfloor}+\delta})$ expected time, for any fixed $\delta > 0$. Their approach has the disadvantage that the hidden constant is at least $d!$ since the algorithm works by recurring on smaller dimensions.

In the first part of this paper we present a simple deterministic algorithm for enumerating the extreme points of a finite set of n points in d dimensions. It is based on an interesting modification of the naive approach to determine the extreme points of P. We enumerate all the extreme points of a point set P of n points in d dimensions in $O(nm)$ time where m is the number of extreme points of P. If $m = o(n)$, then our method improves the previous best known deterministic complexity of $O(n^2)$ for enumerating extreme points in d dimensions where $d \geq 4$ [12]. In many real world applications, like for example a uniform distribution of the points in the d-dimensional unit cube, the number of expected extreme points is considerably less than n [4], in the example of the unit cube $O(\log^{d-1} n)$ [21].

A closely related problem to the enumeration of extreme points is the computation of the *convex layers* of a set P. Starting with the convex hull as the first layer, the ith layer is defined as the convex hull of the set of points remaining after removing all the points from the previous j layers with $j \leq i-1$. The *depth* of a point in P is i if it belongs to the ith convex layer.

The second part of this paper is concerned with the problem of computing the depth of each point p of P in d dimensions. The two dimensional problem was first considered by Overmars and van Leeuwen which provide an $O(n \log^2 n)$ time solution using a planar configuration maintenance technique [19]. This algorithm has been further refined by Chazelle and he has shown that the convex layers and, therefore, the depth of a set of n points can be computed in optimal $O(n \log n)$ time [6]. In 3-dimensional space Agarwal and Matousek give an $O(n^{1+\epsilon})$ time algorithm to compute the convex layers of a point set [1]. For dimensions $d > 3$, the problem has not yet been considered and the existing (naive) deterministic algorithm takes $O(n^3)$ time.

We show in Section 3 that our method of enumerating the extreme points can be extended to compute all the convex layers of P in $O(n^2)$ time. Hence, the depth of all the points of a finite set of n points in d dimensions can be computed in $O(n^2)$ time, thus solving an open problem posed by Edelsbrunner [12, Problem 8.11].

2   Extreme Points

This section concerns the enumeration of extreme points of a finite set P of n points in d dimensions where the dimension d is fixed. We are only interested in the case $d \geq 4$ and we assume that $n \geq d+1$ and that the points are in general position, i.e., no $d+1$ points lie in a common hyperplane. If it cannot be guaranteed that each hyperplane contains at most d points, then the general technique of *simulating simplicity* can be used which ensures that algorithms developed for points in general position produce a correct output even if the point set contains degenerate configurations [12, Section 9.4].

The problem of deciding whether a given point $p \in P$ is an extreme point is equivalent to the problem of determining whether $p \in conv(P \setminus \{p\})$. This problem can be dualized into a linear programming problem that involves n constraints and d variables [9]. Before we give our algorithm, we review the concepts of linear programming in relation to the computation of extreme points.

2.1   Linear Programming and Extreme points

A natural and frequently studied problem regarding convex polyhedra is the linear programming problem. We are given a set H of halfspaces in d dimensions. The halfspaces are called *linear constraints*. In addition, we are given a linear function f which is called the *objective function*. The tuple (H, f) is called a *linear program*. The linear programming problem is to determine a point of the polyhedron formed by the intersection of the given halfspaces at which the maximum of f is attained.

In order to see how linear programming can be employed to determine extreme points we make use of the concept of *duality*. Consider the geometric transform D which maps each point p of $\mathbb{R}^d \setminus \{0\}$ into a halfspace $D(p) = \{x \in \mathbb{R}^d \mid <x, p> \leq 1\}$ ($<x, y>$ denotes the inner product of the two vectors x and y) and vice versa. We denote the halfspace $D(p)$ also by h_p. The point p and the halfspace h_p are called *duals* of each other (see Figure 1).

Let P be a set of n points $p_1, \ldots, p_n$ in d dimensions and H_P be the set $\{h_{p_1}, \ldots, h_{p_n}\}$ of the halfspaces that are dual to the points of P. If H_Q is a subset of H_P, then we assume in the following that Q is the subset of P such that $D(Q) = H_Q$.

We denote the polyhedron formed by the intersection of the halfspaces of H_P by $\Pi(H_P)$, i.e. $\Pi(H_P) = \bigcap H_P$. A halfspace that contains $\Pi(H_P)$ in its

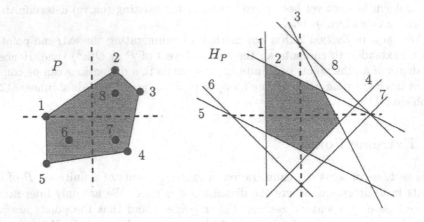

Fig. 1. A point set P and its dual H_P.

interior is called *redundant*. In other words, a halfspace is redundant if it can be discarded without affecting the intersection $\Pi(H_P)$. Otherwise, the halfspace is called *non-redundant*. The hyperplanes bounding non-redundant halfspaces are called *bounding hyperplanes* of $\Pi(H_P)$.

If the origin belongs to $conv(P)$, then p in P is an extreme point of P if and only if h_p is a non-redundant hyperplane of H_P [12, Corollary 1.9]. If the origin does not belong to $conv(P)$, the $d+1$ points $p_1, \ldots, p_{d+1}$ span a d-simplex (since the points are in general position). If we translate P by the vector $-1/(d+1)\sum_{i=1}^{d+1} p_i$, then the convex hull of the translated point set $\overline{P}$ contains the origin while the extreme point of $\overline{P}$ are the translations of the extreme points of P. Since this transformation requires only $O(n)$ additional time we can assume in the following that the origin belongs to $conv(P)$ and to compute the extreme points of P it suffices to decide, for each halfspace h_p in H_P, if the halfspace h_p is redundant or not as we observed above.

In order to do so we make use of linear programming. Let the outer normal of the bounding hyperplane of h_p be denoted by n_p (note that $n_p = p$ if p is considered a vector). Now we consider the linear program (H_P, f_p) where $f_p(x) = \langle n_p, x \rangle$ is the objective function. The problem is to determine the maximum value of the objective function on $\Pi(H_P)$ and also the set of d hyperplanes which determine the maximum value. We denote the value of a linear program with the objective function f_p and the constraints H_P by $f_p(H_P)$. We have the following lemma (see also [7]).

Lemma 1. *The halfspace h_p is non-redundant if and only if $f_p(H_P) = f_p(H_{\{p\}})$.*

Proof: First note that $f_p(H_P) \leq f_p(H_{\{p\}})$ since $\Pi(H_P)$ is contained in h_p. To prove the "only if"-direction we assume that h_p is non-redundant. Hence, there is a least one point q_0 on the bounding hyperplane of h_p that belongs to $\Pi(H_P)$. Note that if q is a point on the bounding hyperplane of h_p, then $<n_p, q> = f_p(H_{\{p\}})$. This implies that $f_p(H_P) \geq <n_p, q_0> = f_p(H_{\{p\}})$ which proves one direction of the claim.

To see the other direction note that the equation $<n_p, x> = f_p(H_{\{p\}}) = f_p(H_P)$ defines a hyperplane which coincides with the bounding hyperplane of h_p. Hence, there is at least one point of $\Pi(H_P)$ on the bounding hyperplane of h_p. This implies that h_p is non-redundant. $\square$

In our algorithm we do not only test a halfspace for redundancy against H_P but also against a suitably chosen subset H_Q of H_P which has a lesser cardinality than H_P.

Corollary 2. *If h_p is a non-redundant halfspace of H_Q, then h_p is a non-redundant halfspace of H_P if and only if $f_p(H_P) = f_p(H_Q)$.*

Proof: The halfspace h_p is a non-redundant halfspace of H_P if and only if $f_p(H_P) = f_p(H_{\{p\}})$ by Lemma 1. Since h_p is a non-redundant halfspace of H_Q, the same lemma implies $f_p(H_Q) = f_p(H_{\{p\}})$. Combining the two equations yields the lemma. $\square$

Hence, if h_p a non-redundant halfspace of H_Q but redundant in H_P, then $f_p(H_P) < f_p(H_Q) = f_p(H_{\{p\}})$.

All of the linear programming algorithms we mentioned before also return a *witness* v^* which is a point of $\Pi(H_P)$ with $f_p(H_P) = f_p(v^*)$ if they are applied to the linear program where the constraints are H_P and the objective function is f_p. This witness is crucial for our algorithm.

Lemma 3. *Let h_p be a halfspace that is non-redundant in H_Q and redundant in H_P. If v^* is a witness of the linear program (H_P, f_p) and $H_R \subseteq H_P$ is the set of halfspaces whose bounding hyperplane contains v^*, then*

- *there is at least one halfspace of H_R that is not contained in H_Q,*
- *all the halfspaces of H_R are non-redundant in H_P, and*
- *$|H_R| \leq d$.*

Proof: To see the first claim note that since h_p is non-redundant in H_Q but redundant in H_P, $f_p(H_P) < f_p(H_Q)$ by Corollary 2. Furthermore, since v^* is contained in the interior of the halfspaces $H_P \setminus H_R$, $f_p(H_P) = f_p(H_R)$. Hence, there is at least one halfspace of H_R that is not contained in H_Q.

To see the second claim just note that v^* is a point on the boundary of $\Pi(H_P)$ that is contained in boundary of each of the halfspaces in H_R. Hence, $\Pi(H_P)$ is not contained in the interior of the halfspaces $h_r \in H_R$.

The third claim of the lemma follows from the general position assumption on P. If more than d hyperplanes intersect in v^*, then there are more than d points of P contained in the hyperplane that is dual to v^*. $\square$

We make use of Lemma 3 to enumerate the extreme points of P in d-dimension. The main idea is to avoid testing the extremality of each point of P against the whole set P by using the set E of the extreme points that have been found so far as a filter. This reduces the complexity of the algorithm from $O(n^2)$ to $O(nm)$.

2.2 The Algorithm

We now present our method of enumerating extreme points of P. We choose $d+1$ linearly independent points such that each point has a maximum coordinate in one of the $2d$ axes-parallel directions. Initially the set E of extreme points of P is created from these $d+1$ points. Let us denote the set $P \setminus E$ by P'. We have to test for every point in P' whether it is an extreme point of P or not. Obviously, a point p in P' is not an extreme point of P if it is not an extreme point of $Q = E \cup \{p\}$, since Q is a subset of P. Therefore, it is sufficient to test the extremality of a point $p \in P'$ in P only if it is an extreme point of Q. In order to do this we first solve the linear program (H_Q, f_p). If $f_p(H_Q) = f_p(H_{\{p\}})$, then h_p is non-redundant in H_Q and p is not contained in $conv(E)$. Only then do we solve the larger linear program (H_P, f_p) which leads to the following two cases.

Case 1: $f_p(H_P) = f_p(H_{\{p\}})$ and p is an extreme point of P. In this case we can update E by adding p to E.

Case 2: $f_p(H_P) < f_p(H_{\{p\}})$ and p is not an extreme point of P. From the algorithm solving the linear program (H_P, f_p) we obtain a witness v^*. Let H_R be the set of halfspaces that contain v^* in their bounding hyperplane. By Lemma 3 $H_R \setminus H_E$ is a subset of the non-redundant halfspaces of H_P. Hence, if we set $E := E \cup R$, then we add only extreme points to E.

More precisely, our algorithm can be described as follows.

> **Algorithm** *Enumeration of extreme points*
> $E := \{p_1, \ldots, p_{d+1}\}$;
> $P' := P \setminus E$;
> **repeat**
>   let p be the next point in P';
> $P' := P' \setminus \{p\}$;
> $Q := E \cup \{p\}$;
> (1)   solve the linear program (H_Q, f_p);
>   **if** $f_p(H_Q) = f_p(H_{\{p\}})$
> (2)   **then** (∗ p is an extreme point of $E \cup \{p\}$ ∗)
>   solve the linear program (H_P, f_p);
>   let v^* be a witness of the solution;
>   **if** $f_p(H_P) = f_p(H_{\{p\}})$
>   **then** (∗ p is an extreme point of P ∗)
> $E := E \cup \{p\}$;
>   **else** (∗ p is not an extreme point of P ∗)
>   let H_R be the subset of halfspaces of H_P whose
>   bounding hyperplane contains v^*;
> $E := E \cup R$;
> $P' := P' \setminus R$;
>   **end if**
>   **end if**
> **until** $P' = \emptyset$;

The correctness of the algorithm follows immediately from the case analysis above.

Now, we analyze the time complexity of our algorithm. Clearly, the execution time of the algorithm is dominated by the time to solve the linear programming problems in Steps (1) and (2). First consider Step (1). The linear program (H_Q, f_p) is solved for each point p in P. The maximum cardinality of H_Q is $|Q| = |E| + 1 \leq m + 1$ if m is the number of extreme points of P. Hence, the total time used for Step (1) is bounded by $O(nm)$.

Now consider Step (2). Step (2) is called for each point p of P' that is an extreme point of E. We claim that each time Step (2) is executed the cardinality of E increases at least by one. If p is an extreme point of P, then p is added to E and the claim obviously holds. If p is not an extreme point of E and v^* a witness of the value of the linear program (H_P, f_p), then there is at least one halfspace of H_P that contains v^* in its bounding hyperplane and that is not contained in H_E by Lemma 3. Clearly, all the halfspaces that contain v^* in its bounding hyperplane can be found in time $O(dn)$. Since all the points that correspond to halfspaces whose bounding hyperplane contains v^* are added to E, the cardinality of E increases by at least one. Hence, a linear program of the form (H_P, f_p) is solved at most $|E| = m$ times which again leads to a time bound of $O(mn)$. Hence, we have shown the following theorem.

Theorem 4. *Given a set of n points in d dimensions, the extreme points can be computed in $O(nm)$ time where m is the number of extreme points of P.*

3 Convex layers

We show in this section that we can efficiently compute the depth of each point in a finite set of n points in d dimensions. The *depth* of a point $p \in P$ is 1 if p is an extreme point. Otherwise, the depth of p in P is one plus the depth of p in P minus the set of extreme points. Let E_1 be the set of extreme points of P. It determines the first convex layer of P. The set E_2 of extreme points of $P \setminus E_1$ is the second convex layer of P. In general E_i, the i the convex layer, is the set of extreme points of $P \setminus (E_1 \cup E_2 \ldots \cup E_{i-1})$.

After the discussion of the algorithm of enumerating the extreme points in the previous section, the procedure for constructing all the convex layers and hence finding the depth of each point of the given set P of finite number of points in d-dimensions is now straightforward.

The first convex layer E_1 of the given set P of n points can be determined in $O(nm_1)$ time where m_1 is the number of points of E_1. The ith convex layer E_i can be obtained in time $O(nm_i)$ after removing points from the first $i - 1$ layers of P, where $|E_i| = m_i$. In each iteration we determine only the extreme points of the set which is obtained from discarding all the extreme points which have been found in the previous iterations. We continue the procedure until we obtain all the convex layers. This procedure for computing all the convex layers of P is known as "shelling" or "peeling".

Theorem 5. *One can determine the convex layers of a finite set of n points in d dimensions by shelling in $O(n^2)$ time.*

Proof: Determining E_i takes $O(nm_i)$ time where $|E_i| = m_i$. Hence, the total time complexity for determining all the layers is $\sum m_i(n - (m_1 + m_2 + \cdots + m_{i-1})) \leq \sum m_i n \leq n \sum m_i$. Since each point is contained in exactly one layer, $\sum m_i = n$ and the sum is bounded by $O(n^2)$. $\qquad\square$

Corollary 6. *The depth of all points in a set of n points in d-dimensions can be computed in time $O(n^2)$.*

4 Conclusions

We have presented a new algorithm for computing the extreme points of a finite set of n points in d-dimensions in $O(n)$ space and $O(nm)$ time where m is the number of extreme points of the set. Using this result, we have achieved an improvement for computing the depth of all the points of a finite set of points in dimensions $d \geq 4$. The method takes $O(n^2)$ time which improves the $O(n^3)$ complexity of the previouly best deterministic algorithm. It also improves the best known randomized algorithm with expected running time $O(n^{3 - \frac{2}{1 + \lfloor d/2 \rfloor} + \delta})$ (for any fixed $\delta > 0$).

One of the main open questions is whether there are faster algorithms than $O(n^2)$ to compute the depth of all points.

References

1. P. Agarwal and J. Matousek. Ray shooting and parametric search. In *Proc. 21st ACM Symp. on Theory of Computing*, pages 517–526, 1992.
2. S. G. Akl and G. T. Toussaint. A fast convex hull algorithm. *Information Processing Letters*, 7(5):219–222, 1978.
3. B. K. Bhattacharya and G. T. Toussaint. Time- and storage-efficient implementation of an optimal convex hull algorithm. *Image Vision Computing*, 1:140–144, 1983.
4. K. H. Borgwardt, N. Gaffke, M. Jünger, and G. Reinelt. Computing the convex hull in the euclidean plane in linear expected time. In *Applied Geometry and Discrete Mathematics THE VICTOR KLEE FESTSCHRIFT*, pages 91–107. DIMACS Series in Discrete Mathematics and Theoretical Computer Science, Volume 4, 1991.
5. B. Chazelle. An optimal convex hull algorithm and new results on cuttings. In *Proc. 32nd IEEE Symp. on Foundations of Computer Science*, pages 29–38, 1991.
6. B. Chazelle. Optimal algorithms for computing depths and layers. In *Proc. 21st Allerton Conference on Communication, Control and Computation*, pages 427–436, 1983.
7. V. Chvátal. *Linear Programming*. W. H. Freeman, New York, NY, 1983.
8. K. L. Clarkson. A Las Vegas algorithm for linear programming when the dimension is small. In *Proc. 29th IEEE Symp. on Foundations of Computer Science*, pages 452–456, 1988.

9. D. P. Dobkin and S. P. Reiss. The complexity of linear programming. *Theoretical Computer Science*, 11:1-18, 1980.

10. M. E. Dyer. Linear time algorithms for two- and three-variable linear programs. *SIAM Journal of Computing*, 13:31-45, 1984.

11. H. Edelsbrunner and W. Shi. An $O(n \log^2 h)$ time algorithm for the three-dimensional convex hull problem. *SIAM Journal of Computing*, 20:259-277, 1991.

12. H. Edelsbrunner. *Algorithms in Combinatorial Geometry*. Springer Verlag, EATCS Monographs on Theoretical Computer Science Edition, 1987.

13. R. L. Graham. An efficient algorithm for determining the convex hull of a finite planar set. *Information Processing Letters*, 1:132-133, 1972.

14. G. H. Johansen and C. Gram. A simple algorithm for building the 3-d convex hull. *BIT*, 23:146-160, 1983.

15. M. Kallay. Convex hull made easy. *Information Processing Letters*, 22:161-163, 1986.

16. D. G. Kirkpatrick and R. Seidel. The ultimate planar convex hull algorithm? *SIAM Journal of Computing*, 15:287-299, 1986.

17. J. Matousek and O. Schwarzkopf. Linear optimization queries. In *Proc. 8th ACM Symp. on Computational Geometry*, pages 16-25, 1992.

18. N. Megiddo. Linear programming in linear time when the dimension is fixed. *Journal of the ACM*, 31:114-127, 1984.

19. M. Overmars and J. van Leeuwen. Maintenance of configurations in the plane. *Journal of Computer and System Sciences*, 23:166-204, 1981.

20. E. Welzl and R. Seidel. referred to in [17], p. 25.

21. A. Rényi and R. Sulanke. Über die konvexe Hülle von n zufällig gewählten Punkten. *Zeitschrift für Wahrscheinlichkeitstheorie und Verwandte Gebiete*, 2:75-84, 1963.

22. R. Seidel. Small-dimensional linear programming and convex hulls made easy. *Discrete & Computational Geometry*, 6:423-434, 1991.

23. M. Sharir and E. Welzl. A combinatorial bound for linear programming and related problems. In *Proc. 9th Symp. on Theoretical Aspects Computer Science*, LNCS 577, pages 569-579. Springer-Verlag, 1992.

The Number of Views of Piecewise-Smooth Algebraic Objects

Sylvain Petitjean

CRIN-CNRS & INRIA Lorraine, Bâtiment LORIA, BP 239
54506 Vandœuvre-les-Nancy cedex, France
email: petitjea@loria.fr

Abstract. A solid object in 3-dimensional space may be described by a collection of all its topologically distinct 2-dimensional appearances, its aspect graph. In this paper, we study the complexity of aspect graphs of piecewise-smooth algebraic objects using the modern tools of algebraic geometry, i.e. intersection theory, multiple-point theory and enumerative geometry. We give a bound on the number of different appearances of such objects, an indication of the computational complexity of aspect graphs.

1 Introduction

In model-based computer vision, one is usually interested in extracting meaningful information from a camera image, in organizing these information into some representation and in matching this representation with models of the scene objects stored off-line in a database. A fundamental example is that of depth discontinuities, the so-called *edges*, organized in a line-drawing, also called an *aspect* or a *view* of an object. To be able to "recognize" and give the orientation of an object present in the scene, one needs to have in the database all the topologically distinct aspects of the object and a viewpoint from which these aspects may be observed. This representation is known as the *aspect graph* or *view graph* [Koenderink and van Doorn, 1979] of the object.

Assuming perspective projection as camera model (the set of viewpoints is the entire 3-dimensional space in which the object lives), the range of possible viewpoints can be partitioned into maximal connected regions that yield identical aspects. The change in aspect at the boundary between regions is called a *visual event*. The maximal regions and their associated aspects form the nodes of an aspect graph, whose arcs correspond to the visual event boundaries between adjacent regions. The main organizers of this partitioning are called *visual event surfaces*.

Recent research has focused on theoretical questions related to the complexity of this representation. Rieger [Rieger, 1993] considered the case of *piecewise-smooth surfaces*, i.e. surfaces consisting of smooth algebraic surfaces intersecting pairwise transversally along crease (*double*) curves and having isolated triple points. He proved that instead of the 5 visual event surfaces in the case of smooth surfaces, one has to consider a set of 19 event surfaces. He obtained bounds for the degrees of these surfaces as well as an upper bound for the number of views of the corresponding aspect graph, all this using tools from singularity theory.

Modern algebraic geometry, though more abstract, provides a nice and constructive setting for studying these questions. What we propose in this paper is to rephrase the problem using the tools of *enumerative geometry* and *intersection theory*. We show how to obtain exact degrees (not just bounds) for all the visual event surfaces in terms of characteristics of the original piecewise-smooth surface, without ever manipulating any of the equations defining these surfaces. Details are left out in this version of the paper to concentrate on the methods to obtain these results.

2 Singularity Theory and Visual Events

For a given viewpoint, the view of a piecewise-smooth surface is the union of its *outline* (projection onto the image of the *contour generator*, defined as the set of points where the line of sight grazes the surface) and of all projected crease curves. Like any other plane curve, the view may have a certain number of singularities. *Singularity theory* tells us exactly which ones can be expected, and how the view structure changes as a function of viewpoint. This is precisely the information needed to handle the visual event surfaces.

2.1 Projection onto a Plane

In 1955, Whitney published a paper that laid the foundations for the theory of singularities of mappings. Here, we are interested in a particular mapping, the projection of a surface onto some image plane. For open subsets of the viewspace V considered, the views of a piecewise-smooth C^∞-surface may only have singular points equivalent to one of six stable types [Rieger, 1987, Tari, 1991], as indicated in Figure 1. A result by [Rieger, 1993] asserts that the set of viewpoints B (called the *bifurcation set*) for which the preceding result does not hold has measure 0. We then use the same term aspect graph to talk about the partitioning of viewpoint space that B induces or about the graph whose nodes are the connected components of $V - B$ and whose edges represent transitions between adjacent cells of the partitioning of V.

Cusps are observed when the viewline is an *asymptotic* tangent to the surface (contact of order 3 with the surface).

2.2 Visual Event Surfaces

If the viewpoint is generic, then the only singularities of the view are the types listed above. However, if one chooses it in a special way, one may also obtain some non-generic (unstable) projections of a piecewise-smooth surface. Rieger proceeded to prove that a view of a piecewise-smooth surface is unstable if the corresponding viewpoint belongs to at least one of 19 sets of visual event ruled surfaces [Rieger, 1993].

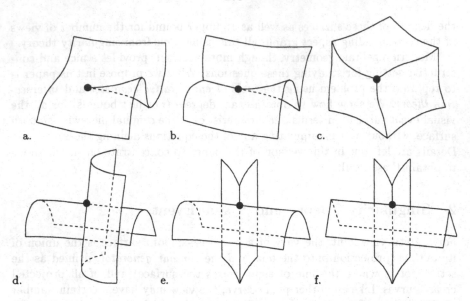

Fig. 1. Stable singularities of projections of piecewise-smooth surfaces. a. Cusp (C). b. Semi-fold (SF). c. Triple point (T). d. Fold crossing. e. Fold-crease crossing. f. Crease crossing.

Letting $+$ denote transversal crossing, $++$ denote tangential superposition, F denote fold and D denote crease, one can easily describe multilocal events (coming from more than one surface point). For instance, $F + +F + F$ stands for lines tritangent to the surface such that in projection two of the contours are tangent and the third is transverse. Then the multilocal events are (using the notations of Figure 1): $F + F + F$, $F + F + D$, $F + D + D$, $D + D + D$, $F + +F$, $F + +D$, $D + +D$, $F + C$, $D + C$, $F + T$, $D + T$, $F + SF$, and $D + SF$. As for local event surfaces, they are made of: lines asymptotic at parabolic points, lines asymptotic at flecnodal points (contact of order 4), lines tangent to the double curve, planes tangent at the triple points, lines asymptotic at double curve points and lines conjugate to lines tangent at double curve points. This classification shows that such visual events will appropriately be handled through the study of lines and planes having prescribed contacts with curves and surfaces.

3 Preliminaries

Our main goal in the rest of this paper is to show how the degrees of the different visual event surfaces can be obtained. As we shall see, this will be done by identifying suitable spaces parameterising lines and planes and applying multiple-point theory to the maps between those spaces.

Throughout the rest of this paper, the base field is C, the field of complex numbers. X will denote a projective algebraic piecewise-smooth surface of degree d, having a double curve of degree b and t isolated triple points, $\mathcal{P}^m$ will stand for the m-dimensional projective space, and a ˇsymbol will mean duality. Though our setup allows to compute exact formulas in terms of d, b and t, we will here put the emphasis on the methods used and for the most part we will give bounds for the degrees of the visual event surfaces. Then, we suppose that X is made of n different surfaces all of degree less than or equal to δ. Thus $d = O(n\delta), b = O(n^2\delta^2)$ and $t = O(n^3\delta^3)$. The symbol $*$ will stand for the class of a point, in whatever space it lives.

3.1 Multiple-Point Theory

Given a map $f : U \to V$ of codimension n, an r-fold point of f is a point u_1 of U such that there exist points $u_2, \cdots, u_r$ of U all having the same image under f. If $u_1, \cdots, u_r$ are all distinct points of U, then we shall say that the point is *ordinary*. On the contrary, if some of the u_i lie *infinitely near* each other, then it is called *stationary*. We can rephrase this a little bit. Let $\mathbf{a}$ be a partition of r, i.e. $\mathbf{a} = (a_1, \cdots, a_k)$ is a k-tuple of positive integers such that $\sum_{g=1}^{k} a_g = r$. We consider the multiple point locus $S_f(\mathbf{a})$ described as follows. $S_f(\mathbf{a})$ consists of points u_1 of U such that there are $r - 1$ other points $u_2, \cdots, u_r$ of U all having the same image under f and also such that the first a_1 points lie infinitely near each other, the next a_2 points lie infinitely near each other, and so on.

The precise definition of "infinitely near" is out of the scope of this paper; we prefer to describe this notion by example, which will also serve as the general philosophy of the remaining sections. Let C be a plane curve, $C \subset \mathcal{P}^2$. Let U be

$$U = \{(x, l) \in C \times \check{\mathcal{P}}^2 \ / \ x \in l\},$$

where $\check{\mathcal{P}}^2$ is the dual projective plane, i.e. the space parameterizing lines in $\mathcal{P}^2$. Now, we consider multiple points of the map $f : U \to \check{\mathcal{P}}^2$. Suppose for instance that we look at the multiple-point locus corresponding to the partition $\mathbf{a} = (1, 1, 1, 1)$. Pictorially this locus is as indicated in the first image of Figure 2. Now, if we allow some points to coalesce (i.e. to lie infinitely near each other), we may get a different picture. Figure 2 illustrates the case where the first two points coalesce and the last two points coalesce (it is the case $\mathbf{a}=(2,2)$). If we allow 3 points to coalesce, then this is the same as imposing that a line has contact of ordre 3 (inflexional) with C. So we see that in this example, the notion of stationarity is very close to that of order of tangency.

We now go back to the general case. Modern multiple-point theory is concerned with characterizing the loci of multiple points of general classes of maps, a topic that has considerable interest in several mathematical domains ranging from differential geometry to topology. In algebraic geometry, it has presently culminated in two basic approaches: the *Hilbert scheme* technique [le Barz, 1987] and an iterative method [Colley, 1987]. We shall here be mainly interested in the latter approach.

In [Colley, 1987], the author defines an intersection-theoretic class $l(\mathbf{a}; n)$ whose geometric support is the multiple point locus $S_f(\mathbf{a})$, up to an overcount factor. Colley gives a set of rules to compute $l(\mathbf{a}; n)$ in terms of Chern classes

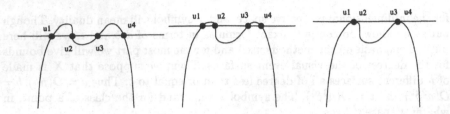

Fig. 2. Deformation of an ordinary 4-fold point into a (2,2)-point.

of the normal sheaf of f, and of n. We have recently implemented this set of rules [Petitjean, 1994] and all the formulas appearing in this paper have been computed using this package.

Note that to be able to use stationary mutiple-point theory on f, one has to impose some conditions on the map, so that the image of the multiple point locus by f has the expected codimension in V. However, the Hilbert schemes method allows to get rid of this unnecessary restriction. What it shows is that every enumerative formula of the kind we will see in a moment must be a certain polynomial in d, b and t, valid for *any* surface X. Since multiple-point theory gives a polynomial valid in "generic" situations, both formulas must coincide and hold in the general case.

3.2 Numerical Invariants of a Surface

Let X be a surface, $Z \to X$ its normalization map, and $\varphi : Z \to \mathcal{P}^3$ the induced map. Let D_b be the double curve on X, Γ_b the corresponding curve on Z. Let also K denote the canonical divisor on Z, $c_2(T_Z)$ the second Chern class of Z, h be the hyperplane class in $\mathcal{P}^3$ and e its pullback to Z. The Chern polynomial of Z is $CP_t(T_Z) = 1 - Kt + c_2(T_Z)t^2$ and that of $\mathcal{P}^3$ is $CP_t(T_{\mathcal{P}^3}) = (1 + ht)^4$ by standard theory. By the exact sequence $0 \to T_Z \to \varphi^* T_{\mathcal{P}^3} \to \mathcal{N}_{Z/\mathcal{P}^3} \to 0$, we get that:

$$\begin{cases} c_1(\mathcal{N}_{Z/\mathcal{P}^3}) = 4e - c_1(T_Z) = 4e + K, \\ c_2(\mathcal{N}_{Z/\mathcal{P}^3}) = 6e^2 + K.c_1(\mathcal{N}_{Z/\mathcal{P}^3}) - c_2(T_Z) = K^2 + 4Ke + 6e^2 - c_2(T_Z). \end{cases}$$

Now, we can apply multiple-point theory to φ. The set of double points of φ is given by (the codimension of this map is 1) $[M_2] = \varphi^* \varphi_* [Z] - c_1(\mathcal{N}_{Z/\mathcal{P}^3})$, and this cycle is precisely $[\Gamma_b]$. Replacing with the value of the first Chern class we have seen and using that $\varphi_*[Z] = dh$, we get $[\Gamma_b] = (d-4)e - K$. Since $\int [\Gamma_b].e = 2b$ (double covering), we have $\int Ke = d(d-4) - 2b = O(n^2 \delta^2)$.

The set of triple points of φ is governed by:

$$[M_3] = \varphi^* \varphi_* [M_2] - 2c_1(\mathcal{N}_{Z/\mathcal{P}^3}).[M_2] + 2c_2(\mathcal{N}_{Z/\mathcal{P}^3}),$$

and its degree is equal to $6t$ (a triple point on X comes from 3 double points on Z and the overcount factor is 2). Thus, since $\varphi_*[M_2] = 2bh^2$,

$$[M_3] = 4K^2 - 2(d-12)Ke + 2(b - 4d + 22)e^2 - 2c_2(T_Z),$$

and taking degrees yields the relation

$$\int (2K^2 - c_2(T_Z)) = d(d^2 - 12d + 26) - 3(d - 8)b + 3t. \qquad (1)$$

The number of pinchpoints ν_2 is the degree of the (finite) ramification locus R of φ. But we have $[R] = c_2(\mathcal{N}_{Z/\mathcal{P}^3})$, so we obtain

$$\int (K^2 - c_2(T_Z)) = -2d(2d - 5) + 8b + \nu_2. \qquad (2)$$

Since in our case $\nu_2 = 0$, we obtain by combining (1) and (2) that

$$\begin{cases} \int K^2 = d(d - 4)^2 - (3d - 16)b + 3t = O(n^3\delta^3), \\ \int c_2(T_Z) = d(d^2 - 4d + 6) - (3d - 8)b + 3t. \end{cases}$$

Another relation comes from the *adjunction formula* applied to Γ_b. Indeed, $2p_a(\Gamma_b) - 2 = \int [\Gamma_b].(K + [\Gamma_b]) = 2(d - 4)b$. D_b has t triple points, which means that Γ_b has $3t$ ordinary double points. Thus, $p_a(\Gamma_b) = g(\Gamma_b) + 3t$. Using the Riemann-Hurwitz theorem, $2(2g(D_b) - 2) = 2g(\Gamma_b) - 2$, so we have $2g(D_b) - 2 = (d - 4)b - 3t = O(n^3\delta^3)$.

3.3 Contacts of Lines with Curves and Surfaces

Inspired by the example we have given for lines having contacts with plane curves, we generalize this procedure to the case of space curves and surfaces. We then consider the following two diagrams:

where F_3 is the point-line flag manifold for $\mathcal{P}^3$, i.e. $F_3 = \{(x, l) \in \mathcal{P}^3 \times G \ / \ x \in l\}$, G is the 4-dimensional Grassmannian of lines in $\mathcal{P}^3$, and F_X and F_{D_b} are the restrictions of F_3 to X and D_b respectively. F_{D_b} is 3-dimensional, while F_X is 4-dimensional.

Considering the example we have given for plane curves, we want to be able to apply stationary multiple-point theory to $\bar{r}$ and $\bar{q}$. For this, we first have to "build" F_{D_b} and F_X, i.e. obtain their Chern classes and their Chow rings. But before that, we have to build F_3 and G. G may be realized as a quadric in $\mathcal{P}^5$, via the Plücker embedding, and its structure follows. Let γ_1 be the *first Schubert cycle* on G, i.e. the cycle of lines meeting a line in general position and γ_2 be the *second Schubert cycle*, i.e. the cycle of lines contained in a plane in arbitrary position. Note that $\gamma_1^2 - \gamma_2$ is the cycle of lines going through a point in general position. Then we have that $\gamma_1^4 = 2*, \gamma_1^2\gamma_2 = \gamma_2^2 = *$ and $\gamma_1^3 = 2\gamma_1\gamma_2$.

Without going into the details, F_3 may be realized both as a projective bundle over $\mathcal{P}^3$ and over G, so that its intersection theory is obtained as a combination of that of $\mathcal{P}^3$ and G. And by inclusion, we get the Chern classes of F_{D_b} and F_X, from which we infer those of the normal sheaves $\mathcal{N}_{F_{D_b}/G}$ and $\mathcal{N}_{F_X/G}$.

Intersection Theory on F_X. Let E and $\mathcal{K}$ respectively be the pullbacks to F_X of the class of a hyperplane section e of X and of the canonical divisor K of X, Γ_1 and Γ_2 the pullbacks of the Schubert cycles. Let also P such that $E^2 = dP$. Then the Chern classes of the normal sheaf of $\bar{q}$ are as follows:

$$c_k = c_k(\mathcal{N}_{F_X/G}) = (\Gamma_1 + \mathcal{K} + 2E)(\Gamma_1 - 2E)^{k-1}.$$

As for the intersection pairings, they go as follows (they are obtained by pulling back analogous relations on X and G). Denoting $\lambda = \int K.e = d(d-4) - 2b$ and $\mu = \int K^2 = d(d-4)^2 - (3d-16)b + 3t$, we have $P^2 = PK = PE = 0, \mathcal{K}E = \lambda P, \mathcal{K}^2 = \mu P, \Gamma_2 = \Gamma_1 E - E^2, \Gamma_1^3 = 2\Gamma_1\Gamma_2, \Gamma_1^4 = 2d*, \Gamma_1^2 E^2 = \Gamma_2^2 = d*, \Gamma_1^3 E = 2\Gamma_1^2 E^2 = 2d*$. As for the projection onto G, we have the following relations ($\bar{q}$ has degree d - X is cut in d points by a line in general position, which means that generically d points of F_X project onto a single point of G - and codimension 0):

$$\begin{cases} \bar{q}_*E = d\gamma_1, \\ \bar{q}_*E^2 = d(\gamma_1^2 - \gamma_2), \\ \bar{q}_*\mathcal{K} = \lambda\gamma_1. \end{cases}$$

Now, let S be one of the visual event surfaces and A the curve that S draws on X. Our goal is to find the fundamental cycle in F_X of a subvariety M of F_X such that the projection of M onto X is A and the projection of M onto G is S. Now, $A^3(F_X)$ the third Chow group of F_X may be realized to be 3-dimensional, and generated by $\Gamma_1^2 E, \Gamma_1^2 \mathcal{K}$ and $\Gamma_1 P$. So suppose we have obtained $[M]$ as follows (that will be our goal in Section 4 for all of the 19 visual event surfaces):

$$[M] = x\Gamma_1^2 E + y\Gamma_1^2 \mathcal{K} + z\Gamma_1 P.$$

The projection onto G yields $[S] = \bar{q}_*[M] = (2xd + 2y\lambda + z)\gamma_1\gamma_2$. The degree of a surface is the number of times in which it is met by a line in general position. But a ruled surface is a 1-dimensional system of lines, so its degree is the number of its generating lines which meet a line in general position. Generating lines of S are represented by $[S]$ in G, and γ_1 is the pullback of the class of a hyperplane section by the Plücker embedding, so that the degree of S is simply

$$\int [S].\gamma_1 = 2xd + 2y\lambda + zd = \sup(O(xd), O(yd^2), O(z)).$$

Note that by projecting $[M]$ onto X, one could also obtain useful information about the curve on X that S draws, but this is not our purpose here.

Intersection Theory on F_{D_b}. Let g_1 and g_2 be the pullbacks to F_{D_b} of respectively γ_1 and γ_2. Let b be the degree of C and g its genus. Let ε be the pullback to F_{D_b} of the class of a point in the Chow ring $A(C)$. Then the Chern classes of the normal sheaf $\mathcal{N}_{F_{D_b}/G}$ are:

$$\begin{cases} c_1' = g_1 + (2b + 2g - 2)\varepsilon), \\ c_2' = g_1^2 + (2g-2)g_1\varepsilon, \\ c_3' = (2g-2)*. \end{cases}$$

As for the intersection pairings, we have $g_1^3 = 2b*, g_1^2\varepsilon = *, g_2 = bg_1\varepsilon$. For the projection onto G, we have $\bar{r}_*1_{F_{D_b}} = b\gamma_1, \bar{r}_*\varepsilon = \gamma_1^2 - \gamma_2$.

Now, suppose that S is a visual event surface for which we have obtained the fundamental cycle $[M]$ in F_{D_b}. F_{D_b} is 3-dimensional and $[M]$ belongs to the second Chow group $A^2(F_{D_b})$. This group is generated by g_1^2 and $g_1\varepsilon$, so we may set $[M] = xg_1^2 + yg_1\varepsilon$. Thus $[S] = \bar{r}_*[M] = (2xb + y)\gamma_1\gamma_2$, so the degree of S is

$$\int [S] = 2xb + y = \sup(O(xb), O(y)).$$

3.4 Contacts of Planes with Curves and Surfaces

The Case of Surfaces. The naive approach would be to imitate what we have done for the case of lines. But in this case, a similar F_X would still be 4-dimensional, but the image space, in this case $\check{\mathcal{P}}^3$ the space parameterizing hyperplanes in $\mathcal{P}^3$, is 3-dimensional, and therefore we cannot apply multiple-point theory to this map. Instead we prefer to work with the *dual map*. Let $\check{X}$ denote the *dual surface* of X, i.e. the closure of the set of tangent planes to X. Assuming X is generic, $\check{X}$ is 2-dimensional and therefore a surface in $\check{\mathcal{P}}^3$. The dual map is the morphism $\check{\pi} : X \to \check{\mathcal{P}}^3$ which sends a point of X to its tangent plane (obviously $\check{\pi}(X) = \check{X}$). If we let $\check{e}$ be the pullback to X of the class of a hyperplane in $\check{\mathcal{P}}^3$, then standard theory shows that $\check{e} = K + 3e$, so that the degree of $\check{X}$ is $\int \check{e}^2 = d(d-1)^2 - (3d-4)b + 3t$.

We will later apply multiple-point theory to the map $\check{\pi}$ and thus we need the Chern classes of the normal sheaf. From the exact sequence $0 \to T_X \to \check{\pi}^*T_{\check{\mathcal{P}}^3} \to \mathcal{N}_{X/\check{\mathcal{P}}^3} \to 0$, we get that

$$\begin{cases} c_1(\mathcal{N}_{X/\check{\mathcal{P}}^3}) = 5K + 12e, \\ c_2(\mathcal{N}_{X/\check{\mathcal{P}}^3}) = 10K^2 + 44Ke + 48e^2, \end{cases}$$

because in our case $c_2(T_X) = K^2 + 4Ke + 6e^2$ and $\check{e} = K + 3e$ as we have seen.

The Case of Space Curves. We construct the point-plane incidence variety for D_b, i.e. $\check{F}_{D_b} = \{(x, H) \in D_b \times \check{\mathcal{P}}^3 \mid x \in H\}$. It is easy to check that $\check{F}_{D_b}$ is 3-dimensional, and thus we may apply multiple-point theory to $\check{s} : \check{F}_{D_b} \to \check{\mathcal{P}}^3$. Letting as before ε be the pullback to $\check{F}_{D_b}$ of the class of a point on D_b and $\check{E}$ be the pullback of $\check{h}$, we then have that the Chern classes of the normal sheaf $\mathcal{N}_{\check{F}_{D_b}/\check{\mathcal{P}}^3}$ are

$$\begin{cases} \check{c}_1 = \check{E} + (b + 2g - 2)\varepsilon, \\ \check{c}_2 = (2g - 2)\check{E}\varepsilon, \\ \check{c}_3 = 0. \end{cases}$$

Intersection pairings are $\varepsilon^2 = 0$, $\int \check{E}^3 = b$, $\int \check{E}^2\varepsilon = 1$, and for the projection onto $\check{\mathcal{P}}^3$, we have $\check{s}_*[\check{F}_{D_b}] = b[\check{\mathcal{P}}^3], \check{s}_*\varepsilon = \check{h}$.

4 Visual Event Surfaces

We are now ready to turn our attention to the actual computation of the degrees of the visual event surfaces. Due to space limitation, we will only here display bounds on these degrees, but it is interesting to note that our method yields *exact* formulas. For similar reasons, we shall not here try to give every detail of the proofs. Rather we choose to indicate how the results may be obtained. Throughout the section, we have choosen to indicate a multiple-point cycle on F_X by a l letter and the relevant Chern classes of $\bar{q}$ by c_k, while the corresponding symbols on F_C (and thus on the map $\bar{r}$) are m and c'_k, and those on $\bar{F}_{D_b}$ (and thus on the map $\bar{s}$) are n and $\check{c}_k$.

Surface $F + F + F$. As we have indicated, contacts of X with lines may be explored by applying multiple-point theory to $\bar{q}$. We want to find those lines that are triply tangent to the surface, and for this we compute the cycle $l(2,2,2;0)$. It turns out that:

$$l(2,2,2;0) = O(n^4\delta^4)\Gamma_1^2 E + O(n^4\delta^4)\Gamma_1^2 \mathcal{K} + O(n^5\delta^5)\Gamma_1 P,$$

so that the degree of this surface is $O(n^6\delta^6)$.

Surface $F + F + D$. The idea here is to consider the cycle $l(1,2,2;0)$ of lines cutting the surface transversally and also bitangent, but rather than just impose that the first point be a surface point, we also impose that it be a double curve point. We have seen that $[\Gamma_b] = (d-4)e - K$, and let ϕ be its pullback to F_X. Thus the cycle we are looking for is $\phi.l(1,2,2;0)$ and it turns out that

$$\phi.l(1,2,2;0) = O(n^5\delta^5)\Gamma_1^2 E + O(n^4\delta^4)\Gamma_1^2 \mathcal{K} + O(n^5\delta^5)\Gamma_1 P,$$

so the surface has degree $O(n^6\delta^6)$.

Surface $F + D + D$. We consider now the cycle $l(1,1,2;0)$ of lines meeting X twice transversally, and further tangentially, and impose that the first two points be double curve points, as above. The result is then

$$O(n^5\delta^5)\Gamma_1^2 E + O(n^4\delta^4)\Gamma_1 \mathcal{K} + O(n^6\delta^6)\Gamma_1 P,$$

so it has degree $O(n^6\delta^6)$.

Surface $D + D + D$. We look at the cycle of triple points of the map $\bar{r}$. It is given by:

$$\begin{aligned}
m(1,1,1) &= \bar{r}^*\bar{r}_*m(1,1) - 2c'_1.m(1,1) + 2c'_2, \\
&= O(n^4\delta^4)g_1^2 + O(n^4\delta^4)g_1\varepsilon,
\end{aligned}$$

so that the degree of this surface is $O(n^6\delta^6)$.

Surface $F++F$. This surface is made of the lines of support of planes bitangent to the surface. Looking at the map $\check{\pi}$, we see that its set of double points is given by $[M_2] = \check{\pi}^*\check{\pi}_*[X] - c_1(\mathcal{N}_{X/\check{p}^3}) = O(n^3\delta^3)K + O(n^3\delta^3)e$. We have to be a little bit careful here because the ramification of $\check{\pi}$ is not finite - $\check{X}$ has a cuspidal curve - and it turns out that this cuspidal curve is the image by $\check{\pi}$ of the parabolic curve P on X, with $[P] = O(1)K + O(1)e$. Thus the curve TC on X corresponding to $F++F$ has degree $O(n^5\delta^5)$.

Then it is easy to realize that a line generating S_5 projects onto a tangent to the double curve of $\check{X}$. Thus the degree of S_5 is the *rank* (number of tangents meeting a general line in space) of this double curve. Finding this rank requires describing the singularities of TC and the final result is that the degree of S_5 is $O(n^5\delta^5)$.

Surface $F++D$. Let $\check{D}$ be the closure of the set of tangent planes of D_b, a surface in $\check{P}^3$. Then the degree of $F++D$ may be seen as the rank of the curve of intersection of $\check{D}$ and $\check{X}$. One first has to compute the projective characters of $\check{D}$, which can be achieved by applying multiple-point theory to $\check{s}$. Then a classical result allows to relate this rank to the degrees and ranks of $\check{X}$ (resp. $O(n^3\delta^3)$ and $O(n^2\delta^2)$) and $\check{D}$ (resp. $O(n^3\delta^3)$ and $O(n^2\delta^2)$), and the end result is that this surface has degree $O(n^5\delta^5)$.

Surface $D++D$. The degree of S_7 is again similarly the rank of the double curve of $\check{D}$. We know the degree of this curve, and it remains to find the number of cusps it has. But this follows from standard theory on developable surfaces. Again we find that S_7 has degree $O(n^5\delta^5)$.

Surface $F+C$. This is the visual event surface generated by lines tangent at one point of X and asymptotic (contact of order 3) at another point. As such, we use $l(2,3;0) = c_1\bar{q}^*\bar{q}_*c_1 - 6c_1^3 - 12c_1c_2 - 6c_3$, or

$$l(2,3;0) = O(n^3\delta^3)\Gamma_1^2 E + O(n^3\delta^3)\Gamma_1^2 \mathcal{K} + O(n^5\delta^5)\Gamma_1 P,$$

and the degree of this surface is $O(n^5\delta^5)$.

Surface $D+C$. As we have done earlier, we start with the cycle $l(1,3;0)$ of lines meeting the surface transversally and asymptotic at another place, and we impose that the first point be a double curve point:

$$\phi.l(1,3;0) = O(n^4\delta^4)\Gamma_1^2 E + O(n^3\delta^3)\Gamma_1^2 \mathcal{K} + O(n^4\delta^4)\Gamma_1 P,$$

so it has degree $O(n^5\delta^5)$.

Surface $F+T$. The idea is again very similar. Consider the cycle $l(1,2;0)$ of lines tangent at one point and tranversal at another, and multiply it by the pullback to F_X of the cycle of triple points on X, i.e. tP. Then $tP.l(1,2;0) = O(n^5\delta^5)\Gamma_1 P$, and this surface has degree $O(n^5\delta^5)$.

Surface $D+T$. We use the cycle $m(1,1;1)$ in $A(F_{D_b})$ of lines bisecants to the double courbe, and multiply it by the cycle $t\varepsilon$ of triple points. We get $m(1,1;1).t\varepsilon = O(n^5\delta^5)g_1\varepsilon$, and the surface has degree $O(n^5\delta^5)$.

Surface $F + SF$. A semi-fold is obtained when the contour generator on the surface touches the double curve. Thus is suffices to look at the cycle $l(2,2;0)$ of bitangent lines and modify it in such a way that the first point also be on the double curve. Thus

$$\phi.l(2,2;0) = O(n^3\delta^3)\Gamma_1^2 E + O(n^2\delta^2)\Gamma_1^2 \mathcal{K} + O(n^5\delta^5)\Gamma_1 P,$$

and it has degree $O(n^5\delta^5)$.

Surface $D + SF$. Again we push the cycle $m(1,1)$ forward to F_X and intersect it with the cycle of tangent lines:

$$w_* m(1,1).l(2) = O(n^3\delta^3)\Gamma_1^2 E + O(n^2\delta^2)\Gamma_1^2 \mathcal{K} + O(n^5\delta^5)\Gamma_1 P.$$

In turn, this means that S_{13} has degree $O(n^5\delta^5)$.

The Parabolic Surface. On X, points of the elliptic region (positive Gaussian curvature) have no asymptotic tangent, point of the parabolic region (vanishing Gaussian curvature) have one, while hyperbolic points (negative Gaussian curvature) have two. Let A_3 be as follows:

$$A_3 = \{(x,l) \in X \times G \ / \ l \text{ has contact of order 3 with } X \text{ at } x\}.$$

A_3 is a subset of F_X and it is easy to realize that the set of parabolic points on X is the image of the ramification curve of the map $A_3 \to X$. To be able to compute this curve, we need a result of [Kulikov, 1983] giving the normal sheaf of A_3 in F_X. The corresponding cycle in F_X is

$$O(1)\Gamma_1^2 E + O(1)\Gamma_1^2 \mathcal{K} + O(n^3\delta^3)\Gamma_1 P,$$

so this surface has degree $O(n^3\delta^3)$.

The Flecnodal Surface. We look at those lines having contact of order 4 with X. The locus is $l(4;0) = c_1^3 + 3c_1 c_2 + 2c_3$ or

$$l(4;0) = O(1)\Gamma_1^2 E + O(1)\Gamma_1^2 \mathcal{K} + O(n^3\delta^3)\Gamma_1 P,$$

so the flecnodal surface has degree $O(n^3\delta^3)$.

Tangents to the Double Curve. The degree here is the rank of the double curve, so it is $O(n^3\delta^3)$.

Planes Tangent at Triple Points. Obviously, we have here a set of $3t$ planes and thus the surface has degree $O(n^3\delta^3)$.

Asymptotic lines at Double Points. We simply have to intersect in F_X the cycle of lines going through the double curve with the cycle of asymptotic lines, yielding

$$\phi.l(3;0) = O(n\delta)\Gamma_1^2 E + O(1)\Gamma_1^2 \mathcal{K} + O(n^3\delta^3)\Gamma_1 P,$$

so that it has degree $O(n^3\delta^3)$.

Lines Conjugate to Double Curve Tangents. We compute the rank of the image on $\tilde{X}$ of the double curve and find $O(n^3\delta^3)$.

5 Conclusion

To conclude on the complexity of the aspect graph, we need only use a result called the *Thom-Milnor bound* [Milnor, 1964] which goes as follows. The number of connected components of a semi-algebraic set of $\mathcal{R}^m$ that is defined by a polynomial equation of degree p is upper bounded by $O(p^m)$. Now, the visual event surfaces having highest degree are the trilocal ones, with a bound of $O(n^6\delta^6)$. In turn, this means that the global visual event locus is formed by a variety of degree $O(n^6\delta^6)$. Using Thom-Milnor's bound, we may conclude that a piecewise-smooth algebraic object has $O(n^{12}\delta^{12})$ views if orthographic projection is assumed (the viewpoint space may be modelled by a unit view sphere) and $O(n^{18}\delta^{18})$ views if perspective projection is assumed (the space of viewpoint is the entire 3-dimensional space). This bound in turn gives a strong indication of the computational complexity of building the aspect graph.

References

[Colley, 1987] Colley, S. (1987). Enumerating Stationary Multiple-Points. *Advances in Mathematics*, 66(2):149–170.

[Koenderink and van Doorn, 1979] Koenderink, J. and van Doorn, A. (1979). The Internal Representation of Solid Shape with Respect to Vision. *Biological Cybernetics*, 32:211–216.

[Kulikov, 1983] Kulikov, V. (1983). The Calculation of the Singularities of the Embedding of a Generic Algebraic Surface in the Projective Space $\mathcal{P}^3$. *Functional Analysis and Applications*, 17:176–186.

[le Barz, 1987] le Barz, P. (1987). Formules pour les trisécantes des surfaces algébriques. *L'Ens. Mathématique*, 33:1–66.

[Milnor, 1964] Milnor, J. (1964). On the Betti Numbers of Real Varieties. In *Proceedings of the American Mathematical Society*, volume 15, pages 275–280.

[Petitjean, 1994] Petitjean, S. (1994). Automating the Construction of Stationary Multiple-Point Classes. In *Proceedings of ISSAC'94 (International Symposium on Symbolic and Algebraic Computation)*, pages 9–14, Oxford, UK. ACM Press.

[Rieger, 1987] Rieger, J. (1987). On the Classification of Views of Piecewise-Smooth Objects. *Image and Vision Computing*, 5:91–97.

[Rieger, 1993] Rieger, J. (1993). On the Complexity and Computation of View Graphs of Piecewise-Smooth Algebraic Surfaces. Technical Report FBI-HH-M-228/93, Universität Hamburg.

[Tari, 1991] Tari, F. (1991). Projections of Piecewise-Smooth Surfaces. *Journal of the London Mathematical Society*, 44:155–172.

On the structure of
log-space probabilistic complexity classes
(Extended abstract)

Ioan I. Macarie

Department of Computer Science
University of Rochester, USA
macarie@cs.rochester.edu

Abstract. We investigate hierarchies of complexity classes defined by log-space probabilistic Turing machines, Arthur-Merlin games and Games against nature with logarithmic space-bounded probabilistic verifiers. We decompose each log-space complexity class into a hierarchy based on corresponding multihead two-way finite-state automata and we prove the separation of the levels of several hierarchies even over a one letter alphabet; furthermore, we show deterministic log-space reductions of each log-space complexity class to low levels of its corresponding hierarchy.

We find probabilistic (and "probabilistic+nondeterministic") variants of Savitch's maze threading problem that are log-space complete for **PL** (and respectively **P**) and that can be recognized by two-head one-way and one-head one-way one-counter finite-state automata with probabilistic (probabilistic and nondeterministic) states.

1 Results

We continue the study from [Ma94b] on connections between classes defined by log-space probabilistic Turing machines that recognize an input string with unbounded-, bounded- or one-sided-error (**PL**, **BPL**, **RPL** respectively), and classes recognized by the corresponding k-head two-way and one-way non-sensing probabilistic finite-state automata (**2PFA**(k), **2BPFA**(k), **2RPFA**(k), and respectively **1PFA**(k), **1BPFA**(k), **1RPFA**(k), where $k \in \mathbf{N}$). We extend these results to the settings of Arthur-Merlin games (**AM**-games) and the unbounded-error version of Arthur-Merlin games (**UAM**-games) (also known as "Games against nature" [Pa85]) having as verifiers log-space probabilistic Turing machines (**AM**$(\log n)$, **UAM**$(\log n)$) or k-head two-way and one-way non-sensing probabilistic finite-state automata (**AM**$(2pfa(k))$, **UAM**$(2pfa(k))$, **AM**$(1pfa(k))$, **UAM**$(1pfa(k))$). Additionally, we make use of the classes of languages recognized by one-way one-counter unbounded-error probabilistic finite-state automata (**1PCM**(1)) and by **UAM**-games with one-way one-counter probabilistic finite-state automata as verifiers (**UAM**$(1pcm(1))$).

For each class of languages **C** defined by some kind of automata, we denote by $\mathbf{C}_{poly}$ the subclass defined by the same automata that run in worst-case polynomial time. Based on the known fact that **AM**- and **UAM**-games can be defined by automata with both nondeterministic and probabilistic states [GS89], we will call the classes of languages defined by these games "probabilistic+nondeterministic" complexity classes.

In these terms, the results presented in this paper are:

- The "equivalence" between the space of log-space Turing machines with probabilistic and nondeterministic states, and the number of heads of multihead finite-state automata with the same kind of states:
  $\mathbf{AM}(\log n) = \bigcup_{k=1}^{\infty} \mathbf{AM}(2pfa(k))$, $\mathbf{UAM}(\log n) = \bigcup_{k=1}^{\infty} \mathbf{UAM}(2pfa(k))$,
  $\mathbf{AM}_{poly}(\log n) = \bigcup_{k=1}^{\infty} \mathbf{AM}_{poly}(2pfa(k))$, and
  $\mathbf{UAM}_{poly}(\log n) = \bigcup_{k=1}^{\infty} \mathbf{UAM}_{poly}(2pfa(k))$.
  These relations parallel those recently noticed in the setting of probabilistic computation [Ma94b]. To prove these relations, we adapt the proofs of their deterministic and nondeterministic versions [Ha72].
- For **AM**-games and **UAM**-games with multihead two-way probabilistic finite-state verifiers the heads hierarchy is proper (even for languages over a one-letter alphabet), i.e., for $k \geq 2$,
  $\mathbf{AM}(2pfa(k)) \subsetneqq \mathbf{AM}(2pfa(k+1))$, $\mathbf{UAM}(2pfa(k)) \subsetneqq \mathbf{UAM}(2pfa(k+1))$,
  $\mathbf{UAM}_{poly}(2pfa(k)) \subsetneqq \mathbf{UAM}_{poly}(2pfa(k+1))$.
  Similar separations hold for multihead unbounded- and one-sided-error probabilistic finite-state automata [Ma94b]. The deterministic and nondeterministic versions of these theorems were obtained by Monien [Mo80]. To prove our results we adapt translational methods to the setting of probabilistic+nondeterministic computation. One example of the strength of these methods is as follows: whereas Dwork and Stockmeyer proved that Pal = $\{x \in \Sigma^* | x = x^R\}$ separates $\mathbf{AM}(2pfa(1))$ from $\mathbf{AM}(\log n) = \mathbf{P}$ [DS92], we refine this separation by proving that there are entire natural hierarchies between $\mathbf{AM}(2pfa(1))$ and $\mathbf{P}$, even over a one-letter alphabet.
- Using varying techniques, we show log-space reductions ($\leq_{log}$) among probabilistic (probabilistic+nondeterministic) complexity classes, as follows:
  - Log-space (bounded- and one-sided-error) complexity classes are reducible to classes of languages recognized by the corresponding two-head two-way finite-state automata, that additionally have sweeping and non-sensing heads: $\mathbf{BPL} \leq_{log} \mathbf{2BPFA}(2)$, $\mathbf{BPL}_{poly} \leq_{log} \mathbf{2BPFA}_{poly}(2)$, $\mathbf{RPL} \leq_{log} \mathbf{2RPFA}(2)$, $\mathbf{RPL}_{poly} \leq_{log} \mathbf{2RPFA}_{poly}(2)$, and $\mathbf{P} = \mathbf{AM}(\log n) \leq_{log} \mathbf{AM}(2pfa(2))$.
  - Polynomial-time log-space (bounded- and one-sided-error) complexity classes are log-space reducible to languages recognized by the corresponding multihead one-way (bounded-error and one-sided-error) finite-state automata, that additionally move at least one head at each computation step: $\mathbf{BPL}_{poly} \leq_{log} \mathbf{1BPFA}(8)$, $\mathbf{RPL}_{poly} \leq_{log} \mathbf{1RPFA}(8)$, and $\mathbf{AM}_{poly}(\log n) \leq_{log} \mathbf{AM}(1pfa(8))$.
  - Log-space unbounded-error complexity classes are reducible to classes of languages recognized by the corresponding two-head one-way finite-state automata and one-head one-way one-counter finite-state automata, that additionally move at least one head at each computation step:

$\mathbf{PL} \leq_{log} \mathbf{1PFA}(2)$, $\mathbf{PL} \leq_{log} \mathbf{1PCM}(1)$ and
$\mathbf{P} = \mathbf{UAM}(\log n) \leq_{log} \mathbf{UAM}(1pfa(2))$, $\mathbf{P} \leq_{log} \mathbf{UAM}(1pcm(1))$.
It follows that $\mathbf{PL}$ (and $\mathbf{P}$) can be defined as the classes of languages
log-space reducible to languages recognized by two-head one-way and
one-head one-way one-counter finite-state automata that recognize with
unbounded-error and have probabilistic (probabilistic+nondeterministic,
respectively) states. Moreover, the log-space reductions of $\mathbf{PL}$ mentioned
above can be regarded as generalizations of the well-known result of Jung
$\mathbf{PL} = \mathbf{PL}_{poly}$ [Ju85].
Some nondeterministic versions of these reductions were proven by Hartmanis [Ha72] and Sudborough [Su75].

- To prove log-space reductions of $\mathbf{PL}$ we design probabilistic variants of Savitch's maze threading problem that are log-space complete for $\mathbf{PL}$, and
surprisingly, have not been remarked so far. (Note that several nondeterministic variants of maze threading problems were already known in early
1970's.) Similarly, to prove log-space reductions of $\mathbf{P}$, we present proba-
bilistic+nondeterministic variants of the maze threading problem that are
log-space complete for $\mathbf{P}$.

2 Introduction

Deterministic and nondeterministic multihead finite-state automata were studied
primarily in the 1970's. Several results were published, including characterizations of hierarchies of multihead finite-state automata, their connections with
log-space Turing machines and transformations of languages recognized by one
type of devices to languages recognized by the same or different types of devices
[Ha72], [Ib73], [Su75],[Mo76], [Se77a], [Se77b], [YR78], [Mo80]. Probabilistic analogues of these results remained unnoticed until recently, when separations for
the heads hierarchies in the cases of multihead unbounded-error and one-sided-
error probabilistic automata were proven [Ma94b].

The goal of this paper is to further investigate properties of log-space probabilistic Turing machines in connection with multihead probabilistic finite-state
automata and to generalize them to the settings of Arthur-Merlin games and
Games against nature having as verifiers log-space probabilistic Turing machines or multihead two-way and one-way non-sensing probabilistic finite-state
automata. Our study follows the next outline: for each log-space complexity class
we are focusing on, we decompose it into a hierarchy based on the corresponding
multihead finite-state automata and, eventually, we prove the separation of the
hierarchy levels even over a one-letter alphabet; furthermore, we show log-space
reductions of the log-space complexity class to low levels of this hierarchy.

In Section 3 we notice the equalities between the classes of languages recognized by Arthur-Merlin games and Games against nature with log-space probabilistic Turing machines as verifiers and the classes of languages recognized by
the same games with multihead two-way probabilistic finite-state verifiers. The
equalities remain true even when the probabilistic verifiers run in polynomial

time. The parallel relations for the settings of deterministic, nondeterministic, and probabilistic computations can be found in [Ha72] and [Ma94b], respectively. Next, we show that for Arthur-Merlin games and Games against nature with multihead two-way (non-sensing) probabilistic finite-state verifiers the heads hierarchies are proper. These results parallel those obtained for multihead two-way unbounded- and one-sided-error probabilistic finite-state automata [Ma94b]. To obtain these separations, we adapt translational methods used in 1970's for separating deterministic and nondeterministic complexity classes [Mo80].

In Section 4 we present log-space reductions of log-space bounded probabilistic complexity classes to classes of languages recognized by simple probabilistic automata. Next, we adapt the techniques used and we show similar reductions in the settings of Arthur-Merlin games and Games against nature. Nondeterministic versions of these theorems were found by Sudborough [Su75]. To prove our results, we design simple probabilistic and probabilistic+nondeterministic variants of Savitch's maze threading problem that are log-space complete for **PL** and respectively **P**.

In this extended abstract we sometimes omit or give only short hints for some of the proofs. More details can be found in the full version of the paper.

In what follows, we present the definitions and notations used by our models.

A *k-head two-way non-sensing probabilistic finite-state automaton* is a probabilistic finite-state automaton having k-heads on the input string, which is delimited by two distinct endmarkers. A configuration of the probabilistic automaton is defined by its state and the positions of the k-heads on the input string. From each configuration the automaton executes transitions to next configurations with probabilities from the set $\{0, 1/2, 1\}$. The transition probability to another configuration depends on the present state and the symbols scanned by the k-heads (and not on the fact that some heads do (or do not) have the same position.) Without loss of generality, sometimes we assume that there is only one accepting state. The acceptance probability of a probabilistic finite-state automaton for an input w is the probability of eventually reaching the accepting state when processing w. The automaton accepts the input string if this probability is $> 1/2$. A formal definition for k-head two-way (non-sensing) probabilistic automata can be found in [Ma94b].

The definition of *probabilistic Turing machine* (PTM) is standard [Gi77]. We recall a classification of probabilistic automata depending on the type of acceptance. If the acceptance probability for the input strings is not necessarily bounded away from $1/2$, then the automaton is called *unbounded-error*; if there is an interval around $1/2$ such that for every input string the acceptance probability never falls inside, then the automaton is called *(two-sided) bounded-error*; if for every input string the acceptance probability is either 0 or above $1/2$, the automaton is called *one-sided error (or randomized)*.

Several equivalent definitions of Arthur-Merlin games (**AM**-games) or interactive proofs with public coins verifiers have been published in the literature [BM88], [GS89]. See [Co93] for a survey of space-bounded interactive proof systems. For our purpose, the most appropriate is the definition based on automata with guess (nondeterministic) states and random (probabilistic) states [GS89]. Such an automaton A accepts an input string x if there is a strategy (i.e., a way to "decide" the nondeterministic transitions) such that if the nondeterministic transitions are decided according to this strategy, then the acceptance probability of x by A is $> 1 - \epsilon$, for some $\epsilon < 1/2$. A rejects x if, for any strategy used to decide the nondeterministic transitions, the acceptance probability of x by A is $\leq 1/2$. If $\epsilon = 1/2$, we obtain an unbounded-error variant of Arthur-Merlin games (**UAM**-games) also known as Games against nature [Pa85]. In this paper, we focus on cases where the machine A is a multihead finite-state automaton or a log-space Turing machine with both nondeterministic and probabilistic states that recognizes with bounded- or unbounded-error.

The formal definitions for a k-head two-way finite-state automaton with both nondeterministic and probabilistic states and of its (nondeterministic) strategy are straightforward generalizations of the definitions for the corresponding one-head finite-state automaton [CHPW94]. We present them in the Appendix.

A multihead automaton has *sweeping* heads if it may reverse the direction of motion of any head only when that head is scanning the right or left endmarker of the input string. In this paper, all the multihead automata have *non-sensing* heads, i.e., they can not detect each other's position. Without creating misunderstanding, we sometimes omit the word "non-sensing".

Our list of notations is as follows:

- 2pfa(k), 2bpfa(k) and 2rpfa(k) (1pfa(k), 1bpfa(k) and 1rpfa(k)) denote k-head two-way (one-way) unbounded-error, bounded-error, and respectively one-sided-error probabilistic finite-state automata;
- **2PFA**(k), **2BPFA**(k) and **2RPFA**(k) (**1PFA**(k), **1BPFA**(k) and **1RPFA**(k)) denote the classes of languages recognized by the corresponding two-way (one-way) probabilistic finite-state automata;
- **1PCM**(1) is the class of languages recognized by (one-head) one-way one-counter unbounded-error probabilistic finite-state automata;
- **1NFA**(k) denotes the class of languages recognized by k-head one-way nondeterministic finite-state automata;
- **DTIME**(t) is the class of languages recognized by $O(t)$-time-bounded deterministic Turing machines.
- **L**, **NL**, **PL**, **BPL**, and **RPL** are the classes of languages recognized by logspace deterministic, nondeterministic, unbounded-error, bounded-error, and one-sided-error probabilistic Turing machines;
- **AM**($2pfa(k)$), **AM**($1pfa(k)$), (**UAM**($2pfa(k)$), **UAM**($1pfa(k)$)) denote **AM**-games (**UAM**-games) with two-way and respectively one-way k-head probabilistic finite-state automata as verifiers;
- **UAM**($1pcm(1)$) is the class of languages recognized by **UAM**-games with one-way one-counter probabilistic finite-state automata as verifiers;
- **AM**(S), **UAM**(S) denote $O(S)$-space-bounded **AM**-games, **UAM**-games;
- **C**$_{poly}$ is the subclass of languages recognized by the machines that define the class **C** but are restricted to work in polynomial time;

- For any complexity class $\mathbf{C}$, $\widehat{\mathbf{C}}$ is the subclass of unary languages defined by $\widehat{\mathbf{C}} = \{L_1 \mid L_1 \subseteq \{1^{2^n} \mid n \in \mathbb{N}\}, L_1 \in \mathbf{C}\}$;
- $\subseteq$ and $\subsetneq$ denote inclusion (possible not proper) and proper inclusion, respectively;
- $|x|$ denotes the length of the string x;
- $\mathbb{N}$ is the set of natural numbers (note that we also use N to denote the set of nondeterministic states of an automaton);
- By probabilistic+nondeterministic automata we mean automata with both probabilistic and nondeterministic states.

3 Heads hierarchy

This section presents analogues, in the setting of probabilistic+nondeterministic computation, of results obtained in [Ma94b] for the setting of probabilistic computation[1]. First, we prove the equality of the class of languages recognized by **AM**- and **UAM**-games with multihead two-way probabilistic finite-state verifiers and the class of languages recognized by the same games with log-space probabilistic Turing machines as verifiers. Next, we separate heads hierarchies for **AM**- and **UAM**-games with multihead two-way probabilistic finite-state verifiers.

Theorem 3 $\quad \mathbf{AM}_{poly}(\log n) = \bigcup_{k=1}^{\infty} \mathbf{AM}_{poly}(2pfa(k))$,
$$\mathbf{UAM}_{poly}(\log n) = \bigcup_{k=1}^{\infty} \mathbf{UAM}_{poly}(2pfa(k)),$$
$$\mathbf{AM}(\log n) = \bigcup_{k=1}^{\infty} \mathbf{AM}(2pfa(k)), \ \mathbf{UAM}(\log n) = \bigcup_{k=1}^{\infty} \mathbf{UAM}(2pfa(k)).$$

Proof. Adapt the proof for the nondeterministic case [Ha72]. □

In what follows, we show: $\widehat{\mathbf{AM}(2pfa(k))} \subsetneq \widehat{\mathbf{AM}(2pfa(k+1))}$, $\forall k \geq 2$.

The proofs for the relations $\widehat{\mathbf{UAM}(2pfa(k))} \subsetneq \widehat{\mathbf{UAM}(2pfa(k+1))}$ and

$\widehat{\mathbf{UAM}_{poly}(2pfa(k))} \subsetneq \widehat{\mathbf{UAM}_{poly}(2pfa(k+1))}$ are similar.

We follow the same outline as in Monien's proof for the deterministic and nondeterministic automata [Mo80]. We use languages $X \subseteq \{1^{2^n} \mid n \in \mathbb{N}\}$ and the family of padding functions

---

[1] More precisely, in [Ma94b] it is shown:

Theorem 1 $\quad \bigcup_{k=1}^{\infty} \mathbf{2PFA}(k) = \bigcup_{k=1}^{\infty} \mathbf{2PFA}_{poly}(k) = \mathbf{PL}$,
$$\bigcup_{k=1}^{\infty} \mathbf{2BPFA}(k) = \mathbf{BPL}, \ \bigcup_{k=1}^{\infty} \mathbf{2BPFA}_{poly}(k) = \mathbf{BPL}_{poly},$$
$$\bigcup_{k=1}^{\infty} \mathbf{2RPFA}(k) = \mathbf{RPL}, \ \bigcup_{k=1}^{\infty} \mathbf{2RPFA}_{poly}(k) = \mathbf{RPL}_{poly}.$$

Theorem 2 *For multihead two-way unbounded- and one-sided-error probabilistic finite-state automata, the heads hierarchies are proper, i.e. for $k \geq 1$, $\mathbf{2PFA}(k) \subsetneq \mathbf{2PFA}(k+1)$, $\mathbf{2PFA}_{poly}(k) \subsetneq \mathbf{2PFA}_{poly}(k+1)$, and $\mathbf{2RPFA}(k) \subsetneq \mathbf{2RPFA}(k+1)$. For $k \geq 2$ the separations are over one letter alphabet.*

$$f_k : \{1^{2^n} \mid n \in \mathbb{N}\} \to \{1^{2^n} \mid n \in N\} \text{ defined by } f_k(1^{2^n}) = 1^{2^{kn}}.$$

The first step of our proof (i.e. the "coarse separation" $\overbrace{\mathbf{AM}(2pfa(k))} \subsetneq$ $\overbrace{\mathbf{AM}(\log n)})$ is specific to probabilistic+nondeterministic computation. The second part of the proof (i.e. how to contradict the "coarse separation" from the assumption "$\overbrace{\mathbf{AM}(2pfa(k))} \subsetneq \overbrace{\mathbf{AM}(2pfa(k+1))}$"), represented by Lemmas 1–3 and Theorem 5, is an adaptation of Monien's proof and it is omitted.

Theorem 4 (Coarse Separation) *For every natural number k,*

$$\overbrace{\mathbf{AM}(2pfa(k))} \subsetneq \overbrace{\mathbf{AM}(\log n)}.$$

Proof. We show that $\exists \alpha > 0$ such that for any $k \in \mathbb{N}, \mathbf{AM}(2pfa(k)) \subseteq$ $\mathbf{DTIME}(n^{k\alpha})$. From $\overbrace{\mathbf{DTIME}(n^{k\alpha})} \subsetneq \overbrace{\mathbf{P}} = \overbrace{\mathbf{AM}(\log n)}$, we obtain the coarse separation.

In what follows we present more details. Let $L \in \mathbf{AM}(2pfa(k))$. Deciding whether a length-n input string x belongs to L is equivalent to solving a linear programming problem with $O(n^k)$ variables. (A detailed proof for the similar case $\mathbf{AM}(\log n) \subset \mathbf{P}$ can be found in [Co89].) Using the result of Khachiyan [Kh79], this can be deterministically done in time $O((n^k)^\alpha)$, for some constant α. It follows $L \in \mathbf{DTIME}(n^{k\alpha})$. We obtain $\mathbf{AM}(2pfa(k)) \subset \mathbf{DTIME}(n^{k\alpha})$. As a corollary, we have $\overbrace{\mathbf{AM}(2pfa(k))} \subset \overbrace{\mathbf{DTIME}(n^{k\alpha})}$. To prove $\overbrace{\mathbf{DTIME}(n^{k\alpha})} \subsetneq$ $\overbrace{\mathbf{P}}$, we use an universal deterministic Turing machine that stops its computation after $n^{2k\alpha+1}$ steps and diagonalizes over all one-tape deterministic Turing machines that run in time less than $n^{2k\alpha+1}$. (We recall that any multi-tape deterministic Turing machine that runs in time $O(n^{k\alpha})$ can be simulated by a one-tape deterministic Turing machine that runs in time $O(n^{2k\alpha})$.) The witness language consists of all the strings of the form 1^{2^m}, where m is a valid encoding of a one-tape deterministic Turing machine M_m, and 1^{2^m} is not accepted by M_m in time $(2^m)^{2k\alpha+1}$. $\square$

Lemma 1 *For all languages $X \in \overbrace{\mathbf{AM}(\log n)}$ there is a natural number u such that:*

$$f_u(X) \in \overbrace{\mathbf{AM}(2pfa(3))}.$$

Lemma 2 *For all languages $X \in \overbrace{\mathbf{AM}(\log n)}$ and for $u, v \geq 1$,*

$$f_u(X) \in \overbrace{\mathbf{AM}(2pfa(v))} \Rightarrow X \in \overbrace{\mathbf{AM}(2pfa(u \cdot v))}.$$

Lemma 3 *For all languages $X \in \overbrace{\mathbf{AM}(\log n)}$ and for $u > v > 1$,*

$$f_{u+1}(X) \in \overbrace{\mathbf{AM}(2pfa(v))} \Rightarrow f_u(X) \in \overbrace{\mathbf{AM}(2pfa(v+1))}.$$

Using the relations $\mathbf{P} = \mathbf{AM}(\log n) = \mathbf{UAM}(\log n) = \mathbf{UAM}_{poly}(\log n)$ [Co89], we can prove that Theorem 4 and Lemmas 1–3 hold for $\mathbf{UAM}$-games as well. Furthermore, by adapting a technique of Monien [Mo80], we obtain:

Theorem 5 *For all $k \in \mathbf{N}$, $k \geq 2$,*

$$\overbrace{\mathbf{AM}(2pfa(k))} \subsetneq \overbrace{\mathbf{AM}(2pfa(k+1))}, \quad \overbrace{\mathbf{UAM}(2pfa(k))} \subsetneq \overbrace{\mathbf{UAM}(2pfa(k+1))},$$
$$\overbrace{\mathbf{UAM}_{poly}(2pfa(k))} \subsetneq \overbrace{\mathbf{UAM}_{poly}(2pfa(k+1))}.$$

4 Log-space reductions of space-bounded probabilistic complexity classes

In this section we present log-space reductions of $O(\log n)$-space-bounded probabilistic (probabilistic+nondeterministic) complexity classes to classes of languages recognized by relatively simple probabilistic (probabilistic+nondeterministic, respectively) automata. Our results parallel some of the results obtained in the nondeterministic setting by Hartmanis [Ha72] and Sudborough [Su75], and in the alternating setting by King [Ki88]. They may help to investigate upper bounds for deterministic space simulation of probabilistic (probabilistic+nondeterministic) automata.

Theorem 6 [Ma94b] $\mathbf{PL} \leq_{log} \mathbf{2PFA}_{poly}(2)$,
  $\mathbf{BPL} \leq_{log} \mathbf{2BPFA}(2)$, $\mathbf{BPL}_{poly} \leq_{log} \mathbf{2BPFA}_{poly}(2)$,
  $\mathbf{RPL} \leq_{log} \mathbf{2RPFA}(2)$, $\mathbf{RPL}_{poly} \leq_{log} \mathbf{2RPFA}_{poly}(2)$.

Proof.(Sketch) The details of the proof can be found in [Ma94b]. The main idea is that any v-head finite-state automaton processing a length-n string $a_1 \ldots a_n$ over an alphabet Σ can be simulated, with only an $O(n^h)$-factor time loss, by a two-head finite-state automaton processing the length-$(n+2)^h$ string $g_{\Sigma,h}(a_1 \ldots a_n)$, where h can be any integer greater than v, and $g_{\Sigma,h}$ is a log-space transformation introduced by Monien [Mo76]. Moreover, using some standard techniques, it is possible to have the two heads *non-sensing* and *sweeping*, a fact that was not pointed out in [Ma94b].□

As in the nondeterministic setting, we can ask whether $\mathbf{PL}$, $\mathbf{BPL}$, $\mathbf{RPL}$ are log-space reducible to classes of languages recognized by the corresponding *one-way* multihead probabilistic finite-state automata. Sudborough proved $\mathbf{NL} \leq_{log} \mathbf{1NFA}(2)$. Unfortunately, his technique uses properties of nondeterministic computation (like particular forms of some log-space complete problems for $\mathbf{NL}$) that are not known to hold for probabilistic computation. However, by refining part of his proofs ([Su75],Theorem 1), we obtain:

Proposition 1 $\mathbf{PL} \leq_{log} \bigcup_{k=1}^{\infty} \mathbf{1PFA}(k)$,
  $\mathbf{BPL}_{poly} \leq_{log} \bigcup_{k=1}^{\infty} \mathbf{1BPFA}(k)$, $\mathbf{RPL}_{poly} \leq_{log} \bigcup_{k=1}^{\infty} \mathbf{1RPFA}(k)$.

Proof. (Sketch) We show that any language recognized by a two-head two-way (sweeping, non-sensing) probabilistic finite-state automaton with run time less than n^i, for some $i \in \mathbf{N}$, is log-space reducible to a language recognized by an $(i + 6)$-head one-way (non-sensing) probabilistic finite-state automaton.□

The log-space reductions from Proposition 1 can be made stronger, as follows from Theorems 7–8.

Theorem 7 $\mathbf{BPL}_{poly} \leq_{log} \mathbf{1BPFA}(8)$, $\mathbf{RPL}_{poly} \leq_{log} \mathbf{1RPFA}(8)$.

Proof. (Sketch) We prove the first relation, the second proof being similar. We show that $\mathbf{BPL}_{poly}$ is log-space reducible to languages recognized by (non-sensing, sweeping) 2bpfa(2) that run in sub-quadratic time. Using the proof of Proposition 1 with $i = 2$ it follows our claim.

For any language $L \in \mathbf{BPL}_{poly}$ over the alphabet Σ, there are two integers p and h, such that there is a 2bpfa(h) called A, that recognizes L in time less than n^p. As in the proof of Theorem 6, we choose a transformation $g_{\Sigma,l}$, where $l >> \max(p, h)$. We denote by B the corresponding (sweeping, non-sensing) 2bpfa(2) that recognizes $g_{\Sigma,l}(L)$. The computation time of B on a length-m input string w is $O(m)$ if $w \neq g_{\Sigma,l}(x)$ for any $x \in \Sigma^*$, and is $O(n^p m)$ if $w = g_{\Sigma,l}(x)$ for some string x such that $n = |x|$. In the later case, from $m = |w| \in \Theta(n^l)$ we obtain that the computation time of B on w is $o(m^2)$.□

Theorem 8 $\mathbf{PL} \leq_{log} \mathbf{1PFA}(2)$, $\mathbf{PL} \leq_{log} \mathbf{1PCM}(1)$.

Proof. It follows from Lemmas 4–5, stated after the following definitions.□

We define two languages that are log-space complete for PL and can be recognized by "simple" probabilistic automata, i.e., by two-head one-way and respectively (one-head) one-way one-counter unbounded-error probabilistic finite-state automata. These languages are probabilistic versions of the maze threading problem of Savitch [Sa70] and of the languages L_P and L_Q of Sudborough [Su75].

Definition 1 PMT_1 is the language over the alphabet $\{[,], a, \#\}$ containing the strings of the following form, denoted by (*):

$$[a^{p_1}\#a^{m_1(1)}\#a^{m_2(1)}]\cdots[a^{p_t}\#a^{m_1(t)}\#a^{m_2(t)}]a^{v_1}\#\ldots\#a^{v_{h_1}}\#\#a^{r_1}\#\ldots\#a^{r_{h_2}}\#$$

with the properties:

$$\sum_{(q,i_1,\ldots,i_q)\in A_{cc}} 1/2^{q-1} > \sum_{(r,i_1,\ldots,i_r)\in R_{ej}} 1/2^{r-1},$$

where A_{cc} and R_{ej} are sets satisfying the relations:

$$(q,i_1,\ldots,i_q) \in A_{cc} \Leftrightarrow \begin{cases} i_1 = 1, i_2 > 1, \text{and } i_k > i_{k-2} \text{ for } 3 \leq k \leq q; \\ \forall k \in \{2,\ldots,q\}, \exists l \in \{1,2\} \text{ such that } p_{i_k} = m_l(i_{k-1}); \\ \exists l \in \{1,2\} \text{ such that } m_l(i_q) \in \{v_1,\ldots,v_{h_1}\}. \end{cases}$$

$$(r,i_1,\ldots,i_r) \in R_{ej} \Leftrightarrow \begin{cases} i_1 = 1, i_2 > 1, \text{and } i_k > i_{k-2} \text{ for } 3 \leq k \leq r; \\ \forall k \in \{2,\ldots,r\}, \exists l \in \{1,2\} \text{ such that } p_{i_k} = m_l(i_{k-1}); \\ \exists l \in \{1,2\} \text{ such that } m_l(i_r) \in \{r_1,\ldots,r_{h_2}\}. \end{cases}$$

For each string of the form (*), p_1 is the initial index, $v_i, i \in \{1, \ldots, h_1\}$ and $r_i, i \in \{1, \ldots, h_2\}$ are the accepting and respectively rejecting indices, and A_{cc} and R_{ej} are all the "almost one-way" paths that connect the index p_1 to the accepting and respectively rejecting indices. A string belongs to PMT_1 if the "weight" of all the "almost one-way" paths connecting the initial index to accepting indices is greater than the "weight" of all the "almost one-way" paths connecting the initial index to rejecting indices.□

Definition 2 PMT_2 is the language over the alphabet $\{[,], a, \#\}$ defined in a similar way as PMT_1 with the following difference: in the definitions of A_{cc} and R_{ej} the conditions "$i_k > i_{k-2}$ for $3 \le k \le q$" and "$i_k > i_{k-2}$ for $3 \le k \le r$" are replaced by "$i_k > i_{k-1}$ for $2 \le k \le q$"and respectively "$i_k > i_{k-1}$ for $2 \le k \le r$". In this case, A_{cc} and R_{ej} contain all the "one-way" paths that connect the index p_1 to the accepting and respectively rejecting indices. □

Lemma 4   **PL** $\le_{log} PMT_1$, **PL** $\le_{log} PMT_2$.

Proof. (Sketch). Using Proposition 1 and some standard techniques from probabilistic computation, it can be easily shown that each language in **PL** is log-space reducible to a language recognized by a multihead one-way probabilistic finite-state automaton that halts with probability 1 in accepting or rejecting configurations, that moves at least one head at every computation step, and that from each non-halting configuration moves with probability 1/2 to two next configurations. For each input string x, the configurations of a multihead one-way finite-state automaton A can be indexed in lexicographically increasing order of input heads positions. (Note that during the computation of A on x, the sequence of indices assigned to consecutive configurations is strictly increasing.) For each configuration we build a "configuration transition block" containing the configuration and its succesors. The log-space transformation f we are looking for maps each string x to the string consisting of the sequence of "configuration transition blocks" (corresponding to all the configurations of A on x, enumerated in increasing order of their indices) concatenated with the sequences of accepting and rejecting configurations of A on x. It ca be checked that $f(x) \in PMT_1$ iff $f(x) \in PMT_2$ iff A accepts x.□

Lemma 5 $PMT_1 \in \mathbf{1PFA}(2)$, $PMT_2 \in \mathbf{1PCM}(1)$.

Proof. We describe an 1pfa(2) B that recognizes PMT_1. In parallel to its "main computation", B checks whether the input string u is of the form (*) from the definition of PMT_1; if not, B rejects u, no matter what is the stage of the main computation. Consequently, in the main computation, described next, we suppose that u is of the form (*). By block-i we mean $[a^{p_i} \# a^{m_1(i)} \# a^{m_2(i)}]$ if $i \le t$ or $a^{v(i-t)}$ if $t < i \le t + h_1$ or $a^{r(i-t-h_1)}$ if $t + h_1 < i \le t + h_1 + h_2$.

Suppose that B has one head ($H1$) on the substring $a^{m_1(i)}$ (inside block $i = [a^{p_i} \# a^{m_1(i)} \# a^{m_2(i)}]$) which is the "current" index, and the second head ($H2$) at the end of some block j. B "probabilistically guesses" a block $q > j$ moving the head $H2$ right and tossing a fair coin for each encountered block; q is the first block for which the outcome of the coin toss is "Tail". If H_2 reaches the right end of u without "guessing" any block then B accepts or rejects with probability $1/2$. If H_2 guesses a block q, then B deterministically compare a^{p_q} with $a^{m_l(i)}$ moving both heads to the right over these substrings.

If $p_q \neq m_l(i)$ (i.e., the probabilistic guess was wrong) then B accepts or rejects with probability $1/2$.

If $p_q = m_l(i)$ and $q \leq t$ (i.e., B found a block describing the transitions from the "current index" $m_l(i)$) then B tosses a coin to select the next index. If the outcome is "Tail", it moves H_2 at the beginning of $a^{m_1(q)}$. Otherwise, B moves the head H_2 at the beginning of $a^{m_2(q)}$ and continues the computation with H_1 and H_2 interchanged.

If $p_q = m_l(i)$ and $t < q \leq t + h_1$ (or $t + h_1 < q \leq t + h_1 + h_2$), i.e., B found an accepting (or rejecting) path, then B performs a procedure that "balances" (for all the "almost one-way" paths) the probability adjustments produced by "probabilistic guesses". It keeps both heads moving to the right end of u, one head at a time, and it tosses a fair coin each time when a head encounters a block. If the outcome in all these tosses is "all Tails" then B accepts (rejects, respectively) u. If not, B accepts or rejects with probability $1/2$. In this way, B makes sure that the probabilities of all accepting and rejecting "almost one-way" paths of the input strings are multiplied by the same number, independently of the length and the structure of the path.

Using a similar technique, we prove that PMT_2 can be recognized by a one-way one-counter probabilistic finite-state automaton B. In this case, the second head is replaced by a counter as follows: B stores into the counter the "current index" $m_l(i)$, and moves its head forward to probabilistically guess the block q describing the transitions from $m_l(i)$. To compare $m_l(i)$ with p_q, B scans a^{p_q} and decrements simultaneously the counter. If $p_q = m_l(i)$ (so B guessed the right block), then B probabilistically selects the next index, located in the block q, and stores its value into the counter. $\Box$

In the settings of **AM**- and **UAM**-games we have the reductions:

Theorem 9 $\mathbf{AM}_{poly}(\log n) \leq_{log} \mathbf{AM}(1pfa(8)), \mathbf{AM}(\log n) \leq_{log} \mathbf{AM}(2pfa(2))$
   $\mathbf{UAM}(\log n) \leq_{log} \mathbf{UAM}(1pfa(2)), \mathbf{UAM}(\log n) \leq_{log} \mathbf{UAM}(1pcm(1))$.

Proof. (Sketch) The proofs for the first two reductions are similar with the proofs of Theorem 7 and Theorem 6, respectively. To prove the next two reductions we use the relations: $\mathbf{P} = \mathbf{AM}(\log n) = \mathbf{UAM}_{poly}(\log n) = \mathbf{UAM}(\log n)$, and $\mathbf{UAM}_{poly}(\log n) \leq_{log} \mathbf{UAM}(1pfa(8))$ (whose proof is similar to the proof of Theorem 7). Furthermore, we design probabilistic+nondeterministic variants of Savitch's maze-threading problem (denoted by $PNMT_1$ and $PNMT_2$) that are log-space complete for $\mathbf{P}$ and can be solved by $\mathbf{UAM}$-games with simple probabilistic verifiers. The claims follow from Lemmas 6–7, stated after the next definitions.$\Box$

Definition 3 $PNMT_1$ is a language over the alphabet $\{[,], a, \#\}$ that has a structure similar to PMT_1 but the "transition" blocks have the form $[a^{p_i}\#a^k\#a^{m_1(i)}\#a^{m_2(i)}]$, where $k = 1$ if p_i is a "nondeterministic" index and

$k = 2$ if p_i is a "probabilistic" index. A "nondeterministic" strategy for such a string is a function that, for each "nondeterministic" index, select its succesor among the two indices from its transition block. For each "nondeterministic" strategy K we define the sets $A_{cc}(K)$ and $R_{ej}(K)$ that contain all "almost one-way" paths that, according to the strategy, connect the (initial) index p_1 to the accepting and respectively rejecting indices. Note that, given a strategy K, $A_{cc}(K)$ and $R_{ej}(K)$ are similar to A_{cc} and respectively R_{ej} from the definition of PMT_1. A string is in $PNMT_1$ if there is a strategy K, such that:

$$\sum_{(q,i_1,\ldots,i_q) \in A_{cc}(K)} 1/2^{q-1} > \sum_{(r,i_1,\ldots,i_r) \in R_{ej}(K)} 1/2^{r-1}.$$

Definition 4 $PNMT_2$ is a language over the alphabet $\{[,],a,\#\}$ that has a structure similar to $PNMT_1$ but for each nondeterministic strategy K, the sets $A_{cc}(K)$ and $R_{ej}(K)$ contain all "one-way" paths connecting the initial index p_1 to the accepting or rejecting indices. For a fixed K, $A_{cc}(K)$ and $R_{ej}(K)$ are similar to the sets A_{cc} and R_{ej} used in the definition of PMT_2.

By adapting the proofs from Lemmas 4–5, we obtain:

Lemma 6 $\mathbf{UAM}(\log n) \leq_{log} PNMT_1$, $\mathbf{UAM}(\log n) \leq_{log} PNMT_2$.

Lemma 7 $PNMT_1 \in \mathbf{UAM}(1pfa(2))$, $PNMT_2 \in \mathbf{UAM}(1pcm(1))$.

References

[BM88] Babai, L. and Moran, S. *Arthur-Merlin games: A randomized proof system and a hierarchy of complexity classes.* J. Comp. and System Sc., Vol. 36, 1988, pp. 254-276.

[Co89] Condon, A. *Computational Models of Games*, MIT Press, 1989.

[Co93] Condon, A. *The Complexity of Space Bounded Interactive Proof Systems.* Complexity Theory: current research, ed. Spies, K.A., Homer, S., and Schoning, U., Cambridge Univ. 1993, pp. 147-189.

[CHPW94] Condon, A., Hellerstein, L., Pottle, S., and Wigderson, A. *On the Power of Finite Automata with both Nondeterministic and Probabilistic States.* Proceedings STOC'94, 1994, pp. 676-685.

[DS92] Dwork, C., and Stockmeyer, L. *Finite state verifiers I: the power of interaction.* J. ACM, Vol. 39, 1992, pp. 800-828.

[Fr81] Freivalds, R. *Probabilistic two-way machines.* Proceedings, Int. Sympos. Math. Found. of Comput. Sci. 1981, LNCS 118, 1981, pp. 33-45.

[Gi77] Gill, J. *Computational complexity of probabilistic Turing machines.* SIAM J. Comput. Vol 6, 1977, pp. 675-695.

[GMR89] Goldwasser, S., Micali, S., and Rackoff, C. *The knowledge complexity of interactive proof systems.* SIAM J. Comput. 18, 1989, pp. 186-208.

[GS89] Goldwasser, S., and Sipser, M. *Public coins vs. private coins in interactive proof systems.* Randomness and Computation, Vol. 5 of Advances in Computing Research, JAI Press, Greenwich, 1989, pp. 73-90.

[Ha72] Hartmanis, J. *On Non-Determinancy in Simple Computing Devices.* Acta Informatica 1, 1972, pp. 336-344

[HS66] Hennie, F. C., and Stearns, R. E. *Two-tape simulation of multitape Turing machines.* J. ACM, Vol. 13, 1966, pp. 533-546.

[Ib73] Ibarra, O. H. *On two-way multihead automata.* J. Comp. and System Sc., Vol. 7, 1973, pp. 28-36.

[Ju85] Jung, H. *On probabilistic time and space.* Proceedings, ICALP 1985, LNCS 194, pp. 310-317.

[Kh79] Khachiyan, L. G. *A polynomial algorithm for linear programming.* Soviet Math Dokl., Vol. 20, 1979, pp. 191-194.

[Ki88] King, K.N. *Alternating multihead finite automata.* Theoretical Computer Science, Vol. 61, 1988, pp. 149-174.

[LSH65] Lewis II, P.M., Stearn, R., and Hartmanis, J. *Memory bounds for recognition of context-free and context-sensitive languages.* IEEE Conference Record on Switching Circuit Theory and Logical Design, 1965, pp. 191-202.

[Ma94a] Macarie, I. I. *Space-efficient deterministic simulations of probabilistic automata.* Proceedings STACS'94, LNCS 775, 1994, pp. 109-122.

[Ma94b] Macarie, I. I. *Multihead two-way probabilistic finite automata.* To appear in Proceedings LATIN'95, 1995; also as *Properties of Multihead Two-Way Probabilistic Finite Automata.* TR 477, August 1994, Dept. of Computer Science, University of Rochester.

[Mo76] Monien, B. *Transformational Methods and their Application to Complexity Problems.* Acta Informatica 6, 1976, pp. 95-108; Corrigendum, Acta Informatica 8, 1977, pp. 383-384.

[Mo80] Monien, B. *Two-way Multihead Automata over a one-letter alphabet.* R.A.I.R.O. Informatique theoretique/ Theoretical Informatics, Vol. 14, No. 1, 1980, pp. 67-82.

[Pa85] Papadimitriou, C. H. *Games against nature.* J. Comp. and System Sc., Vol. 31, 1985, pp. 288-301.

[RF65] Ruby, S., and Fisher, P.C. *Translational methods and computational complexity.* Conf. Rec. IEEE Symp. on Switching Circuit Theory and Logical Design, 1965, pp.173-178.

[RST82] Ruzzo, W., Simon, J.,and Tompa, M. *Space-bounded hierarchies and probabilistic computation.* J. Comp. and System Sc., Vol. 28, 1984, pp. 216-230.

[Sa70] Savitch, W. J. *Relationships between nondeterministic and deterministic tape complexity.* J. Comp. and System Sc., Vol. 4, 1970, pp. 177-192.

[Se77a] Seiferas, J. I. *Relating Refined Space Complexity Classes.* J. Comp. and System Sc., Vol. 14, 1977, pp. 100-129.

[Se77b] Seiferas, J. I. *Techniques for Separating Space Complexity Classes.* J. Comp. and System Sc., Vol. 14, 1977, pp. 73-99.

[SFM78] Seiferas, J. I., Fischer, M.J., and Meyer, A.R. *Separating Nondeterministic Time Complexity Classes.* J. ACM, Vol. 25, 1978, pp. 146-167.

[Su75] Sudborough, I. H. *On Tape-Bounded Complexity Classes and Multihead Finite Automata.* J. Comp. and System Sc., Vol. 10, 1975, pp. 62-76.

[YR78] Yao, A.C. and Rivest, R.L. $K + 1$ *heads are better than* K. J. ACM, Vol. 25, 1978, pp. 337-340.

5 Appendix

Definition 5 A *k-head two-way finite-state automaton with nondeterministic and probabilistic states* is a structure $S = (Q, \Sigma, \delta, q_0, N, R, Q_{acc}, Q_{rej})$, where:

- Q is a finite, nonempty set of states partitioned into the (disjoint) sets N, R, Q_{acc}, Q_{rej};
- Σ is the input alphabet and does not contain the symbols (left and right endmarkers) ¢ and \$;
- $q_0 \in Q$ is the initial state;
- N is the subset of nondeterministic states;
- R is the subset of probabilistic states;
- Q_{acc} and Q_{rej} are the sets of accepting and rejecting states.
- $\delta : Q \times (\Sigma \cup \{¢, \$\})^k \times Q \times (\{-1, 0, 1\})^k \to \{0, 1/2, 1\}$ is the transition function; the meaning of $\delta(q, s_1, \ldots, s_k, q', d_1, \ldots, d_k)$ is as follows: if $q \in R$ and the automaton is in state q reading the symbols $s_1, \ldots, s_k$ then with probability $\delta(q, s_1, \ldots, s_k, q', d_1, \ldots, d_k)$ the automaton enters state q' and moves each head $j \in \{1, \ldots, k\}$ one symbol in direction d_j (left if $d_j = -1$, right if $d_j = 1$, stationary if $d_j = 0$); if the current state is $q \in N$ and the symbols read are $s_1, \ldots, s_k$, then the automaton nondeterministically chooses some q' and $d_1, \ldots, d_k$ such that $\delta(q, s_1, \ldots, s_k, q', d_1, \ldots, d_k) = 1$, enters state q' and moves each head $j \in \{1, \ldots, k\}$ one symbol in direction d_j. There are the following restrictions on δ:
  - $\forall q \in R, \forall(s_1, \ldots, s_k) \in (\Sigma \cup \{¢, \$\})^k$, it holds: $\sum_{q', d_1, \ldots, d_k} \delta(q, s_1, \ldots, s_k, q', d_1, \ldots, d_k) = 1$ (δ is a transition probability function);
  - $\forall q \in N, \forall(s_1, \ldots, s_k) \in (\Sigma \cup \{¢, \$\})^k, \forall(q', d_1, \ldots, d_k) \in Q \times (\Sigma \cup \{¢, \$\})^k$ it holds: $\delta(q, s_1, \ldots, s_k, q', d_1, \ldots, d_k) \in \{0, 1\}$ (δ is a nondeterministic transition);
  - $\delta(q, s_1, \ldots, s_{j-1}, ¢, s_{j+1}, \ldots, s_k, q', d_1, \ldots, d_{j-1}, -1, d_{j+1}, \ldots, d_k) = 0$ (no head can move to the left of the left endmarker ¢) and $\delta(q, s_1, \ldots, s_{j-1}, \$, s_{j+1}, \ldots, s_k, q', d_1, \ldots, d_{j-1}, 1, d_{j+1}, \ldots, d_k) = 0$ (no head can move to the right of the right endmarker \$);

Definition 6 For any input string $x = x_0 x_1 \ldots x_{n+1}$ (where $x_0 = ¢$ and $x_{n+1} = \$$ are the endmarkers), a (nondeterministic) *strategy* on x is a function

$$S_x : N \times (\{0, \ldots, n+1\})^k \to Q \times (\{-1, 0, 1\})^k$$

such that $\delta(q, s_1, \ldots, , \ldots, s_k, q', d_1, \ldots, d_k) = 1$ whenever $S_x(q, p_1, \ldots, p_k) = (q', d_1, \ldots, d_k)$ and $x_{p_l} = s_l, \forall l \in \{1, \ldots, k\}$. (Discussions on other possible definitions for (nondeterministic) strategy and their equivalence can be found in [Co89].)

Resource-Bounded Instance Complexity
(Extended Abstract)

Lance Fortnow *[1] and Martin Kummer[2]

[1] Department of Computer Science, University of Chicago, 1100 E. 58th St.,
Chicago, IL 60637, USA. fortnow@cs.uchicago.edu
[2] Institut für Logik, Komplexität und Deduktionssysteme, Universität Karlsruhe,
D-76128 Karlsruhe, Germany. kummer@ira.uka.de

Abstract. We prove the Instance Complexity Conjecture of Ko, Orponen, Schöning, and Watanabe for all recursive tally sets and for all recursive sets which are NP-hard under honest reductions, in particular it holds for all natural NP-hard problems. On the other hand, the conjecture is shown to be oracle dependent. Additional results concern the nonrecursiveness of the instance complexity measure and a comparison of time-bounded C- and CD-complexity.

1 Introduction

Instance complexity was introduced by Ko, Orponen, Schöning, and Watanabe [6, 14] (see also [8, Section 7.3.3]) as a measure of the complexity of individual instances of a decision problem A. Intuitively, the *instance complexity* $ic(x : A)$ of x with respect to A is the length of the shortest program p which correctly computes $\chi_A(x)$ and does not make any mistakes on other inputs (it is permitted to output "don't know" answers). In this paper we consider the resource-bounded version $ic^t(x : A)$ where the running time of p is bounded by some polynomial t.

The trivial program which contains an encoding of x shows that $ic(x : A)$ is bounded by the Kolmogorov complexity of x. This fact can be transferred to the time-bounded setting. An instance x is called hard if this trivial upper bound is already optimal, i.e., there is no easier way to decide x than to explicitly encode x into the program. The "Instance Complexity Conjecture" of Orponen et al. [14] states informally that every complex set has infinitely many hard instances. More precisely, in the polynomial-time bounded setting it is conjectured that every set $A \notin P$ must have *p-hard instances*, i.e., for every polynomial t there is a polynomial t' such that $ic^t(x : A) \geq C^{t'}(x) + O(1)$ for infinitely many x, where $C^{t'}(x)$ denotes the t'-time bounded Kolmogorov complexity of x.

As a starting point we show that the conjecture holds for all recursive tally sets A. Orponen et al. [14] proved that every set which is NP-complete under honest 1-tt reductions has p-hard instances, unless DEXT = NEXT. We obtain a strong improvement of this result: All sets which are NP-complete under honest Turing reductions have p-hard instances, unless P = NP.

---

* Partially supported by NSF Grant CCR 92-53582.

The Instance Complexity Conjecture cannot be settled with relativizable methods, since we construct relativized worlds where it holds and where it fails. In fact, we even show that the CD-version of the conjecture—where C-complexity is replaced by Sipser's CD-complexity—fails in some relativized world. In [14] a weak form of the conjecture is shown where the time bounds depend on the complexity of A. We show that the dependence on A can be removed. It follows that the polynomial-space bounded and the exponential-time bounded version of the conjecture hold. We also show that the ic-measure is not recursive and we compare time-bounded C- and CD-complexity.

2 Notation and definitions

We consider strings over the alphabet $\Sigma = \{0,1\}$. The length of a string x is denoted by $|x|$; ϵ is the empty string. The characteristic function of A is denoted by χ_A. Recall that $\text{DEXT} = \bigcup_{c>0} \text{DTIME}(2^{cn})$ and $\text{NEXT} = \bigcup_{c>0} \text{NTIME}(2^{cn})$. For further background and unexplained notions we refer the reader to [1, 8].

Our machine model are deterministic Turing machines with three input tapes and an arbitrary number of work tapes. They compute partial functions from $\Sigma^* \times \Sigma^* \times \Sigma^*$ to $\Sigma^* \cup \{\bot\}$. If M is such a machine we denote the output of M on input (p_1, p_2, x) by $M(p_1, p_2, x)$, and the number of steps in the computation by $time_M(p_1, p_2, x)$. We assume that $t(n) > n$ for all time bounds t.

The following notion of time bounded Kolmogorov complexity was introduced by Hartmanis [3] and Sipser [16]. Intuitively, the t-bounded Kolmogorov complexity of x is the length of the shortest program which computes x in $t(|x|)$ steps from the empty input.

Definition 1. For any time bound $t = t(n)$ and $x, y \in \{0,1\}^*$ the t-bounded Kolmogorov complexity of x conditional to y using M is defined as

$$C_M^t(x|y) = \min\{|p| : M(p, \epsilon, y) = x \land time_M(p, \epsilon, y) \le t(|x|)\}.$$

The t-bounded Kolmogorov complexity of x using M is defined as

$$C_M^t(x) = C_M^t(x|\epsilon).$$

Instance complexity was introduced by Ko, Orponen, Schöning and Watanabe [6]. Intuitively, the t-bounded instance complexity of x with respect to A is the length of the shortest program which runs in time $t(n)$, correctly decides whether x is in A, and does not make mistakes on any other input (where it is allowed to output $\bot$ for "don't know").

Definition 2. Let $A \subseteq \{0,1\}^*$. A function $f : \{0,1\}^* \to \{0,1,\bot\}$ is called A-consistent if for all $x \in dom(f)$

$$f(x) = \chi_A(x) \lor f(x) = \bot .$$

For any time bound $t = t(n)$ the t-bounded instance complexity of $x \in \{0,1\}^*$ with respect to A using M is defined as

$$ic_M^t(x:A) = \min\{|p| : \lambda z.M(p,\epsilon,z) \text{ is } A\text{-consistent}, (\forall z)[time_M(p,\epsilon,z) \le t(|z|)],$$
$$\text{and } M(p,\epsilon,x) = \chi_A(x)\}.$$

The CD-version of Kolmogorov complexity was introduced by Sipser [16]. Intuitively, the CD-complexity of x is the shortest program which accepts x and rejects every other string. This notion is only of interest in the time bounded setting, since its unbounded version coincides with the unbounded Kolmogorov complexity.

Definition 3. For any time bound $t = t(n)$ and $x, y \in \{0,1\}^*$ the *t-bounded* CD-*complexity* of x conditional to y using M is defined as

$$CD_M^t(x|y) = \min\{|p| : \lambda z.M(p,y,z) = \chi_{\{x\}} \text{ and } (\forall z)[time_M(p,y,z) \le t(|z|)]\}.$$

The t-bounded CD-complexity of x using M is defined as

$$CD_M^t(x) = CD_M^t(x|\epsilon).$$

Thus, unconditional CD-complexity can be seen as a special case of instance complexity; for all natural interpreters M we have $CD_M^t(x) = ic_M^t(x : \{x\})$.

There is a universal Turing machine U (an "optimal interpreter") such that the following invariance property holds (see [3], [14, Theorem 2.1]).

Fact 1. *For every Turing machine M there is a constant c such that for all sets A, all time bounds t, and all strings x, y:*

$$ic_U^{t'}(x:A) \le ic_M^t(x:A) + c,$$
$$C_U^{t'}(x|y) \le C_M^t(x|y) + c;$$
$$CD_U^{t'}(x|y) \le CD_M^t(x|y) + c,$$

where $t'(n) = ct(n)\log t(n) + c$.

In the following we fix such a U and write C^t, ic^t, CD^t for C_U^t, ic_U^t, CD_U^t. If the context is clear we may write $U(p)$ instead of $U(p,\epsilon,\epsilon)$, and $U(p,x)$ instead of $U(p,\epsilon,x)$, etc.

3 The instance complexity conjecture

The following basic fact shows that the Kolmogorov complexity is an upper bound for the instance complexity.

Fact 2. [14, Proposition 3.1] *For any time constructible function t there is a constant c such that for any set A and string x,*

$$ic^{t'}(x:A) \le C^t(x) + c,$$

where $t'(n) = ct(n)\log t(n) + c$.

Clearly, if $A \in \text{DTIME}(t)$ then ic^t is bounded by a constant. Orponen et al. conjectured that for $A \notin \text{DTIME}(t)$, the instance complexity must be infinitely often as high as the Kolmogorov complexity.

Conjecture 1. [14] *Let t be time-constructible and A recursive. If $A \notin \text{DTIME}(t)$ then there is a constant c and infinitely many x such that*

$$ic^t(x : A) \geq C^{t'}(x) - c,$$

where $t' = O(t \log t)$.

The following observation characterizes the class P.

Fact 3. [14, Proposition 3.2] *A set A is in P iff there is a polynomial t and a constant c such that for all x, $ic^t(x : A) \leq c$.*

Definition 4. [5, 14] A set A has *p-hard instances* if for every polynomial t there exists a polynomial t' and a constant c such that for infinitely many x, $ic^t(x : A) \geq C^{t'}(x) - c$.

This motivates the following interesting special case of Conjecture 1, which is to a larger extent independent of the machine model.

Conjecture 2. *Every recursive set $A \notin \text{P}$ has p-hard instances.*

Clearly, Conjecture 2 follows from Conjecture 1. By definition, the CD-complexity is an upper bound for the instance complexity in the following sense.

Fact 4. *For any time bound t, any set A, and all strings x,*

$$ic^{t'}(x : A) \leq CD^t(x) + O(1),$$

where $t' = O(t \log t)$. (For natural optimal interpreters we even have $t' = t + O(1)$.)

This motivates the following CD-version of Conjecture 2.

Conjecture 3. *For every recursive set $A \notin \text{P}$ and every polynomial t there is a polynomial t' and a constant c such that*

$$ic^t(x : A) \geq CD^{t'}(x) - c \text{ for infinitely many } x.$$

The CD-complexity is less or equal to the Kolmogorov-complexity; for every polynomial t there is a polynomial t' such that for all x, $CD^{t'}(x) \leq C^t(x) + O(1)$ (cf. [8, Theorem 7.2]). Thus, Conjecture 3 is weaker than Conjecture 2.

Remark: Orponen et al. [13, 14] stated an unbounded version of the instance complexity conjecture for all nonrecursive r.e. sets. It is shown in [7] that this conjecture fails.

3.1 Positive results

As partial evidence for Conjecture 2, Orponen et al. [14] show that every DEXT-complete set has p-hard instances, and SAT has p-hard instances unless DEXT = NEXT (see [14, Corollary 5.6, 5.7]). Both results can be deduced from the following new[3] theorem:

Theorem 5. *Every recursive tally set* $A \notin P$ *has p-hard instances.*

Proof. Assume that $A \subseteq 0^*$ is a recursive tally set and $A \notin P$. Let t be a given polynomial of the form $n^k + k$, and let N be a Turing machine which computes χ_A. For $q, \sigma \in \{0,1\}^*$, we say that "q is t-consistent with σ" if for all $m \leq |\sigma|$,

$$U^{t(|x_m|)}(q, x_m) \text{ is defined and } \neq \perp \implies U^{t(|x_m|)}(q, x_m) = \sigma(m).$$

Here x_m is the m-th string in the standard ordering and $\sigma(m)$ denotes the m-th bit of σ.

Now we define an algorithm M to witness that $C_M^{t'}(x) \leq ic^t(x : A)$ for some polynomial t' and infinitely many $x \in 0^*$.

M computes as follows for input p:
Let $I = \{q \in \{0,1\}^* : |q| \leq 2 \cdot |p|\}$. Let $n = |I|$. Goto stage n.
Stage n :
(1) Spend n steps in computing $N(x_i)$ for $i = 1, 2, \ldots$, and let σ be the maximal initial segment of A which has been computed in this way.
(2) Eliminate all q from I which are not t-consistent with σ.
(3) Compute $U^{t(n)}(q, 0^n)$ for all $q \in I$.
  If one of these values is in $\{0,1\}$ then goto stage $n + 1$.
  Else let $M(p) = 0^n$ and halt.

  a.) $M(p)$ terminates for all p: Suppose for a contradiction that $M(p)$ does not terminate. Then n increases infinitely often and σ denotes larger and larger initial segments of A. Let I_0 denote the final value of I, and let n_0 be the stage when this final value is reached. Since σ is unbounded it follows that for all $q \in I_0$ and all m, if $U^{t(m)}(q, 0^m) \in \{0,1\}$ then $U^{t(m)}(q, 0^m) = \chi_A(0^m)$. Since no stage $n \geq n_0$ terminates it follows that for every $0^n, n \geq n_0$ there is $q \in I_0$ with $U^{t(n)}(q, 0^n) = \chi_A(0^n)$. Thus, if we amalgamate the programs in I_0 and patch the finitely many arguments $0^m, m < n_0$, we obtain an $O(t)$ time bounded algorithm for A, so $A \in P$, a contradiction.
  b.) If $M(p) = 0^n$ then the computation of $M(p)$ takes only $O(n^3 \cdot t(n))$ steps. This is obvious since the computation in each stage $m \leq n$ uses $O(m + m|I|t(m) + |I|t(m))$ steps and $|I| \leq n$.
  c.) There are infinitely many n such that $M(p) = 0^n$ for some p.
  d.) If $M(p) = 0^n$ then $ic^t(0^n : A) > 2 \cdot |p|$. This is clear, since the algorithm terminates only if $U^{t(n)}(p, 0^n) \notin \{0,1\}$ for all A-consistent q with $|q| \leq 2 \cdot |p|$.

---

[3] The theorem does not follow from [14, Theorem 5.5] since their result does not apply to p-immune sets, but there exist recursive p-immune tally sets

Hence there is a polynomial t' such that for infinitely many n: $ic^t(0^n : A) > 2 \cdot |p| \geq 2 \cdot C_M^{t'}(0^n)$. By invariance, there is a polynomial t'' and a constant c such that for all x, $C^{t''}(x) \leq C_M^{t'}(x) + c$. Thus, $ic^t(0^n : A) > C^{t''}(0^n)$ for infinitely many n.

Remark: Note that with a slight modification we can even show that for every recursive function f there are infinitely many n such that $ic^t(0^n : A) > f(C^{t''}(0^n))$.

The following Lemma is proved in [14, Lemma 5.8]. Recall that $A \leq_{1\text{-}tt}^p B$ if there is a polynomial-time bounded oracle Turing machine M^B which computes χ_A and queries the oracle at most once for each input. The reduction is *honest* if there is a polynomial r such that if y is queried on input x then $|x| \leq r(|y|)$, i.e., the length of the query has to be within a fixed polynomial of the length of the input.

Lemma 6. *If A has p-hard instances and $A \leq_{1\text{-}tt}^p B$ by an honest[4] reduction, then B has p-hard instances.*

Corollary 7. [14] *Every DEXT-complete set has p-hard instances. SAT has p-hard instances unless DEXT = NEXT.*

Remarks: a.) By a different approach, Buhrman and Orponen [2, Theorem 4.3] proved that every DEXT-complete set has an exponentially dense subset of p-hard instances.

b.) Of course, it also follows that any recursive set A such that $A \cap 0^* \notin P$ has p-hard instances (in particular, any recursive p-bi-immune set). The class of these sets is *p-meager* and has *p-measure 1* [10, 11].

c.) If A is recursive and has a *co-sparse complexity core* (see [1, Vol. II, Definition 6.1]), then A has p-hard instances: We modify the machine M from Theorem 5 and compute in step (3) $U^{t(n)}(q, x)$ for the first $r(n) + 1$ strings x of length n. Here $r(n)$ is polynomial such that $2^n - r(n)$ elements of length n belong to the complexity core.

d.) A set L is called *leftcut* if there is an infinite string $r \in \{0,1\}^\omega$ such that $L = \{x \in \{0,1\}^* : x < r\}$. Here $<$ is the dictionary ordering of strings with 0 less than 1. Every leftcut is p-selective [15] and there are leftcuts which are not p-tt-equivalent to any tally set [12].

Every recursive leftcut $L \notin P$ has p-hard instances: The machine M from Theorem 5 is modified such that in step (3) we perform a binary search assuming that the amalgamation of the programs in I computes the correct characteristic function of L. We search for the lexicographically least $x \in \{0,1\}^n$ such that $x \notin L$ (i.e., x is a prefix of the infinite string which defines L). Since $L \notin P$, we will eventually get n and $z \in \{0,1\}^n$ such that $U^{t(n)}(q, z) = \bot$ for all $q \in I$.

For NP-hard sets we can further exploit the idea of Remark d.) to get the following strong improvement of Corollary 7. We call a p-time Turing reduction *honest* if there is a polynomial r such that for all x, y, if y is queried on input x, then $|x| \leq r(|y|)$.

---

[4] Without this condition the lemma fails in some relativized world.

Theorem 8. *Every recursive set A which is* NP-*hard w.r.t. honest p-time Turing reduction has p-hard instances unless* $A \in$ P.

Proof. For every polynomial t we let L^t be the set of all triples $(x, 0^n, I)$, $x \in \{0,1\}^*$, $n \in \mathcal{N}$, and I a finite subset of $\{0,1\}^*$, such that there is a string $z \in \{0,1\}^n$ which extends $x0$ and $U^{t(n)}(q, z) \notin \{0,1\}$ for all $q \in I$. Clearly $L^t \in$ NP.

Now assume that A is a recursive set which is NP-hard w.r.t. honest Turing reductions and fix a polynomial t. Then $L^t \leq_T A$ via a polynomially time bounded oracle Turing machine M_0 such that $L^t = M_0^A$ and, for all x, y and all oracles X, if M_0^X queries y on input x, then $|x| \leq r(|y|)$, for some polynomial r.

We proceed as in the proof of Theorem 5, i.e., we define an algorithm M to witness that $C_M^{t'}(x) \leq ic^t(x : A)$ for some polynomial t' and infinitely many x. Let N be a decision procedure for A.

M computes as follows for input p:
Let $I = \{q \in \{0,1\}^* : |q| \leq 2 \cdot |p|\}$. Let $n = |I|$. Goto stage n.
Stage n :
(1) Spend n steps in computing $N(x_i)$ for $i = 1, 2, \ldots$ and let σ be the maximal initial segment of A which has been computed in this way.
(2) Eliminate all q from I which are not t-consistent with σ.
(3) Using L^t as an oracle, implement a prefix search for a string z of length n such that $U^{t(n)}(q, z) \notin \{0,1\}$ for all $q \in I$. Queries to L^t are answered by simulating $M_0(x, 0^n, I)$. If in this simulation a string y is queried, then answer according to $\min\{U^{t(n)}(q, y) : q \in I\}$.
If this set does not contain 0 or 1, then let $z = y$ and terminate the search.
If no suitable z is found then goto stage $n + 1$. Else let $M(p) = z$ and halt.

$M(p)$ terminates for all p, unless $A \in$ P: Suppose that $M(p)$ does not terminate. After some stage n_0 all programs in $I = I_0$ are consistent with A. Consider any stage $n > n_0$. If $E_n = \{z \in \{0,1\}^n : (\forall q \in I_0)[U^{t(n)}(q, z) \notin \{0,1\}]\} \neq \emptyset$, then the prefix search finds an element $z \in E_n$. By the consistency of I, every answer of a query in the simulation exists (otherwise we terminate) and is correct. Thus, the only reason, why stage n was not successful, is that $E_n = \emptyset$. Hence if we amalgamate all programs in I_0 and patch finitely many exceptions, we obtain $A \in$ DTIME$(t(n))$, i.e., $A \in$ P.

By the honesty of M_0, it follows that there is a polynomial t' such that if $M(p)$ terminates after s steps with output z, then $s \leq t'(|z|)$. Thus, $C_M^{t'}(z) \leq |p|$ and $ic^t(z : A) > 2|p|$.

So, if $A \notin$ P, then $M(p)$ terminates for all p and there are infinitely many z such that $C^{t''}(z) \leq ic^t(z : A)$ for some polynomial t''.

Corollary 9. *Let* $\mathcal{C} \supseteq$ NP *be any complexity class. Every set A which is $\mathcal{C}$-complete w.r.t. honest p-time Turing reduction has p-hard instances, unless* $\mathcal{C} \subseteq$ P. *In particular,* SAT *and* QBF *have p-hard instances unless* P = NP *or* P = PSPACE.

We can apply the algorithm from the proof of Theorem 5 to arbitrary recursive sets; then we have to consider all x of a given length, hence the running time increases by an exponential factor. However, it does *not* depend on A. Thus we get the following improvement of [14, Theorem 5.1].

Corollary 10. *Let $t(n) \geq n$ be a nondecreasing time constructible function, and let A be a recursive set not in $\mathrm{DTIME}(t)$. Then there exists a constant c such that for infinitely many x, $ic^t(x : A) \geq C^{t'}(x) - c$, where $t'(n) = c2^{2n}t(n)(n + \log t(n))$.*

This shows that a corresponding version of Conjecture 2 holds for DEXT and exponential time bounds: If A is a recursive set not in DEXT then for every $t \in 2^{lin} = \{2^{cn} : c > 0\}$ there is $t' \in 2^{lin}$ such that for infinitely many x, $ic^t(x : A) \geq C^{t'}(x)$.

Similarly, the space-bounded version of the conjecture holds, where P is replaced by PSPACE and ic^t, C^t by their space-bounded analogs.

3.2 Relativized counterexamples

The next result shows that Conjecture 2 cannot be settled with relativizing techniques.

Theorem 11. (a) *If $\mathrm{P} = \mathrm{NP}$ then Conjecture 2 holds (and this relativizes).*
(b) *There is an oracle B such that Conjecture 2 (and hence also Conjecture 1) fails relative to B.*

Proof. (a) This follows at once from Theorem 8.
(b) This argument is based on Hartmanis' idea [3, p. 444] of constructing an oracle B with $\mathrm{P}^B \neq \mathrm{NP}^B$, using Kolmogorov complexity.

Let $tow(0) = 1, tow(i) = 2^{tow(i-1)}$. Let x_i be a Kolmogorov-random string of length $tow(i)$ (i.e., $C(x_i) \geq |x_i|$), and let $B = \{x_i : i \geq 0\}$. Then for every polynomial t and almost all i we have $C^{t,B}(x_i) \geq |x_i|/2$: If x_i is computed by the universal oracle Turing machine U^B in $t(|x_i|)$ steps from a string p, then for sufficiently large i, the machine does not query any string of length $tow(j)$ for $j > i$. Thus we can compute x_i without the oracle, if we are given $p, x_0, \ldots, x_{i-1}$ and the binary representation of the least number $s \leq t(x_i)$ such that $U^B(p)$ queries x_i in step s. This can be coded in a string of length $|p| + O(\log(|x_i|)) \geq C(x_i)$. Since x_i is random, it follows that $|p| \geq |x_i|/2$ for all sufficiently large i.

Now choose any set $A \subseteq B$ such that $A \in \mathrm{DTIME}^B(2^n) - \mathrm{P}^B$. Let $t(n) = n^2$, then there is a constant d such that $ic^{t,B}(x : A) \leq d$ for all $x \notin B$. Furthermore, $ic^{t,B}(x_i : A) \leq \log(|x_i|) + d$ for all i. This is witnessed by a machine which outputs $\perp$ for all $x \neq x_i$ and $\chi_B(x)$ for $x = x_i$. Note that a string of length $\log(|x_i|) + d$ suffices to specify $|x_i|$ and $\chi_B(x)$. Thus for every polynomial t', every constant c, and almost all x we have $ic^{t,B}(x : A) < C^{t',B}(x) - c$.

Remarks: a.) The construction in (b) automatically yields $\mathrm{P}^B \neq \mathrm{UP}^B$ as was noticed in [9, Theorem 4.10].

b.) Note that A is sparse and p-selective (and also 1-cheatable) relative to B. In addition, we may ensure that A is p-immune relative to B. Thus, we cannot improve Theorem 5 in a relativizable way from "tally" to "sparse" or from "leftcut" to "p-selective" or from "p-bi-immune" to "p-immune".

c.) The construction in (b) can be modified such that A is d-self-reducible relative to B. We choose for each length $n = tow(i)$ a random string x_i of length $4n$. Decompose $x_i = q_i r_i$ into two strings q_i, r_i of length $3n$ and n, respectively. Let $B = \{q_i, r_i : i \geq 0\}$ and $A = \{q_i u : u \text{ is prefix of } r_i\}$. Clearly A is d-self-reducible relative to B. If $A \in P^B$ then r_i is computable from q_i in polynomial time relative to B, contradicting the randomness of x_i. All strings not of the form $q_i u$ with $|u| \leq tow(i)$ have constant instance complexity w.r.t. A. Certainly, $ic^{t,B}(q_i u : A) \leq \log(|q_i|) + tow(i) + O(1)$ for some polynomial t. On the other hand, $C^{t,B}(q_i u) \geq |q_i|/2 = (3/2)tow(i)$ for every polynomial t and all sufficiently large i. Thus, A does not have hard instances relative to B.

d.) Orponen et al. [14, Theorem 4.1] proved that for every self-reducible set $A \notin P$ every polynomial t and every c, there are infinitely many x such that $ic^t(x : A) \geq c\log(|x|)$. This result is optimal w.r.t. relativization, because for every function $f(n)$ such that $f(n)/\log n$ is non-decreasing and unbounded there is a relativized world with $P^B \neq NP^B$ and for every $A \in NP^B$ there is a polynomial t such that $ic^{B,t}(x : A) = f(|x|) + O(1)$ for all x. Just take the oracle of Homer and Longpré [4, Theorem 16]. This gives a (relativized) negative answer to a question of Ko [5, p. 335] who asked whether an NP-hard set must have an infinite number of hard instances which have high Kolmogorov complexity.

We might still hope to prove Conjecture 3, the CD-version of Conjecture 2. However, also in this case we can construct a relativized counterexample. The construction may be of independent interest.

Theorem 12. *There is an infinite set B which contains only strings of length $tow(k)$ for all $k \geq 0$ and no other strings, such that for every polynomial t:*

$$CD^{t,B}(x) \geq |x|/4 \text{ for almost all } x \in B.$$

Proof. We define B in stages $k \geq 3$. The construction depends on a constant n_1 which will be determined later. In stage k we define $B \cap \{0,1\}^{tow(k)}$ as follows:

Let $B_k = \{x \in B : |x| < tow(k)\}$, $n = tow(k)$. If $n < n_1$ then let $B \cap \{0,1\}^{tow(k)} = \emptyset$. Otherwise, choose $2^{n/4}$ strings $x_1, \ldots, x_{2^{n/4}}$ such that $C^{B_k}(x_i | x_j) \geq n/4$ for all $i \neq j$. For instance, let x be a random string of length $n2^{n/4}$ with $C^{B_k}(x) \geq |x|$, split it up into $2^{n/4}$ blocks of length n, and let x_i be the i-th block. If $C^{B_k}(x_i | x_j) \leq n/4$ then we could describe x by i, j and the shortened string x where the i-th block is cut out. Thus we get the contradiction $C^{B_k}(x) \leq 3(n/4) + n(2^{n/4} - 1) + O(1) < n2^{n/4}$ for all $n \geq n_1$. Assume that $2^n > n^{\log n}$ for all $n \geq n_1$.

Let $I_n = \{x_1, \ldots, x_{2^{n/4}}\}$ and let P_n be the set of all $2^{n/4} - 1$ programs of length less than $n/4$. If we run any $p \in P_n$ on input $x_i \in I_n$ for at most $n^{\log n}$ steps with any oracle then, by choice of n_1, no string of length $\geq 2^n = tow(k+1)$ can be queried. If the oracle is $M = B_k \cup D$ with $D \subseteq I_n$ then no x_j with $j \neq i$ can be queried. Otherwise, consider the x_j which is queried first, say in step $s \leq n^{\log n}$. Then we can describe x_j from x_i by $\log s + O(1) \leq (\log n)^2 + O(1) < n/4$ bits for $n \geq n_1$, which contradicts the hypothesis $C^{B_k}(x_i|x_j) \geq n/4$. For each $p \in P_n$ let T_p denote the set of all $x \in I_n$ such that $U^{B_k \cup \{x\}}(p, x) = 1$ in at most $n^{\log n}$ steps. By the remarks above, if $x \in D \subseteq I_n$ then the first $n^{\log n}$ steps in the computations of $U^{B_k \cup \{x\}}(p, x)$ and $U^{B_k \cup D}(p, x)$ are identical. (*)

Now we reduce the set I_n by the following procedure: Let $D = I_n, E = P_n$. If there is $x \in D$ and $p \in E$ such that $D \cap T_p = \{x\}$, then let $D = D - \{x\}$, $E = E - \{p\}$, and iterate the procedure.

Since each iteration decreases $|D|$ and $|E|$ by 1, and $|I_n| > |P_n|$, it follows that the procedure stops after finitely many steps with the final values D, E and $|D| > |E| \geq 0$. Let $B \cap \{0,1\}^n = D$. Consider any $p \in P_n$, we argue that p is not a witness for the CD-complexity of any $x \in D$. If $p \in E$ then $|T_p \cap D| \neq 1$; so, using (*), $U^B(p, -)$ does not accept a unique string from D. If $p \in P_n - E$, then no $x \in D$ belongs to T_p, i.e., $U^{B_k \cup \{x\}}(p, x)$ does not halt within $n^{\log n}$ steps with output 1. By (*), $U^B(p, -)$, does not accept any string from D within $n^{\log n}$ steps.

Thus, the construction yields $CD^{t,B}(x) \geq |x|/4$ for all $x \in B$ and $t(n) = n^{\log n}$. Since B is also infinite, the theorem follows.

Corollary 13. *Conjecture 3 fails relative to some oracle.*

Proof. Choose B as in the previous theorem. There is a set $A \subseteq B$ such that A is recursive in B, $A \notin P^B$, and for all k: Either $A \cap \{0,1\}^{tow(k)} = B \cap \{0,1\}^{tow(k)}$ or $A \cap \{0,1\}^{tow(k)} = \emptyset$. Let $t(n) = n^2$. Clearly, $ic^t(x : A) = O(1)$ for all $x \notin B$. If $x \in B, |x| = tow(k)$, consider the B-recursive program p which computes $\chi_B(z)$ for all $z \in \{0,1\}^{tow(k)}$ and otherwise outputs $\perp$. We can choose $|p| \leq k + O(1)$ and assume that the running time of p is bounded by t. Thus, $ic^{t,B}(x : A) \leq \log^*(|x|) + O(1)$ for all $x \in B$. Hence, by the choice of B, $ic^{t,B}(x : A) = o(CD^{t'}(x))$ for every polynomial t'.

4 The *ic*-measure is nonrecursive

While t-bounded Kolmogorov complexity is trivially recursive for each recursive time bound t, Orponen et al. [14] conjectured that t-bounded instance complexity may be nonrecursive. This is confirmed by the following result whose proof we omit.

Theorem 14. *Let t be a recursive time bound. There is a recursive set A such that $\lambda x. ic^t(x : A)$ is nonrecursive.*

5 C versus CD

In the previous sections we have compared instance complexity and Kolmogorov complexity. Since CD-complexity can be seen as a special case of instance complexity, it is natural to investigate the connection between C- and CD-complexity. We consider the question whether, with respect to polynomial time bounds, the C-complexity can be bounded by the CD-complexity. This is formally stated by the following hypotheses.

(H1) For every polynomial t there is a polynomial t' and a constant c
    such that for all x, y: $C^{t'}(x|y) \leq CD^t(x|y) + c$.
(H2) For every polynomial t there is a polynomial t' and a constant c
    such that for all x: $C^{t'}(x) \leq CD^t(x) + c$.

The promise problem (1SAT,SAT) belongs to P iff there is a deterministic polynomial time algorithm which accepts all Boolean formulas with a unique satisfying assignment, and rejects all Boolean formulas which are not satisfiable. It is well-known that (1SAT,SAT) is complete for $\mathcal{UP}$, the promise-version of UP.

Theorem 15. (H1) $\Leftrightarrow$ (1SAT,SAT) $\in$ P.

Proof. ($\Leftarrow$) Let t be a fixed polynomial. If there is a polynomial time algorithm for (1SAT,SAT) then we can determine in polynomial time for each t-time bounded program p, each y, and each n, the unique $x \in \{0,1\}^n$ such that $U(p, y, x) = 1$, if such an x exists. Now (H1) follows easily.
($\Rightarrow$) We assume that assignments a of a Boolean formula ϕ are padded such that $|a| = |\phi|$. There is a program p and a polynomial t such that for every Boolean formula ϕ and assignment a:

$$U(p, \phi, a) = \begin{cases} 1 & \text{if } \phi(a) = true; \\ 0 & \text{otherwise.} \end{cases}$$

Thus, for every Boolean formula with exactly one satisfying assignment a^* we get $CD^t(a^*|\phi) \leq |p|$. By hypothesis there is a polynomial t' and a constant c (independent of ϕ) such that $C^{t'}(a|\phi) \leq c$. Thus, we get a polynomial time algorithm for (1SAT,SAT): On input ϕ, we simulate $U(p', \epsilon, \phi)$ for at most $t'(|\phi|)$ steps for all p' with $|p'| \leq c$. We accept only if one of them outputs a satisfying assignment of ϕ. Since only a constant number of programs is simulated, the computation runs in polynomial time.

Trivially, (H1) implies (H2), but the converse might fail. However, we have the following partial converse.

Proposition 16. (H2) $\Rightarrow$ FewP $\cap$ SPARSE $\subseteq$ P.

Proof. Let A be a sparse set and let M be a nondeterministic Turing machine that accepts A. Let $|A \cap \{0,1\}^n|$, the running time of M, and the number of accepting paths all be bounded by a polynomial. For each n let

$$l_n = \langle x_1, w_{1,1}, \ldots, w_{1,m_1}, \ldots, x_s, w_{s,1}, \ldots, w_{s,m_s} \rangle$$

608

be the list of all elements $x_1 < \cdots < x_s$ in $A \cap \{0,1\}^n$, where $w_{i,1}, \ldots, w_{i,m_i}$ is the list of all accepting paths for x_i in lexicographical ordering (we assume that $|w_{i,j}| > n$). Note that l_n can be uniquely recognized in polynomial time if we are given n and $m_1 + \cdots + m_s$. Thus, $CD^t(l_n) \leq l(\langle n, m_1 + \cdots + m_s \rangle) = O(\log n)$ for some polynomial t. Using (H2) it follows that $C^{t'}(l_n) = O(\log n)$ for all n and some polynomial t'. This means that we can generate all elements in $A \cap \{0,1\}^n$ in polynomial time, hence $A \in P$. In fact, A is even p-printable (cf. [8, Definition 7.13]).

References

1. J. Balcázar, J. Diaz, J. Gabarró. Structural complexity I, II. Spinger-Verlag, Berlin, 1988, 1990.
2. H. Buhrman, P. Orponen. Random strings make hard instances. In: *Proceedings Structure in Complexity Theory, Ninth Annual Conference*, 217–222, 1994.
3. J. Hartmanis. Generalized Kolmogorov complexity and the structure of feasible computation. In: *Proc. 24th IEEE Symp. Foundations of Computer Science*, pp. 439–445, 1983.
4. S. Homer, L. Longpré. On reductions of NP sets to sparse sets. *Journal of Computer and System Sciences* 48, 324–336, 1994.
5. K. Ko. A note on the instance complexity of pseudorandom sets. In: *Proceedings Structure in Complexity Theory, Seventh Annual Conference*, pp. 327–337, 1992.
6. K. Ko, P. Orponen, U. Schöning, O. Watanabe. What is a hard instance of a computational problem? In: *Structure in Complexity Theory (Ed. A. Selman)*, pp. 197–217, Lecture Notes in Computer Science 223, Springer-Verlag, Berlin, 1986.
7. M. Kummer. Kolmogorov complexity and instance complexity of recursively enumerable sets. Submitted for publication.
8. M. Li, P. Vitányi. *An introduction to Kolmogorov complexity and its applications*. Springer-Verlag, Berlin, 1993.
9. L. Longpré, O. Watanabe. On symmetry of information and polynomial time invertibility. Manuscript, 1993.
10. J. Lutz. Category and measure in complexity classes, *SIAM J. Comput.* 19:1100–1131, 1990.
11. E. Mayordomo. Almost every set in exponential time is p-bi-immune. In: *Seventeeth International Symposium on Mathematical Foundations of Computer Science*, pp. 392–400, Lecture Notes in Computer Science 629, Springer-Verlag, Berlin, 1992.
12. A. Naik, M. Ogiwara, A. Selman. P-selective sets, and reducing search to decision vs. self-reducibility. In: *Proceedings Structure in Complexity Theory, Eighth Annual Conference*, pp.52–64, 1993.
13. P. Orponen. On the instance complexity of NP-hard problems. In: *Proceedings Structure in Complexity Theory, Fifth Annual Conference*, pp. 20–27, 1990.
14. P. Orponen, K. Ko, U. Schöning, O. Watanabe. Instance complexity. *J. of the ACM* 41:96–121, 1994.
15. A. Selman. P-selective sets, tally languages, and the behavior of polynomial time reducibilities on NP. *Math. Systems Theory* 13:55–65, 1979.
16. M. Sipser. A complexity theoretic approach to randomness. In: *Proc. 15th ACM Symp. Theory of Computing*, pp. 330–335, 1983.

On the Sparse Set Conjecture for Sets with Low Density

Harry Buhrman*[1] and Montserrat Hermo**[2]

[1] CWI PO Box 94079, 1090 GB Amsterdam, The Netherlands,
buhrman@cwi.nl
[2] Universidad del Pais Vasco, Facultad de Informatica,
Apdo. 649 , 20080, San Sebastian, Spain,
jiphehum@si.ehu.es

Abstract. We study the sparse set conjecture for sets with low density. The sparse set conjecture states that $P = NP$ if and only if there exists a sparse Turing hard set for NP. In this paper we study a weaker variant of the conjecture. We are interested in the consequences of NP having Turing hard sets of density $f(n)$, for (unbounded) functions $f(n)$, that are sub-polynomial, for example $\log(n)$. We establish a connection between Turing hard sets for NP with density $f(n)$ and bounded nondeterminism: We prove that if NP has a Turing hard set of density $f(n)$, then satisfiability is computable in polynomial time with $O(\log(n) * f(n^c))$ many nondeterministic bits for some constant c. As a consequence of the proof technique we obtain absolute results about the density of Turing hard sets for EXP. We show that no Turing hard set for EXP can have sub-polynomial density. On the other hand we show that these results are optimal w.r.t. relativizing computations. For unbounded functions $f(n)$, there exists an oracle relative to which NP has a $f(n)$ dense Turing hard tally set but still $P \neq NP$.

1 Introduction

The density of NP -complete and hard sets has been an early object of study and starts with the seminal paper of Berman and Hartmanis [BH77]. In that paper roughly two lines of research have been initiated: the density of $\leq_m^p$ -complete sets and the density of $\leq_T^p$ -hard sets for NP and other complexity classes.

The study of the $\leq_m^p$ -complete sets for NP becomes apparent in relation with the isomorphism conjecture [BH77]. The conjecture implies that all NP -complete sets are exponentially dense, since SAT, the well known NP -complete

* Part of this research was done while visiting the Univ. Politècnica de Catalunya in Barcelona. Partially suported by the Dutch foundation for scientific research (NWO) through NFI Project ALADDIN, under contract number NF 62-376 and a TALENT stipend.
** Part of this research was done while visiting the Univ. Politècnica de Catalunya in Barcelona.

set, itself is of exponential density. Along these lines it was Mahaney who showed that NP -complete sets can not be polynomially dense unless $P = NP$.

The study of the $\leq_T^p$ -hard sets for NP is motivated by the equivalence between sets that are $\leq_T^p$ -reducible to a sparse set, sets that have polynomial size circuits [BH77] and sets that can be recognized in polynomial time with the additional help of a polynomial amount of advice ($P/poly$) [Pip79]. Hence if there exists a $\leq_T^p$ -hard sets for NP that is sparse, there exists a polynomial time algorithm for SAT that needs the help of a small (polynomial size) table. For practical purposes this would mean that one only had to compute this small table once (for inputs of a certain length) and that from then on NP would equal P for all inputs of this length. Karp and Lipton however showed that the existence of sparse $\leq_T^p$ -hard sets for NP implies an unlikely collapse of the Polynomial Time Hierarchy to its second level [KL80].

Many efforts have been put into improving the Karp and Lipton result to $P = NP$. This improvement also goes by the name "sparse set conjecture". An important step towards this conjecture was obtained by Ogiwara and Watanabe, who showed that indeed the stronger consequence, i.e. $P = NP$, can be obtained if $\leq_{btt}^p$ -reductions are used instead of $\leq_T^p$ -reductions [OW91].

Not only does the sparse set conjecture imply a better understanding of the structure of NP and NP -hard sets, also does it settle the blatant unability to prove that EXP does not have polynomial size circuits. Best known upper bounds on this can be found in [Kan82].

Attempts to prove the sparse set conjecture usually result in studying stronger than Turing reducibility types to sparse sets [OW91, HL94, OL91, AHH+93]. In this paper we follow a different line of attack. Instead of strengthening the reduction type we study the most general Turing reduction and vary the density of the set reduced to. We are in particular interested in the consequences of the existence of $\leq_T^p$ -hard sets for NP that have *smaller* density than sparse sets. In [HOT] a similar approach was taken with respect to log-space-bounded reductions. The analogous question for sets with bigger than polynomial, i.e. super-polynomial, density has been addressed in [BH92].

We study the consequences of the existence of $\leq_T^p$ -hard sets for NP, that contain only $f(n)$ strings of size less than or equal to n, for $f(n)$ a unbounded function that is strictly smaller than any polynomial. We show that there is a link between classes of bounded nondeterminism [KF80, DT90], and NP having hard sets with low density. We prove that under the assumption that NP has a $\leq_T^p$ -hard set with density $f(n)$, SAT can be computed with only $O(\log(n) * f(n^c))$ bits of nondeterminism, for some constant c. Taking for $f(n)$ for example $\log(n)$ results in a collapse of NP to the second level of the Beta Hierarchy[DT90]. This on its turn implies for example that $EXP = NEXP$. Note P can be characterized as the class of sets that are recognized by nondeterministic polynomial time machines that use $O(\log(n))$ bits of nondeterminism.

On the other hand we show that this result is optimal with respect to relativizing computations, even if we consider tally sets. We prove that there exists an oracle relative to which NP does have Turing hard tally sets with $f(n)$ density but $P \neq NP$, for $f(n)$ an unbounded function.

As an application of the developed proof technique we establish absolute results concerning the density of $\leq_T^P$-hard sets for EXP. We prove that Turing hard sets for EXP can not be of sub-polynomial density. This is in some sense optimal, since improvement to polynomial density, would show that EXP does not have polynomial size circuits, and Wilson [Wil85] showed the existence of an oracle where EXP does have polynomial size circuits.

The main results in this paper are:

- We establish a connection between classes of bounded nondeterminism and NP having Turing hard sets with low density.
- We prove that if NP has a Turing hard set with density $f(n)$, for any unbounded function $f(n)$, then SAT can be computed in polynomial time with the use of $O(\log(n) * f(n^c))$ many nondeterministic bits, for c some constant and hence $EXP = NEXP$.
- We show that these results are optimal with respect to relativized computations: there exists an oracle relative to which NP has a Turing hard tally set with density $f(n)$, but $P \neq NP$.
- As a consequence of the developed proof technique we show that Turing hard sets for EXP can not have sub-polynomial density.

The results suggest that it is probably hard to prove the sparse set conjecture even if we consider sets with arbitrary low density. On the other hand this line of research might give a handle on proving the actual sparse set conjecture. It seems more doable to work on non-relativizing proof techniques for proving the sparse set conjecture, for sets with low density than for sparse sets.

2 Preliminaries

We assume the reader familiar with standard notions in structural complexity theory, as are defined e.g. in [BDG88]. We will be using (non)deterministic polynomial time oracle Turing machines. Let M be a (non)deterministic polynomial time oracle Turing machine. We will denote $Q(M, x, A)$ as the set of queries M makes on input x with oracle A. Note that if M is a deterministic machine then $\|Q(M, x, A)\|$ is bounded by a polynomial in the length of x.

Apart from SAT, the well known NP-complete set, we will be using the set K^A as well. Where K^A is defined as follows:

$$K^A = \{ <i, x, 0^{|x|^i}> \mid M_i^A(x) \text{ accepts x within } |x|^i \text{ steps } \}$$

We will be considering efficient reductions of complete sets for various classes to sets of different subpolynomial densities. The following definition specifies our measure of a set's density.

Definition 1. Let f be a nondecreasing function, $f : I\!N \to I\!N$. A set $S \subseteq \Sigma^*$ is $f(n)$ dense or has $f(n)$ density if $\|S^{\leq n}\| < f(n)$ for all n. If F is a class of functions, we say S is F-dense if S is f dense for some $f \in F$.

S is said to be *sparse* if S is P-dense. Where P is the class of all polynomials. S is said to be of *sub-polynomial density* if S is F-dense, where F is a class of functions such that $f \in F$ iff $\forall \epsilon \exists n_0 \forall n > n_0 : f(n) < n^\epsilon$. We will call such a function *sub-polynomial*.

We will be using classes that are defined by limiting the number of nondeterministic moves of a nondeterministic polynomial time Turing machine [KF80, DT90].

Definition 2. [DT90] For any function $f : N \to N$ let

$$\beta_f = \{L \mid \exists A \in P, \exists c, \forall x : x \in L \Leftrightarrow (\exists y, |y| \leq c * f(|x|) \text{ and } <x, y> \in A)\}$$

Will will also use the notation $\beta_f^{\beta_f}$ for the class of sets recognizable by a polynomial time oracle Turing machine that uses at most $f(n)$ nondeterministic moves and has a set in β_f as oracle.

3 Hard sets for NP and Bounded Nondeterminism

In this section we study the consequences of *NP* having Turing hard sets with low density. We are interested in sets with sub-polynomial density.

Let us consider an example of such a set. Let $f(n)$ be $\log(n)$. Consider the assumption that *NP* has a Turing hard tally set T of density $\log(n)$. This means that SAT $\leq_T^p T$, say in time n^c. The following counting argument, together with a nowadays standard technique, yield that SAT is computable in time $DTIME(c^2 * n^{\log(n)})$, for some constant c.

First lets count how many different tally sets $T^{\leq n^c}$ of density $\log(n)$ there exist. Each $T^{\leq n^c}$ may contain at most $c * \log(n)$ strings, that can be placed at n^c many different positions, hence the number of different tally sets up to length n^c is bounded by:

$$\binom{n^c}{c \log(n)} \leq n^{c^2 * \log(n)}$$

Next we will use the fact that it is possible to compute in polynomial time relative to SAT, for any satisfying formula ϕ, using the disjunctive selfreducibility of SAT, a satisfying assignment for ϕ. This property is also called Search Reduces to Decision or Functional Selfreducibility [BD76, BBFG91, NOS93]. Since SAT reduces to some tally set with $\log(n)$ density, it is reducible to one among the $n^{c^2 * \log(n)}$ many different ones. Consider the following algorithm. On input ϕ cycle through all the possible tally sets of $\log(n)$ density. For each one try to compute a satisfying assignment for ϕ and accept if and only if one is found . It is clear that a satisfying assignment will be found this way if and only if $\phi \in$ SAT. Furthermore this procedure runs in time $n^{c^2 * \log(n)}$.

The problem with the previous approach is that it does not work for sets over $\{0, 1\}$. The number of possible sets with density $\log(n)$ is only bounded by $2^{n^{c * \log(n)}}$ and hence will yield that SAT is computable in time $2^{n^{c * \log(n)}}$, but this is not very good since SAT is computable in time 2^n. The following theorem shows that linking the problem to bounded nondeterminism yields even better results than the above approach for non tally sets. We will show that for any function $f(n)$ the assumption that NP has a Turing hard set with density $f(n)$ implies that SAT is computable in polynomial time with $O(\log(n) * f(n^c))$ many nondeterministic bits, for some constant c.

Theorem 3. *Let $f(n)$ be any fully time constructible function. If there exists a set S with density $f(n)$ that is Turing hard for NP then SAT is computable in polynomial time with $O(\log(n) * f(n^c))$ many nondeterministic bits, for some constant c.*

Proof. (Sketch)We have to show that under the assumption that SAT reduces to a set S with density $f(n)$ we can construct a polynomial time algorithm using $O(\log(n) * f(n^c))$ many nondeterministic bits, that decides SAT. Assume that SAT $\leq_T^p S$ via a machine M_c, that runs in time n^c and that M_a witnesses the fact that SAT has Search Reducing to Decision. Simulate the machine M_a, that generates a satisfying assignment relative to SAT on input ϕ. Every time M_a makes a query to SAT simulate the Turing reduction M_c, from A to S, on this query. Every time M_c makes a query q to S either assume that q is out of S or guess that q is in S. Make sure that at most $f(n^c)$ times a query is guessed to be in S and that the decision about q is consistent with previously made decisions about q. Accept if and only if a satisfying assignment for ϕ is found. It should be clear that this construction runs in polynomial time. From this it follows that at most $O(\log(n) * f(n^c))$ many nondeterministic bits are used. The following describes in more detail the above algorithm:

```
input φ
n := |φ|
Guess a set Positions with ≤ f(n^c) pointers of size ≤ log(n^{c+1})
Queries := ∅
Count := 0
z := φ
   while there is at least one variable in z
      let x be the first variable in z
      z' := z|_{x:=0}
      while Simulation of M_c on z' not ended do
         Simulate M_c on z' until it queries q
         Count := Count + 1
         if q ∈ Queries then continue simulation in YES state
         else if Count ∈ Positions then
            Queries := Queries ∪ {q}
            continue simulation in YES state
         else continue simulation in NO state
      end while
      if M_c accepted z' then z := z'
      else z = z|_{x:=1}
```

end while
if z simplifies to "true" **then** accept **else** reject

Where $z|_x := i$ for $i = 0, 1$ means the formula obtained by substituting i for every occurrence of x in z.

The above Theorem shows that although a set S over $\{0, 1\}$ with density $f(n)$ (for $f(n)$ small) contains in some sense more information than a tally set T of the same density, a polynomial time algorithm is not able to extract this information out of S.

Plugging in explicit values for $f(n)$ yields the following corollary:

Corollary 4. *If there exists a set S with density $(\log(n))^k$, that is Turing hard for NP, then:*

1. $NP = \beta_{polylog}$.
2. $EXP = NEXP$.

Proof. Use Theorem 3 together with standard padding arguments.

Another consequence of the proof technique of Theorem 3 is that it yields absolute results about the density of Turing hard sets for EXP. To our knowledge this is the first result concerning the density of $\leq_T^p$ -hard sets for EXP.

Theorem 5. *There do not exist Turing hard sets for EXP that have sub-polynomial density.*

Proof. (Sketch) Assume that there exists a $f(n)$ dense Turing hard set for EXP for some sub-polynomial function f. From this we can conclude [KL80] that $EXP = \Sigma_2^p$. We will see that by extending Theorem 3 we will be able to show that Σ_2^p is computable in time $2^{O(\log(n)*f(n^{O(1)}))}$. Then we will have a contradiction with the hierarchy Theorems for deterministic time, since EXP is not computable in sub-exponential deterministic time. In order to extend Theorem 3 we will make use of the fact that all $\leq_T^p$ -complete sets for Σ_2^p are functional selfreducible [BD76]. Functional selfreducibility is the natural generalization of search reducing to decision for other levels of the Polynomial Time Hierarchy. Consider any set A in Σ_2^p. By definition there exists a polynomial time computable relation R_A such that:

$$x \in A \Leftrightarrow \exists y \forall z : R_A(x, y, z)$$

A set $A \in \Sigma_2^p$ is functional selfreducible if there exists a polynomial time procedure that can compute, relative to A, for all $x \in A$ a y_0 such that $\forall z : R_A(x, y_0, z)$. For all strings not in A such a y_0 does not exists. Borodin and Demers showed that this is always the case if A is $\leq_T^p$ -complete for Σ_2^p [BD76]. We will see that under the assumption of the existence of a $f(n)$ dense hard set for EXP any complete set A for Σ_2^p can be recognized in $\beta_{g(n)}^{\beta_{g(n)}}$, for $g(n) \in O(\log(n) * f(n^{O(1)}))$.

Let A be $\leq_T^p$ -complete for Σ_2^p, M_f be the procedure that witnesses that A is functional selfreducible and M_c be the machine witnessing that $A \leq_T^p S$. Simulate M_f on some input x and every time a query to A is made simulate the reduction M_c, from A to S, on this query. Again, as in the proof of Theorem 3, if M_c makes a query q to S assume either that q is not in S or guess that the query is in the set, making sure that no more than $f(n^c)$ many yes guesses are made and that the decisions are consistent with previously made decisions about q. After this computation some y' has been computed. If nothing is computed, because y_0 does not exists or because some wrong sequence of guesses is used, reject. Next the algorithm checks whether the computed y' indeed satisfies the property that $\forall z : R_A(x, y', z)$. This can be done by one oracle call to SAT. Since SAT $\in \Sigma_2^p$ it follows using Theorem 3 that SAT $\in \beta_{O(\log(n)*f(n^d))}$ for some d. Hence $A \in \beta_{g(n)}^{\beta_{g(n)}}$ and can be decided in deterministic sub-exponential time.

Note that any improvement to the previous theorem will settle the big open question whether EXP has polynomial size circuits. Also does the theorem hint at the possibility that a much weaker form of the sparse set conjecture[3], might settle the circuit issue for EXP.

4 Relativized Optimality

In this section we show that Theorem 3 is optimal with respect to relativized computations.

Theorem 6. *Let $f(n)$ be an unbounded function. There exists an oracle A and a tally set T of density $f(n)$ such that:*

1. $K^A \leq_T^{p,A} T$ *and*
2. $P^A \neq NP^A$.

Proof. (Sketch) W.l.o.g. we assume that $f(n) < n$ and monotone. The construction of the set A consists out of two parts. One to satisfy requirement 1 and the other part to satisfy 2. The set A will be the marked union of QBF, a *PSPACE* $\leq_m^p$ -complete set, and a set B (i.e. A =QBF$\oplus B$). Requirement 2 will be satisfied by showing that the following test language L is in NP^A but not in P^A:

$$L = \{0^n \mid \exists x \in B \text{ and } |x| = n\}$$

Note that for all B, L is in NP^A. We will construct B in such a way that $L \notin P^A$. In order to do this we need a sequence of strings to diagonalize over. Let $\{a_i\}_{i=0}^{\infty}$ be a sequence of natural numbers such that the following things hold:

---

[3] We mean here the following weaker variant: SAT is computable in polynomial time with significantly less than a linear number of nondeterministic bits if and only if there exists a sparse Turing hard set for *NP*.

1. $f(a_i) \geq 2 * f(a_{i-1})$,
2. $f(a_{i-1}) * a_{i-1} < a_i$,
3. $a_i^{f(a_i)} > a_i^i + i$, and
4. a_0 is the first n such that $f(n) \geq 2$.

Since $f(n)$ is unbounded it is not hard to see that $\{a_i\}_{i=0}^{\infty}$ exists and is infinite. In the following let $A = \text{QBF} \oplus B$ and let $M_1, M_2 \ldots$ be an enumeration of polynomial time oracle Turing machines such that M_i runs in time $n^i + i$. The construction of B goes as follows:

stage n:

Let $y_{a_i} = x_1 x_2 \ldots x_k 00 \ldots 0$ be a string such that:

1. $k = \log(a_i) * f(a_i)$,
2. $x_j \in \{0, 1\}$ $(1 \leq j \leq k)$,
3. $|y_{a_i}| = a_i$, and
4. $y_{a_i} \notin Q(M_i, 0^{a_i}, A)$.

Put y_{a_i} into B if and only if $M_i^A(0^{a_i})$ rejects.

end of stage n

From the definition of $\{a_i\}_{i=0}^{\infty}$, the fact that M_i runs in time $n^i + i$, and that $f(n)$ is unbounded it follows that y_{a_i} exists and that $L \notin P^A$. The construction of B satisfies requirement 2. In order to satisfy requirement 1 we need to code B into a $f(n)$ dense tally set. We will show that we can code B into a $2 * f(n)$ dense tally set T, which is sufficient[4] to satisfy requirement 1. First observe the following. If we put, for all n, $f(a_n)$ strings into T at the interval $0^{a_n}, \ldots, 0^{a_n * f(a_n)}$ then T will have density $2 * f(n)$. The observation yields that we have $f(a_n)$ strings to code y_{a_n} into T. To do this divide the interval $0^{a_n}, \ldots, 0^{a_n * f(a_n)}$ into $f(a_n)$ intervals I_k of length a_n such that $I_k = 0^{k * a_n}, \ldots, 0^{((k+1) * a_n - 1)}$ $(1 \leq k < f(a_n))$. Next if we place one string t_k in each I_k we can interpret $t_1 t_1 \ldots t_{f(a_n)}$ as a $f(a_n)$ digit number base a_n. Recall that $y_{a_n} = x_1 x_2 \ldots x_k 00 \ldots 0$ where $k = \log(a_n) * f(a_n)$. The only part of y_{a_n} that matters is $x_1 x_2 \ldots x_k$. Since we can express $x_1 x_2 \ldots x_k$ as a $f(a_n)$ digit number base a_n there is room to code $x_1 x_2 \ldots x_k$ and hence y_{a_n} into T.

This coding argument shows that we can code B into T. To see that $K^A \leq_T^{p,A} T$ we do the following reduction. Let M_j be some nondeterministic polynomial time oracle machine that accepts K^A. In order to know whether $M_j^A(x)$ accepts or rejects, the reduction firsts recovers B up to length $|x|^j$, using T. Next it queries QBF whether $M_j(x)$ with QBF and B up to length $|x|^j$ accepts or rejects.

Note that the above construction actually proves something stronger. It shows that there exists an oracle A such that NP^A has a Turing hard tally set of $f(n)$ density and even $P^A \neq \beta_{\log(n) * f(n)}^A$.

---

[4] This actually only shows that for each unbounded function $f(n)$ there exists a $2 * f(n)$ dense tally set with the desired properties. However starting out with a function $f'(n) = f(n)/2$ will satisfy requirement 1.

5 Conclusions

The oracle result (Theorem 6) shows that the weaker form of the sparse set conjecture needs nonrelativizing proof techniques to be proven. On the other hand it seems more doable to develop non-relativizing techniques for the weaker form of the conjecture than for the actual conjecture.

Another interesting point that comes out of the oracle construction is that the idea behind the coding can be used to show that the class of sets that Turing reduce to a tally set with polylog[5] density and the nonuniform advice class *Full-P/polylog* [Ko87, BHM92] are equal. It seems therefore natural to study the structure of these advice classes in greater detail.

Theorem 5 suggests that the weaker form of the sparse set conjecture, i.e $NP = \beta_f(n)$ iff exists a Turing hard sparse set for NP for some subpolynomial function $f(n)$, implies that EXP is not contained in $P/poly$. It would be interesting to prove this.

Acknowledgements

We would like to thank José Balcázar and Ricard Gavaldà for listening to us with great patience and suggesting interesting ideas. Special thanks are due to Jacobo Torán for pointing out the importance of limited nondeterminism.

References

[AHH+93] V. Arvind, Y. Han, L. Hemachandra, J. Koebler, A. Lozano, M. Mundhenk, M. Ogiwara, U. Schöning, R. Silvestri, and T. Thierauf. Reductions to sets of low information content. In K. Ambos-Spies, S. Homer, and U. Schöning, editors, *Complexity Theory*, pages 1–46. Cambridge University Press, December 1993.

[BBFG91] R. Beigel, M. Bellare, J. Feigenbaum, and S. Goldwasser. Languages that are easier to verify than their proofs. In *Proc. 32nd IEEE Symposium on Foundations of Computer Science*, pages 19–28, 1991.

[BD76] A. Borodin and A. Demers. Some comments on functional self-reducibility and the NP hierarchy. Technical Report TR76-284, Cornell University, Department of Computer Science, Upson Hall, Ithaca, NY 14853, 1976.

[BDG88] J. Balcázar, J. Díaz, and J. Gabarró. *Structural Complexity I*. Springer-Verlag, 1988.

[BH77] L. Berman and H. Hartmanis. On isomorphisms and density of NP and other complete sets. *SIAM J. Comput.*, 6:305–322, 1977.

[BH92] H. Buhrman and S. Homer. Superpolynomial circuits, almost sparse oracles and the exponential hierarchy. In R. Shyamasundar, editor, *Proc. 12th Conference on the Foundations of Software Technology & Theoretical Computerscience, Lecture Notes in Computer Science*, pages 116–127. Springer Verlag, 1992.

---

[5] Polylog stands for the class of functions $\{f \mid \exists i, f(n) = (\log(n))^i\}$.

[BHM92] J.L. Balcázar, M. Hermo, and E. Mayordomo. Characterizations of loga-
         rithmic advice complexity classes. In *Algorithms, Software, Architecture:
         Information Procesing 92*, volume 1, pages 315–321. Elsevier, 1992.

[DT90]   J. Díaz and J. Torán. Classes of bounded nondeterminism. *Math. Systems
         Theory*, 23:21–32, 1990.

[HL94]   S. Homer and L. Longpré. On reductions of NP sets to sparse sets. *J.
         Computer and System Sciences*, 48:324–336, 1994.

[HOT]   L. Hemaspaandra, M. Ogiwara, and S. Toda. Space-efficient recognition of
         sparse self-reducible languages. *Computational Complexity*. In press.

[Kan82] R. Kannan. Circuit-size lower bounds and non-reducibility to sparse
         sets. *Information and Control*, 55(1–3):40–56, October/November/Decem-
         ber 1982.

[KF80]   C. Kintala and P. Fisher. Refining nondeterminism in relativized polynom-
         ial-time bounded computations. *SIAM J. Comput.*, 9(1):46–53, 1980.

[KL80]   R. Karp and R. Lipton. Some connections between nonuniform and uniform
         complexity classes. In *Proc. 12th ACM Symposium on Theory of Computing*,
         pages 302–309, 1980.

[Ko87]   K. Ko. On helping by robust oracle machines that take advice. *Theoretical
         Computer Science*, 52:15–36, 1987.

[NOS93] A.V. Naik, M. Ogiwara, and A.L. Selman. P-selective sets, and reducing
         search to decision vs. self-reducibility. In *Proc. Structure in Complexity
         Theory 8th annual conference*, pages 52–64, San Diego, California, 1993.
         IEEE computer society press.

[OL91]   M. Ogiwara and A. Lozano. On one query self-reducible sets. In *Proc.
         Structure in Complexity Theory 6th annual conference*, pages 139–151,
         Chicago, Ill., 1991. IEEE Computer Society Press.

[OW91]   M. Ogiwara and O. Watanabe. On polynomial time bounded truth-table
         reducibility of NP sets to sparse sets. *SIAM J. Comput.*, 20:471–483, 1991.

[Pip79] N. Pippenger. On simultaneous resource bounds. In *Proc. 20th IEEE Sym-
         posium on Foundations of Computer Science*, pages 307–311, 1979.

[Wil85] C.B. Wilson. Relativized circuit complexity. *J. Comput. System Sci.*,
         31:169–181, 1985.

Beyond $\mathbf{P^{NP}} = \mathbf{NEXP}$

Stephen A. Fenner[1]* and Lance J. Fortnow[2]**

[1] University of Southern Maine, Department of Computer Science 96 Falmouth St.,
Portland, ME 04103, USA
E-mail: fenner@usm.maine.edu, Fax: (207) 780-4933
[2] University of Chicago, Department of Computer Science 1100 E. 58th St., Chicago,
IL 60637, USA
E-mail: fortnow@cs.uchicago.edu, Fax: (312) 702-8487

Abstract. Buhrman and Torenvliet created an oracle relative to which
$\mathbf{P^{NP}} = \mathbf{NEXP}$ and thus $\mathbf{P^{NP}} = \mathbf{P^{NEXP}}$. Their proof uses a delicate finite injury argument that leads to a nonrecursive oracle. We simplify their proof removing the injury to create a recursive oracle making $\mathbf{P^{NP}} = \mathbf{NEXP}$. In addition, in our construction we can make $\mathbf{P} = \mathbf{UP} = \mathbf{NP} \cap \mathbf{coNP}$. This leads to the curious situation where $\mathbf{LOW(NP)} = \mathbf{P}$ but $\mathbf{LOW(P^{NP})} = \mathbf{NEXP}$, and the complete $\leq_m^p$-degree for $\mathbf{P^{NP}}$ collapses to a p-isomorphism type.

1 Introduction

In 1978, Seiferas, Fischer and Meyer [SFM78] showed a very strong separation theorem for nondeterministic time: For time constructible $t_1(n)$ and $t_2(n)$, if $t_1(n + 1) = o(t_2(n))$ then $\mathbf{NTIME}(t_1(n))$ does not contain $\mathbf{NTIME}(t_2(n))$. Thus we have a huge gap between nondeterministic polynomial time ($\mathbf{NP}$) and nondeterministic exponential time ($\mathbf{NEXP}$).

We would also expect then a separation between $\mathbf{P^{NP}}$ and $\mathbf{P^{NEXP}}$. Indeed, we have some evidence for that direction: Mocas [Moc94] (improving upon work of Fu, Li an Zhong [FLZ94]) showed that for any fixed c, $\mathbf{NEXP}$ is not contained in $\mathbf{P^{NP}}$ if the polynomial-time machine can only ask n^c queries to the $\mathbf{NP}$ oracle.

Recently, Buhrman and Torenvliet [BT94] showed the existence of an oracle relative to which $\mathbf{P^{NP}} = \mathbf{NEXP}$ and thus $\mathbf{P^{NP}} = \mathbf{P^{NEXP}}$. This says that we can not prove a separation between $\mathbf{P^{NP}}$ and $\mathbf{P^{NEXP}}$ with relativizable techniques. They prove this result using a difficult finite injury argument where injuries may cascade through the oracle by more than any recursive bound. Their "construction" thus does not lead to a recursive oracle.

In this paper, we simplify the Buhrman and Torenvliet proof. We use their proof as a starting block but remove the finite injury and replace it with an exponential (and thus recursive) search. Thus we end up with a recursive oracle relative to which $\mathbf{P^{NP}} = \mathbf{NEXP}$.

* Partially Supported by NSF Grant CCR-9209833.
** Partially Supported by NSF Grant CCR-9253582.

We use a tree-based construction (see [Soa87, Chapter XIV]) where if we can get an injury from one leaf in a tree we can then throw away that leaf and start using the next one. We arrange our tree so that we have more leaves than injuries.

Also, we can combine our construction with techniques developed by Rackoff [Rac82], Hartmanis and Hemachandra [HH91] and Blum and Impagliazzo [BI87] to also get $\mathbf{P} = \mathbf{UP} = \mathbf{NP} \cap \mathbf{coNP}$ while also having $\mathbf{P^{NP}} = \mathbf{NEXP}$ relative to a recursive oracle. We eliminate machines that do not categorically accept on at most one path by forcing the acceptance on one of the leaves of our tree and then using a future leaf for encoding.

The relativized world we create has two interesting properties. The first is about low sets. The low sets of a class $\mathcal{C}$ consist of those oracles A such that $\mathcal{C}^A = \mathcal{C}$. Essentially the low sets give no help to the class $\mathcal{C}$. Relative to the oracle we construct, we get a surprising relationship between the low sets for $\mathbf{NP}$ and the low sets for $\mathbf{P^{NP}}$: The first consists of exactly those languages in $\mathbf{P}$ while the second consists of those languages in $\mathbf{NEXP}$.

The second property of our relativized world is that the complete $\leq_m^p$-degree for $\mathbf{P^{NP}}$ collapses to a p-isomorphism type. That is, all $\mathbf{P^{NP}}$-complete sets under polynomial-time many-one reductions are polynomial-time isomorphic. This advances a program for getting complete degrees to collapse: if $\mathcal{C} \subseteq \mathbf{NEXP}$ is a class with complete sets, then one can make all $\mathcal{C}$-complete sets p-isomorphic in a relativized world by setting $\mathbf{P} = \mathbf{UP}$ and $\mathcal{C} = \mathbf{EXP}$. Homer and Selman [HS92] were able to do this for $\mathcal{C} = \Sigma_2^p$, and our present oracle works for $\mathcal{C} = \mathbf{P^{NP}}$. An oracle for $\mathcal{C} = \mathbf{NP}$ would affirm the Isomorphism Conjecture [BH77]. Even though oracles making the Conjecture true are known [FFK92], it is still an interesting open question whether there is an oracle relative to which $\mathbf{P} = \mathbf{UP}$ and $\mathbf{NP} = \mathbf{EXP}$.

2 Notation and Definitions

We let $\Sigma = \{0, 1\}$ and identify Σ^* with the natural numbers $0, 1, 2, \ldots$ in the usual way. We will sometimes use the divider symbol, "#", and in fact, our oracles will always be languages over the alphabet $\{0, 1, \#\}$. Inputs to machines will always be taken as strings in Σ^*, however. For any $n \geq 0$, we let Σ^n (resp. $\{0, 1, \#\}^n$) be the set of strings in Σ^* (resp. $\{0, 1, \#\}^*$) of length n. We order strings in Σ^n or $\{0, 1, \#\}^n$ lexicographically according to the order $\# < 0 < 1$ on the symbols. We say "lex less than" for "lexicographically less than." We say a string w extends a string v if v is a prefix of w.

We will also deal with partial characteristic functions $\{0, 1, \#\}^* \to \{0, 1\}$ with finite domain, which usually represent the portion of some oracle we are committed to so far. (We will build our oracles by finite extension at each stage.) We use lower-case Greek letters to denote these finite functions. We identify a language A over $\{0, 1, \#\}$ with its (total) characteristic function $\{0, 1, \#\}^* \to \{0, 1\}$. When dealing with partial functions, we use the relation "extends" in the usual functional sense.

Our notation for machines is standard. See, for example, [HU79]. The only peculiarity in the paper is when a nondeterministic oracle Turing machine M accesses a partial characteristic function σ as its oracle. We say that $M^\sigma(x)$ has *an accepting path* p if and only if p is an accepting path of M on input x where all queries along p are in domain(σ) and are answered according to σ. $M^\sigma(x)$ *accepts* if it has some accepting path (even if other paths make queries outside domain(σ)).

3   Main Results

Theorem 1. *There is a recursive oracle A such that* $\mathbf{P}^{\mathbf{NP}^A} = \mathbf{NEXP}^A$.

Proof. Fix a nondeterministic oracle machine M that accepts some $\mathbf{NEXP}^B$-complete set for all oracles B. We may assume without loss of generality that M asks at most 2^n queries along any path, where n is the length of the input. We define a relativized language L^B as follows: consider any $x \in \Sigma^*$ of length n. Let C_x be the set of all strings of the form

$$w_0 \# w_1 \# \cdots \# w_n \# x \# y,$$

such that $|w_i| = i + 1$ for all $i \leq n$, and $|y| = 2n + 3$. (We identify each w_i with a number in the range from 0 to $2^{i+1} - 1$ in the usual way.) For any oracle B, we define $x \in L^B$ if and only if $C_x \cap B \neq \emptyset$ and the rightmost bit of the lexicographically maximum element of $C_x \cap B$ is 1. We call C_x the *coding region* of x.

We can determine whether a given x is in L^B by binary search, asking questions of the form, "Is there an element of $C_x \cap B$ which is lex no less than z?" These questions are in $\mathbf{NP}^B$ and we only need ask polynomially many of them, so it follows that $L^B \in \mathbf{P}^{\mathbf{NP}^B}$ for all B. Our goal, then, is to construct a recursive A such that $L^A = L(M^A)$.

We construct A in stages $0, 1, \ldots$. Currently, all the work will be done in the even stages; the odd stages will be used later in the proof of Theorem 2. First some notation: if σ and τ are finite characteristic functions and w is a string, then we say that τ is a *w-extension* of σ if τ extends σ and for all strings $z \notin$ domain(σ), if $\tau(z) = 1$ then z extends w. The finite function α, below, represents the committed portion of the oracle so far. Initially, before stage 0, α is the empty function, and α grows by finite extension throughout the construction, so that, for any z, once $\alpha(z)$ is defined it never changes. The numbers m_i will always be identified with binary strings of length $i + 1$. From now on throughout the proof, w stands for the string $m_0 \# m_1 \# \cdots \# m_{2n}$.

Stage $2n$
/* $\alpha, m_0, m_1, \ldots, m_{2n-1}$ are given. */
Phase 1: *Forcing Accepting Computations*
   Let $m_{2n} = 0$.
   Let $S = \Sigma^n$.

Do the following repeatedly until no such x exists:

Find some $x \in S$ such that there is a w-extension β of α making $M^\beta(x)$ accept.

If x exists, then

(i) fix such a β,

(ii) let p be some accepting path of $M^\beta(x)$,

(iii) remove x from S,

(iv) extend α to include the query answers along p, and

(v) increment m_{2n}.

Phase 2: *Coding*

For each x of length n (order is unimportant):

Let y_x be the lex least $y \in \Sigma^{2n+2}$ such that neither $w\#x\#y0$ nor $w\#x\#y1$ is in domain(α). [We show later that y_x always exists.]

If $M^\alpha(x)$ accepts, set $\alpha(w\#x\#y_x 1) = 1$.

Otherwise, set $\alpha(w\#x\#y_x 0) = 1$.

Phase 3: *Cleanup*

Set $\alpha(z) = 0$ for all $z \in \bigcup_{x \in \Sigma^n} C_x - \text{domain}(\alpha)$.

Set $\alpha(z) = 0$ for all $z \in \{0, 1, \#\}^n - \text{domain}(\alpha)$.

End stage $2n$.

Stage $2n + 1$

Let $m_{2n+1} = 0$.

End stage $2n + 1$.

Note that in the Forcing phase, m_{2n} is incremented at most 2^n times, so there is no possibility of overflow. In the Coding phase, for each x, the unique string z for which $\alpha(z)$ is set to 1 we will call x's *coding string*.

Define the oracle $A \subseteq \{0, 1, \#\}^*$ such that $w \in A$ if and only if $\alpha(w)$ is set to 1 at some stage. The three claims below finish the proof.

Claim 1. *A is recursive.*

Proof. The stage-by-stage construction is recursive, α is finite at every stage, and every $z \in \{0, 1, \#\}^*$ enters domain(α) at some stage. □ Claim 1

Claim 2. *The string y_x exists for all $x \in \Sigma^*$.*

Proof. Fix x of length n. It suffices to show that at the start of the Coding phase of Stage $2n$, $|\text{domain}(\alpha) \cap C_x| < 2^{2n+2}$. Note that all strings in C_x are strictly longer than n, and all the other coding regions are disjoint from C_x. This means that we can ignore the elements entering domain(α) in the Coding and Cleanup phases of stages 0 through $2n - 1$. That is, the strings contributing to $|\text{domain}(\alpha) \cap C_x|$ must have entered domain(α) during Phase 1 of these stages. Taken together, these phases add at most 2^n queries to domain(α) for each x' with $|x'| \leq n$. This makes at most $2^n(2^{n+1} - 1) < 2^{2n+2}$ elements in all. (The overkill in the bound will be useful in the proof of Theorem 2.) □ Claim 2

Claim 3. *For all x of length n, $x \in L^A$ if and only if $M^A(x)$ accepts.*

Proof. Let $\alpha, m_0, \ldots, m_{2n}$ be as at the end of phase 1 of stage $2n$. We need to show two things: (1) the coding string of x is the lex maximum element of $C_x \cap A$, and (2) the accept/reject behavior of $M^\alpha(x)$ at the Coding phase is not disturbed by any later changes to α, i.e., $M^\alpha(x) = M^A(x)$.

No strings enter A in the Cleanup phases of any stage. The coding strings for all $x' \neq x$ are not in C_x, and hence do not affect (1). Also, the Cleanup phase of stage $2n$ ensures that no strings enter $C_x \cap A$ after stage $2n$. What is left is the Forcing phases of stages $0, \ldots, 2n$. If a string enters A during the Forcing phase of some stage $n' \leq 2n$, then it must be some query extending $m_0 \# \cdots m_{n'-1} \# m$ made along some accepting path of M, for some $m < m_{n'}$. This is because all queries not extending this prefix were answered "no" and kept out of A (except if they were already in domain(α)), and m was incremented immediately afterwards. Thus any strings in C_x that enter A are lex less than x's coding string. This shows (1).

If $M^\alpha(x)$ accepts, then $M^A(x)$ accepts because A extends α. Suppose $M^\alpha(x)$ rejects. Since the loop in phase 1 has ended, there is no w-extension β of α such that $M^\beta(x)$ accepts. It is clear by the construction that all strings put into A beyond this point in the construction have w as a prefix. Therefore, $M^A(x)$ must still reject. $\qquad\qquad$ □ **Claim 3**

$\qquad\qquad\qquad\qquad\qquad\qquad\qquad\qquad\qquad\qquad\qquad$ □ **Theorem 1**

We can now flesh out the odd stages of the construction above to get $\mathbf{P}^A = \mathbf{UP}^A$ and $\mathbf{P}^A = \mathbf{NP}^A \cap \mathbf{coNP}^A$ as well. For simplicity, we only show how to get $\mathbf{P}^A = \mathbf{UP}^A$ here. Also getting $\mathbf{P}^A = \mathbf{NP}^A \cap \mathbf{coNP}^A$ is accomplished in an entirely similar way, which we describe briefly afterwards.

Theorem 2. *There is a recursive oracle A such that $\mathbf{P}^{\mathbf{NP}^A} = \mathbf{NEXP}^A$ and $\mathbf{P}^A = \mathbf{UP}^A$.*

Proof. We build A in stages just as in the proof of Theorem 1. In fact, the even-numbered stages are exactly as they were before, but we now use the odd-numbered stages to force **NP** machines to be illegal as **UP** machines (i.e., to have more than one accepting path on some input). This is done very much like the forcing of acceptances of M in the even stages.

Fix a standard enumeration $N_1, N_2, \ldots$ of all ptime nondeterministic oracle TMs, where N_i runs in time n^i. The set-up for the construction is identical with that of Theorem 1. In stage $2n + 1$ we always use w to denote the string $m_0 \# m_1 \# \cdots \# m_{2n+1}$.

Stage $2n$
This is identical with stage $2n$ of Theorem 1.
End stage $2n$.

Stage $2n + 1$

Let $m_{2n+1} = 0$.

For $i = 1$ to n:

Find the least string y with $|y| \leq 2^{n/i}$ such that there is a w-extension β of α where $N_i^\beta(y)$ has at least two accepting paths p_1 and p_2.

If y, β, p_1, and p_2 exist, then:

(i) extend α to include the query answers along p_1 and p_2,

(ii) increment m_{2n+1}.

End stage $2n + 1$.

The oracle A is defined as before, and it is clearly recursive. The proof that $\mathbf{P^{NP^A}} = \mathbf{NEXP^A}$ requires little change from the previous proof: Since the odd stages closely resemble the Forcing phases of the even stages, the proof of Claim 3 still applies in the present case. We only need check that Claim 2 is still valid by bounding $|\text{domain}(\alpha) \cap C_x|$ at the start of the Coding phase of stage $2n$. At most $2^n(2^{n+1} - 1)$ strings are contributed by the even stages, and each odd stage contributes at most $n \cdot 2|y|^i \leq n2^{n+1}$ strings. There are n odd stages before stage $2n$, so we have

$$|\text{domain}(\alpha) \cap C_x| \leq 2^n(2^{n+1} - 1) + n^2 2^{n+1} < 2^{2n+2}.$$

Therefore, Claim 2 holds.

It remains to show that $\mathbf{P^A} = \mathbf{UP^A}$. First, it is important to note that this entire proof, including the construction, can be recast relative to an oracle that makes $\mathbf{P} = \mathbf{PSPACE}$, e.g., some $\mathbf{PSPACE}$-complete set H. This recasting clearly alters the definition of A, but not the facts we establish. We will therefore assume for the rest of the proof that $\mathbf{P} = \mathbf{PSPACE}$ (unrelativized). We can discharge this assumption by recasting everything relative to H.

Let i be such that N_i^A is a $\mathbf{UP^A}$ machine. We describe a $\mathbf{P^A}$ procedure to compute $L(N_i^A)$. For input x, let $n = i \cdot \lceil \log |x| \rceil$ and run the construction through stage $2n + 1$, obtaining an α and $w = m_0 \# \cdots m_{2n+1}$ at the end of this stage. Note that α and w can be computed and stored using polynomial space.[3] Hence α and w can be computed in time polynomial in $|x|$. Moreover, by the construction and the fact that N_i^A is a $\mathbf{UP^A}$ machine, $N_i^\beta(x)$ has at most one accepting path for every β which is a w-extension of α. We can now adapt a standard technique developed and used by Rackoff [Rac82], Hartmanis & Hemachandra [HH91], and Blum & Impagliazzo [BI87] to compute $N_i^A(x)$.

ALGORITHM FOR $N_i^A(x)$.

Compute α and w as above.

Repeat the following $|x|^i$ times:

If there is a w-extension β of α where $N_i^\beta(x)$ accepts, then:

---

[3] Actually, $|\text{domain}(\alpha)|$ is superpolynomial by virtue of the Cleanup phases. We can compress α, however, by only retaining the single coding string, and omitting the other strings added in the Cleanup phase.

Let p be some accepting path of $N_i^\beta(x)$.

Extend α to include all queries along p *answered according to* A.

Accept iff $N_i^\alpha(x)$ accepts.

END OF ALGORITHM.

The algorithm can clearly be run using polynomial space, and hence polynomial time by our assumptions.

Note that throughout the algorithm, α agrees with A. Thus if $N_i^A(x)$ rejects, then the algorithm rejects. Suppose $N_i^A(x)$ accepts along the unique path p^*. At the start of any given loop iteration, suppose that domain(α) does not include all the queries made along p^*. Some β and p must be found in the iteration, since A is itself a w-extension of α by our construction. If $p = p^*$, then the algorithm will clearly accept. If $p \neq p^*$, then they must share a common query that is answered differently along each path; otherwise, there is a single w-extension of α yielding two distinct accepting paths for $N_i(x)$, which violates our construction. If q is such a common query, then $q \notin$ domain(α) before the iteration but enters domain(α) during the iteration. Thus, the number of queries along p^* not in domain(α) decreases by one on each iteration. Since there are at most $|x|^i$ queries along p^*, by the end of the loop α includes all such queries, and the algorithm accepts. $\qquad\square$

To get $\mathbf{P}^A = \mathbf{NP}^A \cap \mathbf{coNP}^A$, we can easily interleave $\mathbf{P}^A = \mathbf{UP}^A$ stages with $\mathbf{P}^A = \mathbf{NP}^A \cap \mathbf{coNP}^A$ stages. In the latter stages, which are handled similarly, we consider each N_i^X as a proper $\mathbf{NP}^X \cap \mathbf{coNP}^X$ machine if, for each input, it has at least one accepting path, and either all accepting paths start with a left branch or they all start with a right branch. N_i^X accepts an input iff it has an accepting path starting with a left branch. In the $\mathbf{P}^A = \mathbf{NP}^A \cap \mathbf{coNP}^A$ stages of the construction we look for w-extensions that force both types of accepting path for the same input. In corresponding $\mathbf{P}^A$ algorithm, the main difference is that we now search for pairs of w-extensions that yield both types of accepting path. We thus have the following theorem:

Theorem 3. *There is a recursive oracle* A *such that* $\mathbf{P}^{\mathbf{NP}^A} = \mathbf{NEXP}^A$ *and* $\mathbf{P}^A = \mathbf{UP}^A = \mathbf{NP}^A \cap \mathbf{coNP}^A$.

3.1 Lowness and Collapsing Degrees

For any relativizable class $\mathcal{C}$, we let $\mathbf{LOW}(\mathcal{C})$ denote the class of all $\mathcal{C}$-low sets, i.e., the class of all B such that $\mathcal{C}^B = \mathcal{C}$. This concept itself relativizes, i.e., we say a set B is low for $\mathcal{C}$ relative to an oracle A if $\mathcal{C}^{A \oplus B} = \mathcal{C}^A$.

Since the classes $\mathbf{NP}$ and $\mathbf{P}^{\mathbf{NP}}$ are "close" to each other, one might expect that $\mathbf{LOW}(\mathbf{NP})$ should likewise be close to $\mathbf{LOW}(\mathbf{P}^{\mathbf{NP}})$, but instead we get the following curious lowness property relative to the oracle A of Theorem 3:

Corollary 4. *Relative to the set* A *of Theorem 3,*

$$\mathbf{LOW}(\mathbf{NP}) = \mathbf{P} \ and \ \mathbf{LOW}(\mathbf{P}^{\mathbf{NP}}) = \mathbf{NEXP}.$$

Proof. It is well-known (see [Sel79]) that $\mathbf{LOW(NP)} = \mathbf{NP} \cap \mathbf{coNP}$, and the proof relativizes; thus, $\mathbf{LOW(NP)} = \mathbf{P}$ relative to A. Moreover, relative to A we have

$$(\mathbf{P^{NP}})^{\mathbf{NEXP}} = (\mathbf{P^{NP}})^{\mathbf{P^{NP}}} \subseteq \mathbf{PH} \subseteq \mathbf{NEXP} = \mathbf{P^{NP}},$$

and thus $\mathbf{NEXP} \subseteq \mathbf{LOW(P^{NP})} \subseteq \mathbf{P^{NP}} = \mathbf{NEXP}$. □

Homer and Selman [HS92] produced an oracle relative to which $\mathbf{P} = \mathbf{UP}$ and $\Sigma_2^p = \mathbf{EXP}$, and thus the complete $\leq_m^p$-degree for Σ_2^p collapses. The oracle A of Theorem 3 brings the collapse further down in the polynomial hierarchy.

Corollary 5. *Relative to the set A of Theorem 3, all $\leq_m^p$-complete sets for $\mathbf{P^{NP}}$ are polynomial-time isomorphic.*

Proof. Berman [Ber77] showed via a relativizable proof that the complete $\leq_m^p$-degree for $\mathbf{EXP}$ collapses to a 1-li-degree (one-to-one, length-increasing m-reductions). By results in [GS88, KLD87], all 1-li-degrees collapse if and only if $\mathbf{P} = \mathbf{UP}$, again by a relativizable proof. Relative to A, we have $\mathbf{P} = \mathbf{UP}$ and $\mathbf{P^{NP}} = \mathbf{EXP}$. □

4 Open Questions

Of course we would like to see the $\mathbf{P^{NP}} = \mathbf{NEXP}$ question answered in the unrelativized world. We conjecture that the classes are in fact different but such a proof will require vastly new techniques.

In the relativized setting, we would like to see an oracle relative to which $\mathbf{P^{NP}} = \mathbf{NEXP}$ but $\mathbf{P} = \mathbf{BPP}$. We think a proof similar to the proof of Theorem 2 may work but trying to force all $\mathbf{BPP}$ machines to be categorical may put too many strings in the oracle.

Is there an oracle relative to which $\mathbf{P} = \mathbf{UP}$ and $\mathbf{NP} = \mathbf{EXP}$?

5 Acknowledgment

We would like to thank Harry Buhrman for Corollary 5.

References

[Ber77] L. Berman. *Polynomial Reducibilities and Complete Sets.* PhD thesis, Cornell University, 1977.

[BH77] L. Berman and J. Hartmanis. On isomorphism and density of NP and other complete sets. *SIAM Journal on Computing*, 1:305–322, 1977.

[BI87] M. Blum and R. Impagliazzo. Generic oracles and oracle classes. In *Proceedings of the 28th IEEE Symposium on Foundations of Computer Science*, pages 118–126, New York, 1987. IEEE.

[BT94]   H. Buhrman and L. Torenvliet. On the cutting edge of relativization: The re-
          source bounded injury method. In *Proceedings of the 21st International Col-
          loquium on Automata, Languages and Programming*, Lecture Notes in Com-
          puter Science. Springer-Verlag, 1994. To appear.

[FFK92]   S. Fenner, L. Fortnow, and S. Kurtz. The isomorphism conjecture holds rela-
          tive to an oracle. In *Proceedings of the 33rd IEEE Symposium on Foundations
          of Computer Science*, pages 30–39, 1992. To appear in SIAM J. Comp.

[FLZ94]   B. Fu, H. Li, and Y. Zhong. An application of the translational method.
          Mathematical Systems Theory, 27:183–186, 1994.

[GS88]   J. Grollmann and A. Selman. Complexity measures for public-key cryptosys-
          tems. *SIAM Journal on Computing*, 17:309–335, 1988.

[HH91]   J. Hartmanis and L. Hemachandra. One-way functions and the nonisomor-
          phism of NP-complete sets. *Theoretical Computer Science*, 81(1):155–163,
          1991.

[HS92]   S. Homer and A. Selman. Oracles for structural properties: The isomorphism
          problem and public-key cryptography. *Journal of Computer and System Sci-
          ences*, 44(2):287–301, 1992.

[HU79]   J. E. Hopcroft and J. D. Ullman. *Introduction to Automata Theory, Lan-
          guages, and Computation*. Addison-Wesley, Reading, Mass., 1979.

[KLD87]   K. Ko, T. Long, and D. Du. A note on one-way functions and polynomial-
          time isomorphisms. *Theoretical Computer Science*, 47:263–276, 1987.

[Moc94]   S. Mocas. Using bounded query classes to separate classes in the exponential
          time hierarchy from classes in PH. In *Proceedings of the 9th IEEE Structure
          in Complexity Theory Conference*, pages 53–58. IEEE, New York, 1994.

[Rac82]   C. Rackoff. Relativized questions involving probabilistic algorithms. *Journal
          of the ACM*, 29(1):261–268, 1982.

[Sel79]   A. Selman. P-selective sets, tally languages, and the behavior of polynomial-
          time reducibilities on NP. *Mathematical Systems Theory*, 13:55–65, 1979.

[SFM78]   J. Seiferas, M. Fischer, and A. Meyer. Separating nondeterministic time
          complexity classes. *Journal of the ACM*, 25(1):146–167, 1978.

[Soa87]   R. I. Soare. *Recursively Enumerable Sets and Degrees*. Springer-Verlag,
          Berlin, 1987.

Malign Distributions for Average Case Circuit Complexity

Andreas Jakoby   Rüdiger Reischuk   Christian Schindelhauer

Med. Universität zu Lübeck*

Abstract. In contrast to machine models like Turing machines or random access machines, circuits are a rigid computational model. The internal information flow of a computation is fixed in advance, independent of the actual input. Therefore, in complexity theory only worst case complexity measures have been used to analyse this model. In [JRS94] we have defined an average case measure for the time complexity of circuits. Using this notion tight upper and lower bounds could be obtained for the average case complexity of several basic Boolean functions.

In this paper we will examine the asymptotic average case complexity of the set of n-input Boolean functions. In contrast to the worst case a simple counting argument does not work. We prove that almost all Boolean function require at least $n - \log n - \text{llog} \, n$ expected time even for the uniform probability distribution. On the other hand, we show that there are significant subsets of functions that can be computed with a constant average delay.

Finally, the worst case and average case complexity of a Boolean function will be compared. We show that for each function that requires circuit depth d, the expected time complexity will be at least $d - \log n - \log d$ with respect to an explicitly defined probability distribution. A nontrivial bound on the complexity of such a distribution is obtained.

Key words: average case complexity, circuit complexity, delay, distribution.

1   Introduction

Complexity theory is traditionally based on worst case measures. Until recently, the average amount of resources necessary to solve a computational problems has been analysed only in a few cases. The average case measure considered there is mostly the expectation with respect to a uniform distribution over the input space. Levin observed that this simple analysis has serious drawbacks from a complexity theoretic point of view, and made a proposal how these difficulties could be overcome [Levi86]. One particular point is to deal with broader classes of distributions, and it turned out that for this purpose a complexity measure for the distributions themselves was needed.

Levin's ideas have been further developed in [Gure91, BCGL92, ReSc93] to define various average case complexity classes based on the time complexity of

---

* Institut für Theoretische Informatik, Wallstraße 40, 23560 Lübeck, Germany
  email: jakoby / reischuk / schindel @ informatik.mu-luebeck.de

Turing machine computations. This was motivated by the question whether computationally hard problems – that means problems difficult in the worst case – might efficiently be solvable at least on the average (see also the discussion in [WaBe92]). However, it was shown that certain $\mathcal{NP}$-complete problems are likely to remain infeasible on the average. As in the worst case analysis this was done with the help of a reducibility notion between distributional problems and the existence of complete problems in this sense. If the Tiling problem, for example, could be solved in average polynomial time with respect to the uniform distribution then every $\mathcal{NP}$-complete problem has polynomial average case complexity with respect to any distribution that can be computed in polynomial time [Levi86].

In [JRS94] we have developed an average case measure for parallel time, which is based on the Boolean circuit model. For machine models even when fixing the problem size the length of a computation in general depends on the specific input data, whereas the information flow in circuits is fixed. Thus, it is not obvious how an average case consideration could decrease computational resources in the circuit model. In particular, due to the trivial logarithmic lower bound on circuit depth that holds for almost all n-argument Boolean functions, is there any way how to speedup the computation time below the logarithm? Indeed, in certain favourable cases the result of an output gate may be available much earlier. For example, for an OR-gate this happens as soon as one of its predecessors delivers the value 1. If this predecessor does not lie on a critical path (a path of maximal length between input and output gates) the computational delay is actually smaller than the circuit depth (see also [Krap78]).

We have shown how this timing information can be used to define the notion of delay for a circuit with respect to each input vector. This way, one obtains a meaningful average case measure for the circuit delay. The timing information can also be made explicit and then be used in actual circuit designs. Hardware designers have exploited a similar technique when dealing with so called *self-timed circuits* [DGY89, LBS93]. Thus, good average case upper bounds for the circuit model have important practical implications.

For a number of basic Boolean functions we have obtained an exponential speed-up going from the worst case to the average delay measure, most significantly for the addition of two binary numbers [JRS94]. On the other hand the parity function has been proved to require logarithmic delay even on the average. It is well known that the addition is basically equivalent to compute all prefixes of a linear formula over a specific semigroup. In [JRSW94] we have investigated the average case complexity of the parallel prefix problem for arbitrary semigroups. By proving matching upper and lower bound it is shown that the complexity depends only on algebraic properties of the semigroup and that only two different situations are possible. The average delay is either of order $\log \log n$ as for the addition, or of order $\log n$ like for the parity function.

For the Turing machine as well as for the circuit model the average case complexity of computational problems depends to some extent on the set of distributions that may occur. Restricting an average case analysis to just the uniform distribution is of limited value. But it has been observed that allowing arbitrary distributions the average case complexity equals the worst case complexity for uniform computational models. Li/Vitanyi have shown that one particular distribution, called *universal* or *Solomonoff-Levin distribution*, has the property that the average complexity of any machine is at most a constant factor smaller than its worst case complexity, where the constant depends on the particular machine [LiVi92], see also [Koba93]. This distribution is closely related to the Kolmogorov complexity of strings [LiVi89], and thus not recursive.

Fortunately, one may therefore argue that in real computations such input distributions do not occur. In order to restrict the set of allowable distributions one has considered time and space limits for a Turing machine to provide information about the individual distribution. The notion *computable* was proposed by Levin [Levi86]. It requires that the corresponding distribution function can be approximated in polynomial time. A weaker notion based on probabilistic machines called *sampleable* has been investigated by Ben-David/Chor/Goldreich/Luby in [BCGL92]. Reischuk/Schindelhauer have defined another natural notion called *rankable* [ReSc93], and have obtained tight hierarchies for average case complexity classes with respect to the time bounds of the machines as well as with respect to the complexity of the distributions.

Milterson has extended the result of [LiVi92] to subclasses C of machines with a fixed upper time bound. He calls a distribution with the property that the average case complexity of any machine in C is at most a constant factor smaller than its worst case complexity *malign* for C. His main result in [Milt91] is that there exists a distribution computable in exponential time that is malign for the class $\mathcal{P}$ of all polynomial time bounded machines (see also Prop. 2 in [BCGL92] for a similar result). Furthermore, no distribution computable in polynomial time has this property if we make the technical assumption that the probabilities of the input strings do not decrease too fast to 0 with respect to their length. When computing a malign distribution for machines with a fixed polynomial time bound the exponential time bound can be improved to a polynomial time bounded generator with a Σ_2 oracle [Milt91], and in a slightly different model even to a generator with an $\mathcal{NP}$-oracle [ReSc93].

If computability is replaced by the weaker notion of sampleability it has been shown that the class $\mathcal{NP}$ has malign distributions that can be generated, i.e. probabilistically sampled, in polynomial time [BCGL92]. Grape [Grap90] has proved that $\mathcal{P}$ and $\mathcal{NL}$ have malign distributions that are sampleable in logarithmic space.

In this paper we will study the question of *maligness* for the nonuniform circuit model. Recursion theoretic tools like the universal distribution will not be of any help in this case. Instead, completely different and explicit constructions are necessary to obtain hardness results.

We will show that for this nonuniform model malign distributions do not exist for the class of all Boolean functions. For any distribution there exist Boolean functions whose average delay is significantly smaller than their worst case delay. Next the asymptotic behaviour of the delay measure will be studied. In the worst case the so called Shannon effect holds: Almost all n-argument Boolean function require depth $n - \log\log n$ [Weg87] and this lower bound is optimal since it can be achieved up to a small additive constant [Gask78]. The situation for the average delay is more complicated. For a large portion of functions we can almost achieve this bound even for the uniform distribution. On the other hand, there are significant subsets of functions that can be computed with a constant average delay.

The last result of this paper shows that for any Boolean function f with a given worst case complexity one can explicitly construct a distribution that is malign for all circuits realizing f. Their average case delay will be smaller by at most an additive term of order $\log n$ compared to the worst case delay. We will also determine the complexity of such distributions. In [ReSc93] the tradeoff between average time and the complexity of distributions has been studied for the Turing machine model. In the circuit model, for specific functions like the OR or PARITY the tradeoff could be determined for the whole range of distributions exactly [JRS94]. In particular, the cutpoint where average and worst case complexity become identical has been located precisely in these cases. The results here solve the asymptotic question. They imply that allowing complex distributions for each function one can find distributions that make the average case complexity almost identical to the worst case complexity.

2 An Average Case Measure for Circuits

For combinatorial circuits the depth is usually taken as a measure for the computational delay. A close relationship between circuit depth and the time of several parallel machine models has been shown. Note that depth as well as the parallel time considered so far are worst case measures.

Definition 1 *Let B_n denote the set of Boolean functions $f : \{0,1\}^n \to \{0,1\}$. $\mathcal{D}_n$ denotes the set of all probability distributions μ on $\{0,1\}^n$. The uniform distribution on $\{0,1\}^n$ that gives equal probability to each of the 2^n possible input vectors is denoted by $\mu_{n,\text{uni}}$.*
Circuits will be defined over the standard basis of AND, OR and NOT gates. Let $Cir(f)$ denote the set of all circuits that compute f and $\text{CirDepth}_n(d)$ all functions in B_n that can be computed by a circuit of depth at most d.

Fact 1 *[Gask78, Weg87] $B_n = CirDepth_n(n - \log\log n + O(1))$. This bound is best possible (up to a small additive term) for almost all functions in B_n.*

Information can be propagated faster in a circuit if, for example, one of the inputs of an OR-gate is already available and has the value 1. Then its output is determined as 1 independent of the value of the other input. More formally, we define a function $time : \{0,1\}^n \to \mathbb{N}$ for each gate v of a circuit C. It specifies for each input x the step when v can compute its result $\text{res}_v(x)$ using the values of its predecessors.

Definition 2 *Let C be a circuit and v be a gate of C. For input gates and constant gates v set $time_v(x) := 0$. For an internal nonconstant gate v with k direct predecessors $v_1, \ldots, v_k$ define*

$$time_v(x) := 1 + \min\{t \mid \text{the values } res_{v_i}(x) \text{ with } time_{v_i}(x) \leq t$$
$$\text{uniquely determine } res_v(x)\} .$$

For the circuit C itself with output gates $y_1, \ldots, y_m$ we define the global time function by $time_C(x) := \max_i time_{y_i}(x)$.

For example, the delay of an OR-gate v with predecessors v_1, v_2 is given by

$$time_v(x) := 1 + \begin{cases} \max\{time_{v_1}(x), time_{v_2}(x)\} & \text{if } res_{v_1}(x) = res_{v_2}(x) = 0, \\ \min\{time_{v_i}(x) \mid res(v_i) = 1\} & \text{else.} \end{cases}$$

This notion of time is so far defined only implicitly. In [JRS94] we have shown how this information can also be generated explicitly within the same delay increasing the circuit size by at most a constant factor.

Definition 3 *For a function $t : \{0,1\}^n \to \mathbb{N}$ and a probability distribution $\mu : \{0,1\}^n \to [0;1]$ let $E_\mu(t) := \sum t(x)\, \mu(x)$ be the expectation of t with respect to μ. If D is a set of probability distributions we define*

$$etime(f, D) := \max_{\mu \in D} \min_{C \in Cir_\mu(f)} E_\mu(time_C)$$

*as the optimal **expected circuit delay** of f with respect to distributions in D.*

A simple example of a Boolean function that can be computed significantly faster in the average case compared to the worst case (for which the trivial logarithmic lower bound for the depth holds) is the OR-function. In [JRS94] we have shown

$$etime(OR_n, \mu_{n,\text{uni}}) = 2 - 2^{-(n-2)} .$$

The complexity class of all functions that can be computed within expected time at most t with respect to distributions in D will be denoted by

$$\text{CirETime}_n(t, D) := \{f \in B_n \mid etime(f, D) \leq t\} .$$

3 The Complexity of Distributions

For the average case analysis of circuits we also have to define a complexity measure for the distributions that generate the random inputs. The complexity will be measured by the circuit model itself, that is by the complexity of a circuit that starting with a vector of truly random bits generates the specific distribution. This may be considered as the circuit analog of the notion sampleable for Turing machines.

Definition 4 *A circuit C with r input gates and n output gates performs a transformation of a random variable Z defined over $\{0,1\}^r$ into a random variable X over $\{0,1\}^n$ as follows. The input vector for C is chosen according to Z. Then X equals the distribution of the values obtained at the output gates. If Z is the uniform distribution over $\{0,1\}^r$ such a circuit will be called a **distribution generating circuit, DG-circuit**, that generates the distribution of X.*

In the following we will identify a distribution μ with a random variable X that is distributed according to μ. Let $X = X_1, \ldots, X_n$. DG-circuits are required to have a constant fan-out, let us say fan-out 2. With the notion of DG-circuits we classify distributions as follows:

Definition 5
$\mathcal{DD}\mathrm{epth}_n(d) := \{ \mu \in \mathcal{D}_n \mid \exists$ *an r-input and n-output DG-circuit C of depth d that transforms a random variable Z over $\{0,1\}^r$ with distribution $\mu_{r,\mathrm{uni}}$ into a random variable X over $\{0,1\}^n$ with distribution $\mu \}$.*

In [JRS94] the following precise estimations for the average complexity of some basic Boolean functions have been obtained. Let AND_n denote the n-ary AND-function, EQUAL_n the test for equality of 2 binary strings of length n, $\mathrm{ADDITION}_n$ the addition of 2 binary numbers of length n, etc.

$$etime(f, \mathcal{DD}\mathrm{epth}(d)) = \Theta(\min(2^d, \log n)) \quad \text{for } f = \mathrm{OR}_n, \mathrm{AND}_n, \mathrm{EQUAL}_n,$$
$$etime(f, \mu_{n,\mathrm{uni}}) = \Theta(\log n) \quad \text{for } f = \mathrm{PARITY}_n, \mathrm{MAJORITY}_n,$$
$$etime(\mathrm{ADDITION}_n, \mathcal{DD}\mathrm{epth}(d)) = \Theta(\min(\log\log n + 2^d, \log n)),$$
$$etime(\mathrm{THRESHOLD}_n^a, \mathcal{DD}\mathrm{epth}(d)) = \Theta(\min(\log a + 2^d, \log n)).$$

For slightly restricted classes of distributions one can even construct universal circuit designs in case of addition [JRSW94] and OR_n [BHPS94].

4   Circuits Do Not Have Malign Distributions

For a Boolean variable x and constant α let x^α equal x if $\alpha = 1$, and $\neg x$ else. $\mathrm{OR}(x_1, \ldots, x_n)$ denotes the n-ary Boolean OR-function over the variables $x_1, \ldots, x_n$. The following result can easily be shown by induction.

Lemma 1 *Let $X = x_1, \ldots, x_n$ be a random variable on $\{0,1\}^n$ with an arbitrary distribution and let $\{i_1, i_2, \ldots, i_l\} \subseteq [1..n]$. Then there exists Boolean constants $\alpha_1, \ldots, \alpha_l$ such that $\Pr[\mathrm{OR}(x_{i_1}^{\alpha_1}, \ldots x_{i_l}^{\alpha_l}) = 1] \geq 1 - 2^{-l}$.*

Thus already for a small subset of variables one can select values that make the disjunction of these literals quite likely. Using this property we can prove

Theorem 1 *For every probability distributions μ over $\{0,1\}^n$ there exists an n-ary Boolean function f with*

$$depth(f) \geq n - \log n - \mathrm{llog}\, n \quad \text{and} \quad etime(f, \mu) \leq 4.$$

Proof: Given μ the function f is defined as follows. Let $l := \log n$ and apply the lemma above to the random subvector $x_1, \ldots, x_l$ of a random variable $X = x_1, \ldots, x_n$ that is distributed according to μ. Choose $g \in B_{n-\log n}$ with $g \notin$ CirDepth$(n - \log n - \mathrm{llog}\, n - 1)$. Due to the Shannon bound such a g exists (Fact 1). Then $f(x_1, \ldots, x_n) := \mathrm{OR}(x_1^{\alpha_1}, \ldots, x_l^{\alpha_l}, g(x_{l+1}, \ldots, x_n))$. The OR-subfunction is realized by the average case optimal design presented in [JRS94] with average delay less than 2. ∎

Hence, the class B_n of all n-argument Boolean functions does not have malign distributions. The proof actually shows that already a small set of at most n functions has the property that for any distribution it possesses at least one example with a maximal difference between the average case and the worst case complexity, that is from constant to linear.

In section 6 we will therefore switch sides by considering an arbitrary Boolean function f and ask how complex a distribution μ has to be in order to make the average complexity of this specific f with respect to μ almost as large as its worst case complexity.

5 Asymptotic Bounds with respect to the Uniform Distribution

We will now study the question how far the Shannon effect remains valid for the average case complexity. For a circuit C and a natural number t define

$$I[C, t] := \{x \in \{0,1\}^n \mid time_C(x) > t\} .$$

It is easy to see that $|I[C, t]| \leq \frac{2^n}{t+1} E_{\mu_{n,uni}}(time_C)$.

Theorem 2 *Almost all functions $f \in B_n$ have average complexity larger than $n - \log n - \log\log n - 1$ w.r.t. the uniform distribution.*

Proof: Let $d := n - \log n - \log\log n - 1$. Assume that with respect to the uniform distribution $f \in B_n$ can be computed by an expected d-time bounded circuit C. We allow that input gates of C may also be set to the negation $\overline{x_i}$ of a variable. This way, internal gates can be restricted to AND and OR gates. Without increasing the delay C can be transformed into an equivalent circuit C' with fanout 1 — simply duplicate gates with larger fanout. Thus C' looks like a binary tree.

We extend the Boolean domain by a new symbol "?". The OR and AND function is then defined by the following tables:

OR	?	0	1
?	?	?	1
0	?	0	1
1	1	1	1

AND	?	0	1
?	?	0	?
0	0	0	0
1	?	0	1

Cutting off all gates with distance larger than d from the output gate and replacing noninput gates at distance d by "?" we get a binary tree C'' of depth at most d where internal gates are labelled with AND or OR and input gates with $x_i, \overline{x_i}$ or "?". By adding redundant gates we may assume that C'' is a complete binary tree. There are less than $\exp(2^d(1 + \log(2n + 1)))$ different such C'', thus each such circuit can be encoded by a binary string of length at most $2^d(1 + \log(2n + 1))$.

Comparing C and C'' the definition of *time* implies that on all inputs x that do not belong to $I[C, d]$ C'' yields the same result as C. For $x \in I[C, d]$, however, C'' yields the result "?". Thus the set $I[C, d]$ is uniquely determined by C''. Then the function f can be described by C'' and a list of values $f(x)$ for $x \in I[C, d]$. The length of this description is bounded by

$$2^d(1 + \log(2n + 1)) + 2^n \frac{d}{d+1} \leq 2^n \left(1 - \frac{1}{\Theta(n)}\right) .$$

But it is well known that for almost all n-ary Boolean functions their Kolmogorov complexity is larger than the last bound.   ∎
Because of the worst case depth upper bound $n - \log\log n$ this lower bound is guaranteed to be best possible up to at most an additive logarithmic term.
On the other hand, it is not difficult to construct a set of $2^{2^{n-\log n}}$ n-ary Boolean functions with average delay at most 3 with respect to the uniform distribution. The proportion of such efficiently computable functions in the average case can be made even larger if we increase the delay bound moderately. Compare this result to the worst case where any set of $2^{2^{n-\log n}}$ n-ary Boolean functions contains functions that requires depth $n - 2\log n$.

6   Constructing Hard Distributions

Although we have just proved that most functions have large average case complexity even with respect to the uniform distribution we do not have any specific example. Simply from the property that a function has large worst case delay, let's say larger than $2\log n$, we cannot deduce much information concerning its expected behaviour for the uniform distribution.
But it will be shown in the following that for every such function f there exist distributions μ_f that make the average case complexity of f almost as large as its worst case complexity. This means, even in this nonuniform model there is no way to exploit information about the likelihood of different input patterns. This contrast to the result of section 4 where for each distribution a Boolean function has been constructed that had only constant average delay with respect to this distribution. This function depended heavily on the probabilities of individual input vectors.
We will show that there are circuits that can generate such hard distributions. Since there is little known about distribution generating circuits, we introduce a special family of distributions. Each one gives weight to a particular set of the input domain and zero weight to the complement. A collection of such distributions, which can be approximated by different circuit types, will form the final distribution μ_f. Note that contrary to the linear depth bound for Boolean functions there is no a priori bound known for the depth of circuits that generate arbitrary distributions.
A lot of effort in the following construction will be devoted to keeping the complexity of the distribution μ_f as small as possible. It is not surprising that the complexity of μ_f will grow with the complexity of f. Let f require depth d. Then it is not too hard to find a distribution μ_f with complexity $n + O(d)$. We will construct a distribution with an upper bound of the form $\frac{1}{2}(n + d)$. Although the saving of a factor 2 does not seem to be much at first glance a closer look shows that a simple diagonalization technique like enumerating all 2^n different input patterns cannot be used to obtain such a bound. Instead, a much more involved construction will be necessary.
First, we will investigate distributions that are almost uniform on subsets of $\{0,1\}^n$.

Definition 6 *For a nonempty set $A \subseteq \{0,1\}^n$ define the A-uniform proba-*
bility distribution μ_A by
$$\mu_A(x) \ := \ \begin{cases} |A|^{-1} & \text{if } x \in A, \\ 0 & \text{else.} \end{cases}$$

If $|A|$ is not a power of 2 this distribution cannot be generated by a DG-circuit since all probabilities of such distributions are (negative) powers of 2. In this case define $a \in \mathbb{N}$ by $2^a \le |A| < 2^{a+1}$. Probability distributions μ are called **nearly A-uniform** *iff $\mu(x)$ for $x \in A$ is either 2^{-a} or $2^{-(a+1)}$.*

It is not obvious how nearly uniform distributions can be generated efficiently.

Lemma 2 *Any nearly A-uniform distribution of a nonempty set $A \subseteq \{0,1\}^n$ can be generated in depth $\log|A| + \log(\log|A| + 1) + \log n + 3$.*

Proof: For an integer n let $\hat{n}$ be the smallest power of 2 which is at least as large as n. Then, let $\alpha := \widehat{|A|}$. First consider the following circuit C with unbounded fan-out. Its inputs are inputs constants $y_0, \ldots, y_{a-1}$, for which holds: $y_0, \ldots, y_{|A|-1}$ are all elements of A and $y_{|A|+i} := y_i$, for $i \ge 0$. Further we need random bits $r_1, \ldots, r_{\log|A|}$. The multiplexer circuit C with r and $y_0, \ldots, y_{\alpha-1}$ as inputs outputs the string $z = y_{\mathrm{bin}^{-1}(r)}$. This can be achieved by a design using
$$z[k] \ := \ \bigvee_{i=0}^{\alpha-1} \left(y_i[k] \wedge \bigwedge_{j=1}^{\log|A|} r_j^{\mathrm{bin}(i,\log|A|)[j]} \right),$$
for all $k \le n$, where $s[i]$ for a string s and an integer i denotes the ith bit of s and $\mathrm{bin}(i,n)$ for integer $i \le 2^n - 1$ denotes the binary representation of i of length n. Clearly the depth of C is $\log|A| + \log(\log|A| + 1) + 1$.

But note that every random bit r_i is used $|A| \cdot n$ times. To obtain a circuit with constant fan-out we can duplicate these bits using trees. Such a straightforward modification increases the depth by $\log|A| + \log n$. In this modified circuit the inputs y_i are used in depth $\log|A| + \log n + l\log|A| + 1$ for the first time. Alternatively we can construct a circuit that selects the elements in A iteratively using multiplexers of various depth. Recursively we duplicate random bits of a multiplexer and select elements of A using smaller multiplexers in parallel. It can be shown that this leads to a total depth of $\log|A| + \log(\log|A| + 1) + \log n + 3$. ∎

If A is relatively large one could approximate the A-uniform distribution also by generating n-bit strings at random and select one of them that belongs to A. We therefore make the following

Definition 7 *The (A,k)-uniform distribution is given by*
$$\mu(x) \ := \ \begin{cases} (1 - (1 - |A| \cdot 2^{-n})^k) \, |A|^{-1}, & \text{if } x \in A, \\ (1 - |A| \cdot 2^{-n})^k) \, (2^n - |A|)^{-1}, & \text{else.} \end{cases}$$

Lemma 3 *Let $C \in Cir(f)$ and $t \in \mathbb{N}$. With the help of the set $I[C,t]$ from above define functions $f_t^{(1)}$ and $f_t^{(0)}$ by $f_t^{(1)}(x) := f(x) \vee [\, x \in I[C,t] \,]$, $f_t^{(0)}(x) := f(x) \wedge [\, x \notin I[C,t] \,]$. Both functions can be computed in depth t.*

Let $\chi_{C,t}$ be the characteristic function for the complement of $I[C,t]$. Therefore $\chi_{C,t}$ can be computed in depth $t+3$ using $f_t^{(0)}$ and $f_t^{(1)}$.

Lemma 4 *Let $A := f^{-1}(1)$ and $f \in CirDepth(d)$. Then the (A,k)-uniform distribution μ can be generated in depth $d + \log k + \lceil \sqrt{8 \log k} \rceil + \log n + 1$.*

Proof: Generate k n-bit strings $R_0, \ldots, R_{k-1}$ at random and check for each of them whether they belong to A. If at least one test succeeds output the first such string. Otherwise output the last string.

The probability that this circuit outputs a string not in A is $(1 - |A|/2^n)^k$. All strings in A occur with the same probability. The same holds for the strings in $\overline{A}$. Thus this construction generates a (A,k)-uniform distribution.

In parallel all random strings are tested using a circuit for $\chi_{C,t}$ of depth d. It remains to select one of the strings. A straightforward implementation of a multiplexer circuit requires depth $2 \log k$. Since we need the parameter k up to size 2^n the factor 2 implies a substantial loss of efficiency. This result can be improved by dividing the multiplexer into $\lceil \log k / \delta \rceil + 2$ levels with $\delta := \lceil \sqrt{\log k/2} \rceil$, and evaluating these levels in parallel. ∎

These almost uniform distributions share the following property.

Lemma 5 *Let $t \in \mathbb{N}$ and μ be a nearly A-uniform distribution or a (A,k)-uniform distribution where $k \geq \ln(2t+1)\, 2^n |A|^{-1}$. Further let $h : \{0,1\} \to \mathbb{N}$ be a function with expectation bounded by t, that is $\mathrm{E}_\mu(h) \leq t$. Then for the set $A[h,t] := \{x \in A \mid h(y) \leq t\}$ holds $|A[h,t]| \geq |A| \cdot (2 \cdot (t+1))^{-1}$.*

Theorem 3 *For any $t \in \mathbb{N}$ holds:*
$$CirETime\left(t, \mathcal{D}Depth\left(\tfrac{(t+n)}{2} + \sqrt{n-t} + \log n + 4\right)\right)$$
$$\subseteq CirDepth(t + \log n + \log t + 3) .$$

Proof: Let $\tau := \frac{t+n}{2} + \sqrt{n-t} + \log(n+t) + 3$ and $f \in \mathrm{CirETime}(T, \mathcal{D}Depth(\tau))$. The strategy to compute f by a circuit of small depth is as follows.

1. We select $p \leq O(n \cdot t)$ circuits $C_1, \ldots, C_p$ in $\mathrm{Cir}(f)$ such that the sets $X_i := \overline{I[C_i,t]} = \{x \mid time_{C_i} \leq t\}$ completely cover the input set $\{0,1\}^n$.
2. Using lemma 3 one can find circuits $S_1, \ldots, S_p$ of depth at most t that compute the functions $f_i(x) := f(x) \lor [x \notin X_i]$. Obviously, $f(x) = \bigwedge_i f_i(x)$. Thus f can be computed by combining the p circuits S_i by a binary tree yielding a circuit of total depth $t + \log p$.

To get X_1 let μ_1 be the uniform distribution over the whole input space $Z_1 := \{0,1\}^n$. Since by assumption $f \in \mathrm{CirETime}(t, \mathcal{D}Depth(\tau))$ there exists a circuit $C_1 \in \mathrm{Cir}(f)$ such that $\mathrm{E}_{\mu_1}(time_{C_1}) \leq t$. Define $X_1 := \{x \mid time_{C_1}(x) \leq t\}$ and $Z_2 := Z_1 \setminus X_1$.

To construct X_m consider $Z_m := Z_{m-1} \setminus X_{m-1}$ and a distribution μ_m on Z_m. If $\log |Z_m| \leq (t+n)/2 + \sqrt{n-t}$ we choose μ_m to be a nearly Z_m-uniform distribution, otherwise as a $(Z_m, \ln(2t+1)\frac{2^n}{|X|})$-uniform distribution. Let $C_m \in \mathrm{Cir}(f)$ be of average complexity at most t with respect to μ_m and obtain X_m as $I[C_m,t]$.

638

Applying lemma 2 and lemma 4 the distributions μ_m can be generated in depth τ. Using lemma 5 we get

$$|X_m| \geq \frac{|Z_{m-1}|}{2(t+1)} \quad \text{and thus} \quad |Z_m| \leq |Z_{m-1}| \left(1 - \frac{1}{2(t+1)}\right) .$$

This implies $\quad |Z_m| \leq 2^n \cdot \left(1 - (2t+2)^{-1}\right)^m$.

For $m = p := (t+1) \cdot n \cdot \ln 4$ this gives $|Z_p| < 1$. Since for all $m \leq p$ by construction $\{0,1\}^n = X_1 \cup \ldots \cup X_m \cup Z_m$ the sets $X_1, \ldots, X_p$ cover all inputs. ∎

Corollary 1 *For all Boolean functions $f \in CirDepth(d)$ there exists a probability distribution μ_f computable in depth $\frac{1}{2}(n+d) + \sqrt{n-d} + O(\log n)$ such that all circuits for f have an expected delay of at least $d - \log n - \log d - 3$ with respect to μ_f.*

7 Conclusion

These results together with previous upper and lower bounds provide a detailed understanding of average case complexity in a nonuniform setting given by the Boolean circuit model. For simple probability distributions there are functions like OR, AND, THRESHOLD and ADDITION [JRS94] with substantially smaller average case complexity. On the other hand for other functions like PARITY it has been shown in [JRS94, JRSW94] that average case and worst case complexity are asymptotically identical for any distribution.

In this paper we have shown that most functions are hard in the average case even for the uniform distributions, thus the Shannon effect also holds for the average case. But the boundary is not as sharp as in the worst case. For every fixed distribution the number of functions with constant expected delay is quite large (larger than the number of functions with depth at most $n - 2\log n$).

Finally, we have shown that there is no function for which the worst case behavior is substantially worse than the average case behavior for every distribution. But what is the threshold for the complexity of distributions to make the average case complexity as hard as the worst case complexity? From [JRS94] and Theorem 3 it follows that it is between $\textrm{llog} n$ and $n + O(\log n)$. Narrowing this gap would yield a better understanding of average case complexity for a broader class of functions and distributions.

References

[BCGL92] S. Ben-David, B. Chor, O. Goldreich, M. Luby, *On the Theory of Average Case Complexity*, J. CSS 44, 1992, 193-219.

[BHPS94] B. Bollig, M. Hühne, S. Pölt, P. Savický, *On the Average Case Circuit Delay of Disjunction*, Technical Report, University of Dortmund, 1994.

[DGY89] I. David, R. Ginosar, M. Yoelli, *An Efficient Implementation of Boolean Functions and Finite State Machines as Self-Timed Circuits*, ACM SIG-ARCH, 1989, 91-104.

[Gask78] Gaskov, *The Depth of Boolean Functions*, Prob. Kybernet. 34, 1978, 265-268.

639

[Grap90]   P. Grape, *Complete Problems with L-sampleable Distributions*, Proc. 2.
           SWAT 90, 360-367.
[Gure91]   Y. Gurevich *Average Case Completeness*, J. CSS 42, 1991, 346-398.
[JRS94]   A. Jakoby, R. Reischuk, C. Schindelhauer, *Circuit Complexity: from the
           Worst Case to the Average Case*, Proc. 26. STOC, 1994, 58-67.
[JRSW94]   A. Jakoby, R. Reischuk, C. Schindelhauer, S. Weis *The Average Case
           Complexity of the Parallel Prefix Problem*, Proc. 21. ICALP, 1994, 593-604.
[Koba93]   K. Kobayashi, *On Malign Input Distributions for Algorithms*, IEICE
           Trans. Inf. & Syst. 76, 1993, 634-640.
[Krap78]   V. Krapchenko, Depth and Delay in a Network, Soviet Math. Dokl. 19,
           1978, 1006-1009.
[LBS93]   W. Lam, R. Brayton, A. Sangiovanni-Vincentelli, *Circuit Delay Models and
           Their Exact Computation Using Timed Boolean Functions*, ACM/IEEE,
           Design Automation Conference, 1993, 128-133.
[Levi86]   L. Levin, *Average Case Complete Problems*, SIAM J. Computing 15, 1986,
           285-286.
[LiVi89]   M. Li, P. Vitanyi, *Inductive Reasoning and Kolmogorov Complexity*, Proc.
           4. Structure, 1989, 165-185.
[LiVi92]   M. Li, P. Vitanyi, *Average Case Complexity under the Universal Distribu-
           tion Equals Worst-Case Complexity*, IPL 42, 1992, 145-149.
[Milt91]   P. Miltersen, *The Complexity of Malign Ensembles*, Proc. 6. Structure in
           Complexity Theory, 1991, 164-171, see also SIAM. J. Comput. 22, 1993,
           147-156.
[ReSc93]   R. Reischuk, C. Schindelhauer, *Precise Average Case Complexity*, Proc.
           10. GI-AFCET Symposium on Theoretical Aspects of Computer Science,
           STACS 1993, Springer Lecture Notes, 650-661.
[Weg87]   I. Wegener, *The Complexity of Boolean Functions*, Wiley–Teubner, 1987.
[WaBe92]   J. Wang, J. Belanger, *On Average $\mathcal{P}$ vs. Average $\mathcal{NP}$*, Proc. 7. Structure,
           1992, 318-326.

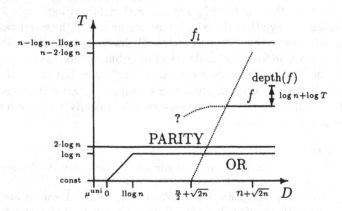

Fig. 1. Lower bounds for the average complexity of OR, PARITY and an arbitrary
function f with respect to the complexity of the distributions. F denotes a functions
of maximal asymptotic complexity as described in theorem 1.

A POSSIBLE CODE
IN THE GENETIC CODE

Didier G. Arquès and Christian J. Michel

Institut Gaspard Monge, Université de Marne-la-Vallée,
2 rue de la butte verte, 93660 Noisy le Grand, France
Tel: (33) 1 49329082, Email : arques@univ-mlv.fr

Abstract. In order to analyse the genetic code, the distribution of the 64 trinucleotides w (words of 3 letters on the gene alphabet {A,C,G,T}, $w \in \mathcal{T} = \{AAA, \ldots, TTT\}$) in the prokaryotic protein coding genes (words of large sizes) is studied with autocorrelation functions. The trinucleotides w^p can be read in 3 frames p (p=0: reference frame, p=1: reference frame shifted by 1 letter, p=2: reference frame shifted by 2 letters) in coding genes. Then, the autocorrelation function $w^p(N)_i w'$ analyses the occurrence probability of the i-motif $w^p(N)_i w'$, i.e. 2 trinucleotides w^p in frame p and w' in any frame ($w, w' \in \mathcal{T}$) which are separated by any i bases N (N=A, C, G or T). The $64^2 \times 3 = 12288$ autocorrelation functions applied to the prokaryotic protein coding genes are almost all non-random and have a modulo 3 periodicity among the 3 following types: 0 modulo 3, 1 modulo 3 and 2 modulo 3. The classification of 12288 i-motifs $w^p(N)_i w'$ according to the type of periodicity implies a constant preferential occurrence frame for w' independent of w and p. Three sub-sets of trinucleotides are identified: 22 trinucleotides in frame 0 forming the sub-set $\mathcal{T}_0 = \{$AAA, AAC, AAT, ACC, ATC, ATT, CAG, CTC, CTG, GAA, GAC, GAG, GAT, GCC, GGC, GGT, GTA, GTC, GTT, TAC, TTC, TTT$\}$ and 21 trinucleotides in each of the frames 1 and 2 forming the sub-sets $\mathcal{T}_1$ and $\mathcal{T}_2$ respectively. Except for AAA, CCC, GGG and TTT, the sub-sets $\mathcal{T}_1$ and $\mathcal{T}_2$ are generated by a circular permutation P of $\mathcal{T}_0$: $P(\mathcal{T}_0) = \mathcal{T}_1$ and $P(\mathcal{T}_1) = \mathcal{T}_2$. Furthermore, the complementarity property $\mathcal{C}$ of the DNA double helix (i.e. $\mathcal{C}$(A)=T, $\mathcal{C}$(C)=G, $\mathcal{C}$(G)=C, $\mathcal{C}$(T)=A and if $w = l_1 l_2 l_3$ then $\mathcal{C}(w) = \mathcal{C}(l_3)\mathcal{C}(l_2)\mathcal{C}(l_1)$ with $l_1, l_2, l_3 \in$ {A,C,G,T}) is observed in these 3 sub-sets: $\mathcal{C}(\mathcal{T}_0) = \mathcal{T}_0$, $\mathcal{C}(\mathcal{T}_1) = \mathcal{T}_2$ and $\mathcal{C}(\mathcal{T}_2) = \mathcal{T}_1$.

1 INTRODUCTION

The distribution of nucleotides in genes is not random. Indeed, several non-random statistical properties were identified with the autocorrelation function $w(N)_i w'$ (defined in [1] and generalized for a frame below in Section 2.1) analysing in gene populations, the occurrence probability of the i-motif $w(N)_i w'$, e.g. 2 trinucleotides w and w' separated by any i bases N. On the purine/pyrimidine alphabet (R=purine=Adenine or Guanine, Y=pyrimidine=Cytosine or Thymine) and with the i-motif $YRY(N)_i YRY$ (w=w'=YRY and N=R or Y), the autocorrelation function $YRY(N)_i YRY$ identifies in genes periodicities (modulo 2 and 3), sub-periodicities (modulo 6), maximum, local maxima, etc [1, 2, 3]. For example, in the protein coding genes of eukaryotes, prokaryotes and viruses, the autocorrelation function $YRY(N)_i YRY$ shows the classical periodicity 0 modulo 3 (maximal values of the function at i=0, 3, 6, etc). In order to understand this periodicity 0 modulo 3, the 64 i-motifs obtained by specifying on the alphabet {A,C,G,T} the trinucleotide YRY of $YRY(N)_i YRY$ (8 trinucleotides {CAC,CAT,...,TGT}), are studied with the autocorrelation functions in the protein coding genes of eukaryotes, prokaryotes and viruses. Most of the autocorrelation functions have the expected periodicity 0 modulo 3. Surprisingly, a few autocorrelation functions have a periodicity 1 modulo 3 (maximal values of the function at i=1, 4, 7, etc) and a periodicity 2 modulo 3 (maximal values of the function at i=2, 5, 8, etc). Furthermore, the classification of i-motifs according to the type of periodicity demonstrates the same strong coherence relation between the 64 i-motifs in the protein coding genes of eukaryotes, prokaryotes as well as viruses (given in [4]). This relation might be related to the genetic code and/or to the complementarity property of the DNA double helix.

In order to deepen this relation, the previous approach is generalized here to the study of the 64 trinucleotides w ($w \in \mathcal{T}$={AAA,...,TTT}) in the 3 frames p noted p=0 (reference frame established by the ATG initiation codon), p=1 (reference frame shifted by 1 base in the 5'-3' direction) and p=2 (reference frame shifted by 2 bases in the 5'-3' direction). There are $64^2 \times 3$=12288 autocorrelation functions noted $w^p(N)_i w'$ with w^p in frame p (p=0, 1, 2) and w' in any frame. The 12288 autocorrelation functions applied to the prokaryotic protein coding genes are non-random and have a modulo 3 periodicity among the 3 following types: 0 modulo 3, 1 modulo 3 and 2 modulo 3. The classification of 12288 i-motifs $w^p(N)_i w'$ according to the type of periodicity identifies 3 properties leading to a possible code in the genetic code (Section 2):

i) The trinucleotides w' have a constant preferential occurrence frame independent of w and p. Three sub-sets of trinucleotides are identified: $\mathcal{T}_0$ composed of 22 trinucleotides in frame 0, $\mathcal{T}_1$ and $\mathcal{T}_2$ composed of 21 trinucleotides in frames 1 and 2 respectively.

ii) The sub-sets $\mathcal{T}_1$ and $\mathcal{T}_2$ are generated by a circular permutation of $\mathcal{T}_0$.

iii) The complementarity property of the DNA double helix is observed in these 3 sub-sets $\mathcal{T}_0$, $\mathcal{T}_1$ and $\mathcal{T}_2$.

In order to verify that the 22 trinucleotides belonging to $\mathcal{T}_0$ can explain the 3 types of periodicities correctly associated with the 12288 i-motifs, a population of simulated genes is generated by an independent mixing of these 22 trinucleotides with equiprobability. The classification of 12288 autocorrelation functions according to the type of periodicity in these simulated genes retrieves the 3 sub-sets of trinucleotides per frame (Section 3).

In Discussion, a consequence of the identified code is given. It shows a strong correlation between the usage of this identified code and the amino acid frequencies in prokaryotes.

2 IDENTIFICATION OF SEVERAL PROPERTIES WITH THE TRINUCLEOTIDES

2.1 METHOD

A correspondence between the computer theory of languages and the gene structure.

The computer theory of languages is well adapted to the study of gene structure and thereby to the formalization of concepts in molecular genetics. Table 1 gives a few basic concepts in correspondence between these 2 fields.

Gene structure	Computer theory of languages
4 nucleotides (or bases): A=Adenine, C=Cytosine, G=Guanine, T=Thymine	Letter of the gene alphabet B={A,C,G,T}
Trinucleotide	Word of 3 letters of B*
Gene (or DNA sequence)	Word of a large size (>100 letters) of B*
Gene population	Language B*

Table1: A few concepts in correspondence between the gene structure and the computer theory of languages.

Definition of the autocorrelation function in frame.

This method generalizes the previous autocorrelation function definition on the alphabet {R,Y} without frame (R=purine=A or G, Y=pyrimidine=C or T) [1] to the alphabet {A,C,G,T} for a given frame.

Let F be a gene population (language) with $n(F)$ protein coding genes(words). Let s be a protein coding gene in F of length $l(s)$. Let w be a trinucleotide (word of 3 letters) on the alphabet {A,C,G,T} (64 trinucleotides $w \in T = \{AAA, \ldots, TTT\}$). A trinucleotide w read in frame p (p=0, 1, 2) in a coding gene is noted w^p. Let the i-motif $m_i^p = w^p(N)_i w'$ be 2 trinucleotides w^p in frame p and w' in any frame $(w, w' \in T)$ separated by any i bases N, $i \in [0, 99]$ and N=A, C, G or T. There are $3*4096 = 12288$ i-motifs $m_i^p \in \{AAA^p(N)_i AAA, AAA^p(N)_i AAC, \ldots, TTT^p(N)_i TTT\}$. For each s of F, the counter $c_i^p(s)$ counts the occurrences of m_i^p in s. The occurrence probability $o_i^p(s)$ of m_i^p for s, is then equal to the ratio of the counter by the total number $t(s)$ of trinucleotides read in frame p, i.e. $o_i^p(s) = c_i^p(s)/t(s)$ $(t(s) = (l(s)-104)/3)$. The occurrence probability $A_{w,w'}^p(i,F)$ of the i-motif m_i^p for a gene population F, is : $A_{w,w'}^p(i,F) = \sum_{s \in F} o_i^p(s)/n(F)$. For a gene population F, the function $i \rightarrow A_{w,w'}^p(i,F)$ giving the occurrence probability that w' occurs i bases after w^p, is called autocorrelation function $w^p(N)_i w'$ (associated with the i-motif $w^p(N)_i w'$) and represented as a curve as follows:

(i) the abscissa shows the number i of bases N between w^p and w', by varying i between 0 and 99;

(ii) the ordinate gives the occurrence probability of $w^p(N)_i w'$ in a gene population F.

Note: in order to have significant statistical results, the autocorrelation functions are applied to sequences having a minimal length of 200 bases.

Data acquisition.

The gene population F analysed here with the 12288 autocorrelation functions is the prokaryotic protein coding genes (13686 sequences of length greater than 200 bases, 14167332 kb) obtained from the release 39 of the EMBL Nucleotide Sequence Data Library as described in previous studies (see e.g. [2, 3] for a description of data acquisition).

2.2 RESULTS

Identification of shifted periodicities.

The 12288 autocorrelation functions applied to the prokaryotic protein coding genes are almost all non-random. Indeed, almost all autocorrelation functions have a modulo 3 periodicity among the 3 following types:

i) Type 0: a periodicity 0 modulo 3 (maximal values of the function at i=0, 3, 6, etc);

ii) Type 1: a periodicity 1 modulo 3 (maximal values of the function at i=1, 4, 7, etc);

iii) Type 2: a periodicity 2 modulo 3 (maximal values of the function at i=2, 5, 8, etc).

The method for classifying an autocorrelation function $w^p(N)_i w'$ (w, w' in T and p in $\{0,1,2\}$) consists of determining the number of points of each modulo 3 type which are greater than the 2 adjacents. There is a maximum of 33 points for a curve with 100 points (i$\in$[0,99]). If the number of points is greater than 22 (corresponding to a level of significance $<10^{-4}$), then the autocorrelation function is said classifiable according to the type p. With the statistical level chosen, an autocorrelation function can only be classifiable according to one type. For example, an autocorrelation function associated with an i-motif containing a stop codon (the 3 trinucleotides TAA, TAG or TGA are absent in frame 0) is equal to 0 and is not classifiable.

These 3 types of periodicities exist whatever the frame p of the word w^p. Indeed, the periodicity 0 modulo 3 can be observed in frame 0 (e.g. the autocorrelation function $CGC^0(N)_i GTC$: Fig. 1a), in frame 1 (e.g. the autocorrelation function $ATC^1(N)_i TCG$: Fig. 1b) and in frame 2 (e.g. the autocorrelation function $CCC^2(N)_i CGT$: Fig. 1c). Similarly, the periodicity 1 (resp. 2) modulo 3 can be observed in frame 0 (e.g., resp. the autocorrelation functions $ATC^0(N)_i TCG$: Fig. 2a and $CCC^0(N)_i CGT$: Fig. 3a), in frame 1 (e.g., resp. the autocorrelation functions $CCC^1(N)_i CGT$: Fig. 2b and $CGC^1(N)_i GTC$: Fig. 3b) and in frame 2 (e.g., resp. the autocorrelation functions $CGC^2(N)_i GTC$: Fig. 2c and $ATC^2(N)_i TCG$: Fig. 3c).

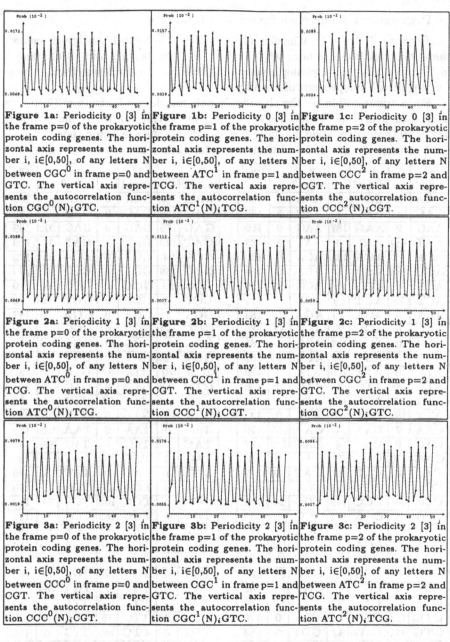

Figure 1a: Periodicity 0 [3] in the frame p=0 of the prokaryotic protein coding genes. The horizontal axis represents the number i, i∈[0,50], of any letters N between CGC[0] in frame p=0 and GTC. The vertical axis represents the autocorrelation function CGC[0](N)$_i$GTC.

Figure 1b: Periodicity 0 [3] in the frame p=1 of the prokaryotic protein coding genes. The horizontal axis represents the number i, i∈[0,50], of any letters N between ATC[1] in frame p=1 and TCG. The vertical axis represents the autocorrelation function ATC[1](N)$_i$TCG.

Figure 1c: Periodicity 0 [3] in the frame p=2 of the prokaryotic protein coding genes. The horizontal axis represents the number i, i∈[0,50], of any letters N between CCC[2] in frame p=2 and CGT. The vertical axis represents the autocorrelation function CCC[2](N)$_i$CGT.

Figure 2a: Periodicity 1 [3] in the frame p=0 of the prokaryotic protein coding genes. The horizontal axis represents the number i, i∈[0,50], of any letters N between ATC[0] in frame p=0 and TCG. The vertical axis represents the autocorrelation function ATC[0](N)$_i$TCG.

Figure 2b: Periodicity 1 [3] in the frame p=1 of the prokaryotic protein coding genes. The horizontal axis represents the number i, i∈[0,50], of any letters N between CCC[1] in frame p=1 and CGT. The vertical axis represents the autocorrelation function CCC[1](N)$_i$CGT.

Figure 2c: Periodicity 1 [3] in the frame p=2 of the prokaryotic protein coding genes. The horizontal axis represents the number i, i∈[0,50], of any letters N between CGC[2] in frame p=2 and GTC. The vertical axis represents the autocorrelation function CGC[2](N)$_i$GTC.

Figure 3a: Periodicity 2 [3] in the frame p=0 of the prokaryotic protein coding genes. The horizontal axis represents the number i, i∈[0,50], of any letters N between CCC[0] in frame p=0 and CGT. The vertical axis represents the autocorrelation function CCC[0](N)$_i$CGT.

Figure 3b: Periodicity 2 [3] in the frame p=1 of the prokaryotic protein coding genes. The horizontal axis represents the number i, i∈[0,50], of any letters N between CGC[1] in frame p=1 and GTC. The vertical axis represents the autocorrelation function CGC[1](N)$_i$GTC.

Figure 3c: Periodicity 2 [3] in the frame p=2 of the prokaryotic protein coding genes. The horizontal axis represents the number i, i∈[0,50], of any letters N between ATC[2] in frame p=2 and TCG. The vertical axis represents the autocorrelation function ATC[2](N)$_i$TCG.

If an autocorrelation function $w^p(N)_i w'$ has the periodicity j modulo 3 then w' preferentially occurs in frame q(w,p)=p+j after w in frame p. For example, the autocorrelation function CCC[0](N)$_i$CGT (Fig. 3a) with a periodicity 2 modulo 3 means that CGT occurs preferentially in frame 0+2=2 after CCC in frame 0.

Preferential occurrence frame of a trinucleotide.

Property 1: For each trinucleotide w' (with a few exceptions given below), the autocorrelation functions $w^p(N)_i w'$ obtained by varying p in $\{0,1,2\}$ and w in T, have a type j implying a constant preferential occurrence frame q(w,p) (=p+j) for w' independent of w and p.

For a trinucleotide w', the classifiable autocorrelation function $w^p(N)_i w'$ (w in T and p in $\{0,1,2\}$) implies a frame q in $\{0,1,2\}$ for w'. A maximum of 64*3=192 autocorrelation functions are classifiable. As the 3 stop codons cannot exist in frame 0, only 192-3=189 autocorrelation functions are classifiable.

w' in q=0		w' in q=1		w' in q=2		Total
AAA	189	AAA	0	AAA	0	189
AAC	161	AAC	3	AAC	5	169
AAG	2	**AAG**	187	AAG	0	189
AAT	189	AAT	0	AAT	0	189
ACA	19	**ACA**	161	ACA	0	180
ACC	188	ACC	0	ACC	0	188
ACG	0	**ACG**	189	ACG	0	189
ACT	75	**ACT**	79	ACT	17	171
AGA	0	AGA	29	**AGA**	154	183
AGC	0	**AGC**	99	AGC	87	186
AGG	0	**AGG**	127	AGG	54	181
AGT	0	AGT	53	**AGT**	129	182
ATA	0	**ATA**	189	ATA	0	189
ATC	185	ATC	1	ATC	0	186
ATG	17	**ATG**	163	ATG	0	180
ATT	189	ATT	0	ATT	0	189
CAA	7	CAA	4	**CAA**	165	176
CAC	0	CAC	4	**CAC**	183	187
CAG	110	CAG	78	CAG	0	188
CAT	0	CAT	0	**CAT**	189	189
CCA	5	**CCA**	179	CCA	0	184
CCC	0	**CCC**	146	CCC	20	166
CCG	0	**CCG**	189	CCG	0	189
CCT	22	CCT	0	**CCT**	155	177
CGA	0	CGA	0	**CGA**	189	189
CGC	0	CGC	0	**CGC**	189	189
CGG	0	CGG	0	**CGG**	188	188
CGT	4	CGT	0	**CGT**	178	182
CTA	0	CTA	97	*CTA*	92	189
CTC	123	CTC	53	CTC	0	176
CTG	141	CTG	42	CTG	0	183
CTT	30	CTT	0	**CTT**	136	166

w' in q=0		w' in q=1		w' in q=2		Total
GAA	189	GAA	0	GAA	0	189
GAC	189	GAC	0	GAC	0	189
GAG	189	GAG	0	GAG	0	189
GAT	149	GAT	0	GAT	31	180
GCA	94	GCA	37	*GCA*	39	170
GCC	189	GCC	0	GCC	0	189
GCG	59	**GCG**	81	GCG	0	140
GCT	74	GCT	0	**GCT**	108	182
GGA	4	GGA	0	**GGA**	183	187
GGC	184	GGC	0	GGC	4	188
GGG	0	GGG	0	**GGG**	186	186
GGT	98	GGT	0	GGT	88	186
GTA	70	GTA	82	GTA	0	152
GTC	189	GTC	0	GTC	0	189
GTG	110	*GTG*	72	GTG	0	182
GTT	115	GTT	0	GTT	70	185
TAA	0	TAA	0	**TAA**	189	189
TAC	98	TAC	0	TAC	88	186
TAG	0	**TAG**	189	TAG	0	189
TAT	1	TAT	0	**TAT**	185	186
TCA	0	**TCA**	156	TCA	14	170
TCC	0	**TCC**	105	TCC	78	183
TCG	0	**TCG**	189	TCG	0	189
TCT	23	*TCT*	51	TCT	80	154
TGA	0	TGA	30	**TGA**	154	184
TGC	0	*TGC*	91	TGC	95	186
TGG	0	TGG	170	*TGG*	12	182
TGT	0	TGT	2	**TGT**	184	186
TTA	2	**TTA**	180	TTA	0	182
TTC	120	TTC	16	TTC	16	152
TTG	0	**TTG**	189	TTG	0	189
TTT	69	TTT	0	TTT	78	147

Table 2: For each trinucleotide w' and for each frame q in the prokaryotic protein coding genes, the number of classifiable autocorrelation functions $w^p(N)_i w'$ implying the frame q for w' is given. The last column gives the total number of classifiable functions. The trinucleotides in bold have a preferential occurrence frame, the 8 trinucleotides in italics are exceptions.

For each trinucleotide w' and for each frame q in the prokaryotic protein coding genes, Table 2 gives the number of autocorrelation functions $w^p(N)_i w'$ implying the frame q for w'. Table 2 shows that almost all the trinucleotides w' can easily be classified in 3 sub-sets according to the frame. 8 trinucleotides (CTA, GCA, GTA, GTG, TCT, TGC, TGG, TTT) have been assigned to the frame according to the properties followed by the 56 other trinucleotides.

Table 3 shows that there are 22 trinucleotides in frame 0 forming the sub-set T_0 and 21 trinucleotides in each of the frames 1 and 2 forming the sub-sets T_1 and T_2 respectively, $T = T_0 \cup T_1 \cup T_2$:

q=0:	AAA	AAC	AAT	ACC	ATC	ATT	CAG	CTC	CTG	GAA	GAC
	GAG	GAT	GCC	GGC	GGT	GTA	GTC	GTT	TAC	TTC	TTT
q=1:	AAG	ACA	ACG	ACT	AGC	AGG	ATA	ATG	CCA	CCC	CCG
	GCG	GTG	TAG	TCA	TCC	TCG	TCT	TGC	TTA	TTG	
q=2:	AGA	AGT	CAA	CAC	CAT	CCT	CGA	CGC	CGG	CGT	CTA
	CTT	GCA	GCT	GGA	GGG	TAA	TAT	TGA	TGG	TGT	

Table 3: List of the trinucleotides per frame in lexicographical order deduced from the Table 2.

Complementarity property.

Recall of the DNA structure [9]:

i) The DNA double helix is formed of 2 nucleotide sequences s_1 and s_2 connected with the nucleotide pairing according to the biological complementarity rule C : the nucleotide A (resp. C, G, T) in s_1 pairs with the complementary nucleotide $C(A)=T$ (resp. $C(C)=G$, $C(G)=C$, $C(T)=A$) in s_2.

ii) The 2 nucleotide sequences s_1 and s_2 run in opposite directions (called antiparallel) in the DNA double helix: the trinucleotide w formed of 3 nucleotides $w=l_1 l_2 l_3$ ($l_1, l_2, l_3 \in \{A,C,G,T\}$) in s_1 pairs with the complementary trinucleotide $C(w)=C(l_3)C(l_2)C(l_1)$ in s_2.

Property 2: If the trinucleotide w belongs to the frame 0 then the complementary trinucleotide $C(w)$ also belongs to the frame 0: $C(T_0)=T_0$. If the trinucleotide w belongs to the frame 1 (resp. 2) then the complementary trinucleotide $C(w)$ belongs to the frame 2 (resp. 1): $C(T_1)=T_2$ and $C(T_2)=T_1$ (Table 4).

q=0:	AAA	AAC	AAT	ACC	ATC	CAG	CTC	GAA	GAC	GCC	GTA
q=0:	TTT	GTT	ATT	GGT	GAT	CTG	GAG	TTC	GTC	GGC	TAC
q=1:	AAG	ACA	ACG	ACT	AGC	AGG	ATA	ATG	CCA	CCC	CCG
q=2:	CTT	TGT	CGT	AGT	GCT	CCT	TAT	CAT	TGG	GGG	CGG
q=1:	GCG	GTG	TAG	TCA	TCC	TCG	TCT	TGC	TTA	TTG	
q=2:	CGC	CAC	CTA	TGA	GGA	CGA	AGA	GCA	TAA	CAA	

Table 4: Complementarity property of the trinucleotides identified in Table 3.

Circularity property.

Property 3: The 20 trinucleotides in frame 0 (without AAA and TTT) generate by circular permutation P the 20 trinucleotides in frame 1 (without CCC) and by another circular permutation the 20 trinucleotides in frame 2 (without GGG) : $P(\mathcal{T}_0)=\mathcal{T}_1$ and $P(\mathcal{T}_1)=\mathcal{T}_2$ (Table 5).

q=0:	AAC	AAT	ACC	ATC	ATT	CAG	CTC	CTG	GAA	GAC
q=1:	ACA	ATA	CCA	TCA	TTA	AGC	TCC	TGC	AAG	ACG
q=2:	CAA	TAA	CAC	CAT	TAT	GCA	CCT	GCT	AGA	CGA
q=0:	GAG	GAT	GCC	GGC	GGT	GTA	GTC	GTT	TAC	TTC
q=1:	AGG	ATG	CCG	GCG	GTG	TAG	TCG	TTG	ACT	TCT
q=2:	GGA	TGA	CGC	CGG	TGG	AGT	CGT	TGT	CTA	CTT

Table 5: Circularity property of the trinucleotides identified in Table 3.

3 SIMULATION OF TRINUCLEOTIDE PROPERTIES

3.1 METHOD

In order to verify the 22 trinucleotides identified in frame 0 can explain the 3 types of periodicities correctly associated with the 12288 i-motifs, a population S of 200 simulated genes of 1000 base length is generated by an independent mixing of these 22 trinucleotides with equiprobability. Note: The computations obtained with such a sample of 200000 bases are precise and stable (i.e. there is no random fluctuations in the probability calculus of i-motifs: a sample having for example 50 simulated genes of 1000 base length leads to similar results). The 12288 autocorrelation functions in the 3 frames are computed in this simulated population S as defined in Section 2.1. Then, they are classified according to the 3 types of modulo 3 periodicity with the method given in Section 2.2.

3.2 RESULTS

Similarly to the Table 2 for the prokaryotic protein coding genes, Table 6 gives, for each trinucleotide w' and for each frame q in the simulated genes by an independent mixing of the 22 trinucleotides identified in frame 0, the number of autocorrelation functions $w^p(N)_i w'$ (w in $\mathcal{T}$ and p in {0,1,2}) implying the frame q for w'. This simple simulation leads to the same 3 sub-sets of trinucleotides per frame which are proposed, except for GCA and TGC which are wrongly classified and for AGA which cannot be classified. Note: As this simulation is based on only 22 trinucleotides, the number of classifiable autocorrelation functions in the simulated genes is obviously less than the one in the prokaryotic protein coding genes (the maximal number is equal to 110 in the simulated genes while it is equal to 189 in the prokaryotic protein coding genes). The concatenation of a trinucleotide with itself generated by this mixing, explains the circularity property.

w' in q=0		w' in q=1		w' in q=2		w' in q=0		w' in q=1		w' in q=2	
AAA	110	AAA	0	AAA	0	**GAA**	110	GAA	0	GAA	0
AAC	110	AAC	0	AAC	0	**GAC**	110	GAC	0	GAC	0
AAG	0	**AAG**	110	AAG	0	**GAG**	110	GAG	0	GAG	0
AAT	110	AAT	0	AAT	0	**GAT**	110	GAT	0	GAT	0
ACA	0	**ACA**	110	ACA	0	GCA	0	**GCA**	86	GCA	0
ACC	110	ACC	0	ACC	0	**GCC**	110	GCC	0	GCC	0
ACG	0	**ACG**	110	ACG	0	GCG	0	**GCG**	110	GCG	0
ACT	0	**ACT**	92	ACT	0	GCT	0	GCT	0	**GCT**	90
AGA	0	AGA	2	AGA	0	GGA	0	GGA	0	**GGA**	110
AGC	0	**AGC**	97	AGC	0	**GGC**	110	GGC	0	GGC	0
AGG	0	**AGG**	110	AGG	0	GGG	0	GGG	0	**GGG**	110
AGT	0	AGT	0	**AGT**	82	**GGT**	110	GGT	0	GGT	0
ATA	0	**ATA**	110	ATA	0	**GTA**	110	GTA	0	GTA	0
ATC	110	ATC	0	ATC	0	**GTC**	110	GTC	0	GTC	0
ATG	0	**ATG**	110	ATG	0	GTG	0	**GTG**	110	GTG	0
ATT	110	ATT	0	ATT	0	**GTT**	110	GTT	0	GTT	0
CAA	0	CAA	0	**CAA**	110	TAA	0	TAA	0	**TAA**	110
CAC	0	CAC	0	**CAC**	110	**TAC**	110	TAC	0	TAC	0
CAG	110	CAG	0	CAG	0	TAG	0	**TAG**	110	TAG	0
CAT	0	CAT	0	**CAT**	110	TAT	0	TAT	0	**TAT**	110
CCA	0	**CCA**	25	CCA	0	TCA	0	**TCA**	110	TCA	0
CCC	0	**CCC**	110	CCC	0	TCC	0	**TCC**	110	TCC	0
CCG	0	**CCG**	110	CCG	0	TCG	0	**TCG**	110	TCG	0
CCT	0	CCT	0	**CCT**	110	TCT	0	**TCT**	18	TCT	0
CGA	0	CGA	0	**CGA**	110	TGA	0	TGA	0	**TGA**	110
CGC	0	CGC	0	**CGC**	110	TGC	0	TGC	0	**TGC**	86
CGG	0	CGG	0	**CGG**	110	TGG	0	TGG	0	**TGG**	43
CGT	0	CGT	0	**CGT**	110	TGT	0	TGT	0	**TGT**	110
CTA	0	CTA	0	**CTA**	110	TTA	0	**TTA**	110	TTA	0
CTC	110	CTC	0	CTC	0	**TTC**	110	TTC	0	TTC	0
CTG	110	CTG	0	CTG	0	TTG	0	**TTG**	110	TTG	0
CTT	0	CTT	0	**CTT**	110	**TTT**	110	TTT	0	TTT	0

Table 6: For each trinucleotide w' and for each frame q in the simulated genes by an independent mixing of the 22 trinucleotides identified in frame 0, the number of classifiable autocorrelation functions $w^p(N)_i$ w' implying the frame q for w' is given. The trinucleotides in bold have a preferential occurrence frame.

4 DISCUSSION

A trinucleotide in frame 0 is called codon in biology as it codes for an amino acid. In the actual universal genetic code, 61 non-stop codons code for 20 amino acids (Table 7). Therefore, several codons code for the same amino acids explaining the "degeneracy" of the genetic code.

The analysis of the 12288 i-motifs in the prokaryotic protein coding genes with autocorrelation functions identifies 22 codons (trinucleotides in frame 0: Table 3). The 22 codons can generate 40 other codons by circular permutation

(Table 3) forming with CCC and GGG the complete set of 64 codons. The concept of a circular permutation of codons has been already proposed from a theoretical point of view in order to assign one codon per amino acid by excluding AAA, CCC, GGG and TTT [5]. However, no set of 20 codons was proposed. This hypothesis was later abandoned after the discovery that an "excluded" codon TTT codes for phenylalanine [8]. Our method has allowed to identify a set of 22 codons having the circularity property. However, several codons in this set code for the same amino acids and 7 amino acids cannot be assigned: arginine, cysteine, histidine, methionine, proline, serine and tryptophan (Table 7).

Codon	Amino acid	Codon	Amino acid	Codon	Amino acid	Codon	Amino acid
TTT	**Phenylalanine**	TCT	Serine	TAT	Tyrosine	TGT	Cysteine
TTC	**Phenylalanine**	TCC	Serine	**TAC**	**Tyrosine**	TGC	Cysteine
TTA	Leucine	TCA	Serine	TAA	Stop codon	TGA	Stop codon
TTG	Leucine	TCG	Serine	TAG	Stop codon	TGG	Tryptophan
CTT	Leucine	CCT	Proline	CAT	Histidine	CGT	Arginine
CTC	**Leucine**	CCC	Proline	CAC	Histidine	CGC	Arginine
CTA	Leucine	CCA	Proline	CAA	Glutamine	CGA	Arginine
CTG	**Leucine**	CCG	Proline	**CAG**	**Glutamine**	CGG	Arginine
ATT	**Isoleucine**	ACT	Threonine	**AAT**	**Asparagine**	AGT	Serine
ATC	**Isoleucine**	**ACC**	**Threonine**	AAC	Asparagine	AGC	Serine
ATA	Isoleucine	ACA	Threonine	**AAA**	**Lysine**	AGA	Arginine
ATG	Methionine	ACG	Threonine	AAC	Lysine	AGG	Arginine
GTT	**Valine**	GCT	Alanine	**GAT**	**Aspartic acid**	**GGT**	**Glycine**
GTC	**Valine**	**GCC**	**Alanine**	GAC	Aspartic acid	**GGC**	**Glycine**
GTA	**Valine**	GCA	Alanine	**GAA**	**Glutamic acid**	GGA	Glycine
GTG	Valine	GCG	Alanine	**GAG**	**Glutamic acid**	GGG	Glycine

Table 7: The universal genetic code. The 22 identified codons (trinucleotides in frame 0) and their associated amino acids are in bold.

These 7 amino acids should have a low frequency in the prokaryotic proteins. In order to verify the consequence of this identified code, the prokaryotic proteins are extracted from the protein data base SWISS-PROT (release 29 from June 1994). The frequencies of the 20 amino acids are computed in 9510 prokaryotic proteins representing 3044028 amino acids and compared with their expected frequencies (number of codons coding for a given amino acid divided by the total number of non-stop codons, i.e. 61). Table 8 shows that except for methionine, the 6 other amino acids arginine, cysteine, histidine, proline, serine and tryptophan have as expected the lowest observed/expected frequency ratio ($<$ 0.8) in the prokaryotic proteins. A difference between the amino acid composition of proteins and the one expected from the genetic code has been already observed for arginine [6]. The unique codon ATG coding for methionine is also the start codon of protein synthesis and explain the identified code avoids this particular codon. This result shows a strong correlation between the usage of this identified code and the amino acid frequencies in prokaryotes.

The complementarity property in the identified code suggests that the 2 nucleotide sequences of the DNA helix code for amino acids. This concept has been recently investigated from an informational theoretical point of view [7].

In summary, a complete statistical study of 12288 i-motifs in the prokaryotic protein coding genes and its simulation allow to deduce a possible code in the genetic code which is both circular and complementary. The genetic code of eukaryotes is currently in investigation and the preliminary results confirm the existence of a circular and complementary code.

Amino acid	Expected frequency (% rounded)	Observed number in prokaryotic proteins	Observed frequency in prokaryotic proteins	Observed frequency/ Expected frequency
Alanine: 4/61 codons	6.56	287360	9.44	1.44
Arginine: 6/61 codons	9.84	164498	5.40	0.55
Asparagine: 2/61 codons	3.28	127874	4.20	1.28
Aspartic acid: 2/61 codons	3.28	170363	5.60	1.71
Cysteine: 2/61 codons	3.28	30213	0.99	0.30
Glutamine: 2/61 codons	3.28	119579	3.93	1.20
Glutamic acid: 2/61 codons	3.28	190544	6.26	1.91
Glycine: 4/61 codons	6.56	234665	7.71	1.18
Histidine: 2/61 codons	3.28	63907	2.10	0.64
Isoleucine: 3/61 codons	4.92	180442	5.93	1.21
Leucine: 6/61 codons	9.84	288009	9.46	0.96
Lysine: 2/61 codons	3.28	158728	5.21	1.59
Methionine: 1/61 codons	1.64	74134	2.44	1.49
Phenylalanine: 2/61 codons	3.28	114989	3.78	1.15
Proline: 4/61 codons	6.56	132643	4.36	0.66
Serine: 6/61 codons	9.84	183680	6.03	0.61
Threonine: 4/61 codons	6.56	173058	5.69	0.87
Tryptophan: 1/61 codons	1.64	38564	1.27	0.77
Tyrosine: 2/61 codons	3.28	94076	3.09	0.94
Valine: 4/61 codons	6.56	216702	7.11	1.09

Table 8: Arginine, cysteine, histidine, proline, serine and tryptophan have the lowest observed/expected frequency ratio in the prokaryotic proteins.

ACKNOWLEDGEMENTS

We thank Dr Nouchine Soltanifar and Stéphane Aubert for their advice. This work was supported by GIP GREG grant (Groupement d'Intérêt Public, Groupement de Recherches et d'Etudes sur les Génomes) and by INSERM grant (Contrat de Recherche Externe N° 930101).

References

1. Arquès, D.G. & Michel, C.J. (1987). A purine-pyrimidine motif verifying an identical presence in almost all gene taxonomic groups. *J. Theor. Biol.* **128**, 457-461.
2. Arquès, D.G. & Michel, C.J. (1990). Periodicities in coding and noncoding regions of the genes. *J. Theor. Biol.* **143**, 307-318.
3. Arquès, D.G. & Michel, C.J. (1990). A model of DNA sequence evolution, Part 1: Statistical features and classification of gene populations, Part 2: Simulation model, Part 3: Return of the model to the reality. *Bull. Math. Biol.* **52**, 741-772.

4. Arquès, D.G., Lapayre, J.-C. & Michel, C.J. (1994). Identification and simulation of shifted periodicities common to protein coding genes of eukaryotes, prokaryotes and viruses. *J. Theor. Biol.* in press.
5. Crick, F.H.C., Griffith, J.S. & Orgel, L.E. (1957). Codes without commas. *Proc. Natl. Acad. Sci.* **43**, 416-421.
6. Jukes, T.H., Holmquist, R. & Moise, H. (1975). Amino acid composition of proteins: selection against the genetic code. *Science* **189**, 50-51.
7. Konecny, J., Eckert, M., Schöniger, M. & Hofacker, G.L. (1993). Neutral adaptation of the genetic code to double-strand coding. *J. Mol. Evol.* **36**, 407-416.
8. Nirenberg, M.W. & Matthaei, J.H. (1961). The dependance of cell-free protein synthesis in *E. Coli* upon naturally occurring or synthetic polyribonucleotides. *Proc. Natl. Acad. Sci.* **47**, 1588-1602.
9. Watson, J.D. & Crick, F.H.C. (1953). A structure for deoxyribose nucleic acid. *Nature* **171**, 737-738.

List of Authors

Springer-Verlag
and the Environment

We at Springer-Verlag firmly believe that an international science publisher has a special obligation to the environment, and our corporate policies consistently reflect this conviction.

We also expect our business partners – paper mills, printers, packaging manufacturers, etc. – to commit themselves to using environmentally friendly materials and production processes.

The paper in this book is made from low- or no-chlorine pulp and is acid free, in conformance with international standards for paper permanency.

Lecture Notes in Computer Science

For information about Vols. 1–821
please contact your bookseller or Springer-Verlag

Vol. 858: E. Bertino, S. Urban (Eds.), Object-Oriented Methodologies and Systems. Proceedings, 1994. X, 386 pages. 1994.

Vol. 859: T. F. Melham, J. Camilleri (Eds.), Higher Order Logic Theorem Proving and Its Applications. Proceedings, 1994. IX, 470 pages. 1994.

Vol. 860: W. L. Zagler, G. Busby, R. R. Wagner (Eds.), Computers for Handicapped Persons. Proceedings, 1994. XX, 625 pages. 1994.

Vol: 861: B. Nebel, L. Dreschler-Fischer (Eds.), KI-94: Advances in Artificial Intelligence. Proceedings, 1994. IX, 401 pages. 1994. (Subseries LNAI).

Vol. 862: R. C. Carrasco, J. Oncina (Eds.), Grammatical Inference and Applications. Proceedings, 1994. VIII, 290 pages. 1994. (Subseries LNAI).

Vol. 863: H. Langmaack, W.-P. de Roever, J. Vytopil (Eds.), Formal Techniques in Real-Time and Fault-Tolerant Systems. Proceedings, 1994. XIV, 787 pages. 1994.

Vol. 864: B. Le Charlier (Ed.), Static Analysis. Proceedings, 1994. XII, 465 pages. 1994.

Vol. 865: T. C. Fogarty (Ed.), Evolutionary Computing. Proceedings, 1994. XII, 332 pages. 1994.

Vol. 866: Y. Davidor, H.-P. Schwefel, R. Männer (Eds.), Parallel Problem Solving from Nature - PPSN III. Proceedings, 1994. XV, 642 pages. 1994.

Vol 867: L. Steels, G. Schreiber, W. Van de Velde (Eds.), A Future for Knowledge Acquisition. Proceedings, 1994. XII, 414 pages. 1994. (Subseries LNAI).

Vol. 868: R. Steinmetz (Ed.), Multimedia: Advanced Teleservices and High-Speed Communication Architectures. Proceedings, 1994. IX, 451 pages. 1994.

Vol. 869: Z. W. Raś, Zemankova (Eds.), Methodologies for Intelligent Systems. Proceedings, 1994. X, 613 pages. 1994. (Subseries LNAI).

Vol. 870: J. S. Greenfield, Distributed Programming Paradigms with Cryptography Applications. XI, 182 pages. 1994.

Vol. 871: J. P. Lee, G. G. Grinstein (Eds.), Database Issues for Data Visualization. Proceedings, 1993. XIV, 229 pages. 1994.

Vol. 872: S Arikawa, K. P. Jantke (Eds.), Algorithmic Learning Theory. Proceedings, 1994. XIV, 575 pages. 1994.

Vol. 873: M. Naftalin, T. Denvir, M. Bertran (Eds.), FME '94: Industrial Benefit of Formal Methods. Proceedings, 1994. XI, 723 pages. 1994.

Vol. 874: A. Borning (Ed.), Principles and Practice of Constraint Programming. Proceedings, 1994. IX, 361 pages. 1994.

Vol. 875: D. Gollmann (Ed.), Computer Security – ESORICS 94. Proceedings, 1994. XI, 469 pages. 1994.

Vol. 876: B. Blumenthal, J. Gornostaev, C. Unger (Eds.), Human-Computer Interaction. Proceedings, 1994. IX, 239 pages. 1994.

Vol. 877: L. M. Adleman, M.-D. Huang (Eds.), Algorithmic Number Theory. Proceedings, 1994. IX, 323 pages. 1994.

Vol. 878: T. Ishida; Parallel, Distributed and Multiagent Production Systems. XVII, 166 pages. 1994. (Subseries LNAI).

Vol. 879: J. Dongarra, J. Waśniewski (Eds.), Parallel Scientific Computing. Proceedings, 1994. XI, 566 pages. 1994.

Vol. 880: P. S. Thiagarajan (Ed.), Foundations of Software Technology and Theoretical Computer Science. Proceedings, 1994. XI, 451 pages. 1994.

Vol. 881: P. Loucopoulos (Ed.), Entity-Relationship Approach – ER'94. Proceedings, 1994. XIII, 579 pages. 1994.

Vol. 882: D. Hutchison, A. Danthine, H. Leopold, G. Coulson (Eds.), Multimedia Transport and Teleservices. Proceedings, 1994. XI, 380 pages. 1994.

Vol. 883: L. Fribourg, F. Turini (Eds.), Logic Program Synthesis and Transformation – Meta-Programming in Logic. Proceedings, 1994. IX, 451 pages. 1994.

Vol. 884: J. Nievergelt, T. Roos, H.-J. Schek, P. Widmayer (Eds.), IGIS '94: Geographic Information Systems. Proceedings, 1994. VIII, 292 pages. 19944.

Vol. 885: R. C. Veltkamp, Closed Objects Boundaries from Scattered Points. VIII, 144 pages. 1994.

Vol. 886: M. M. Veloso, Planning and Learning by Analogical Reasoning. XIII, 181 pages. 1994. (Subseries LNAI).

Vol. 887: M. Toussaint (Ed.), Ada in Europe. Proceedings, 1994. XII, 521 pages. 1994.

Vol. 888: S. A. Andersson (Ed.), Analysis of Dynamical and Cognitive Systems. Proceedings, 1993. VII, 260 pages. 1995.

Vol. 889: H. P. Lubich, Towards a CSCW Framework for Scientific Cooperation in Europe. X, 268 pages. 1995.

Vol. 890: M. J. Wooldridge, N. R. Jennings (Eds.), Intelligent Agents. Proceedings, 1994. VIII, 407 pages. 1995. (Subseries LNAI).

Vol. 891: C. Lewerentz, T. Lindner (Eds.), Formal Development of Reactive Systems. XI, 394 pages. 1995.

Vol. 892: K. Pingali, U. Banerjee, D. Gelernter, A. Nicolau, D. Padua (Eds.), Languages and Compilers for Parallel Computing. Proceedings, 1994. XI, 496 pages. 1995.

Vol. 893: G. Gottlob, M. Y. Vardi (Eds.), Database Theory – ICDT '95. Proceedings, 1995. XI, 454 pages. 1995.

Vol. 894: R. Tamassia, I. G. Tollis (Eds.), Graph Drawing. Proceedings, 1994. X, 471 pages. 1995.

Vol. 895: R. L. Ibrahim (Ed.), Software Engineering Education. Proceedings, 1995. XII, 449 pages. 1995.

Vol. 896: R. M. Taylor, J. Coutaz (Eds.), Software Engineering and Human-Computer Interaction. Proceedings, 1994. X, 281 pages. 1995.

Vol. 898: P. Steffens (Ed.), Machine Translation and the Lexicon. Proceedings, 1993. X, 251 pages. 1995. (Subseries LNAI).

Vol. 899: W. Banzhaf, F. H. Eeckman (Eds.), Evolution and Biocomputation. VII, 277 pages. 1995.

Vol. 900: E. W. Mayr, C. Puech (Eds.), STACS 95. Proceedings, 1995. XIII, 654 pages. 1995.

Vol. 901: R. Kumar, T. Kropf (Eds.), Theorem Provers in Circuit Design. Proceedings, 1994. VIII, 303 pages. 1995.

Vol. 902: M. Dezani-Ciancaglini, G. Plotkin (Eds.), Typed Labda, Calculi and Applications. Proceedings, 1995. VIII, 443 pages. 1995.